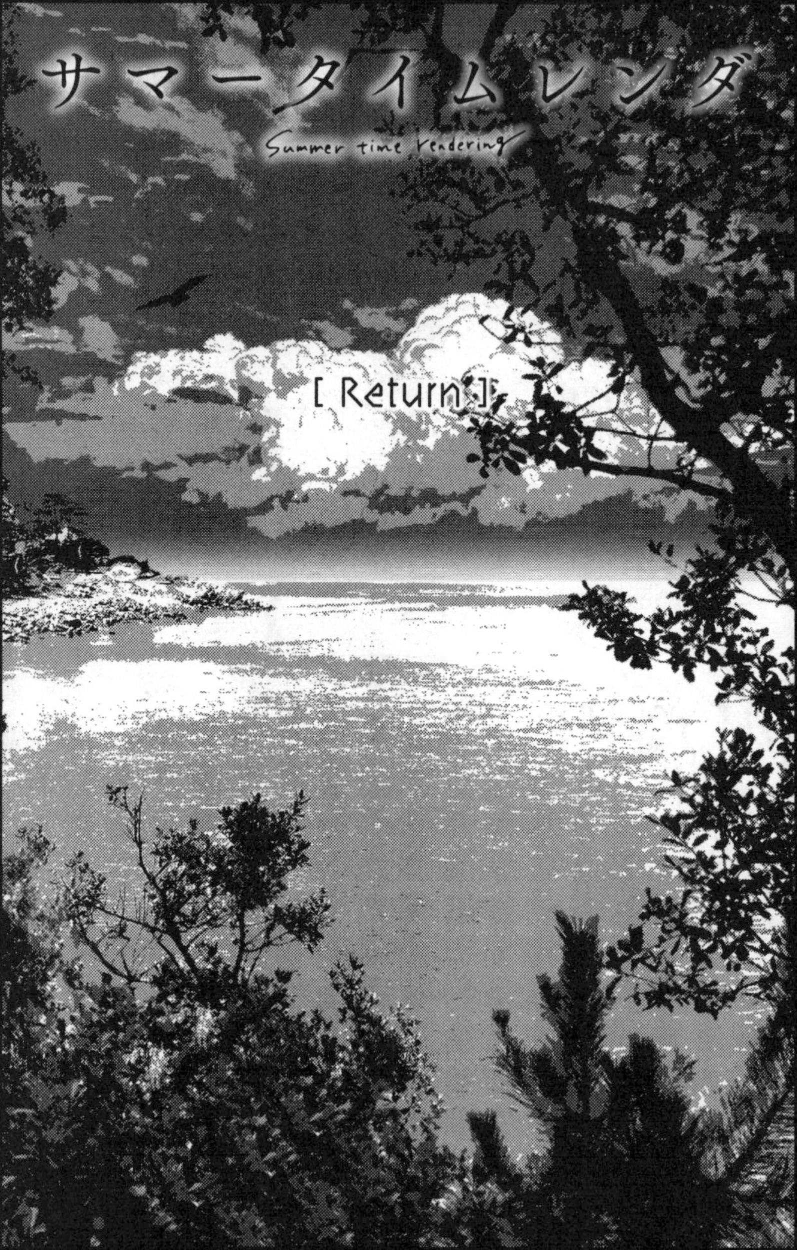
サマータイムレンダ
Summer time rendering
[Return]

田中靖規
TANAKA YASUKI

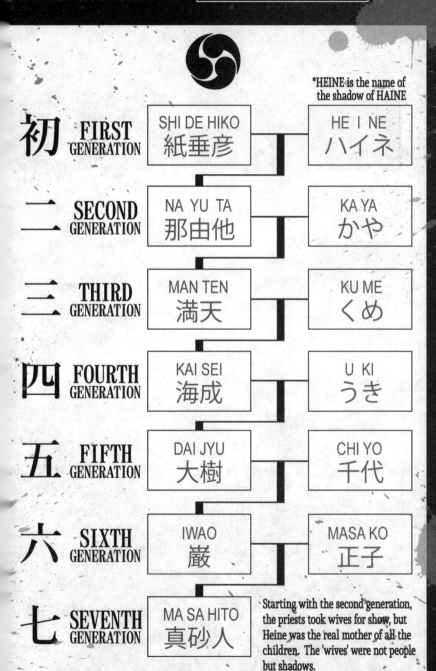

MEMO#021

KARIKIRI FAMILY TREE

*HEINE is the name of the shadow of HAINE

初	**FIRST** GENERATION	SHI DE HIKO 紙垂彦		HE I NE ハイネ
二	**SECOND** GENERATION	NA YU TA 那由他		KA YA かや
三	**THIRD** GENERATION	MAN TEN 満天		KU ME くめ
四	**FOURTH** GENERATION	KAI SEI 海成		U KI うき
五	**FIFTH** GENERATION	DAI JYU 大樹		CHI YO 千代
六	**SIXTH** GENERATION	IWAO 巌		MASA KO 正子
七	**SEVENTH** GENERATION	MA SA HITO 真砂人		

Starting with the second generation, the priests took wives for show, but Heine was the real mother of all the children. The 'wives' were not people but shadows.

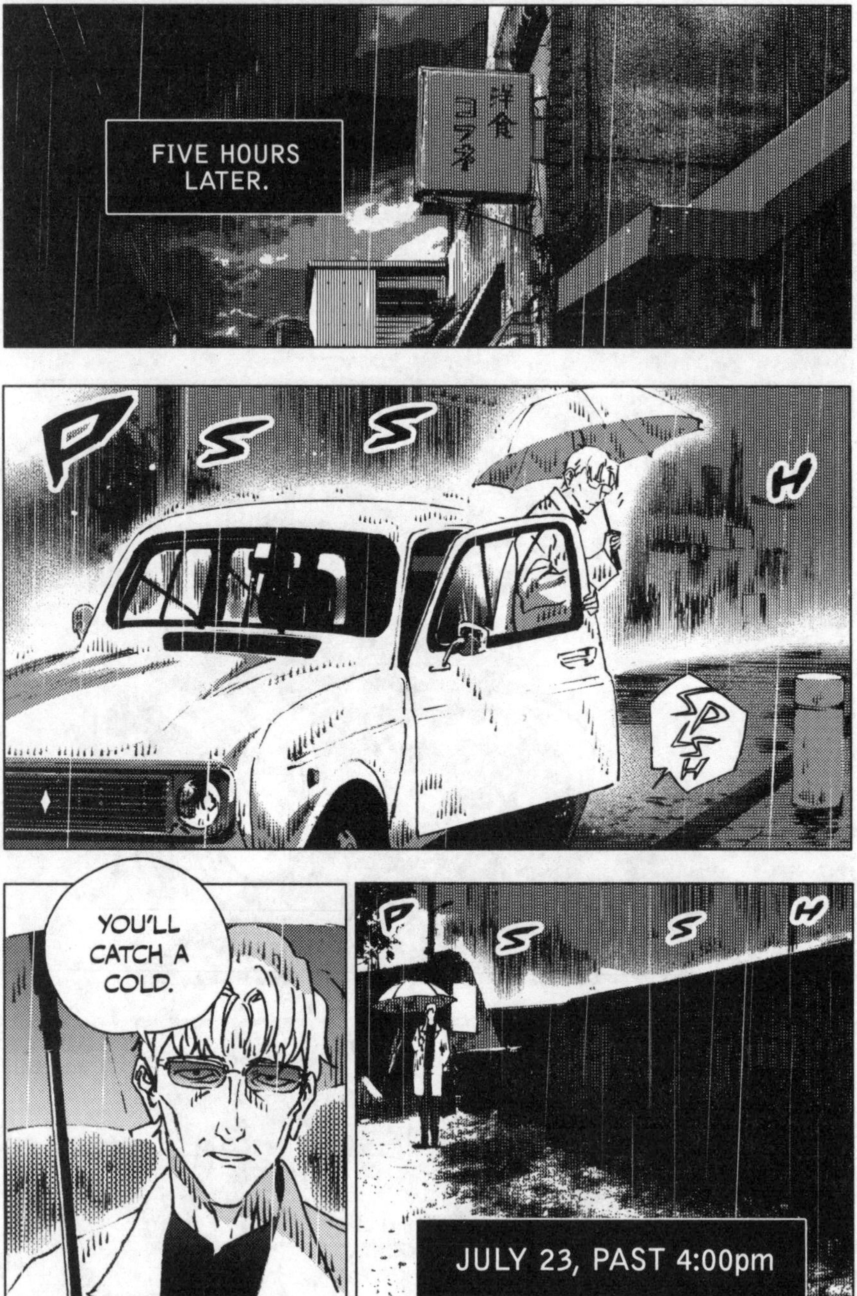
FIVE HOURS LATER.
PSSH
SPLSH
PSSH
JULY 23, PAST 4:00pm
YOU'LL CATCH A COLD.

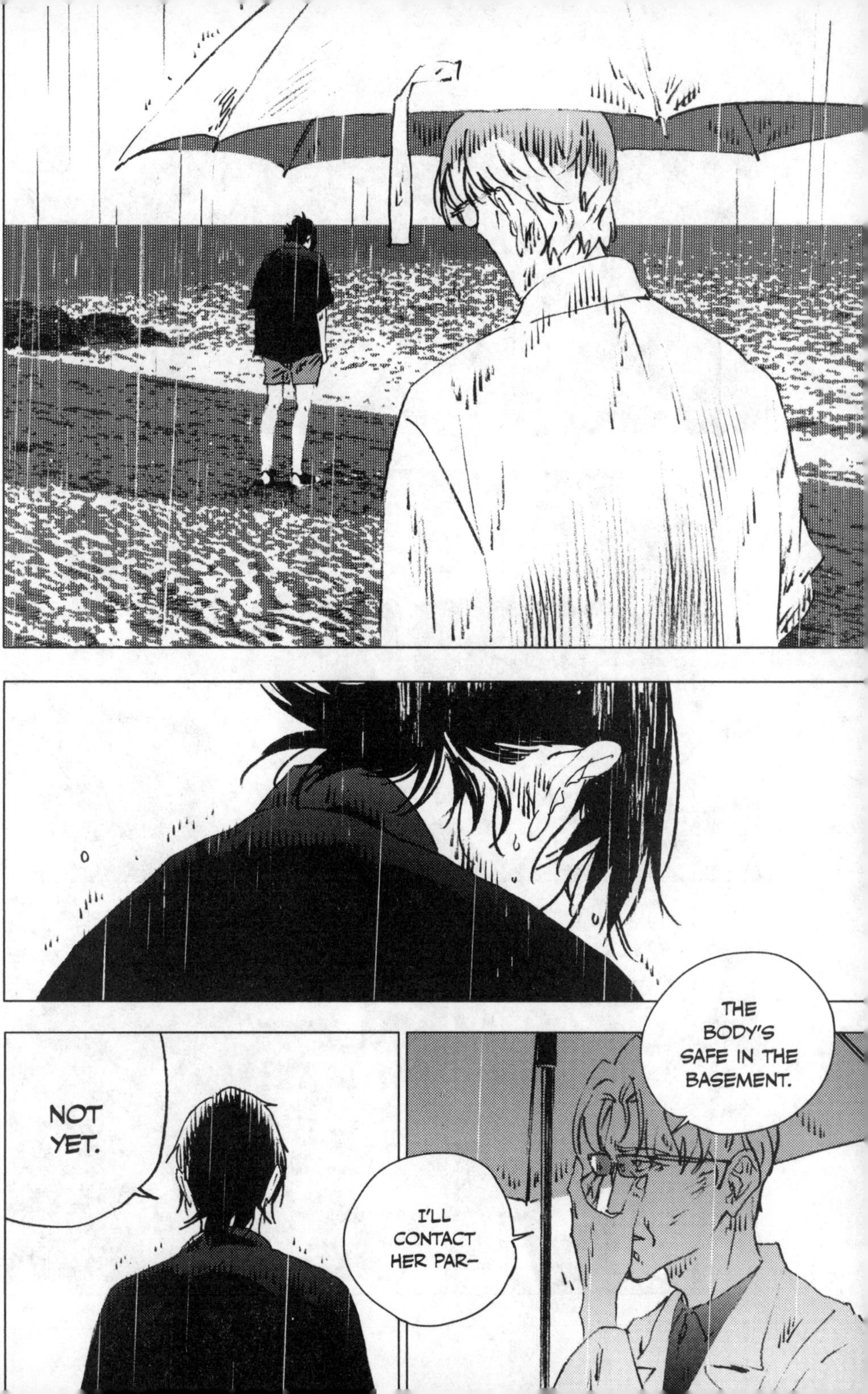
THE BODY'S SAFE IN THE BASEMENT.
I'LL CONTACT HER PAR–
NOT YET.

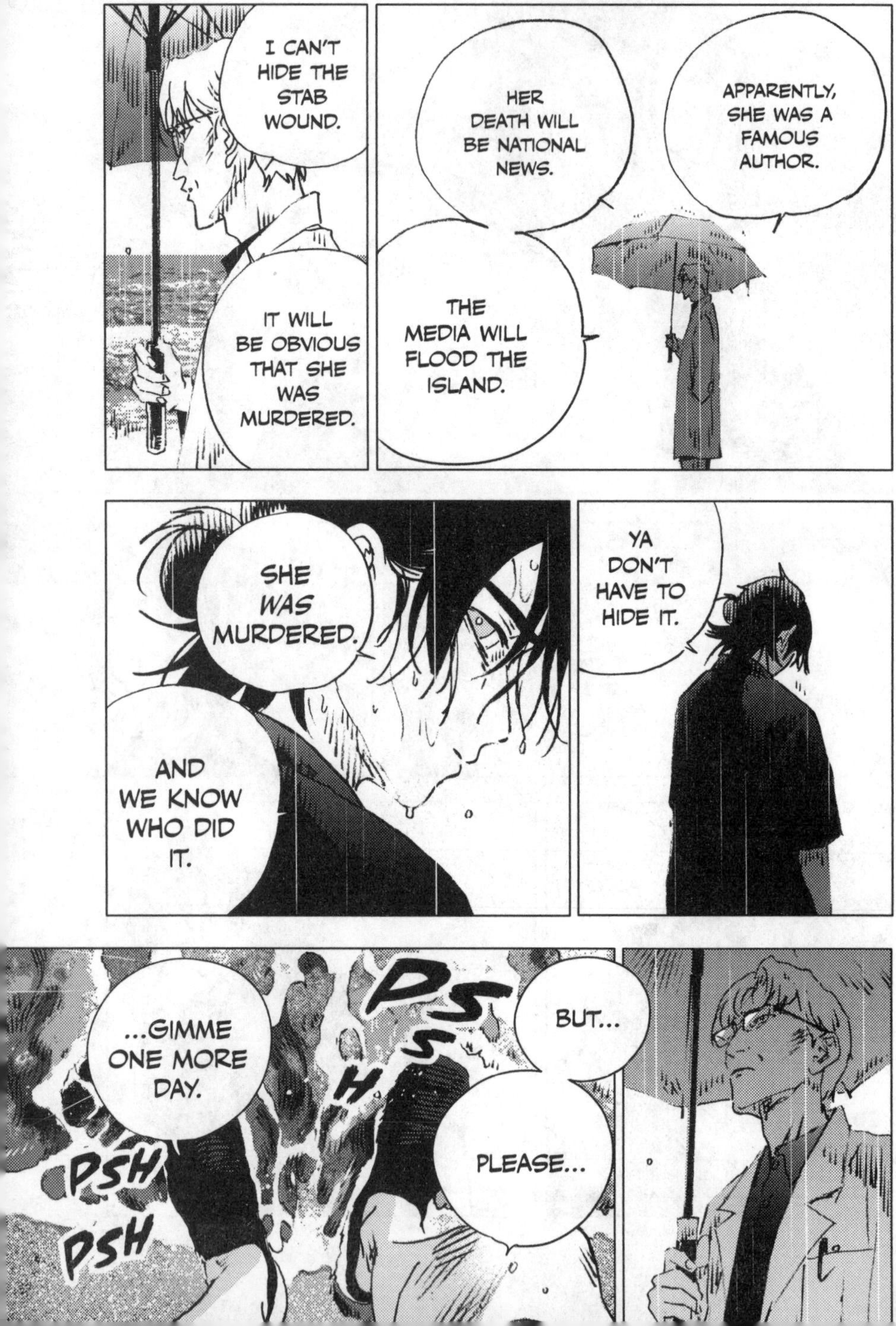
APPARENTLY, SHE WAS A FAMOUS AUTHOR.
HER DEATH WILL BE NATIONAL NEWS.
THE MEDIA WILL FLOOD THE ISLAND.
I CAN'T HIDE THE STAB WOUND.
IT WILL BE OBVIOUS THAT SHE WAS MURDERED.
YA DON'T HAVE TO HIDE IT.
SHE *WAS* MURDERED.
AND WE KNOW WHO DID IT.
BUT...
PSSH
...GIMME ONE MORE DAY.
PLEASE...
PSH
PSH

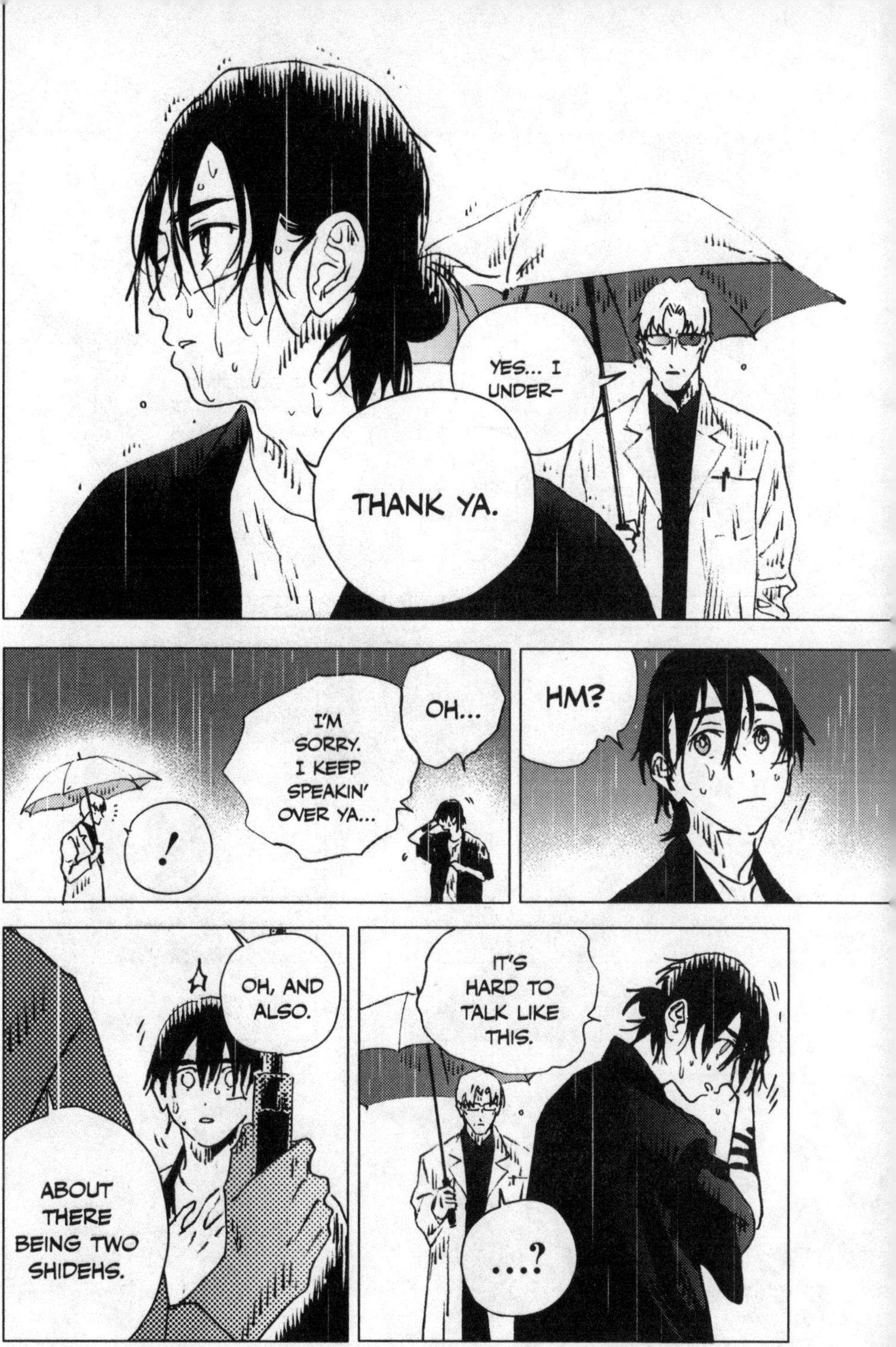
YES... I UNDER–
THANK YA.
HM?
OH...
I'M SORRY. I KEEP SPEAKIN' OVER YA...
!
IT'S HARD TO TALK LIKE THIS.
...?
OH, AND ALSO.
ABOUT THERE BEING TWO SHIDEHS.

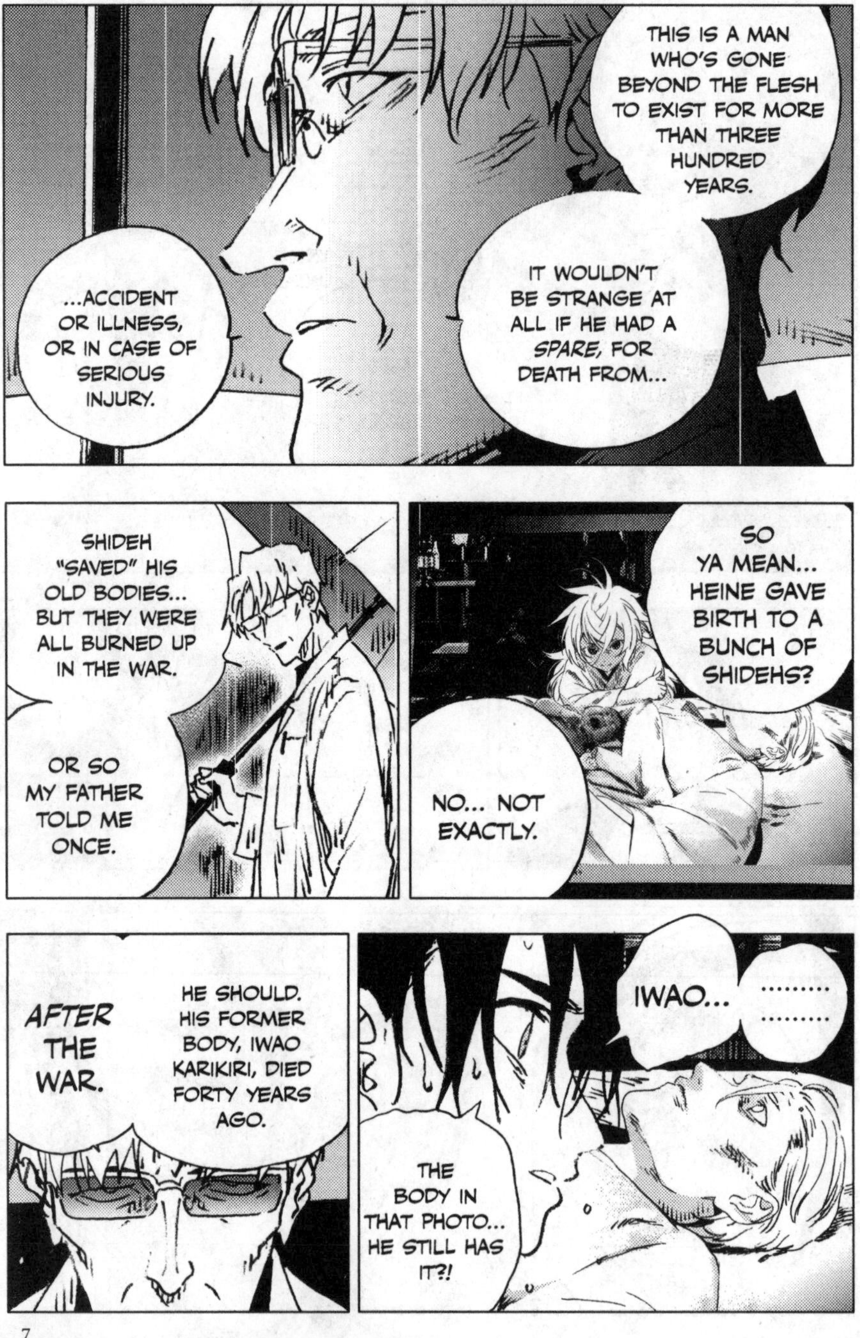
THIS IS A MAN WHO'S GONE BEYOND THE FLESH TO EXIST FOR MORE THAN THREE HUNDRED YEARS.
IT WOULDN'T BE STRANGE AT ALL IF HE HAD A *SPARE*, FOR DEATH FROM...
...ACCIDENT OR ILLNESS, OR IN CASE OF SERIOUS INJURY.
SO YA MEAN... HEINE GAVE BIRTH TO A BUNCH OF SHIDEHS?
NO... NOT EXACTLY.
SHIDEH "SAVED" HIS OLD BODIES... BUT THEY WERE ALL BURNED UP IN THE WAR.
OR SO MY FATHER TOLD ME ONCE.
....
IWAO...
THE BODY IN THAT PHOTO... HE STILL HAS IT?!
HE SHOULD. HIS FORMER BODY, IWAO KARIKIRI, DIED FORTY YEARS AGO.
AFTER THE WAR.

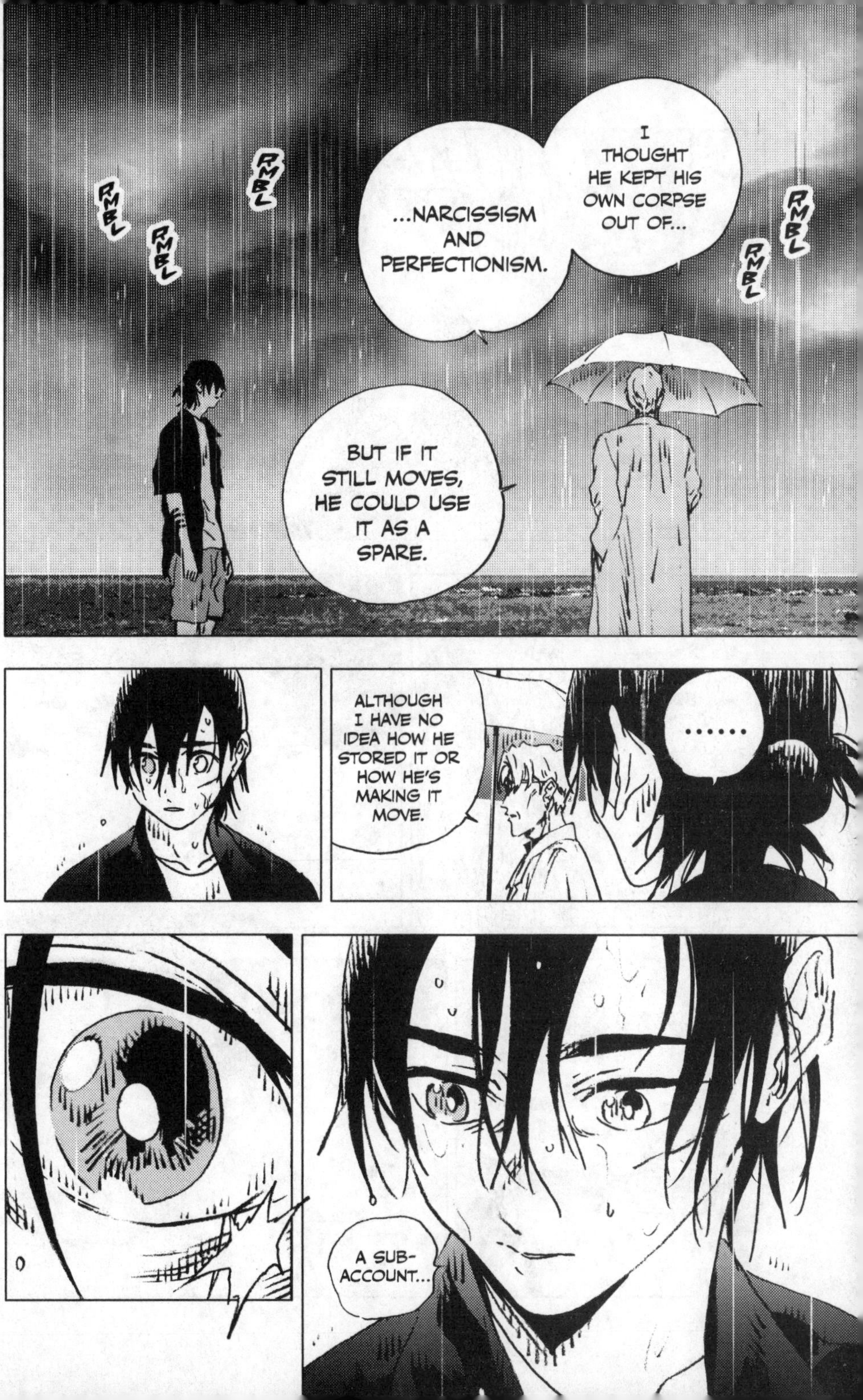
RMBL
RMBL
I THOUGHT HE KEPT HIS OWN CORPSE OUT OF...
...NARCISSISM AND PERFECTIONISM.
RMBL
RMBL
RMBL
BUT IF IT STILL MOVES, HE COULD USE IT AS A SPARE.
......
ALTHOUGH I HAVE NO IDEA HOW HE STORED IT OR HOW HE'S MAKING IT MOVE.
A SUB-ACCOUNT...

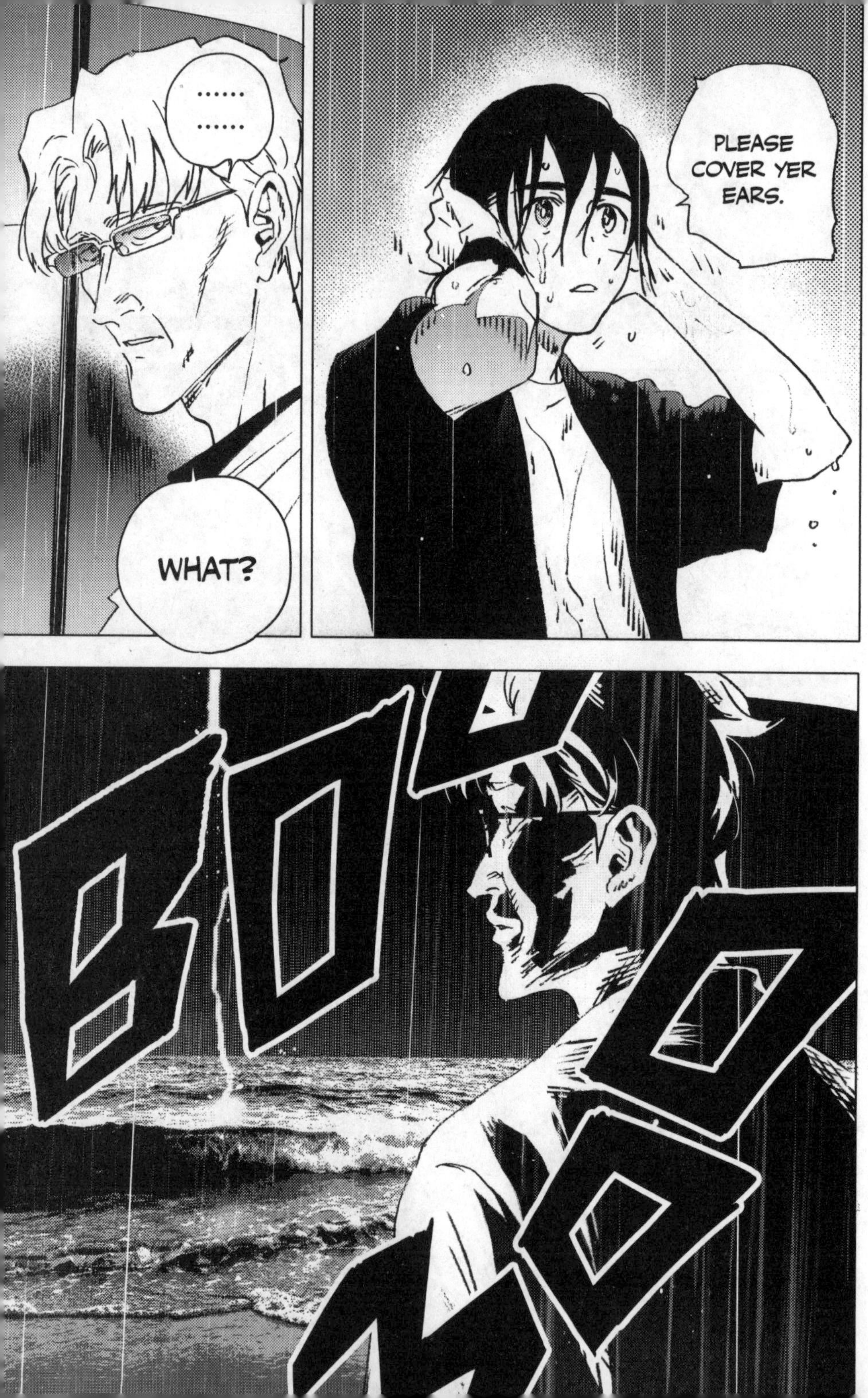
PLEASE COVER YER EARS.
......
......
WHAT?

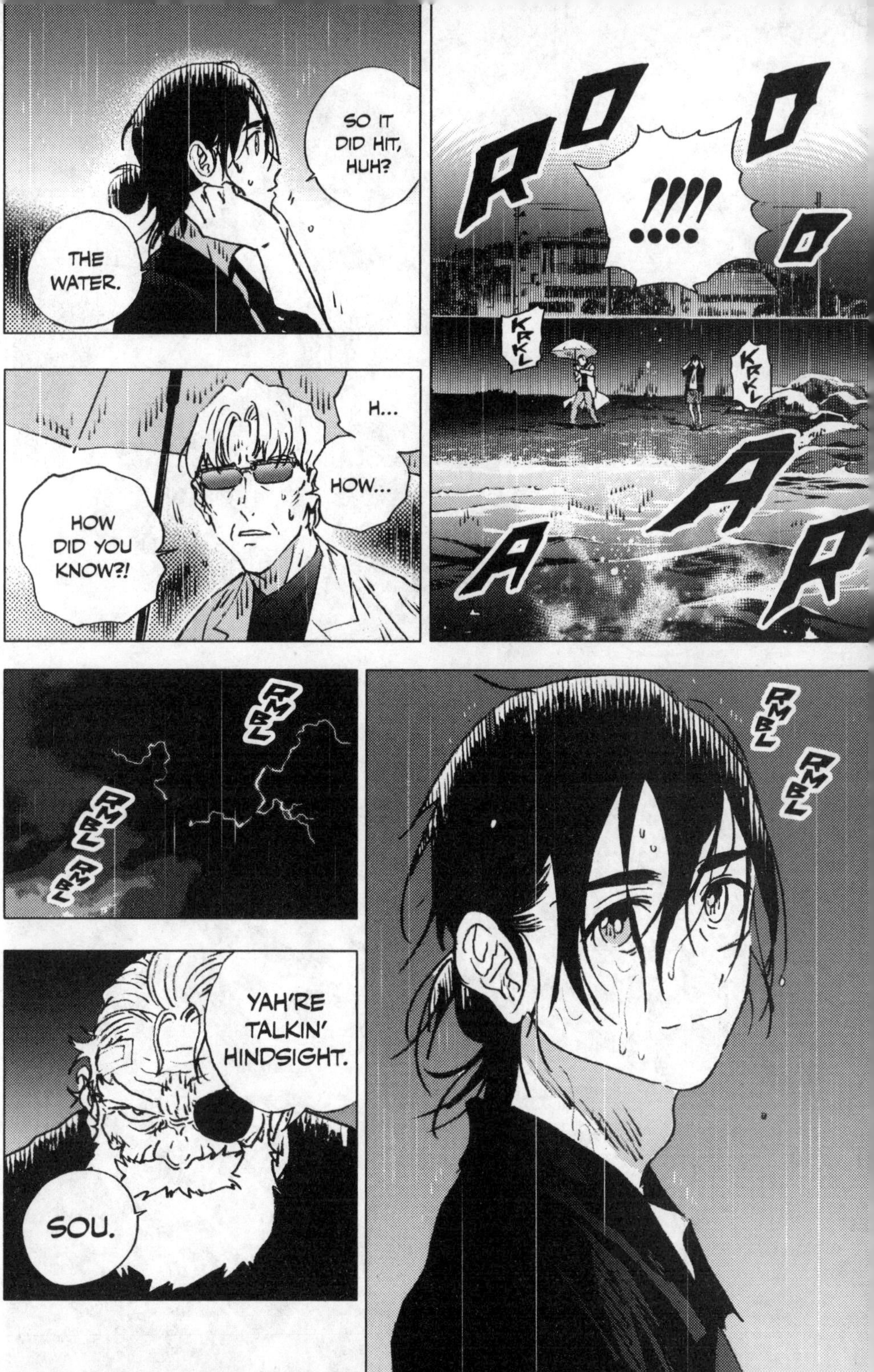
ROOOAAR
!!!!....
KRKL
KRKL
SO IT DID HIT, HUH?
THE WATER.
H...
HOW...
HOW DID YOU KNOW?!
RMBL
RMBL
RMBL
RMBL RMBL
YAH'RE TALKIN' HINDSIGHT.
SOU.

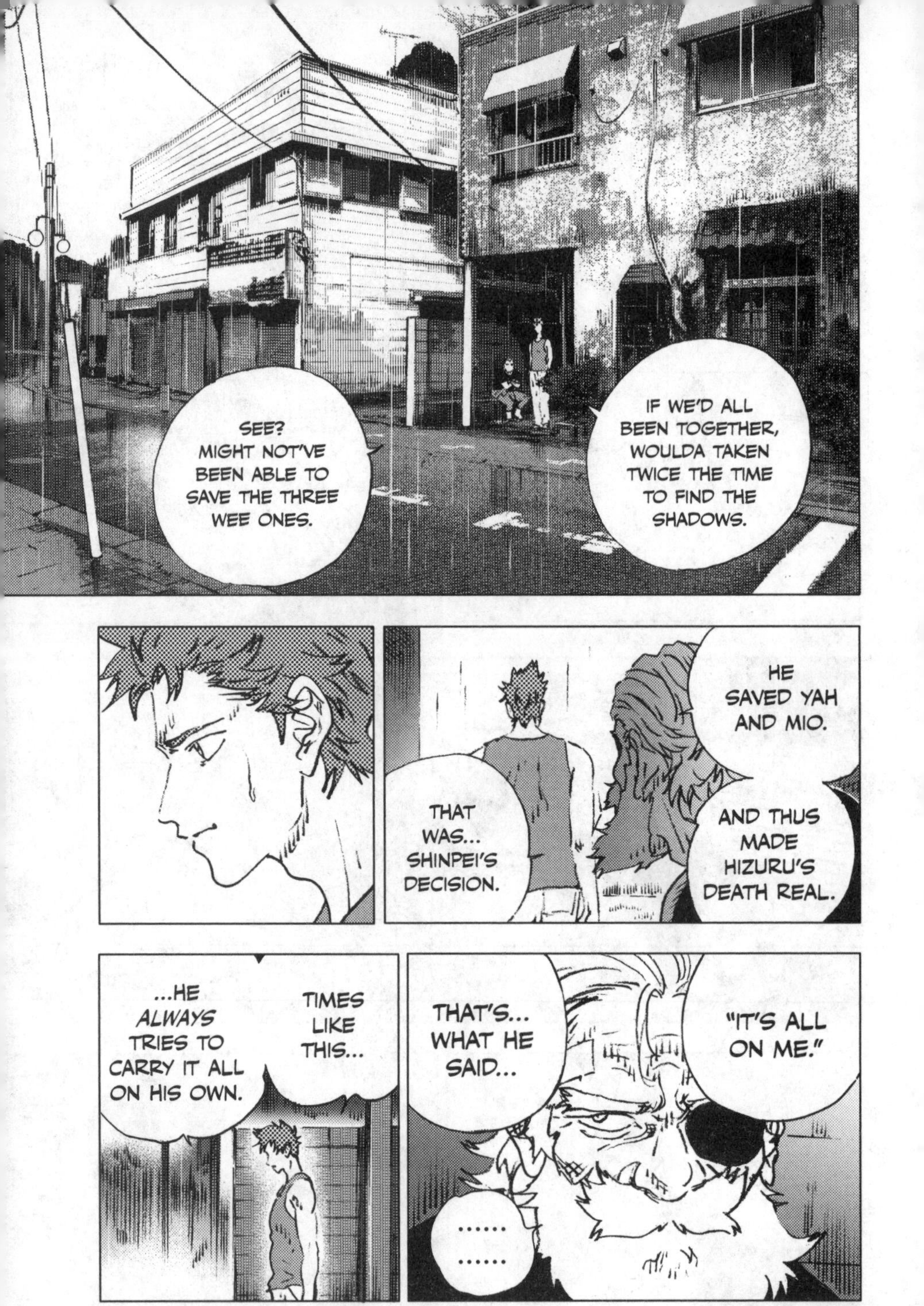
IF WE'D ALL BEEN TOGETHER, WOULDA TAKEN TWICE THE TIME TO FIND THE SHADOWS.
SEE? MIGHT NOT'VE BEEN ABLE TO SAVE THE THREE WEE ONES.
HE SAVED YAH AND MIO.
AND THUS MADE HIZURU'S DEATH REAL.
THAT WAS... SHINPEI'S DECISION.
"IT'S ALL ON ME."
THAT'S... WHAT HE SAID...
....
TIMES LIKE THIS...
...HE *ALWAYS* TRIES TO CARRY IT ALL ON HIS OWN.

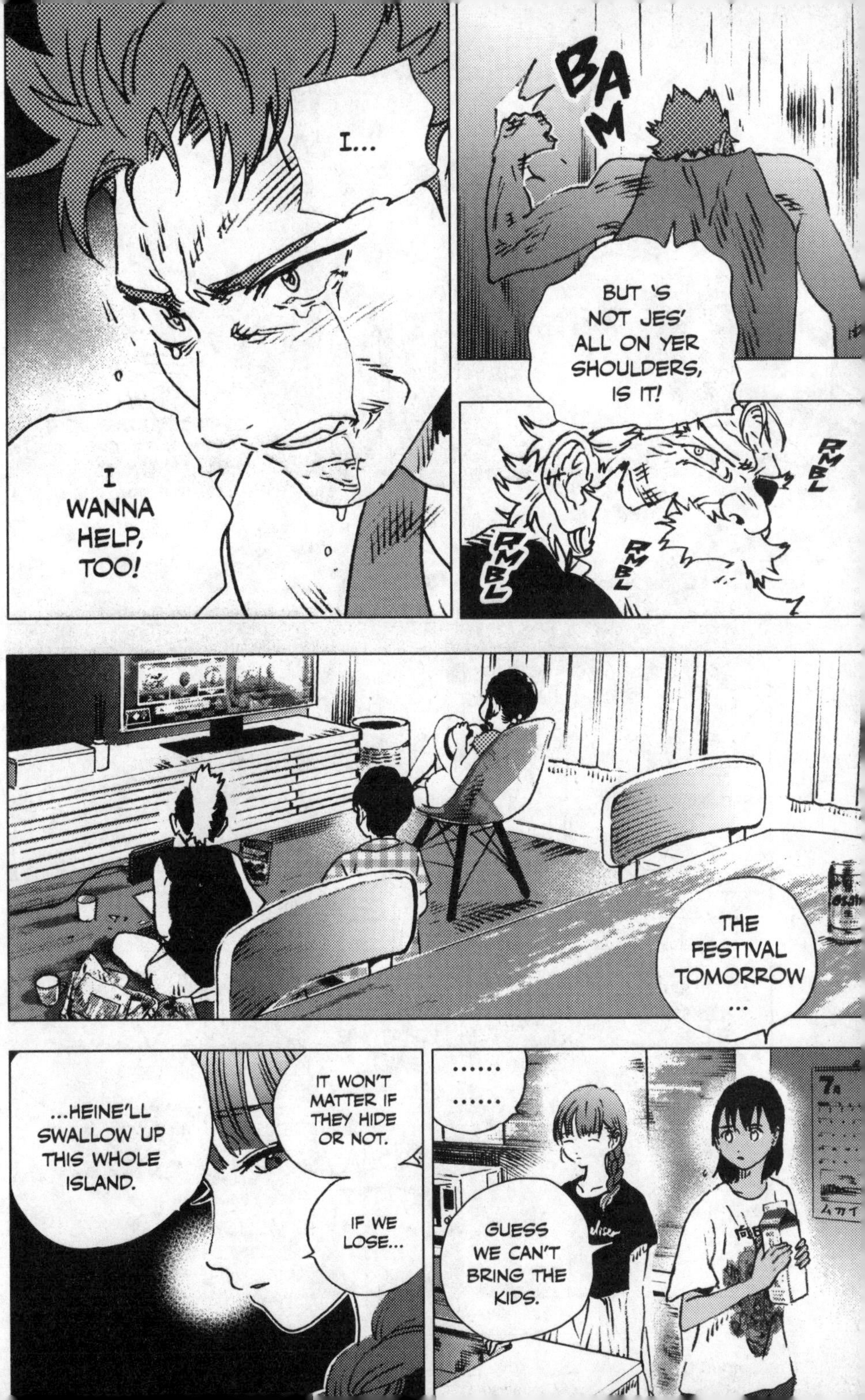
BAM
BUT 'S NOT JES' ALL ON YER SHOULDERS, IS IT!
RMBL
RMBL
RMBL
I...
I WANNA HELP, TOO!
THE FESTIVAL TOMORROW ...
......
......
GUESS WE CAN'T BRING THE KIDS.
IT WON'T MATTER IF THEY HIDE OR NOT.
...HEINE'LL SWALLOW UP THIS WHOLE ISLAND.
IF WE LOSE...

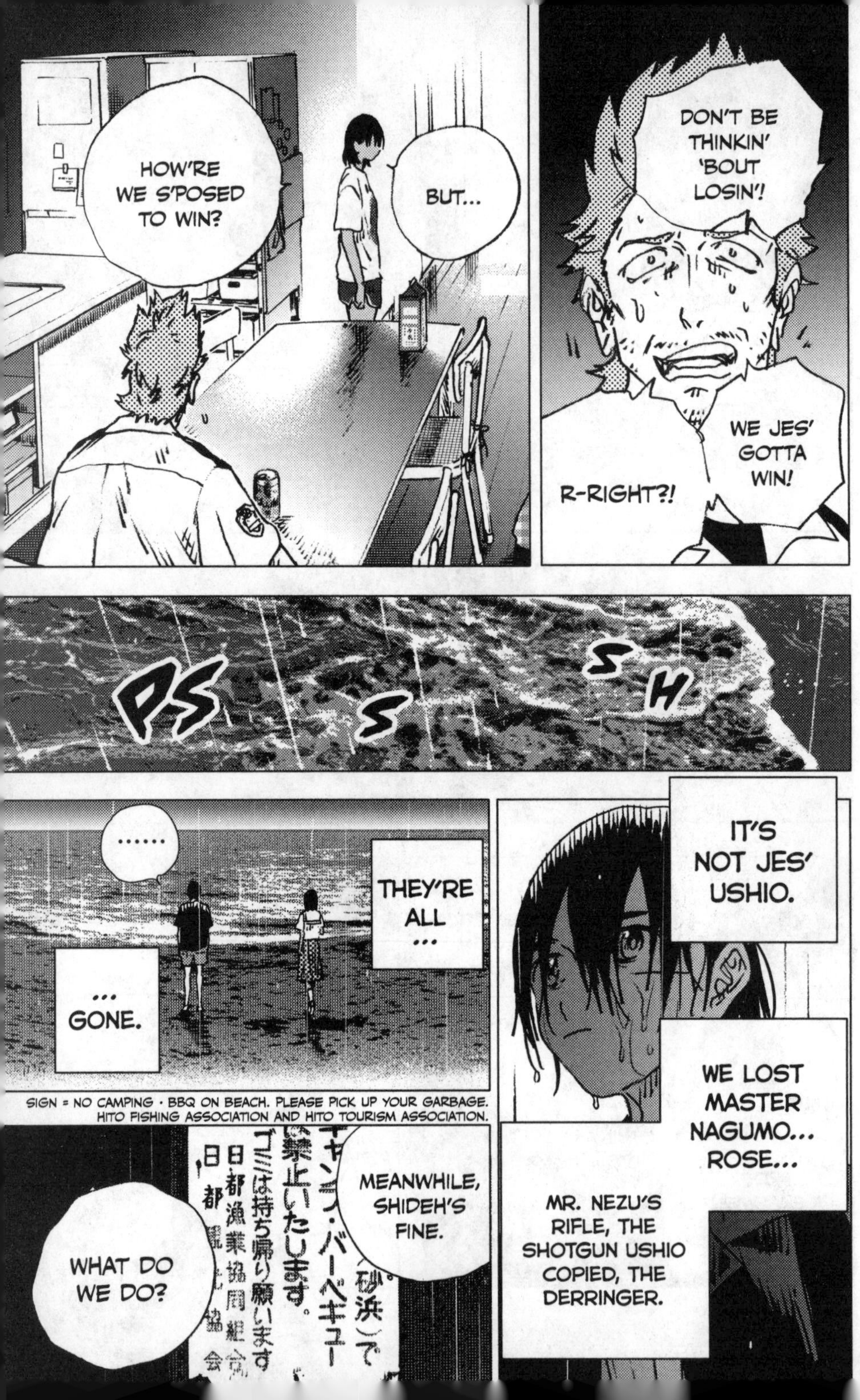
DON'T BE THINKIN' 'BOUT LOSIN'!
WE JES' GOTTA WIN!
R-RIGHT?!
BUT...
HOW'RE WE S'POSED TO WIN?
PSSSH
IT'S NOT JES' USHIO.
WE LOST MASTER NAGUMO... ROSE...
MR. NEZU'S RIFLE, THE SHOTGUN USHIO COPIED, THE DERRINGER.
......
THEY'RE ALL ...
... GONE.
SIGN = NO CAMPING · BBQ ON BEACH. PLEASE PICK UP YOUR GARBAGE. HITO FISHING ASSOCIATION AND HITO TOURISM ASSOCIATION.
MEANWHILE, SHIDEH'S FINE.
WHAT DO WE DO?
ャンプ・バーベキュー（砂浜）で
禁止いたします。
ゴミは持ち帰り願います
日都漁業協同組合

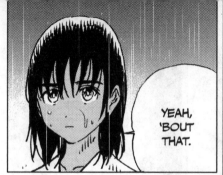

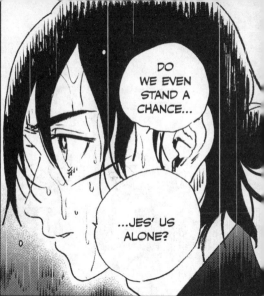

DO WE EVEN STAND A CHANCE...
...JES' US ALONE?
YEAH, 'BOUT THAT.
!
YER POCKET.
WHAT'S IN THERE?
OHH.
THIS...
I GET NO REACTION WHEN I SPEAK TO IT.
I THINK IT'S...
...PROB'LY A FRAGMENT OF USHIO.

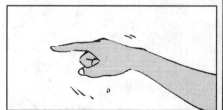

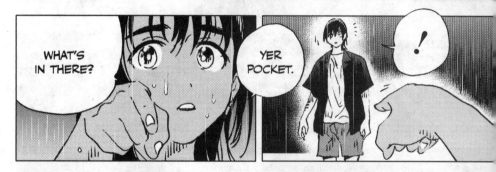

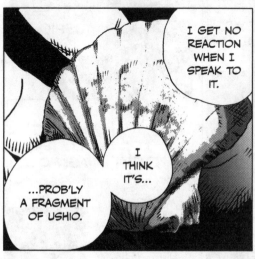

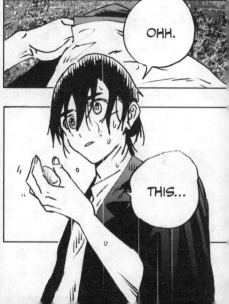

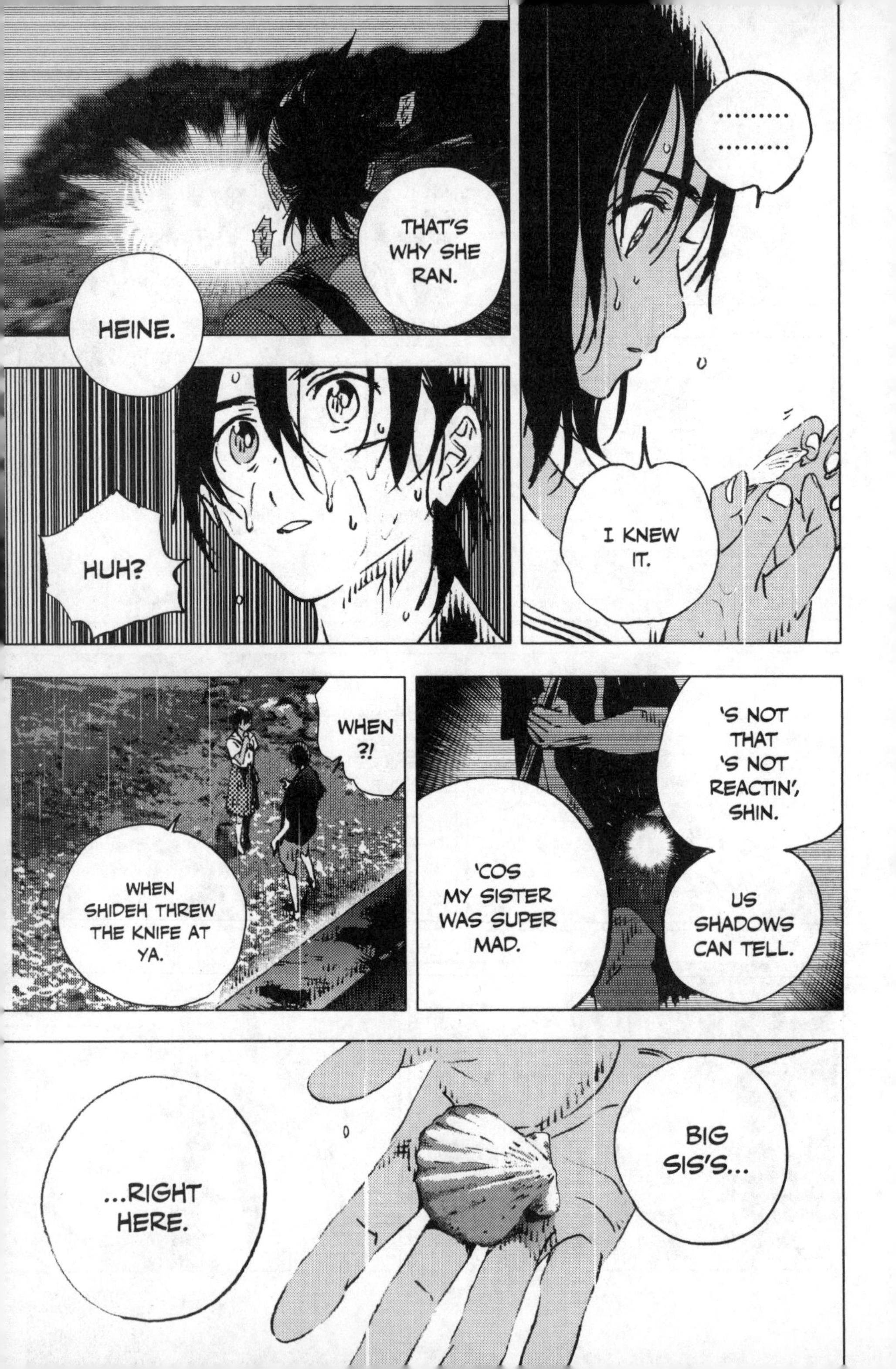
....
....
I KNEW IT.
THAT'S WHY SHE RAN.
HEINE.
HUH?
'S NOT THAT 'S NOT REACTIN', SHIN.
US SHADOWS CAN TELL.
'COS MY SISTER WAS SUPER MAD.
WHEN ?!
WHEN SHIDEH THREW THE KNIFE AT YA.
BIG SIS'S...
...RIGHT HERE.

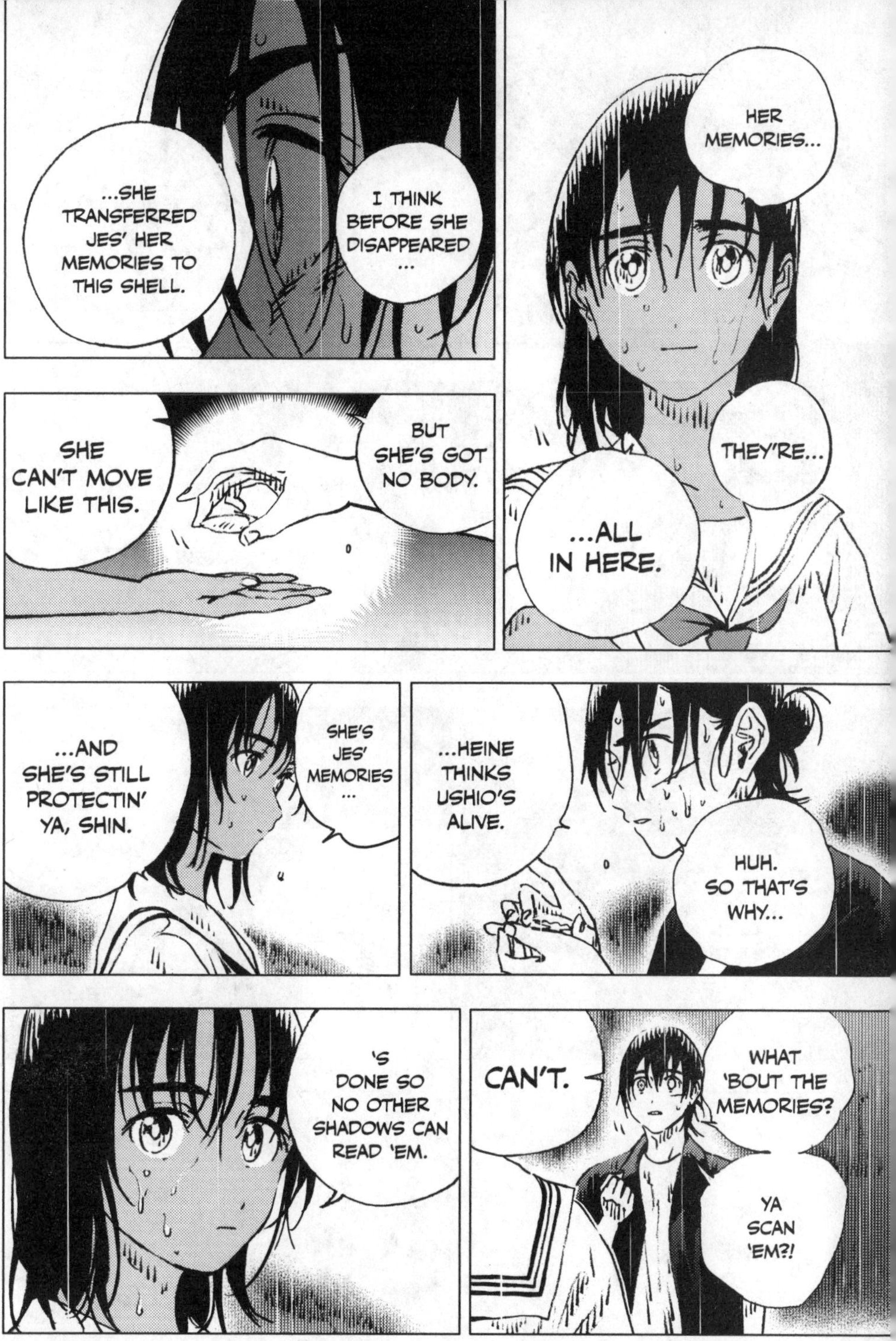
HER MEMORIES...
THEY'RE...
...ALL IN HERE.
I THINK BEFORE SHE DISAPPEARED ...
...SHE TRANSFERRED JES' HER MEMORIES TO THIS SHELL.
BUT SHE'S GOT NO BODY.
SHE CAN'T MOVE LIKE THIS.
HUH. SO THAT'S WHY...
...HEINE THINKS USHIO'S ALIVE.
SHE'S JES' MEMORIES ...
...AND SHE'S STILL PROTECTIN' YA, SHIN.
WHAT 'BOUT THE MEMORIES?
YA SCAN 'EM?!
CAN'T.
'S DONE SO NO OTHER SHADOWS CAN READ 'EM.

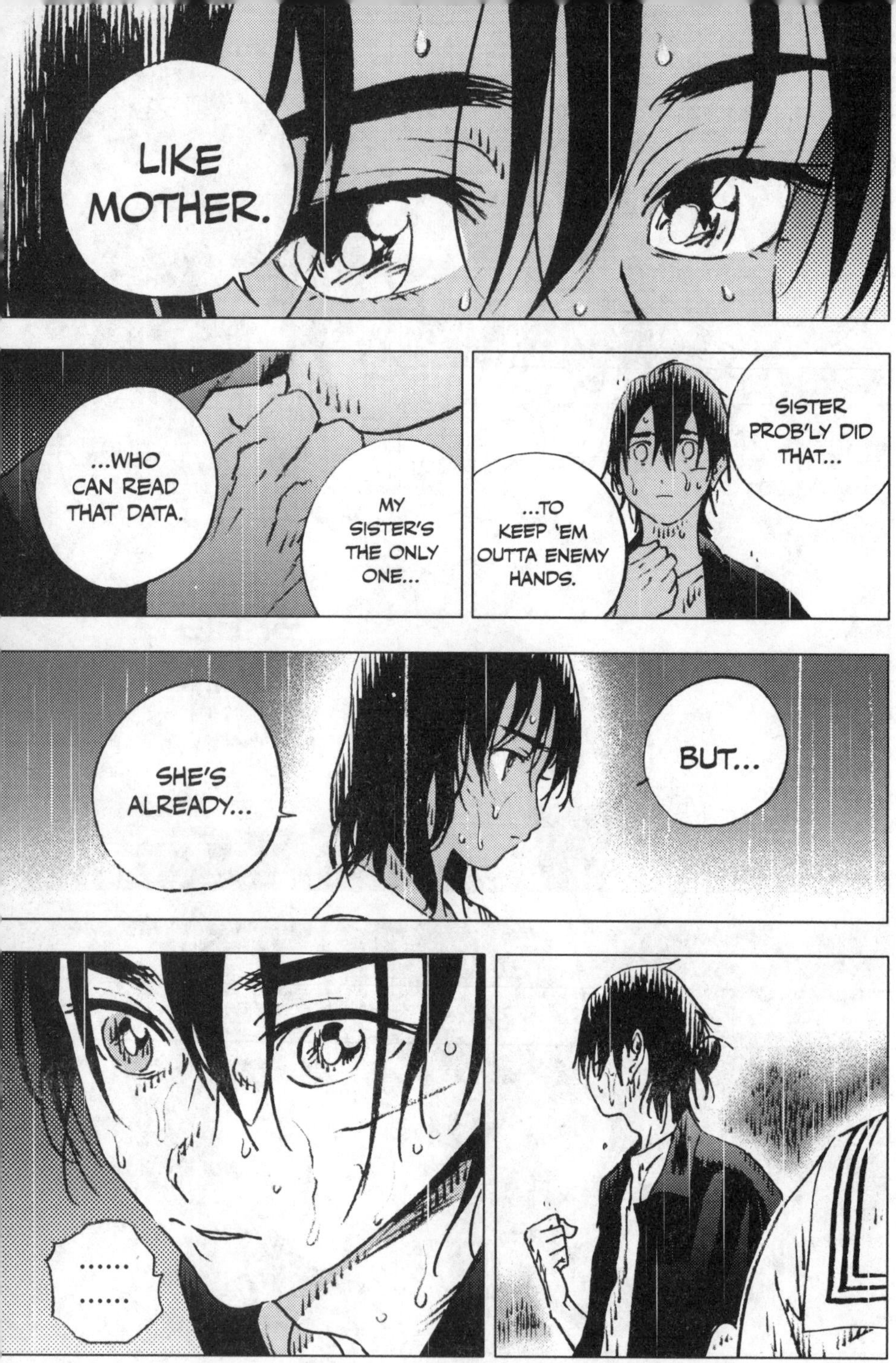
LIKE MOTHER.
SISTER PROB'LY DID THAT...
...TO KEEP 'EM OUTTA ENEMY HANDS.
MY SISTER'S THE ONLY ONE...
...WHO CAN READ THAT DATA.
BUT...
SHE'S ALREADY...
....

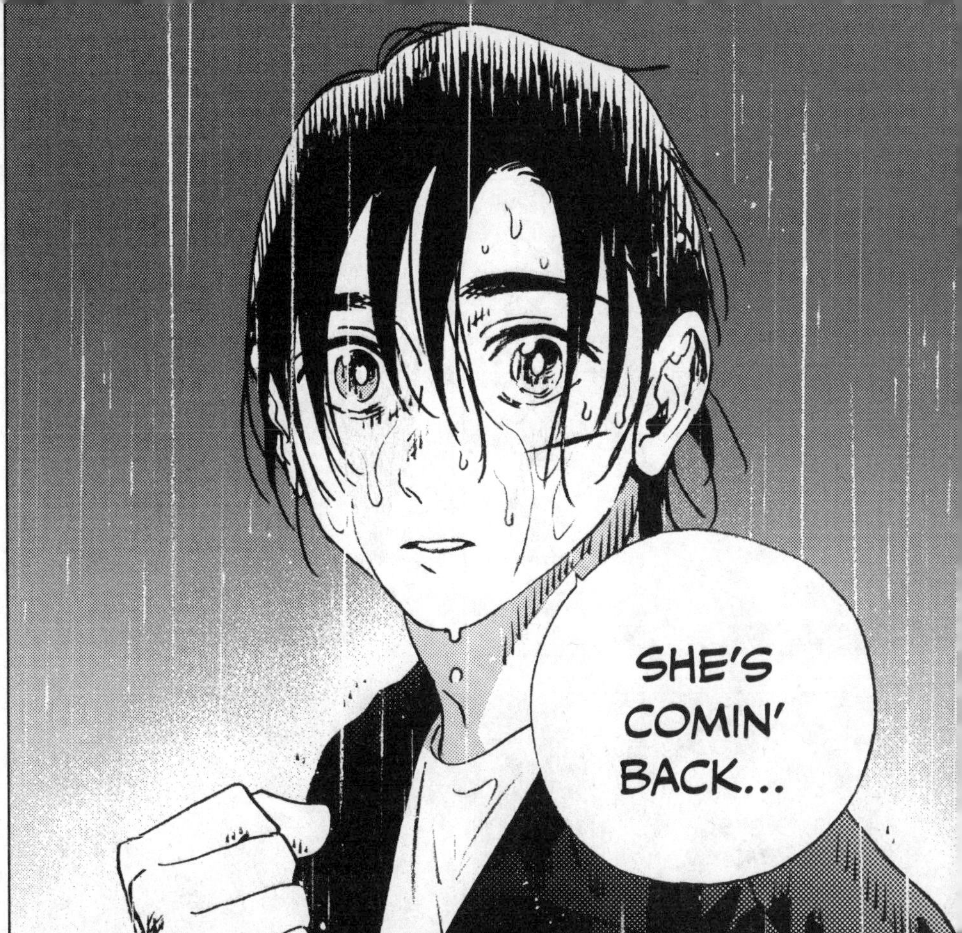
SHE'S COMIN' BACK...
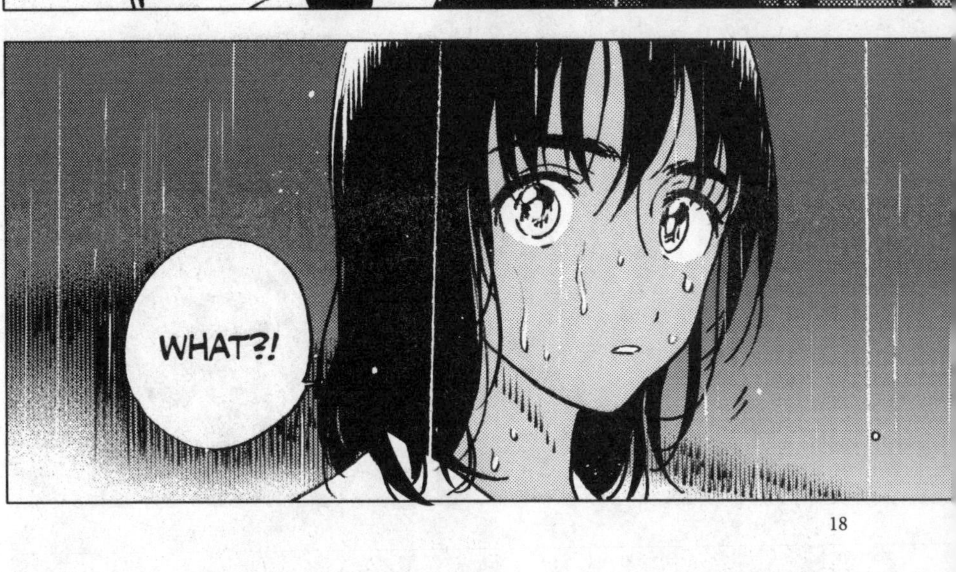
WHAT?!

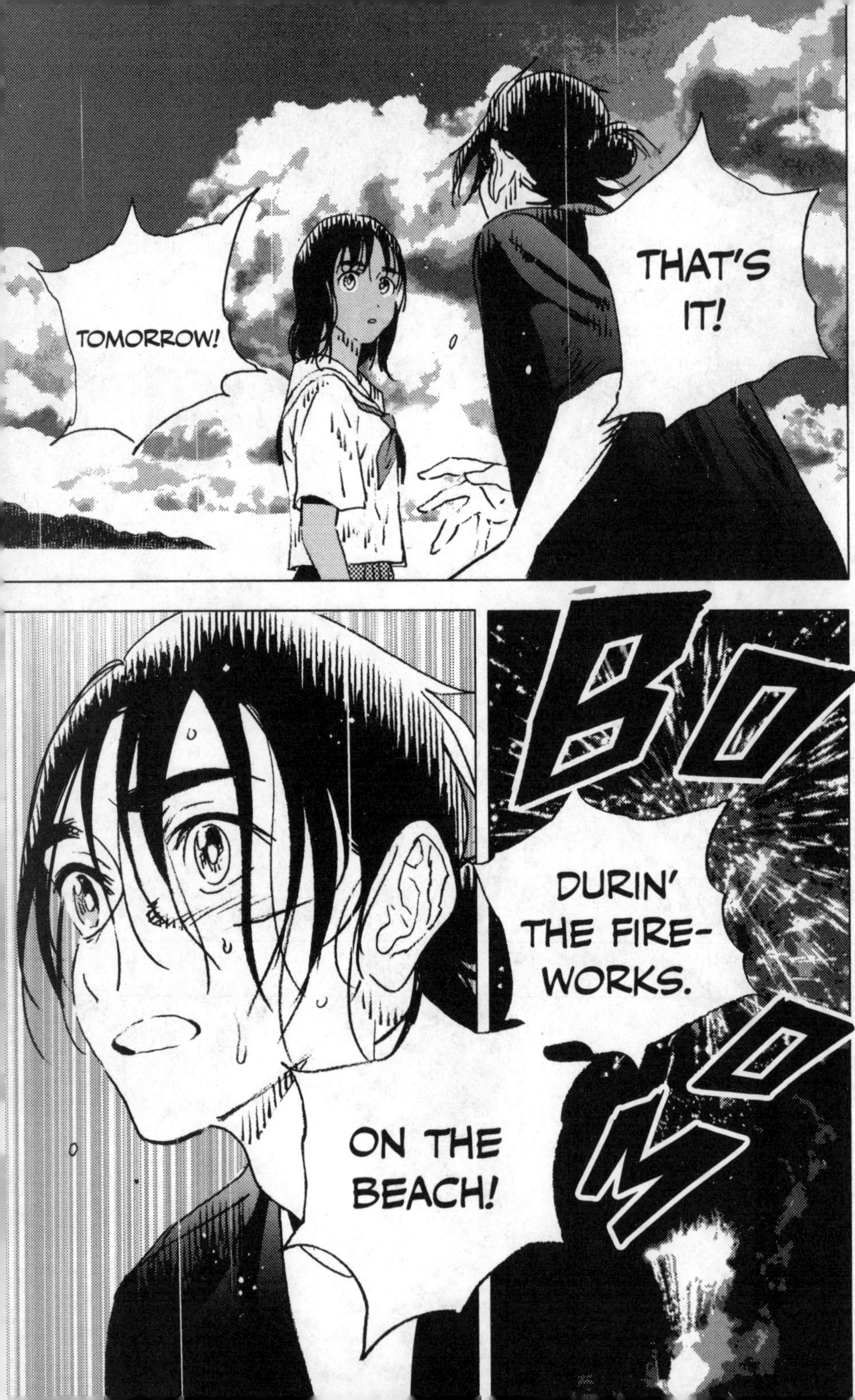
THAT'S IT!
TOMORROW!
BOOM
DURIN' THE FIRE-WORKS.
ON THE BEACH!

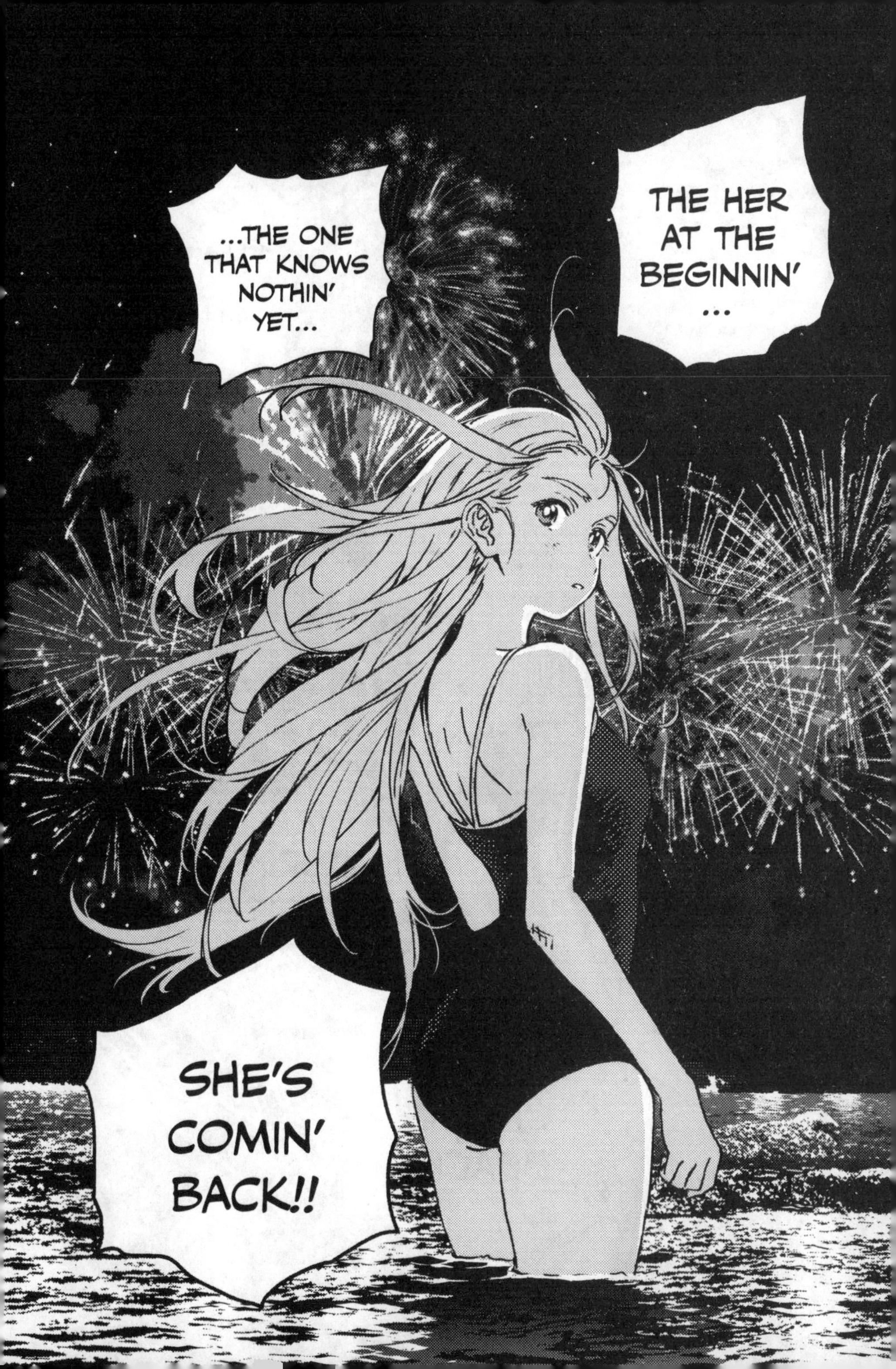
THE HER AT THE BEGINNIN' ...
...THE ONE THAT KNOWS NOTHIN' YET...
SHE'S COMIN' BACK!!

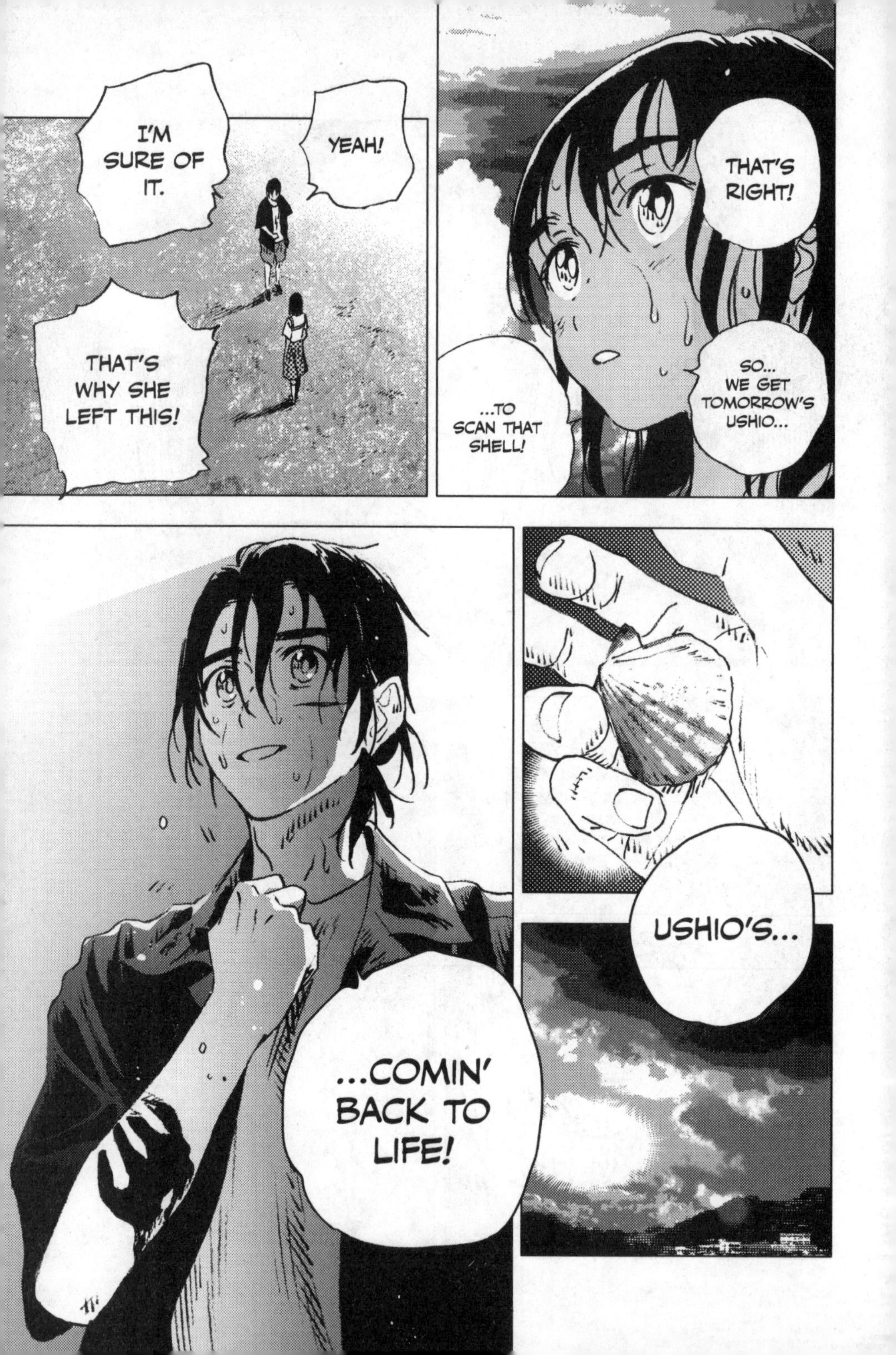
THAT'S RIGHT!
SO... WE GET TOMORROW'S USHIO...
...TO SCAN THAT SHELL!
YEAH!
I'M SURE OF IT.
THAT'S WHY SHE LEFT THIS!
USHIO'S...
...COMIN' BACK TO LIFE!

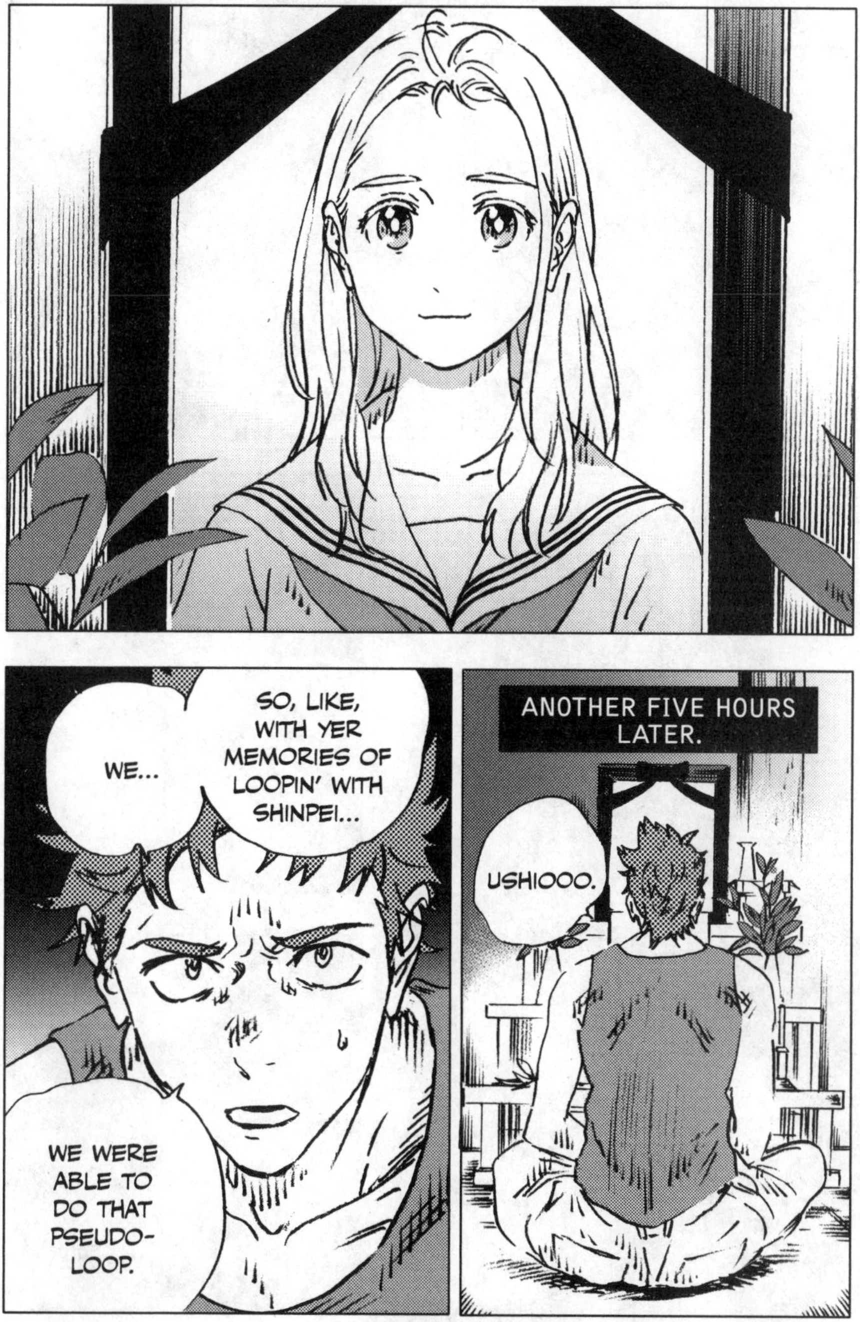
ANOTHER FIVE HOURS LATER.
USHIOOO.
SO, LIKE, WITH YER MEMORIES OF LOOPIN' WITH SHINPEI...
WE...
WE WERE ABLE TO DO THAT PSEUDO-LOOP.

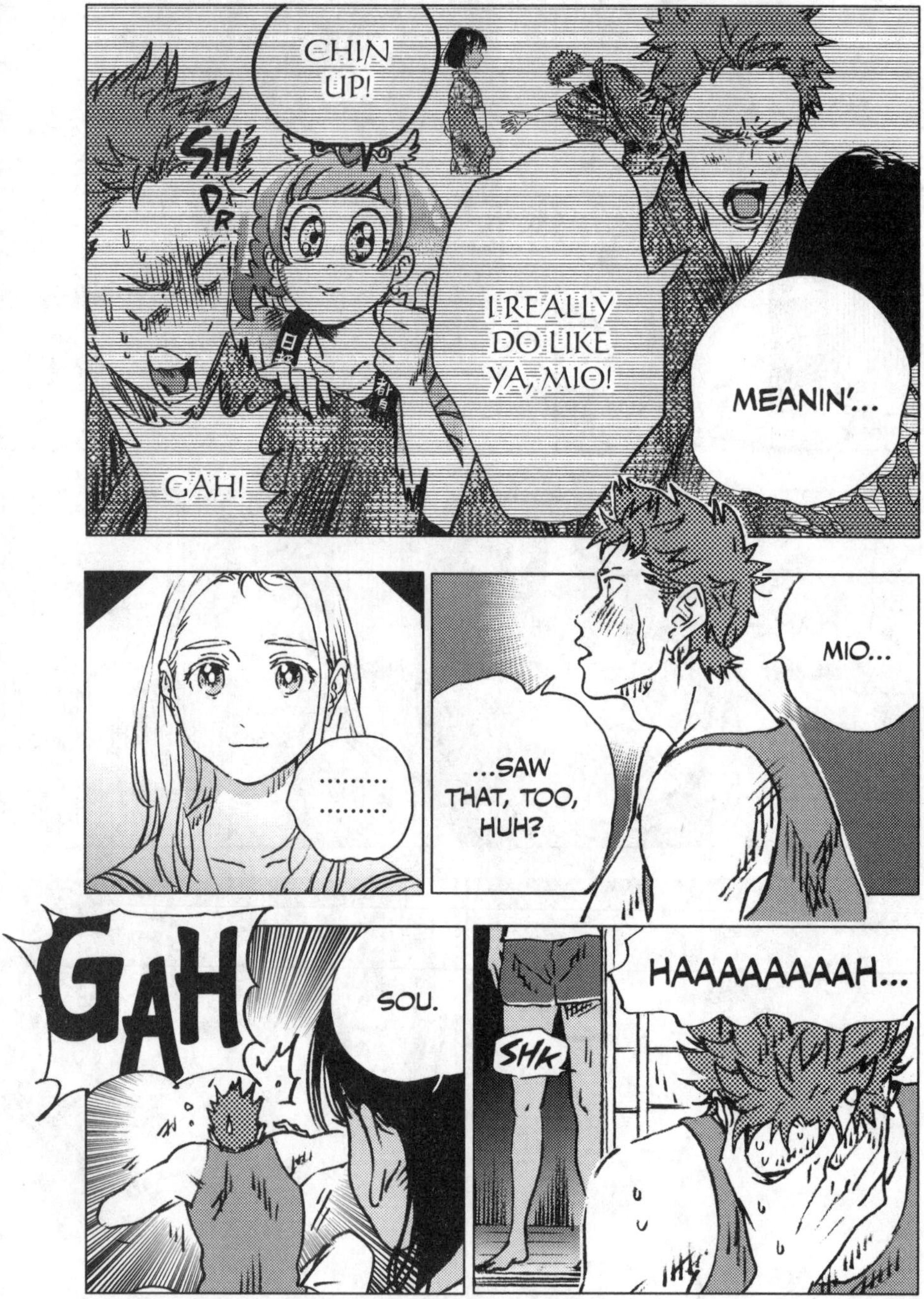
MEANIN'...
I REALLY DO LIKE YA, MIO!
CHIN UP!
SH
DR
GAH!
MIO...
...SAW THAT, TOO, HUH?
....
....
HAAAAAAAAH...
SHK
SOU.
GAH

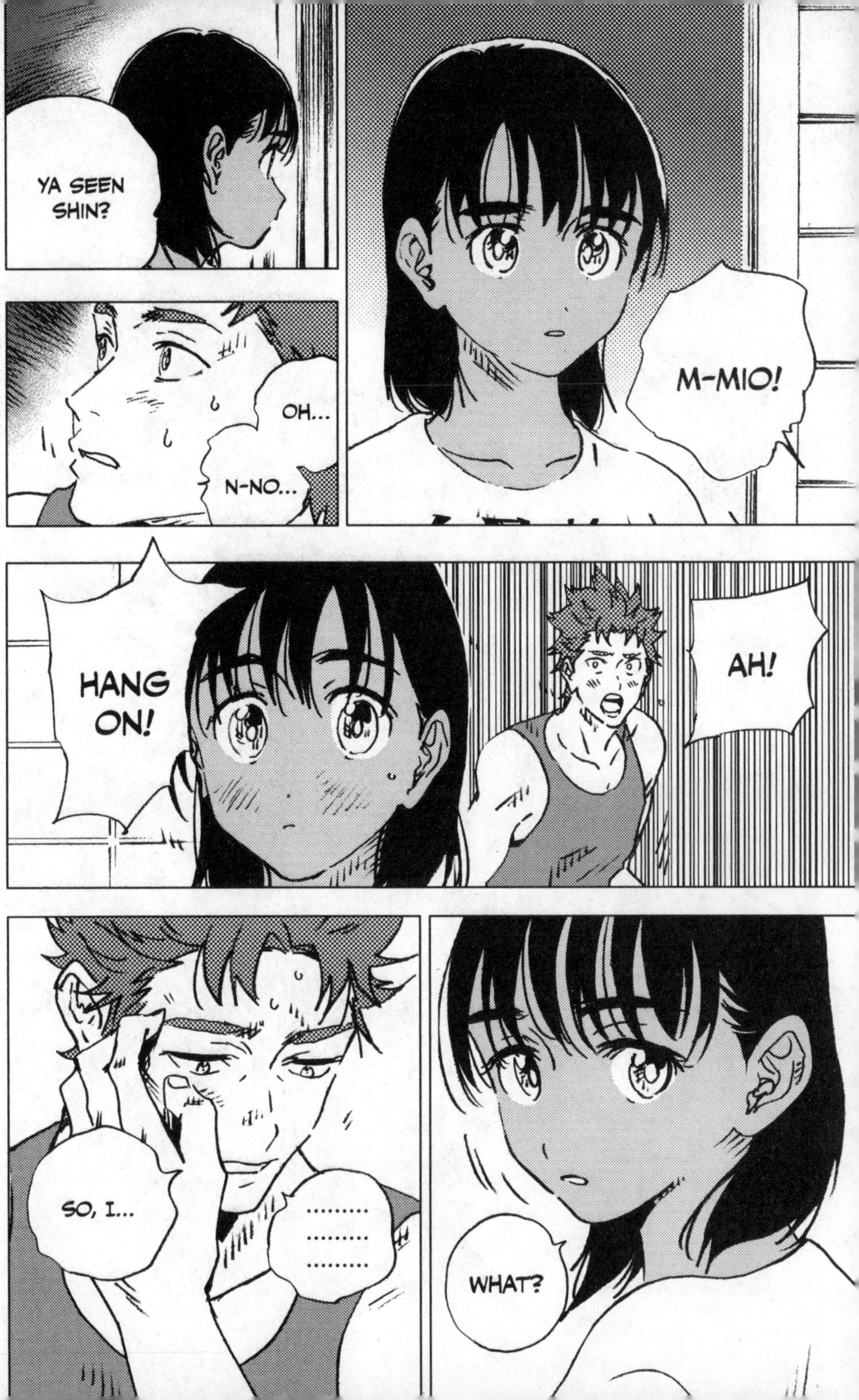
M-MIO!
YA SEEN SHIN?
OH...
N-NO...
AH!
HANG ON!
WHAT?
....
....
....
SO, I...

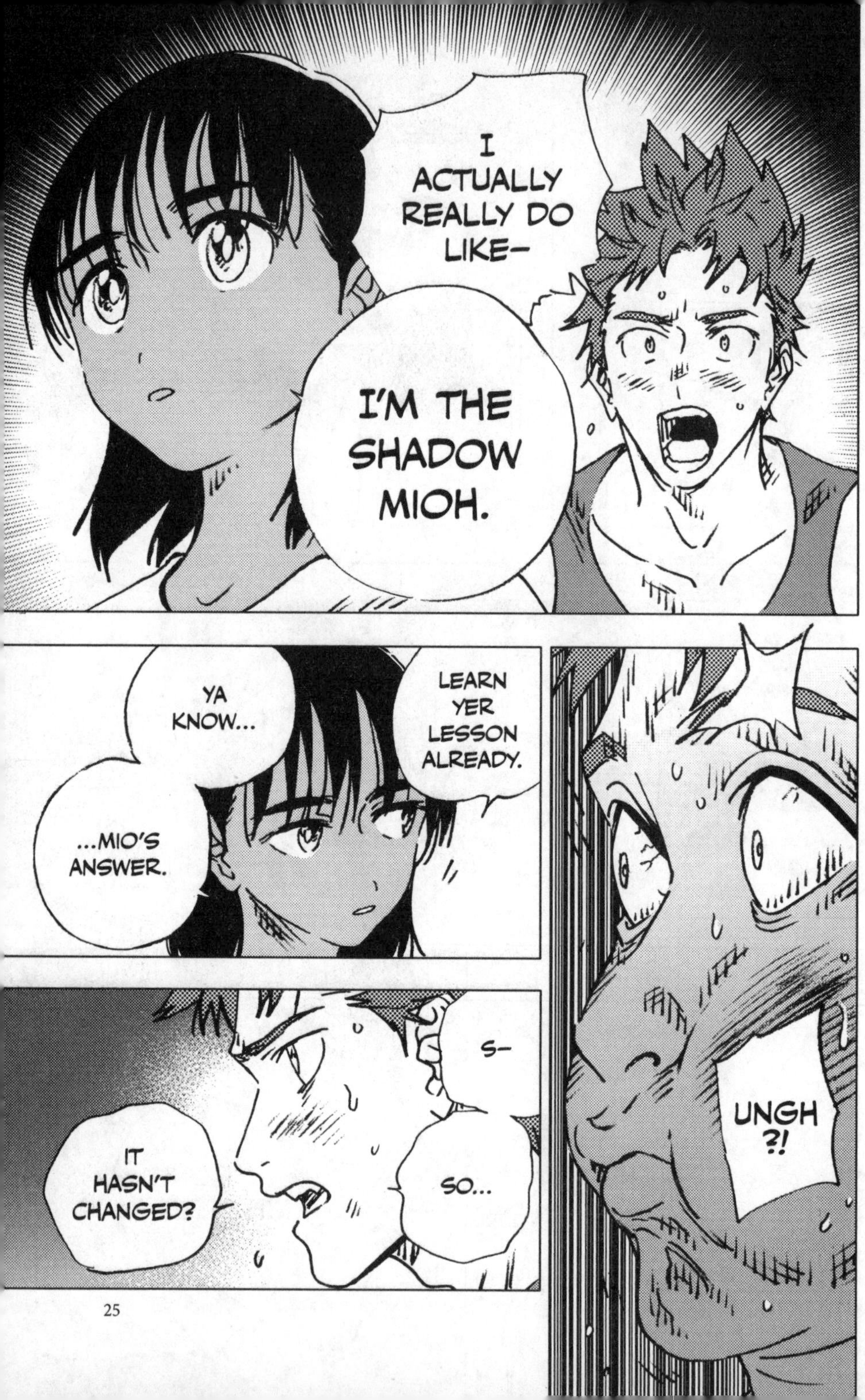
I ACTUALLY REALLY DO LIKE–
I'M THE SHADOW MIOH.
UNGH ?!
LEARN YER LESSON ALREADY.
YA KNOW...
...MIO'S ANSWER.
S–
SO...
IT HASN'T CHANGED?

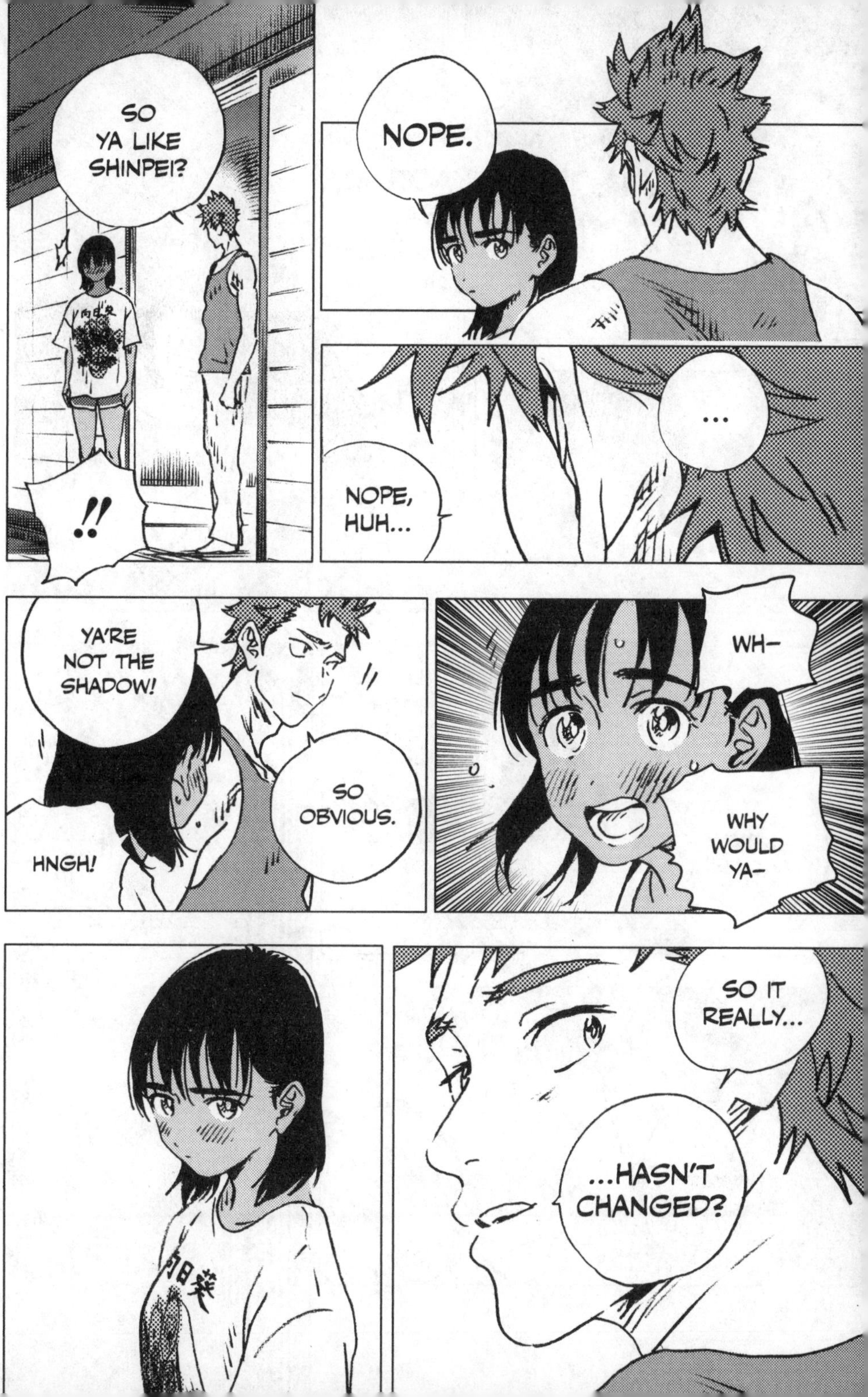
NOPE.
...
NOPE, HUH...
SO YA LIKE SHINPEI?
!!
WH-
WHY WOULD YA-
YA'RE NOT THE SHADOW!
SO OBVIOUS.
HNGH!
SO IT REALLY...
...HASN'T CHANGED?

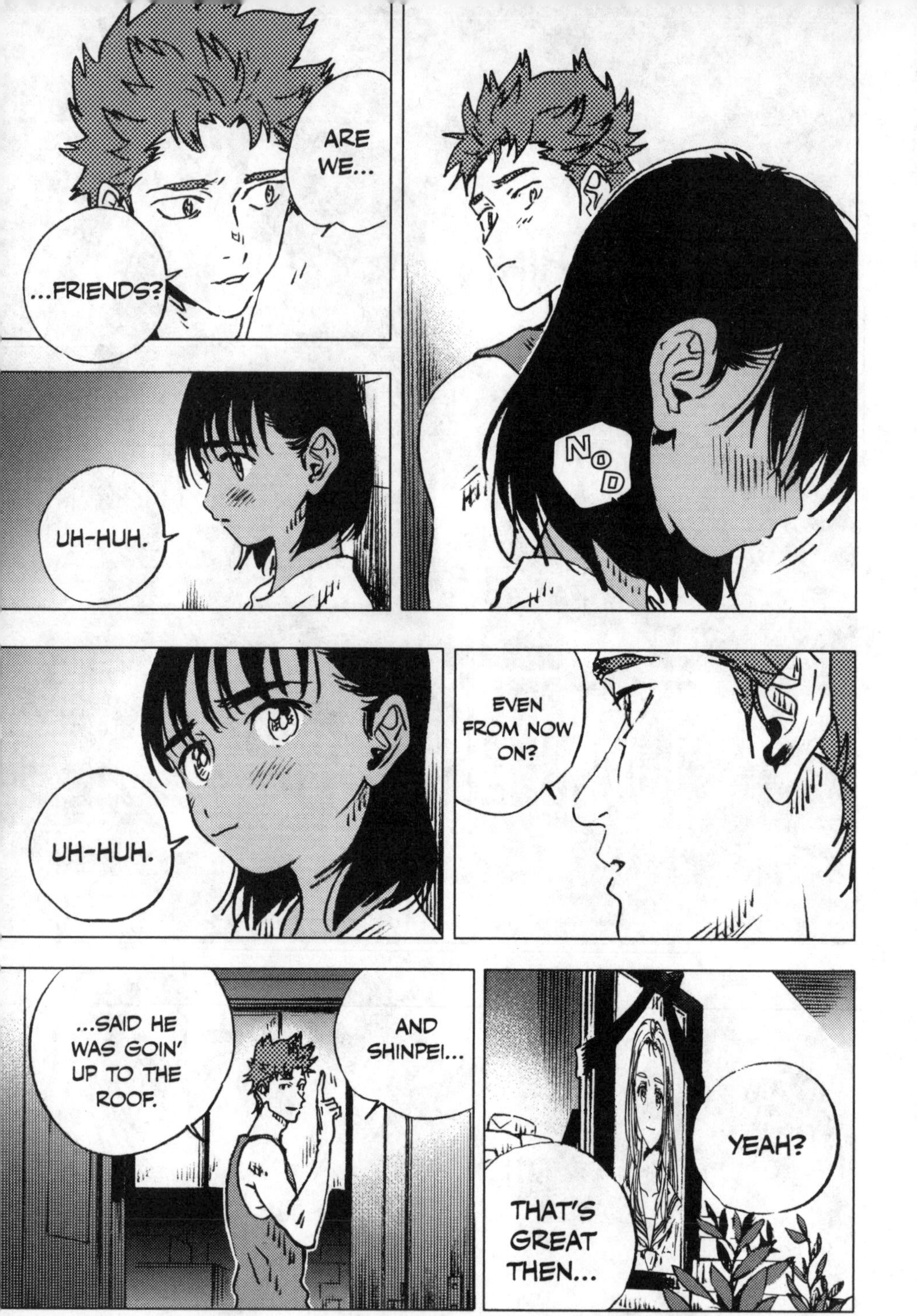

NOD
ARE WE...
...FRIENDS?
UH-HUH.
EVEN FROM NOW ON?
UH-HUH.
YEAH?
THAT'S GREAT THEN...
AND SHINPEI...
...SAID HE WAS GOIN' UP TO THE ROOF.

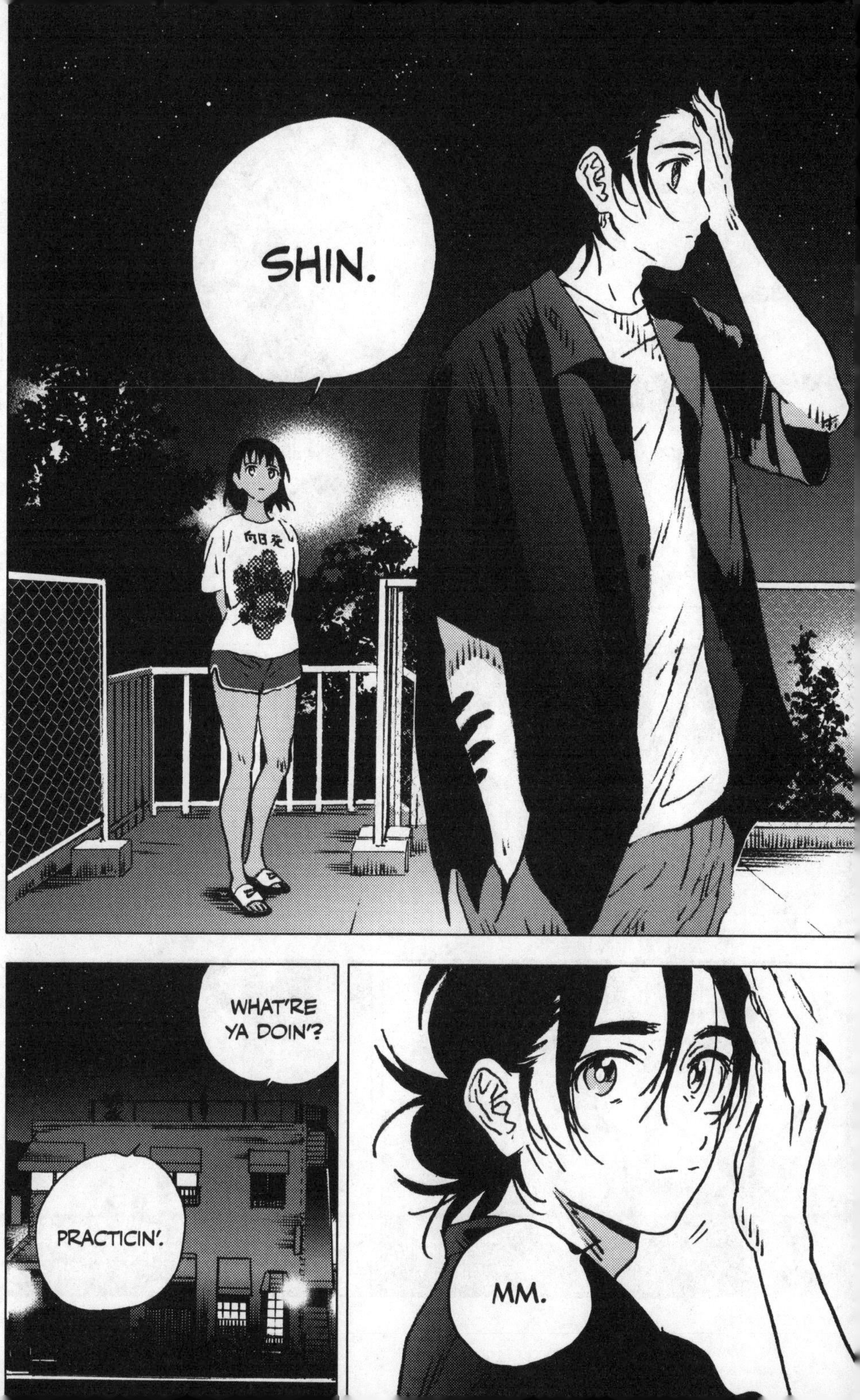
SHIN.
MM.
WHAT'RE YA DOIN'?
PRACTICIN'.

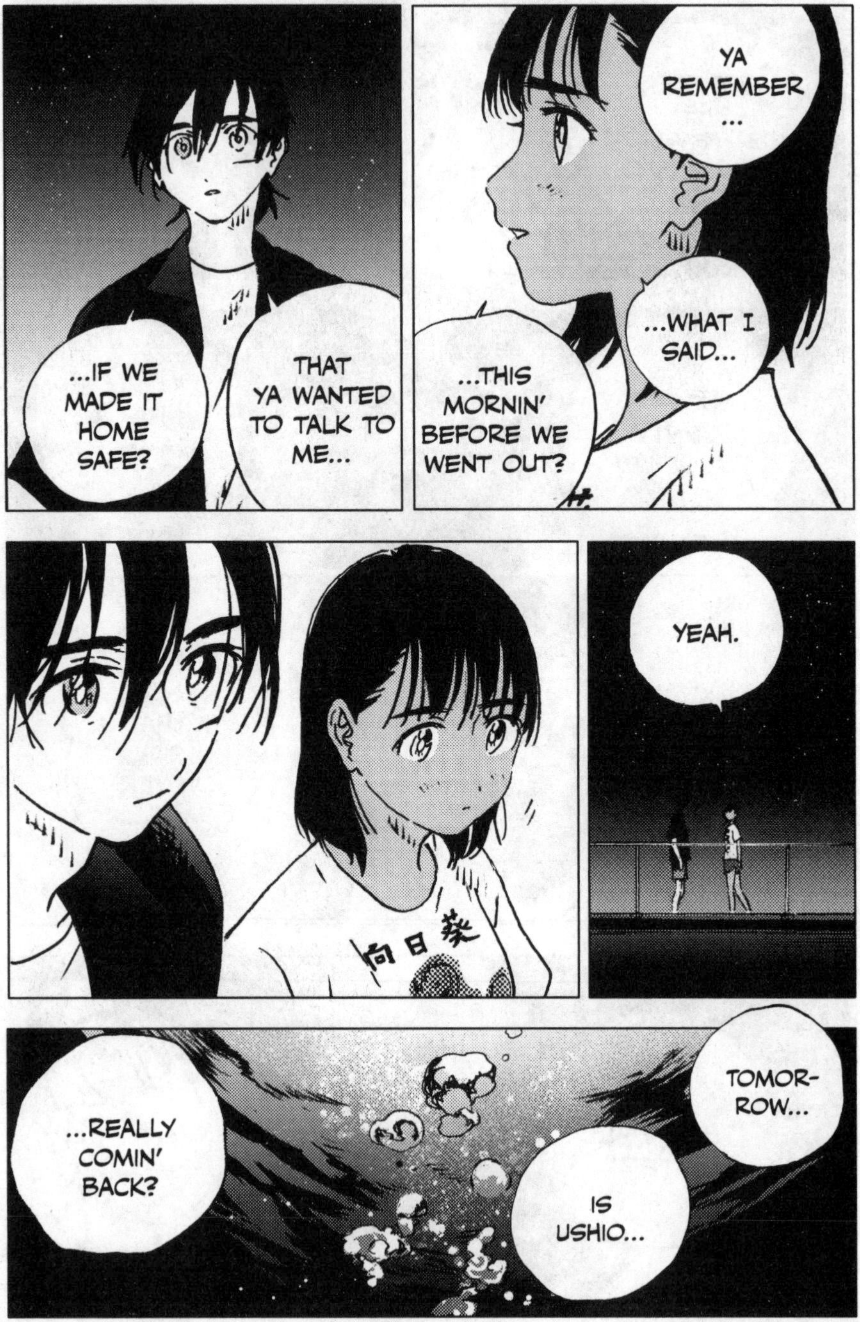
YA REMEMBER ...
...WHAT I SAID...
...THIS MORNIN' BEFORE WE WENT OUT?
THAT YA WANTED TO TALK TO ME...
...IF WE MADE IT HOME SAFE?
YEAH.
向日葵
TOMOR-ROW...
IS USHIO...
...REALLY COMIN' BACK?

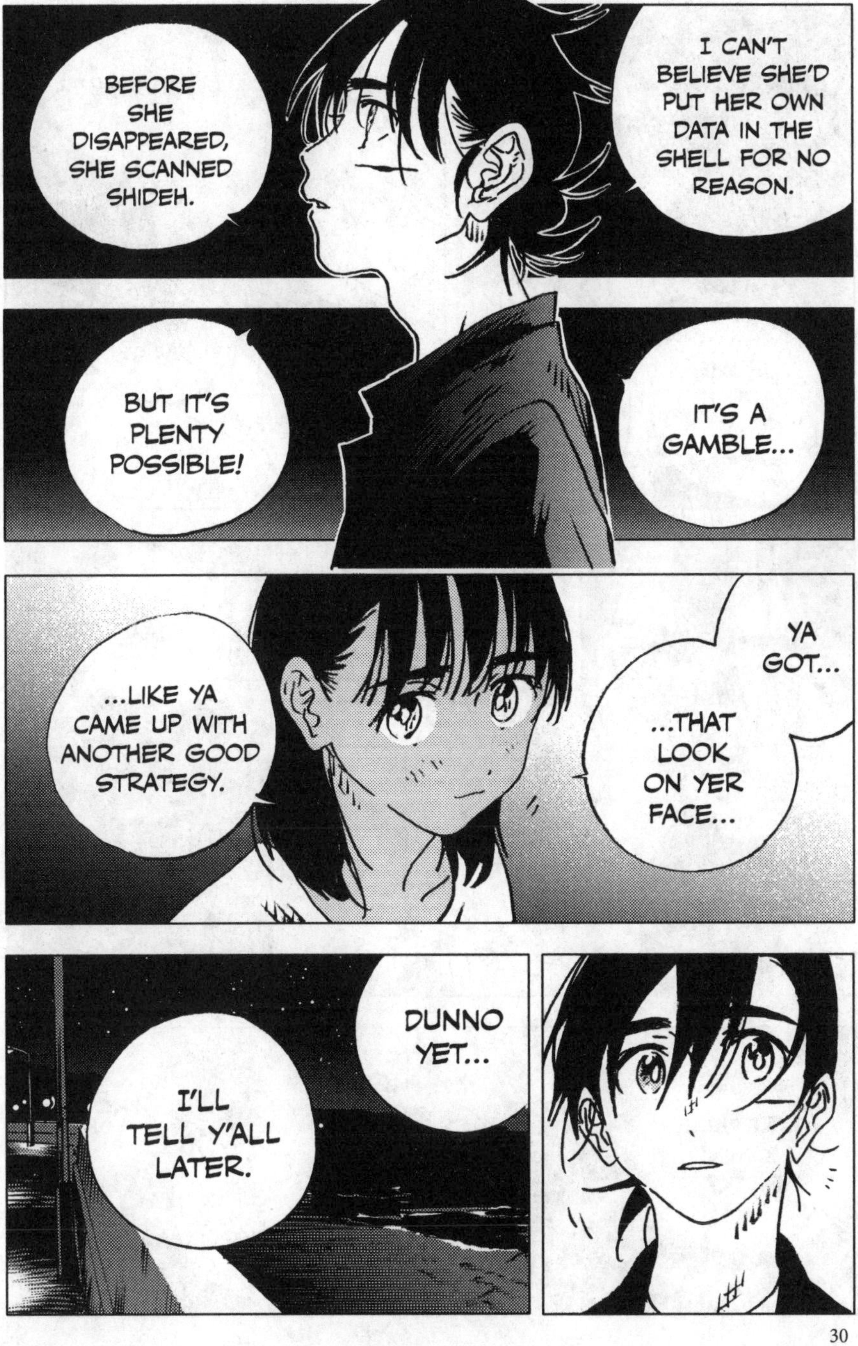
I CAN'T BELIEVE SHE'D PUT HER OWN DATA IN THE SHELL FOR NO REASON.
BEFORE SHE DISAPPEARED, SHE SCANNED SHIDEH.
IT'S A GAMBLE...
BUT IT'S PLENTY POSSIBLE!
YA GOT...
...THAT LOOK ON YER FACE...
...LIKE YA CAME UP WITH ANOTHER GOOD STRATEGY.
DUNNO YET...
I'LL TELL Y'ALL LATER.

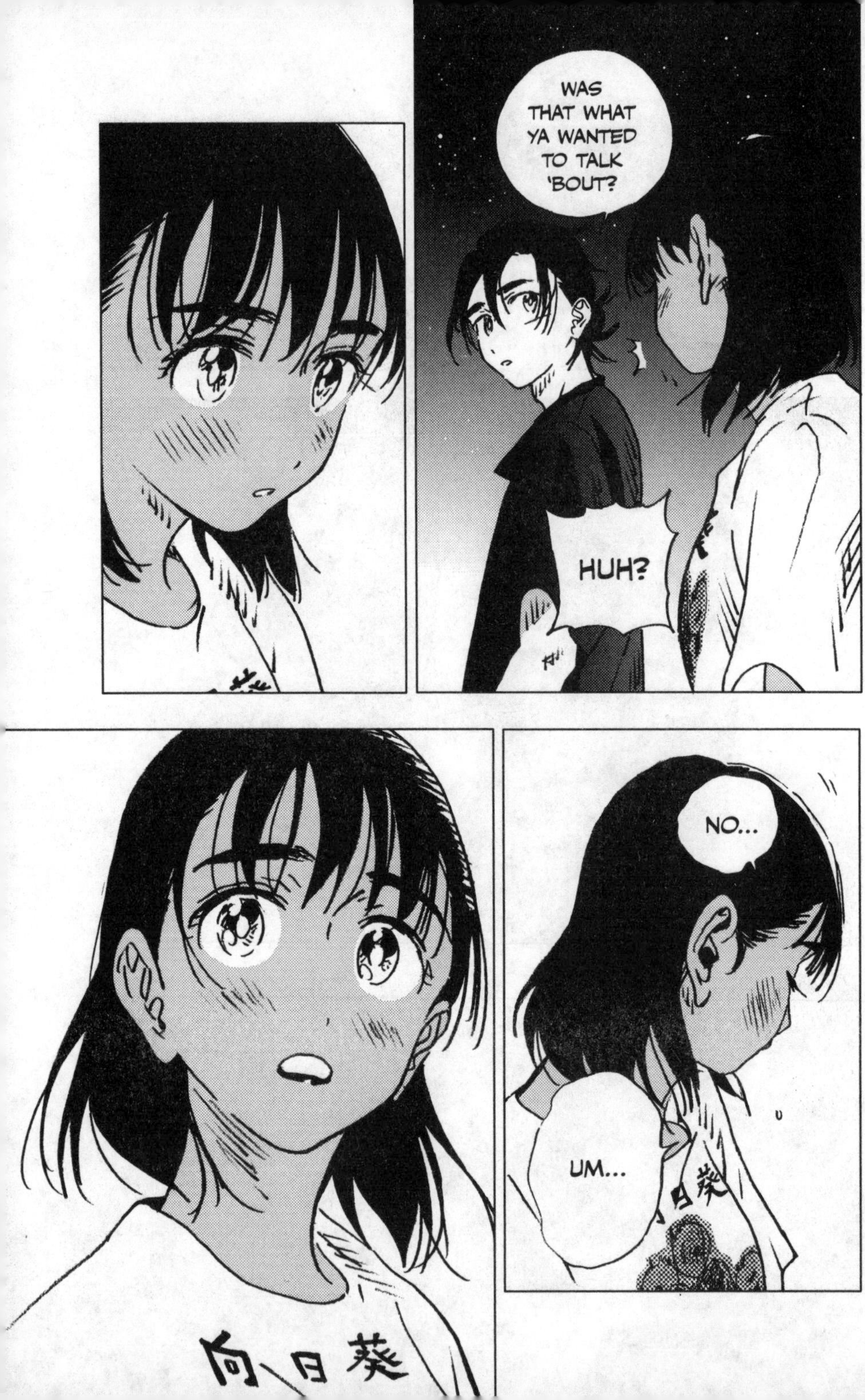
WAS THAT WHAT YA WANTED TO TALK 'BOUT?
HUH?
NO...
UM...
向日葵

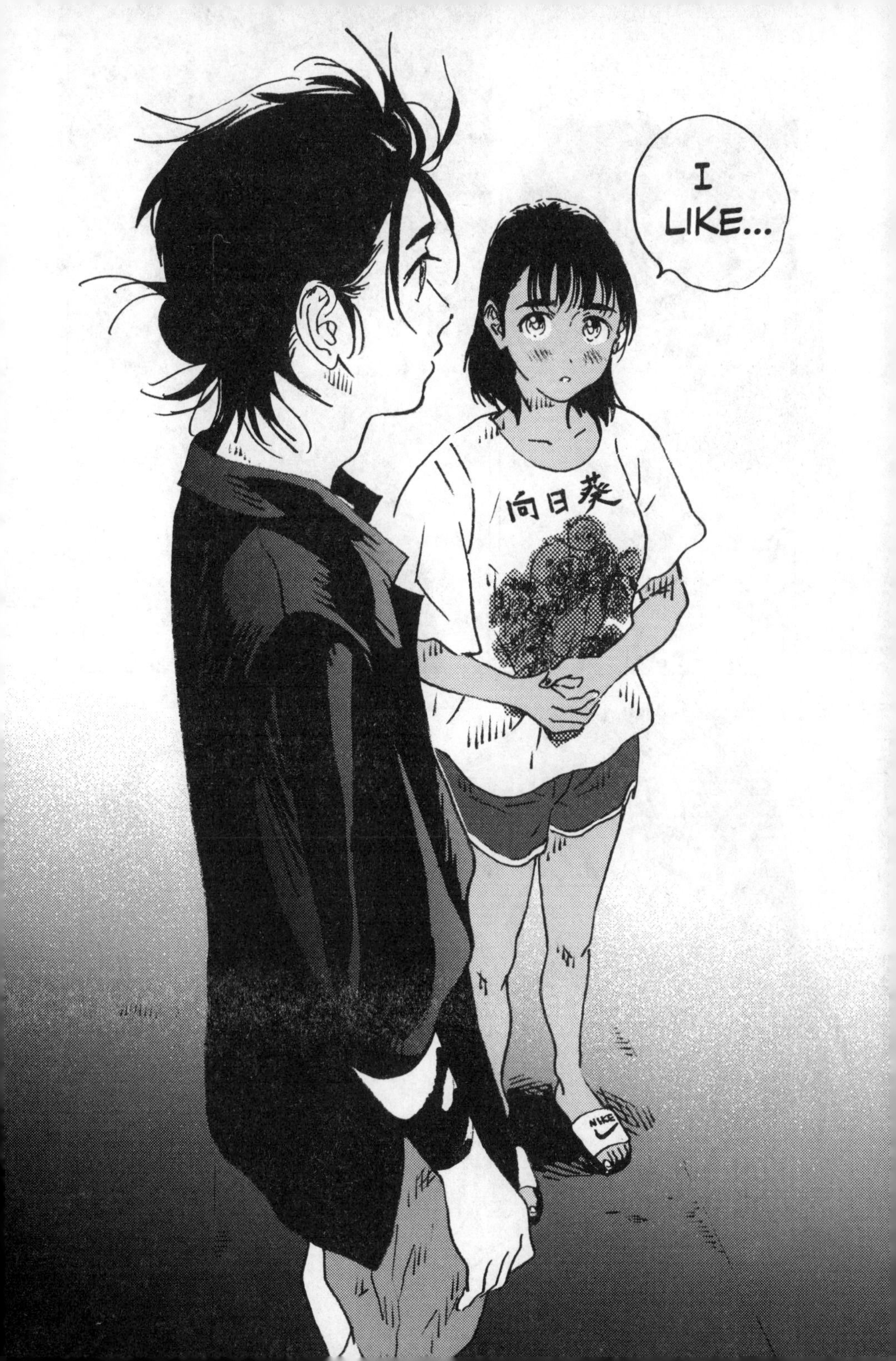
I LIKE...
向日葵
NIKE

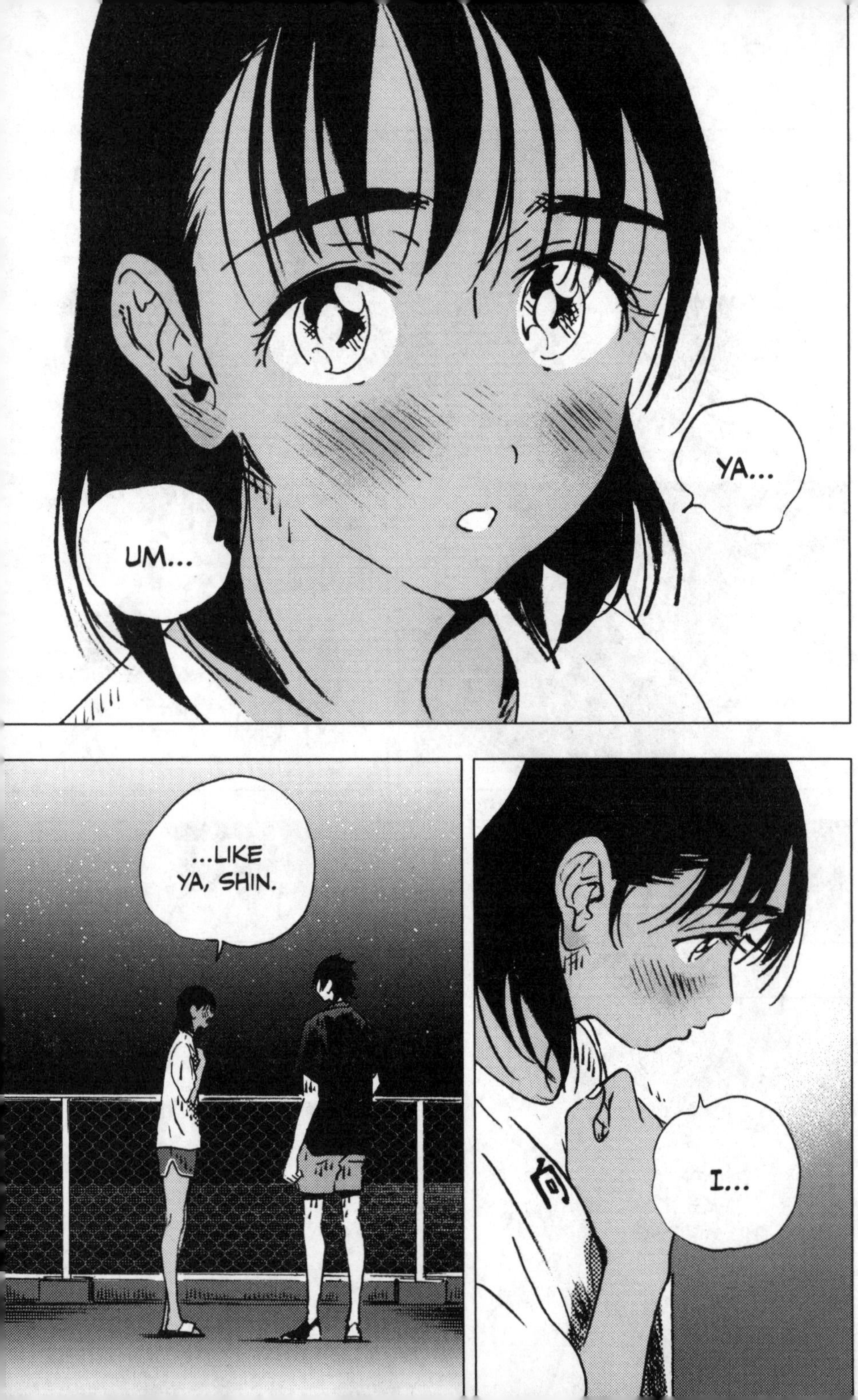
YA...
UM...
I...
...LIKE YA, SHIN.

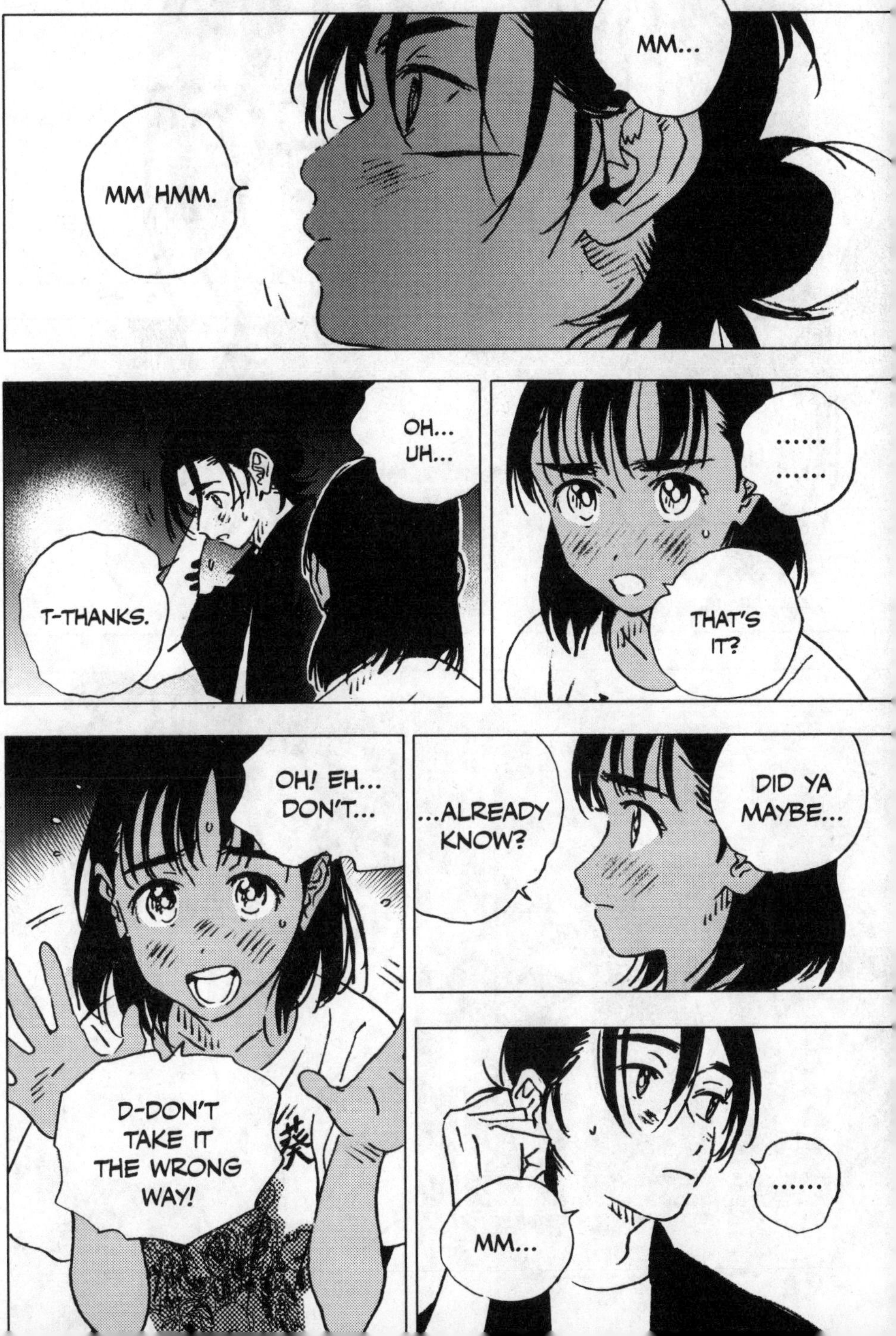
MM...
MM HMM.
......
......
THAT'S IT?
OH... UH...
T-THANKS.
DID YA MAYBE...
...ALREADY KNOW?
......
MM...
OH! EH... DON'T...
D-DON'T TAKE IT THE WRONG WAY!

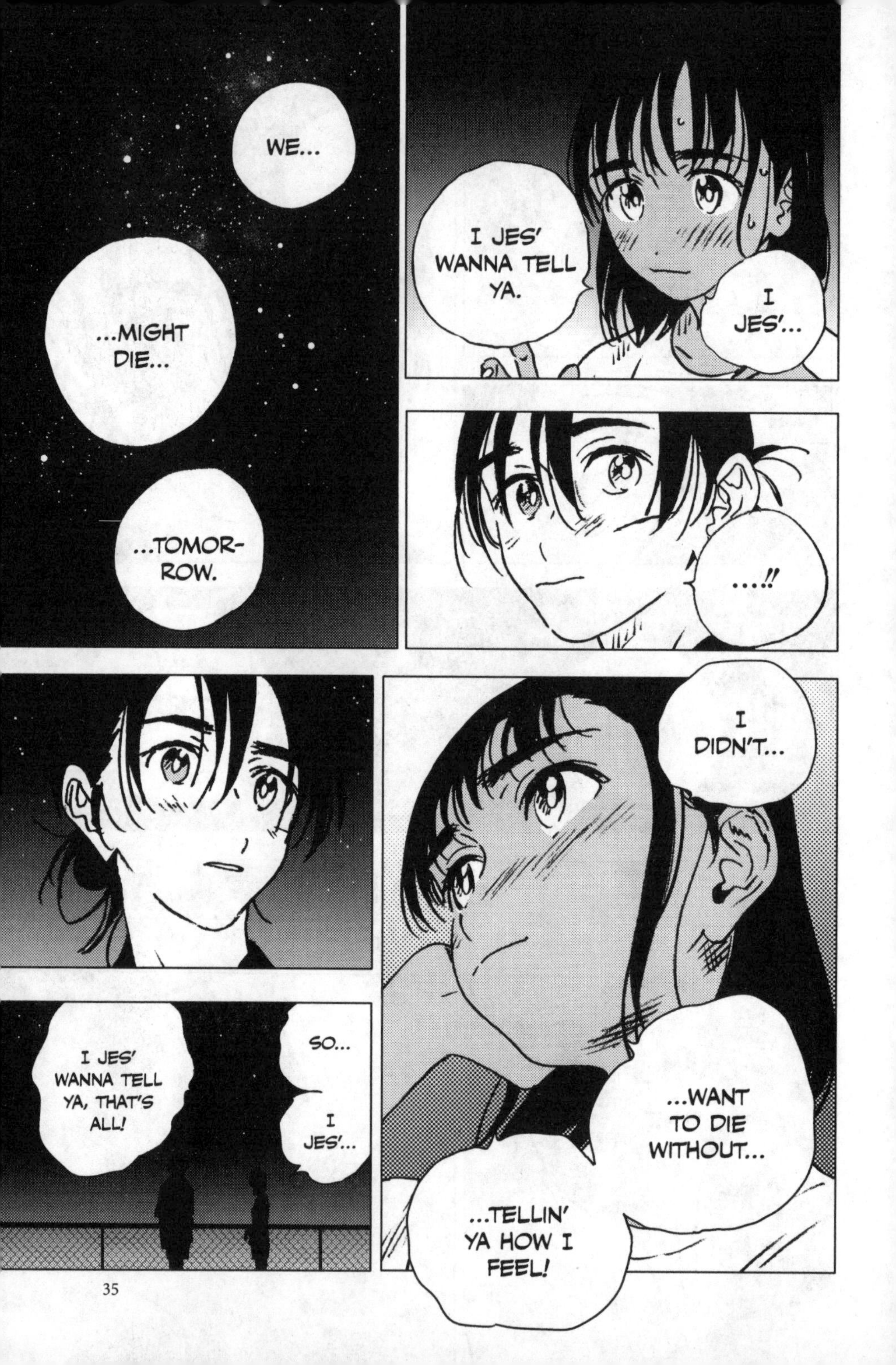
I JES'...
I JES' WANNA TELL YA.
...!!
WE...
...MIGHT DIE...
...TOMORROW.
I DIDN'T...
...WANT TO DIE WITHOUT...
...TELLIN' YA HOW I FEEL!
SO...
I JES'...
I JES' WANNA TELL YA, THAT'S ALL!

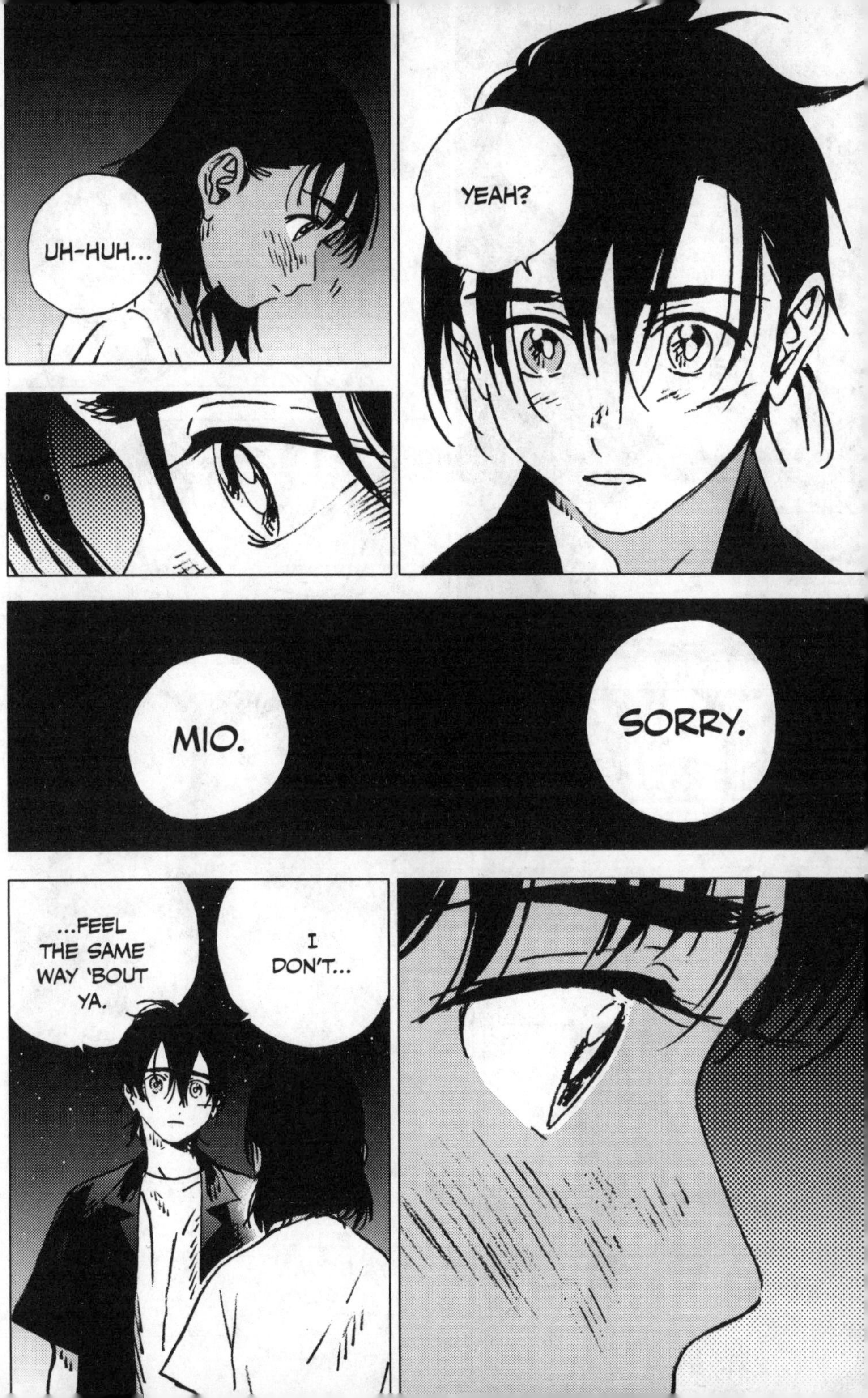
YEAH?
UH-HUH...
SORRY.
MIO.
I DON'T...
...FEEL THE SAME WAY 'BOUT YA.

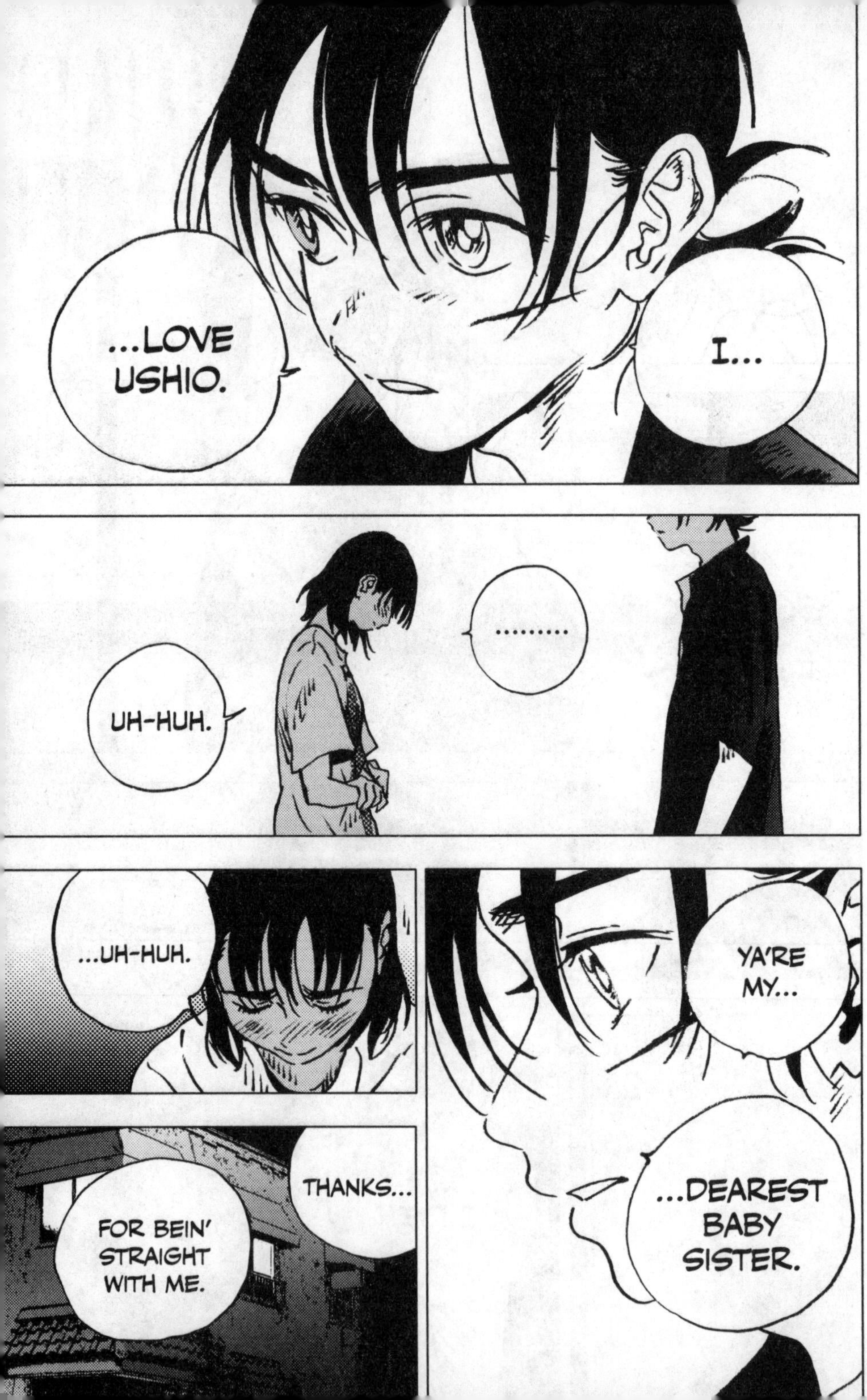
I...
...LOVE USHIO.
....
UH-HUH.
YA'RE MY...
...DEAREST BABY SISTER.
...UH-HUH.
THANKS...
FOR BEIN' STRAIGHT WITH ME.

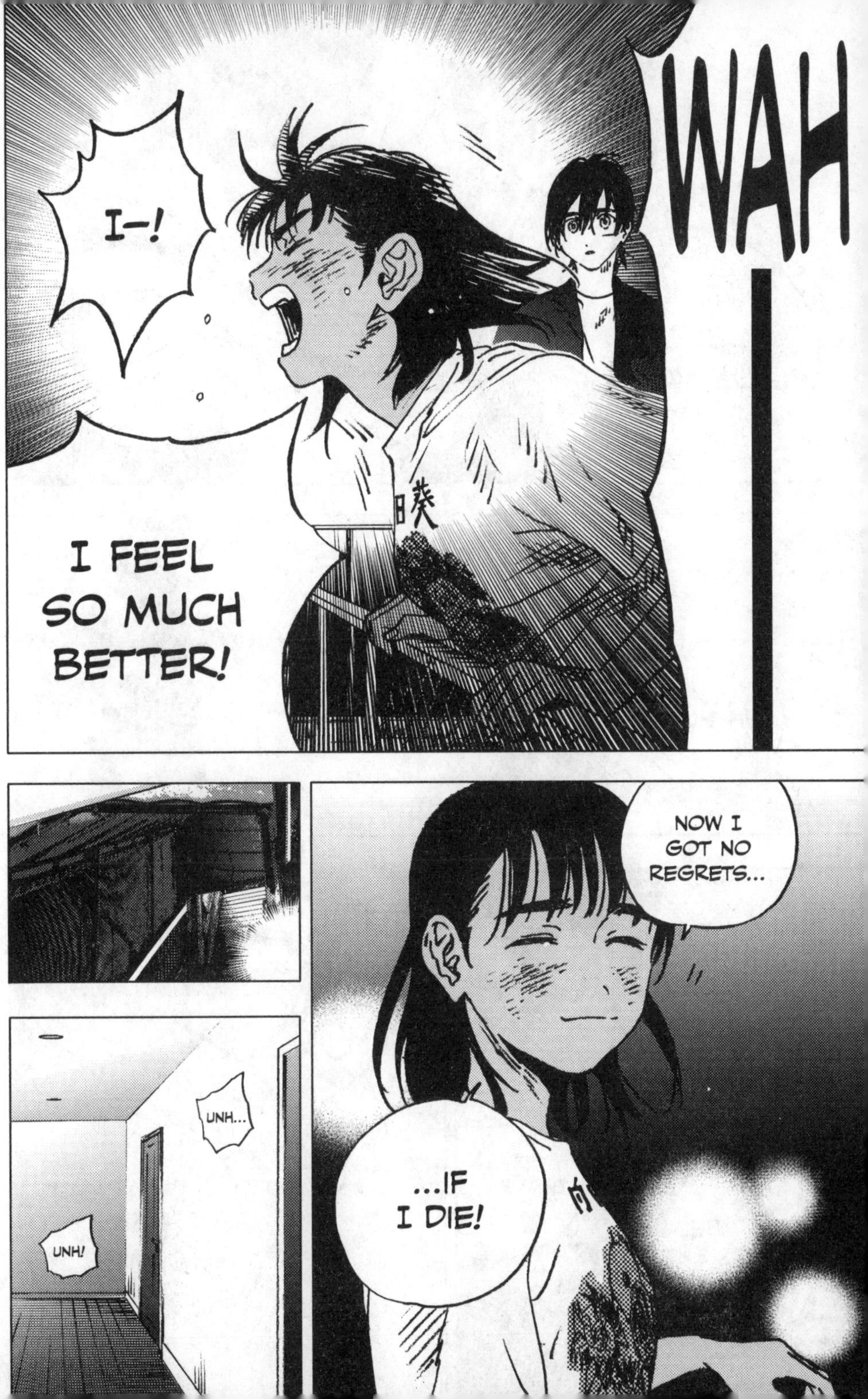
WAH
I—!
I FEEL SO MUCH BETTER!
NOW I GOT NO REGRETS...
...IF I DIE!
UNH...
UNH!

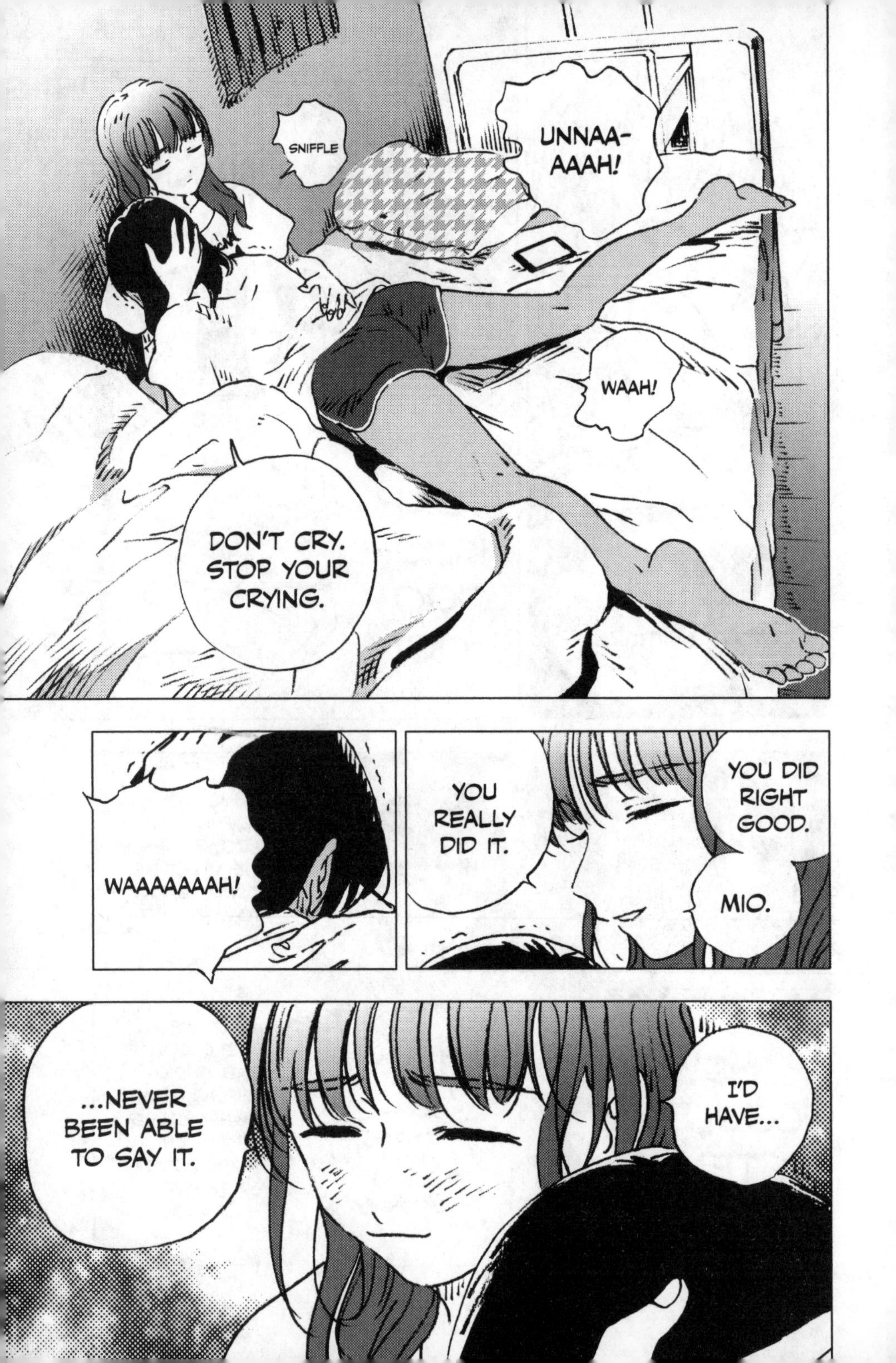
UNNAA-AAAH!
SNIFFLE
WAAH!
DON'T CRY. STOP YOUR CRYING.
YOU DID RIGHT GOOD.
MIO.
YOU REALLY DID IT.
WAAAAAAAH!
I'D HAVE...
...NEVER BEEN ABLE TO SAY IT.

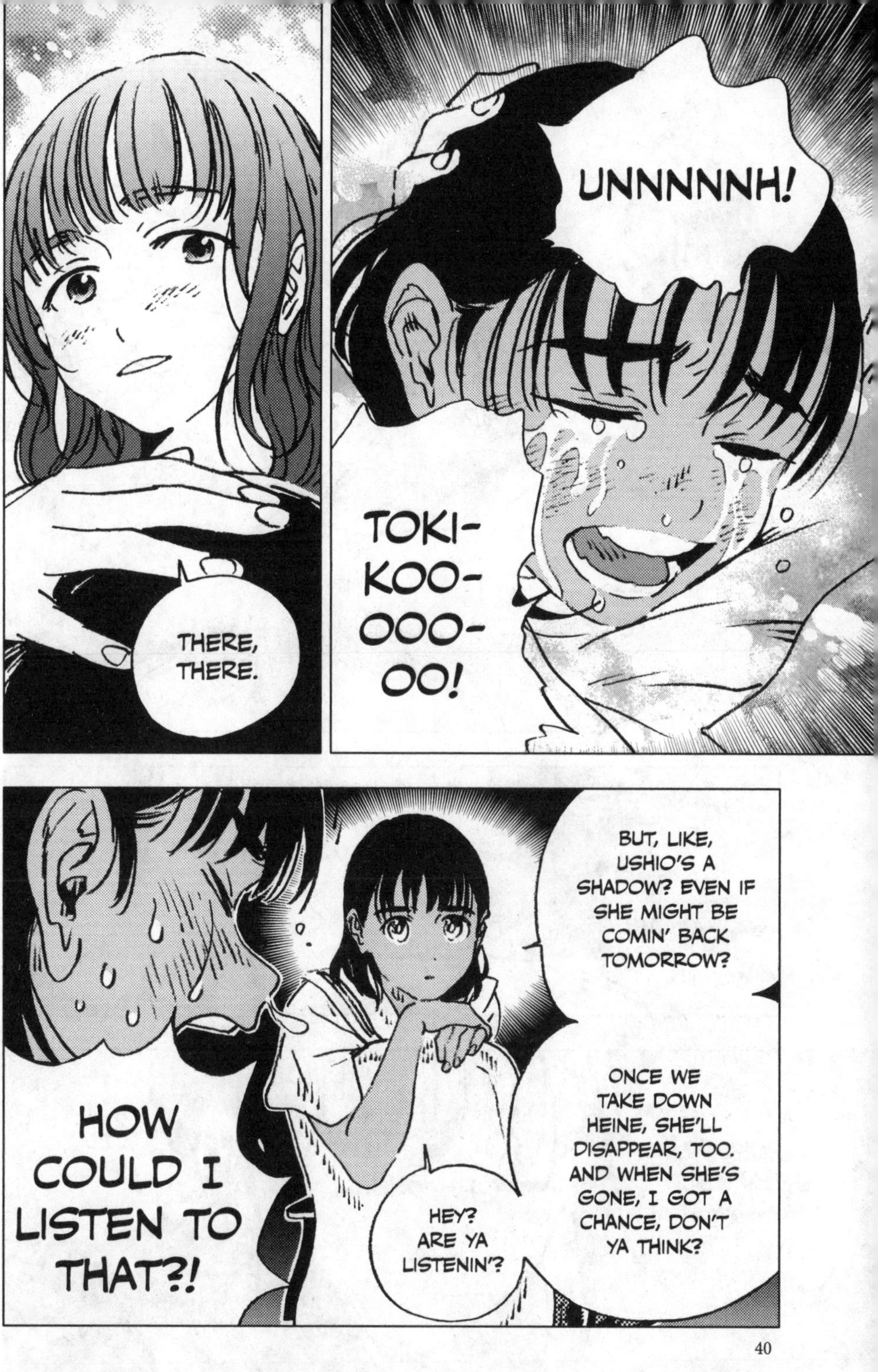
UNNNNNH!
TOKI-KOO-OOO-OO!
THERE, THERE.
BUT, LIKE, USHIO'S A SHADOW? EVEN IF SHE MIGHT BE COMIN' BACK TOMORROW?
ONCE WE TAKE DOWN HEINE, SHE'LL DISAPPEAR, TOO. AND WHEN SHE'S GONE, I GOT A CHANCE, DON'T YA THINK?
HEY? ARE YA LISTENIN'?
HOW COULD I LISTEN TO THAT?!

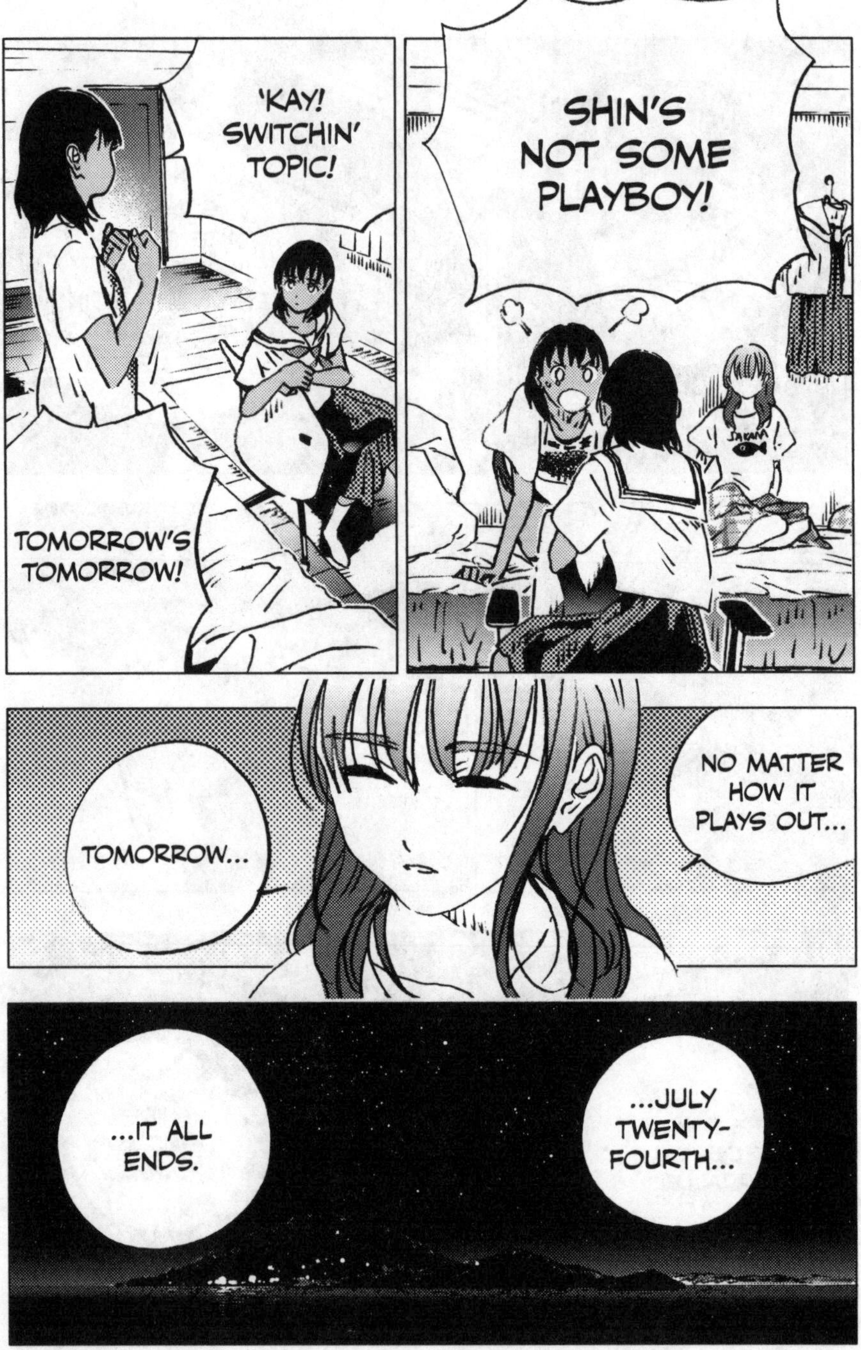
SHIN'S NOT SOME PLAYBOY!
'KAY! SWITCHIN' TOPIC!
TOMORROW'S TOMORROW!
NO MATTER HOW IT PLAYS OUT...
TOMORROW...
...JULY TWENTY-FOURTH...
...IT ALL ENDS.

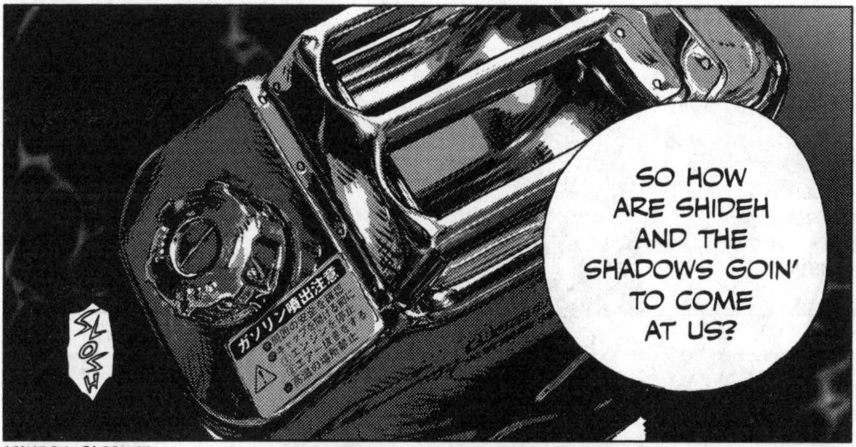
SO HOW ARE SHIDEH AND THE SHADOWS GOIN' TO COME AT US?
SLOSH
ガソリン噴出注意

*CAUTION: GASOLINE

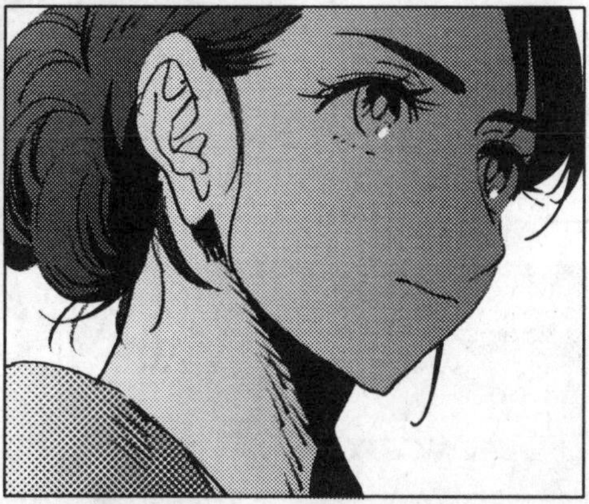

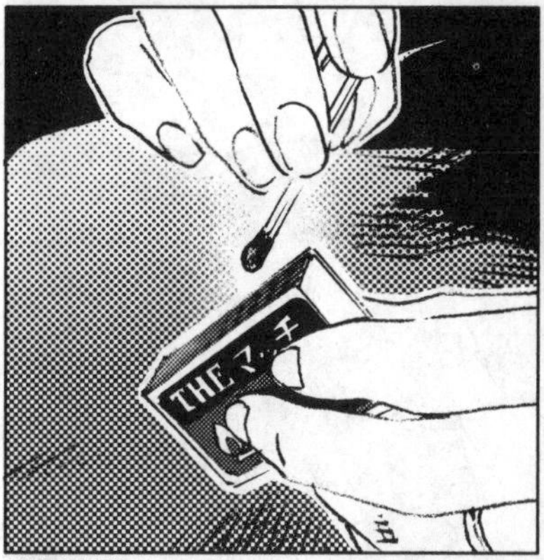
THE

**THE* MATCH

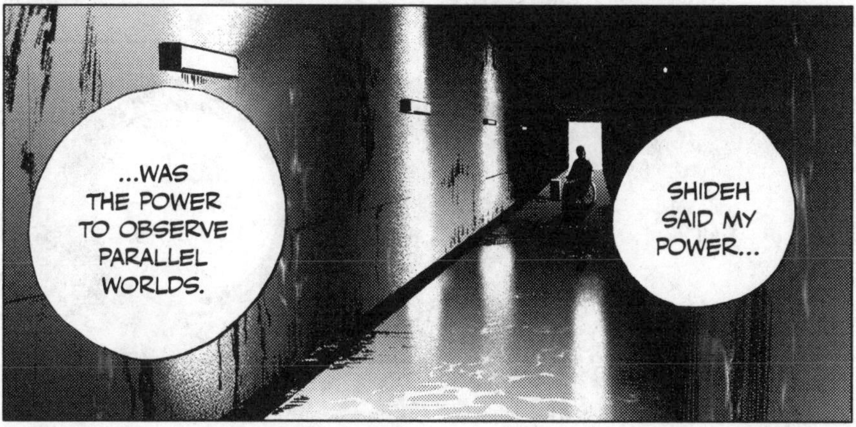
SHIDEH SAID MY POWER...
...WAS THE POWER TO OBSERVE PARALLEL WORLDS.

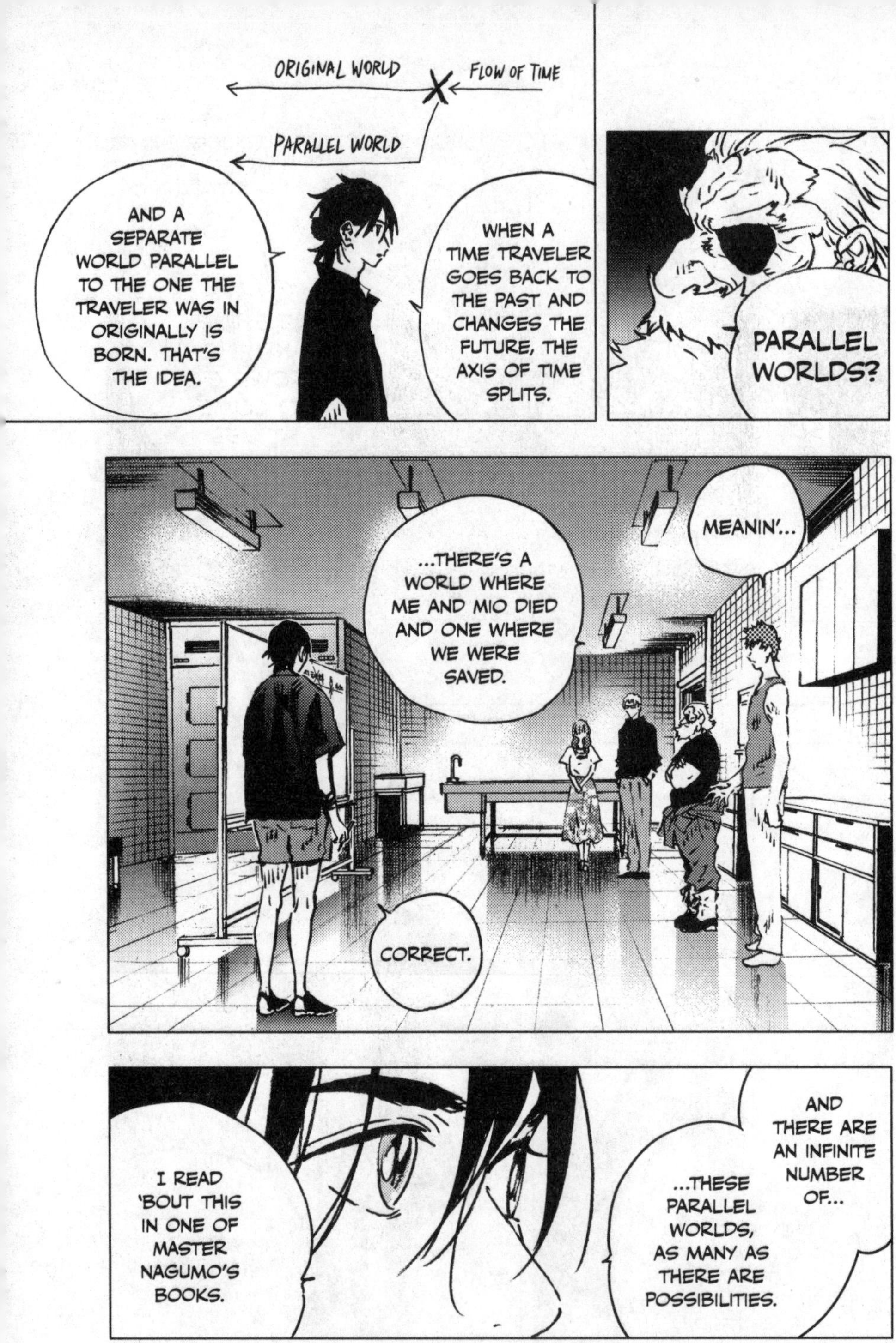
PARALLEL WORLDS?
FLOW OF TIME
ORIGINAL WORLD
PARALLEL WORLD
WHEN A TIME TRAVELER GOES BACK TO THE PAST AND CHANGES THE FUTURE, THE AXIS OF TIME SPLITS.
AND A SEPARATE WORLD PARALLEL TO THE ONE THE TRAVELER WAS IN ORIGINALLY IS BORN. THAT'S THE IDEA.
MEANIN'...
...THERE'S A WORLD WHERE ME AND MIO DIED AND ONE WHERE WE WERE SAVED.
CORRECT.
AND THERE ARE AN INFINITE NUMBER OF...
...THESE PARALLEL WORLDS, AS MANY AS THERE ARE POSSIBILITIES.
I READ 'BOUT THIS IN ONE OF MASTER NAGUMO'S BOOKS.

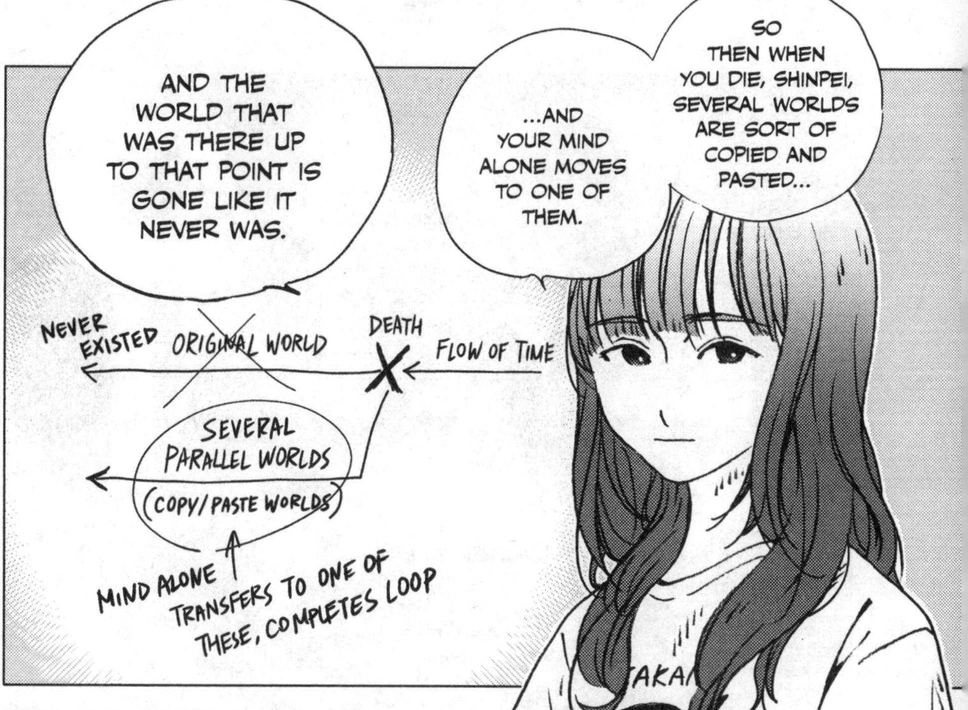
SO THEN WHEN YOU DIE, SHINPEI, SEVERAL WORLDS ARE SORT OF COPIED AND PASTED...
...AND YOUR MIND ALONE MOVES TO ONE OF THEM.
AND THE WORLD THAT WAS THERE UP TO THAT POINT IS GONE LIKE IT NEVER WAS.
NEVER EXISTED
ORIGINAL WORLD
DEATH
FLOW OF TIME
SEVERAL PARALLEL WORLDS (COPY/PASTE WORLDS)
MIND ALONE TRANSFERS TO ONE OF THESE, COMPLETES LOOP

*BOARD = 24TH - O-USHIOH

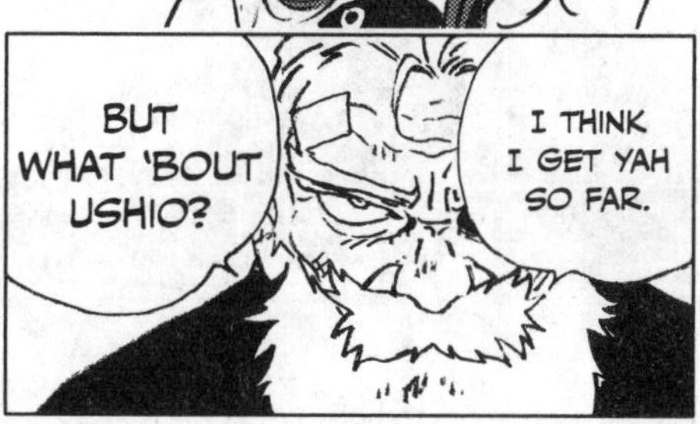
I THINK I GET YAH SO FAR.
BUT WHAT 'BOUT USHIO?

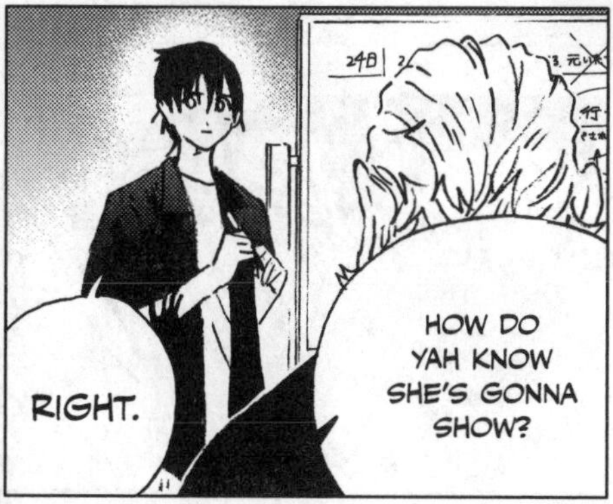
HOW DO YAH KNOW SHE'S GONNA SHOW?
RIGHT.

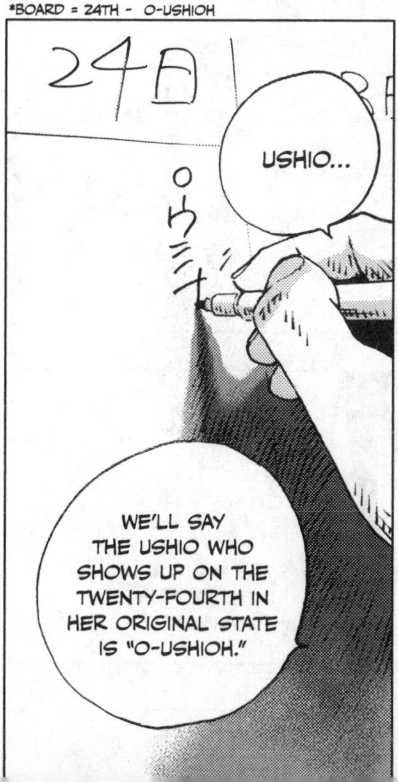
USHIO...
WE'LL SAY THE USHIO WHO SHOWS UP ON THE TWENTY-FOURTH IN HER ORIGINAL STATE IS "O-USHIOH."

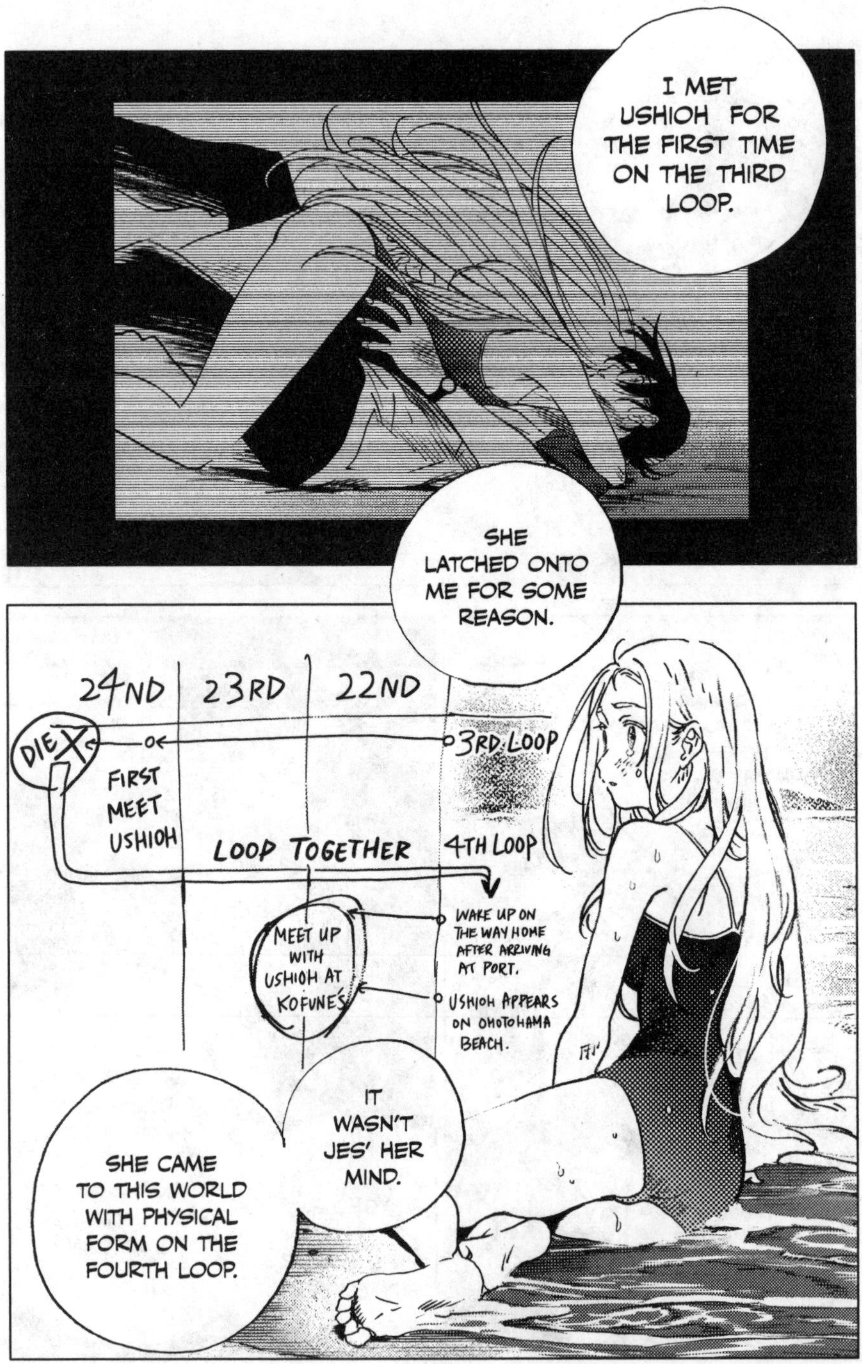
I MET USHIOH FOR THE FIRST TIME ON THE THIRD LOOP.
SHE LATCHED ONTO ME FOR SOME REASON.
24ND
23RD
22ND
DIE X
FIRST MEET USHIOH
3RD LOOP
LOOP TOGETHER
4TH LOOP
MEET UP WITH USHIOH AT KOFUNE'S
WAKE UP ON THE WAY HOME AFTER ARRIVING AT PORT.
USHIOH APPEARS ON OHOTOHAMA BEACH.
IT WASN'T JES' HER MIND.
SHE CAME TO THIS WORLD WITH PHYSICAL FORM ON THE FOURTH LOOP.

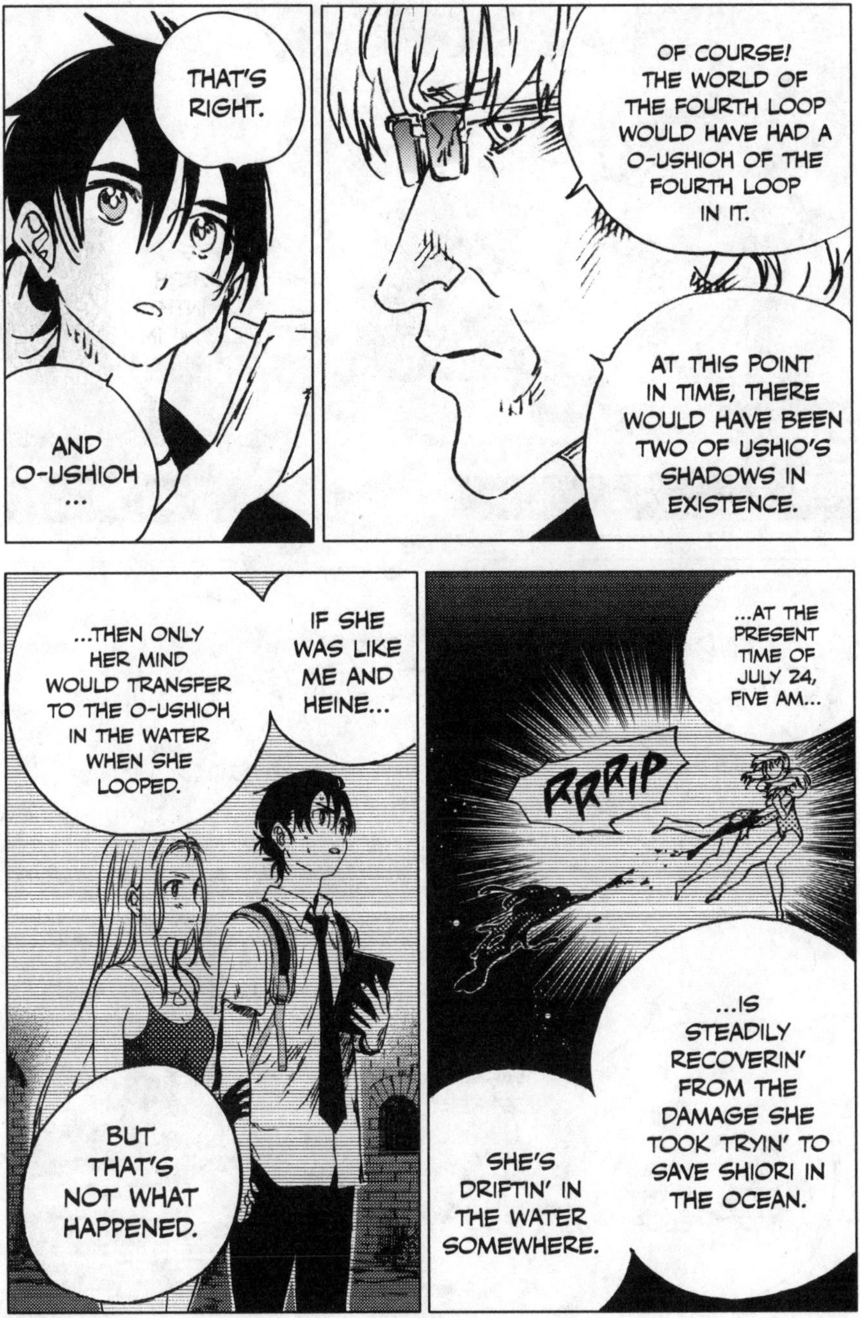
OF COURSE! THE WORLD OF THE FOURTH LOOP WOULD HAVE HAD A O-USHIOH OF THE FOURTH LOOP IN IT.
AT THIS POINT IN TIME, THERE WOULD HAVE BEEN TWO OF USHIO'S SHADOWS IN EXISTENCE.
THAT'S RIGHT.
AND O-USHIOH ...
...AT THE PRESENT TIME OF JULY 24, FIVE AM...
RRRIP
...IS STEADILY RECOVERIN' FROM THE DAMAGE SHE TOOK TRYIN' TO SAVE SHIORI IN THE OCEAN.
SHE'S DRIFTIN' IN THE WATER SOMEWHERE.
IF SHE WAS LIKE ME AND HEINE...
...THEN ONLY HER MIND WOULD TRANSFER TO THE O-USHIOH IN THE WATER WHEN SHE LOOPED.
BUT THAT'S NOT WHAT HAPPENED.

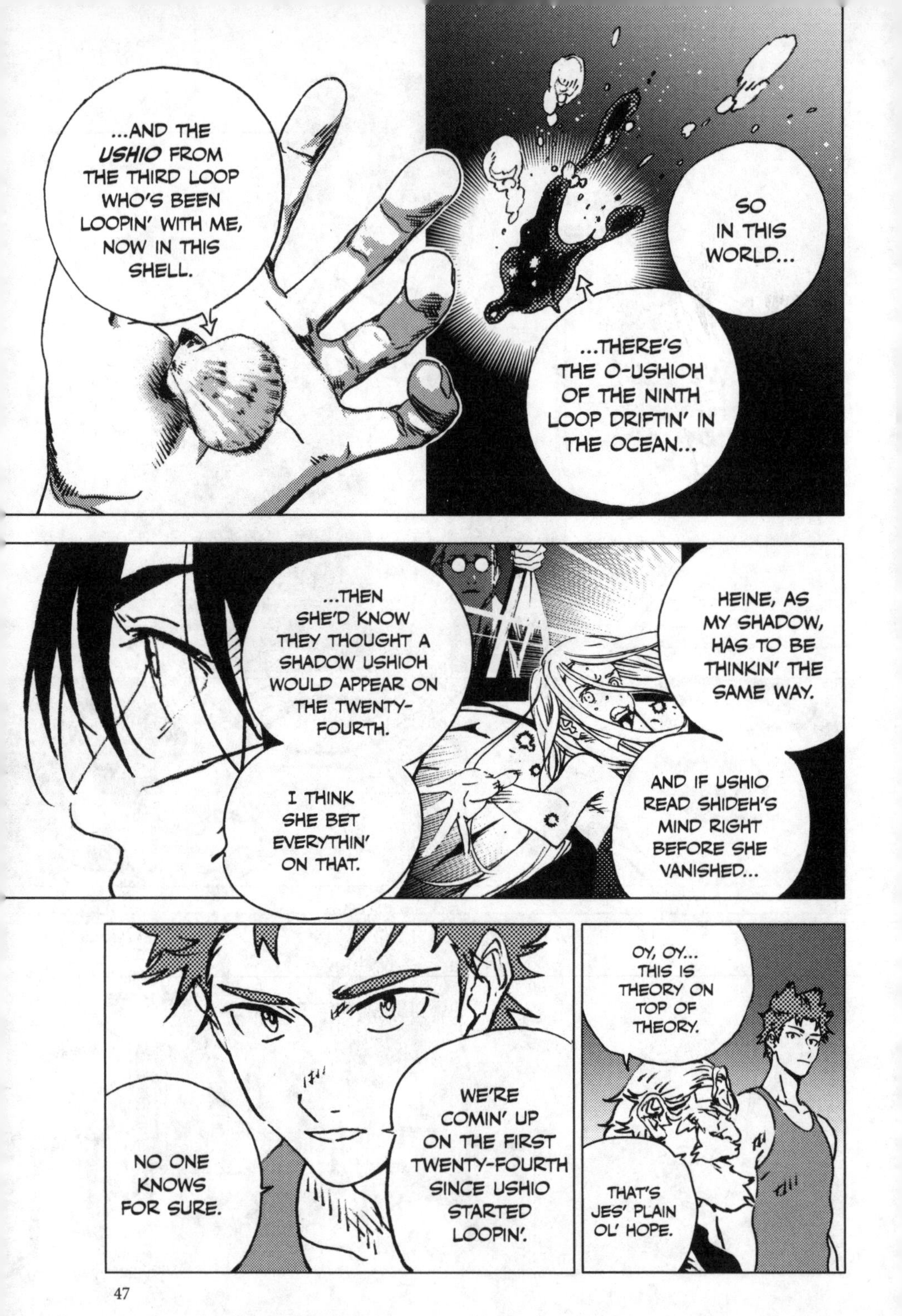
SO IN THIS WORLD...
...THERE'S THE O-USHIOH OF THE NINTH LOOP DRIFTIN' IN THE OCEAN...
...AND THE *USHIO* FROM THE THIRD LOOP WHO'S BEEN LOOPIN' WITH ME, NOW IN THIS SHELL.
HEINE, AS MY SHADOW, HAS TO BE THINKIN' THE SAME WAY.
AND IF USHIO READ SHIDEH'S MIND RIGHT BEFORE SHE VANISHED...
...THEN SHE'D KNOW THEY THOUGHT A SHADOW USHIOH WOULD APPEAR ON THE TWENTY-FOURTH.
I THINK SHE BET EVERYTHIN' ON THAT.
OY, OY... THIS IS THEORY ON TOP OF THEORY.
THAT'S JES' PLAIN OL' HOPE.
WE'RE COMIN' UP ON THE FIRST TWENTY-FOURTH SINCE USHIO STARTED LOOPIN'.
NO ONE KNOWS FOR SURE.

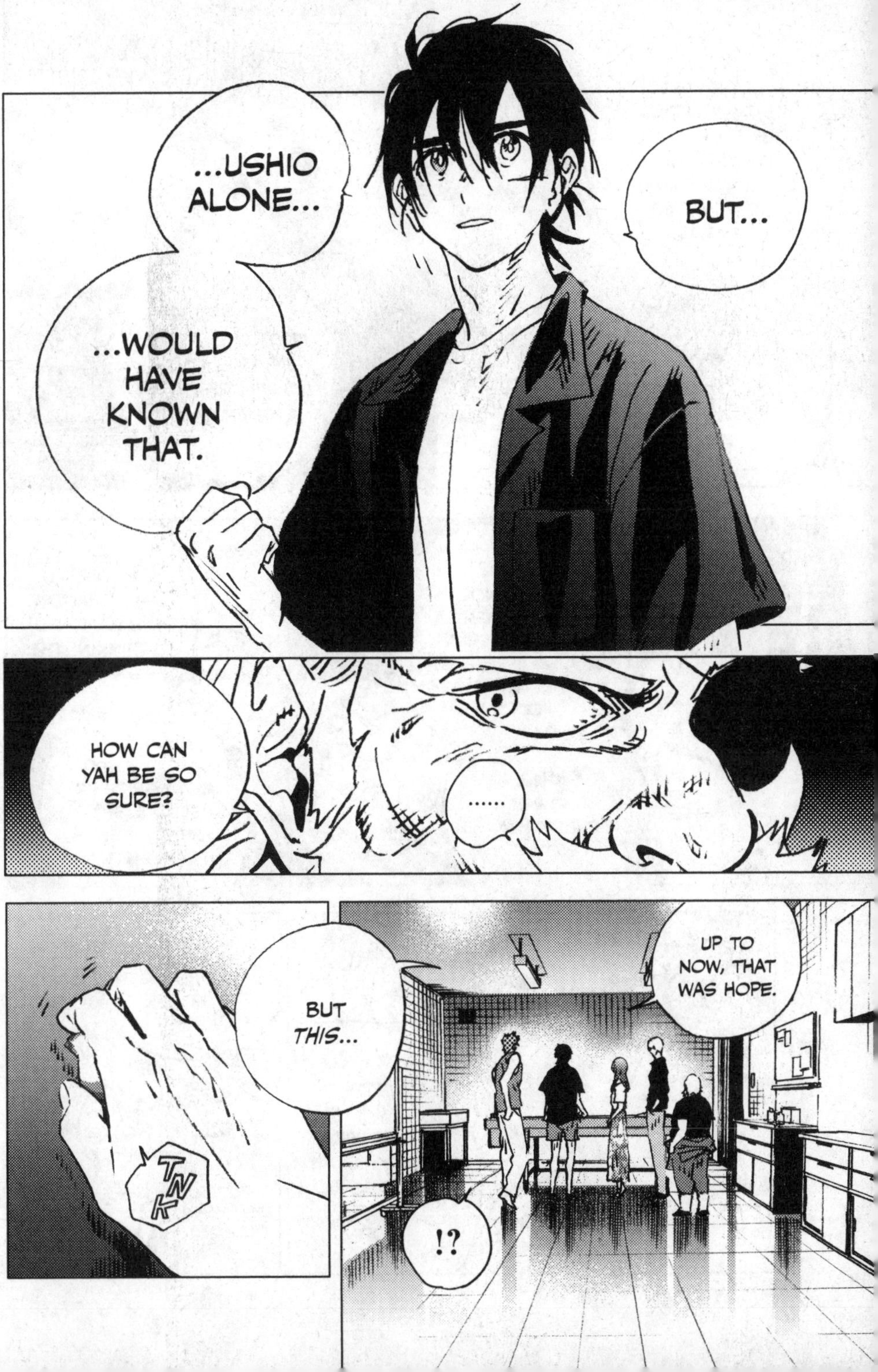

BUT...
...USHIO ALONE...
...WOULD HAVE KNOWN THAT.
......
HOW CAN YAH BE SO SURE?
UP TO NOW, THAT WAS HOPE.
!?
BUT THIS...
TNK

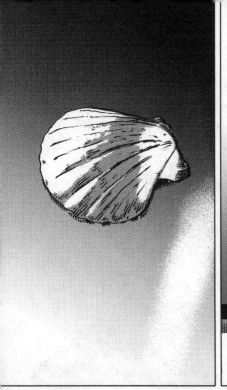

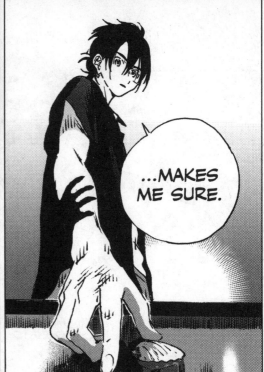

...MAKES ME SURE.

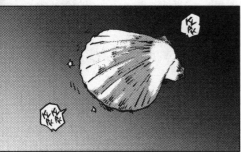

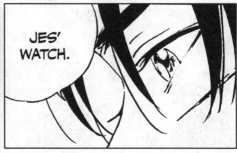

JES' WATCH.

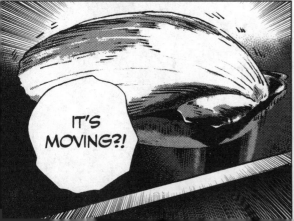

IT'S MOVING?!

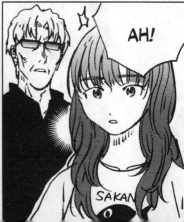

AH!

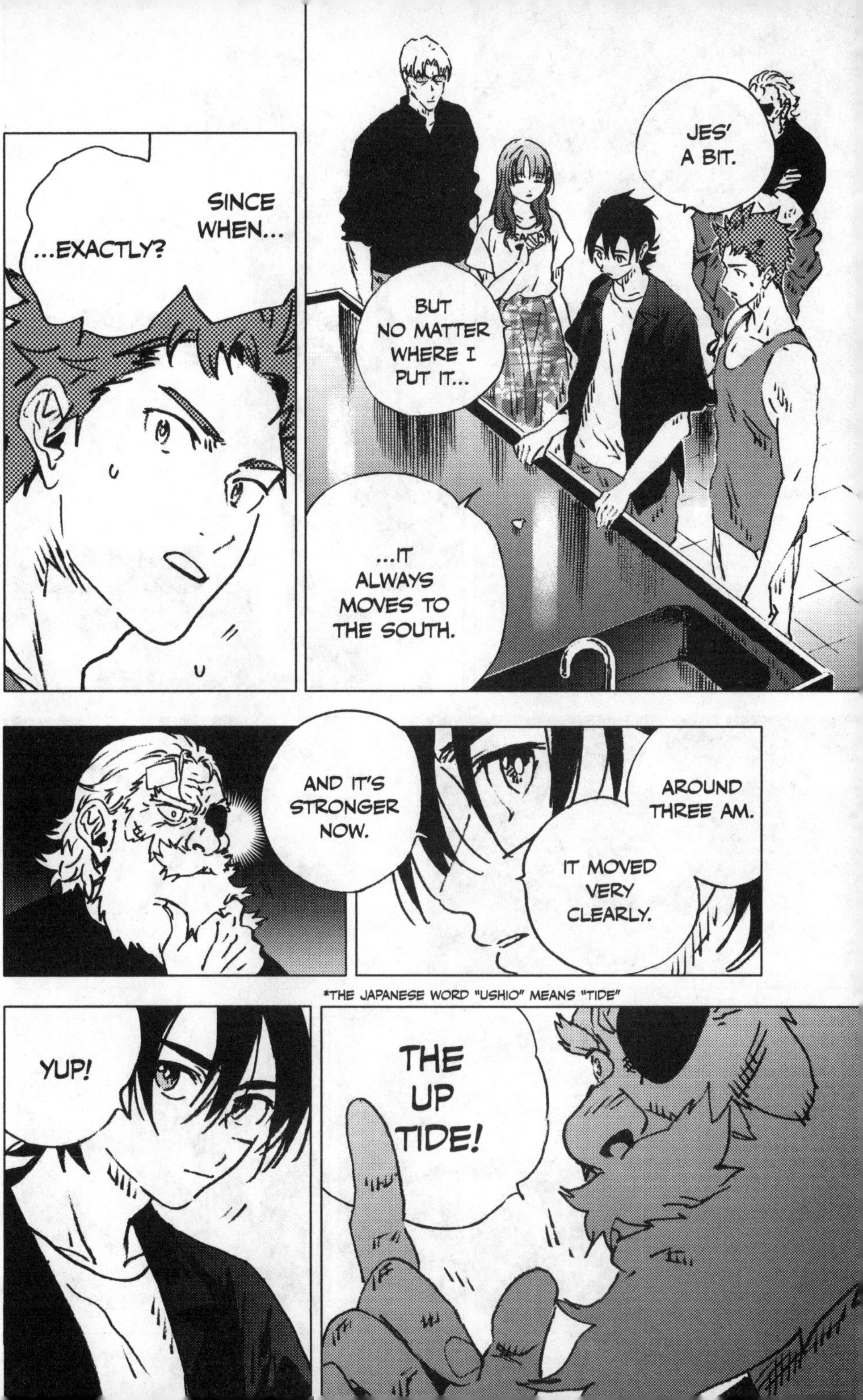
JES' A BIT.
BUT NO MATTER WHERE I PUT IT...
...IT ALWAYS MOVES TO THE SOUTH.
SINCE WHEN...
...EXACTLY?
AROUND THREE AM.
IT MOVED VERY CLEARLY.
AND IT'S STRONGER NOW.
THE UP TIDE!
YUP!

*THE JAPANESE WORD "USHIO" MEANS "TIDE"

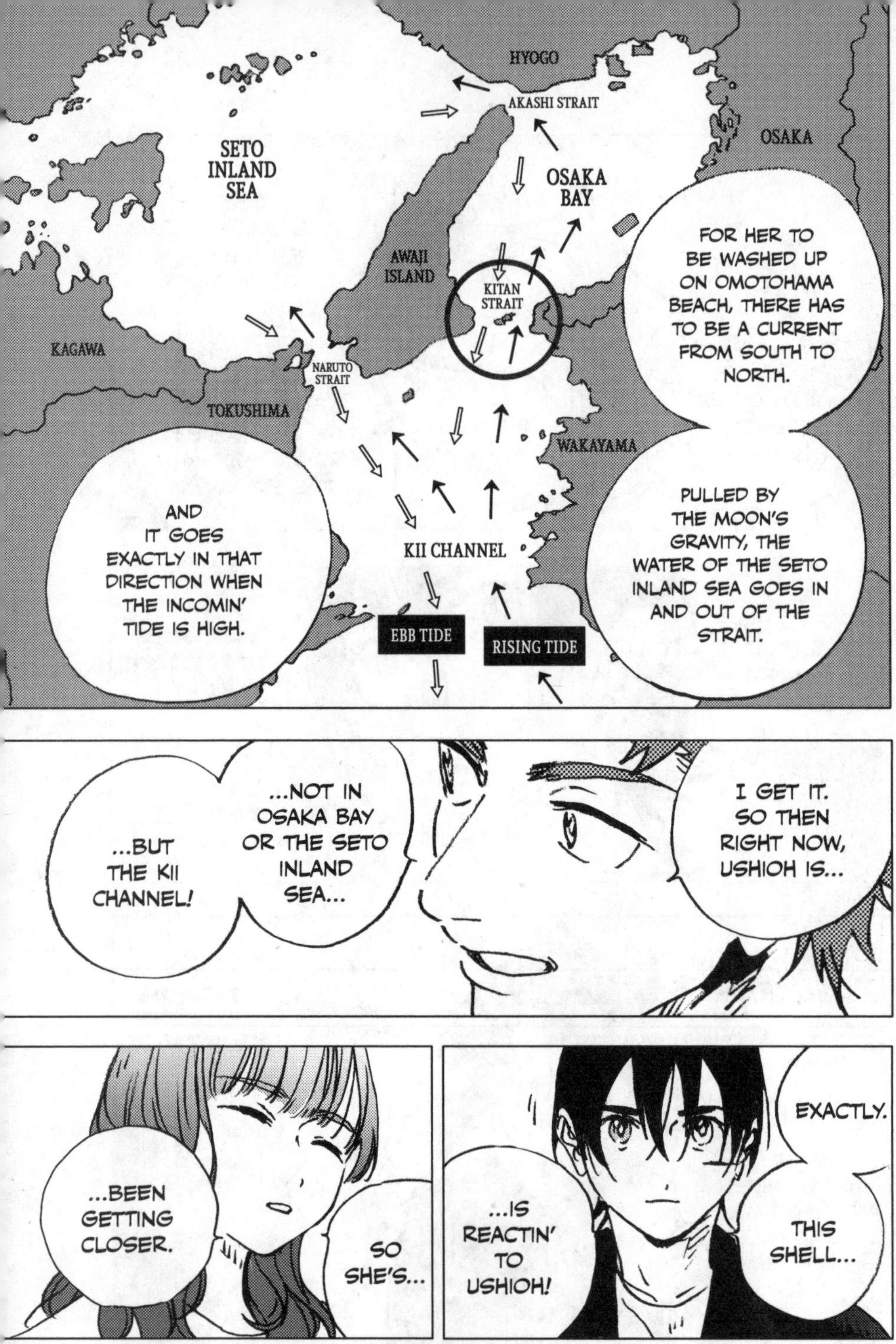
HYOGO
AKASHI STRAIT
OSAKA
SETO INLAND SEA
OSAKA BAY
AWAJI ISLAND
KITAN STRAIT
KAGAWA
NARUTO STRAIT
TOKUSHIMA
WAKAYAMA
KII CHANNEL
EBB TIDE
RISING TIDE
FOR HER TO BE WASHED UP ON OMOTOHAMA BEACH, THERE HAS TO BE A CURRENT FROM SOUTH TO NORTH.
PULLED BY THE MOON'S GRAVITY, THE WATER OF THE SETO INLAND SEA GOES IN AND OUT OF THE STRAIT.
AND IT GOES EXACTLY IN THAT DIRECTION WHEN THE INCOMIN' TIDE IS HIGH.
I GET IT. SO THEN RIGHT NOW, USHIOH IS...
...NOT IN OSAKA BAY OR THE SETO INLAND SEA...
...BUT THE KII CHANNEL!
EXACTLY.
THIS SHELL...
...IS REACTIN' TO USHIOH!
SO SHE'S...
...BEEN GETTING CLOSER.

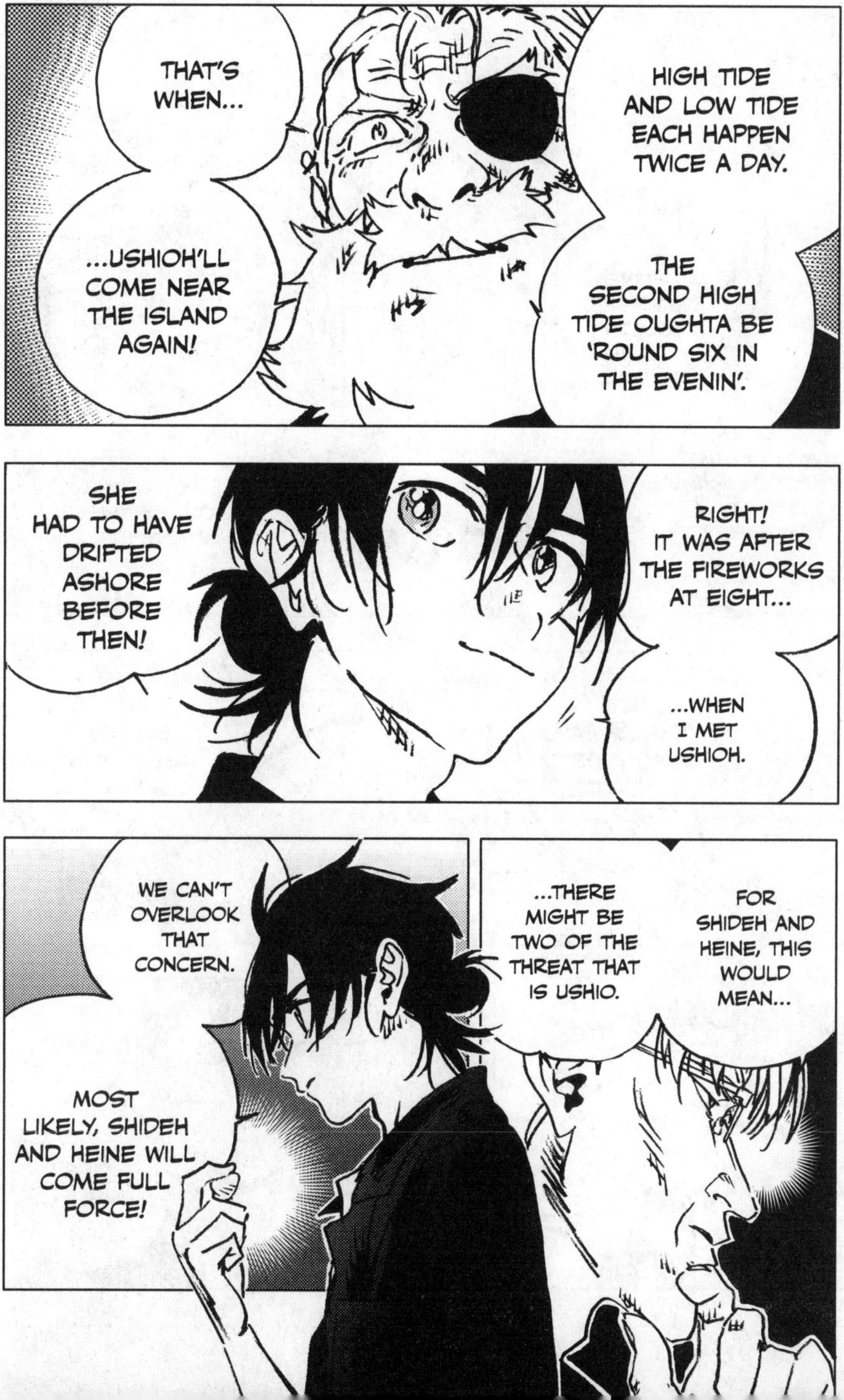
HIGH TIDE AND LOW TIDE EACH HAPPEN TWICE A DAY.
THE SECOND HIGH TIDE OUGHTA BE 'ROUND SIX IN THE EVENIN'.
THAT'S WHEN...
...USHIOH'LL COME NEAR THE ISLAND AGAIN!
RIGHT! IT WAS AFTER THE FIREWORKS AT EIGHT...
...WHEN I MET USHIOH.
SHE HAD TO HAVE DRIFTED ASHORE BEFORE THEN!
FOR SHIDEH AND HEINE, THIS WOULD MEAN...
...THERE MIGHT BE TWO OF THE THREAT THAT IS USHIO.
WE CAN'T OVERLOOK THAT CONCERN.
MOST LIKELY, SHIDEH AND HEINE WILL COME FULL FORCE!

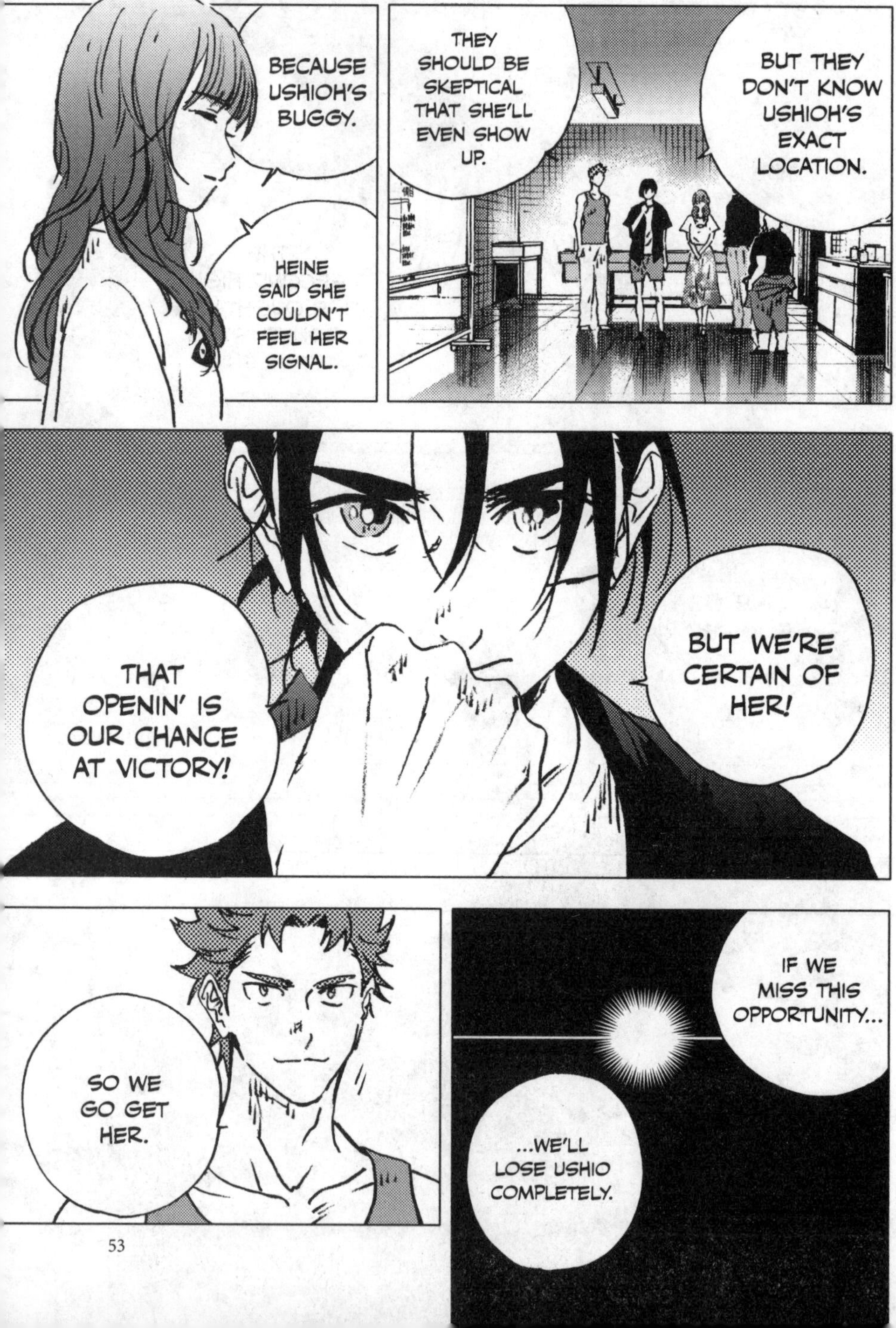
BUT THEY DON'T KNOW USHIOH'S EXACT LOCATION.
THEY SHOULD BE SKEPTICAL THAT SHE'LL EVEN SHOW UP.
BECAUSE USHIOH'S BUGGY.
HEINE SAID SHE COULDN'T FEEL HER SIGNAL.
BUT WE'RE CERTAIN OF HER!
THAT OPENIN' IS OUR CHANCE AT VICTORY!
IF WE MISS THIS OPPORTUNITY...
...WE'LL LOSE USHIO COMPLETELY.
SO WE GO GET HER.

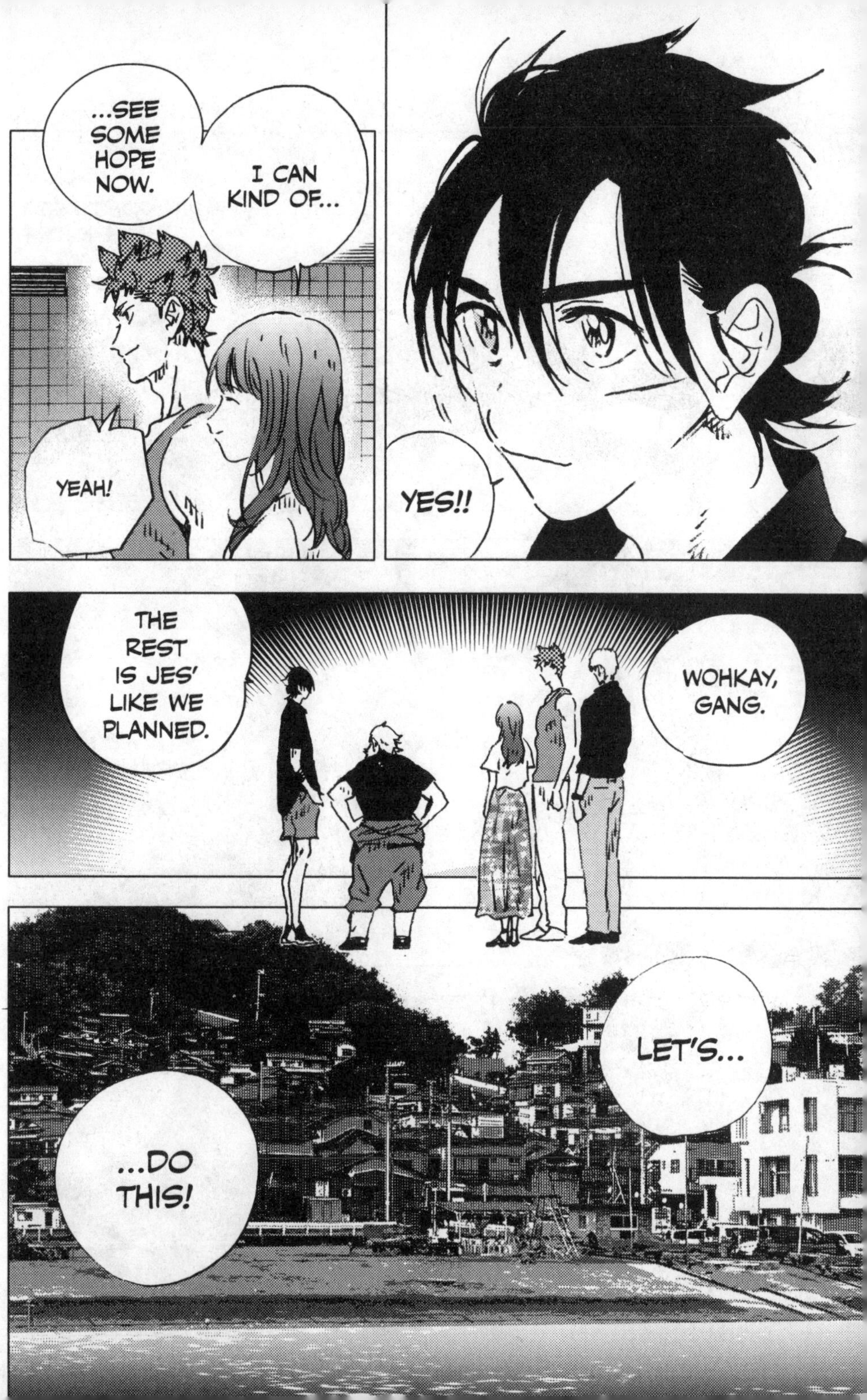
YES!!
I CAN KIND OF...
...SEE SOME HOPE NOW.
YEAH!
WOHKAY, GANG.
THE REST IS JES' LIKE WE PLANNED.
LET'S...
...DO THIS!

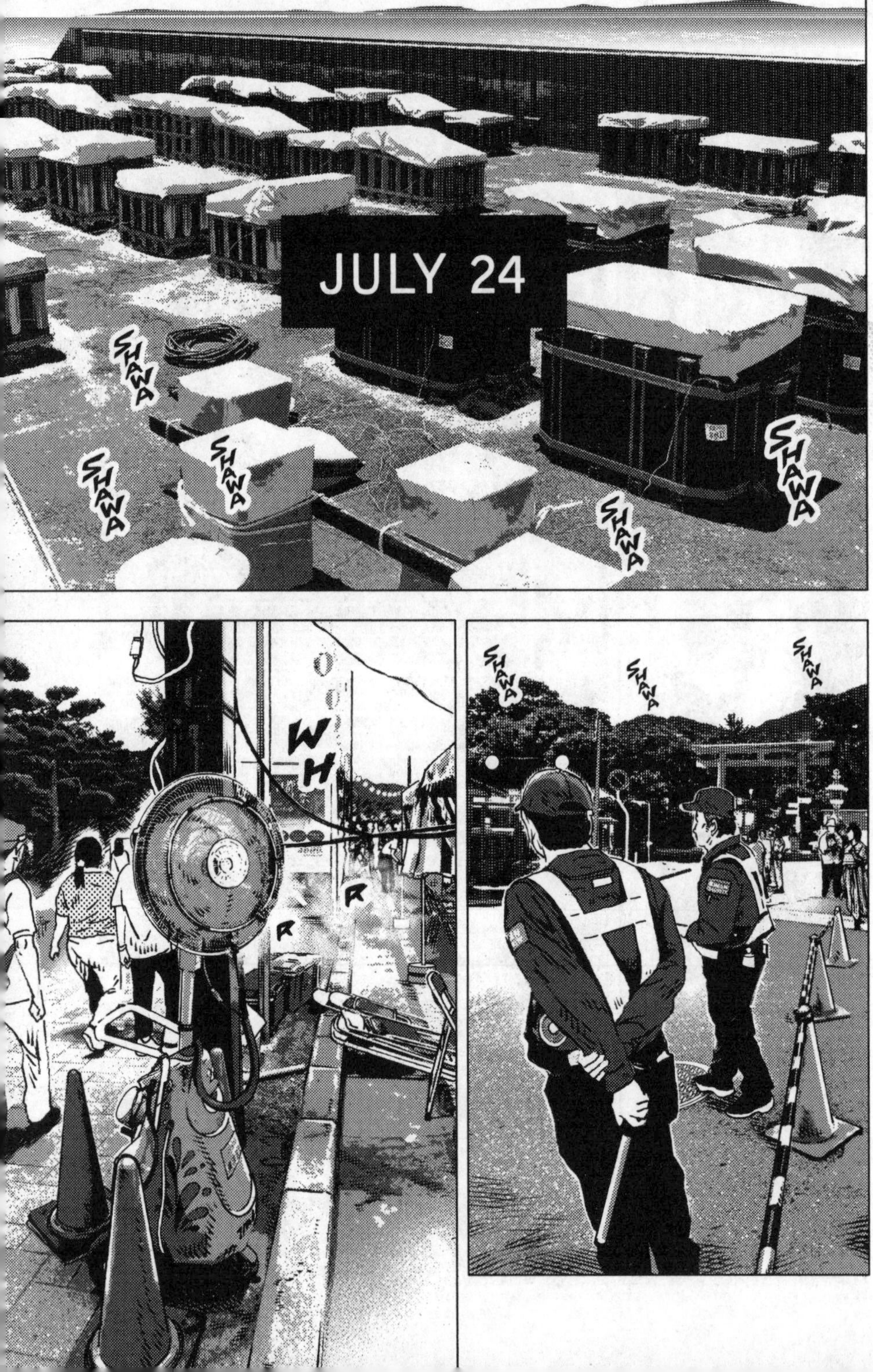
JULY 24
SHAWA
SHAWA
SHAWA
SHAWA
SHAWA
SHAWA
SHAWA
SHAWA
WHRR

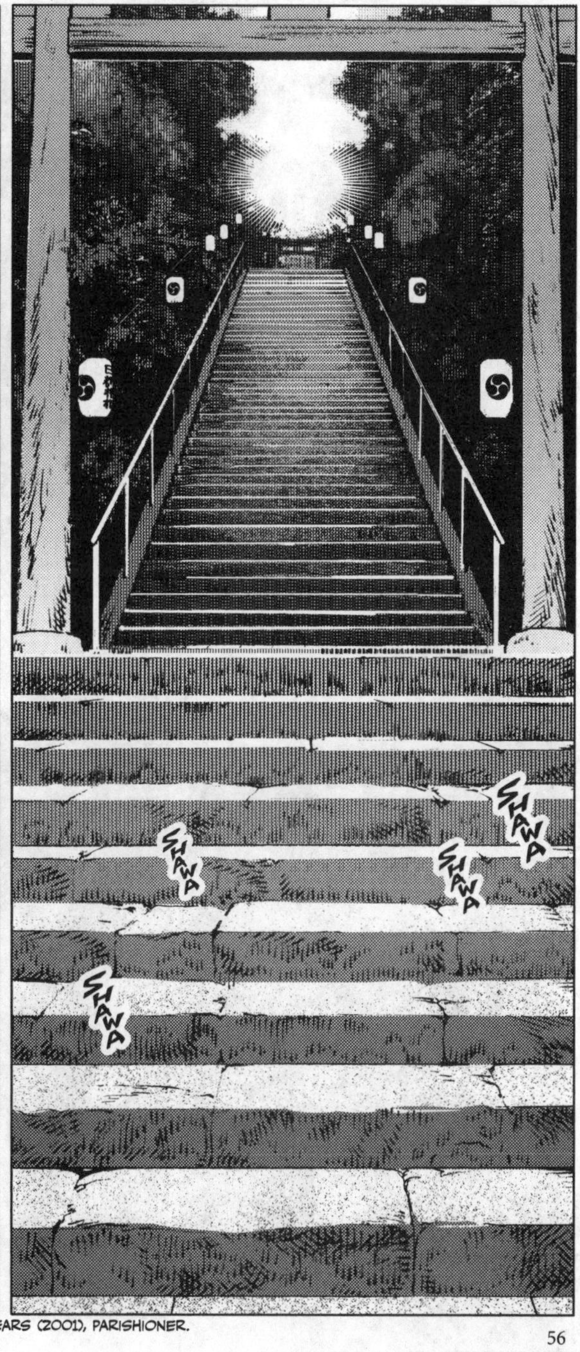
SHAWA
SHAWA
SHAWA
SHAWA

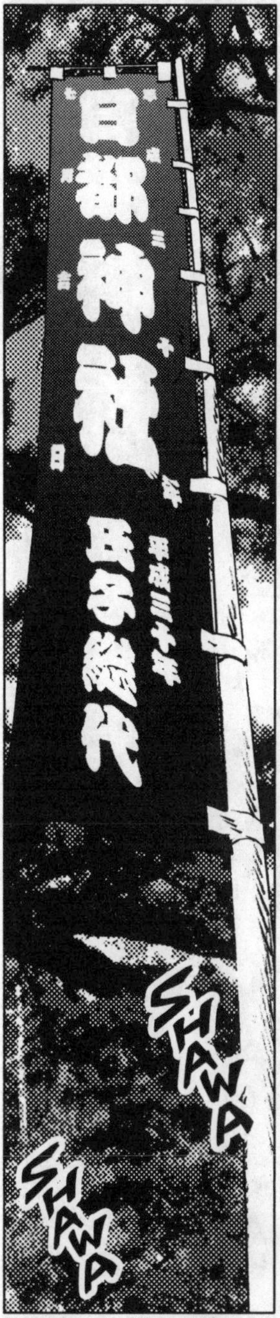
日都神社
平成三十年
氏子総代
SHAWA
SHAWA

*BANNER = HITO SHRINE, HEISEI 30 YEARS (2001), PARISHIONER.

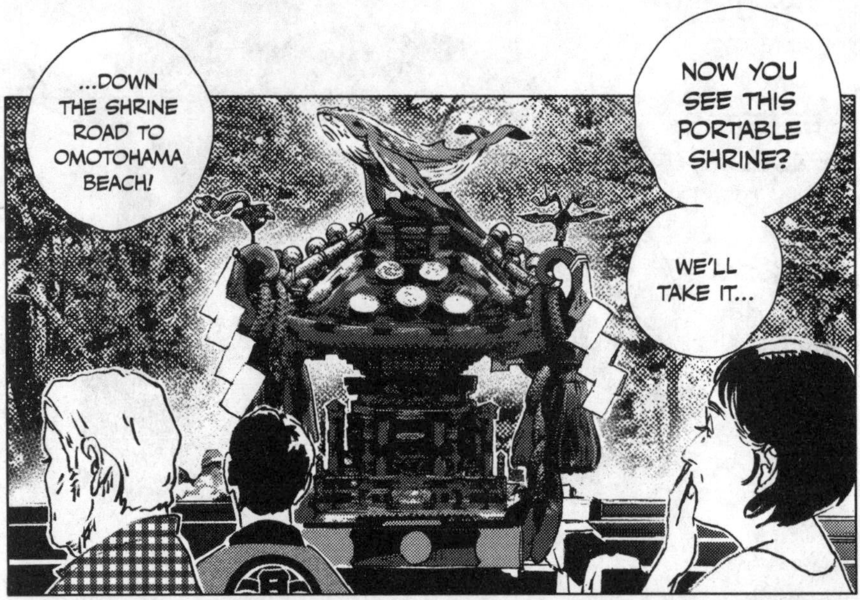
NOW YOU SEE THIS PORTABLE SHRINE?
WE'LL TAKE IT...
...DOWN THE SHRINE ROAD TO OMOTOHAMA BEACH!

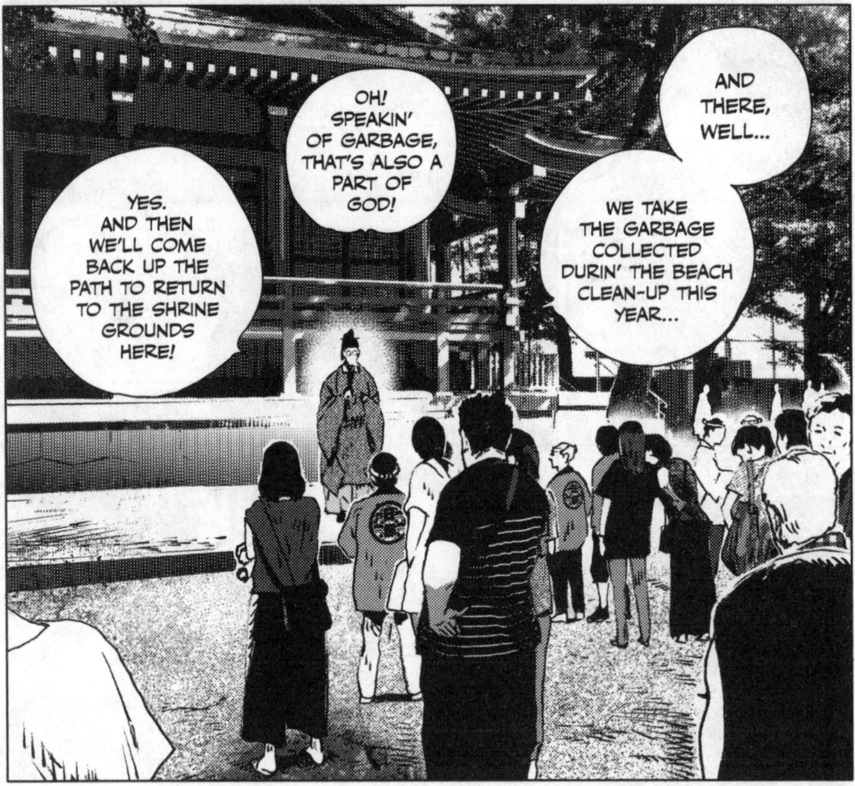
AND THERE, WELL...
WE TAKE THE GARBAGE COLLECTED DURIN' THE BEACH CLEAN-UP THIS YEAR...
OH! SPEAKIN' OF GARBAGE, THAT'S ALSO A PART OF GOD!
YES. AND THEN WE'LL COME BACK UP THE PATH TO RETURN TO THE SHRINE GROUNDS HERE!

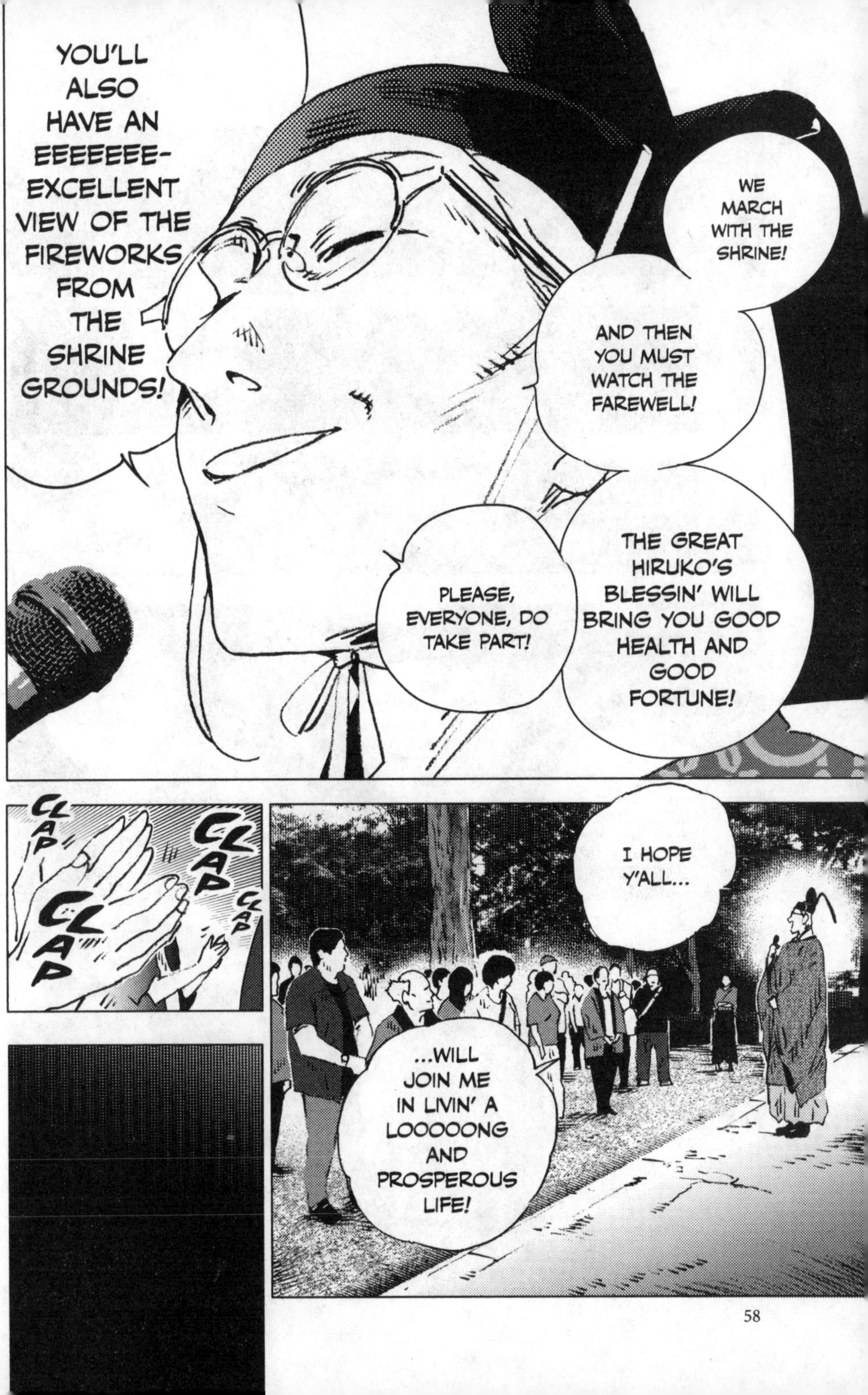
WE MARCH WITH THE SHRINE!
AND THEN YOU MUST WATCH THE FAREWELL!
THE GREAT HIRUKO'S BLESSIN' WILL BRING YOU GOOD HEALTH AND GOOD FORTUNE!
PLEASE, EVERYONE, DO TAKE PART!
YOU'LL ALSO HAVE AN EEEEEEE-EXCELLENT VIEW OF THE FIREWORKS FROM THE SHRINE GROUNDS!
I HOPE Y'ALL...
...WILL JOIN ME IN LIVIN' A LOOOOONG AND PROSPEROUS LIFE!
CLAP
CLAP
CLAP
CLAP
CLAP

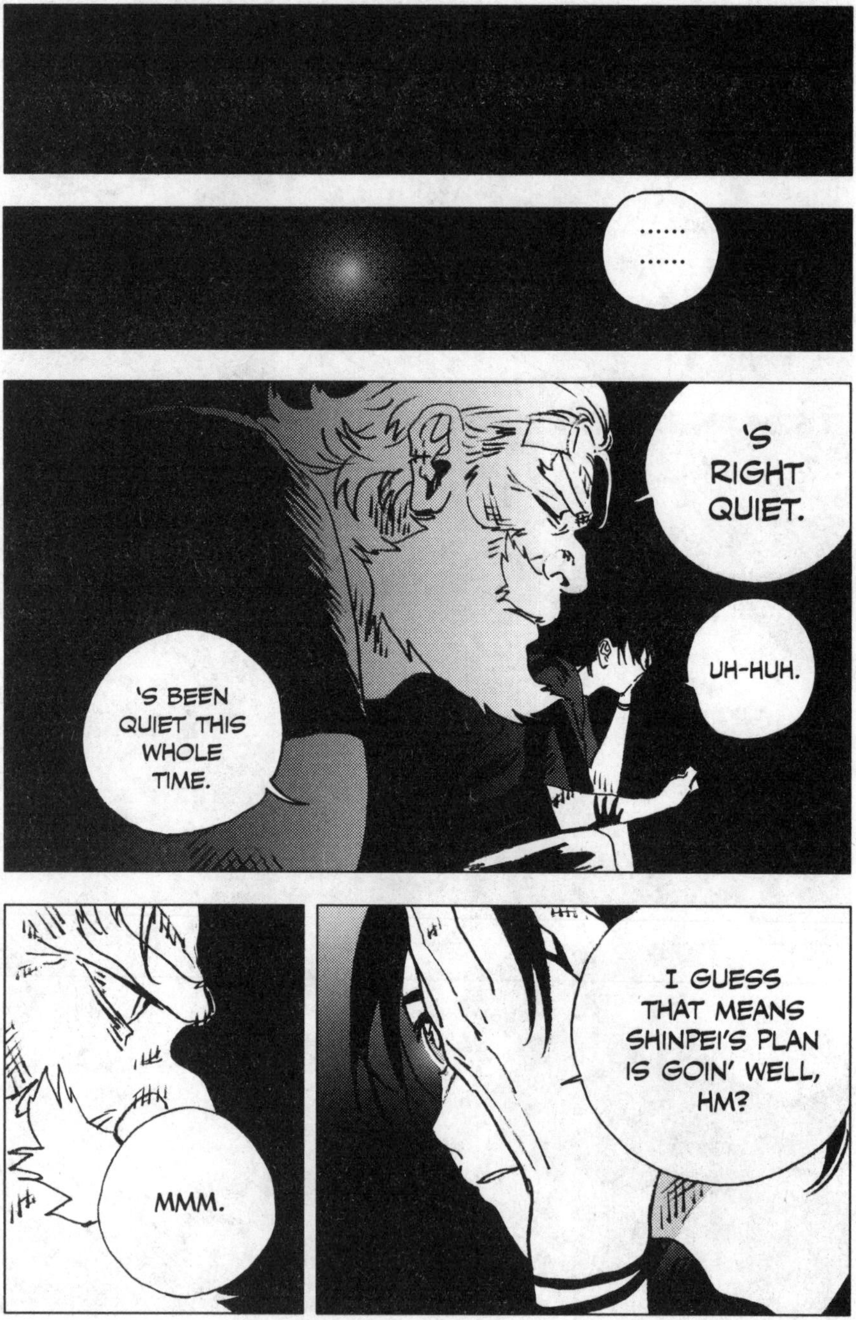
......
......
'S RIGHT QUIET.
UH-HUH.
'S BEEN QUIET THIS WHOLE TIME.
I GUESS THAT MEANS SHINPEI'S PLAN IS GOIN' WELL, HM?
MMM.

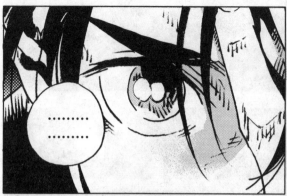

....
....

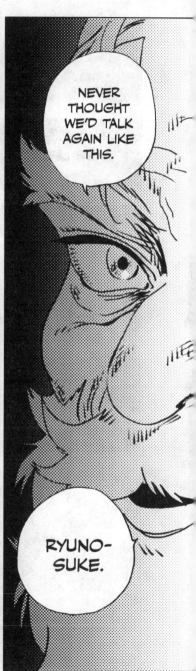

NEVER THOUGHT WE'D TALK AGAIN LIKE THIS.

RYUNO-SUKE.

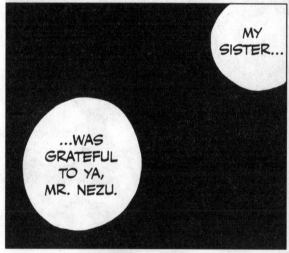

MY SISTER...

...WAS GRATEFUL TO YA, MR. NEZU.

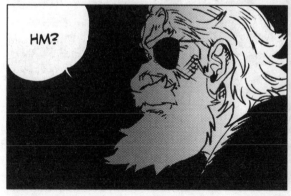

HM?

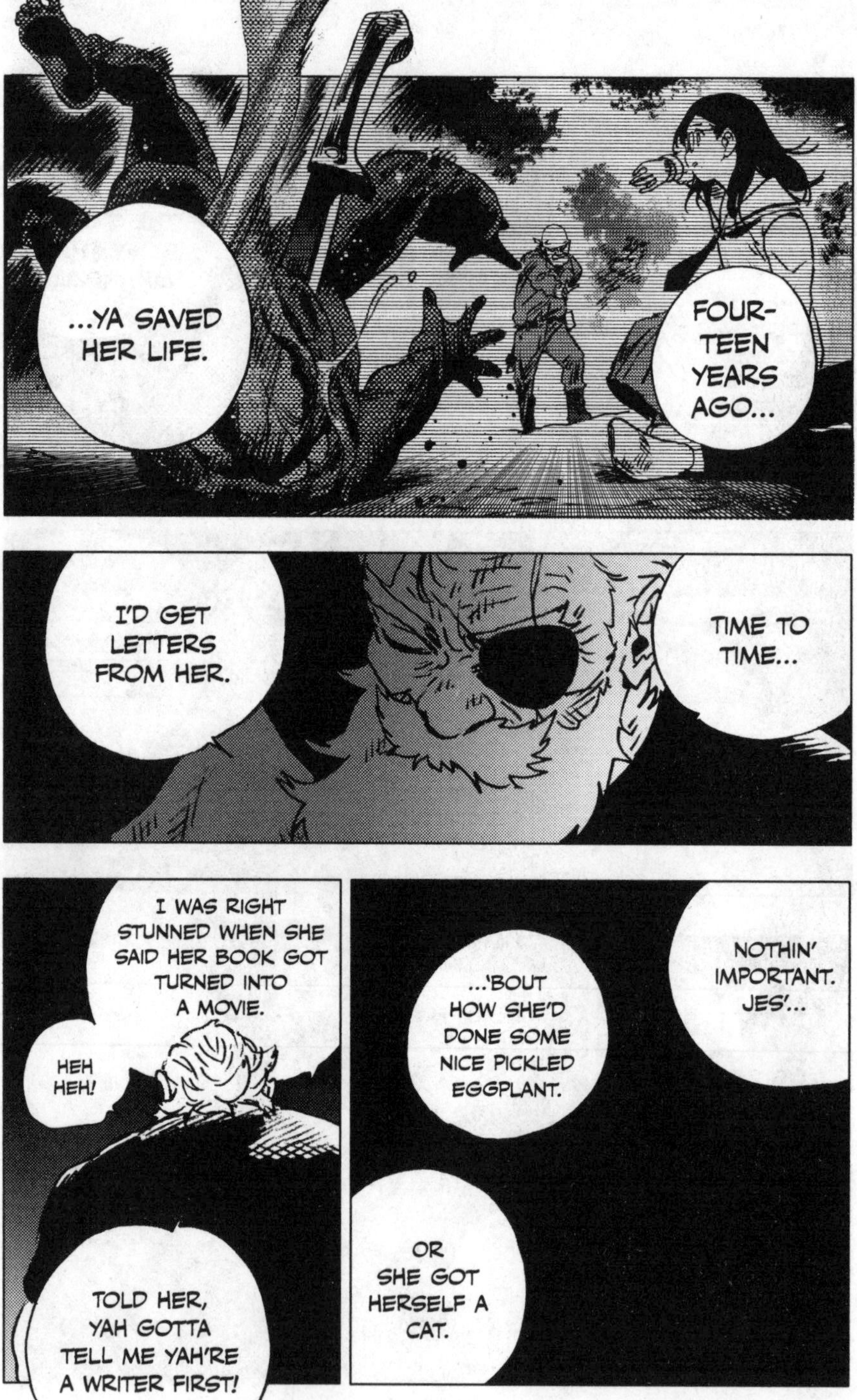
FOUR-TEEN YEARS AGO...
...YA SAVED HER LIFE.
TIME TO TIME...
I'D GET LETTERS FROM HER.
NOTHIN' IMPORTANT. JES'...
...'BOUT HOW SHE'D DONE SOME NICE PICKLED EGGPLANT.
OR SHE GOT HERSELF A CAT.
I WAS RIGHT STUNNED WHEN SHE SAID HER BOOK GOT TURNED INTO A MOVIE.
HEH HEH!
TOLD HER, YAH GOTTA TELL ME YAH'RE A WRITER FIRST!

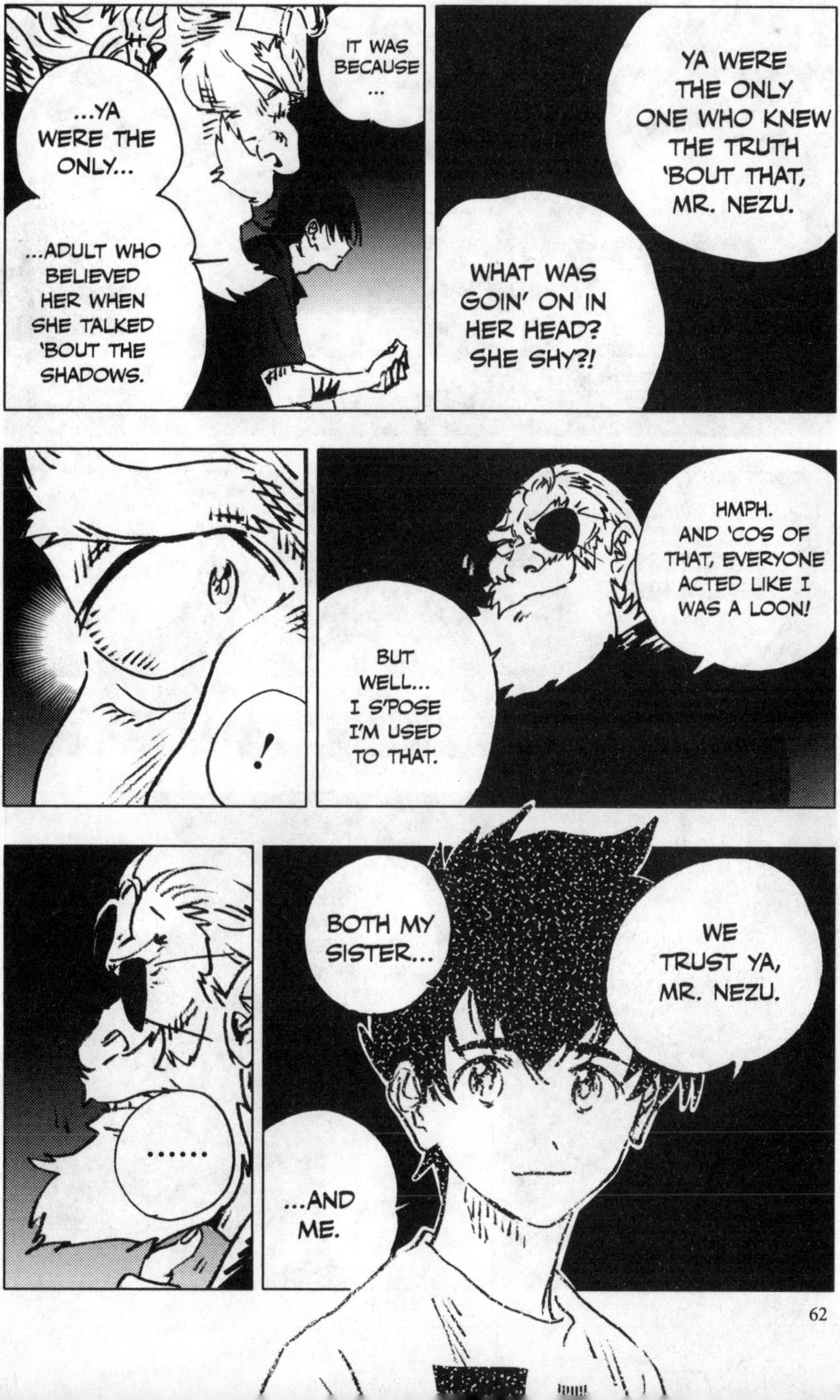
YA WERE THE ONLY ONE WHO KNEW THE TRUTH 'BOUT THAT, MR. NEZU.
WHAT WAS GOIN' ON IN HER HEAD? SHE SHY?!
IT WAS BECAUSE ...
...YA WERE THE ONLY...
...ADULT WHO BELIEVED HER WHEN SHE TALKED 'BOUT THE SHADOWS.
HMPH. AND 'COS OF THAT, EVERYONE ACTED LIKE I WAS A LOON!
BUT WELL... I S'POSE I'M USED TO THAT.
!
WE TRUST YA, MR. NEZU.
BOTH MY SISTER...
...AND ME.
......

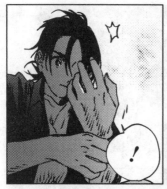

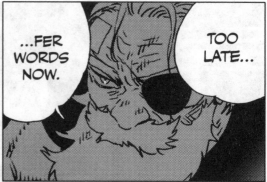

...FER WORDS NOW.

TOO LATE...

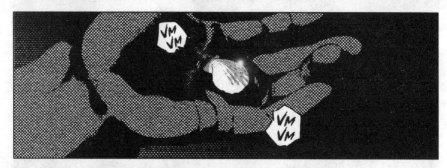

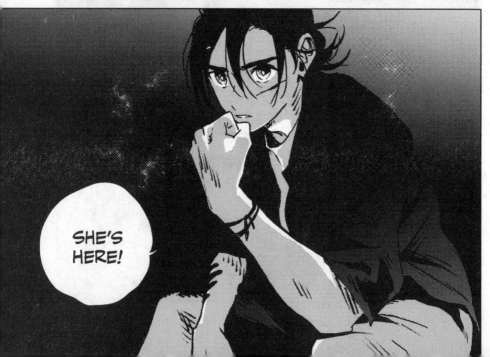

SHE'S HERE!

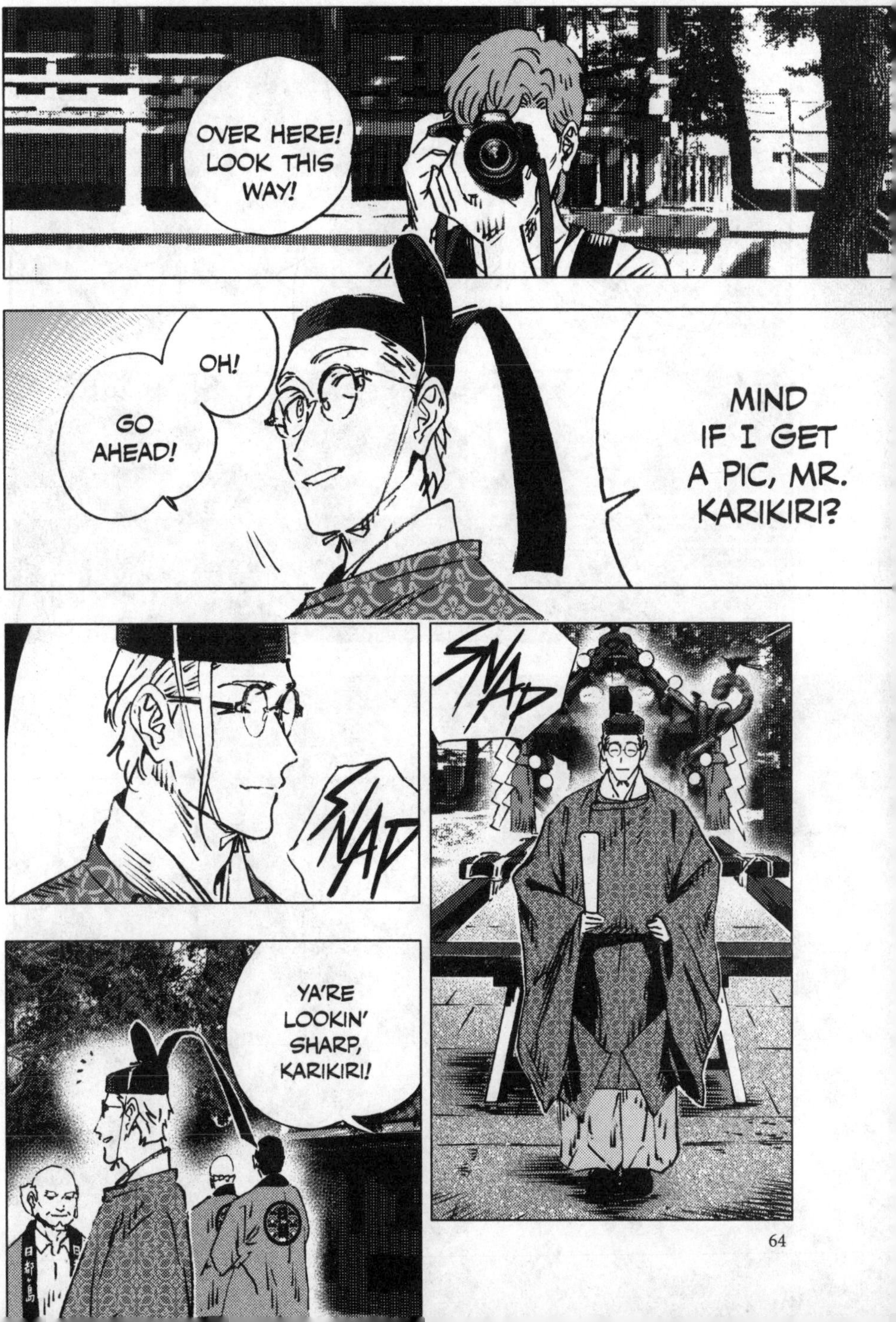

OVER HERE! LOOK THIS WAY!
MIND IF I GET A PIC, MR. KARIKIRI?
OH!
GO AHEAD!
SNAP
SNAP
YA'RE LOOKIN' SHARP, KARIKIRI!

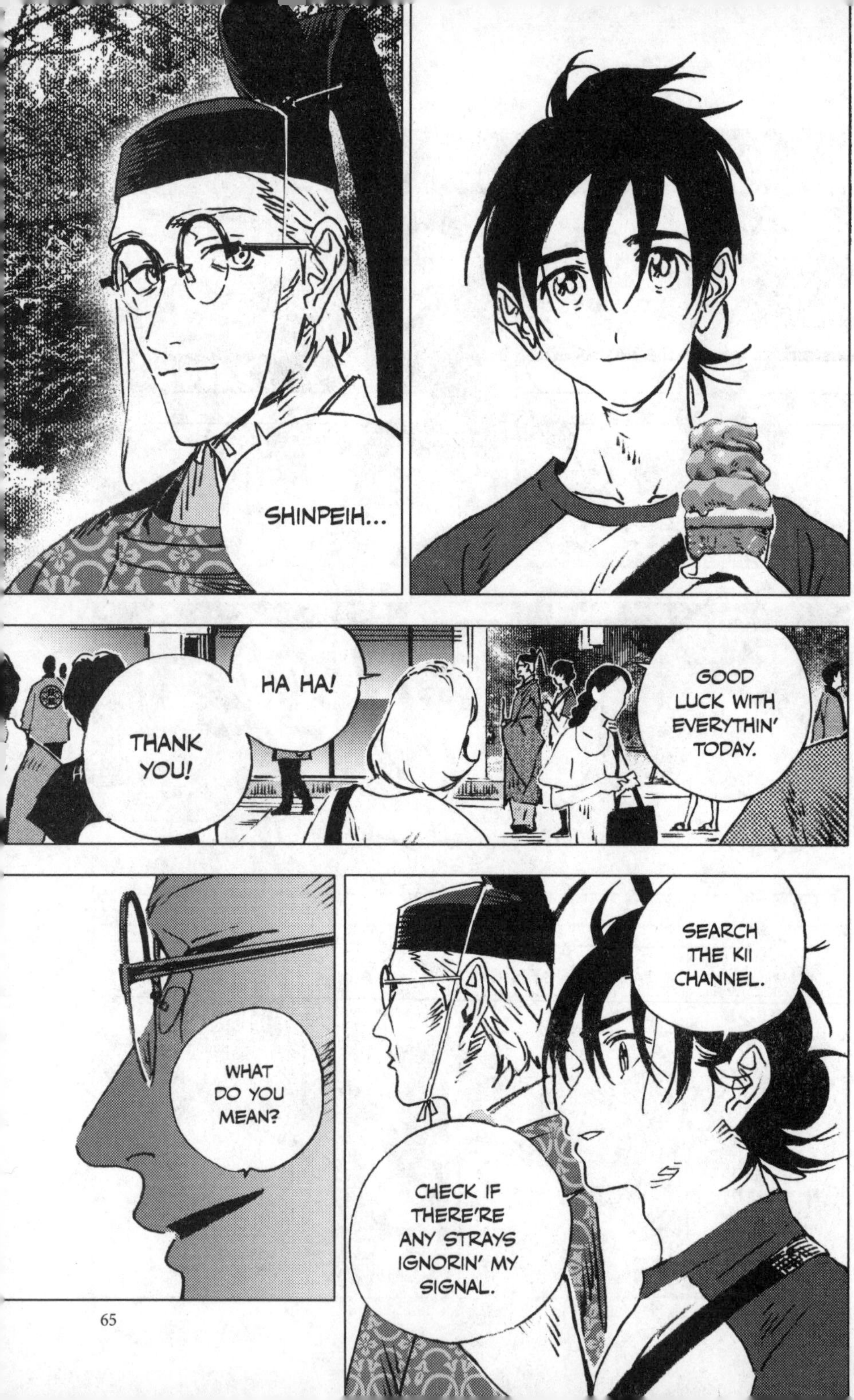
SHINPEIH...
GOOD LUCK WITH EVERYTHIN' TODAY.
HA HA!
THANK YOU!
SEARCH THE KII CHANNEL.
CHECK IF THERE'RE ANY STRAYS IGNORIN' MY SIGNAL.
WHAT DO YOU MEAN?

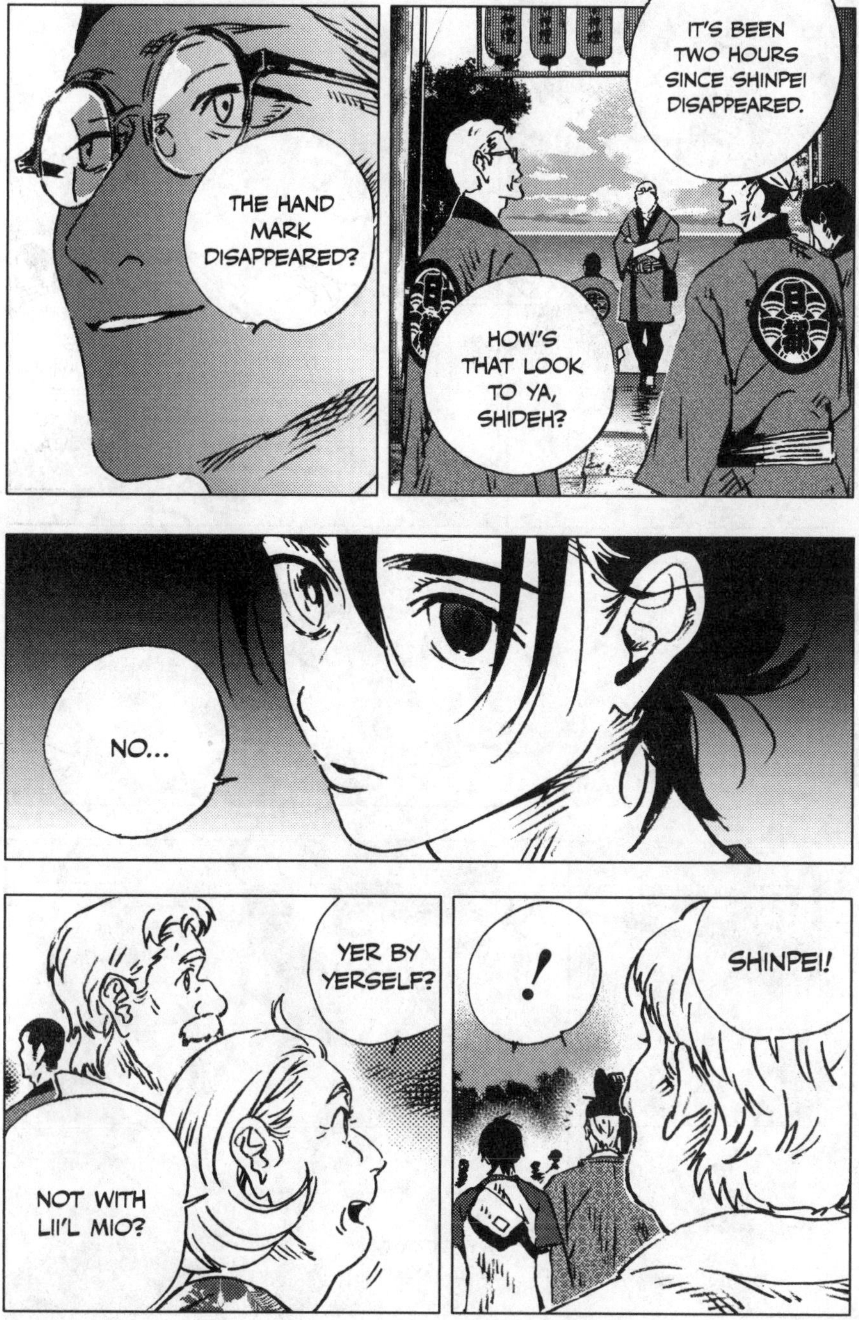
IT'S BEEN TWO HOURS SINCE SHINPEI DISAPPEARED.
HOW'S THAT LOOK TO YA, SHIDEH?
THE HAND MARK DISAPPEARED?
NO...
SHINPEI!
!
YER BY YERSELF?
NOT WITH LII'L MIO?

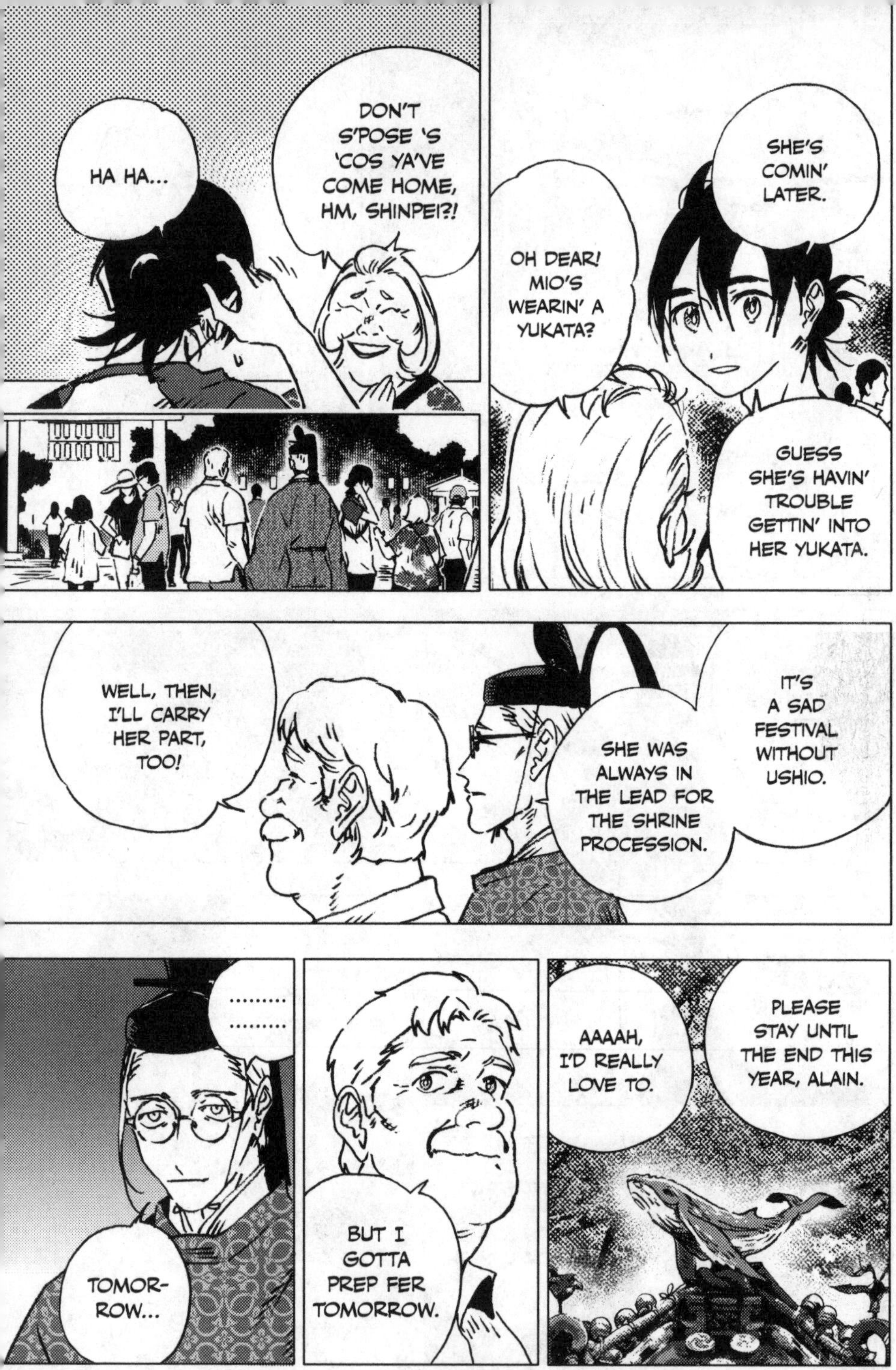
SHE'S COMIN' LATER.
OH DEAR! MIO'S WEARIN' A YUKATA?
GUESS SHE'S HAVIN' TROUBLE GETTIN' INTO HER YUKATA.
DON'T S'POSE 'S 'COS YA'VE COME HOME, HM, SHINPEI?!
HA HA...
IT'S A SAD FESTIVAL WITHOUT USHIO.
SHE WAS ALWAYS IN THE LEAD FOR THE SHRINE PROCESSION.
WELL, THEN, I'LL CARRY HER PART, TOO!
PLEASE STAY UNTIL THE END THIS YEAR, ALAIN.
AAAAH, I'D REALLY LOVE TO.
BUT I GOTTA PREP FER TOMORROW.
....
....
TOMOR-ROW...

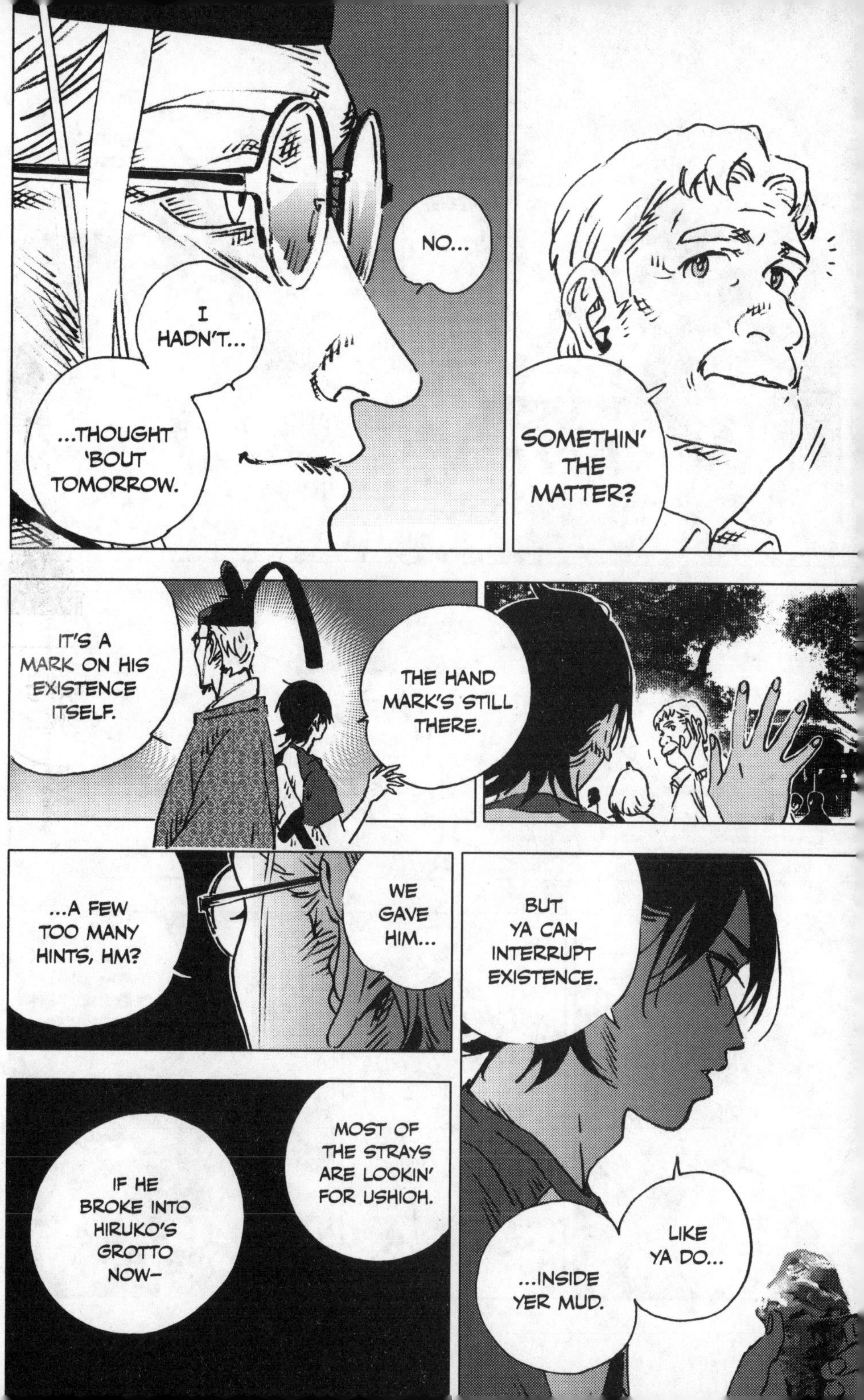
SOMETHIN' THE MATTER?
NO...
I HADN'T...
...THOUGHT 'BOUT TOMORROW.
THE HAND MARK'S STILL THERE.
IT'S A MARK ON HIS EXISTENCE ITSELF.
BUT YA CAN INTERRUPT EXISTENCE.
LIKE YA DO...
...INSIDE YER MUD.
WE GAVE HIM...
...A FEW TOO MANY HINTS, HM?
MOST OF THE STRAYS ARE LOOKIN' FOR USHIOH.
IF HE BROKE INTO HIRUKO'S GROTTO NOW–

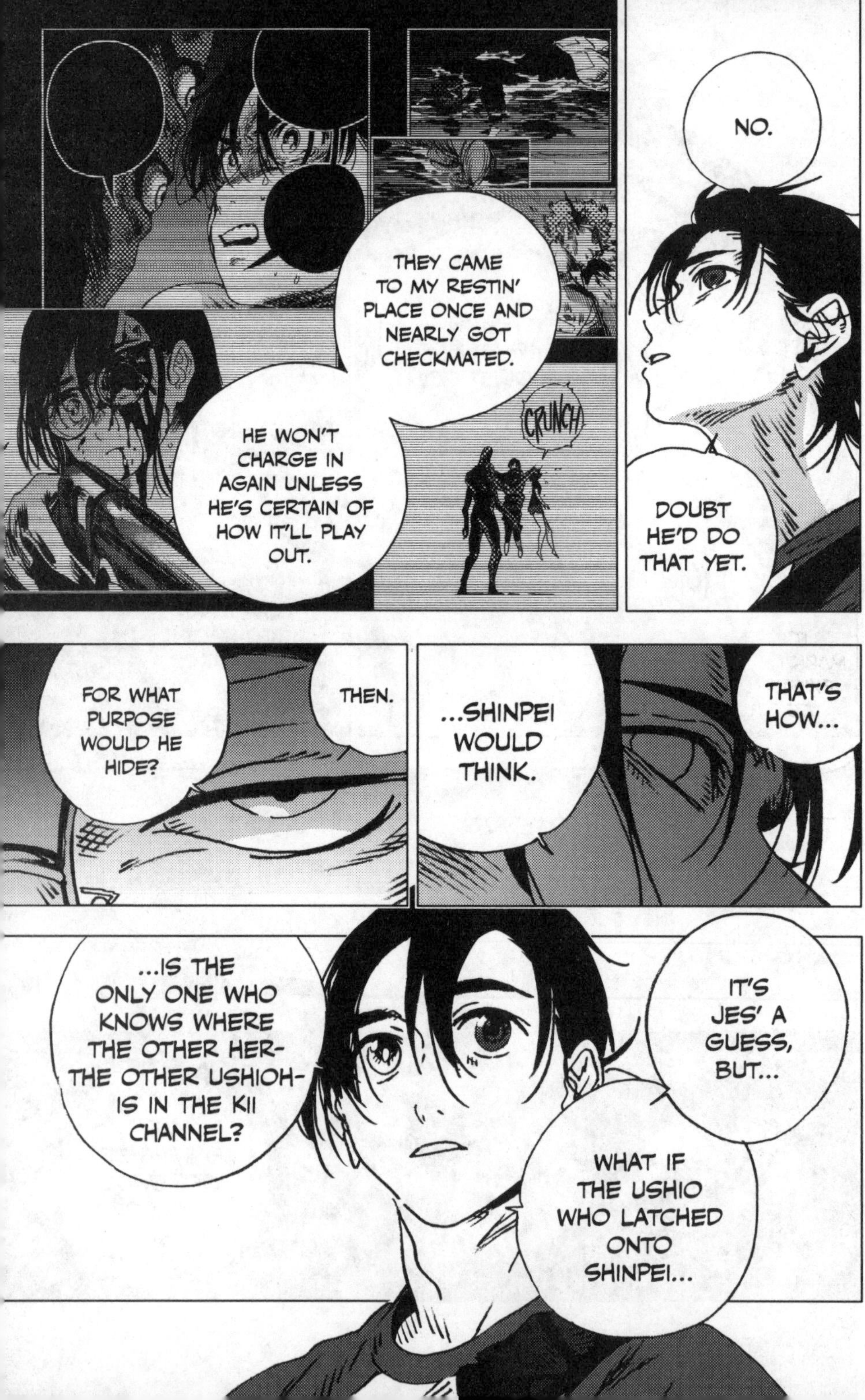
NO.
DOUBT HE'D DO THAT YET.
THEY CAME TO MY RESTIN' PLACE ONCE AND NEARLY GOT CHECKMATED.
CRUNCH
HE WON'T CHARGE IN AGAIN UNLESS HE'S CERTAIN OF HOW IT'LL PLAY OUT.
THAT'S HOW...
...SHINPEI WOULD THINK.
THEN.
FOR WHAT PURPOSE WOULD HE HIDE?
IT'S JES' A GUESS, BUT...
WHAT IF THE USHIO WHO LATCHED ONTO SHINPEI...
...IS THE ONLY ONE WHO KNOWS WHERE THE OTHER HER- THE OTHER USHIOH- IS IN THE KII CHANNEL?

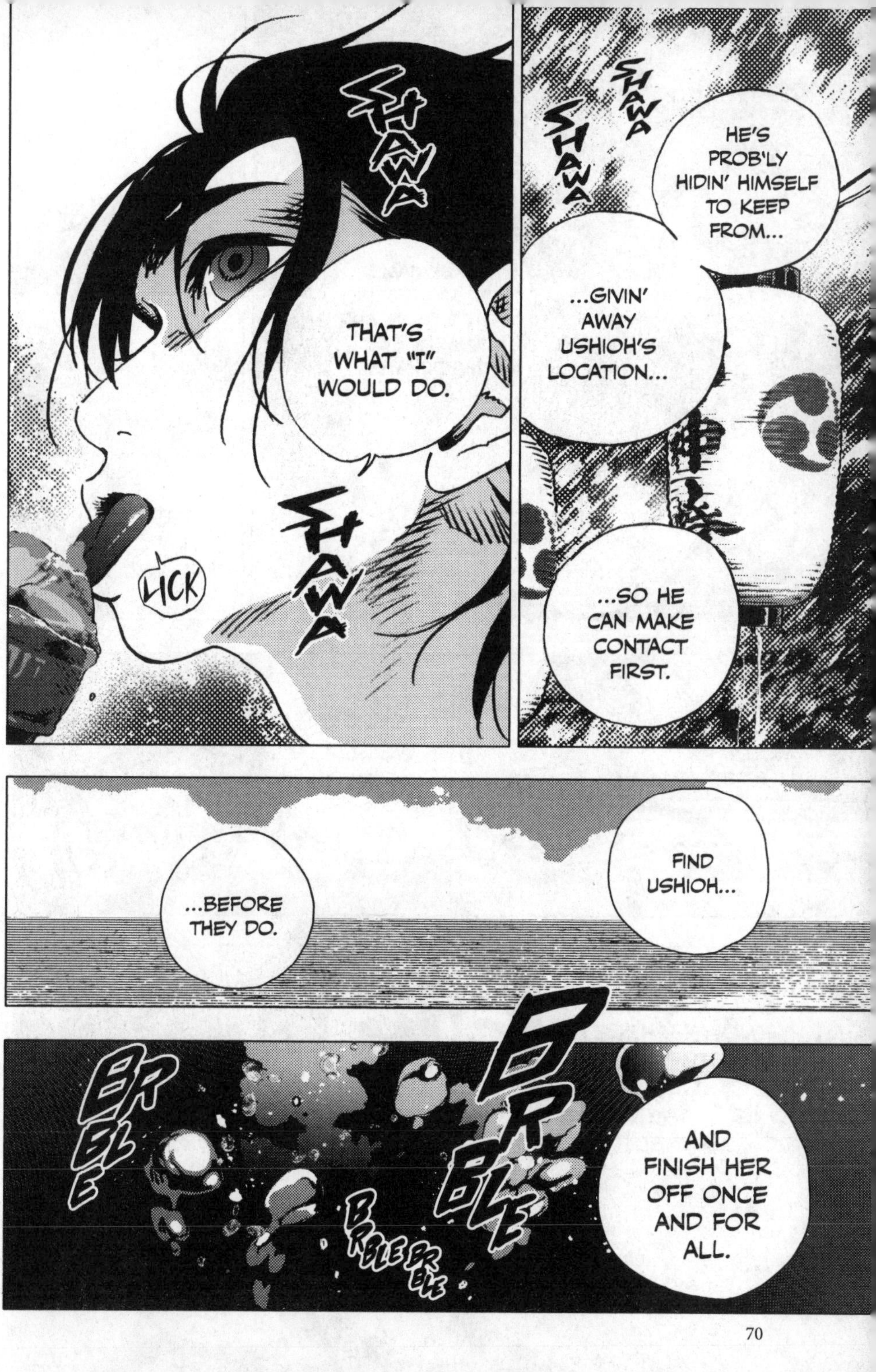
SHAWA
SHAWA
HE'S PROB'LY HIDIN' HIMSELF TO KEEP FROM...
...GIVIN' AWAY USHIOH'S LOCATION...
...SO HE CAN MAKE CONTACT FIRST.
SHAWA
THAT'S WHAT "I" WOULD DO.
SHAWA
LICK
FIND USHIOH...
...BEFORE THEY DO.
AND FINISH HER OFF ONCE AND FOR ALL.
BRBLE
BRBLE BRBLE
BRBLE

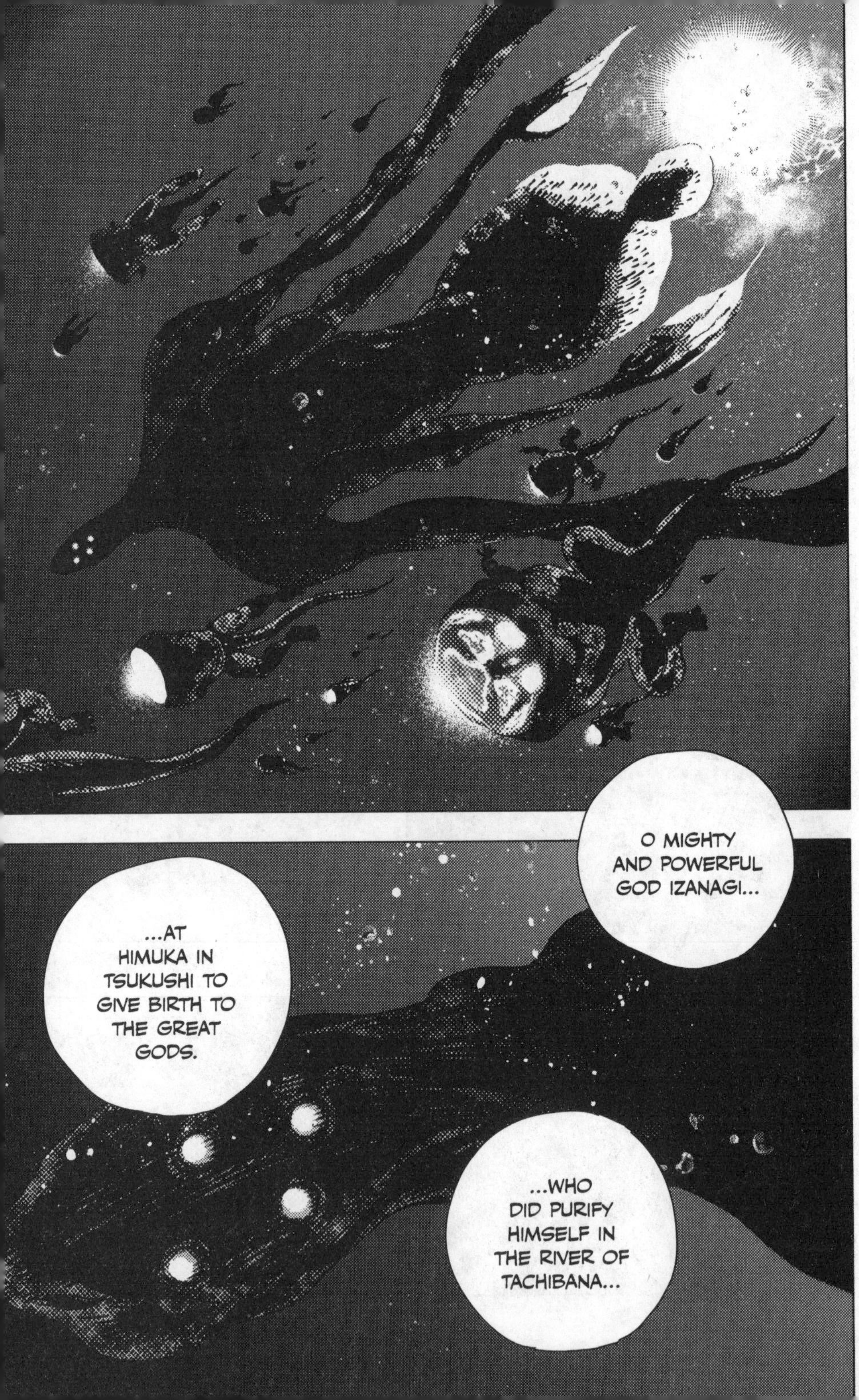
O MIGHTY AND POWERFUL GOD IZANAGI...
...WHO DID PURIFY HIMSELF IN THE RIVER OF TACHIBANA...
...AT HIMUKA IN TSUKUSHI TO GIVE BIRTH TO THE GREAT GODS.

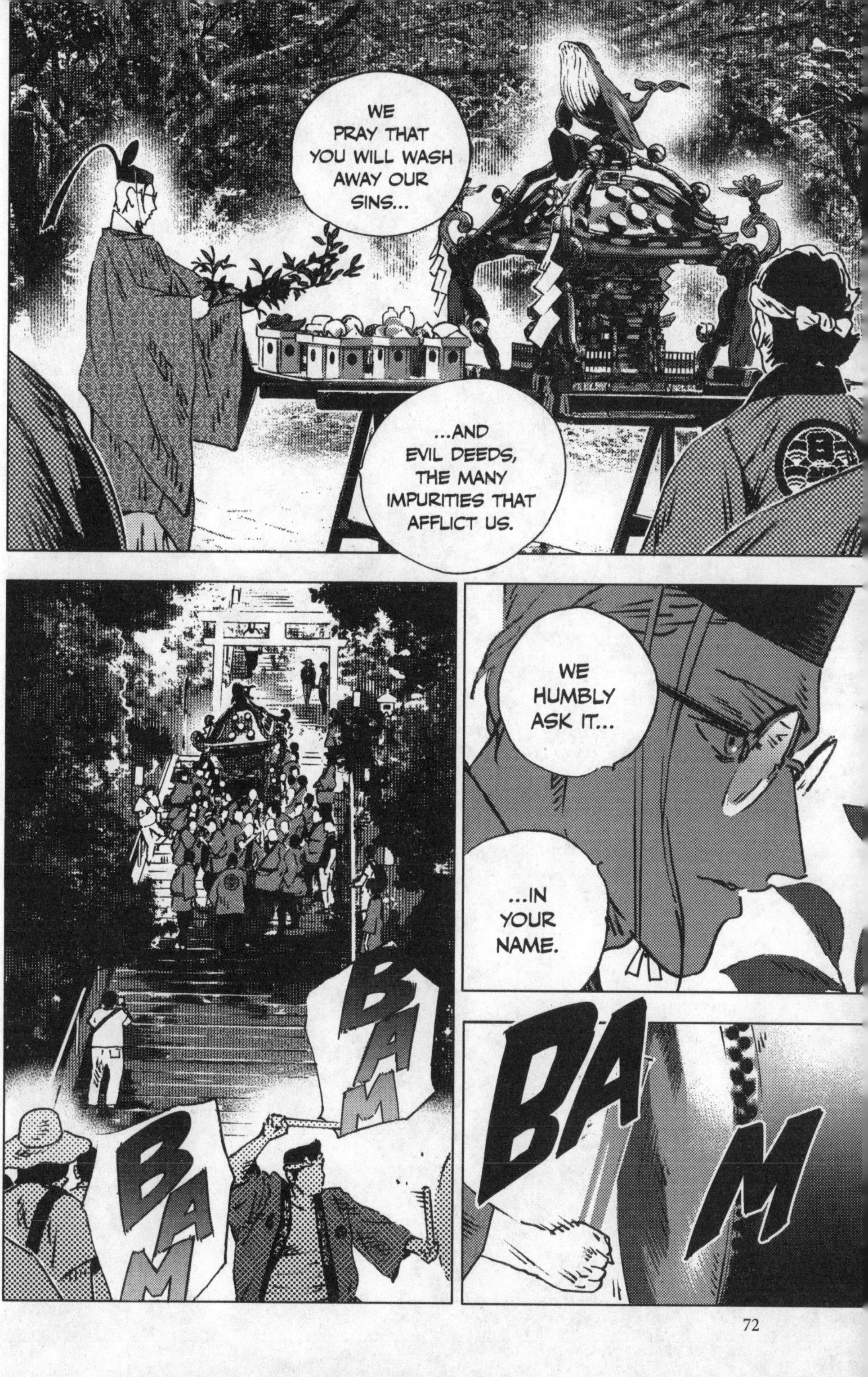
WE PRAY THAT YOU WILL WASH AWAY OUR SINS...
...AND EVIL DEEDS, THE MANY IMPURITIES THAT AFFLICT US.
WE HUMBLY ASK IT...
...IN YOUR NAME.
BAM
BAM
BAM

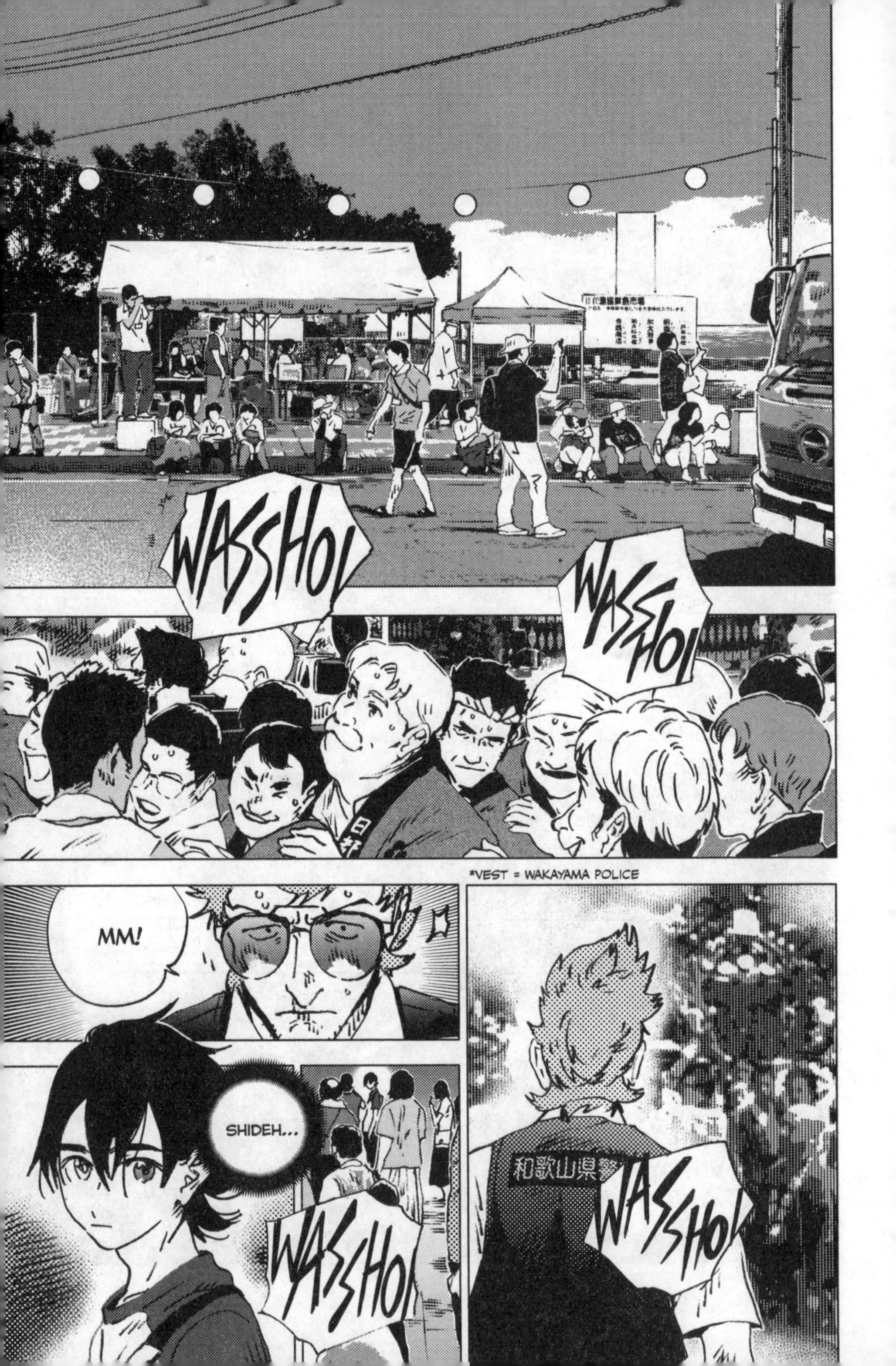
WASSHOI
WASSHOI
*VEST = WAKAYAMA POLICE
和歌山県
WASSHOI
MM!
SHIDEH...
WASSHOI

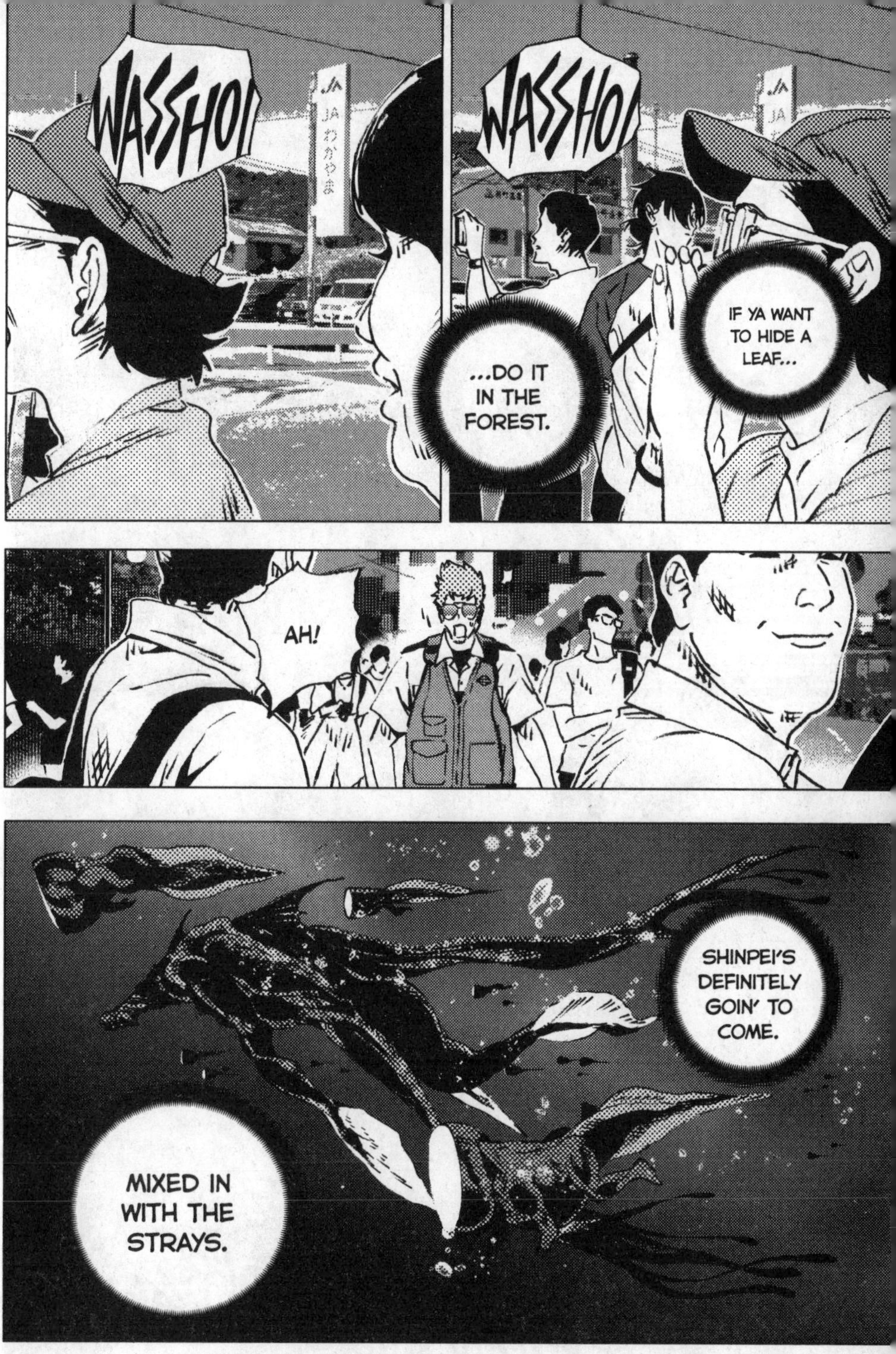
WASSHOI
JA
IF YA WANT TO HIDE A LEAF...
...DO IT IN THE FOREST.
WASSHOI
JA わかやま
AH!
SHINPEI'S DEFINITELY GOIN' TO COME.
MIXED IN WITH THE STRAYS.

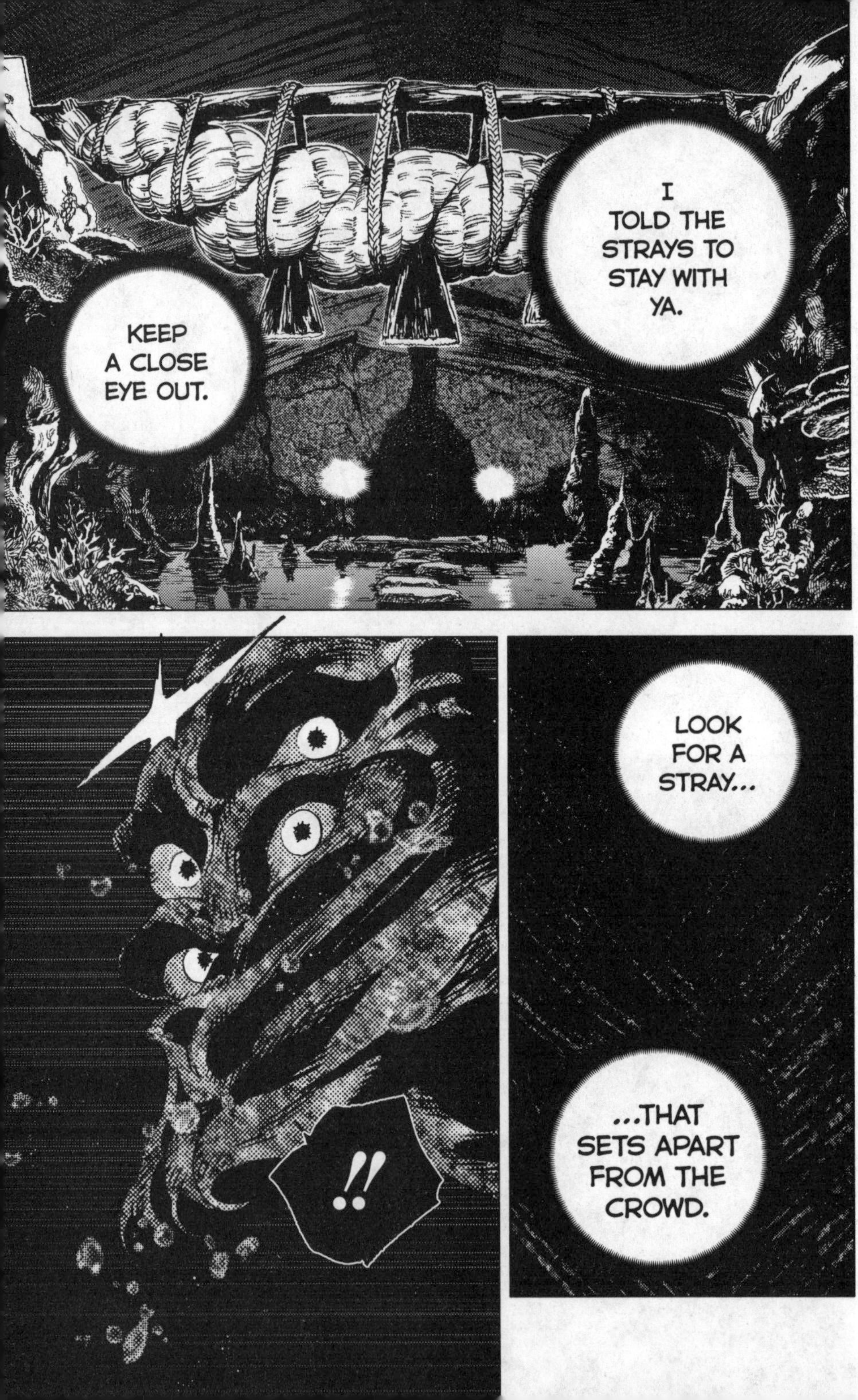
I TOLD THE STRAYS TO STAY WITH YA.
KEEP A CLOSE EYE OUT.
LOOK FOR A STRAY...
...THAT SETS APART FROM THE CROWD.
!!

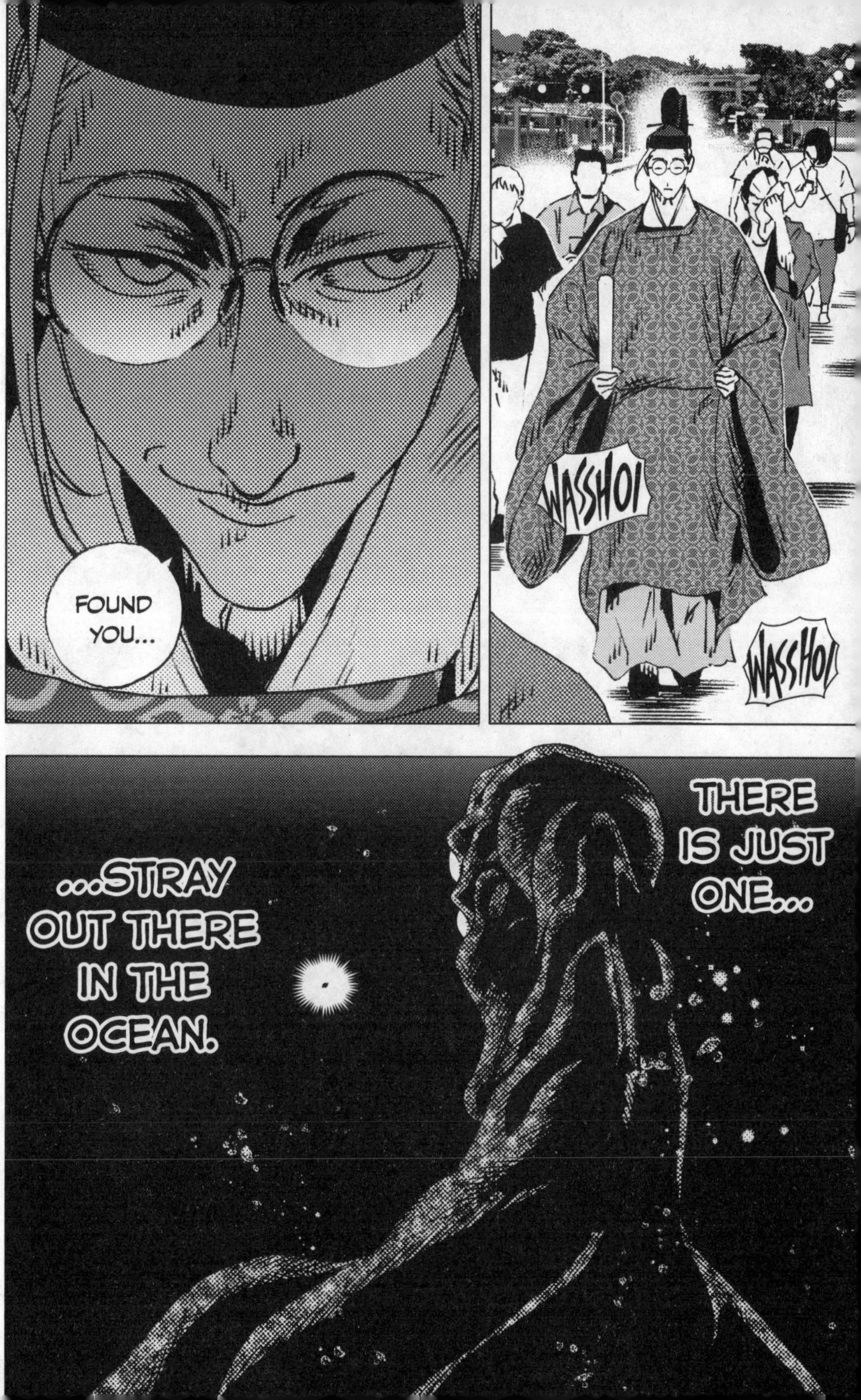
WASSHOI
WASSHOI
FOUND YOU...
THERE IS JUST ONE...
...STRAY OUT THERE IN THE OCEAN.

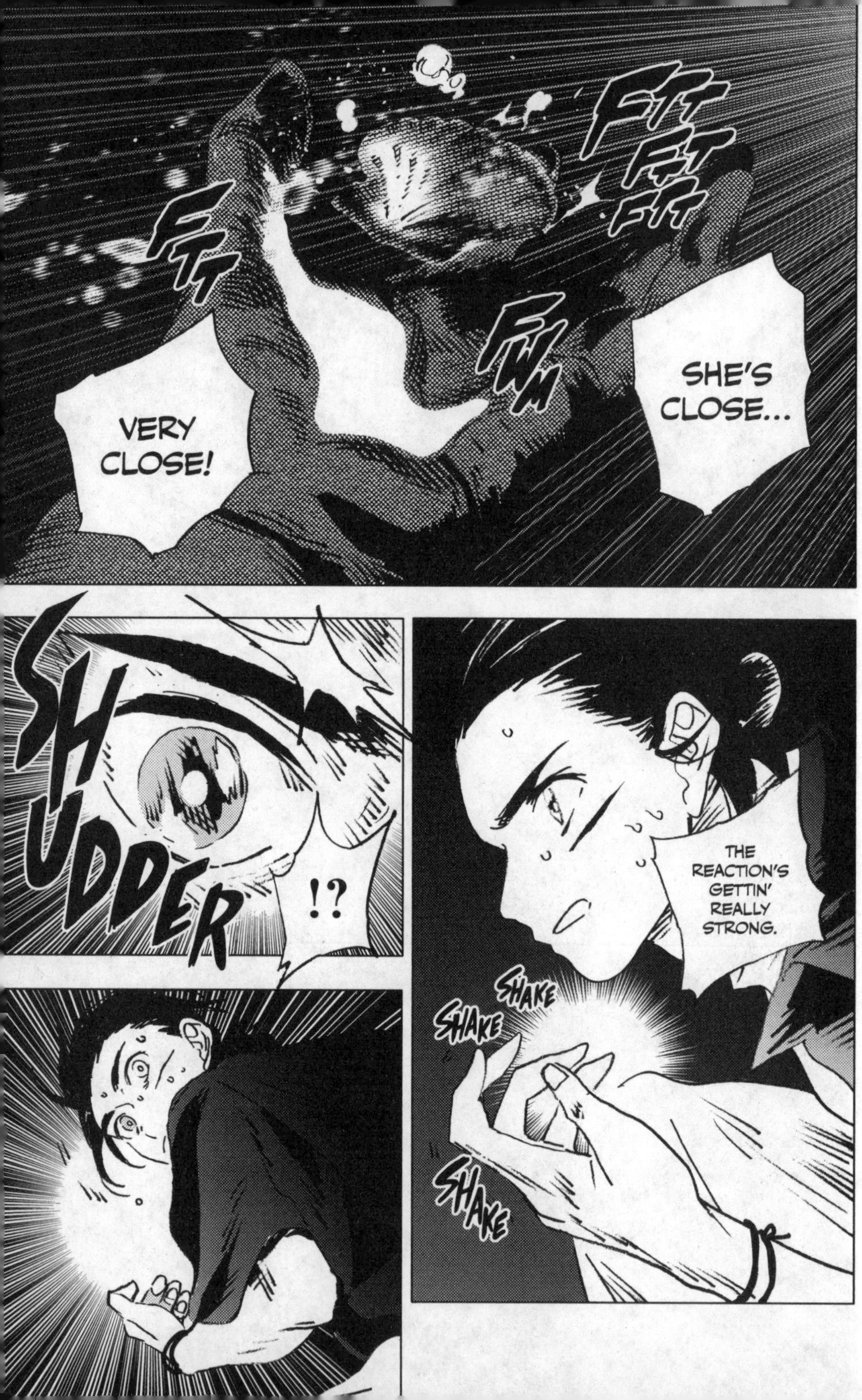
FTT
FTT
FTT
SHE'S CLOSE...
FWM
FTT
VERY CLOSE!
THE REACTION'S GETTIN' REALLY STRONG.
SHAKE
SHAKE
SHAKE
SHUDDER
!?

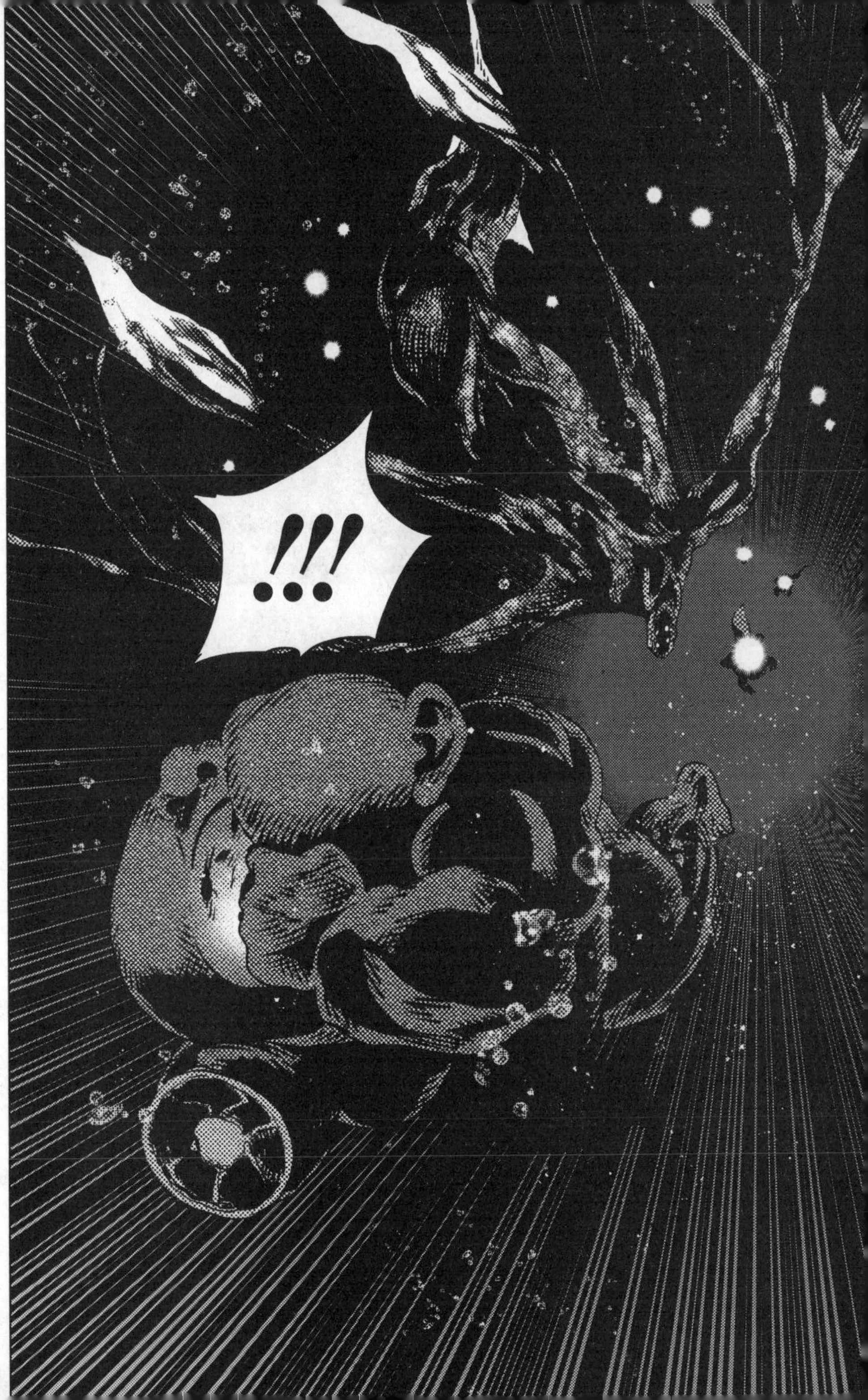
!!!

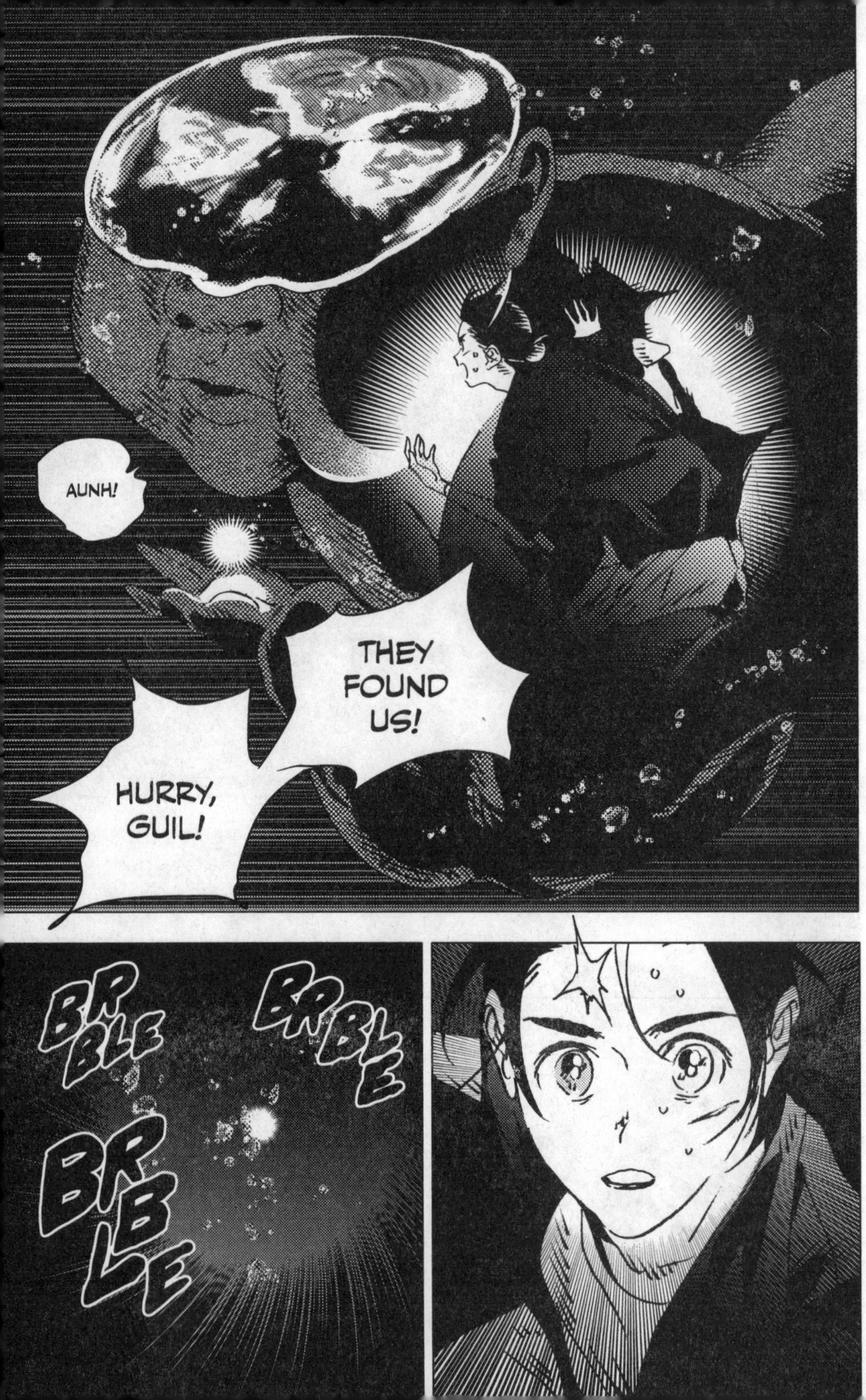
AUNH!
THEY FOUND US!
HURRY, GUIL!
BRBLE
BRBLE
BRBLE

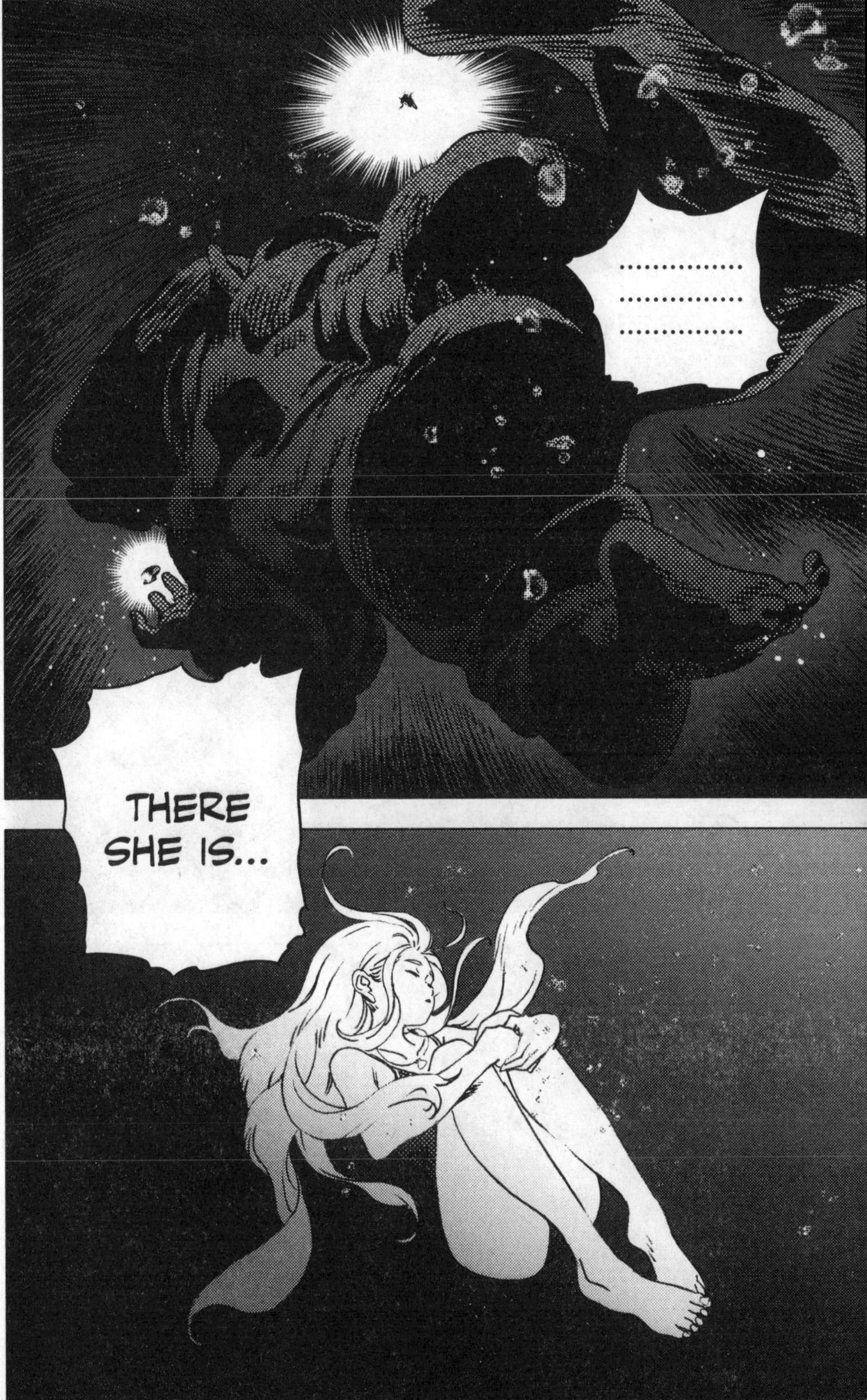
………………
………………
………………
THERE SHE IS...

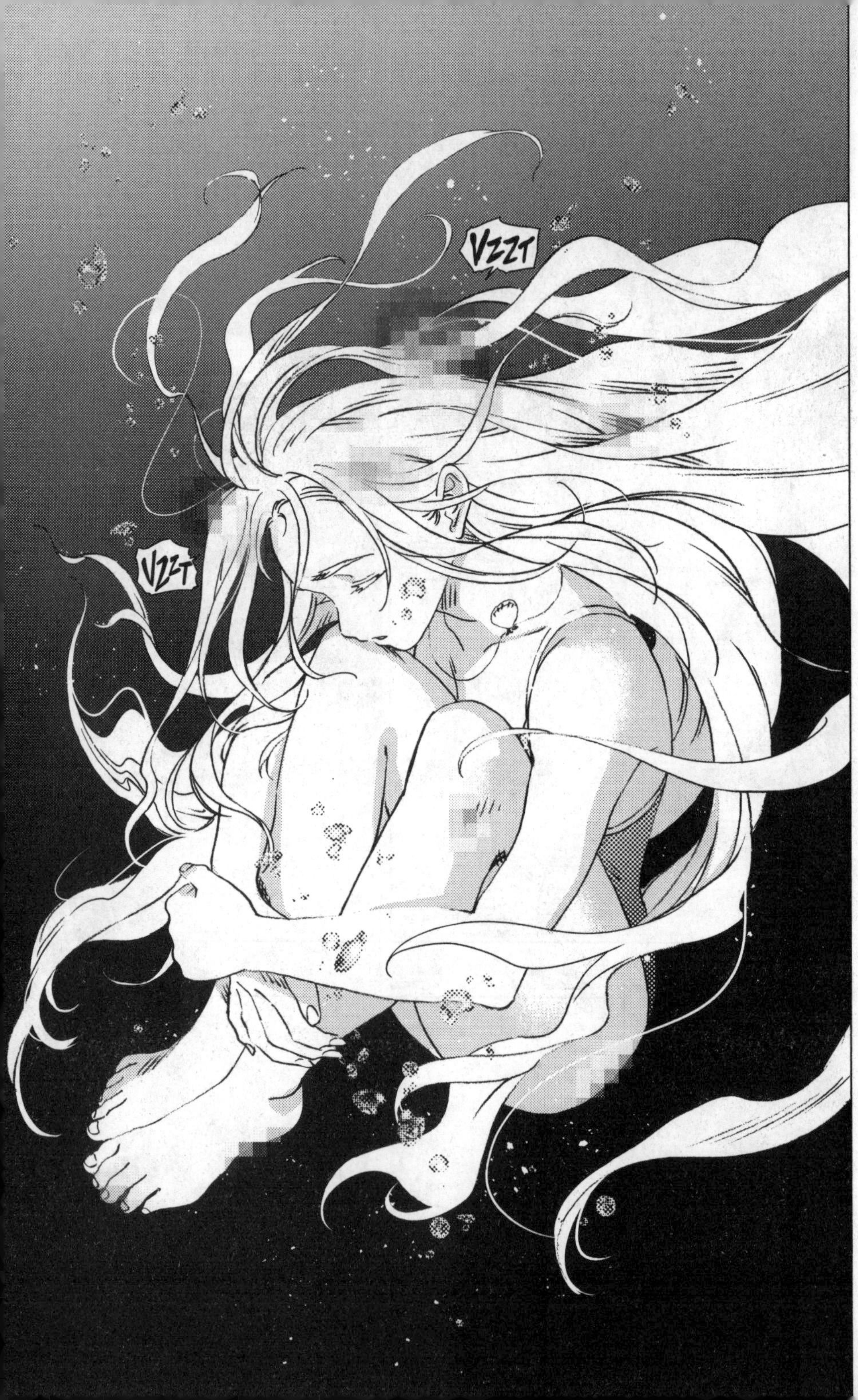
VZZT
VZZT

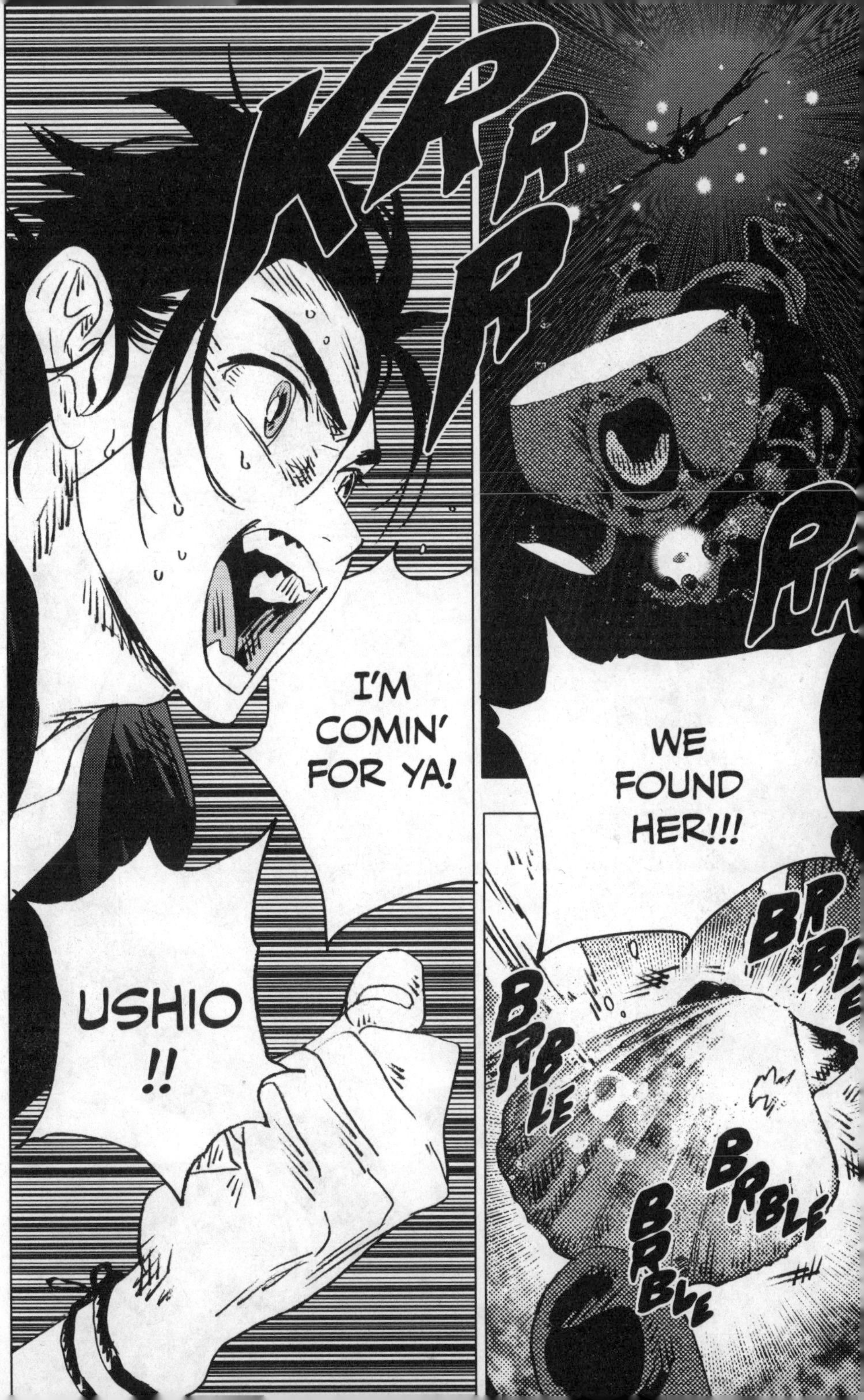
WE FOUND HER!!!
BRBLE
BRRBLE
BRBLE
BRBLE
KIRRR
I'M COMIN' FOR YA!
USHIO !!

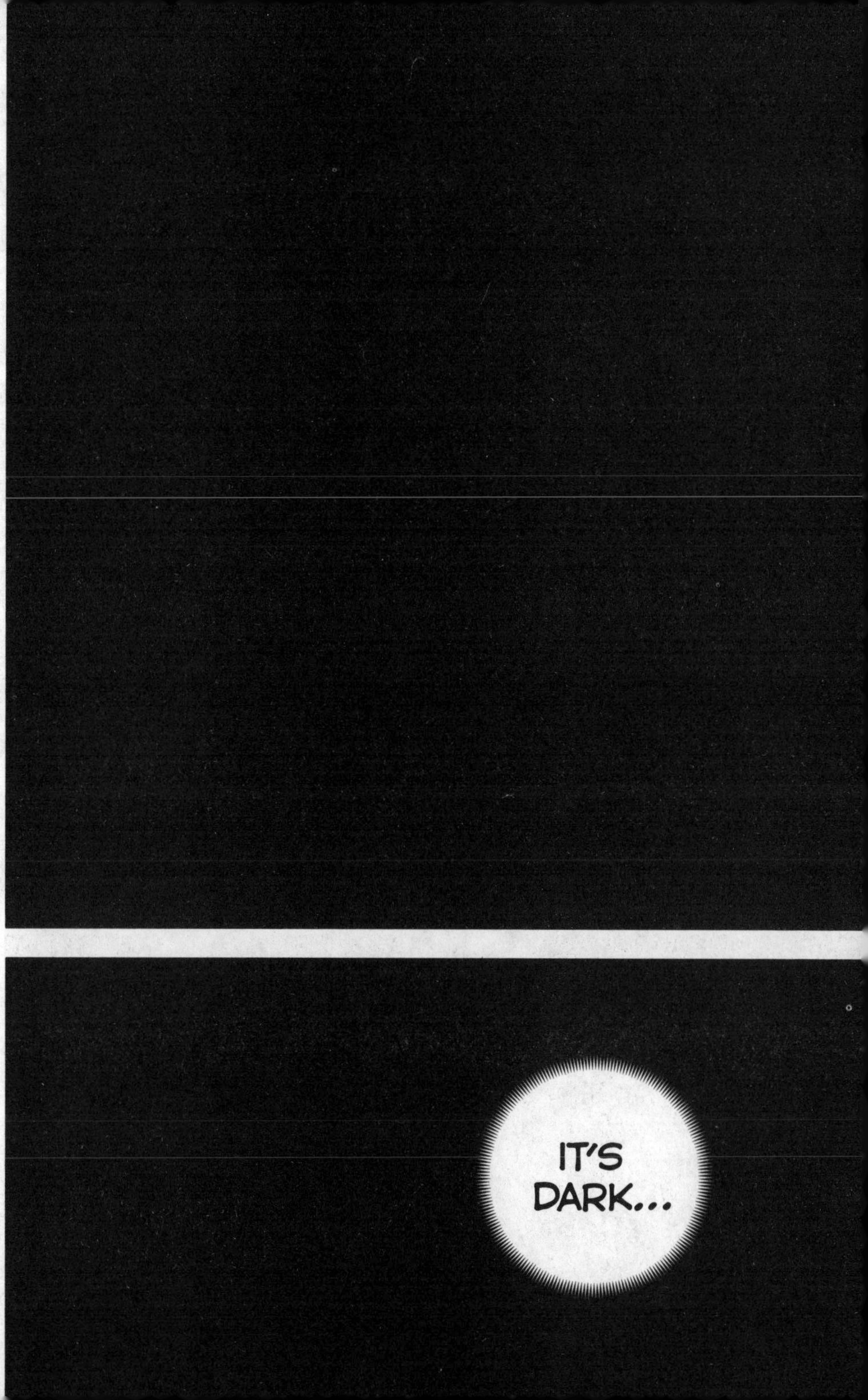
IT'S DARK...

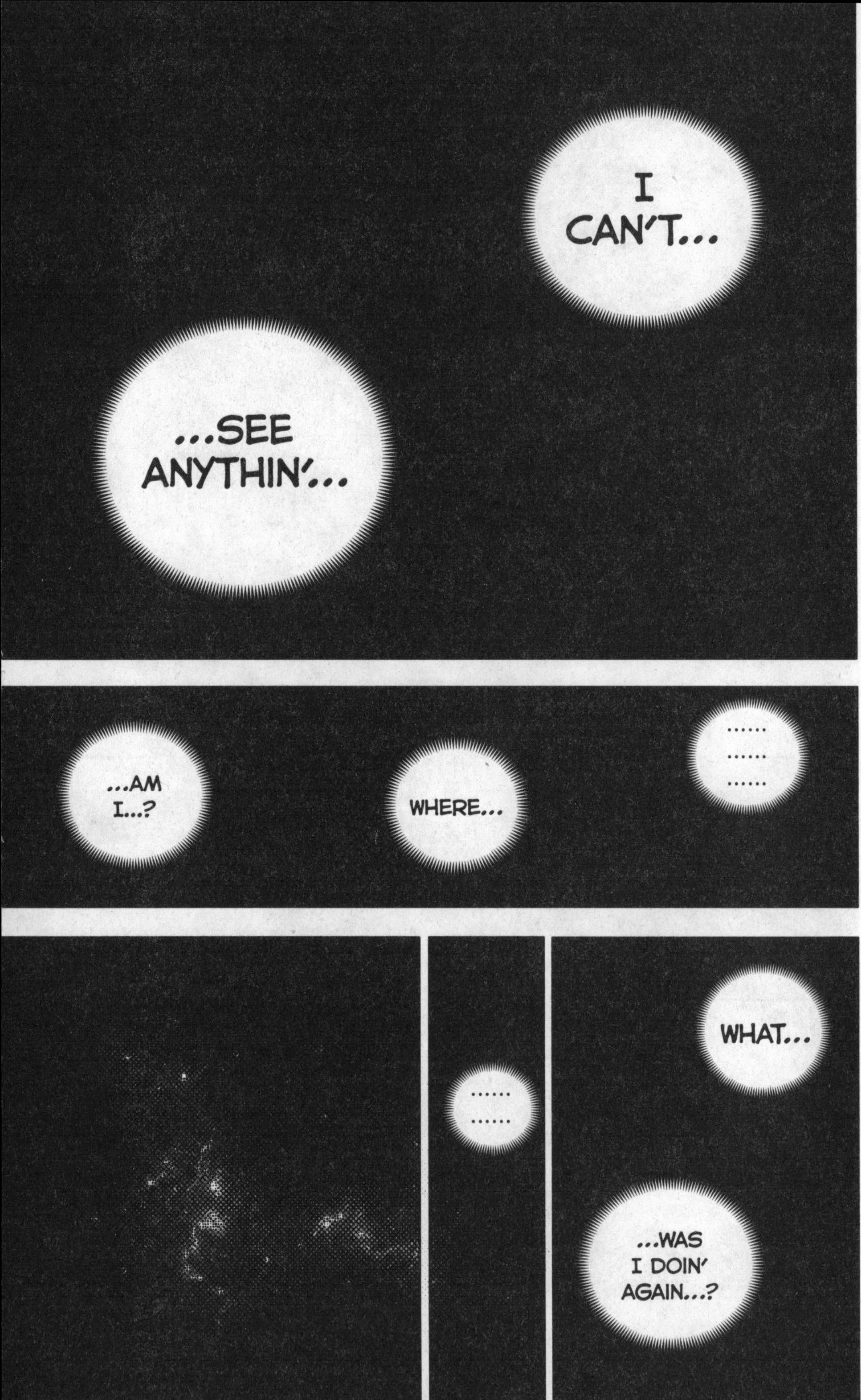
I CAN'T...
...SEE ANYTHIN'...
......
......
......
WHERE...
...AM I...?
WHAT...
...WAS I DOIN' AGAIN...?
......
......

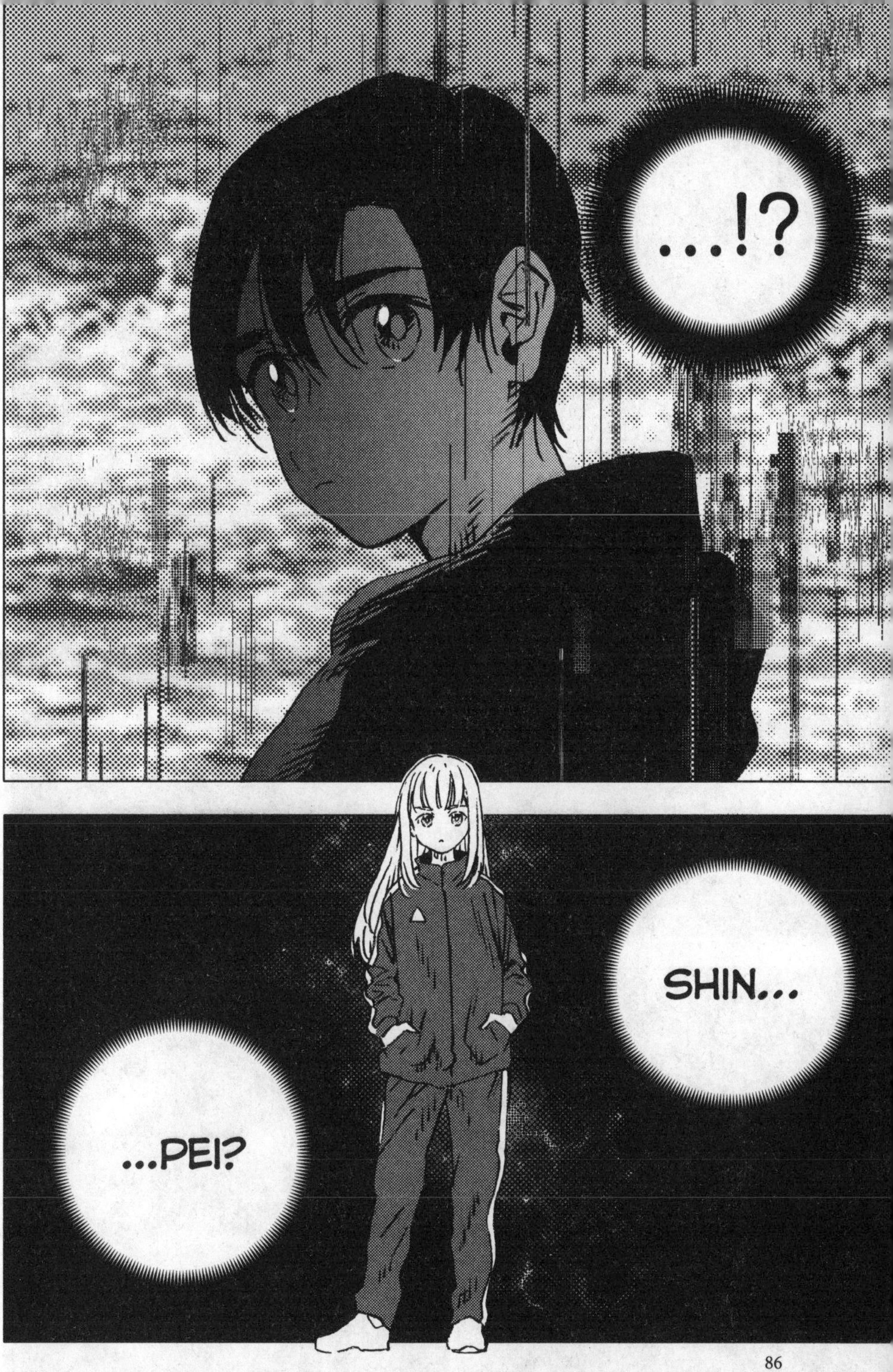
...!?
SHIN...
...PEI?

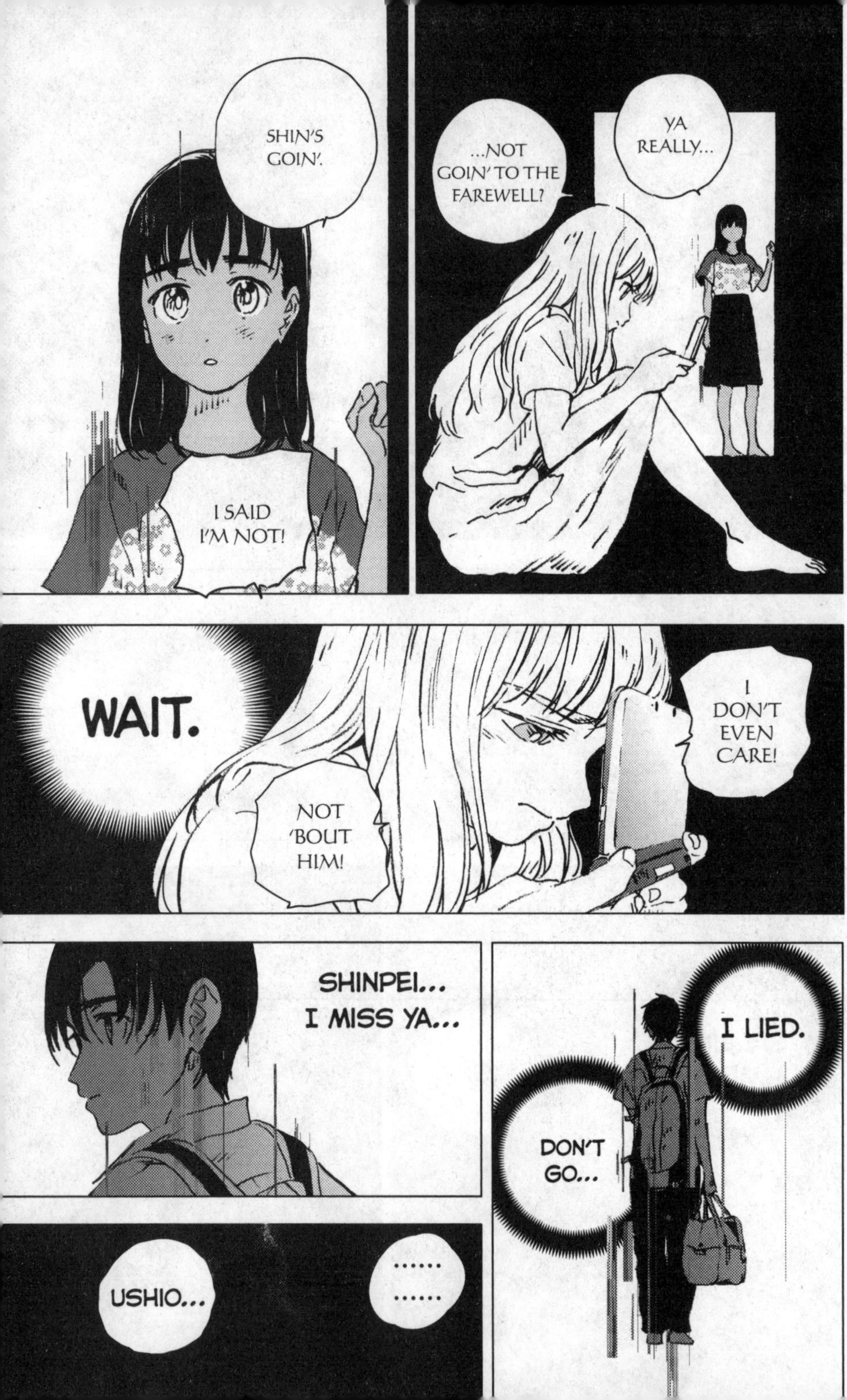
YA REALLY...
...NOT GOIN' TO THE FAREWELL?
SHIN'S GOIN'.
I SAID I'M NOT!
I DON'T EVEN CARE!
NOT 'BOUT HIM!
WAIT.
I LIED.
DON'T GO...
SHINPEI... I MISS YA...
......
......
USHIO...

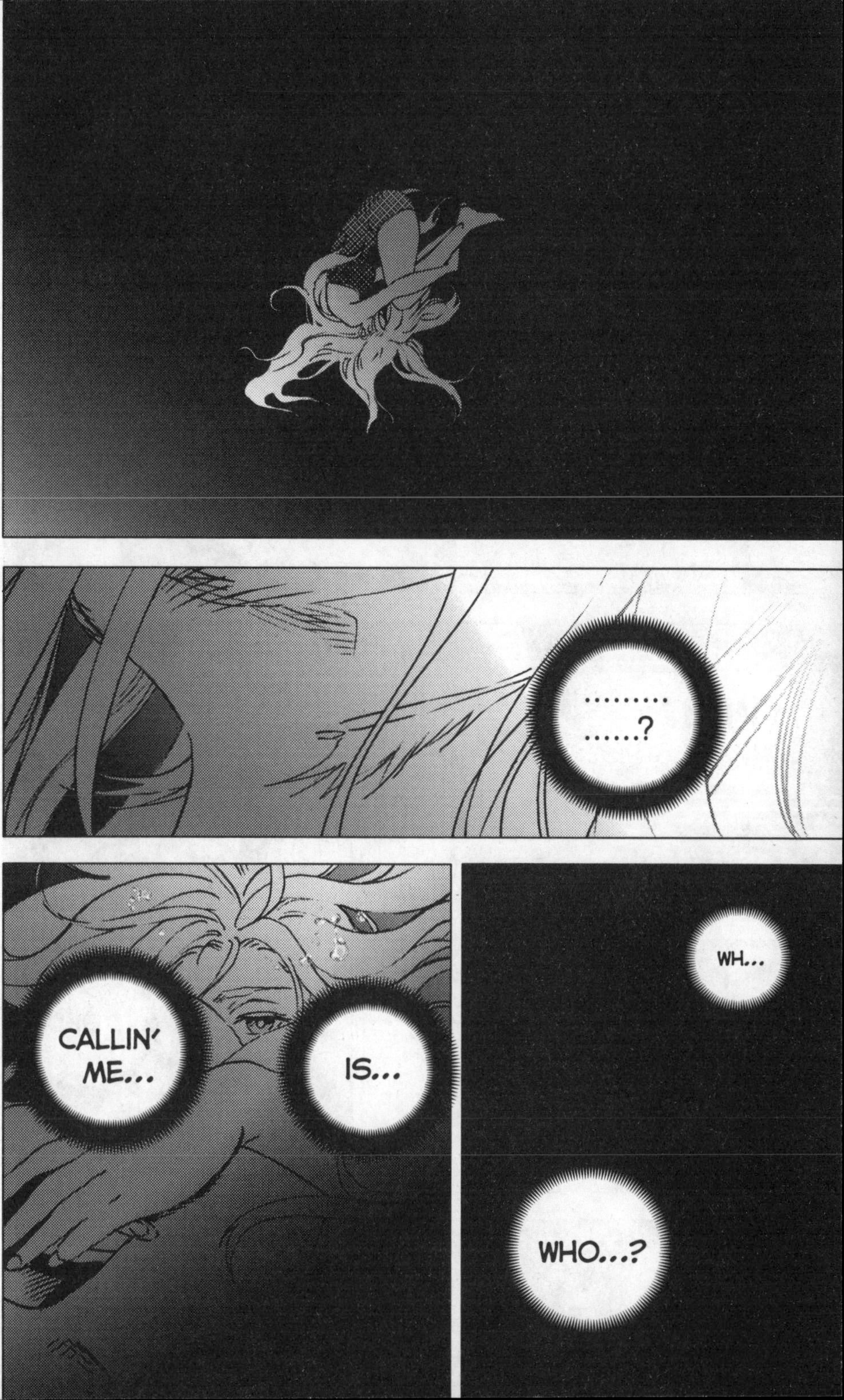
....
......?
WH...
WHO...?
IS...
CALLIN' ME...

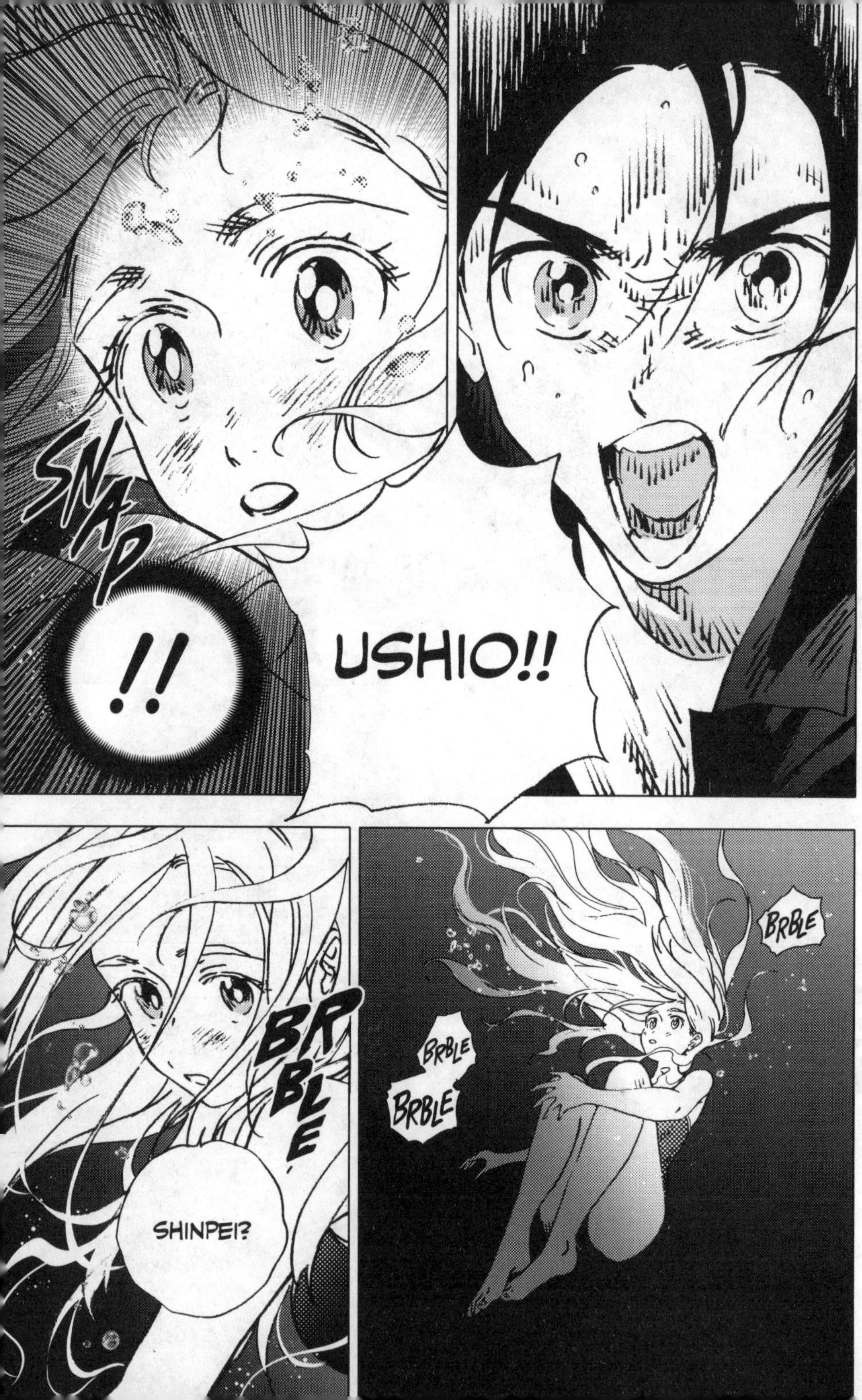

USHIO!!
SNAP
!!
BRBLE
BRBLE
BRBLE
BRBLE
SHINPEI?

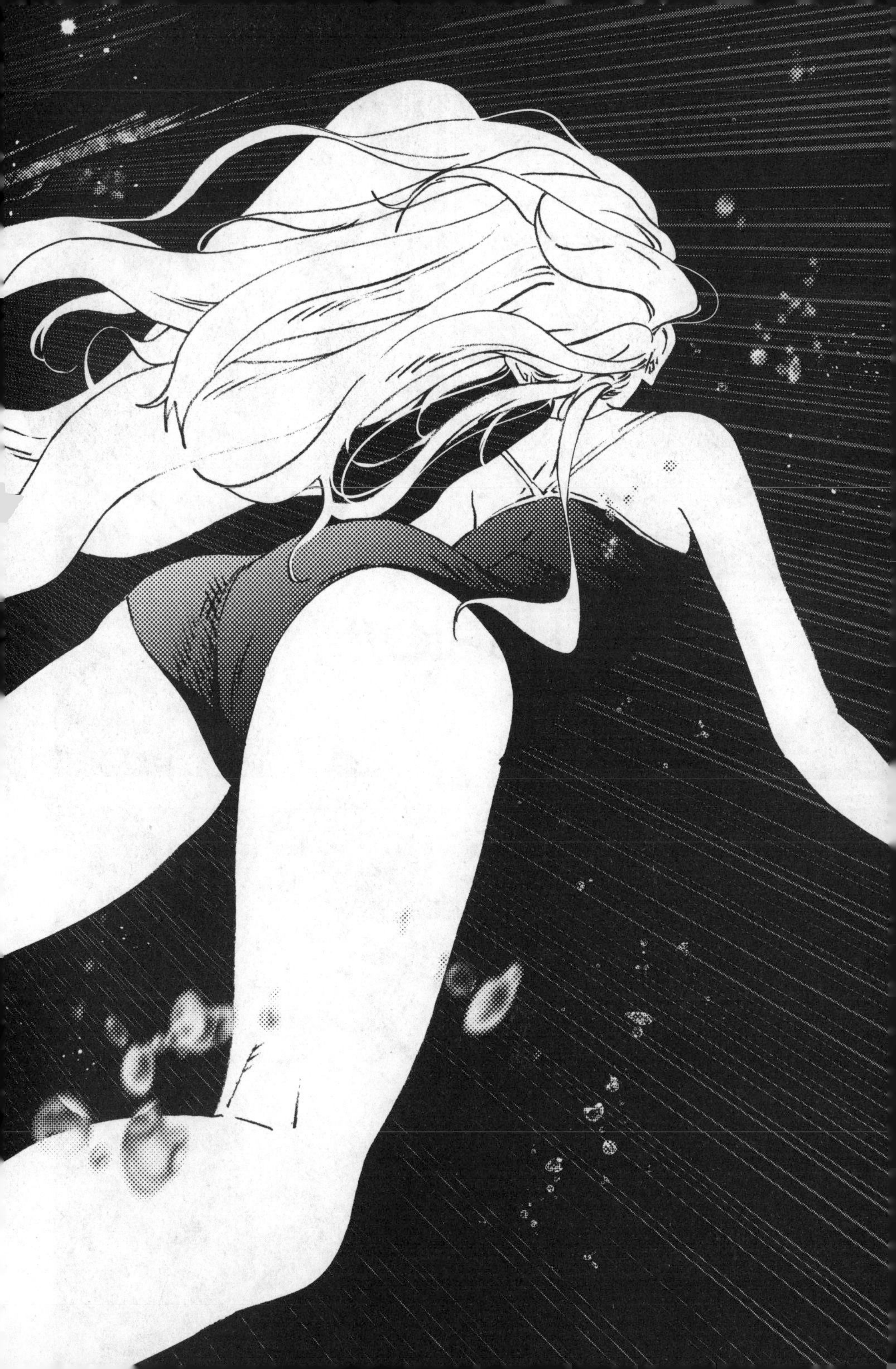

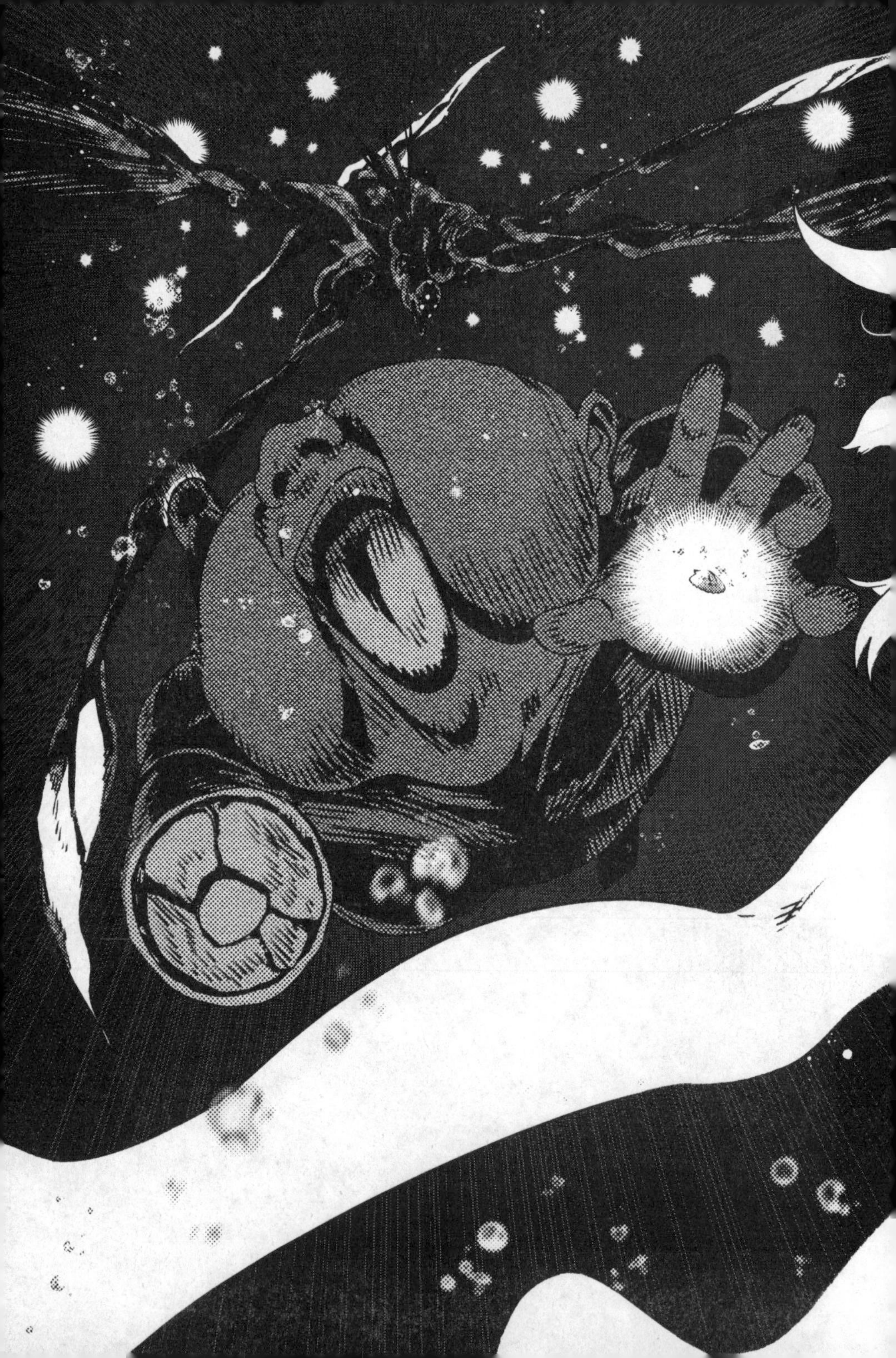

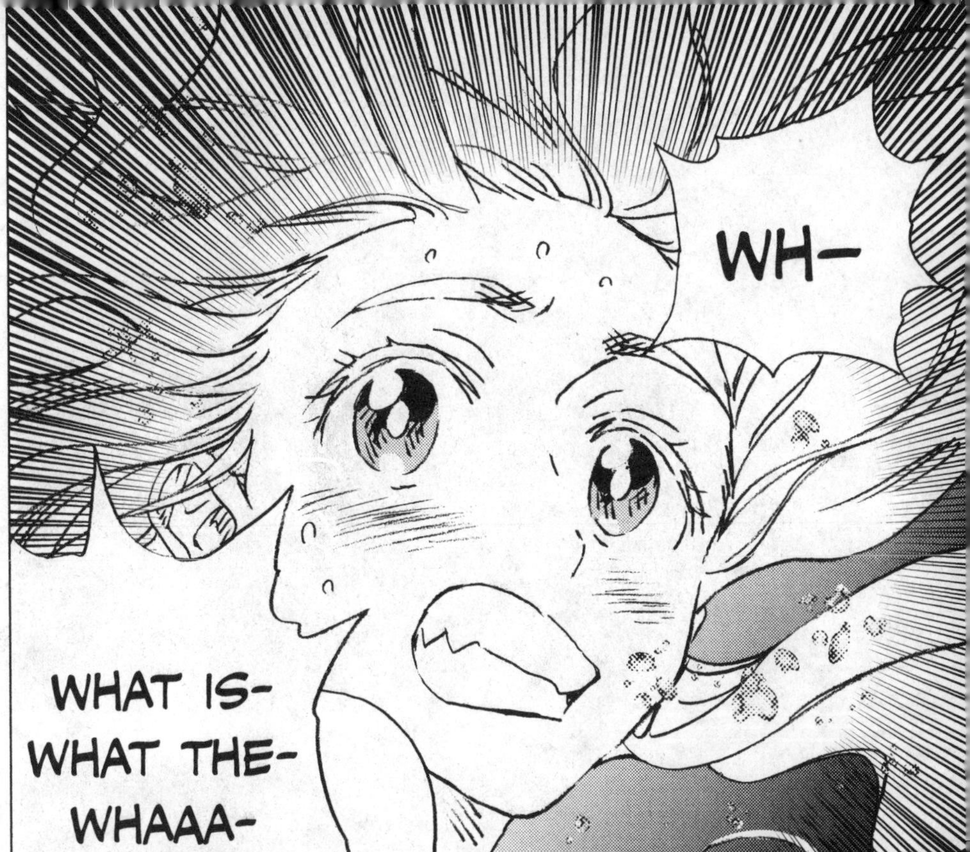
WH-
WHAT IS- WHAT THE- WHAAA- AAT?!

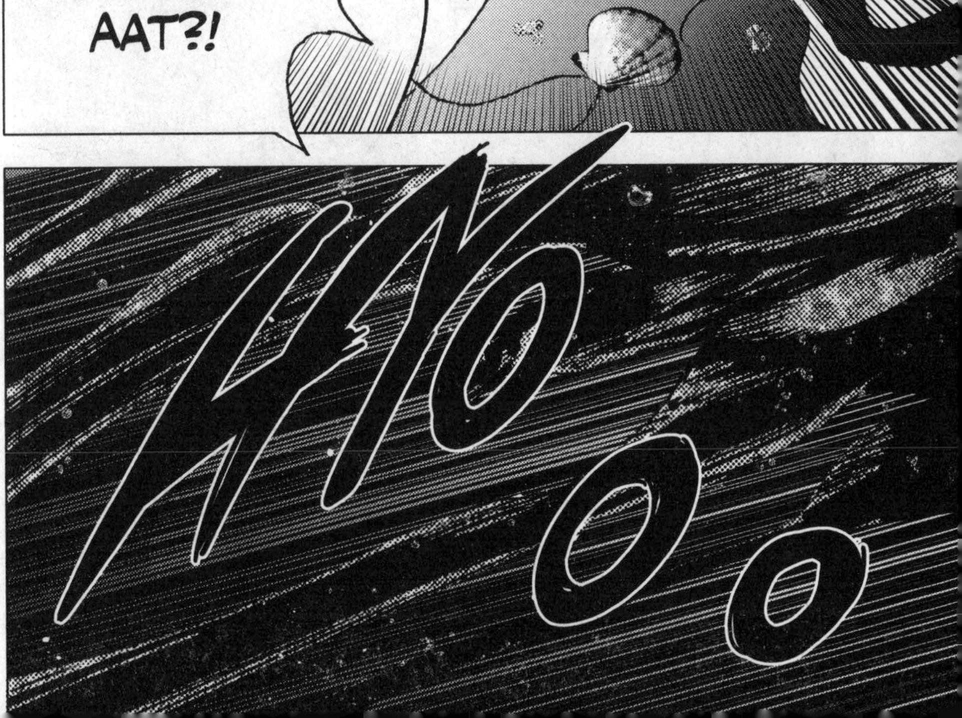

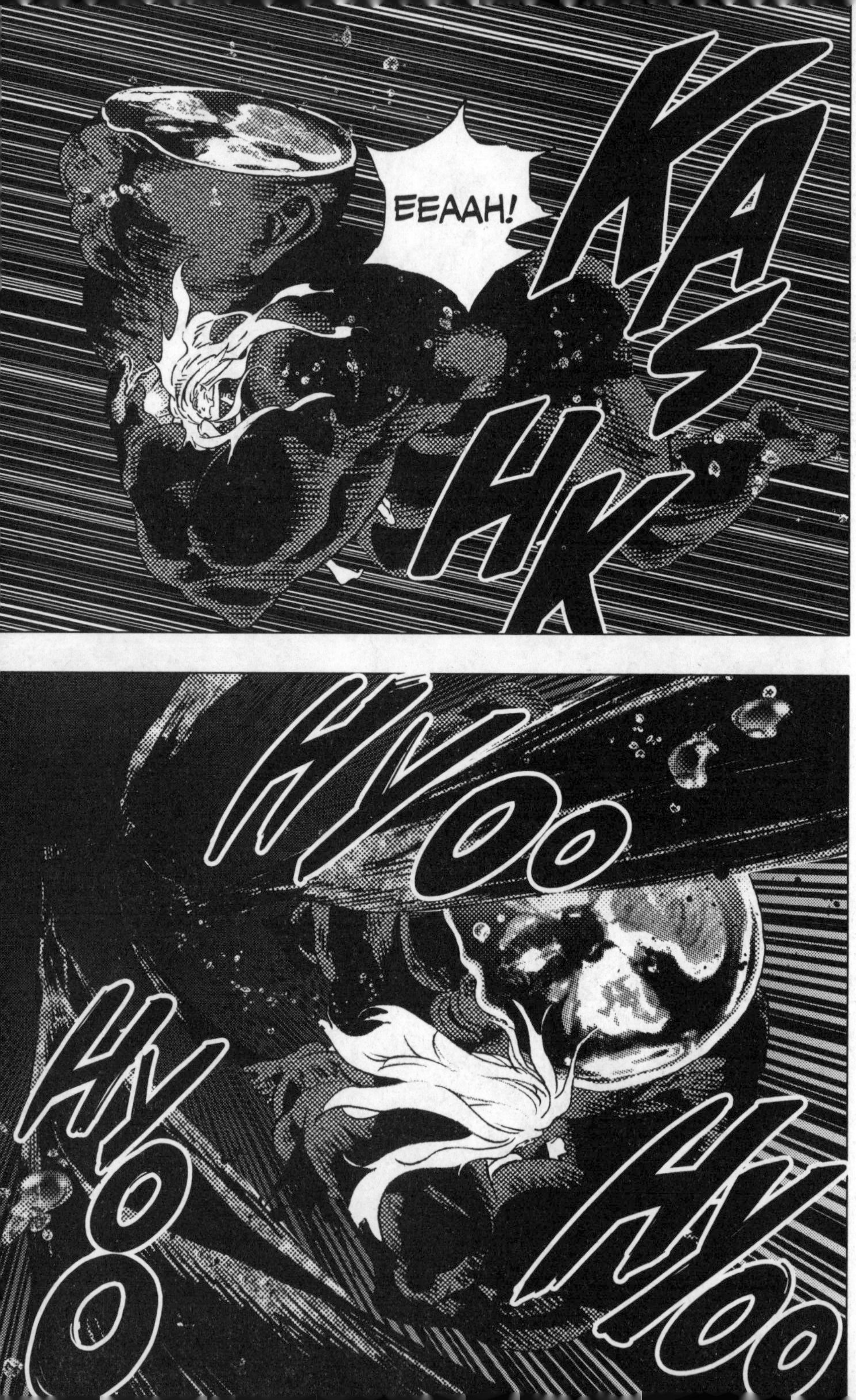
KASHK
EEAAH!
HYOO
HYOO
HYOO

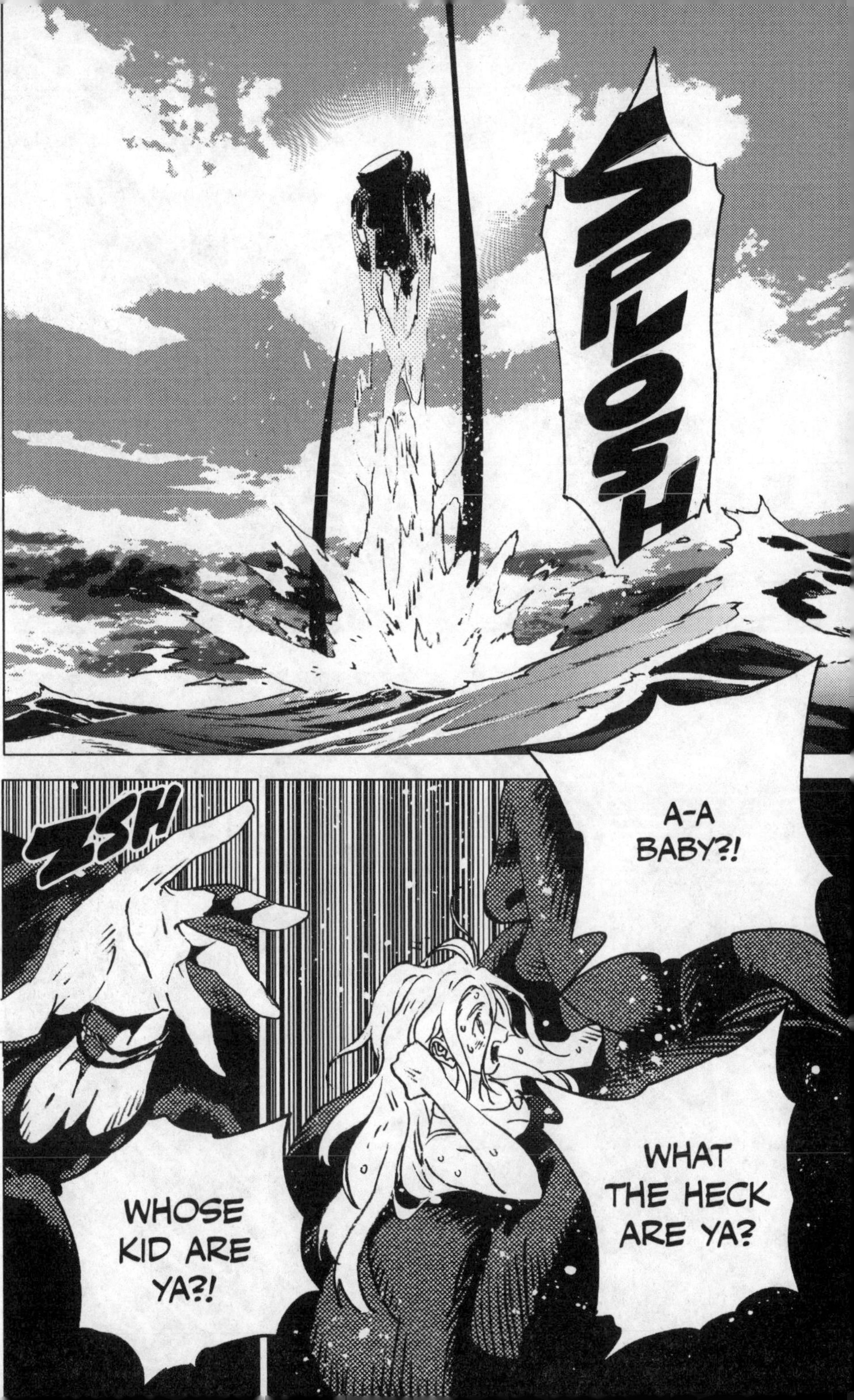
SPLOSH
A-A BABY?!
WHAT THE HECK ARE YA?
WHOSE KID ARE YA?!
ZSH

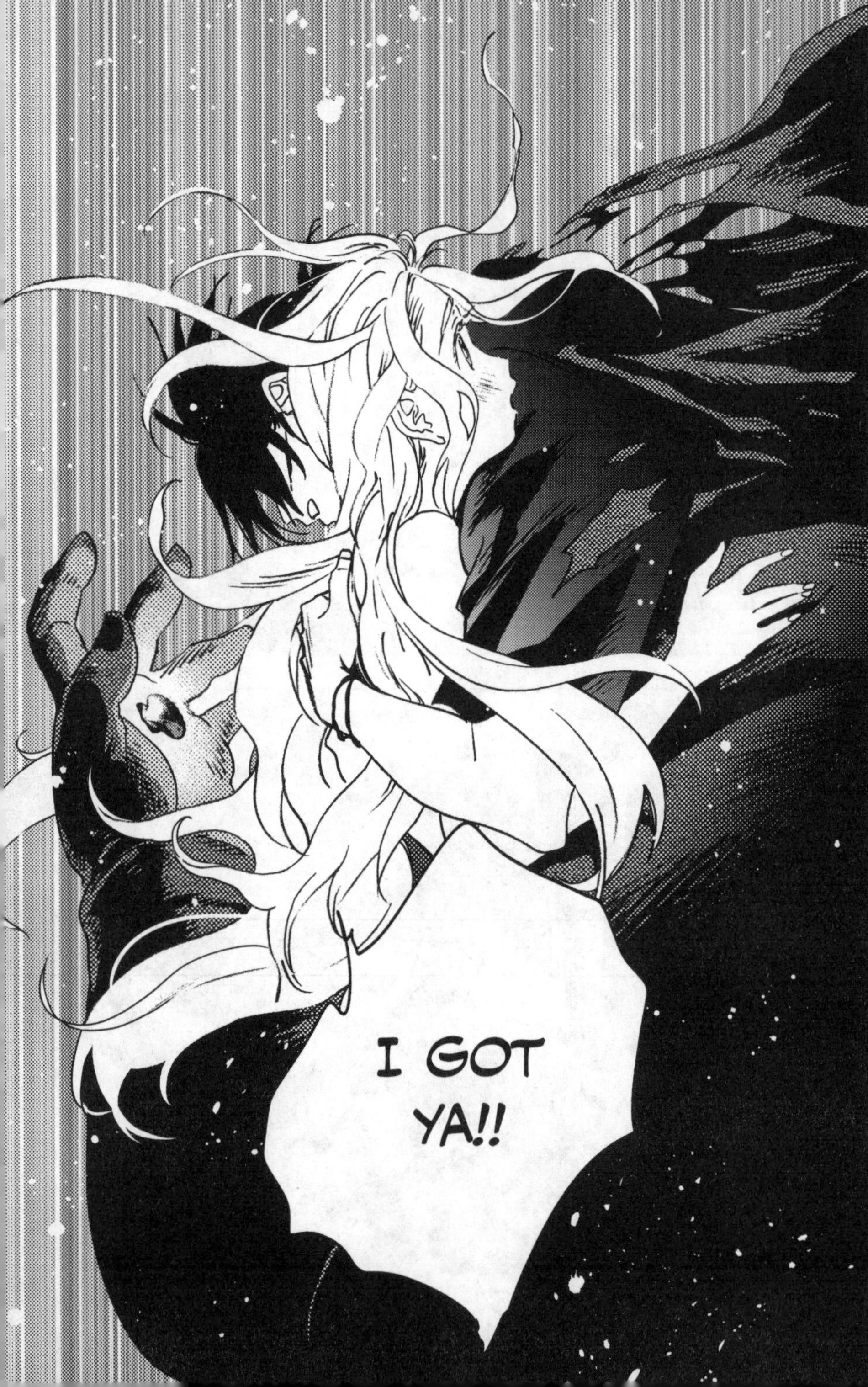
I GOT YA!!

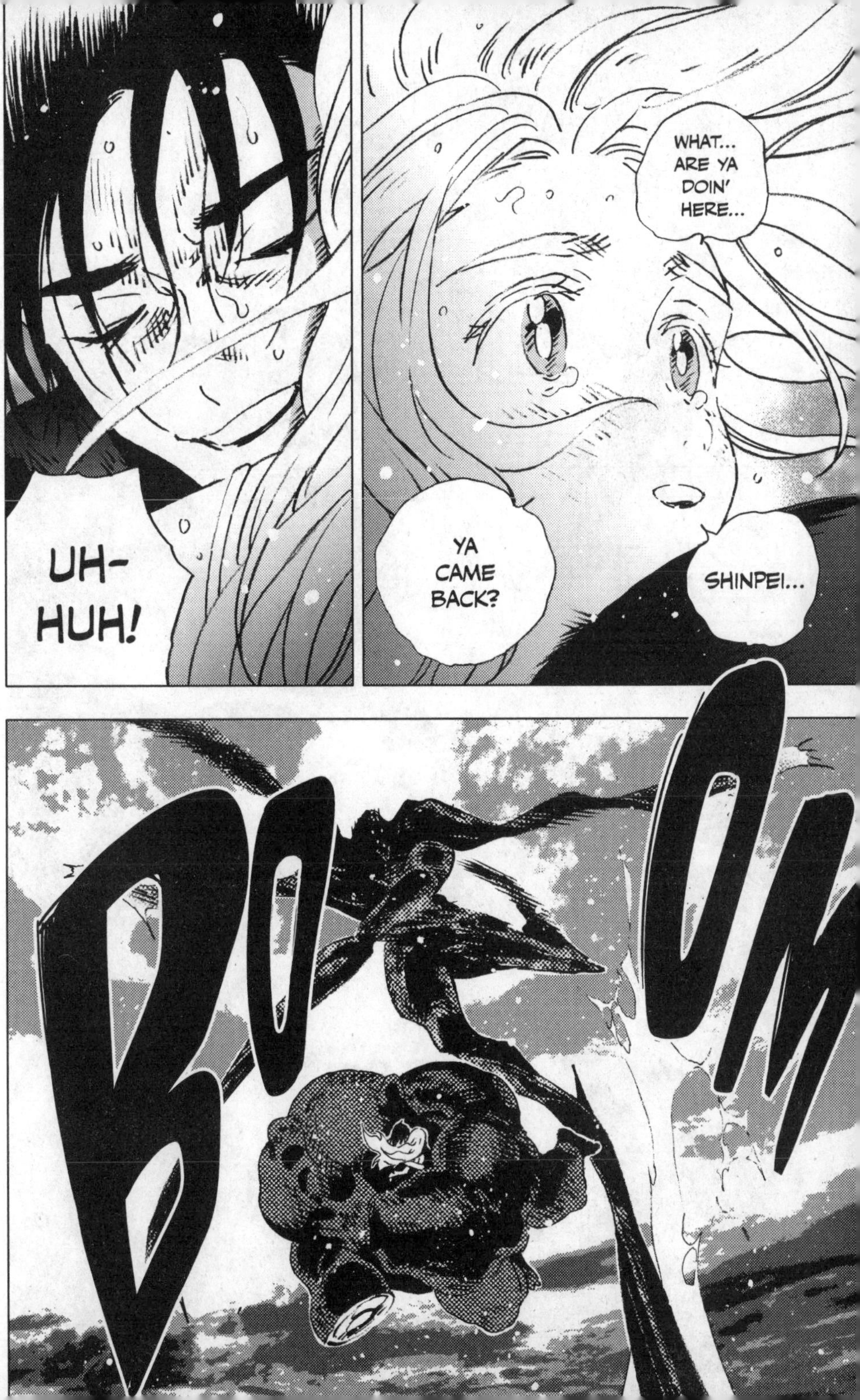
WHAT... ARE YA DOIN' HERE...
SHINPEI...
YA CAME BACK?
UH-HUH!
BOOM

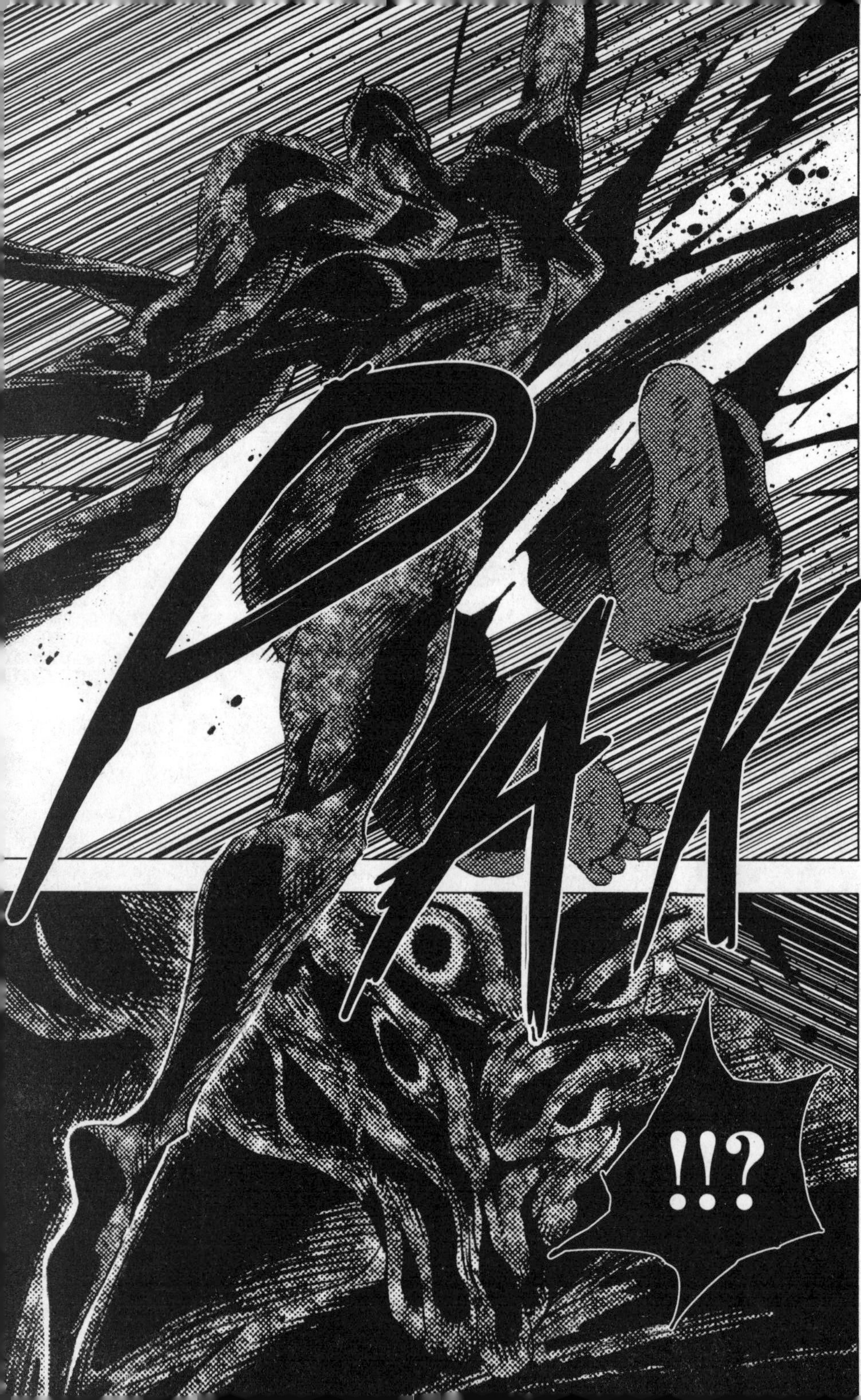
!!?

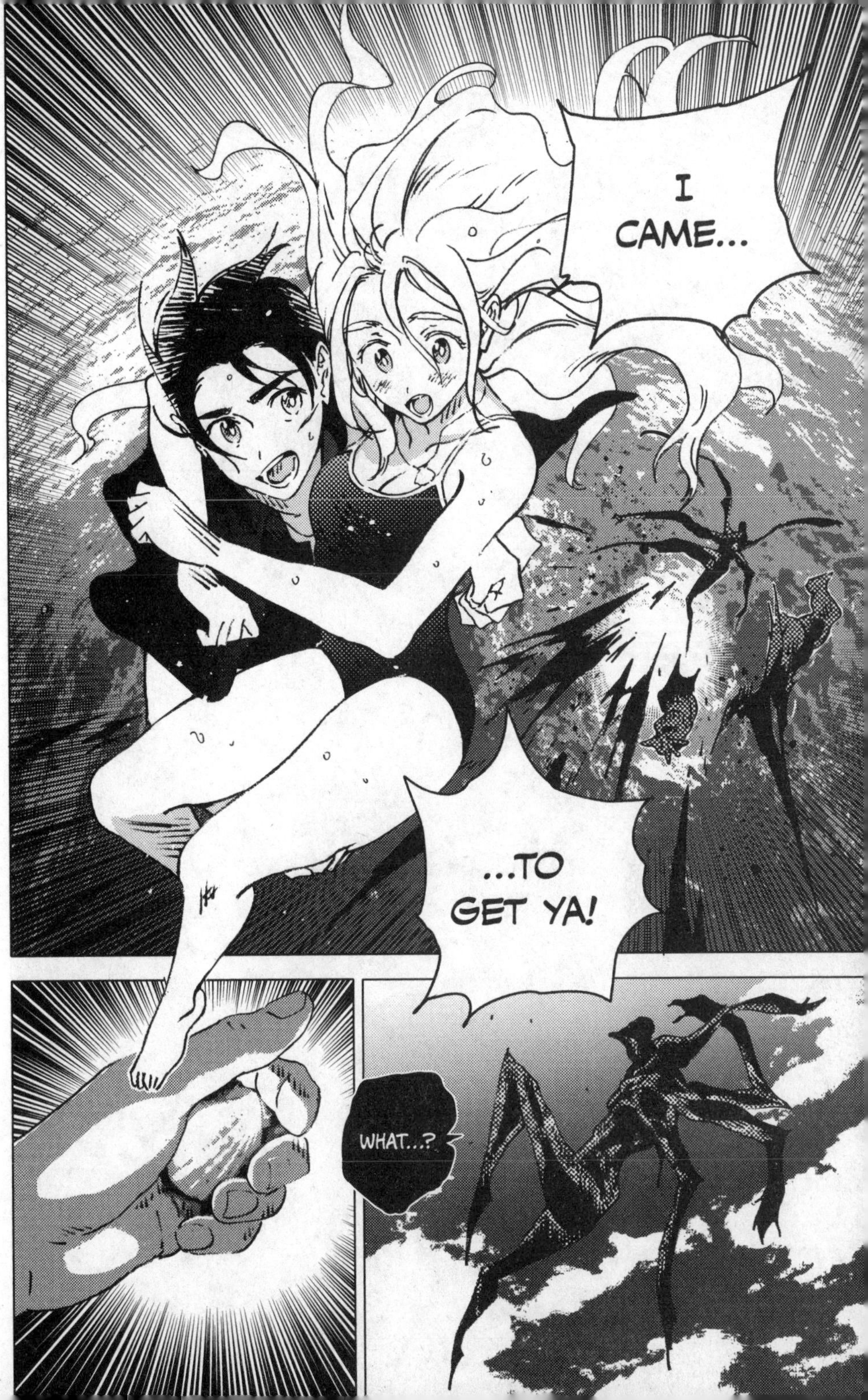
I CAME...
...TO GET YA!
WHAT...?

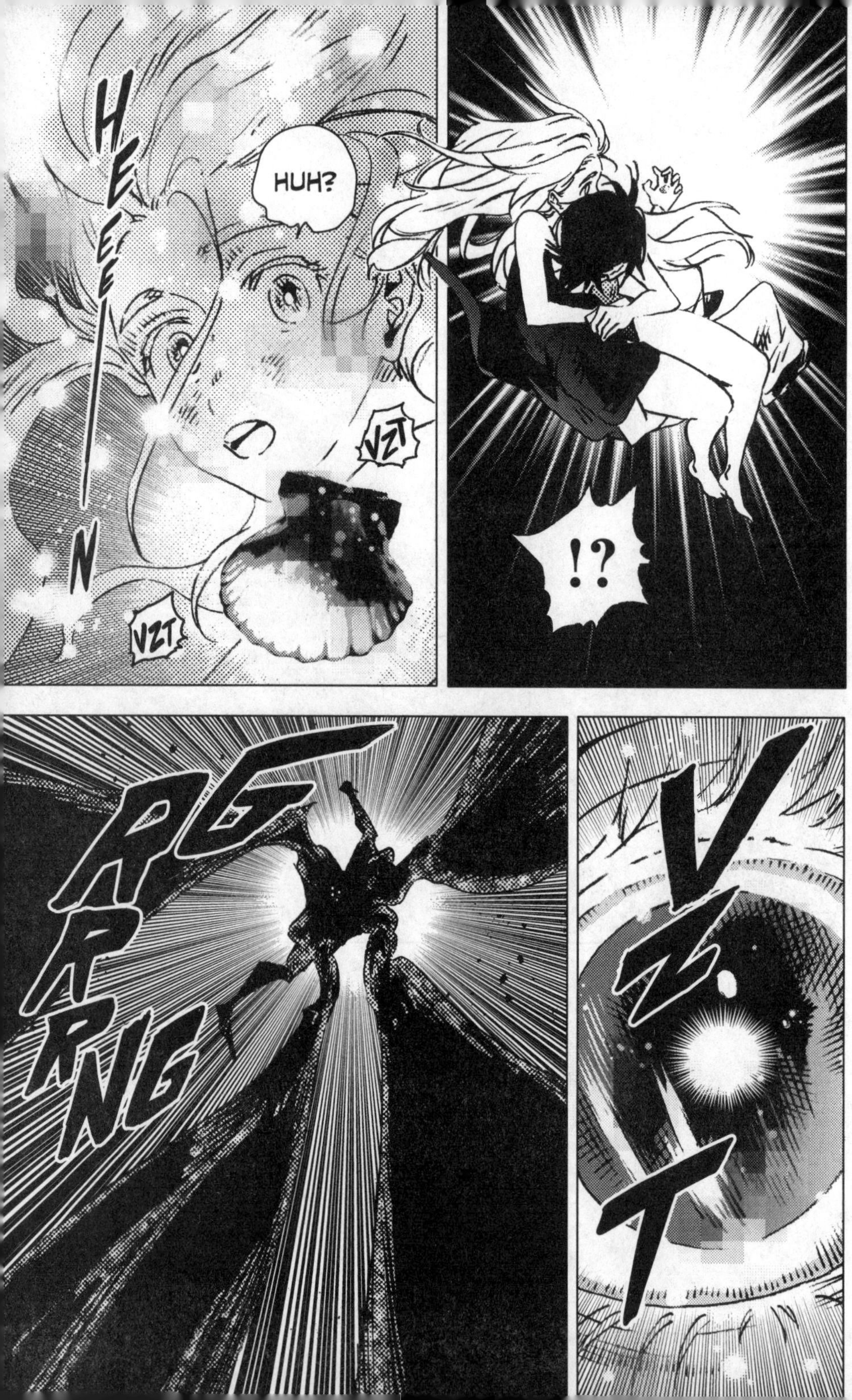
!?
HUH?
HEEE—N
VZT
VZT
VZZT

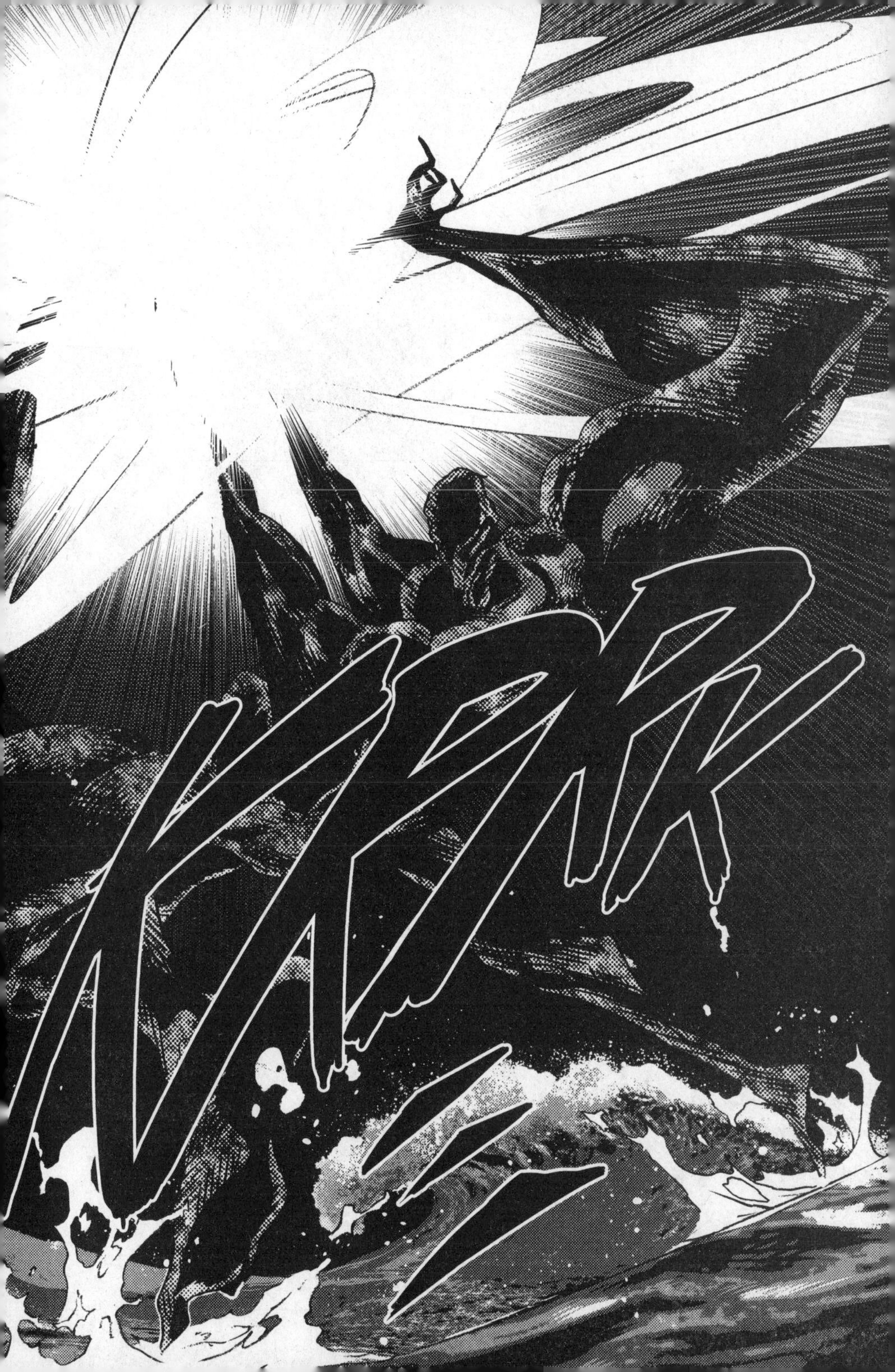

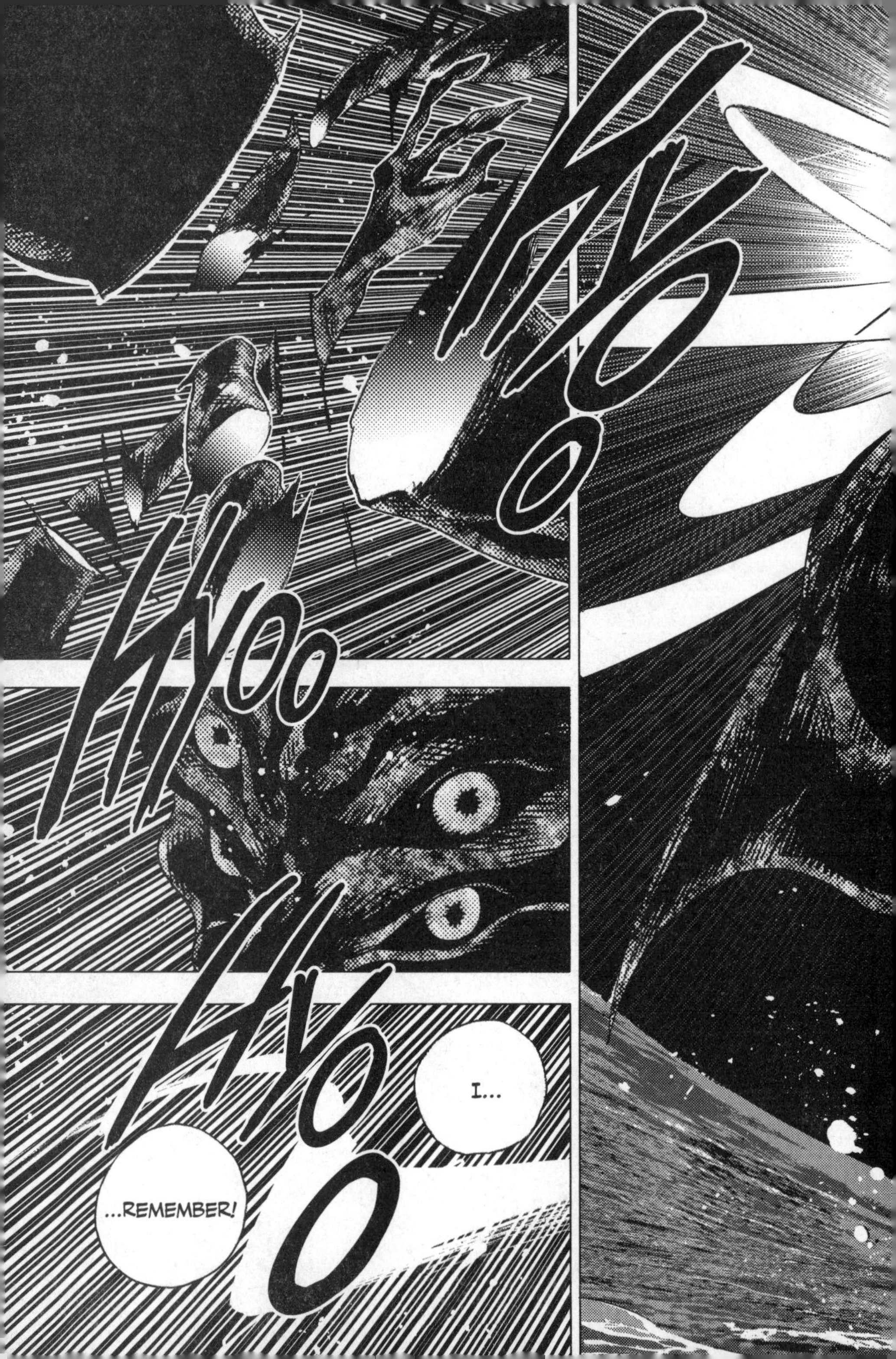
HYOO
HYOO
HYOOO
I...
...REMEMBER!

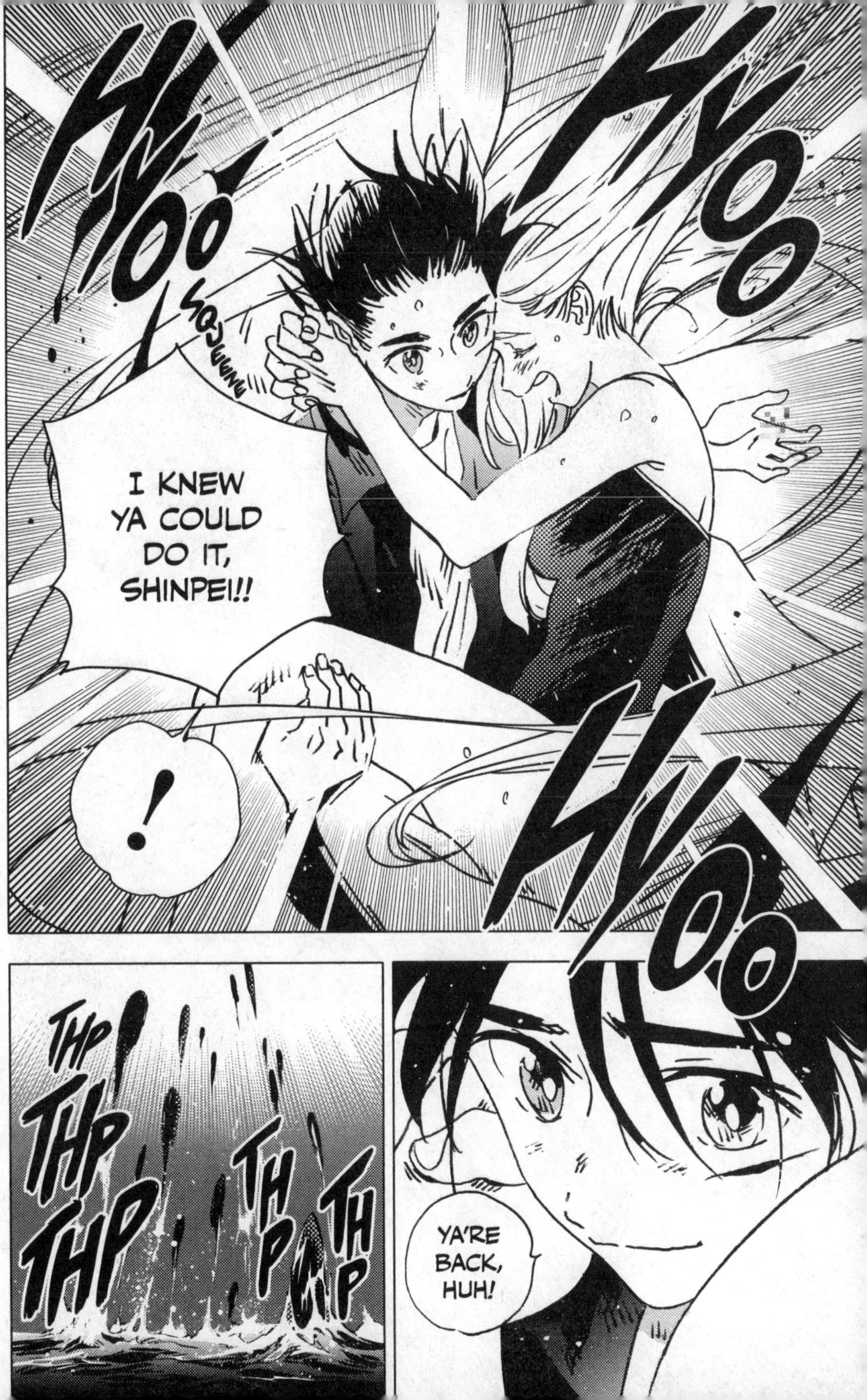
HYOO
HYOO
I KNEW YA COULD DO IT, SHINPEI!!
!
HYOO
YA'RE BACK, HUH!
THP THP THP
TH P
TH P

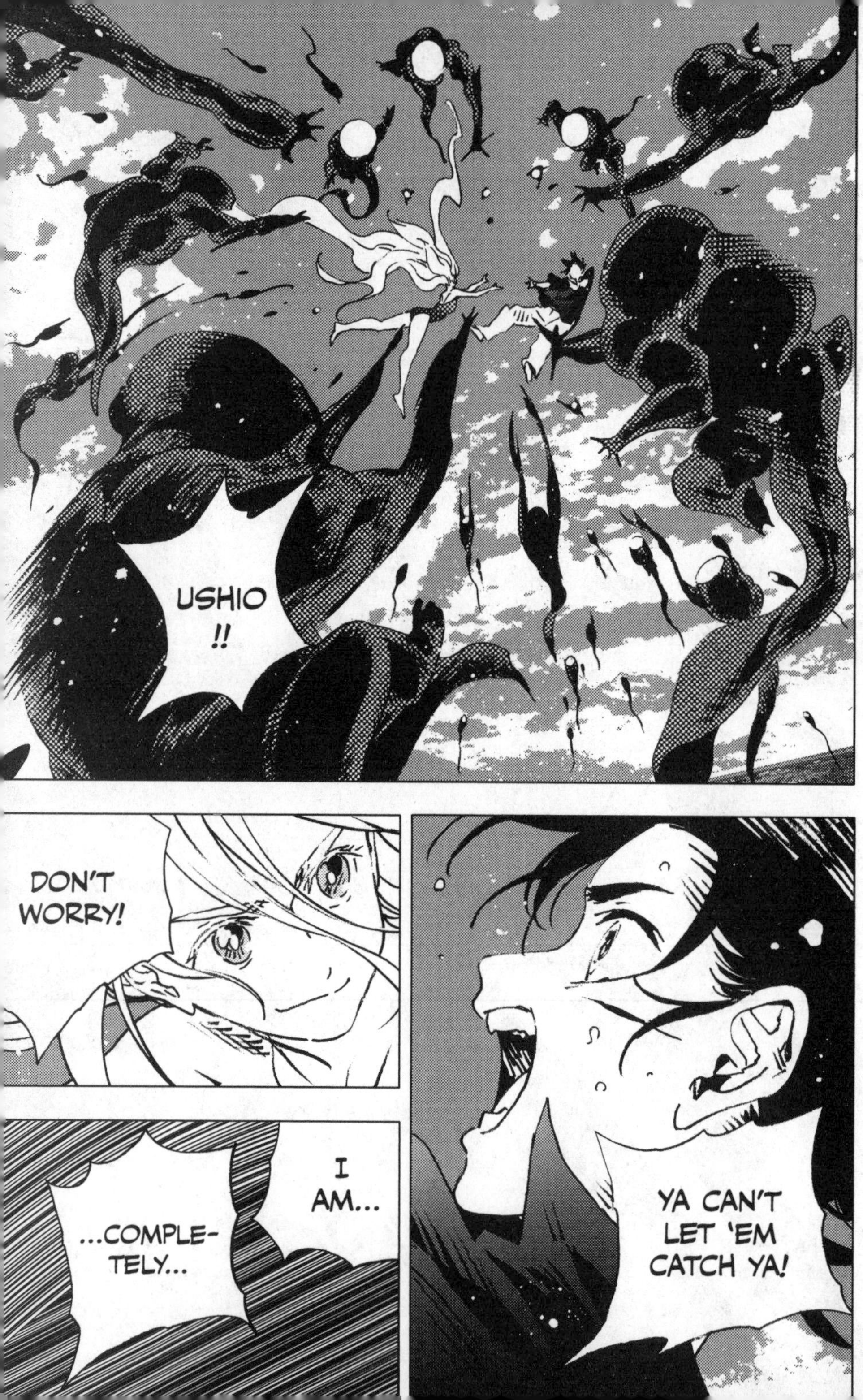
USHIO !!
YA CAN'T LET 'EM CATCH YA!
DON'T WORRY!
I AM...
...COMPLETELY...

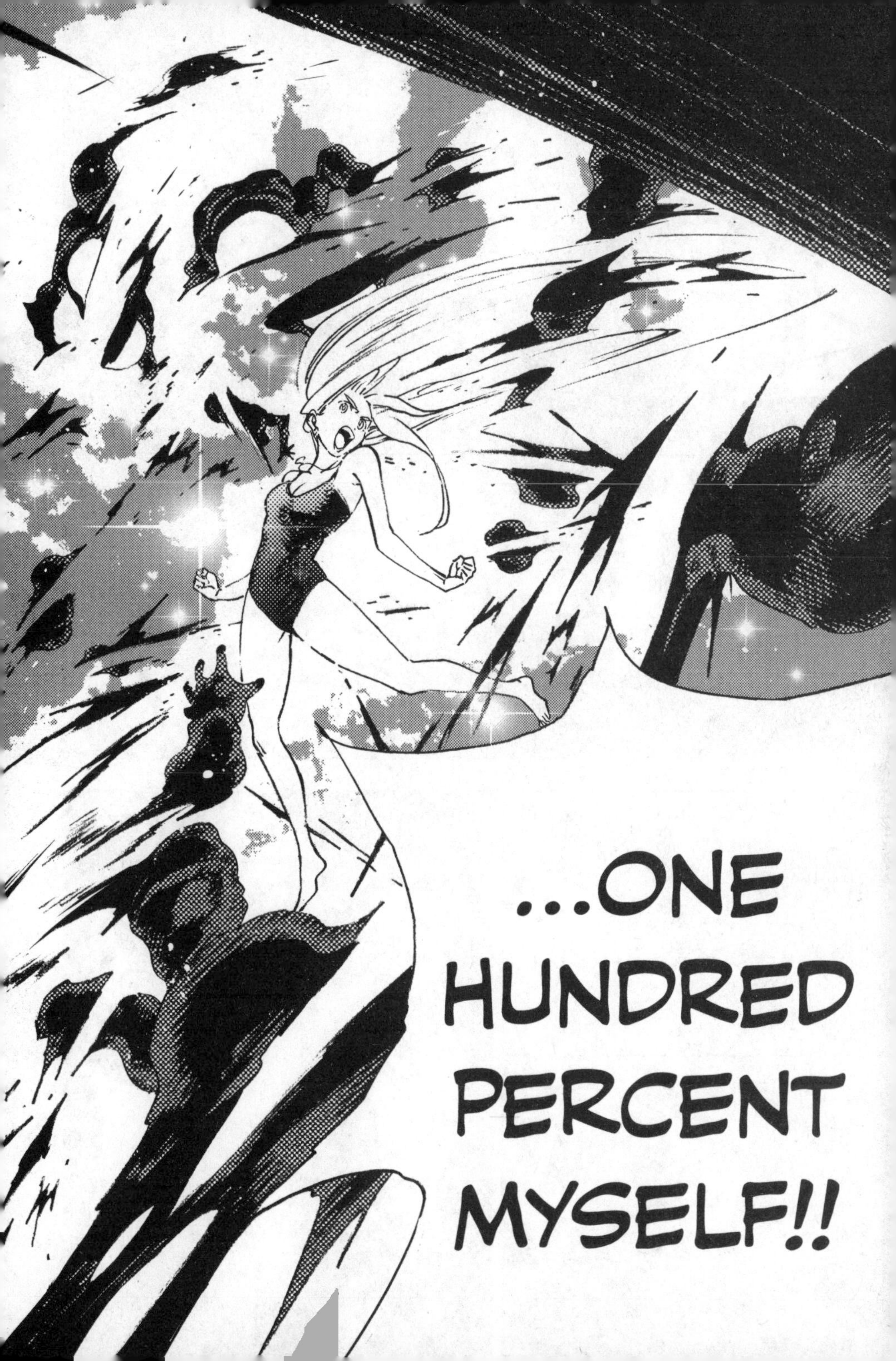
...ONE HUNDRED PERCENT MYSELF!!

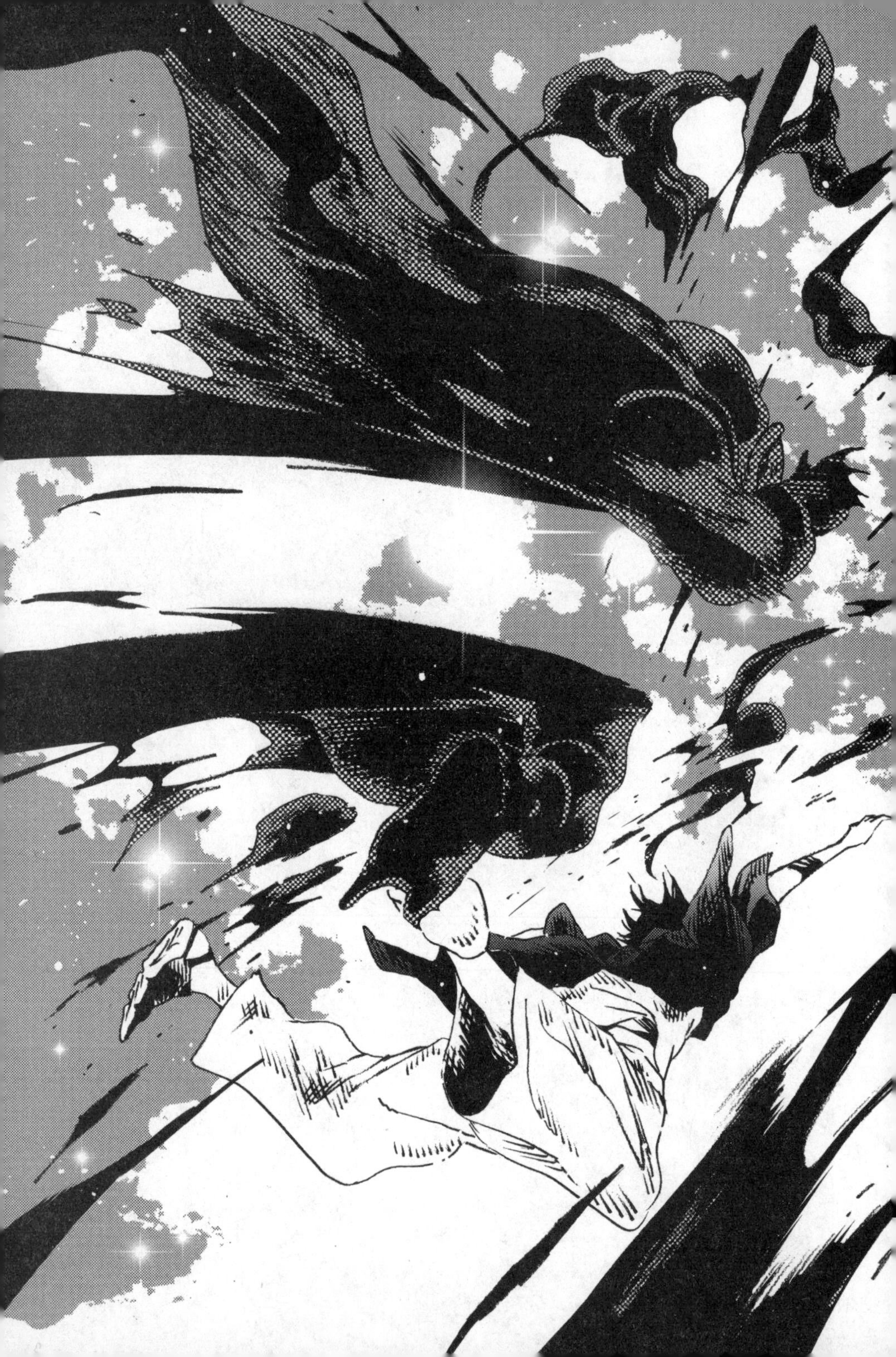

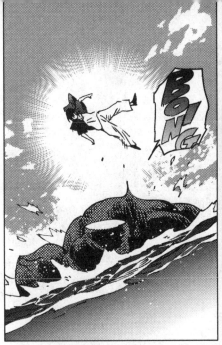

BOING

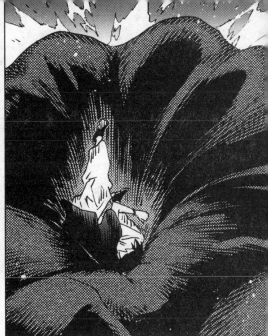

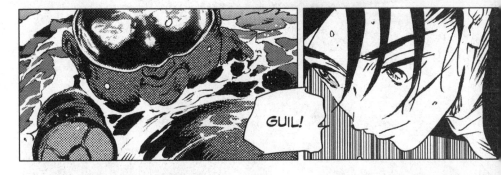

GUIL!

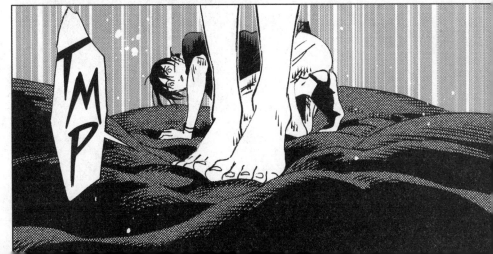

TMP

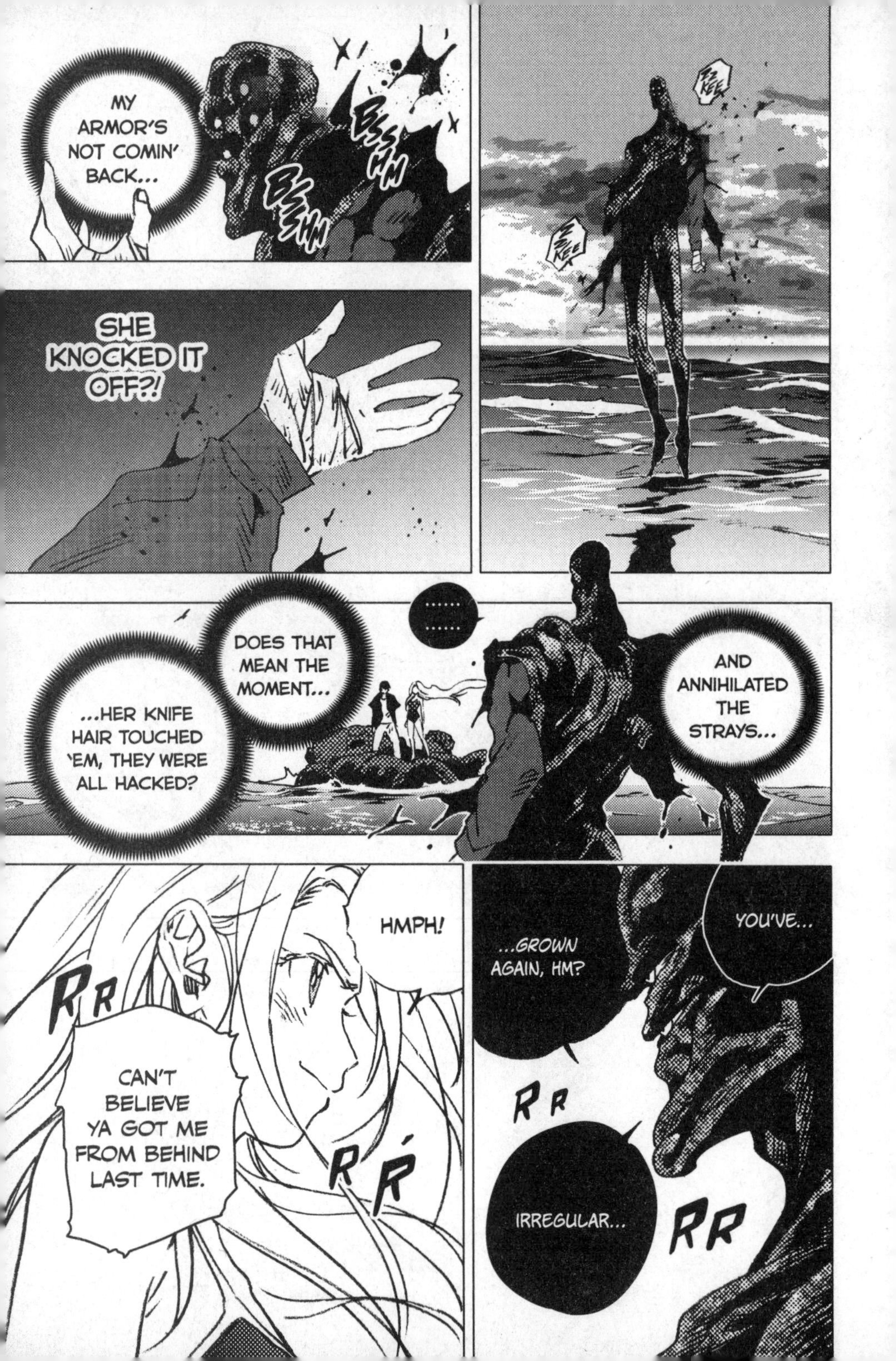
MY ARMOR'S NOT COMIN' BACK...
BSSHM
BSSHM
SHE KNOCKED IT OFF?!
AND ANNIHILATED THE STRAYS...
......
DOES THAT MEAN THE MOMENT...
...HER KNIFE HAIR TOUCHED 'EM, THEY WERE ALL HACKED?
YOU'VE...
...GROWN AGAIN, HM?
RR
IRREGULAR...
RR
HMPH!
RR
CAN'T BELIEVE YA GOT ME FROM BEHIND LAST TIME.
RR

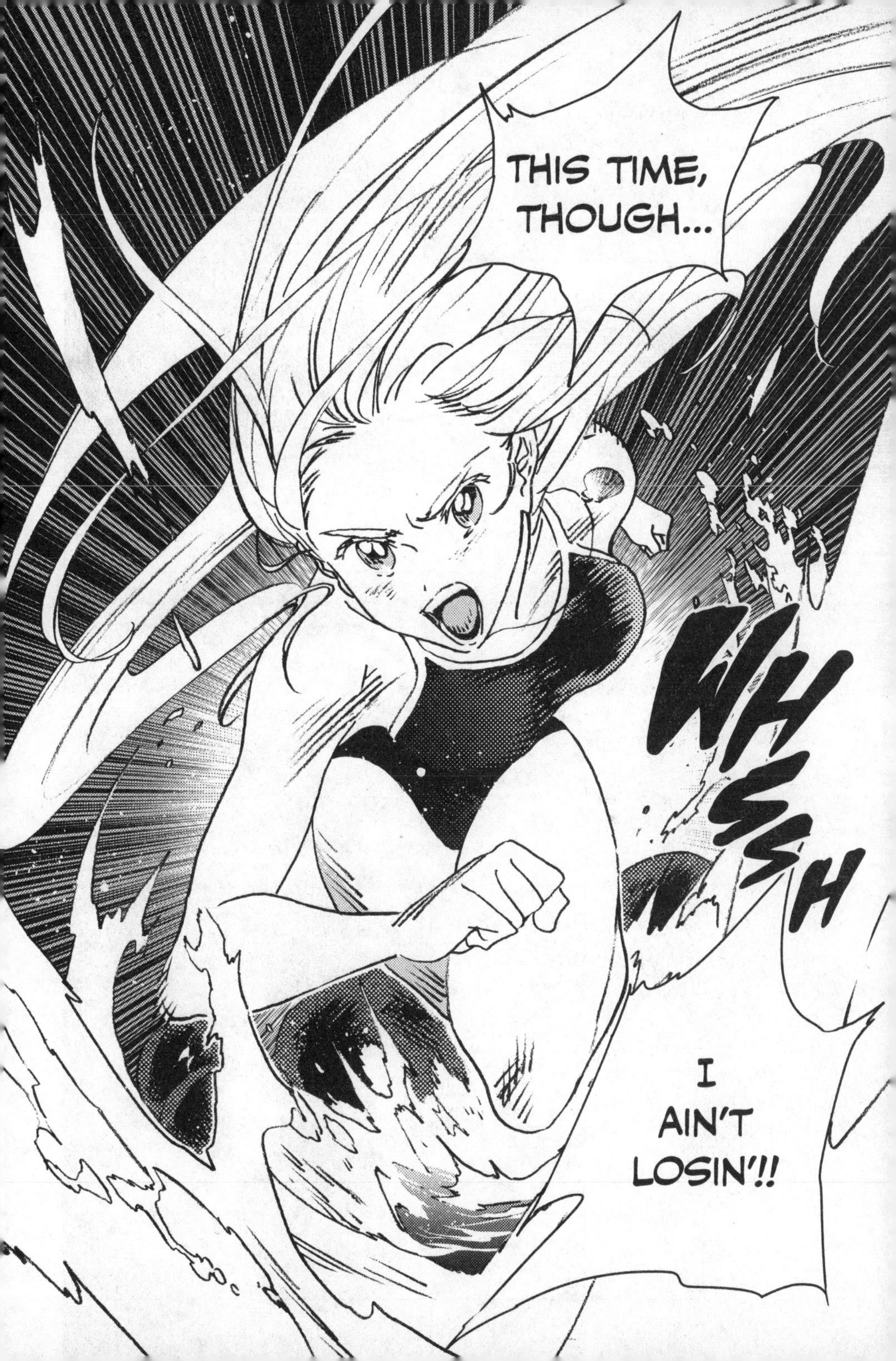
THIS TIME, THOUGH...
WHSSH
I AIN'T LOSIN'!!

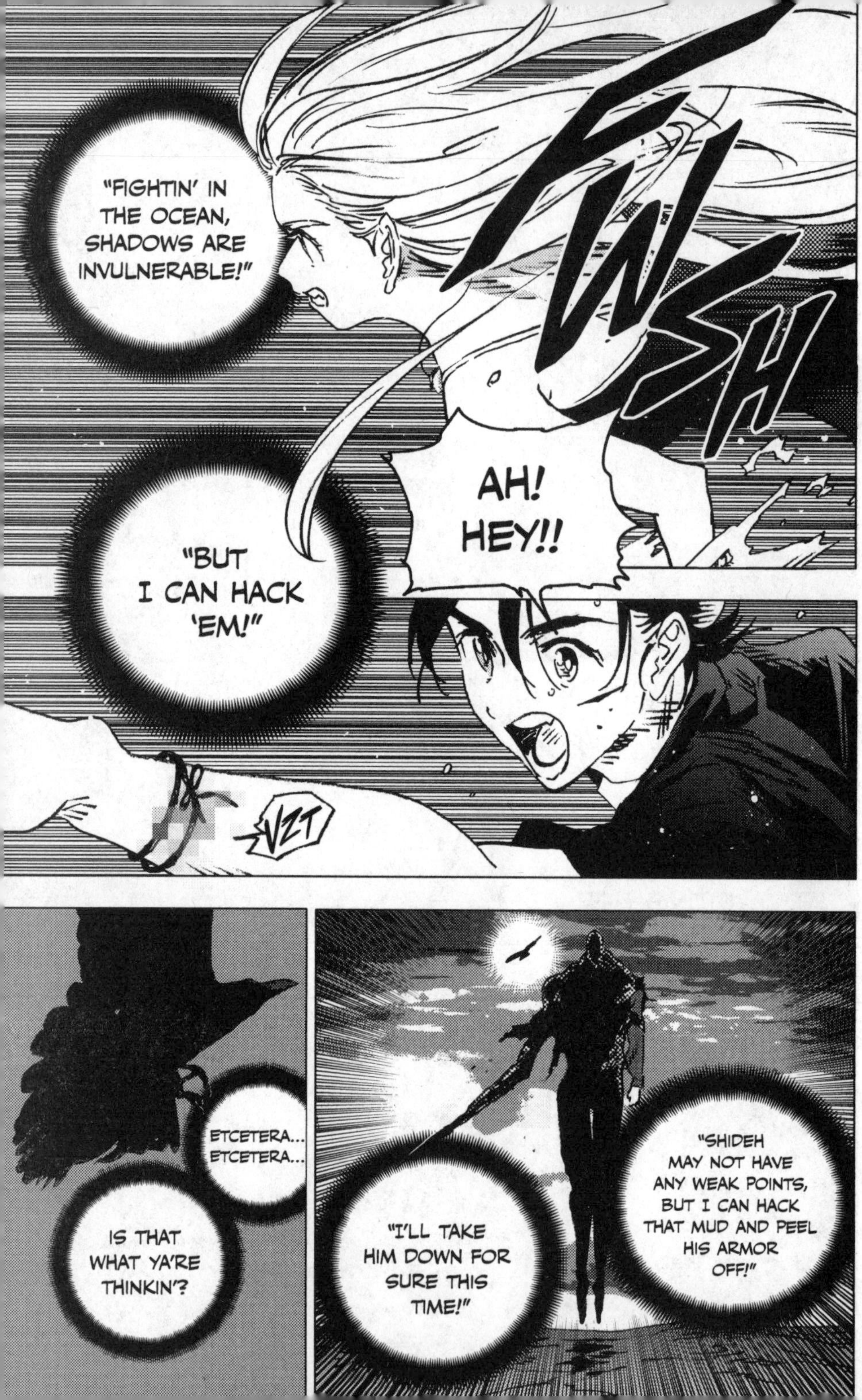
FWSH
"FIGHTIN' IN THE OCEAN, SHADOWS ARE INVULNERABLE!"
AH! HEY!!
"BUT I CAN HACK 'EM!"
VZT
"SHIDEH MAY NOT HAVE ANY WEAK POINTS, BUT I CAN HACK THAT MUD AND PEEL HIS ARMOR OFF!"
"I'LL TAKE HIM DOWN FOR SURE THIS TIME!"
ETCETERA... ETCETERA...
IS THAT WHAT YA'RE THINKIN'?

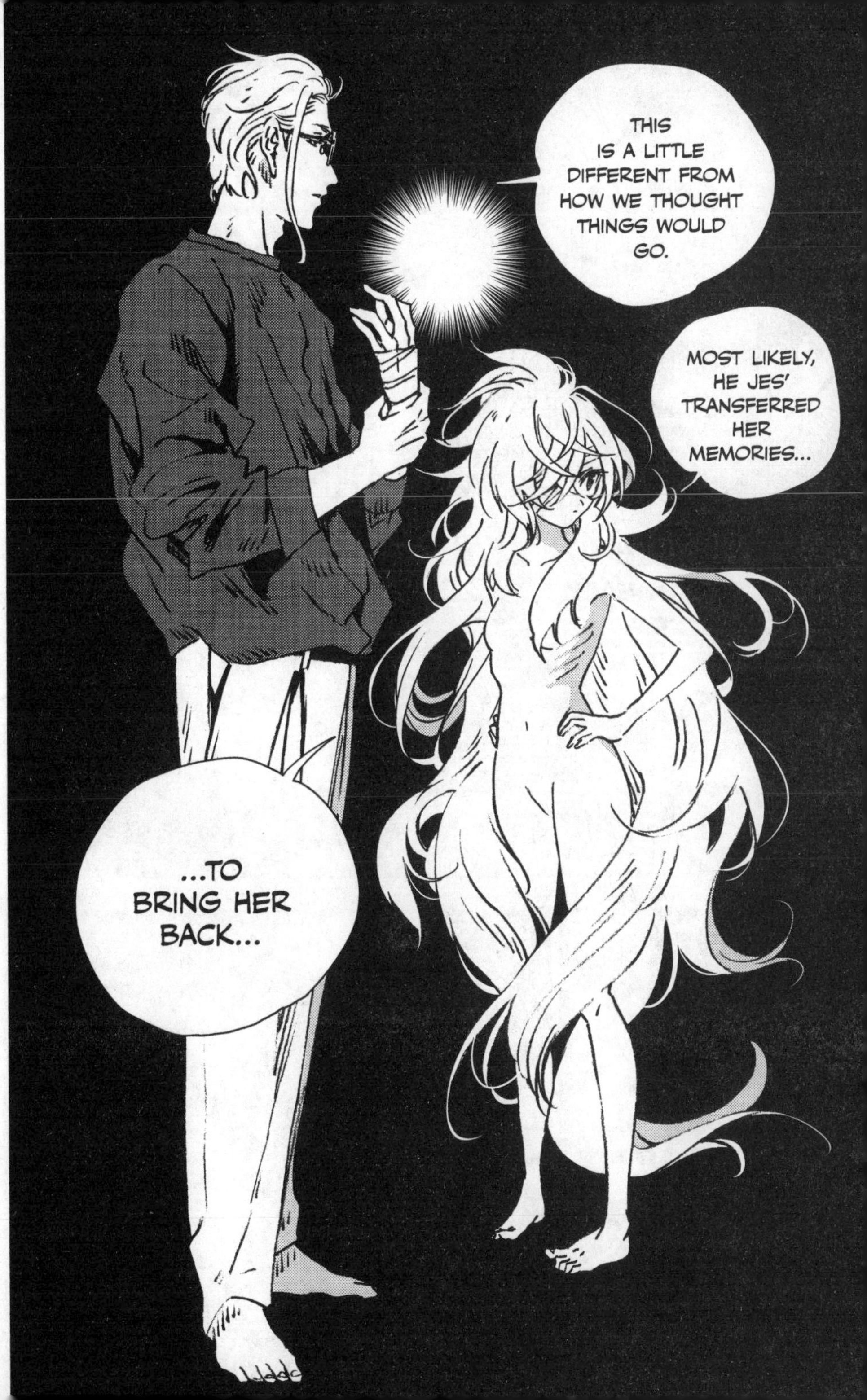
THIS IS A LITTLE DIFFERENT FROM HOW WE THOUGHT THINGS WOULD GO.
MOST LIKELY, HE JES' TRANSFERRED HER MEMORIES...
...TO BRING HER BACK...

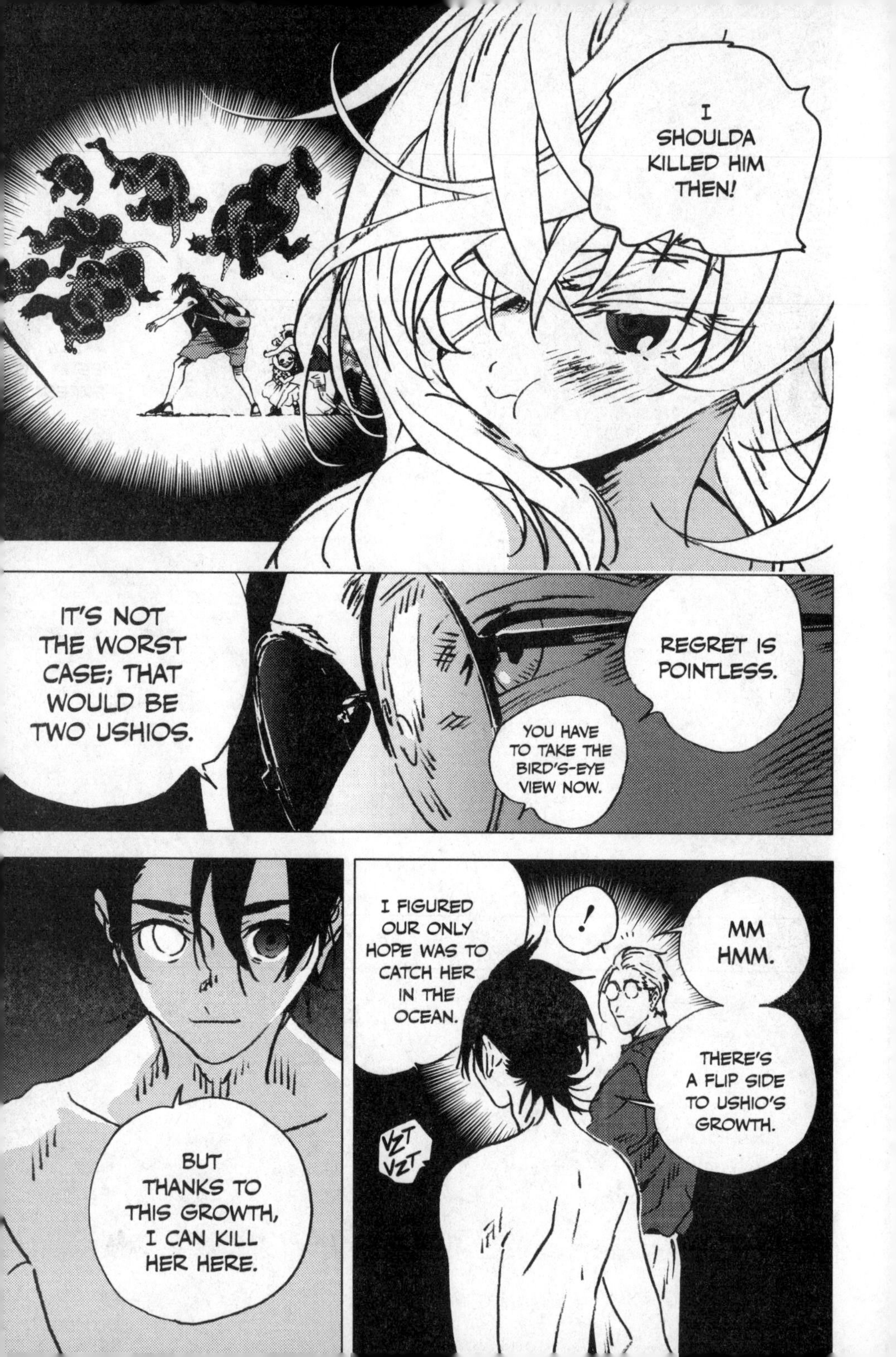
I SHOULDA KILLED HIM THEN!
REGRET IS POINTLESS.
YOU HAVE TO TAKE THE BIRD'S-EYE VIEW NOW.
IT'S NOT THE WORST CASE; THAT WOULD BE TWO USHIOS.
MM HMM.
!
I FIGURED OUR ONLY HOPE WAS TO CATCH HER IN THE OCEAN.
THERE'S A FLIP SIDE TO USHIO'S GROWTH.
VZT VZT
BUT THANKS TO THIS GROWTH, I CAN KILL HER HERE.

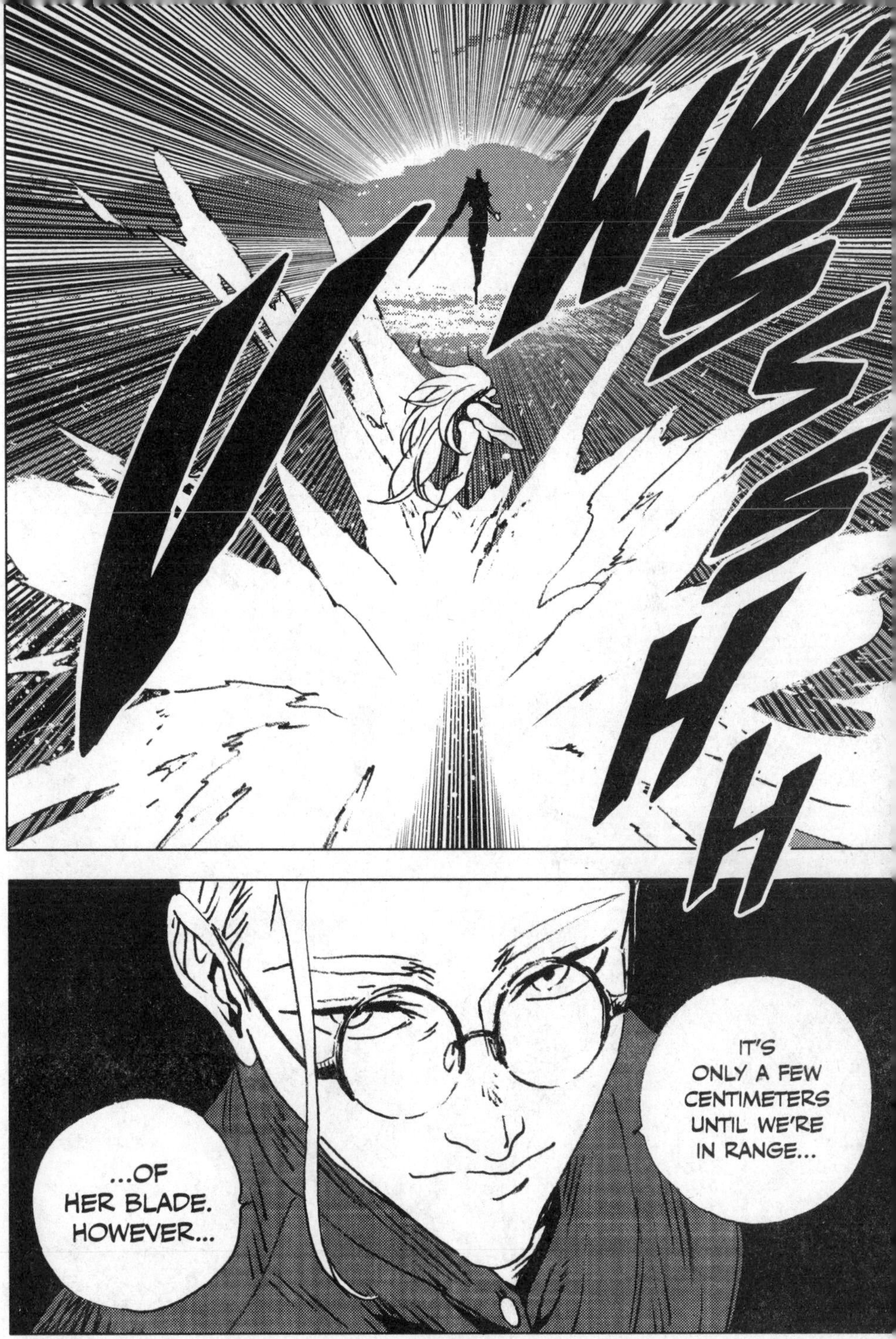
IT'S ONLY A FEW CENTIMETERS UNTIL WE'RE IN RANGE...
...OF HER BLADE. HOWEVER...

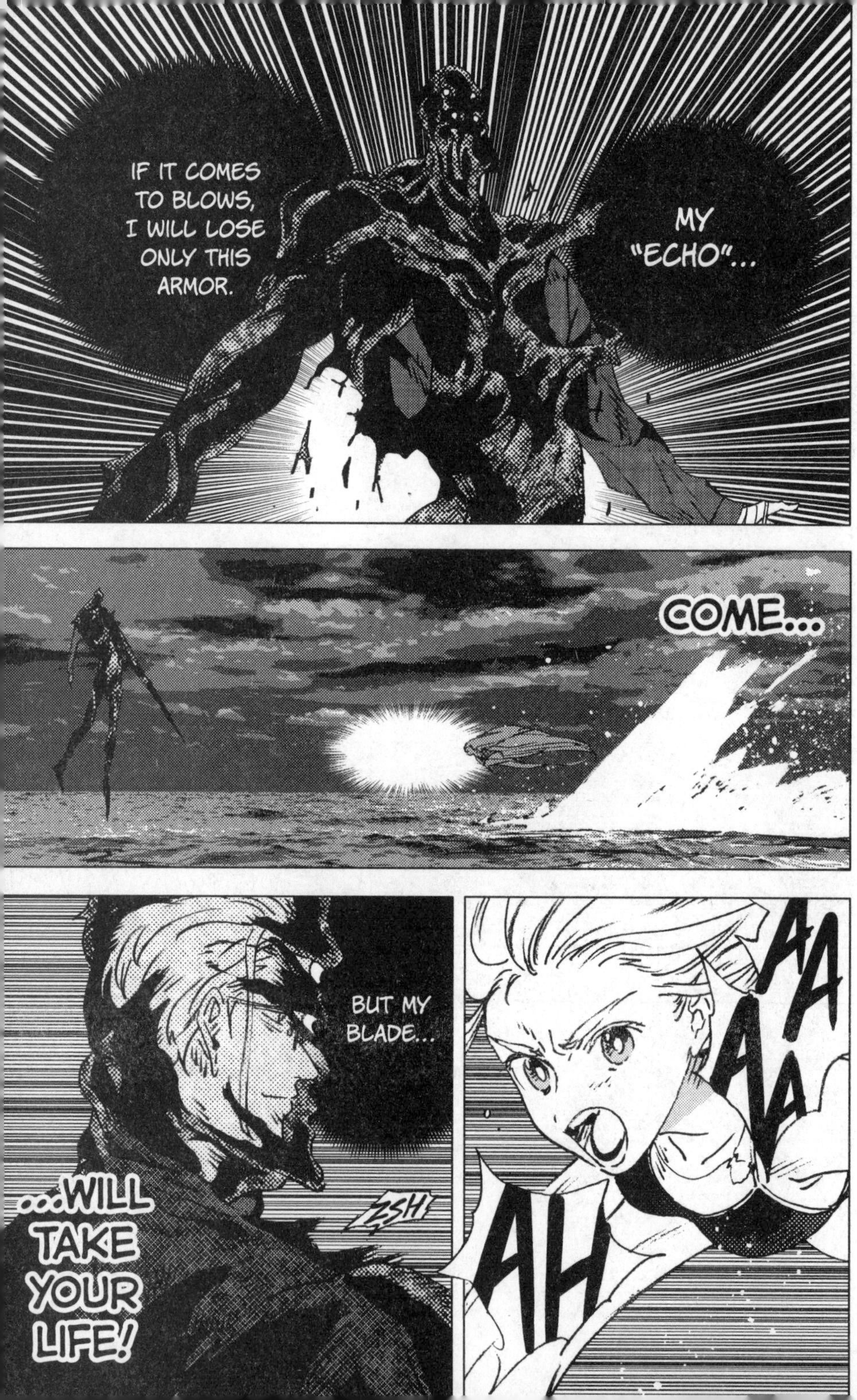
MY "ECHO"...
IF IT COMES TO BLOWS, I WILL LOSE ONLY THIS ARMOR.
COME...
AAAA
AH
BUT MY BLADE...
ZSH
...WILL TAKE YOUR LIFE!

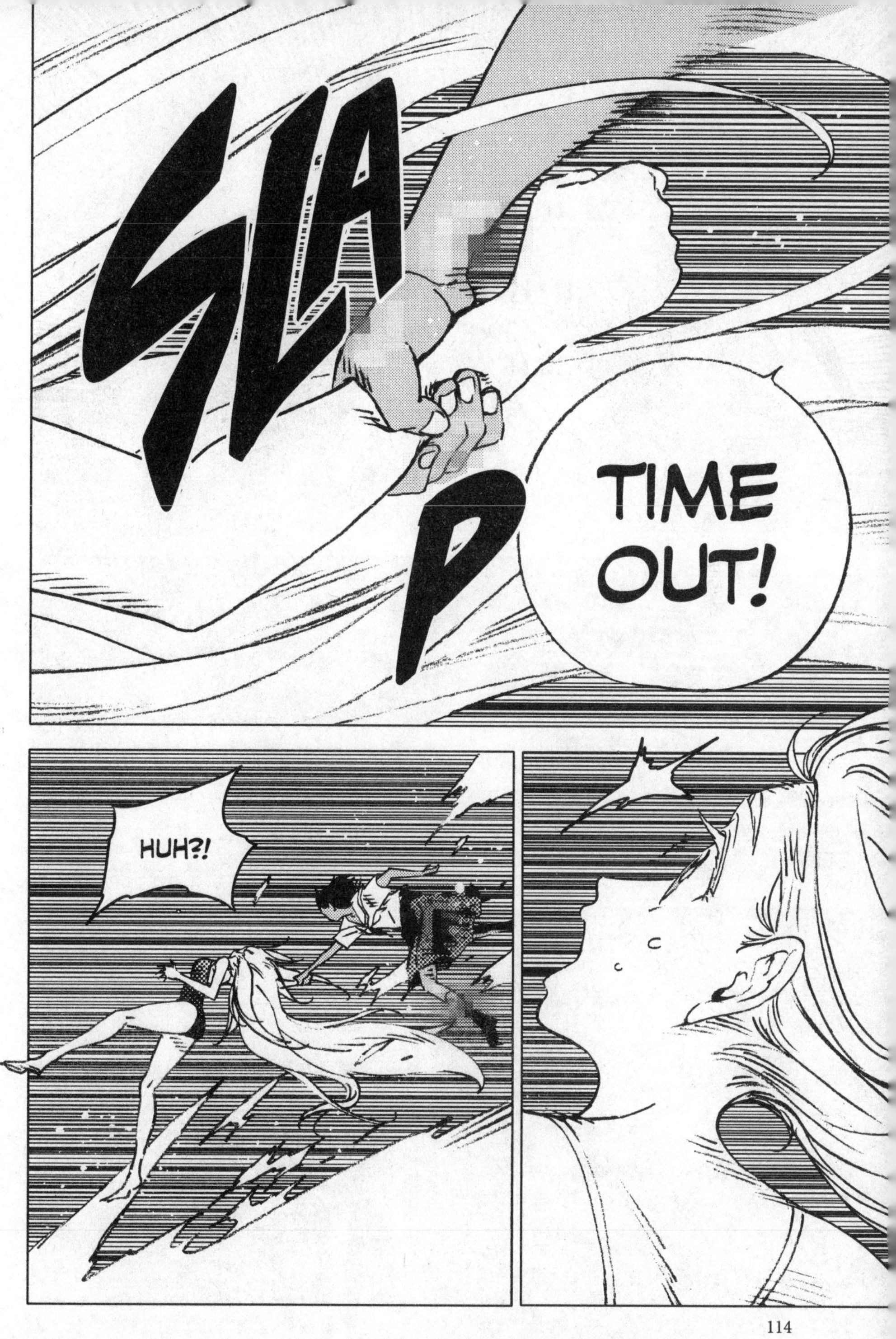
TIME OUT!
SLAP
HUH?!

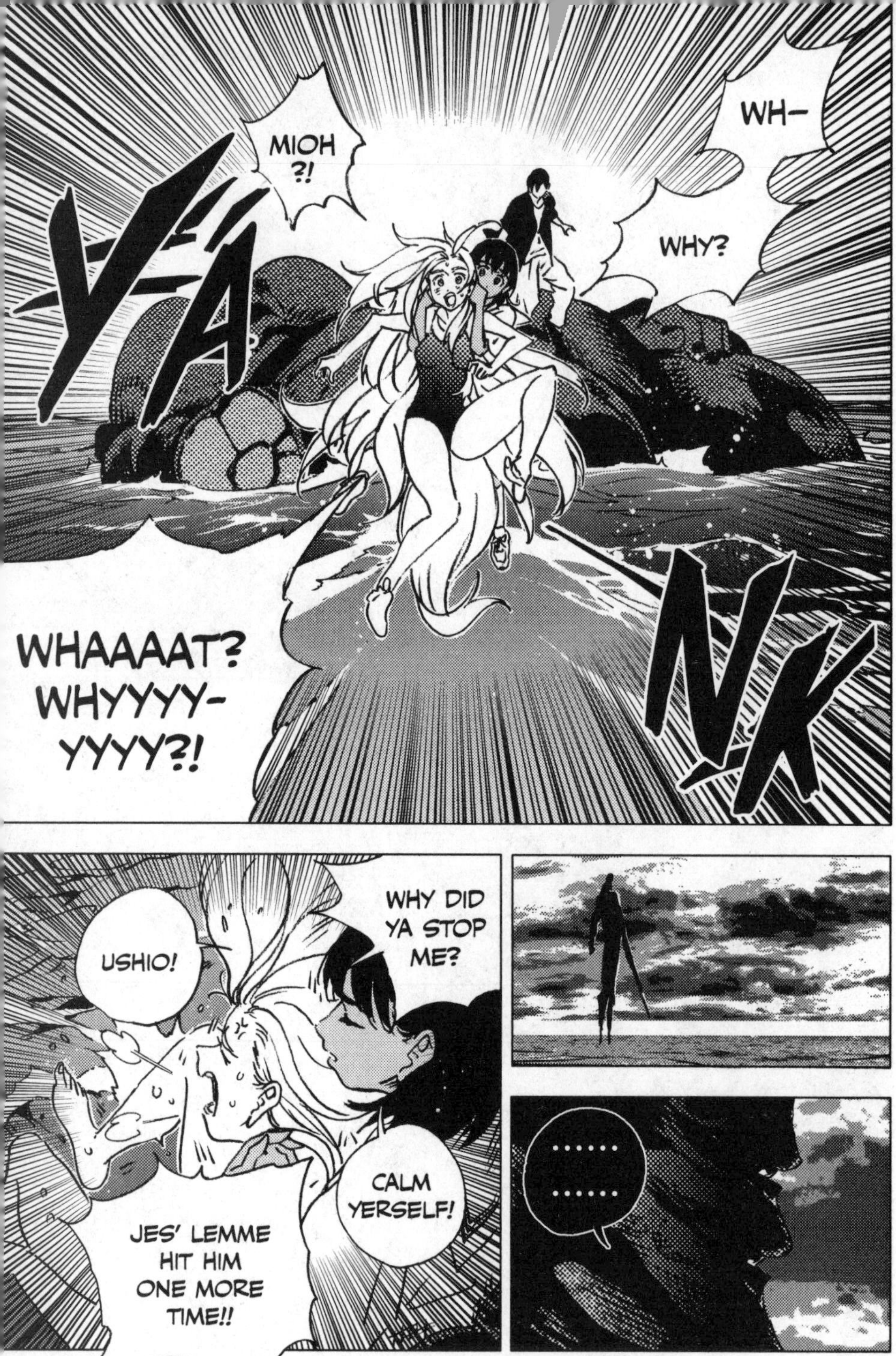
WH-
WHY?
MIOH ?!
YA
NK
WHAAAAT? WHYYYY-YYYY?!
…… ……
WHY DID YA STOP ME?
USHIO!
CALM YERSELF!
JES' LEMME HIT HIM ONE MORE TIME!!

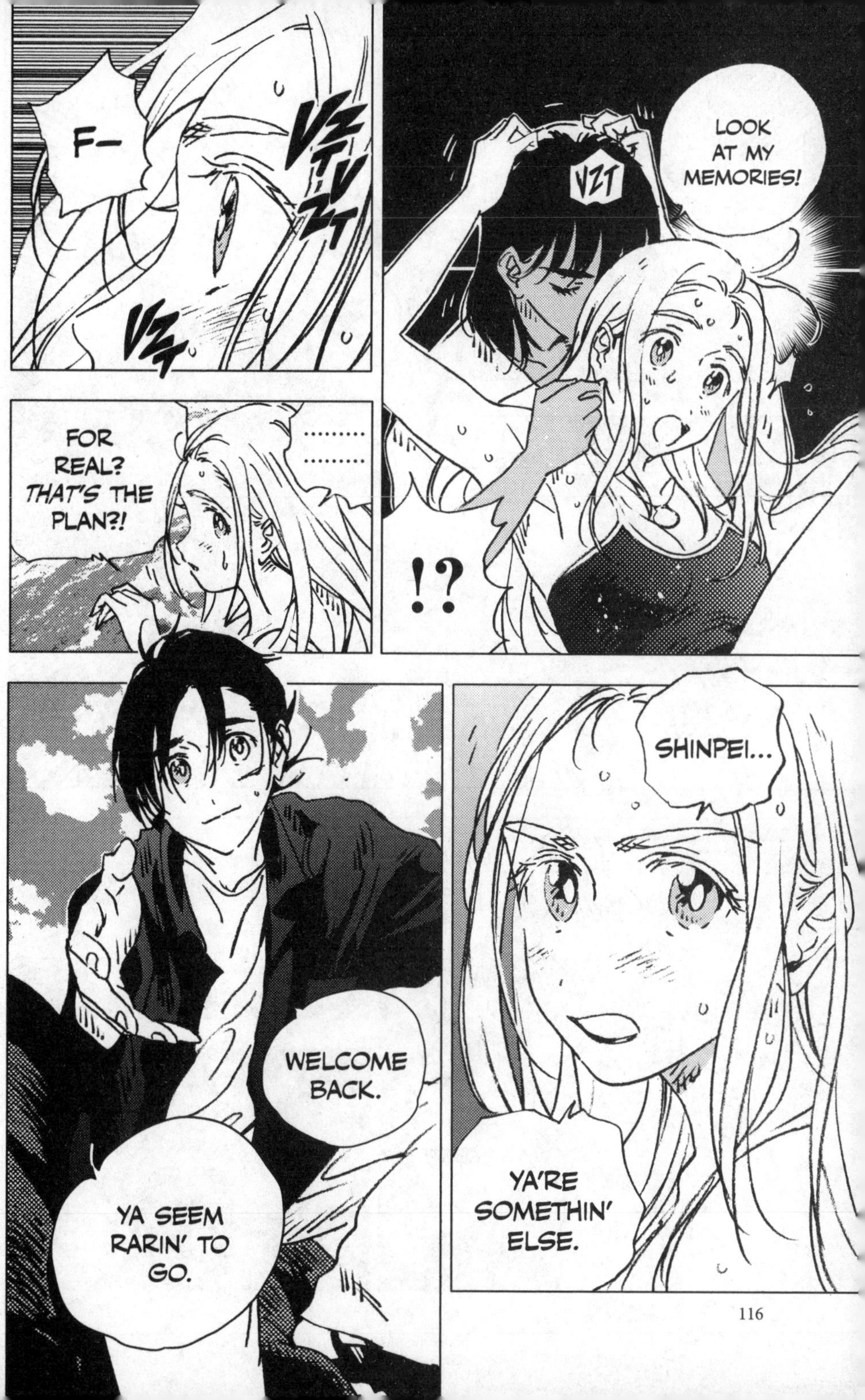

LOOK AT MY MEMORIES!
VZT
!?
F—
....
....
FOR REAL? *THAT'S* THE PLAN?!
SHINPEI...
YA'RE SOMETHIN' ELSE.
WELCOME BACK.
YA SEEM RARIN' TO GO.

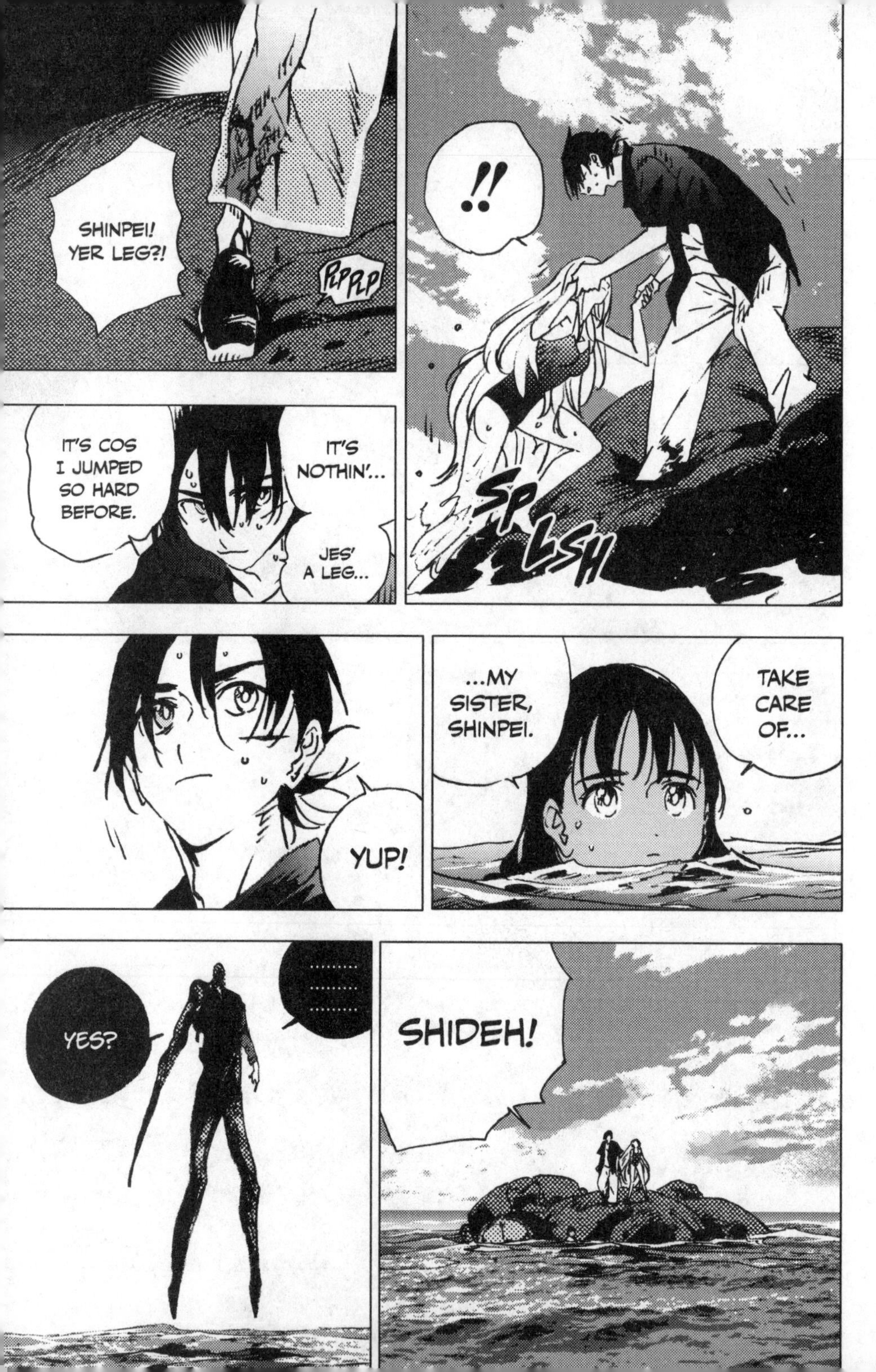
!!
SPLSH
SHINPEI! YER LEG?!
PLPPLP
IT'S NOTHIN'...
JES' A LEG...
IT'S COS I JUMPED SO HARD BEFORE.
TAKE CARE OF...
...MY SISTER, SHINPEI.
YUP!
SHIDEH!
....
YES?

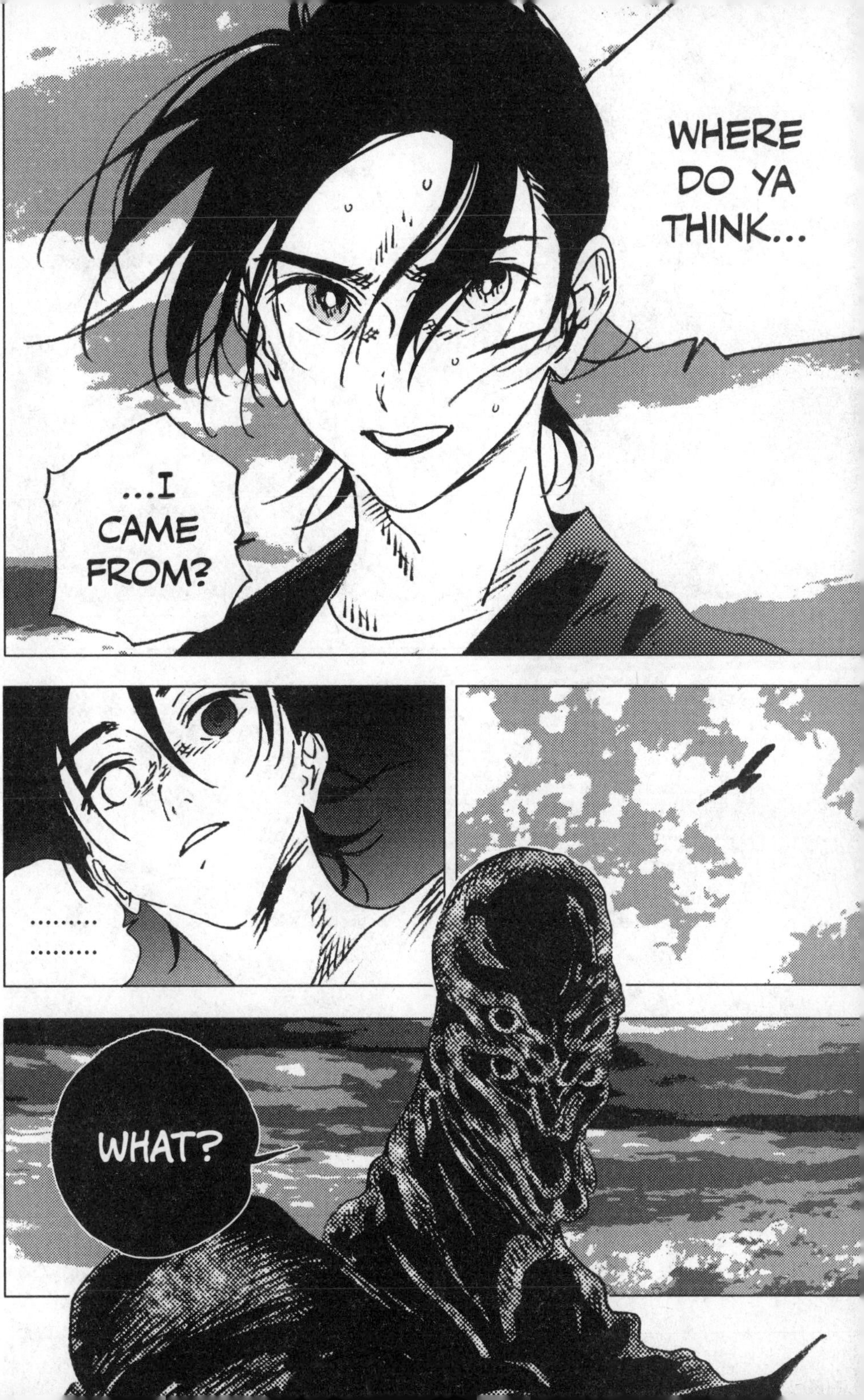

WHERE DO YA THINK...
...I CAME FROM?
....
....
WHAT?

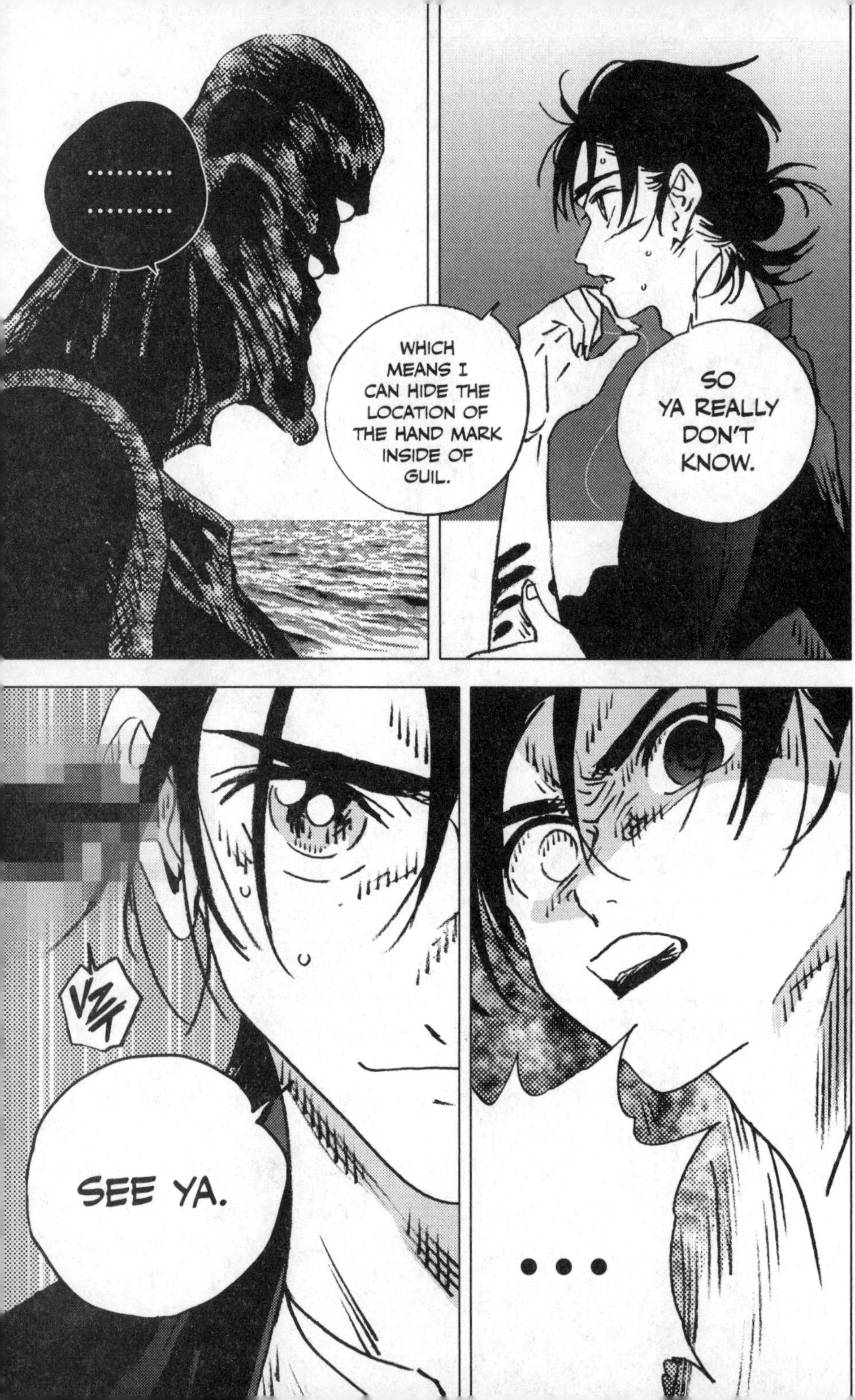
SO YA REALLY DON'T KNOW.
WHICH MEANS I CAN HIDE THE LOCATION OF THE HAND MARK INSIDE OF GUIL.
....
....
...
VZK
SEE YA.

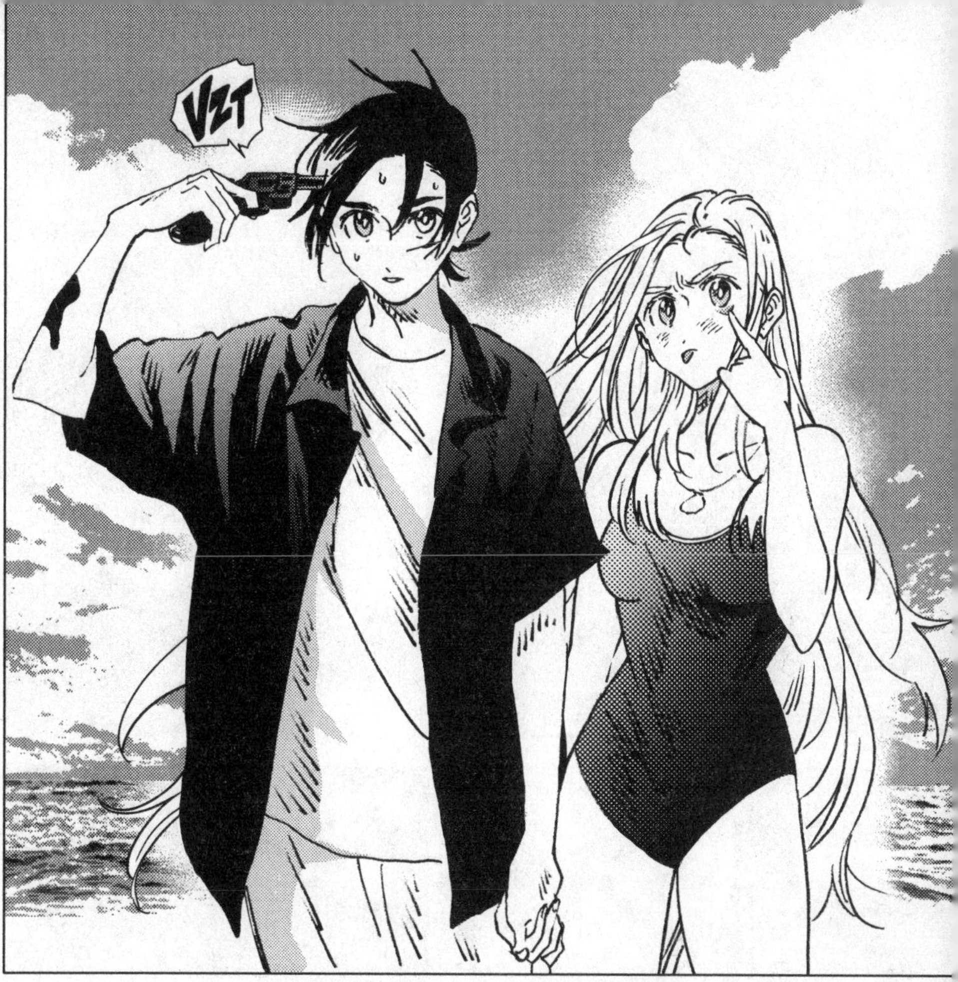
VZT
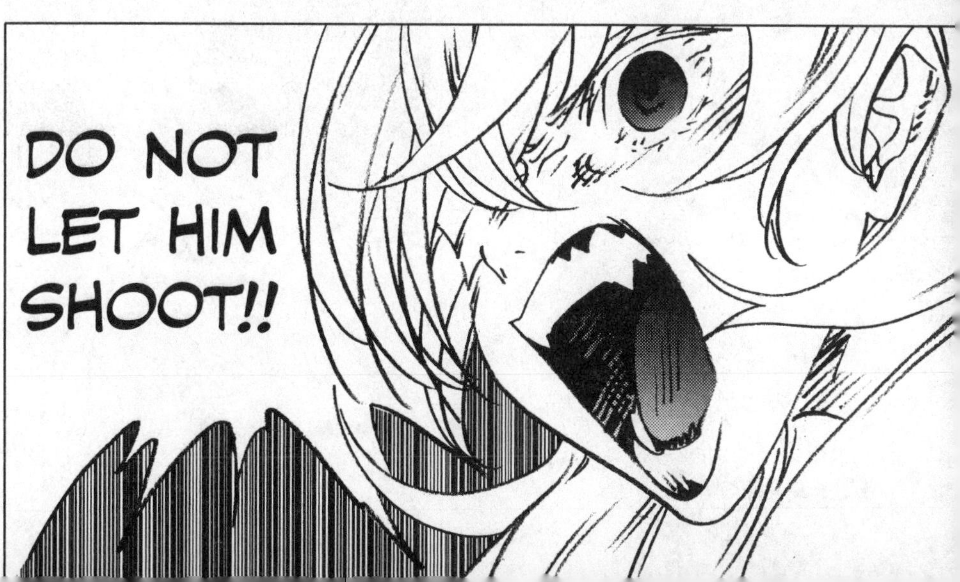
DO NOT
LET HIM
SHOOT!!

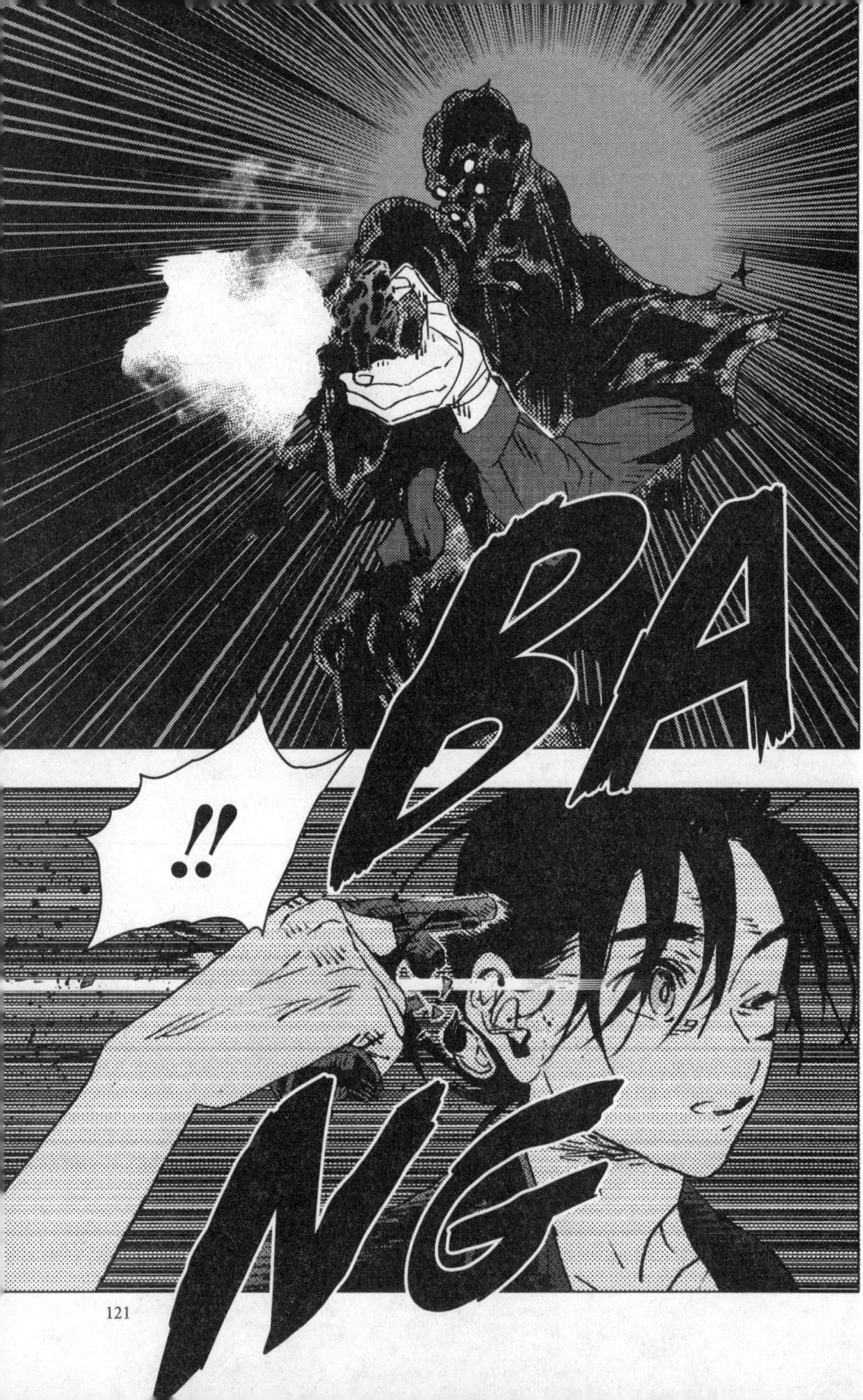
BA
!!
NG

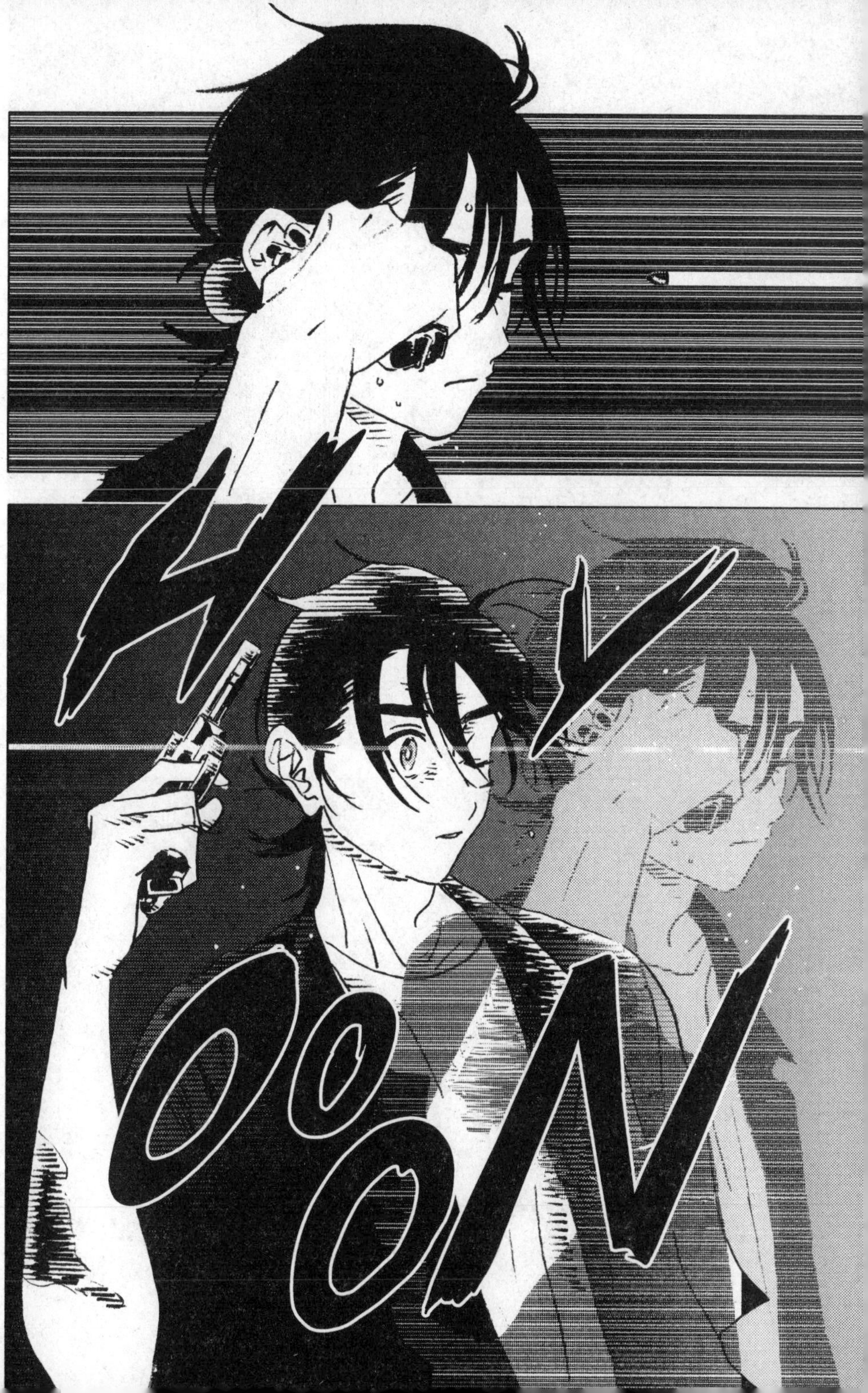

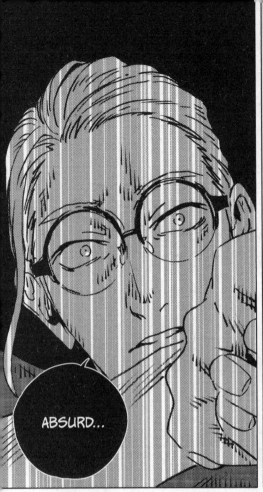

ABSURD...

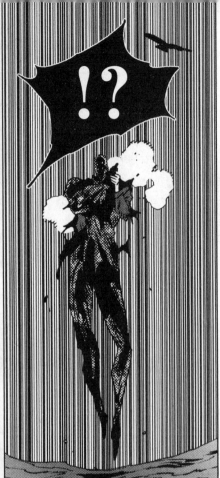

!?

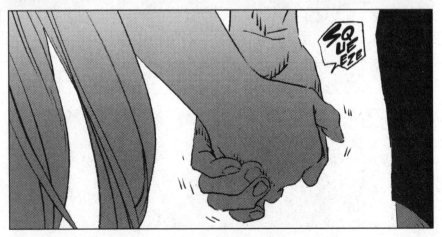

SQUEEZE

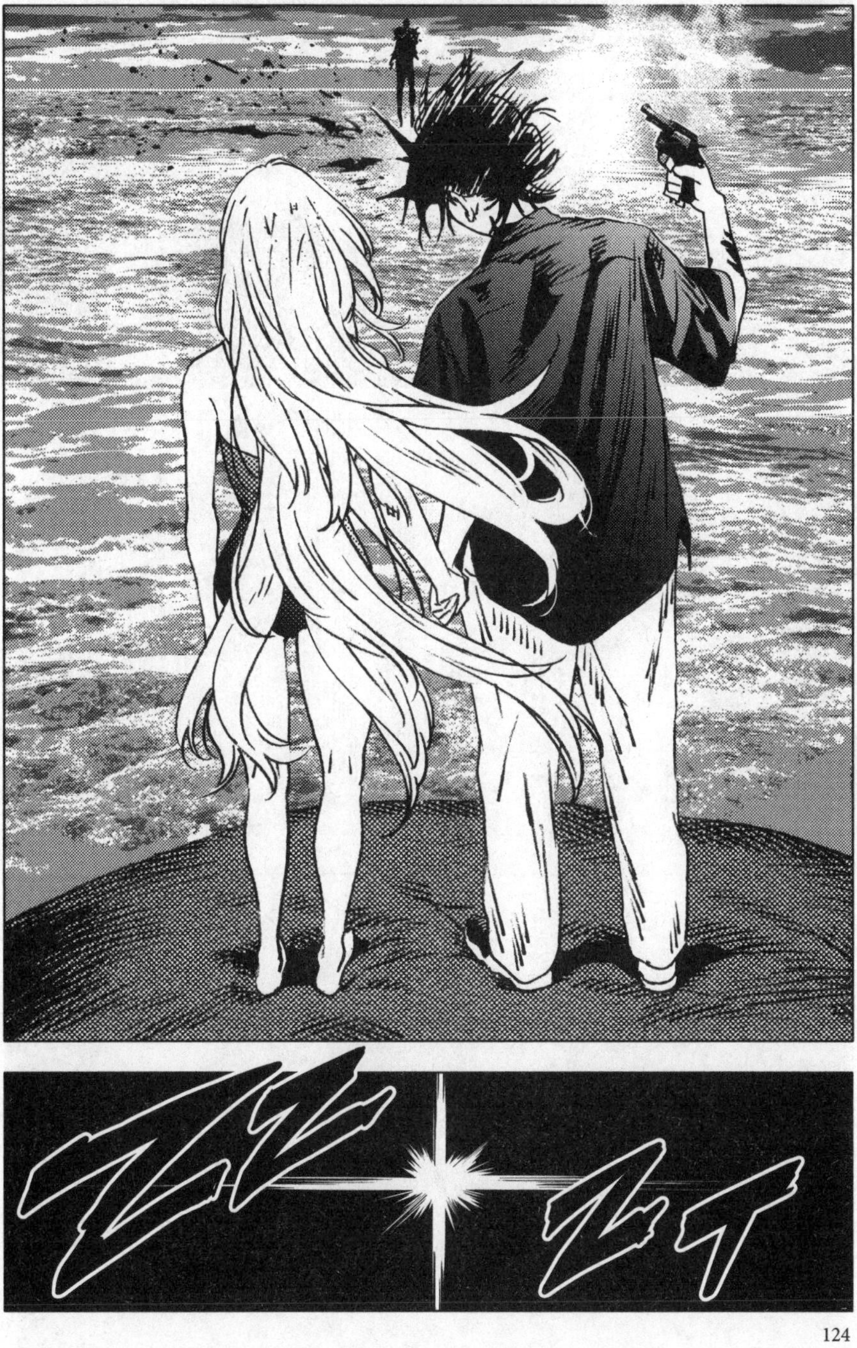

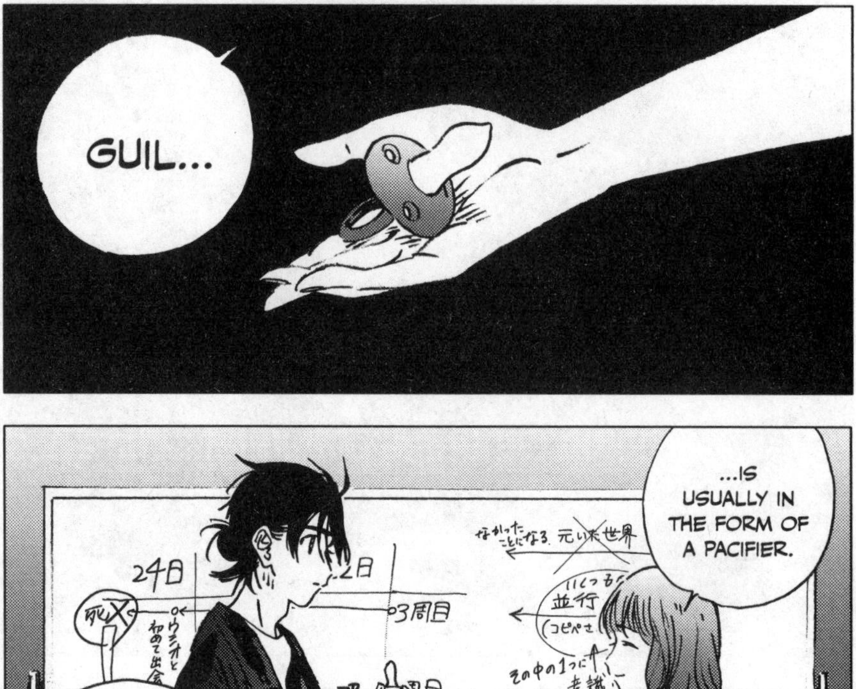
GUIL...
...IS USUALLY IN THE FORM OF A PACIFIER.
IF YOU TOSS IT, HE'LL TAKE ON HIS BATTLE FORM.

*TO READ THE CONTENTS ON THIS BOARD, PLEASE REFERENCE PAGES 44 AND 45 OF THIS VOLUME.

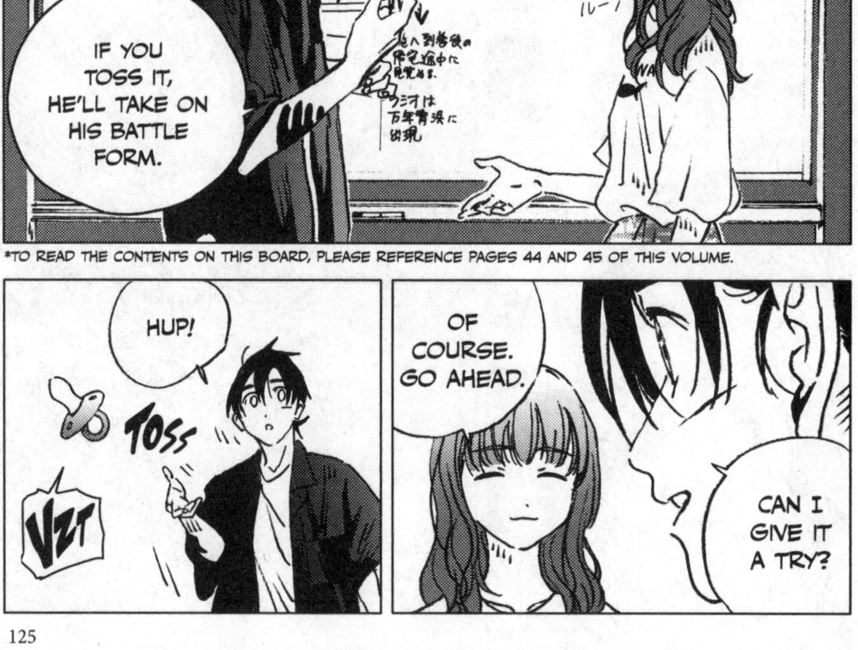
CAN I GIVE IT A TRY?
OF COURSE. GO AHEAD.
HUP!
TOSS
VZT

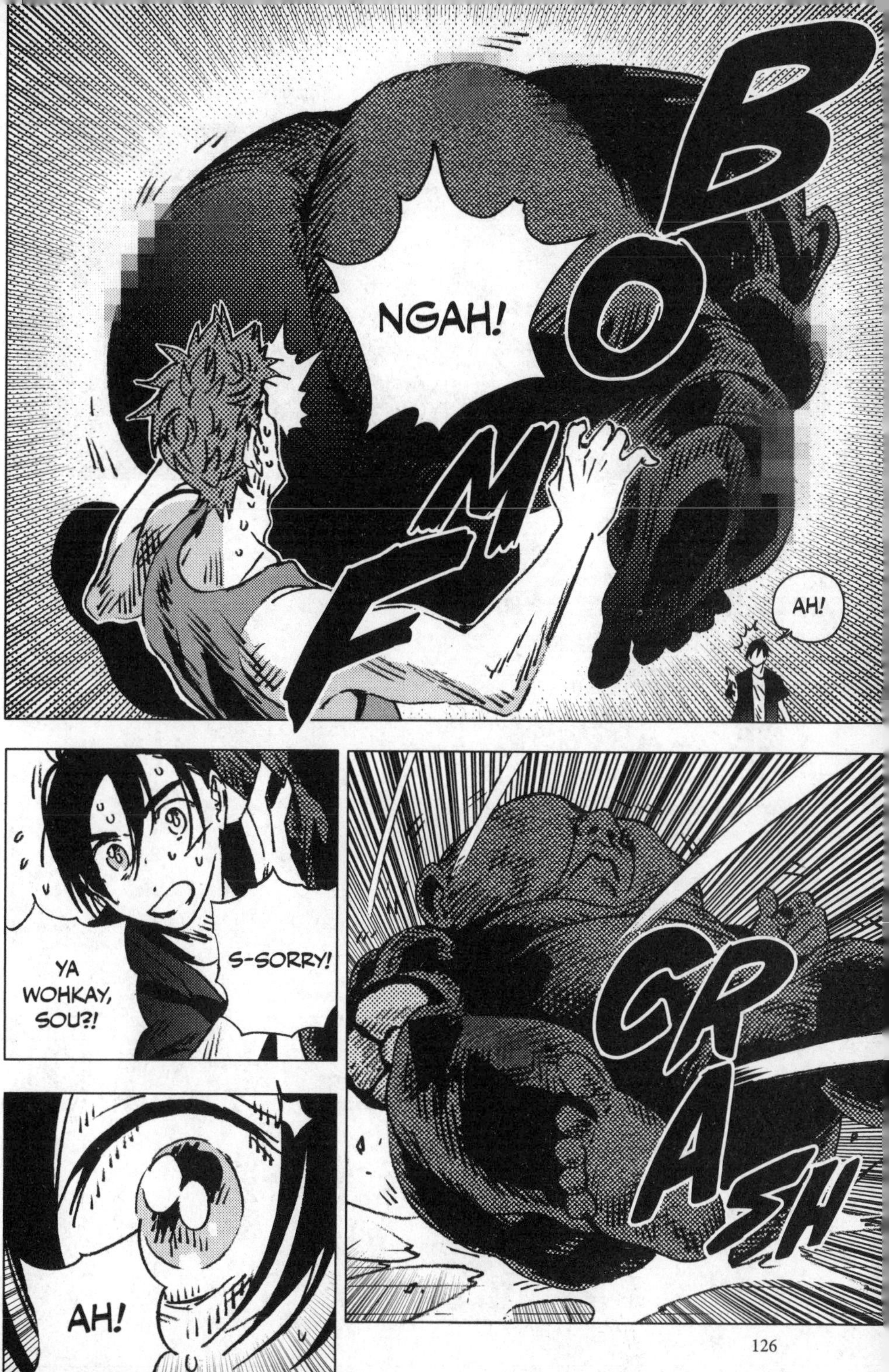
BOM
NGAH!
AH!
CRASH
S-SORRY!
YA WOHKAY, SOU?!
AH!

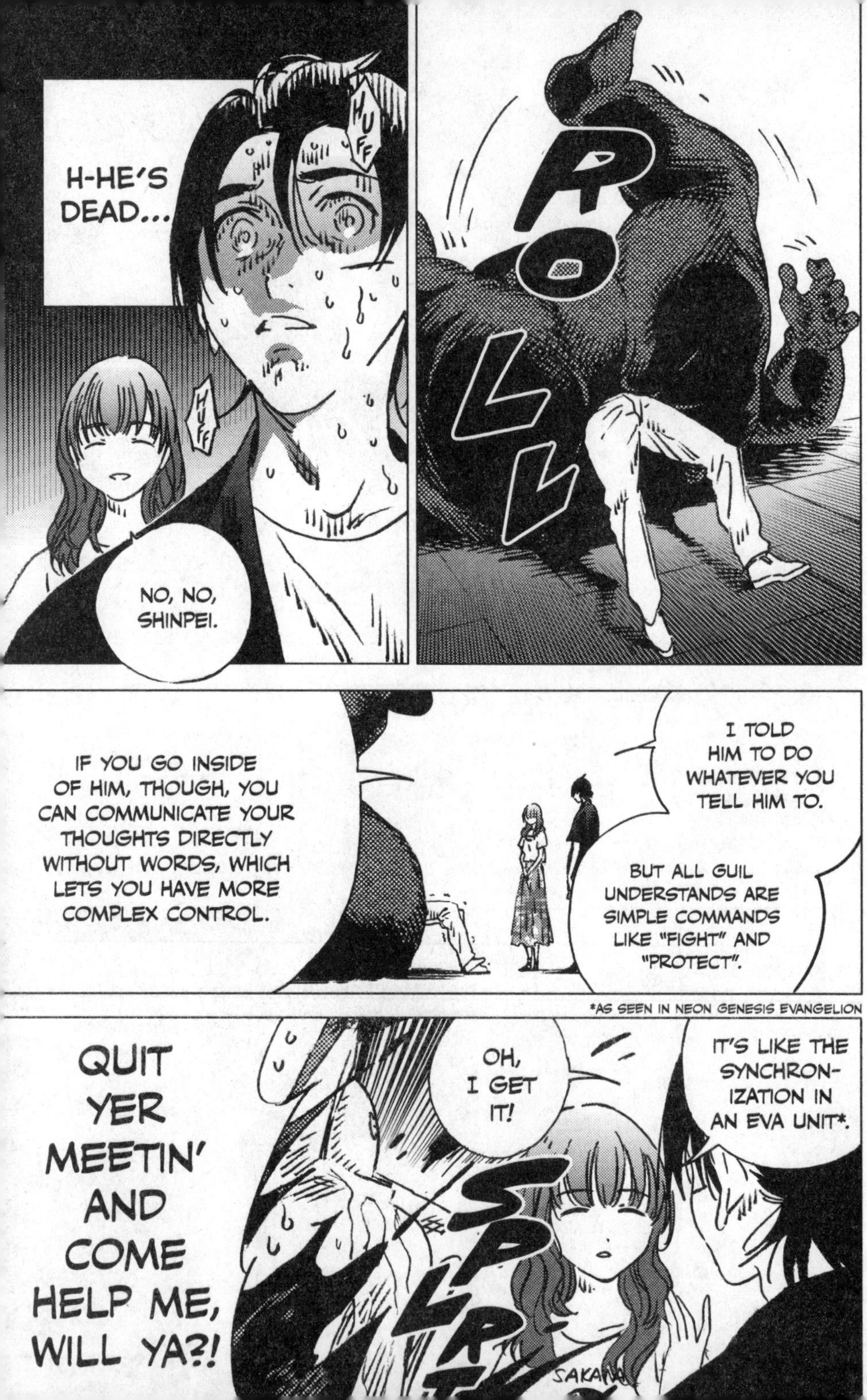
ROLL
HUFF
H-HE'S DEAD...
HUFF
NO, NO, SHINPEI.
I TOLD HIM TO DO WHATEVER YOU TELL HIM TO.
BUT ALL GUIL UNDERSTANDS ARE SIMPLE COMMANDS LIKE "FIGHT" AND "PROTECT".
IF YOU GO INSIDE OF HIM, THOUGH, YOU CAN COMMUNICATE YOUR THOUGHTS DIRECTLY WITHOUT WORDS, WHICH LETS YOU HAVE MORE COMPLEX CONTROL.
IT'S LIKE THE SYNCHRON-IZATION IN AN EVA UNIT*.
OH, I GET IT!
SPLRT
QUIT YER MEETIN' AND COME HELP ME, WILL YA?!
*AS SEEN IN NEON GENESIS EVANGELION

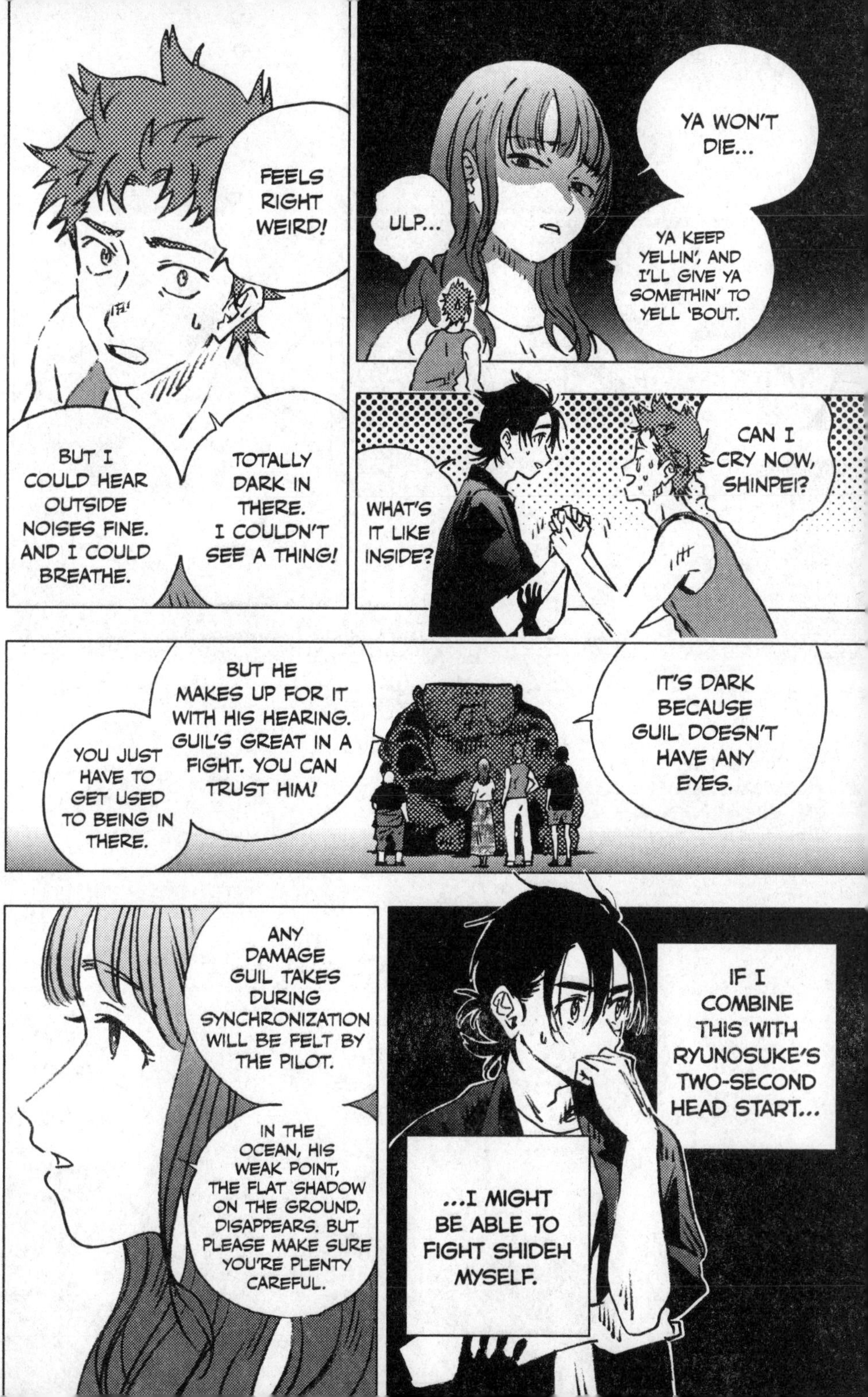
YA WON'T DIE...
YA KEEP YELLIN', AND I'LL GIVE YA SOMETHIN' TO YELL 'BOUT.
ULP...
CAN I CRY NOW, SHINPEI?
WHAT'S IT LIKE INSIDE?
FEELS RIGHT WEIRD!
TOTALLY DARK IN THERE. I COULDN'T SEE A THING!
BUT I COULD HEAR OUTSIDE NOISES FINE. AND I COULD BREATHE.
IT'S DARK BECAUSE GUIL DOESN'T HAVE ANY EYES.
BUT HE MAKES UP FOR IT WITH HIS HEARING. GUIL'S GREAT IN A FIGHT. YOU CAN TRUST HIM!
YOU JUST HAVE TO GET USED TO BEING IN THERE.
IF I COMBINE THIS WITH RYUNOSUKE'S TWO-SECOND HEAD START...
...I MIGHT BE ABLE TO FIGHT SHIDEH MYSELF.
ANY DAMAGE GUIL TAKES DURING SYNCHRONIZATION WILL BE FELT BY THE PILOT.
IN THE OCEAN, HIS WEAK POINT, THE FLAT SHADOW ON THE GROUND, DISAPPEARS. BUT PLEASE MAKE SURE YOU'RE PLENTY CAREFUL.

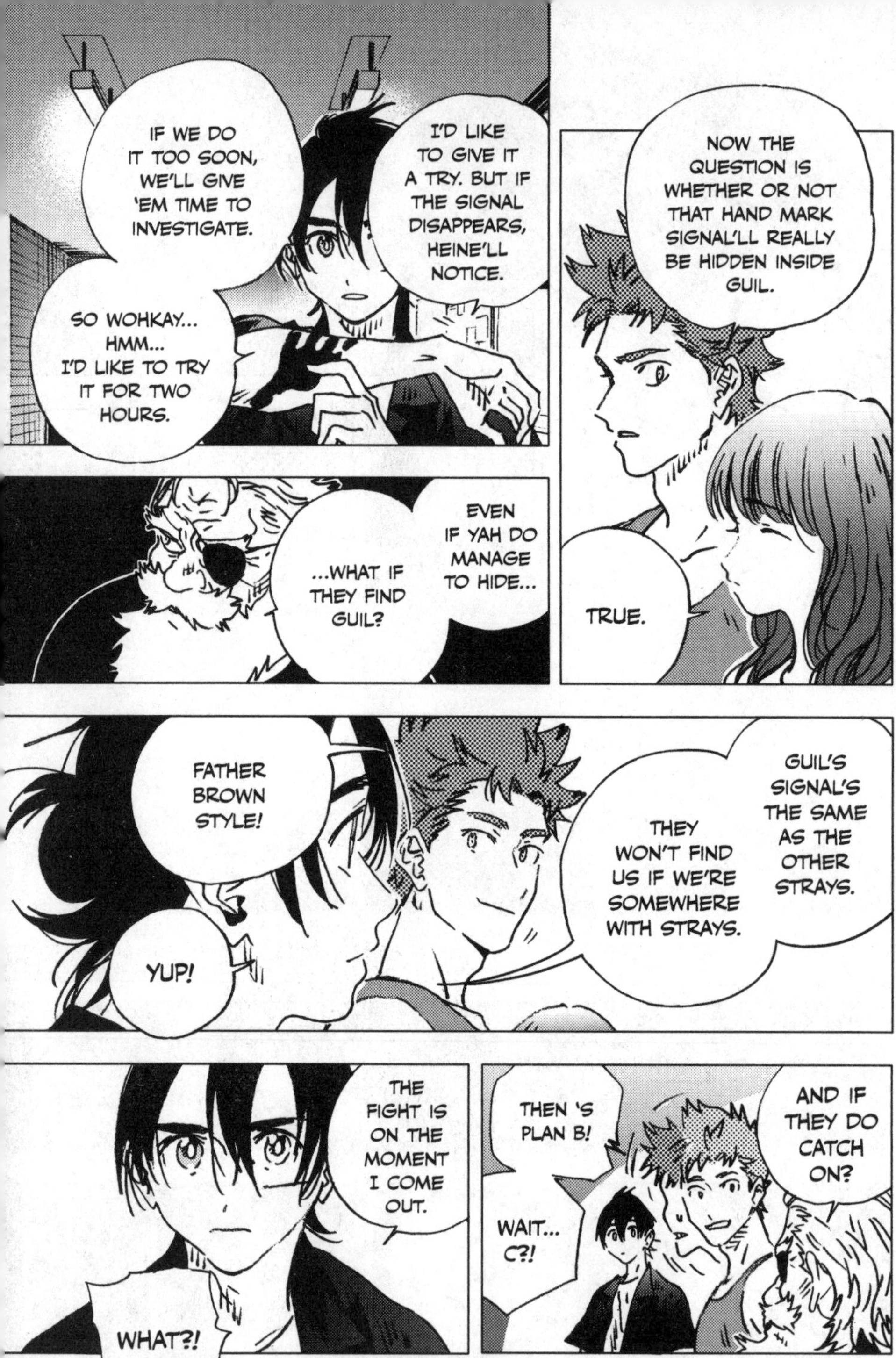
NOW THE QUESTION IS WHETHER OR NOT THAT HAND MARK SIGNAL'LL REALLY BE HIDDEN INSIDE GUIL.
TRUE.
I'D LIKE TO GIVE IT A TRY. BUT IF THE SIGNAL DISAPPEARS, HEINE'LL NOTICE.
IF WE DO IT TOO SOON, WE'LL GIVE 'EM TIME TO INVESTIGATE.
SO WOHKAY... HMM... I'D LIKE TO TRY IT FOR TWO HOURS.
EVEN IF YAH DO MANAGE TO HIDE...
...WHAT IF THEY FIND GUIL?
GUIL'S SIGNAL'S THE SAME AS THE OTHER STRAYS.
THEY WON'T FIND US IF WE'RE SOMEWHERE WITH STRAYS.
FATHER BROWN STYLE!
YUP!
AND IF THEY DO CATCH ON?
THEN 'S PLAN B!
WAIT... C?!
THE FIGHT IS ON THE MOMENT I COME OUT.
WHAT?!

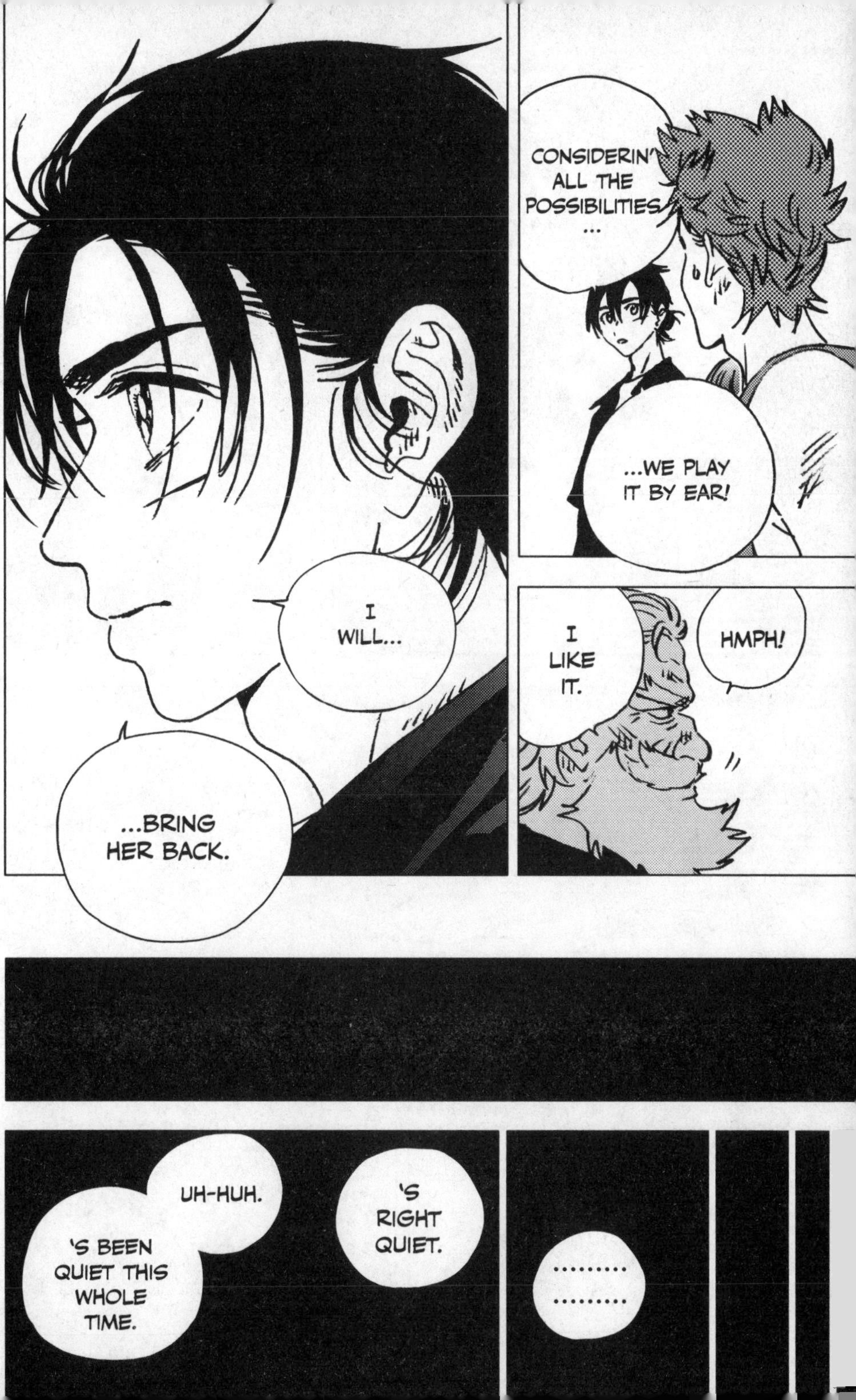
CONSIDERIN' ALL THE POSSIBILITIES...
...WE PLAY IT BY EAR!
HMPH!
I LIKE IT.
I WILL...
...BRING HER BACK.
....
....
'S RIGHT QUIET.
UH-HUH.
'S BEEN QUIET THIS WHOLE TIME.

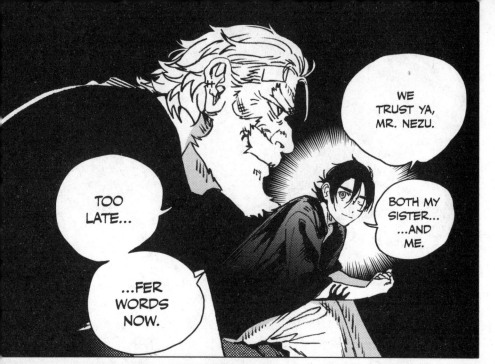

WE TRUST YA, MR. NEZU.

BOTH MY SISTER... ...AND ME.

TOO LATE...

...FER WORDS NOW.

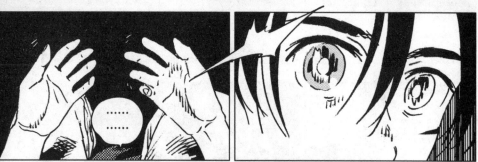

......
......

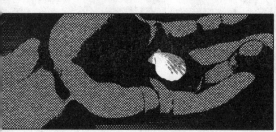

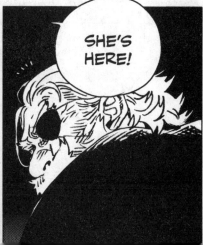

SHE'S HERE!

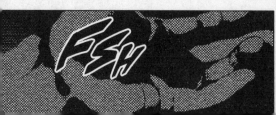

FSH

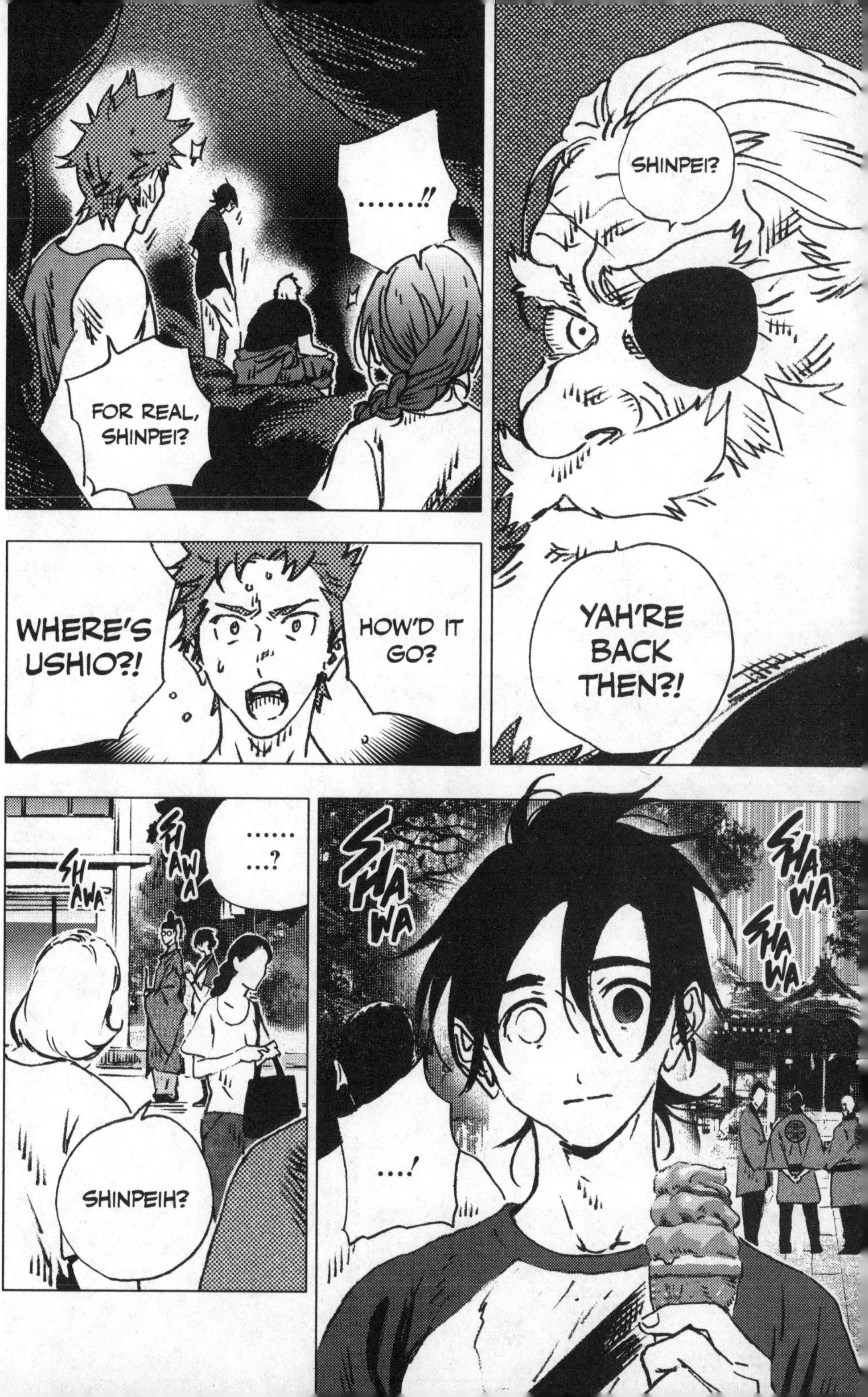

SHINPEI?
YAH'RE BACK THEN?!
……!!
FOR REAL, SHINPEI?
HOW'D IT GO?
WHERE'S USHIO?!
SHAWA WA SHAWA WA
SHAWA WA
…./
SHAWA
…… …?
SHAWA
SHINPEIH?

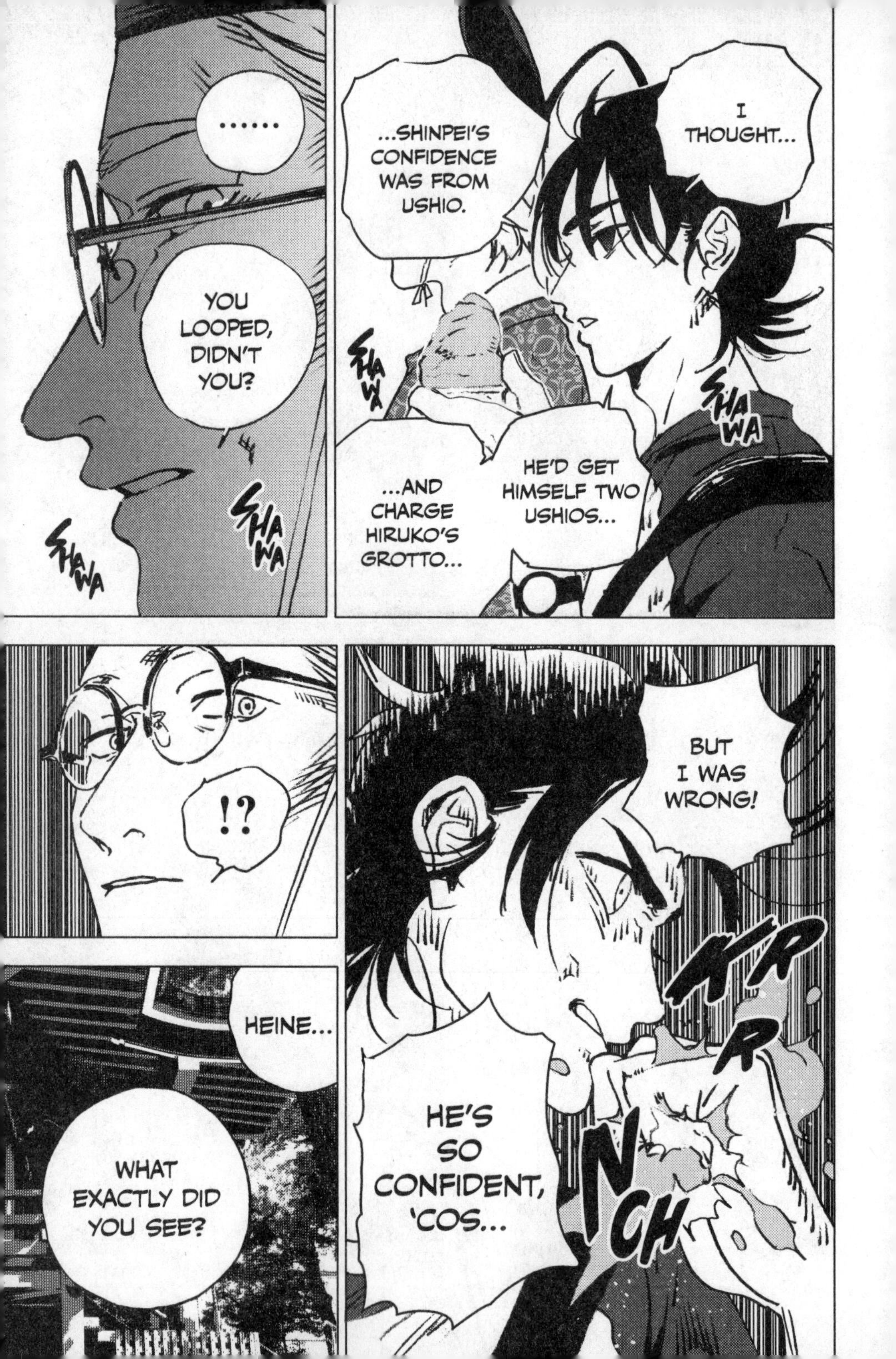
I THOUGHT...
...SHINPEI'S CONFIDENCE WAS FROM USHIO.
SHAWA
SHAWA
HE'D GET HIMSELF TWO USHIOS...
...AND CHARGE HIRUKO'S GROTTO...
......
YOU LOOPED, DIDN'T YOU?
SHAWA
SHAWA
BUT I WAS WRONG!
KRRNCH
HE'S SO CONFIDENT, 'COS...
!?
HEINE...
WHAT EXACTLY DID YOU SEE?

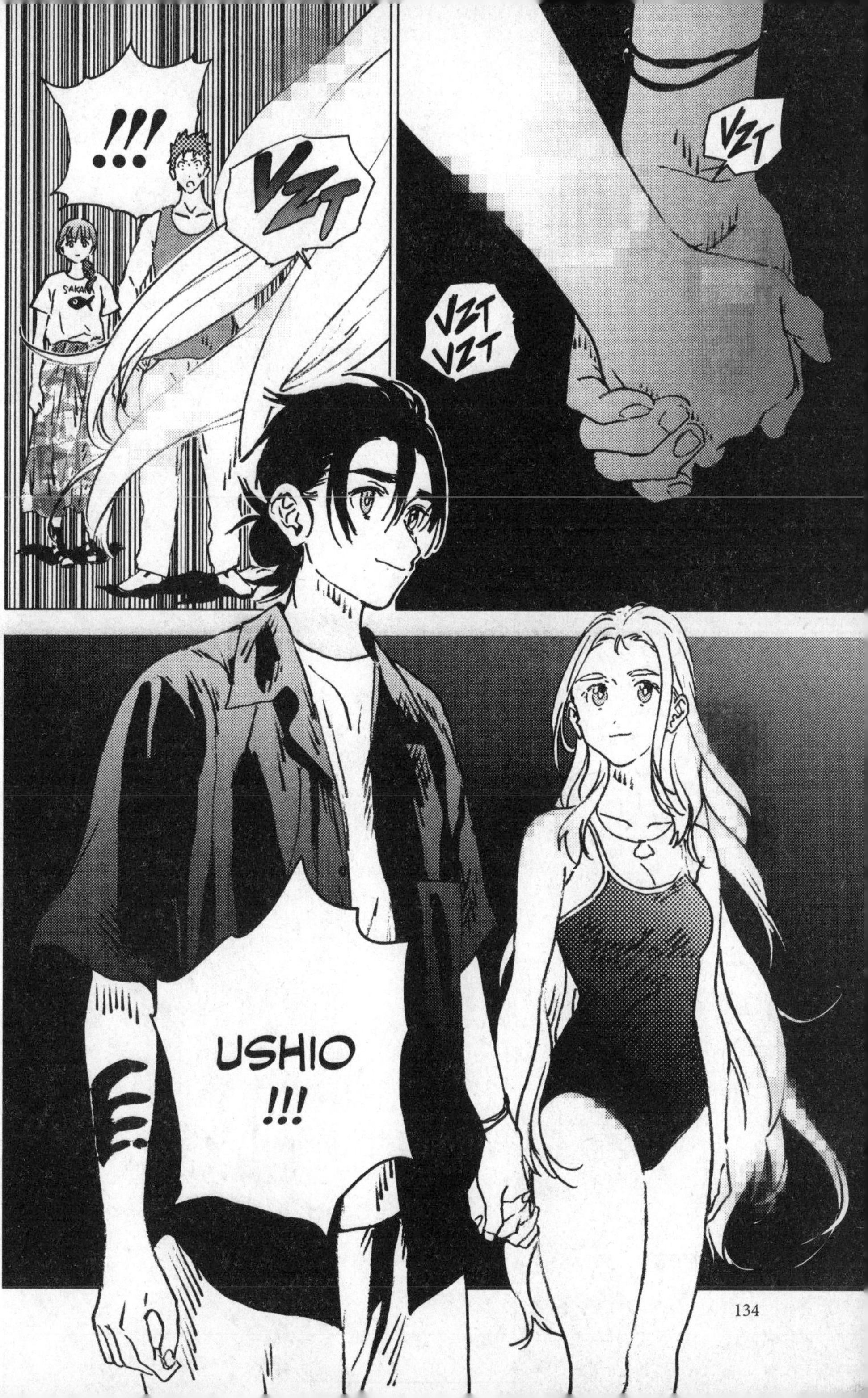
VZT
VZT VZT
!!!
VZT
USHIO !!!

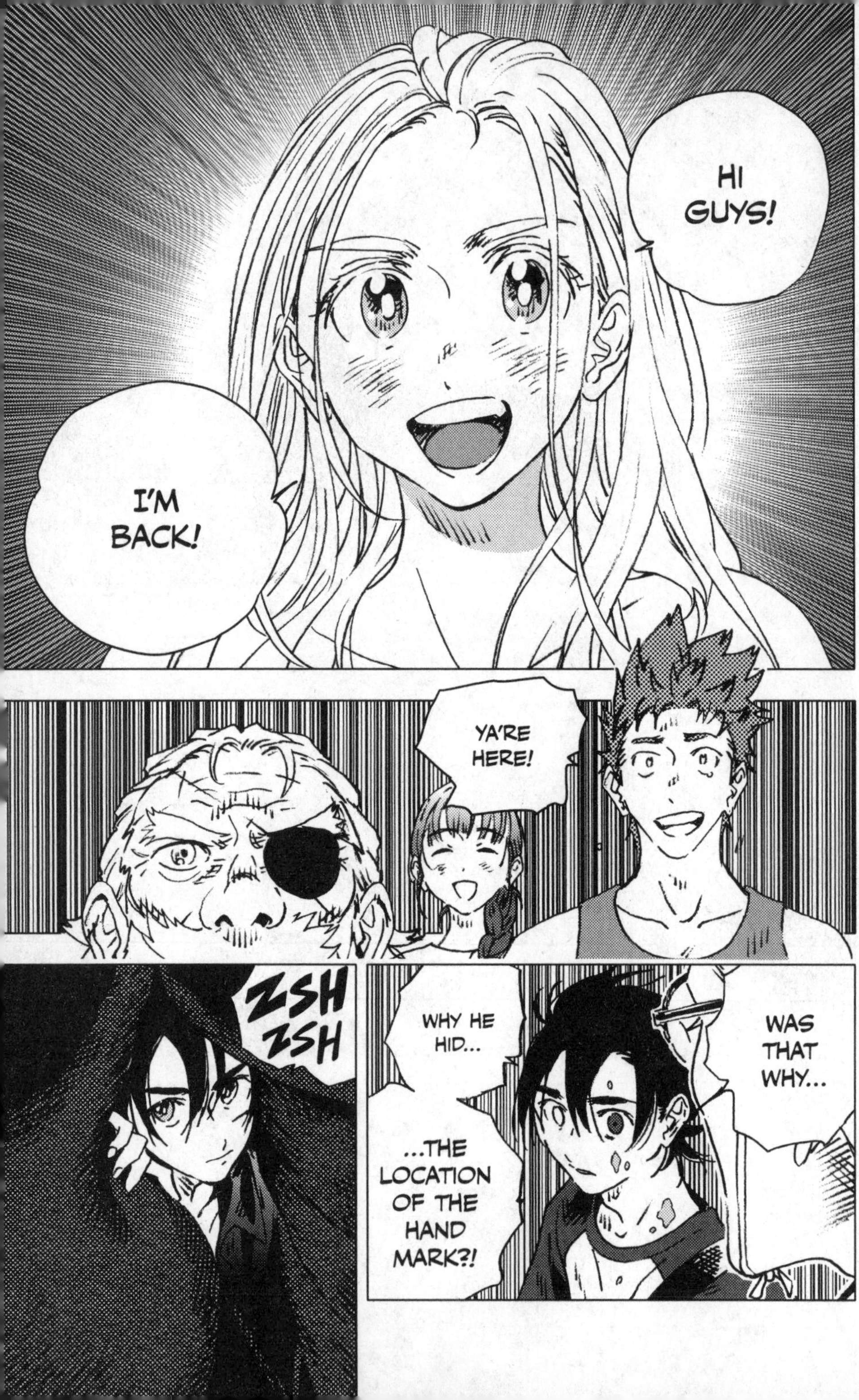
HI GUYS!
I'M BACK!
YA'RE HERE!
WAS THAT WHY...
WHY HE HID...
...THE LOCATION OF THE HAND MARK?!
ZSH ZSH

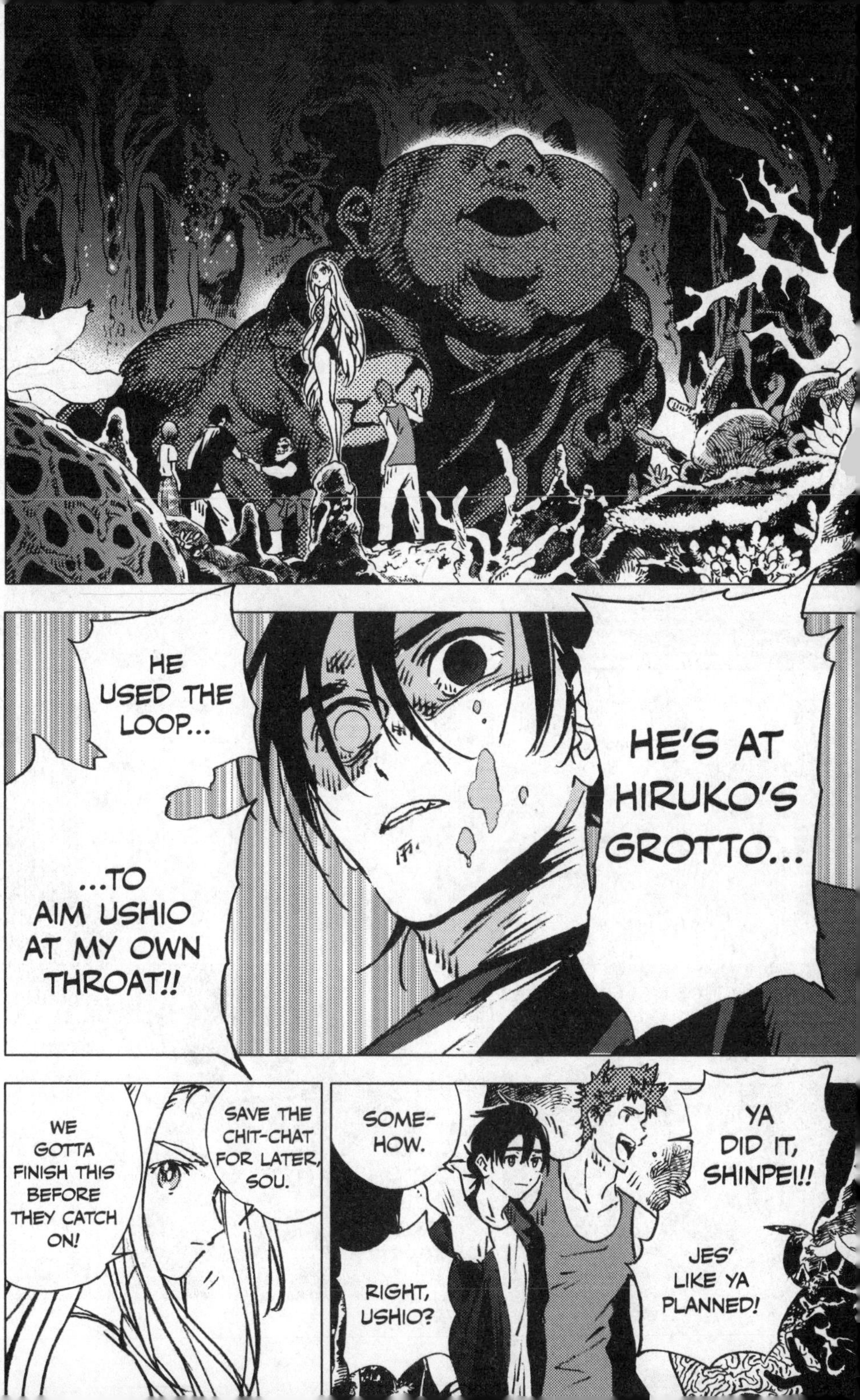
HE'S AT HIRUKO'S GROTTO...
HE USED THE LOOP...
...TO AIM USHIO AT MY OWN THROAT!!
YA DID IT, SHINPEI!!
SOME-HOW.
JES' LIKE YA PLANNED!
RIGHT, USHIO?
SAVE THE CHIT-CHAT FOR LATER, SOU.
WE GOTTA FINISH THIS BEFORE THEY CATCH ON!

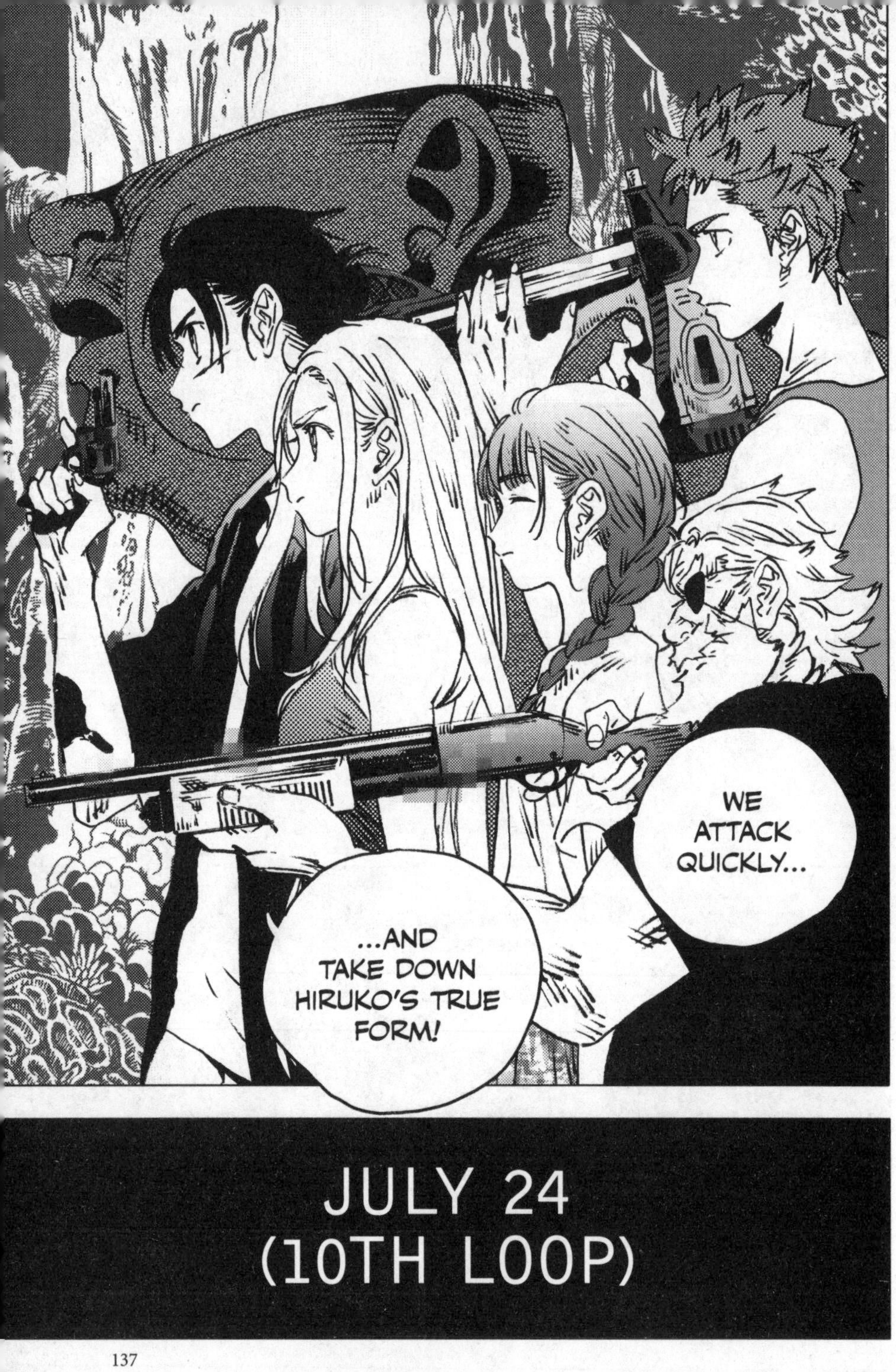
WE ATTACK QUICKLY...
...AND TAKE DOWN HIRUKO'S TRUE FORM!

JULY 24
(10TH LOOP)

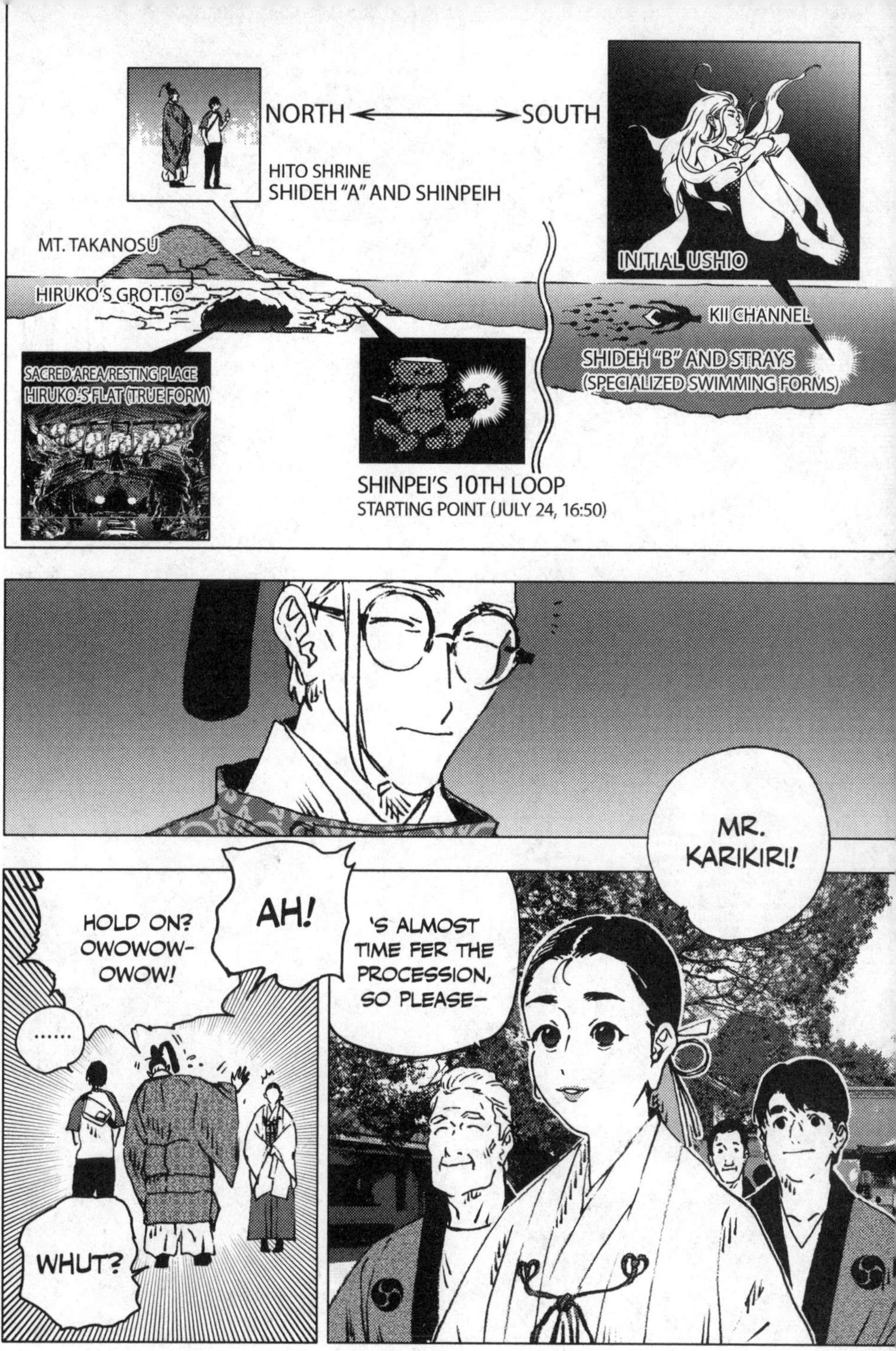
NORTH ⟷ SOUTH
INITIAL USHIO
KII CHANNEL
SHIDEH "B" AND STRAYS
(SPECIALIZED SWIMMING FORMS)
HITO SHRINE
SHIDEH "A" AND SHINPEIH
MT. TAKANOSU
HIRUKO'S GROTTO
SACRED AREA/RESTING PLACE
HIRUKO'S FLAT (TRUE FORM)
SHINPEI'S 10TH LOOP
STARTING POINT (JULY 24, 16:50)
MR. KARIKIRI!
'S ALMOST TIME FER THE PROCESSION, SO PLEASE–
AH!
HOLD ON? OWOWOW-OWOW!
....
WHUT?

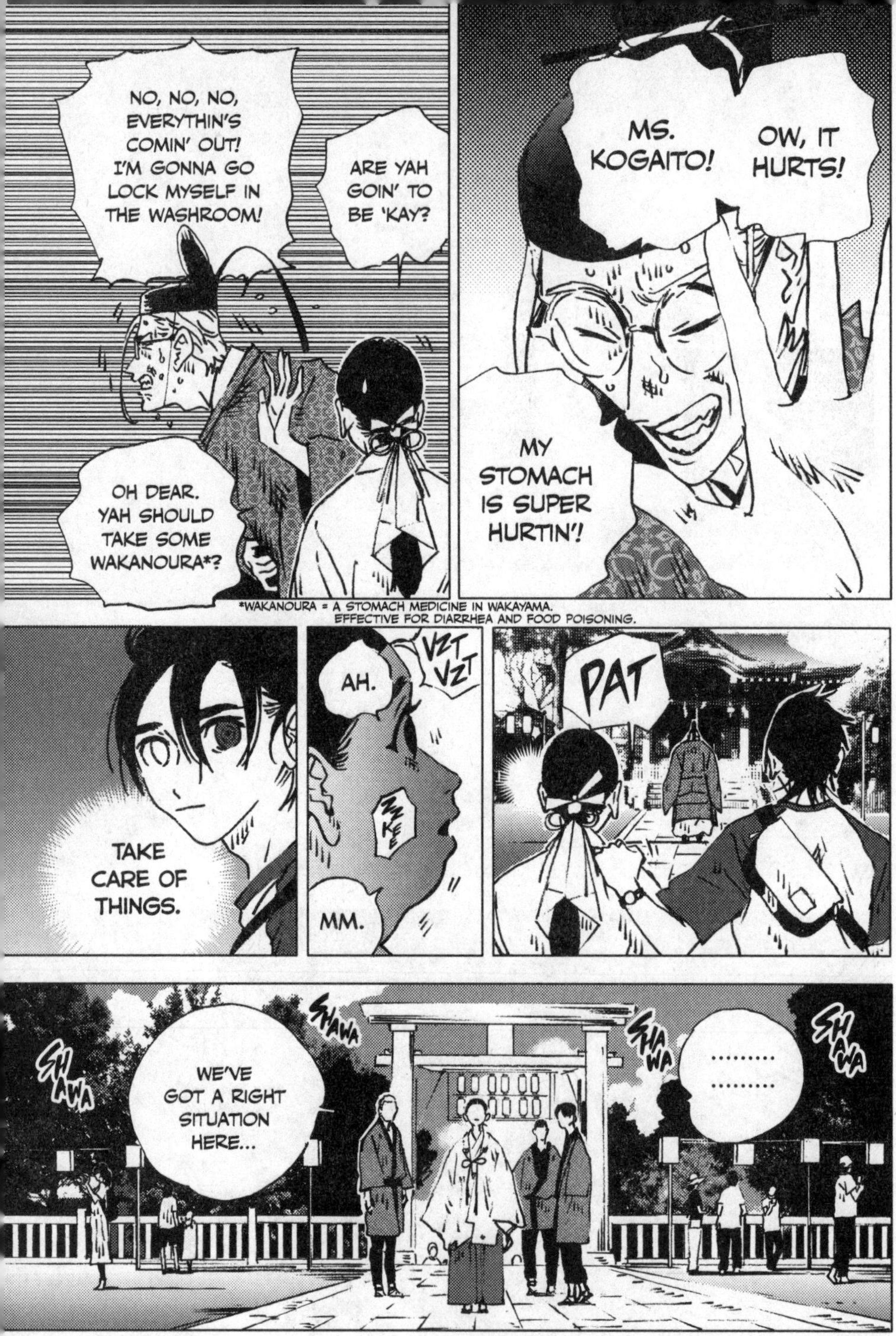
OW, IT HURTS!
MS. KOGAITO!
MY STOMACH IS SUPER HURTIN'!
ARE YAH GOIN' TO BE 'KAY?
NO, NO, NO, EVERYTHIN'S COMIN' OUT! I'M GONNA GO LOCK MYSELF IN THE WASHROOM!
OH DEAR. YAH SHOULD TAKE SOME WAKANOURA*?
PAT
VZT VZT
AH.
MM.
TAKE CARE OF THINGS.
SHAWA
....
....
SHAWA
SHAWA
WE'VE GOT A RIGHT SITUATION HERE...
SHAWA

*WAKANOURA = A STOMACH MEDICINE IN WAKAYAMA. EFFECTIVE FOR DIARRHEA AND FOOD POISONING.

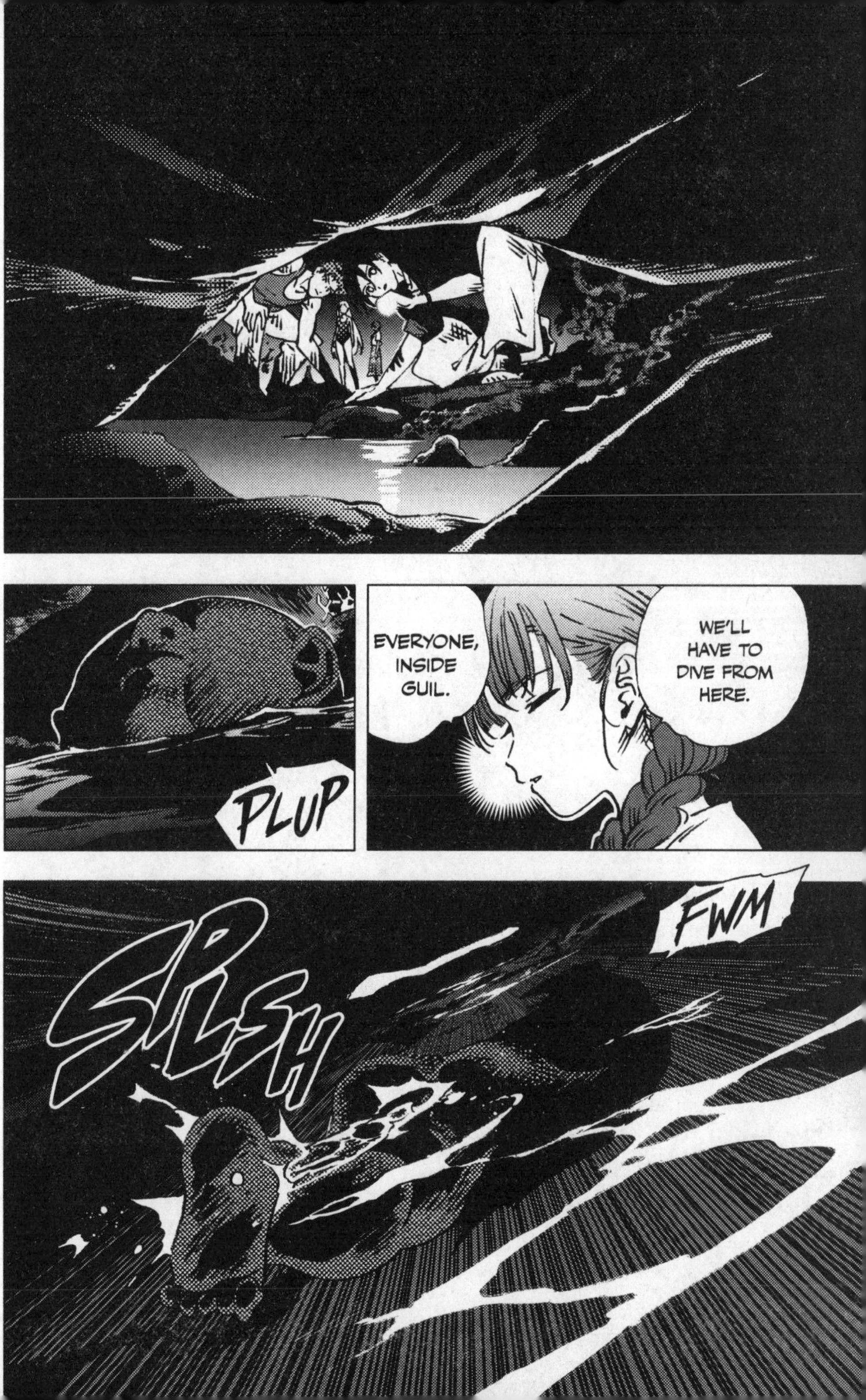
WE'LL HAVE TO DIVE FROM HERE.
EVERYONE, INSIDE GUIL.
PLUP
FWM
SPLSH

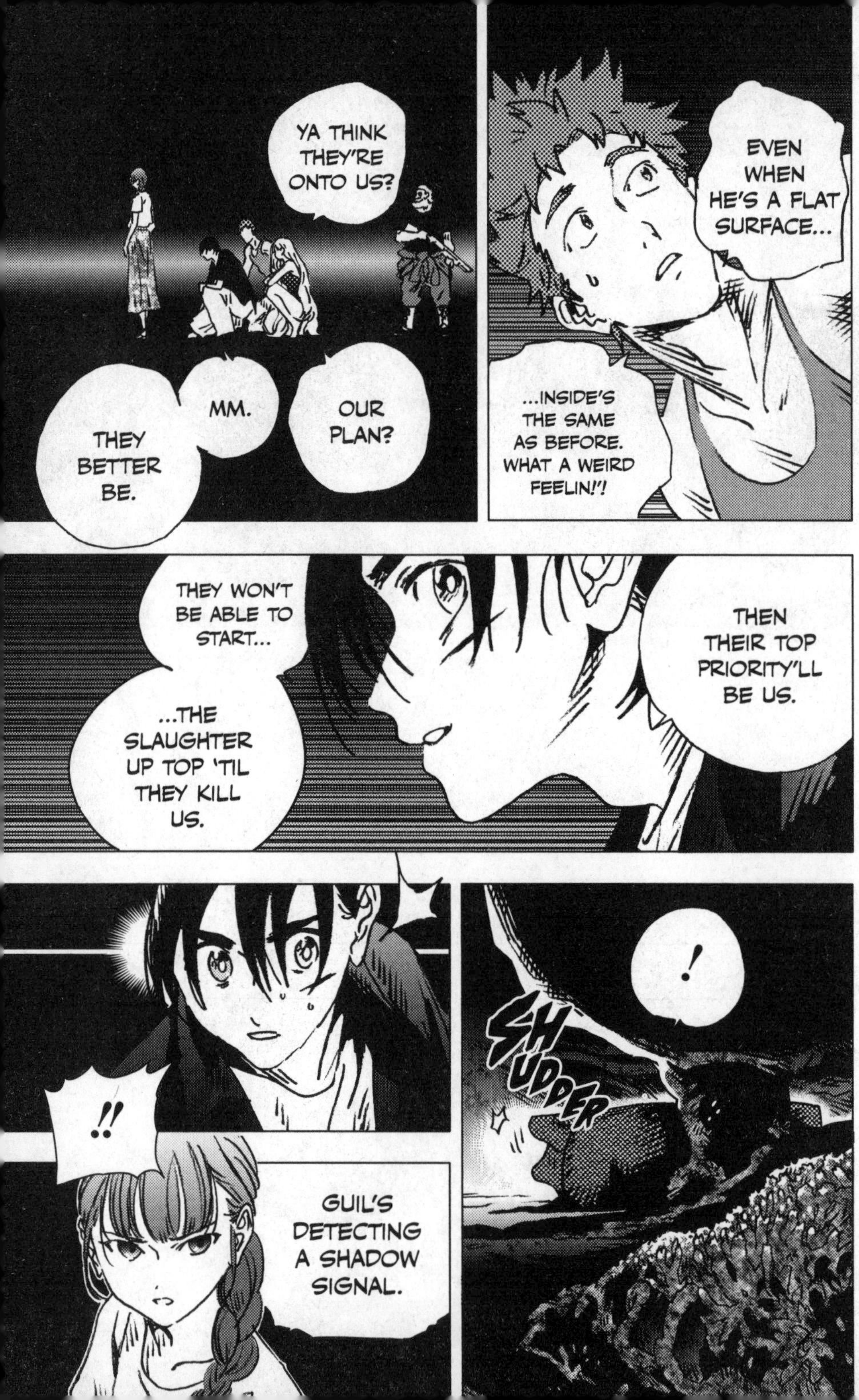
EVEN WHEN HE'S A FLAT SURFACE...
...INSIDE'S THE SAME AS BEFORE. WHAT A WEIRD FEELIN'!
YA THINK THEY'RE ONTO US?
OUR PLAN?
MM.
THEY BETTER BE.
THEN THEIR TOP PRIORITY'LL BE US.
THEY WON'T BE ABLE TO START...
...THE SLAUGHTER UP TOP 'TIL THEY KILL US.
!
SHUDDER
!!
GUIL'S DETECTING A SHADOW SIGNAL.

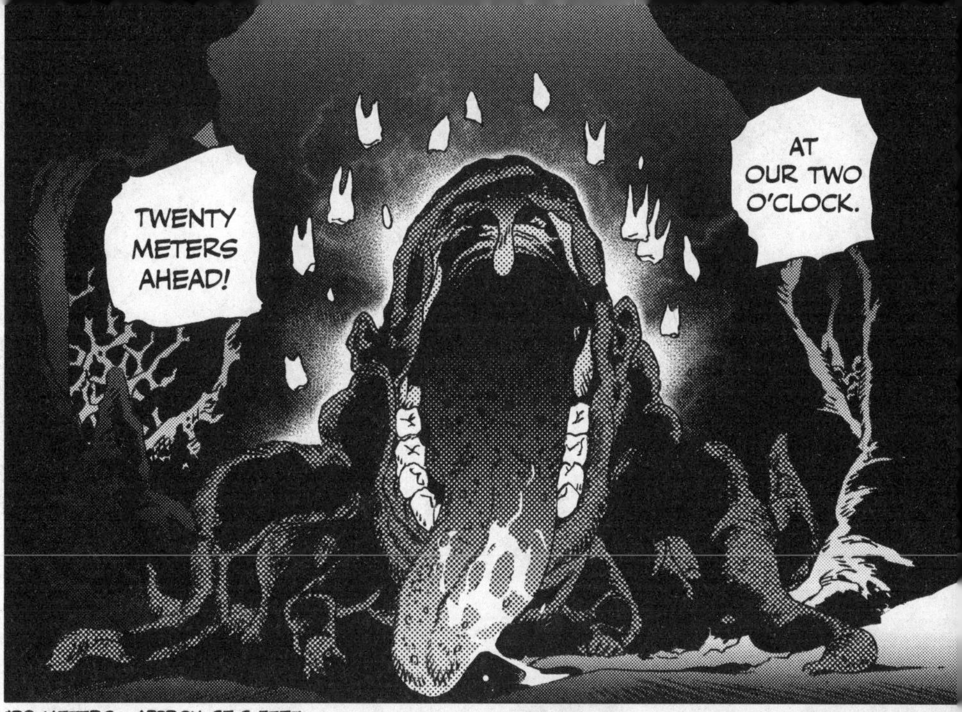
AT OUR TWO O'CLOCK.
TWENTY METERS AHEAD!

*20 METERS = APPROX 65.6 FEET.

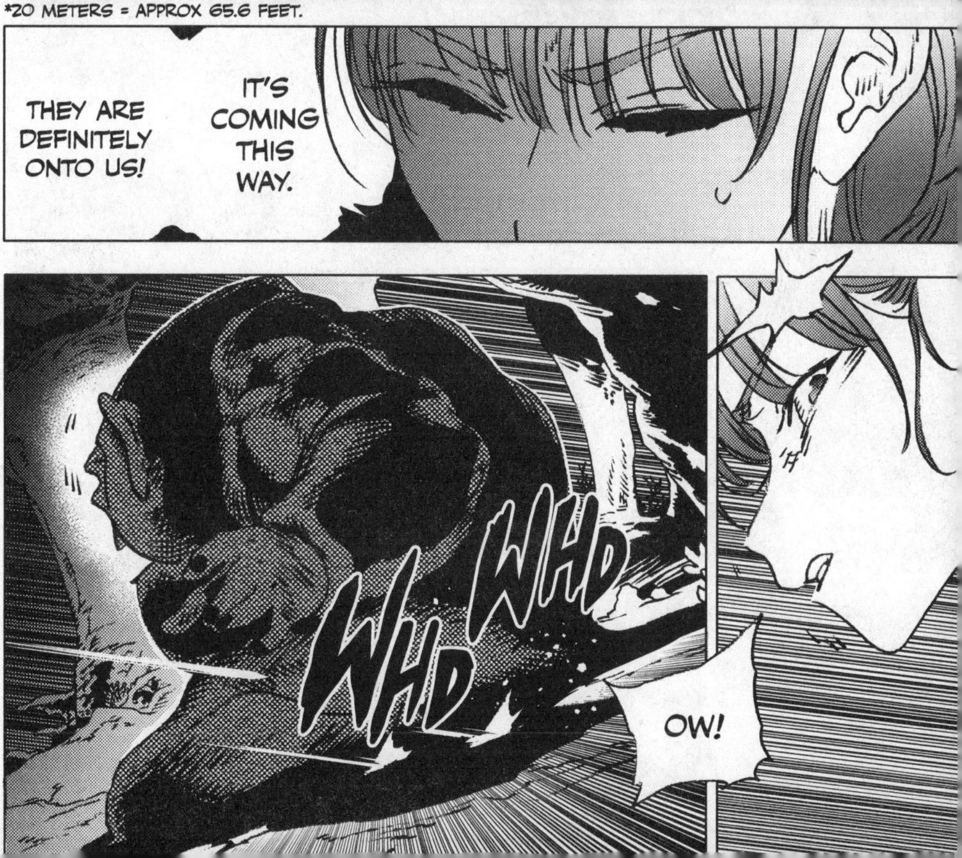
IT'S COMING THIS WAY.
THEY ARE DEFINITELY ONTO US!
OW!
WHD WHD

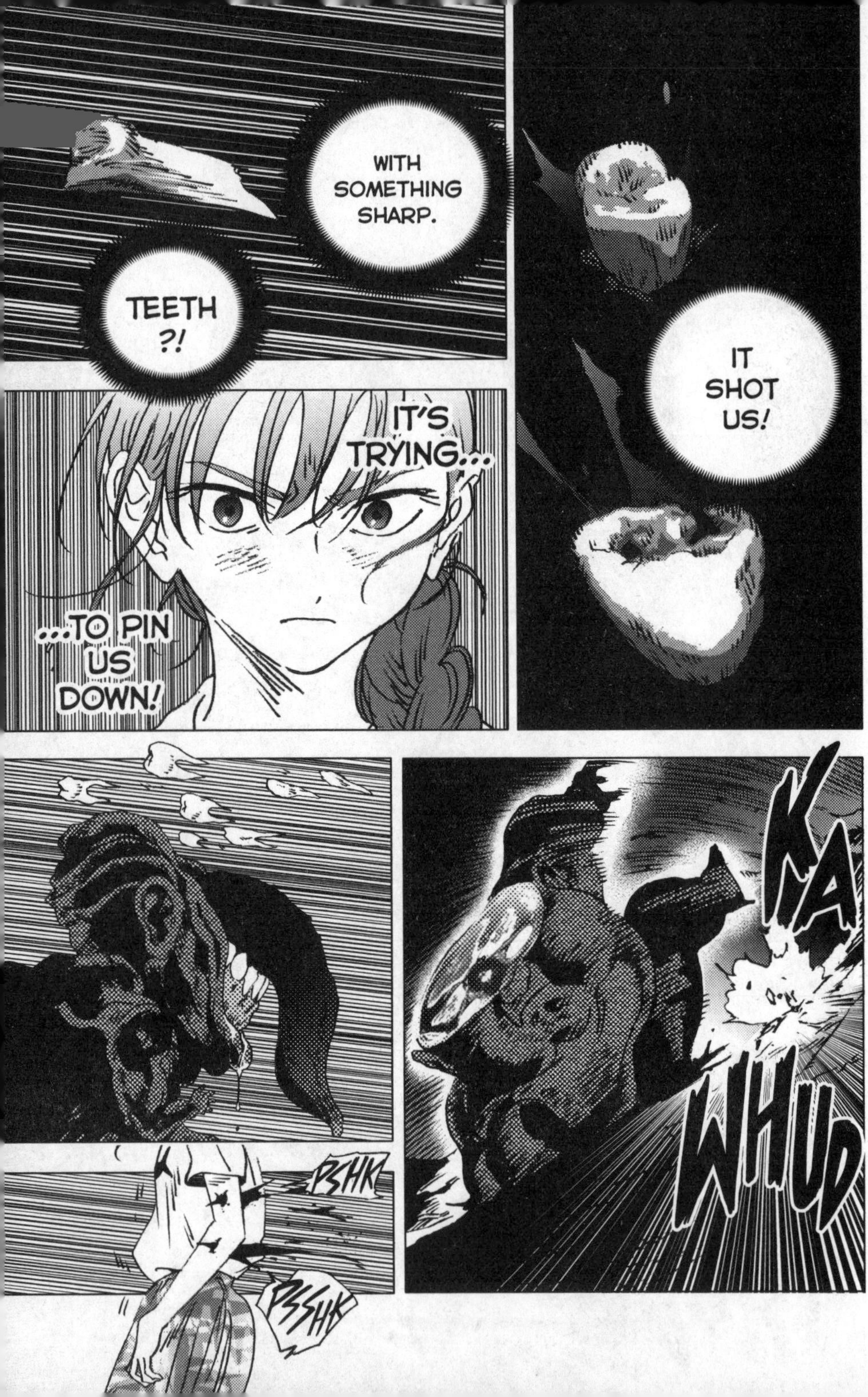
IT SHOT US!
WITH SOMETHING SHARP.
TEETH ?!
IT'S TRYING...
...TO PIN US DOWN!
KA
WHUD
PSHK
PSSHK

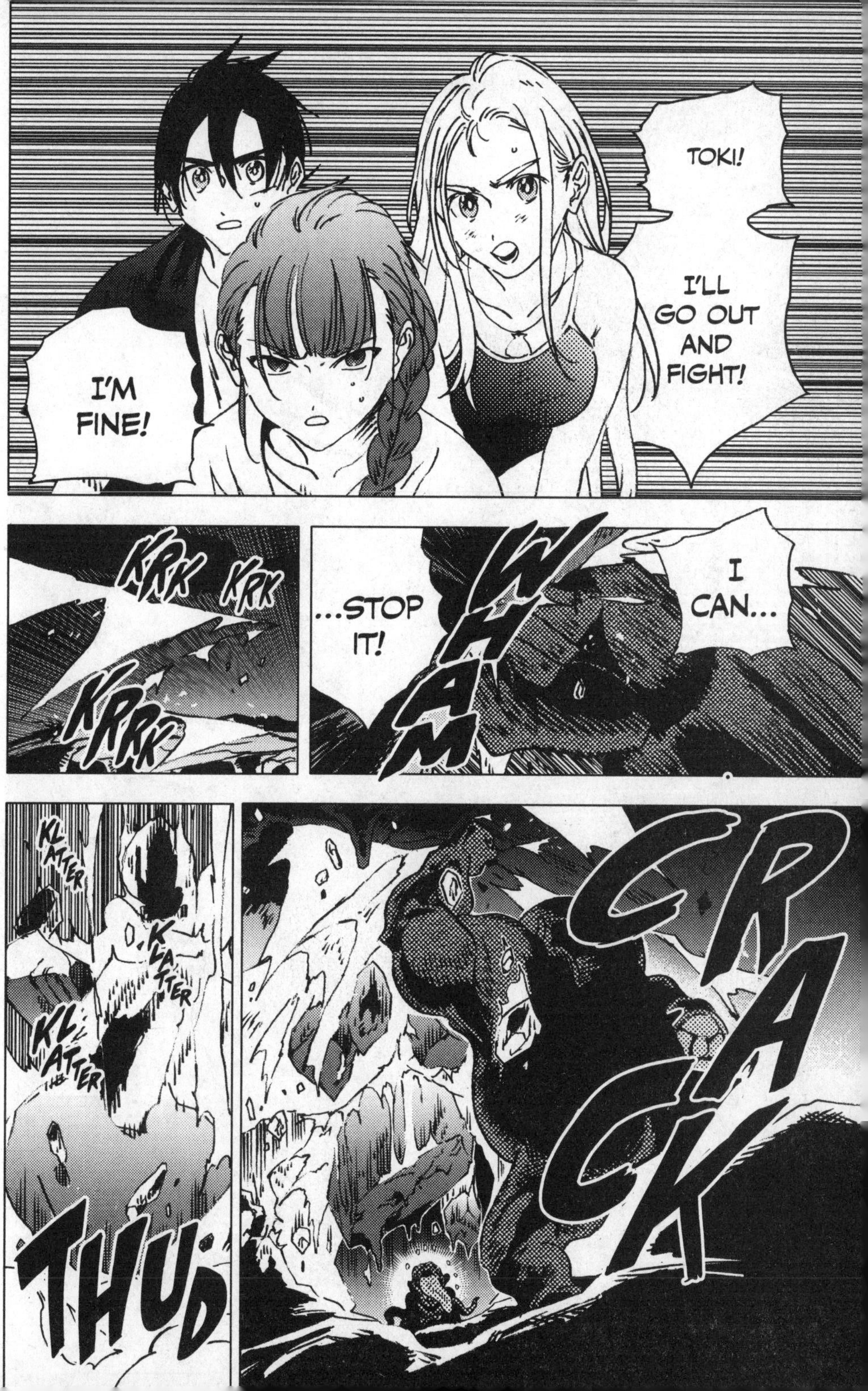
TOKI!
I'LL GO OUT AND FIGHT!
I'M FINE!
I CAN...
WHAM
...STOP IT!
KRK KRK
KRRRK
CRACK
KLATTER
KLATTER
KLATTER
THUD

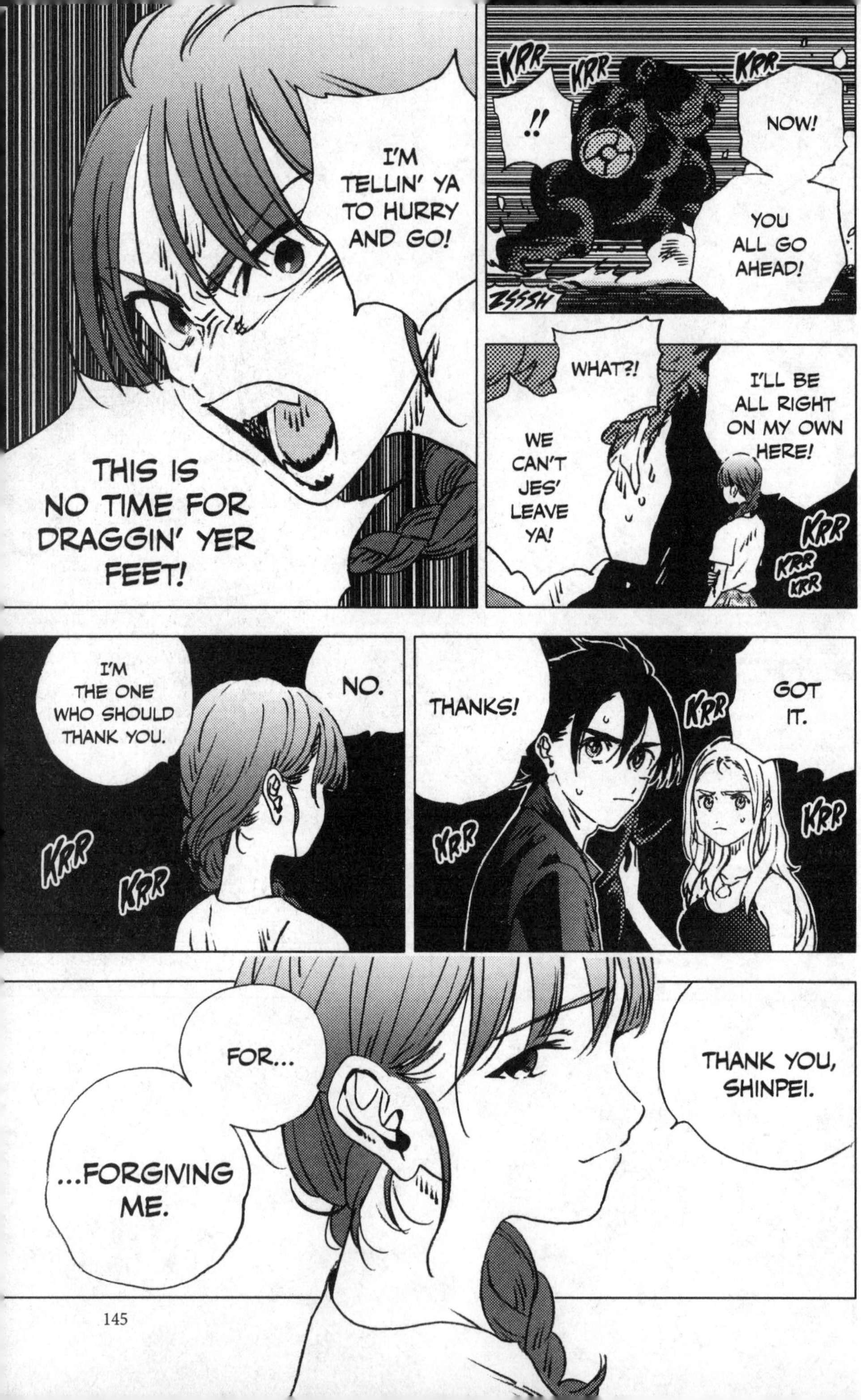
KRR
KRR
KRR
NOW!
YOU ALL GO AHEAD!
!!
ZSSSH
I'LL BE ALL RIGHT ON MY OWN HERE!
WHAT?!
WE CAN'T JES' LEAVE YA!
KRR
KRR KRR
I'M TELLIN' YA TO HURRY AND GO!
THIS IS NO TIME FOR DRAGGIN' YER FEET!
GOT IT.
KRR
THANKS!
KRR
KRR
NO.
I'M THE ONE WHO SHOULD THANK YOU.
KRR
KRR
THANK YOU, SHINPEI.
FOR...
...FORGIVING ME.

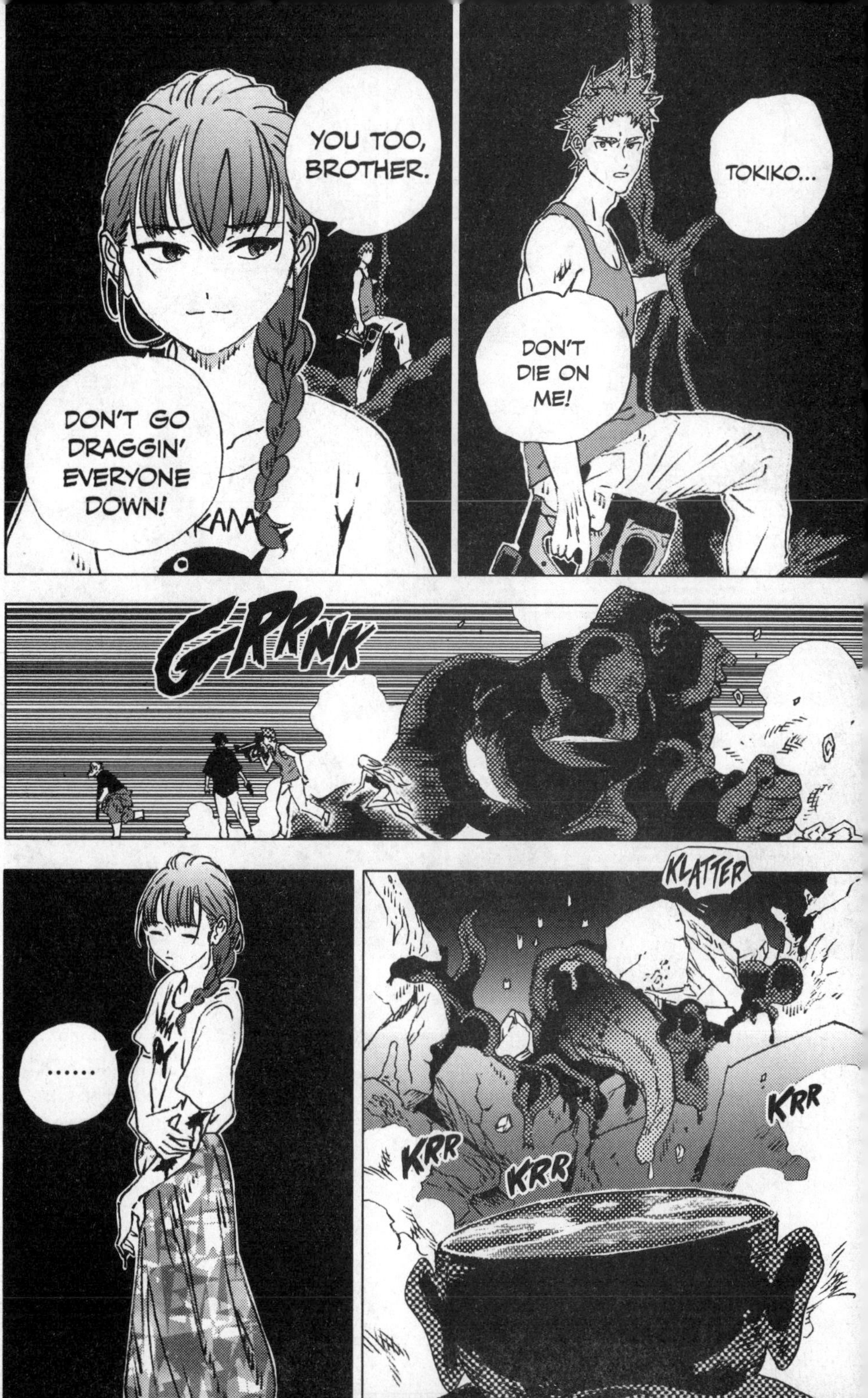
TOKIKO...
DON'T DIE ON ME!
YOU TOO, BROTHER.
DON'T GO DRAGGIN' EVERYONE DOWN!
GRRNK
KLATTER
KRR
KRR
KRR
......

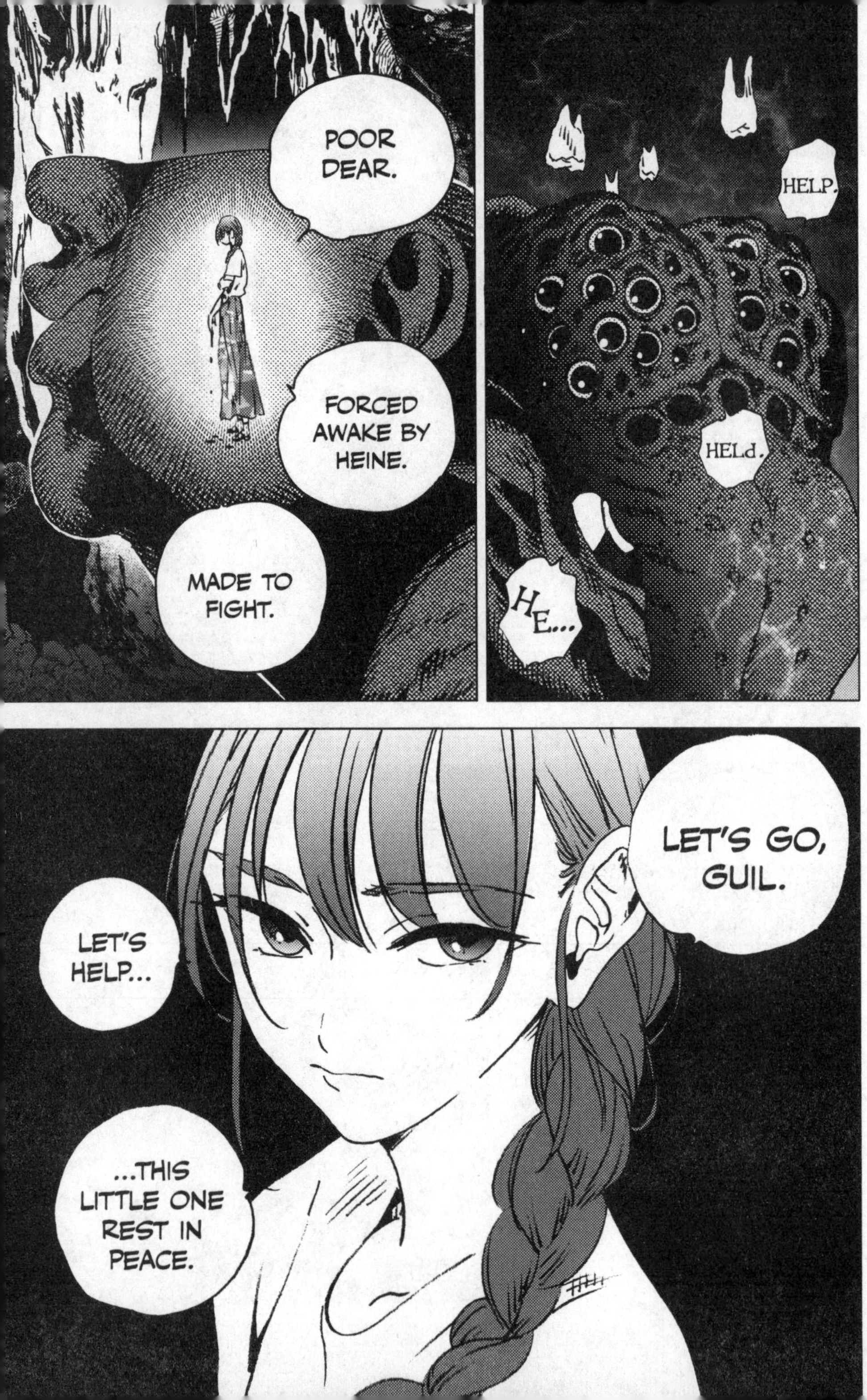
HELP.
HELd.
HE...
POOR DEAR.
FORCED AWAKE BY HEINE.
MADE TO FIGHT.
LET'S GO, GUIL.
LET'S HELP...
...THIS LITTLE ONE REST IN PEACE.

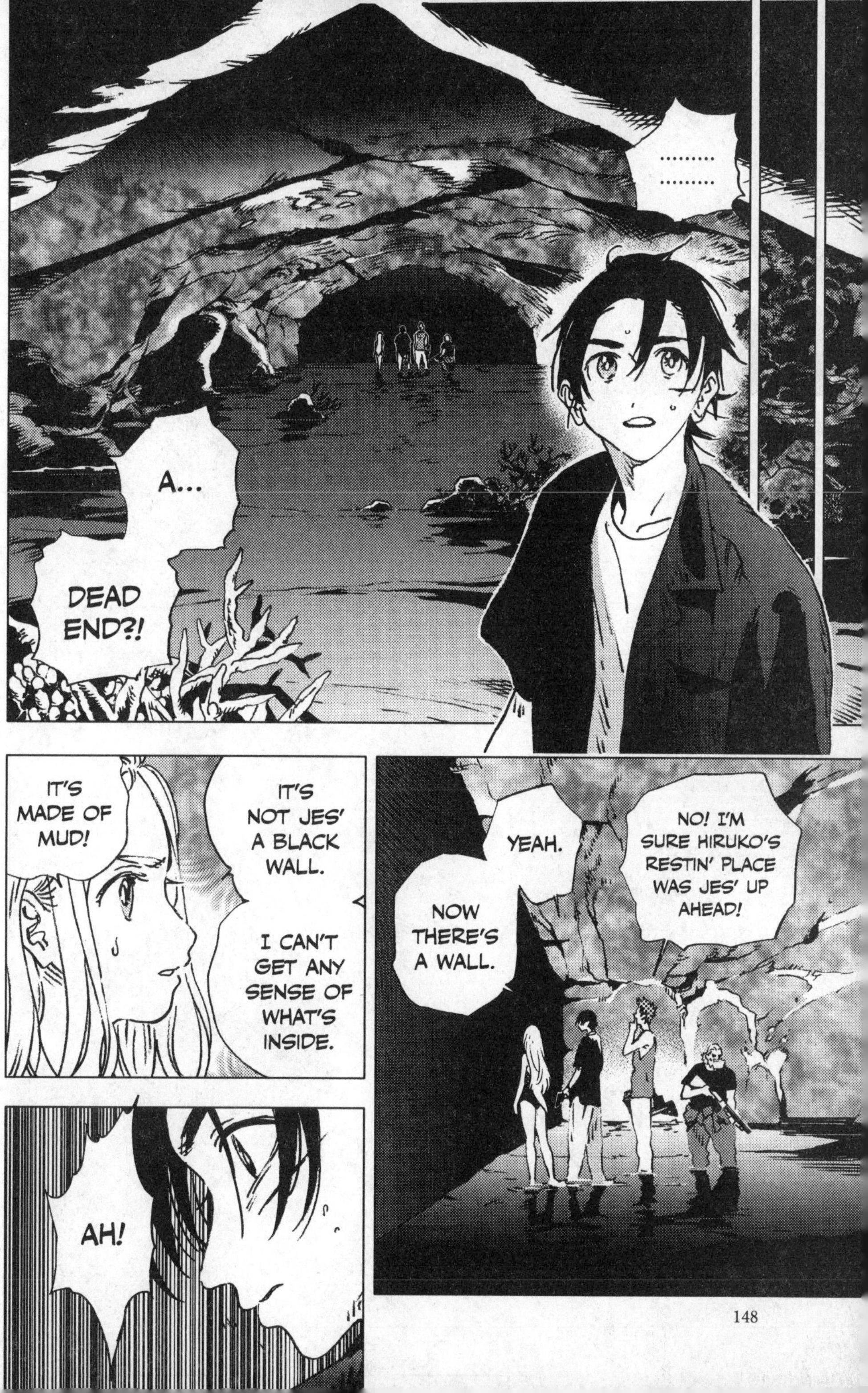
....
....
A...
DEAD END?!
NO! I'M SURE HIRUKO'S RESTIN' PLACE WAS JES' UP AHEAD!
YEAH.
NOW THERE'S A WALL.
IT'S NOT JES' A BLACK WALL.
I CAN'T GET ANY SENSE OF WHAT'S INSIDE.
IT'S MADE OF MUD!
AH!

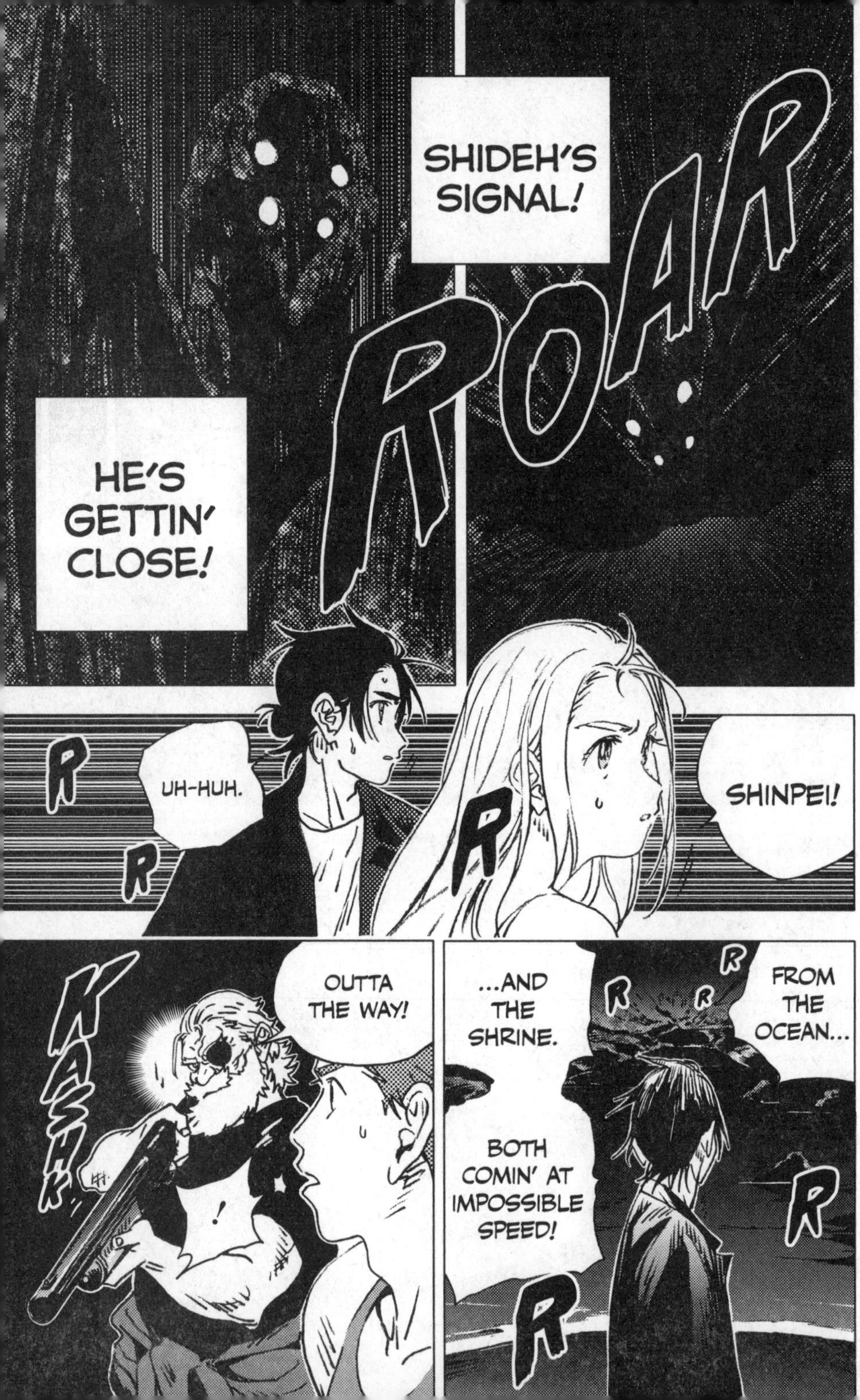
SHIDEH'S SIGNAL!
ROAR
HE'S GETTIN' CLOSE!
SHINPEI!
R
UH-HUH.
R
R
R
R
R
FROM THE OCEAN...
...AND THE SHRINE.
BOTH COMIN' AT IMPOSSIBLE SPEED!
R
R
OUTTA THE WAY!
KASHAK
!

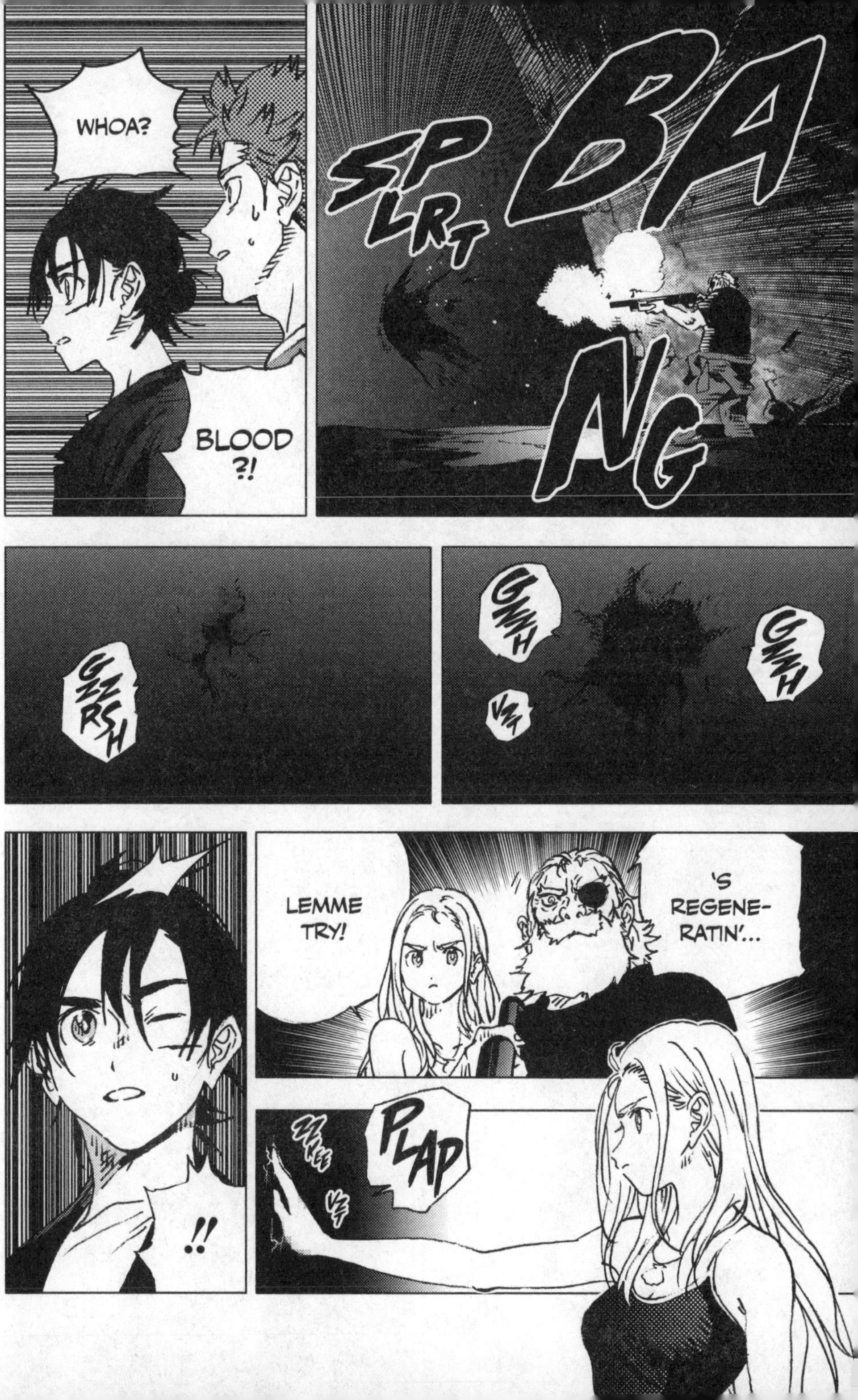
BANG
SPLRT
WHOA?
BLOOD ?!
GMMH
GMMH
GZZRSH
'S REGENE-RATIN'...
LEMME TRY!
PLAP
!!

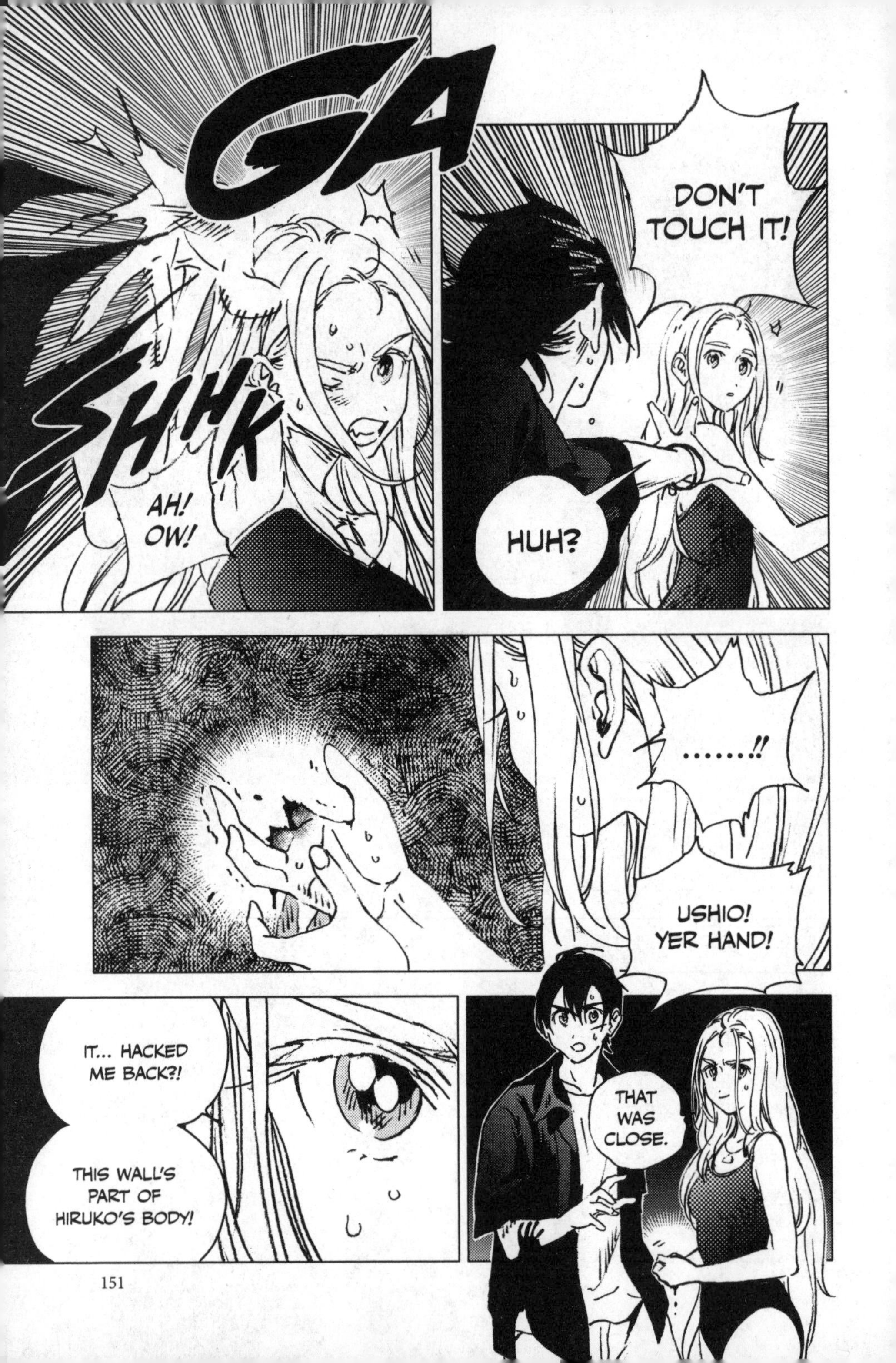
DON'T TOUCH IT!
HUH?
GA
SHHK
AH! OW!
.......!!
USHIO! YER HAND!
THAT WAS CLOSE.
IT... HACKED ME BACK?!
THIS WALL'S PART OF HIRUKO'S BODY!

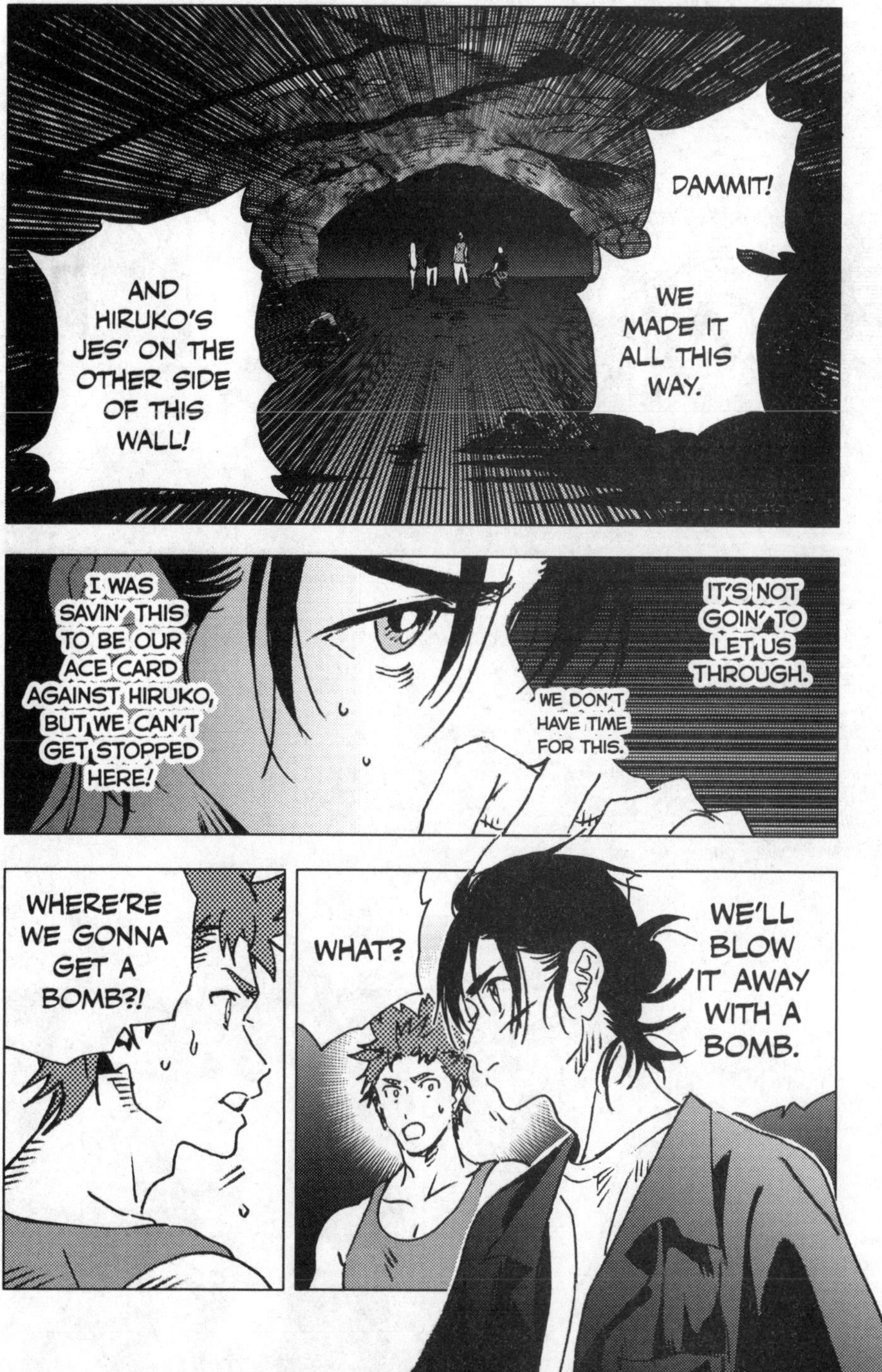
DAMMIT!
WE MADE IT ALL THIS WAY.
AND HIRUKO'S JES' ON THE OTHER SIDE OF THIS WALL!
IT'S NOT GOIN' TO LET US THROUGH.
WE DON'T HAVE TIME FOR THIS.
I WAS SAVIN' THIS TO BE OUR ACE CARD AGAINST HIRUKO, BUT WE CAN'T GET STOPPED HERE!
WE'LL BLOW IT AWAY WITH A BOMB.
WHAT?
WHERE'RE WE GONNA GET A BOMB?!

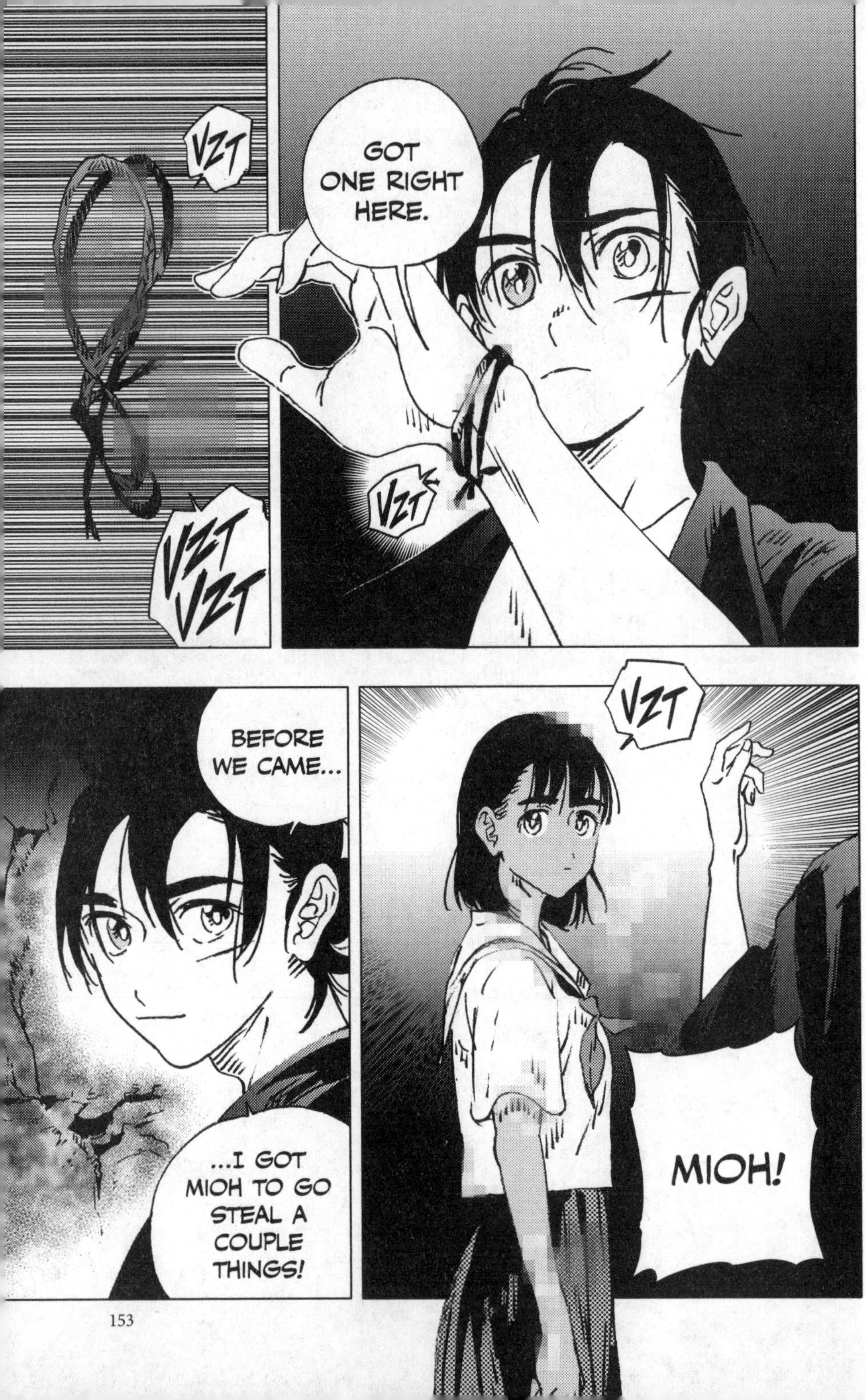
GOT ONE RIGHT HERE.
VZT
VZT
VZT VZT
VZT
MIOH!
BEFORE WE CAME...
...I GOT MIOH TO GO STEAL A COUPLE THINGS!

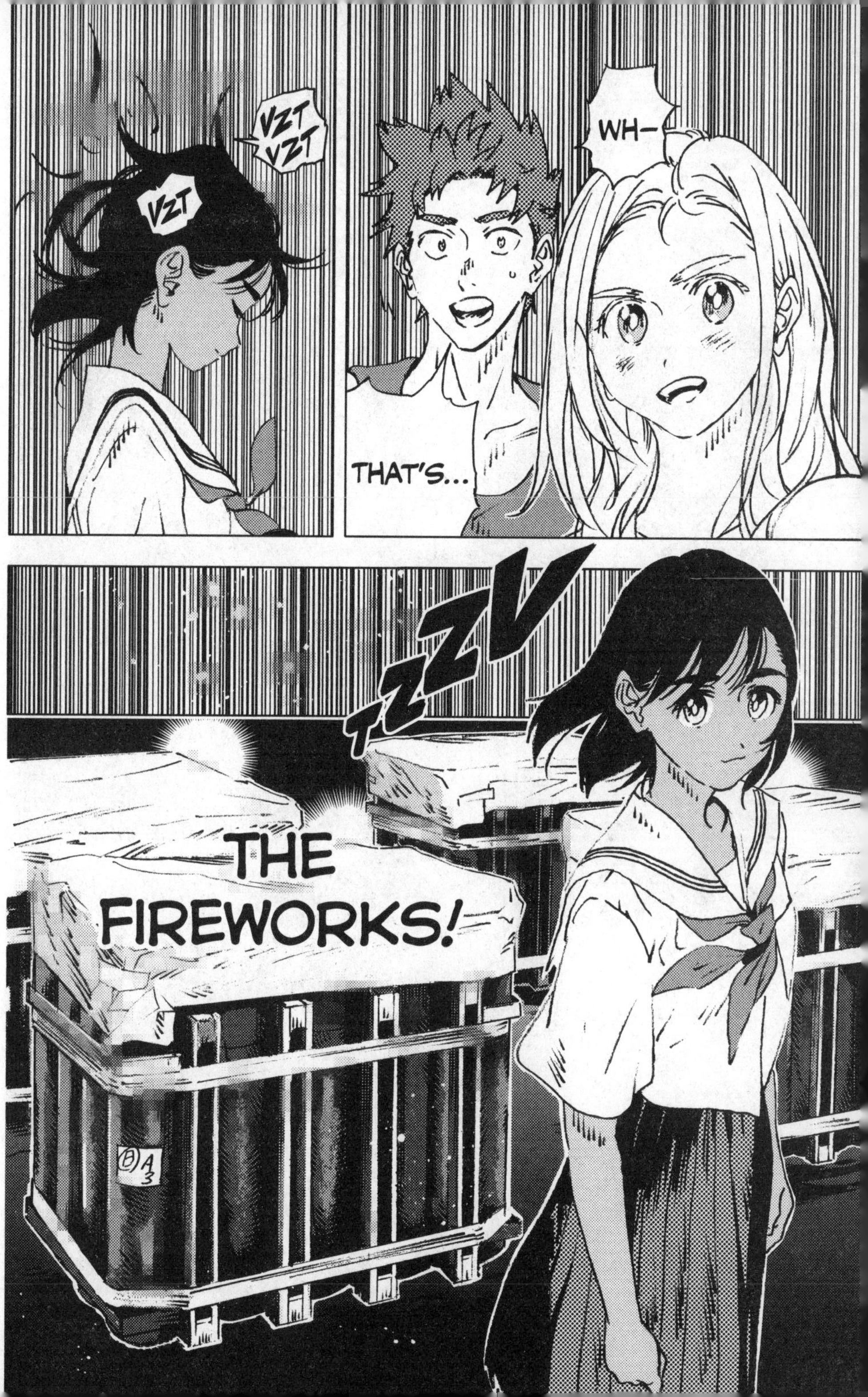
WH-
THAT'S...
VZT VZT
VZT
TZZV
THE FIREWORKS!

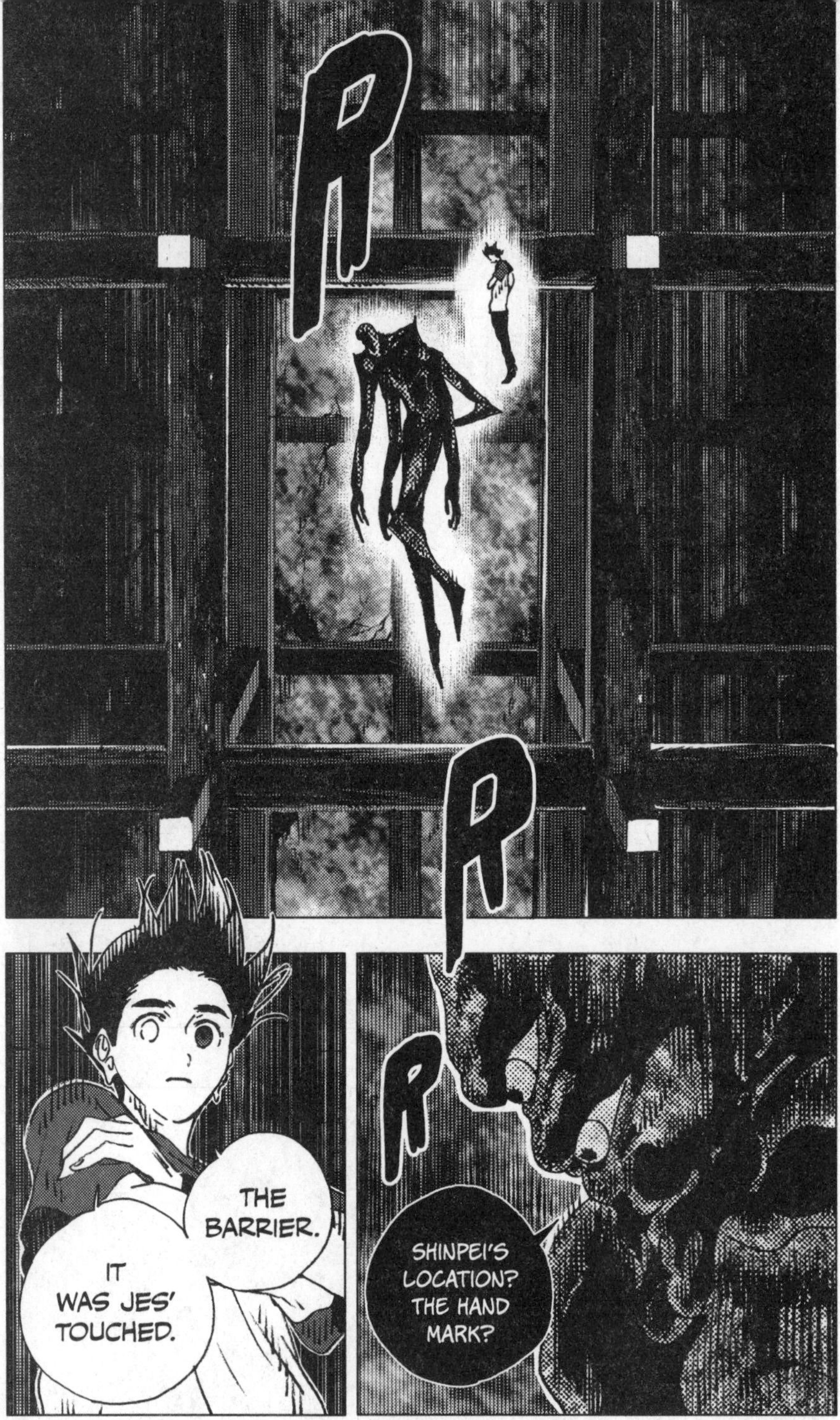
R
R
R
SHINPEI'S LOCATION? THE HAND MARK?
THE BARRIER.
IT WAS JES' TOUCHED.

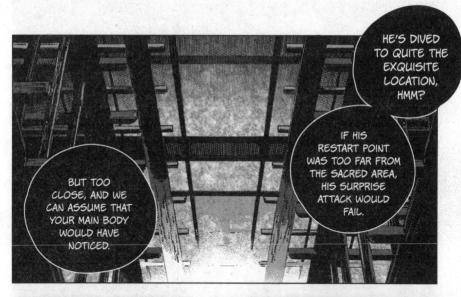

HE'S DIVED TO QUITE THE EXQUISITE LOCATION, HMM?

IF HIS RESTART POINT WAS TOO FAR FROM THE SACRED AREA, HIS SURPRISE ATTACK WOULD FAIL.

BUT TOO CLOSE, AND WE CAN ASSUME THAT YOUR MAIN BODY WOULD HAVE NOTICED.

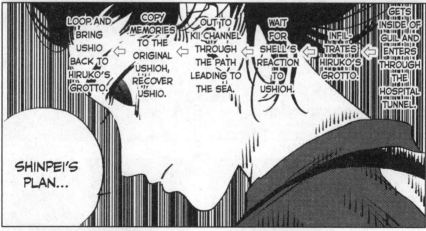

GETS INSIDE OF GUIL AND ENTERS THROUGH THE HOSPITAL TUNNEL.

INFIL-TRATES HIRUKO'S GROTTO.

WAIT FOR SHELL'S REACTION TO USHIOH.

OUT TO KII CHANNEL THROUGH THE PATH LEADING TO THE SEA.

COPY MEMORIES TO THE ORIGINAL USHIOH, RECOVER USHIO.

LOOP, AND BRING USHIO BACK TO HIRUKO'S GROTTO.

SHINPEI'S PLAN...

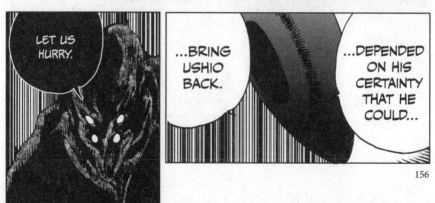

LET US HURRY.

...BRING USHIO BACK.

...DEPENDED ON HIS CERTAINTY THAT HE COULD...

156

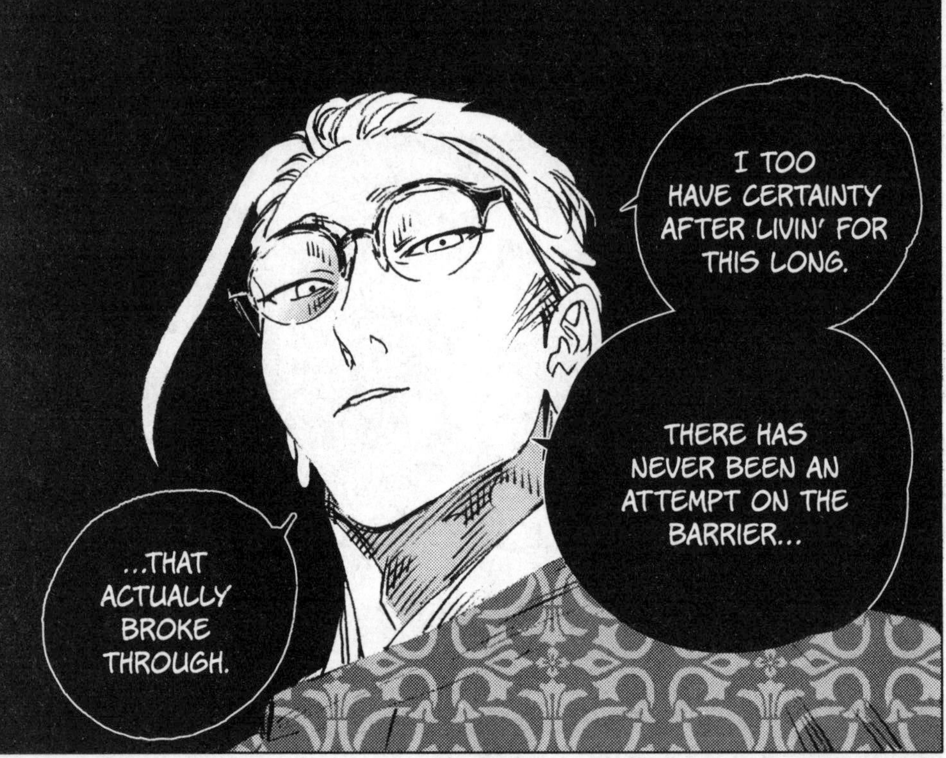
I TOO HAVE CERTAINTY AFTER LIVIN' FOR THIS LONG.
THERE HAS NEVER BEEN AN ATTEMPT ON THE BARRIER...
...THAT ACTUALLY BROKE THROUGH.

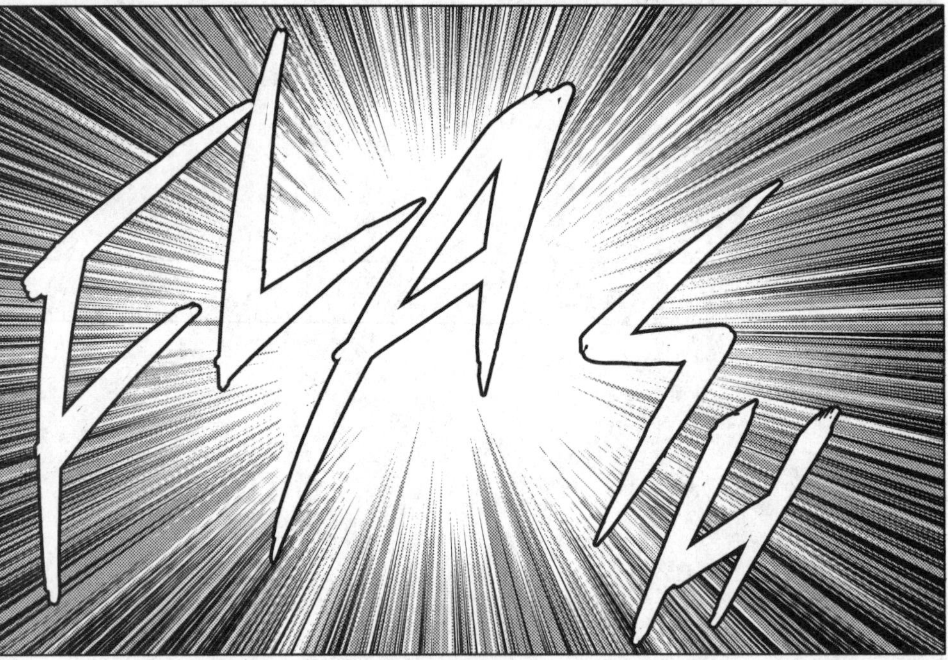
FLASH

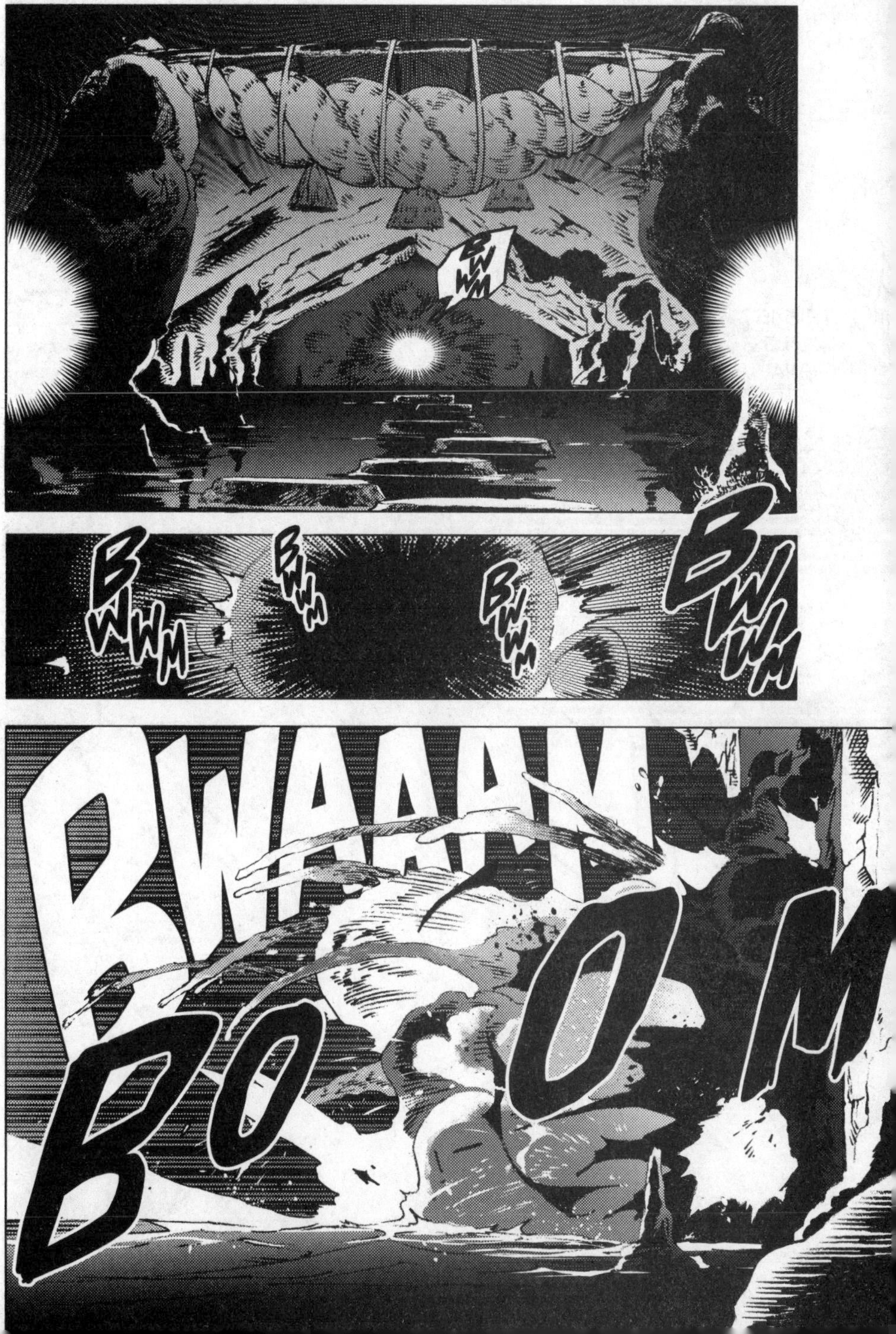
BWWM
BWWM
BWWM
BWWM
BWWM
BWAAM
BO-O-M

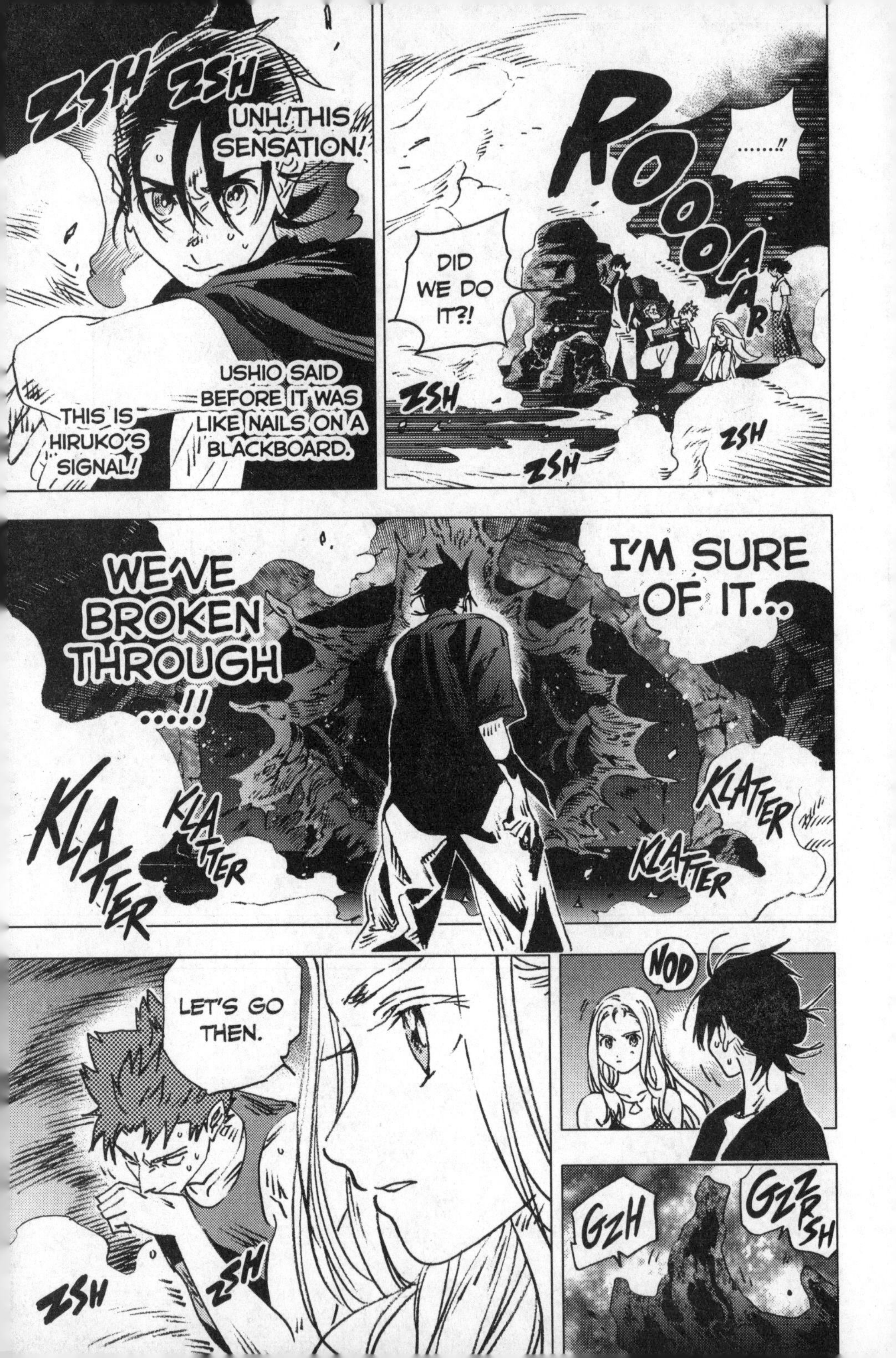
ROOOOAAR
......!!
DID WE DO IT?!
ZSH
ZSH
ZSH
ZSH ZSH
UNH! THIS SENSATION!
USHIO SAID BEFORE IT WAS LIKE NAILS ON A BLACKBOARD.
THIS IS HIRUKO'S SIGNAL!
I'M SURE OF IT...
WE'VE BROKEN THROUGH ...!!
KLATTER
KLATTER
KLATTER
KLATTER
NOD
GZZRSH
GZH
LET'S GO THEN.
ZSH
ZSH

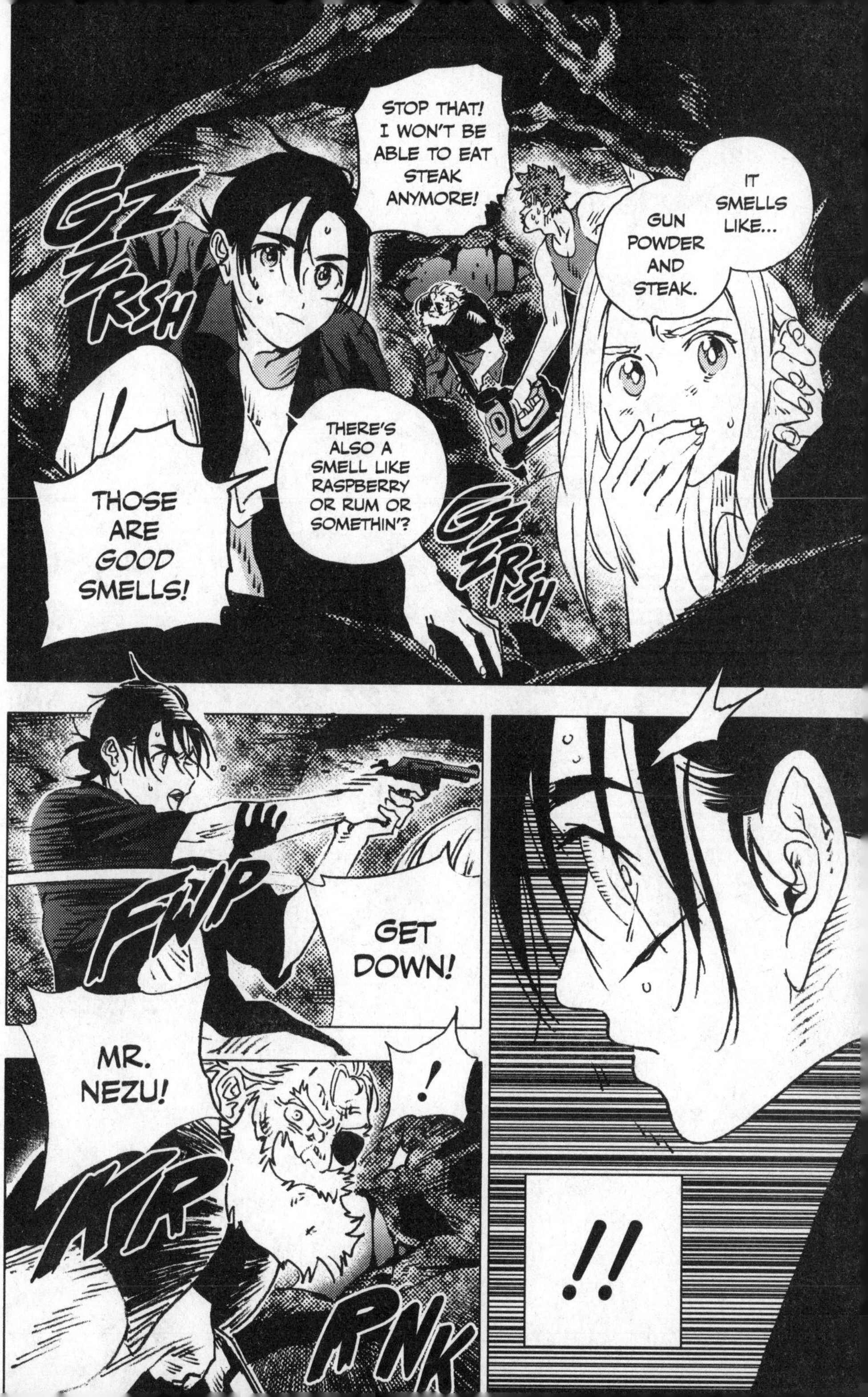
IT SMELLS LIKE...
GUN POWDER AND STEAK.
STOP THAT! I WON'T BE ABLE TO EAT STEAK ANYMORE!
GZZRSH
GZZRSH
THERE'S ALSO A SMELL LIKE RASPBERRY OR RUM OR SOMETHIN'?
THOSE ARE GOOD SMELLS!
!!
FWIP
GET DOWN!
!
MR. NEZU!
WKR
RNK

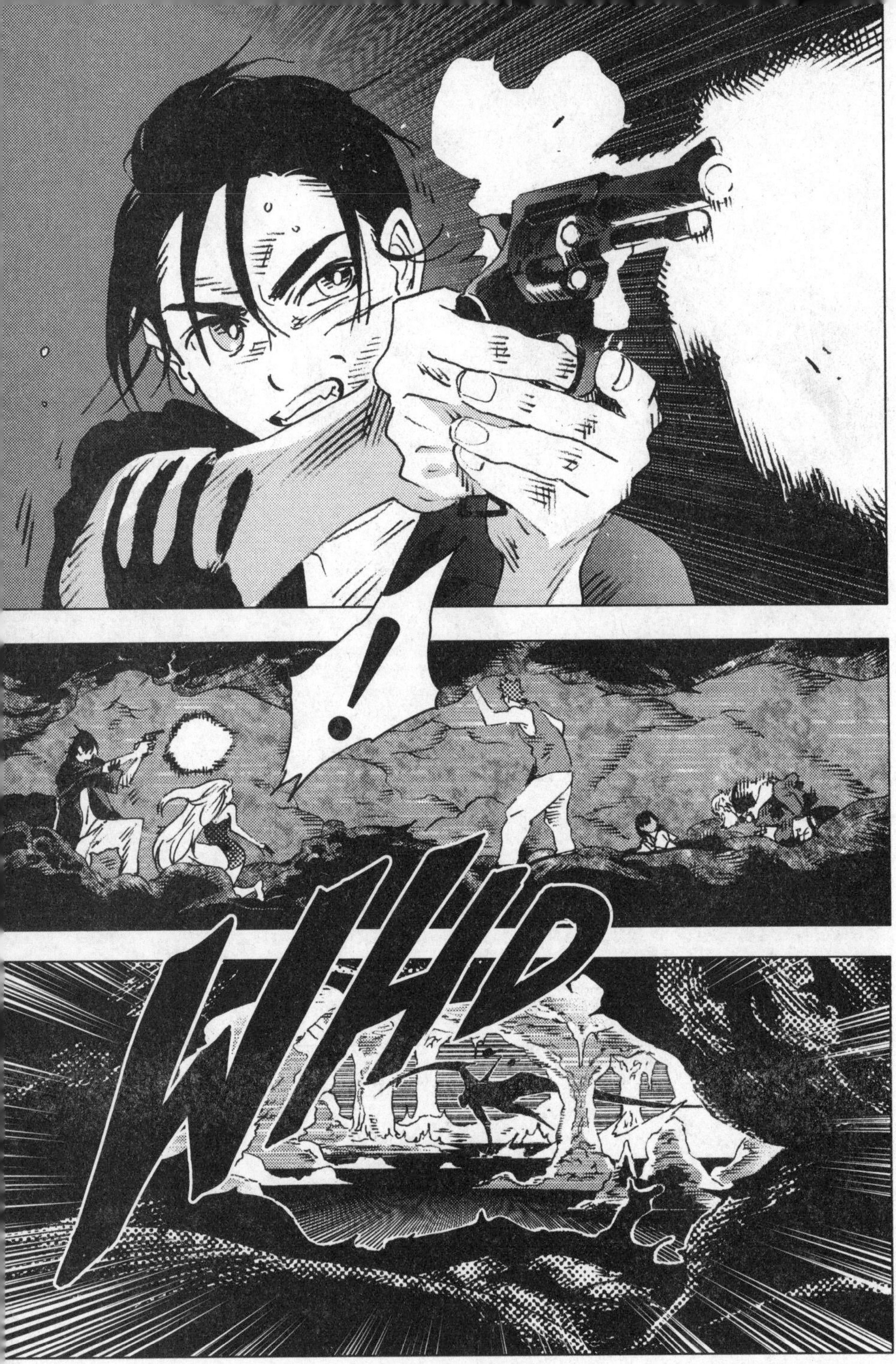
!
WHIP

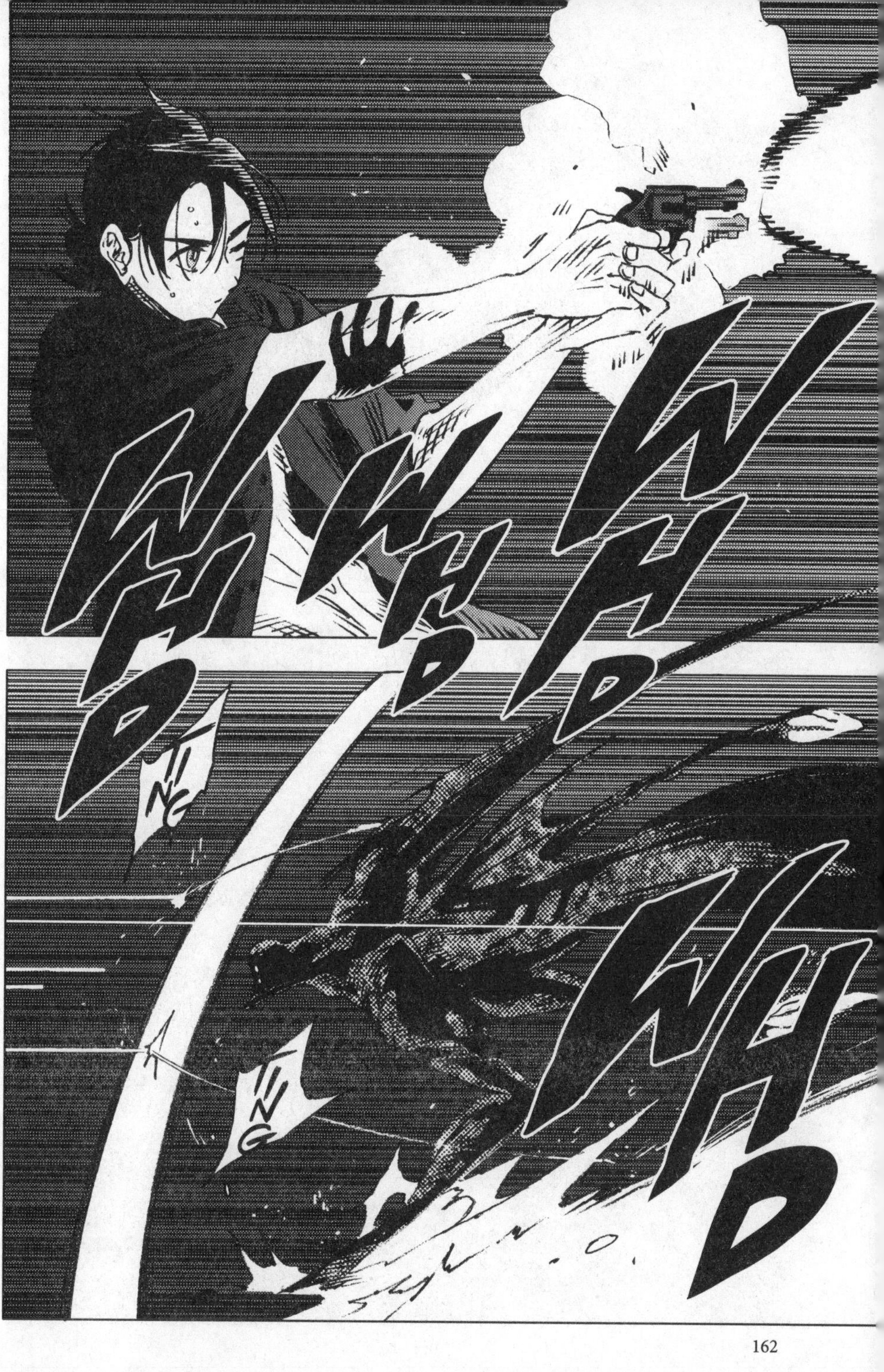
WHUD
WHUD
WHUD
TING
WHUD
TING

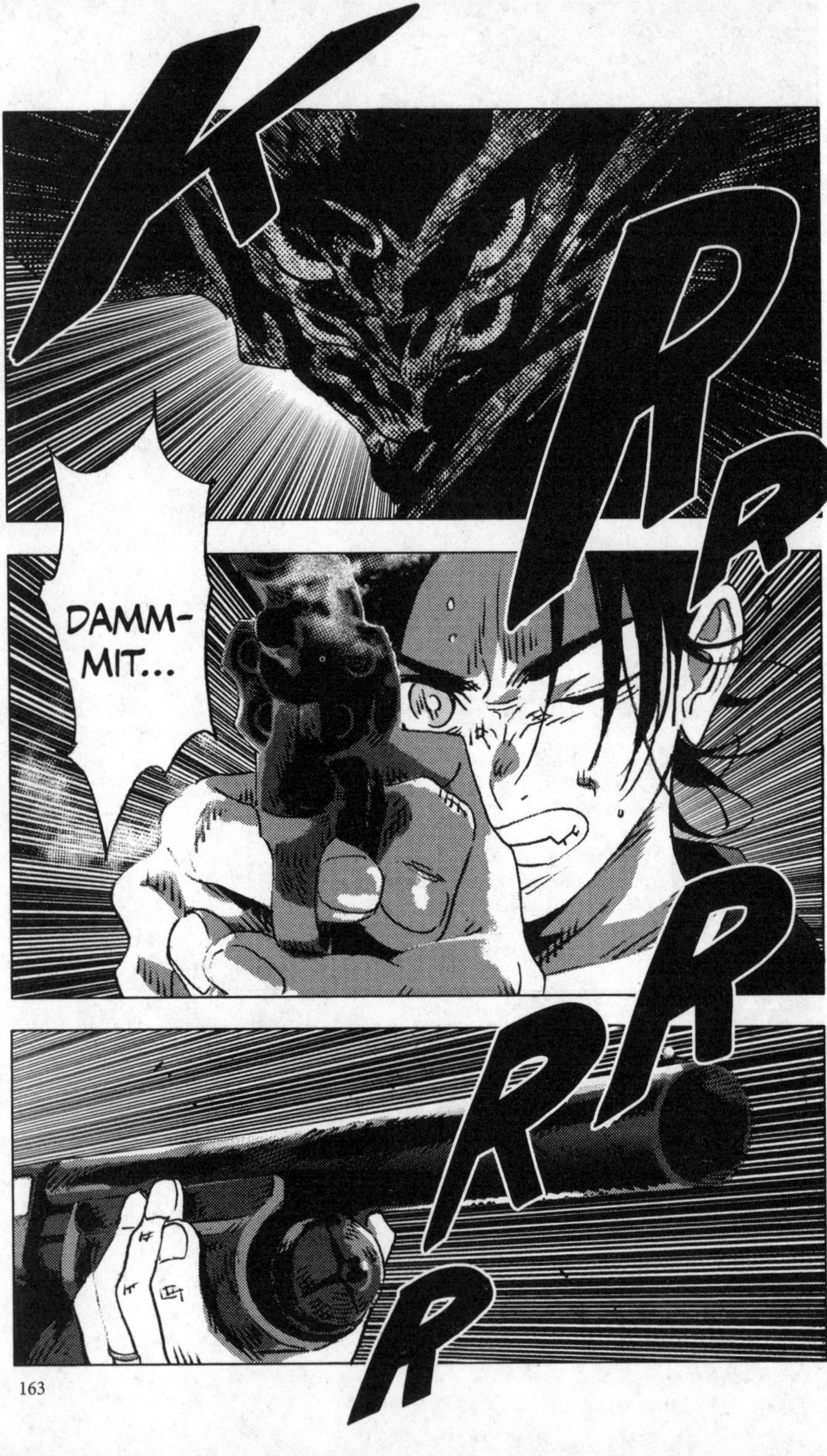
KRRRRRRR
DAMM-
MIT...

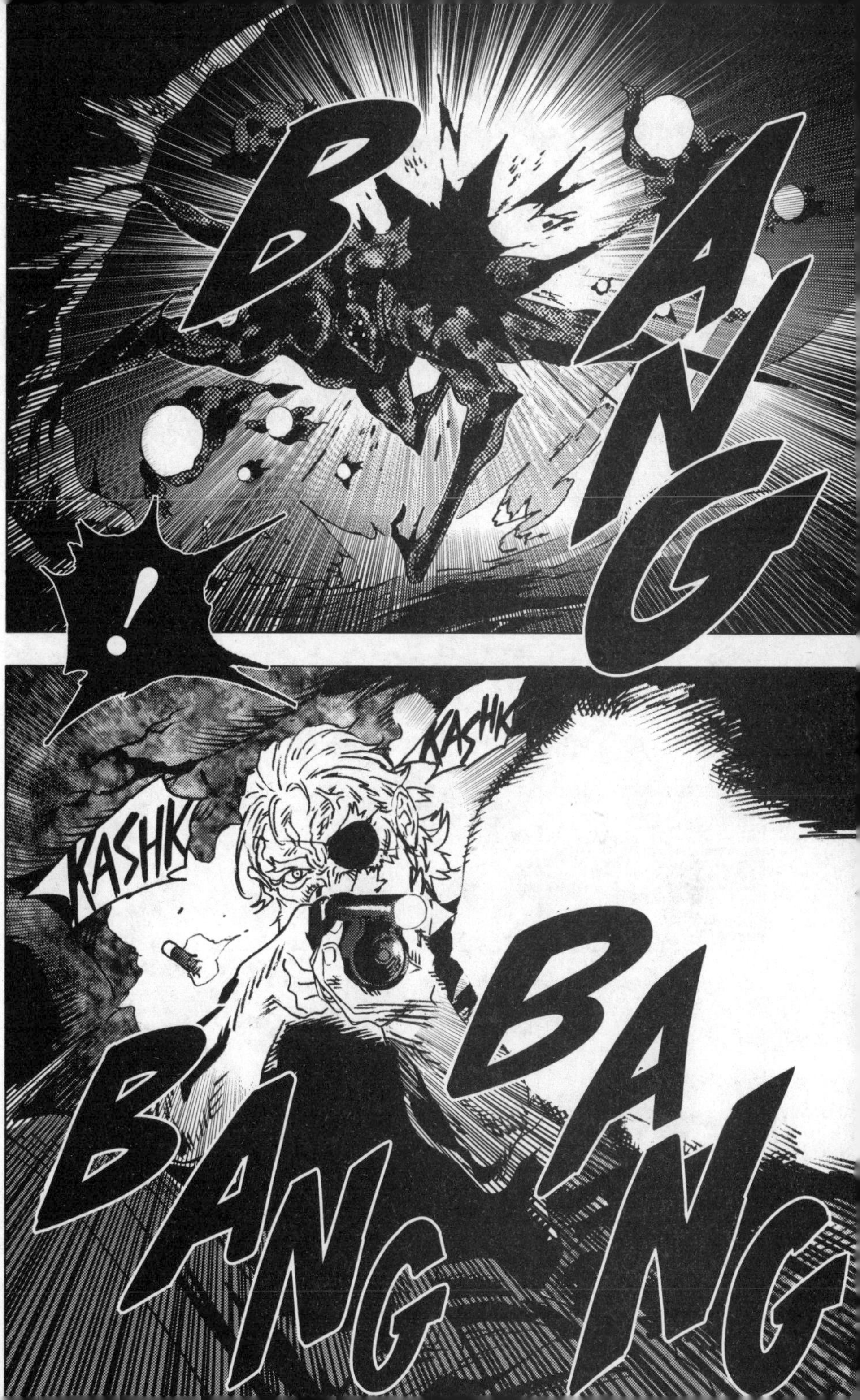
BANG
!
KASHK
KASHK
BANG
BANG

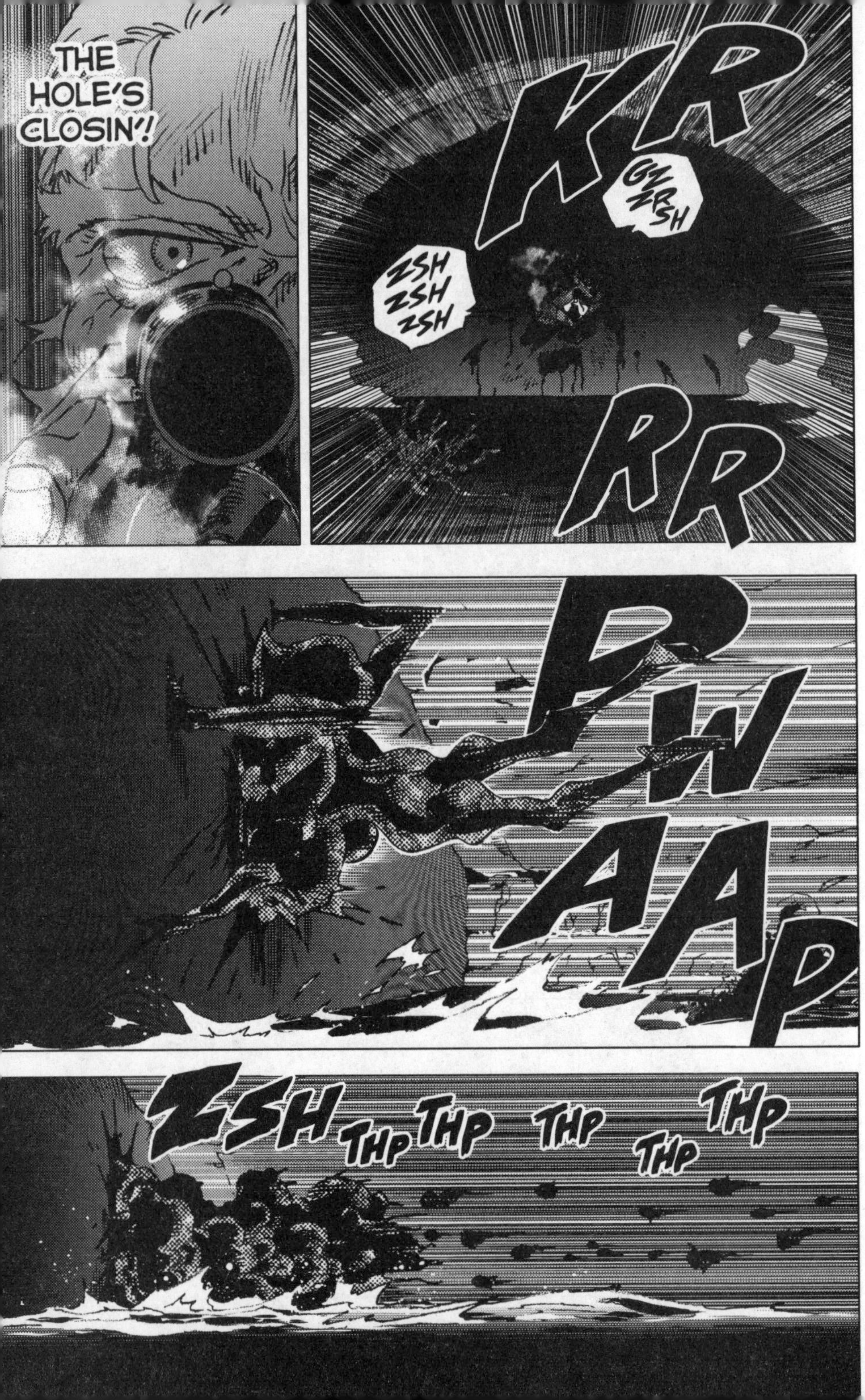

KRRR
GZZRSH
ZSH ZSH ZSH
THE HOLE'S CLOSIN'!
PWAAP
ZSH
THP THP THP THP THP

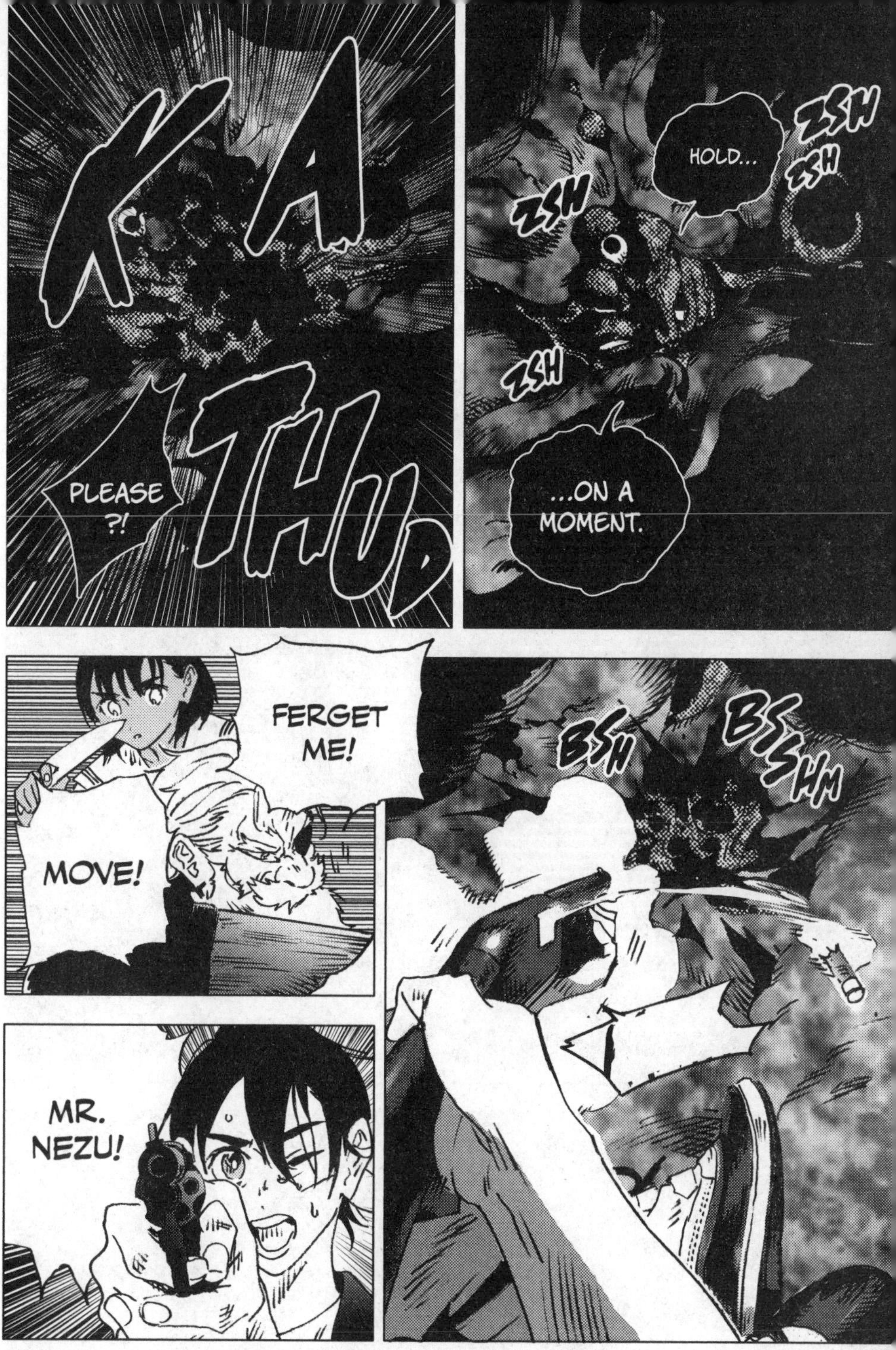
ZSH
ZSH
HOLD...
ZSH
ZSH
...ON A MOMENT.
KA
PLEASE ?!
THUD
BSSHM
BSH
FERGET ME!
MOVE!
MR. NEZU!

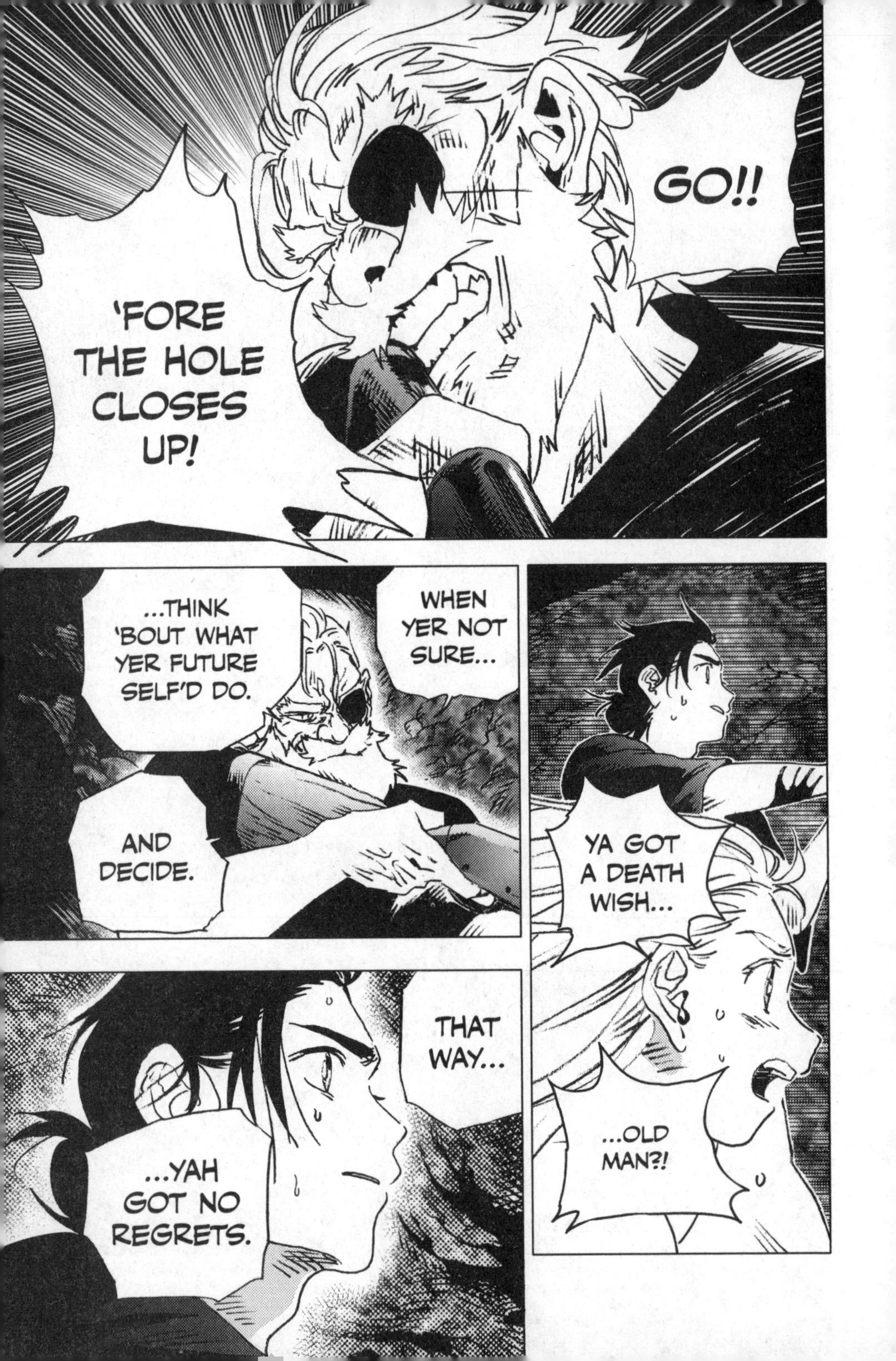
GO!!
'FORE THE HOLE CLOSES UP!
YA GOT A DEATH WISH...
...OLD MAN?!
WHEN YER NOT SURE...
...THINK 'BOUT WHAT YER FUTURE SELF'D DO.
AND DECIDE.
THAT WAY...
...YAH GOT NO REGRETS.

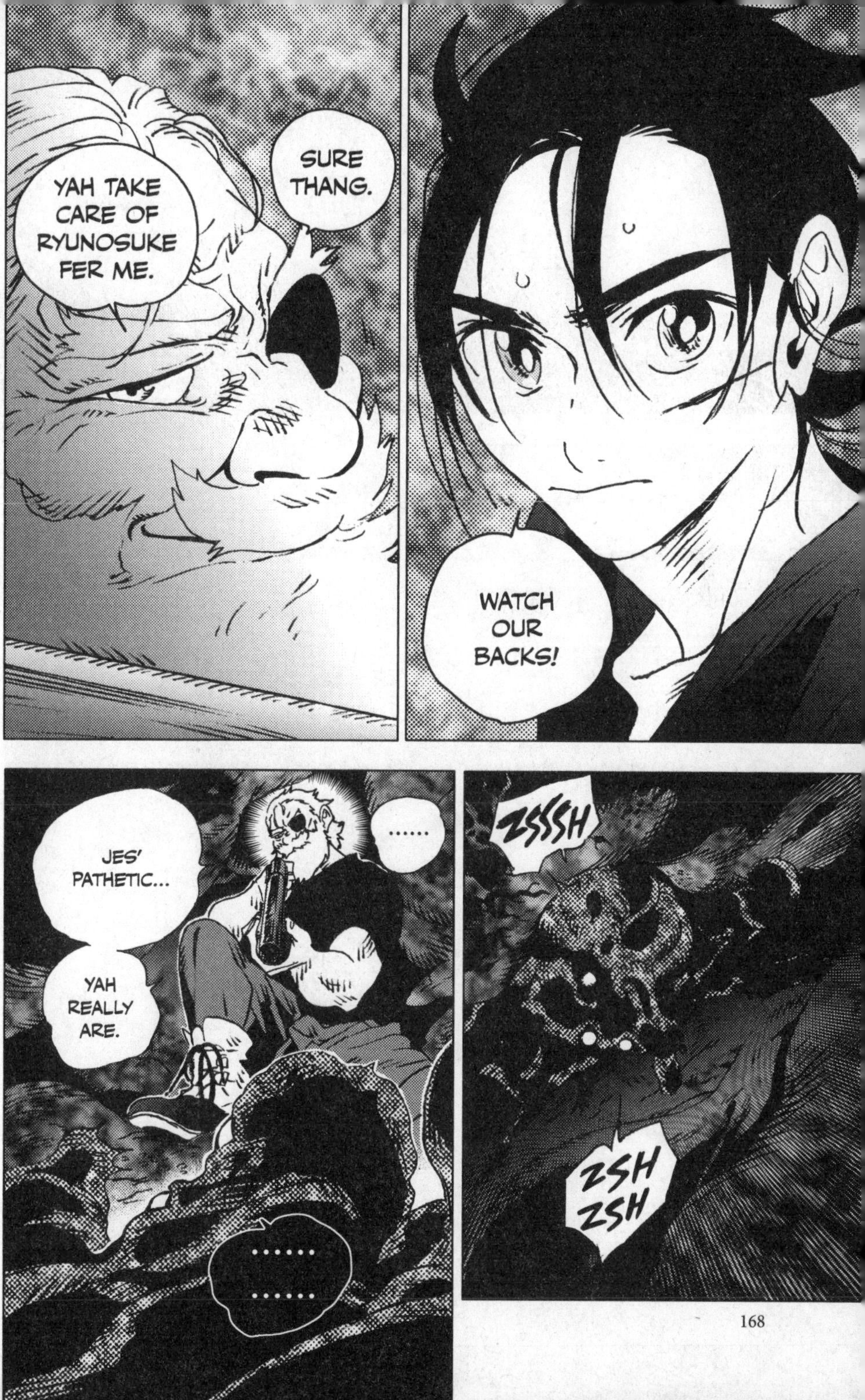
WATCH OUR BACKS!
SURE THANG.
YAH TAKE CARE OF RYUNOSUKE FER ME.
ZSSSH
ZSH ZSH
......
JES' PATHETIC...
YAH REALLY ARE.
....

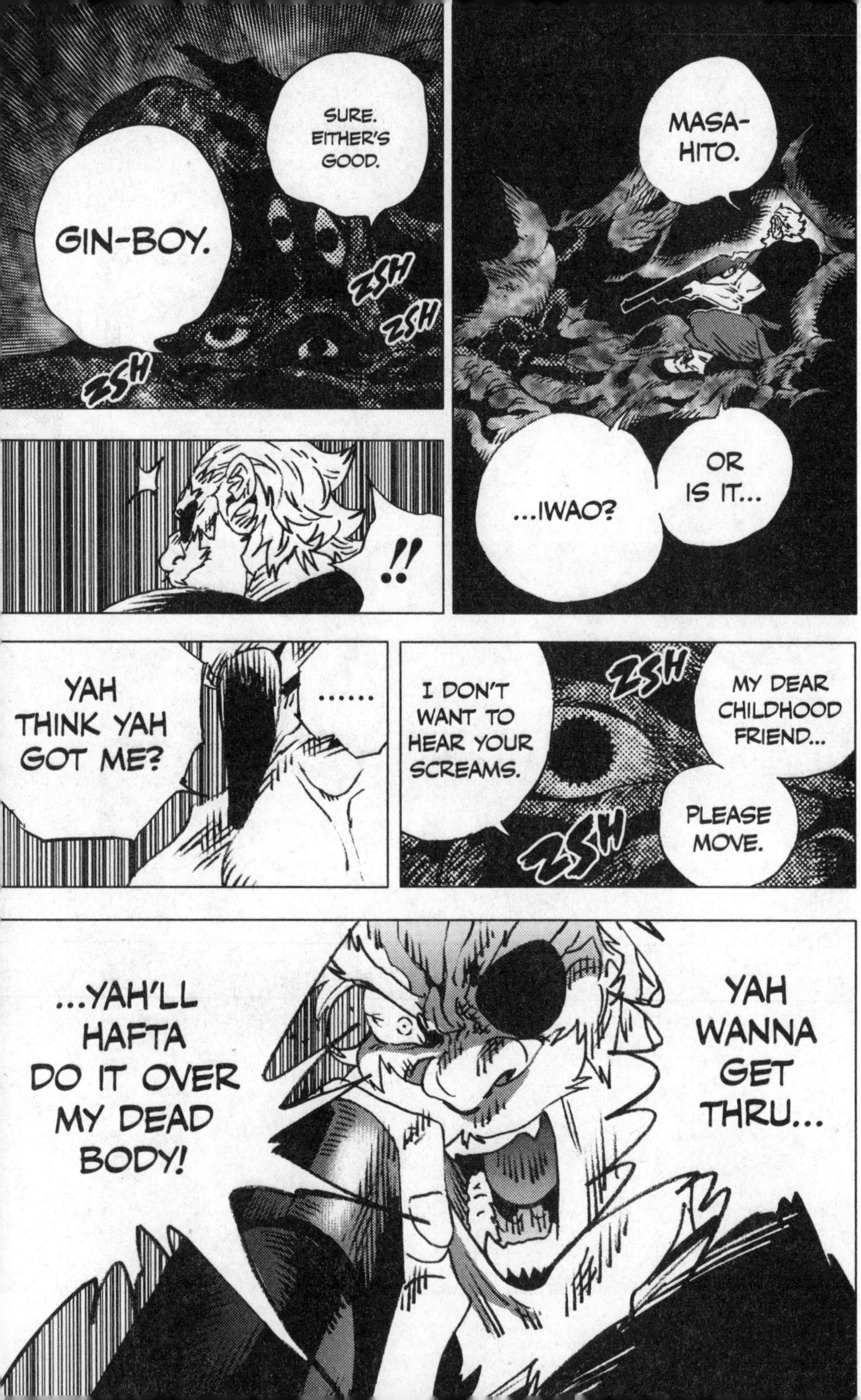

MASA-HITO.
OR IS IT...
...IWAO?
ZSH
ZSH
SURE. EITHER'S GOOD.
GIN-BOY.
ZSH
!!
MY DEAR CHILDHOOD FRIEND...
ZSH
PLEASE MOVE.
I DON'T WANT TO HEAR YOUR SCREAMS.
ZSH
......
YAH THINK YAH GOT ME?
YAH WANNA GET THRU...
...YAH'LL HAFTA DO IT OVER MY DEAD BODY!

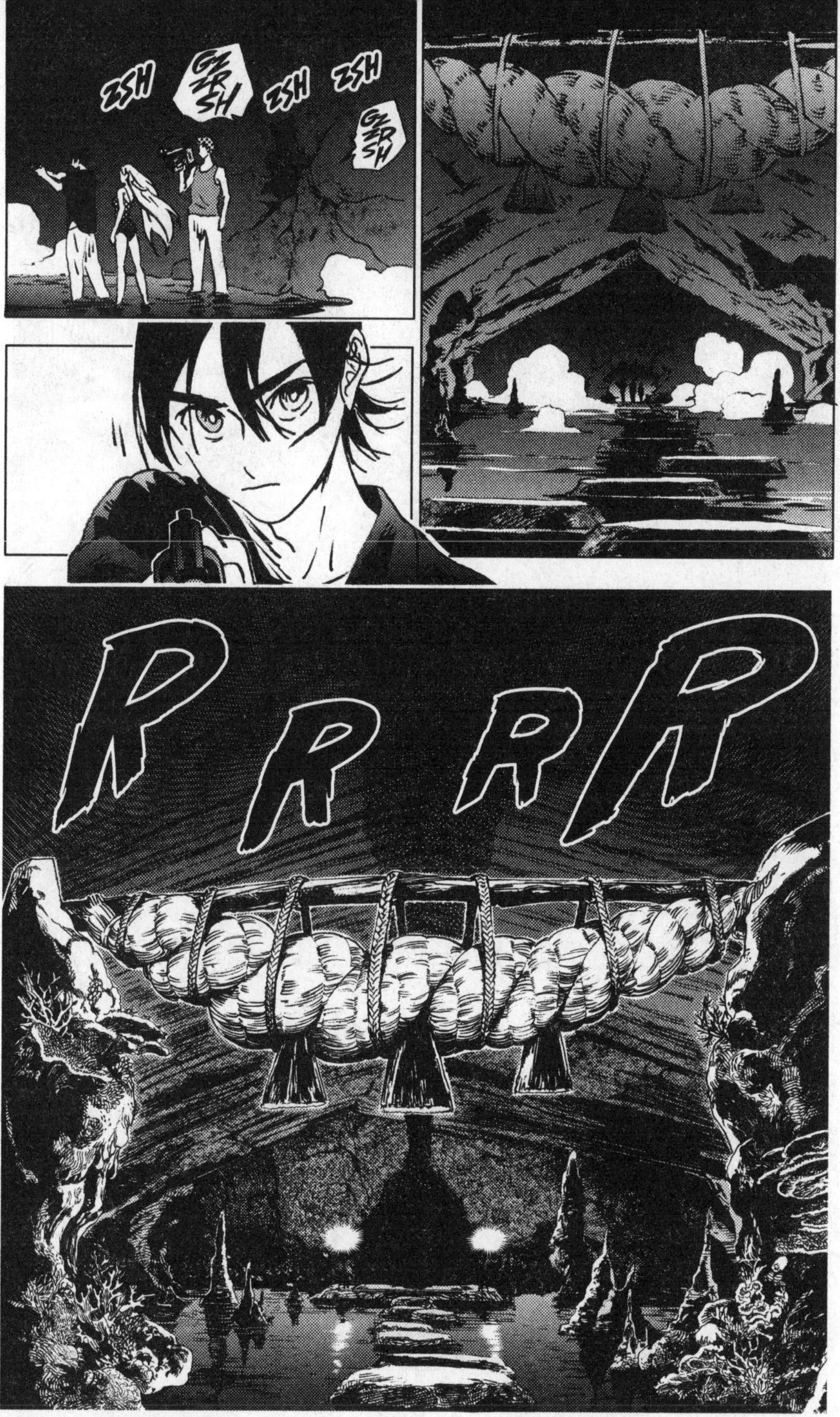
ZSH
ZSH
GZRSH
GZRSH
ZSH
RRRR

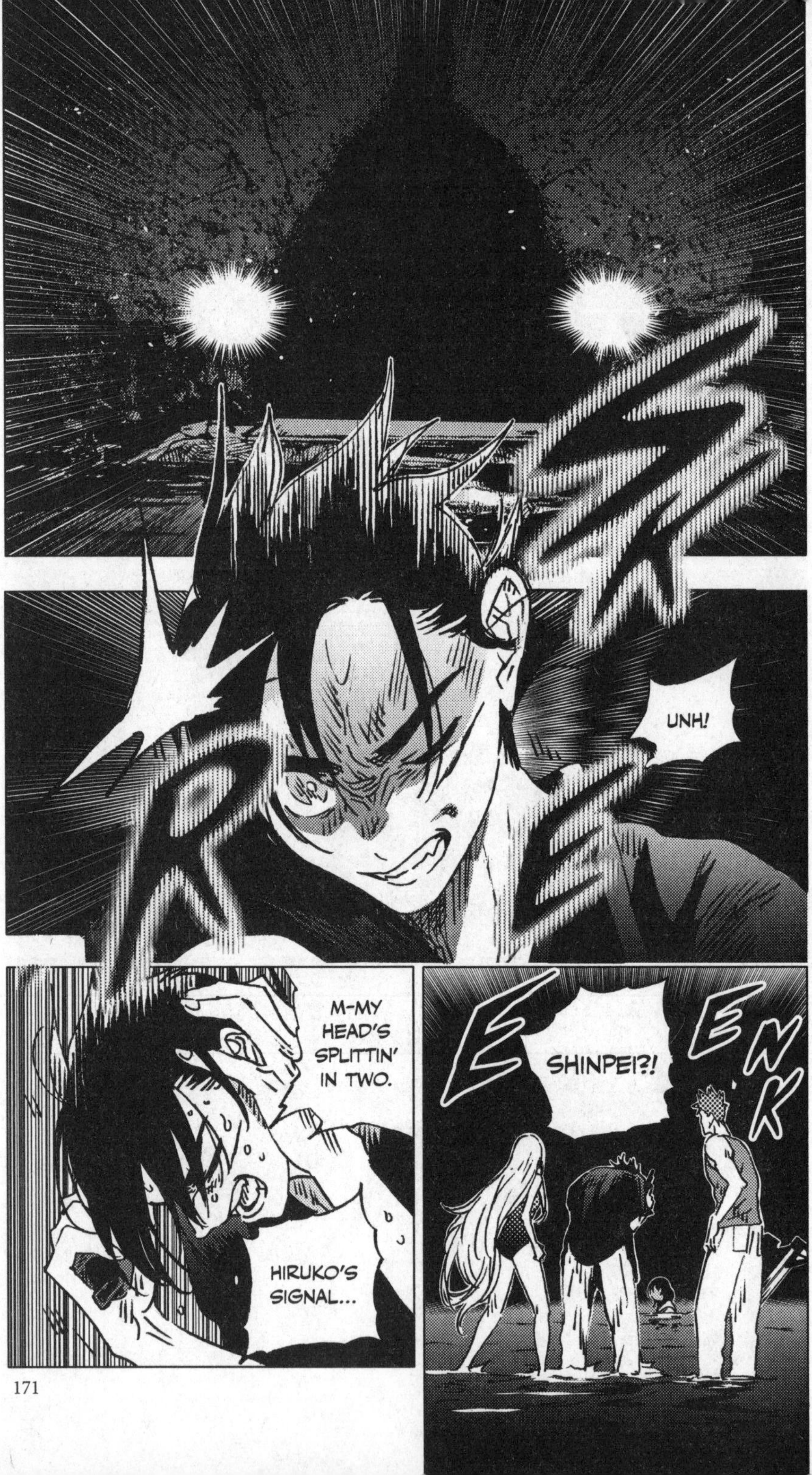
UNH!
SHINPEI?!
M-MY HEAD'S SPLITTIN' IN TWO.
HIRUKO'S SIGNAL...

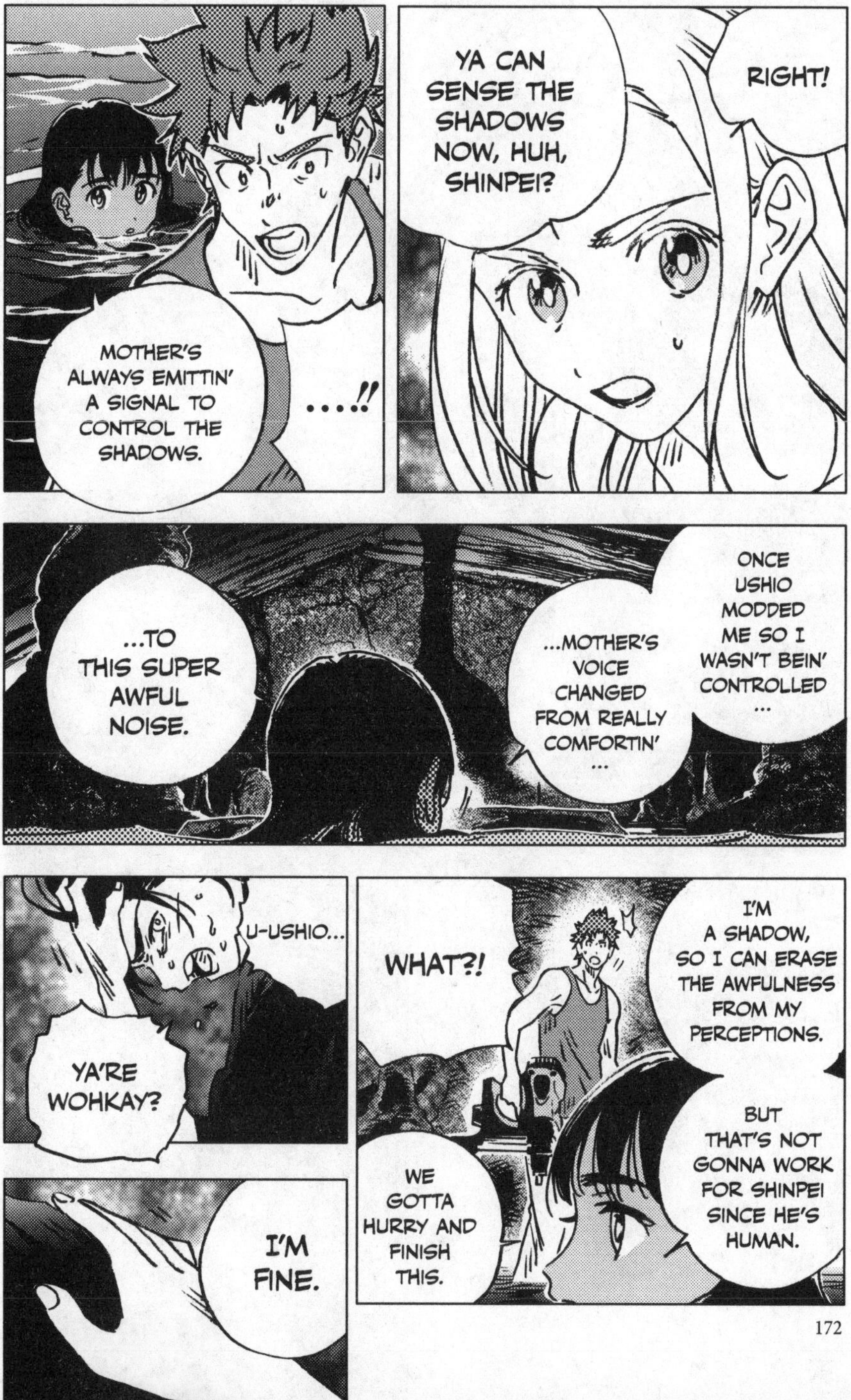
RIGHT!
YA CAN SENSE THE SHADOWS NOW, HUH, SHINPEI?
....!!
MOTHER'S ALWAYS EMITTIN' A SIGNAL TO CONTROL THE SHADOWS.
ONCE USHIO MODDED ME SO I WASN'T BEIN' CONTROLLED ...
...MOTHER'S VOICE CHANGED FROM REALLY COMFORTIN' ...
...TO THIS SUPER AWFUL NOISE.
I'M A SHADOW, SO I CAN ERASE THE AWFULNESS FROM MY PERCEPTIONS.
WHAT?!
BUT THAT'S NOT GONNA WORK FOR SHINPEI SINCE HE'S HUMAN.
WE GOTTA HURRY AND FINISH THIS.
U-USHIO...
YA'RE WOHKAY?
I'M FINE.

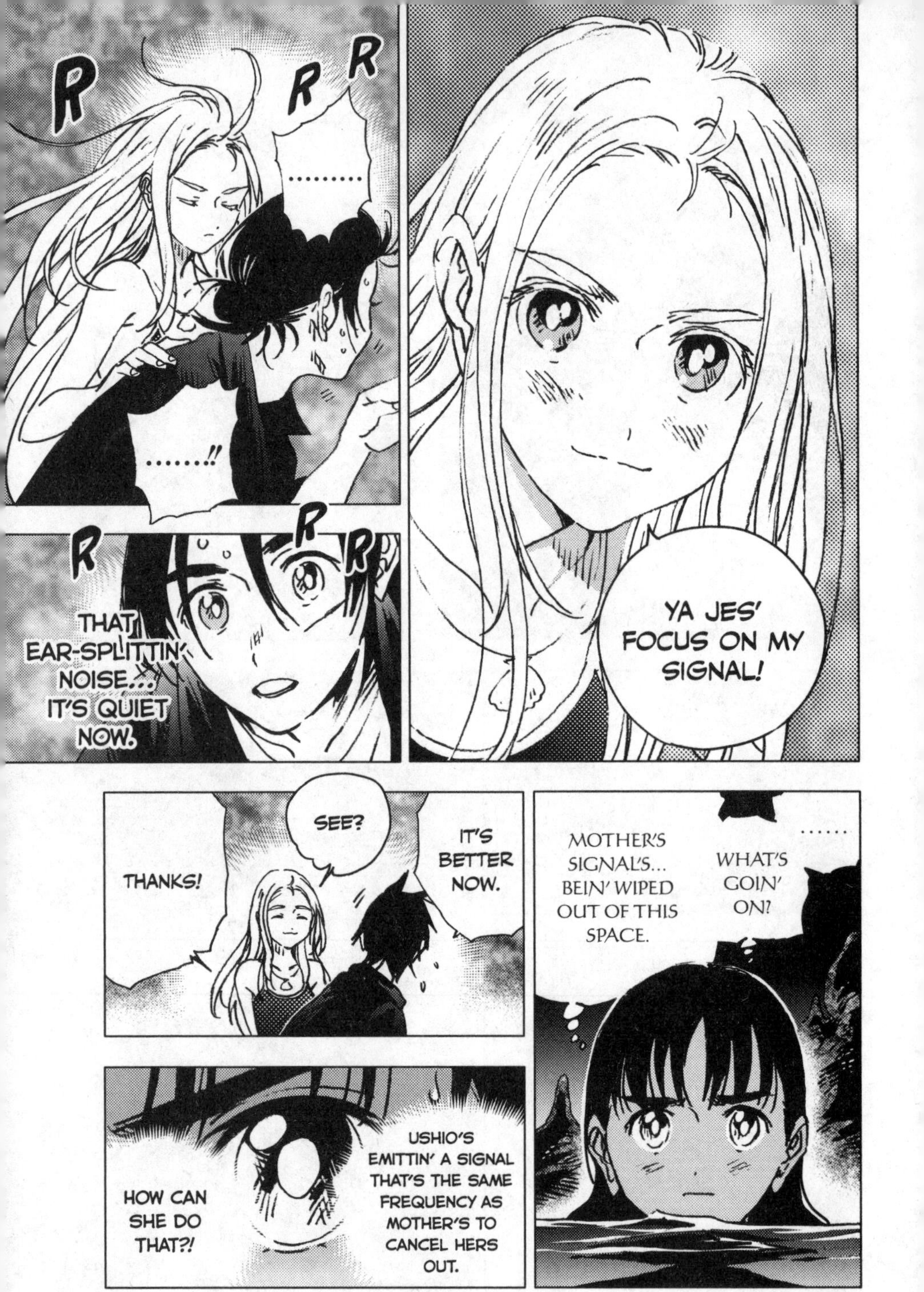
YA JES' FOCUS ON MY SIGNAL!
R R R
....
.......!!
R R R
THAT EAR-SPLITTIN' NOISE... IT'S QUIET NOW.
......
WHAT'S GOIN' ON?
MOTHER'S SIGNAL'S... BEIN' WIPED OUT OF THIS SPACE.
IT'S BETTER NOW.
SEE?
THANKS!
USHIO'S EMITTIN' A SIGNAL THAT'S THE SAME FREQUENCY AS MOTHER'S TO CANCEL HERS OUT.
HOW CAN SHE DO THAT?!

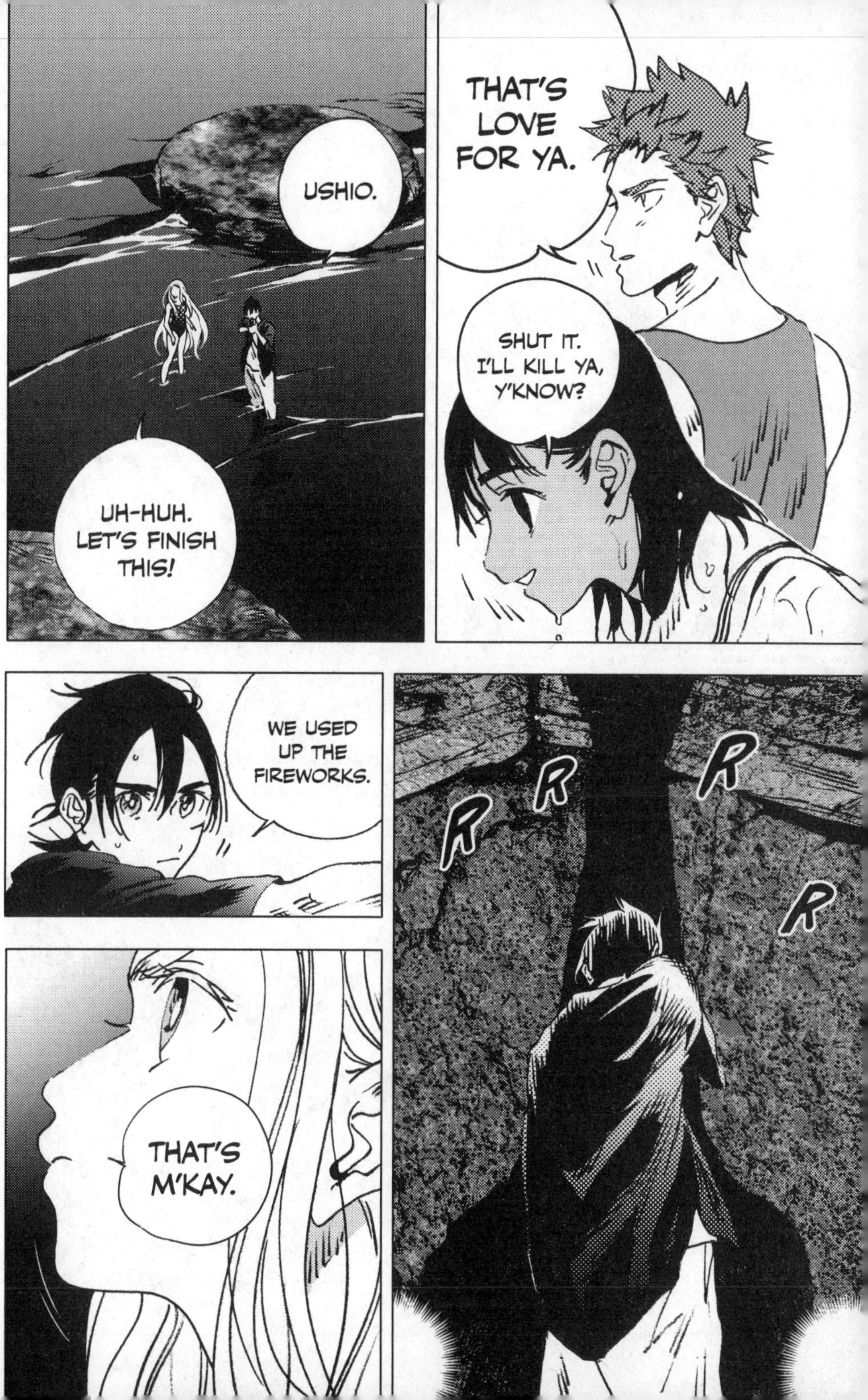
THAT'S LOVE FOR YA.
SHUT IT. I'LL KILL YA, Y'KNOW?
USHIO.
UH-HUH. LET'S FINISH THIS!
R
R
R
R
WE USED UP THE FIREWORKS.
THAT'S M'KAY.

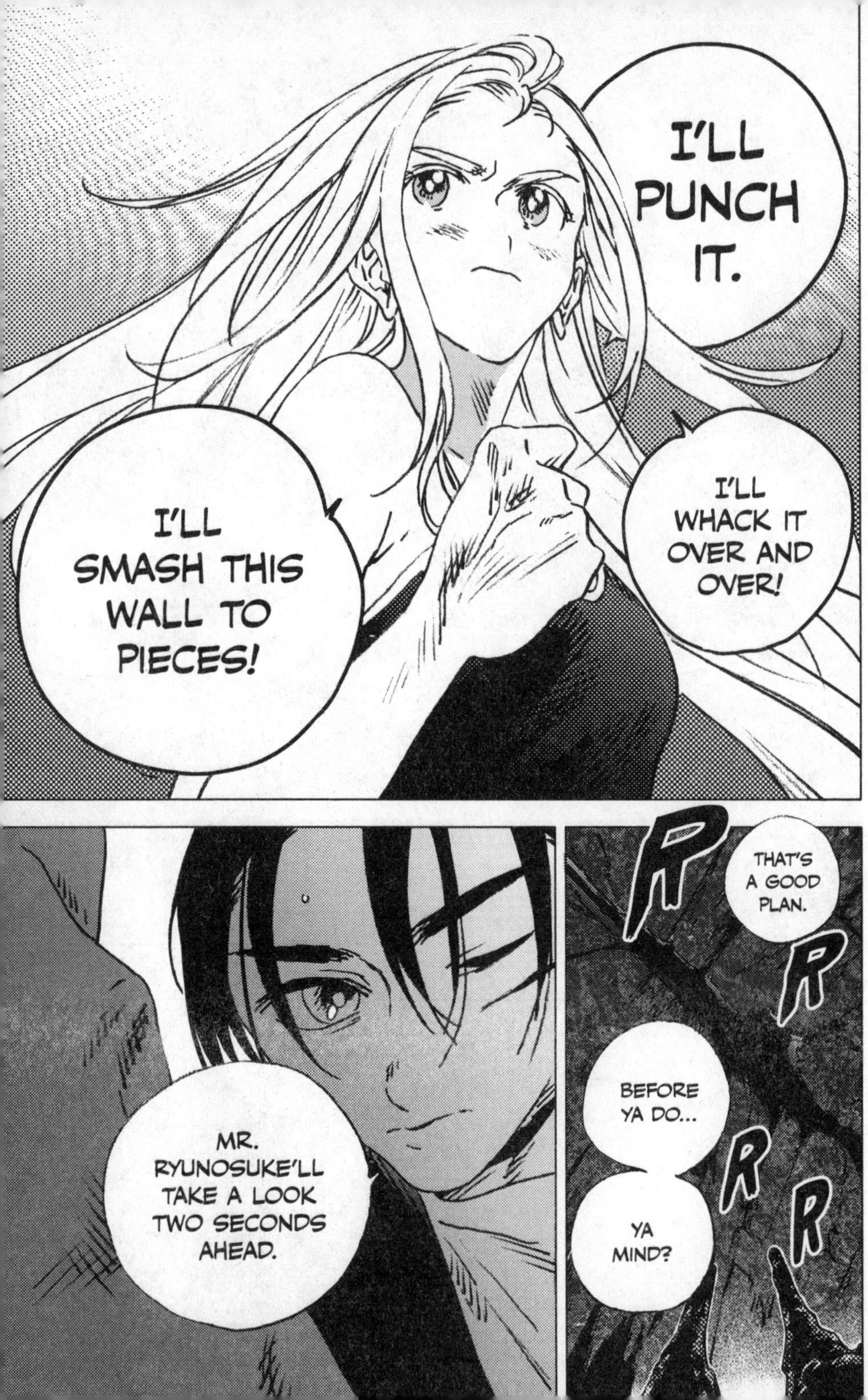
I'LL PUNCH IT.
I'LL WHACK IT OVER AND OVER!
I'LL SMASH THIS WALL TO PIECES!
R
THAT'S A GOOD PLAN.
R
BEFORE YA DO...
YA MIND?
R
R
MR. RYUNOSUKE'LL TAKE A LOOK TWO SECONDS AHEAD.

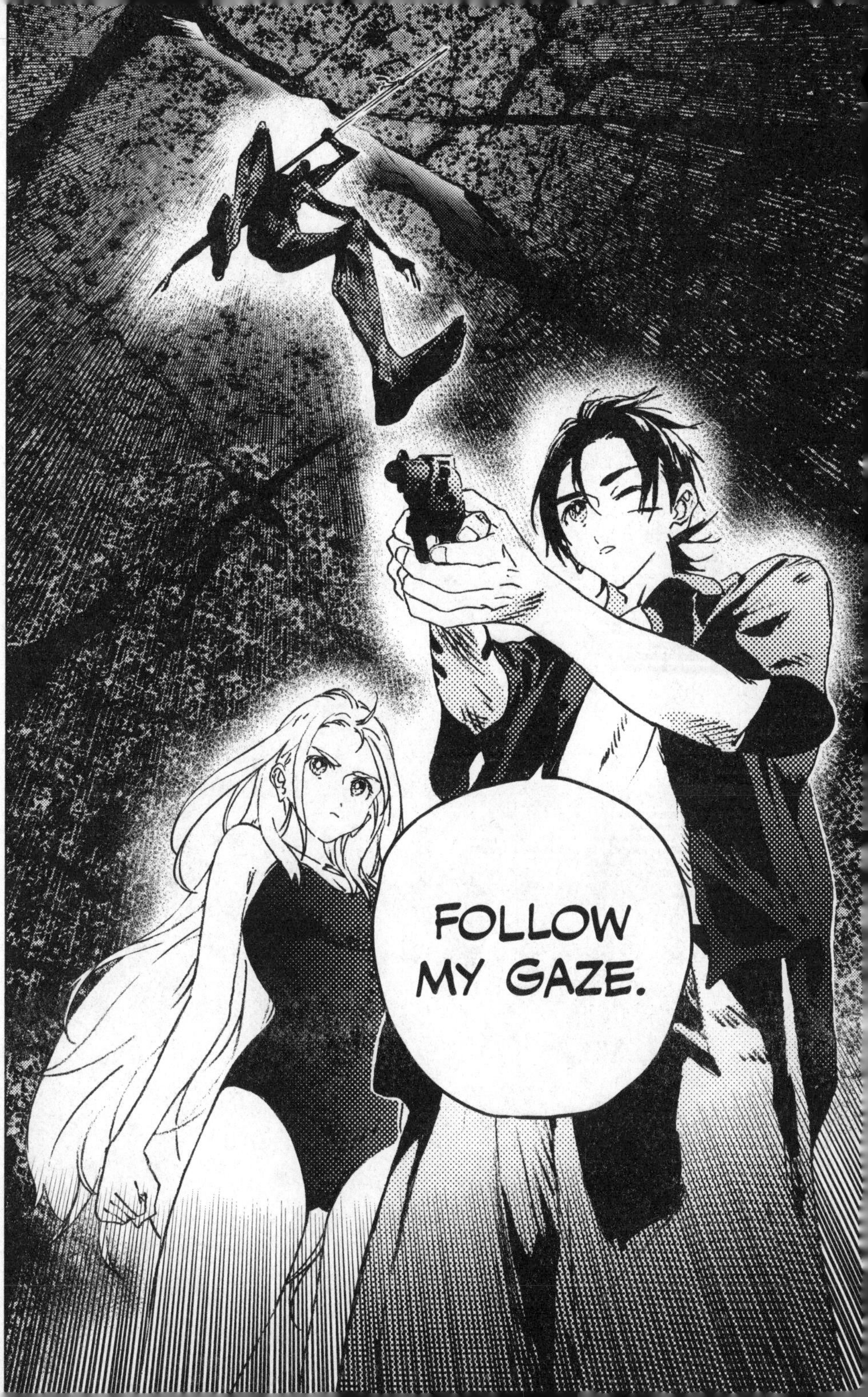
FOLLOW MY GAZE.

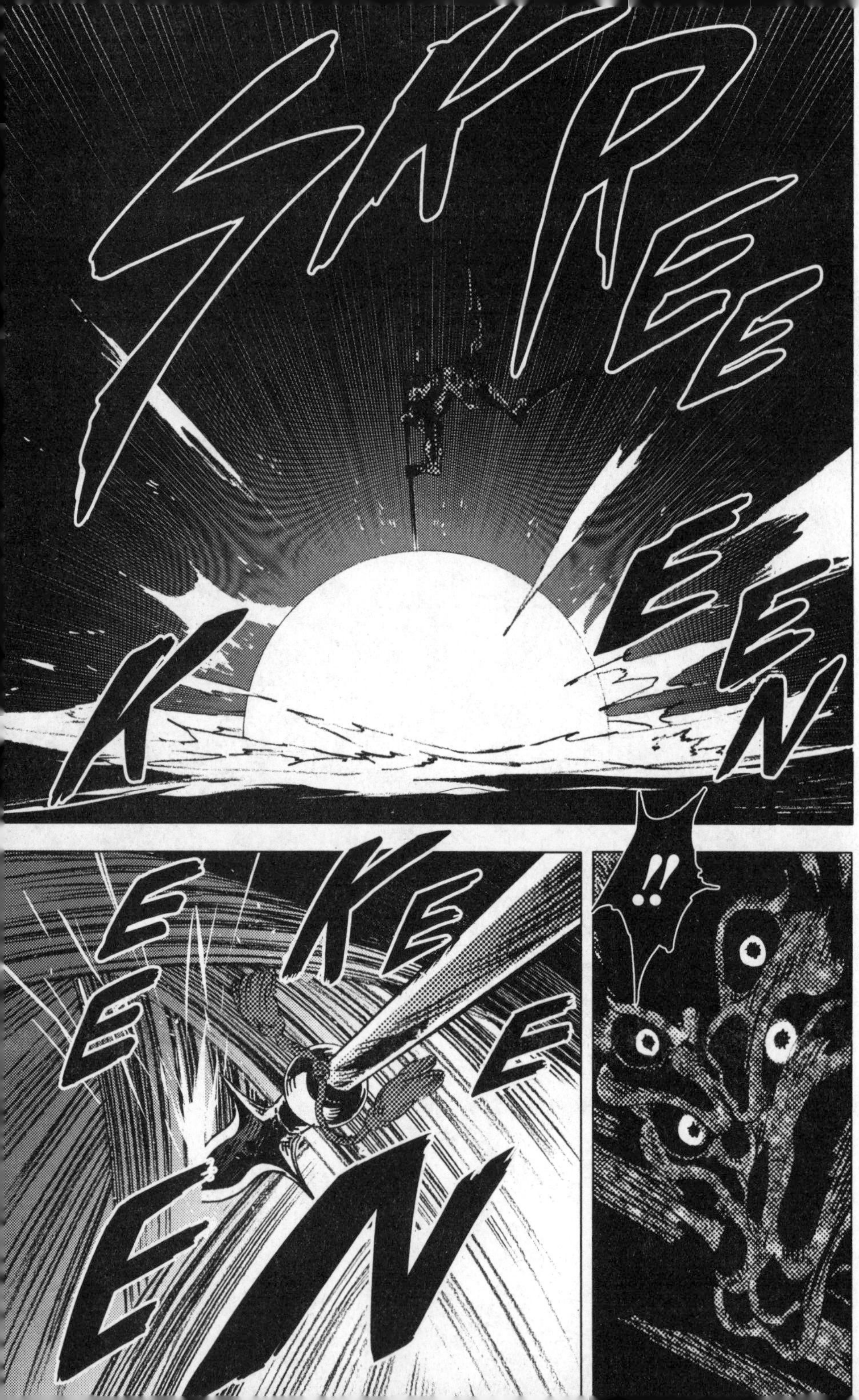
!!

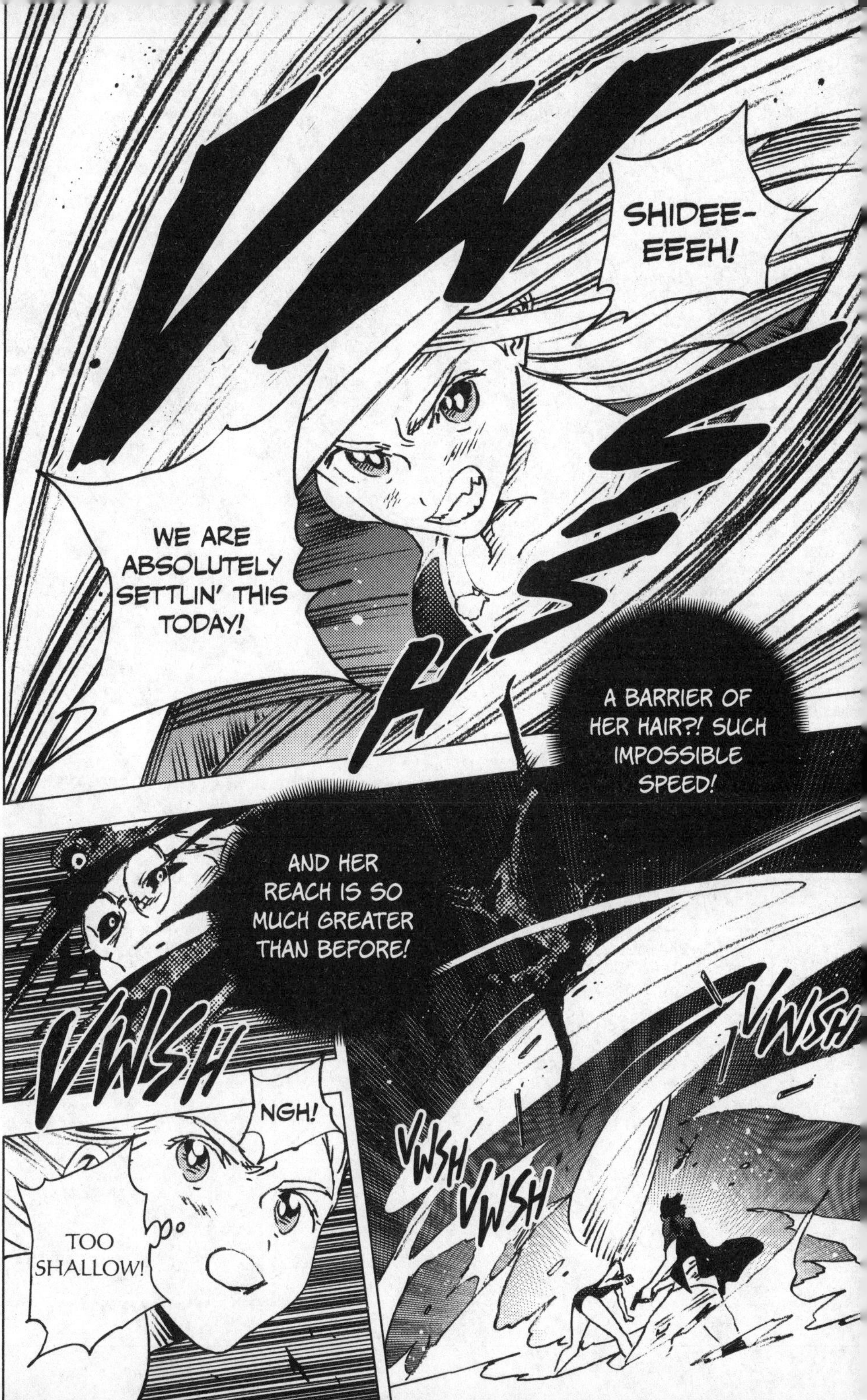
SHIDEE-EEEH!
WE ARE ABSOLUTELY SETTLIN' THIS TODAY!
A BARRIER OF HER HAIR?! SUCH IMPOSSIBLE SPEED!
AND HER REACH IS SO MUCH GREATER THAN BEFORE!
VWSH
VWSH
VWSH
VWSH
NGH!
TOO SHALLOW!

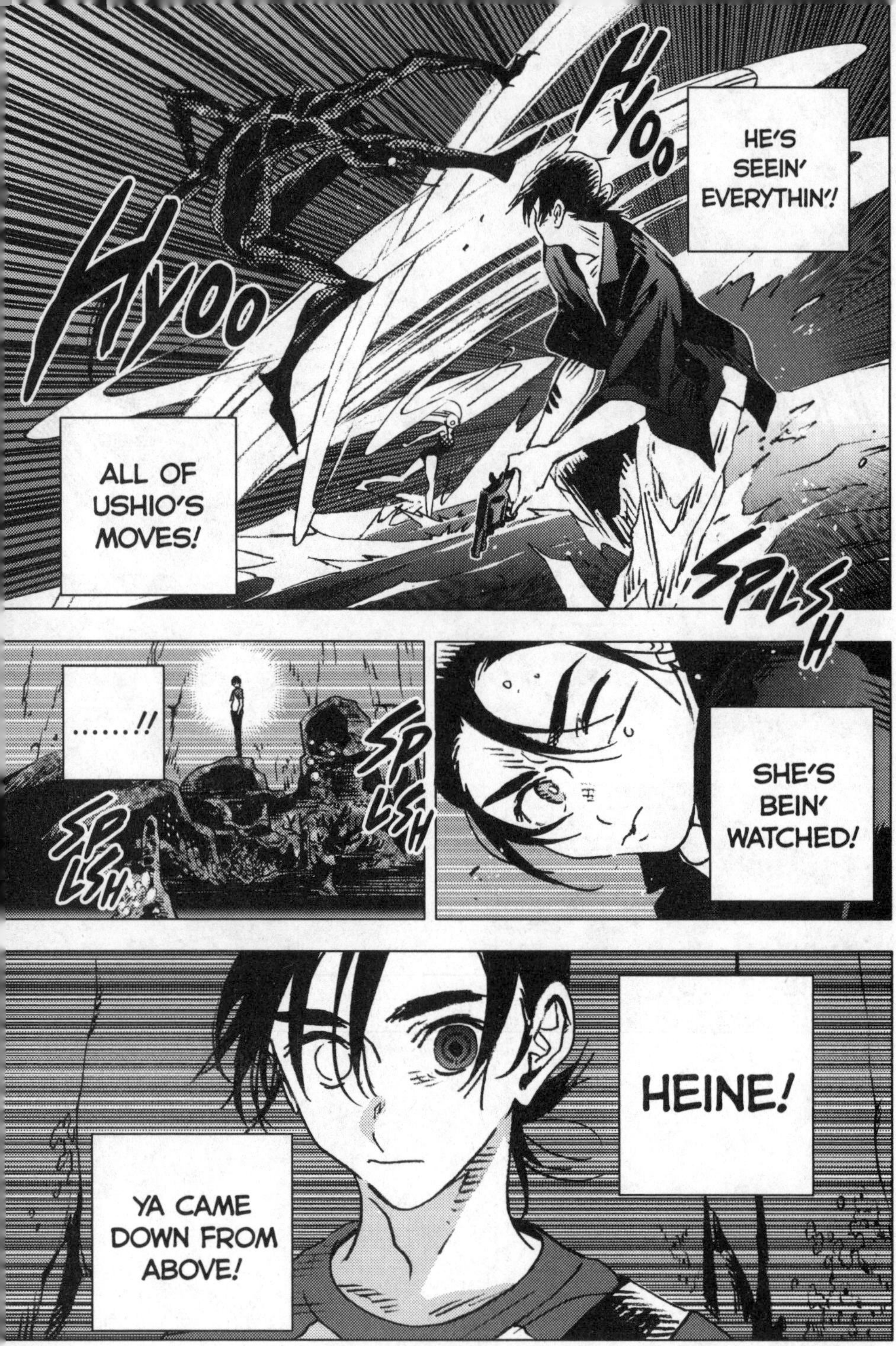
HYOO
HE'S SEEIN' EVERYTHIN'!
HYOO
ALL OF USHIO'S MOVES!
SPLSH
SHE'S BEIN' WATCHED!
......!!
SPLSH
SPLSH
HEINE!
YA CAME DOWN FROM ABOVE!

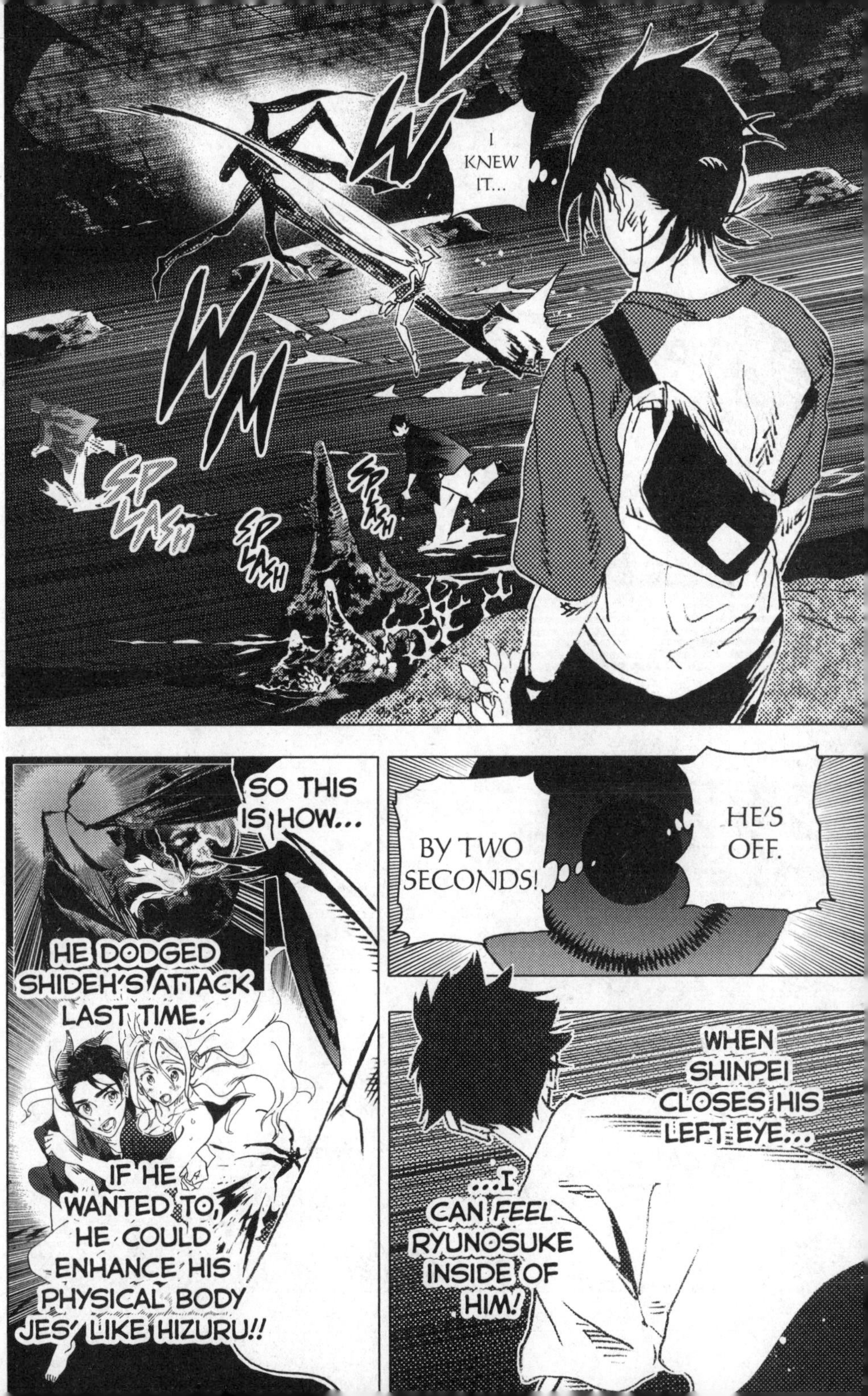
I KNEW IT...
SPLASH
SPLASH
SPLASH
HE'S OFF.
BY TWO SECONDS!
SO THIS IS HOW...
HE DODGED SHIDEH'S ATTACK LAST TIME.
WHEN SHINPEI CLOSES HIS LEFT EYE...
...I CAN FEEL RYUNOSUKE INSIDE OF HIM!
IF HE WANTED TO, HE COULD ENHANCE HIS PHYSICAL BODY JES' LIKE HIZURU!!

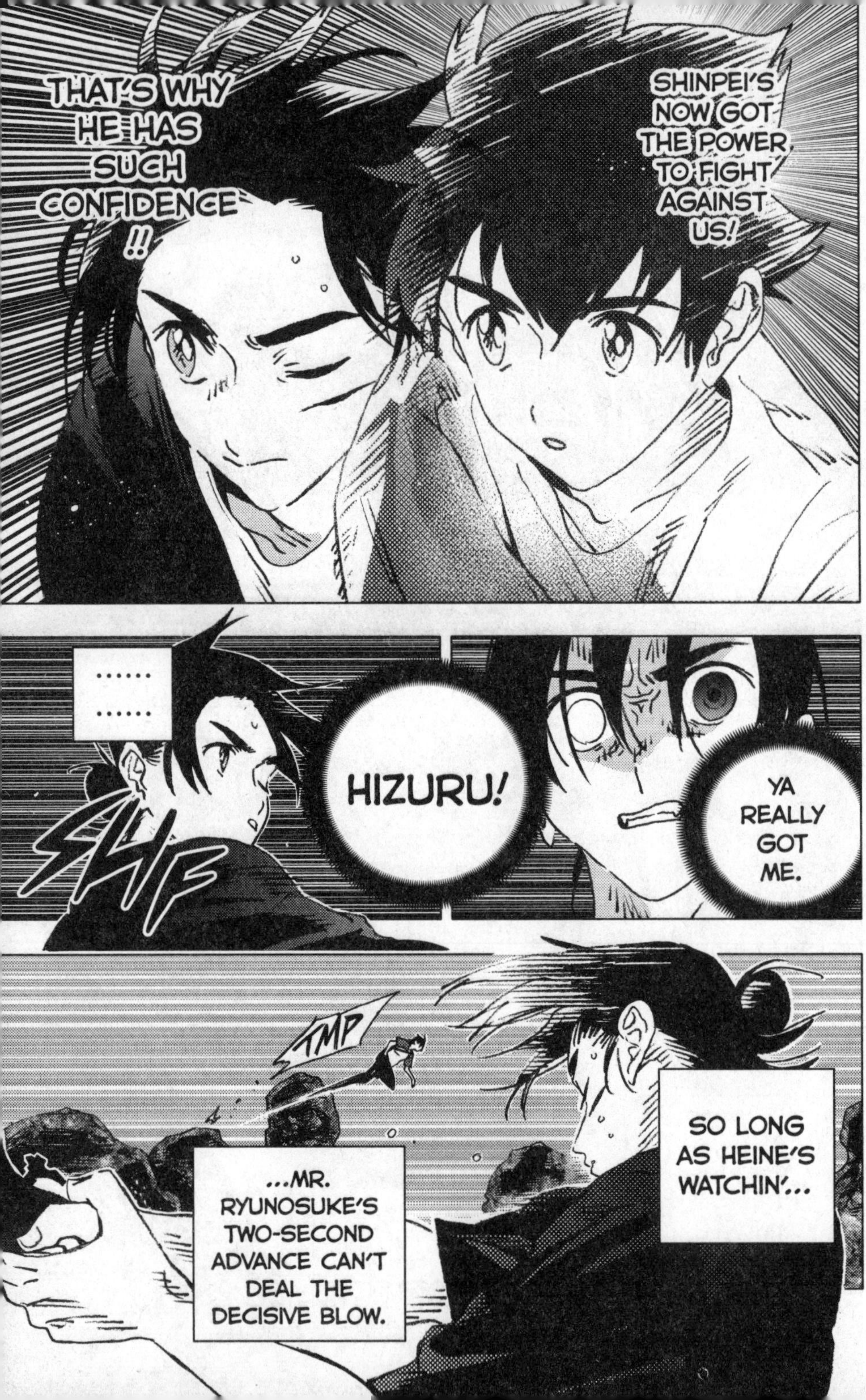

SHINPEI'S NOW GOT THE POWER TO FIGHT AGAINST US!
THAT'S WHY HE HAS SUCH CONFIDENCE !!
HIZURU!
YA REALLY GOT ME.
……
……
SHF
TMP
SO LONG AS HEINE'S WATCHIN'...
...MR. RYUNOSUKE'S TWO-SECOND ADVANCE CAN'T DEAL THE DECISIVE BLOW.

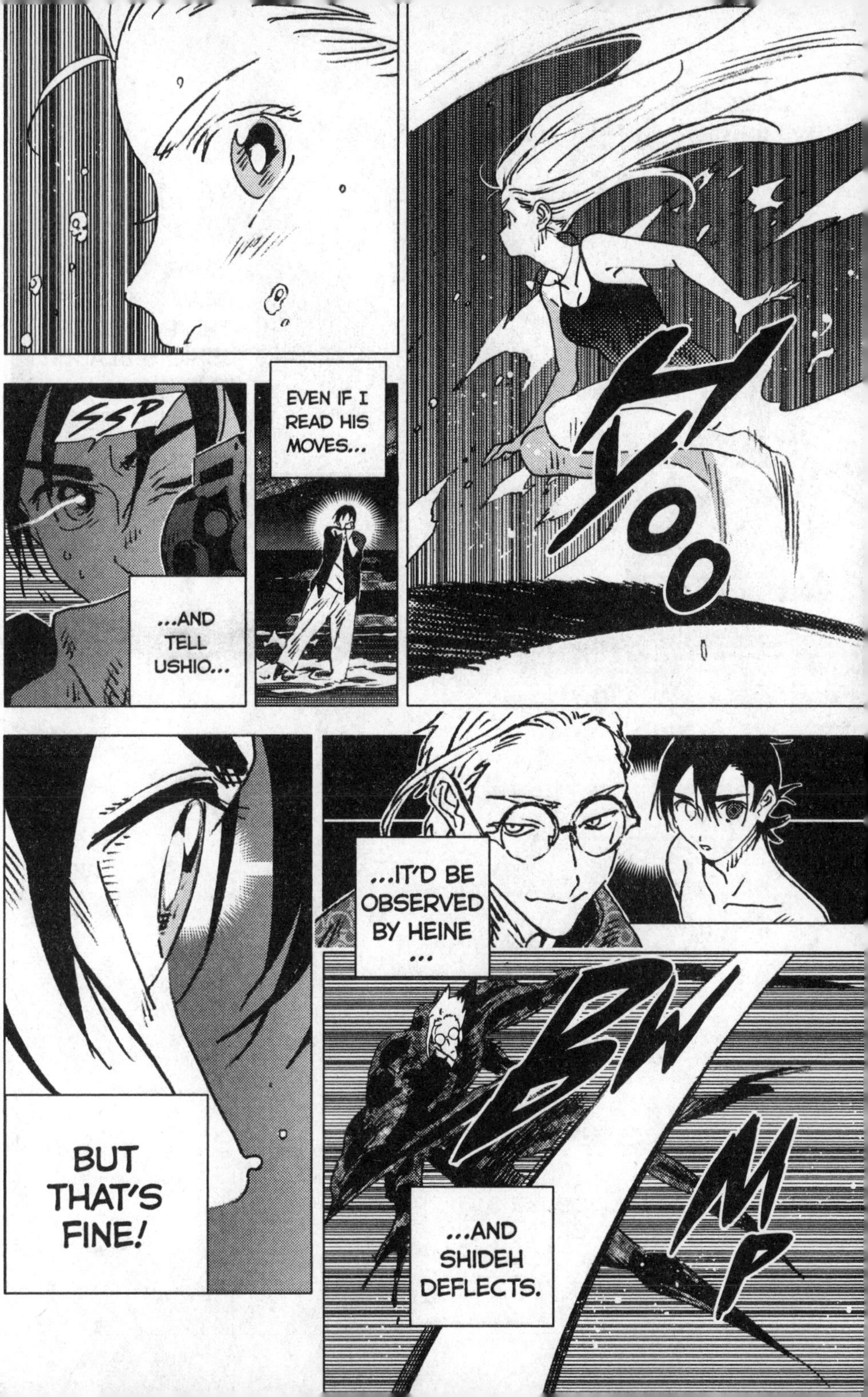
VYOO
EVEN IF I READ HIS MOVES...
SSP
...AND TELL USHIO...
...IT'D BE OBSERVED BY HEINE ...
BWMP
...AND SHIDEH DEFLECTS.
BUT THAT'S FINE!

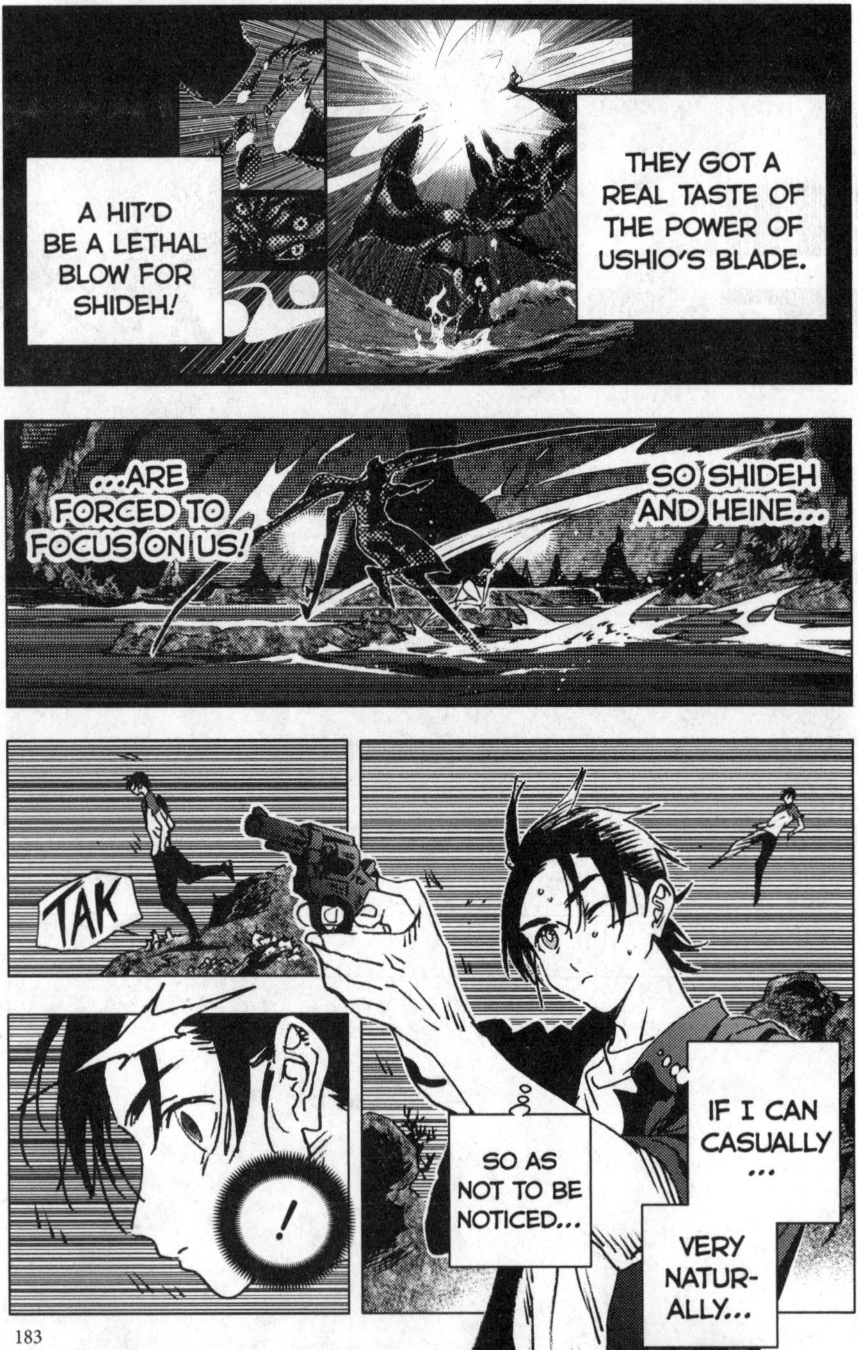
THEY GOT A REAL TASTE OF THE POWER OF USHIO'S BLADE.
A HIT'D BE A LETHAL BLOW FOR SHIDEH!
SO SHIDEH AND HEINE...
...ARE FORCED TO FOCUS ON US!
IF I CAN CASUALLY...
VERY NATUR-ALLY...
SO AS NOT TO BE NOTICED...
TAK
!

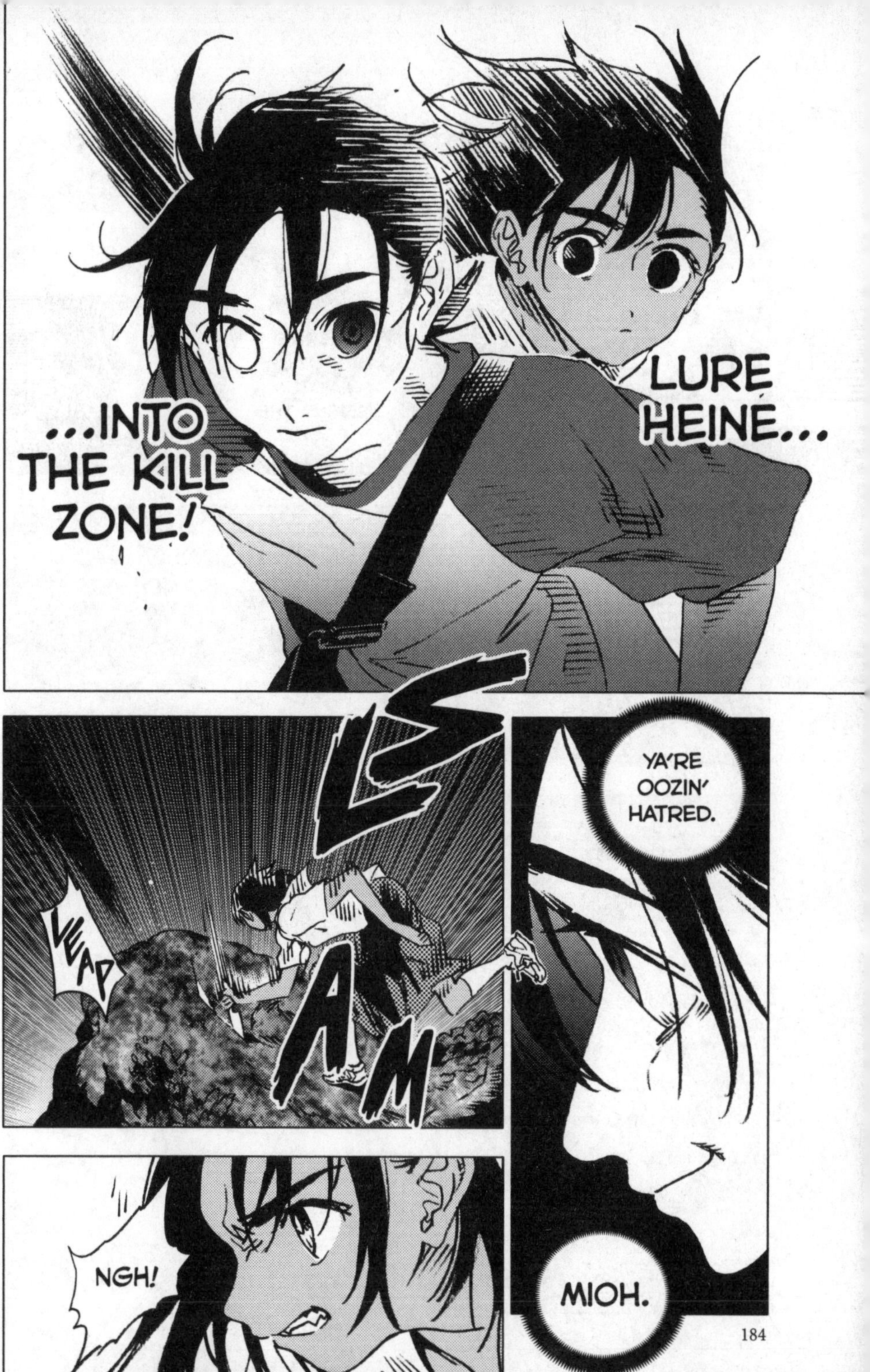
LURE HEINE...
...INTO THE KILL ZONE!
YA'RE OOZIN' HATRED.
MIOH.
SLAM
LEAP
NGH!

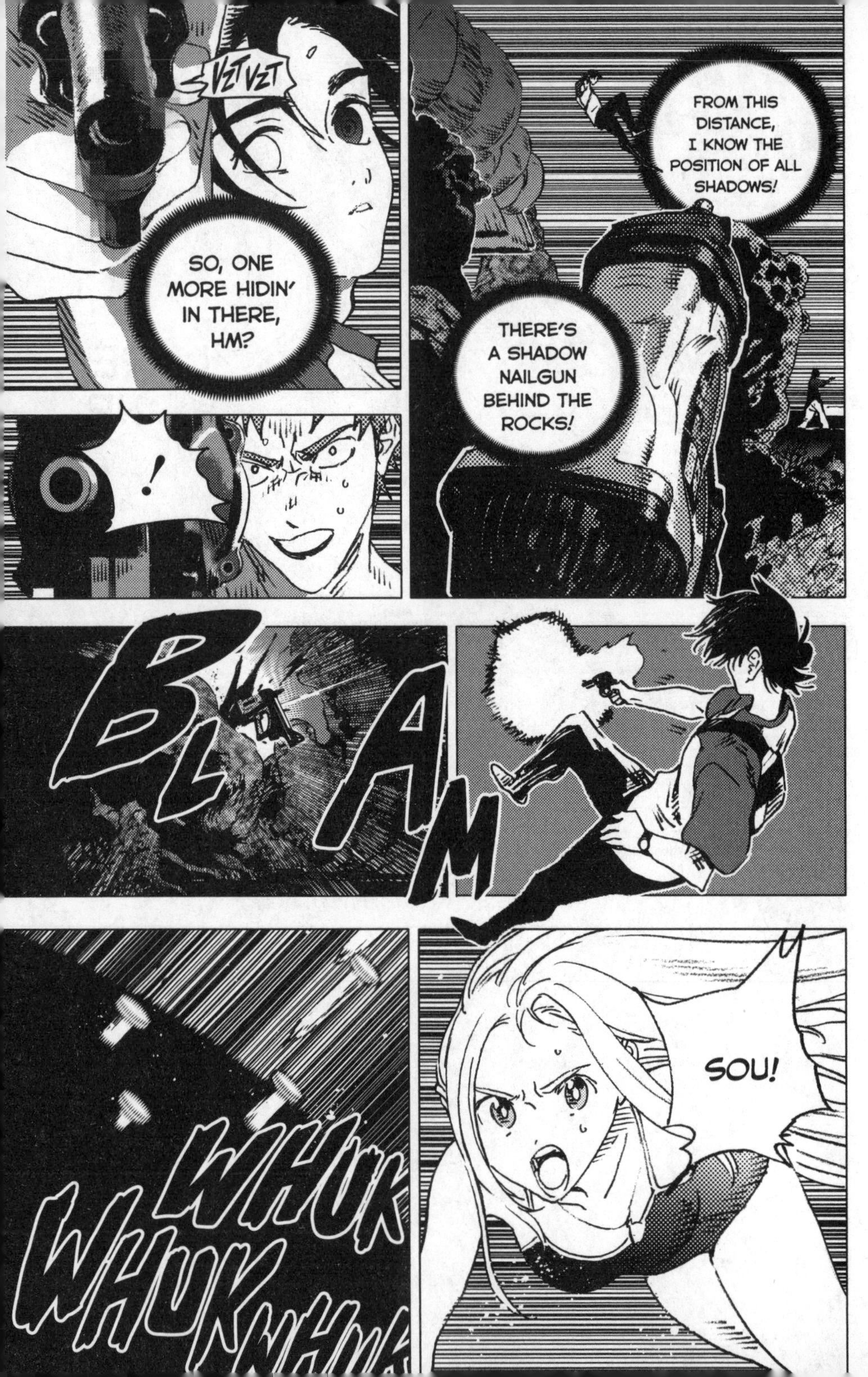
FROM THIS DISTANCE, I KNOW THE POSITION OF ALL SHADOWS!
THERE'S A SHADOW NAILGUN BEHIND THE ROCKS!
VZT VZT
SO, ONE MORE HIDIN' IN THERE, HM?
!
BLAM
SOU!
WHUK
WHUK WHUK WHUK

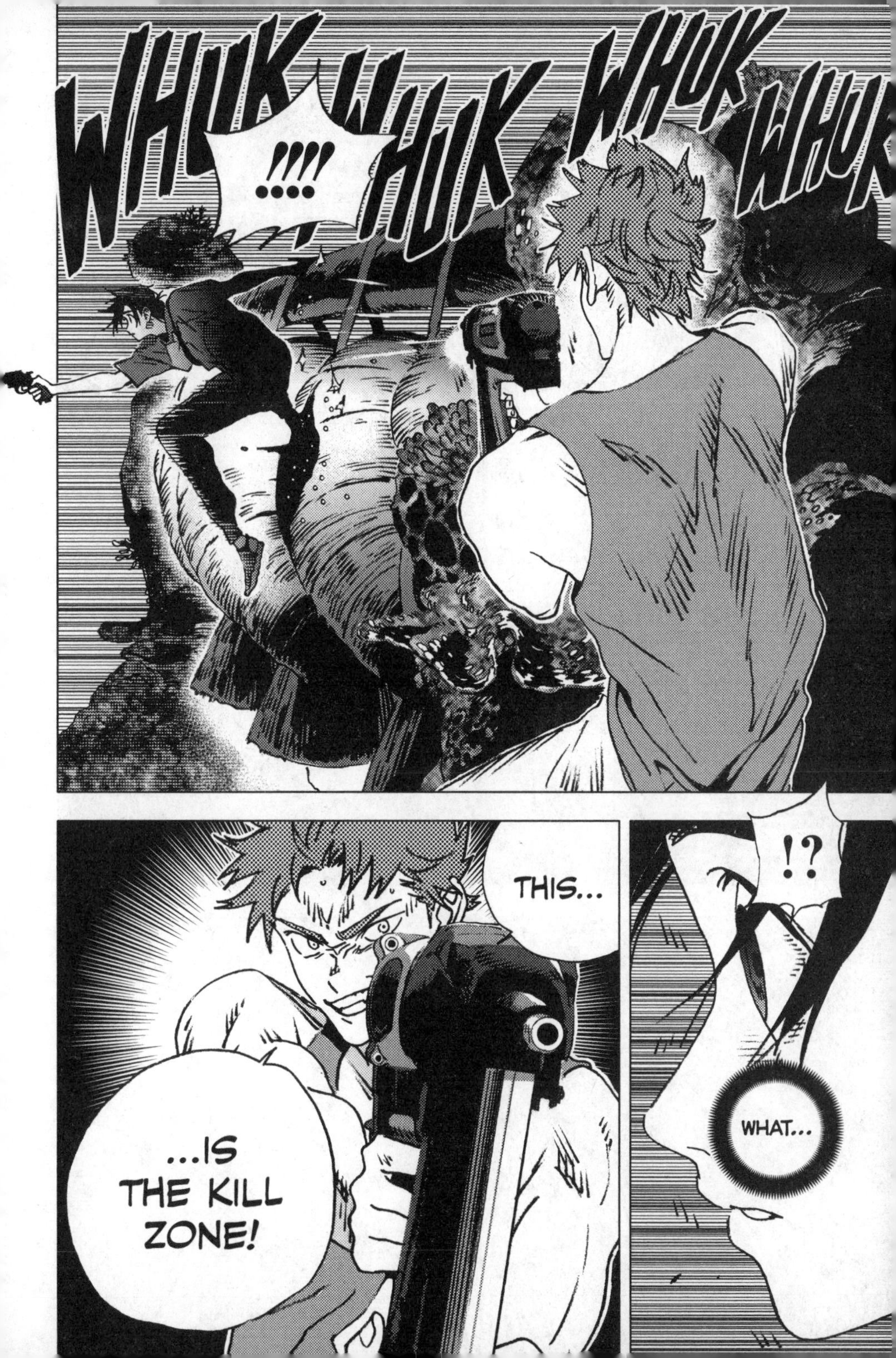
WHUK WHUK WHUK WHUK
!!!!
!?
WHAT...
THIS...
...IS THE KILL ZONE!

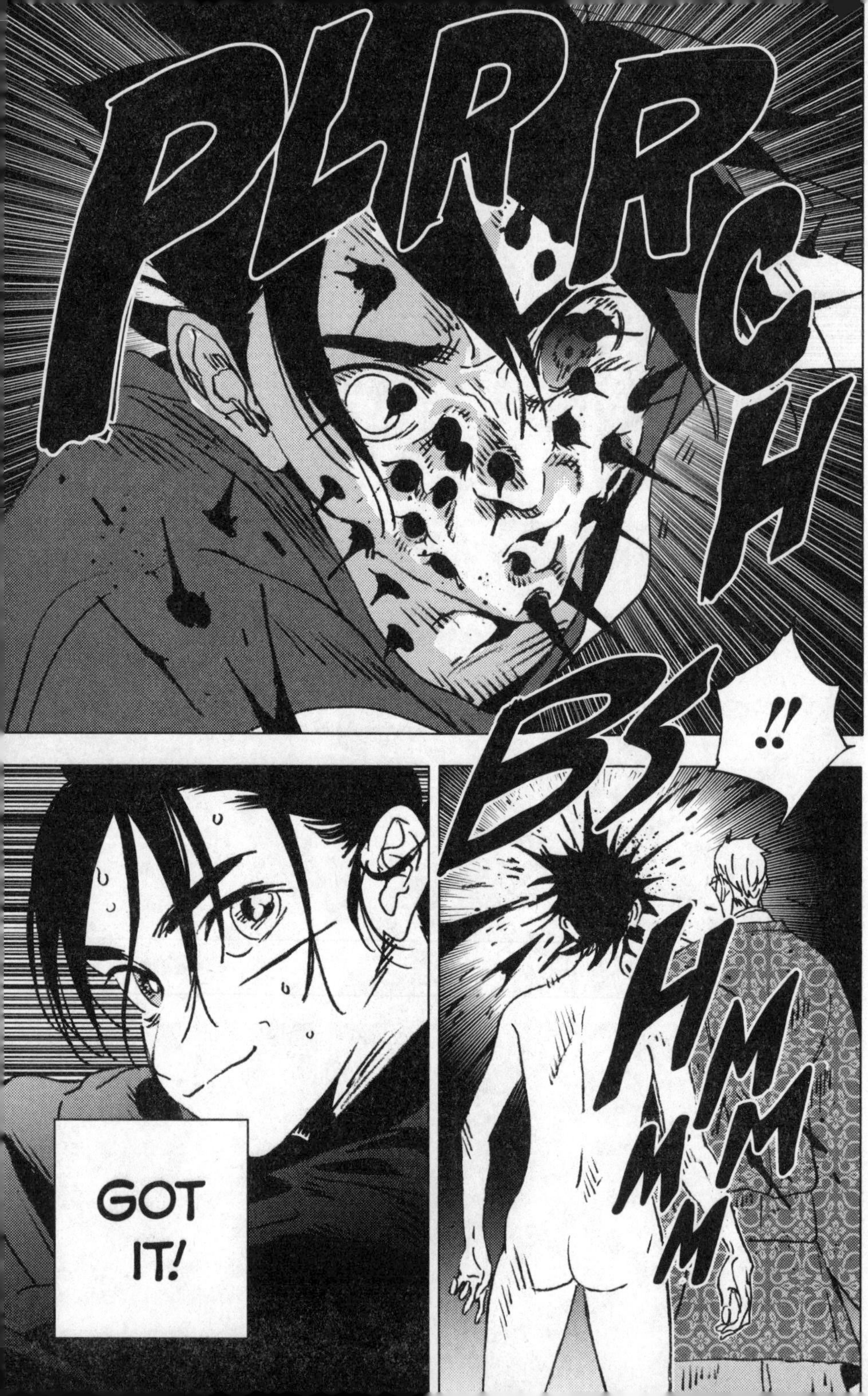
PLRRCH
!!
BSHMMMMM
GOT IT!

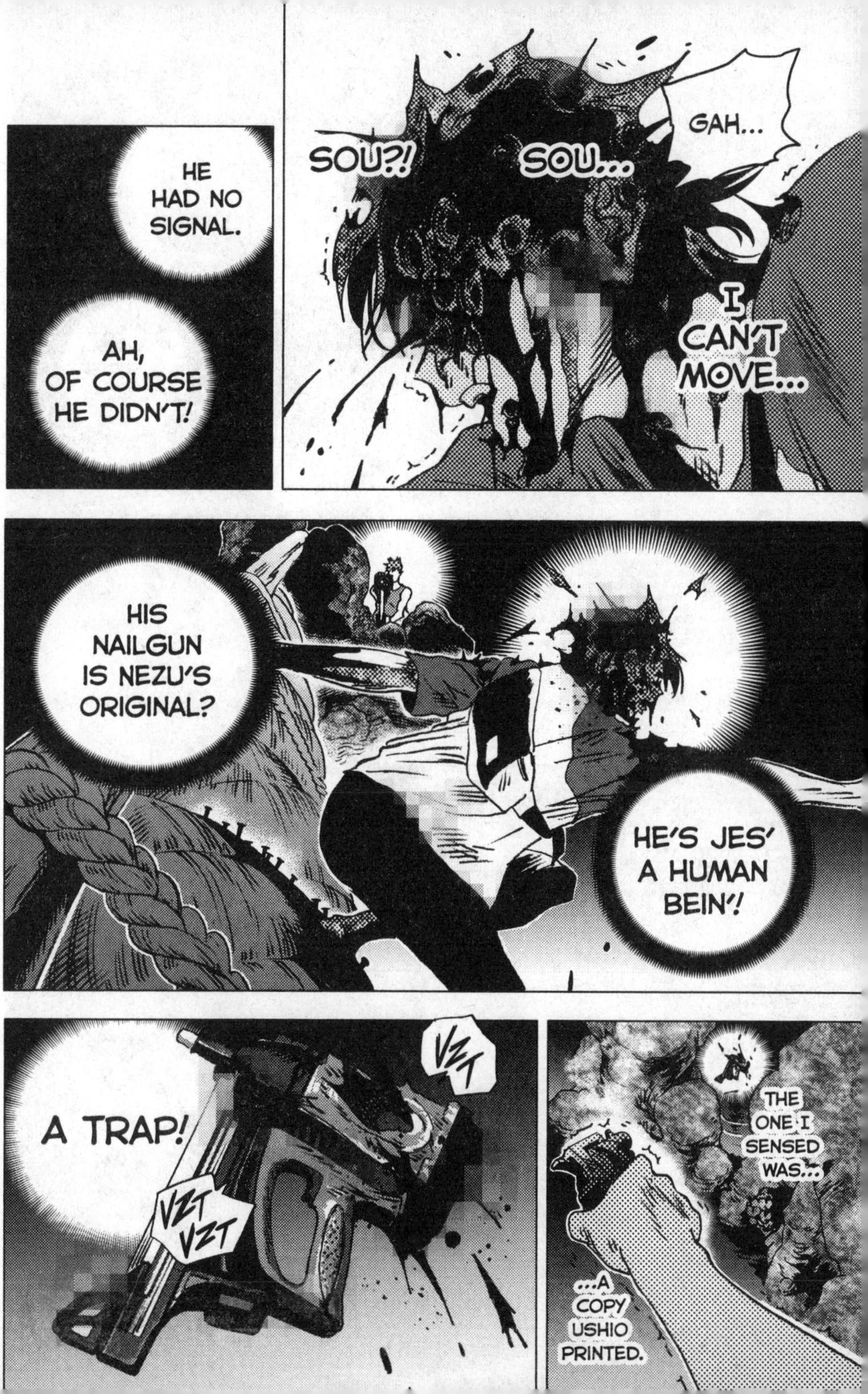
GAH...
SOU...
SOU?!
I CAN'T MOVE...
HE HAD NO SIGNAL.
AH, OF COURSE HE DIDN'T!
HIS NAILGUN IS NEZU'S ORIGINAL?
HE'S JES' A HUMAN BEIN'!
THE ONE I SENSED WAS...
...A COPY USHIO PRINTED.
VZT
A TRAP!
VZT VZT

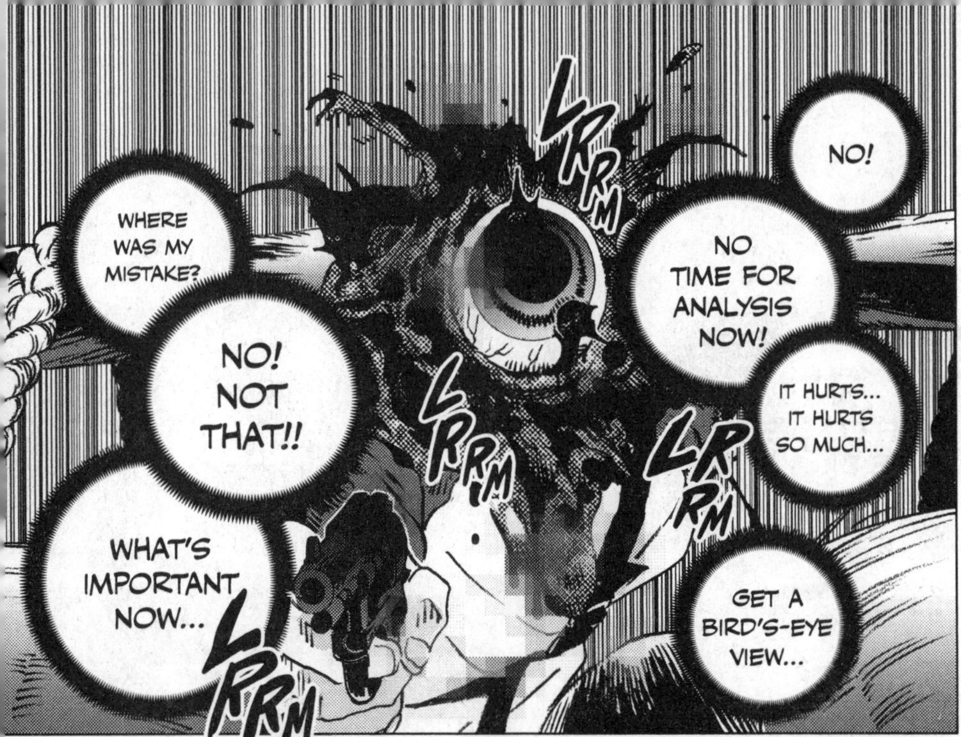
NO!
LRRM
NO TIME FOR ANALYSIS NOW!
WHERE WAS MY MISTAKE?
IT HURTS... IT HURTS SO MUCH...
LRRM
NO! NOT THAT!!
LRRM
GET A BIRD'S-EYE VIEW...
WHAT'S IMPORTANT NOW...
LRRM

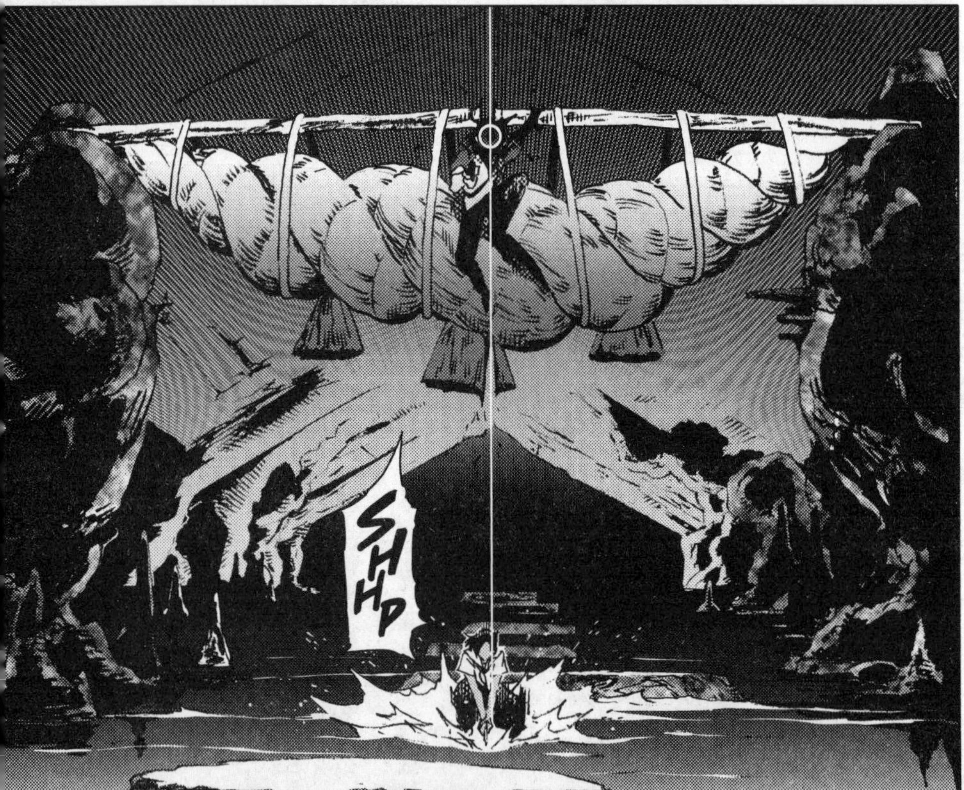
SHHP

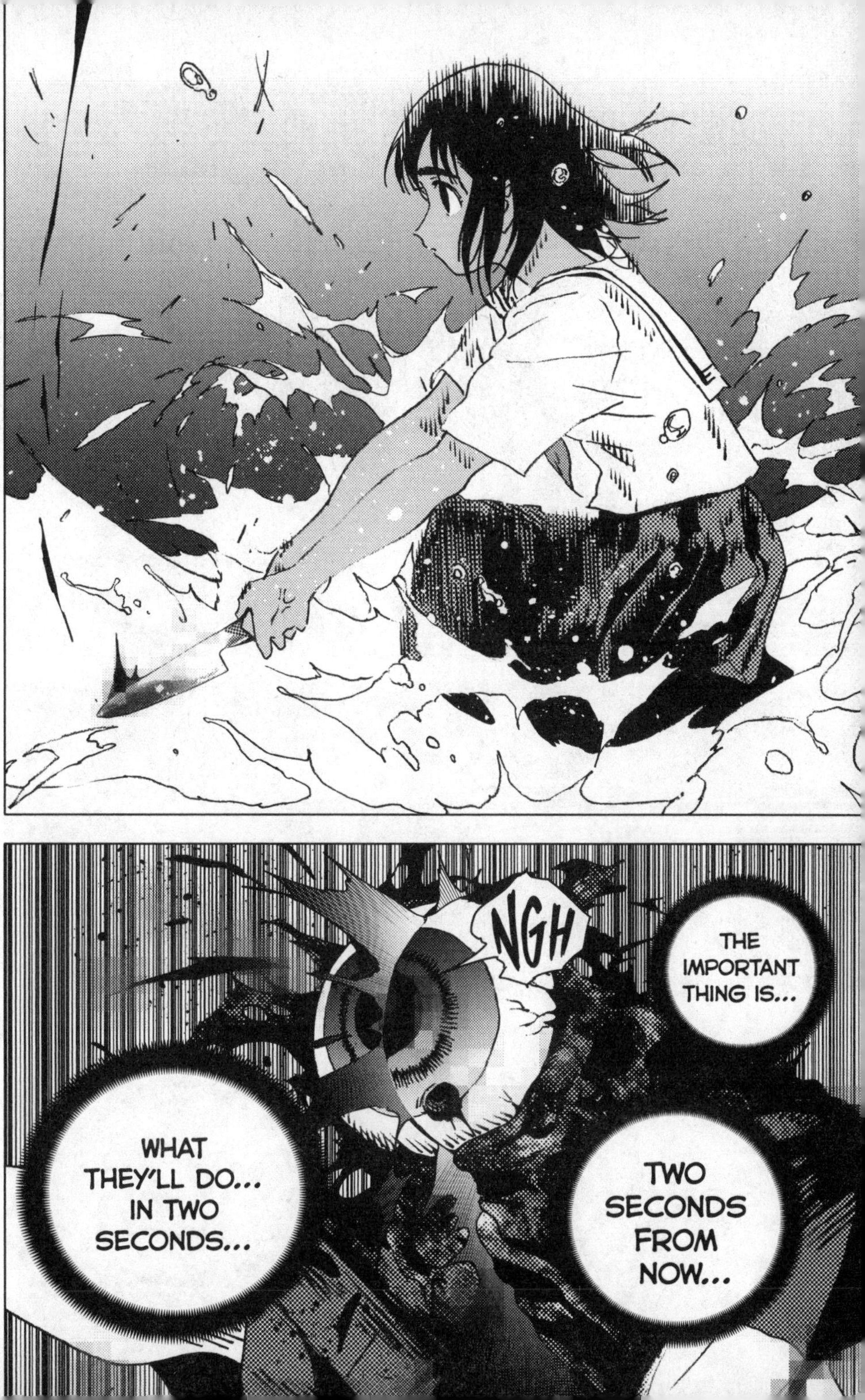
NGH
THE IMPORTANT THING IS...
TWO SECONDS FROM NOW...
WHAT THEY'LL DO... IN TWO SECONDS...

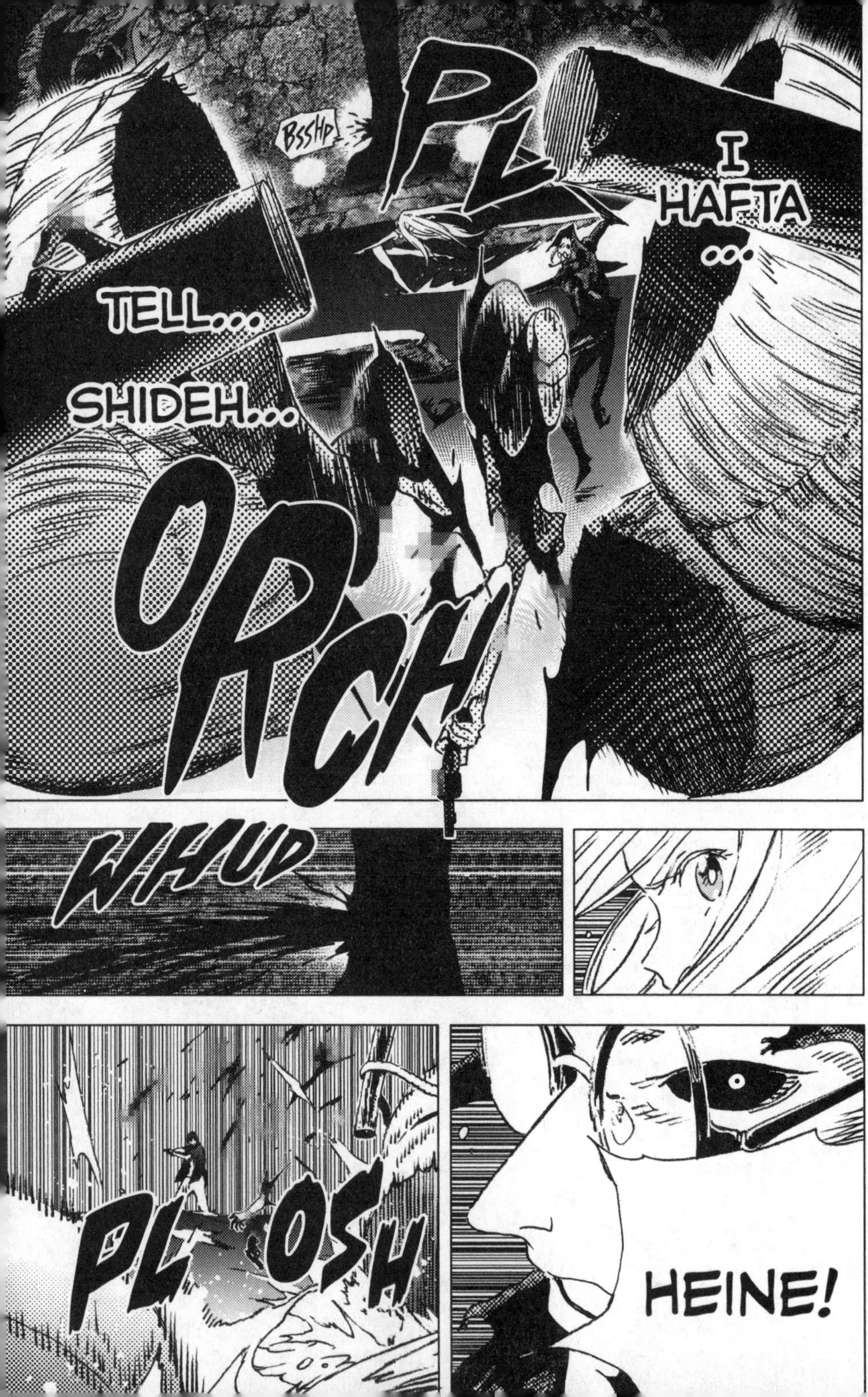
I HAFTA...
PL
BSSHP
TELL...
SHIDEH...
ORCH
WHUD
HEINE!
PLOSH

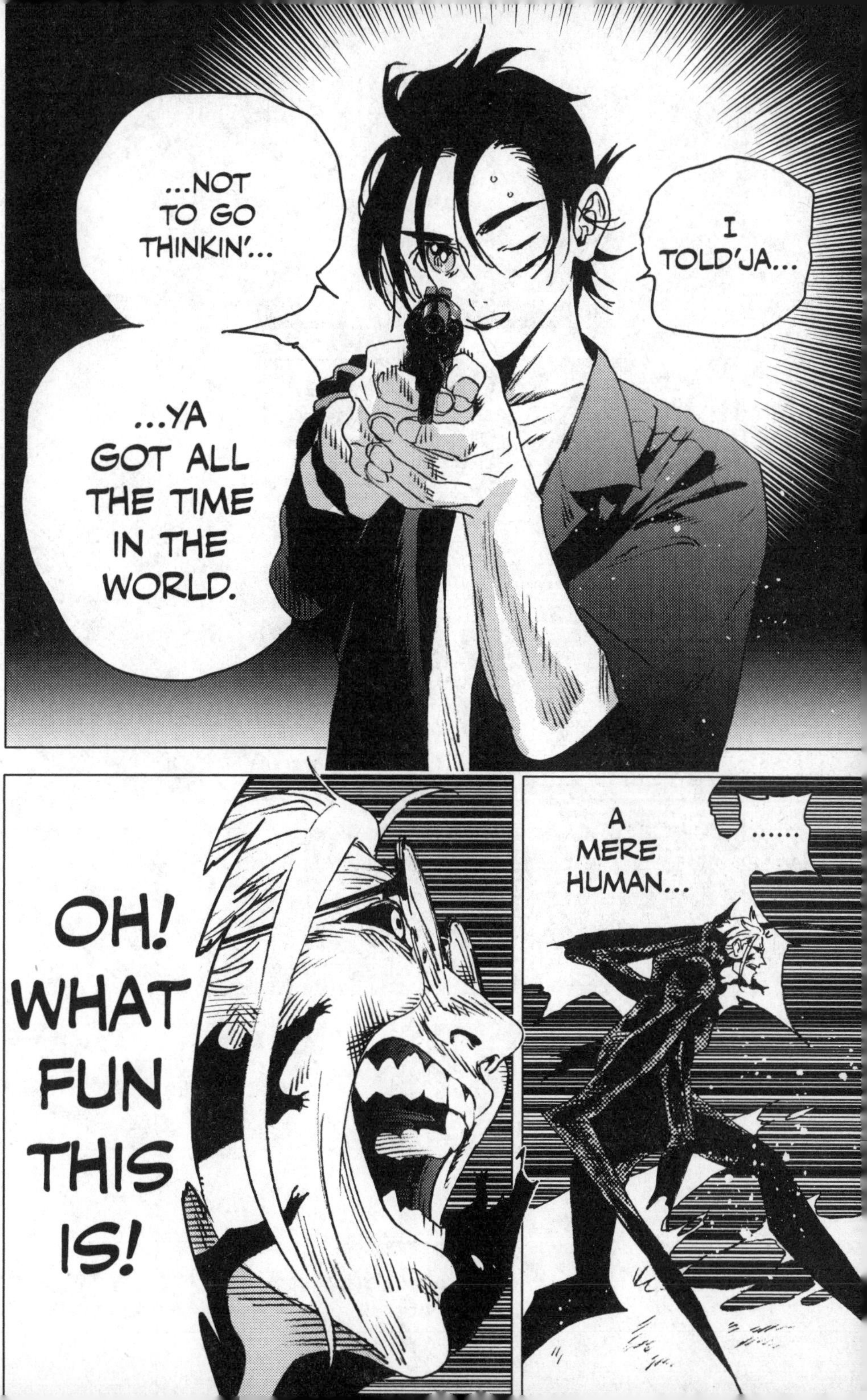
I TOLD'JA...
...NOT TO GO THINKIN'...
...YA GOT ALL THE TIME IN THE WORLD.
......
A MERE HUMAN...
OH! WHAT FUN THIS IS!

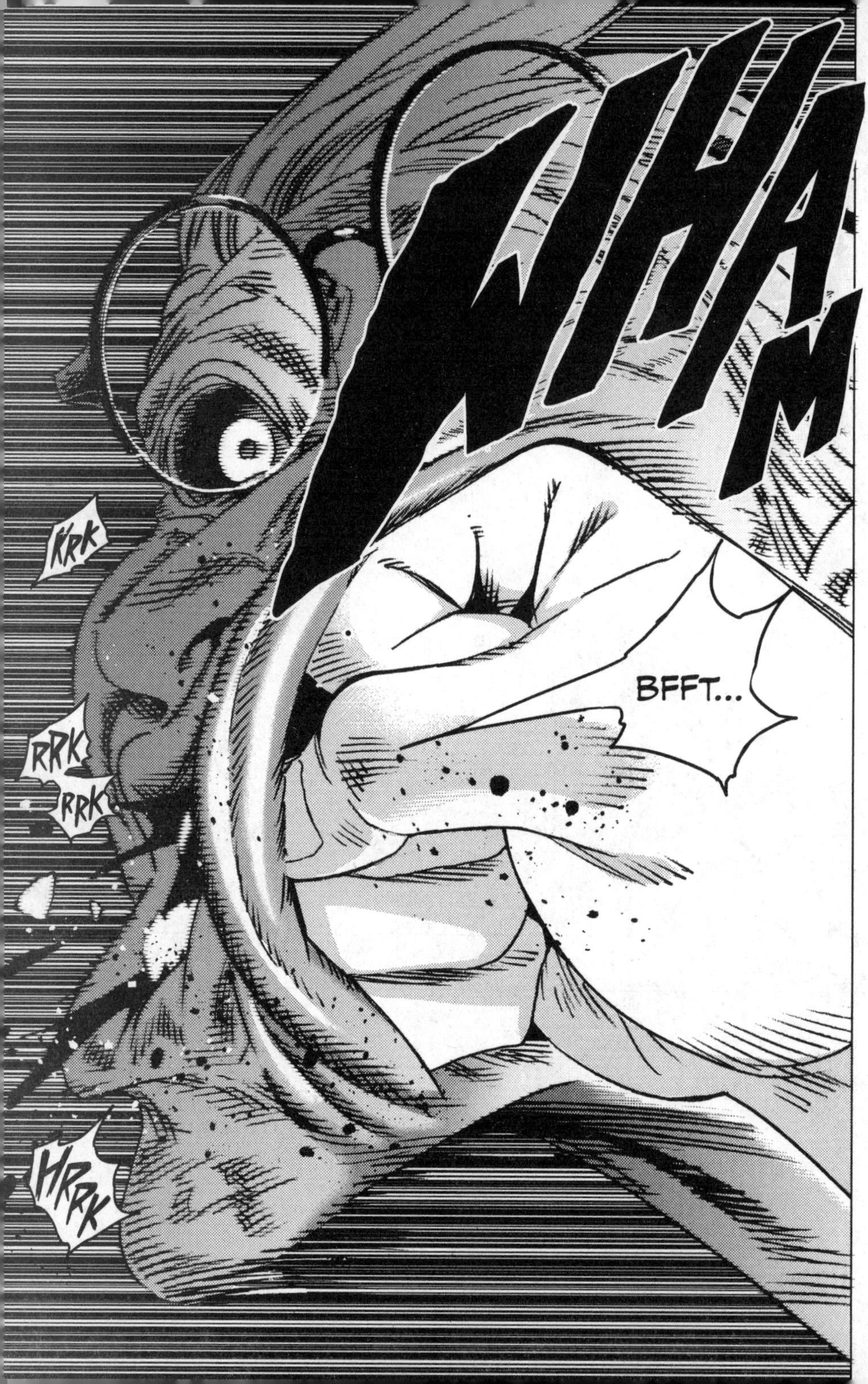
WHAM
BFFT...
KRK
RRK
RRK
HRRK

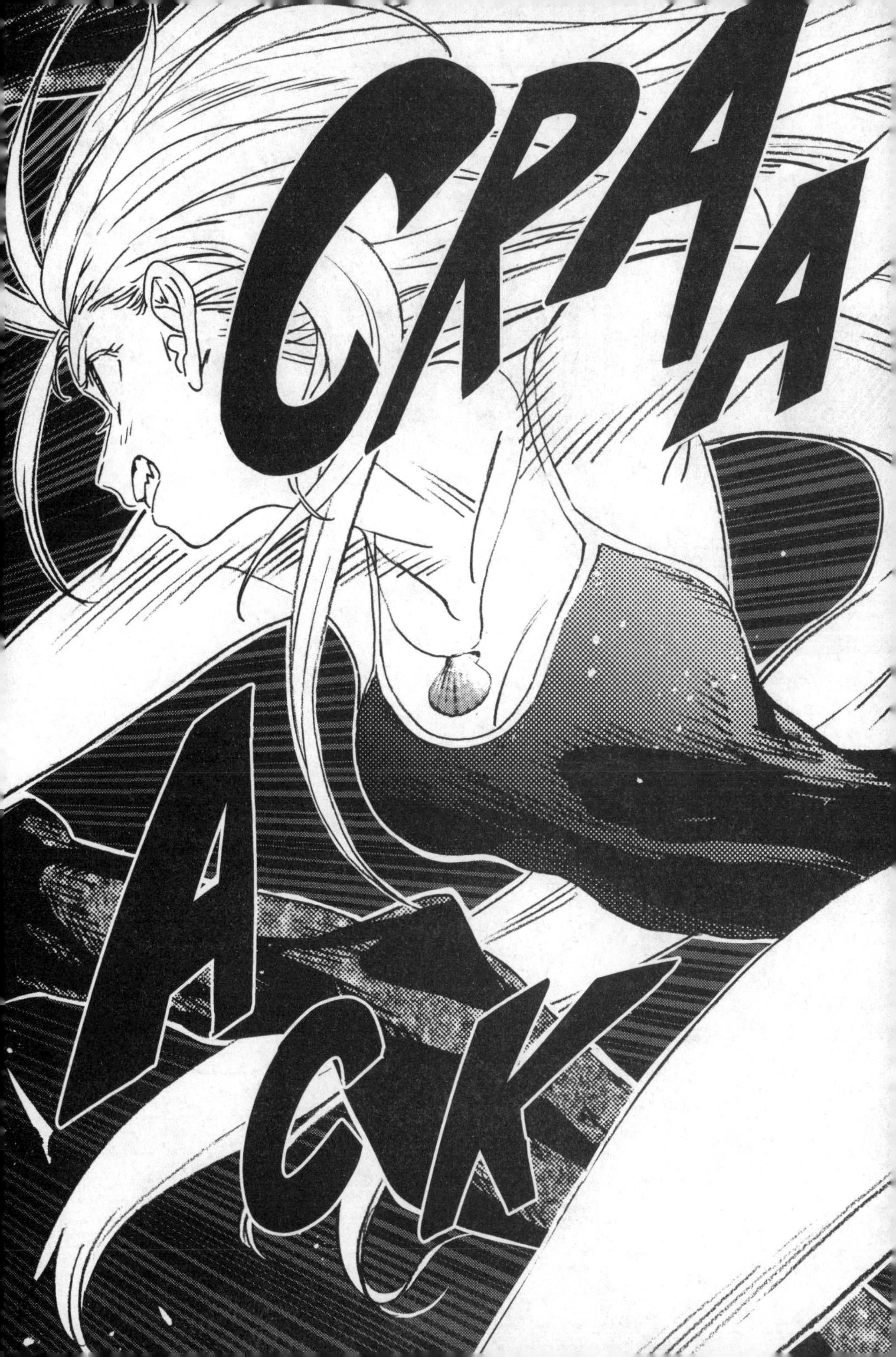
CRAAACK

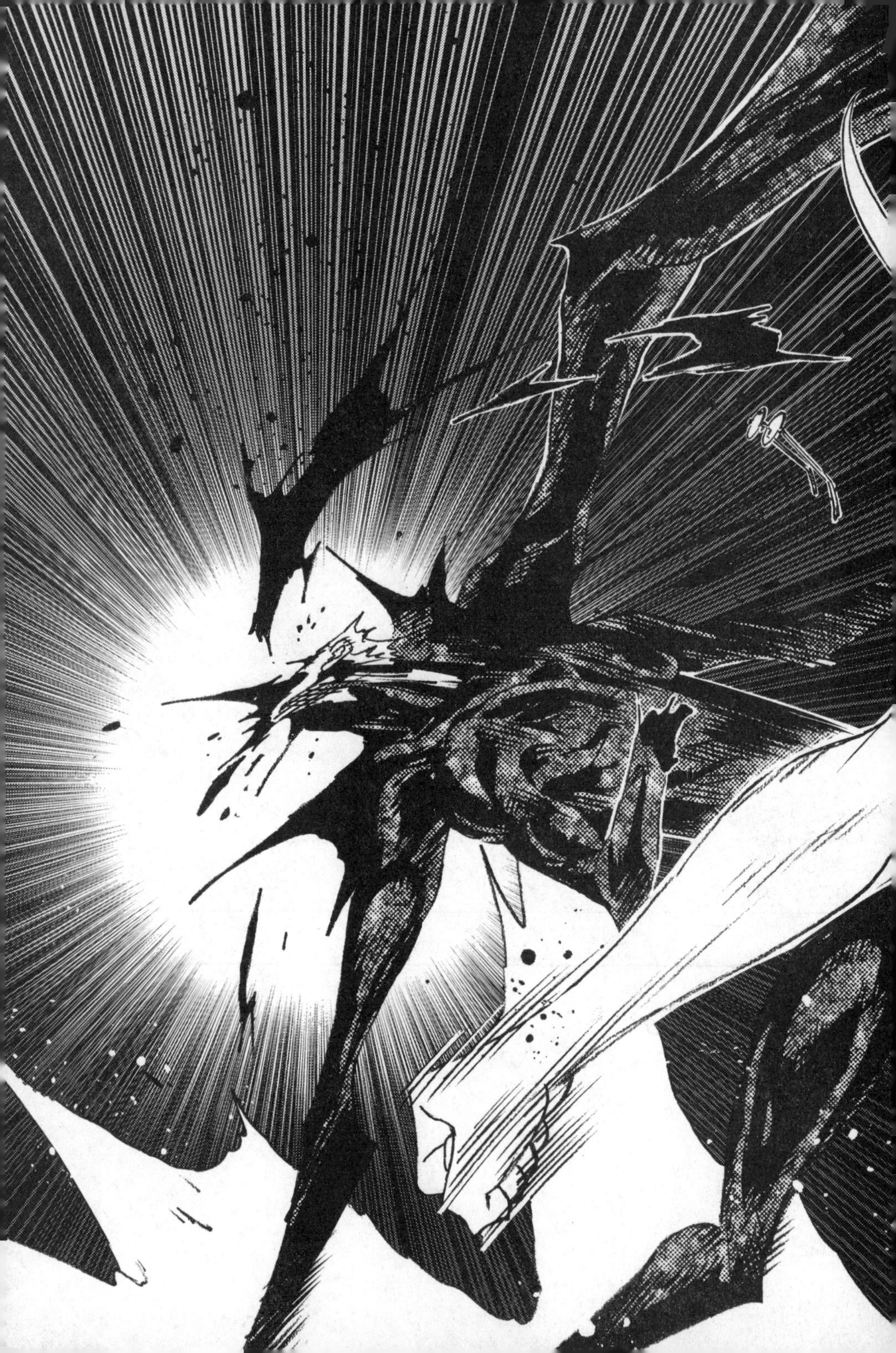

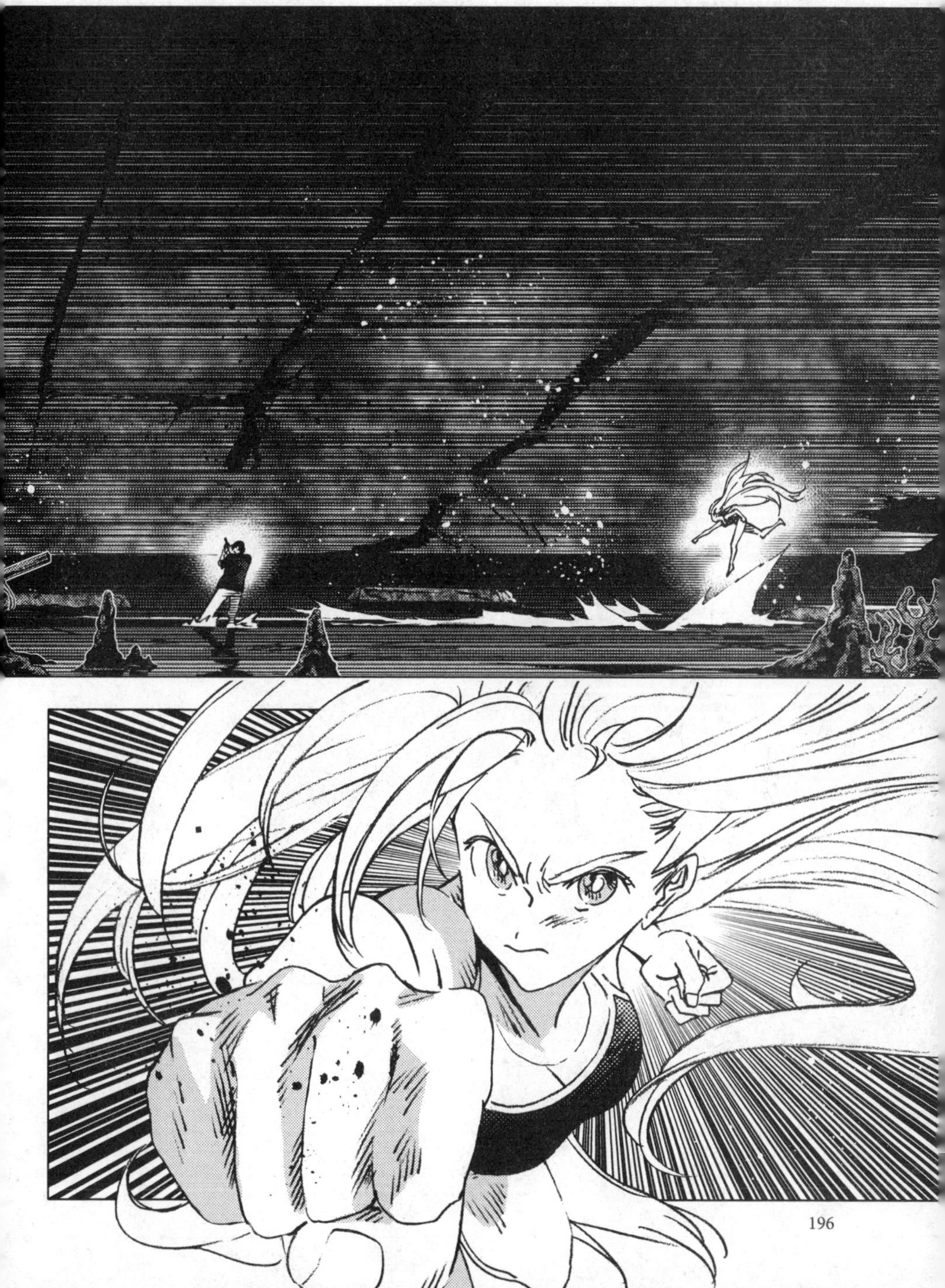

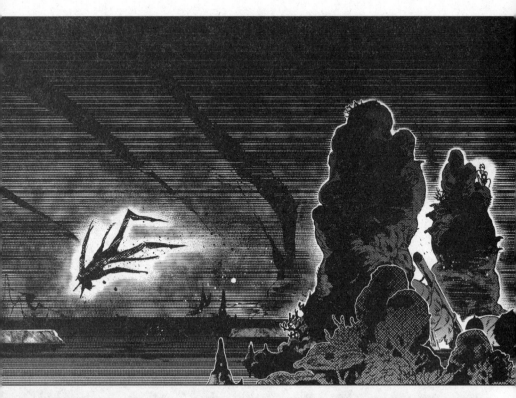

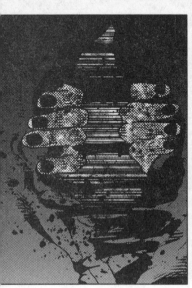

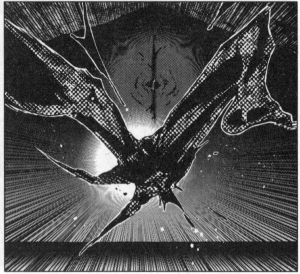

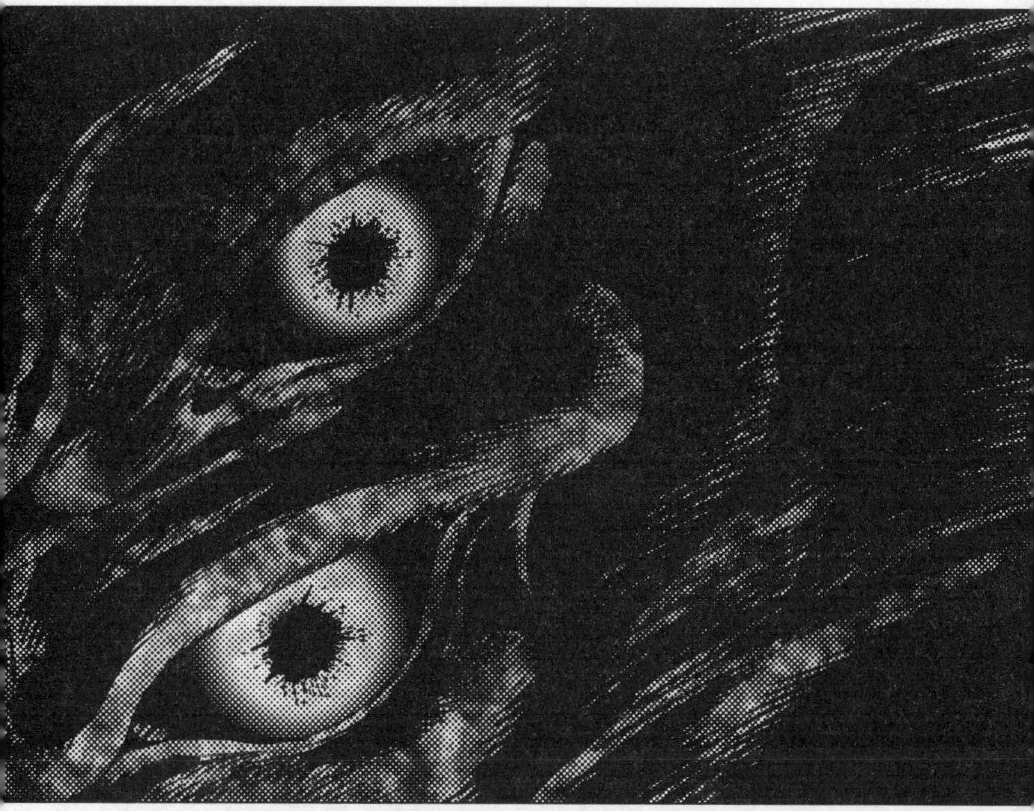
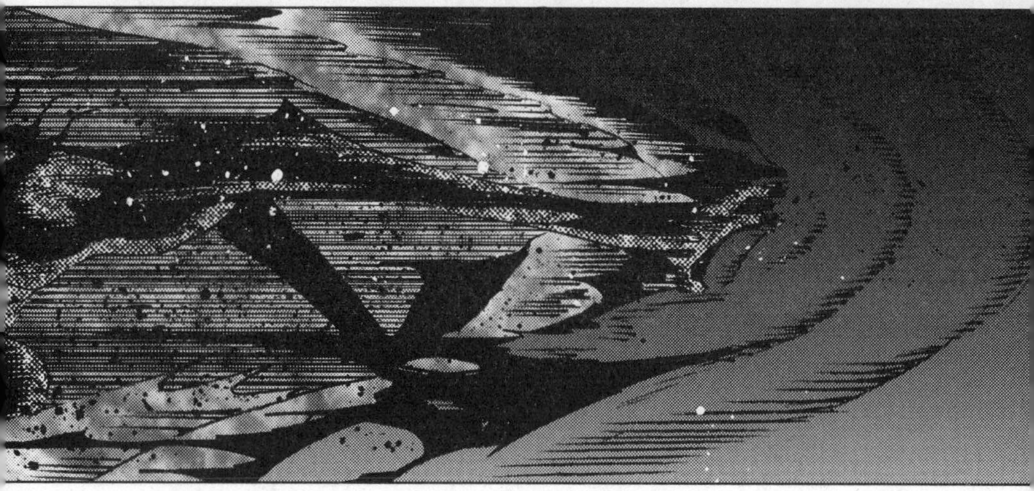

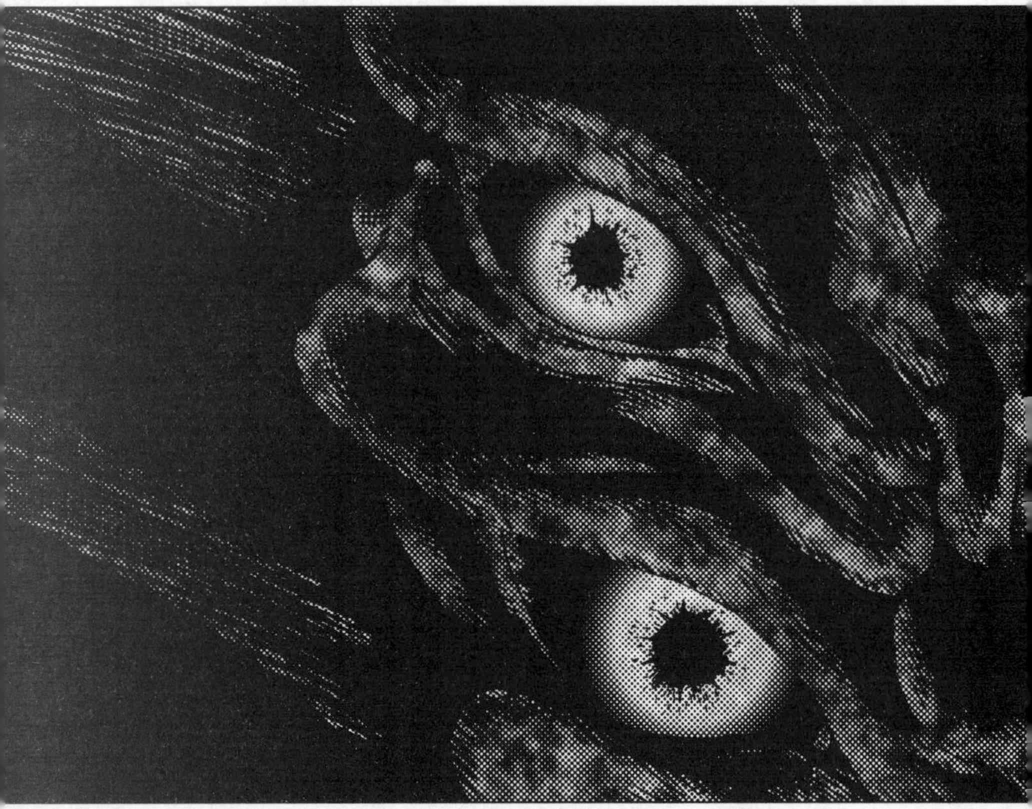
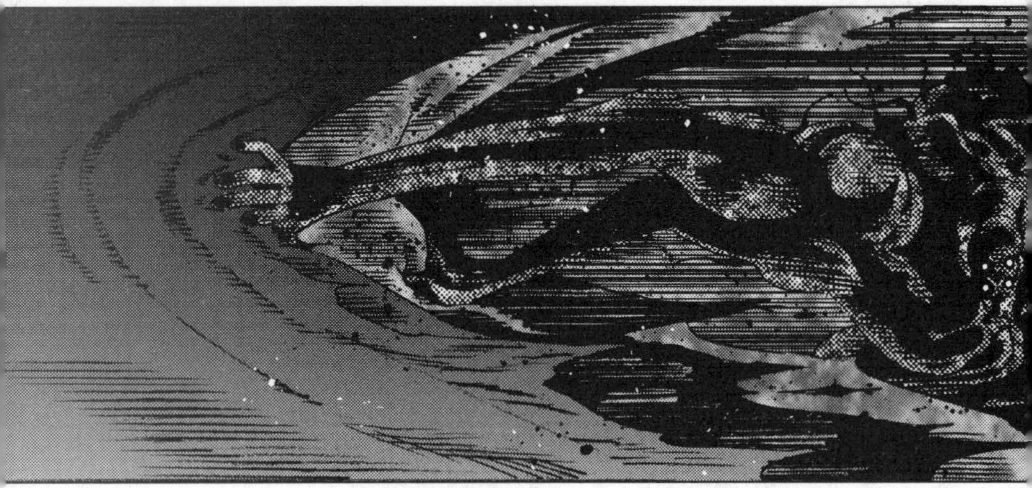

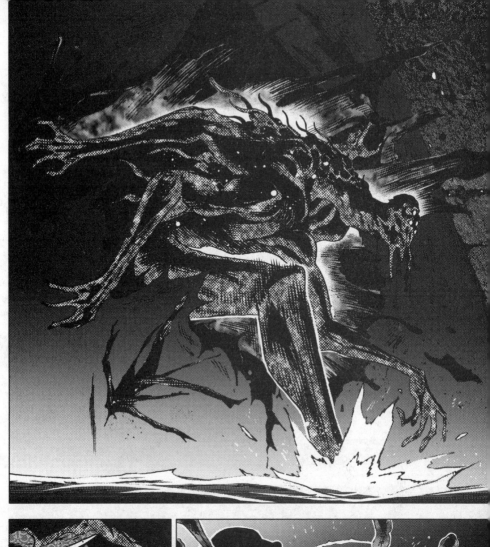

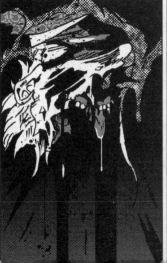

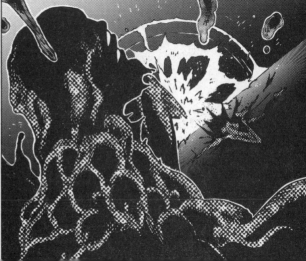

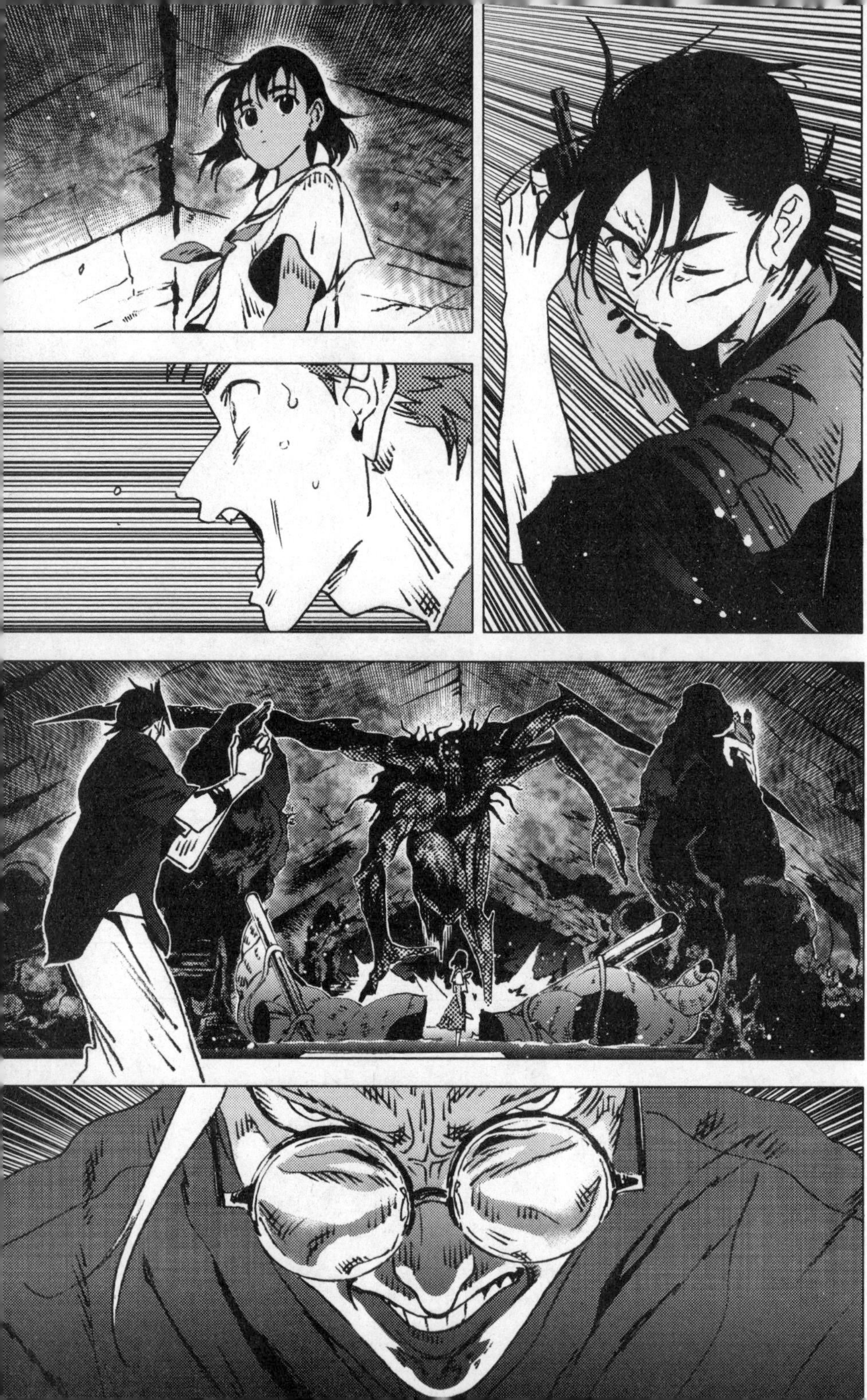

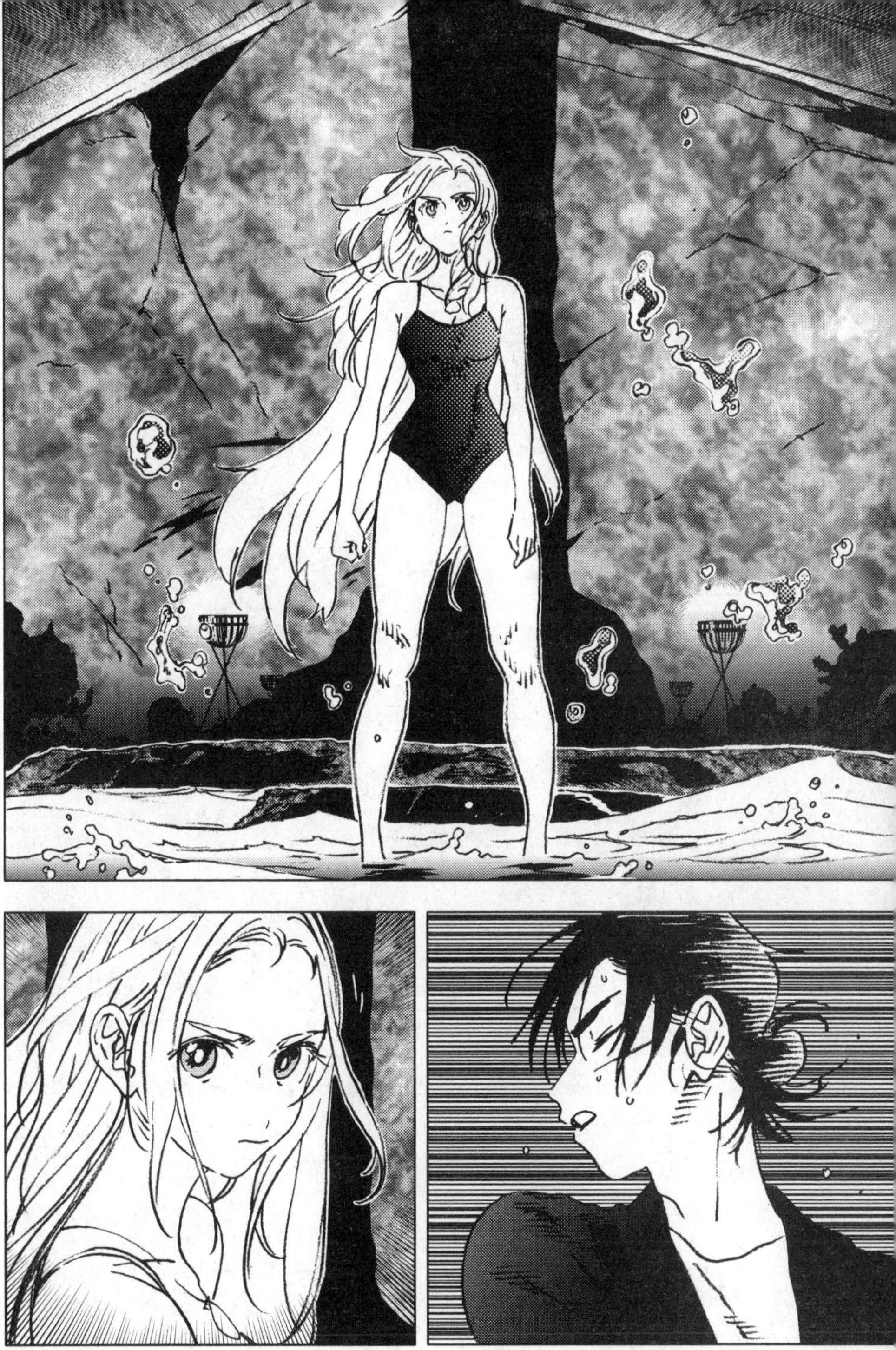

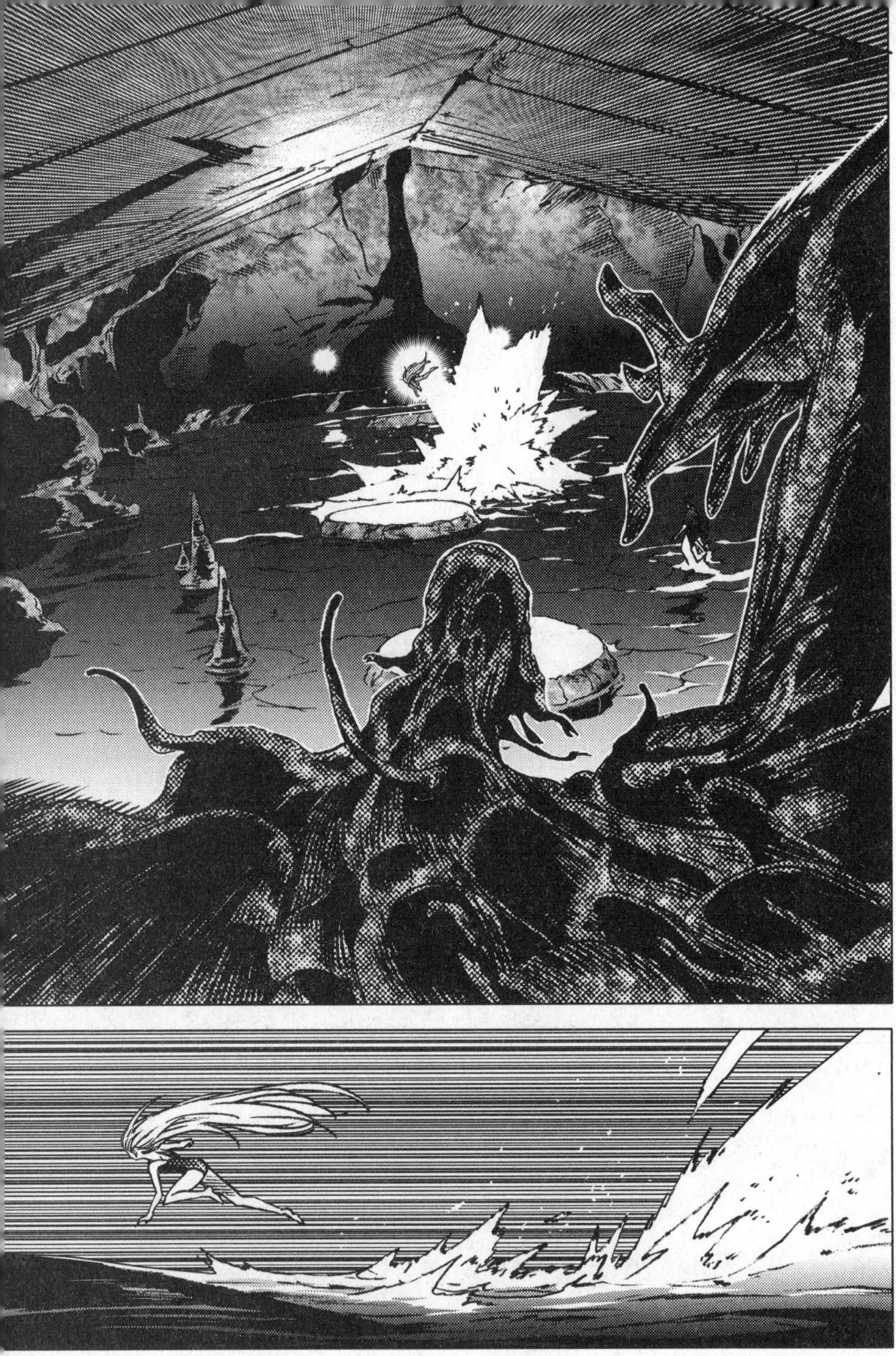

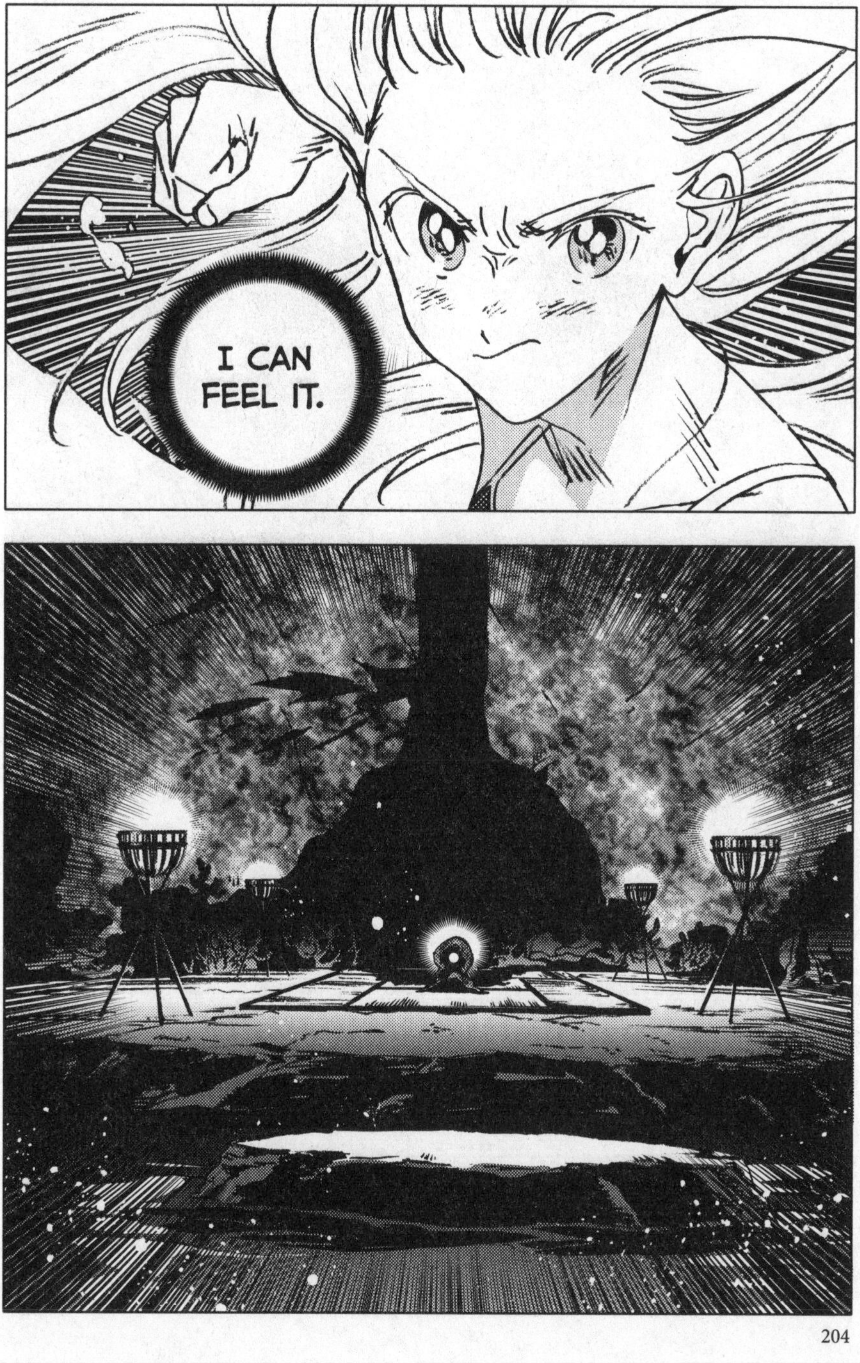
I CAN
FEEL IT.

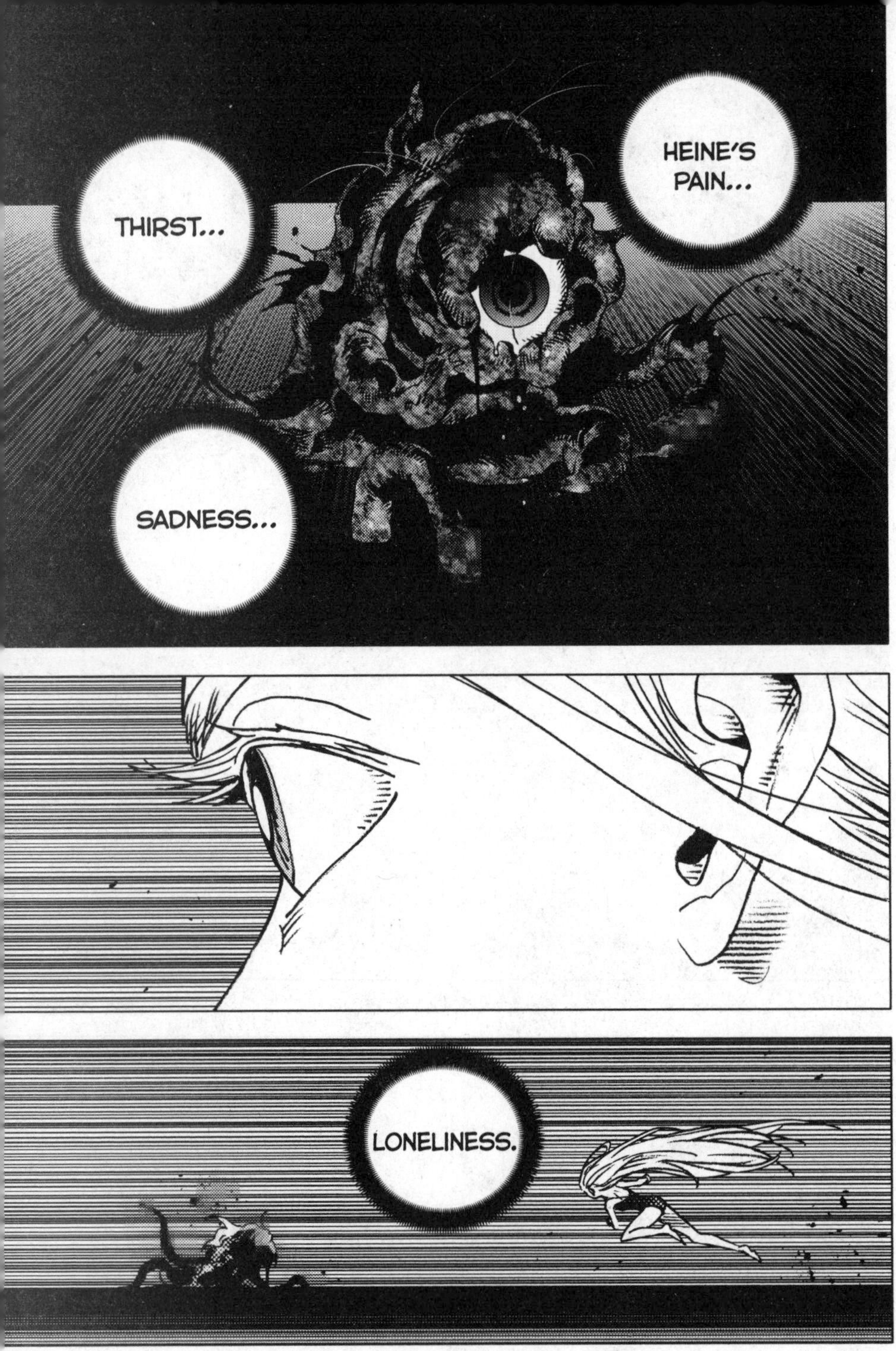
HEINE'S PAIN...
THIRST...
SADNESS...
LONELINESS.

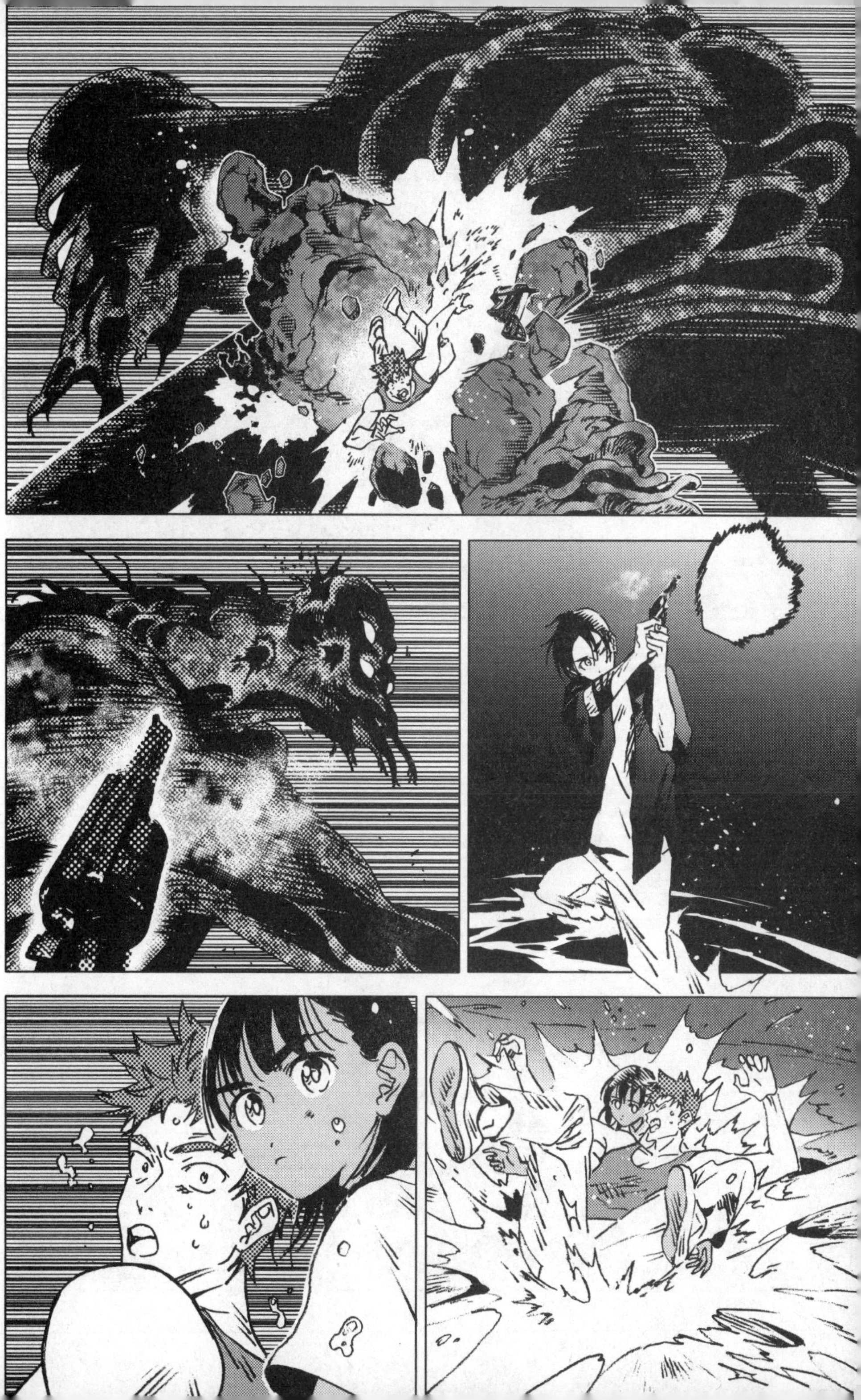

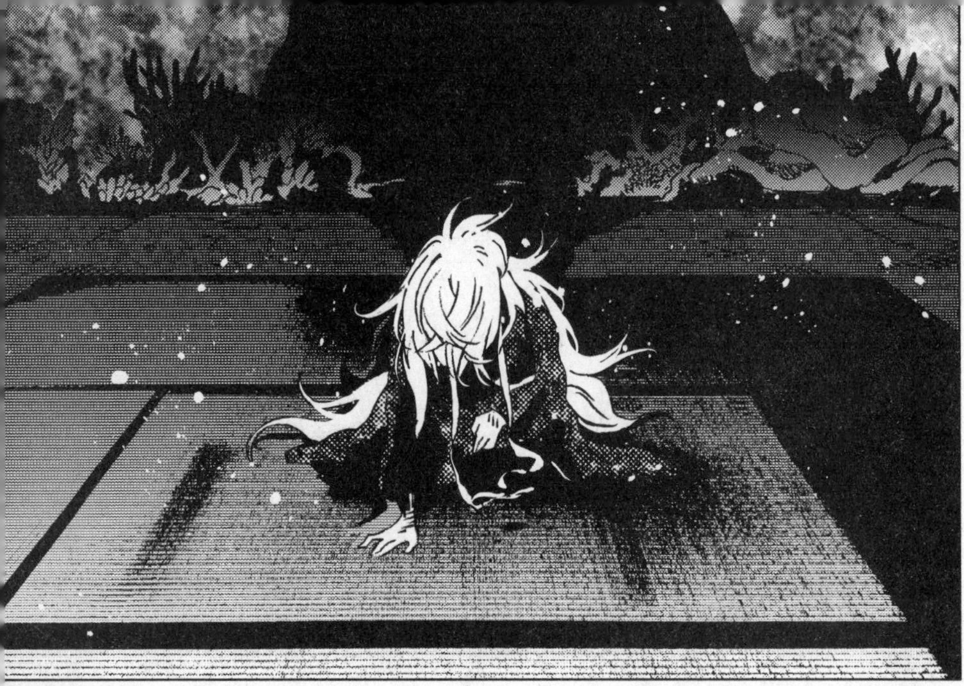
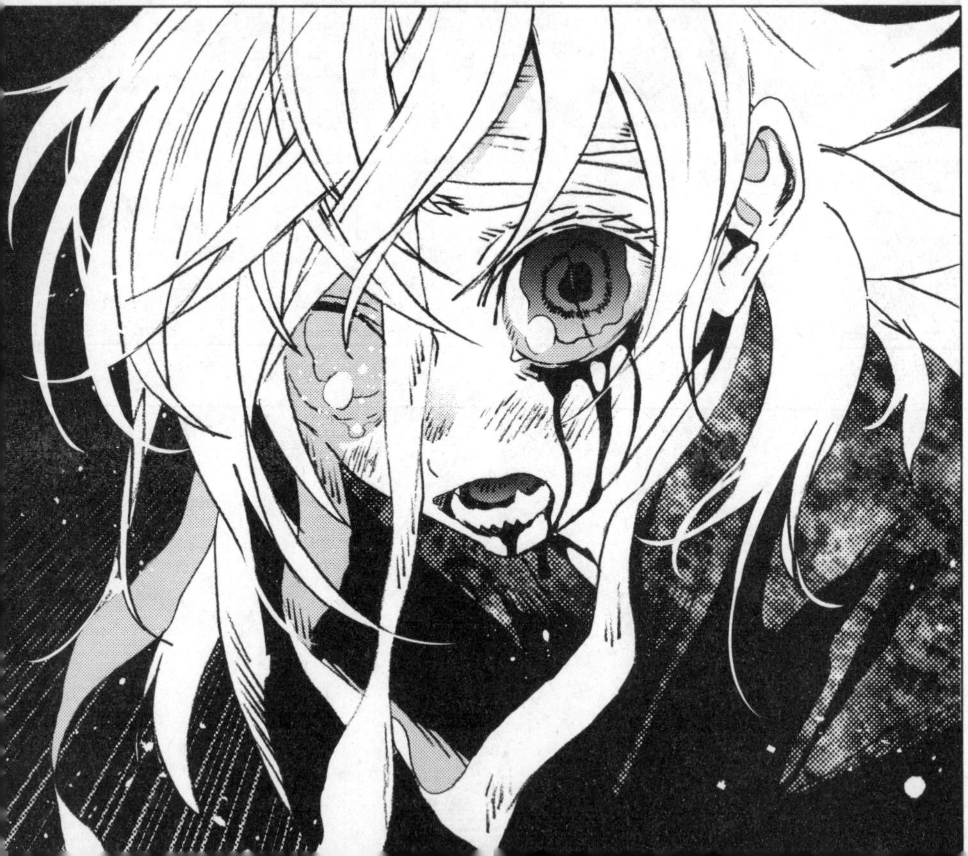

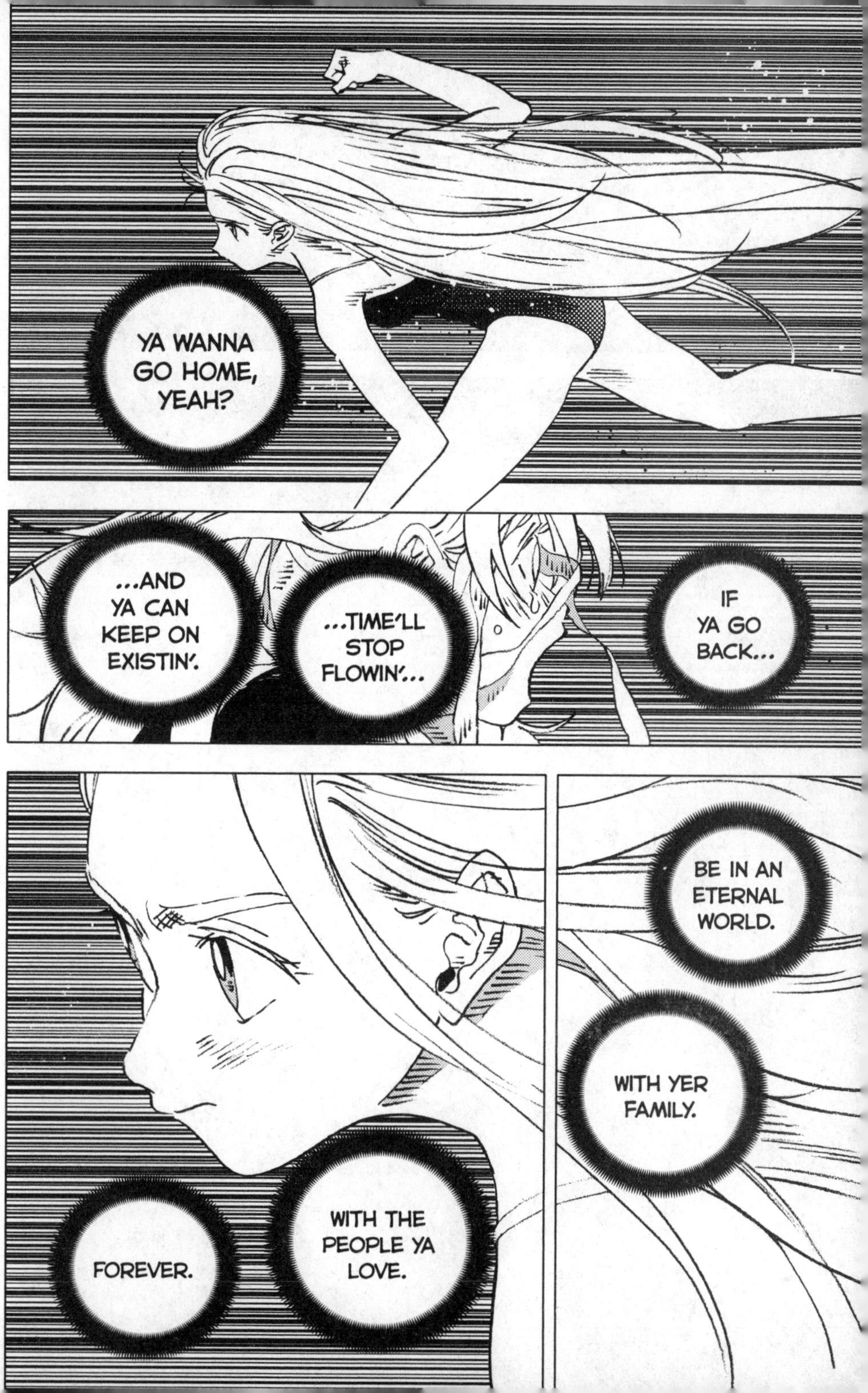
YA WANNA GO HOME, YEAH?
IF YA GO BACK...
...TIME'LL STOP FLOWIN'...
...AND YA CAN KEEP ON EXISTIN'.
BE IN AN ETERNAL WORLD.
WITH YER FAMILY.
WITH THE PEOPLE YA LOVE.
FOREVER.

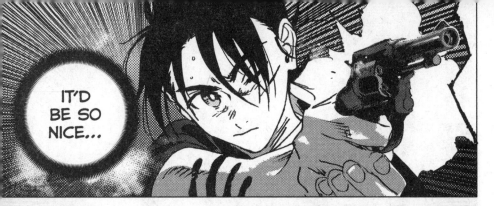

IT'D BE SO NICE...

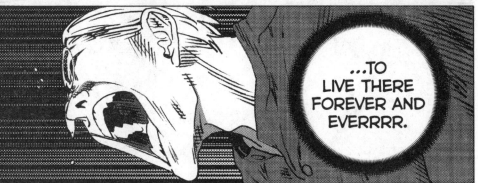

...TO LIVE THERE FOREVER AND EVERRRR.

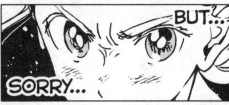

BUT...

SORRY...

WE'LL NEVER...

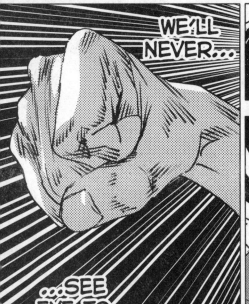

...SEE EYE TO EYE HERE.

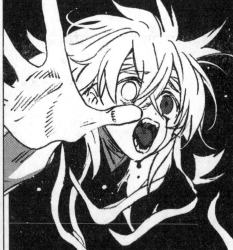

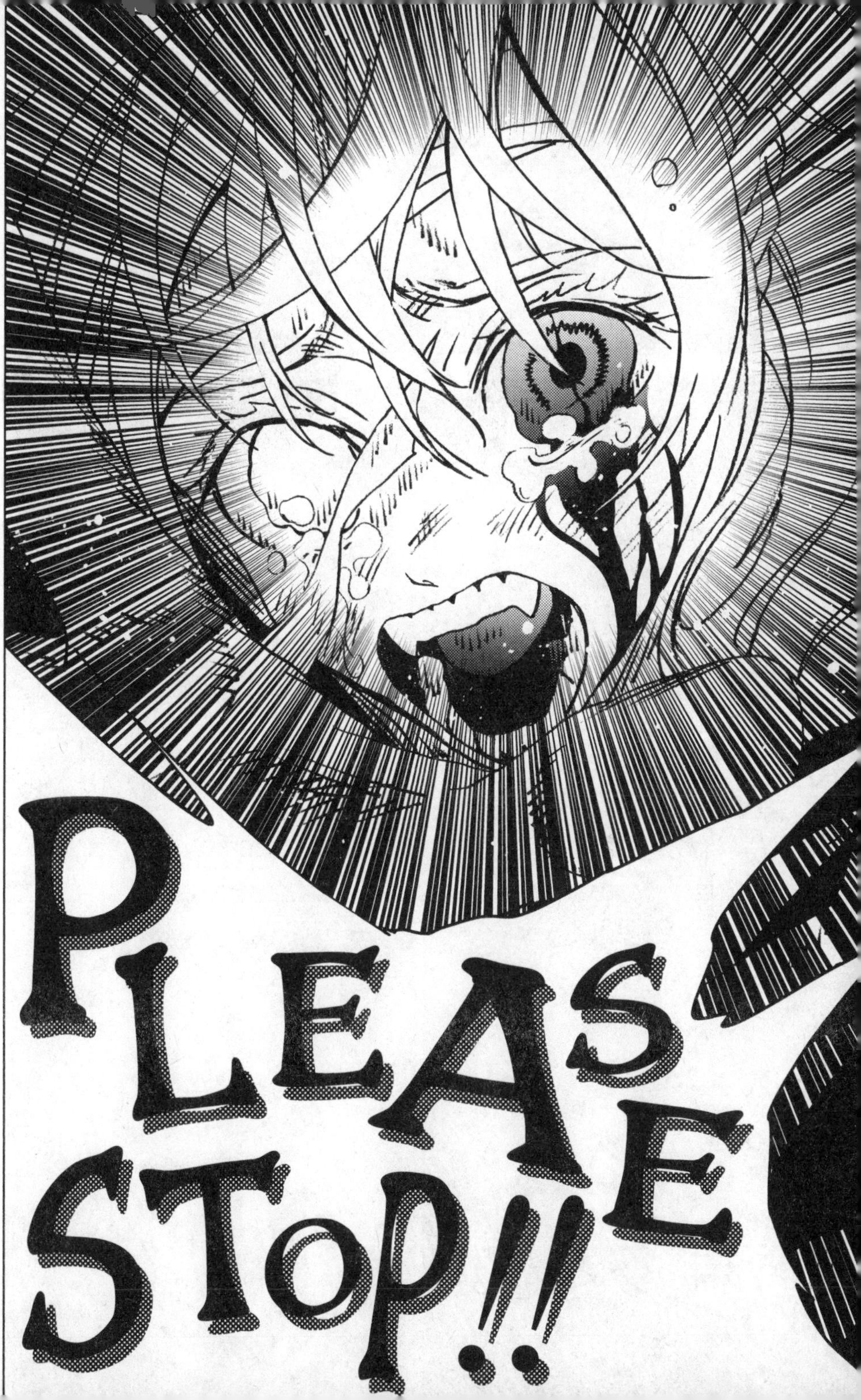
PLEASE STOP!!

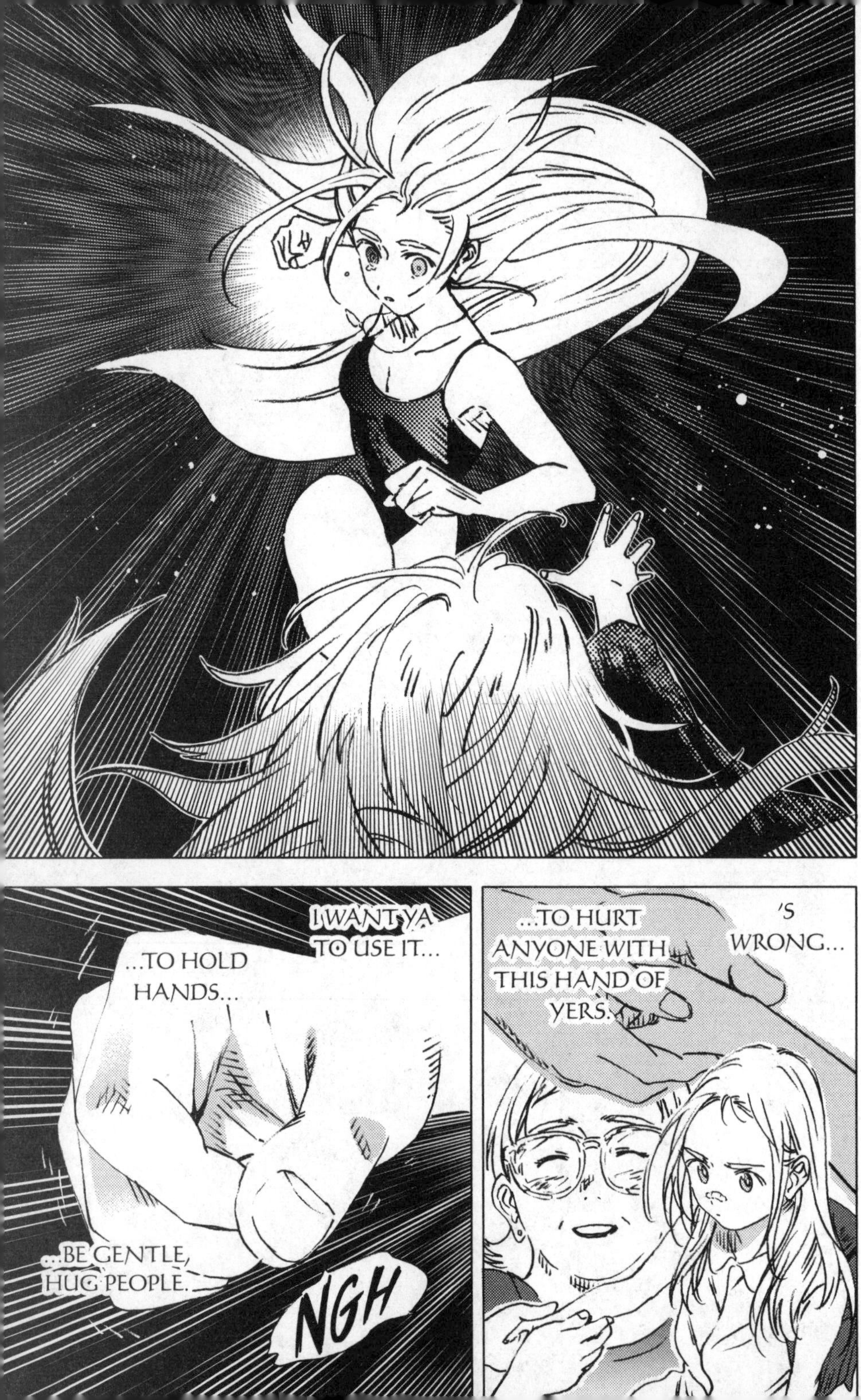
'S WRONG...
...TO HURT ANYONE WITH THIS HAND OF YERS.
I WANT YA TO USE IT...
...TO HOLD HANDS...
...BE GENTLE, HUG PEOPLE.
NGH

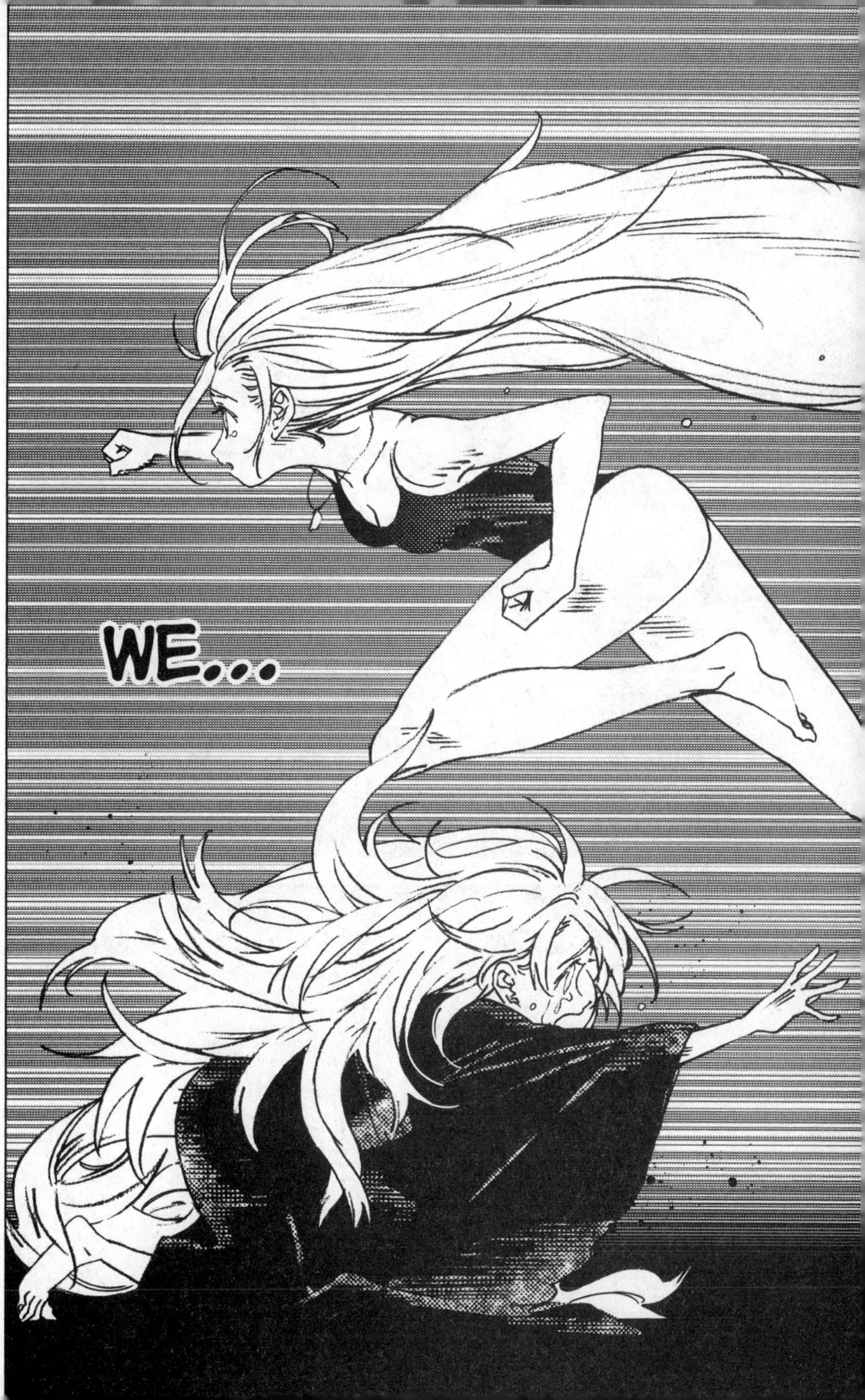
WE...

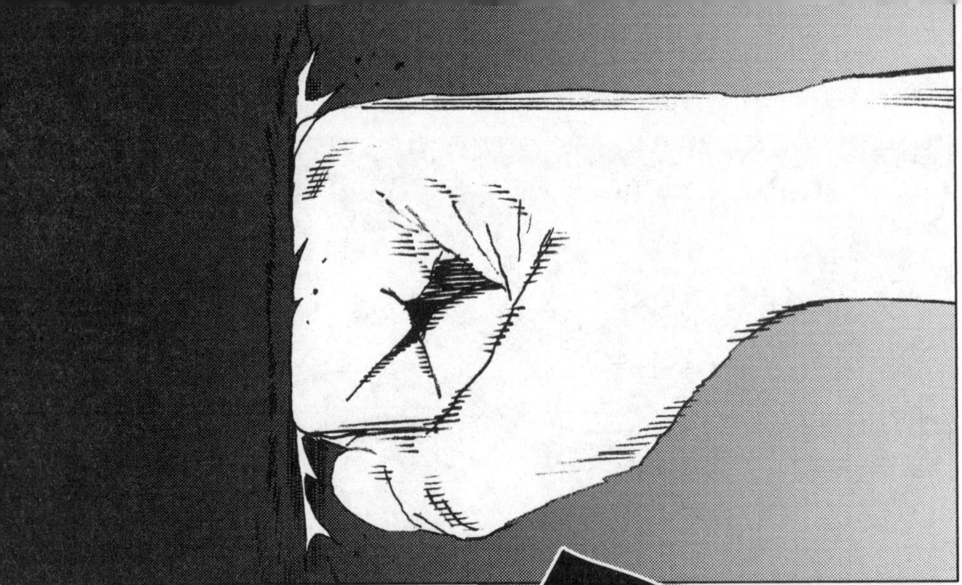

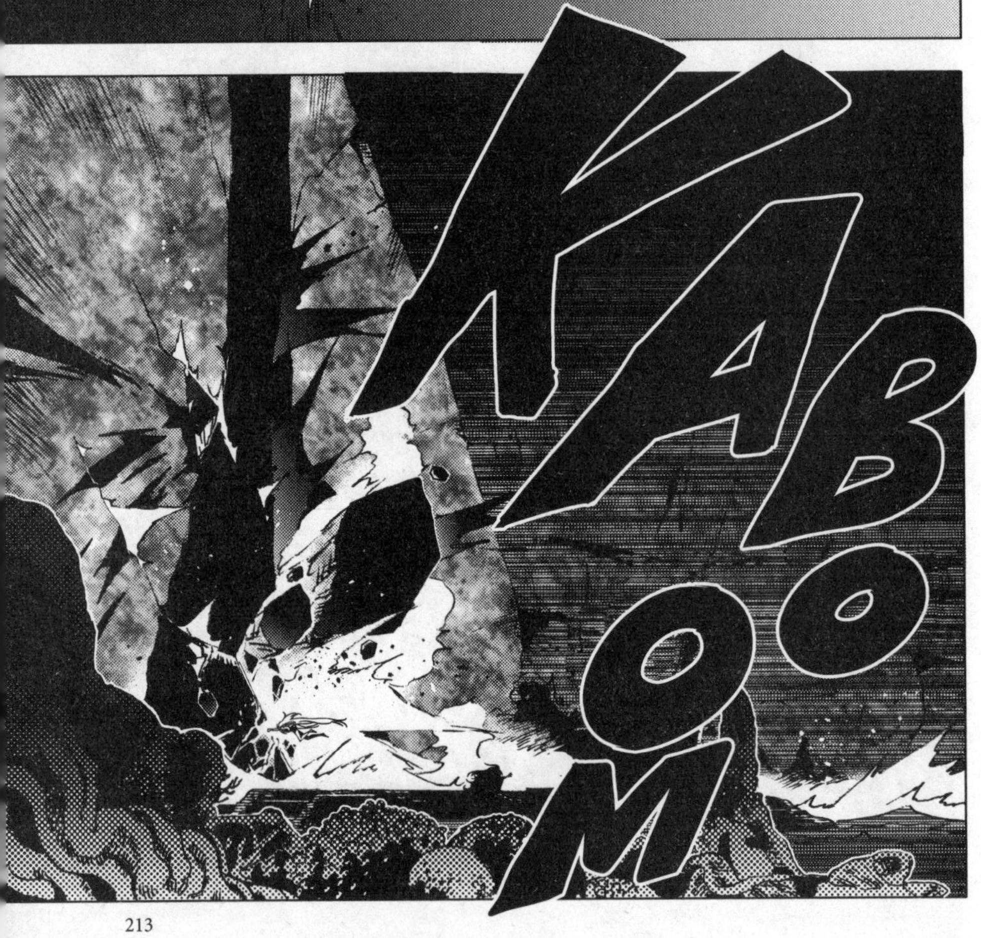
KABOOM

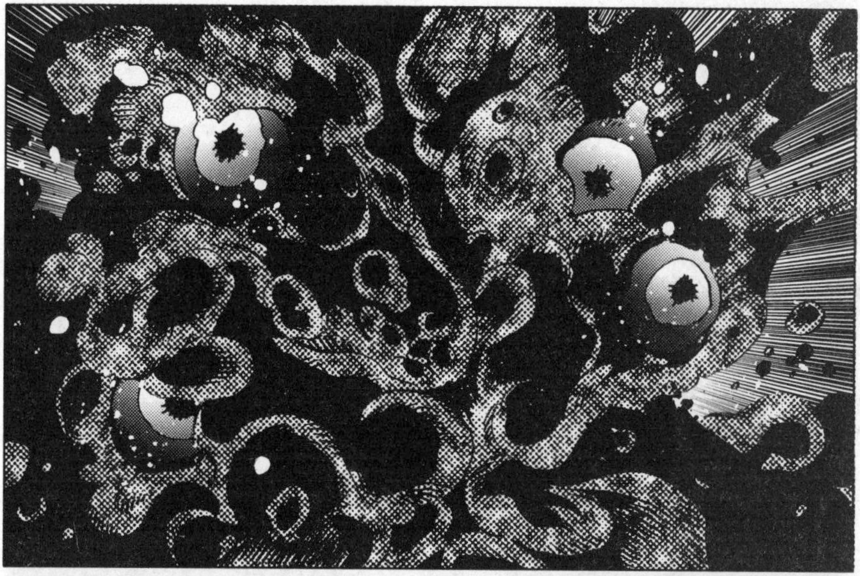

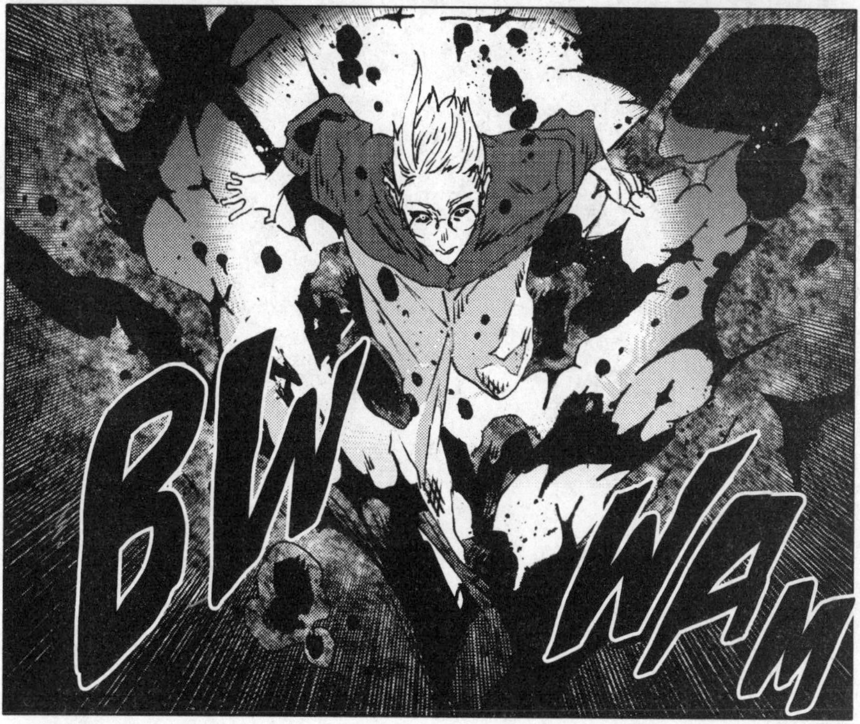
BWWAM

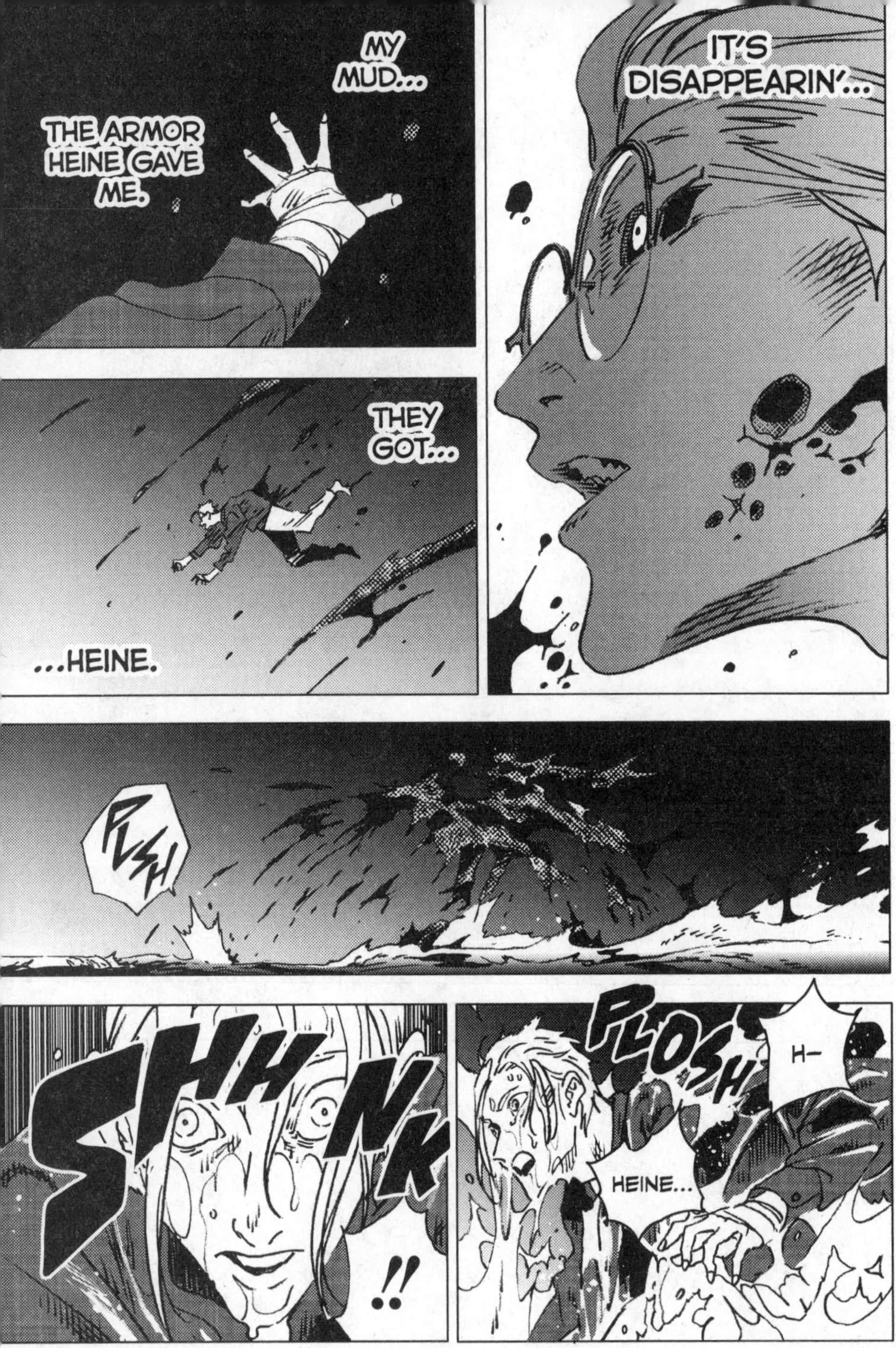

IT'S DISAPPEARIN'...
MY MUD...
THE ARMOR HEINE GAVE ME.
THEY GOT...
...HEINE.
PLSH
PLOSH
H—
HEINE...
SHHNK
!!

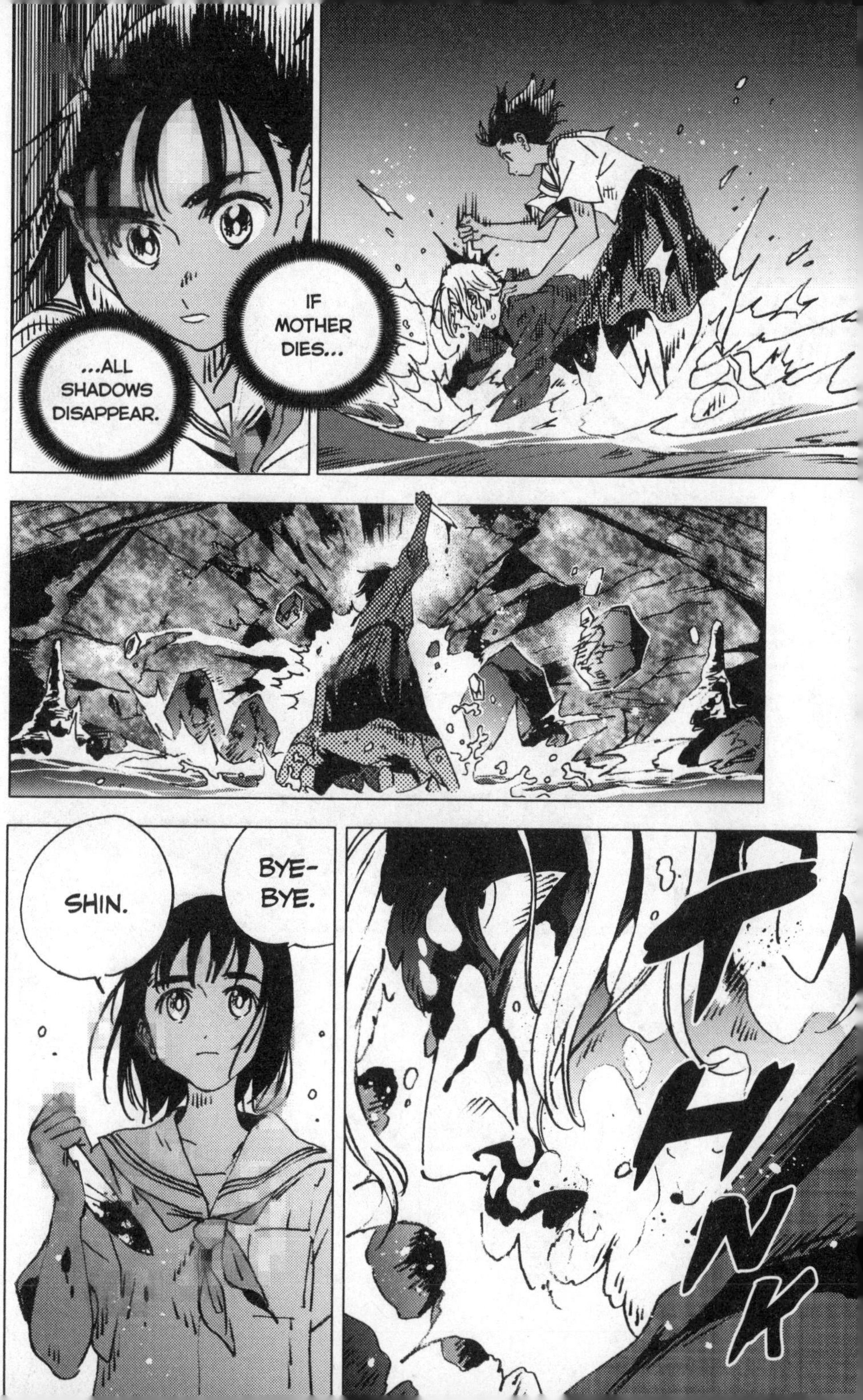
IF MOTHER DIES...
...ALL SHADOWS DISAPPEAR.
THNK
BYE-BYE.
SHIN.

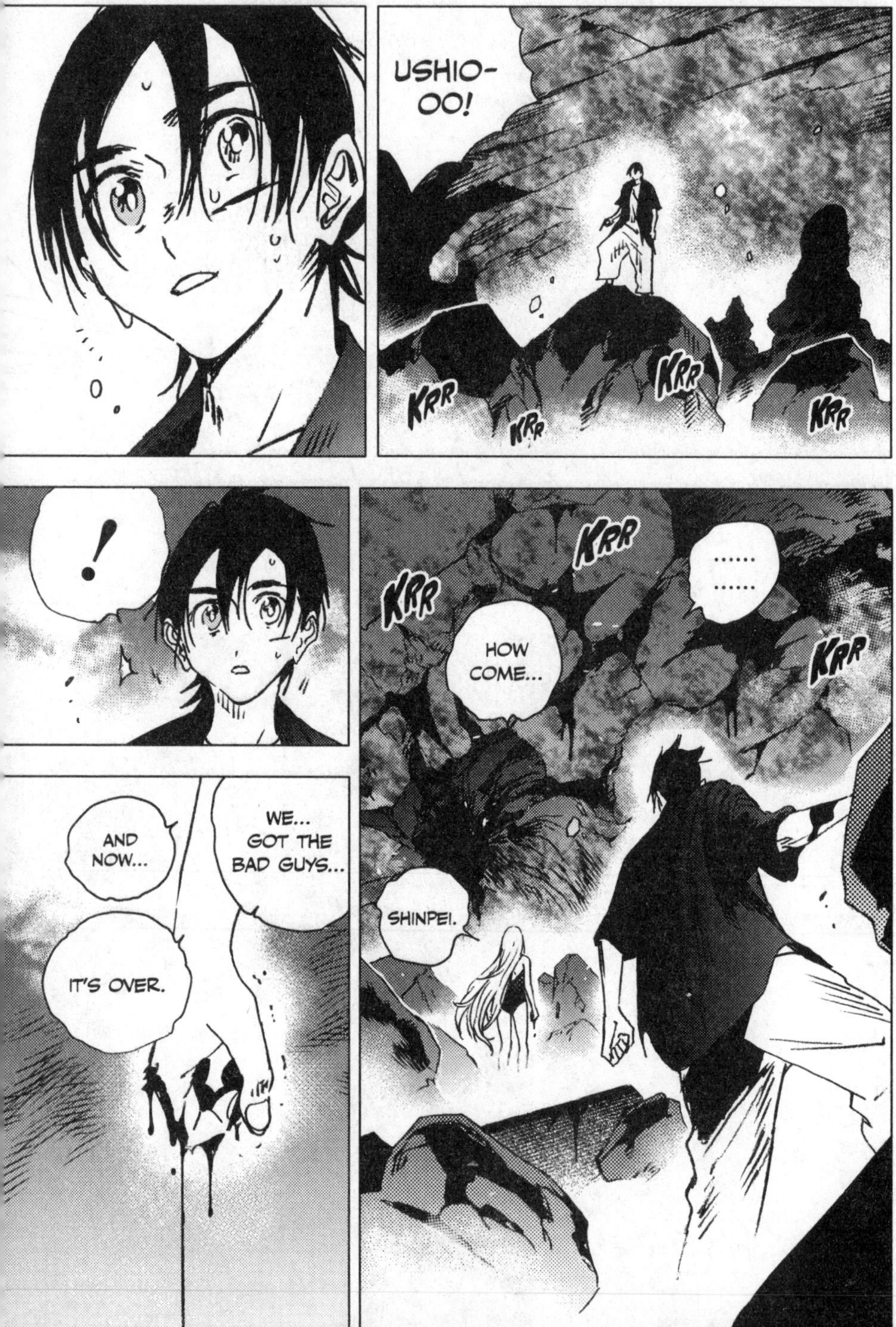
USHIO-OO!
KRR
KRR
KRR
KRR
KRR
......
......
KRR
KRR
HOW COME...
SHINPEI.
!
WE... GOT THE BAD GUYS...
AND NOW...
IT'S OVER.

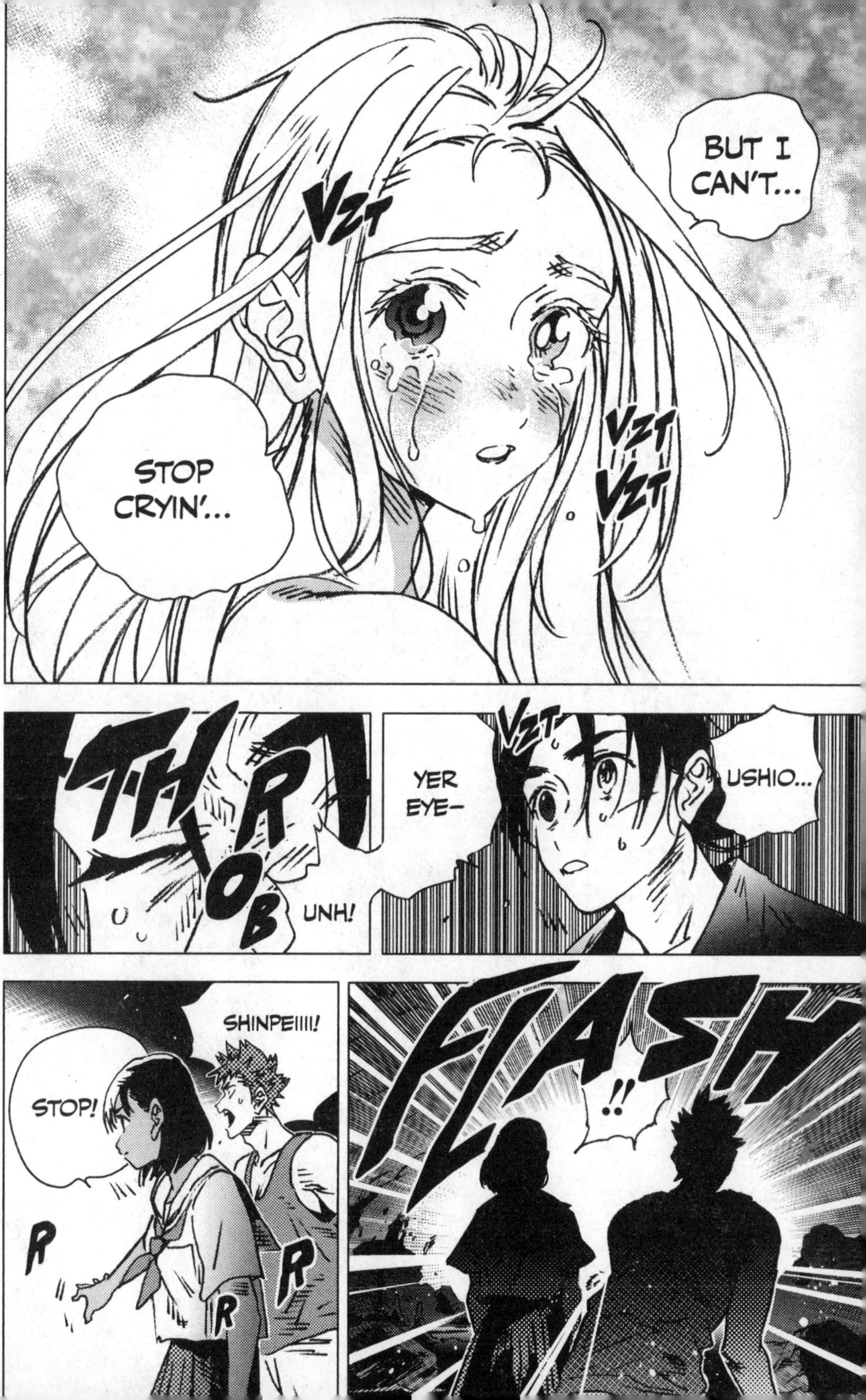
BUT I CAN'T...
VZT
VZT
VZT
STOP CRYIN'...
VZT
USHIO...
YER EYE-
THROB
UNH!
FLASH
!!
SHINPEIIII!
STOP!
RRRR

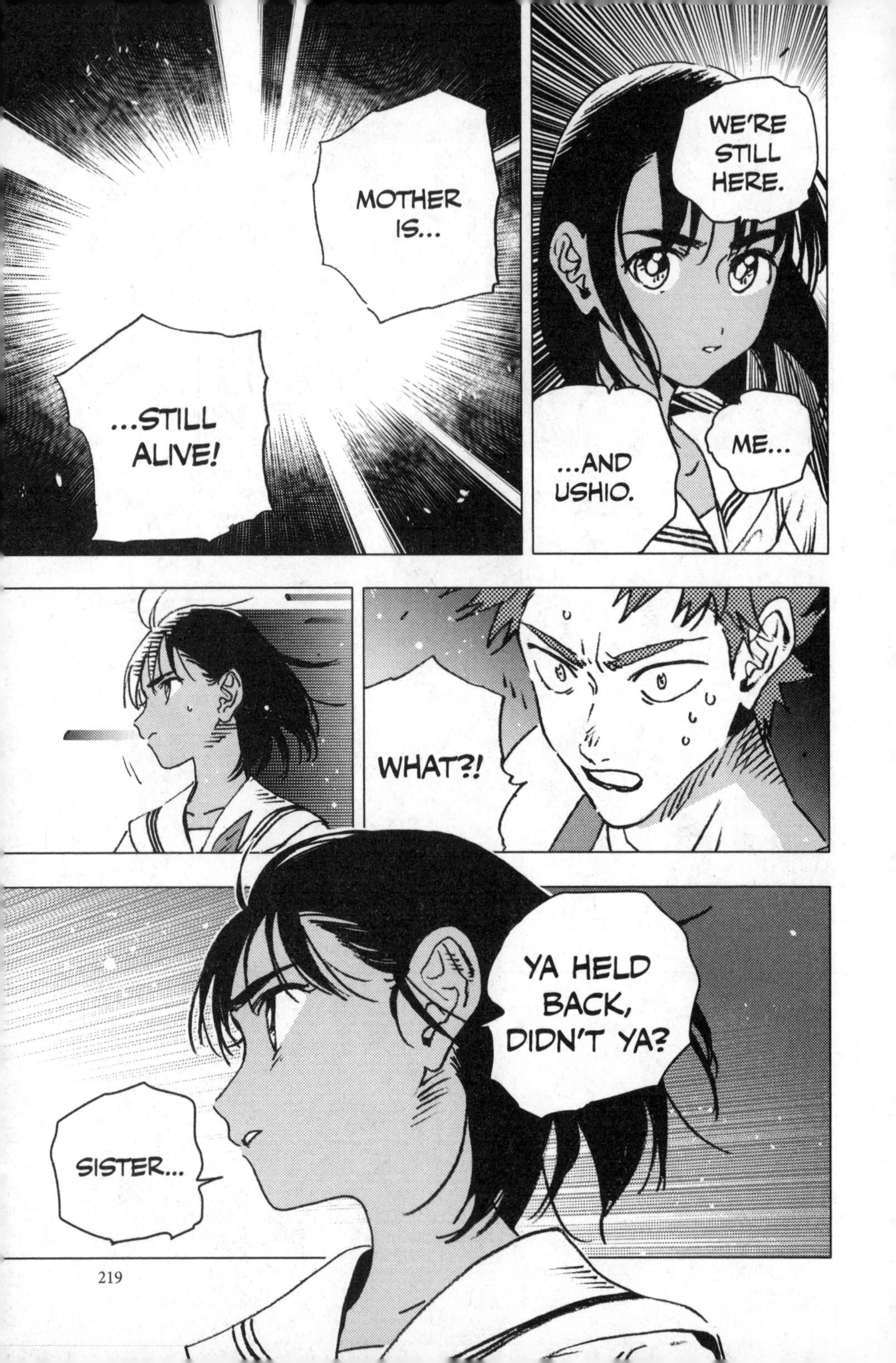
WE'RE STILL HERE.
ME...
...AND USHIO.
MOTHER IS...
...STILL ALIVE!
WHAT?!
YA HELD BACK, DIDN'T YA?
SISTER...

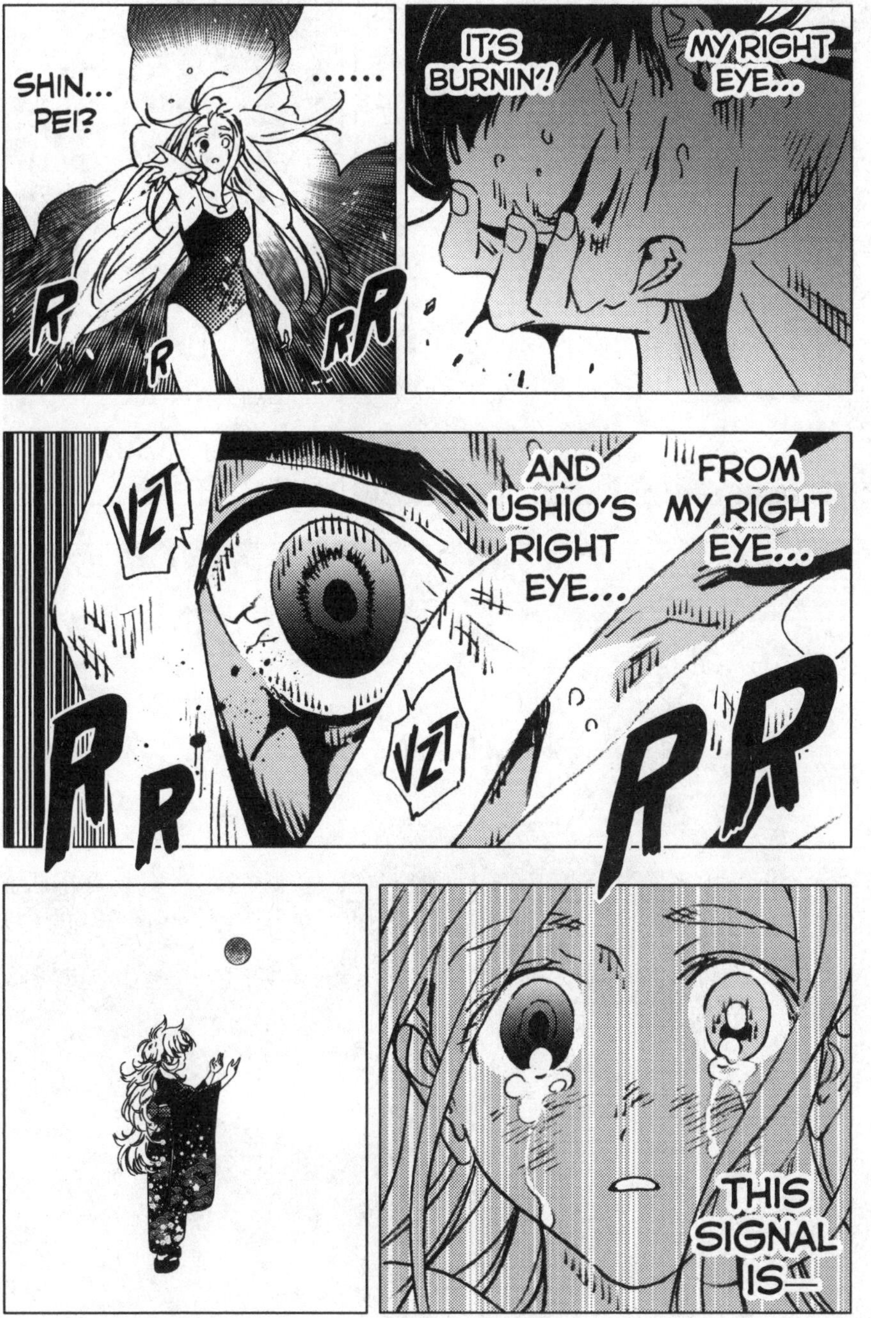
MY RIGHT EYE...
IT'S BURNIN'!
......
SHIN... PEI?
R
R
RR
FROM MY RIGHT EYE...
AND USHIO'S RIGHT EYE...
VZT
VZT
RR
RR
THIS SIGNAL IS—

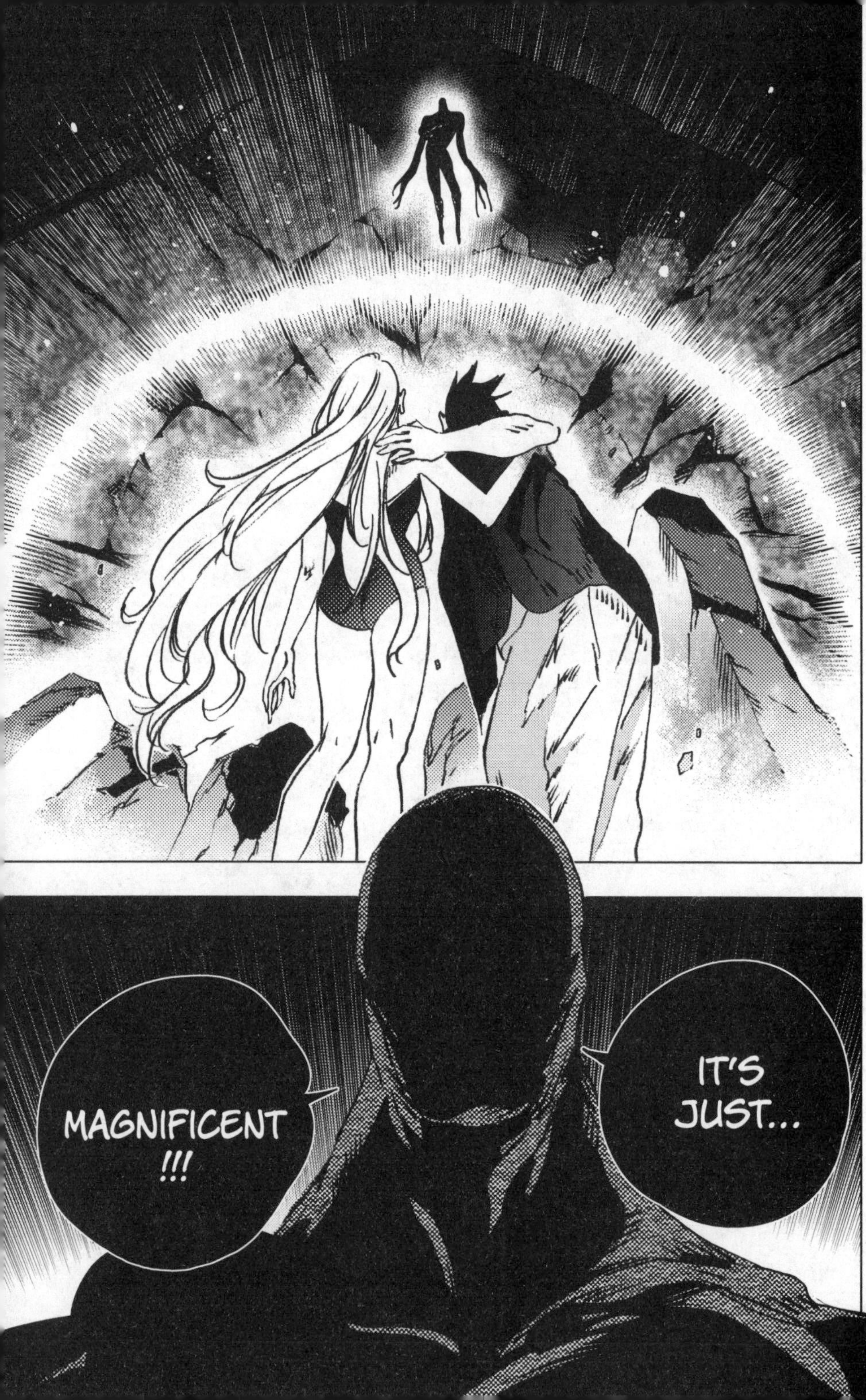
IT'S JUST...
MAGNIFICENT !!!

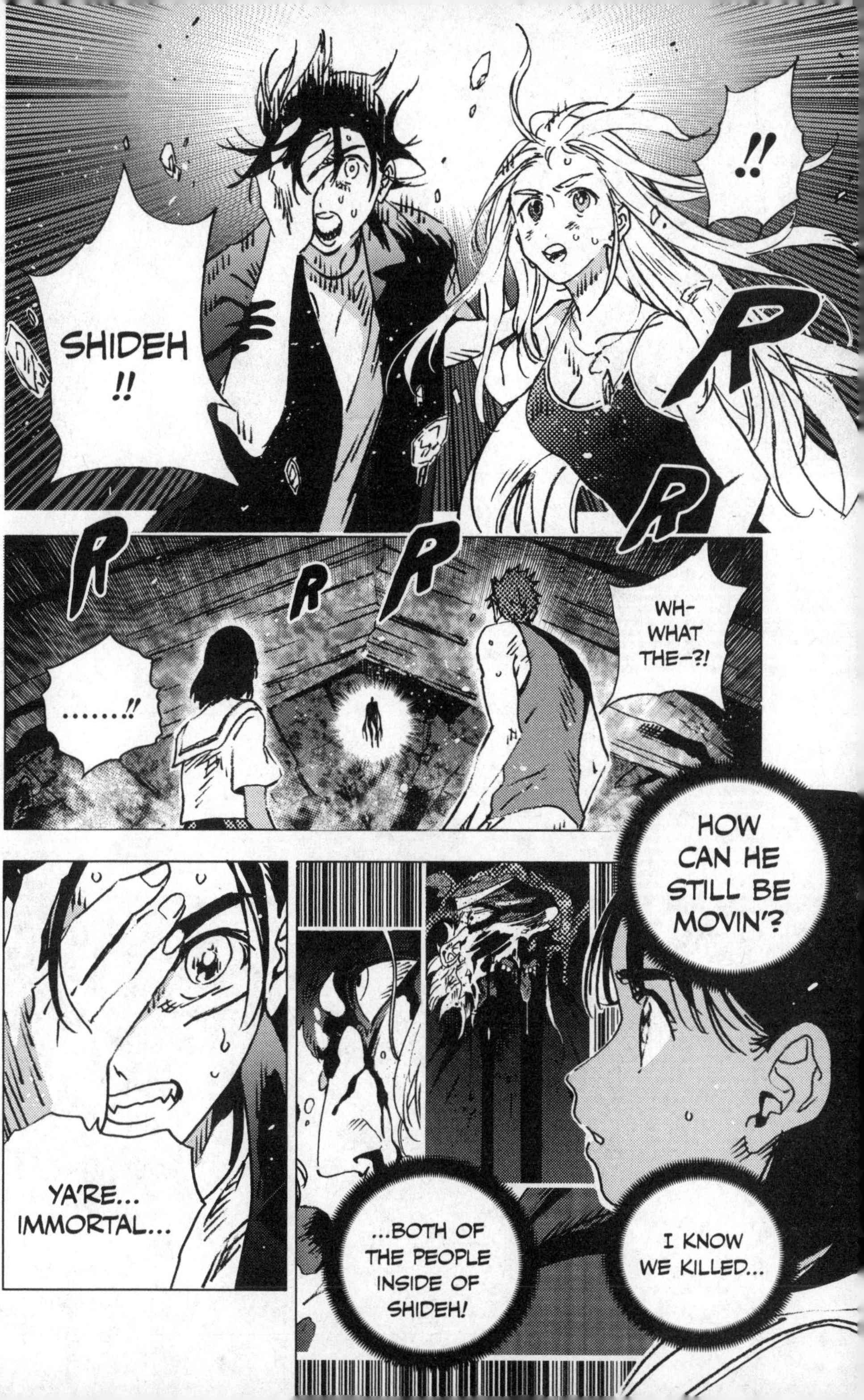
!!
SHIDEH !!
R R R R R
WH- WHAT THE-?!
.......!!
HOW CAN HE STILL BE MOVIN'?
I KNOW WE KILLED...
...BOTH OF THE PEOPLE INSIDE OF SHIDEH!
YA'RE... IMMORTAL...

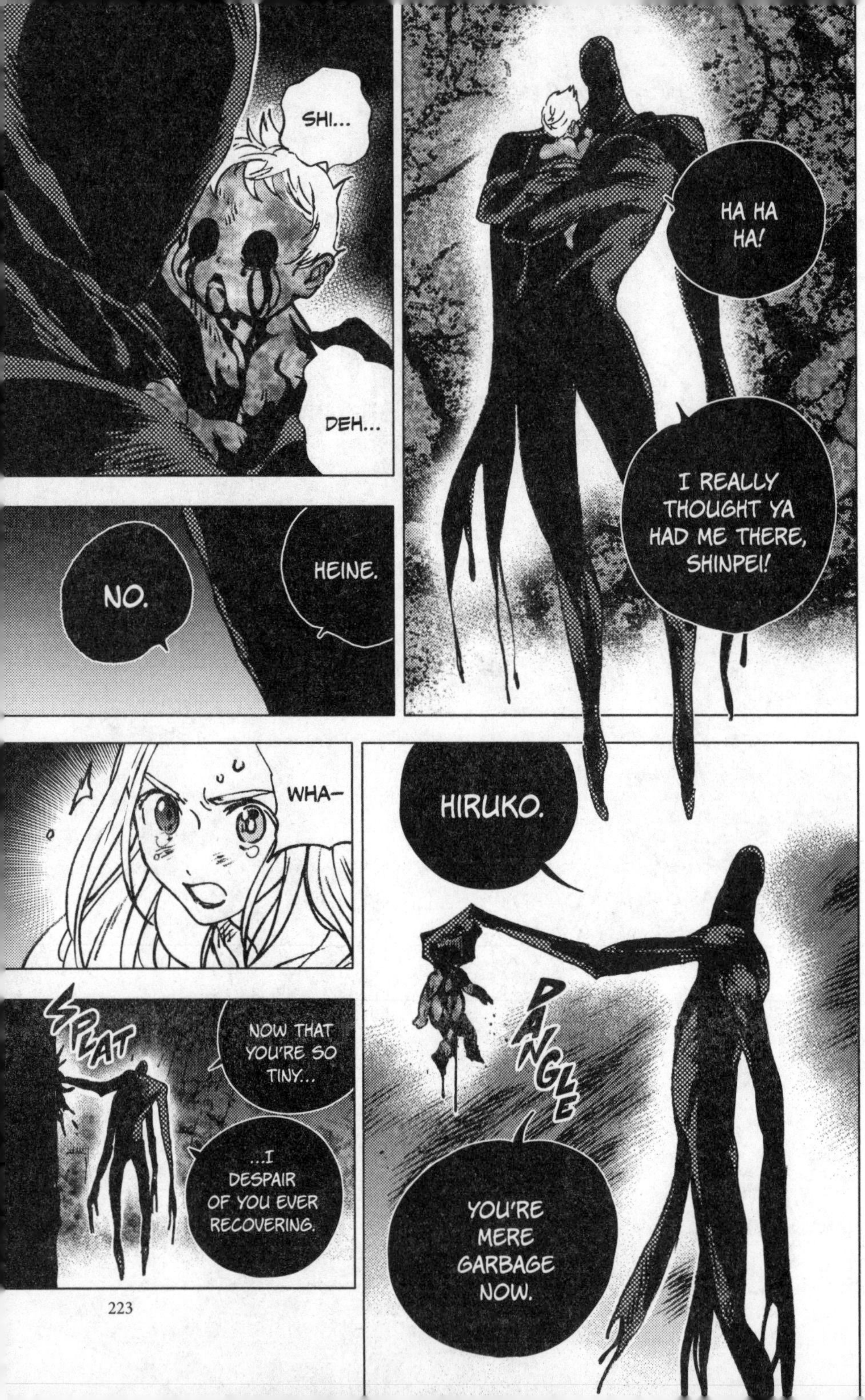
HA HA HA!
I REALLY THOUGHT YA HAD ME THERE, SHINPEI!
SHI...
DEH...
HEINE.
NO.
HIRUKO.
DANGLE
YOU'RE MERE GARBAGE NOW.
WHA-
SPLAT
NOW THAT YOU'RE SO TINY...
...I DESPAIR OF YOU EVER RECOVERING.

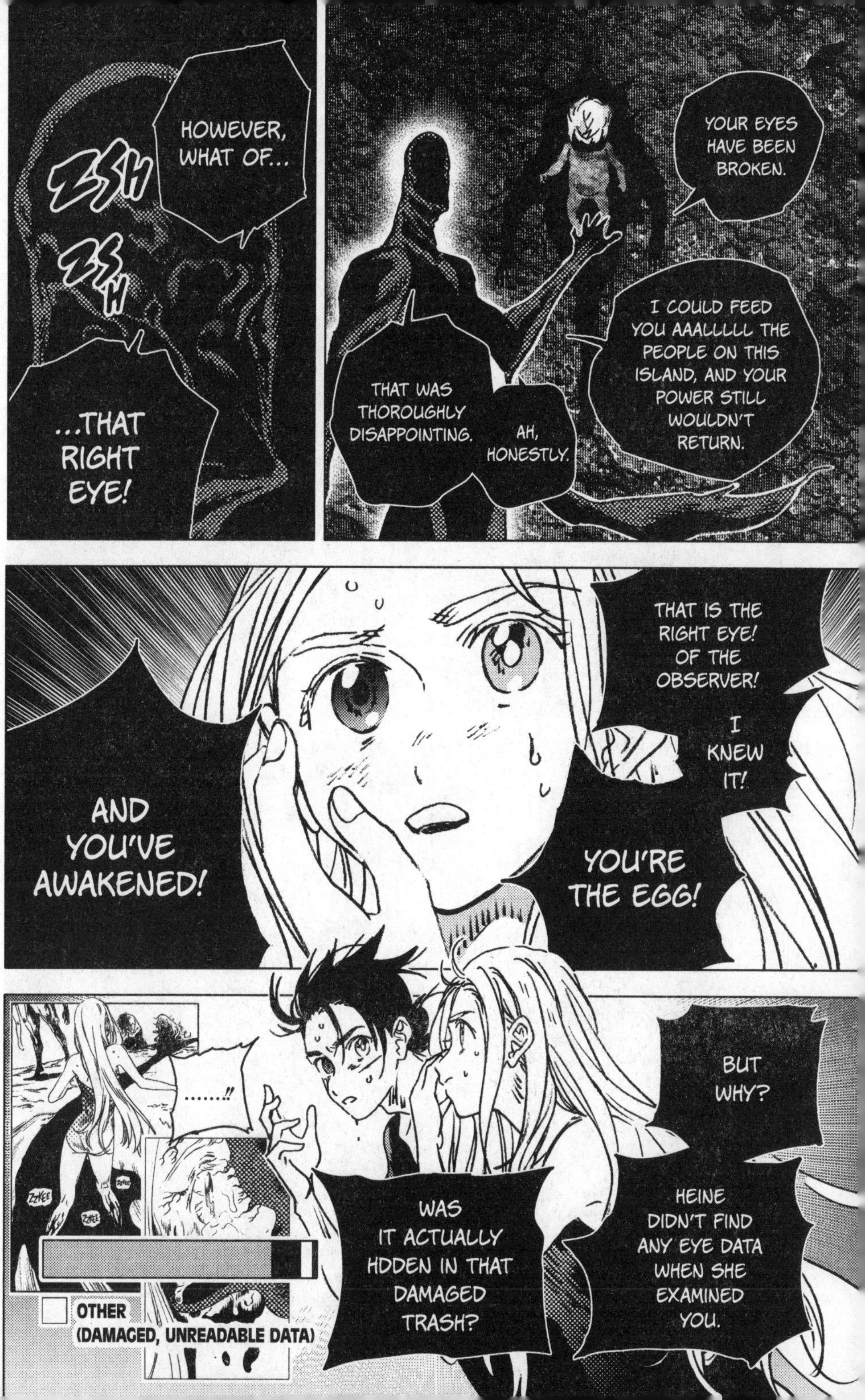
YOUR EYES HAVE BEEN BROKEN.
I COULD FEED YOU AAALLLLL THE PEOPLE ON THIS ISLAND, AND YOUR POWER STILL WOULDN'T RETURN.
AH, HONESTLY.
THAT WAS THOROUGHLY DISAPPOINTING.
HOWEVER, WHAT OF...
ZSH
ZSH
...THAT RIGHT EYE!
THAT IS THE RIGHT EYE! OF THE OBSERVER!
I KNEW IT!
YOU'RE THE EGG!
AND YOU'VE AWAKENED!
BUT WHY?
HEINE DIDN'T FIND ANY EYE DATA WHEN SHE EXAMINED YOU.
WAS IT ACTUALLY HDDEN IN THAT DAMAGED TRASH?
.......!!
ZZKEE
ZZKEE
ZZKEE
OTHER
(DAMAGED, UNREADABLE DATA)

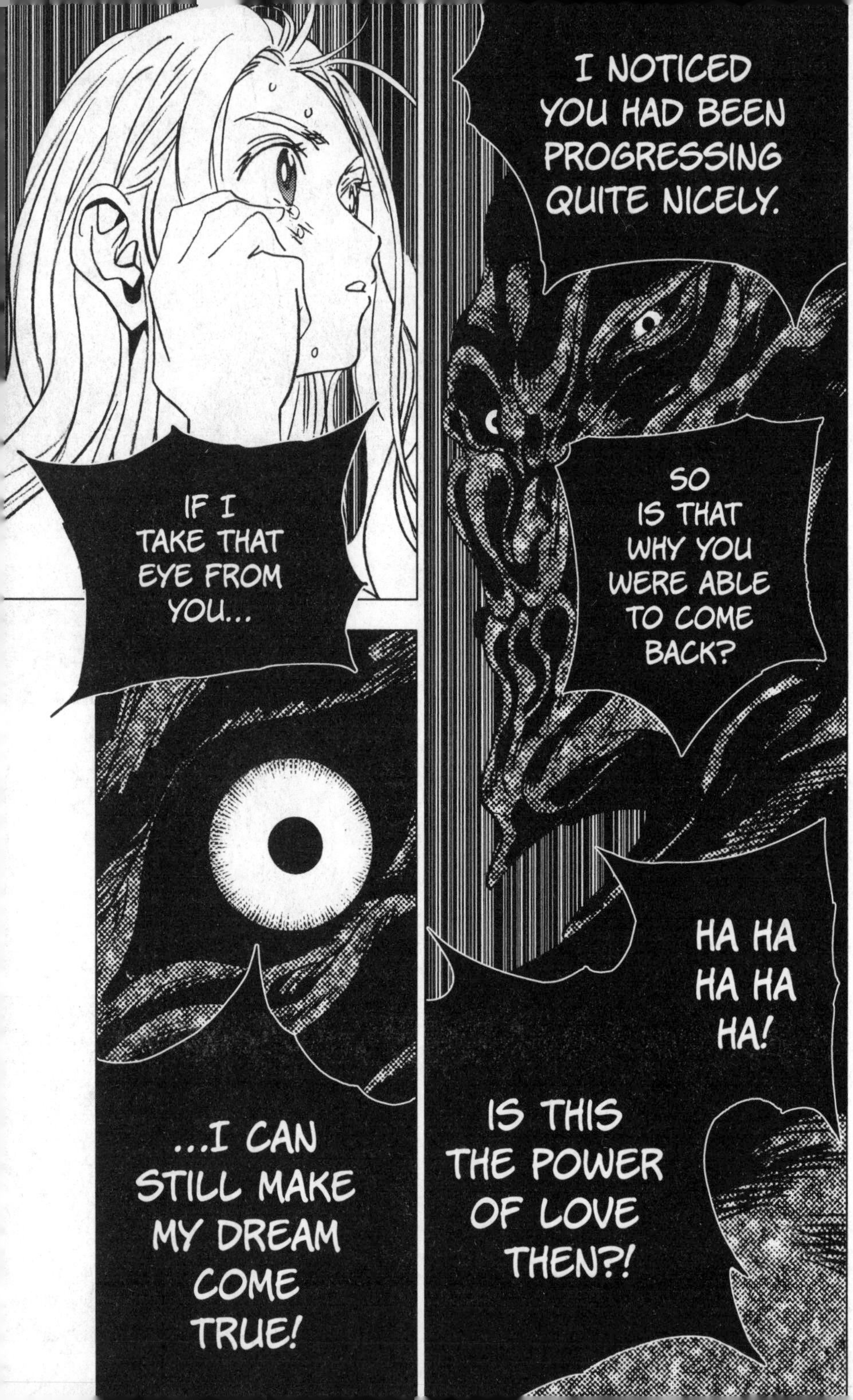
I NOTICED YOU HAD BEEN PROGRESSING QUITE NICELY.
SO IS THAT WHY YOU WERE ABLE TO COME BACK?
HA HA HA HA HA!
IS THIS THE POWER OF LOVE THEN?!
IF I TAKE THAT EYE FROM YOU...
...I CAN STILL MAKE MY DREAM COME TRUE!

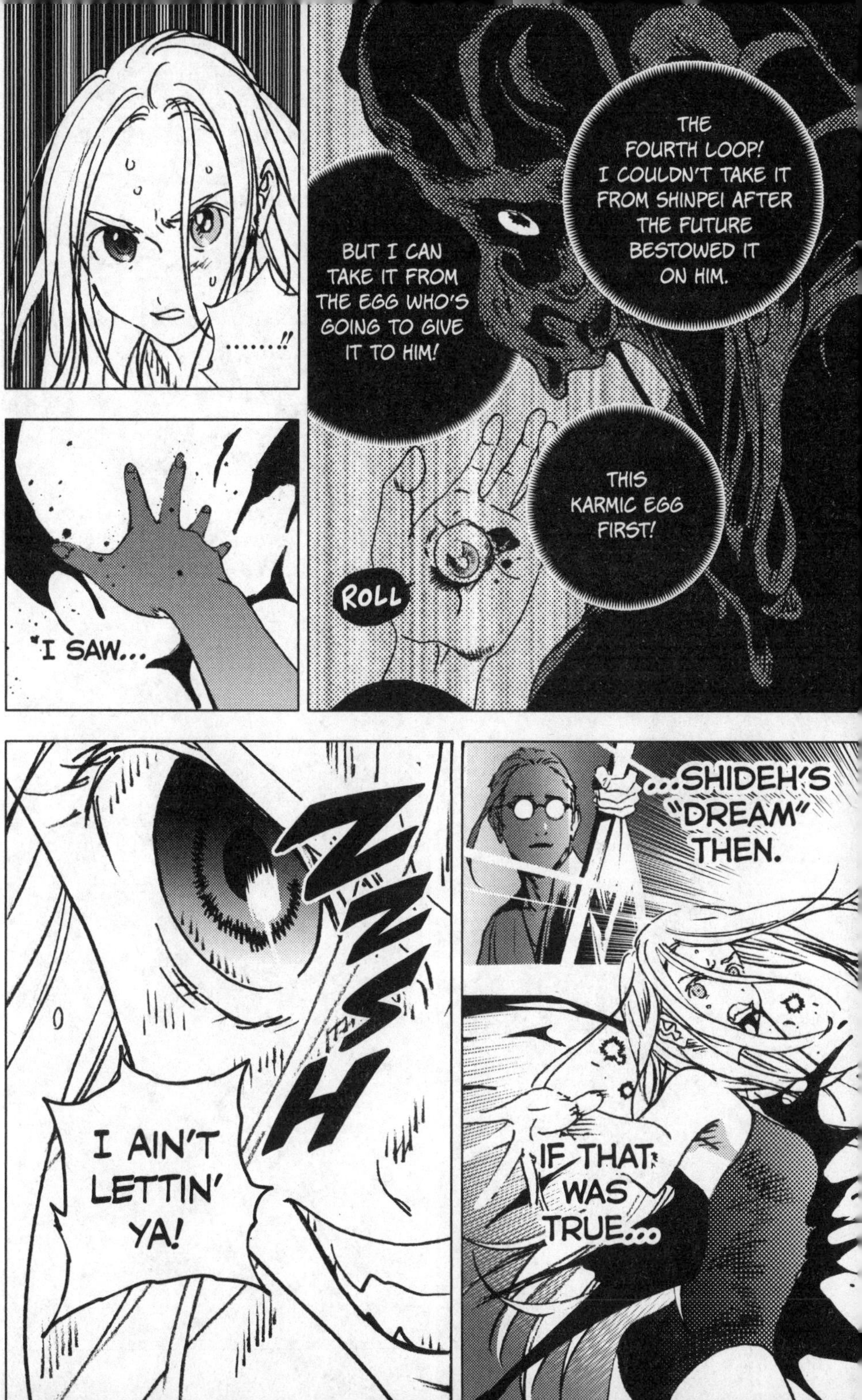

THE FOURTH LOOP! I COULDN'T TAKE IT FROM SHINPEI AFTER THE FUTURE BESTOWED IT ON HIM.
BUT I CAN TAKE IT FROM THE EGG WHO'S GOING TO GIVE IT TO HIM!
THIS KARMIC EGG FIRST!
ROLL
.......!!
"I SAW...
...SHIDEH'S "DREAM" THEN.
IF THAT WAS TRUE...
I AIN'T LETTIN' YA!

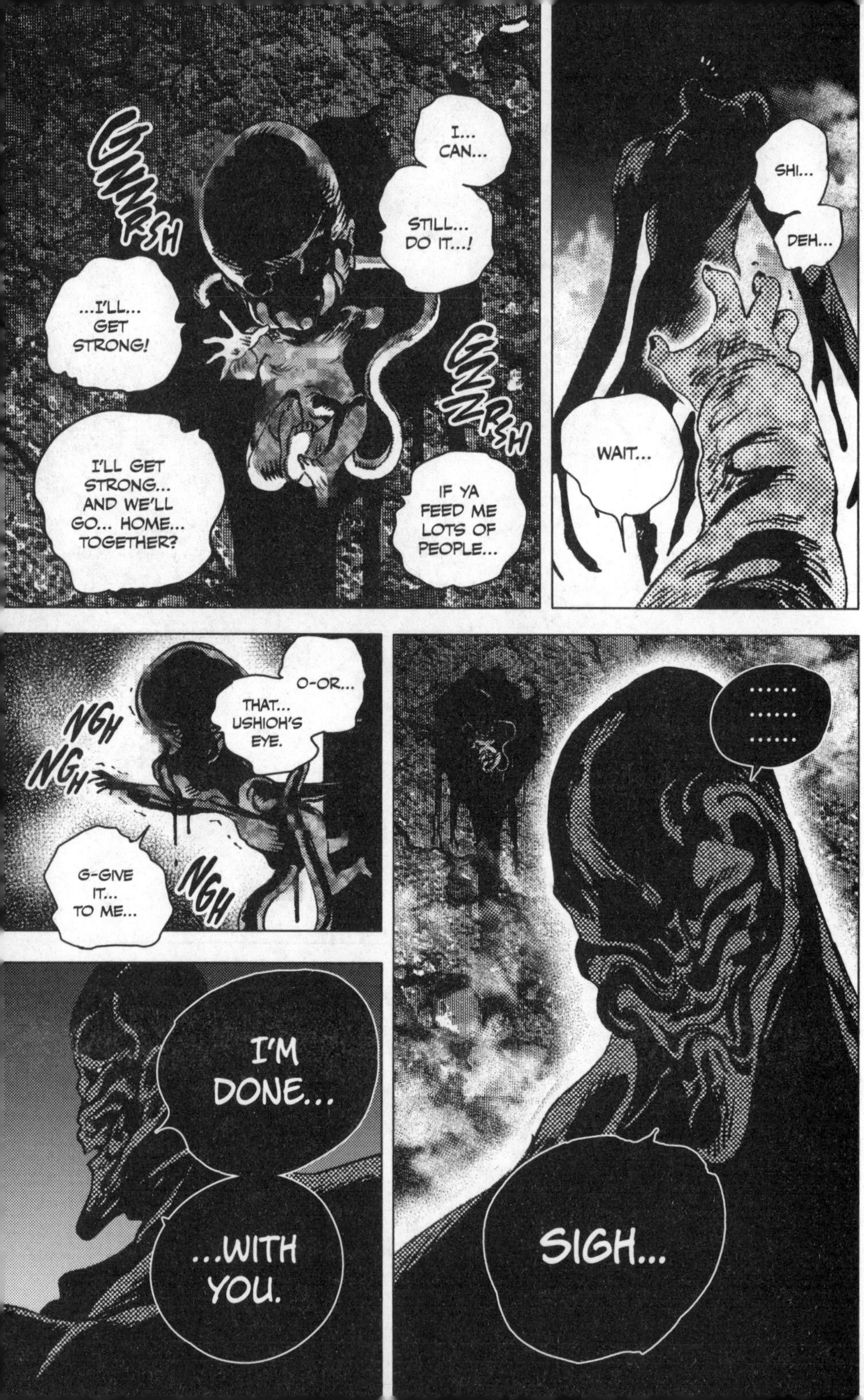
SHI...
DEH...
WAIT...
I... CAN...
STILL... DO IT...!
GNNRSH
...I'LL... GET STRONG!
GNNRSH
IF YA FEED ME LOTS OF PEOPLE...
I'LL GET STRONG... AND WE'LL GO... HOME... TOGETHER?
......
SIGH...
O-OR... THAT... USHIOH'S EYE.
NGH NGH
G-GIVE IT... TO ME...
NGH
I'M DONE...
...WITH YOU.

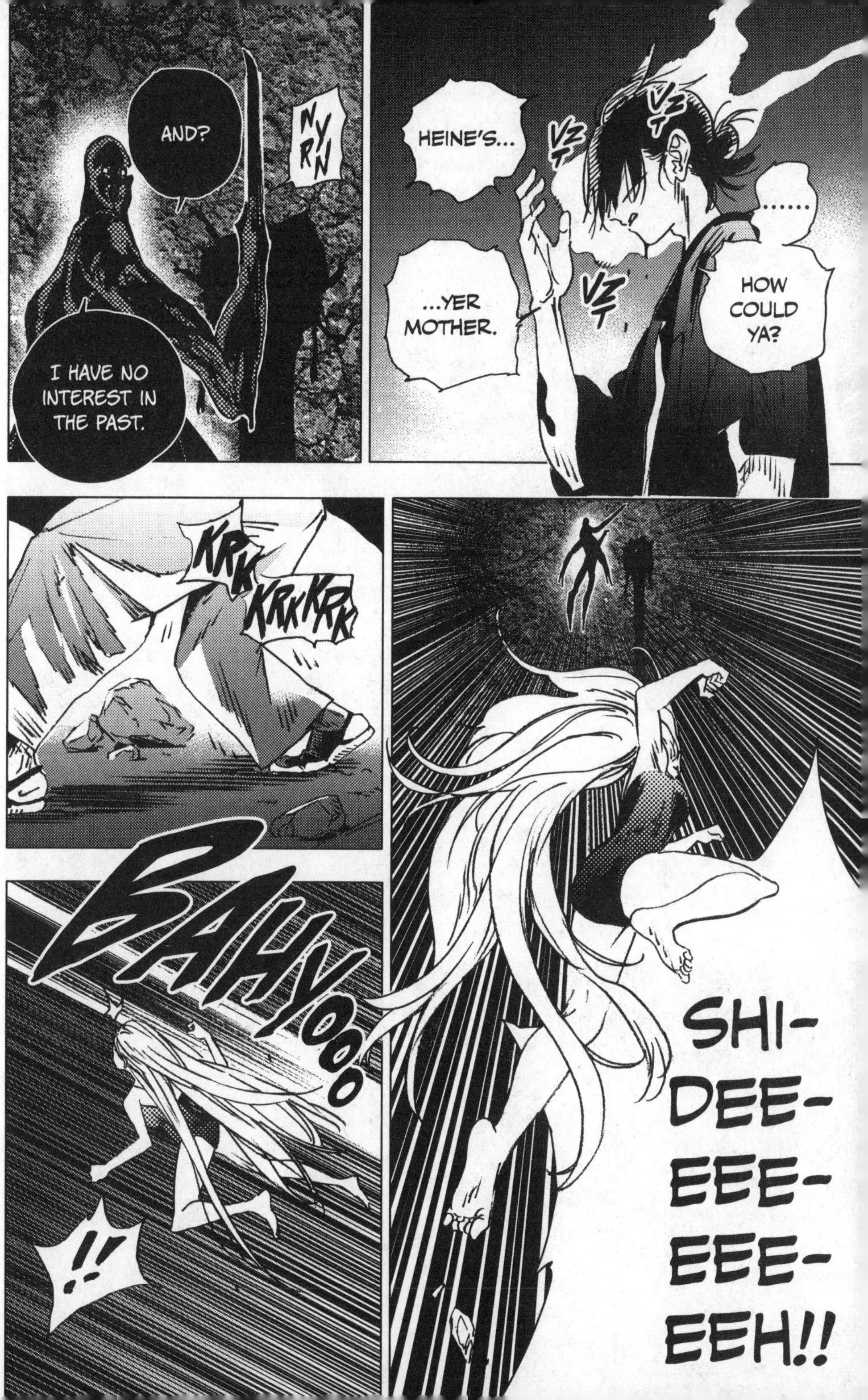
VZT
......
HOW COULD YA?
HEINE'S...
VZT
VZT
...YER MOTHER.
NYRN
AND?
I HAVE NO INTEREST IN THE PAST.
SHI-DEEE-EEE-EEE-EEH!!
KRK
KRKKRK
BAHYOOO
!!

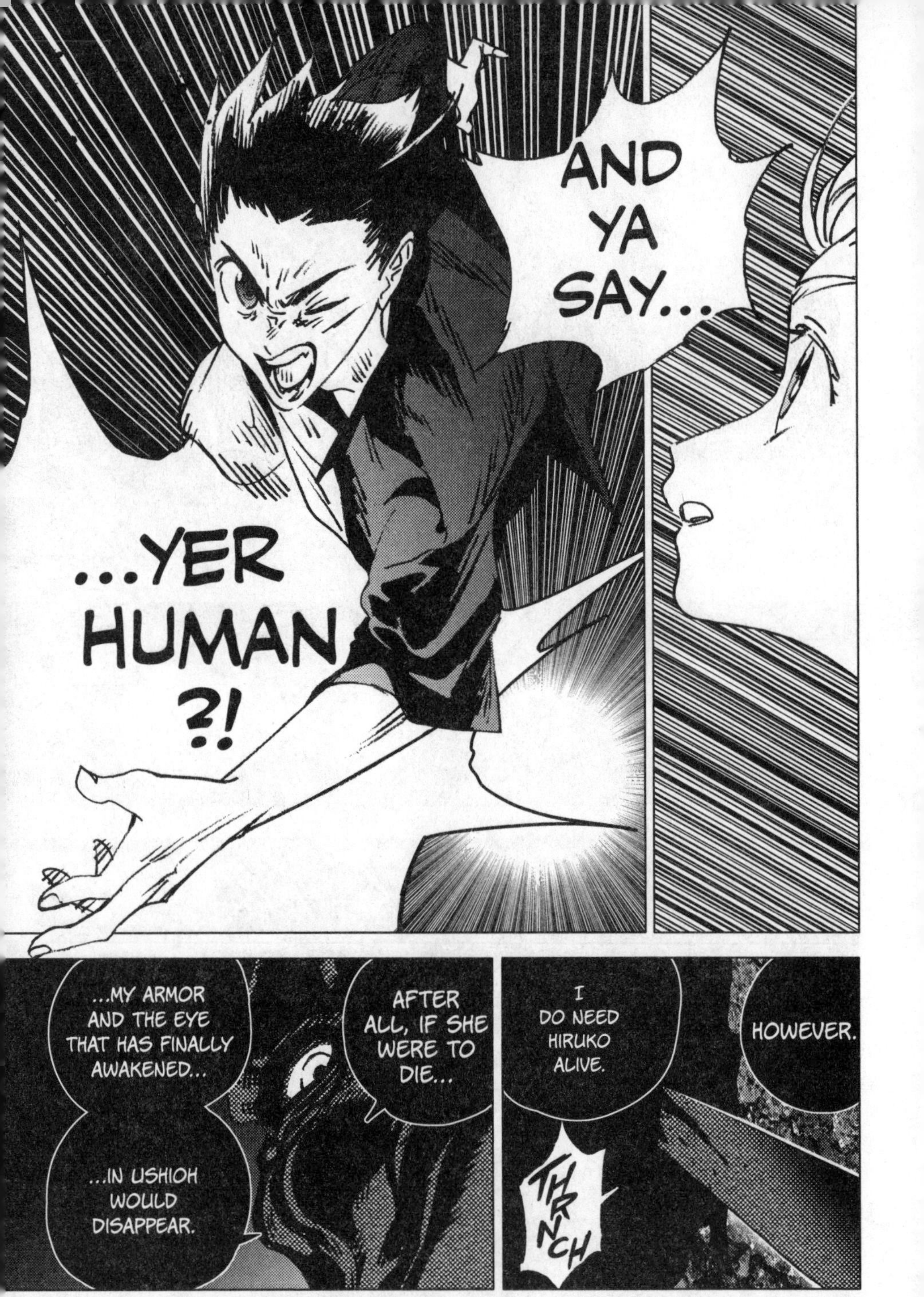
AND YA SAY...
...YER HUMAN ?!
HOWEVER.
I DO NEED HIRUKO ALIVE.
THRNCH
AFTER ALL, IF SHE WERE TO DIE...
...MY ARMOR AND THE EYE THAT HAS FINALLY AWAKENED...
...IN USHIOH WOULD DISAPPEAR.

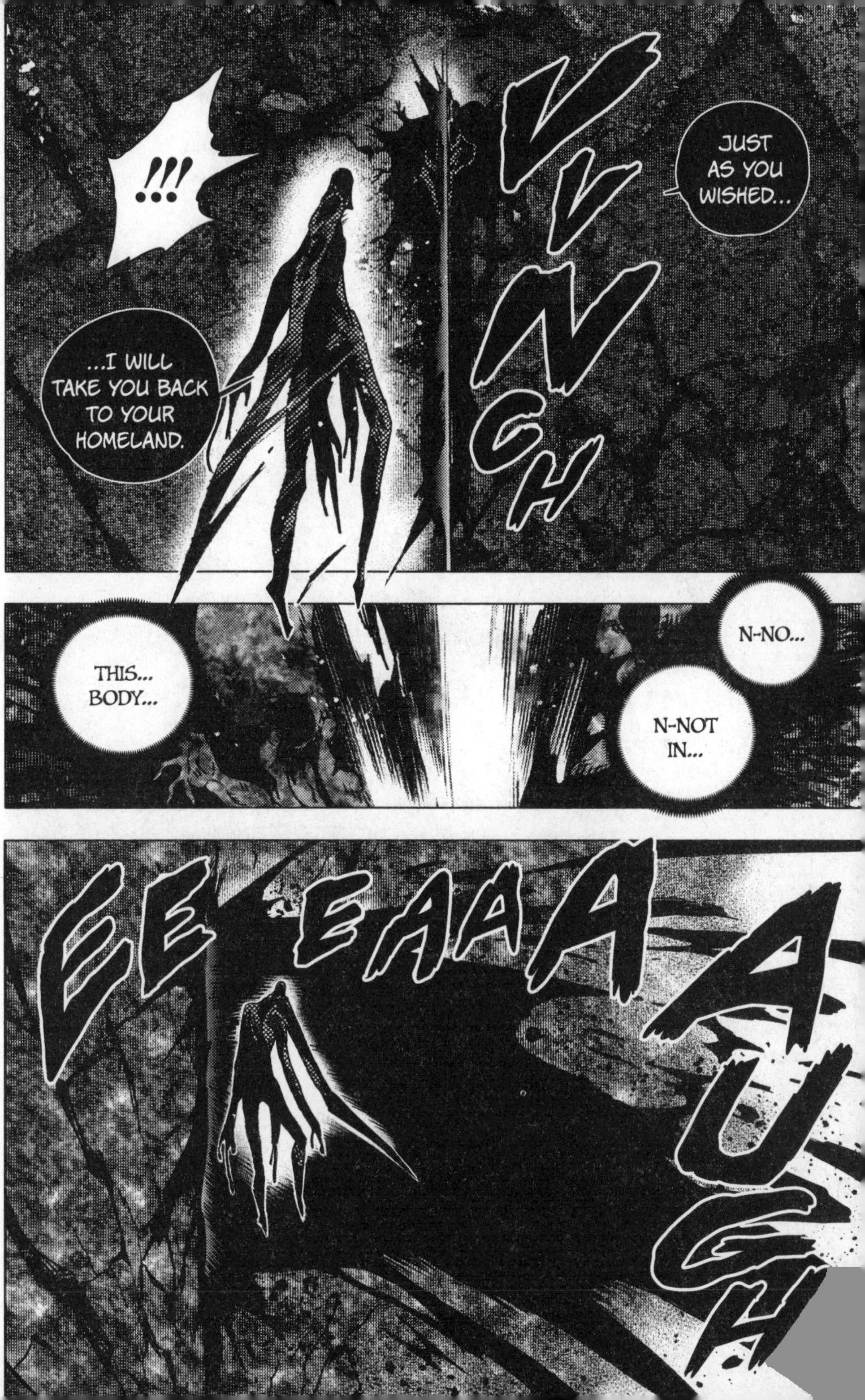
JUST AS YOU WISHED...
VVNNCH
!!!
...I WILL TAKE YOU BACK TO YOUR HOMELAND.
N-NO...
N-NOT IN...
THIS... BODY...
EEEAAAAAUGH

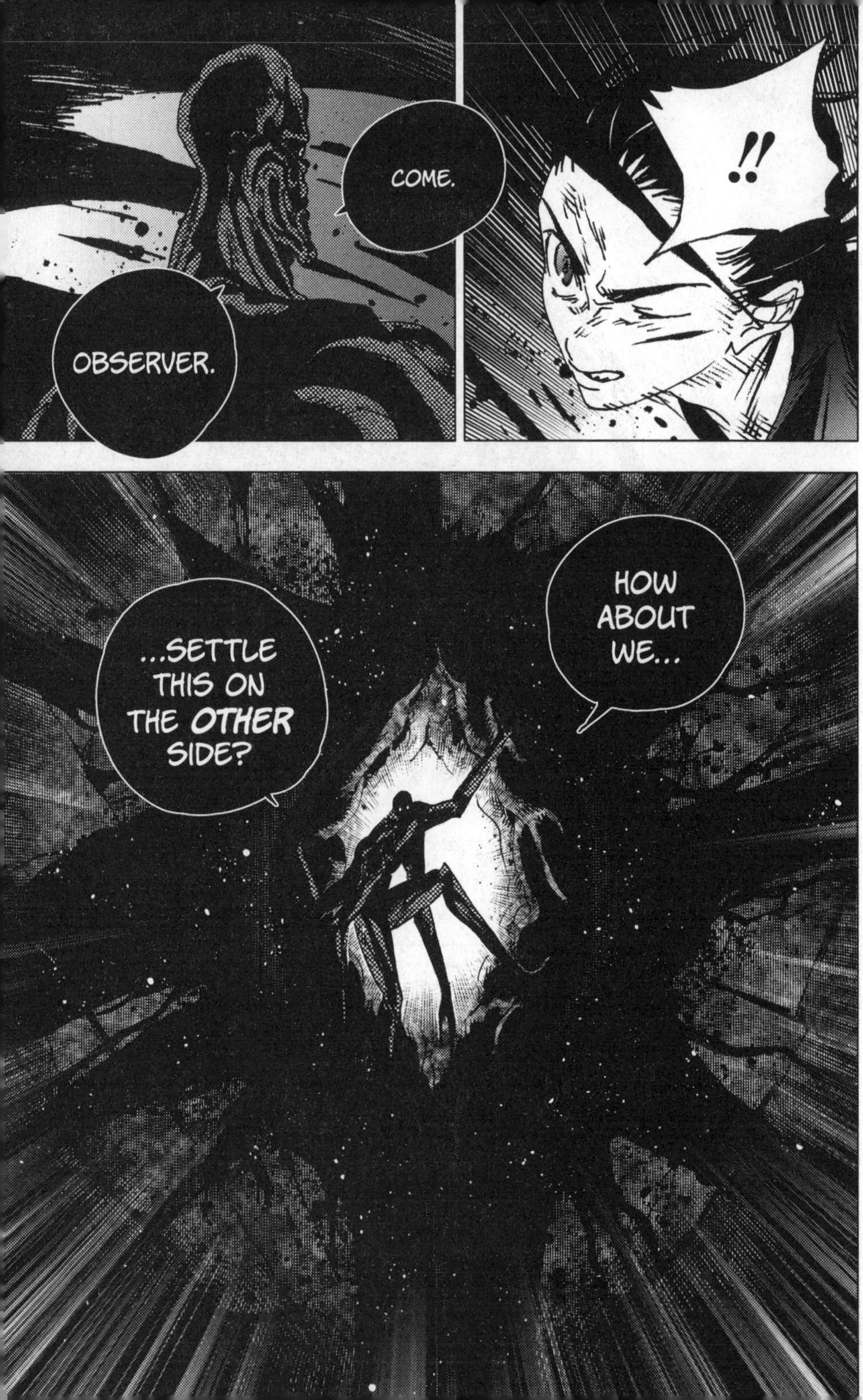
!!
COME.
OBSERVER.
HOW ABOUT WE...
...SETTLE THIS ON THE OTHER SIDE?

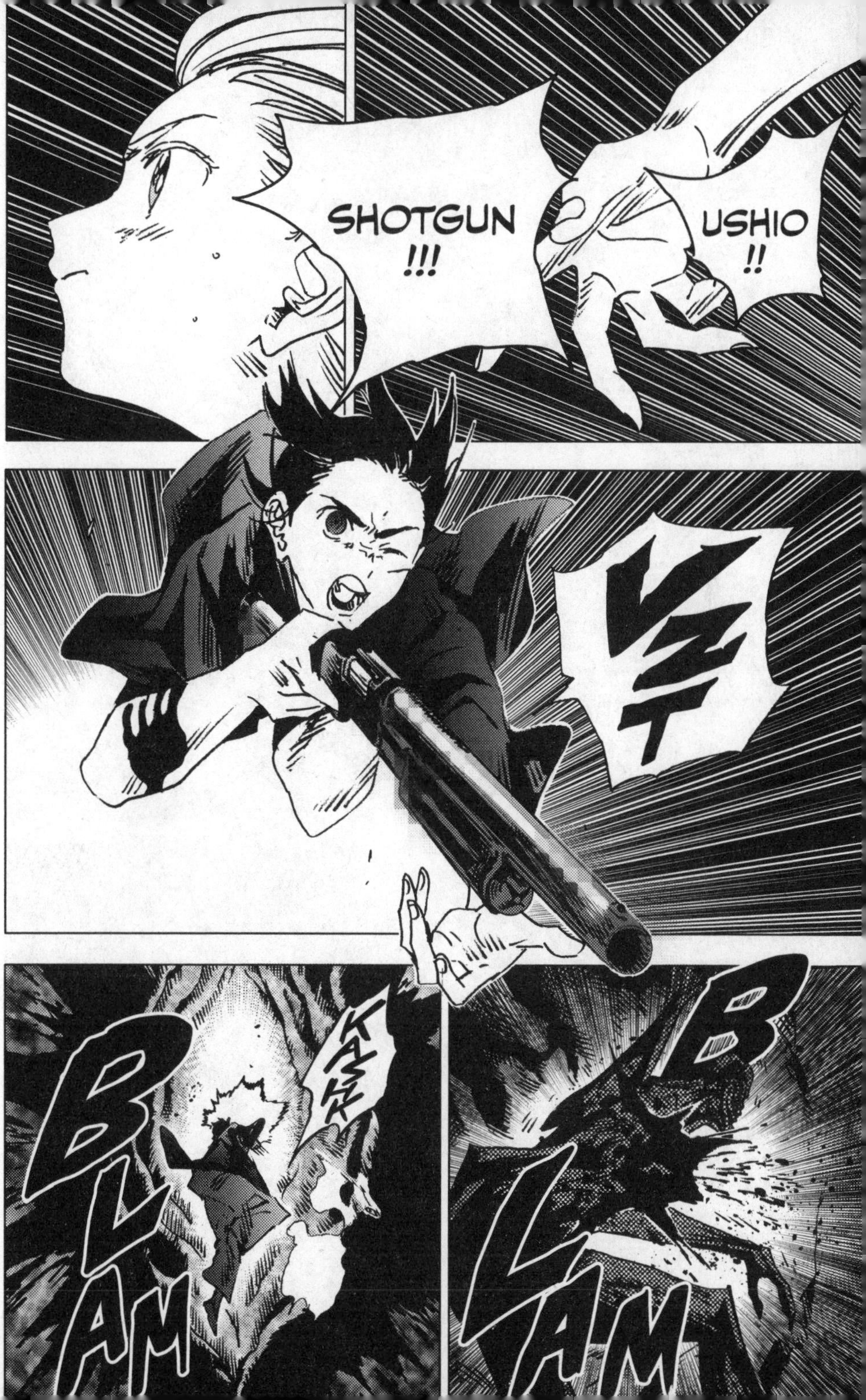
USHIO
!!
SHOTGUN
!!!
BLAM
KASHK
BLAM

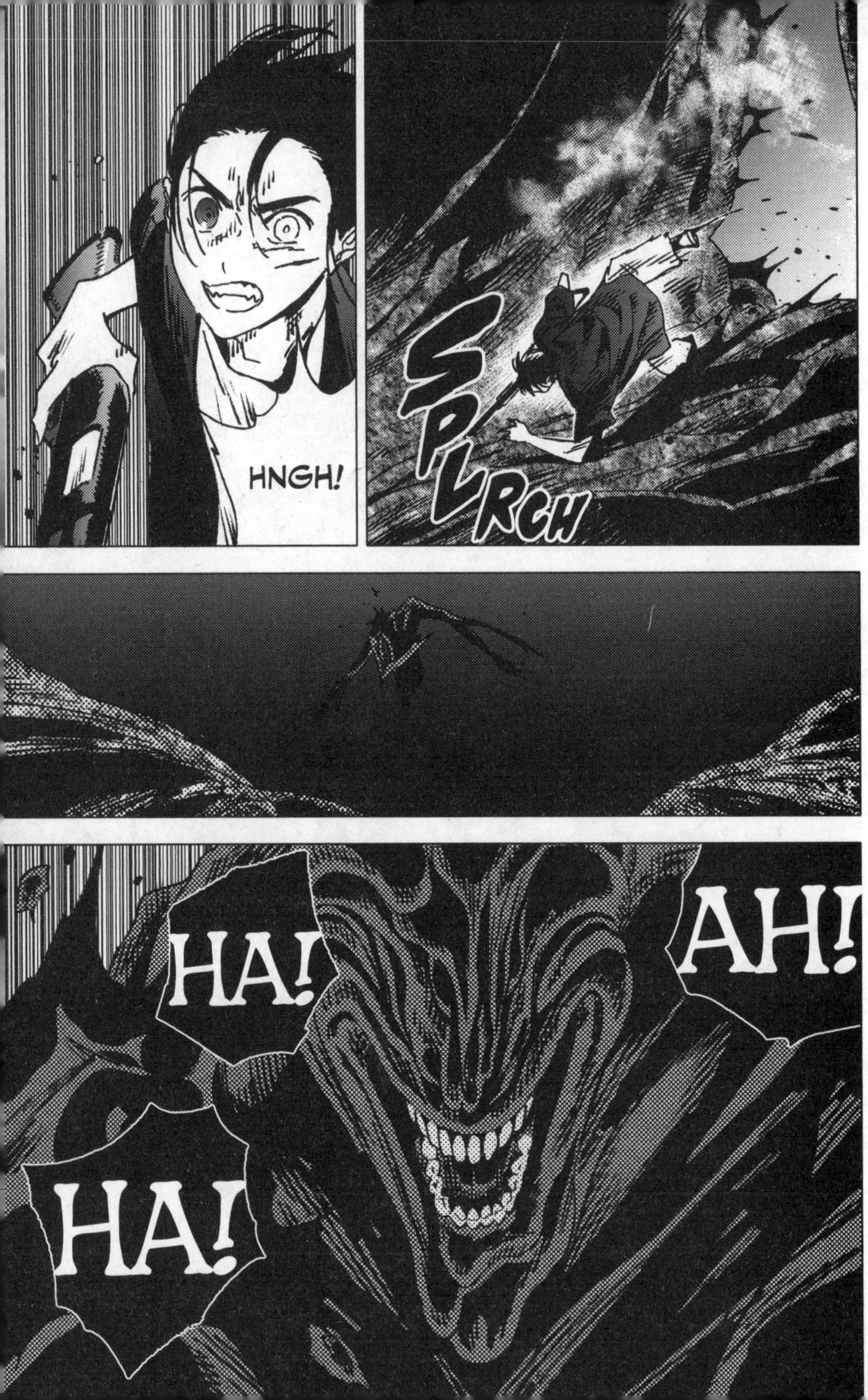
SPLRCH
HNGH!
AH!
HA!
HA!

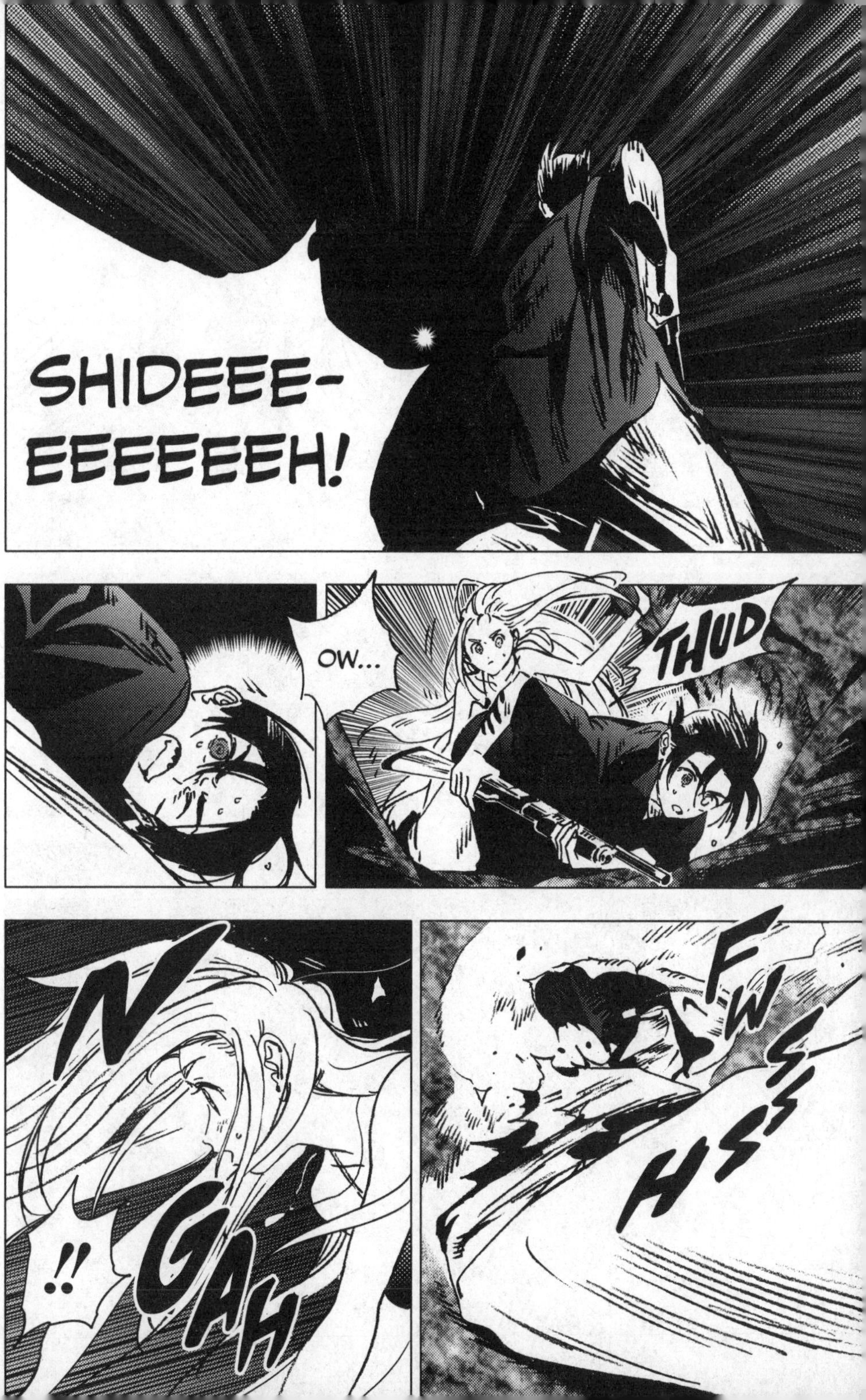
SHIDEEEE-
EEEEEEEH!
THUD
OW...
FWSSSH
!!
NGAH

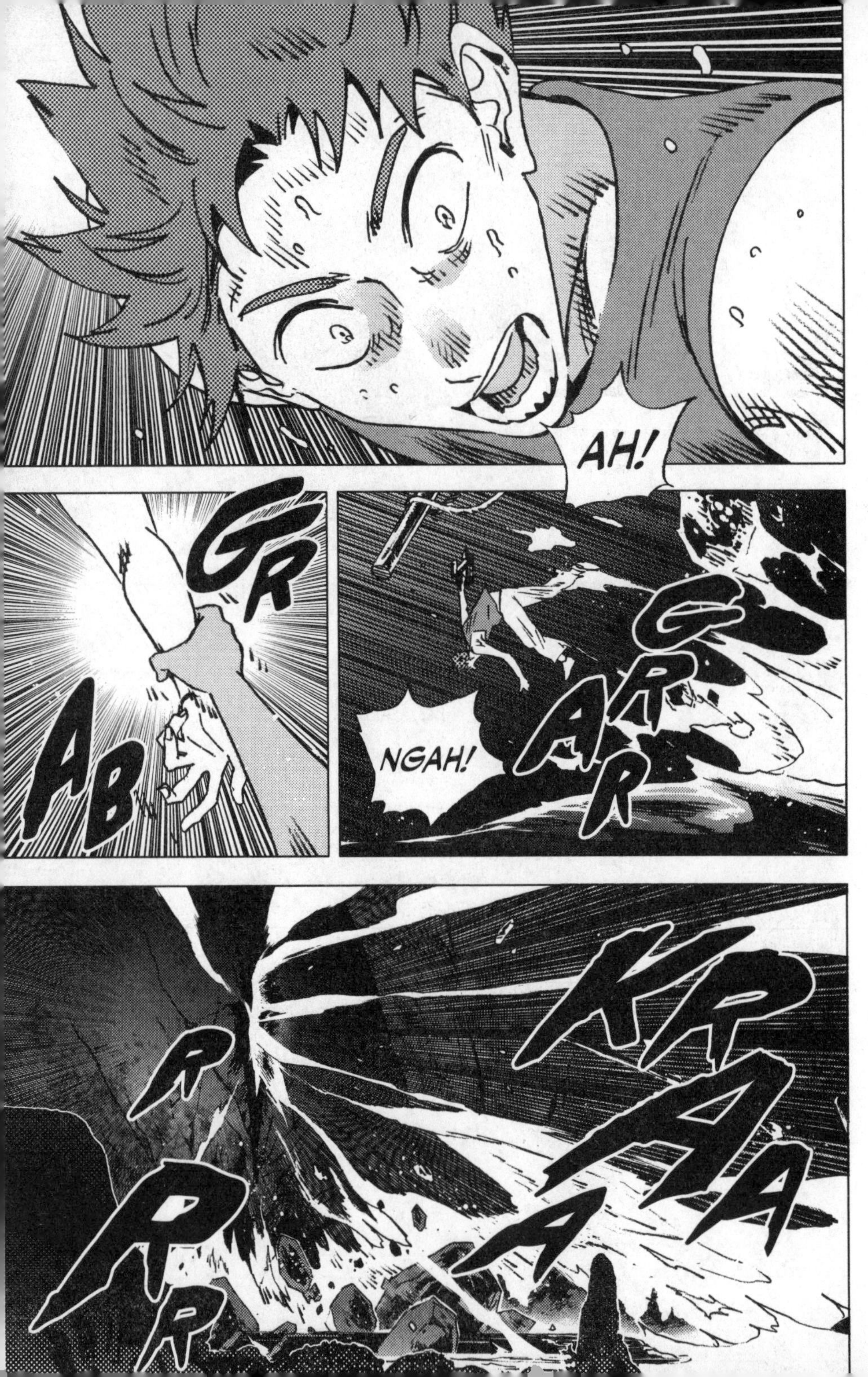
AH!
GRARR
NGAH!
GR
AB
KRAAAA
RRRR

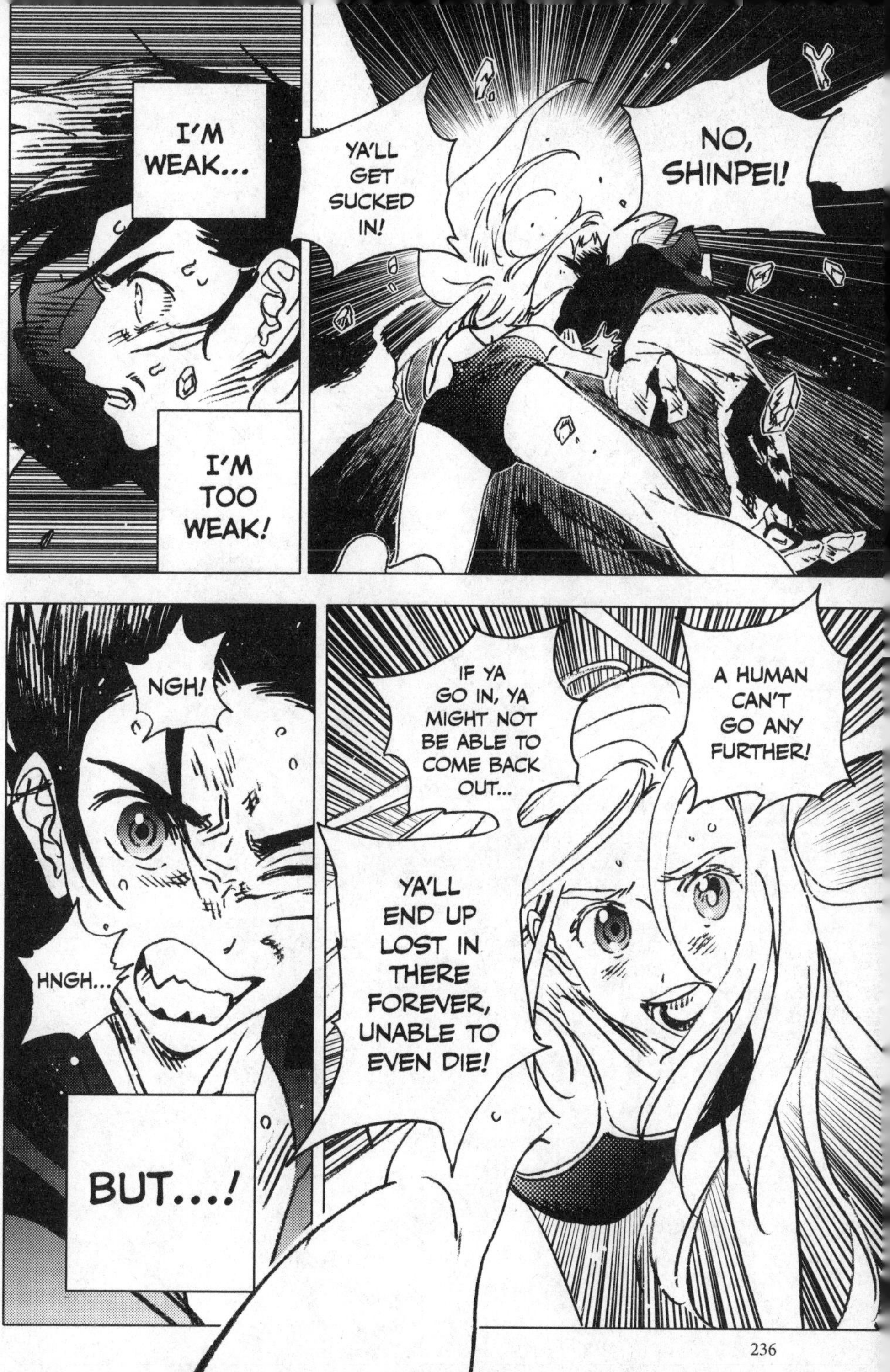
NO, SHINPEI!
YA'LL GET SUCKED IN!
I'M WEAK...
I'M TOO WEAK!
A HUMAN CAN'T GO ANY FURTHER!
IF YA GO IN, YA MIGHT NOT BE ABLE TO COME BACK OUT...
YA'LL END UP LOST IN THERE FOREVER, UNABLE TO EVEN DIE!
NGH!
HNGH...
BUT...!

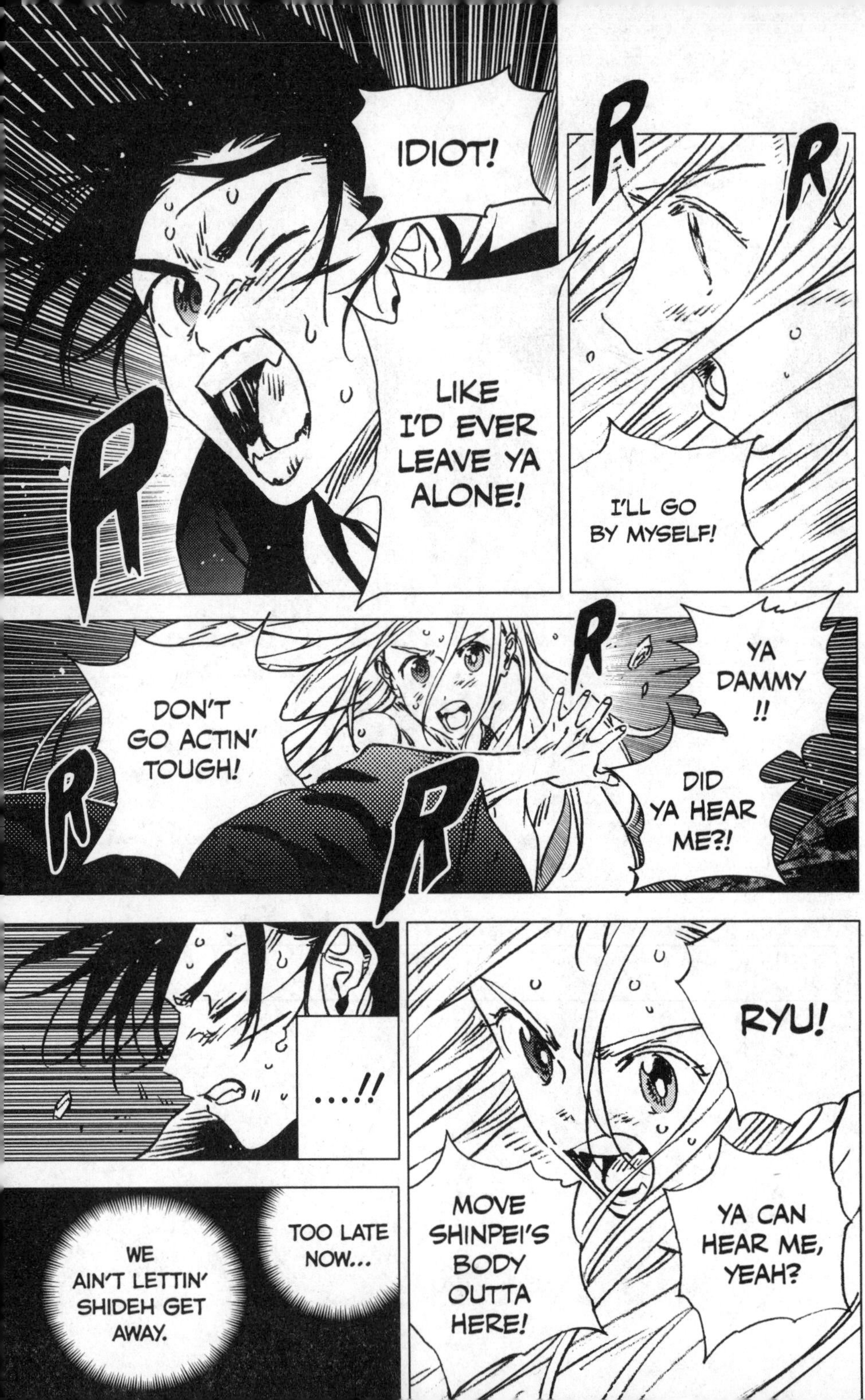
R
R
I'LL GO BY MYSELF!
IDIOT!
LIKE I'D EVER LEAVE YA ALONE!
R
YA DAMMY !!
DID YA HEAR ME?!
R
DON'T GO ACTIN' TOUGH!
R
R
RYU!
YA CAN HEAR ME, YEAH?
MOVE SHINPEI'S BODY OUTTA HERE!
...!!
TOO LATE NOW...
WE AIN'T LETTIN' SHIDEH GET AWAY.

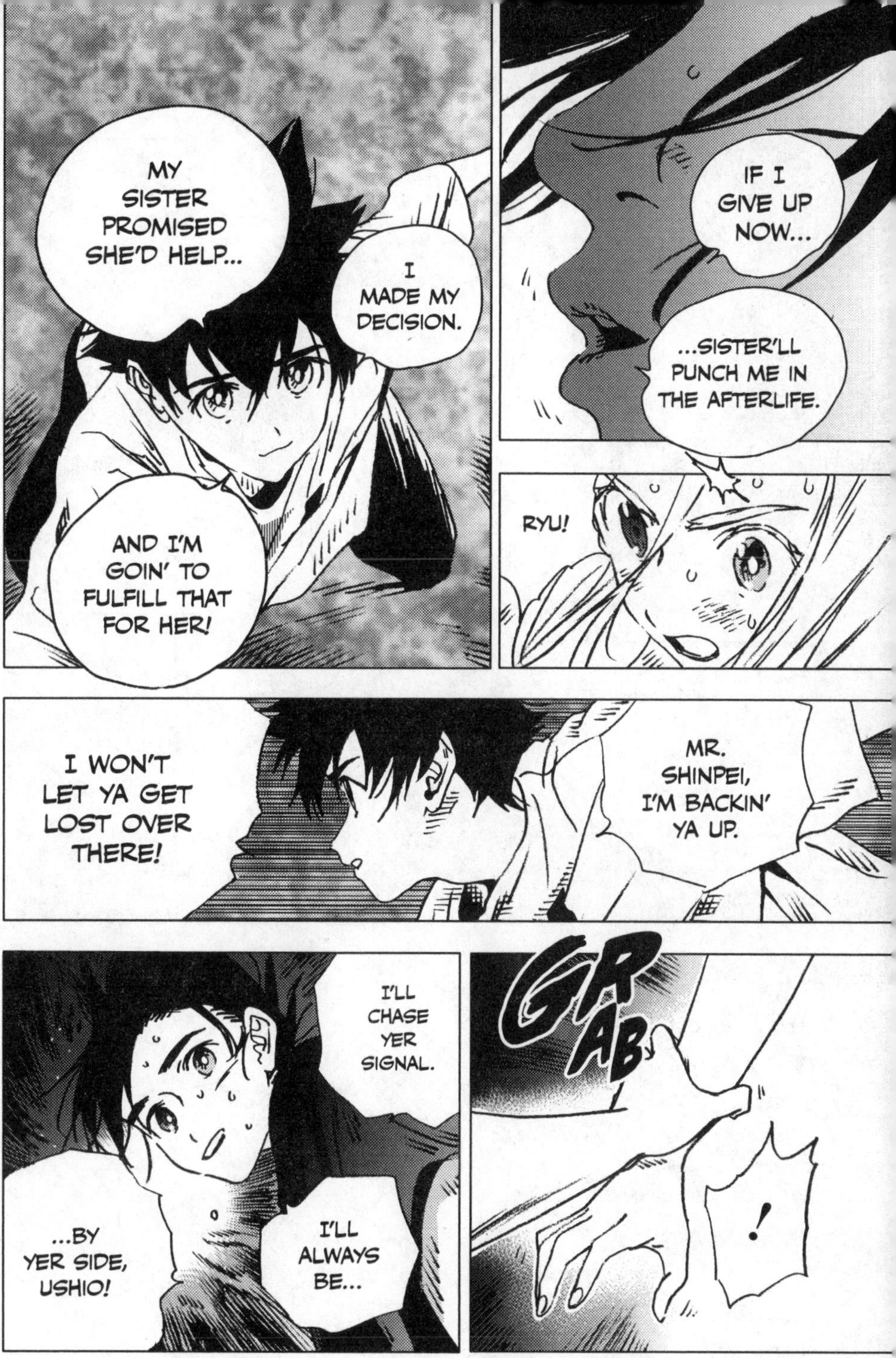
IF I GIVE UP NOW...
...SISTER'LL PUNCH ME IN THE AFTERLIFE.
RYU!
MY SISTER PROMISED SHE'D HELP...
I MADE MY DECISION.
AND I'M GOIN' TO FULFILL THAT FOR HER!
MR. SHINPEI, I'M BACKIN' YA UP.
I WON'T LET YA GET LOST OVER THERE!
GRAB
!
I'LL CHASE YER SIGNAL.
I'LL ALWAYS BE...
...BY YER SIDE, USHIO!

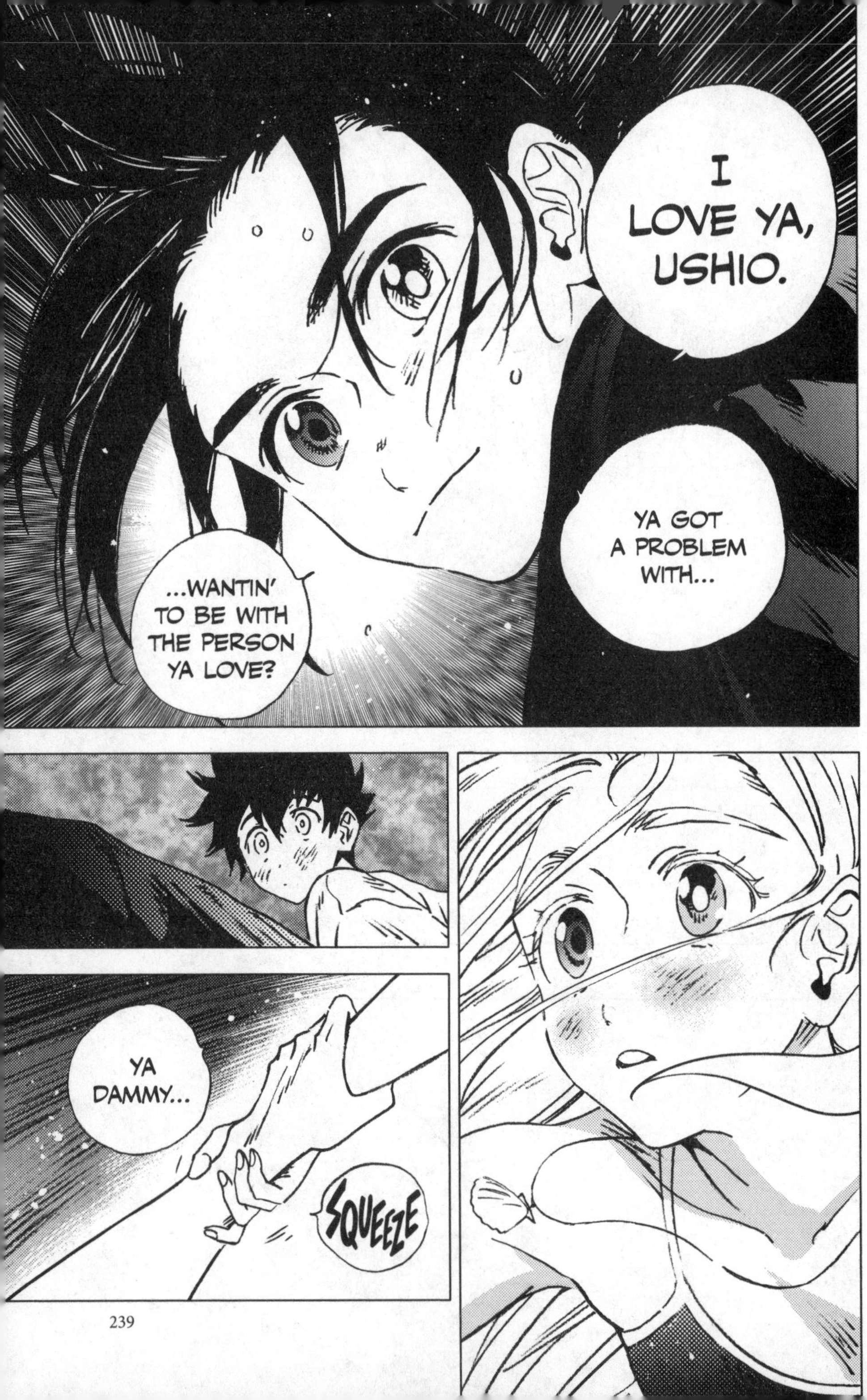
I LOVE YA, USHIO.
YA GOT A PROBLEM WITH...
...WANTIN' TO BE WITH THE PERSON YA LOVE?
YA DAMMY...
SQUEEZE

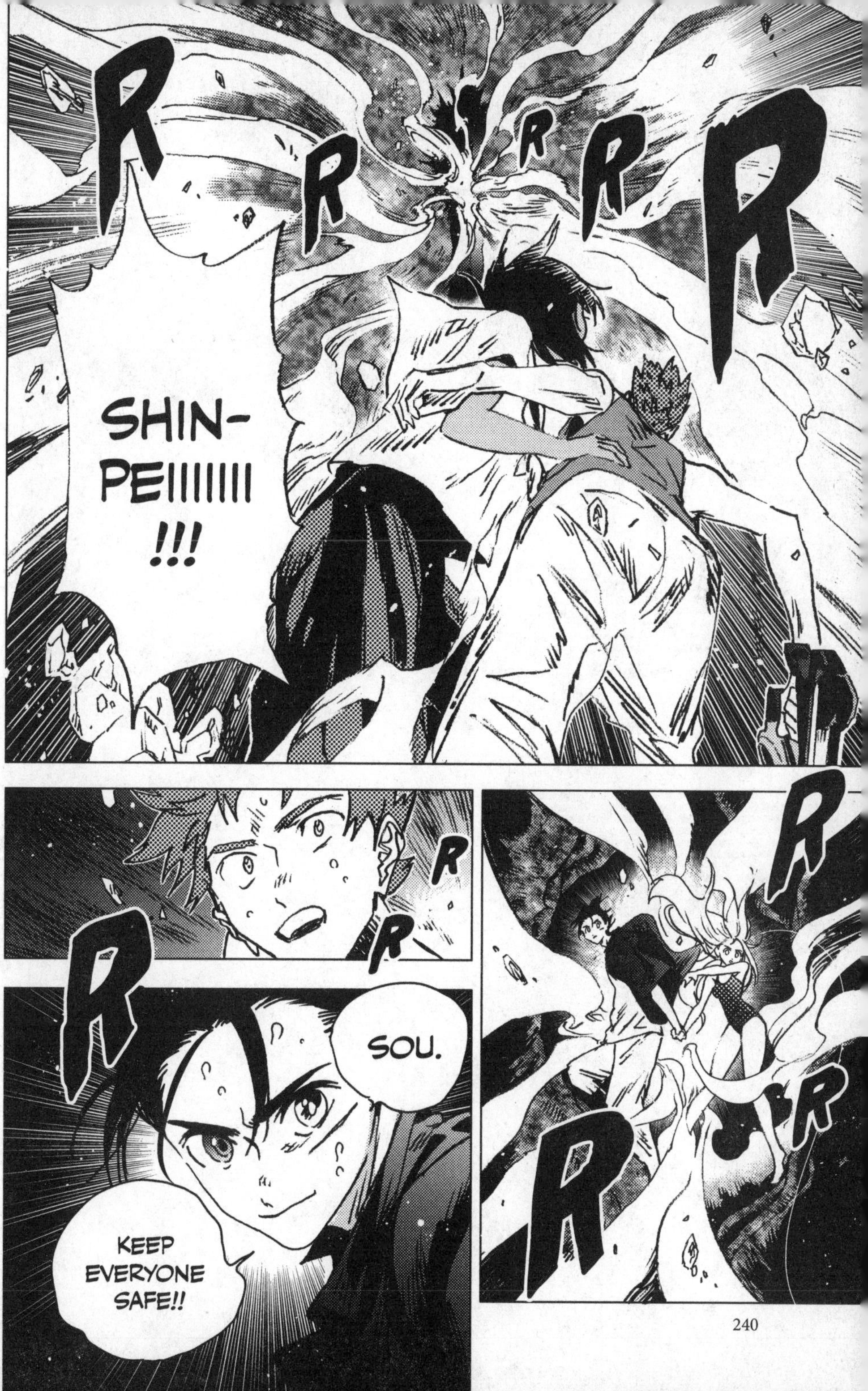
RRRRRR
SHIN-PEIIIIIIIII!!!
RRRR
RR
R
SOU.
KEEP EVERYONE SAFE!!

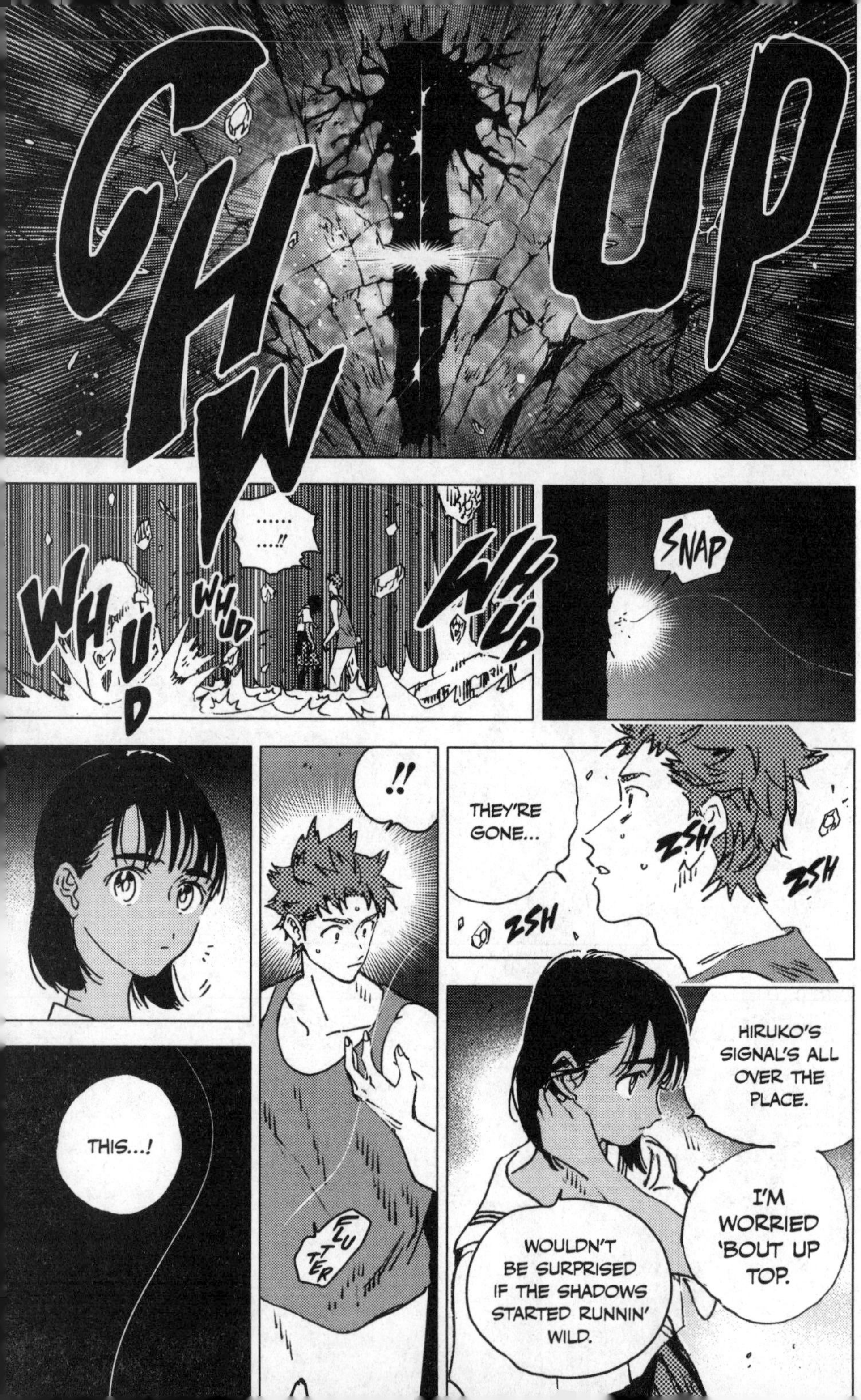
SNAP
WHUD
......
...!!
WHUD
WHUUD
ZSH
ZSH
THEY'RE GONE...
ZSH
!!
HIRUKO'S SIGNAL'S ALL OVER THE PLACE.
I'M WORRIED 'BOUT UP TOP.
WOULDN'T BE SURPRISED IF THE SHADOWS STARTED RUNNIN' WILD.
FLUTTER
THIS...!

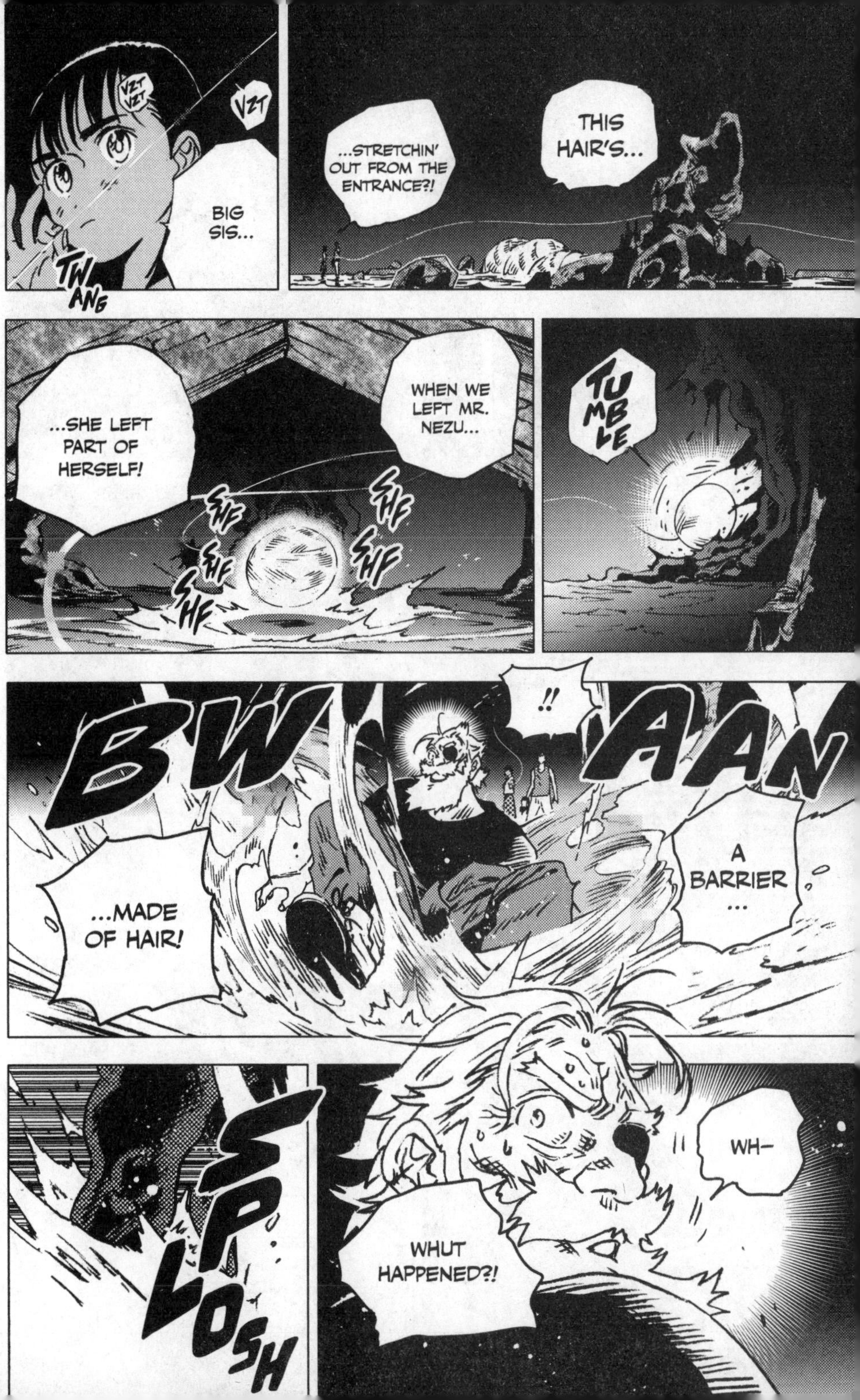
THIS HAIR'S...
...STRETCHIN' OUT FROM THE ENTRANCE?!
VZT VZT
VZT
BIG SIS...
TWANG
TUMBLE
WHEN WE LEFT MR. NEZU...
...SHE LEFT PART OF HERSELF!
SHF SHF SHF SHF SHF
BWAAN
!!
A BARRIER...
...MADE OF HAIR!
WH-
WHUT HAPPENED?!
SPLOSH

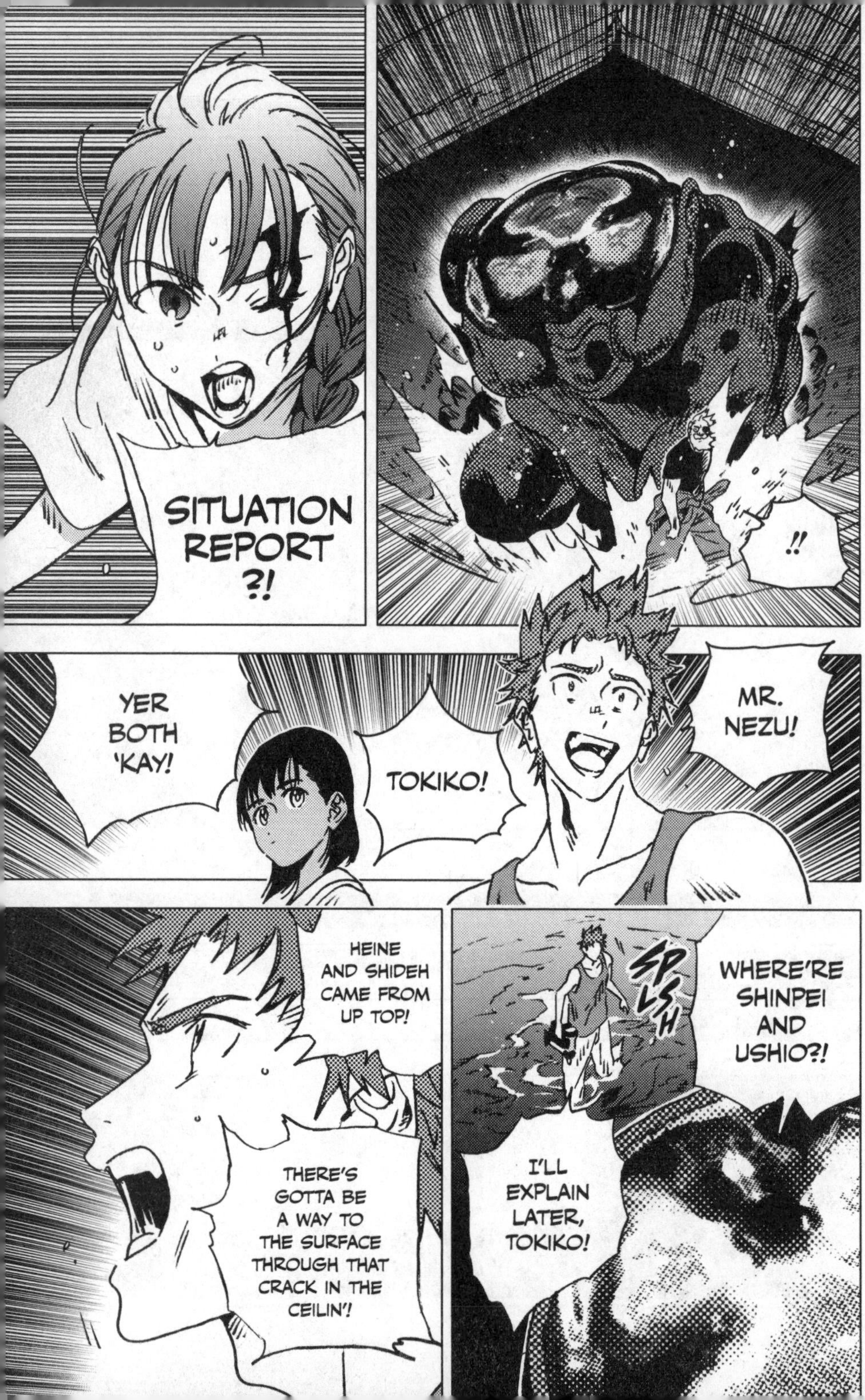
!!
SITUATION REPORT ?!
MR. NEZU!
TOKIKO!
YER BOTH 'KAY!
WHERE'RE SHINPEI AND USHIO?!
SPLSH
I'LL EXPLAIN LATER, TOKIKO!
HEINE AND SHIDEH CAME FROM UP TOP!
THERE'S GOTTA BE A WAY TO THE SURFACE THROUGH THAT CRACK IN THE CEILIN'!

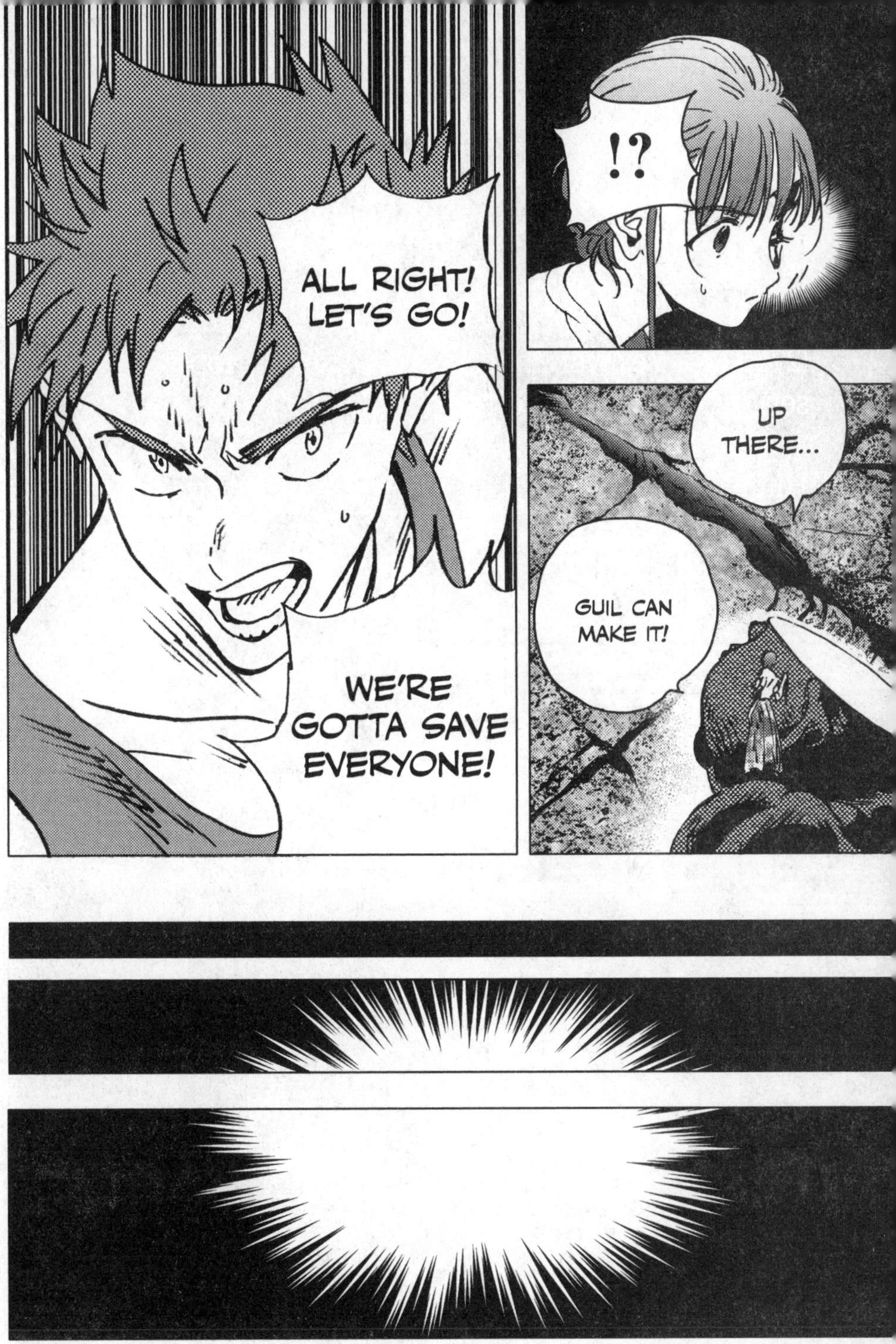
!?
UP THERE...
GUIL CAN MAKE IT!
ALL RIGHT! LET'S GO!
WE'RE GOTTA SAVE EVERYONE!

MEMO#022

WAKAYAMA AIR RAID

Wakayama was hit by dozens of air raids during World War II. Above all, the greatest damage was caused by the Great Wakayama Air Raid on July 9th , 1945. 108 B29s arrived and dropped over 800 tons of incendiary bombs (27402 houses were burned down, 4438 people were seriously injured, and 1101 people died).

Hitogashima, which was a fortress, was also damaged. Hitogashima Shrine was burnt down and Heine herself was seriously damaged. This was the direct cause of her weakening.

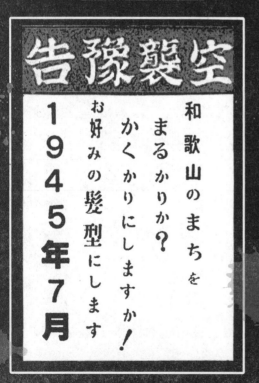

空襲豫告

和歌山のまちを
まるかりか？
かくかりにしますか！
お好みの髪型にします
1945年7月

AIR RAID NOTICE

Are they going to shave Wakayama's head?

Crew cut?

Choose your favorite hair style!

July, 1945

Air raid notice flyer dropped from the American army air-plane.

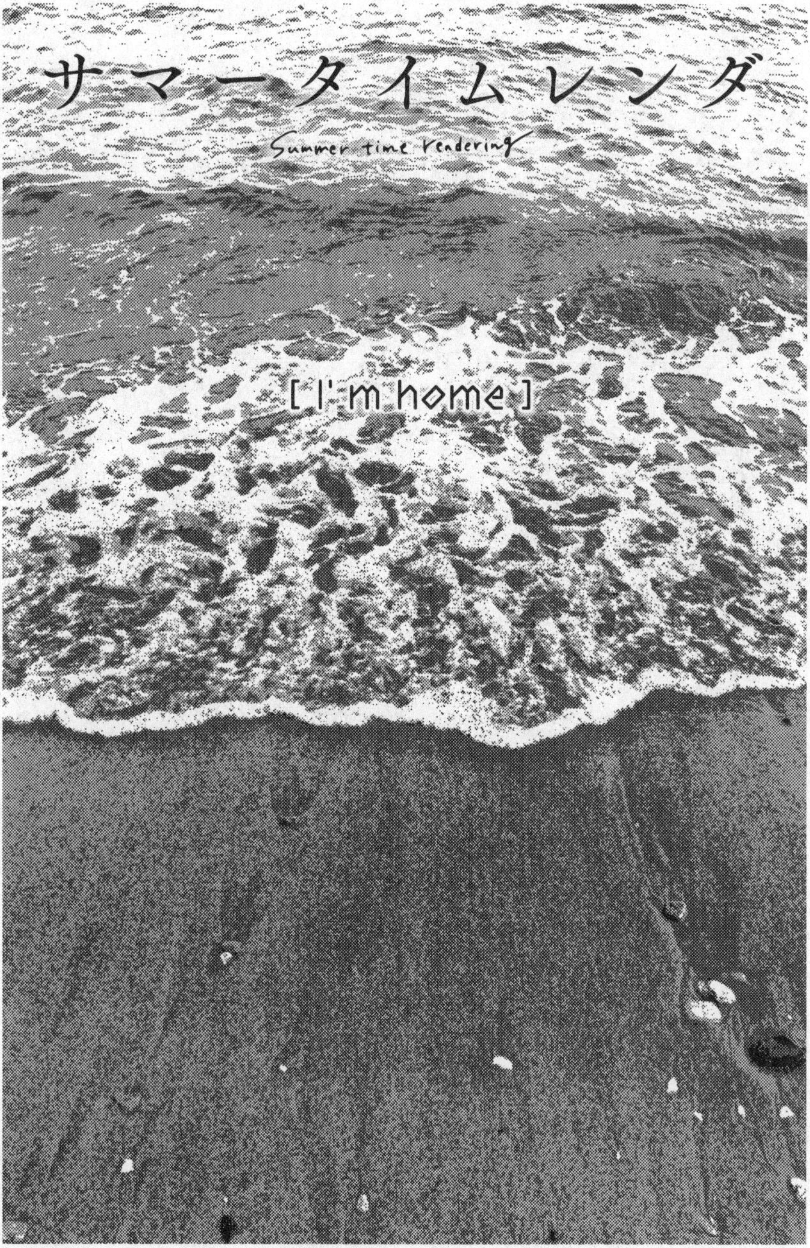
サマータイムレンダ
Summer time rendering
[I'm home]

田中靖規
TANAKA YASUKI

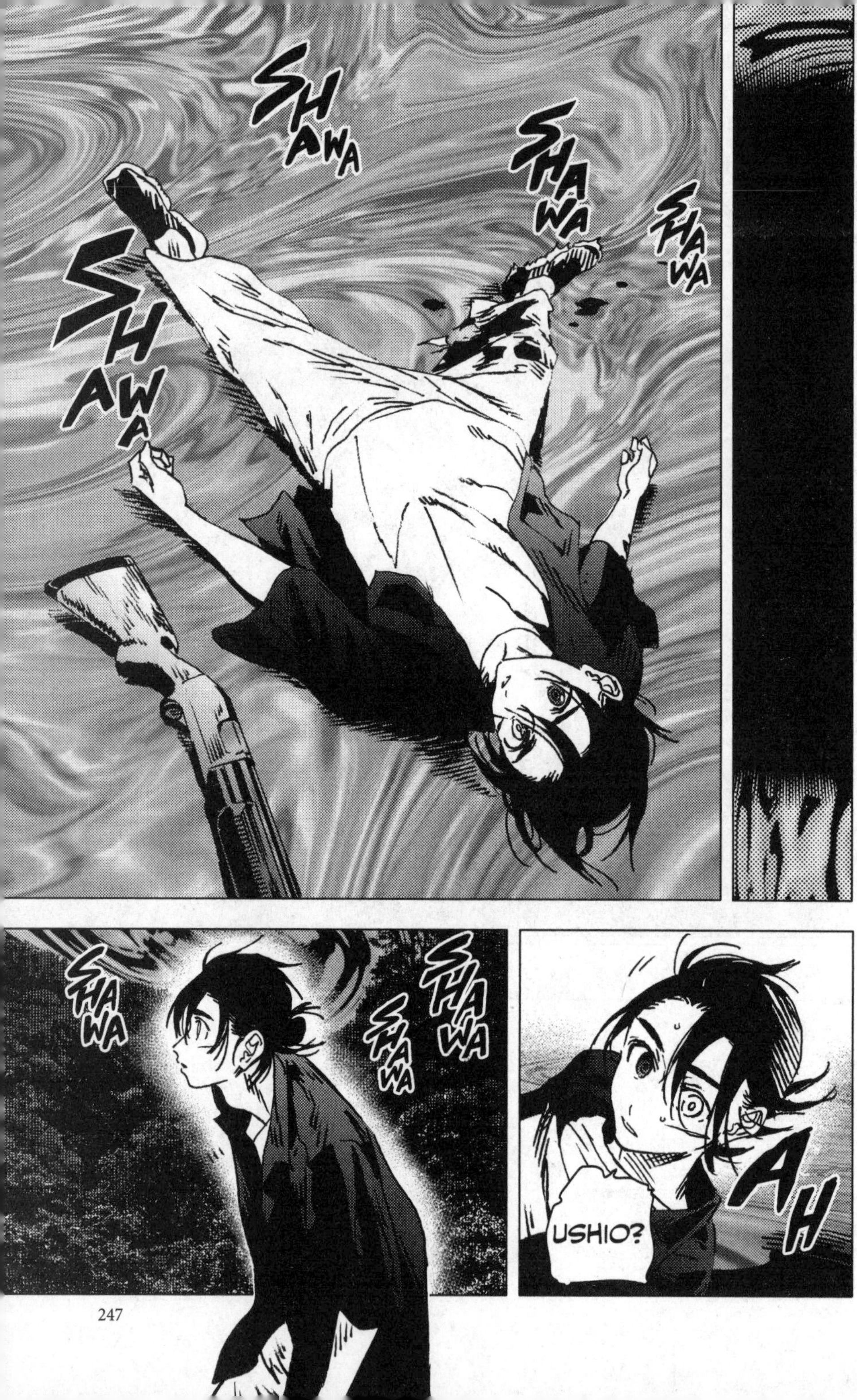
SHAWA
SHAWAWA
SHAWA
SHAWAWA
AH
USHIO?
SHAWA
SHAWA
SHAWA

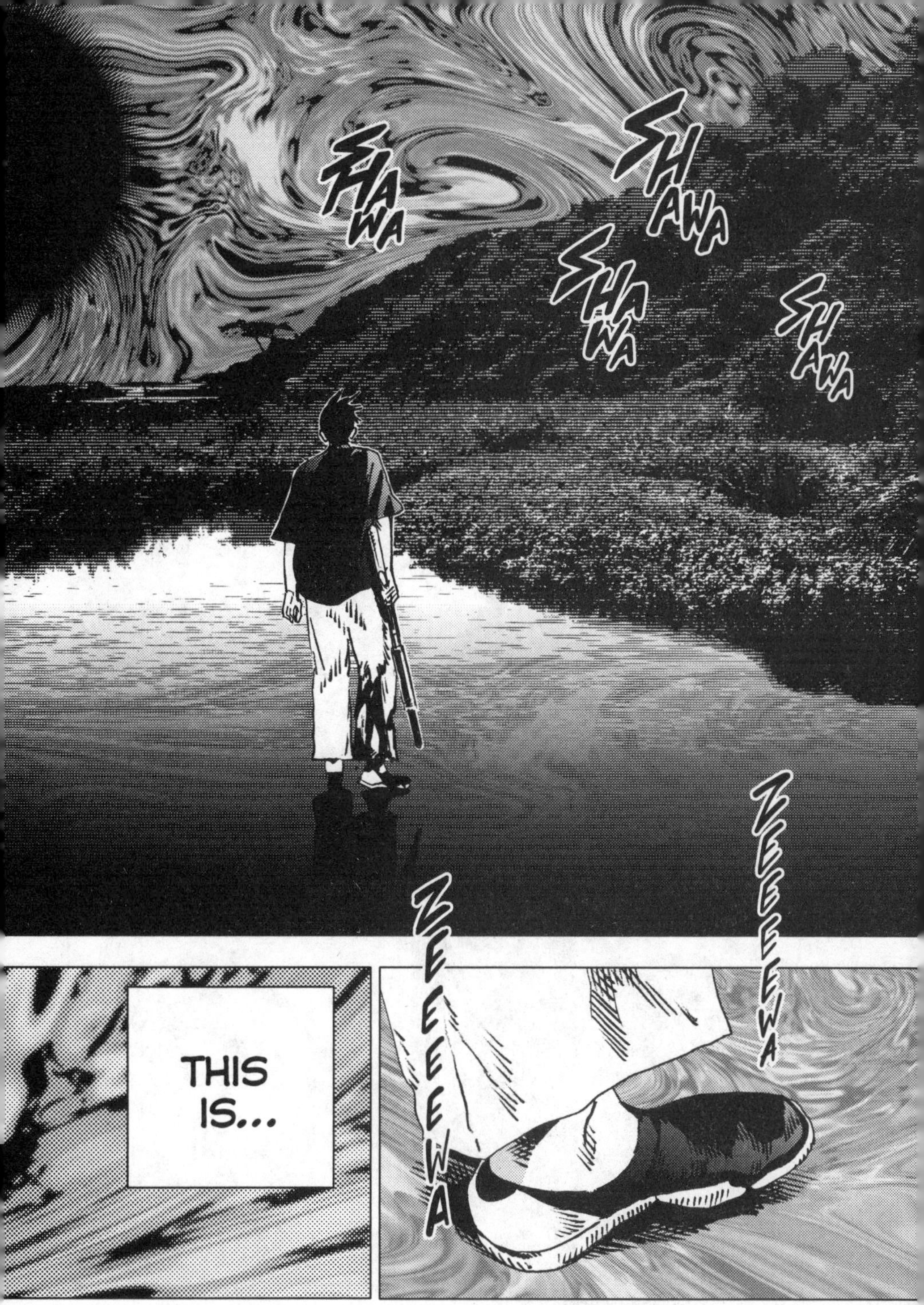
SHAWA
SHAWA
SHAWA
SHAWA
ZEEEEEWA
ZEEEEEWA
THIS IS...

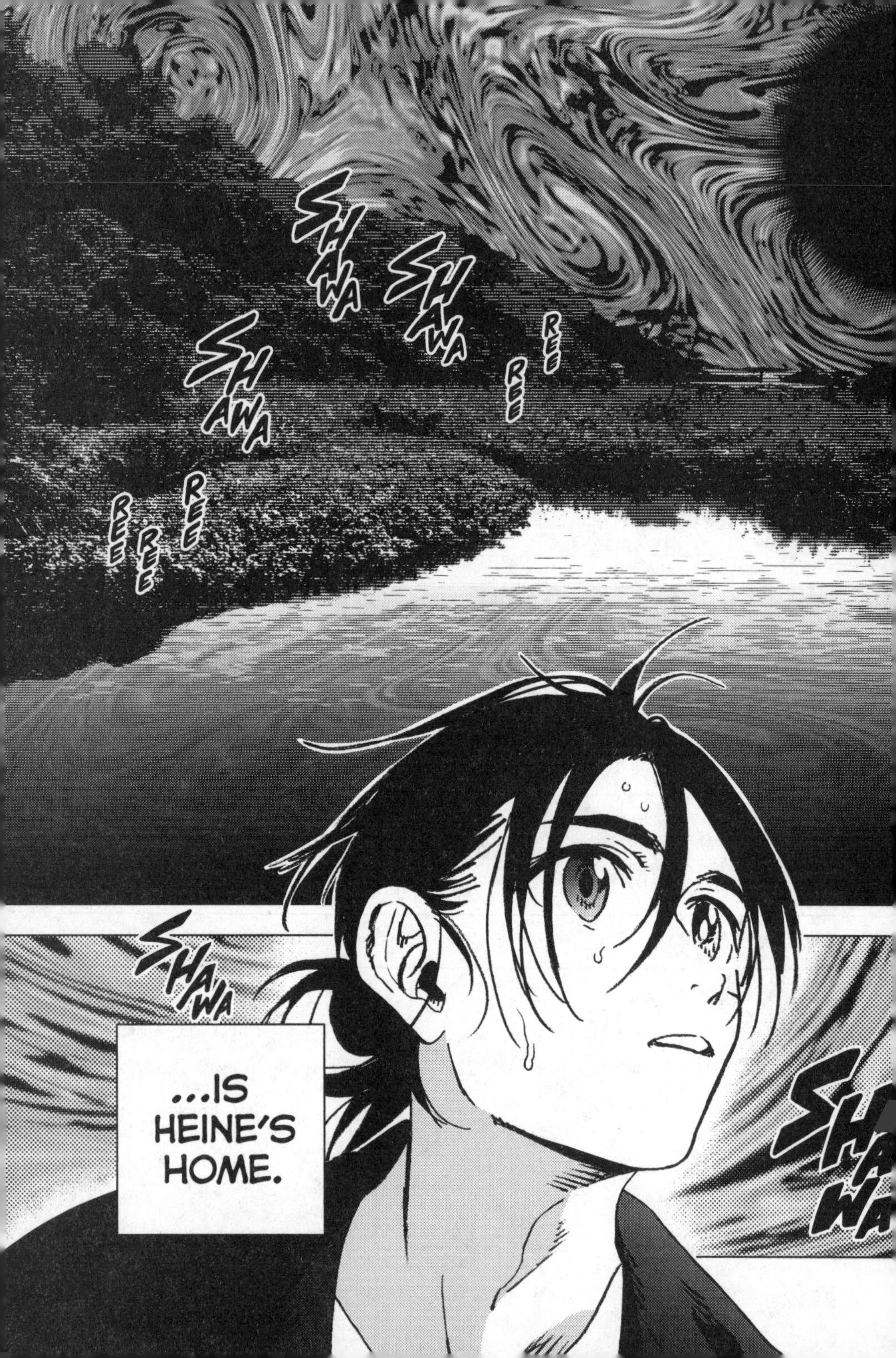
REE REE
SHAWA
SHAWA
SHAWA
REE
REE REE
SHAWA
...IS HEINE'S HOME.
SHAWA

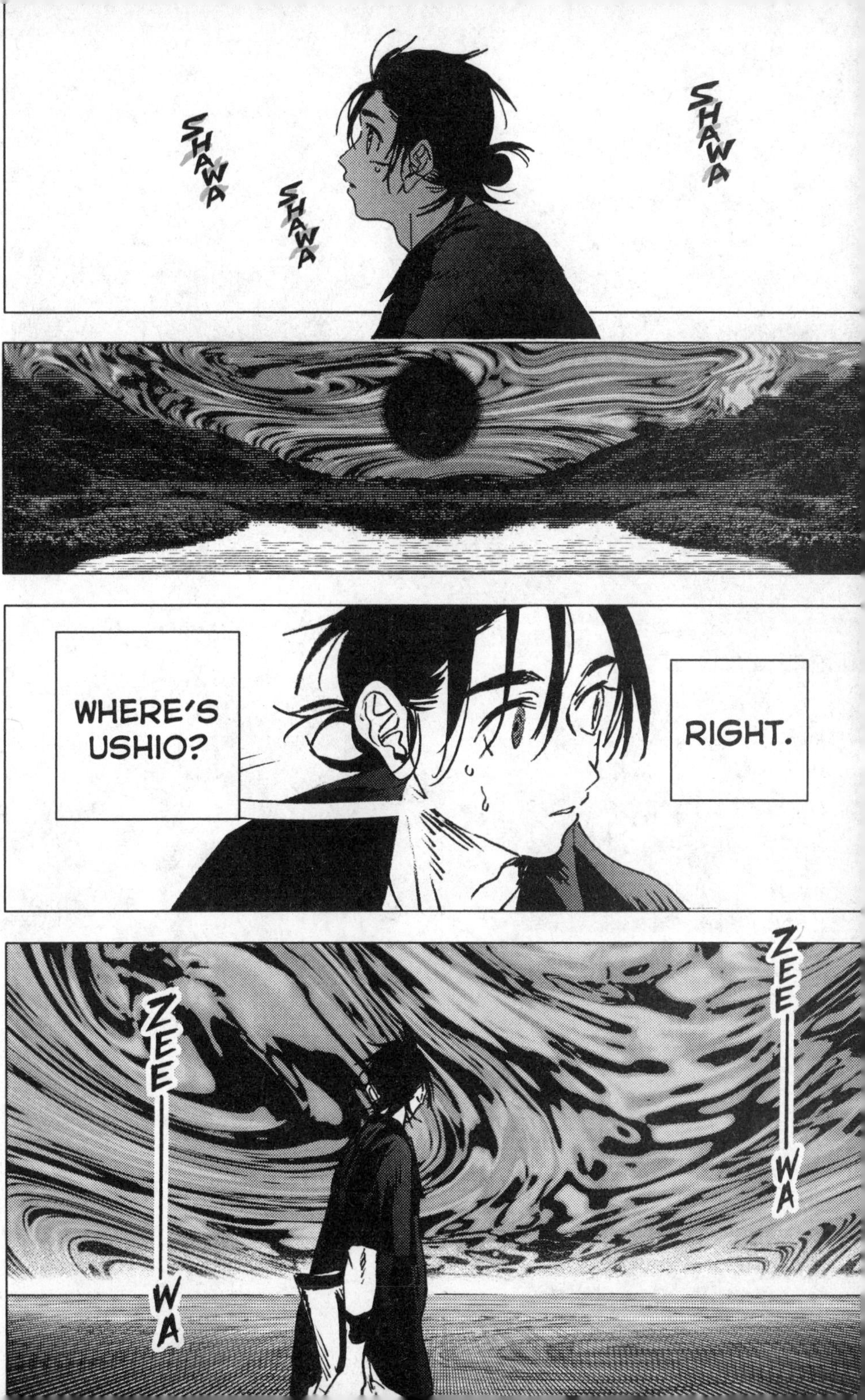
SHAWA
SHAWA
SHAWA
RIGHT.
WHERE'S USHIO?
ZEE—WA
ZEE—WA

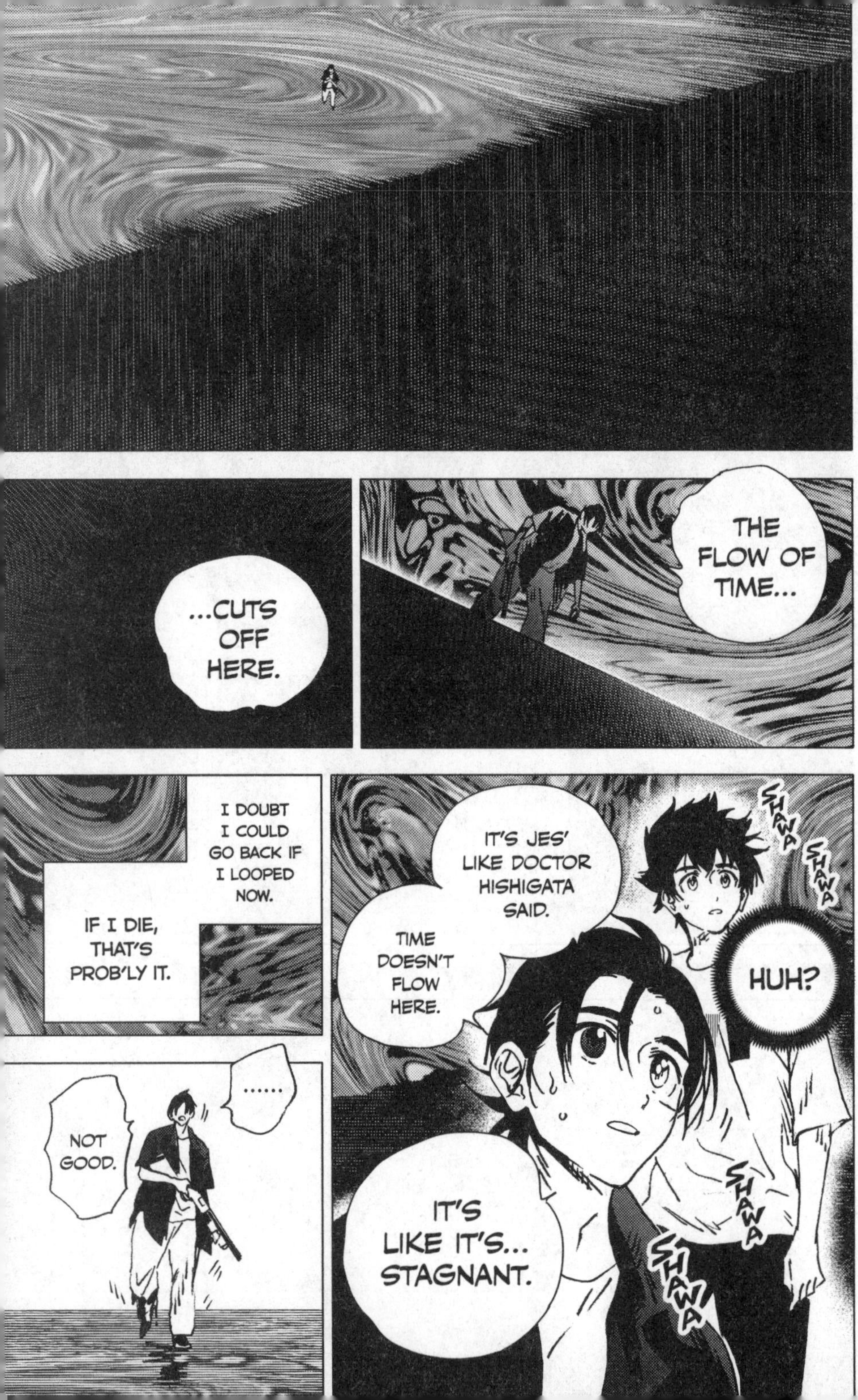
THE FLOW OF TIME...
...CUTS OFF HERE.
SHAWA SHAWA
IT'S JES' LIKE DOCTOR HISHIGATA SAID.
HUH?
TIME DOESN'T FLOW HERE.
SHAWA SHAWA
IT'S LIKE IT'S... STAGNANT.
I DOUBT I COULD GO BACK IF I LOOPED NOW.
IF I DIE, THAT'S PROB'LY IT.
......
NOT GOOD.

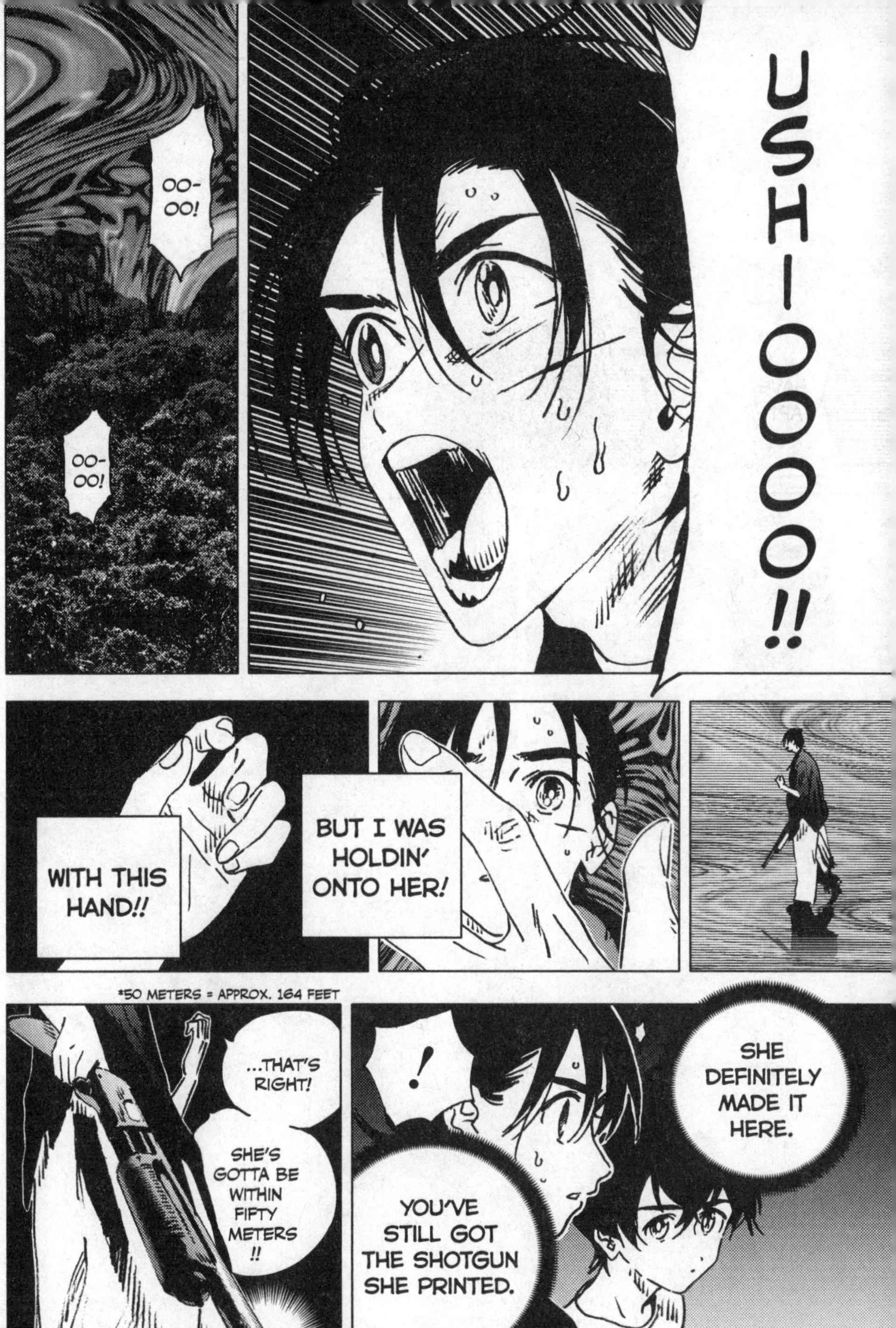
USHIOOOO!!
OO-OO!
OO-OO!
BUT I WAS HOLDIN' ONTO HER!
WITH THIS HAND!!
!
SHE DEFINITELY MADE IT HERE.
YOU'VE STILL GOT THE SHOTGUN SHE PRINTED.
...THAT'S RIGHT!
SHE'S GOTTA BE WITHIN FIFTY METERS!!

*50 METERS = APPROX. 164 FEET

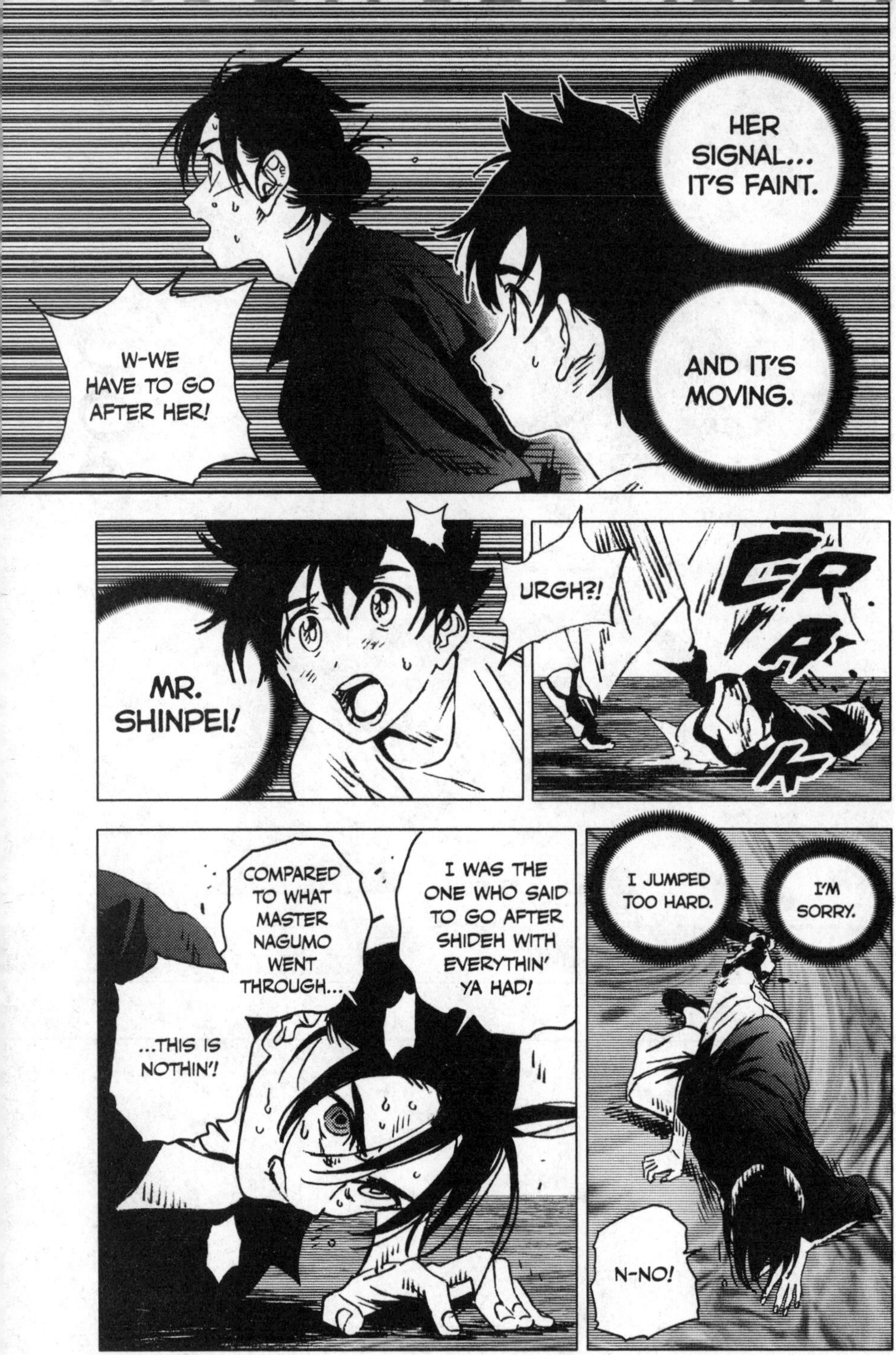
HER SIGNAL... IT'S FAINT.
AND IT'S MOVING.
W-WE HAVE TO GO AFTER HER!
URGH?!
CRAK
MR. SHINPEI!
I'M SORRY.
I JUMPED TOO HARD.
N-NO!
I WAS THE ONE WHO SAID TO GO AFTER SHIDEH WITH EVERYTHIN' YA HAD!
COMPARED TO WHAT MASTER NAGUMO WENT THROUGH...
...THIS IS NOTHIN'!

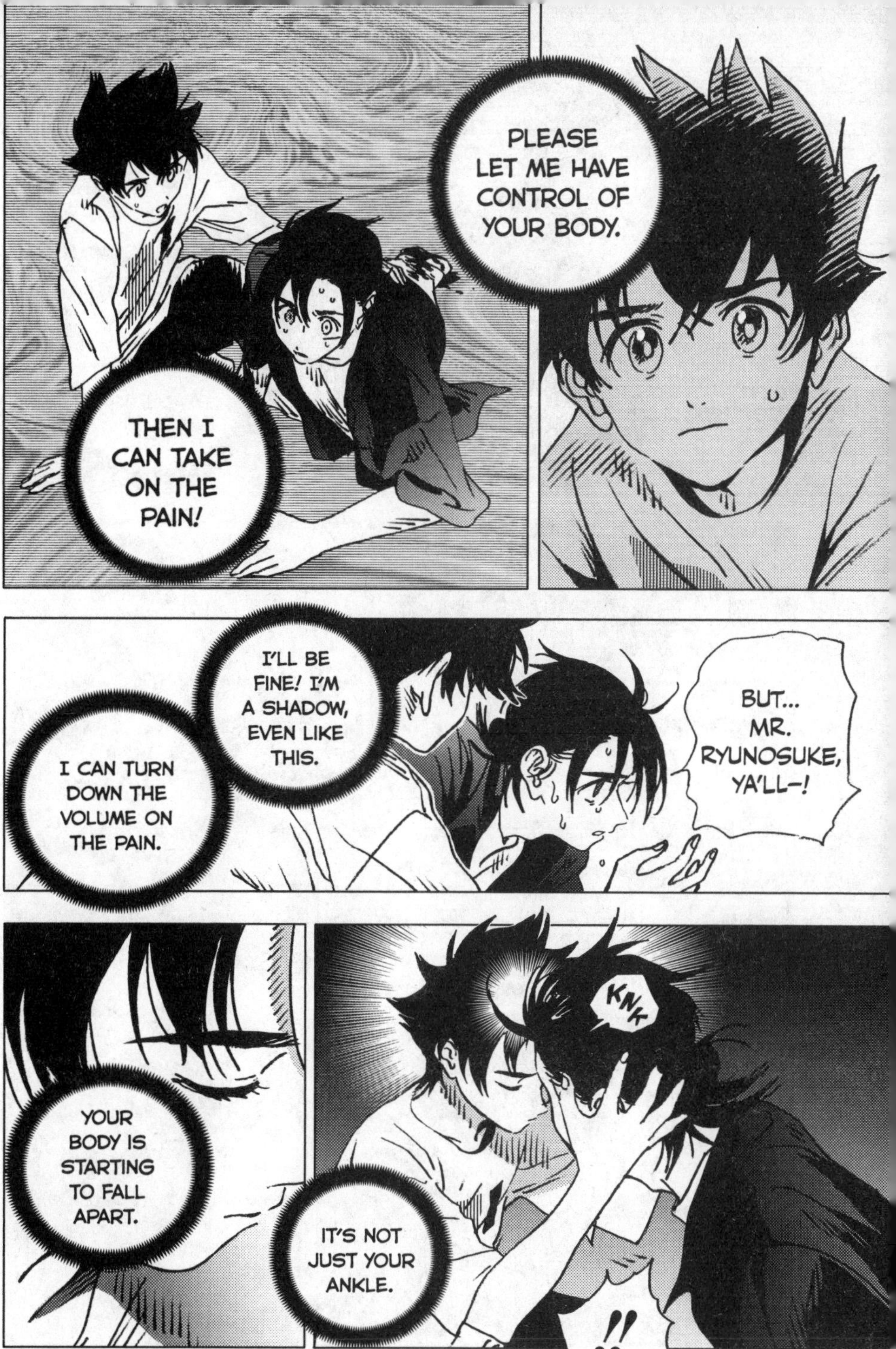
PLEASE LET ME HAVE CONTROL OF YOUR BODY.
THEN I CAN TAKE ON THE PAIN!
BUT... MR. RYUNOSUKE, YA'LL–!
I'LL BE FINE! I'M A SHADOW, EVEN LIKE THIS.
I CAN TURN DOWN THE VOLUME ON THE PAIN.
KNK
IT'S NOT JUST YOUR ANKLE.
!!
YOUR BODY IS STARTING TO FALL APART.

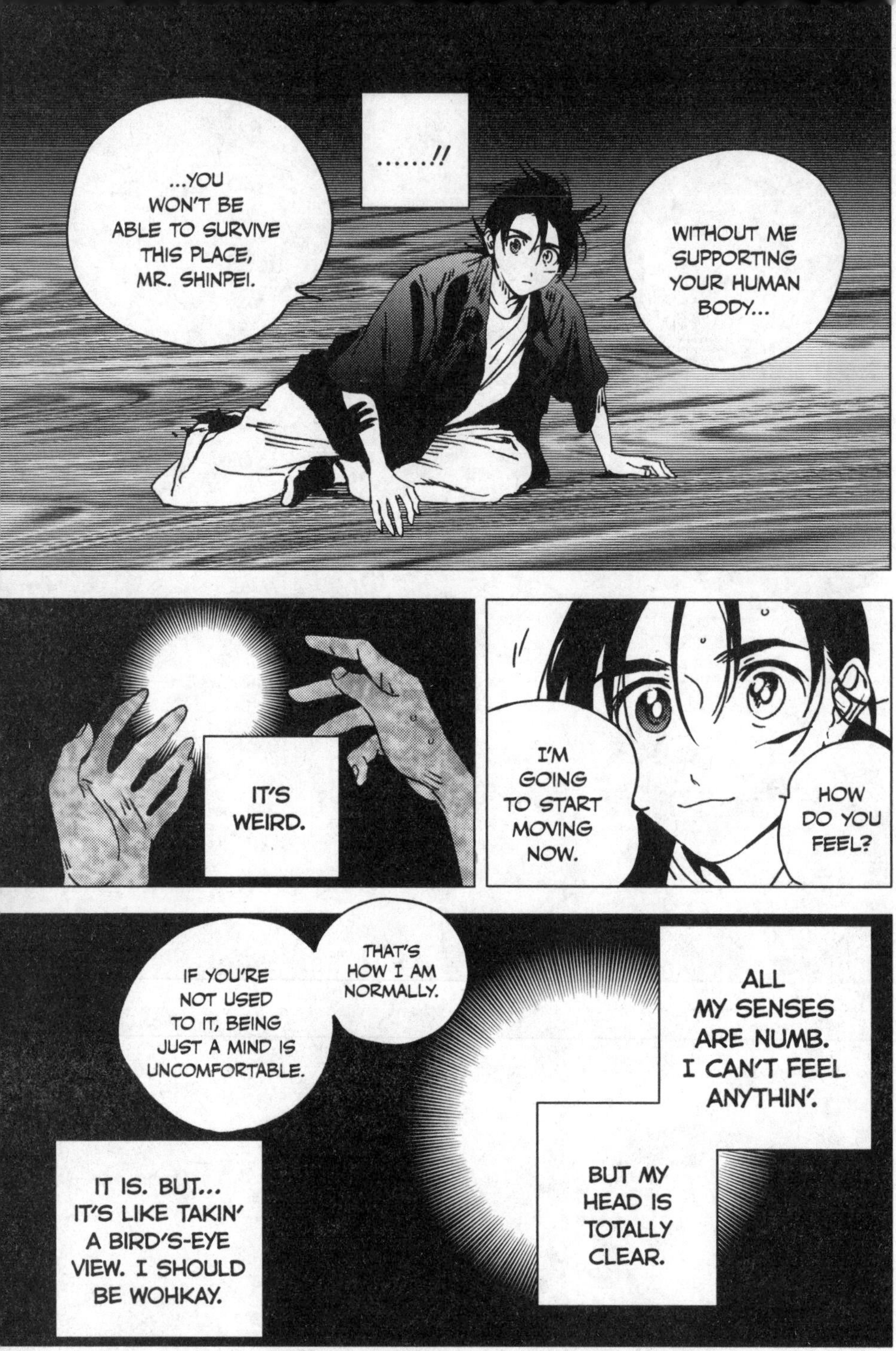
WITHOUT ME SUPPORTING YOUR HUMAN BODY...
...YOU WON'T BE ABLE TO SURVIVE THIS PLACE, MR. SHINPEI.
......!!
HOW DO YOU FEEL?
I'M GOING TO START MOVING NOW.
IT'S WEIRD.
ALL MY SENSES ARE NUMB. I CAN'T FEEL ANYTHIN'.
BUT MY HEAD IS TOTALLY CLEAR.
THAT'S HOW I AM NORMALLY.
IF YOU'RE NOT USED TO IT, BEING JUST A MIND IS UNCOMFORTABLE.
IT IS. BUT... IT'S LIKE TAKIN' A BIRD'S-EYE VIEW. I SHOULD BE WOHKAY.

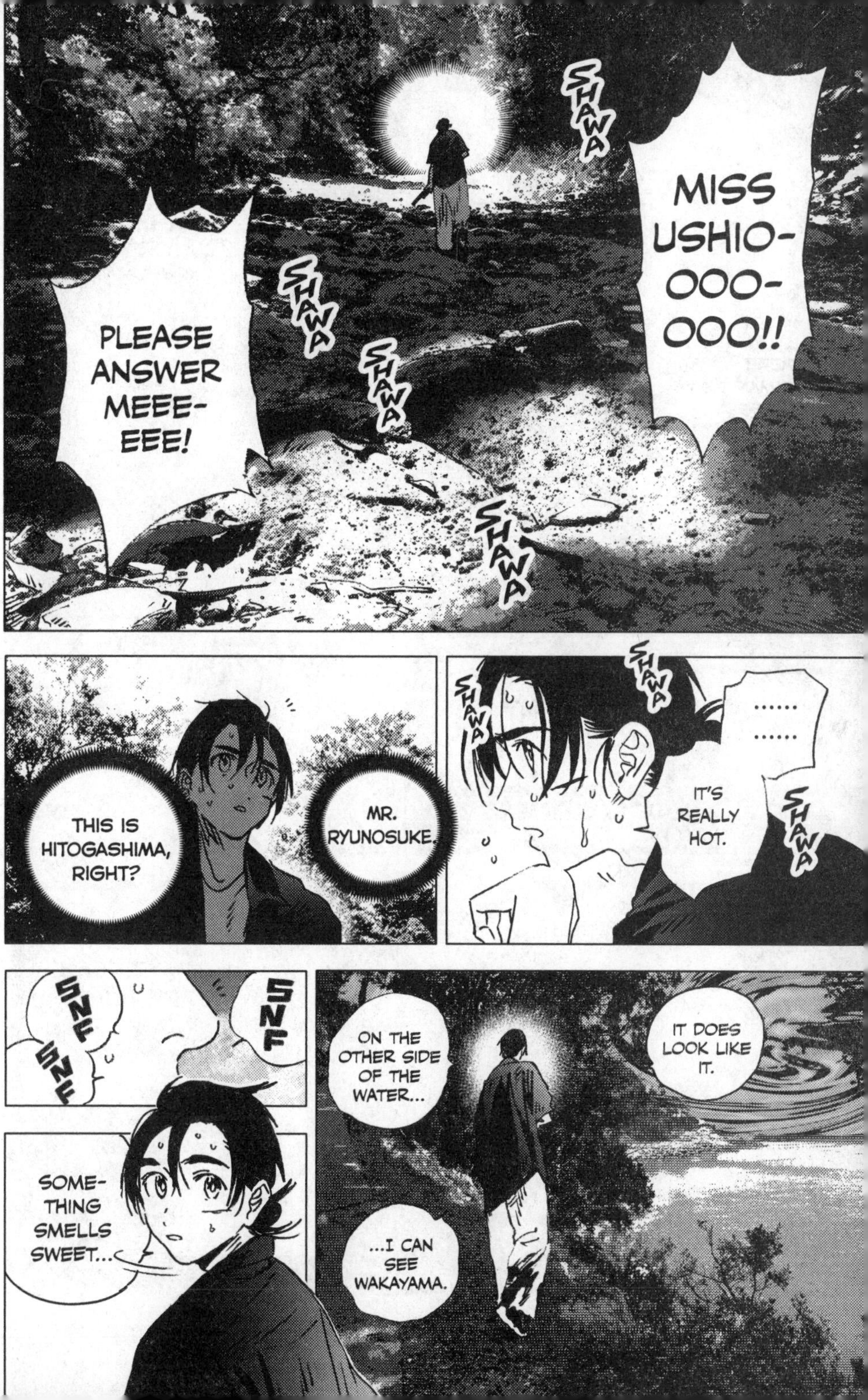
MISS USHIO-OOO-OOO!!
SHAWA
SHAWA
SHAWA
SHAWA
PLEASE ANSWER MEEEE-EEE!
......
......
SHAWA
SHAWA
IT'S REALLY HOT.
SHAWA
MR. RYUNOSUKE.
THIS IS HITOGASHIMA, RIGHT?
IT DOES LOOK LIKE IT.
ON THE OTHER SIDE OF THE WATER...
...I CAN SEE WAKAYAMA.
SNF
SNF
SNF
SOME-THING SMELLS SWEET...

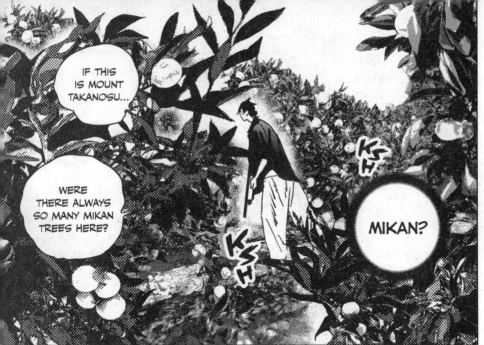

IF THIS IS MOUNT TAKANOSU...

WERE THERE ALWAYS SO MANY MIKAN TREES HERE?

KSH

KSH

MIKAN?

*MIKAN = TANGERINES

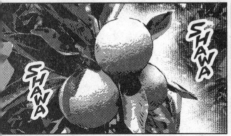

SHAWA

SHAWA

SHAWA

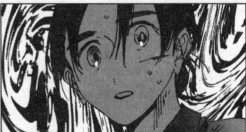

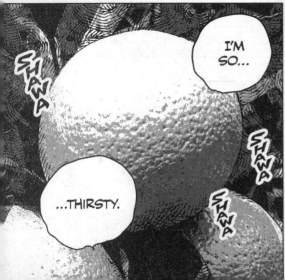

SHAWA

I'M SO...

...THIRSTY.

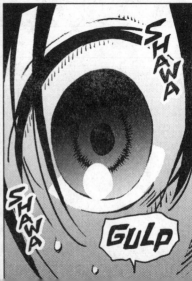

SHAWA

SHAWA

SHAWA

GULP

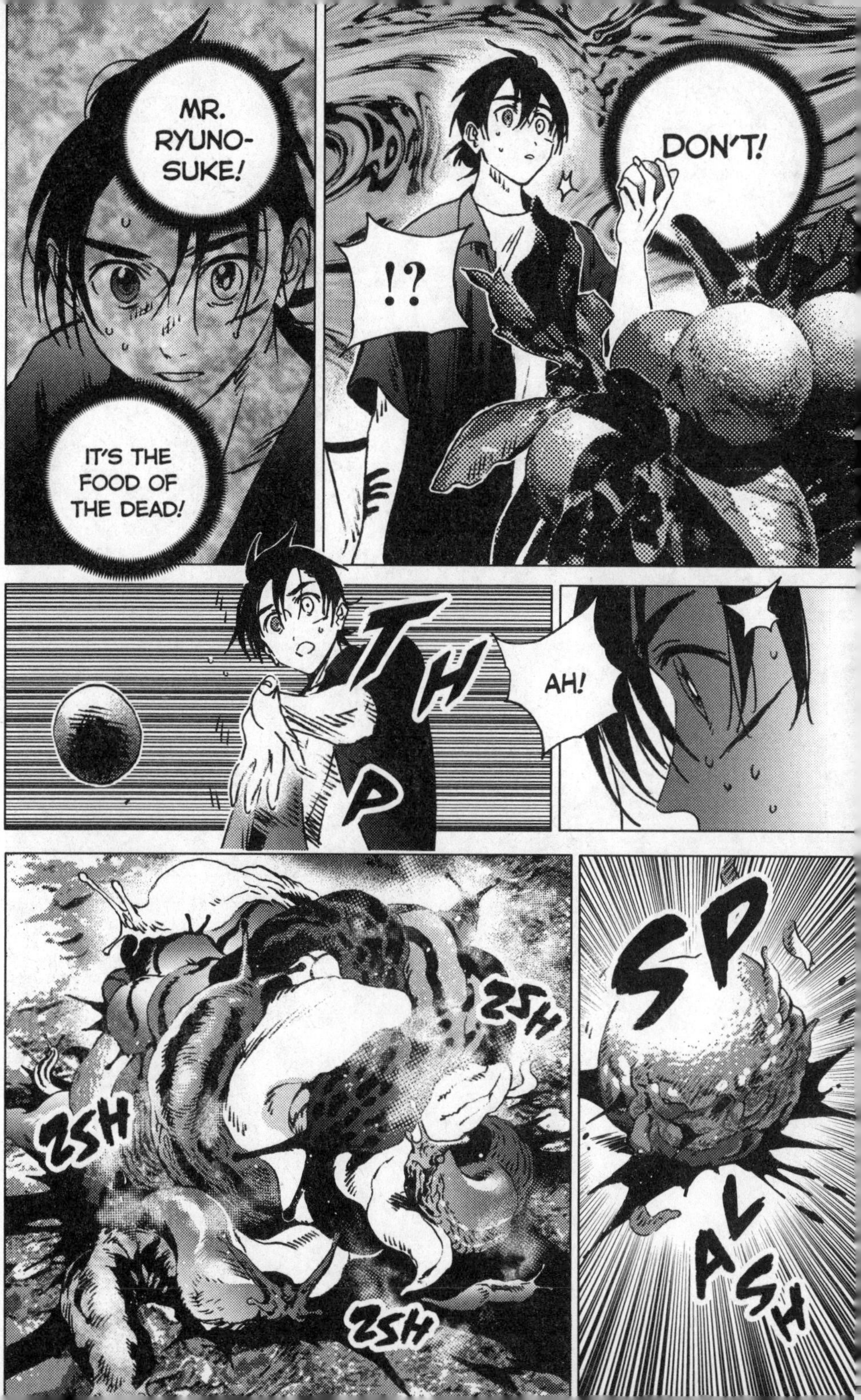

DON'T!
!?
MR. RYUNO-SUKE!
IT'S THE FOOD OF THE DEAD!
AH!
THWP
SPLASH
ZSH
ZSH
ZSH

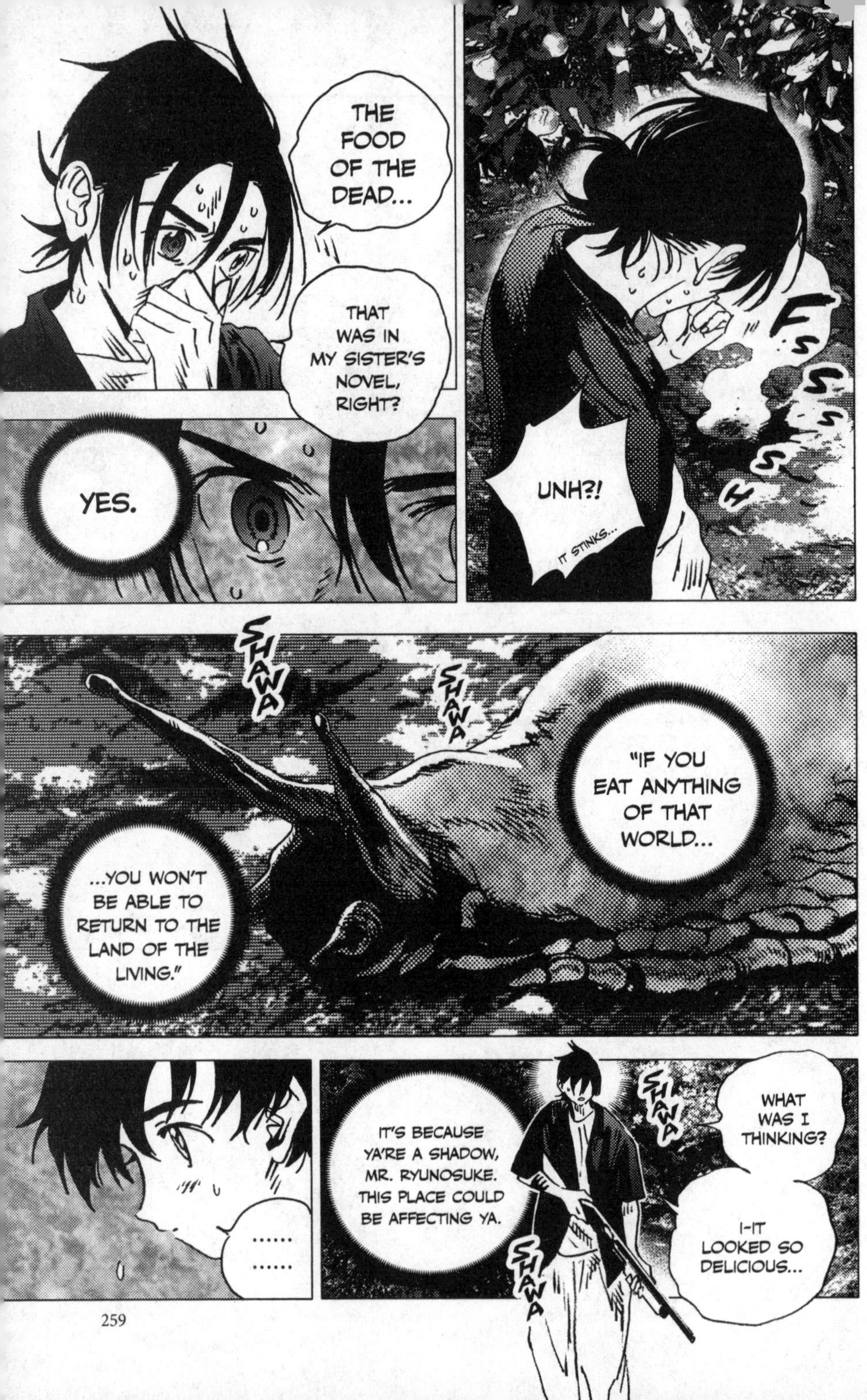
FSSSSH
UNH?!
IT STINKS...
THE FOOD OF THE DEAD...
THAT WAS IN MY SISTER'S NOVEL, RIGHT?
YES.
SHAWA
SHAWA
"IF YOU EAT ANYTHING OF THAT WORLD...
...YOU WON'T BE ABLE TO RETURN TO THE LAND OF THE LIVING."
WHAT WAS I THINKING?
SHAWA
I-IT LOOKED SO DELICIOUS...
IT'S BECAUSE YA'RE A SHADOW, MR. RYUNOSUKE. THIS PLACE COULD BE AFFECTING YA.
SHAWA
......
......

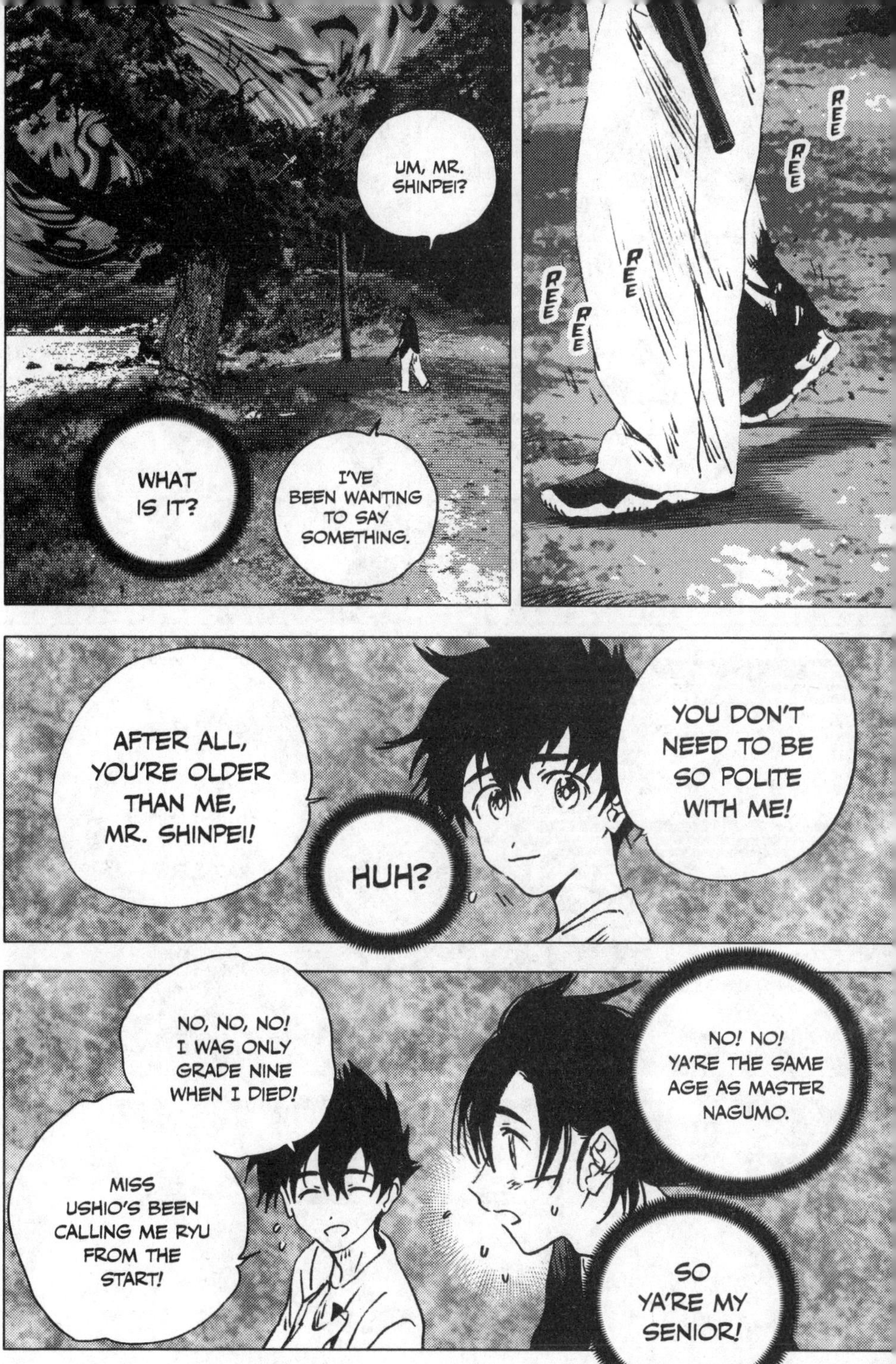
REE REE
REE REE REE
UM, MR. SHINPEI?
WHAT IS IT?
I'VE BEEN WANTING TO SAY SOMETHING.
YOU DON'T NEED TO BE SO POLITE WITH ME!
HUH?
AFTER ALL, YOU'RE OLDER THAN ME, MR. SHINPEI!
NO! NO! YA'RE THE SAME AGE AS MASTER NAGUMO.
SO YA'RE MY SENIOR!
NO, NO, NO! I WAS ONLY GRADE NINE WHEN I DIED!
MISS USHIO'S BEEN CALLING ME RYU FROM THE START!

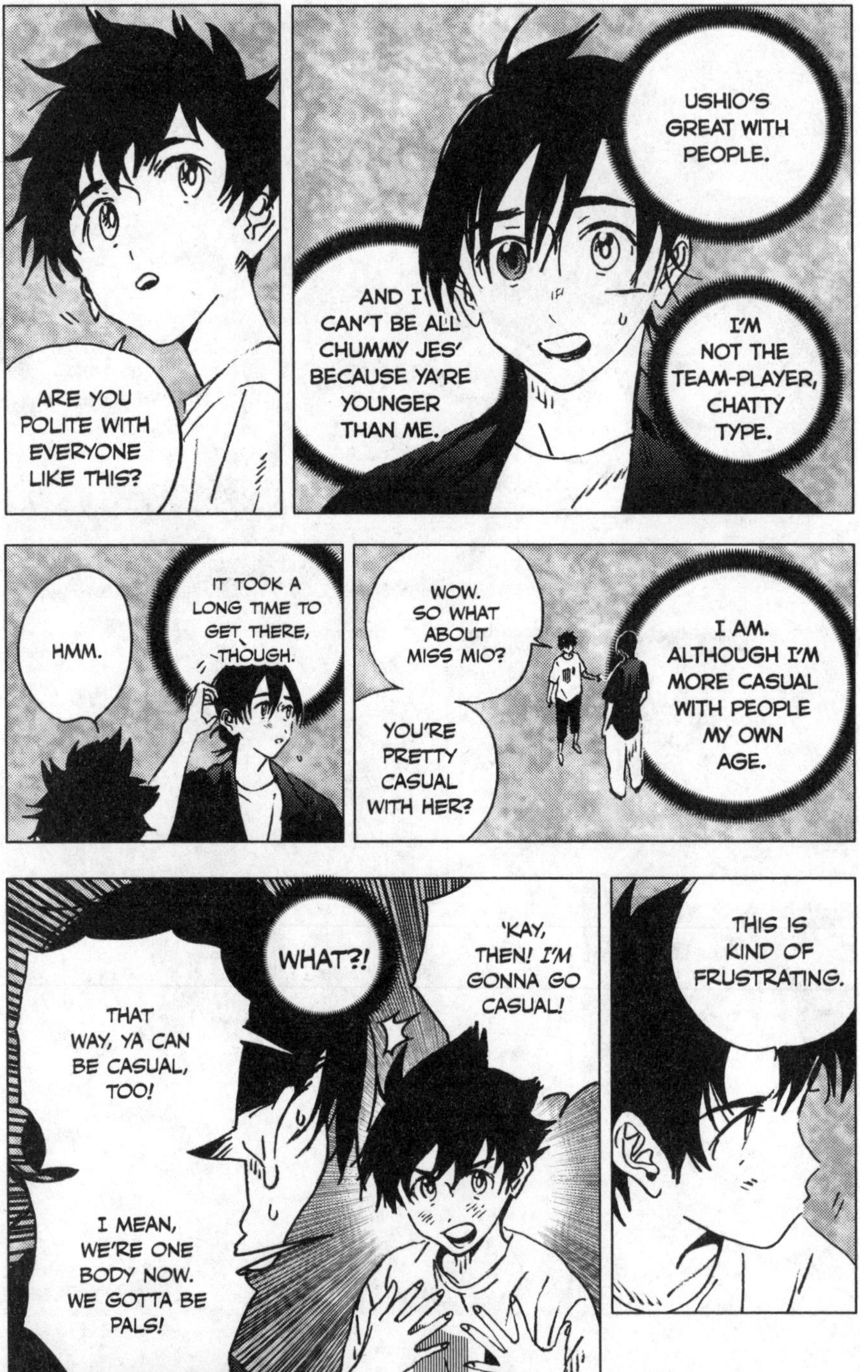
USHIO'S GREAT WITH PEOPLE.
I'M NOT THE TEAM-PLAYER, CHATTY TYPE.
AND I CAN'T BE ALL CHUMMY JES' BECAUSE YA'RE YOUNGER THAN ME.
ARE YOU POLITE WITH EVERYONE LIKE THIS?
WOW. SO WHAT ABOUT MISS MIO?
YOU'RE PRETTY CASUAL WITH HER?
I AM. ALTHOUGH I'M MORE CASUAL WITH PEOPLE MY OWN AGE.
IT TOOK A LONG TIME TO GET THERE, THOUGH.
HMM.
THIS IS KIND OF FRUSTRATING.
'KAY, THEN! *I'M* GONNA GO CASUAL!
WHAT?!
THAT WAY, YA CAN BE CASUAL, TOO!
I MEAN, WE'RE ONE BODY NOW. WE GOTTA BE PALS!

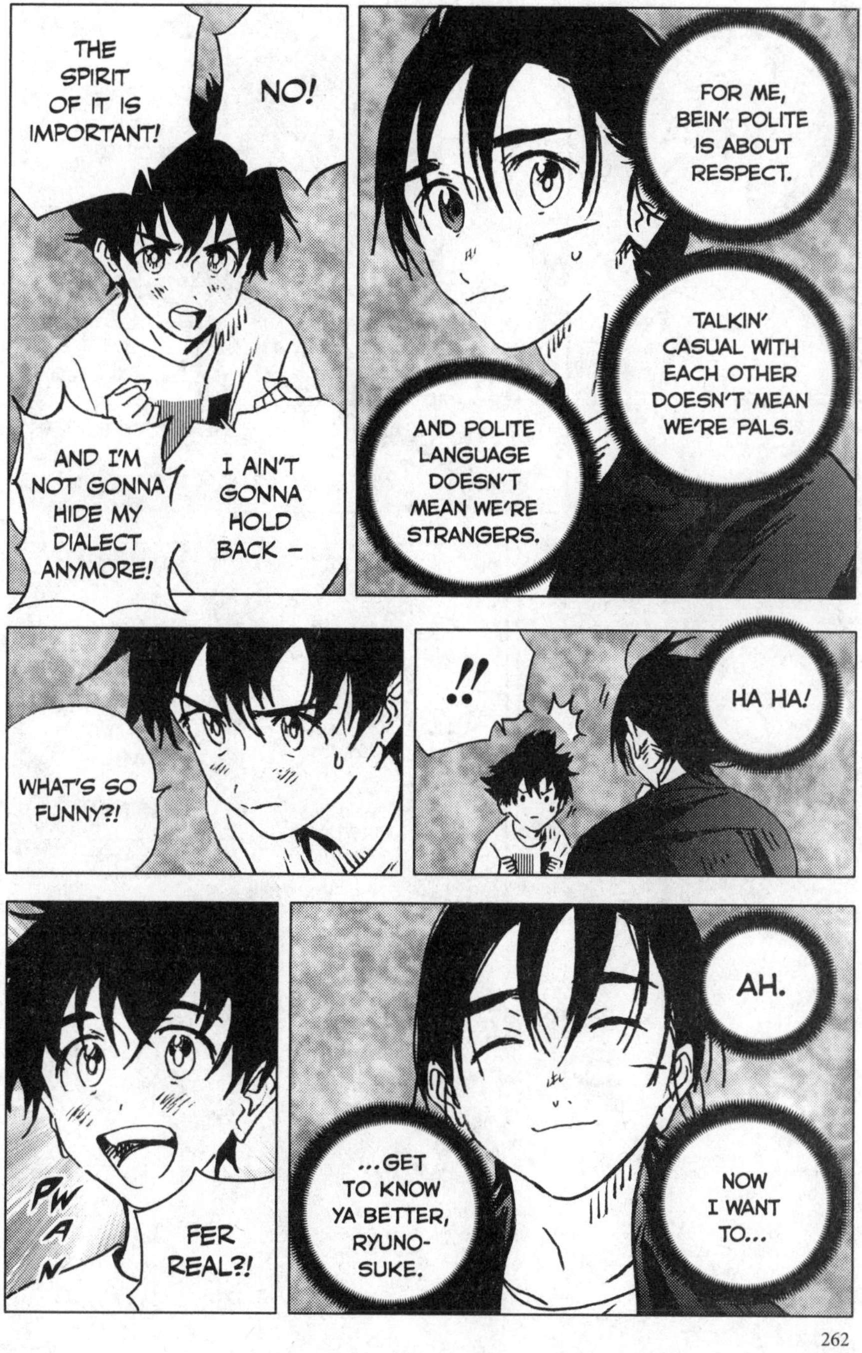

FOR ME, BEIN' POLITE IS ABOUT RESPECT.
TALKIN' CASUAL WITH EACH OTHER DOESN'T MEAN WE'RE PALS.
AND POLITE LANGUAGE DOESN'T MEAN WE'RE STRANGERS.
NO!
THE SPIRIT OF IT IS IMPORTANT!
I AIN'T GONNA HOLD BACK –
AND I'M NOT GONNA HIDE MY DIALECT ANYMORE!
HA HA!
!!
WHAT'S SO FUNNY?!
AH.
NOW I WANT TO...
...GET TO KNOW YA BETTER, RYUNO-SUKE.
PWAN
FER REAL?!

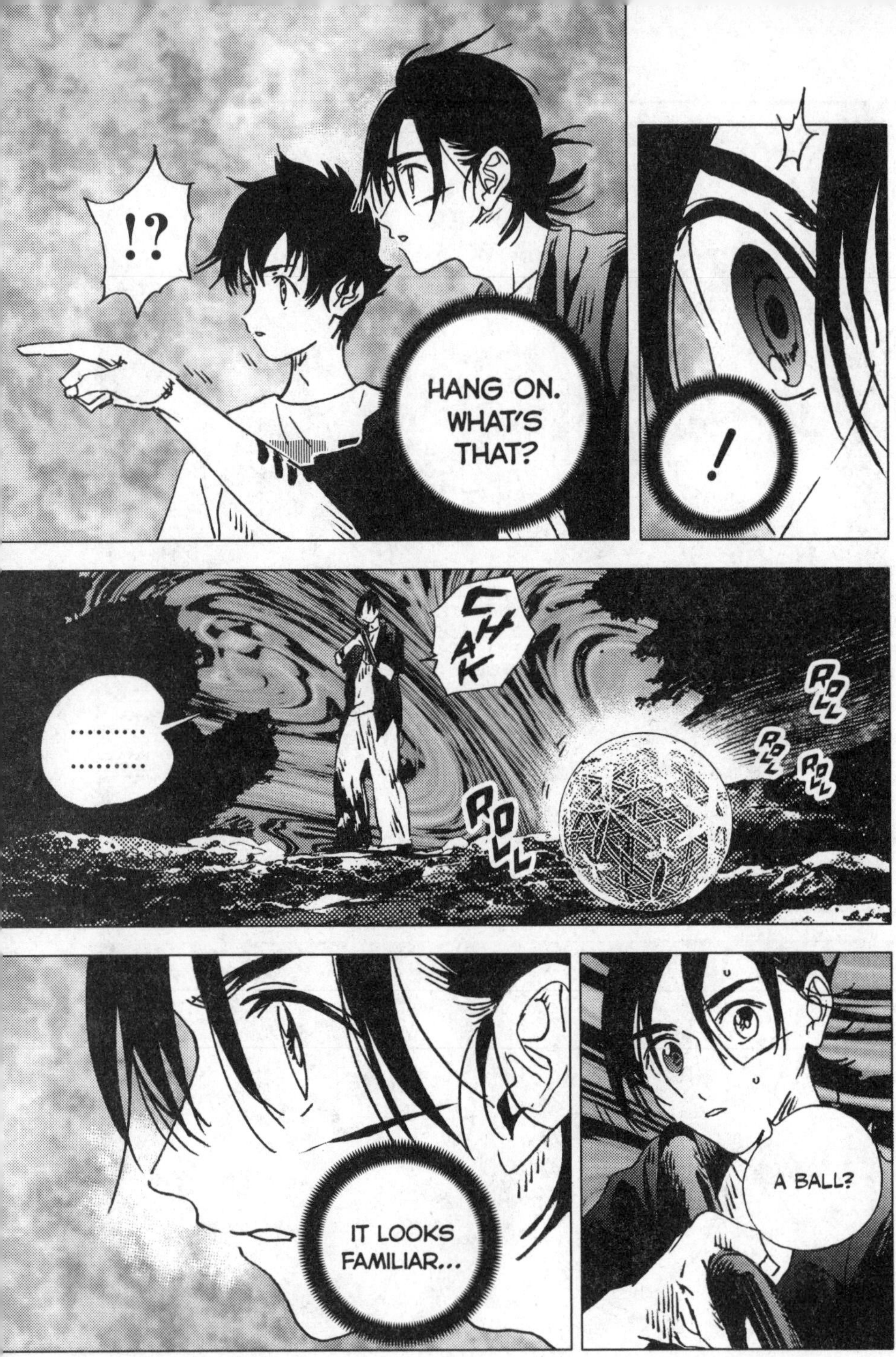
!
HANG ON. WHAT'S THAT?
!?
CHAK
ROLL
ROLL
ROLL
ROLL
....
....
A BALL?
IT LOOKS FAMILIAR...

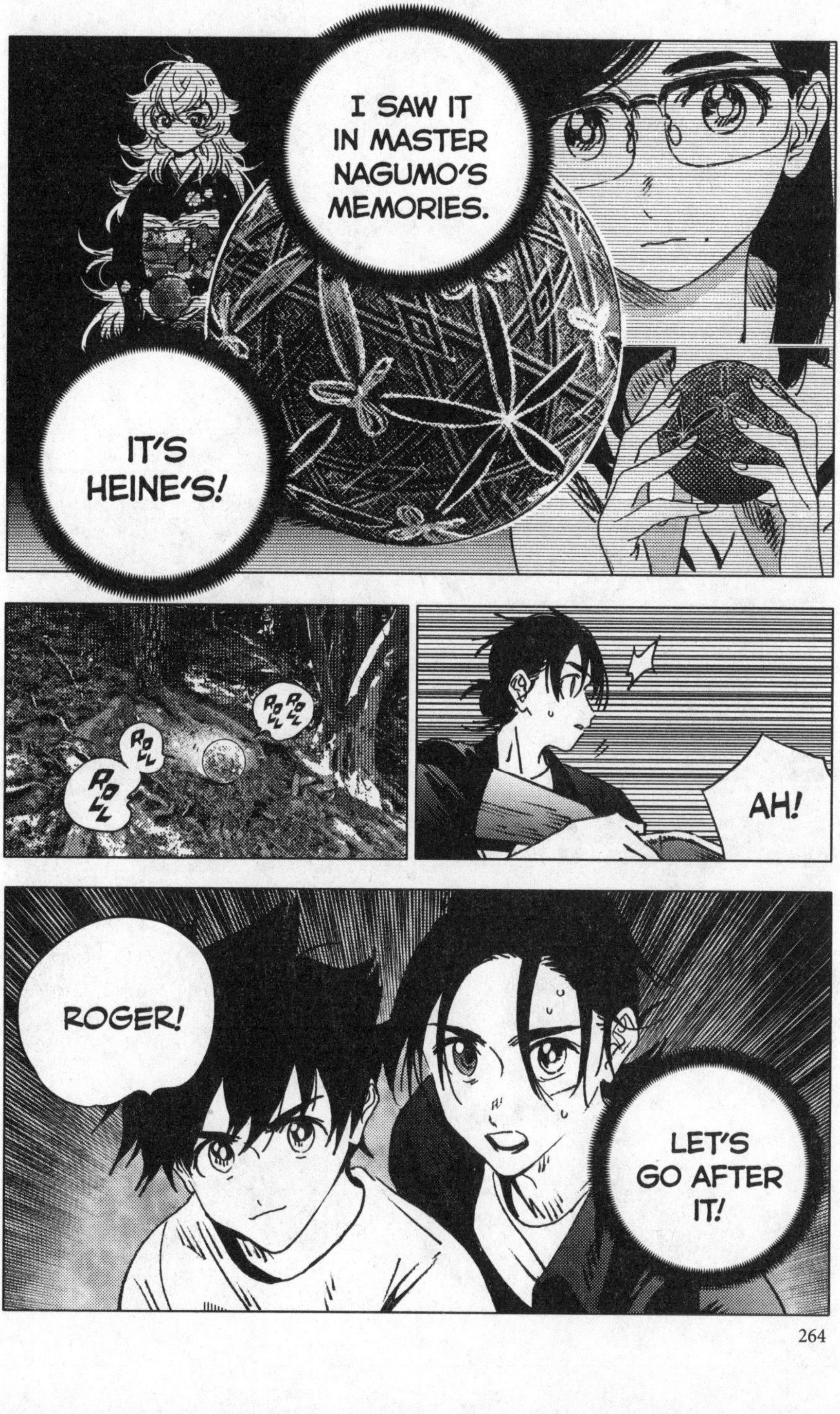
I SAW IT IN MASTER NAGUMO'S MEMORIES.
IT'S HEINE'S!
AH!
ROLL ROLL
ROLL
ROLL
LET'S GO AFTER IT!
ROGER!

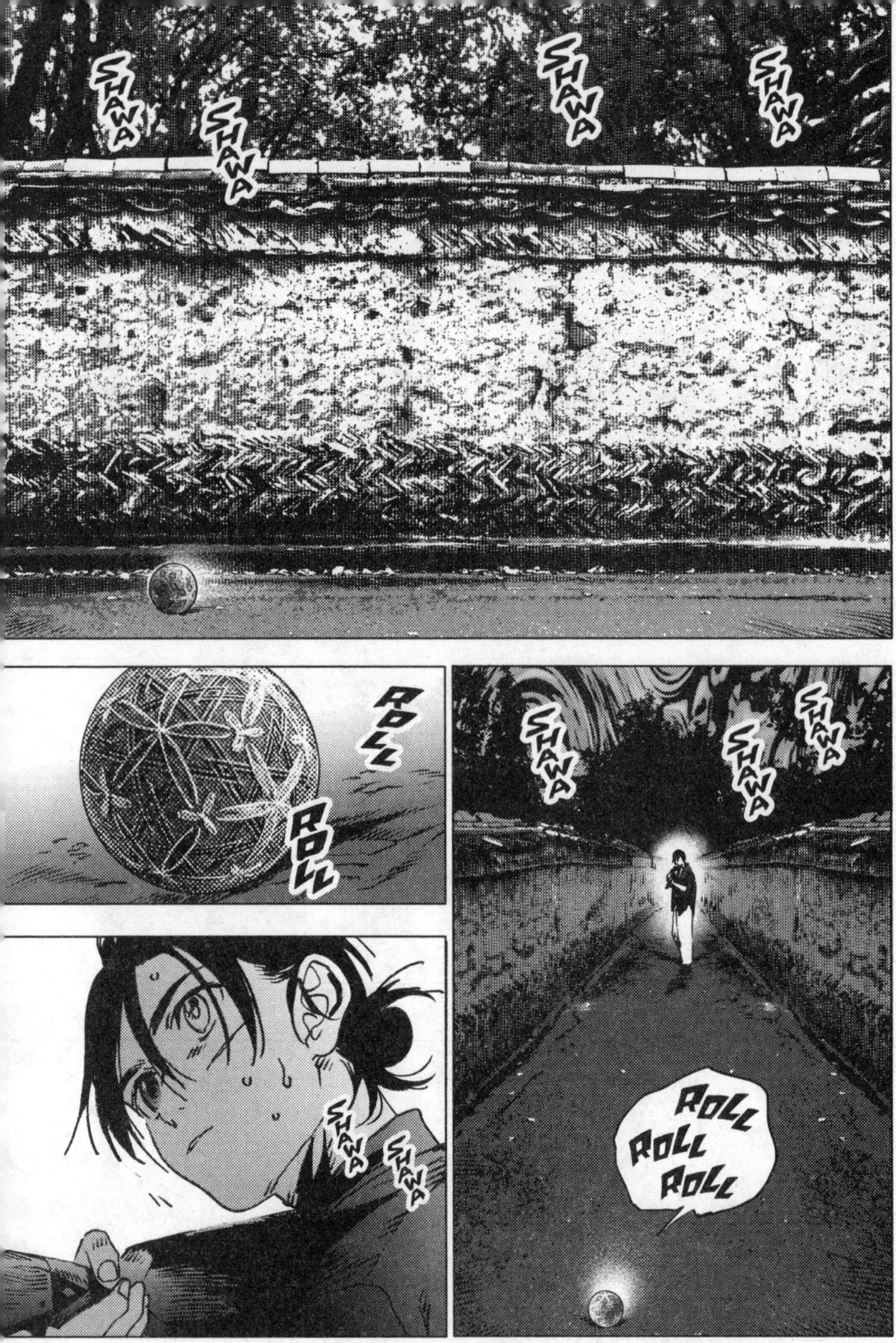
SHAWA
SHAWA
SHAWA
SHAWA
SHAWA
SHAWA
SHAWA
ROLL ROLL ROLL
ROLL ROLL
SHAWA
SHAWA

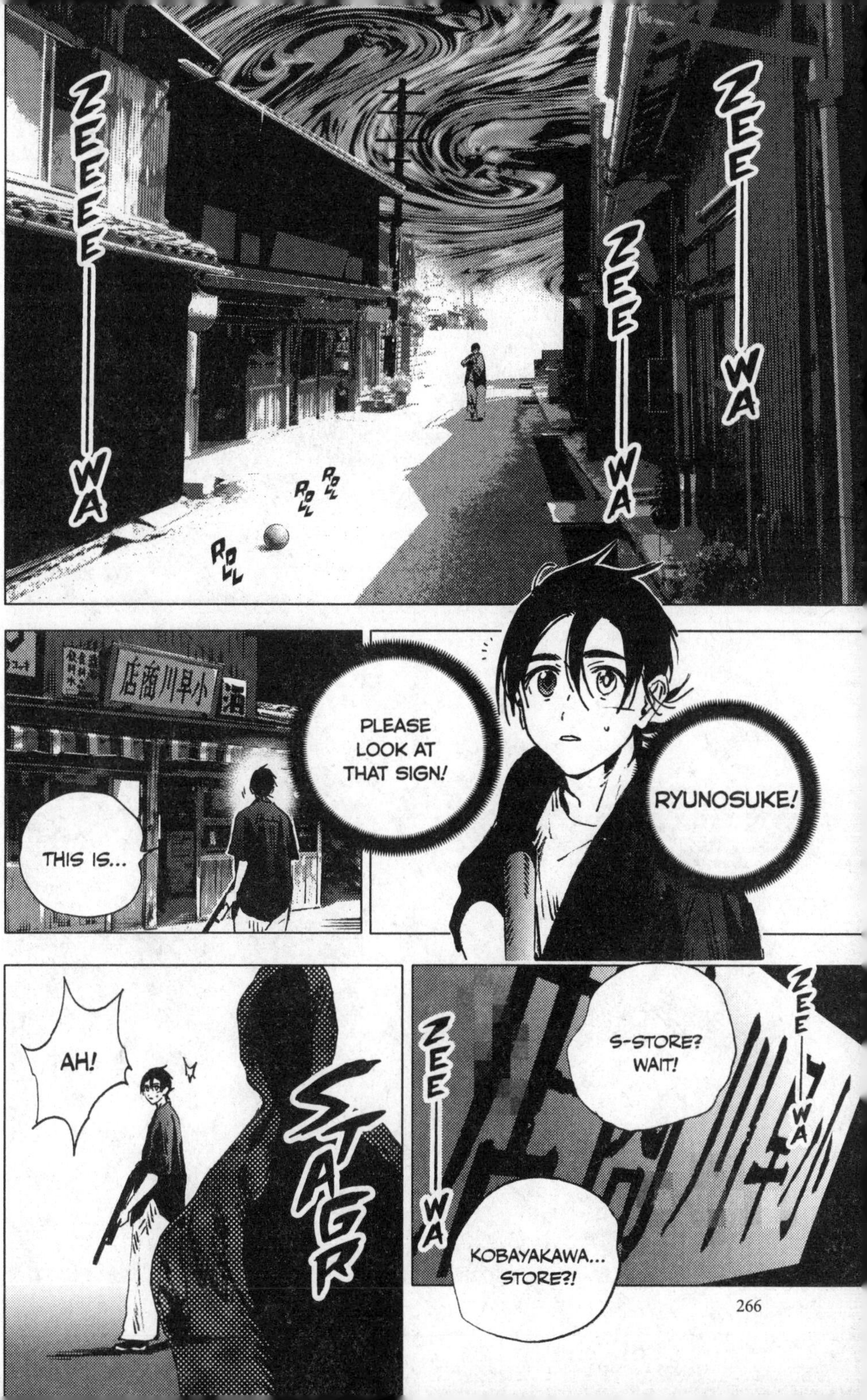
ZEE WA
ZEE WA
ZEEEE WA
ROLL
ROLL
ROLL
RYUNOSUKE!
PLEASE LOOK AT THAT SIGN!
小早川商店
酒
THIS IS...
ZEE WA
S-STORE? WAIT!
ZEE WA
KOBAYAKAWA... STORE?!
STAGR
AH!

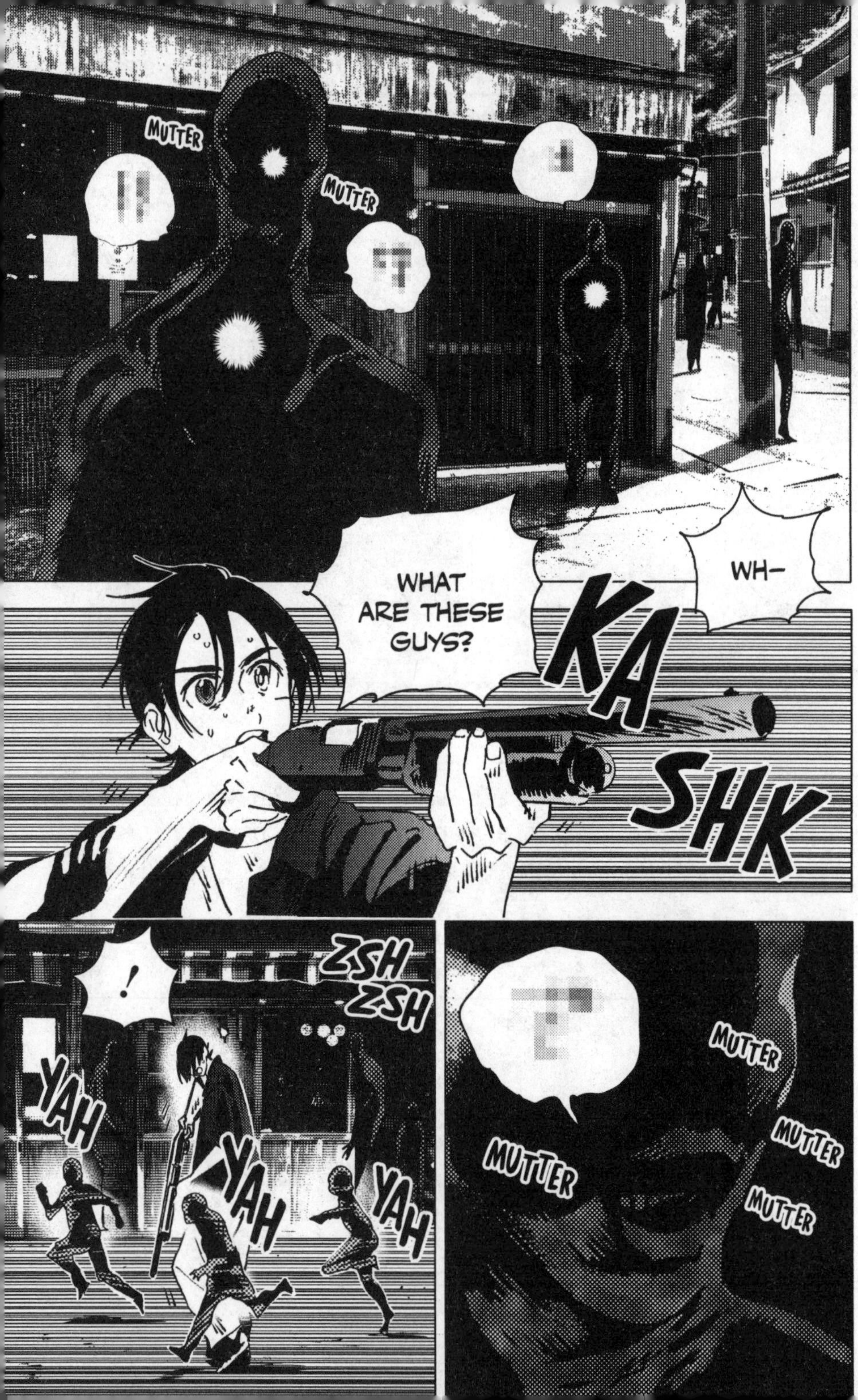
MUTTER
MUTTER
WH-
WHAT ARE THESE GUYS?
KA SHK
MUTTER
MUTTER
MUTTER
MUTTER
!
ZSH ZSH
YAH
YAH
YAH

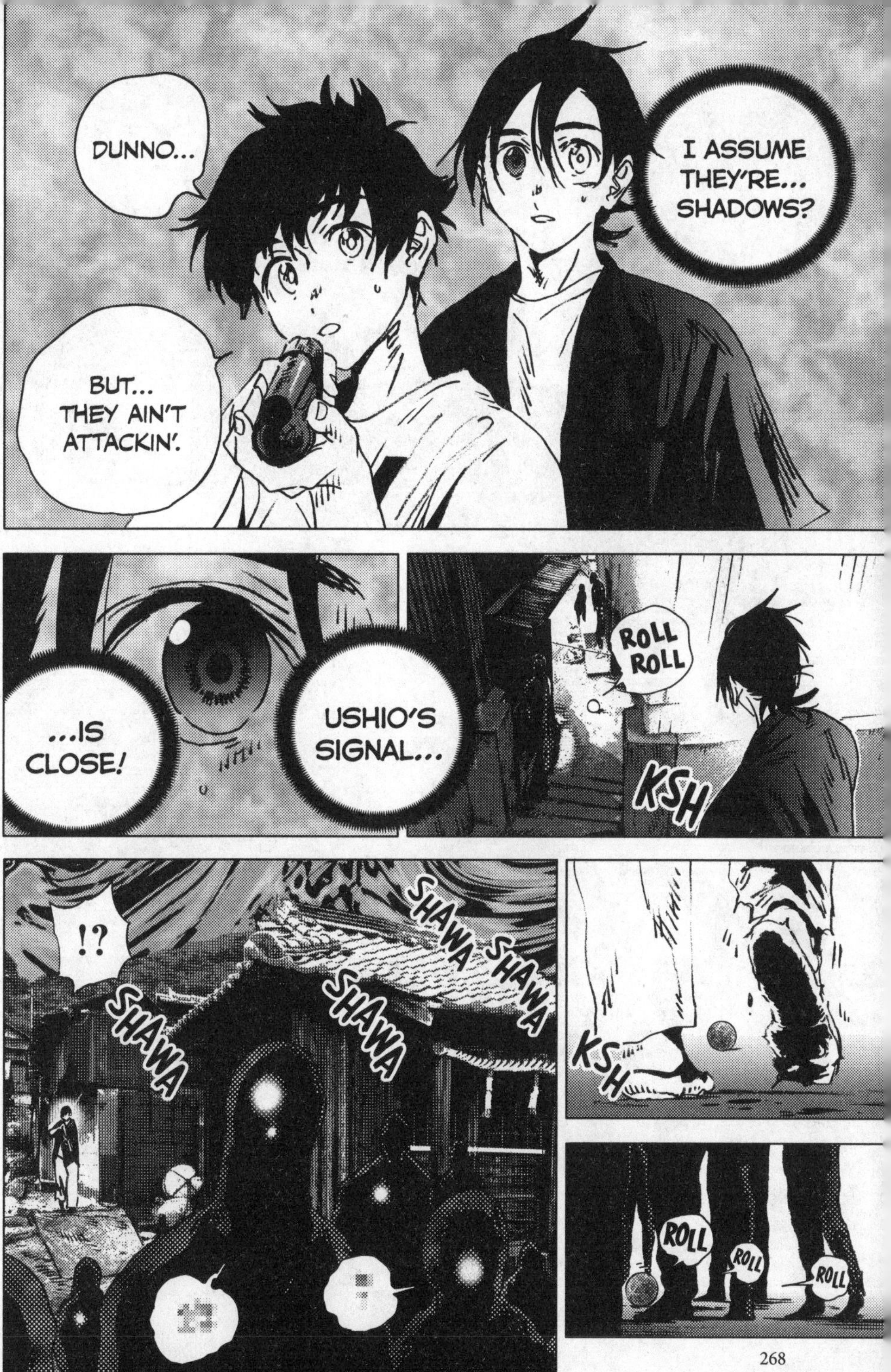
I ASSUME THEY'RE... SHADOWS?
DUNNO...
BUT... THEY AIN'T ATTACKIN'.
ROLL ROLL
KSH
USHIO'S SIGNAL...
...IS CLOSE!
KSH
ROLL
ROLL
ROLL
!?
SHAWA
SHAWA
SHAWA
SHAWA

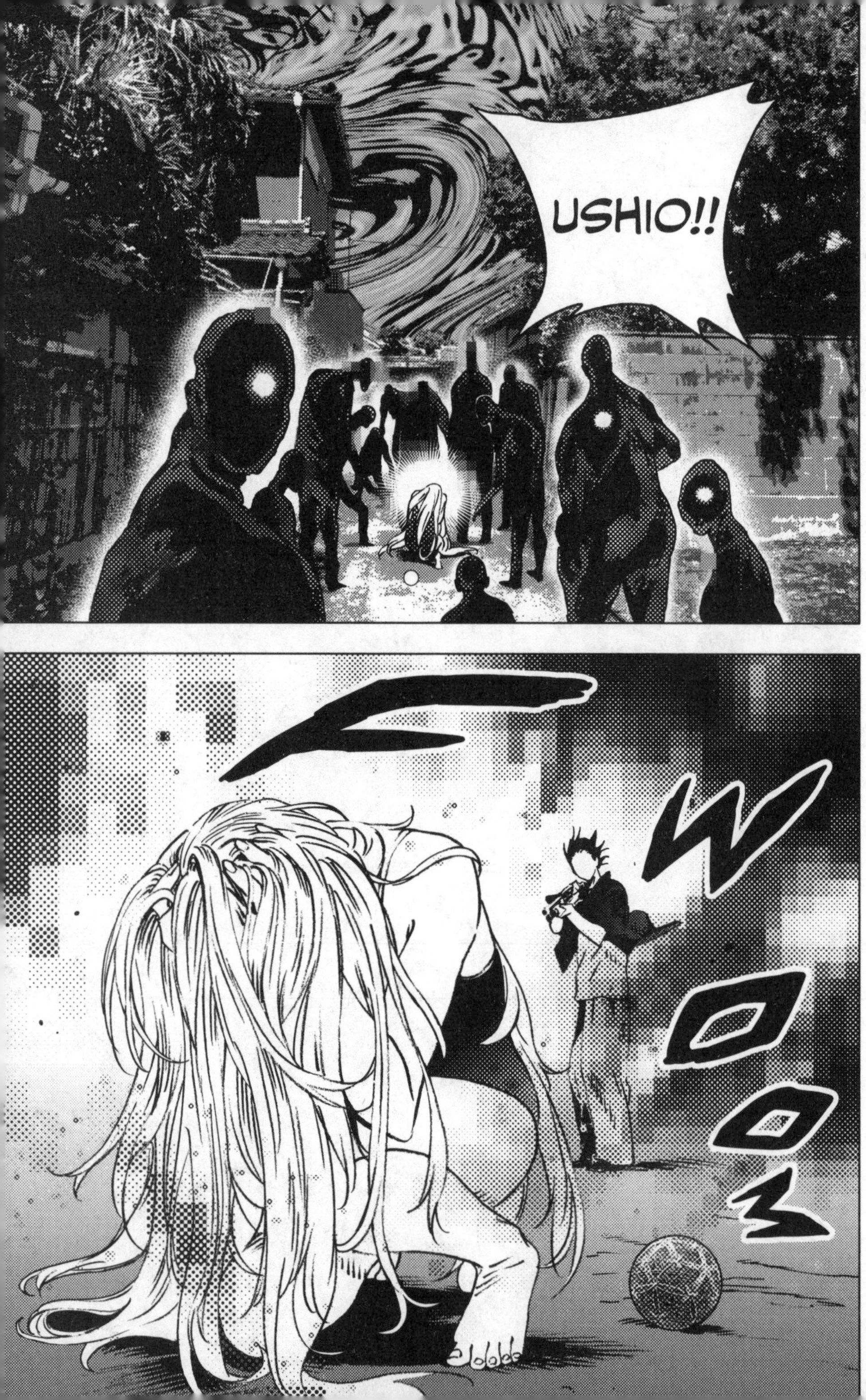
USHIO!!
FWOOM

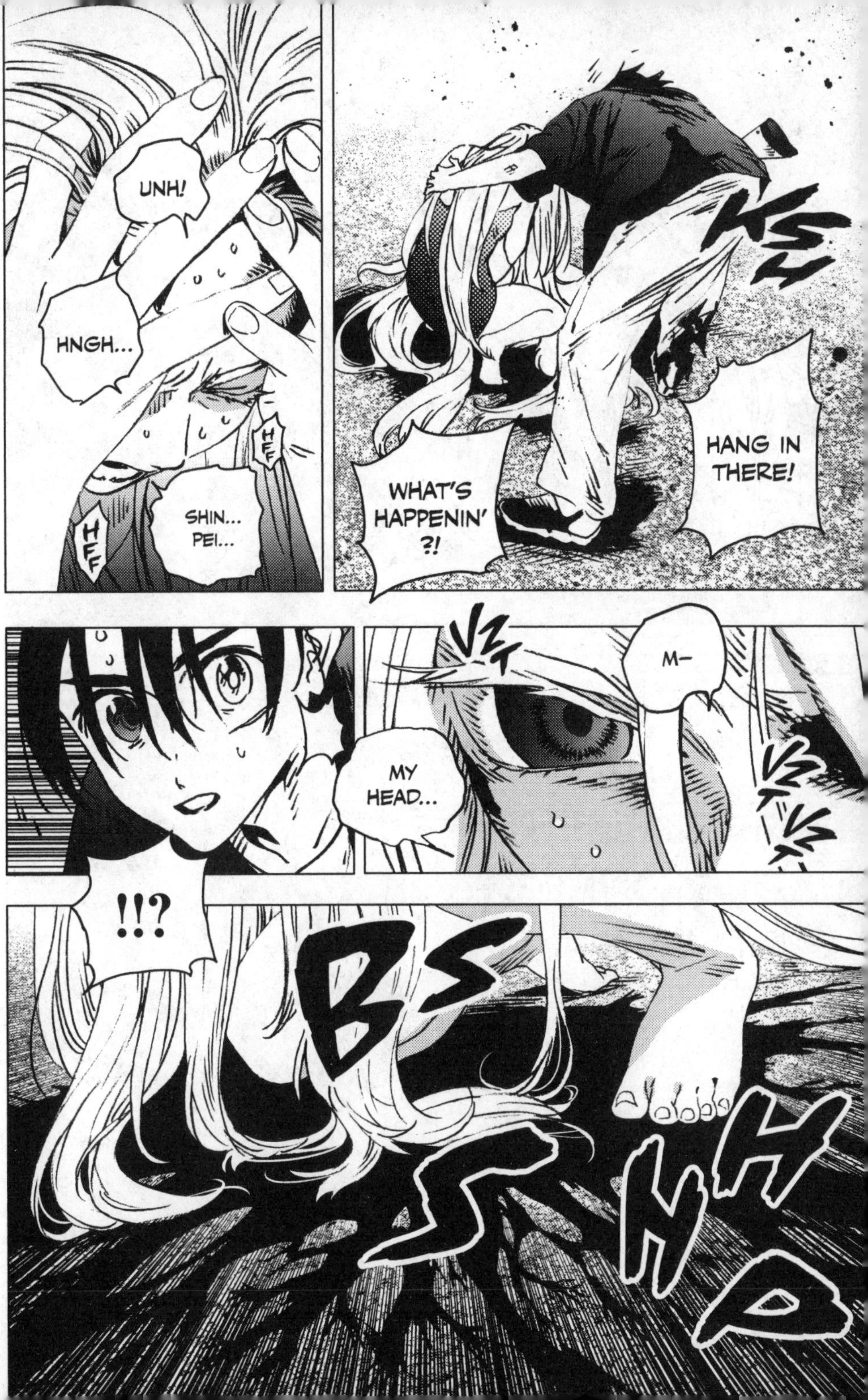
KSH
HANG IN THERE!
WHAT'S HAPPENIN' ?!
UNH!
HNGH...
HFF
SHIN... PEI...
HFF
M–
VZT
VZT
VZT
MY HEAD...
!!?
BSSHHHP

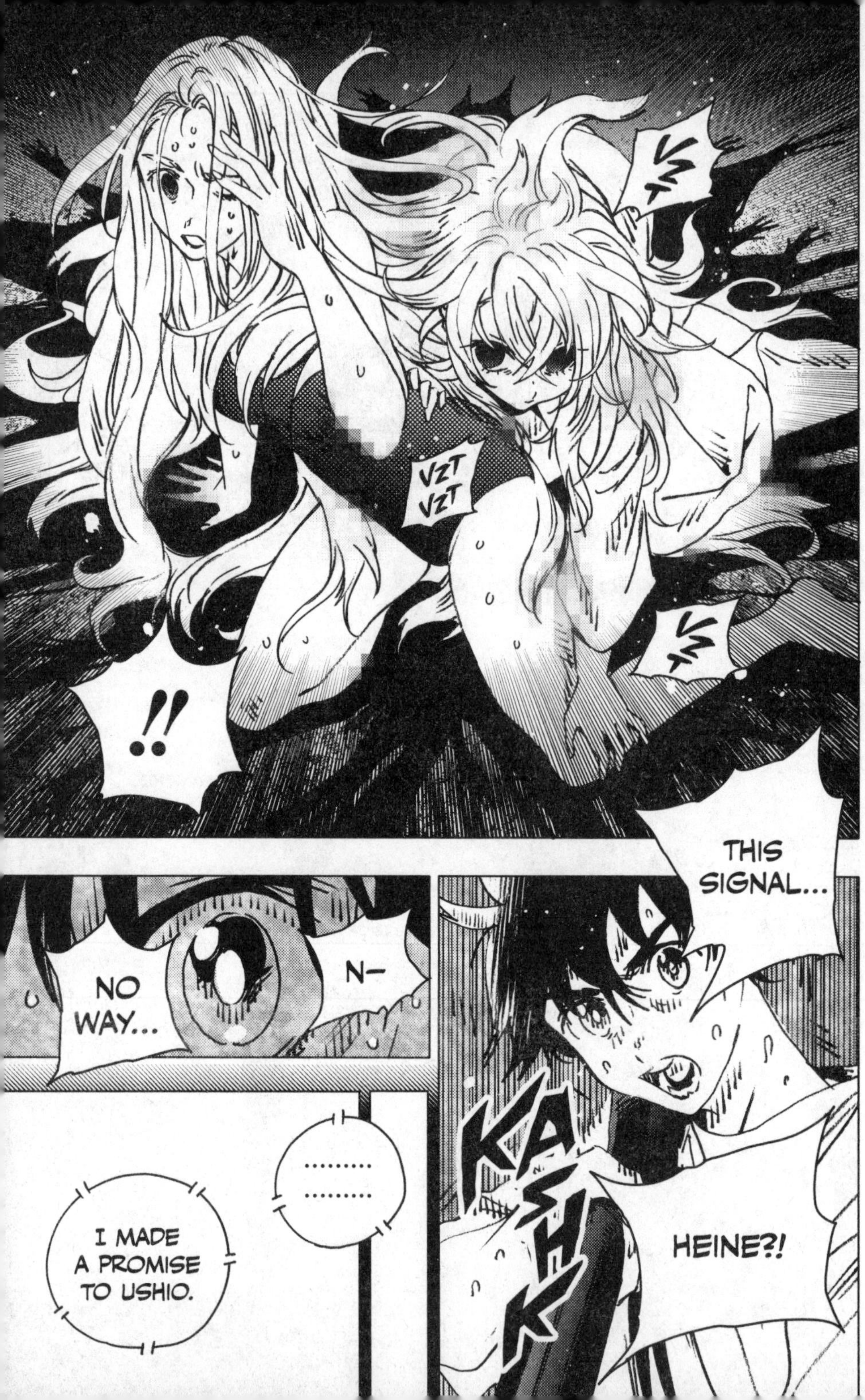
VZT
VZT VZT
VZT
!!
THIS SIGNAL...
N–
NO WAY...
HEINE?!
KASHK
....
....
I MADE A PROMISE TO USHIO.

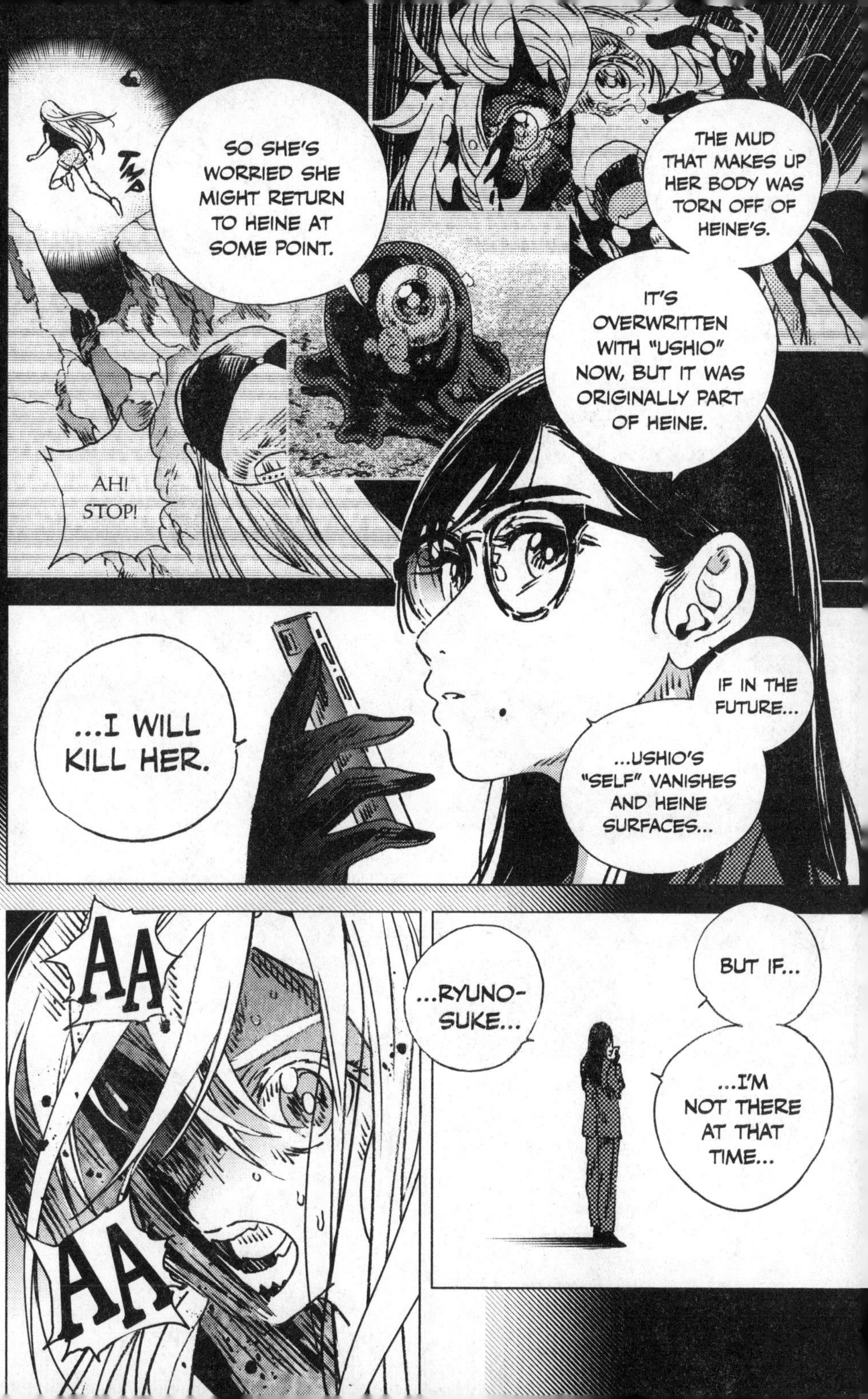
THE MUD THAT MAKES UP HER BODY WAS TORN OFF OF HEINE'S.
IT'S OVERWRITTEN WITH "USHIO" NOW, BUT IT WAS ORIGINALLY PART OF HEINE.
SO SHE'S WORRIED SHE MIGHT RETURN TO HEINE AT SOME POINT.
TMP
AH! STOP!
IF IN THE FUTURE...
...USHIO'S "SELF" VANISHES AND HEINE SURFACES...
...I WILL KILL HER.
BUT IF...
...I'M NOT THERE AT THAT TIME...
...RYUNO-SUKE...
AA
AA

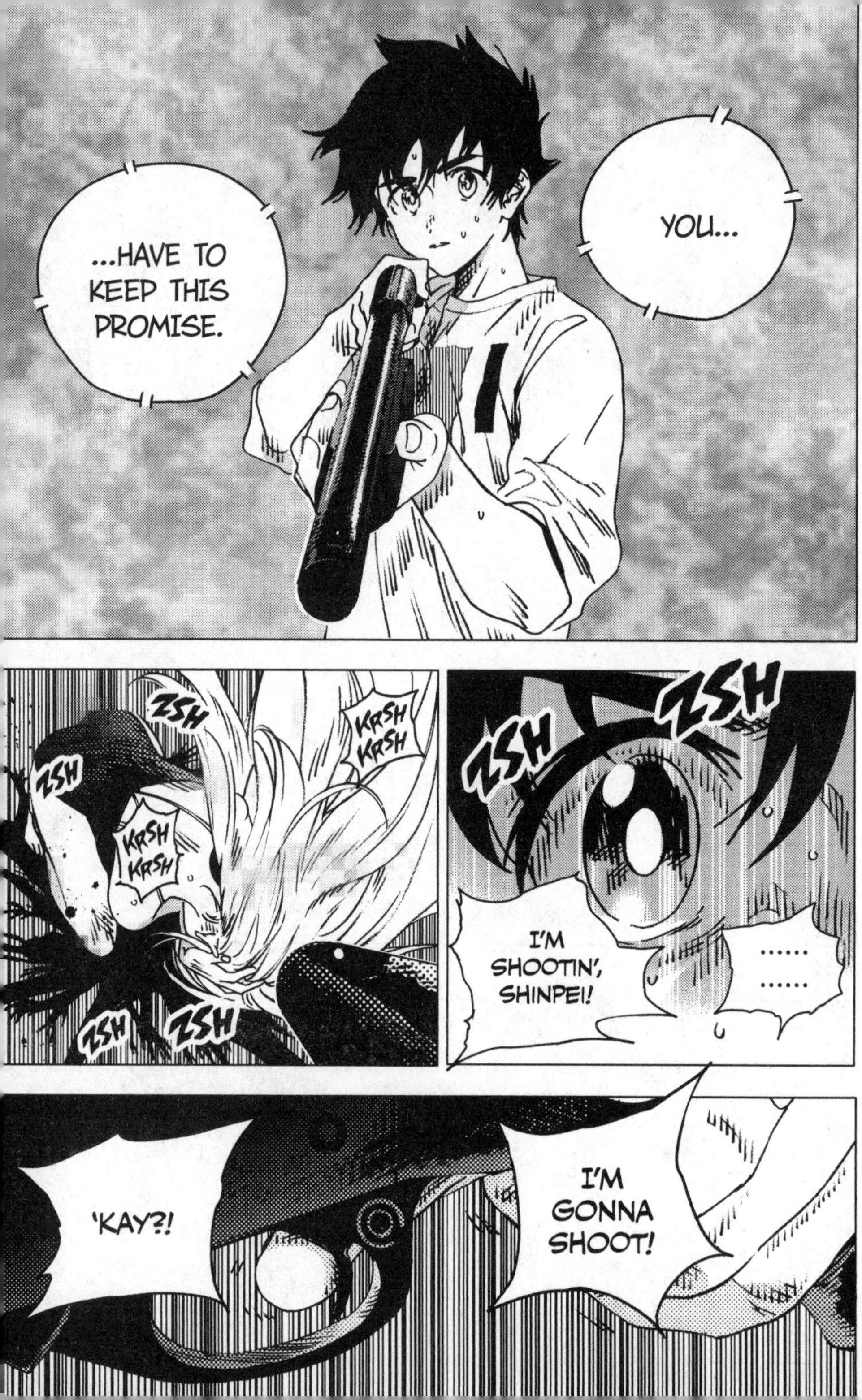
YOU...
...HAVE TO KEEP THIS PROMISE.
ZSH ZSH
......
......
I'M SHOOTIN', SHINPEI!
KRSH KRSH
ZSH
ZSH
KRSH KRSH
ZSH ZSH
I'M GONNA SHOOT!
'KAY?!

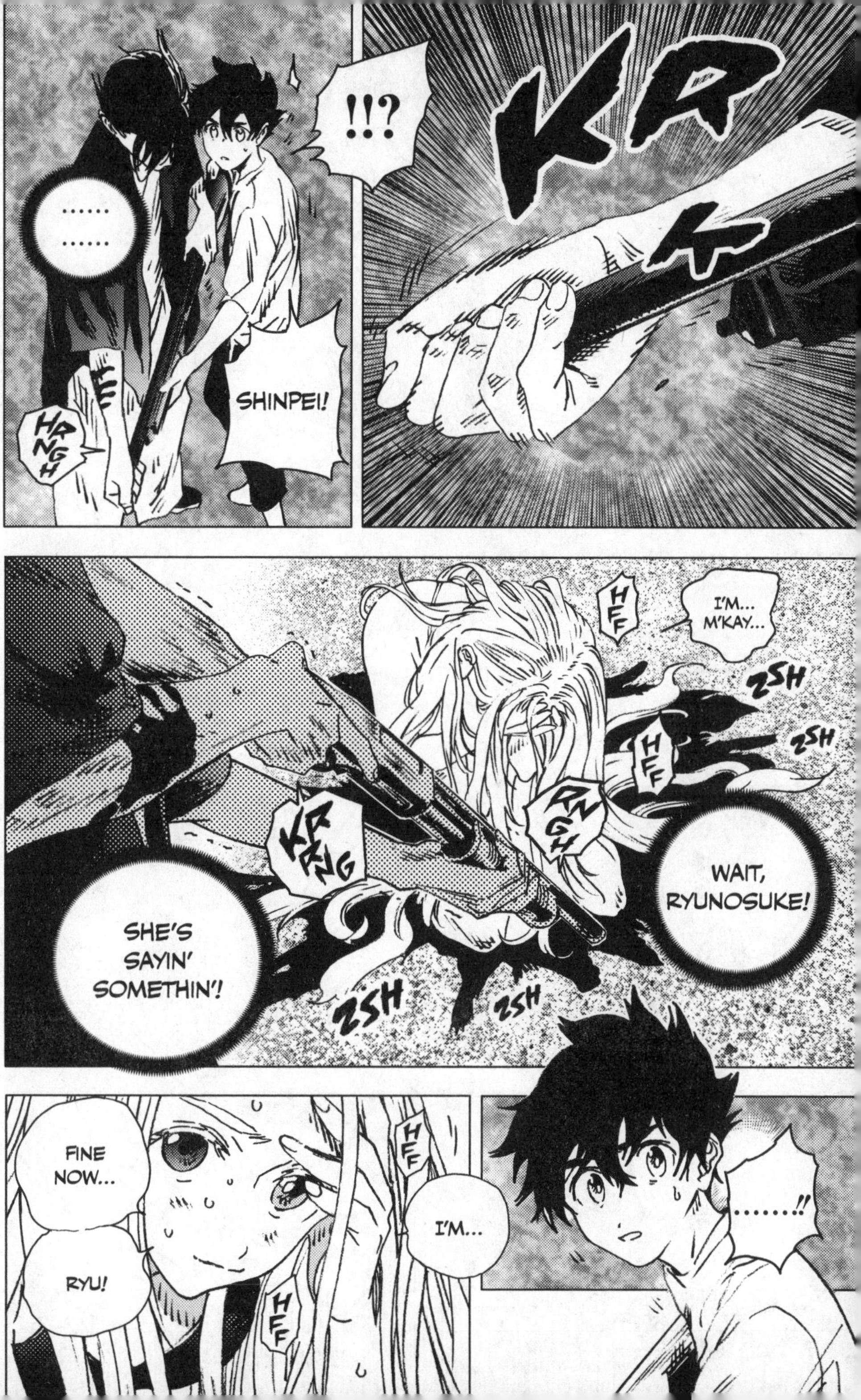
KR
K
!!?
SHINPEI!
......
......
HRNGH
I'M...
M'KAY...
HFF
ZSH
ZSH
HFF
WAIT, RYUNOSUKE!
RNGH
KRRNG
SHE'S SAYIN' SOMETHIN'!
ZSH
ZSH
........!!
HFF
I'M...
FINE NOW...
RYU!
HFF

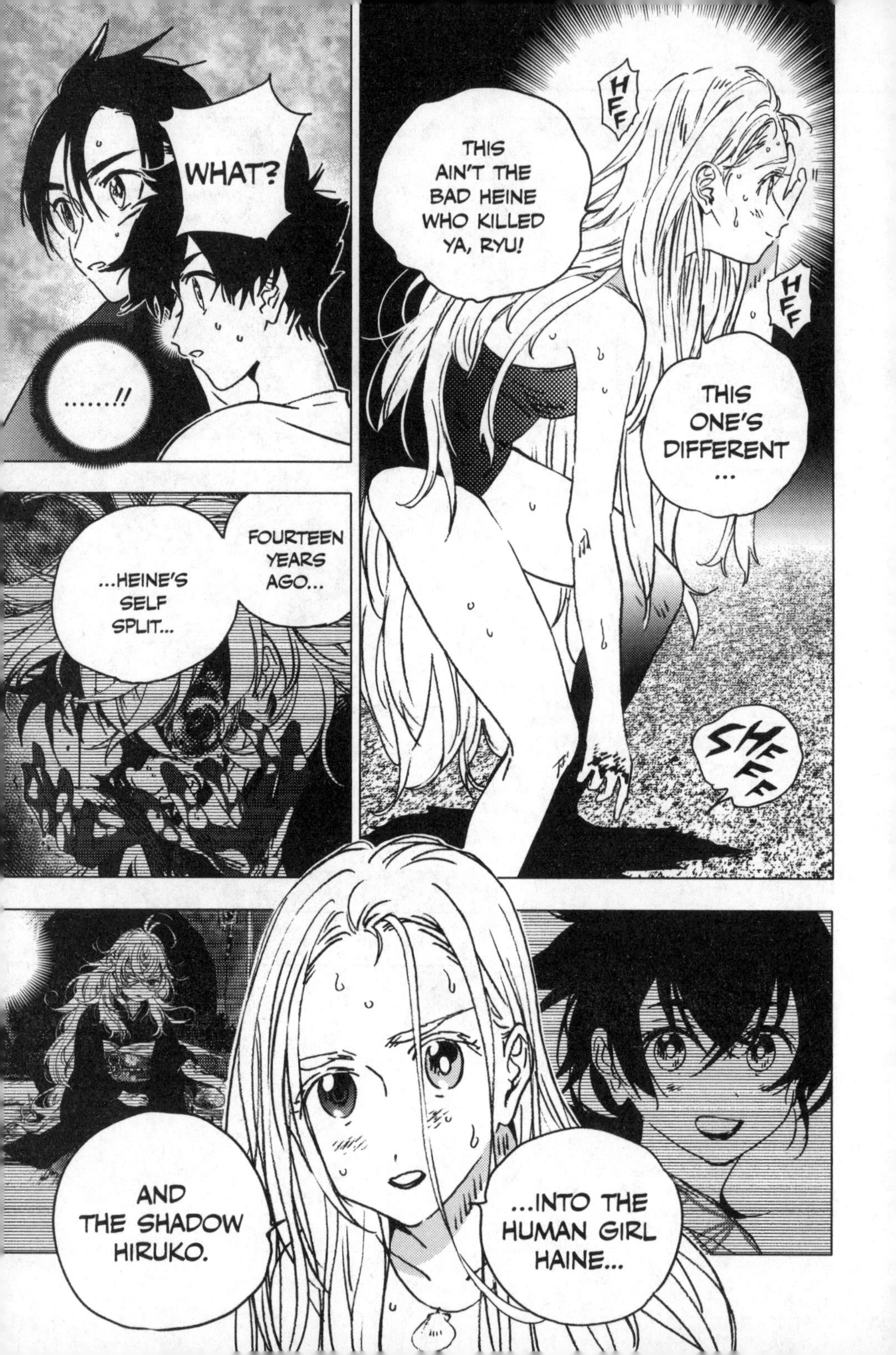
HFF
THIS AIN'T THE BAD HEINE WHO KILLED YA, RYU!
HEFF
THIS ONE'S DIFFERENT ...
SHEFF
WHAT?
......!!
FOURTEEN YEARS AGO...
...HEINE'S SELF SPLIT...
...INTO THE HUMAN GIRL HAINE...
AND THE SHADOW HIRUKO.

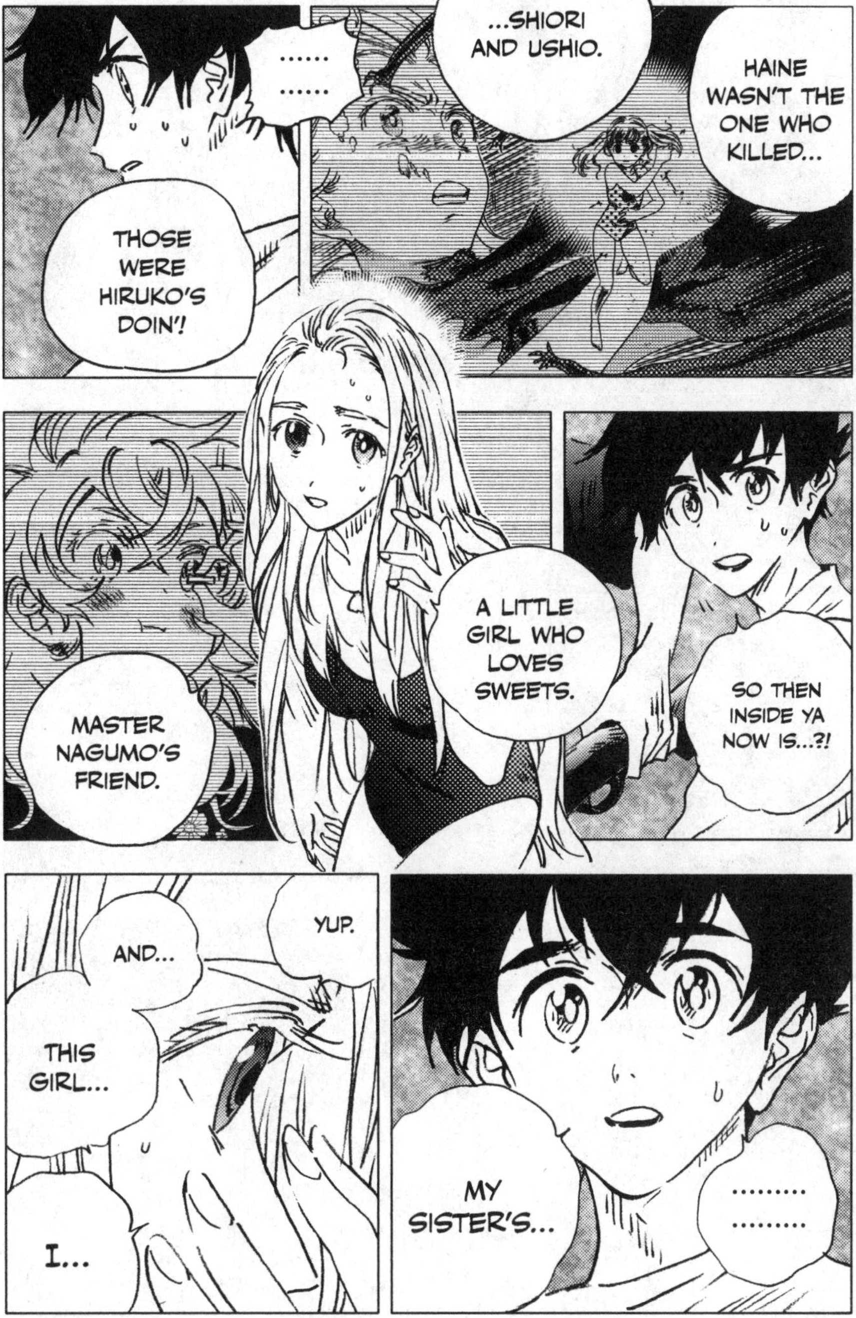
HAINE WASN'T THE ONE WHO KILLED...
...SHIORI AND USHIO.
......
......
THOSE WERE HIRUKO'S DOIN'!
SO THEN INSIDE YA NOW IS...?!
A LITTLE GIRL WHO LOVES SWEETS.
MASTER NAGUMO'S FRIEND.
....
....
MY SISTER'S...
YUP.
AND...
THIS GIRL...
I...

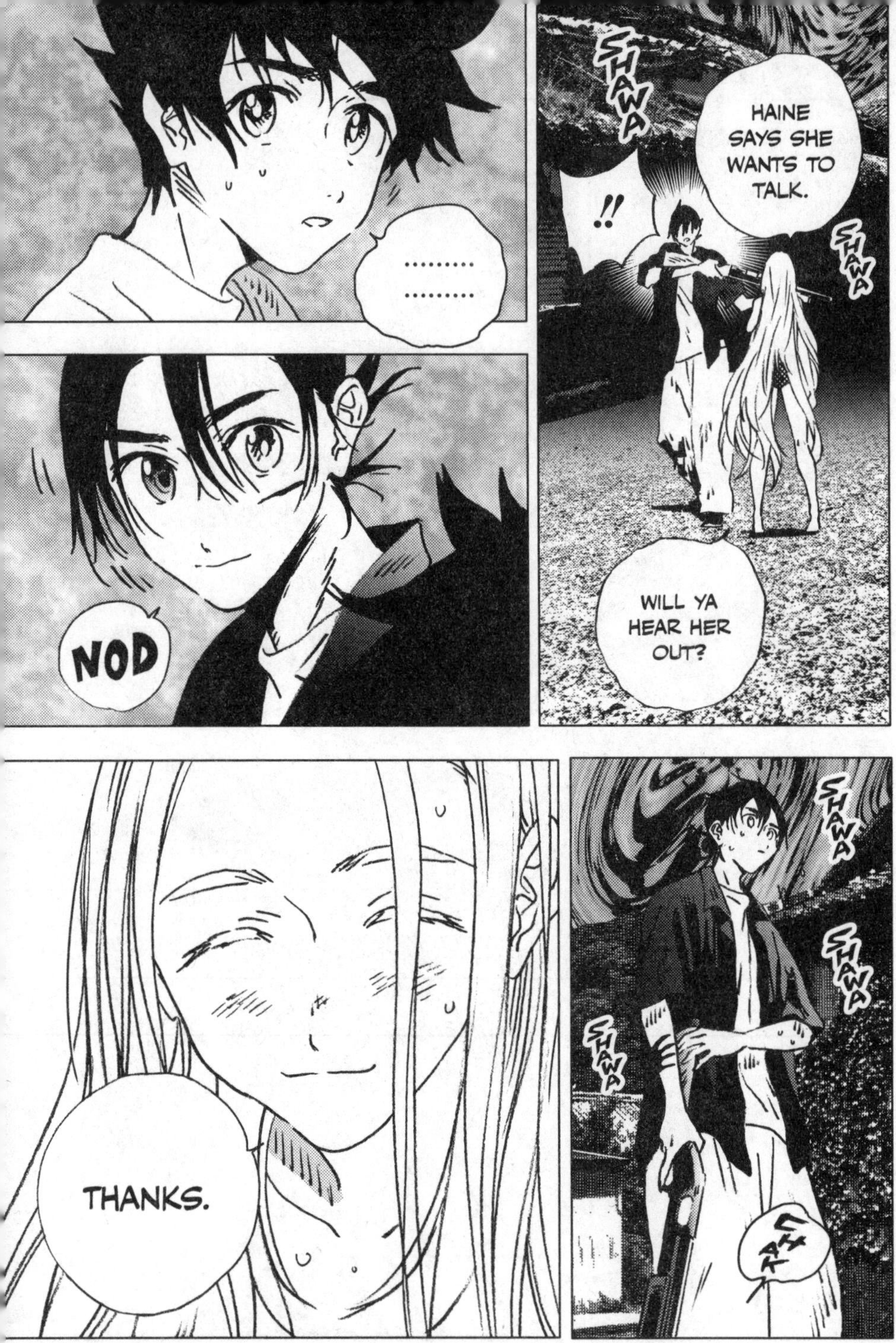
SHAWA
HAINE SAYS SHE WANTS TO TALK.
!!
SHAWA
WILL YA HEAR HER OUT?
....
....
NOD
SHAWA
SHAWA
SHAWA
CHAK
THANKS.

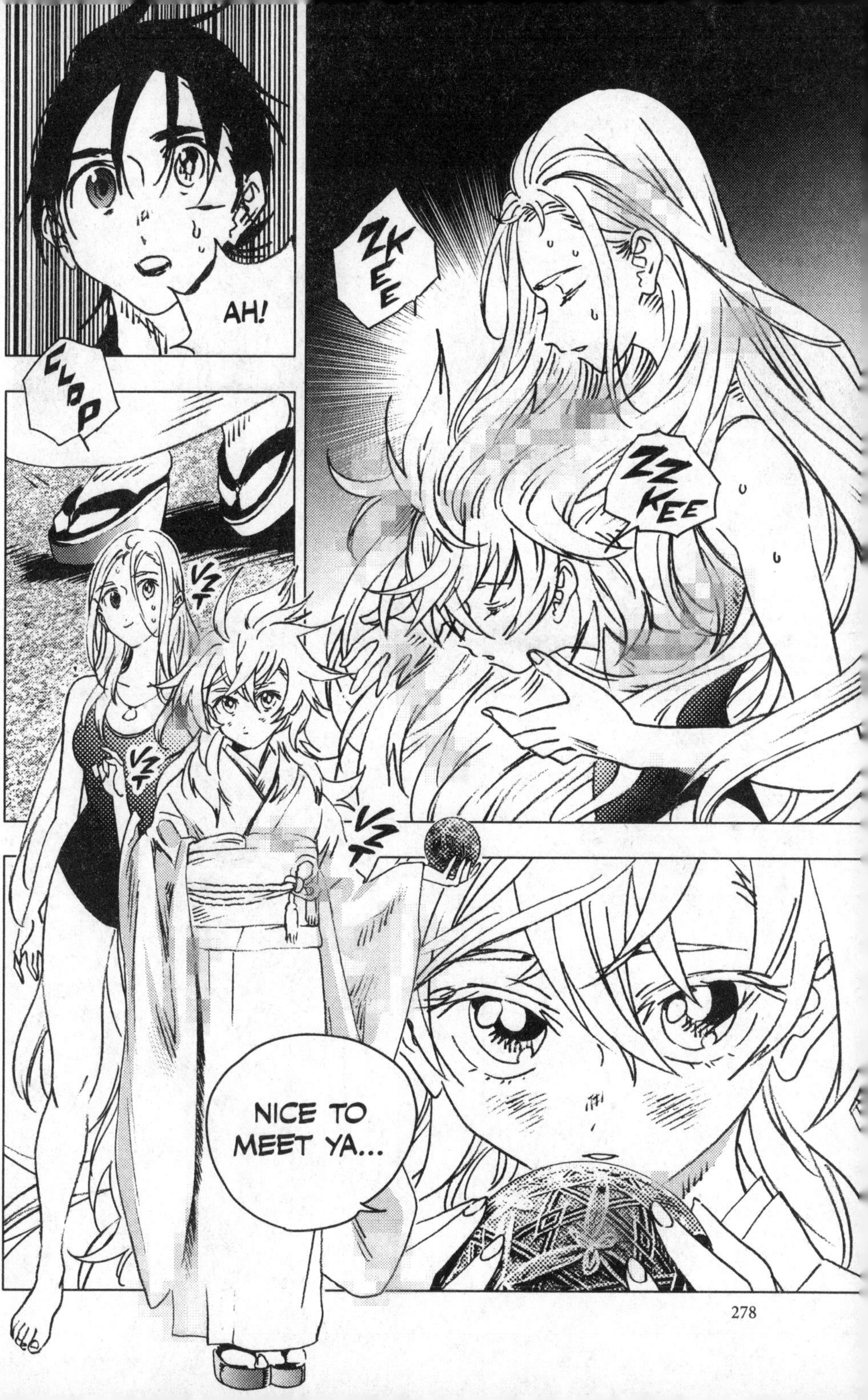
ZKEE
ZZKEE
AH!
GLOP
VZT
VZT
VZT
NICE TO MEET YA...

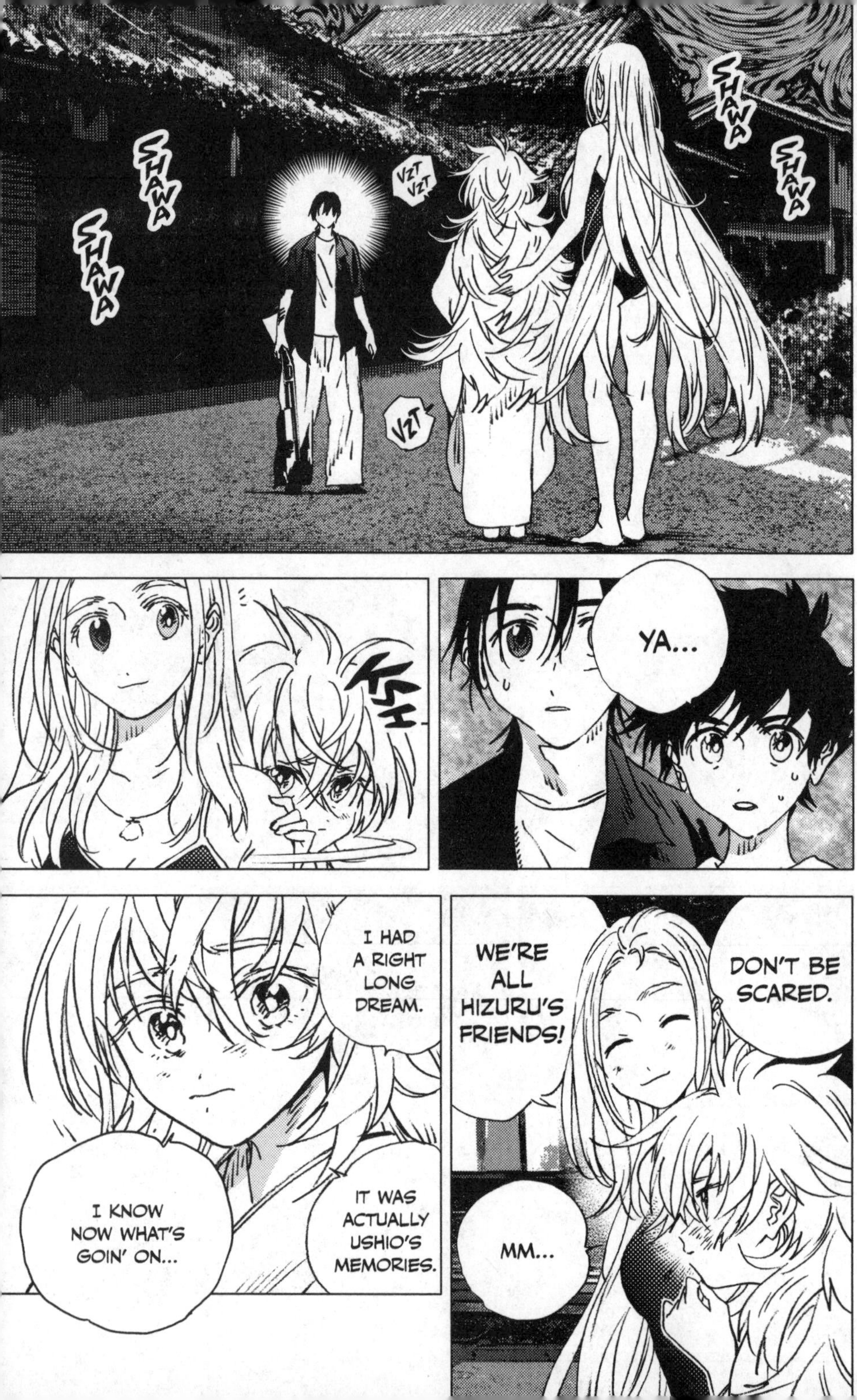
SHAWA
SHAWA
VZT VZT
SHAWA
SHAWA
VZT
YA...
KSH
DON'T BE SCARED.
WE'RE ALL HIZURU'S FRIENDS!
MM...
I HAD A RIGHT LONG DREAM.
IT WAS ACTUALLY USHIO'S MEMORIES.
I KNOW NOW WHAT'S GOIN' ON...

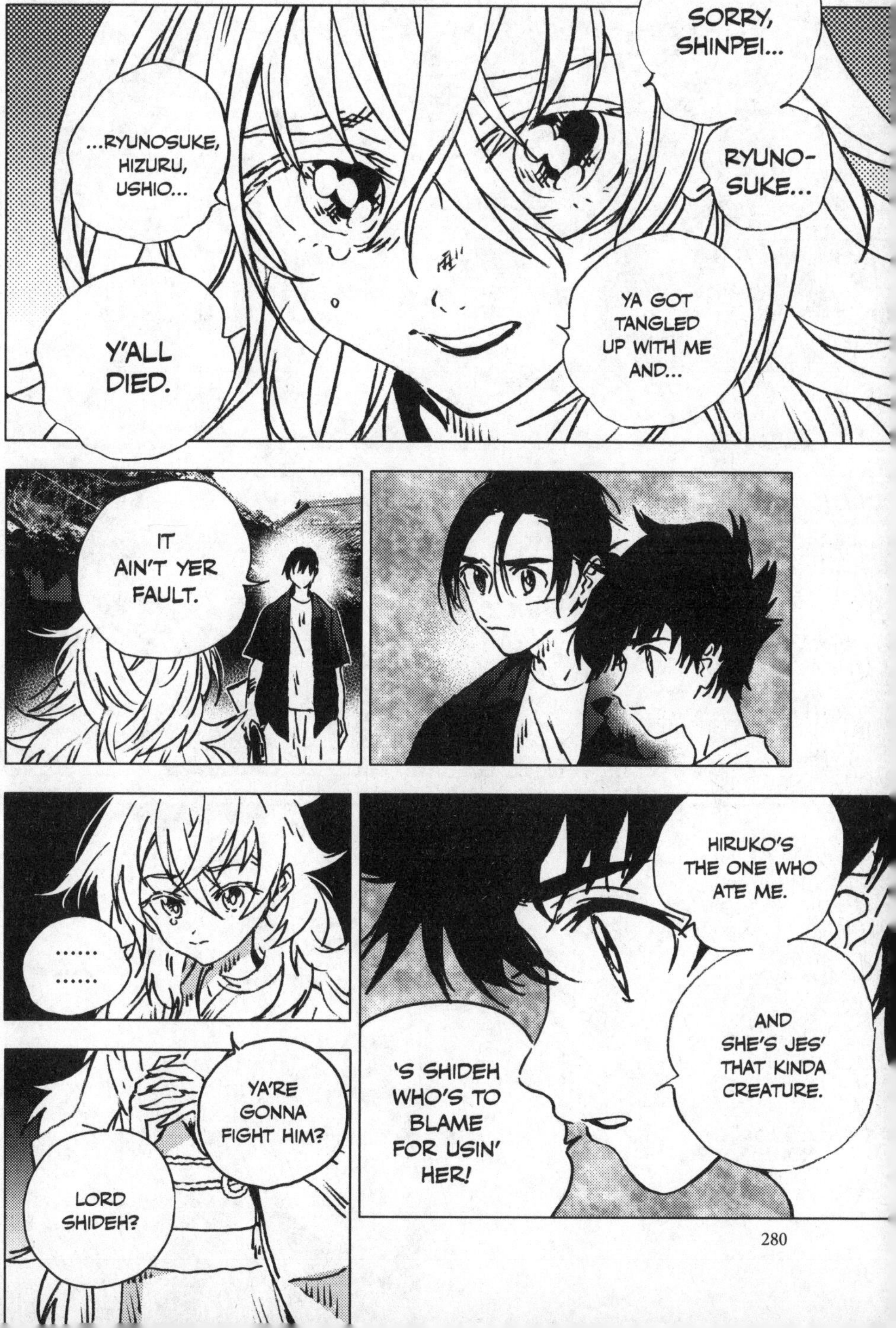
SORRY, SHINPEI...
RYUNO-SUKE...
...RYUNOSUKE, HIZURU, USHIO...
YA GOT TANGLED UP WITH ME AND...
Y'ALL DIED.
IT AIN'T YER FAULT.
HIRUKO'S THE ONE WHO ATE ME.
AND SHE'S JES' THAT KINDA CREATURE.
'S SHIDEH WHO'S TO BLAME FOR USIN' HER!
......
......
YA'RE GONNA FIGHT HIM?
LORD SHIDEH?

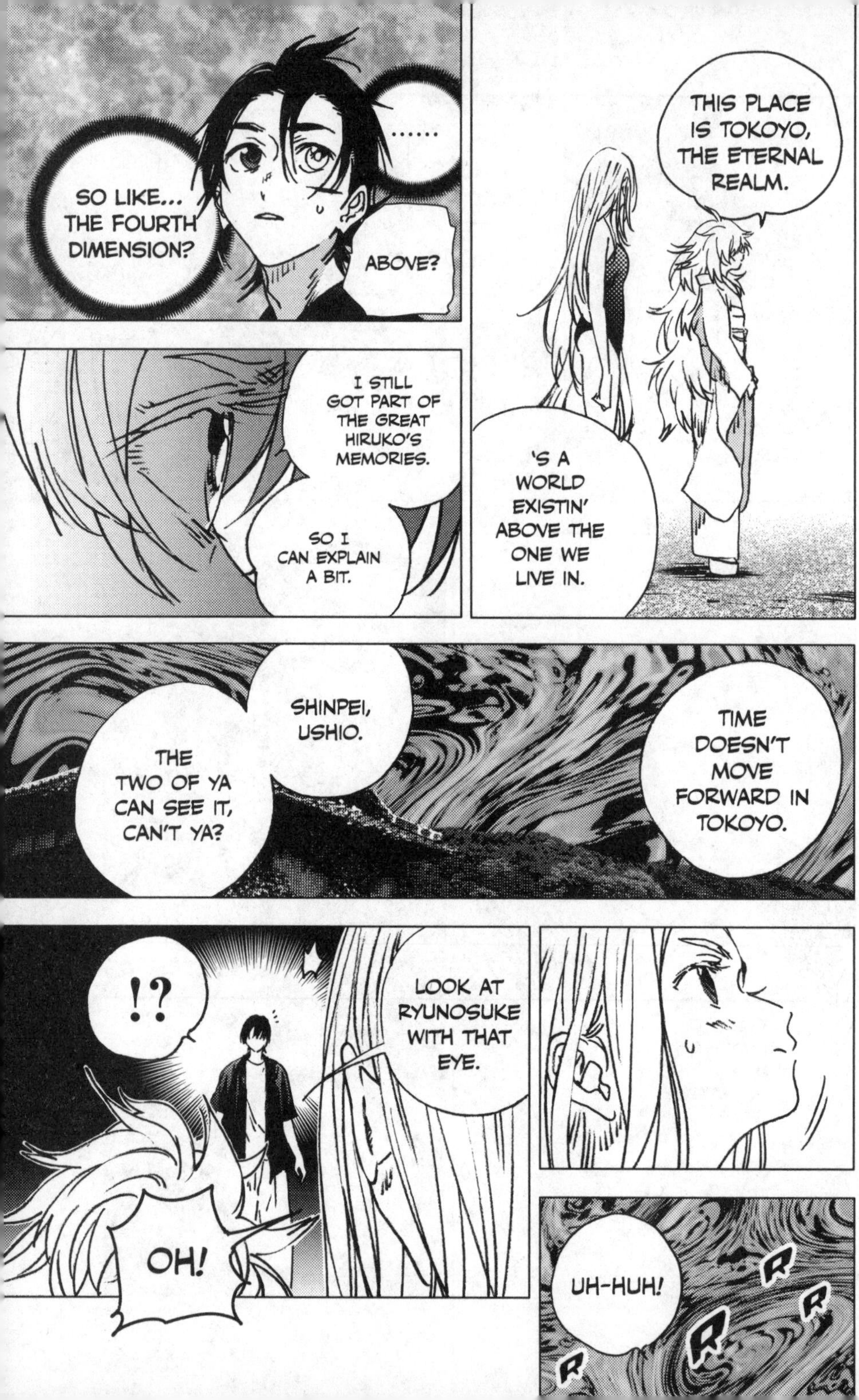
THIS PLACE IS TOKOYO, THE ETERNAL REALM.
'S A WORLD EXISTIN' ABOVE THE ONE WE LIVE IN.
......
ABOVE?
SO LIKE... THE FOURTH DIMENSION?
I STILL GOT PART OF THE GREAT HIRUKO'S MEMORIES.
SO I CAN EXPLAIN A BIT.
TIME DOESN'T MOVE FORWARD IN TOKOYO.
SHINPEI, USHIO.
THE TWO OF YA CAN SEE IT, CAN'T YA?
UH-HUH!
R R R R R
LOOK AT RYUNOSUKE WITH THAT EYE.
!?
OH!

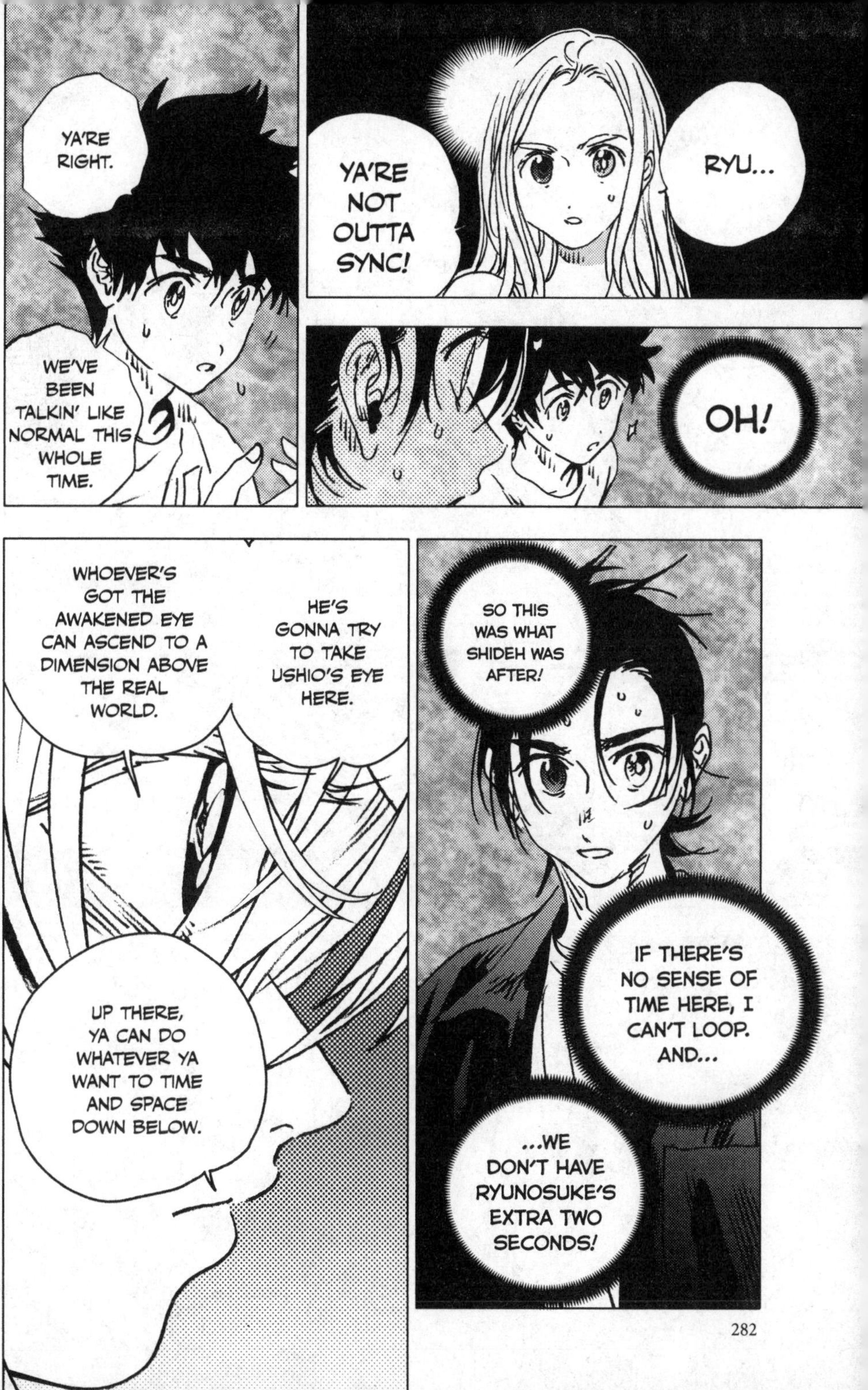
RYU...
YA'RE NOT OUTTA SYNC!
OH!
YA'RE RIGHT.
WE'VE BEEN TALKIN' LIKE NORMAL THIS WHOLE TIME.
SO THIS WAS WHAT SHIDEH WAS AFTER!
IF THERE'S NO SENSE OF TIME HERE, I CAN'T LOOP. AND...
...WE DON'T HAVE RYUNOSUKE'S EXTRA TWO SECONDS!
HE'S GONNA TRY TO TAKE USHIO'S EYE HERE.
WHOEVER'S GOT THE AWAKENED EYE CAN ASCEND TO A DIMENSION ABOVE THE REAL WORLD.
UP THERE, YA CAN DO WHATEVER YA WANT TO TIME AND SPACE DOWN BELOW.

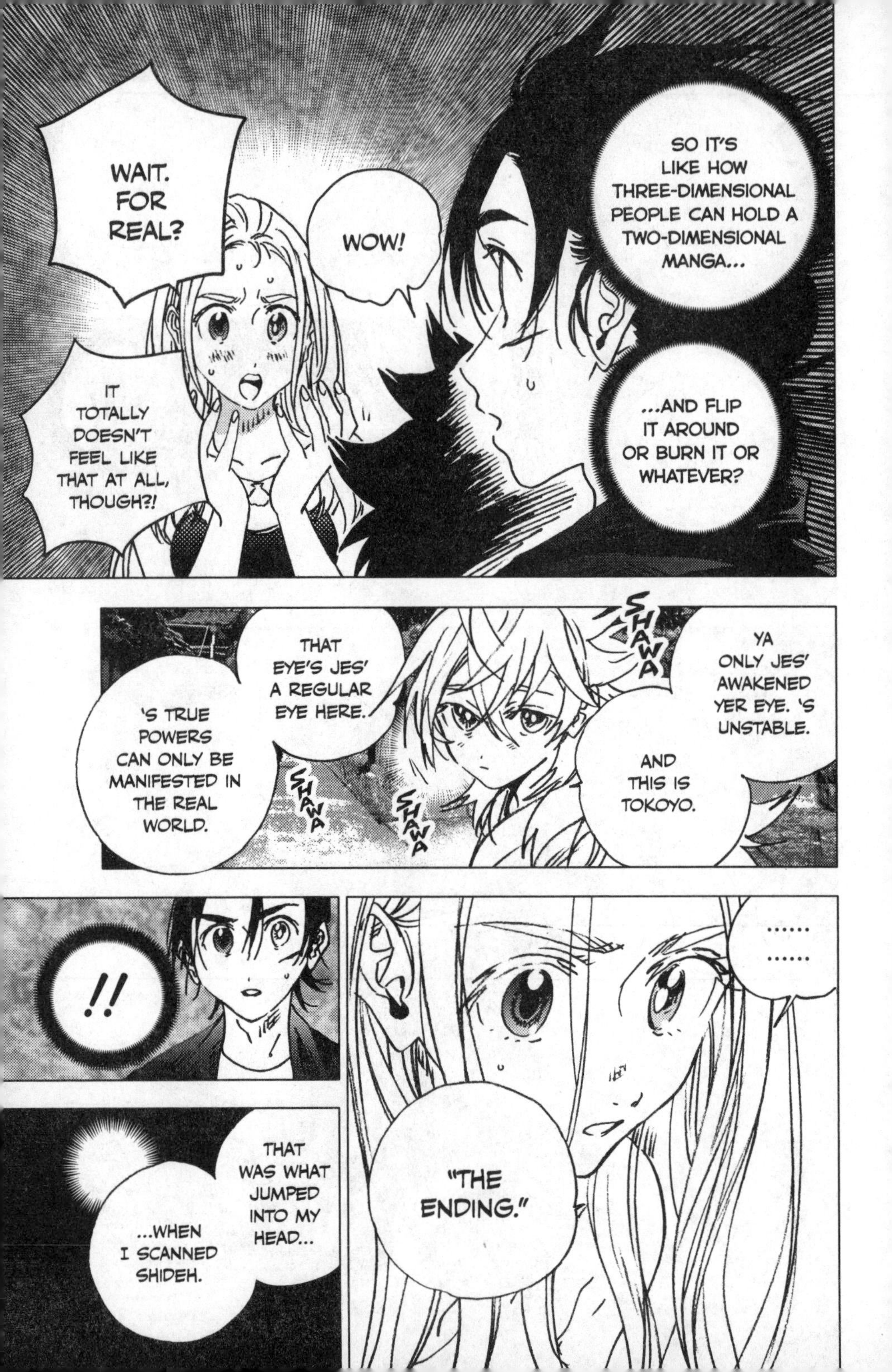
SO IT'S LIKE HOW THREE-DIMENSIONAL PEOPLE CAN HOLD A TWO-DIMENSIONAL MANGA...
...AND FLIP IT AROUND OR BURN IT OR WHATEVER?
WOW!
WAIT. FOR REAL?
IT TOTALLY DOESN'T FEEL LIKE THAT AT ALL, THOUGH?!
SHAWA
YA ONLY JES' AWAKENED YER EYE. 'S UNSTABLE.
AND THIS IS TOKOYO.
SHAWA
SHAWA
THAT EYE'S JES' A REGULAR EYE HERE.
'S TRUE POWERS CAN ONLY BE MANIFESTED IN THE REAL WORLD.
....
"THE ENDING."
!!
THAT WAS WHAT JUMPED INTO MY HEAD...
...WHEN I SCANNED SHIDEH.

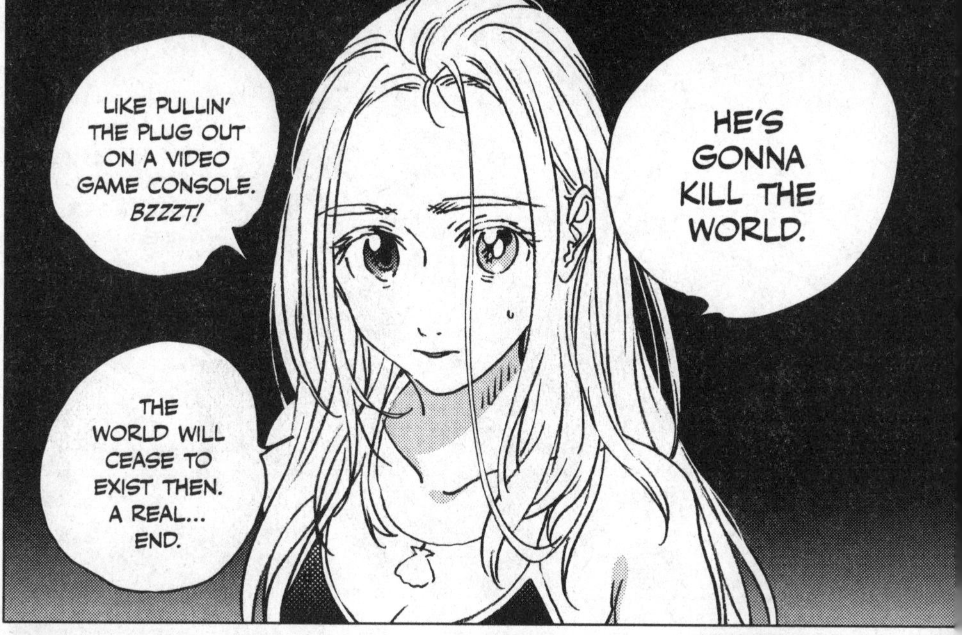
HE'S GONNA KILL THE WORLD.
LIKE PULLIN' THE PLUG OUT ON A VIDEO GAME CONSOLE. *BZZZT!*
THE WORLD WILL CEASE TO EXIST THEN. A REAL... END.

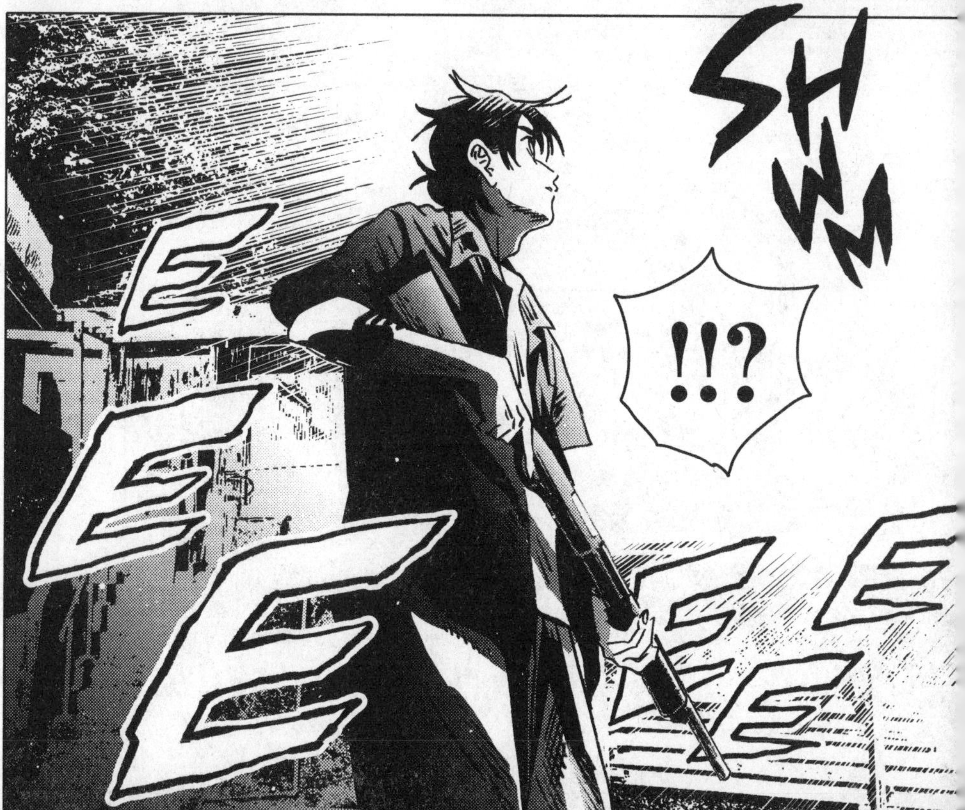
SHWWM
!!?
EEEEE
EEEEE

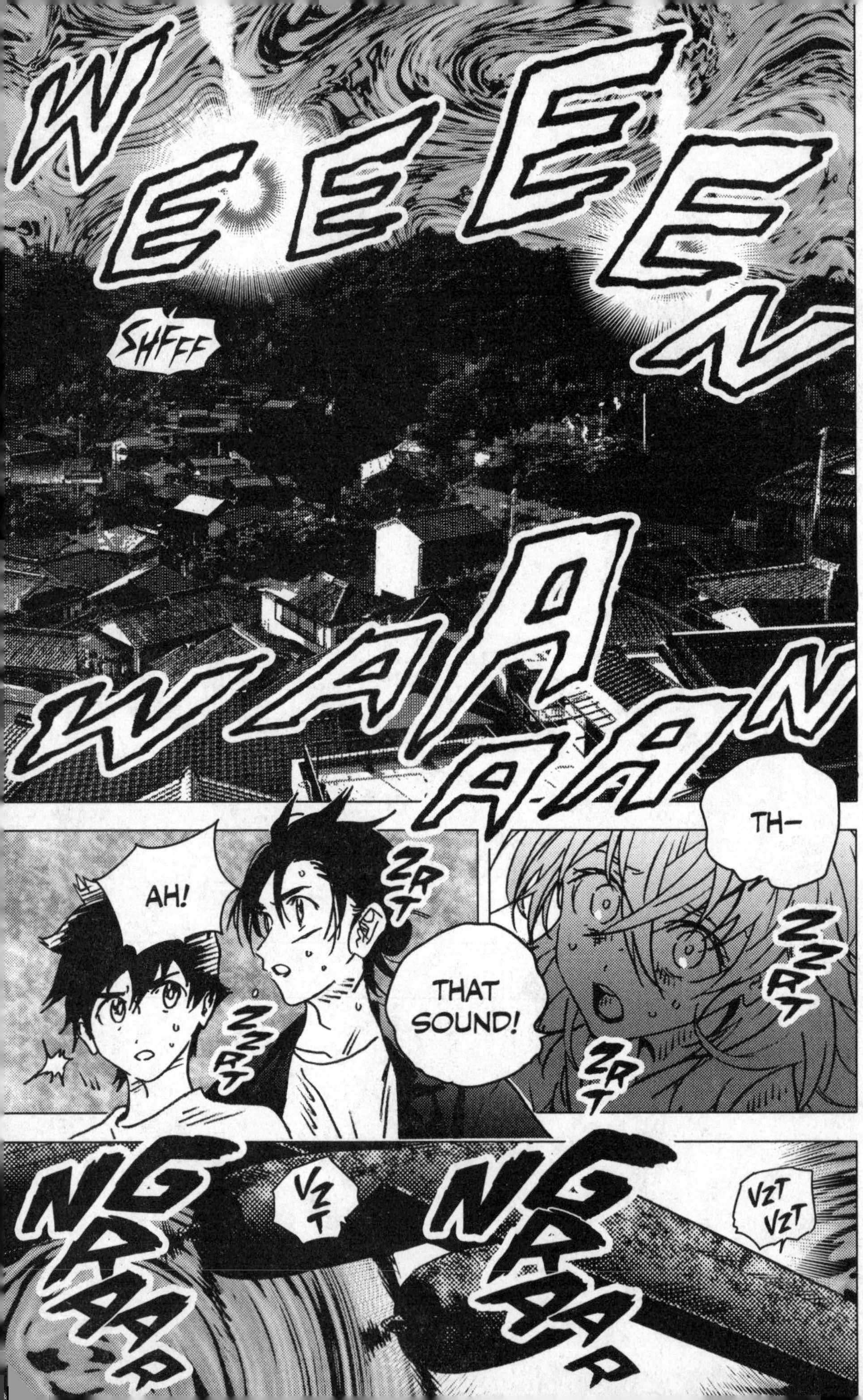
WEEEEN
SHFFF
WAAAAN
TH-
ZZRT
ZRT
THAT SOUND!
ZRT
AH!
ZZRT
VZT VZT
NGNAAR
VZT
NGNAAR

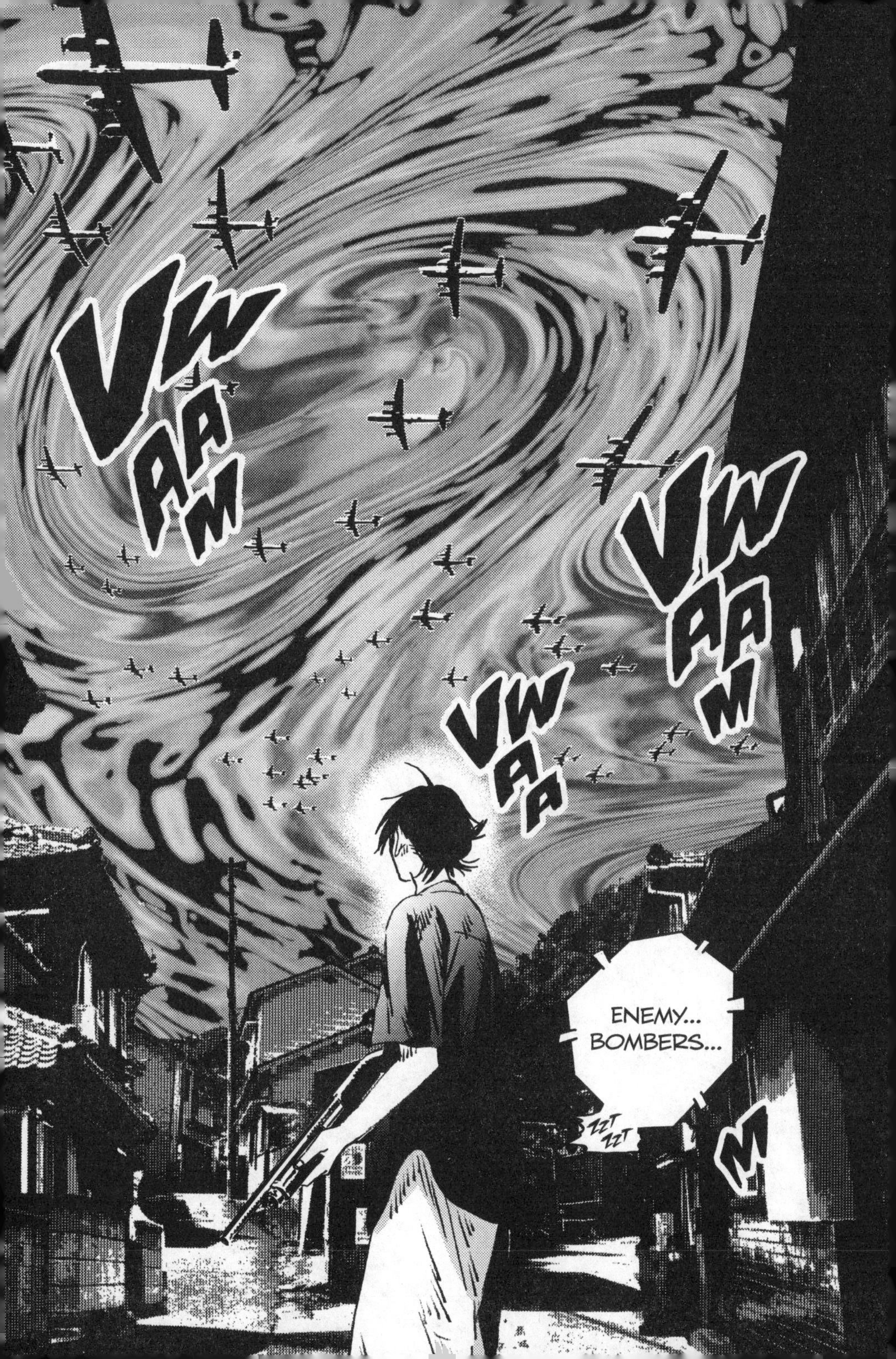
VWAAM
VWAAM
VWAA
ENEMY... BOMBERS...
ZZT ZZT
M

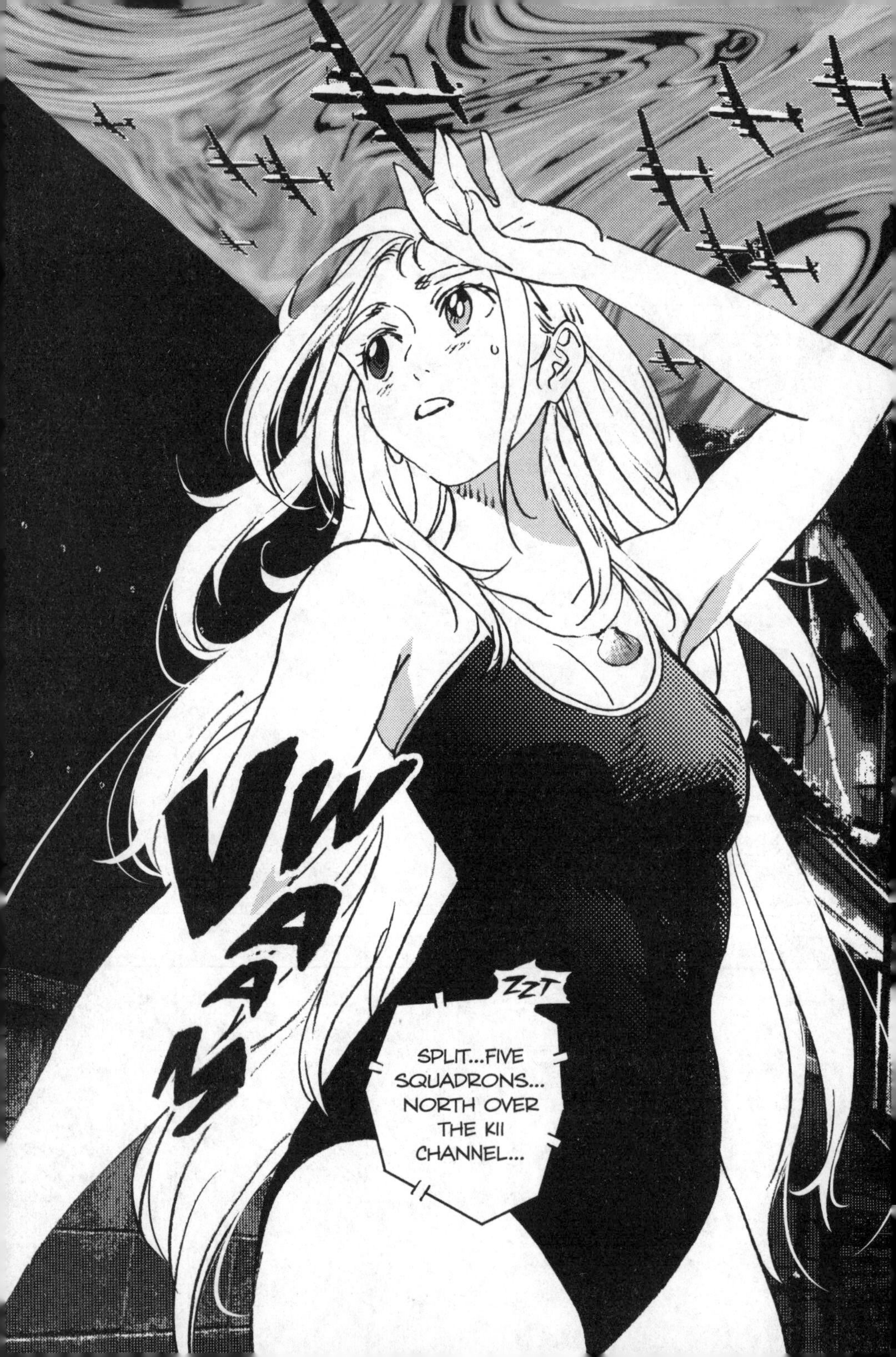
VWAAM
ZZT
SPLIT...FIVE SQUADRONS... NORTH OVER THE KII CHANNEL...

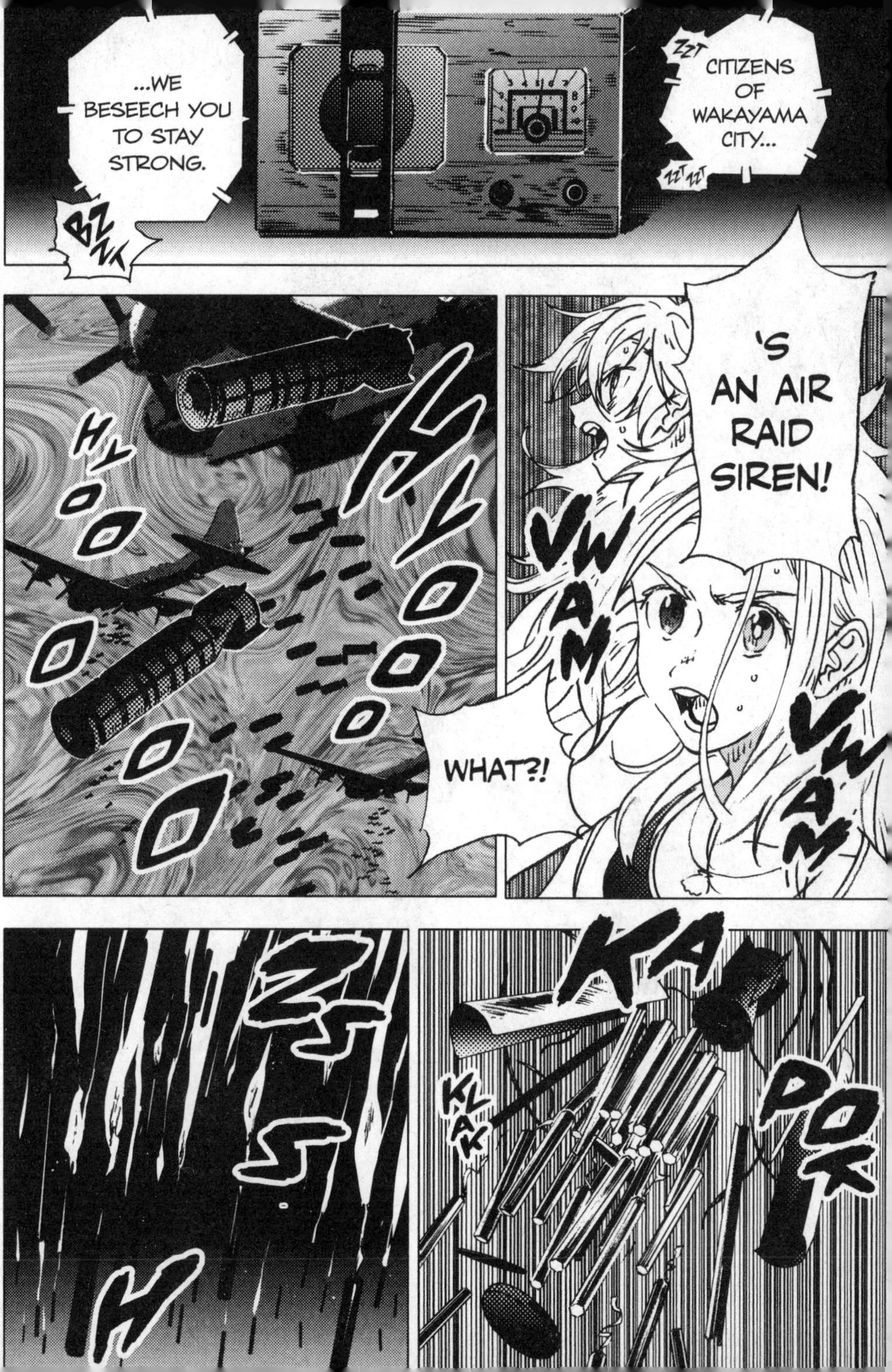
ZZT
CITIZENS OF WAKAYAMA CITY...
ZZT ZZT
...WE BESEECH YOU TO STAY STRONG.
'S AN AIR RAID SIREN!
VWAM
WHAT?!
VWAM
HYOOOO
HYOOOOOO
KA DOK
KLAK

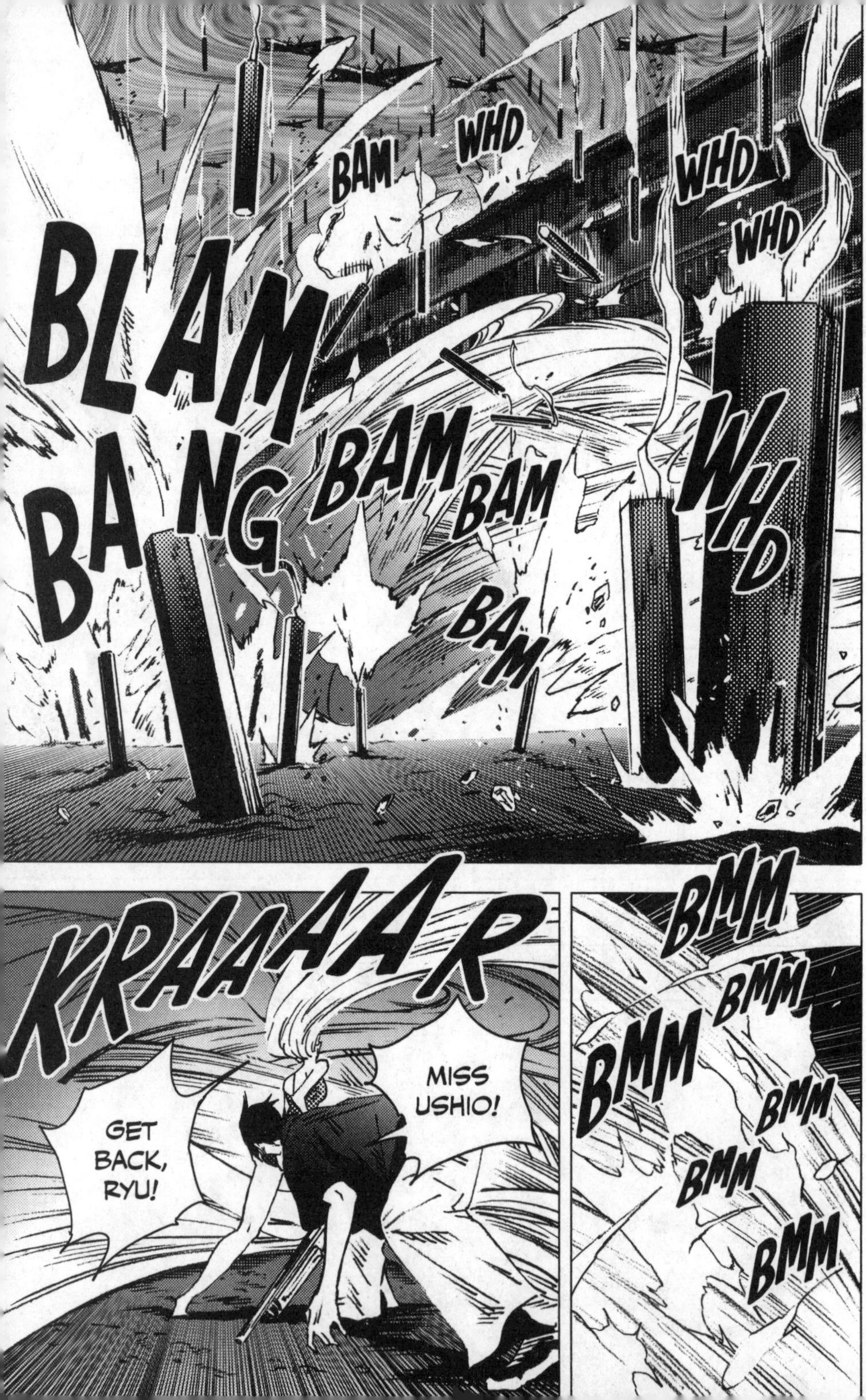
WHD
WHD
WHD
WHD
BAM
BLAM
WHD
BAM
BAM
BAM
BANG
BMM
BMM
BMM
BMM
BMM
BMM
KRAAAAAR
MISS USHIO!
GET BACK, RYU!

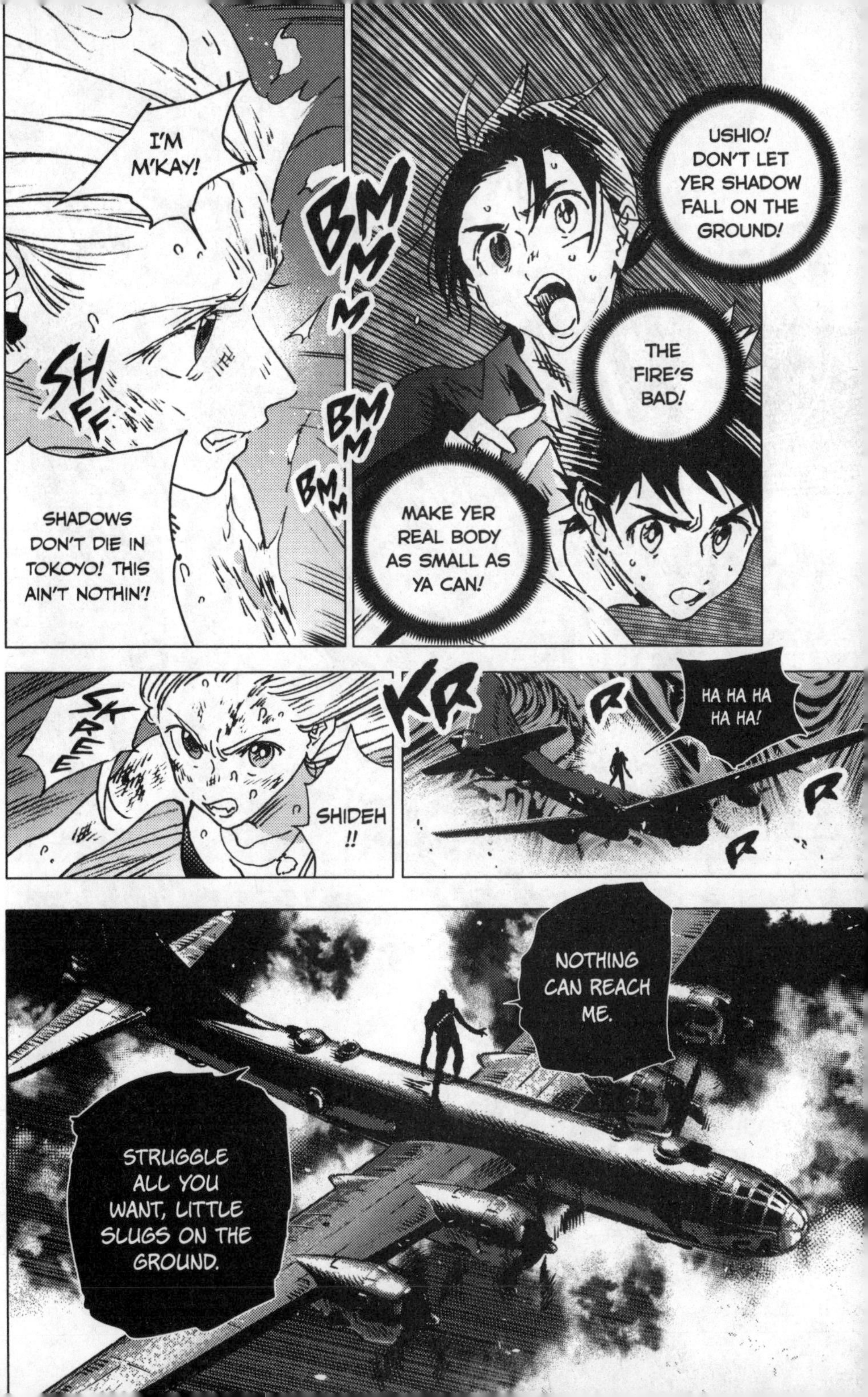
USHIO! DON'T LET YER SHADOW FALL ON THE GROUND!
THE FIRE'S BAD!
MAKE YER REAL BODY AS SMALL AS YA CAN!
BMMM
BMM
BMM
I'M M'KAY!
SHFF
SHADOWS DON'T DIE IN TOKOYO! THIS AIN'T NOTHIN'!
KRRRRR
HA HA HA HA HA!
SKREE
SHIDEH !!
NOTHING CAN REACH ME.
STRUGGLE ALL YOU WANT, LITTLE SLUGS ON THE GROUND.

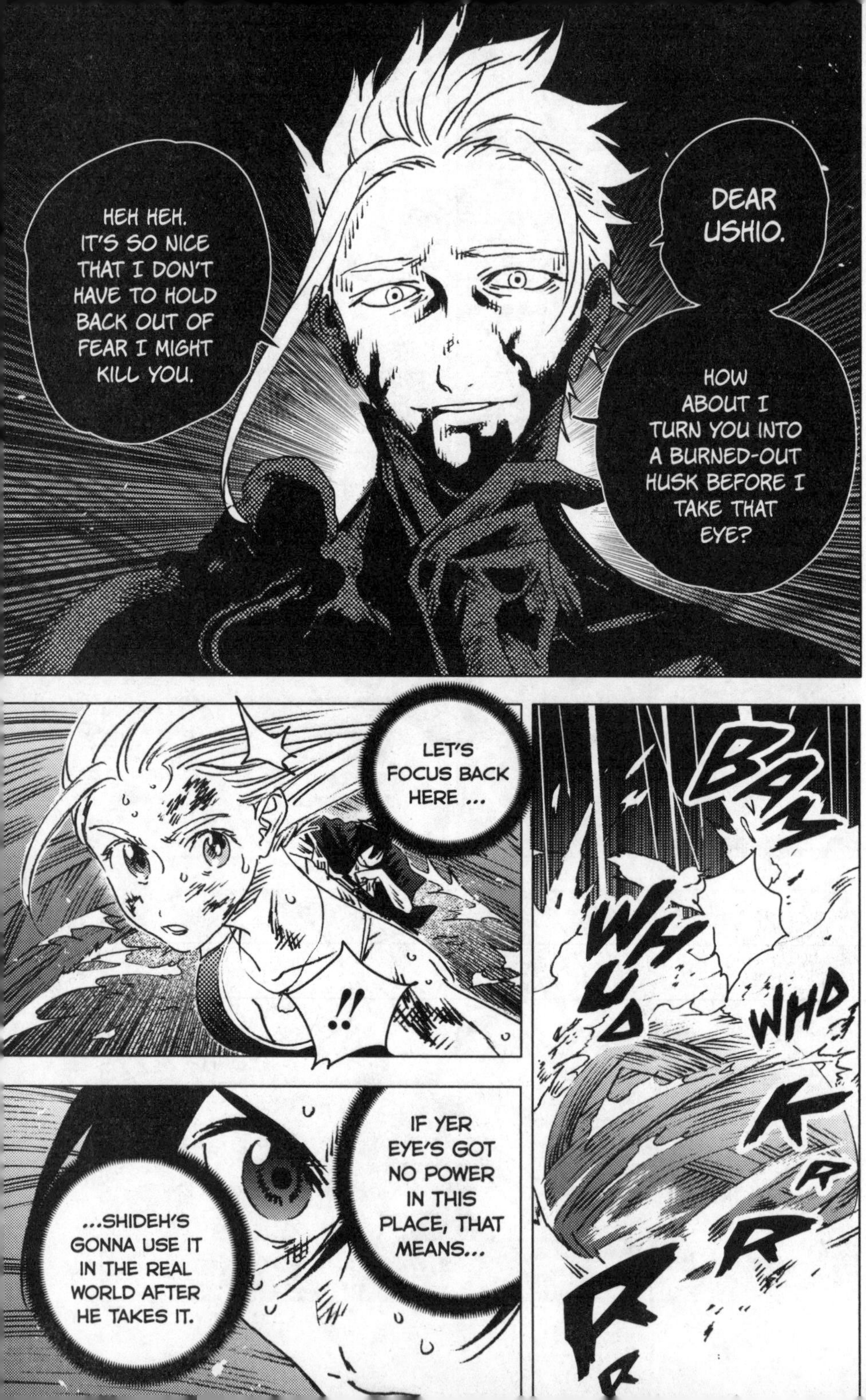
DEAR USHIO.
HOW ABOUT I TURN YOU INTO A BURNED-OUT HUSK BEFORE I TAKE THAT EYE?
HEH HEH. IT'S SO NICE THAT I DON'T HAVE TO HOLD BACK OUT OF FEAR I MIGHT KILL YOU.
BAM
WHUD
WHD
KRRRRR
LET'S FOCUS BACK HERE ...
!!
IF YER EYE'S GOT NO POWER IN THIS PLACE, THAT MEANS...
...SHIDEH'S GONNA USE IT IN THE REAL WORLD AFTER HE TAKES IT.

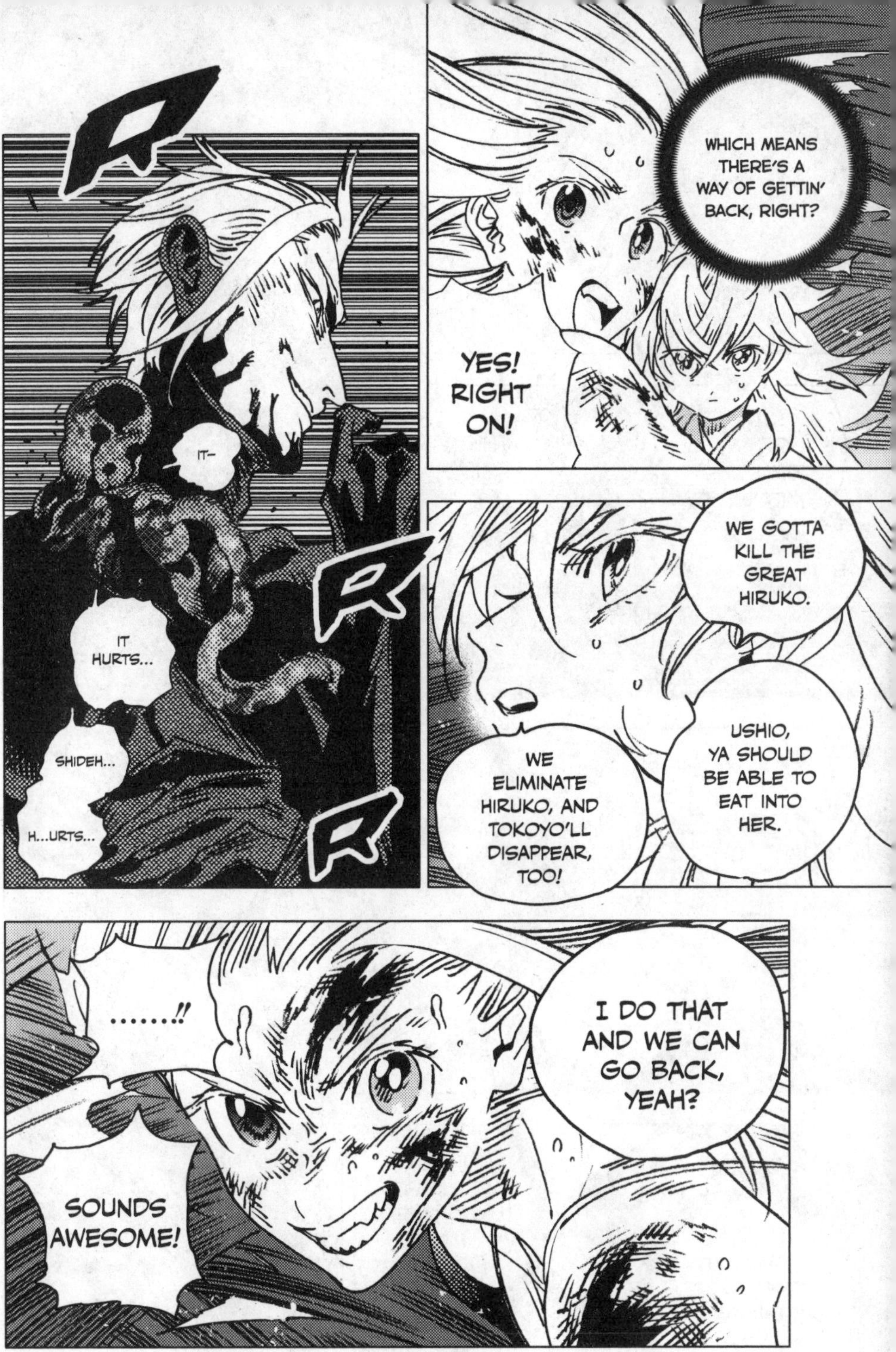
WHICH MEANS THERE'S A WAY OF GETTIN' BACK, RIGHT?
YES! RIGHT ON!
WE GOTTA KILL THE GREAT HIRUKO.
USHIO, YA SHOULD BE ABLE TO EAT INTO HER.
WE ELIMINATE HIRUKO, AND TOKOYO'LL DISAPPEAR, TOO!
IT-
IT HURTS...
SHIDEH...
H...URTS...
I DO THAT AND WE CAN GO BACK, YEAH?
.......!!
SOUNDS AWESOME!

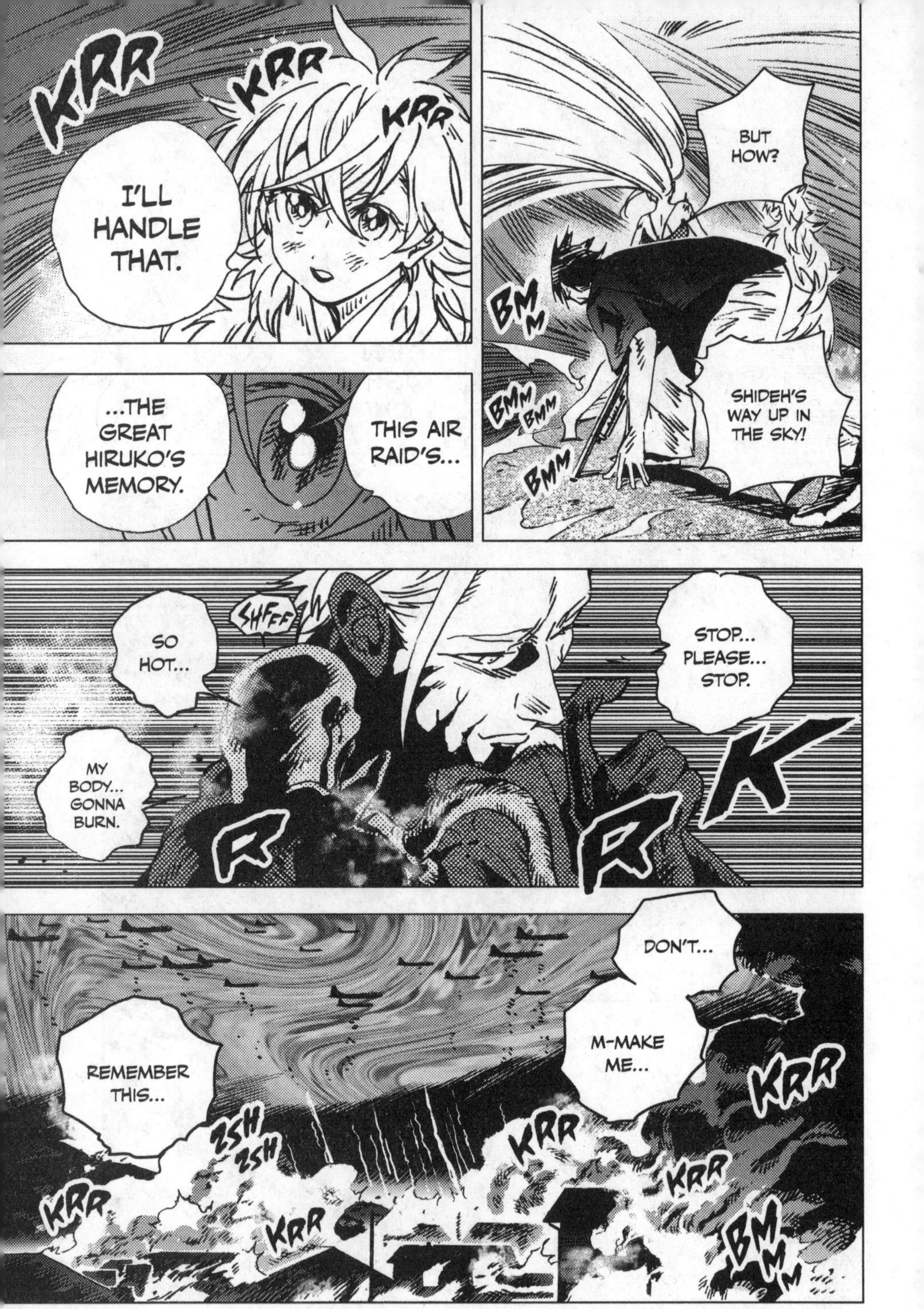
BUT HOW?
SHIDEH'S WAY UP IN THE SKY!
BMM
BMM BMM
BMM
KRR KRR KRR
I'LL HANDLE THAT.
THIS AIR RAID'S...
...THE GREAT HIRUKO'S MEMORY.
STOP... PLEASE... STOP.
KRRK
SHFFF
SO HOT...
MY BODY... GONNA BURN.
DON'T...
M-MAKE ME...
KRR
KRR
KRR
BMM
REMEMBER THIS...
ZSH ZSH
KRR
KRR

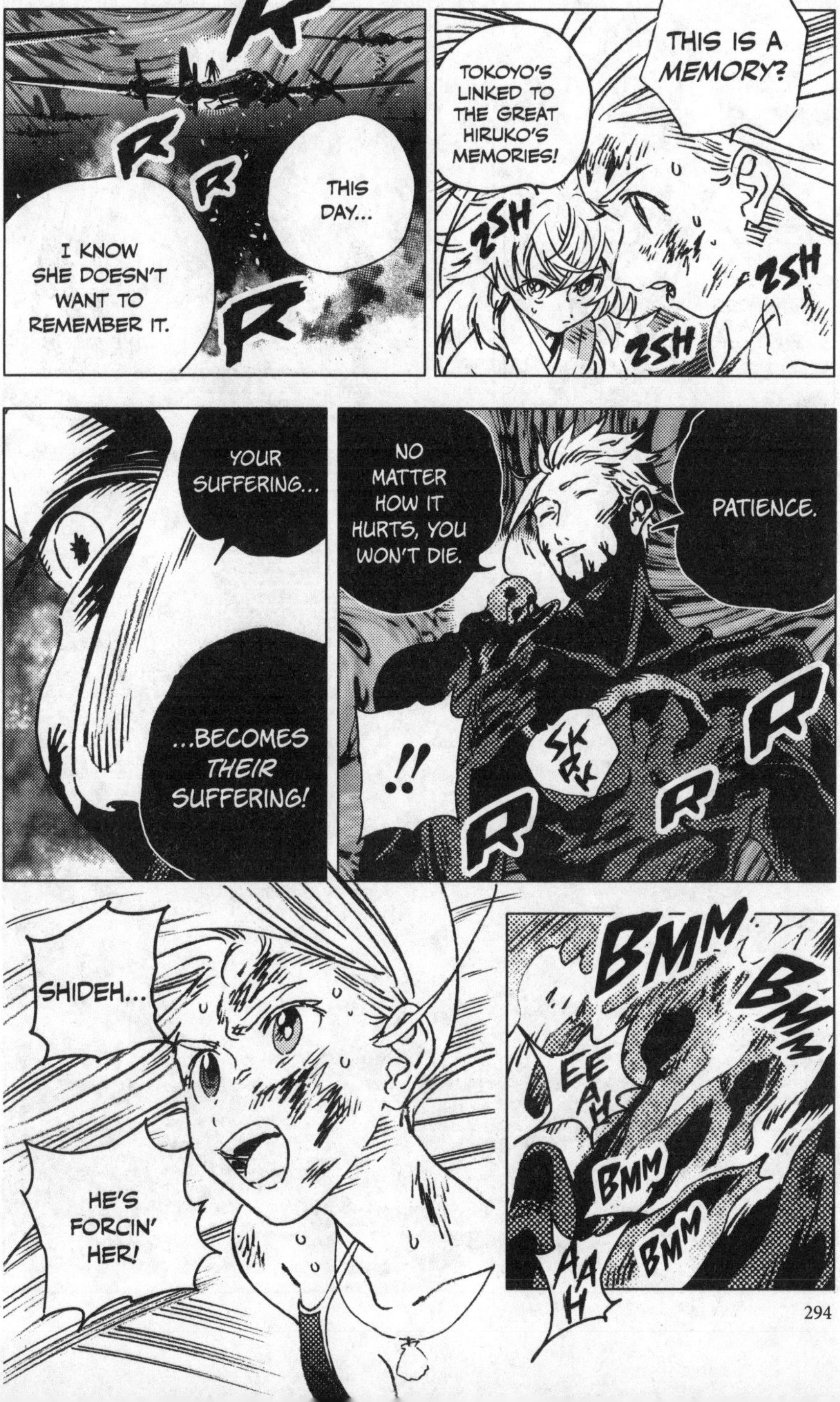
THIS IS A MEMORY?
TOKOYO'S LINKED TO THE GREAT HIRUKO'S MEMORIES!
ZSH
ZSH
ZSH
K
R
R
THIS DAY...
I KNOW SHE DOESN'T WANT TO REMEMBER IT.
R
PATIENCE.
NO MATTER HOW IT HURTS, YOU WON'T DIE.
R
R
R
!!
YOUR SUFFERING...
...BECOMES THEIR SUFFERING!
BMM
BMM
EEAH
BMM
BMM
AAH
SHIDEH...
HE'S FORCIN' HER!

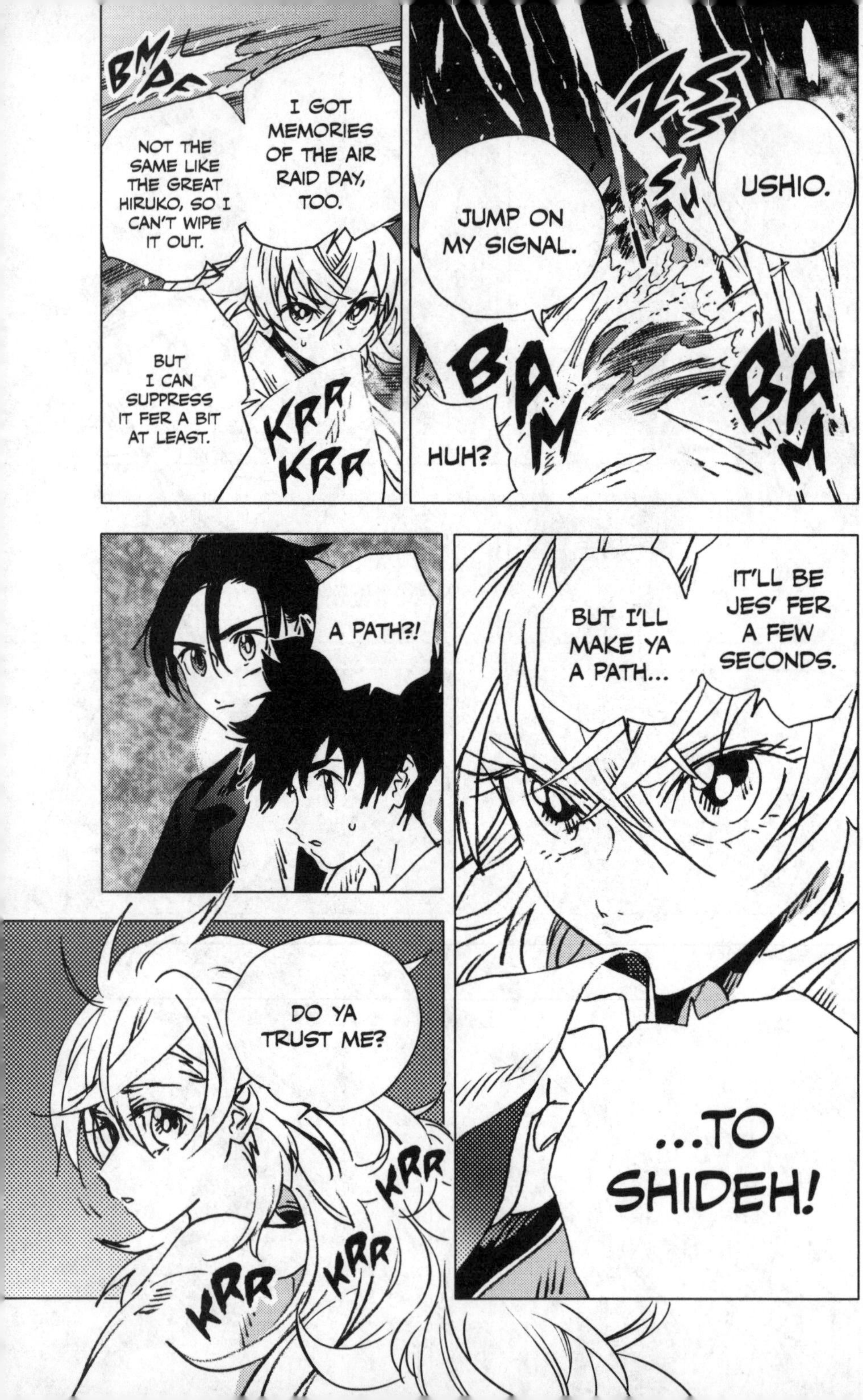
ZSS
SU
USHIO.
JUMP ON MY SIGNAL.
BAM
BAM
HUH?
BMPF
I GOT MEMORIES OF THE AIR RAID DAY, TOO.
NOT THE SAME LIKE THE GREAT HIRUKO, SO I CAN'T WIPE IT OUT.
BUT I CAN SUPPRESS IT FER A BIT AT LEAST.
KRR KRR
IT'LL BE JES' FER A FEW SECONDS.
BUT I'LL MAKE YA A PATH...
...TO SHIDEH!
A PATH?!
DO YA TRUST ME?
KRR
KRR
KRR

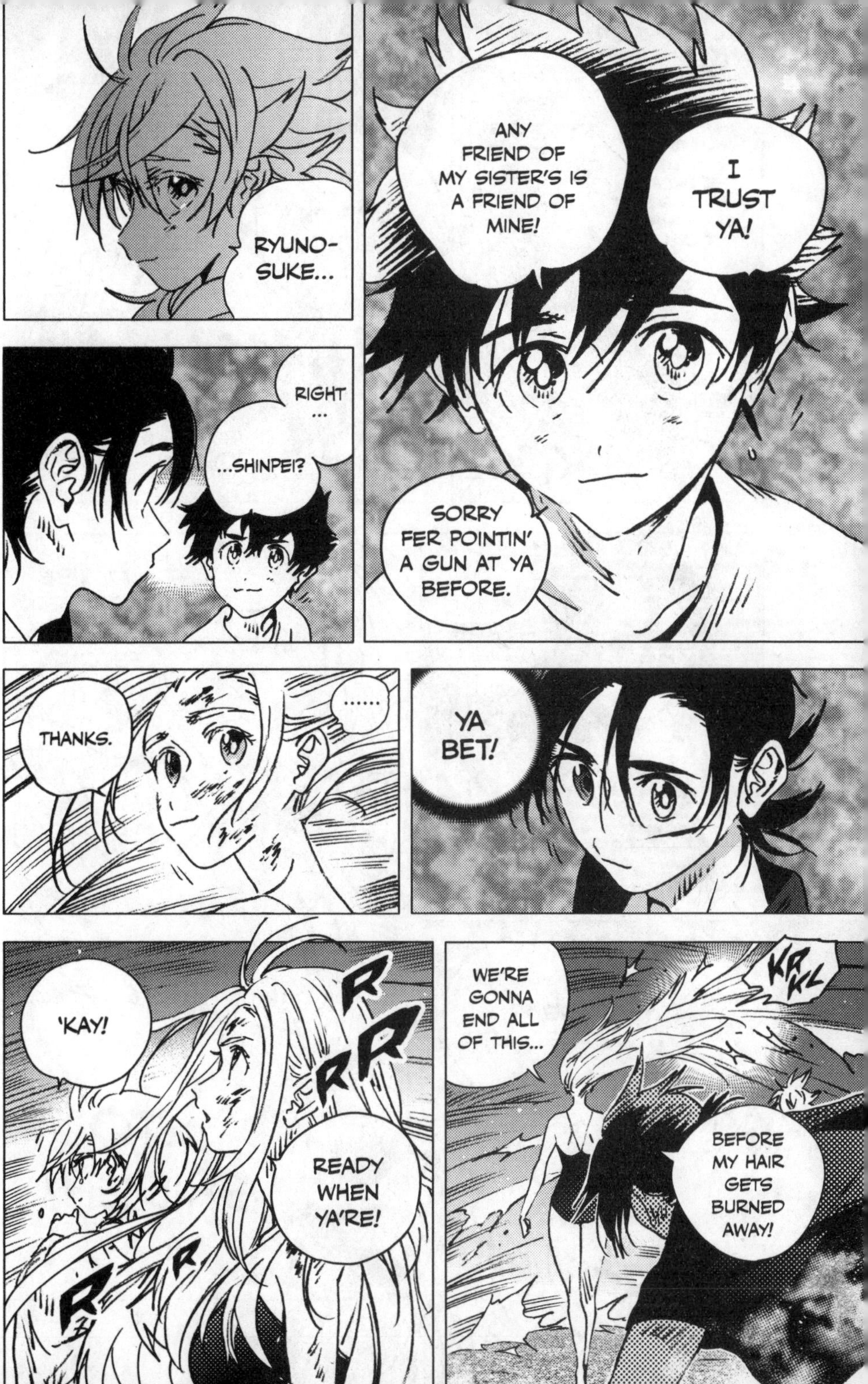
I TRUST YA!
ANY FRIEND OF MY SISTER'S IS A FRIEND OF MINE!
SORRY FER POINTIN' A GUN AT YA BEFORE.
RYUNO-SUKE...
RIGHT ...
...SHINPEI?
YA BET!
....
THANKS.
KRKL
WE'RE GONNA END ALL OF THIS...
BEFORE MY HAIR GETS BURNED AWAY!
RRRR
'KAY!
READY WHEN YA'RE!
RR

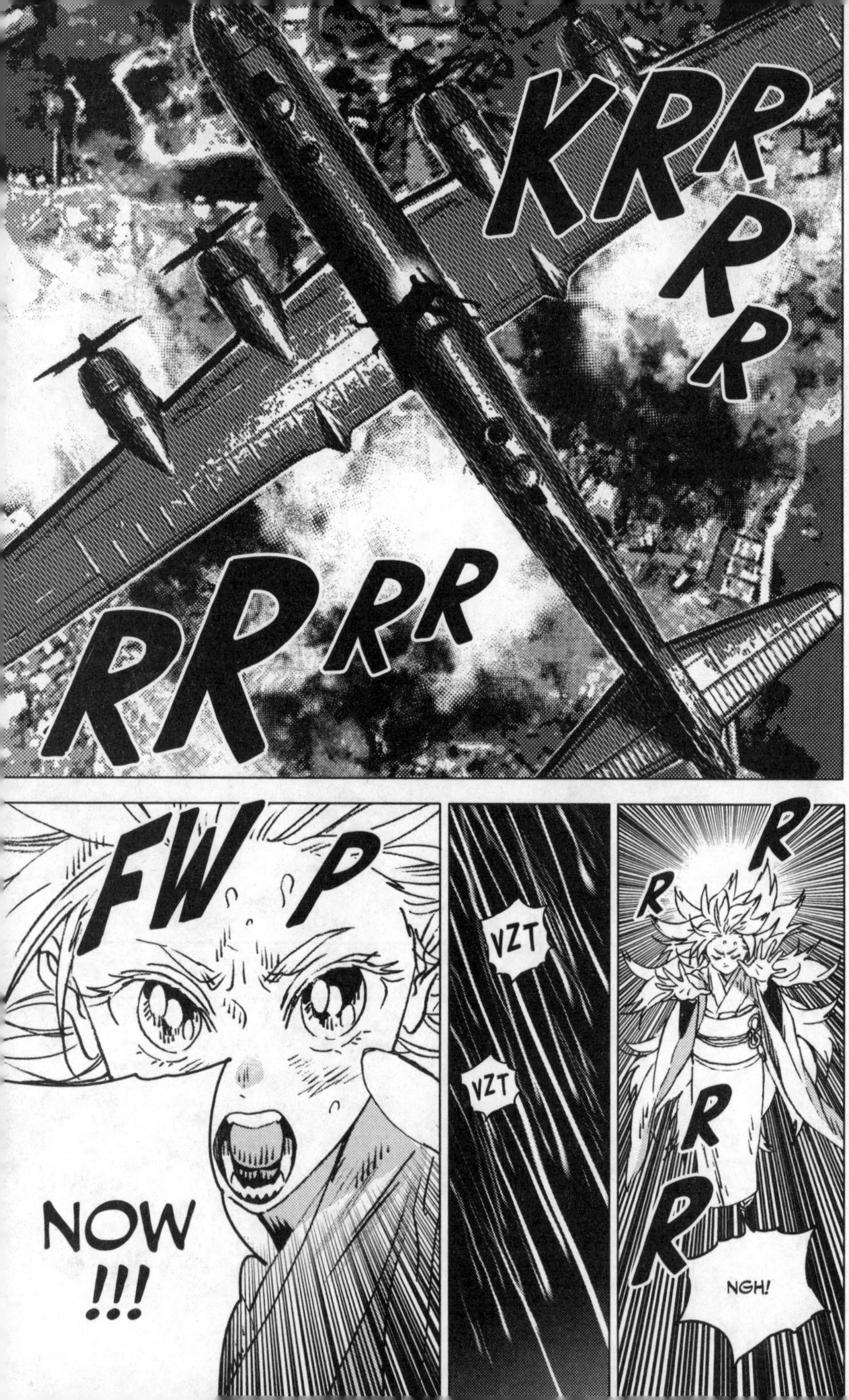
KRRRR
RRRR
R R
R R R
NGH!
VZT
VZT
FWP
NOW!!!

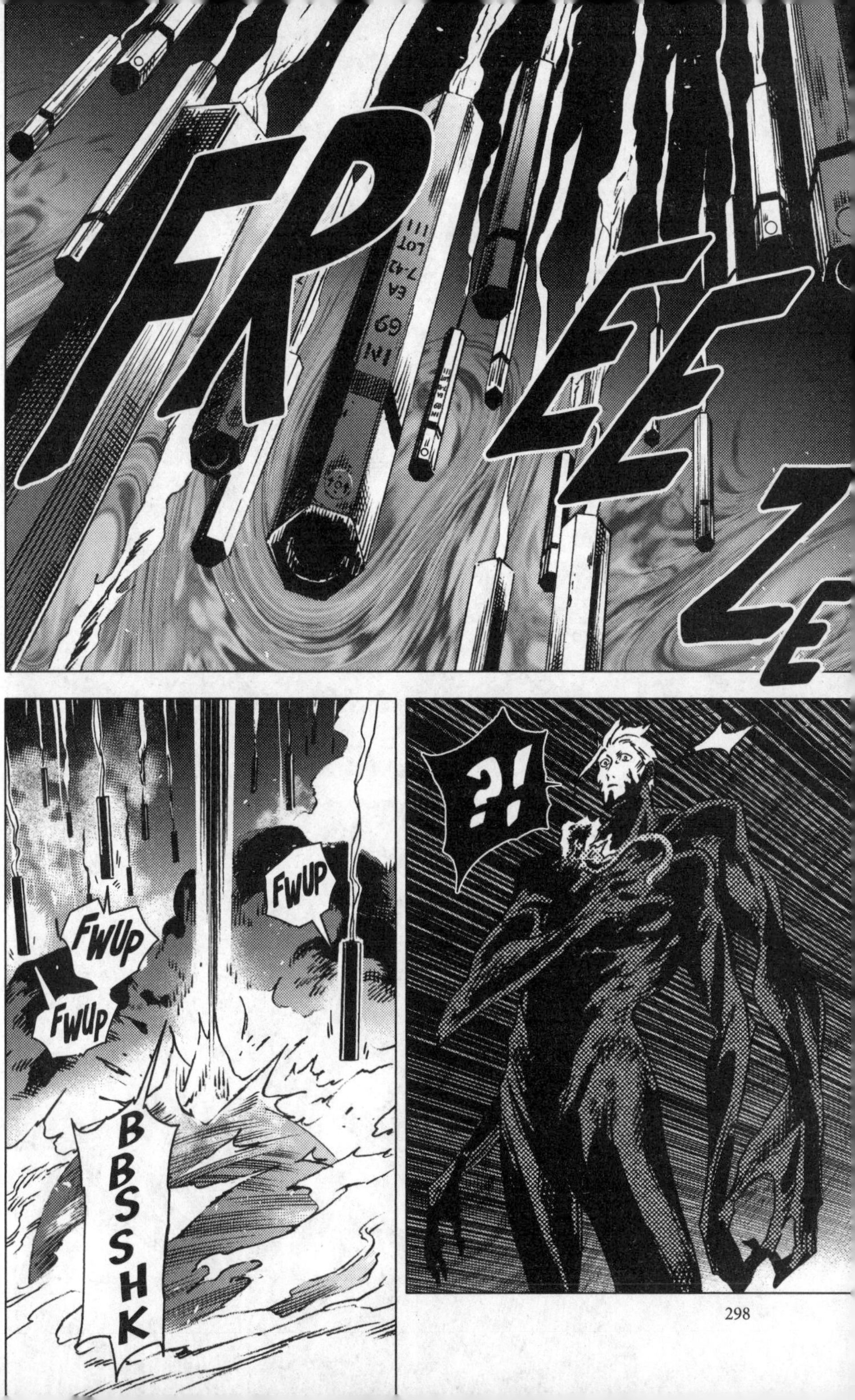

FREEZE
IN 69 EA 7-42 LOT 111
?!
FWUP
FWUP
FWUP
BBSSHK

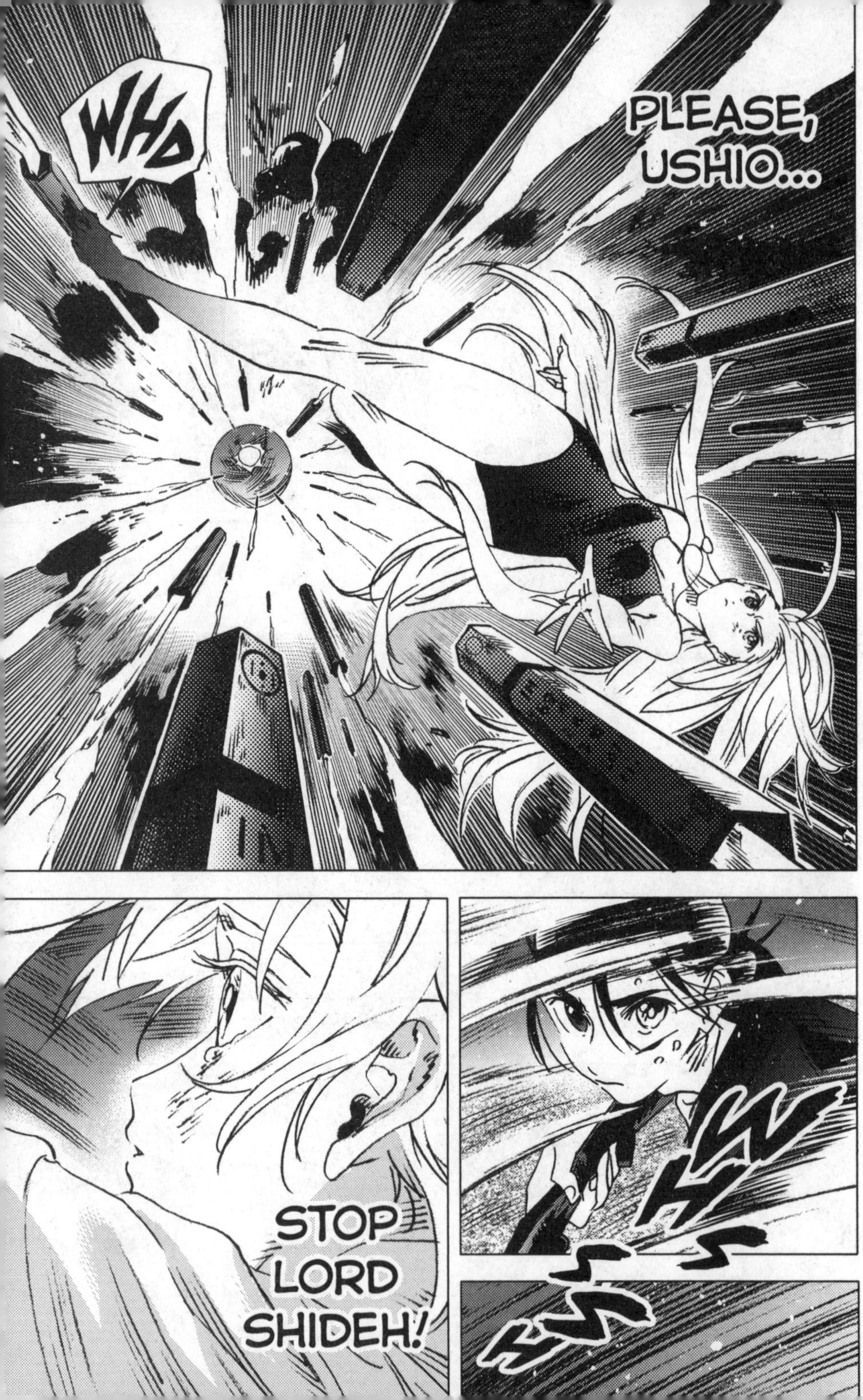
PLEASE, USHIO...
WHD
STOP LORD SHIDEH!

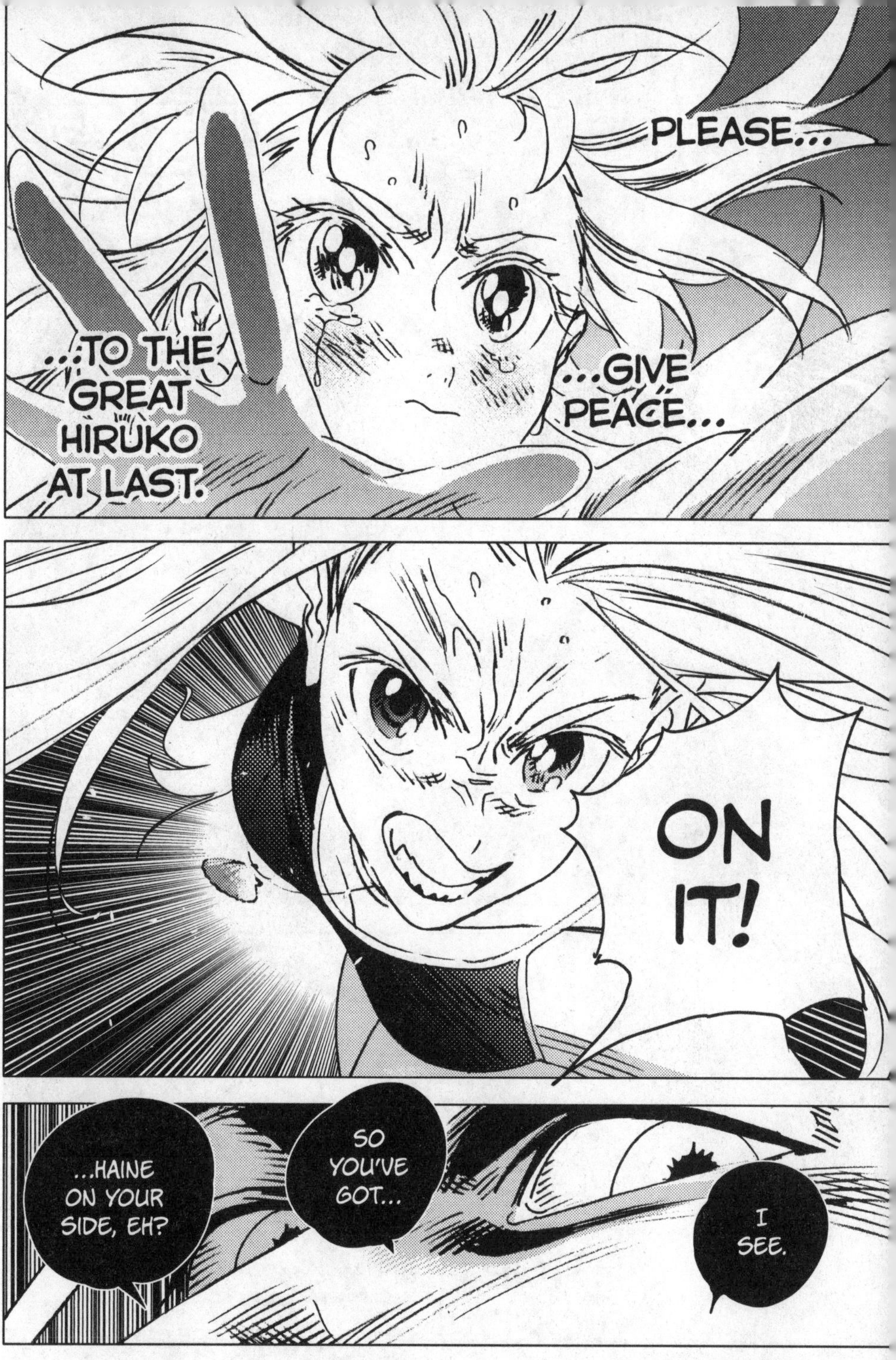
PLEASE...
...GIVE PEACE...
...TO THE GREAT HIRUKO AT LAST.
ON IT!
I SEE.
SO YOU'VE GOT...
...HAINE ON YOUR SIDE, EH?

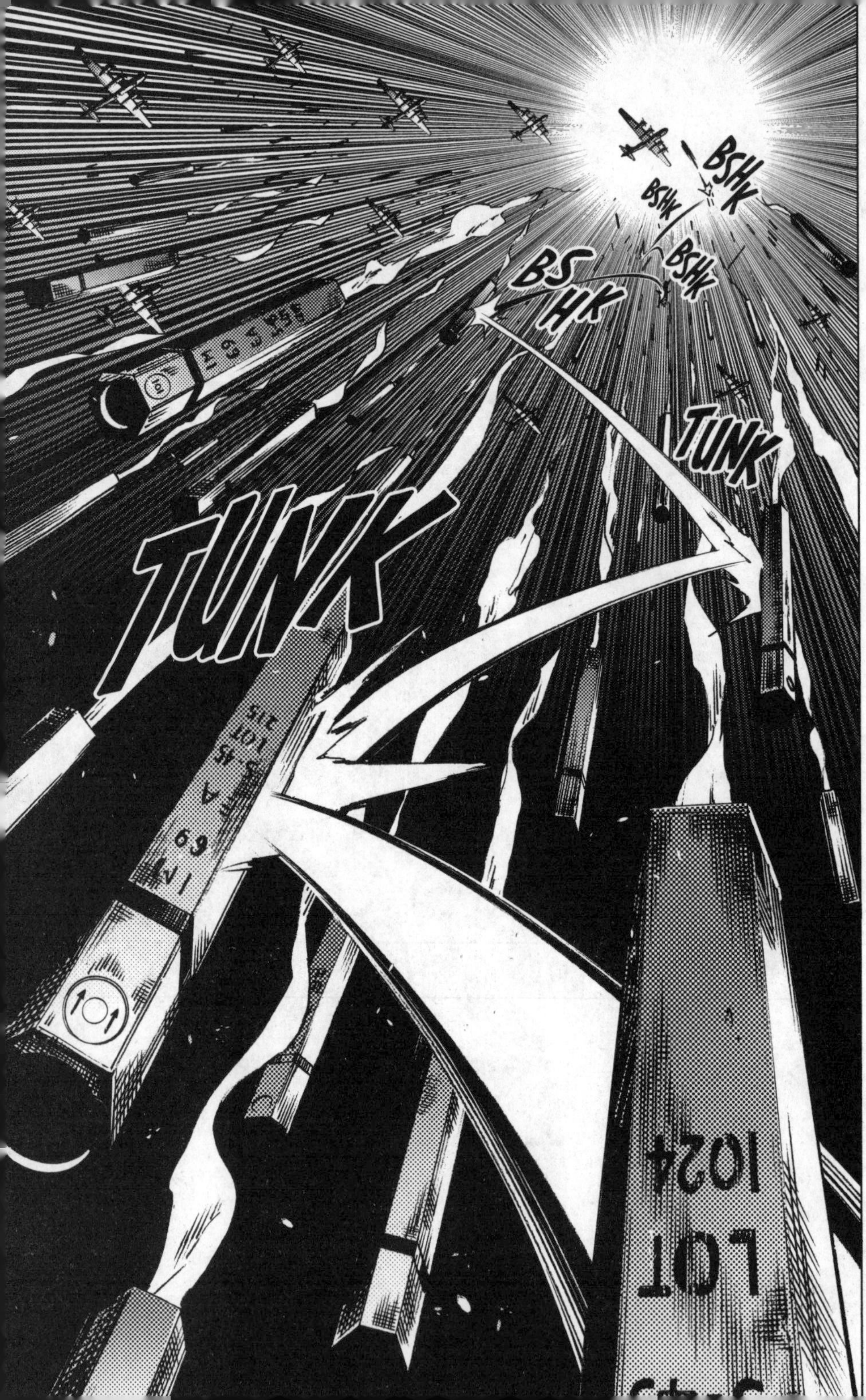
BSHK
BSHK
BSHK
BSHK
TUNK
TUNK
LOT 1024

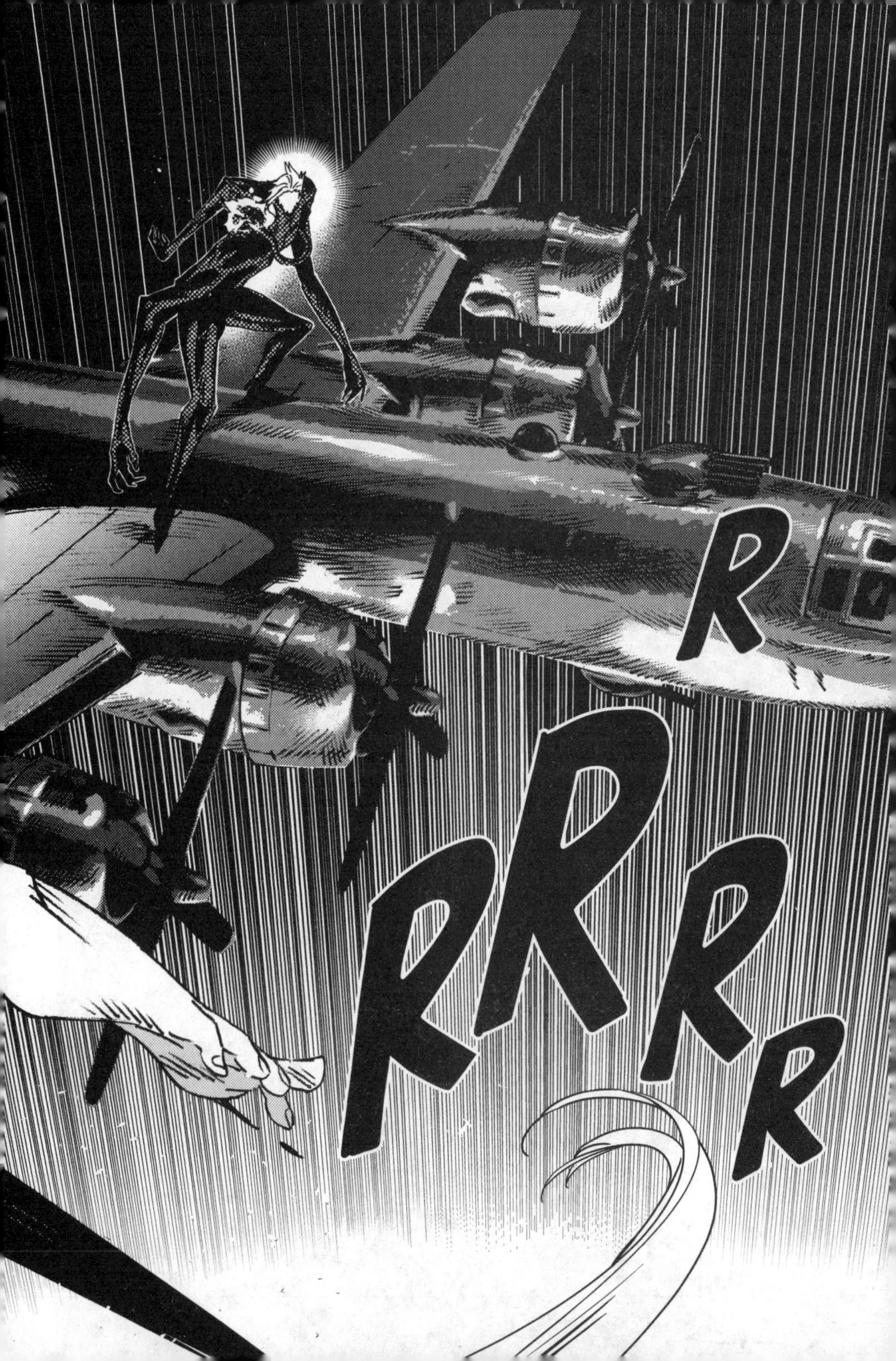
RRRRRR

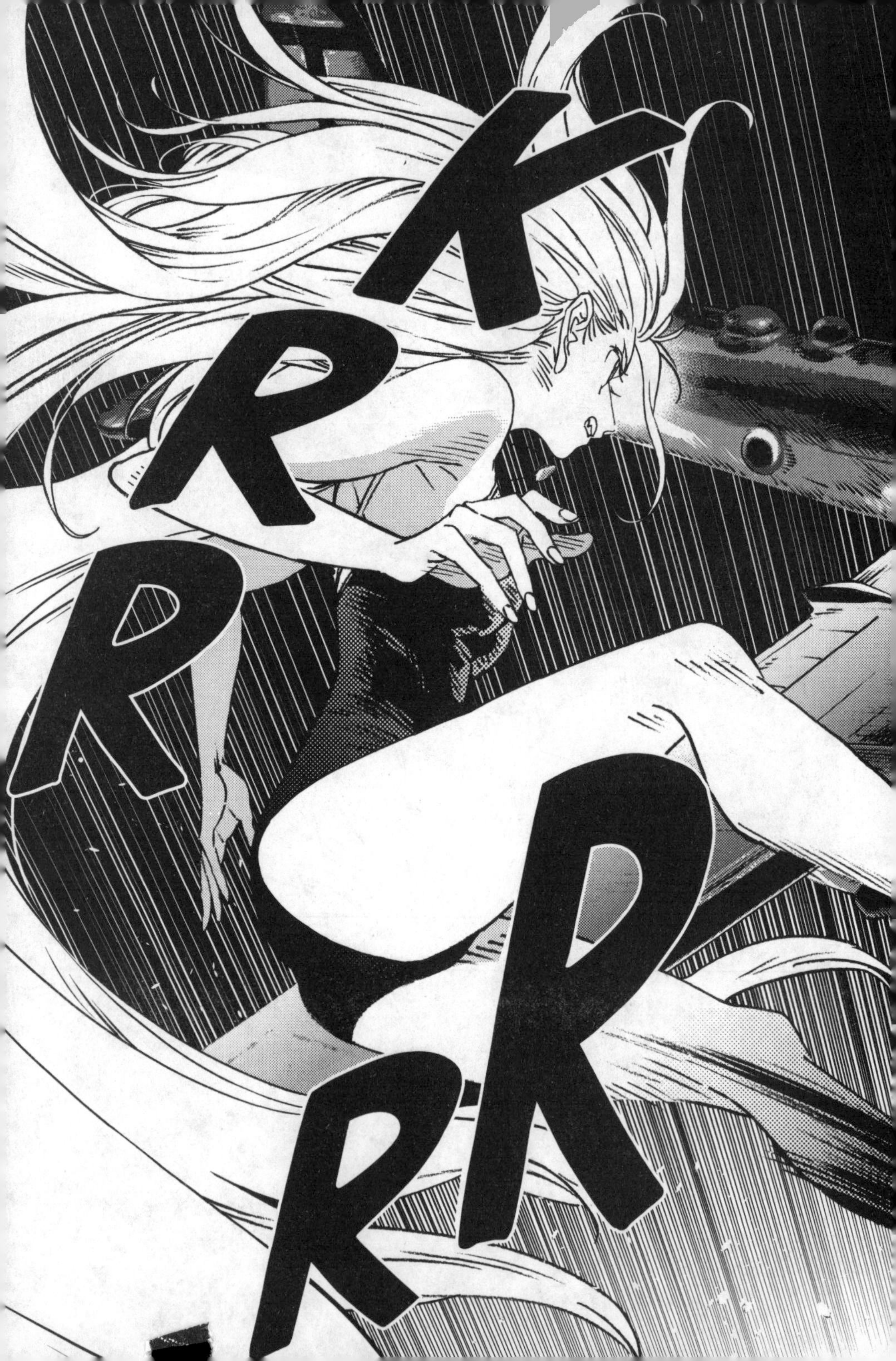
KRRRR

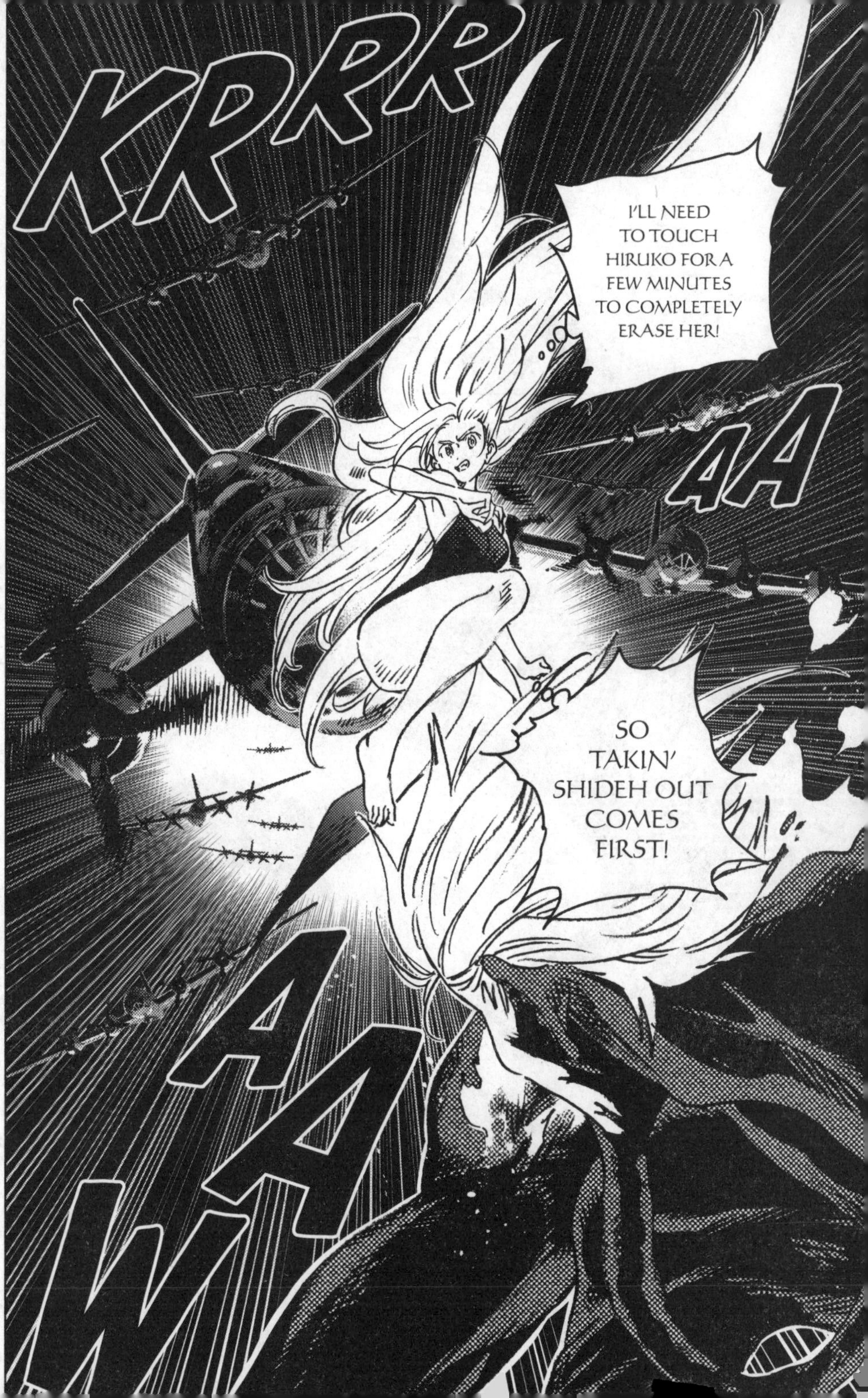

I'LL NEED TO TOUCH HIRUKO FOR A FEW MINUTES TO COMPLETELY ERASE HER!
KRRR
AA
SO TAKIN' SHIDEH OUT COMES FIRST!
WAAAA

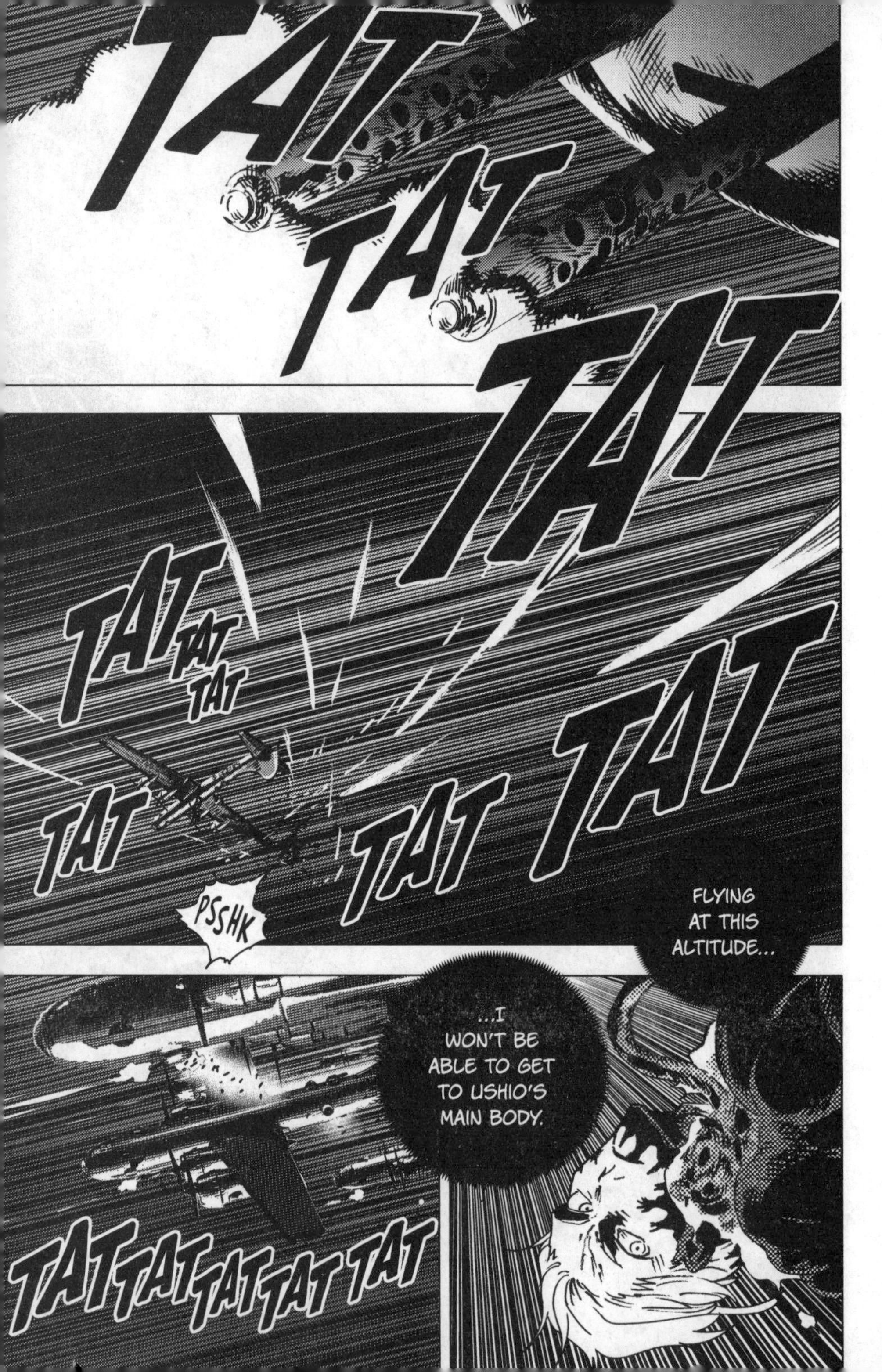
TAT TAT
TAT
TAT
TAT TAT
TAT TAT TAT
TAT
PSSHK
FLYING AT THIS ALTITUDE...
...I WON'T BE ABLE TO GET TO USHIO'S MAIN BODY.
TAT TAT TAT TAT TAT

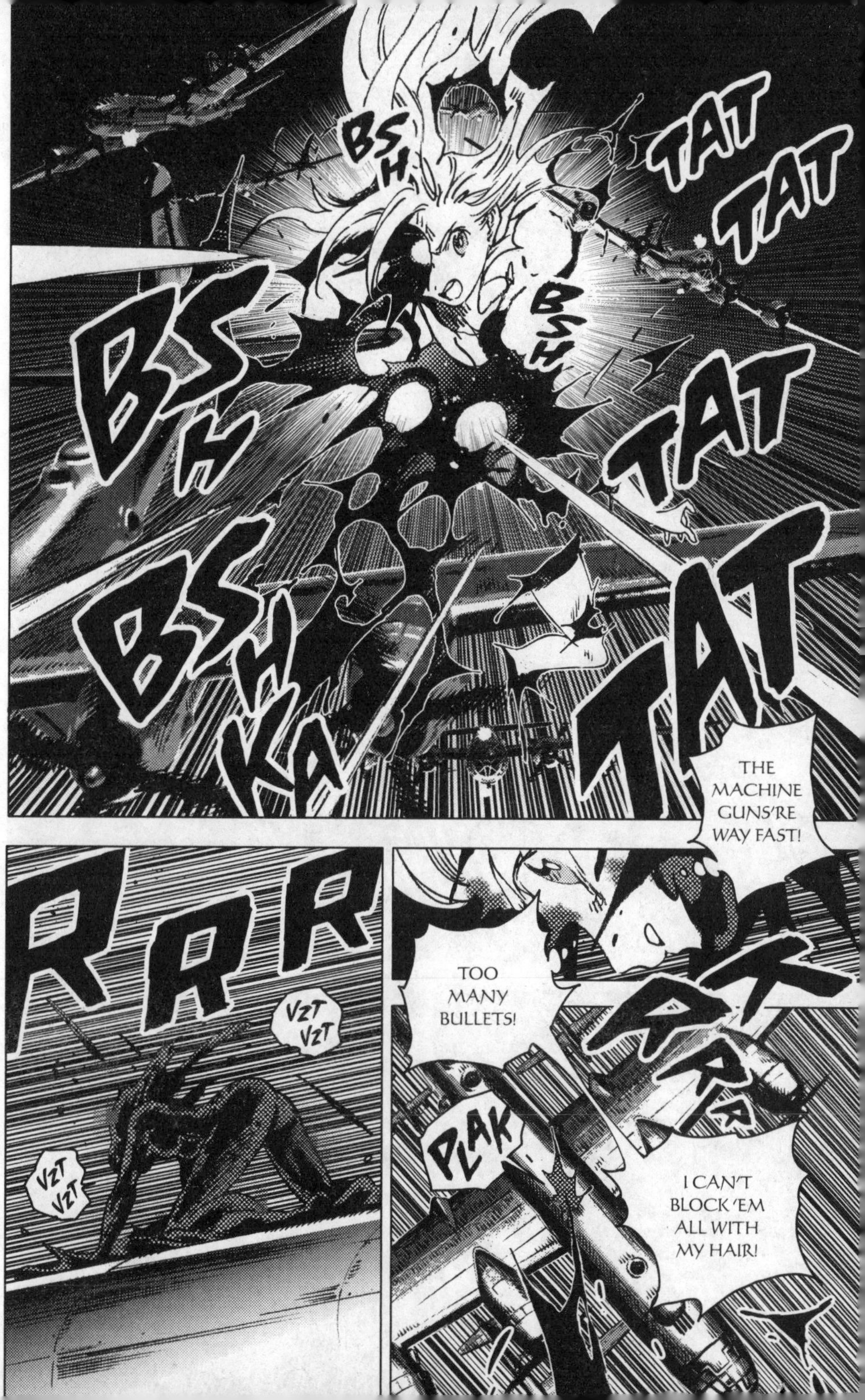
BSH
TAT TAT
BSH
BSH
TAT
BSH
KA
TAT
THE MACHINE GUNS'RE WAY FAST!
RRR
VZT VZT
VZT VZT
TOO MANY BULLETS!
RAT
RAR
PLAK
I CAN'T BLOCK 'EM ALL WITH MY HAIR!

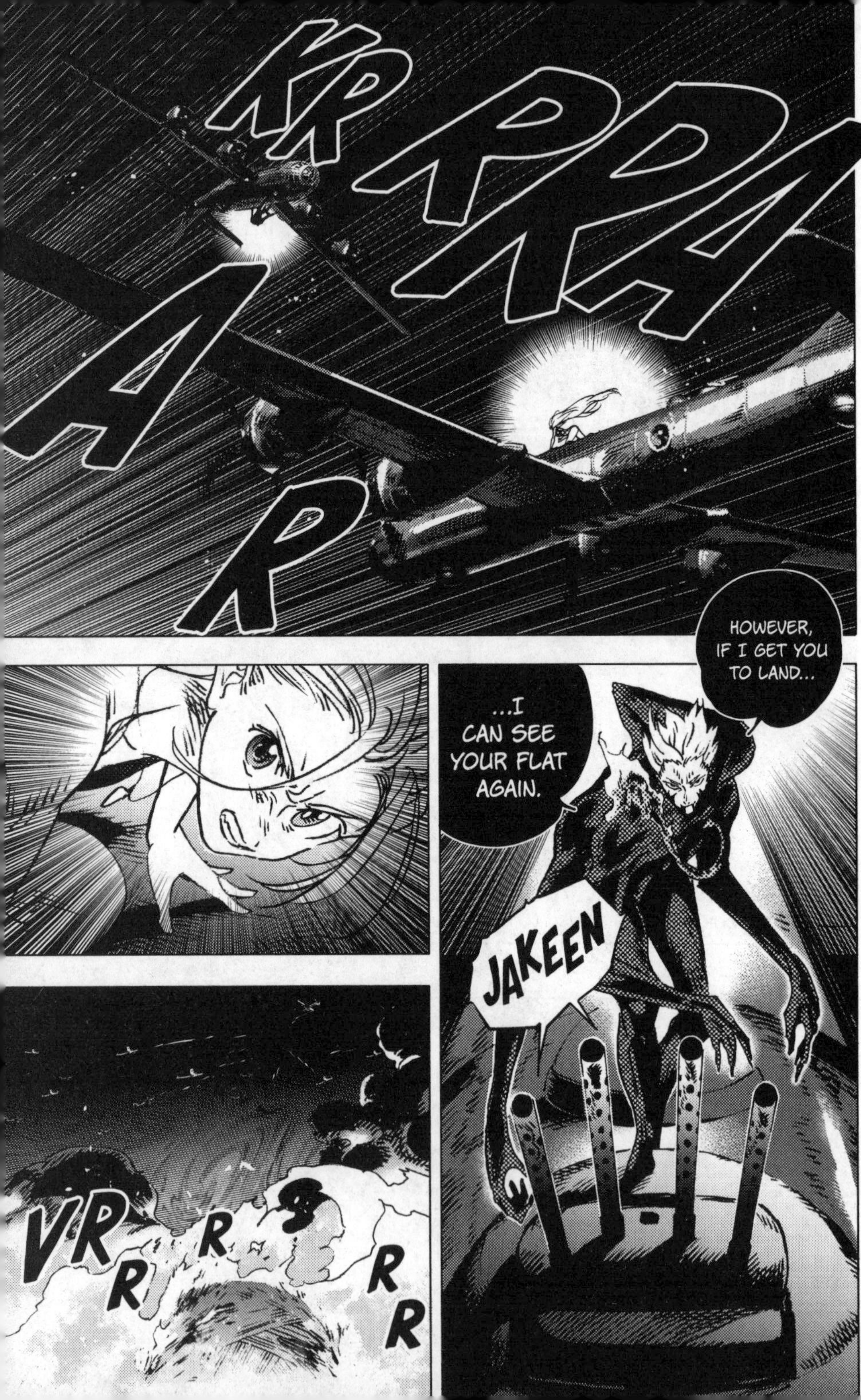
KRRRAAAAR
HOWEVER, IF I GET YOU TO LAND...
...I CAN SEE YOUR FLAT AGAIN.
JAKEEN
VRRRRRRR

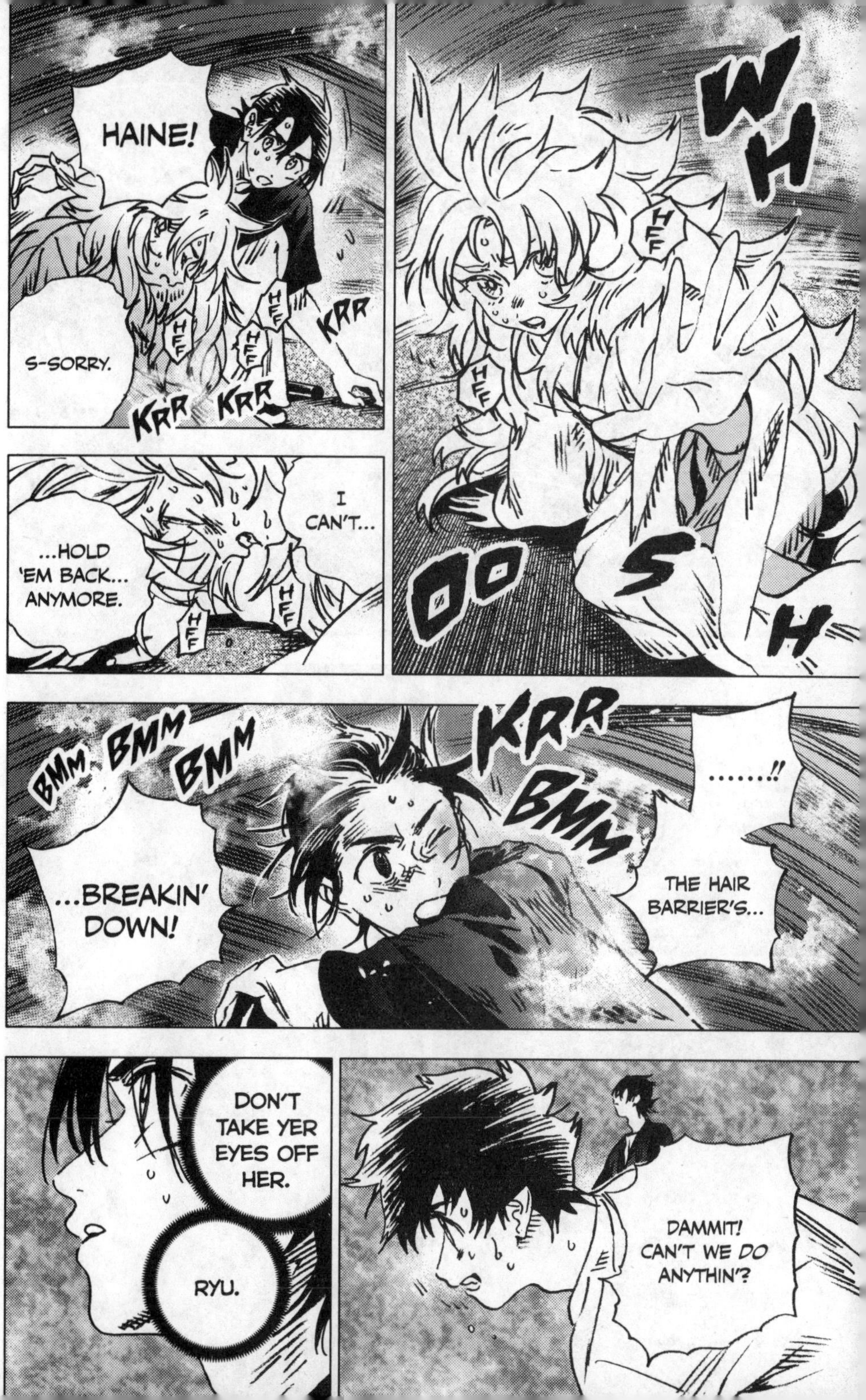
WHOOSH
HFF
HFF
HAINE!
HFF
HFF
HFF
KRR
S-SORRY.
KRR
KRR
I CAN'T...
...HOLD 'EM BACK... ANYMORE.
HFF
HFF
KRR
BMM
.......!!
THE HAIR BARRIER'S...
...BREAKIN' DOWN!
BMM
BMM
BMM
DAMMIT! CAN'T WE *DO* ANYTHIN'?
DON'T TAKE YER EYES OFF HER.
RYU.

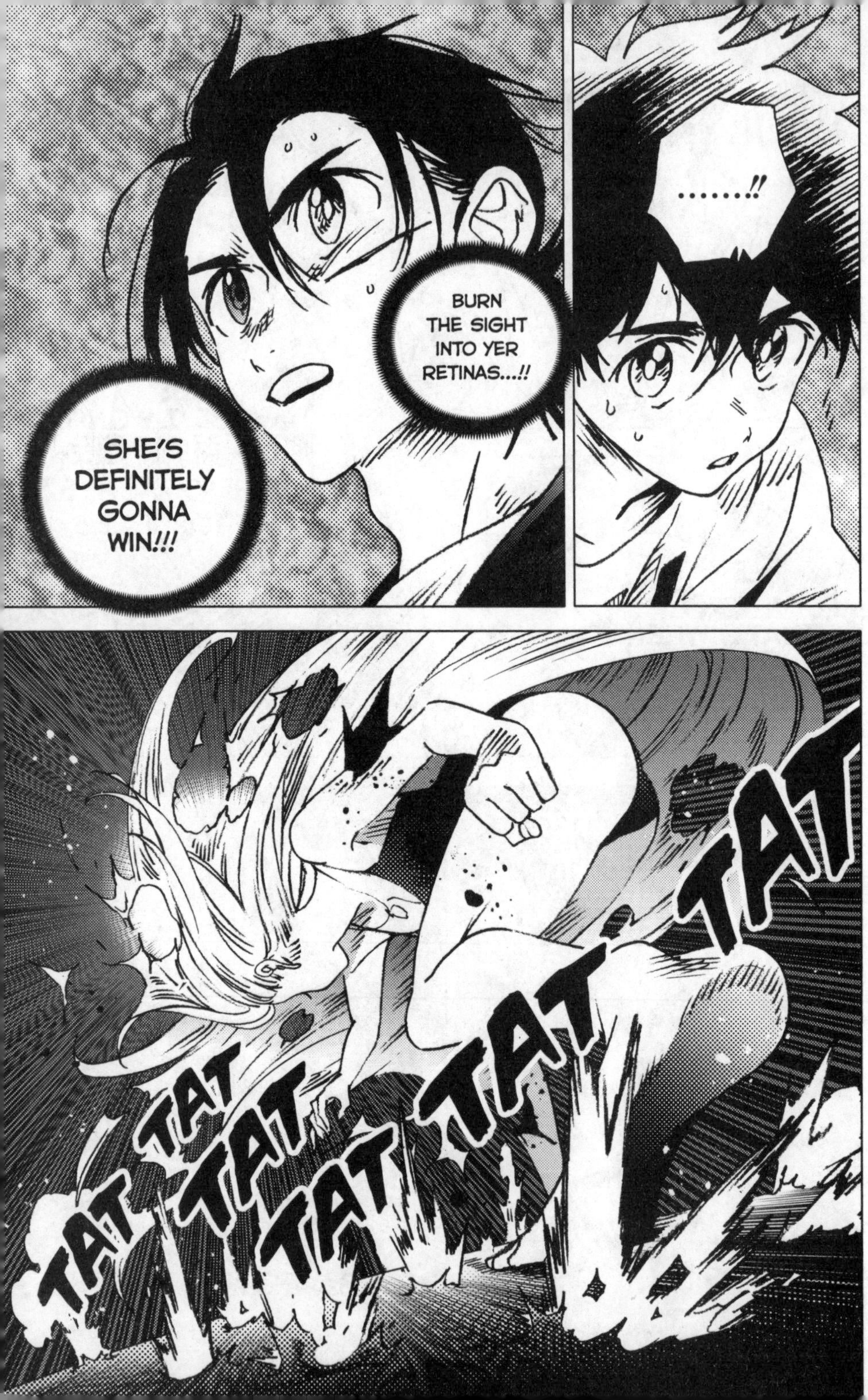

.......!!
BURN THE SIGHT INTO YER RETINAS...!!
SHE'S DEFINITELY GONNA WIN!!!
TAT TAT TAT TAT TAT TAT TAT

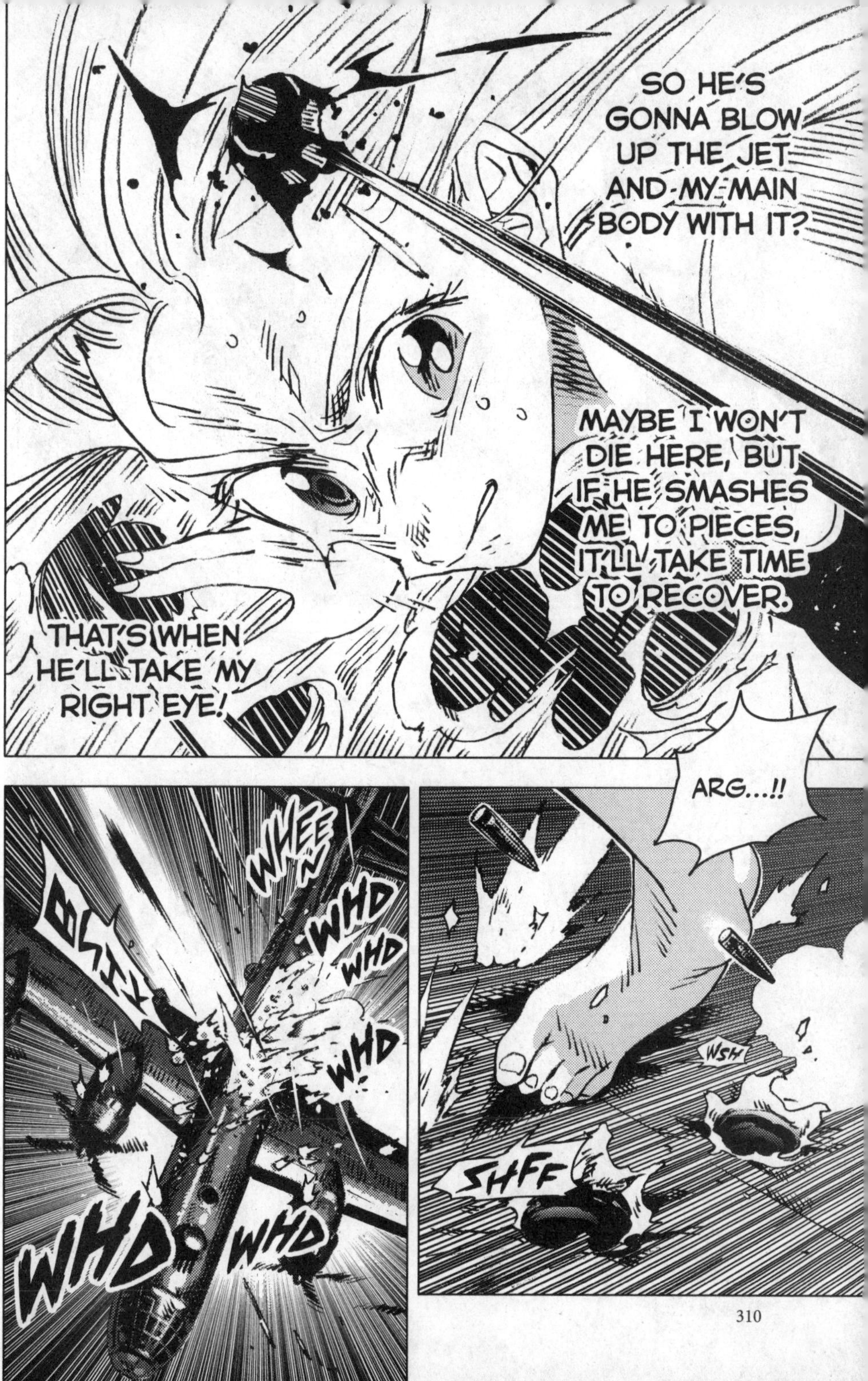
SO HE'S GONNA BLOW UP THE JET AND MY MAIN BODY WITH IT?
MAYBE I WON'T DIE HERE, BUT IF HE SMASHES ME TO PIECES, IT'LL TAKE TIME TO RECOVER.
THAT'S WHEN HE'LL TAKE MY RIGHT EYE!
ARG...!!
WSH
SHFF
WHEE
WHD
WHD
WHD
WHD
WHD

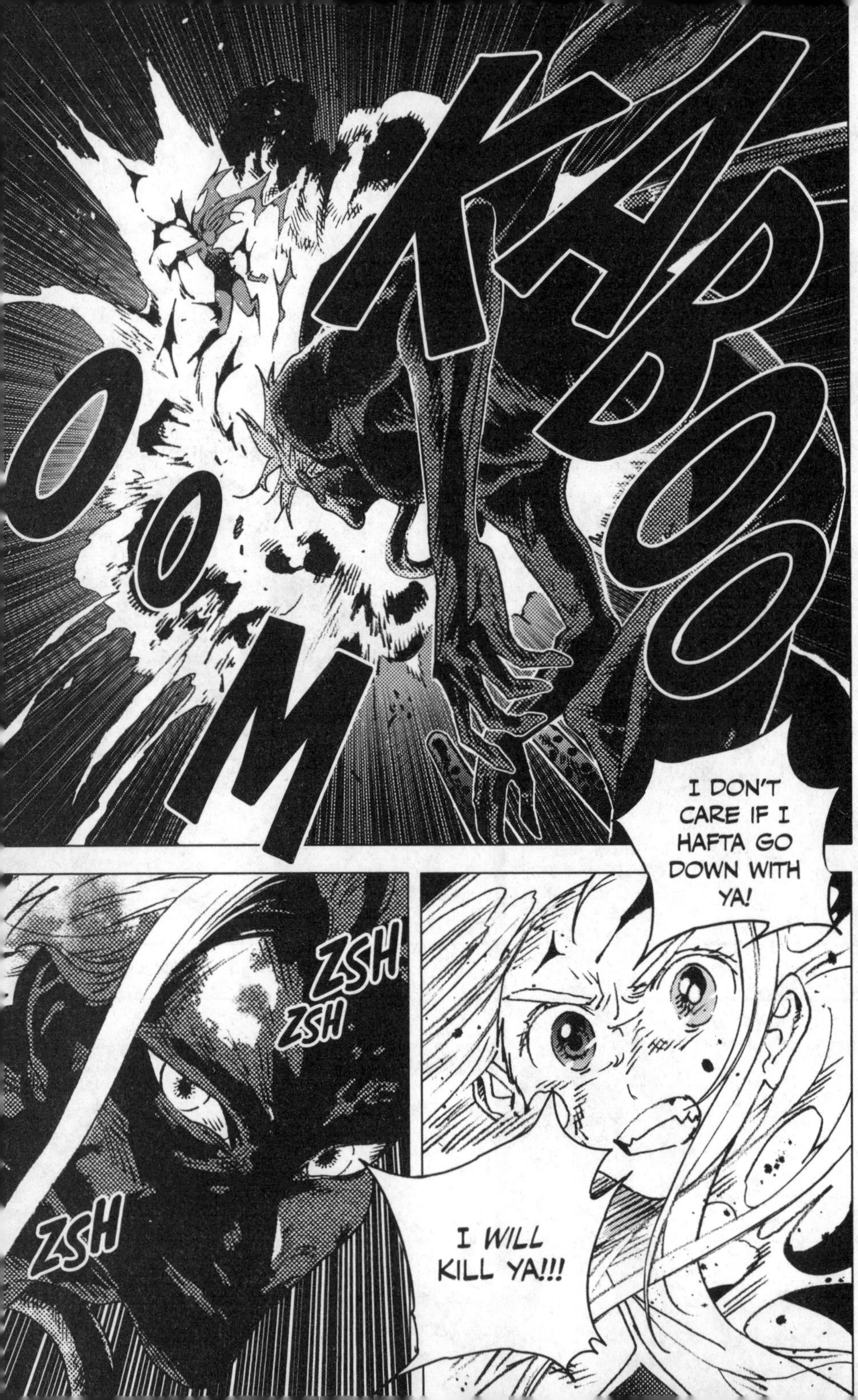
KABOOOOM
I DON'T CARE IF I HAFTA GO DOWN WITH YA!
I WILL KILL YA!!!
ZSH
ZSH
ZSH

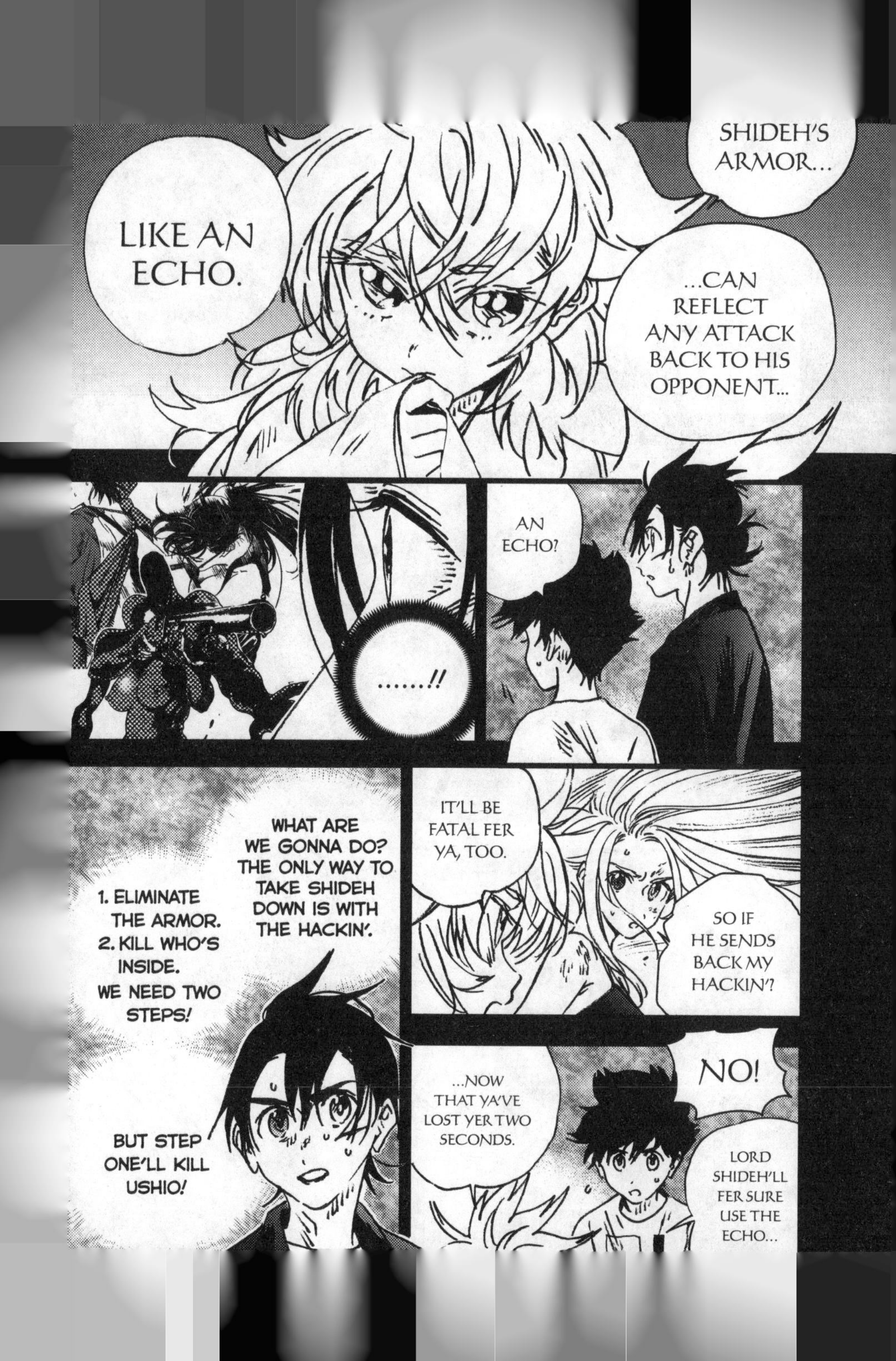
SHIDEH'S ARMOR...
...CAN REFLECT ANY ATTACK BACK TO HIS OPPONENT...
LIKE AN ECHO.
AN ECHO?
......!!
SO IF HE SENDS BACK MY HACKIN'?
IT'LL BE FATAL FER YA, TOO.
NO!
LORD SHIDEH'LL FER SURE USE THE ECHO...
...NOW THAT YA'VE LOST YER TWO SECONDS.
WHAT ARE WE GONNA DO? THE ONLY WAY TO TAKE SHIDEH DOWN IS WITH THE HACKIN'.
1. ELIMINATE THE ARMOR. 2. KILL WHO'S INSIDE. WE NEED TWO STEPS!
BUT STEP ONE'LL KILL USHIO!

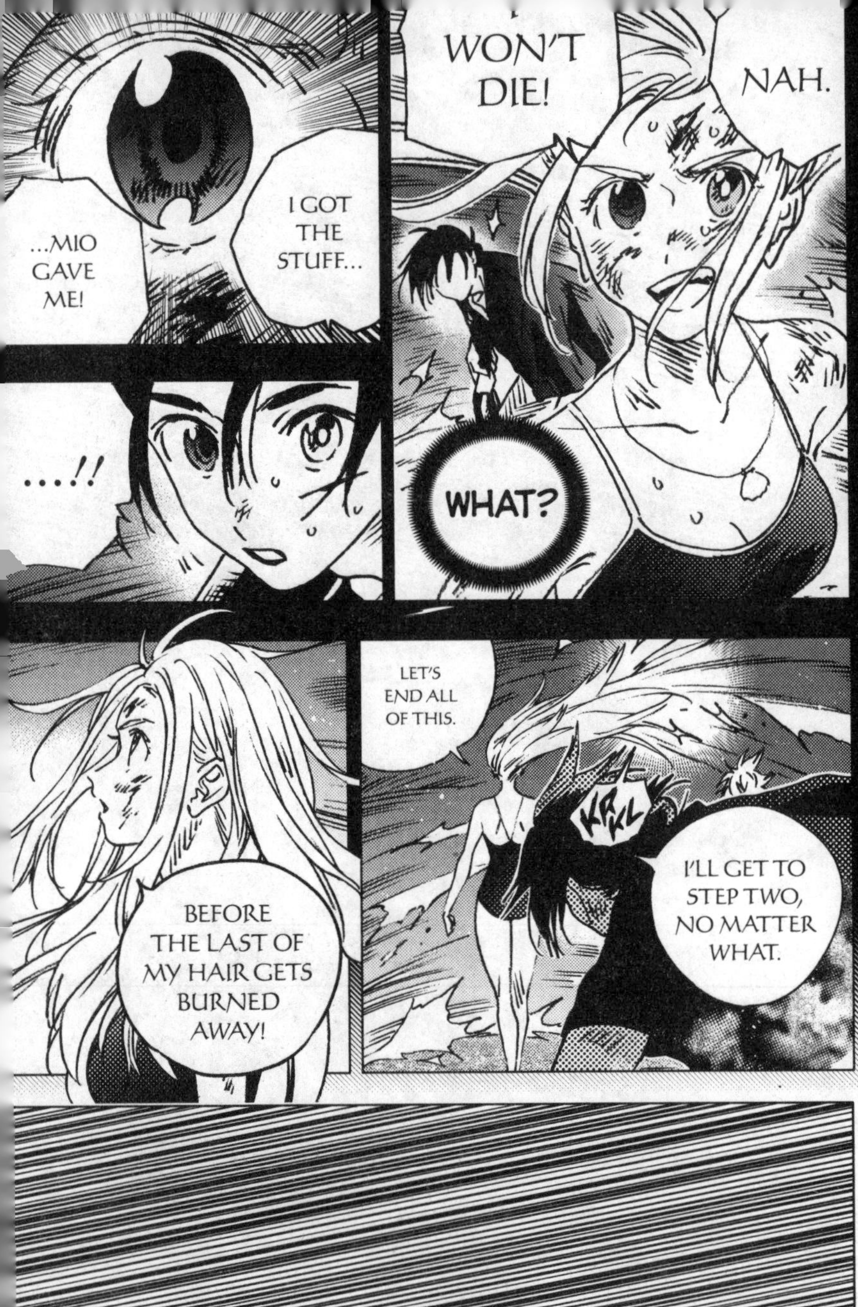
WON'T DIE!
NAH.
WHAT?
I GOT THE STUFF...
...MIO GAVE ME!
...!!
LET'S END ALL OF THIS.
KRKL
I'LL GET TO STEP TWO, NO MATTER WHAT.
BEFORE THE LAST OF MY HAIR GETS BURNED AWAY!

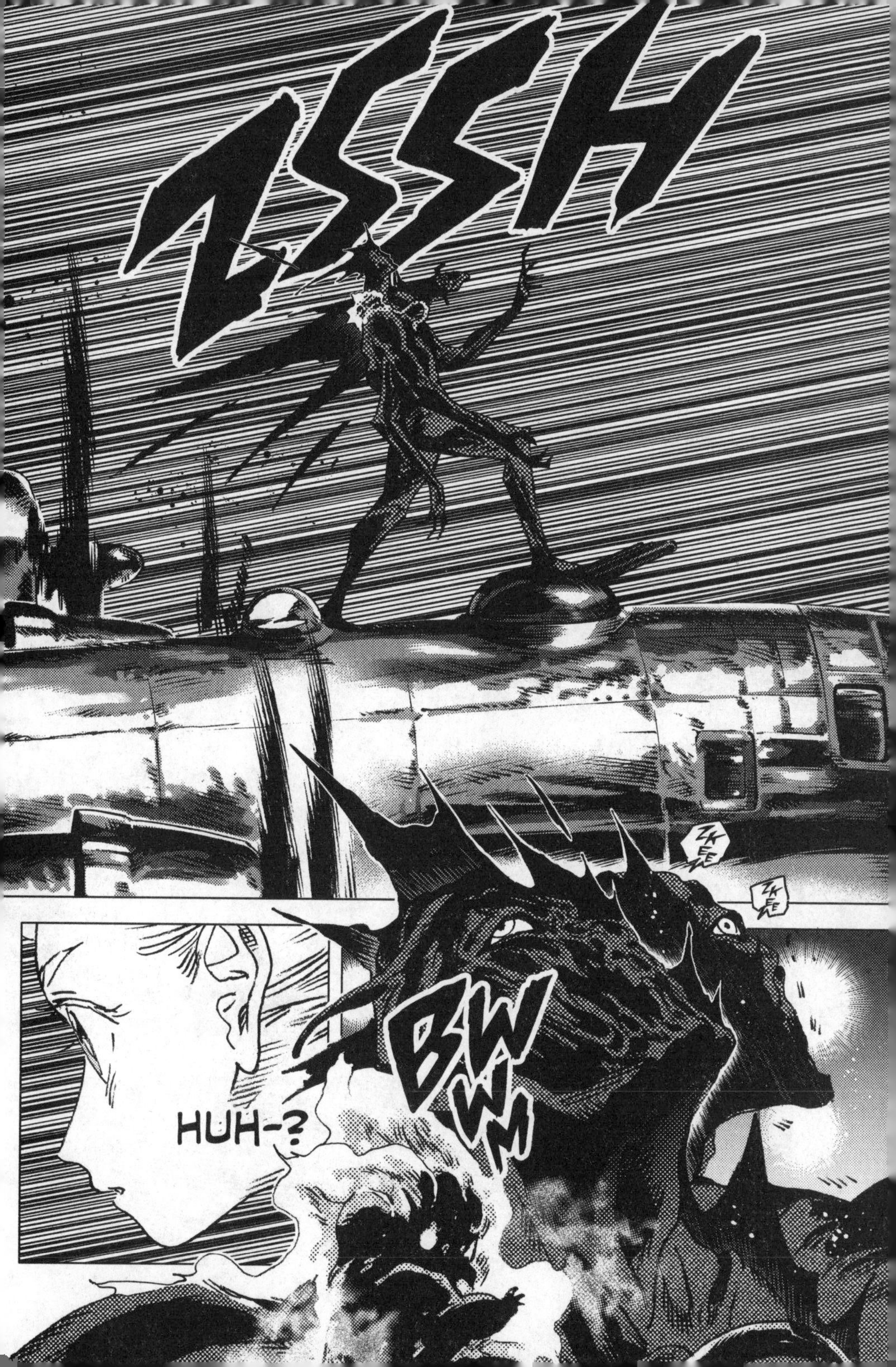
ZSSH
ZKEE
ZKEE
BWWM
HUH-?

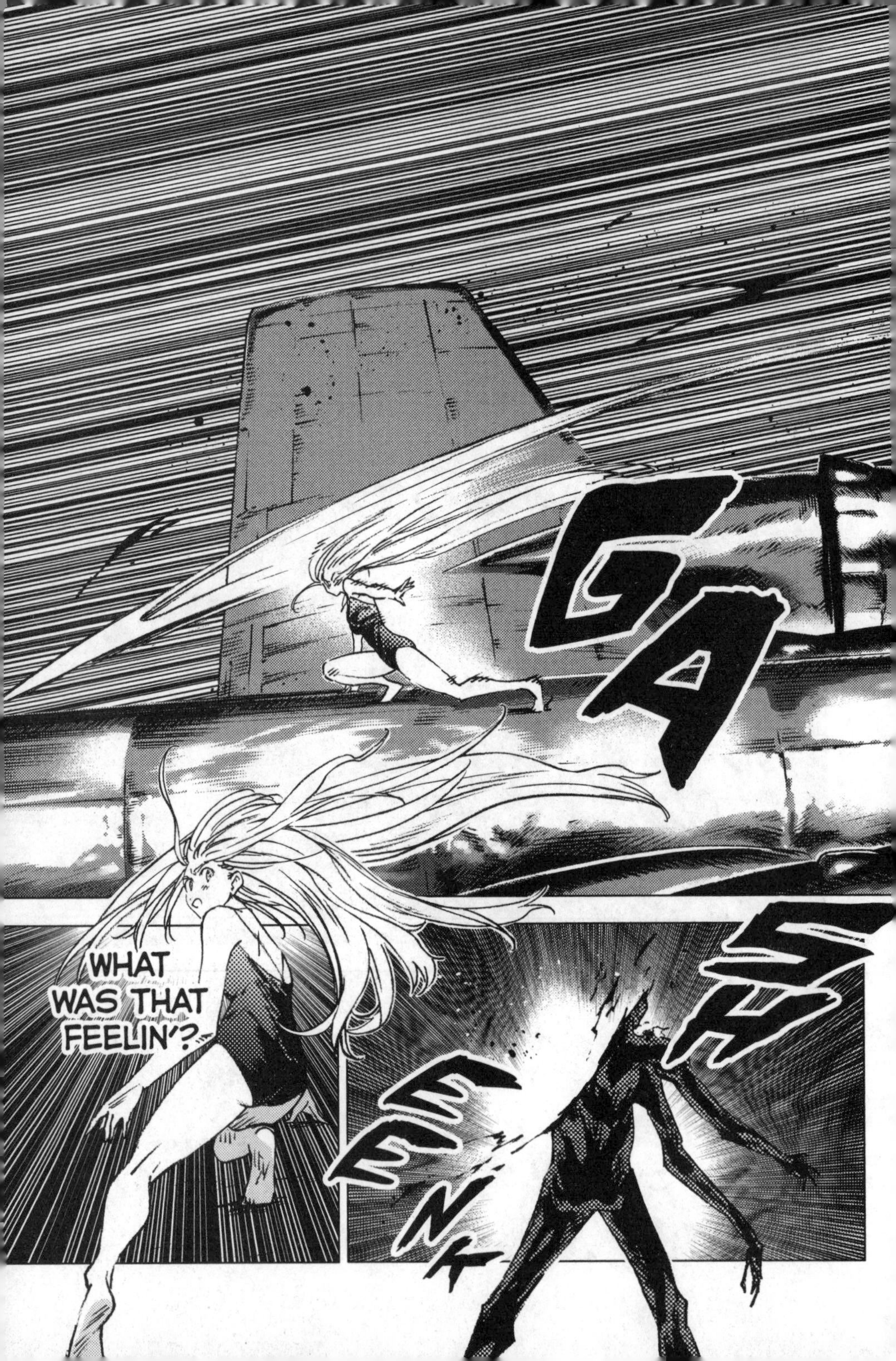
GA
SHEENK
WHAT WAS THAT FEELIN'?

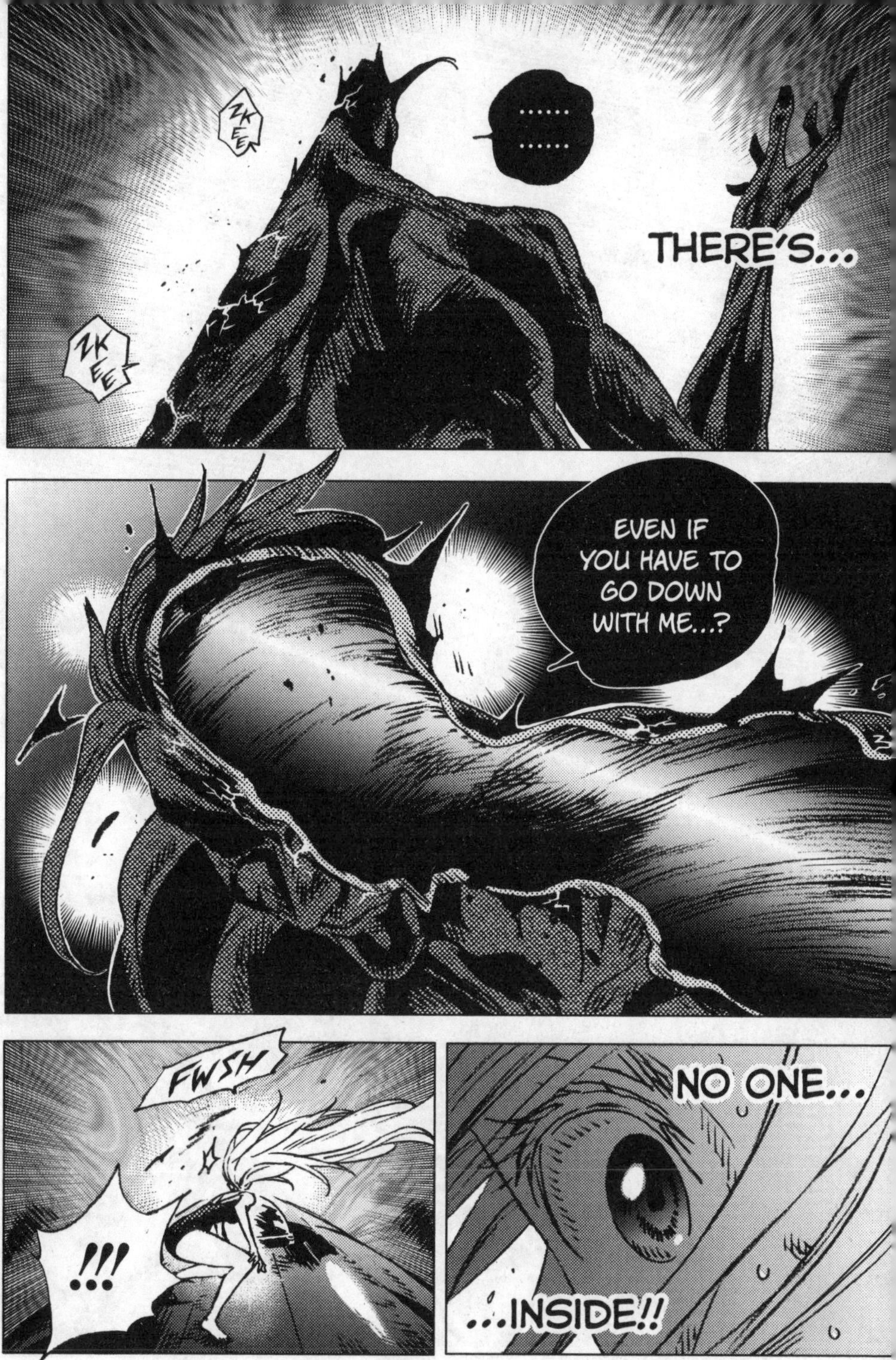
……
……
THERE'S...
ZKEE
ZKEE
EVEN IF YOU HAVE TO GO DOWN WITH ME...?
NO ONE...
...INSIDE!!
FWSH
!!!

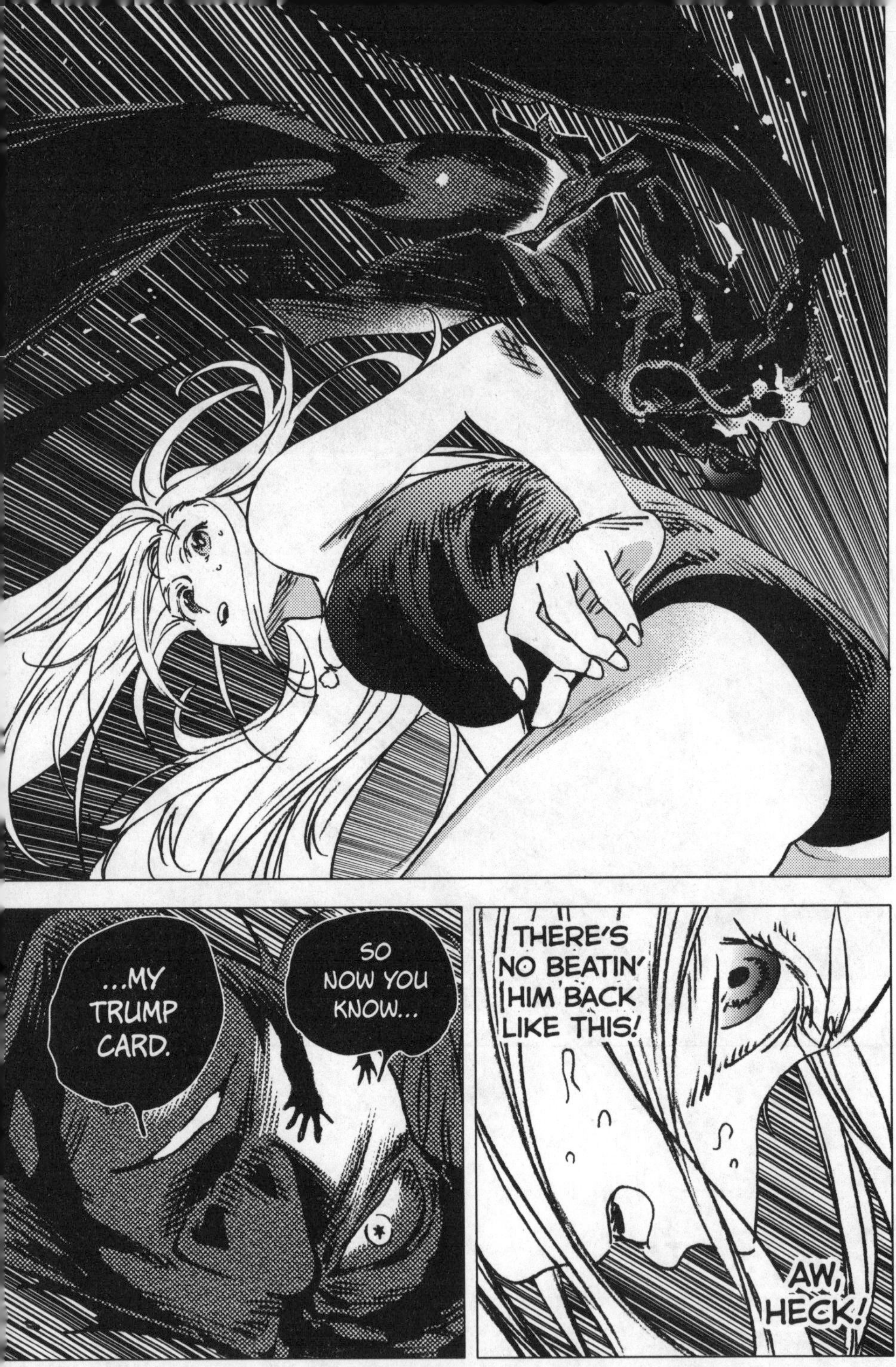
THERE'S NO BEATIN' HIM BACK LIKE THIS!
AW, HECK!
SO NOW YOU KNOW...
...MY TRUMP CARD.

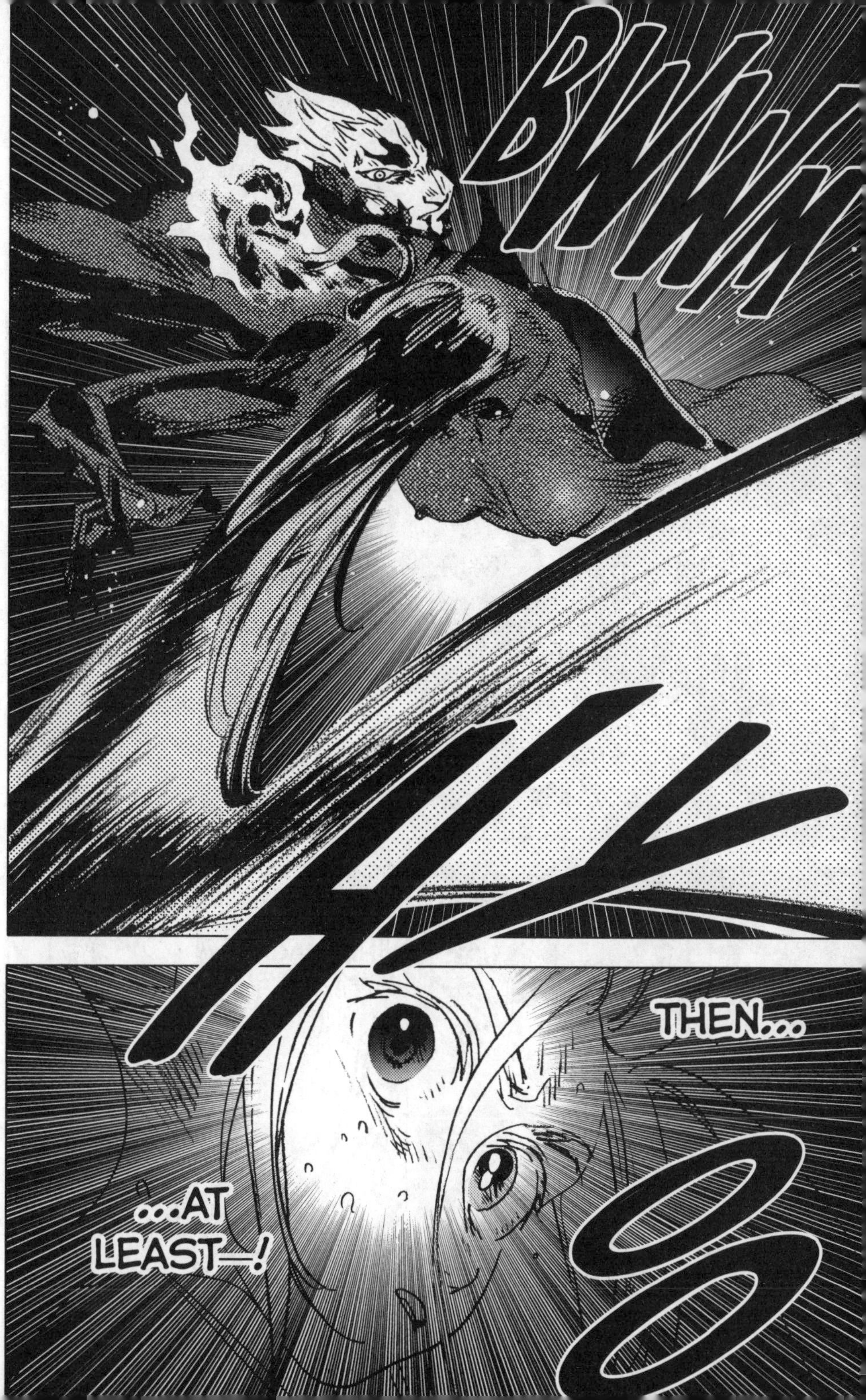
THEN...
...AT LEAST—!

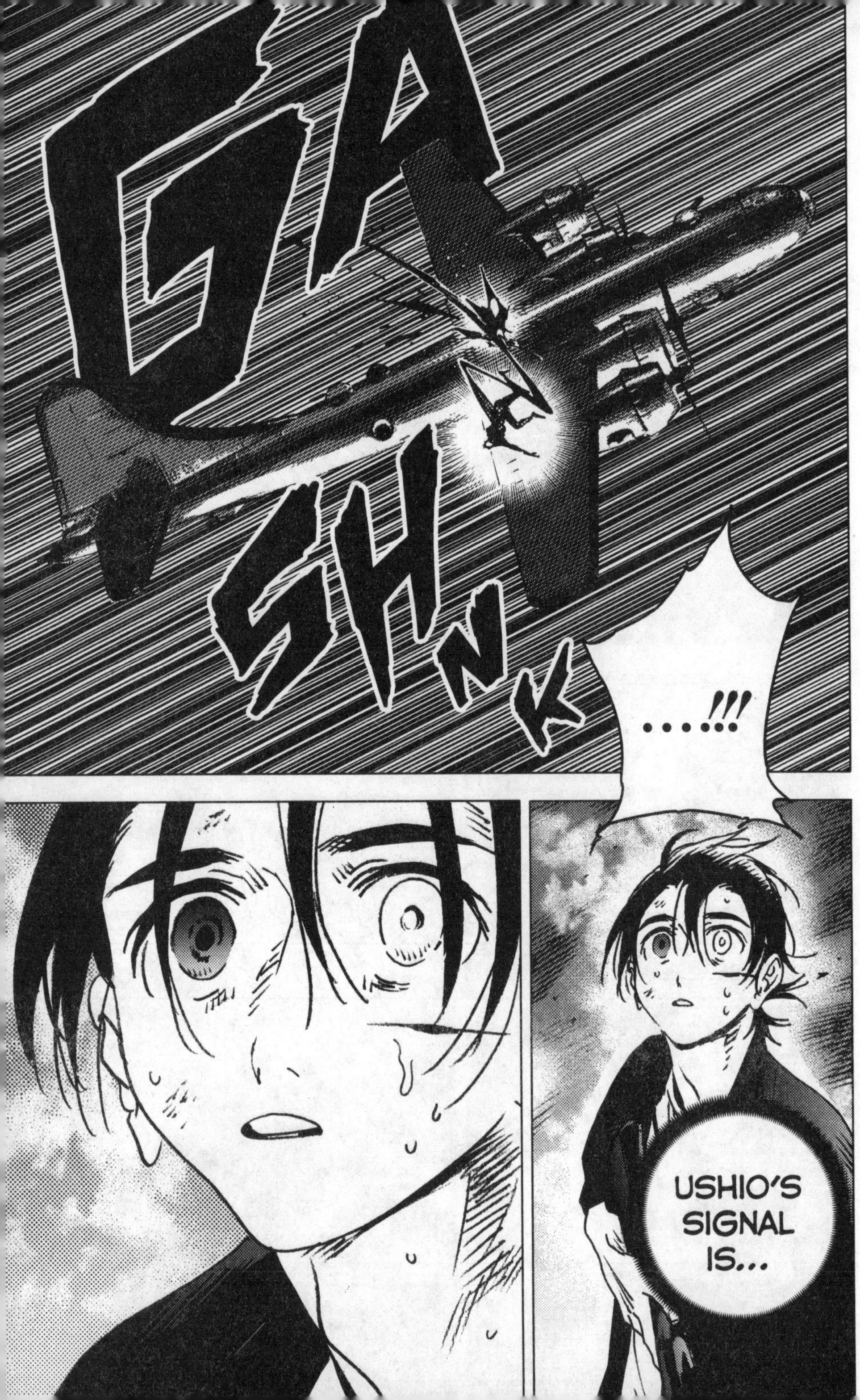
GASHUNK
....!!!
USHIO'S SIGNAL IS...

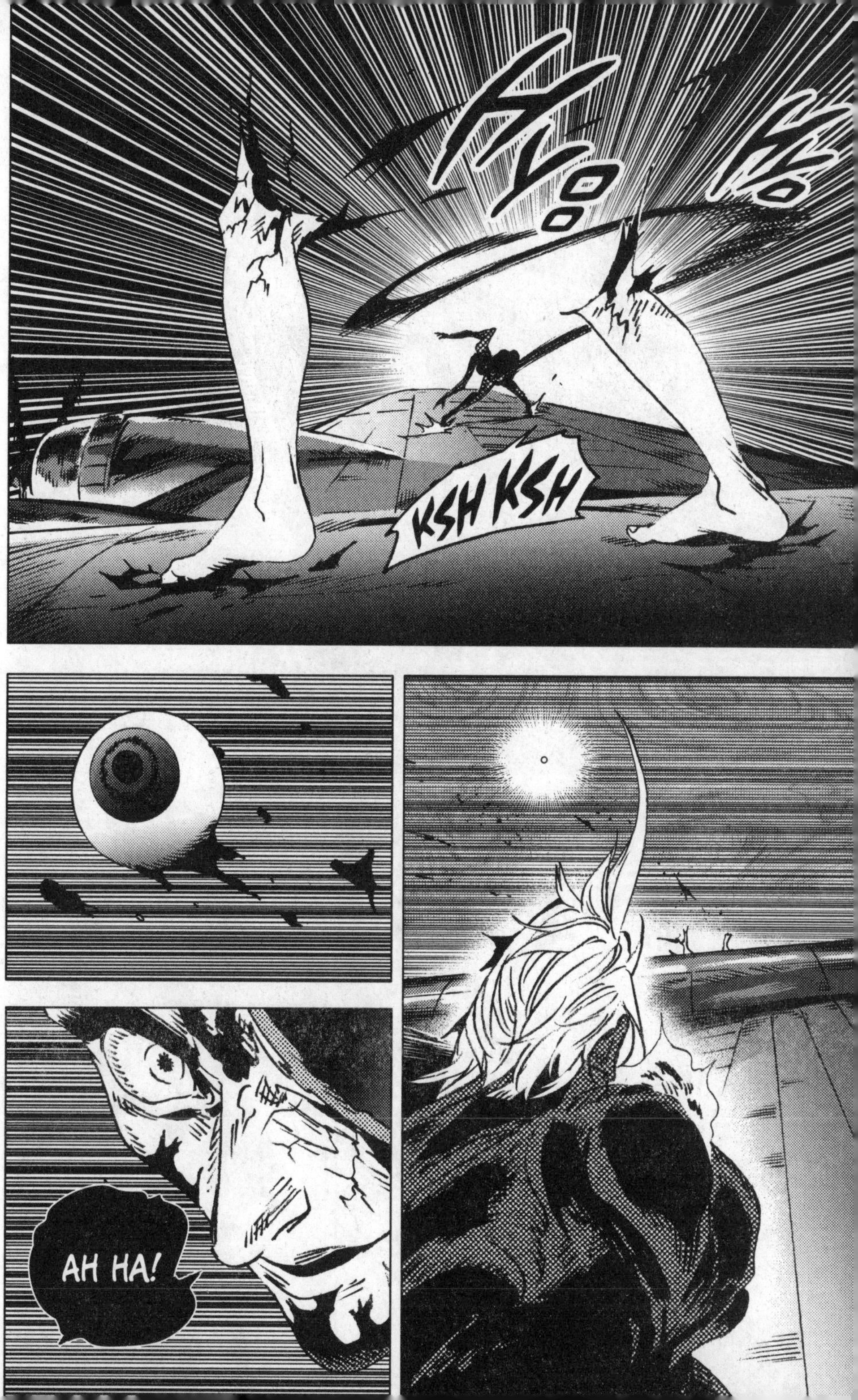
HYOO
KSH KSH
AH HA!

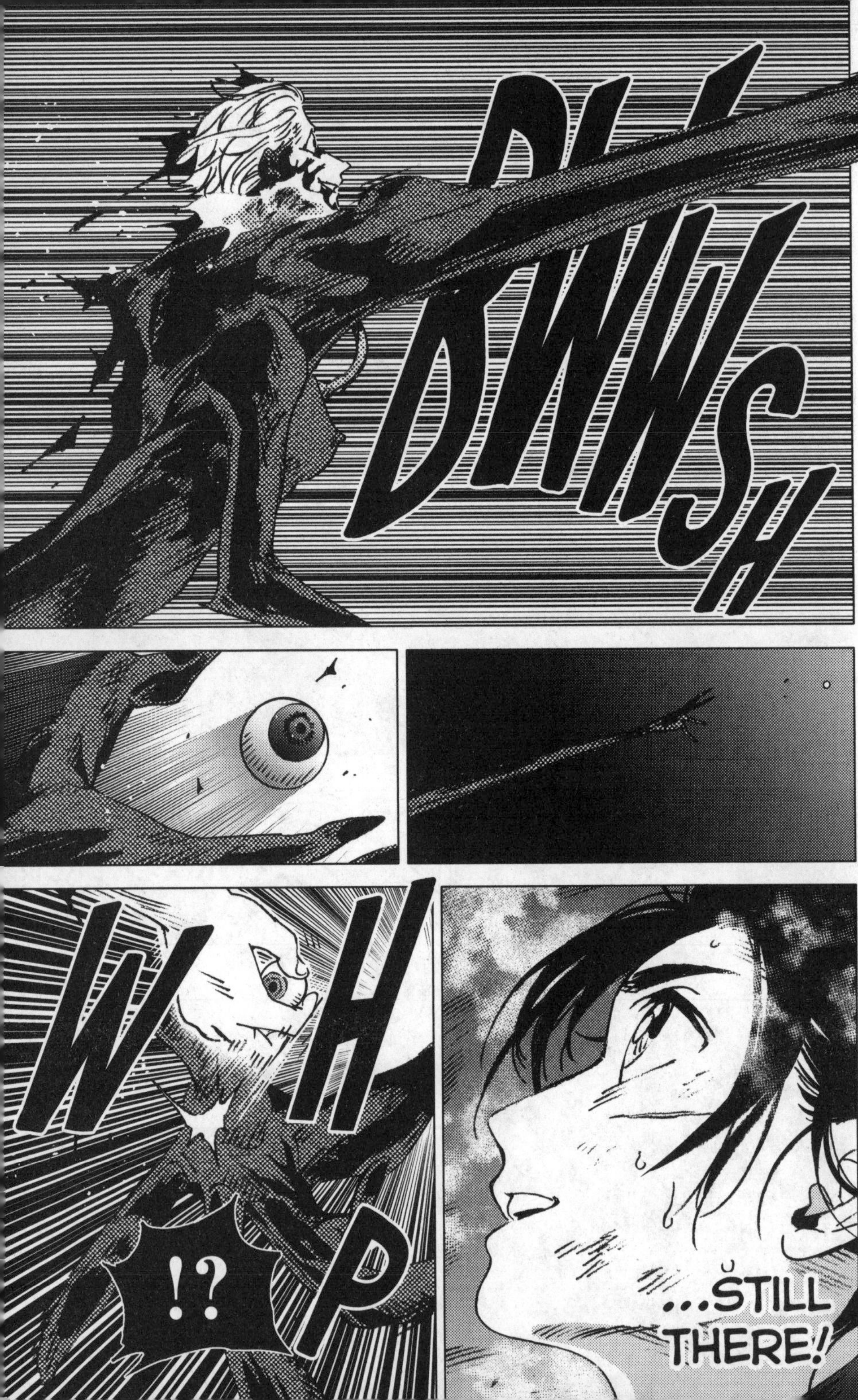
DWWSH
...STILL THERE!
!?
WHP

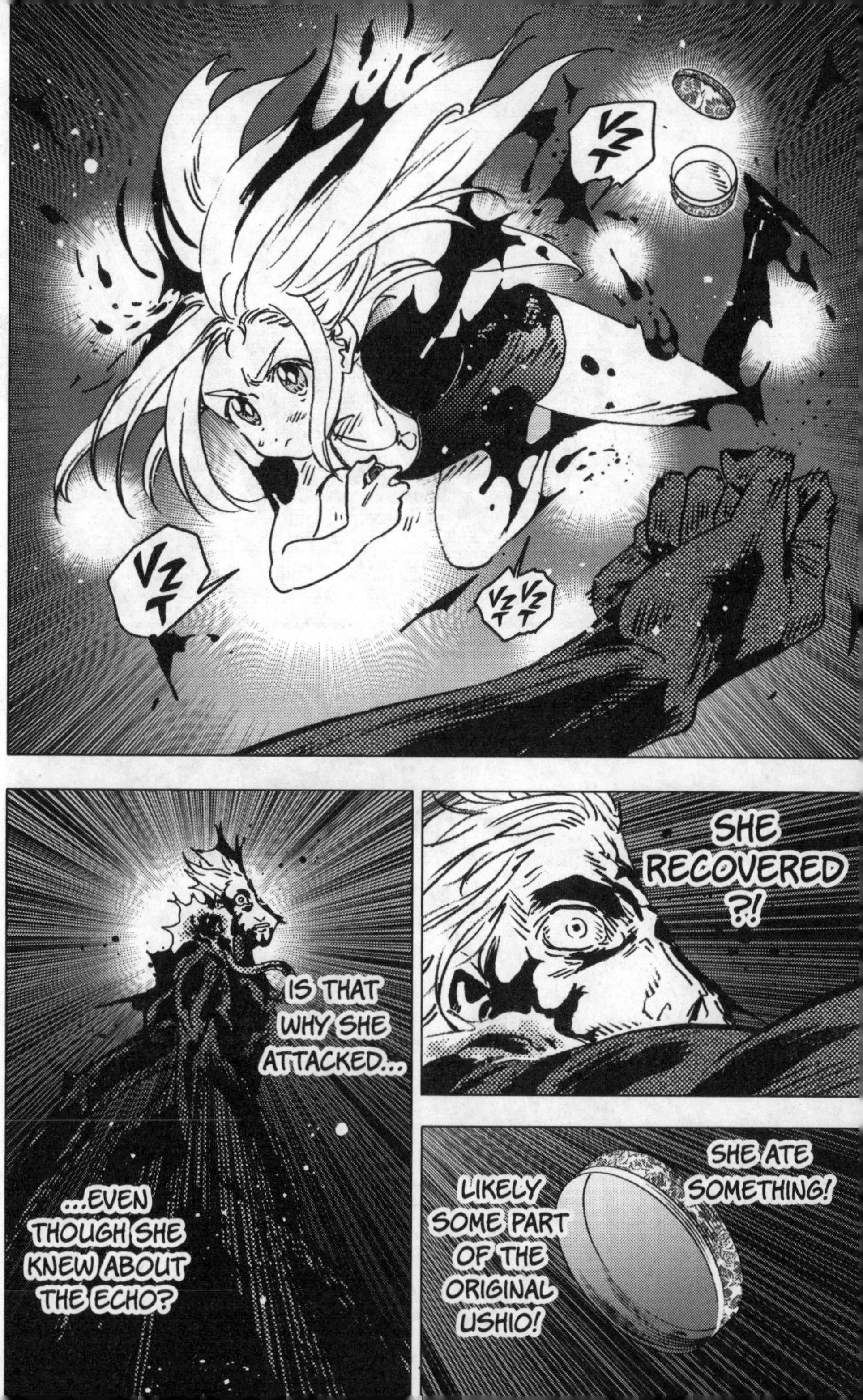

VZT
VZT VZT
VZT
SHE RECOVERED?!
SHE ATE SOMETHING!
LIKELY SOME PART OF THE ORIGINAL USHIO!
IS THAT WHY SHE ATTACKED...
...EVEN THOUGH SHE KNEW ABOUT THE ECHO?

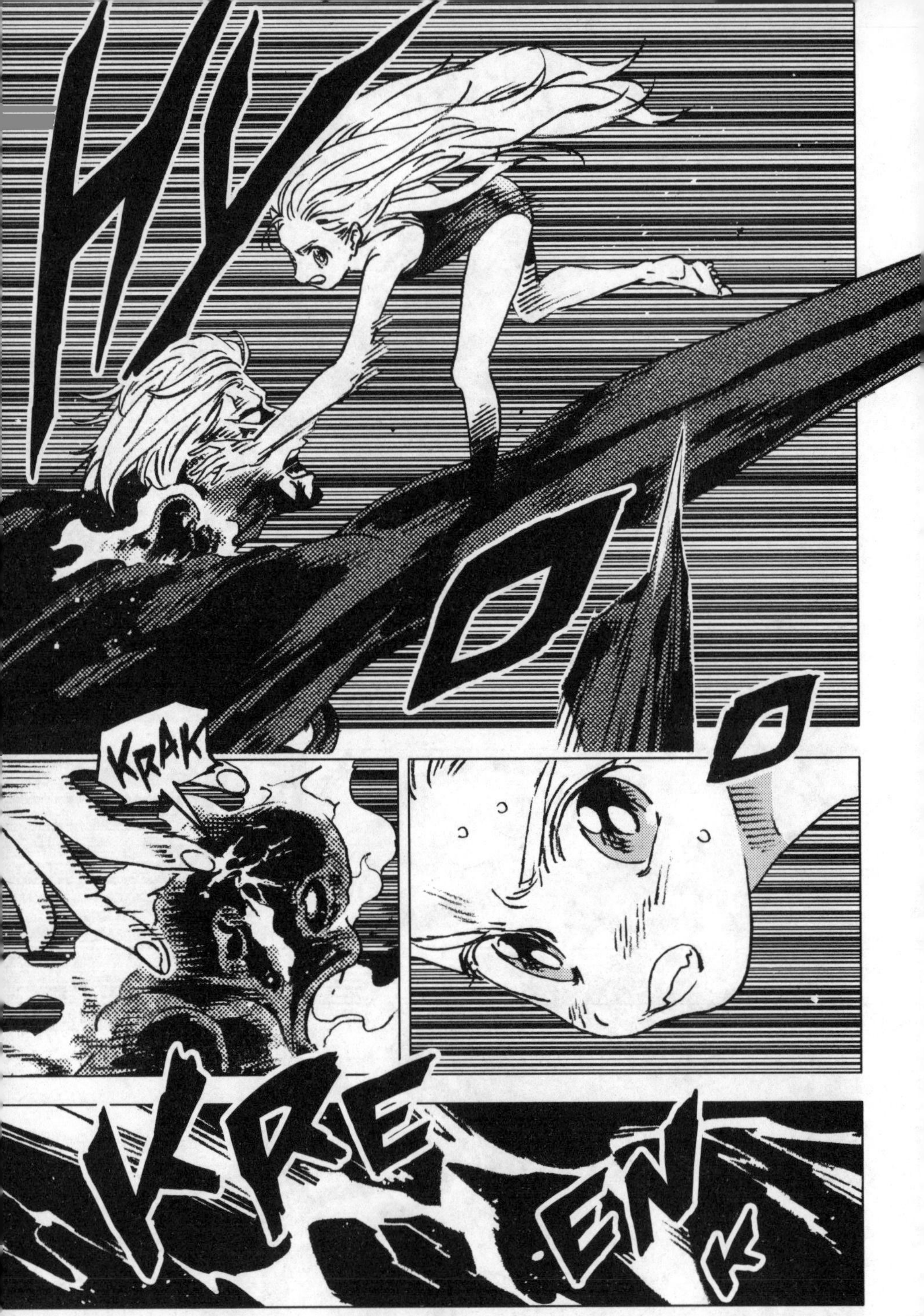
KRAK

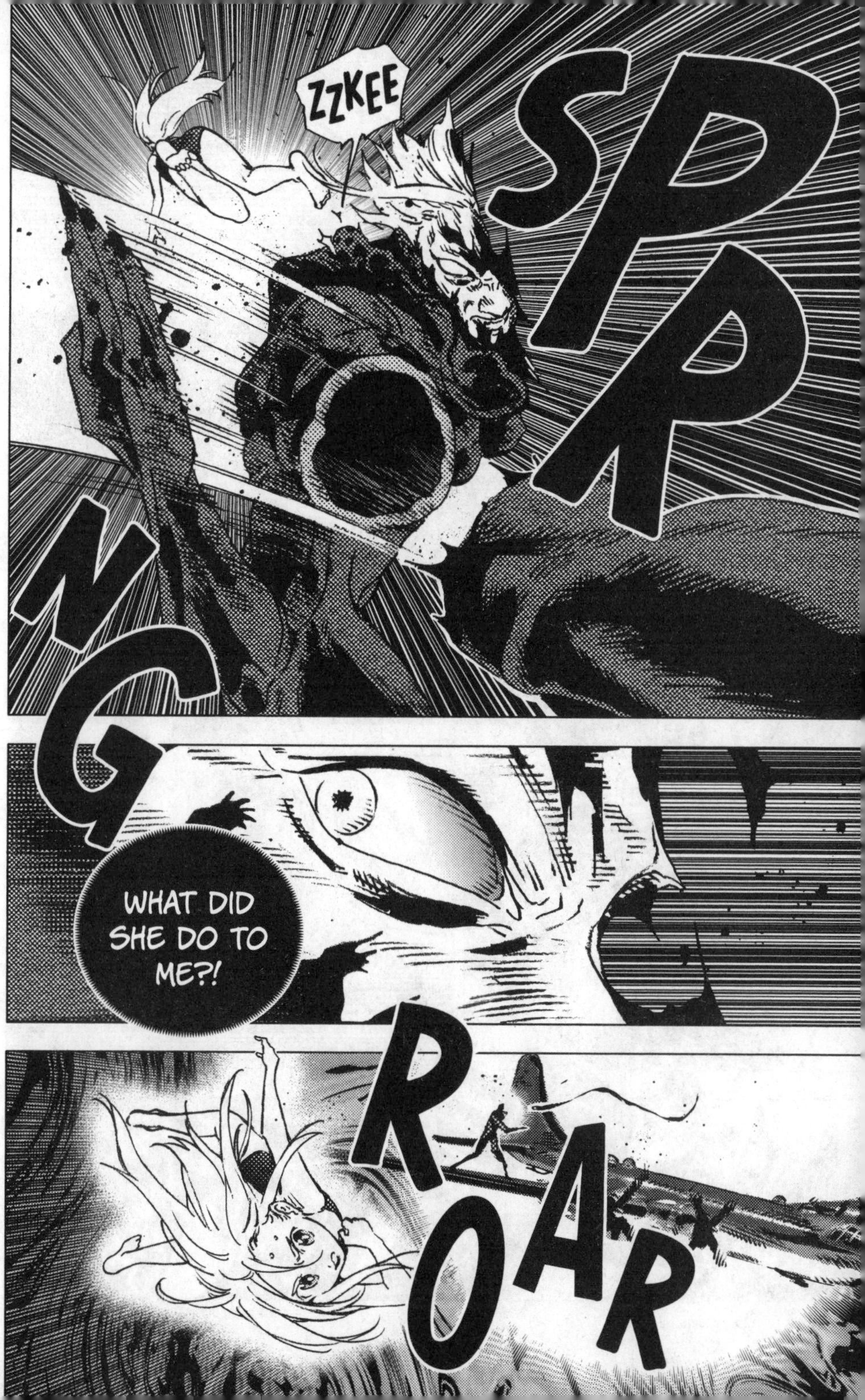
SPRNG
ZZKEE
WHAT DID SHE DO TO ME?!
ROAR

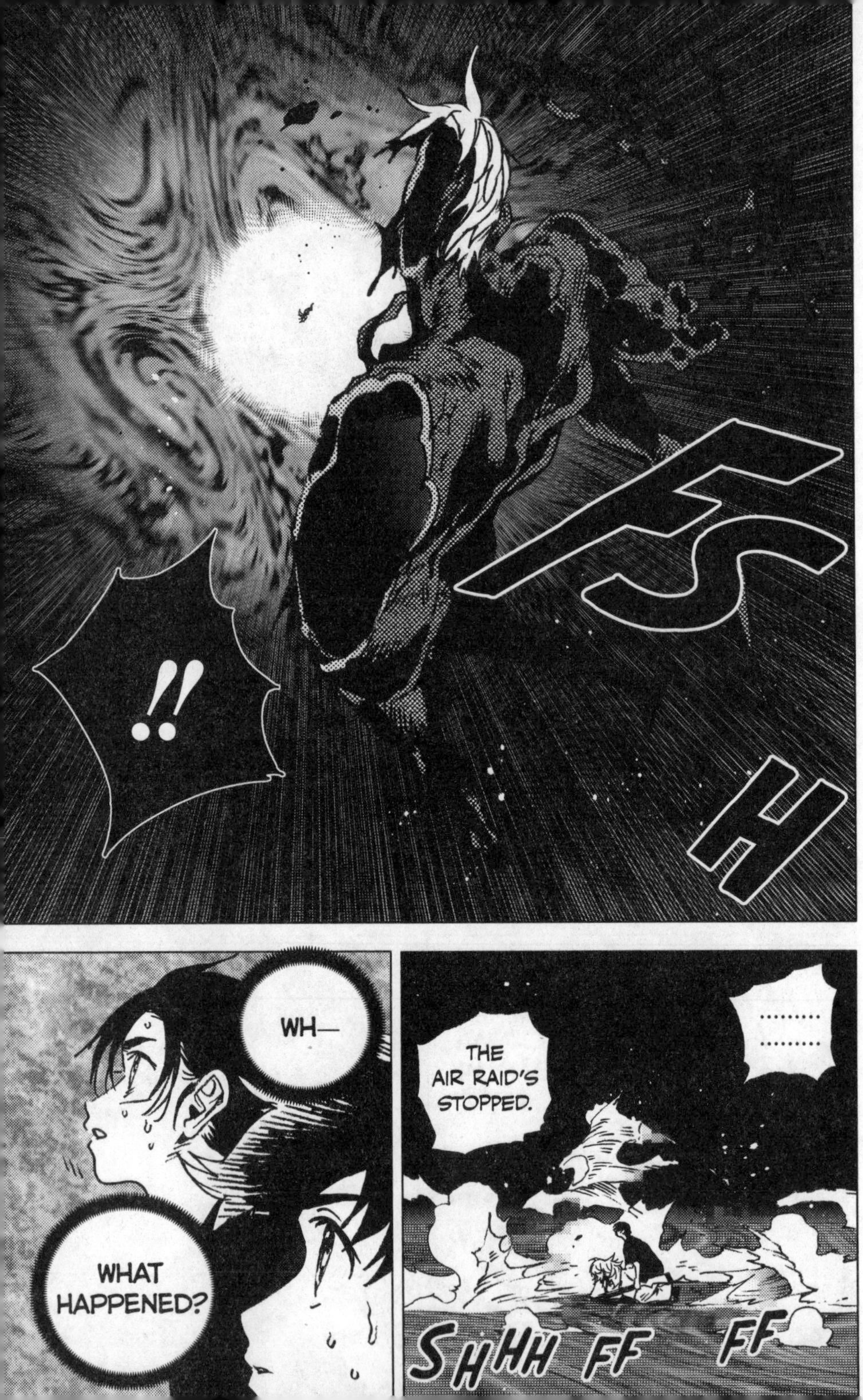
FSH
!!
....
....
THE AIR RAID'S STOPPED.
SHHH FF
FF
WH—
WHAT HAPPENED?

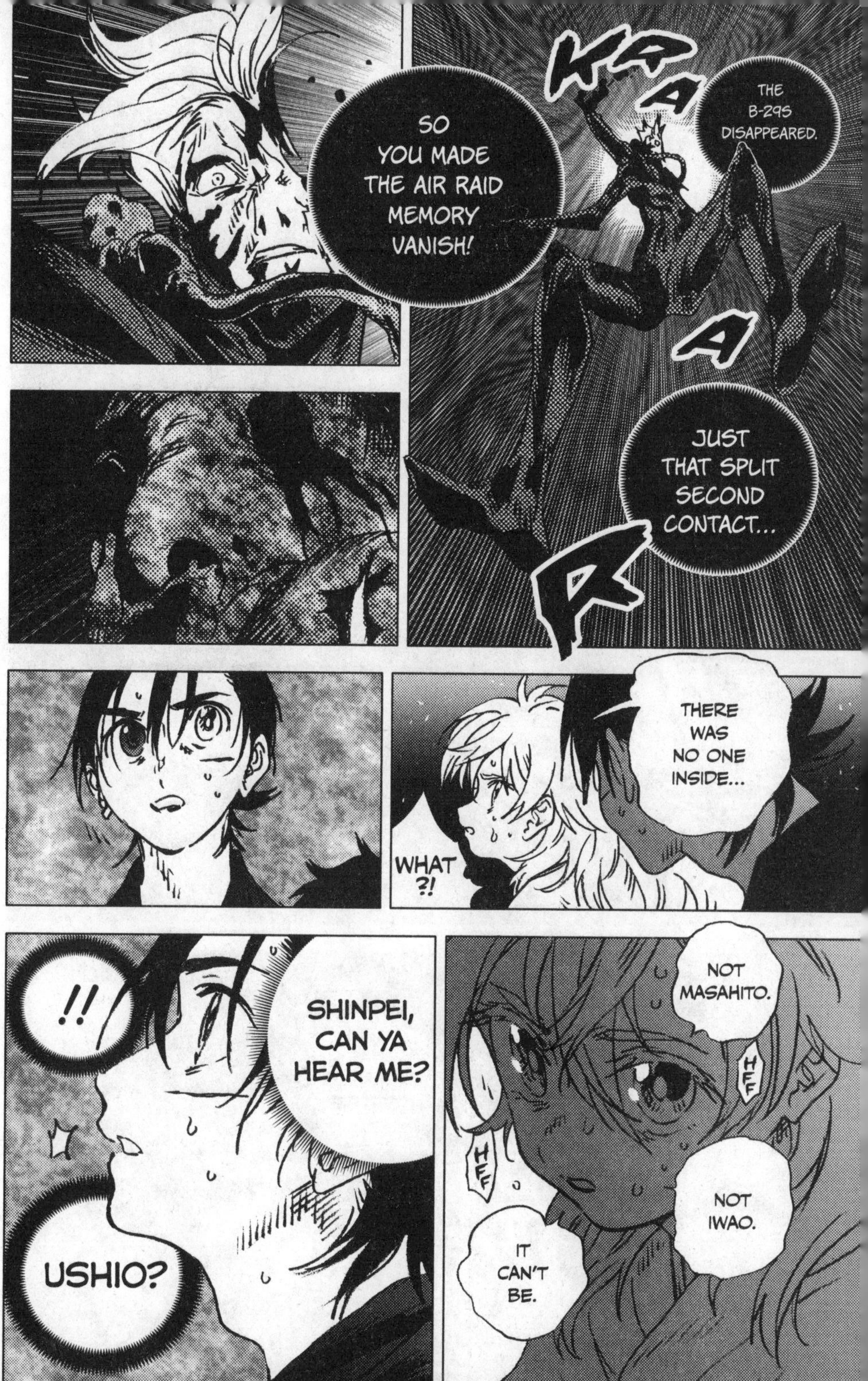

KRAAA
THE B-29S DISAPPEARED.
JUST THAT SPLIT SECOND CONTACT...
SO YOU MADE THE AIR RAID MEMORY VANISH!
THERE WAS NO ONE INSIDE...
WHAT?!
NOT MASAHITO.
HFF
NOT IWAO.
HFF
IT CAN'T BE.
SHINPEI, CAN YA HEAR ME?
!!
USHIO?

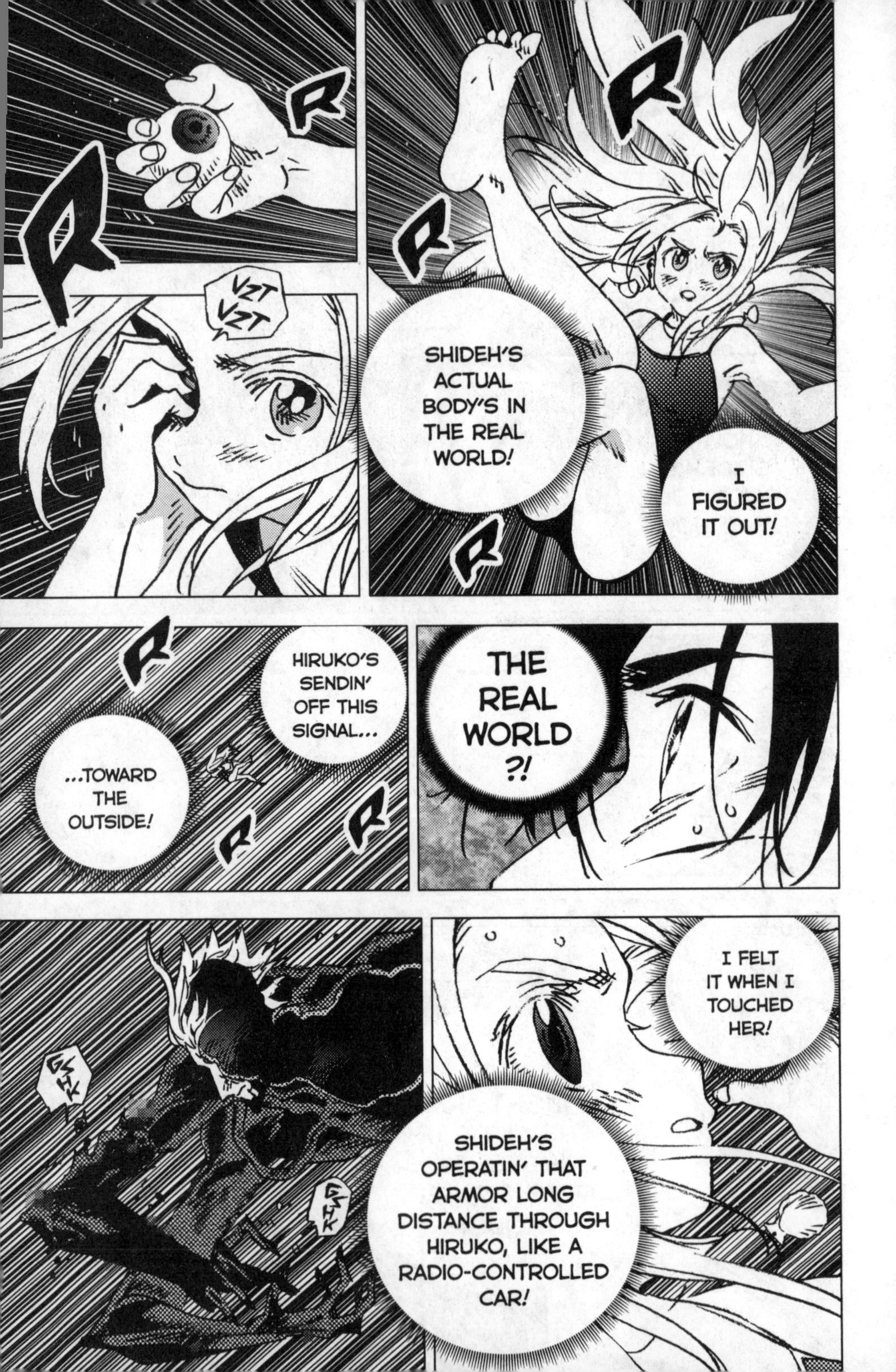
R
R
R
I FIGURED IT OUT!
SHIDEH'S ACTUAL BODY'S IN THE REAL WORLD!
R
R
R
VZT VZT
THE REAL WORLD ?!
R
HIRUKO'S SENDIN' OFF THIS SIGNAL...
...TOWARD THE OUTSIDE!
R
R
I FELT IT WHEN I TOUCHED HER!
SHIDEH'S OPERATIN' THAT ARMOR LONG DISTANCE THROUGH HIRUKO, LIKE A RADIO-CONTROLLED CAR!
GSHK
GSHK

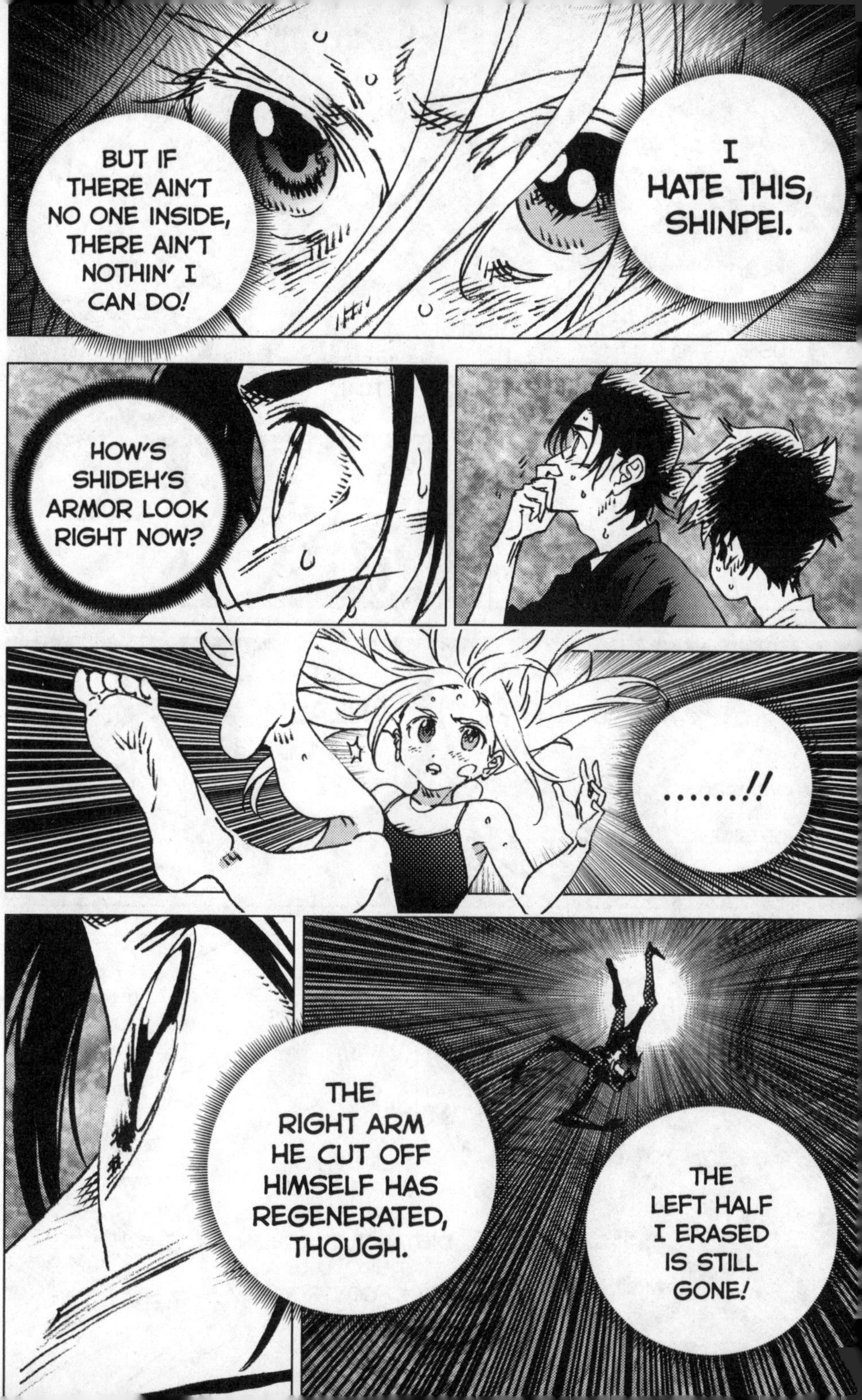
I HATE THIS, SHINPEI.
BUT IF THERE AIN'T NO ONE INSIDE, THERE AIN'T NOTHIN' I CAN DO!
HOW'S SHIDEH'S ARMOR LOOK RIGHT NOW?
......!!
THE LEFT HALF I ERASED IS STILL GONE!
THE RIGHT ARM HE CUT OFF HIMSELF HAS REGENERATED, THOUGH.

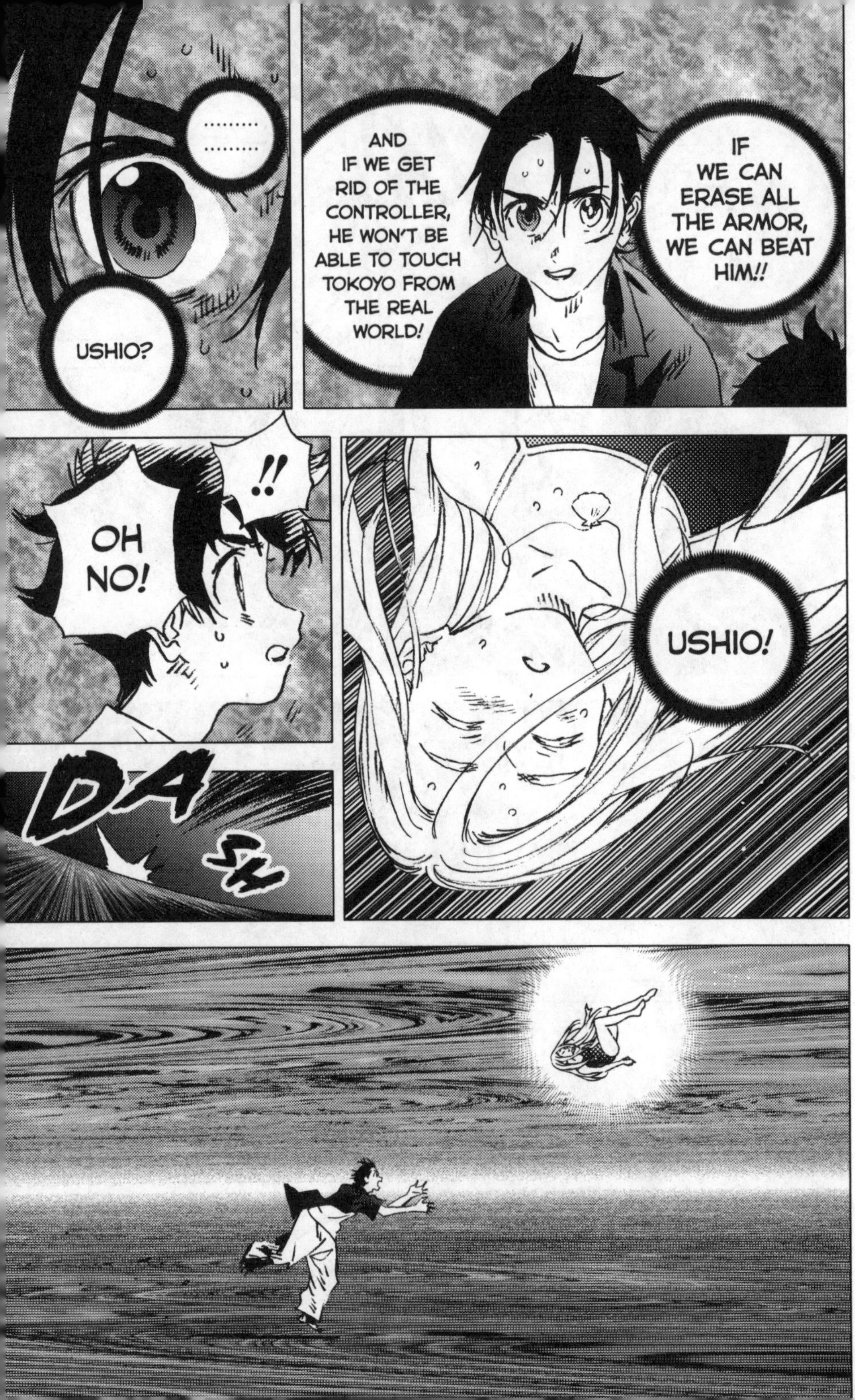
IF WE CAN ERASE ALL THE ARMOR, WE CAN BEAT HIM!!
AND IF WE GET RID OF THE CONTROLLER, HE WON'T BE ABLE TO TOUCH TOKOYO FROM THE REAL WORLD!
....
....
USHIO?
USHIO!
!!
OH NO!
DASH

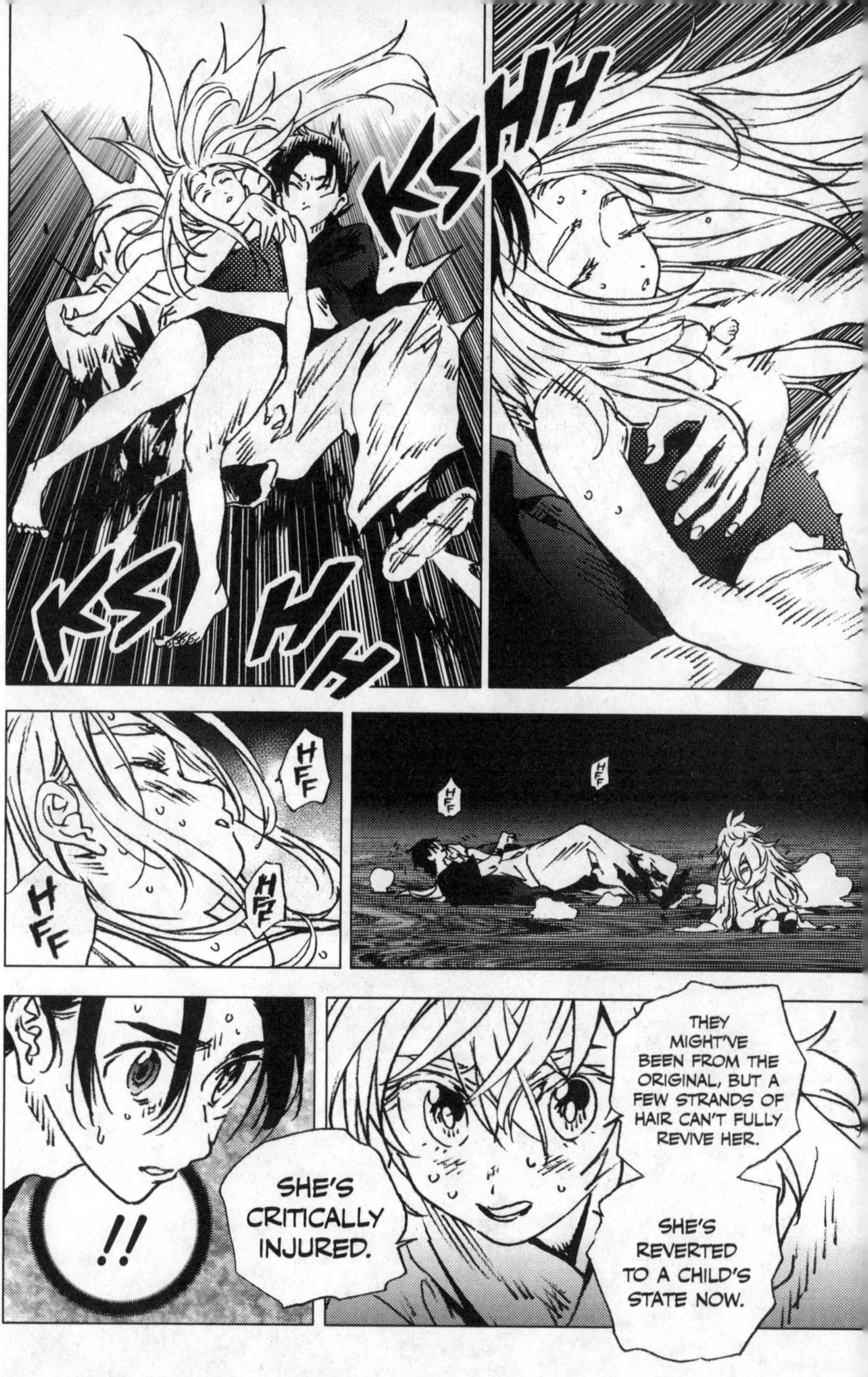
KSHH
KSHH
HFF
HFF
HFF
HFF
THEY MIGHT'VE BEEN FROM THE ORIGINAL, BUT A FEW STRANDS OF HAIR CAN'T FULLY REVIVE HER.
SHE'S REVERTED TO A CHILD'S STATE NOW.
SHE'S CRITICALLY INJURED.
!!

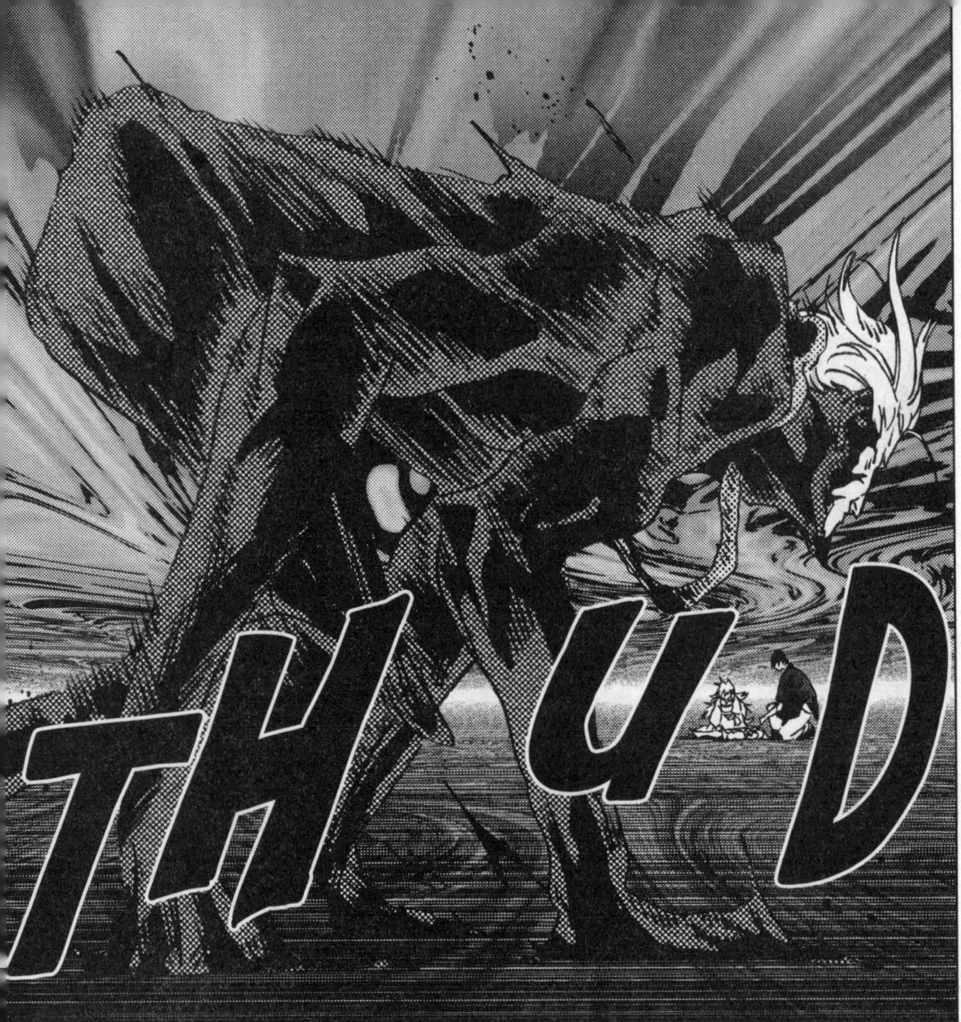
THUD

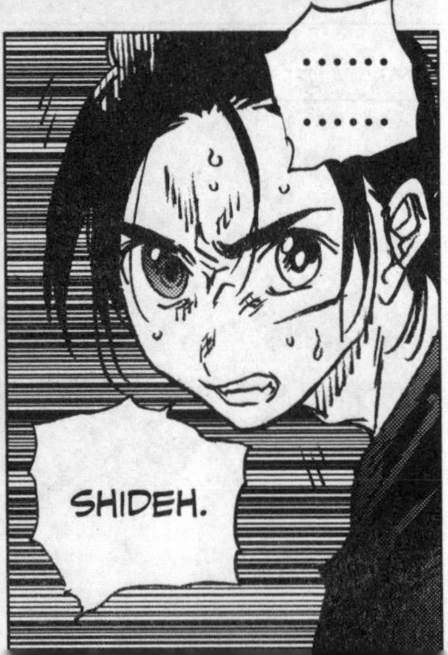
……
……
SHIDEH.

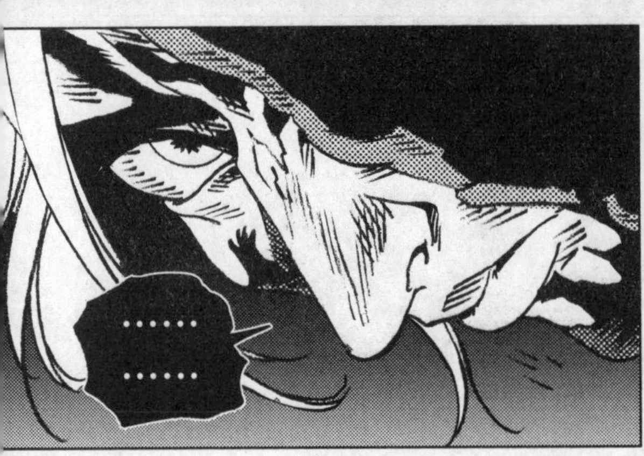
……
……

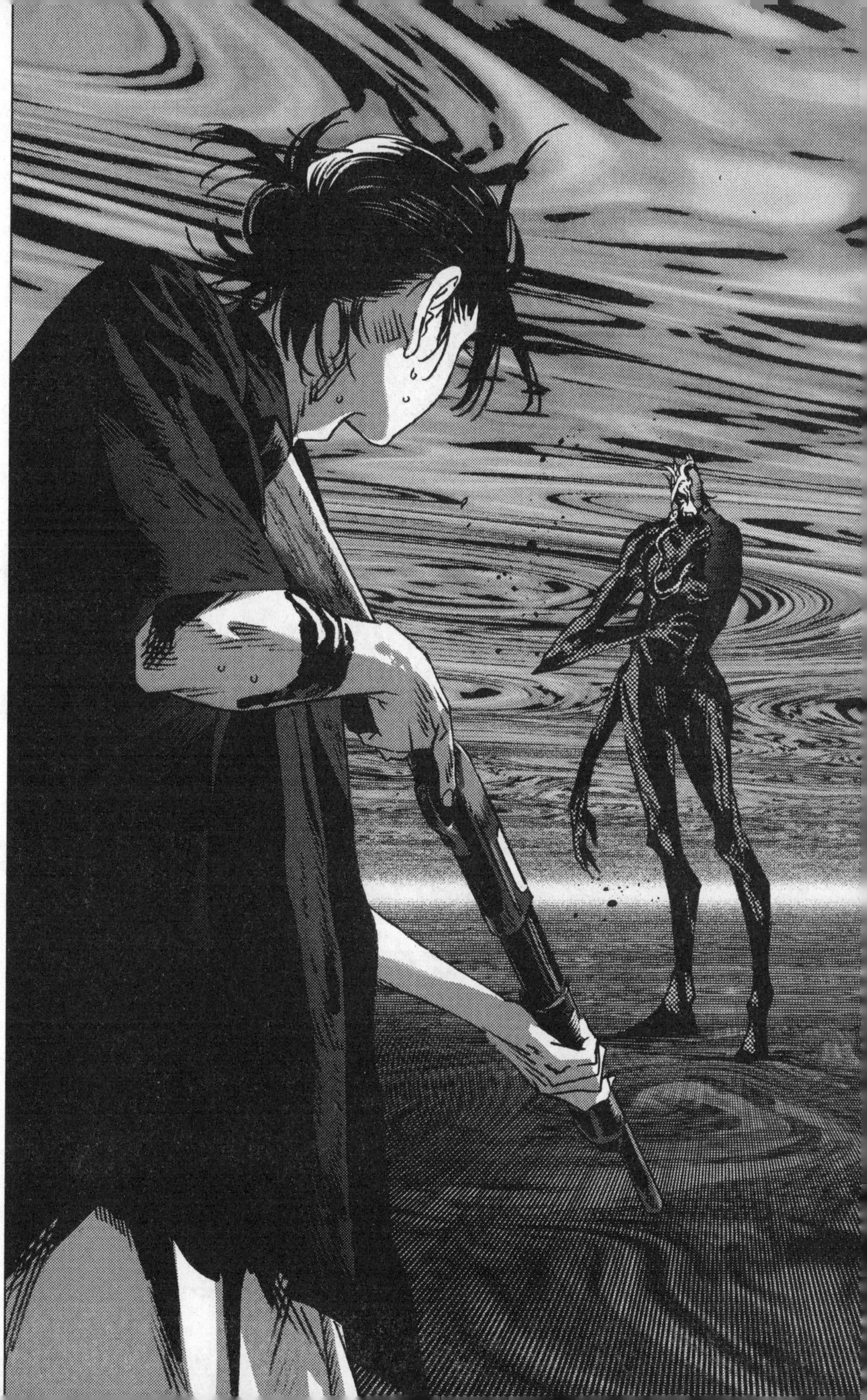

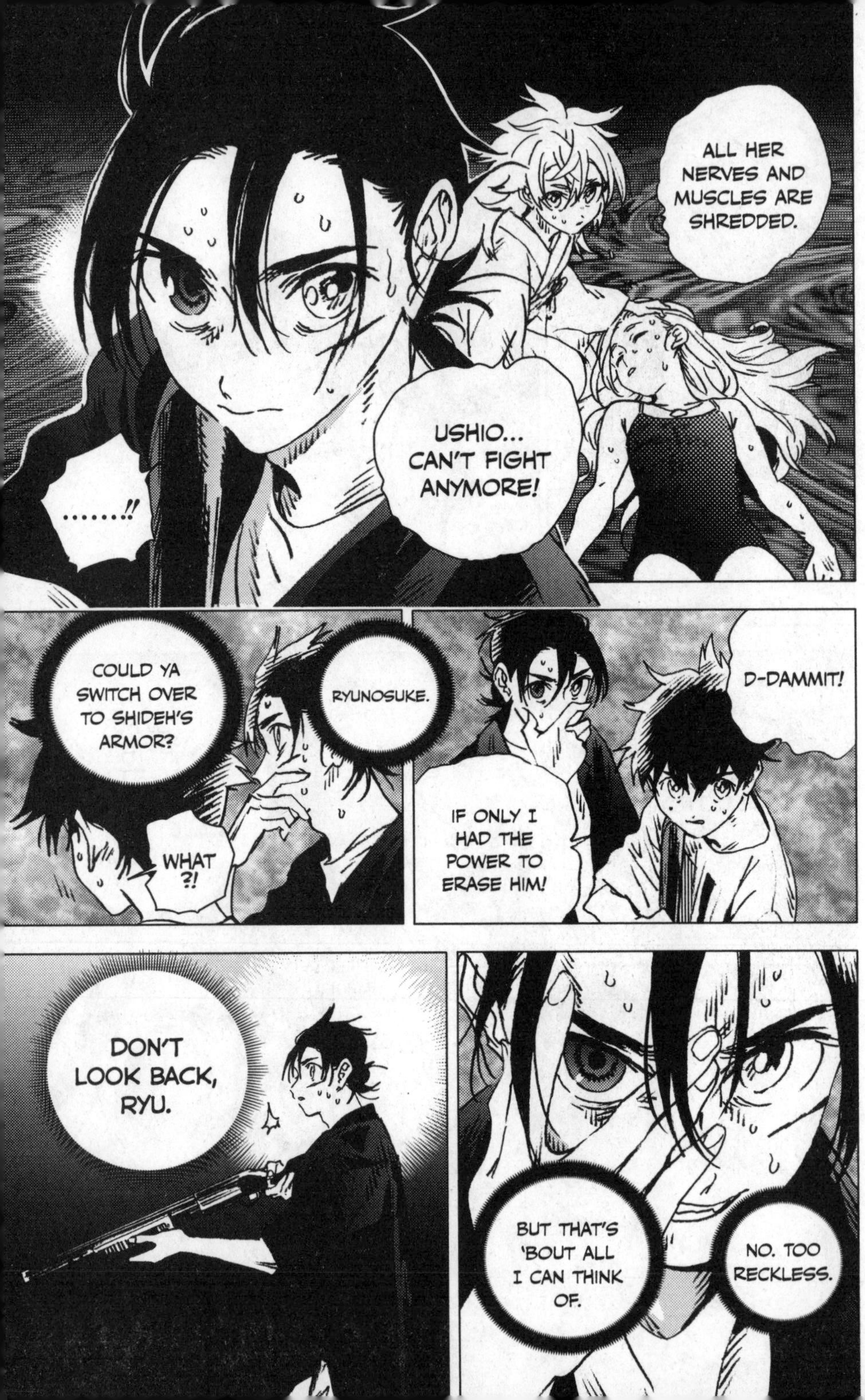
ALL HER NERVES AND MUSCLES ARE SHREDDED.
USHIO... CAN'T FIGHT ANYMORE!
.......!!
D-DAMMIT!
IF ONLY I HAD THE POWER TO ERASE HIM!
RYUNOSUKE.
COULD YA SWITCH OVER TO SHIDEH'S ARMOR?
WHAT ?!
NO. TOO RECKLESS.
BUT THAT'S 'BOUT ALL I CAN THINK OF.
DON'T LOOK BACK, RYU.

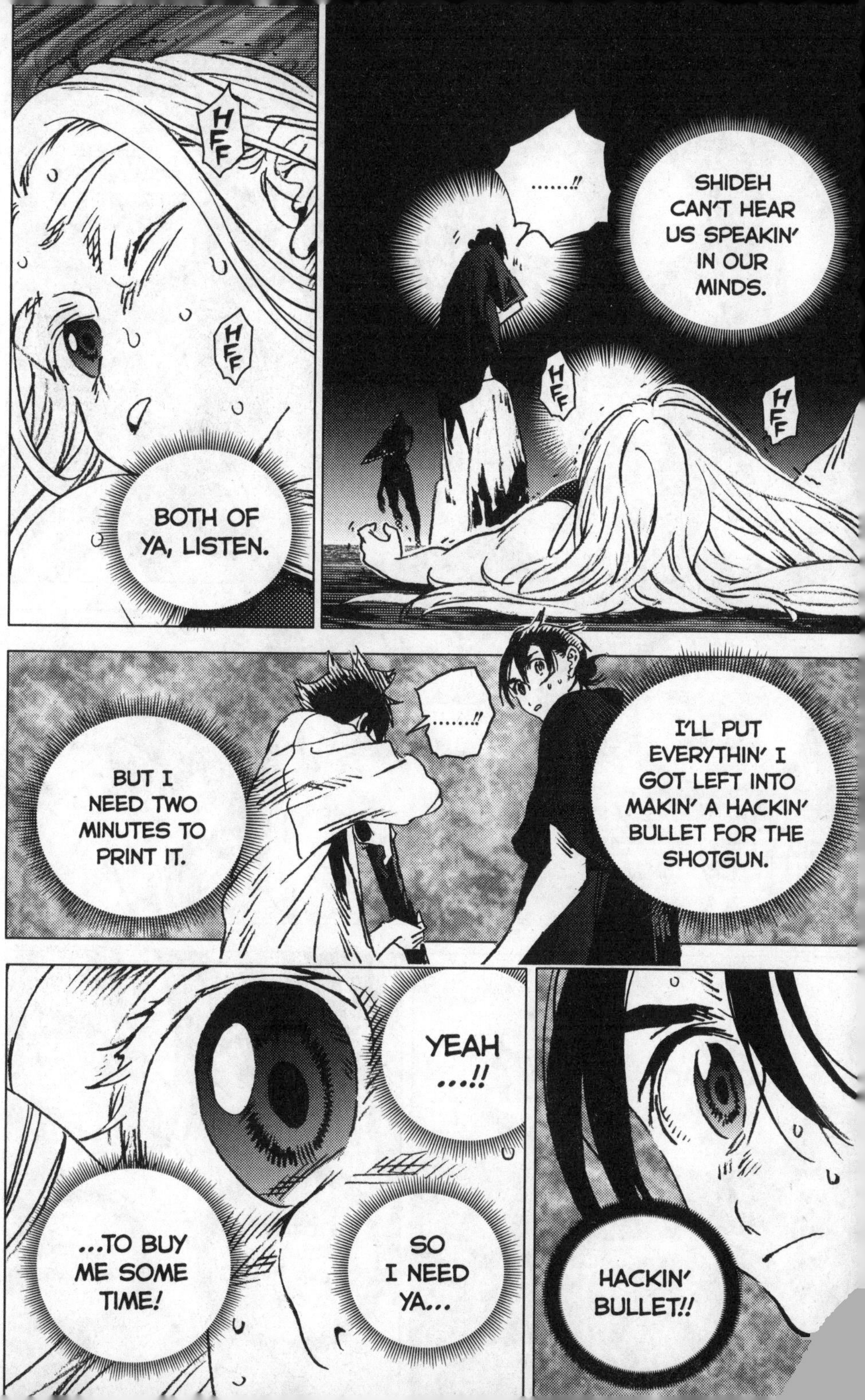
SHIDEH CAN'T HEAR US SPEAKIN' IN OUR MINDS.
......!!
HFF
HFF
HFF
HFF
BOTH OF YA, LISTEN.
I'LL PUT EVERYTHIN' I GOT LEFT INTO MAKIN' A HACKIN' BULLET FOR THE SHOTGUN.
......!!
BUT I NEED TWO MINUTES TO PRINT IT.
HACKIN' BULLET!!
YEAH ...!!
SO I NEED YA...
...TO BUY ME SOME TIME!

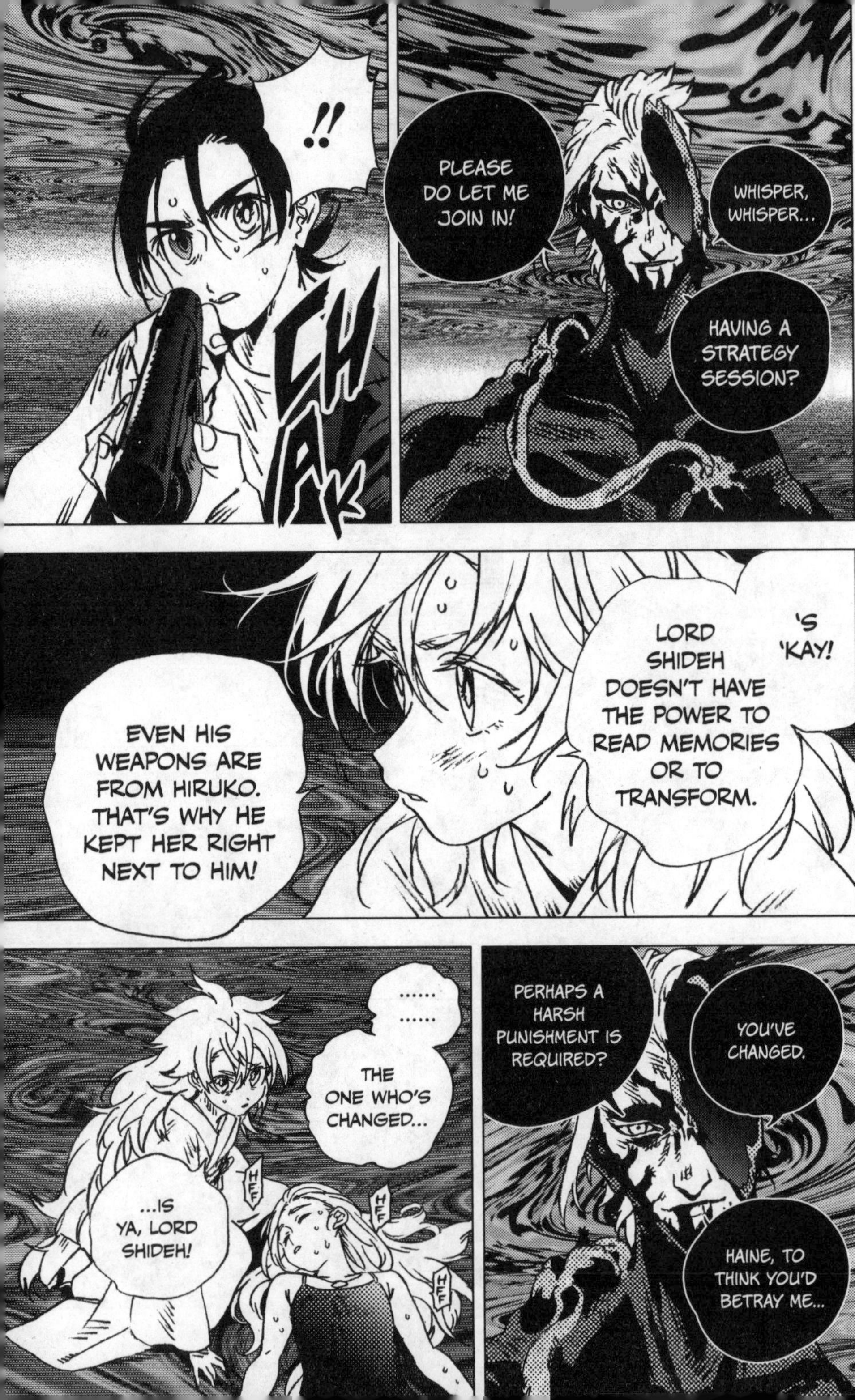
WHISPER, WHISPER...
PLEASE DO LET ME JOIN IN!
HAVING A STRATEGY SESSION?
!!
CHAK
'S 'KAY!
LORD SHIDEH DOESN'T HAVE THE POWER TO READ MEMORIES OR TO TRANSFORM.
EVEN HIS WEAPONS ARE FROM HIRUKO. THAT'S WHY HE KEPT HER RIGHT NEXT TO HIM!
YOU'VE CHANGED.
PERHAPS A HARSH PUNISHMENT IS REQUIRED?
HAINE, TO THINK YOU'D BETRAY ME...
......
......
THE ONE WHO'S CHANGED...
HFF
HFF
...IS YA, LORD SHIDEH!
HFF

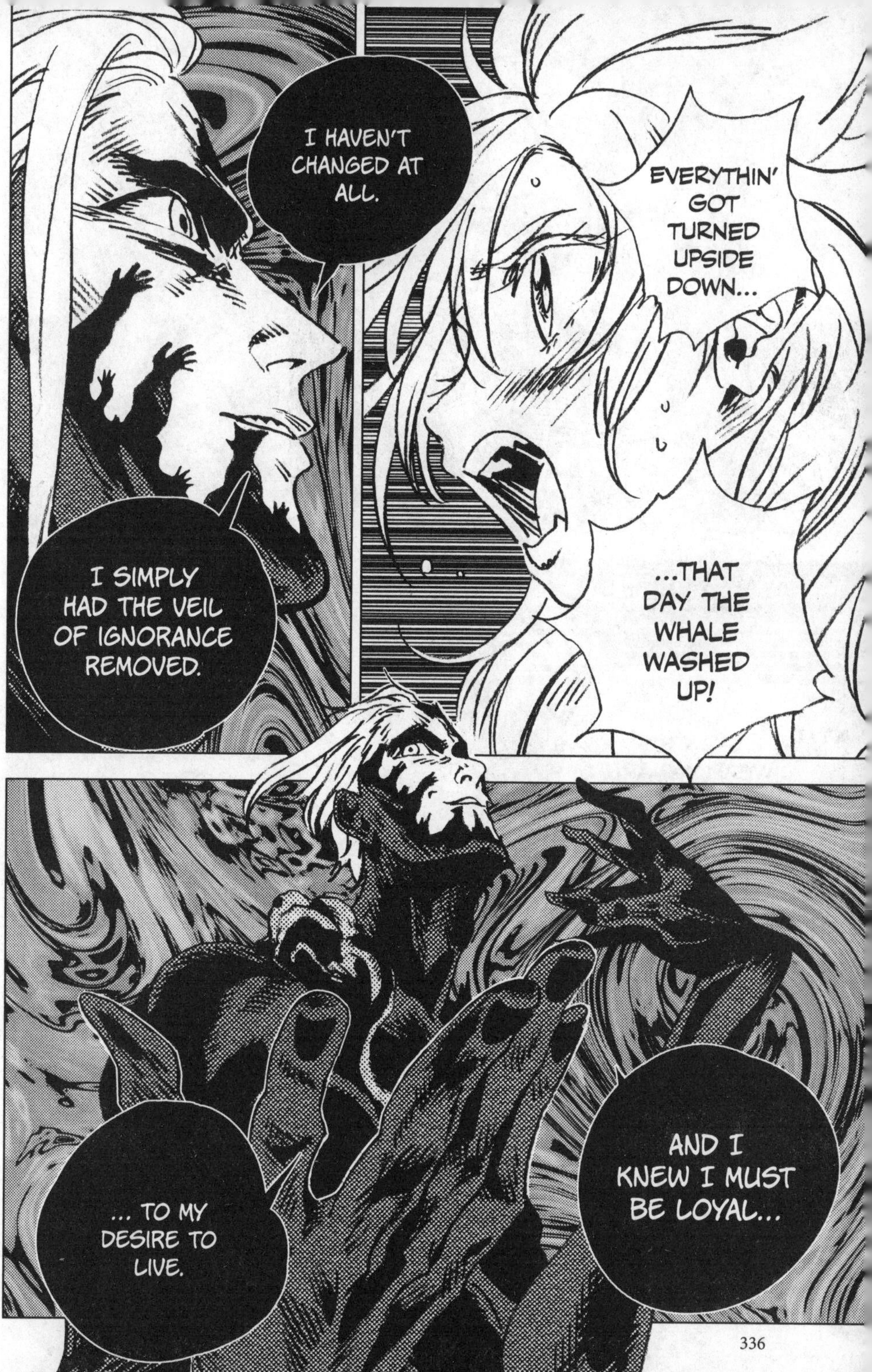
EVERYTHIN' GOT TURNED UPSIDE DOWN...
...THAT DAY THE WHALE WASHED UP!
I HAVEN'T CHANGED AT ALL.
I SIMPLY HAD THE VEIL OF IGNORANCE REMOVED.
AND I KNEW I MUST BE LOYAL...
... TO MY DESIRE TO LIVE.

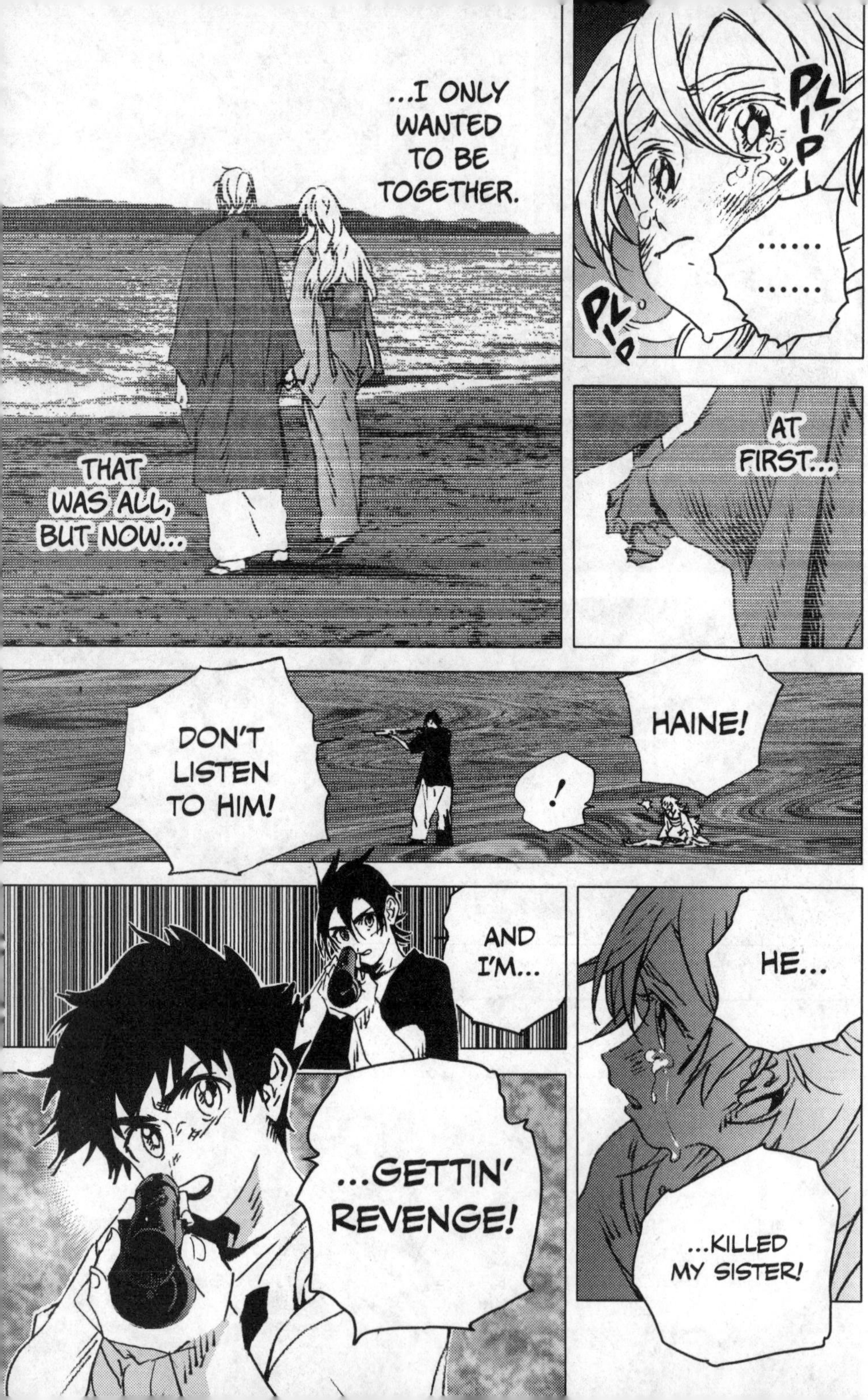
PLIP
......
......
PLIP
AT FIRST...
...I ONLY WANTED TO BE TOGETHER.
THAT WAS ALL, BUT NOW...
HAINE!
!
DON'T LISTEN TO HIM!
HE...
...KILLED MY SISTER!
AND I'M...
...GETTIN' REVENGE!

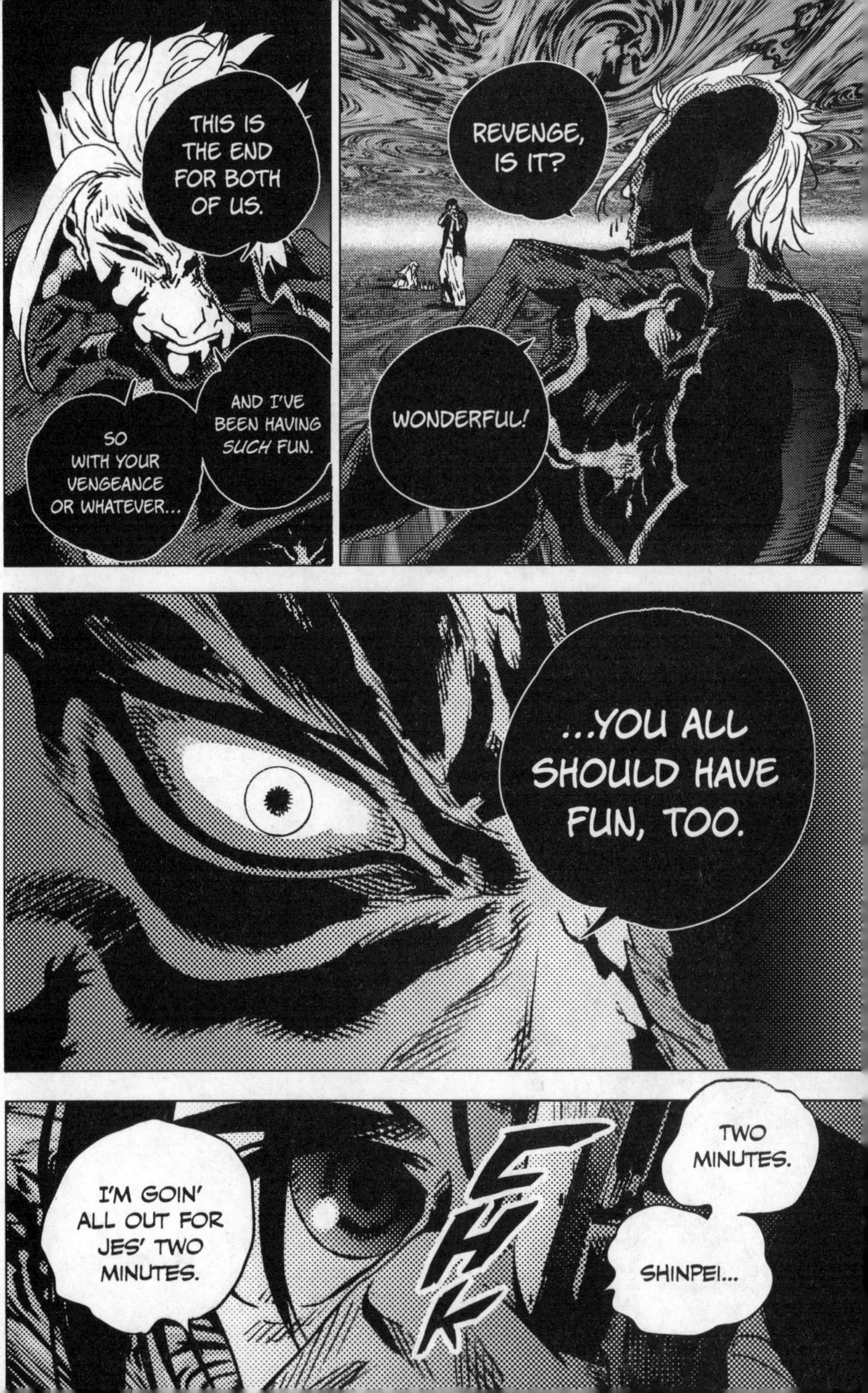
REVENGE, IS IT?
WONDERFUL!
THIS IS THE END FOR BOTH OF US.
AND I'VE BEEN HAVING *SUCH* FUN.
SO WITH YOUR VENGEANCE OR WHATEVER...
...YOU ALL SHOULD HAVE FUN, TOO.
TWO MINUTES.
SHINPEI...
SHK
I'M GOIN' ALL OUT FOR JES' TWO MINUTES.

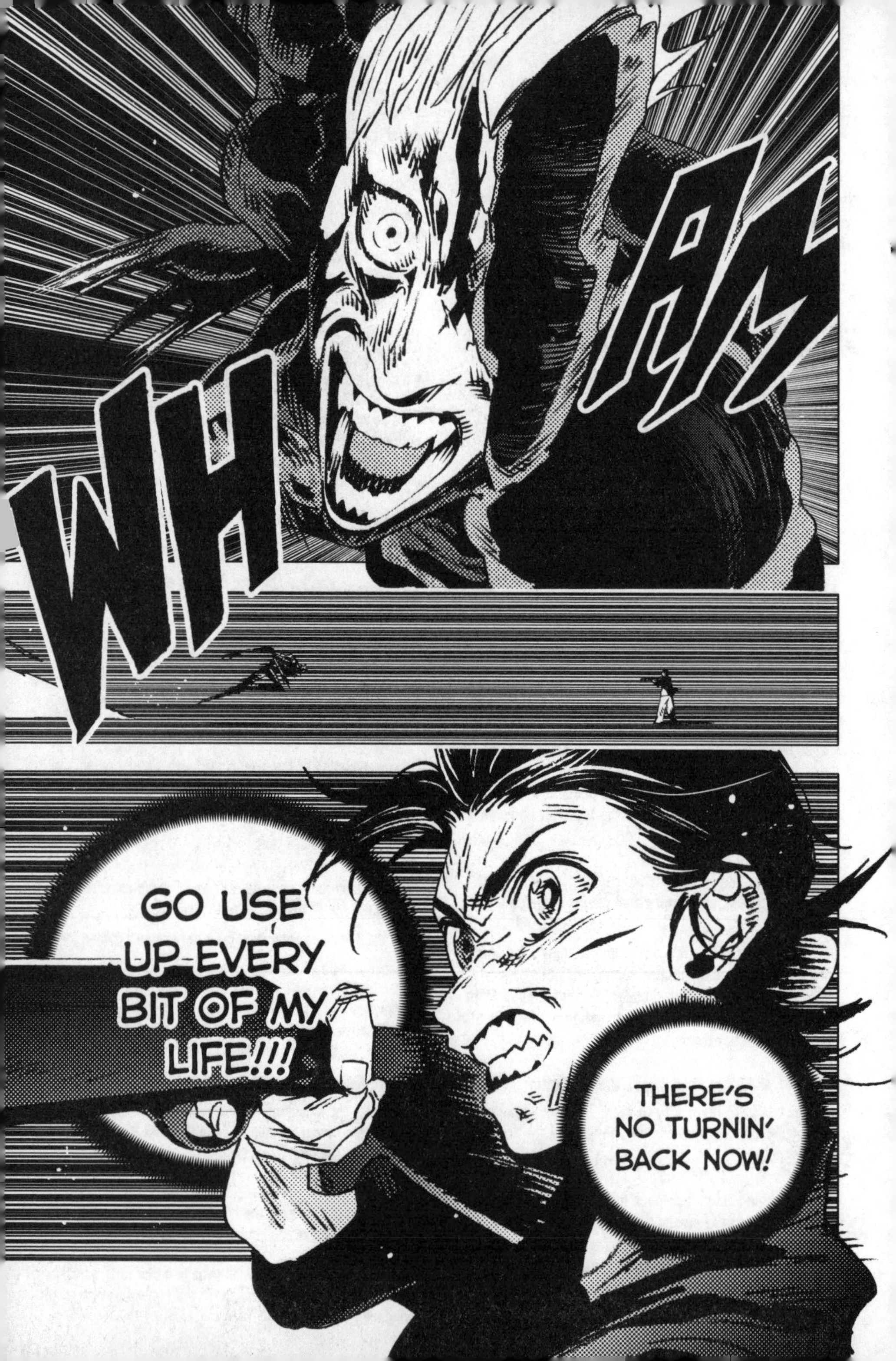
WHAM
THERE'S NO TURNIN' BACK NOW!
GO USE UP EVERY BIT OF MY LIFE!!!

MEMO#023

CARCASS ARMOR

Ryunosuke named it the "Carcass Armor", but since Shinpei was not present when it happened, this name disappeared with the loop.

Shide simply calls it armor.

Due to Ushio and Heine becoming one, the details about Shideh's armor were communicated to Ushio. Below is the information that Ushio found out, in her own words.

- The second-generation heir of Hito Shrine, Nayuta Karikiri, invented this armor in preparation for the recurring war. It was consistently upgraded by each succeeding Karikiri throughout the generations.

- The armor is made of "mud", which is the same matter that makes up the physical form of a shadow.

  Essentially, a shadow's "mud" is a projection of its true body, which is on a flat surface. (This is the opposite of people: a person's true form is their physical body and their projection is the shadow at their feet.)

  Normally, when the true body on the flat surface is destroyed, the shadow is defeated. However, the carcass armor's mud doesn't belong to any body, and it has no data!!

  A shadow deteriorates when it starts to lose its identity data. In the end, all data would be lost and it would not be able to produce the 3D mud. The projected body would turn into muddy liquid and the true flat body would disappear.

- Shideh is not your typical human being. He can transmit his consciousness into empty mud, giving it shape and commanding it to move. That is an amazing skill!

  Because Shideh (who's human) is inside controlling the body, the weakness of the flat surface does not apply. There is a shadow projected underfoot, but it belongs to Shideh, so it is essentially a human shadow. Therefore it is meaningless to attack it.

- Unlike me and other shadows, he cannot flatten himself.

  He does not have the ability to copy, thus also cannot read memories. He also cannot change into the forms of other people.

- There is some kind of subspace inside the mud. Damage to the outside of the armor cannot pass through to Shideh on the inside (even if the armor loses one of its arms, it will not hurt Shideh inside) and Shideh can quickly repair the armor just by imagining it in its original form.

(The inside of Guildenstern is also a subspace. However, because Guil still retains some human identity data, it still has a flat surface weakness. Since Tokiko is mentally linked to Guil, she will feel any damage done to Guil while controlling him.)

- Even if the armor is blown to pieces, it will simply enter a bubbling state and reform again and come back to life. It is hard to believe, but even when the armor is in the bubbling state, Shideh still cannot be hurt inside the bubbles! I do not understand how this works!!

- The armor has 4 arms, which doubles its fighting abilities. This is the maximum number of arms Shideh can control with his consciousness.

- The reason there are 4 eyes is to share the armor's vision with both Masahito and Iwao. When Masahito was inside the armor, Iwao (who was at a different location) could apparently also see through the armor's eyes. And vice versa!

- Even though both Masahito (who was inside) and Iwao were killed, the armor is still moving! This is really crazy!

- The armor is elastic. The arms can stretch to several times their normal length.

- The arms can change form into the shape of a blade.

- The armor can absorb shadows nearby and increase its total amount of mud, growing to giant sizes! Like that time in the gymnasium when it became like a spider!

- Energy projected at the armor can be totally deflected back to the opponent like an echo. This is a special ability called "yamabiko".

- Three ways to defeat Shideh:

1. Kill his human form when he isn't wearing the armor. That time at the shrine was a failure!

2. Hack the armor, erasing it, and kill the exposed human form.

3. If Hiruko can be killed, then all the shadows (including Shideh's armor) will disappear, so after killing Hiruko, kill the exposed human form. The only way to kill Hiruko for good is to hack and erase her. But since Shideh has assimilated with Hiruko and is protecting her, method 3 is not feasible.

- At this point, method 2 seems to be the only viable method. But peeling the armor off reveals that there is nothing inside! Shideh's solid form seemed to be in the Real World somewhere, remotely controlling the armor in the Eternal Realm. What the hell?!

- I have given up on killing the human body. The new goal is to use a hacking bullet and completely erase the armor!!

- When his armor is gone, Shideh (who is in the Real World) won't be able to cause a problem in the Eternal Realm--and in the meantime, I will erase Hiruko and end all this!!

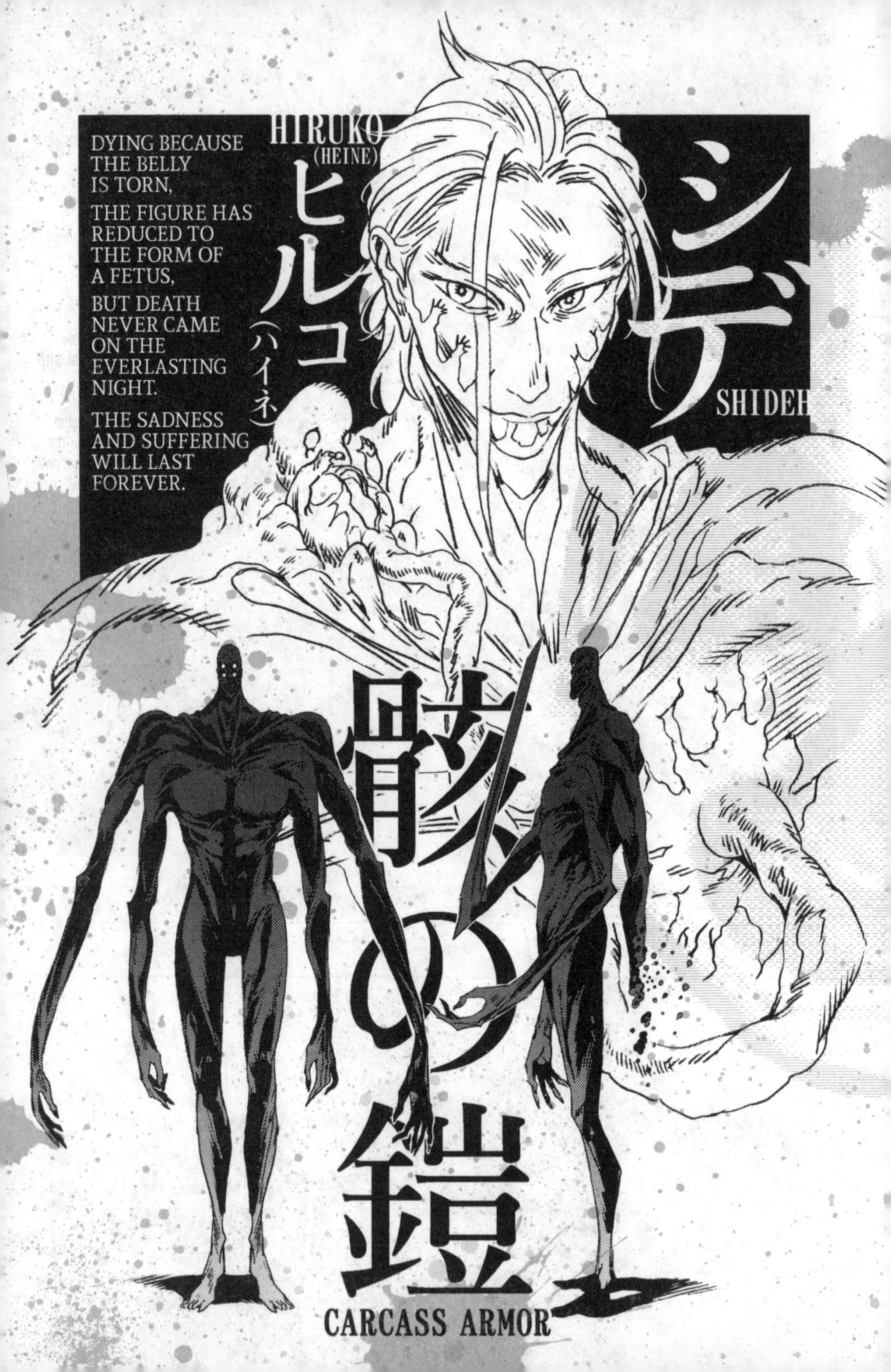
HIRUKO
(HEINE)
ヒルコ(ハイネ)
DYING BECAUSE THE BELLY IS TORN,
THE FIGURE HAS REDUCED TO THE FORM OF A FETUS,
BUT DEATH NEVER CAME ON THE EVERLASTING NIGHT.
THE SADNESS AND SUFFERING WILL LAST FOREVER.
シデ
SHIDEH
骸の鎧
CARCASS ARMOR

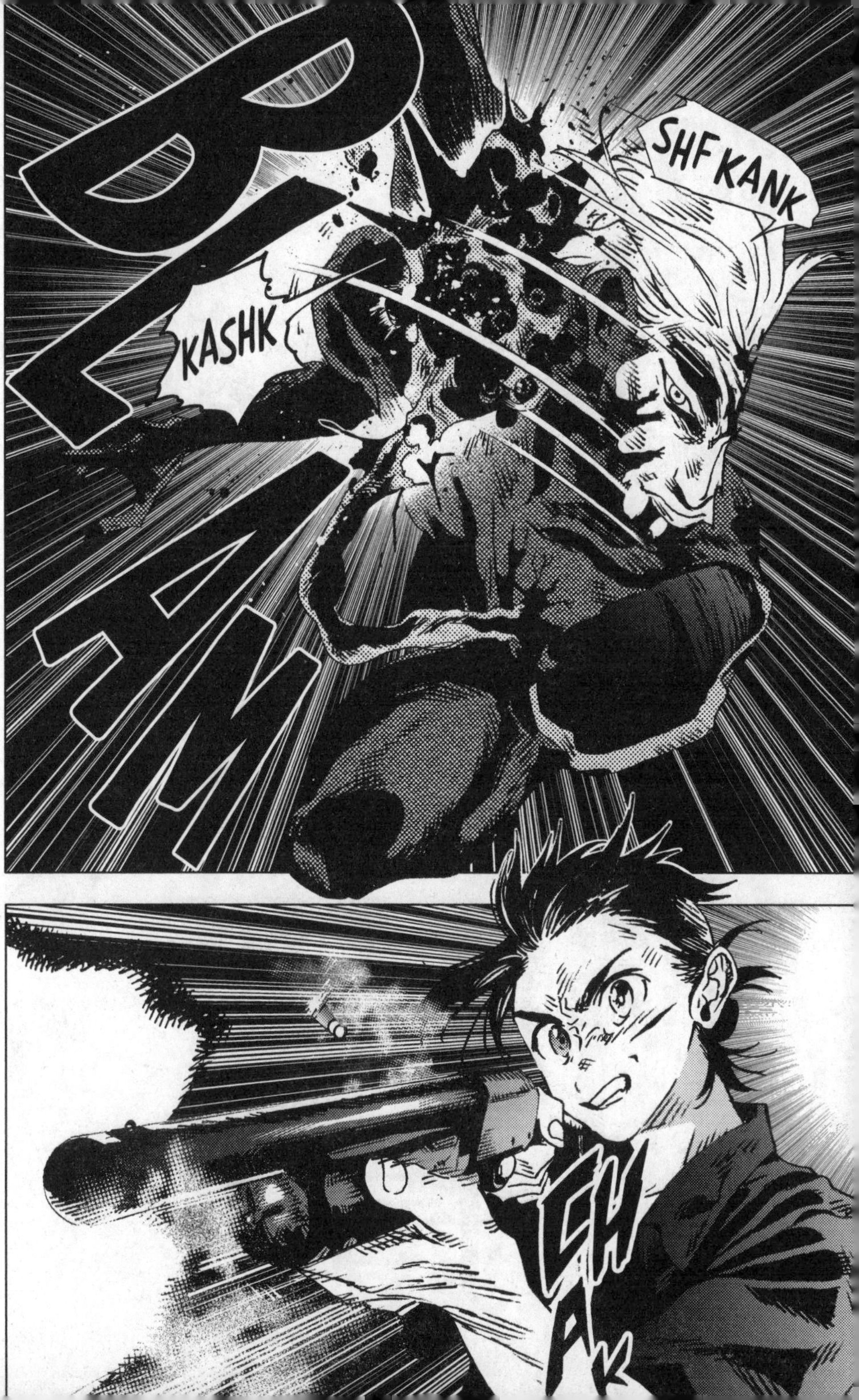
SHF KANK
KASHK

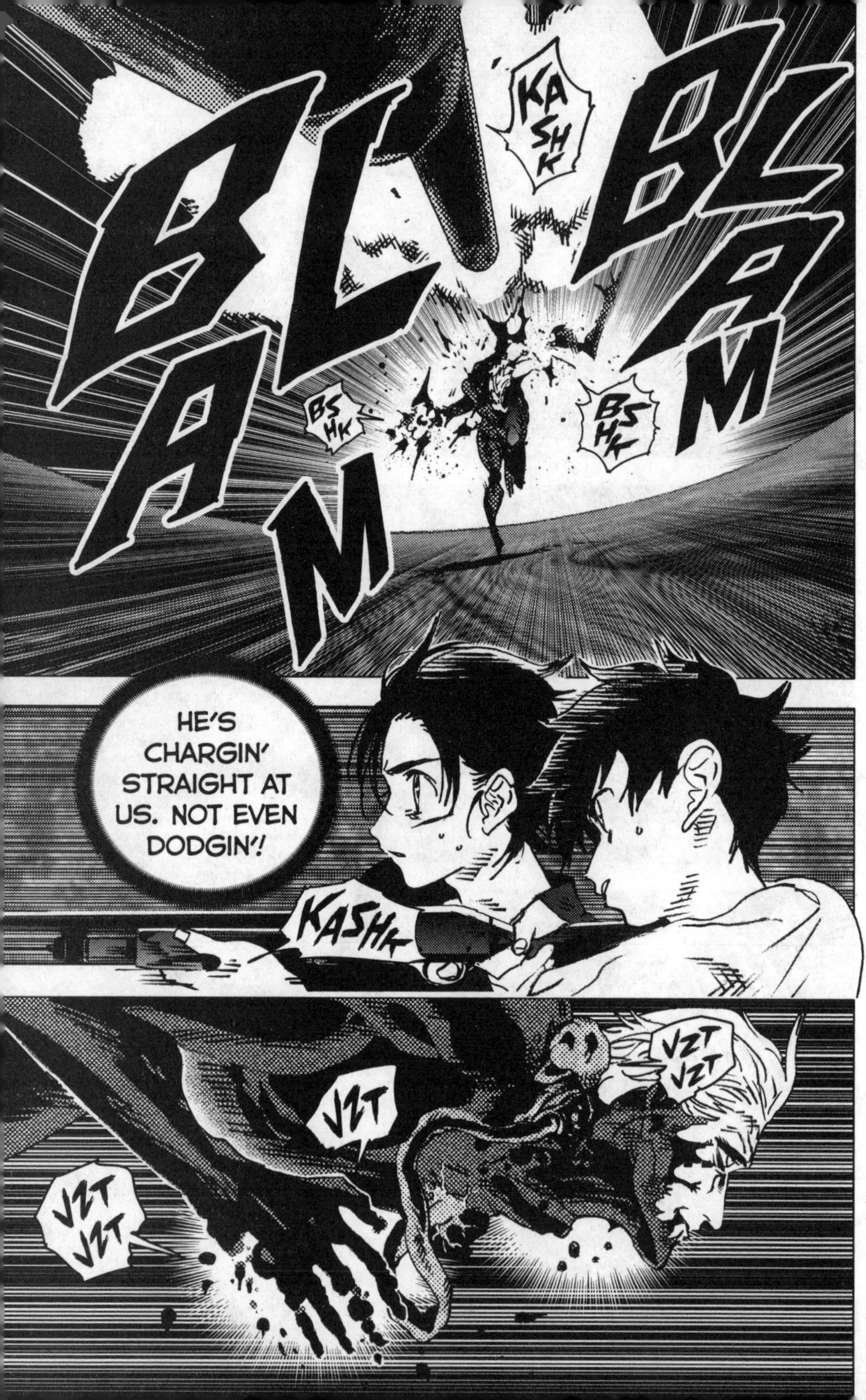
BLAM
KASHK
BLAM
BSHK
BSHK
HE'S CHARGIN' STRAIGHT AT US. NOT EVEN DODGIN'!
KASHK
VZT VZT
VZT
VZT VZT

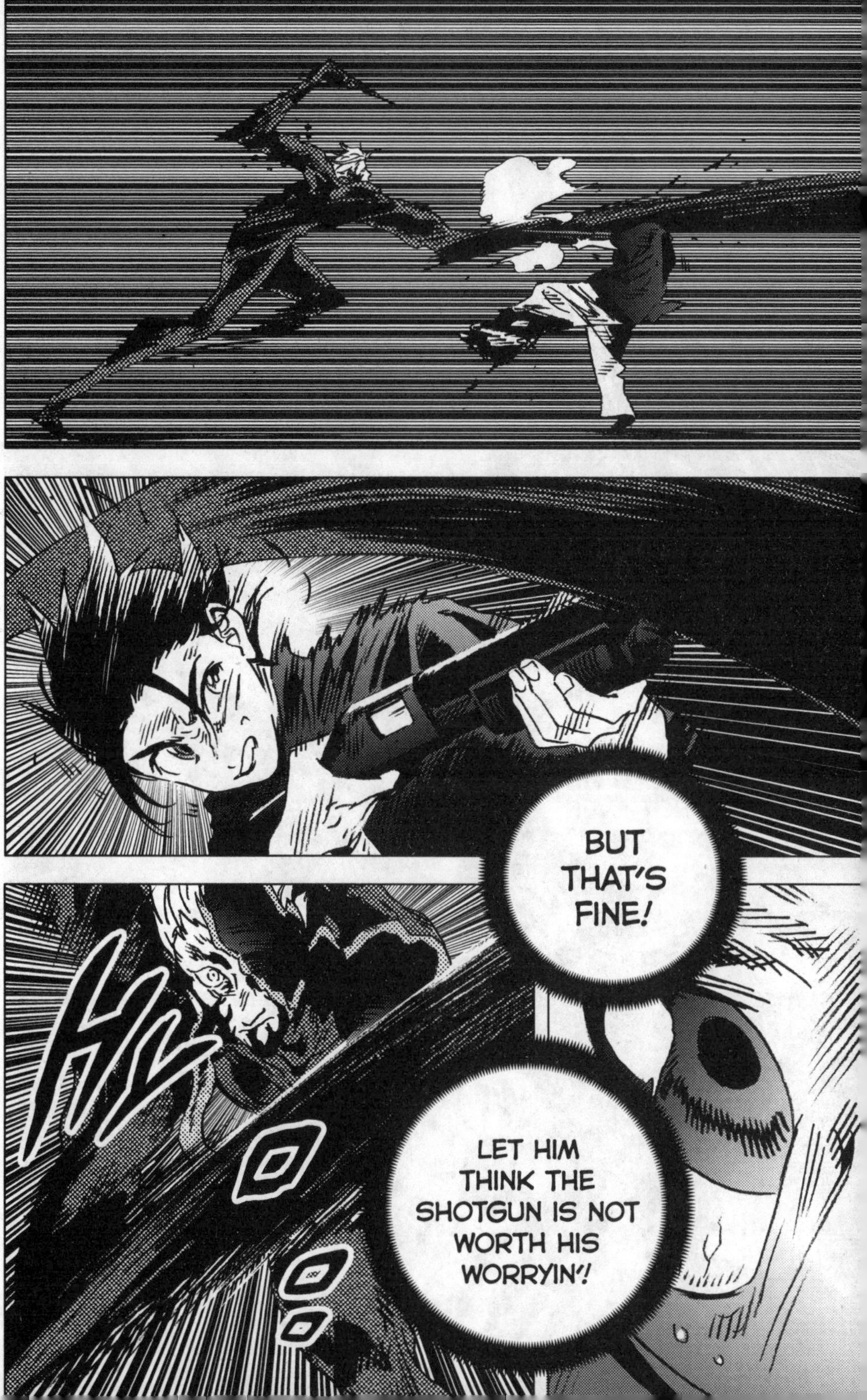
BUT THAT'S FINE!
LET HIM THINK THE SHOTGUN IS NOT WORTH HIS WORRYIN'!

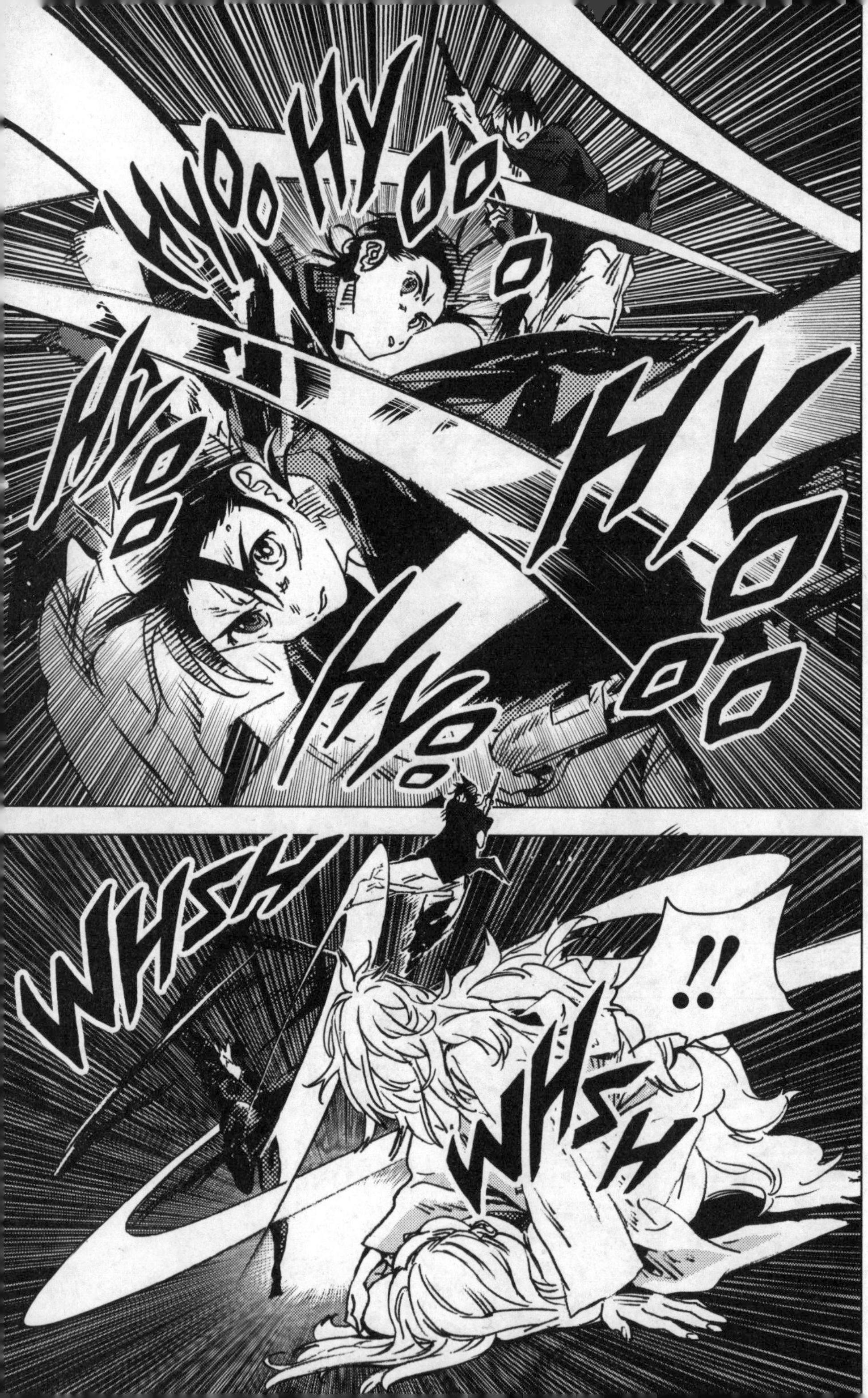
HYOO HYOOO
HYOOO
HYOOO
HYOOO
!!
WHSH
WHSH

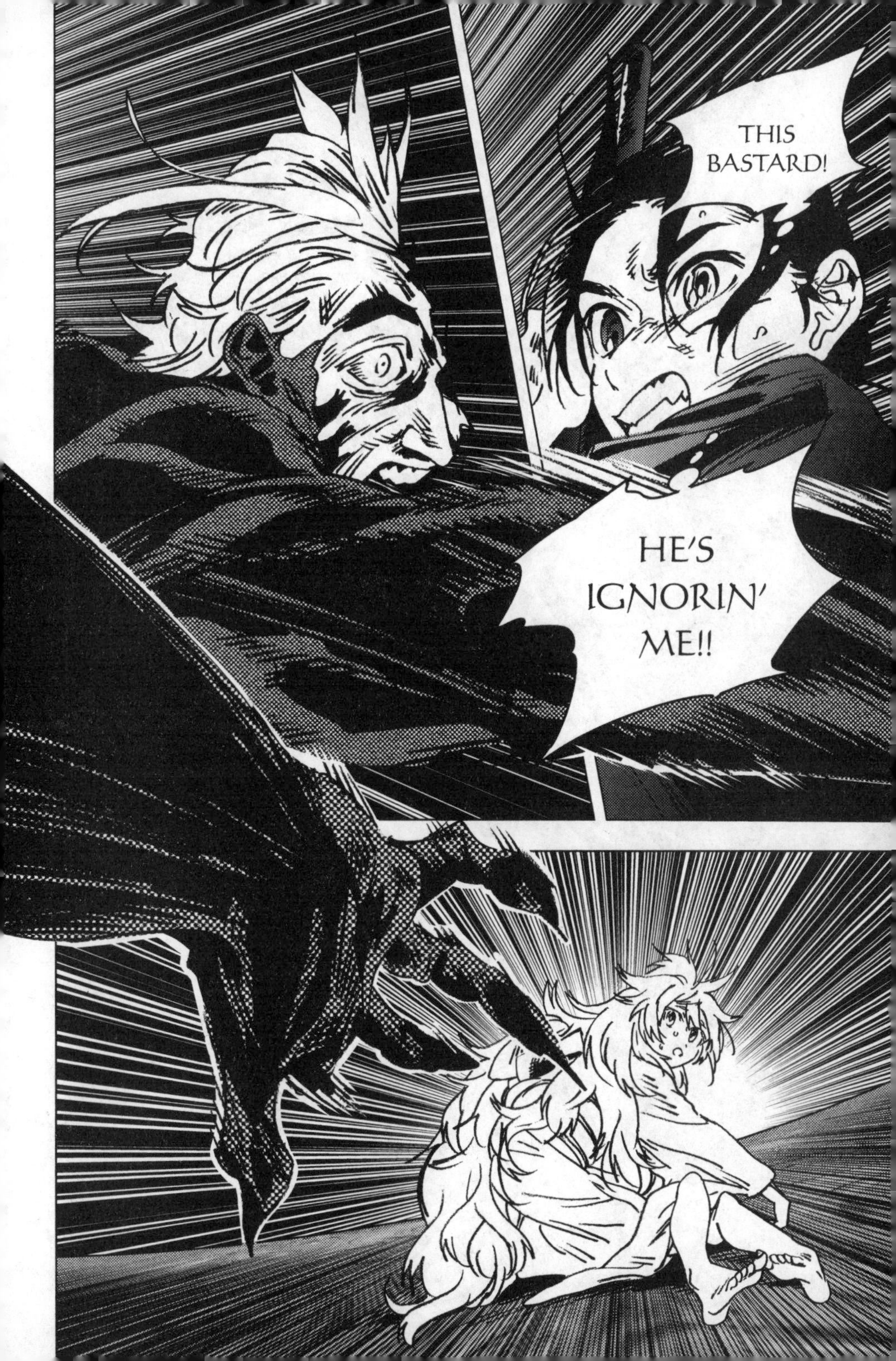
THIS BASTARD!
HE'S IGNORIN' ME!!

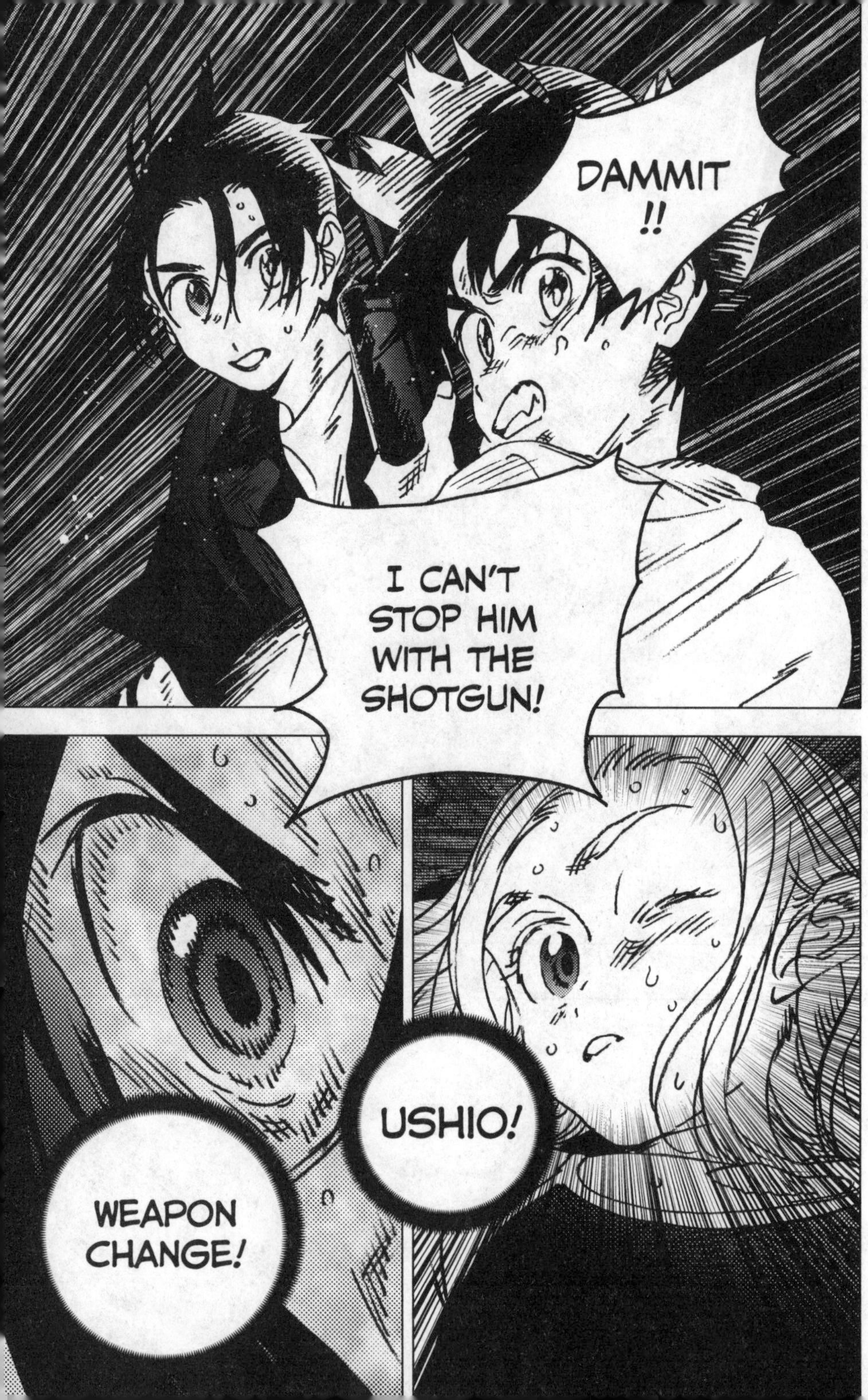
DAMMIT !!
I CAN'T STOP HIM WITH THE SHOTGUN!
USHIO!
WEAPON CHANGE!

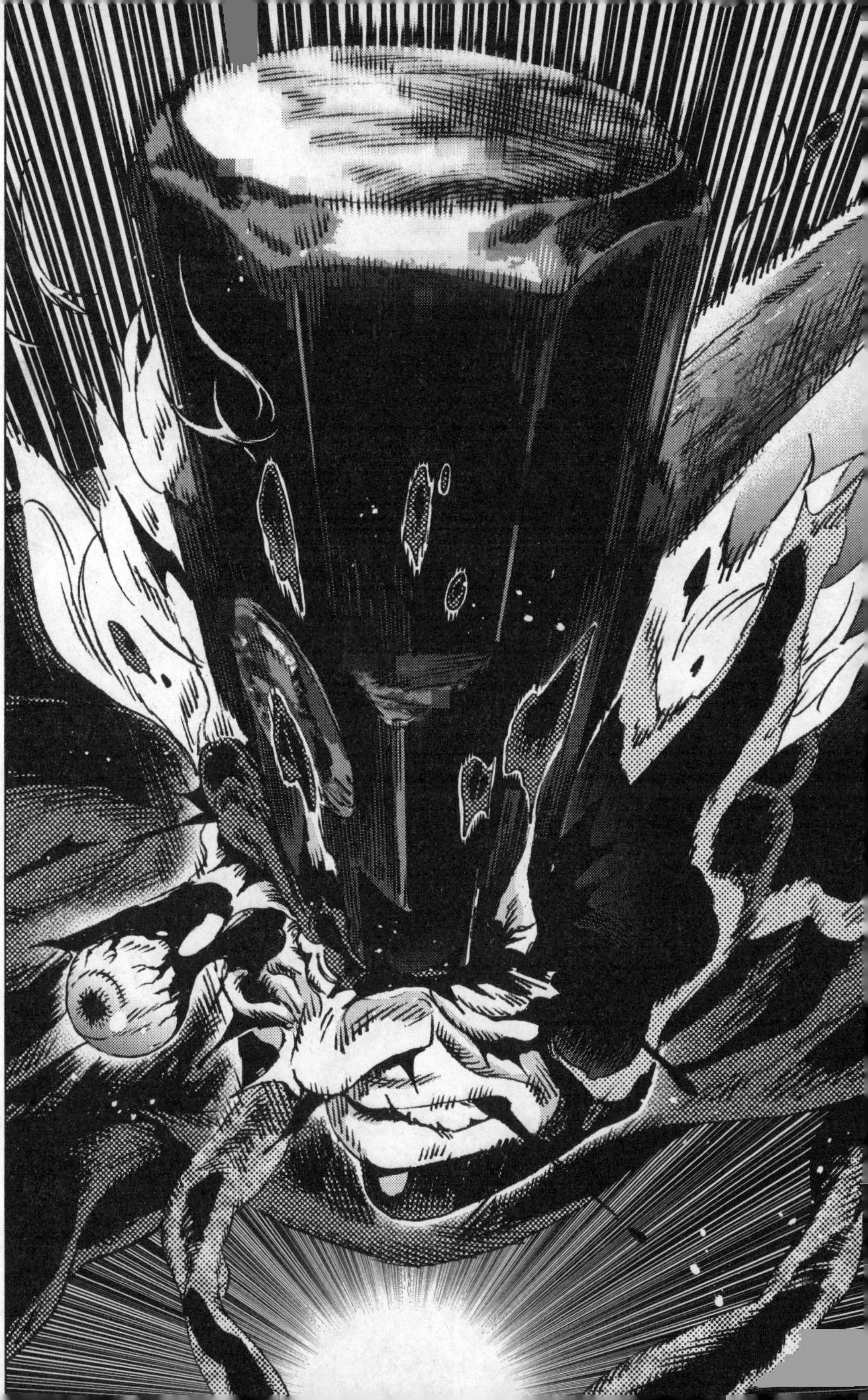

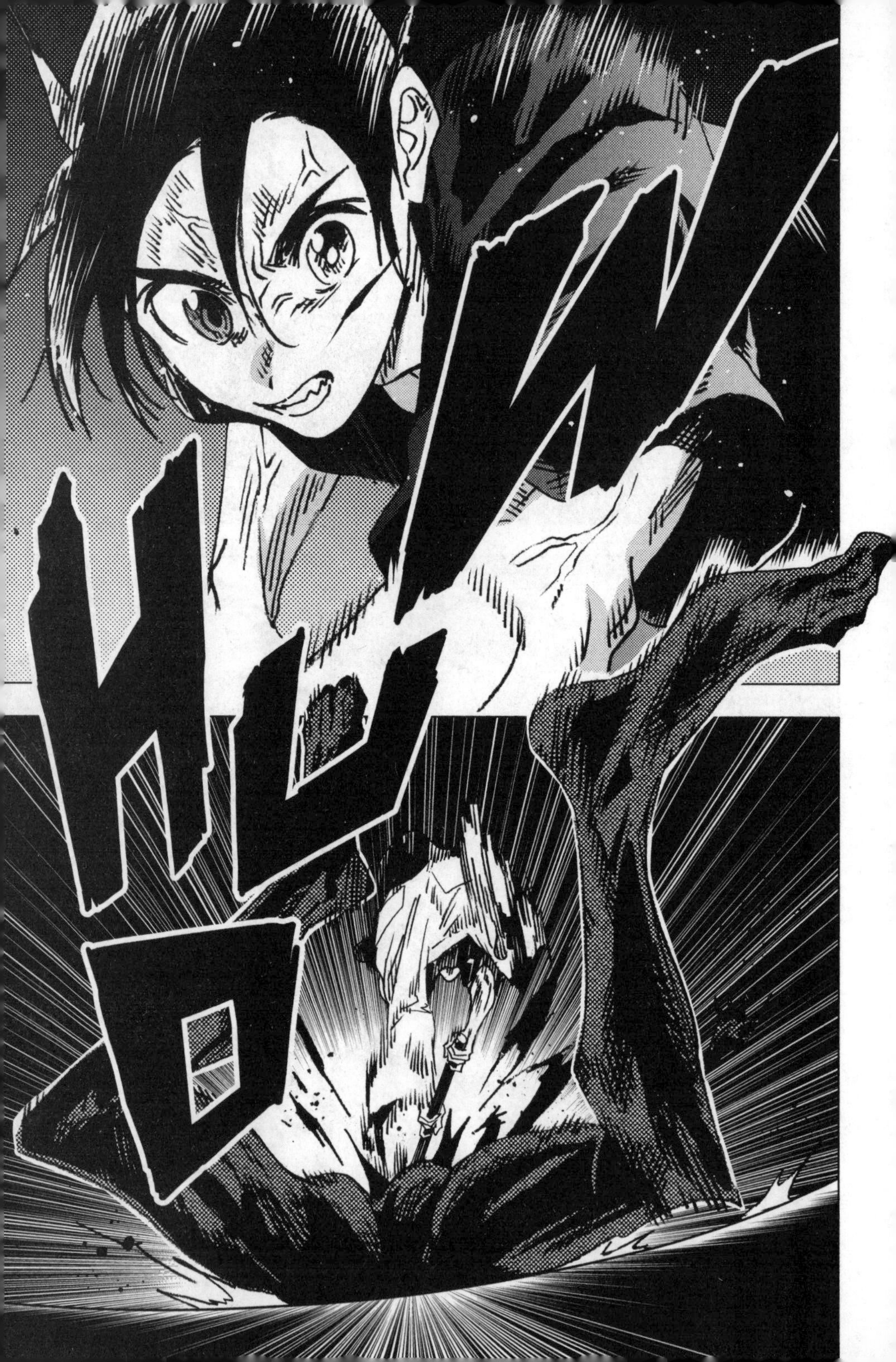

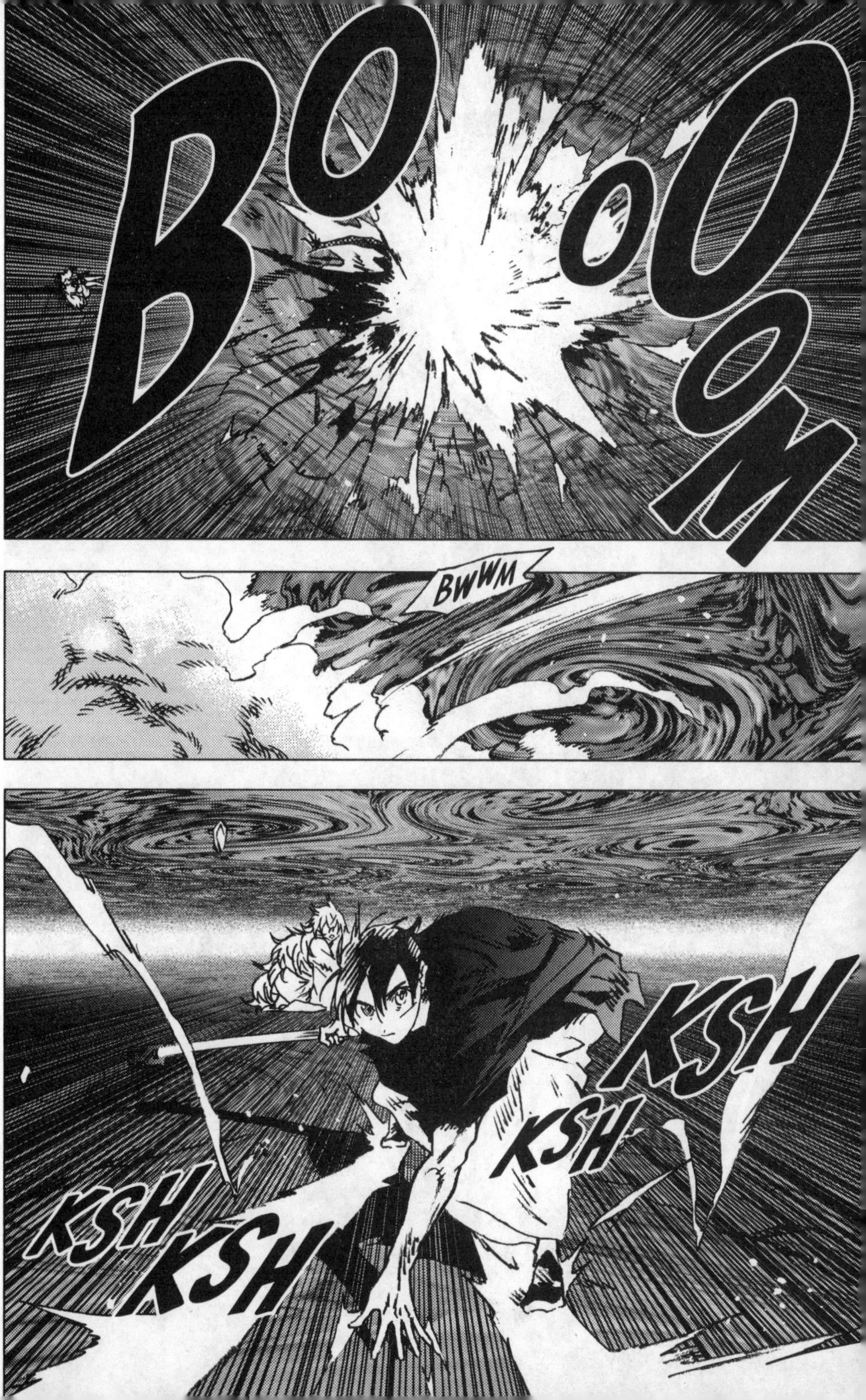
BOOOOM
BWWM
KSH
KSH
KSH
KSH

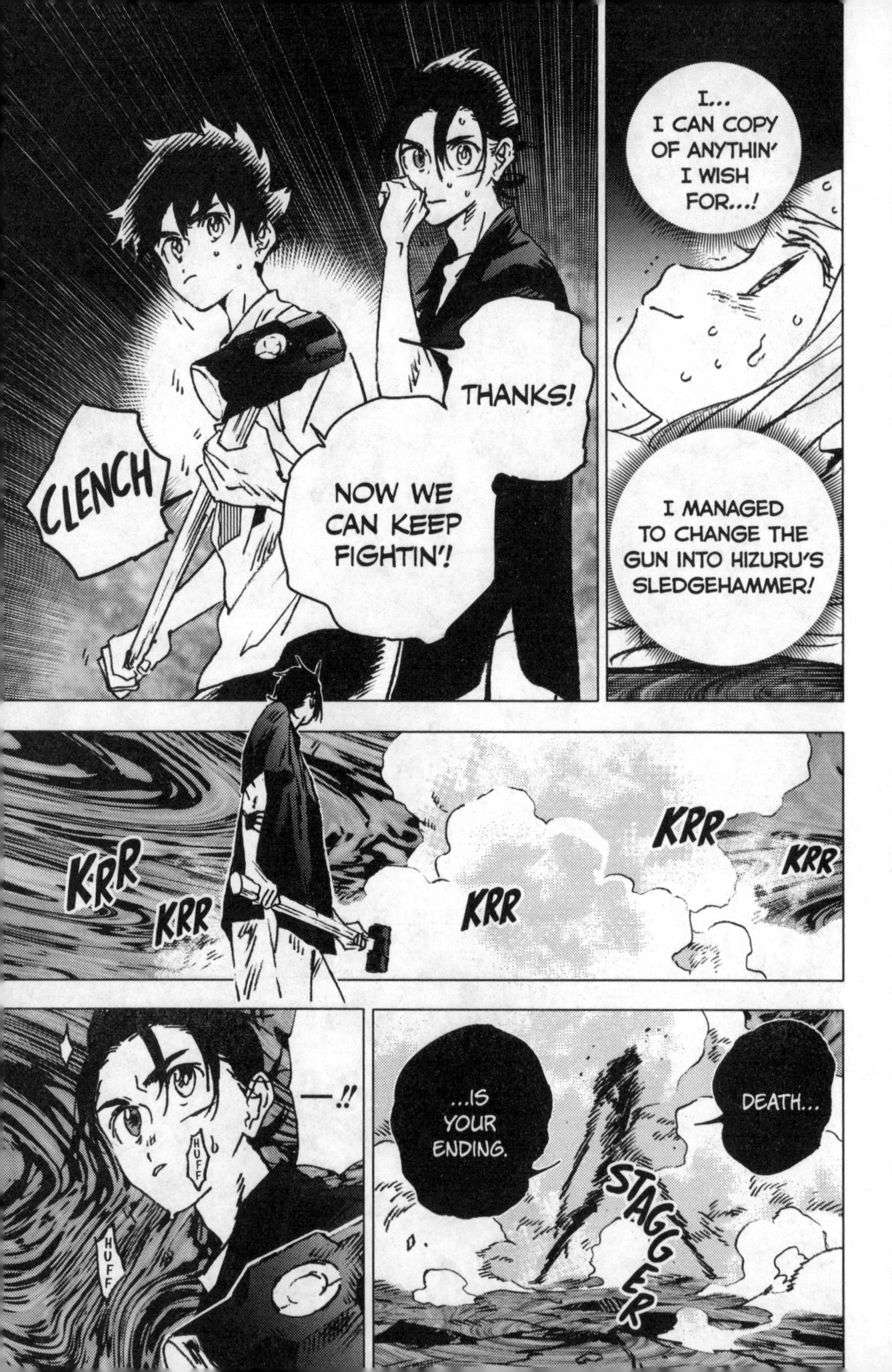
I...
I CAN COPY OF ANYTHIN' I WISH FOR...!
I MANAGED TO CHANGE THE GUN INTO HIZURU'S SLEDGEHAMMER!
THANKS!
NOW WE CAN KEEP FIGHTIN'!
CLENCH
KRR
KRR
KRR
KRR
KRR
DEATH...
...IS YOUR ENDING.
STAGGER
—!!
HUFF
HUFF

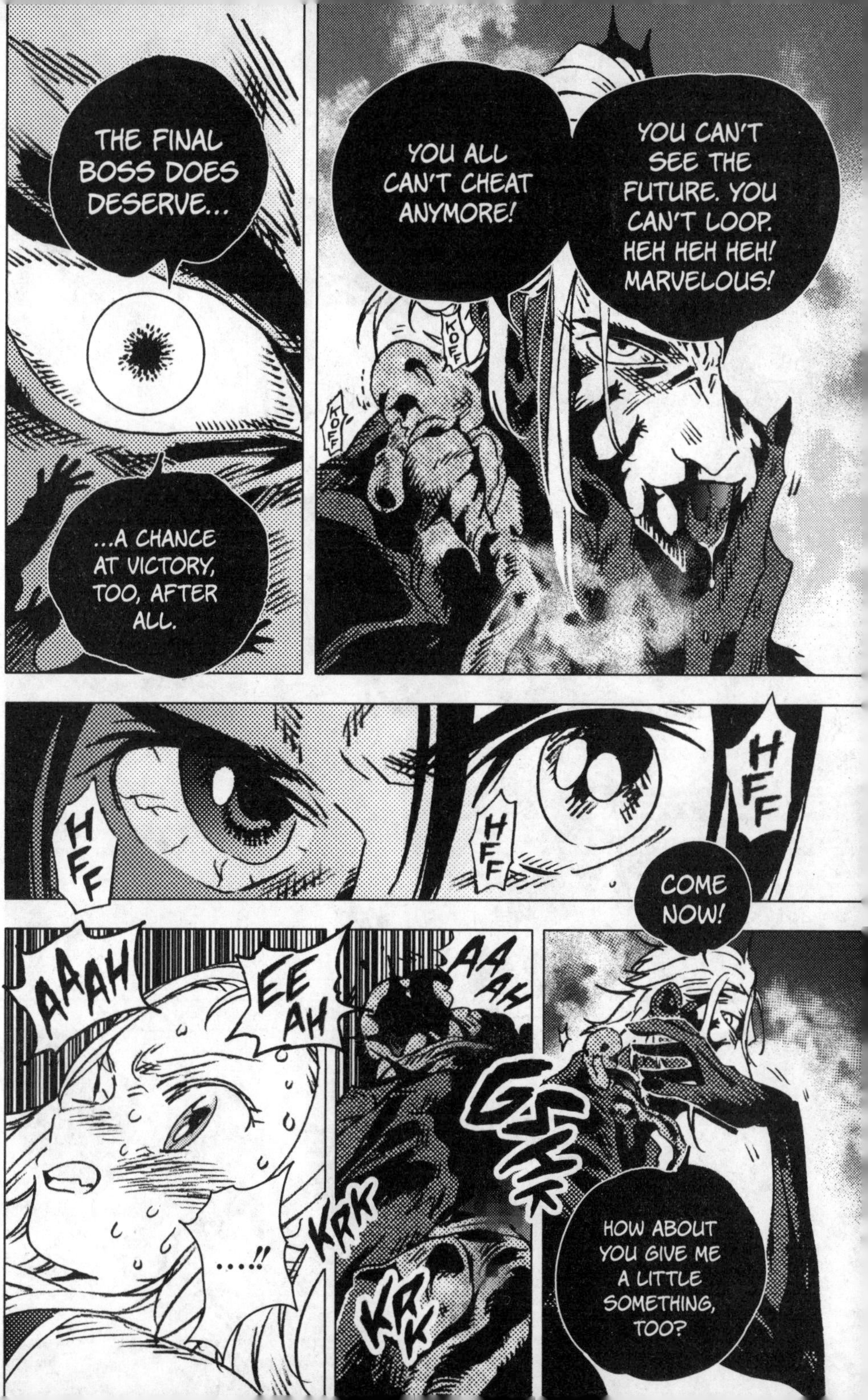
YOU CAN'T SEE THE FUTURE. YOU CAN'T LOOP. HEH HEH HEH! MARVELOUS!
YOU ALL CAN'T CHEAT ANYMORE!
KOFF
KOFF
THE FINAL BOSS DOES DESERVE...
...A CHANCE AT VICTORY, TOO, AFTER ALL.
HFF
HFF
HFF
COME NOW!
GSHK
HOW ABOUT YOU GIVE ME A LITTLE SOMETHING, TOO?
AAAAH
KRK
KRK
EEAH
AAAH
....!!

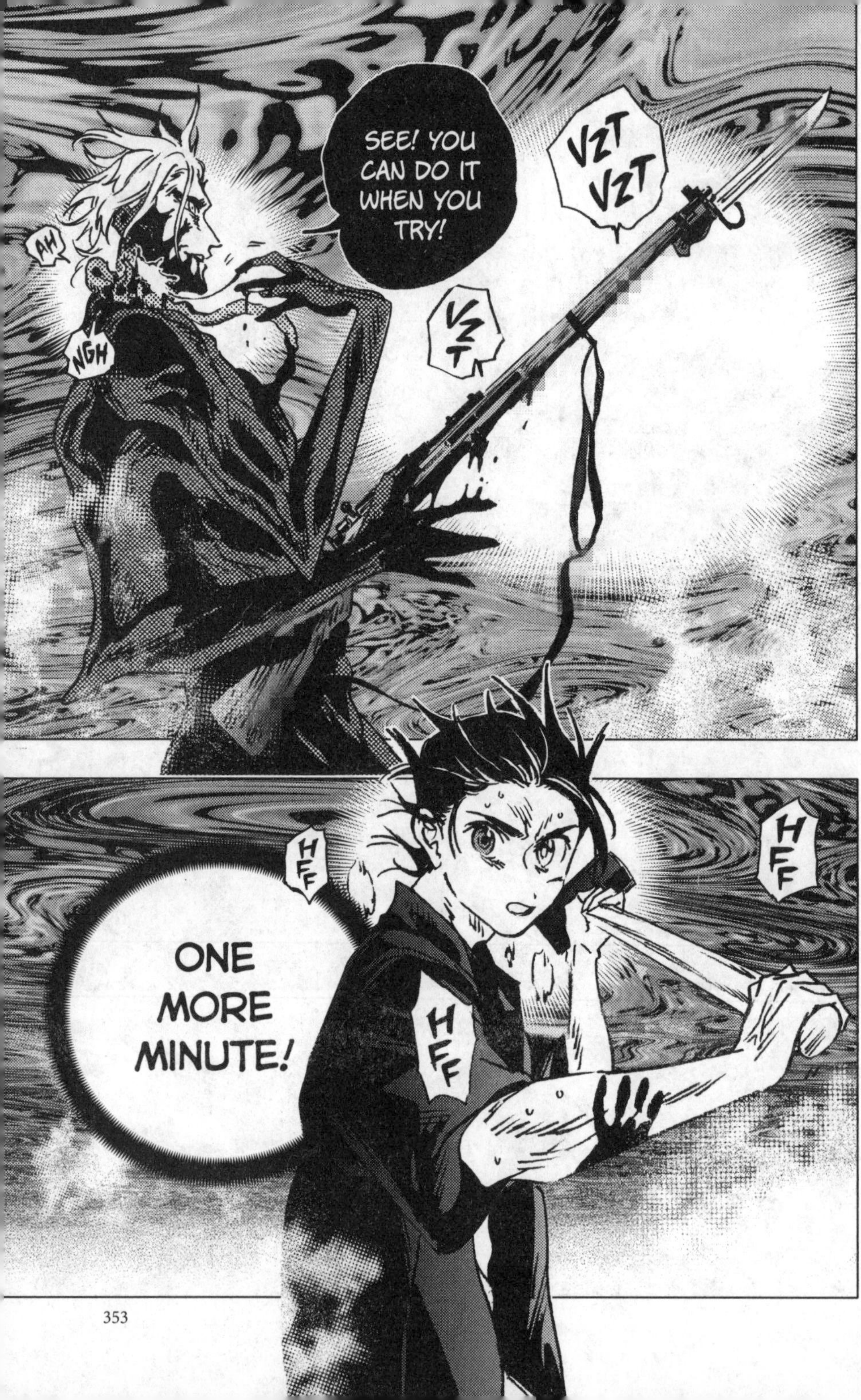
VZT VZT
SEE! YOU CAN DO IT WHEN YOU TRY!
VZT
AH
NGH
HFF
HFF
ONE MORE MINUTE!
HFF

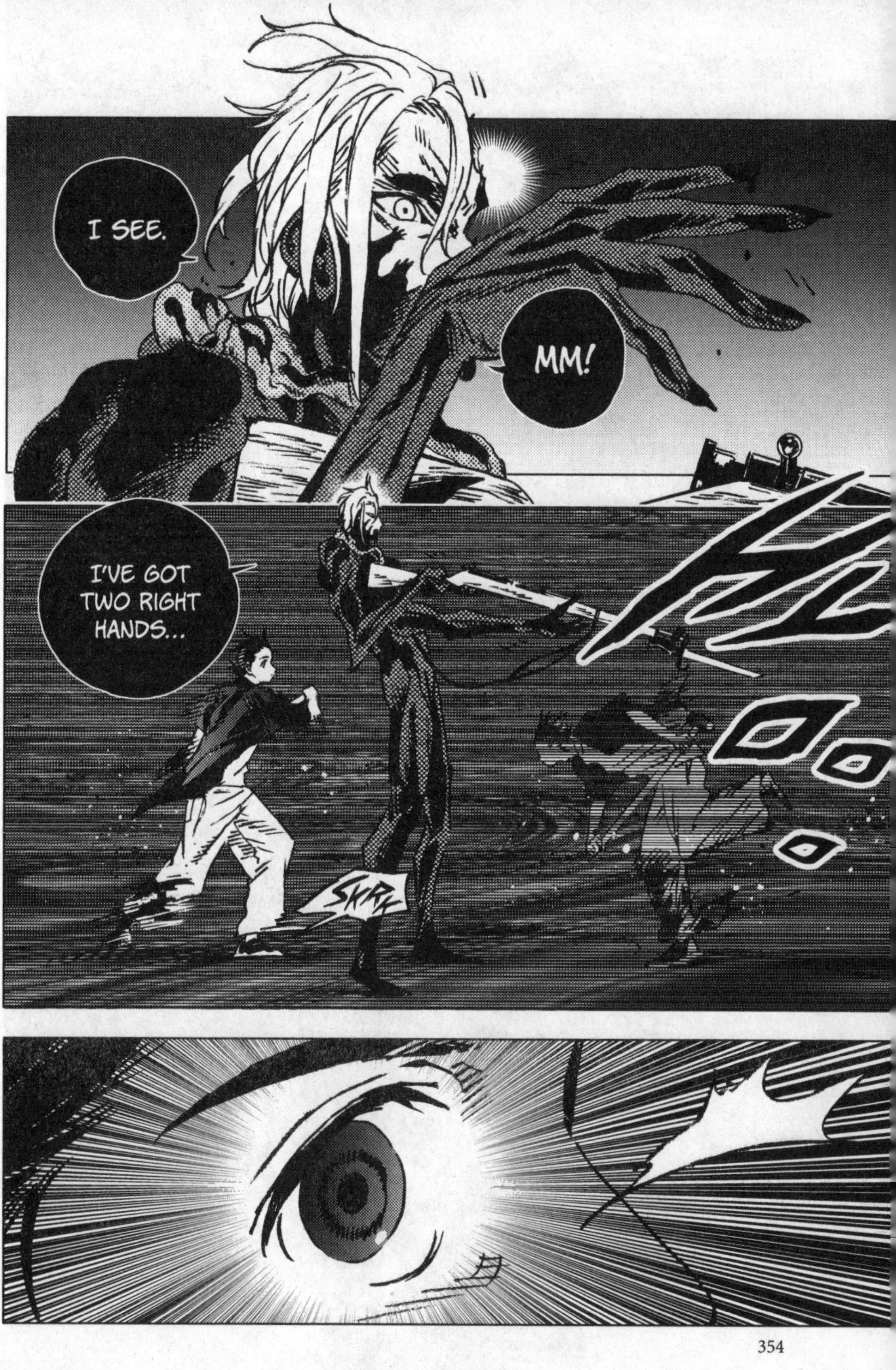
MM!
I SEE.
I'VE GOT TWO RIGHT HANDS...
SKRK

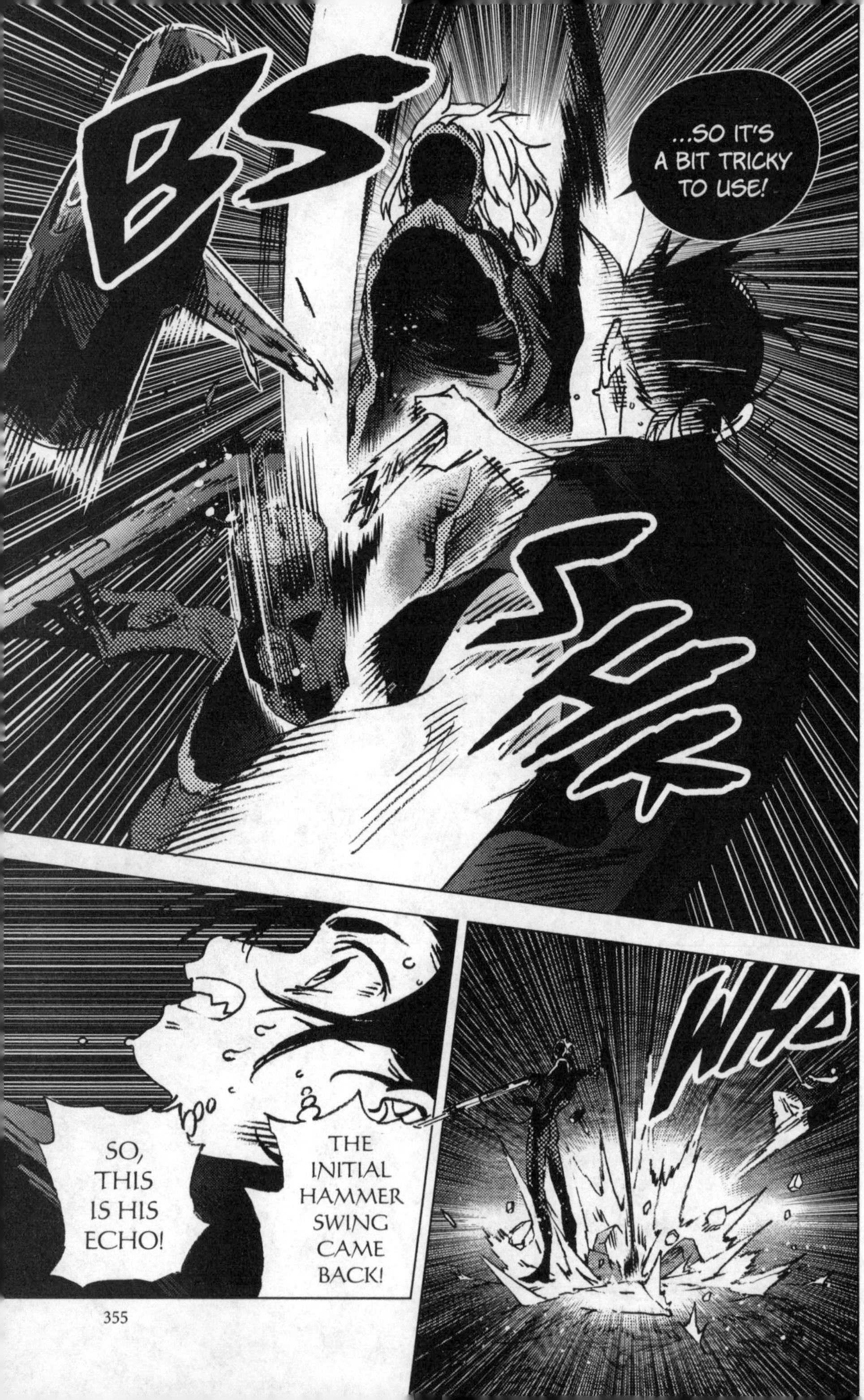
...SO IT'S A BIT TRICKY TO USE!
BS
SHK
WHD
THE INITIAL HAMMER SWING CAME BACK!
SO, THIS IS HIS ECHO!

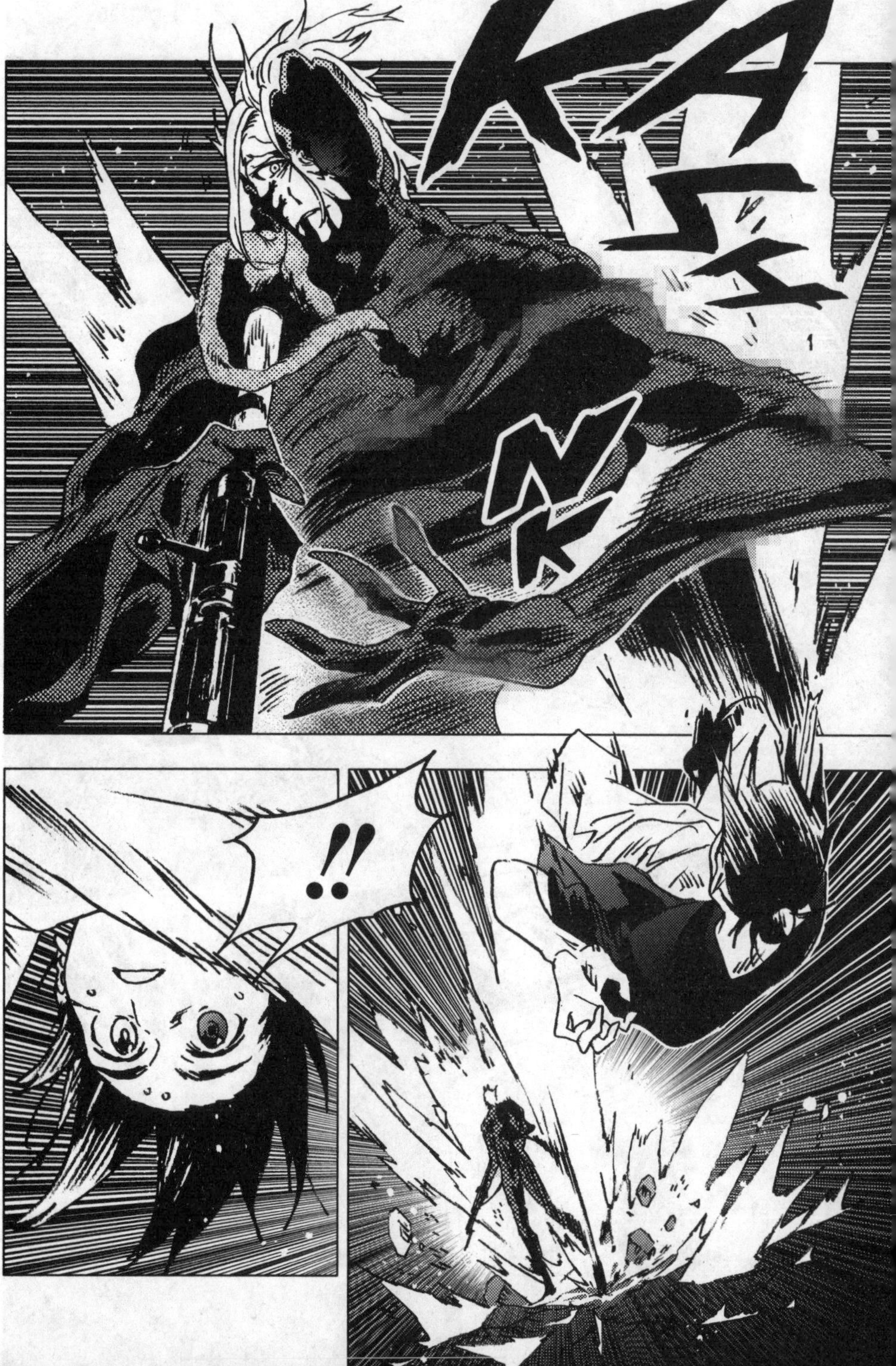
KASHNK
!!

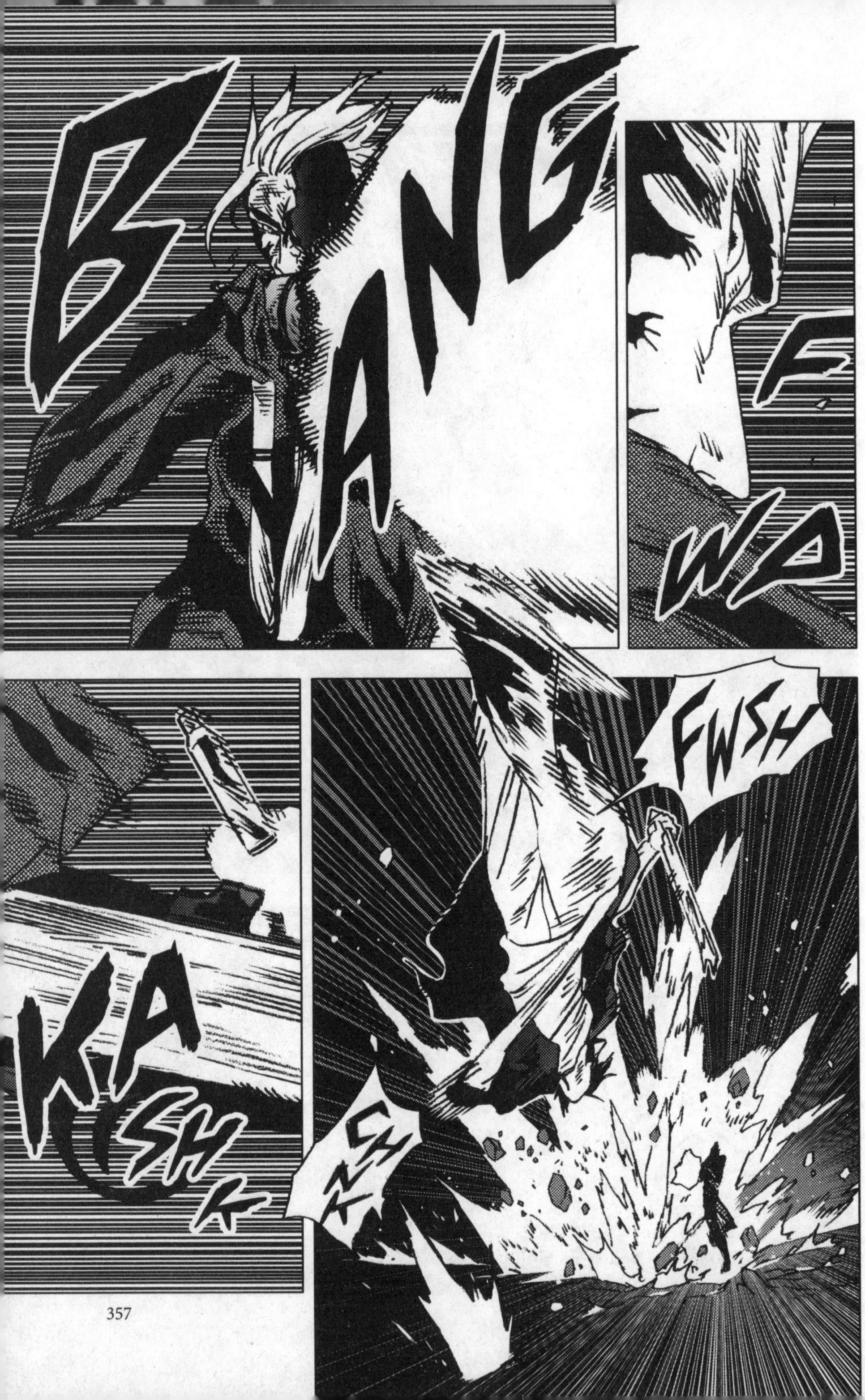
FWA
BANG
FWSH
CHNK
KASHK

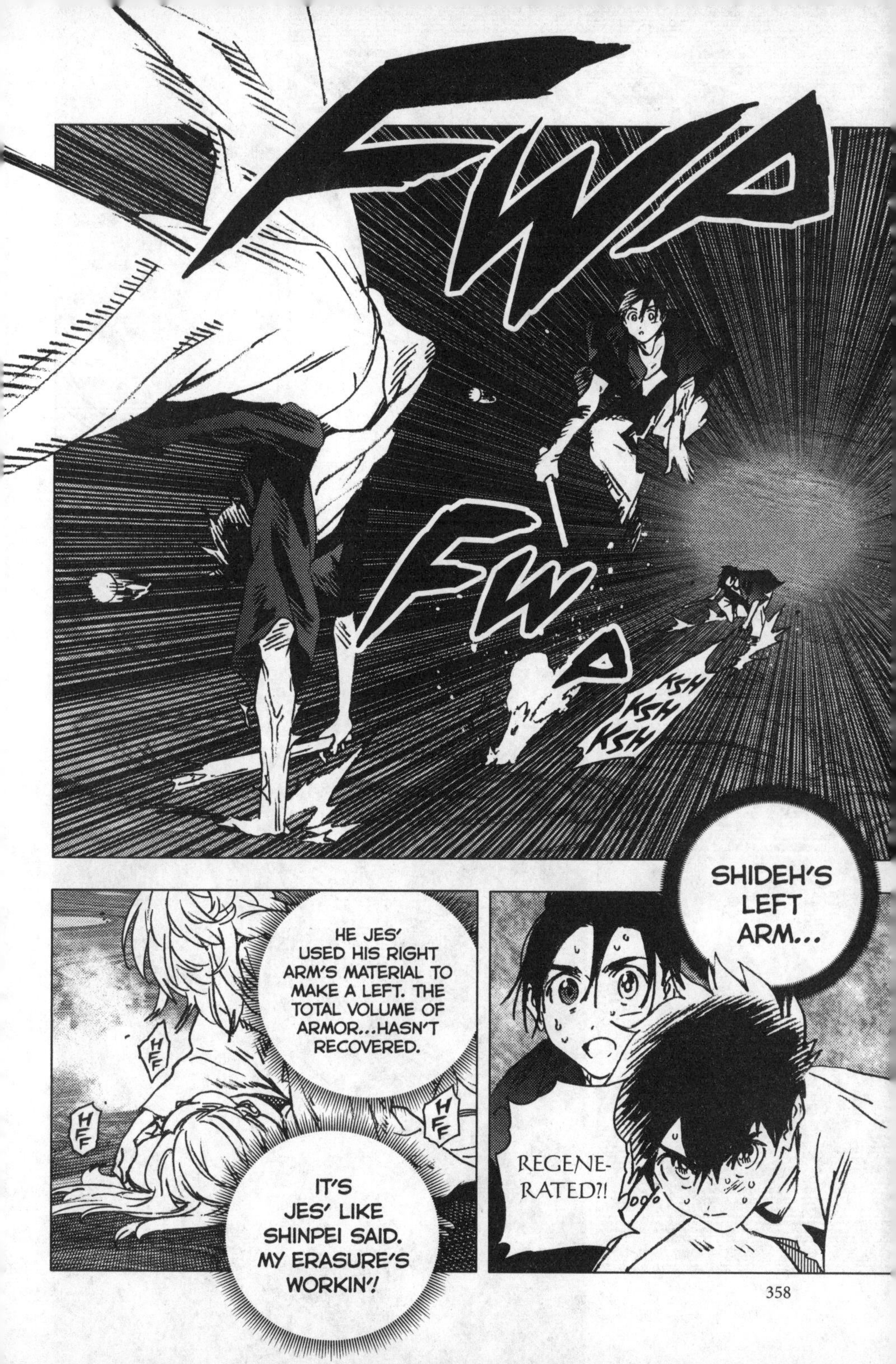
FWIP
FWIP
KSH KSH KSH
SHIDEH'S LEFT ARM...
REGENERATED?!
HE JES' USED HIS RIGHT ARM'S MATERIAL TO MAKE A LEFT. THE TOTAL VOLUME OF ARMOR...HASN'T RECOVERED.
HFF
HFF
HFF
IT'S JES' LIKE SHINPEI SAID. MY ERASURE'S WORKIN'!

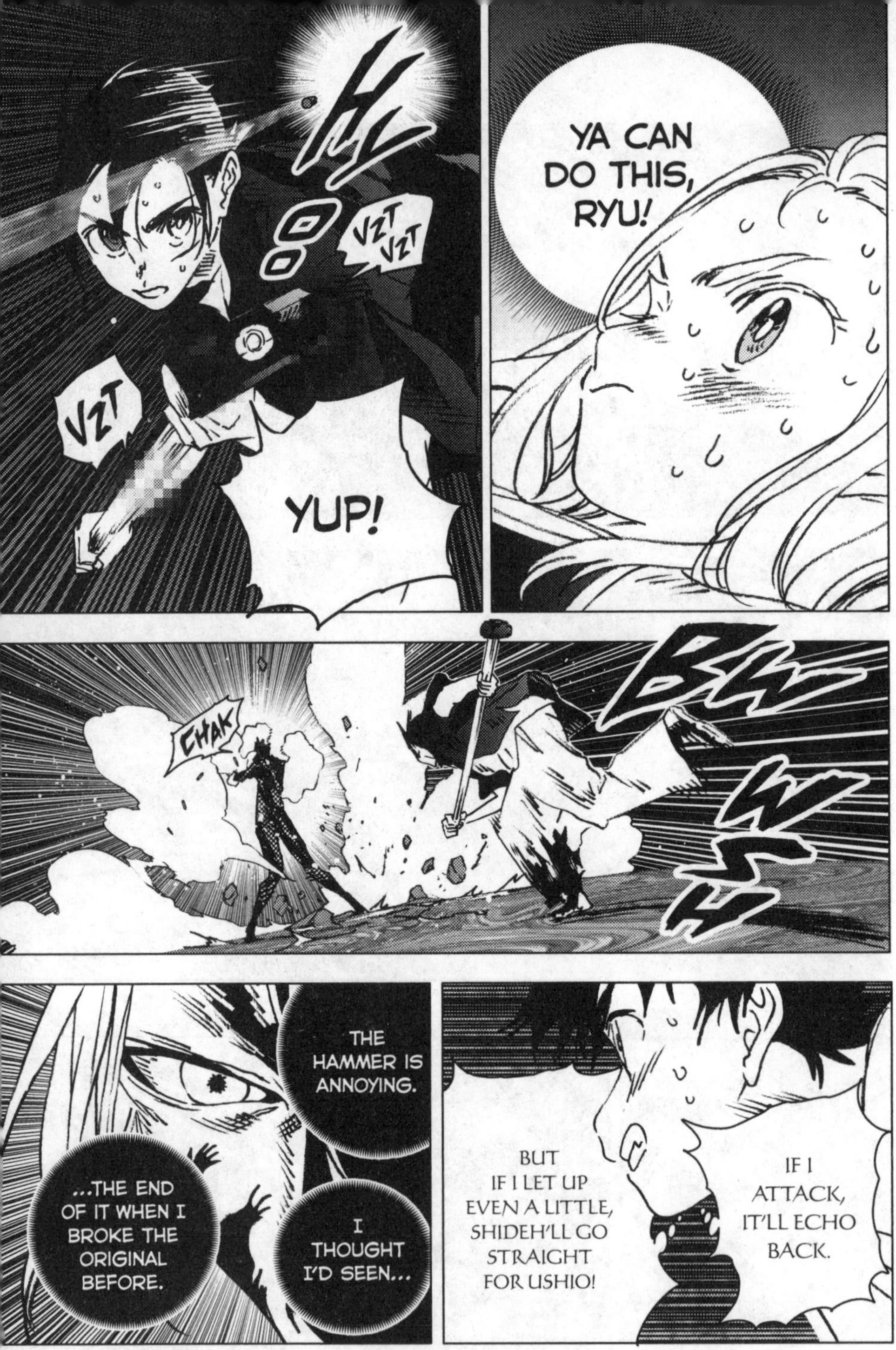
YA CAN DO THIS, RYU!
VZT VZT
VZT
YUP!
CHAK
IF I ATTACK, IT'LL ECHO BACK.
BUT IF I LET UP EVEN A LITTLE, SHIDEH'LL GO STRAIGHT FOR USHIO!
THE HAMMER IS ANNOYING.
I THOUGHT I'D SEEN...
...THE END OF IT WHEN I BROKE THE ORIGINAL BEFORE.

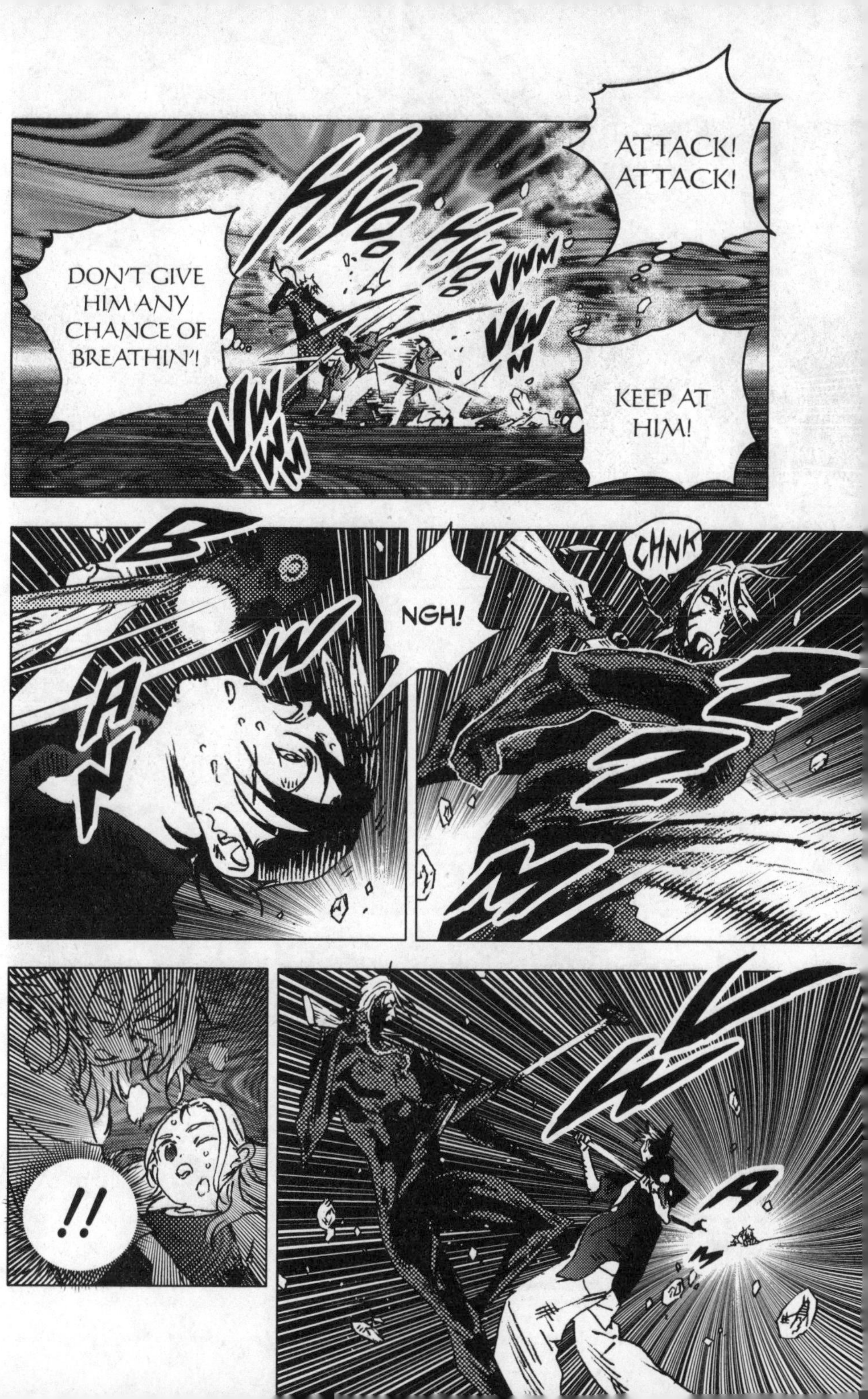
ATTACK! ATTACK!
KEEP AT HIM!
DON'T GIVE HIM ANY CHANCE OF BREATHIN'!
VWM
VWM
CHNK
NGH!
!!

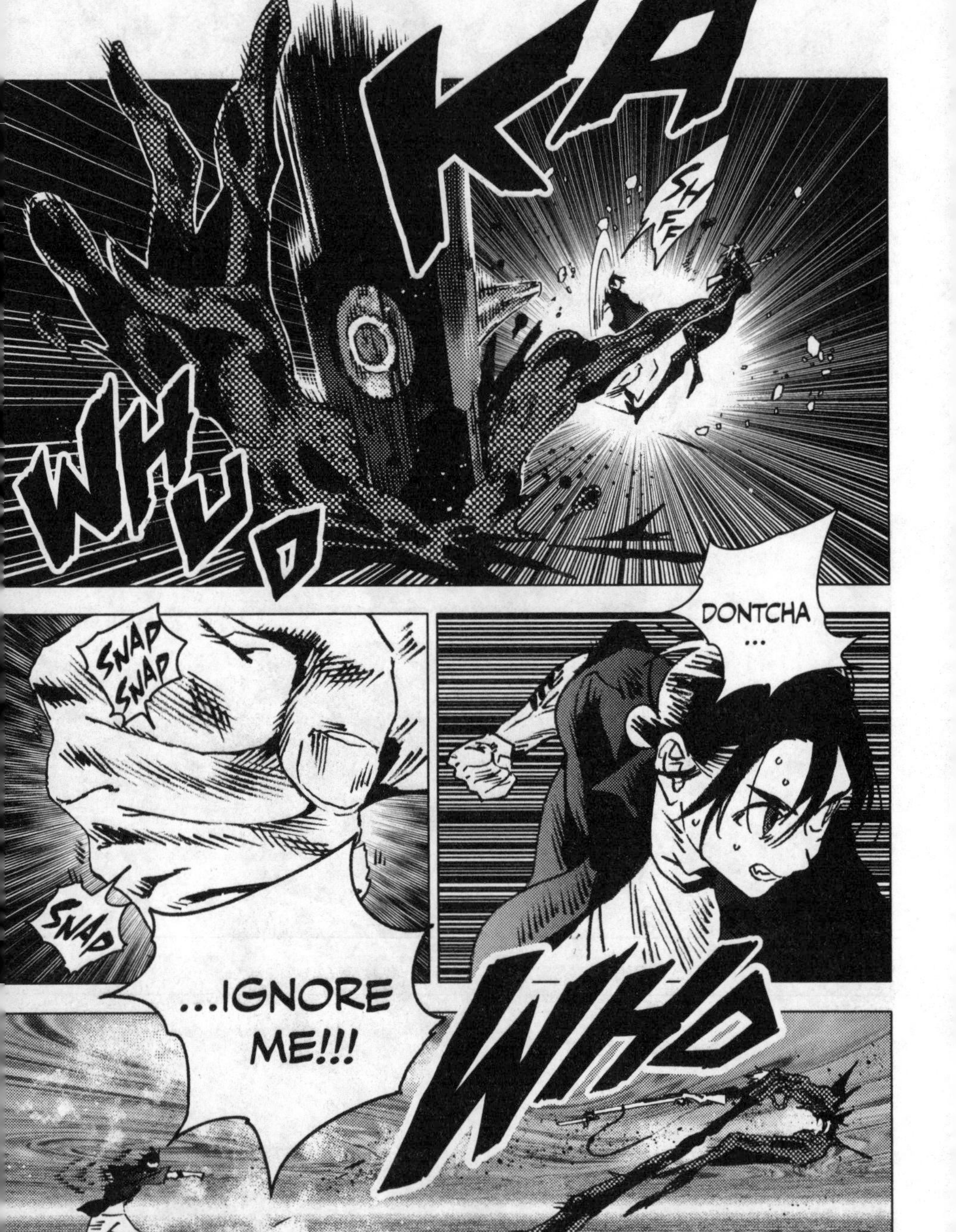
KA
SHFF
WHUD
DONTCHA
...
SNAP
SNAP
SNAP
...IGNORE
ME!!!

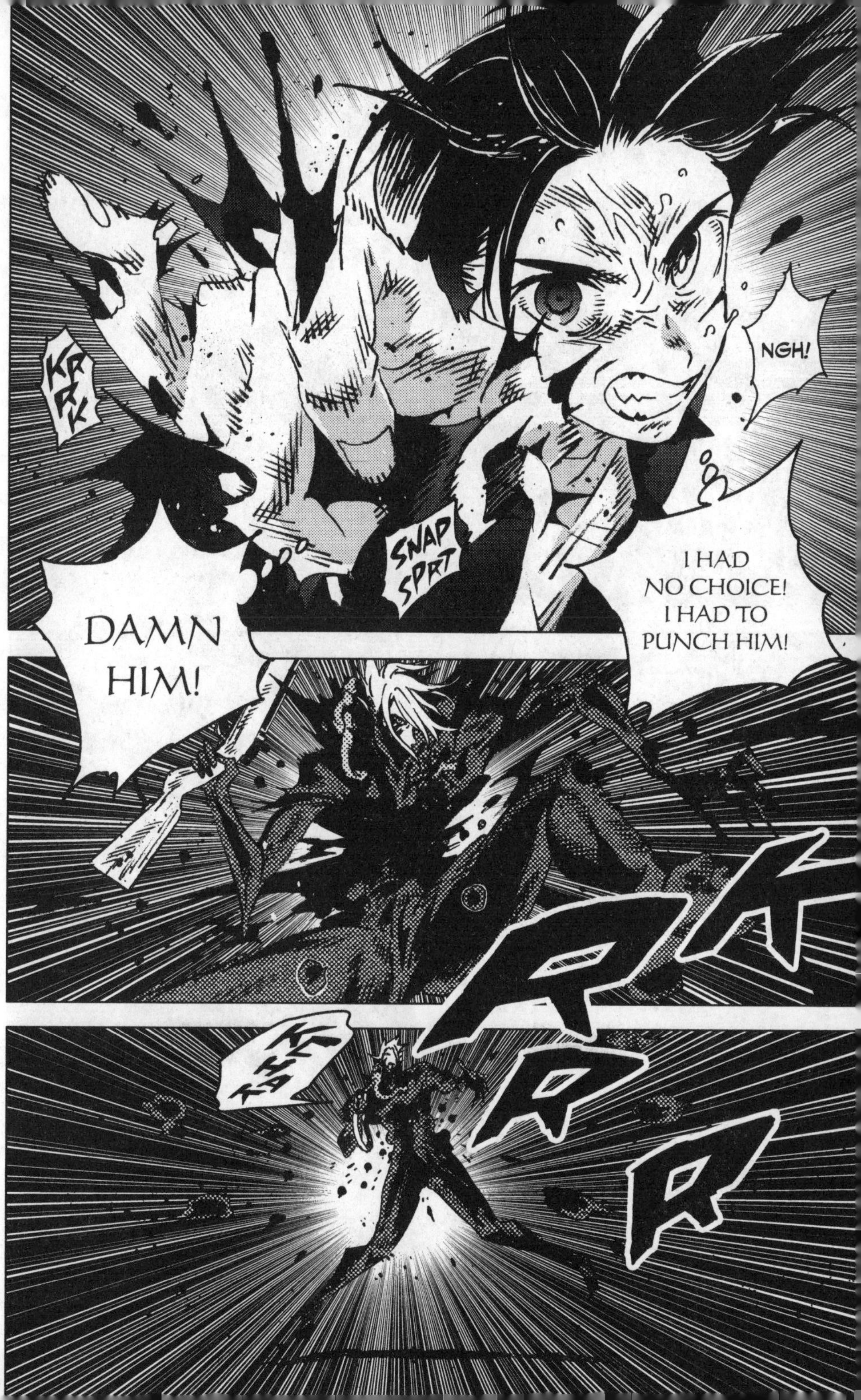
NGH!
KRRK
SNAP SPRT
I HAD NO CHOICE! I HAD TO PUNCH HIM!
DAMN HIM!
KHAK

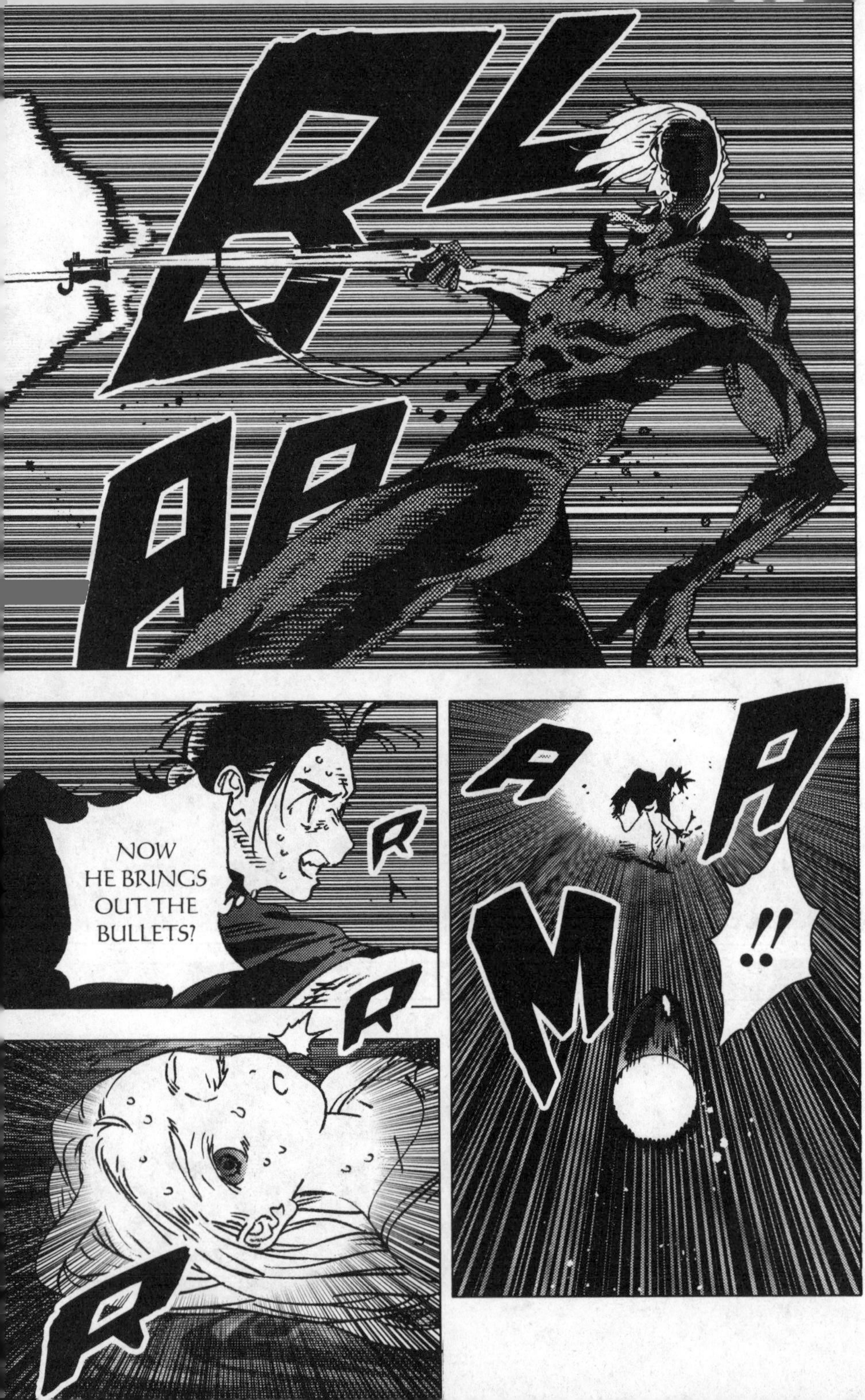
!!
NOW HE BRINGS OUT THE BULLETS?

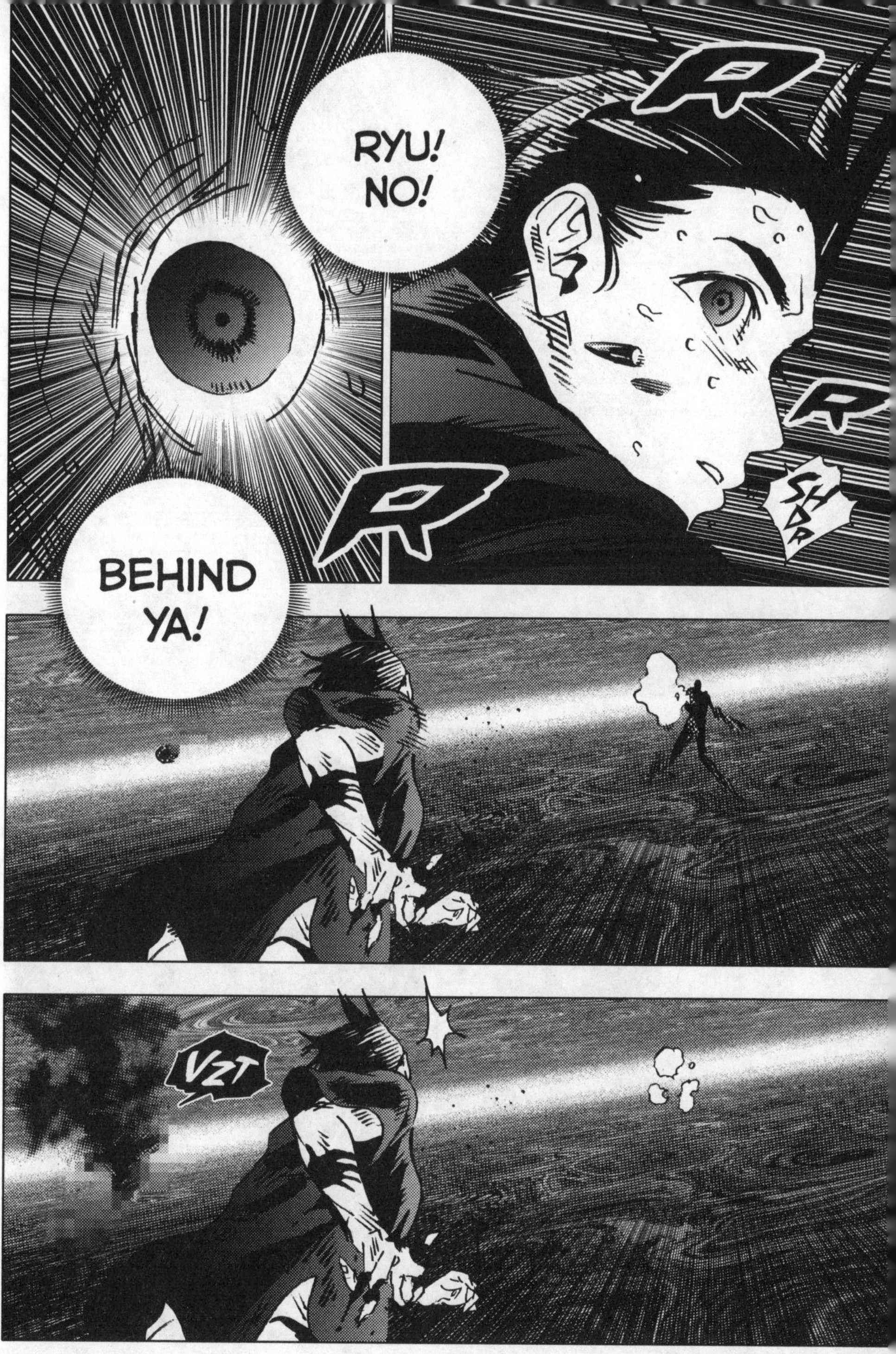
R
R
SHDR
R
RYU! NO!
BEHIND YA!
VZT

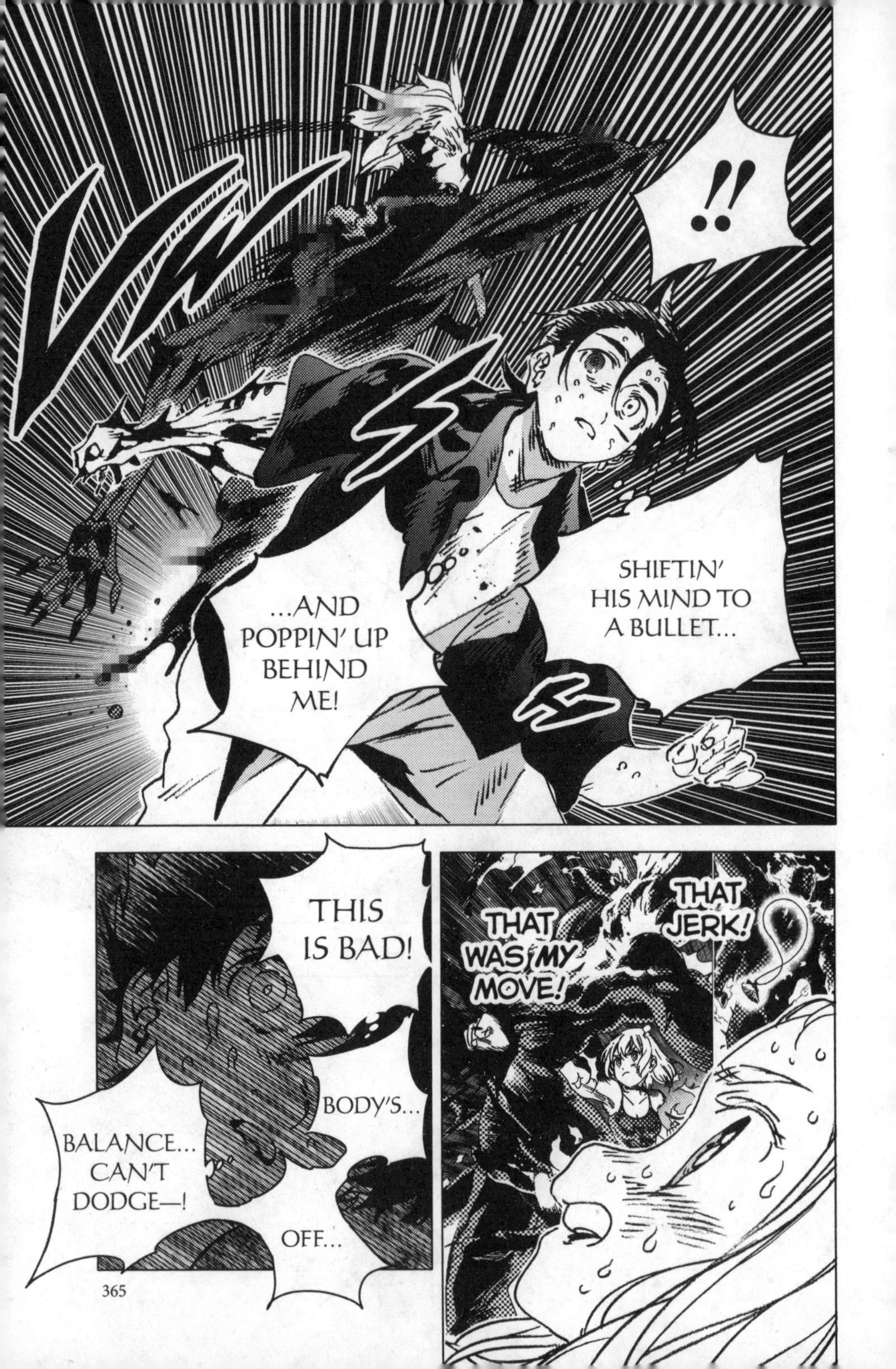
!!
SHIFTIN' HIS MIND TO A BULLET...
...AND POPPIN' UP BEHIND ME!
THAT JERK!
THAT WAS MY MOVE!
THIS IS BAD!
BODY'S...
BALANCE... CAN'T DODGE—!
OFF...

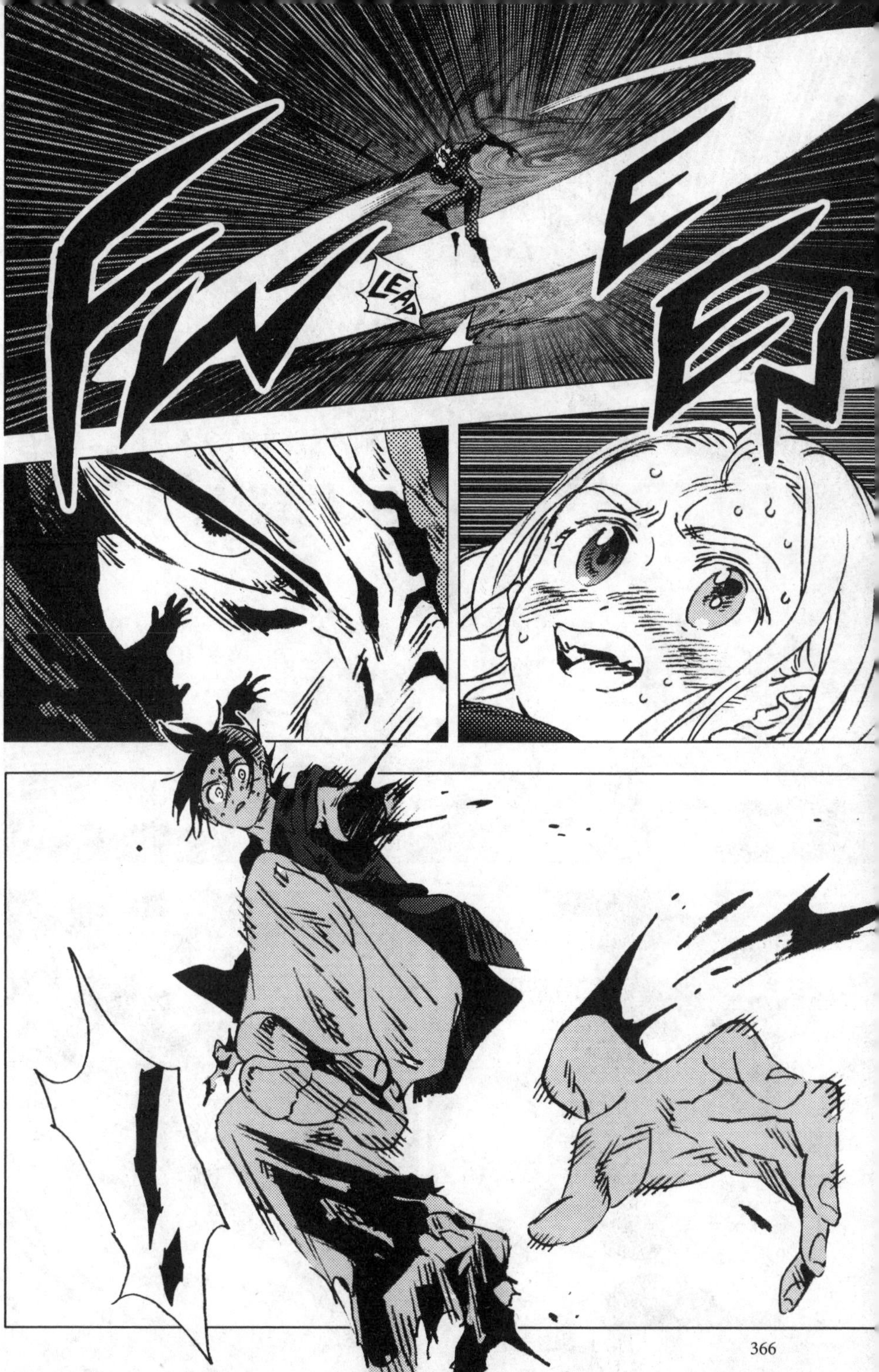
FWEEN
LEAD

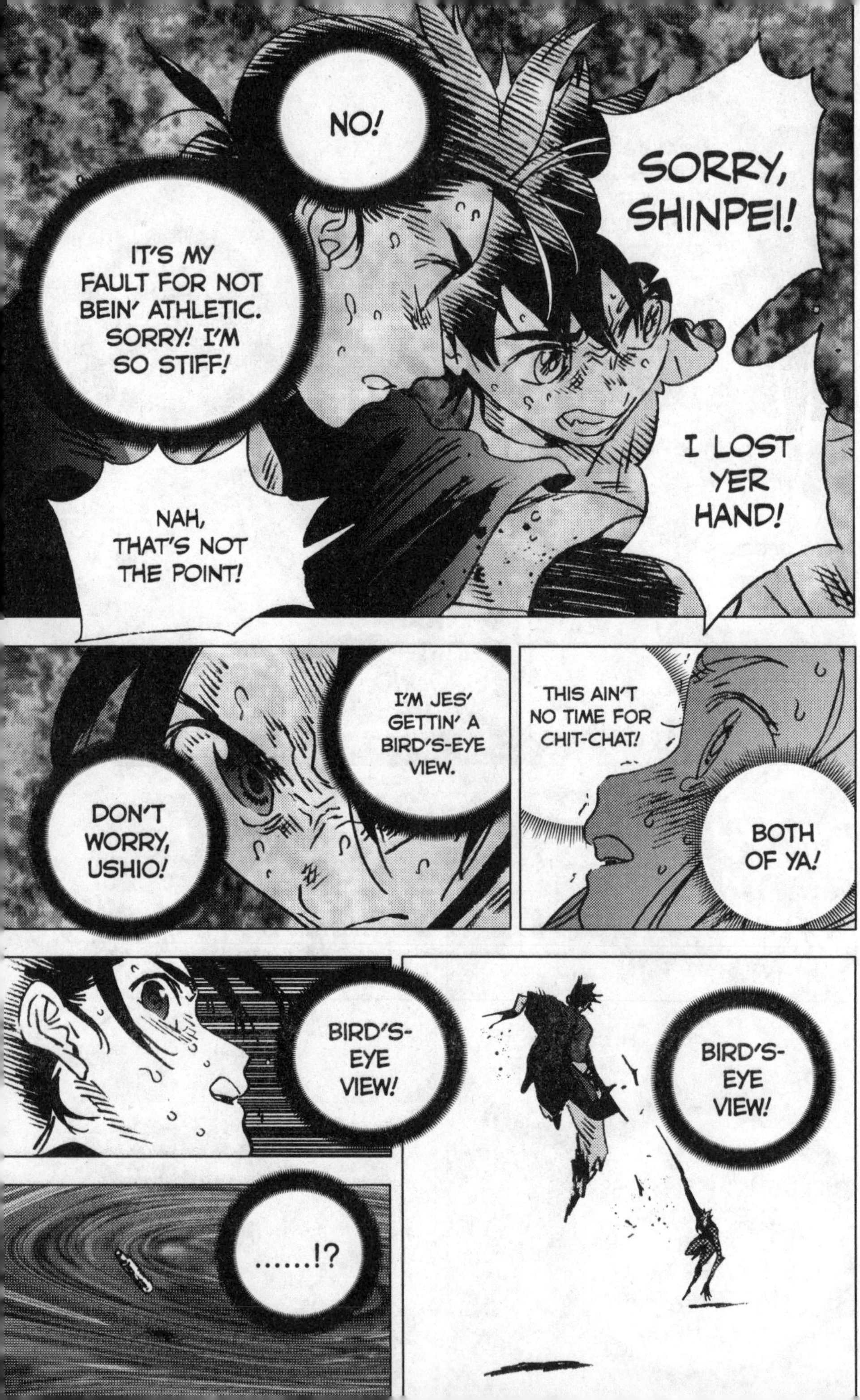
SORRY, SHINPEI!
NO!
I LOST YER HAND!
IT'S MY FAULT FOR NOT BEIN' ATHLETIC. SORRY! I'M SO STIFF!
NAH, THAT'S NOT THE POINT!
THIS AIN'T NO TIME FOR CHIT-CHAT!
BOTH OF YA!
I'M JES' GETTIN' A BIRD'S-EYE VIEW.
DON'T WORRY, USHIO!
BIRD'S-EYE VIEW!
BIRD'S-EYE VIEW!
......!?

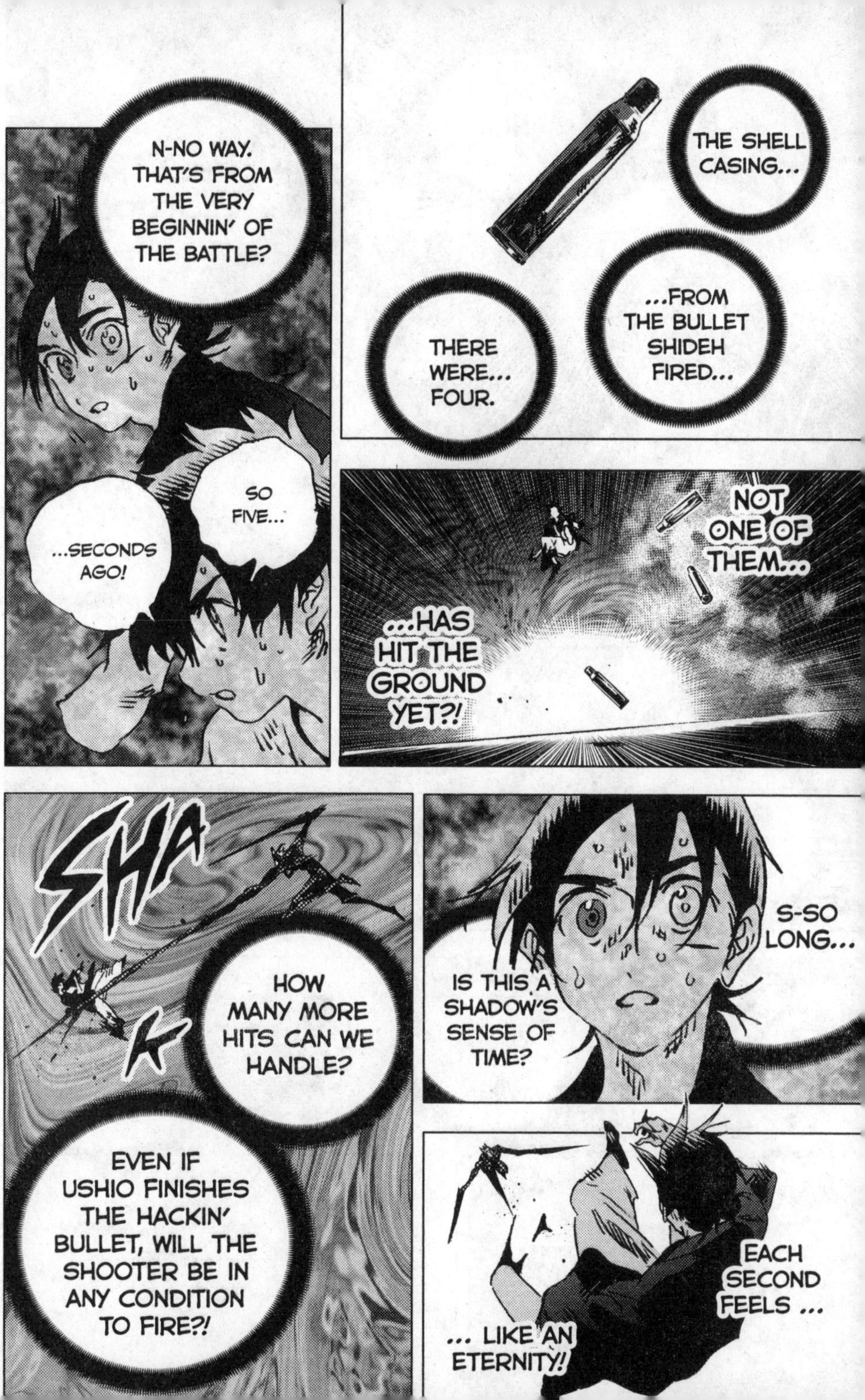
THE SHELL CASING...
...FROM THE BULLET SHIDEH FIRED...
THERE WERE... FOUR.
NOT ONE OF THEM...
...HAS HIT THE GROUND YET?!
N-NO WAY. THAT'S FROM THE VERY BEGINNIN' OF THE BATTLE?
SO FIVE...
...SECONDS AGO!
S-SO LONG...
IS THIS A SHADOW'S SENSE OF TIME?
EACH SECOND FEELS ...
... LIKE AN ETERNITY!
SHA
K
HOW MANY MORE HITS CAN WE HANDLE?
EVEN IF USHIO FINISHES THE HACKIN' BULLET, WILL THE SHOOTER BE IN ANY CONDITION TO FIRE?!

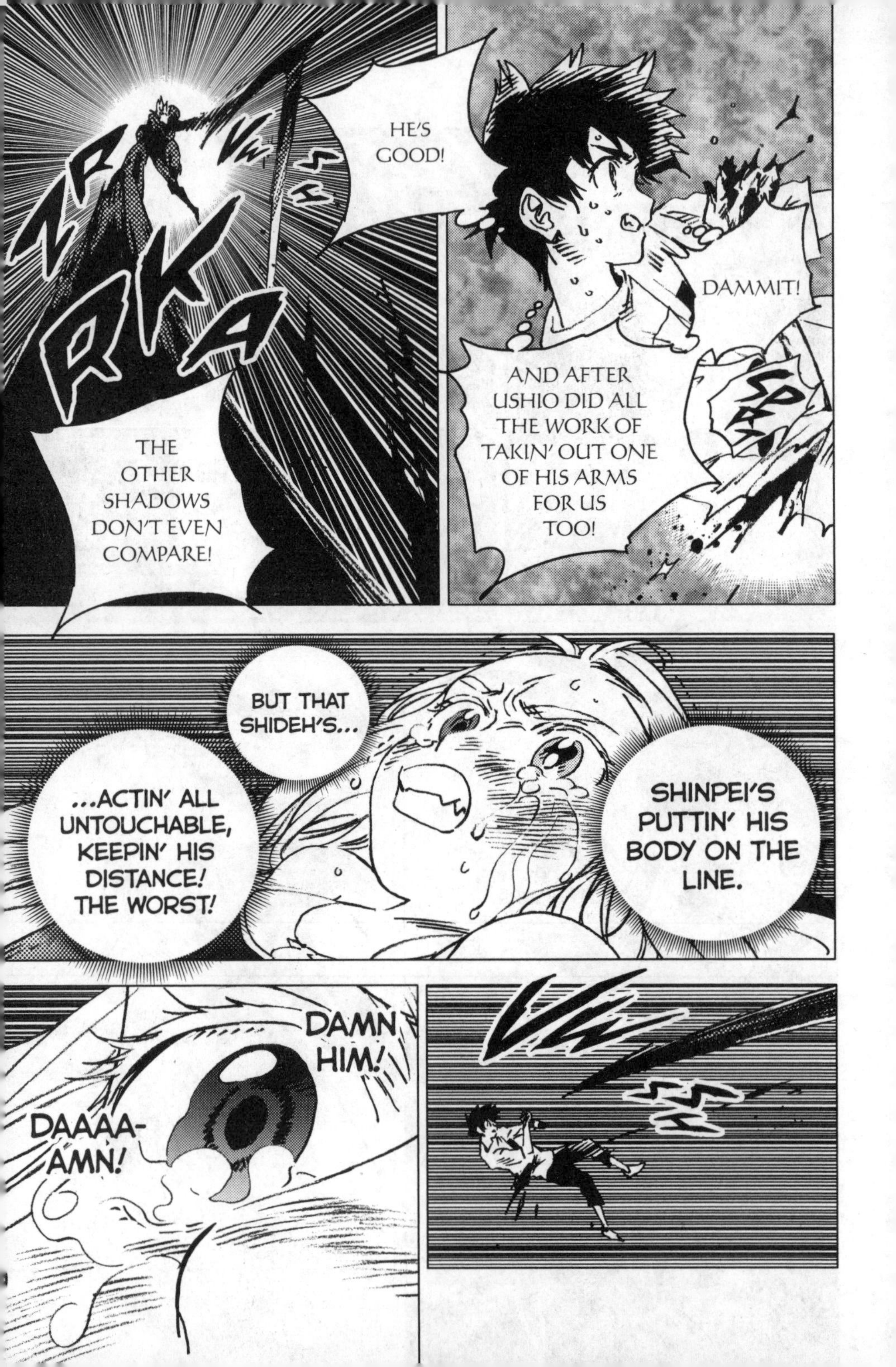
DAMMIT!
AND AFTER USHIO DID ALL THE WORK OF TAKIN' OUT ONE OF HIS ARMS FOR US TOO!
HE'S GOOD!
ZRRKA
THE OTHER SHADOWS DON'T EVEN COMPARE!
SHINPEI'S PUTTIN' HIS BODY ON THE LINE.
BUT THAT SHIDEH'S...
...ACTIN' ALL UNTOUCHABLE, KEEPIN' HIS DISTANCE! THE WORST!
DAMN HIM!
DAAAA-AMN!

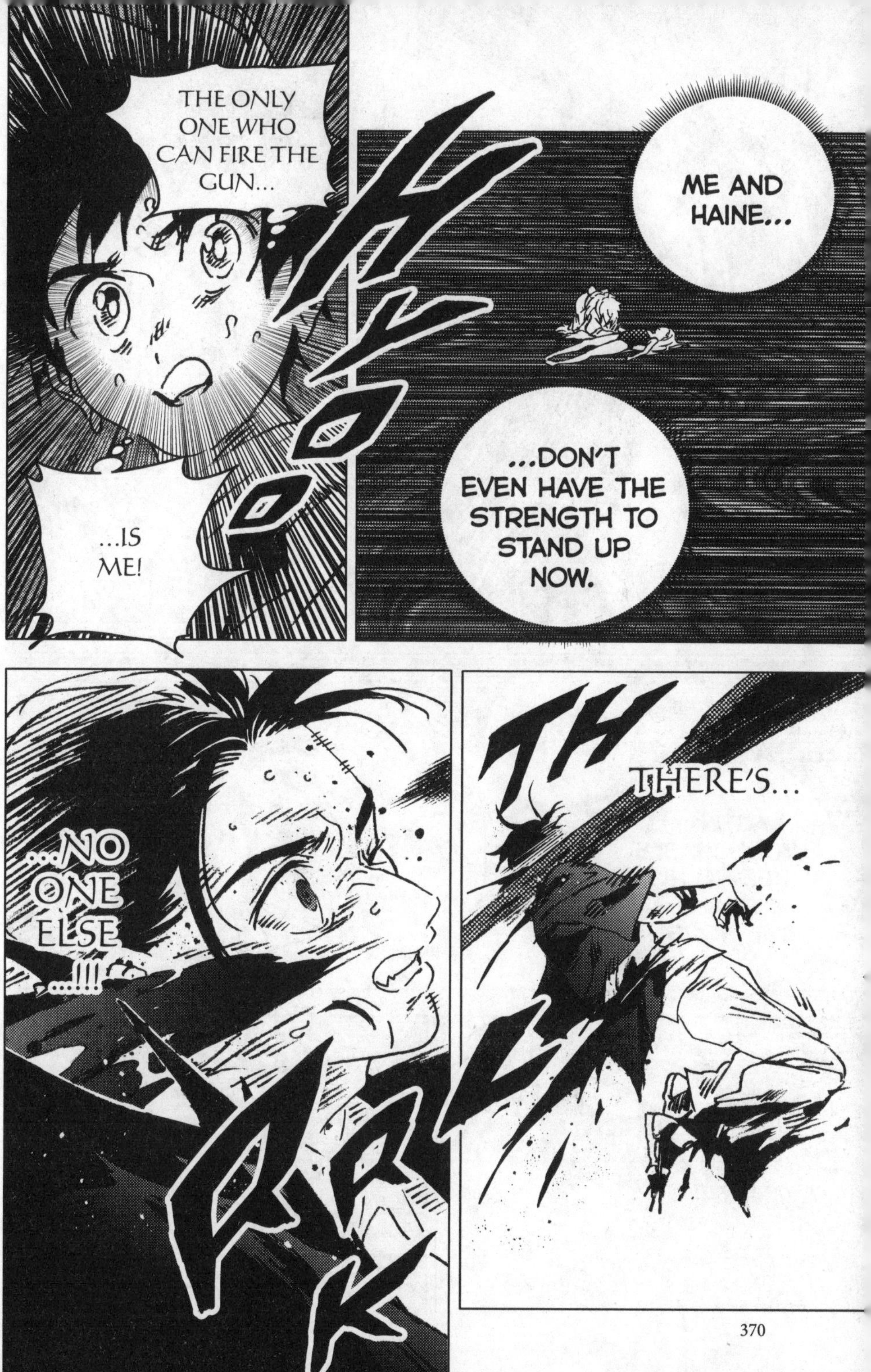
ME AND HAINE...
...DON'T EVEN HAVE THE STRENGTH TO STAND UP NOW.
THE ONLY ONE WHO CAN FIRE THE GUN...
...IS ME!
THERE'S...
...NO ONE ELSE ...!!!

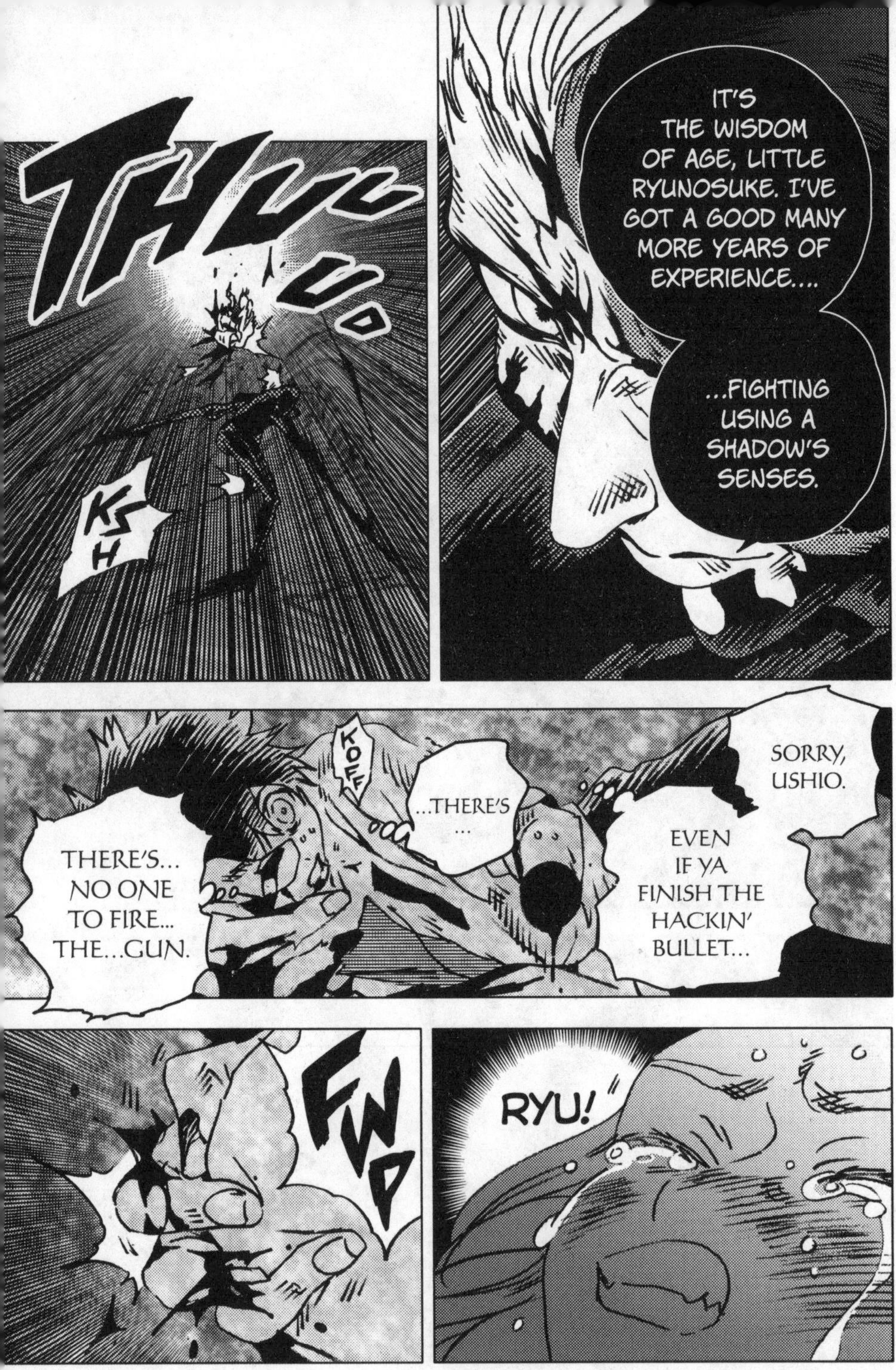
IT'S THE WISDOM OF AGE, LITTLE RYUNOSUKE. I'VE GOT A GOOD MANY MORE YEARS OF EXPERIENCE....
...FIGHTING USING A SHADOW'S SENSES.
THUD
KSH
SORRY, USHIO.
EVEN IF YA FINISH THE HACKIN' BULLET...
KOFF
...THERE'S...
THERE'S... NO ONE TO FIRE... THE...GUN.
RYU!
FWD

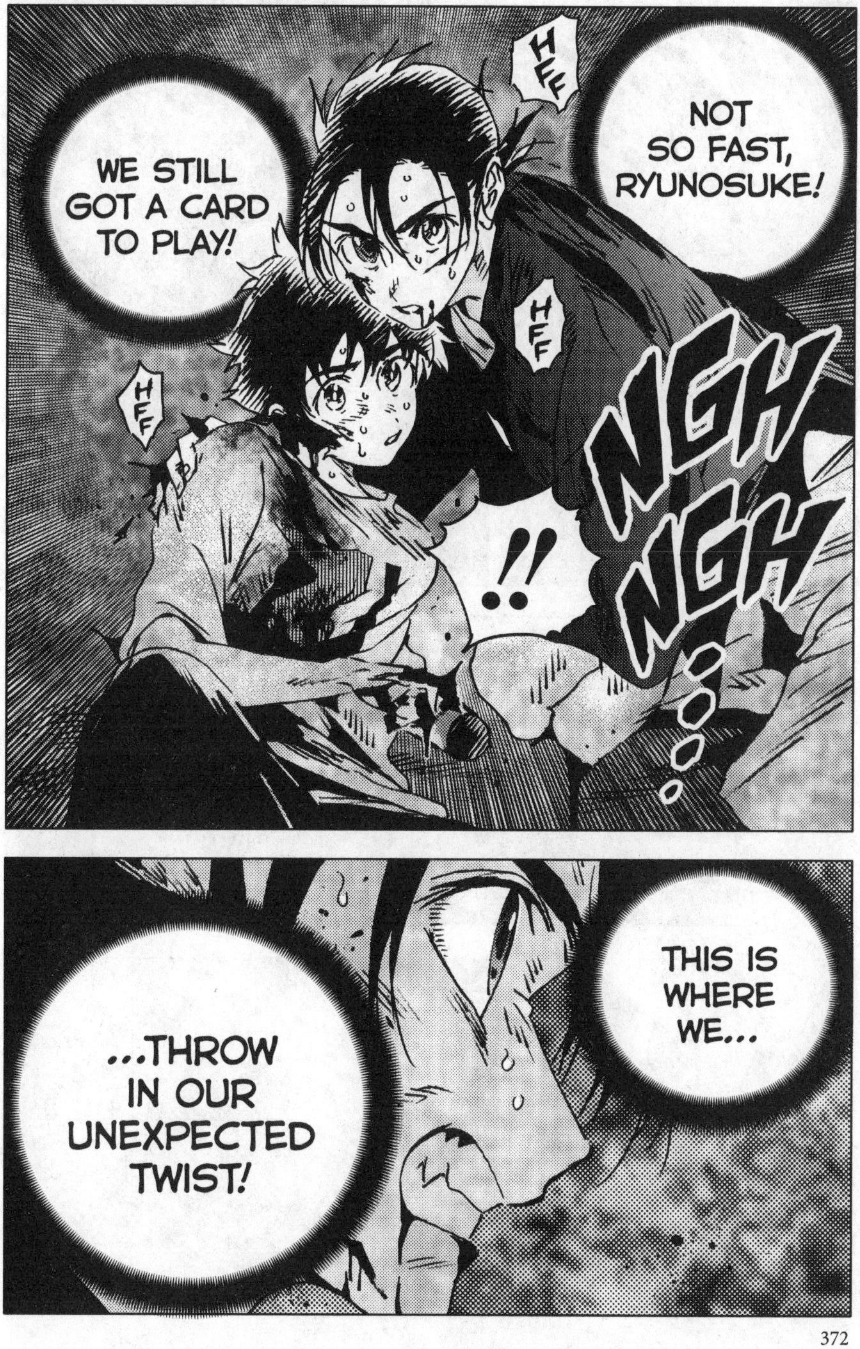
HFF
NOT SO FAST, RYUNOSUKE!
WE STILL GOT A CARD TO PLAY!
HFF
HFF
NGH NGH
!!
THIS IS WHERE WE...
...THROW IN OUR UNEXPECTED TWIST!

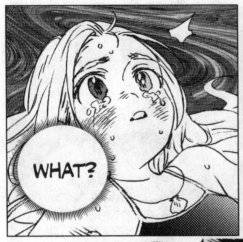

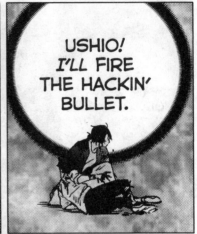

USHIO! I'LL FIRE THE HACKIN' BULLET.
WHAT?
I THINK IT WAS THE END OF THE FIFTH LOOP.
YA SAID YA SCANNED HIS ARMOR?
AND THERE WAS NO DATA. IT WAS EMPTY.
SHINPEI.
WHAT'RE YA THINKIN'?!
HEF
HEF
HEF
RYUNOSUKE.
YA'RE PRETTY GOOD AT TAKIN' OVER A PERSON'S BODY, RIGHT?

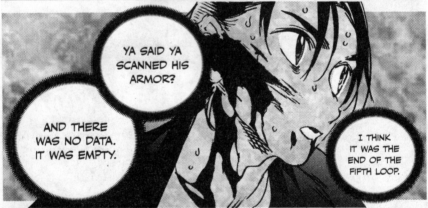

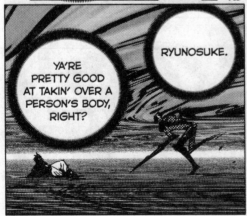

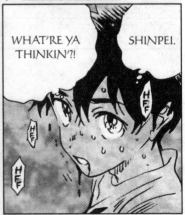

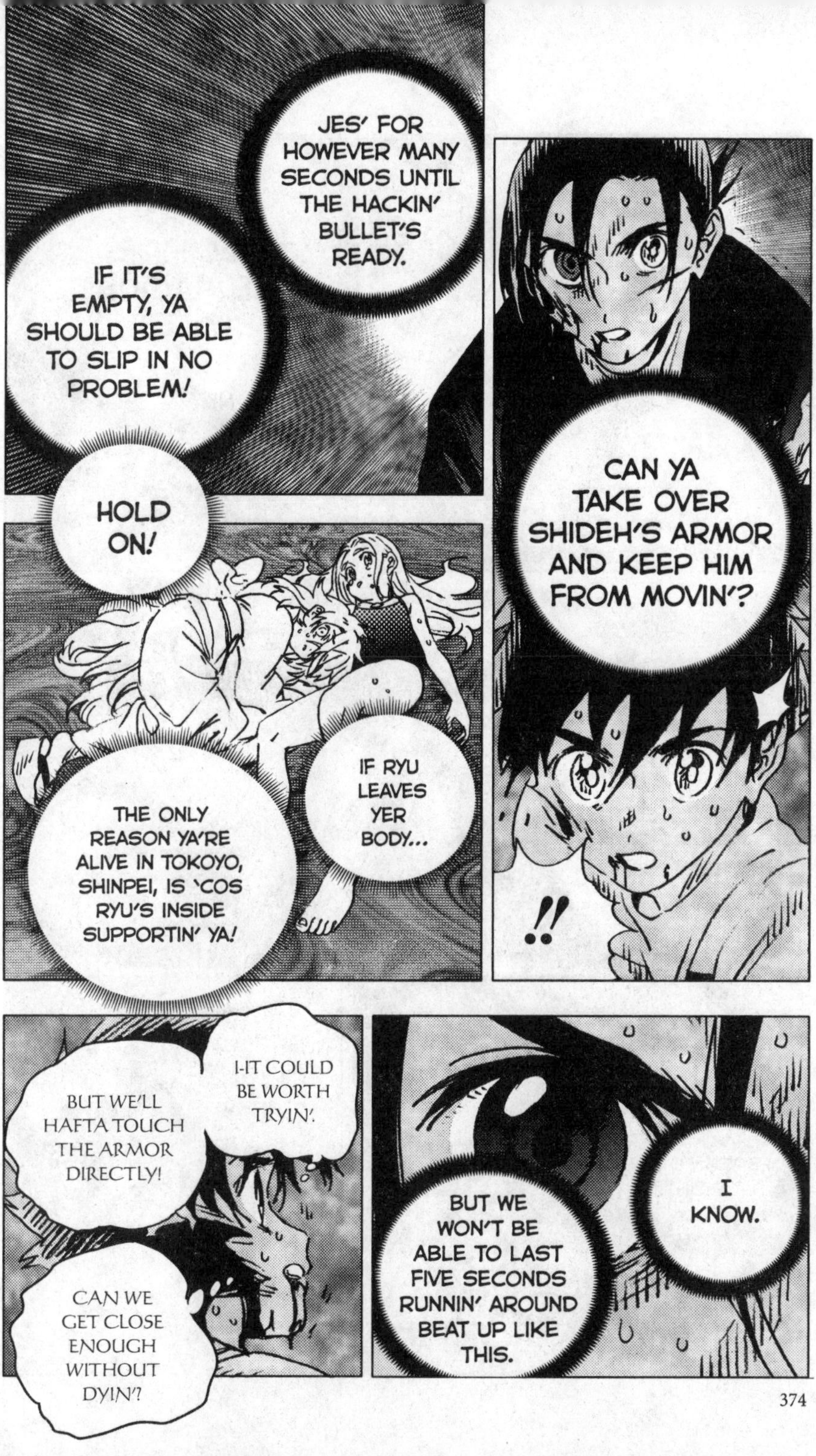
CAN YA TAKE OVER SHIDEH'S ARMOR AND KEEP HIM FROM MOVIN'?
!!
JES' FOR HOWEVER MANY SECONDS UNTIL THE HACKIN' BULLET'S READY.
IF IT'S EMPTY, YA SHOULD BE ABLE TO SLIP IN NO PROBLEM!
HOLD ON!
IF RYU LEAVES YER BODY...
THE ONLY REASON YA'RE ALIVE IN TOKOYO, SHINPEI, IS 'COS RYU'S INSIDE SUPPORTIN' YA!
I KNOW.
BUT WE WON'T BE ABLE TO LAST FIVE SECONDS RUNNIN' AROUND BEAT UP LIKE THIS.
I-IT COULD BE WORTH TRYIN'.
BUT WE'LL HAFTA TOUCH THE ARMOR DIRECTLY!
CAN WE GET CLOSE ENOUGH WITHOUT DYIN'?

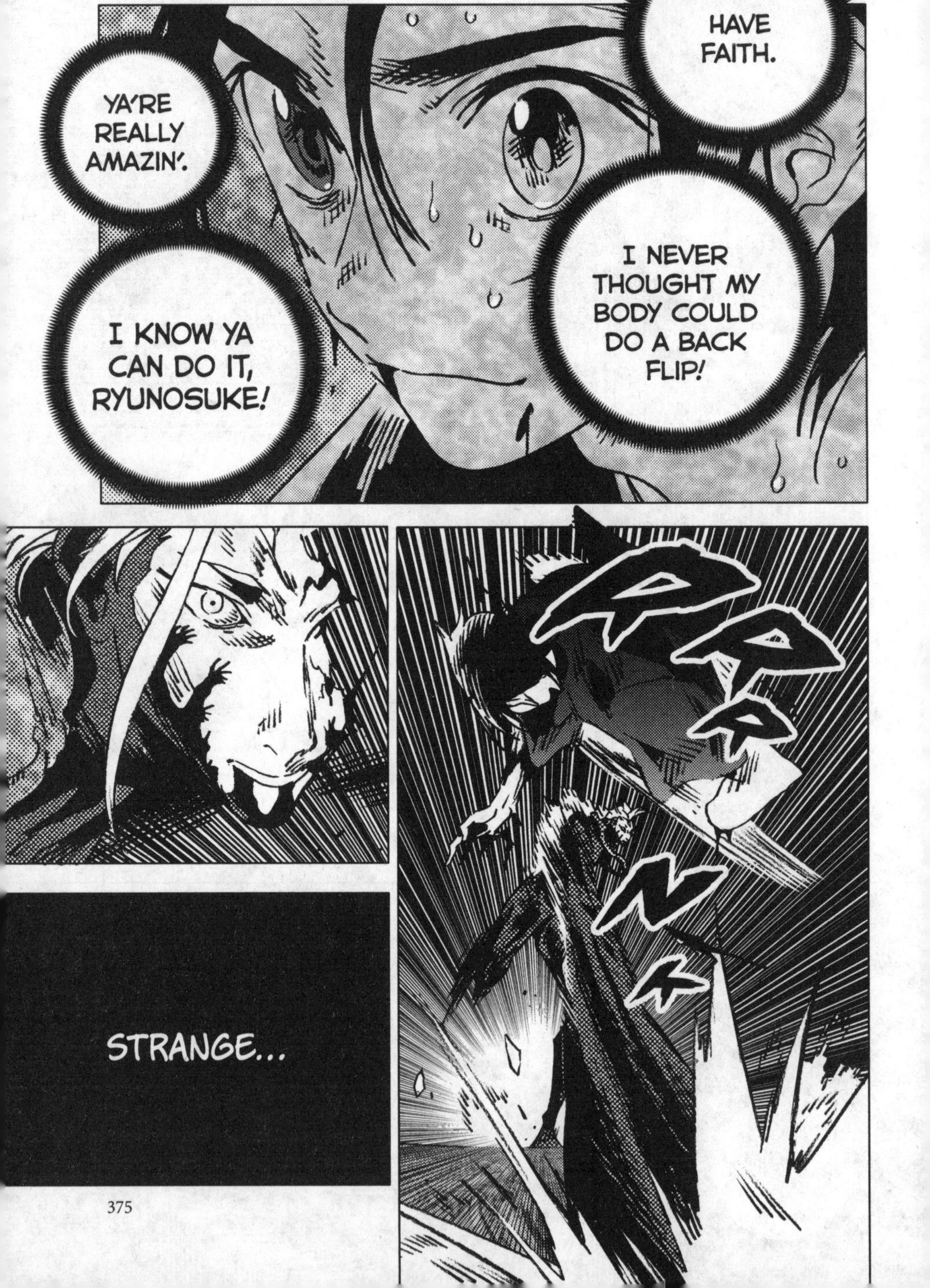
HAVE FAITH.
YA'RE REALLY AMAZIN'.
I NEVER THOUGHT MY BODY COULD DO A BACK FLIP!
I KNOW YA CAN DO IT, RYUNOSUKE!
STRANGE...

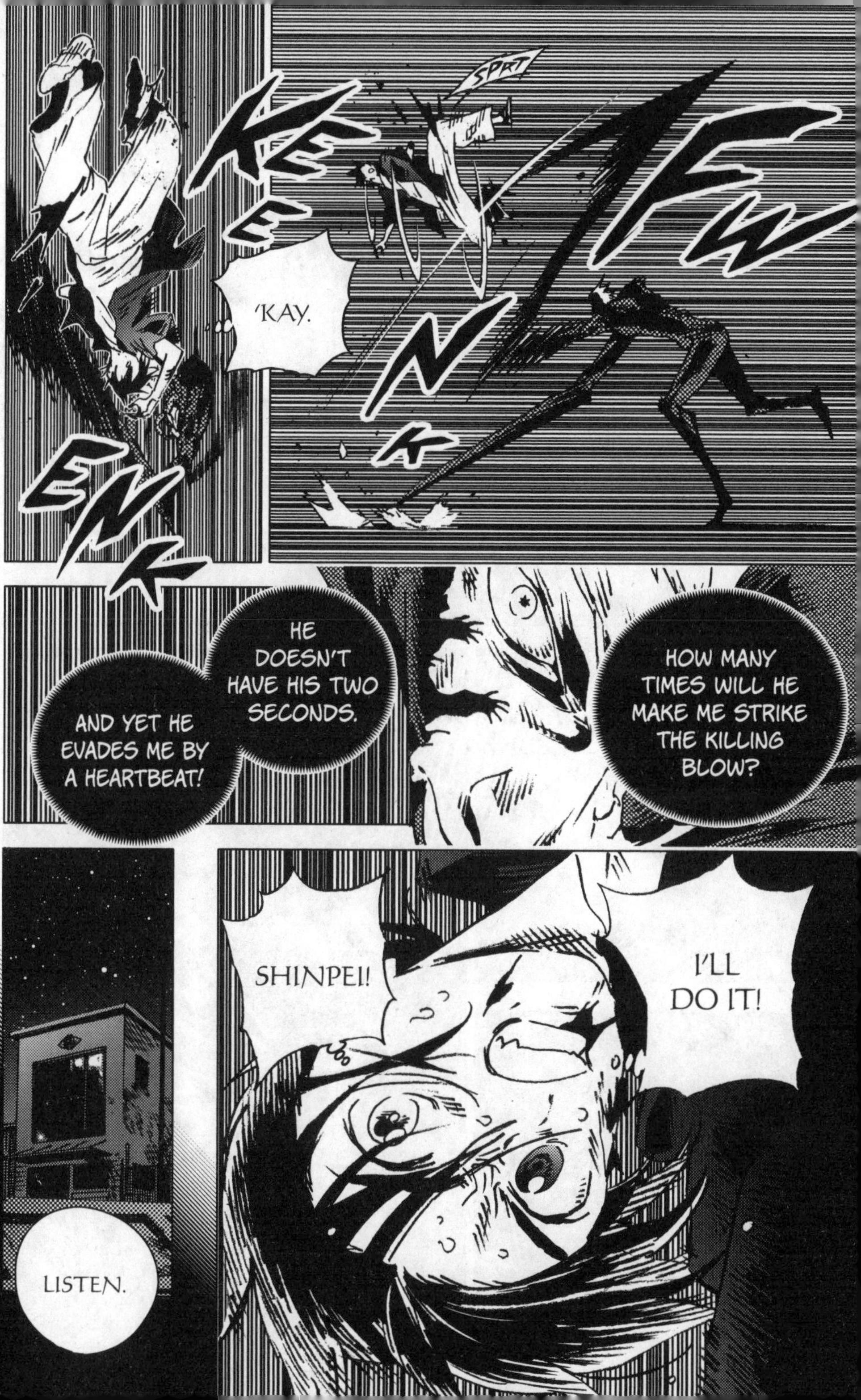
SPRT
KEENK
'KAY.
ENK
HOW MANY TIMES WILL HE MAKE ME STRIKE THE KILLING BLOW?
HE DOESN'T HAVE HIS TWO SECONDS.
AND YET HE EVADES ME BY A HEARTBEAT!
I'LL DO IT!
SHINPEI!
LISTEN.

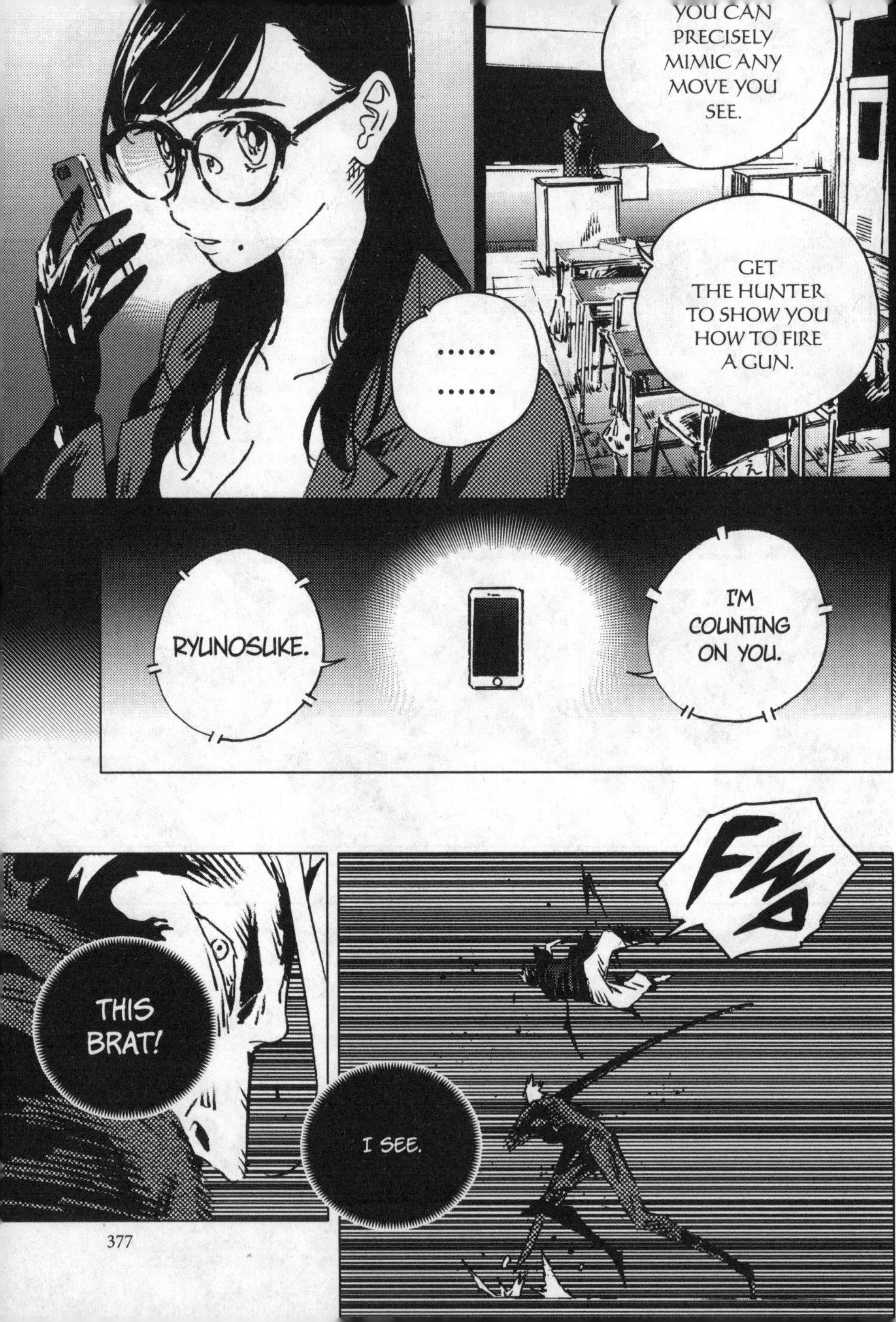
YOU CAN PRECISELY MIMIC ANY MOVE YOU SEE.
GET THE HUNTER TO SHOW YOU HOW TO FIRE A GUN.
……
……
I'M COUNTING ON YOU.
RYUNOSUKE.
FWP
THIS BRAT!
I SEE.

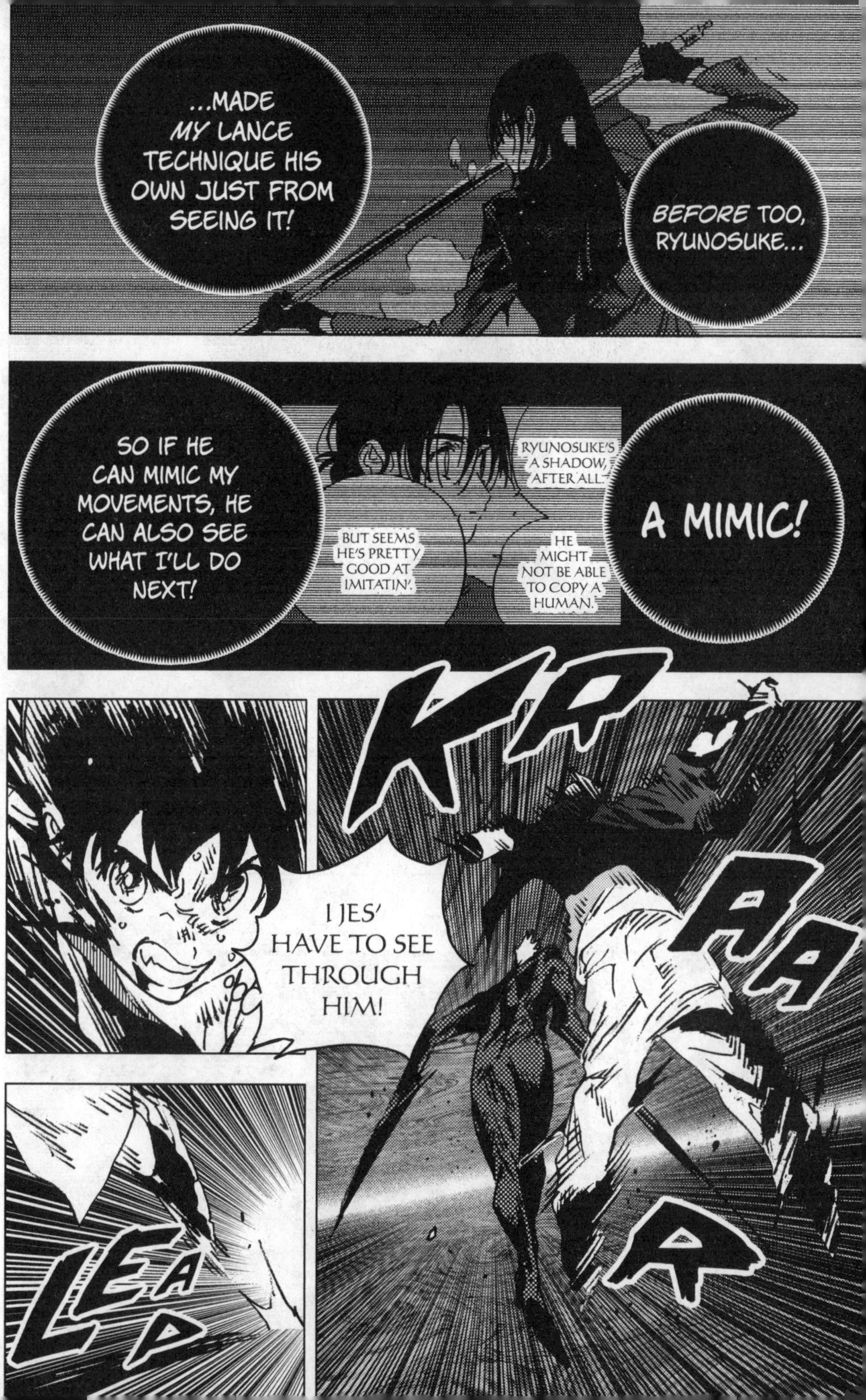
BEFORE TOO, RYUNOSUKE...
...MADE MY LANCE TECHNIQUE HIS OWN JUST FROM SEEING IT!
A MIMIC!
RYUNOSUKE'S A SHADOW, AFTER ALL.
HE MIGHT NOT BE ABLE TO COPY A HUMAN.
BUT SEEMS HE'S PRETTY GOOD AT IMITATIN'.
SO IF HE CAN MIMIC MY MOVEMENTS, HE CAN ALSO SEE WHAT I'LL DO NEXT!
KRAAA
I JES' HAVE TO SEE THROUGH HIM!
LEAP

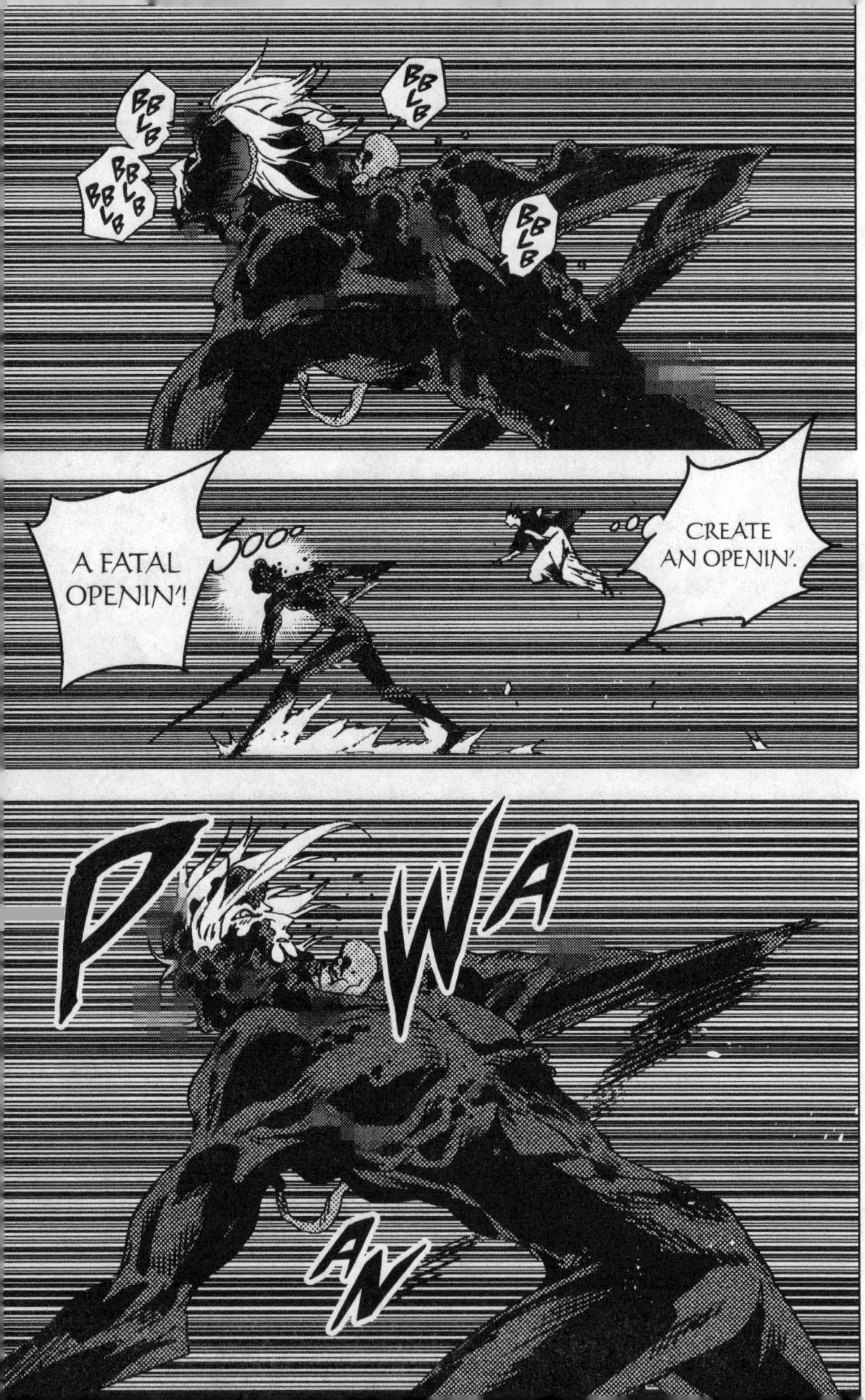
BBLB
BBLB
BBLB
BBLB BBLB
CREATE AN OPENIN'.
A FATAL OPENIN'!
P WA AN

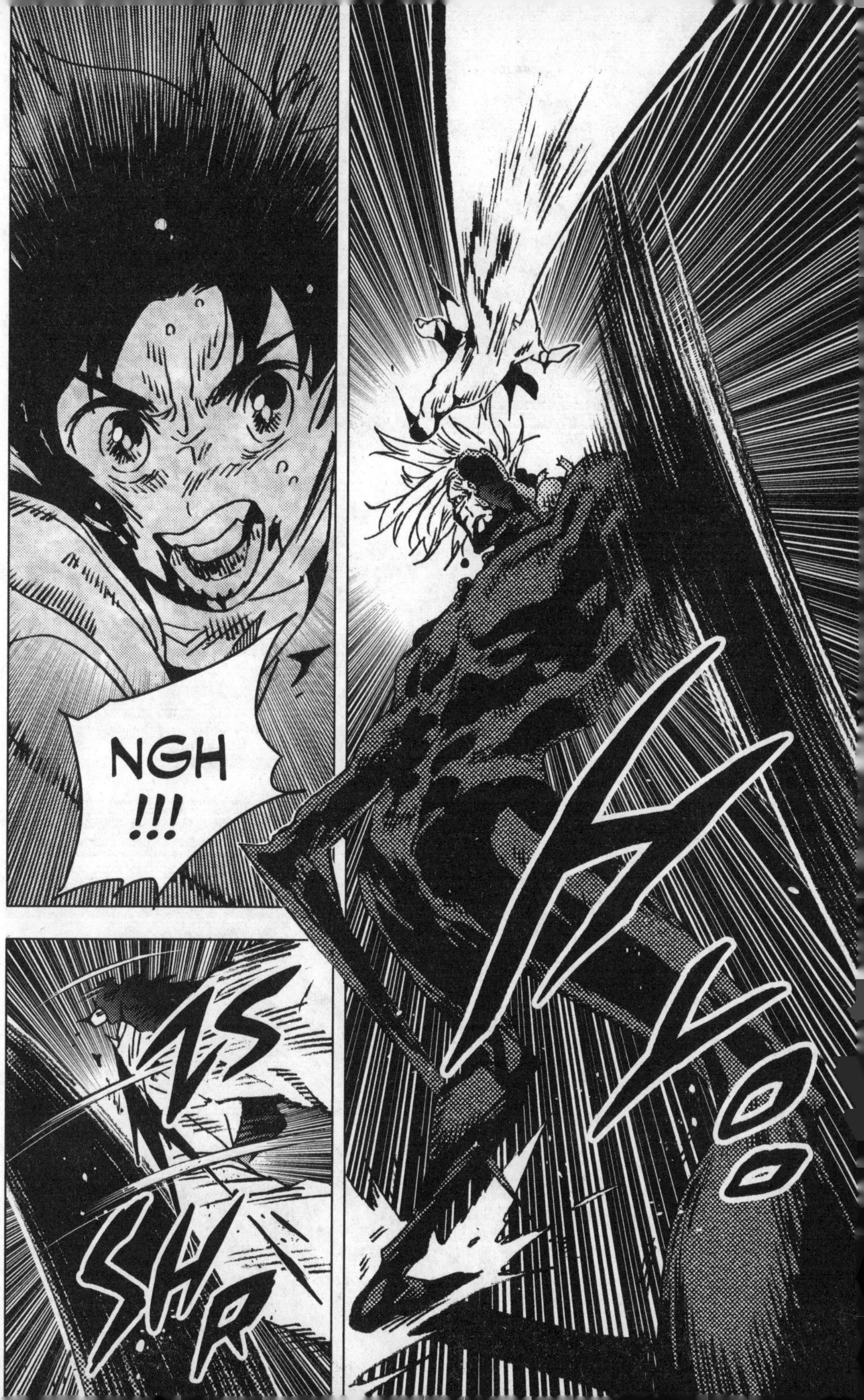
NGH !!!

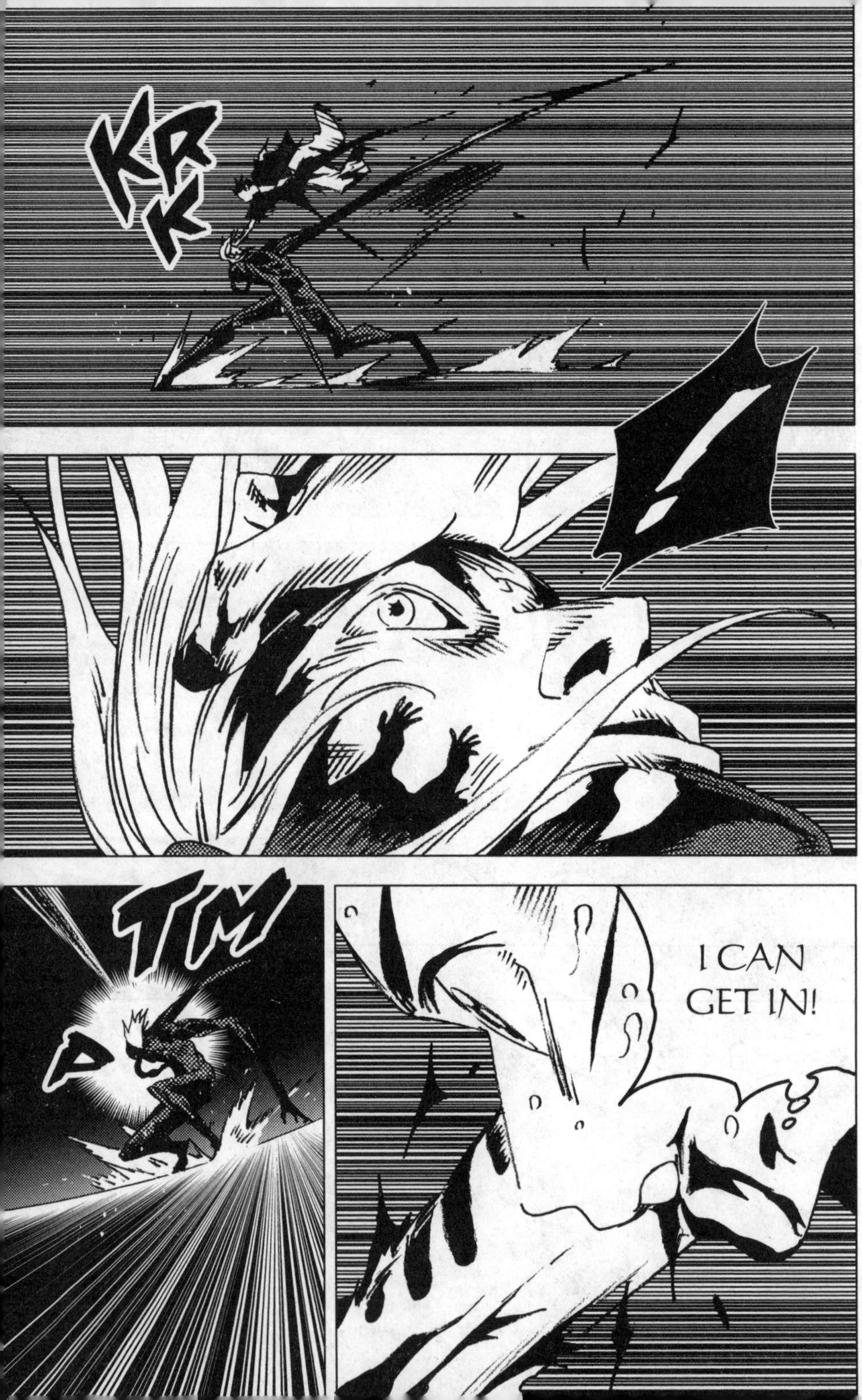
KRK
I CAN GET IN!
TMP

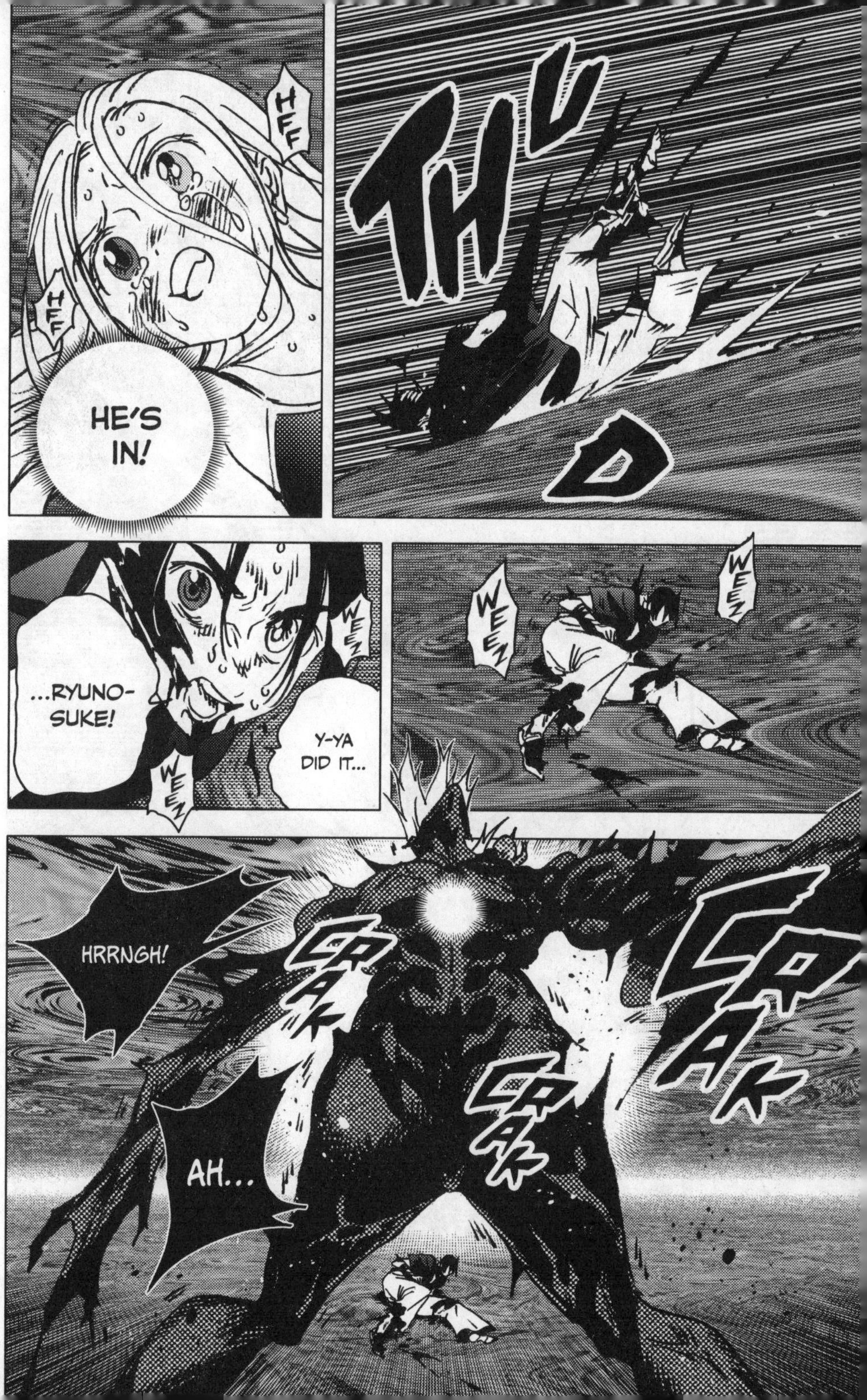
THUD
HEFF
HEFF
HE'S IN!
WEEZ
WEEZ
Y-YA DID IT...
...RYUNO-SUKE!
WEEZ
WEEZ
CRAK
CRAK
HRRNGH!
CRAK
AH...

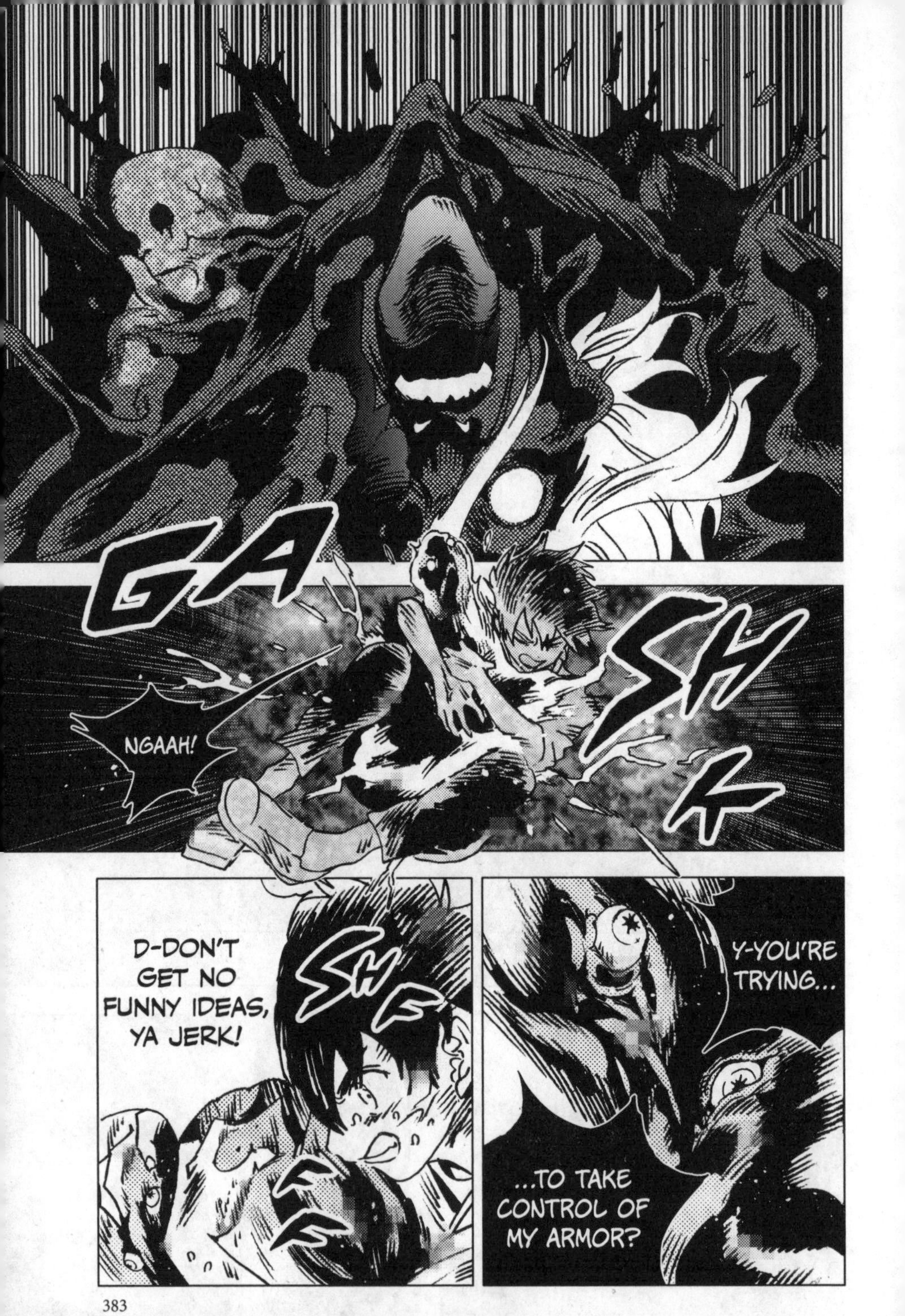
GA
SHK
NGAAH!
Y-YOU'RE TRYING...
...TO TAKE CONTROL OF MY ARMOR?
D-DON'T GET NO FUNNY IDEAS, YA JERK!
SHF

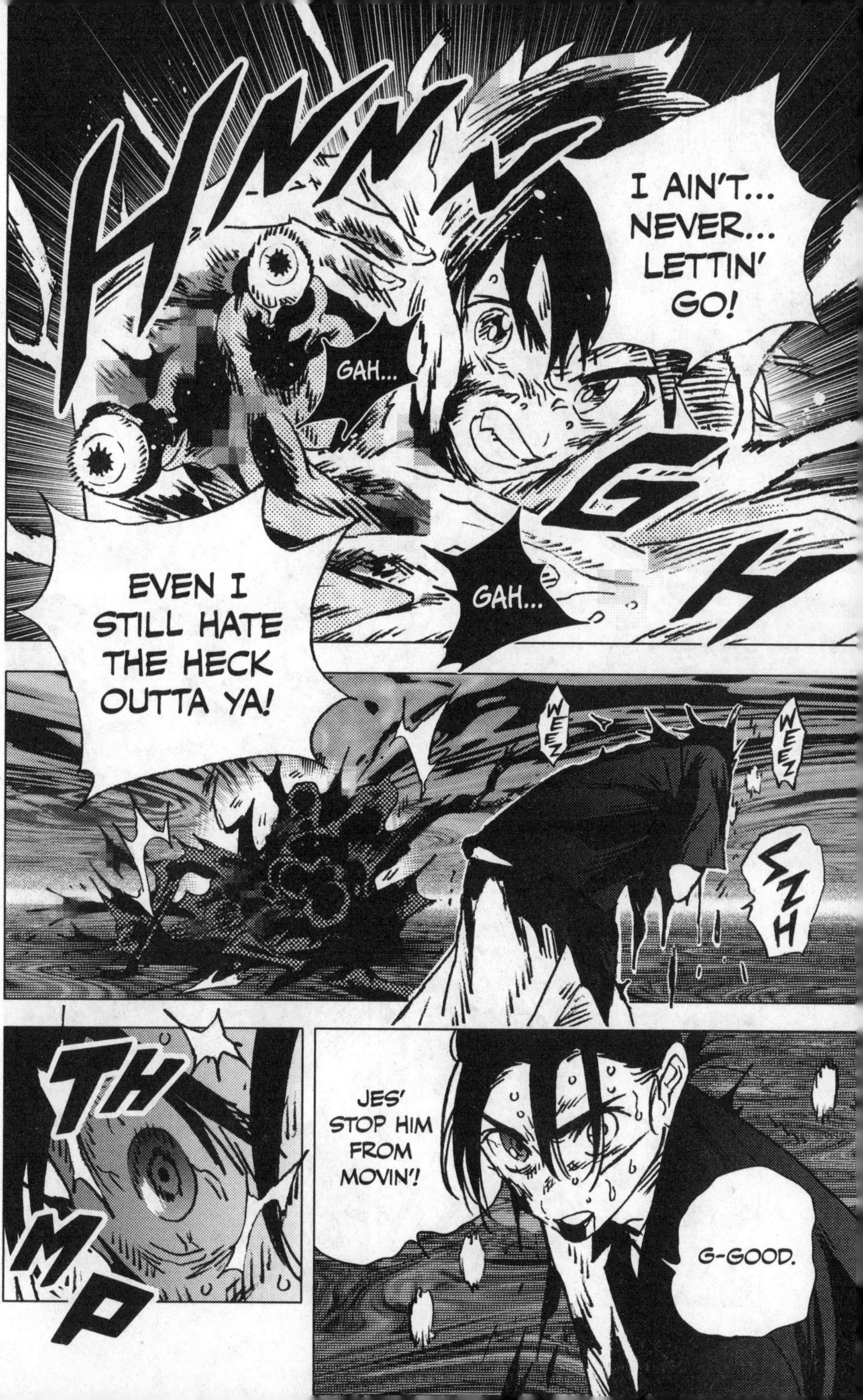

I AIN'T... NEVER... LETTIN' GO!
GAH...
GAH...
EVEN I STILL HATE THE HECK OUTTA YA!
WEEZ
WEEZ
JES' STOP HIM FROM MOVIN'!
G-GOOD.
THMP

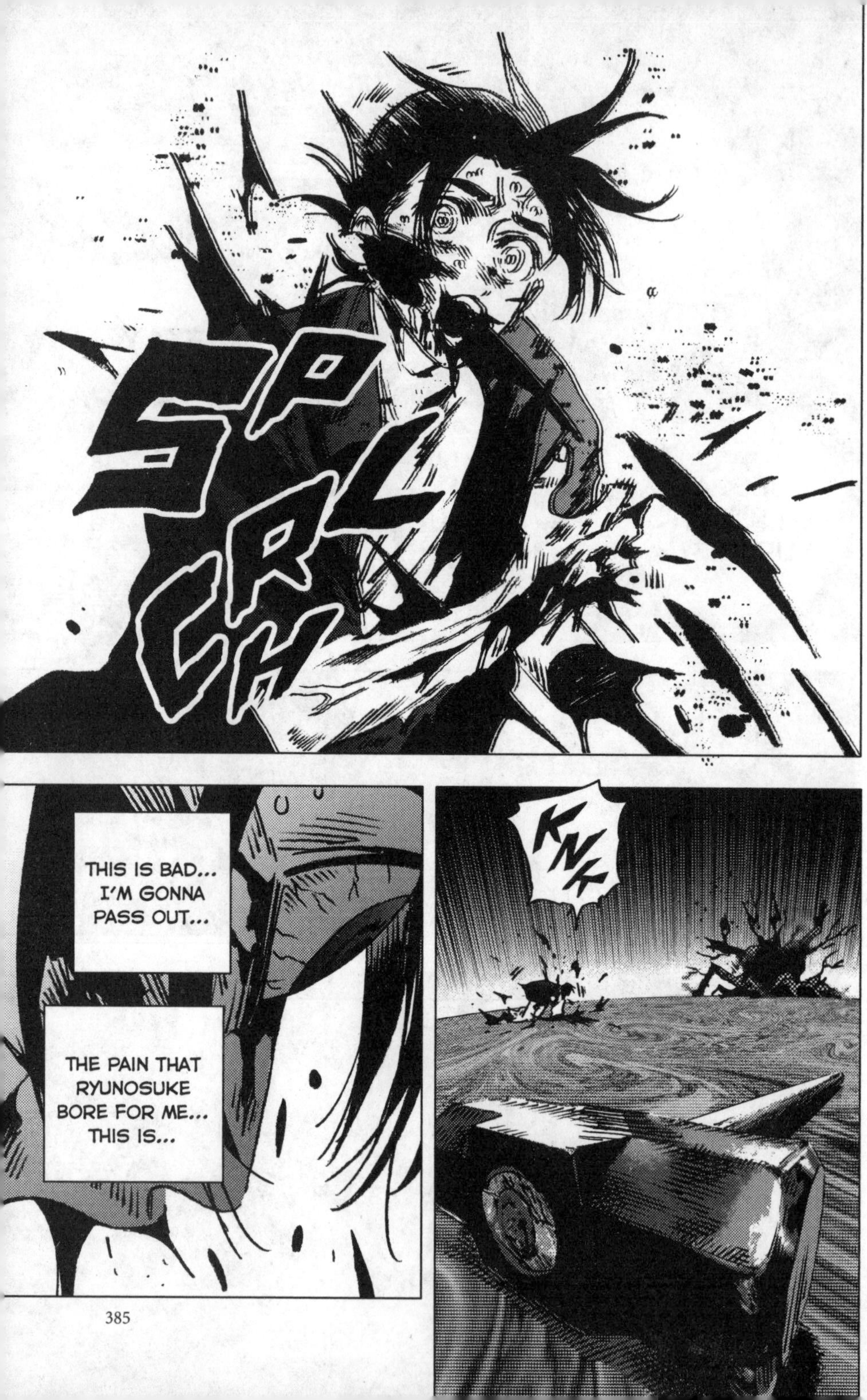
SPLRCH
KNK
THIS IS BAD... I'M GONNA PASS OUT...
THE PAIN THAT RYUNOSUKE BORE FOR ME... THIS IS...

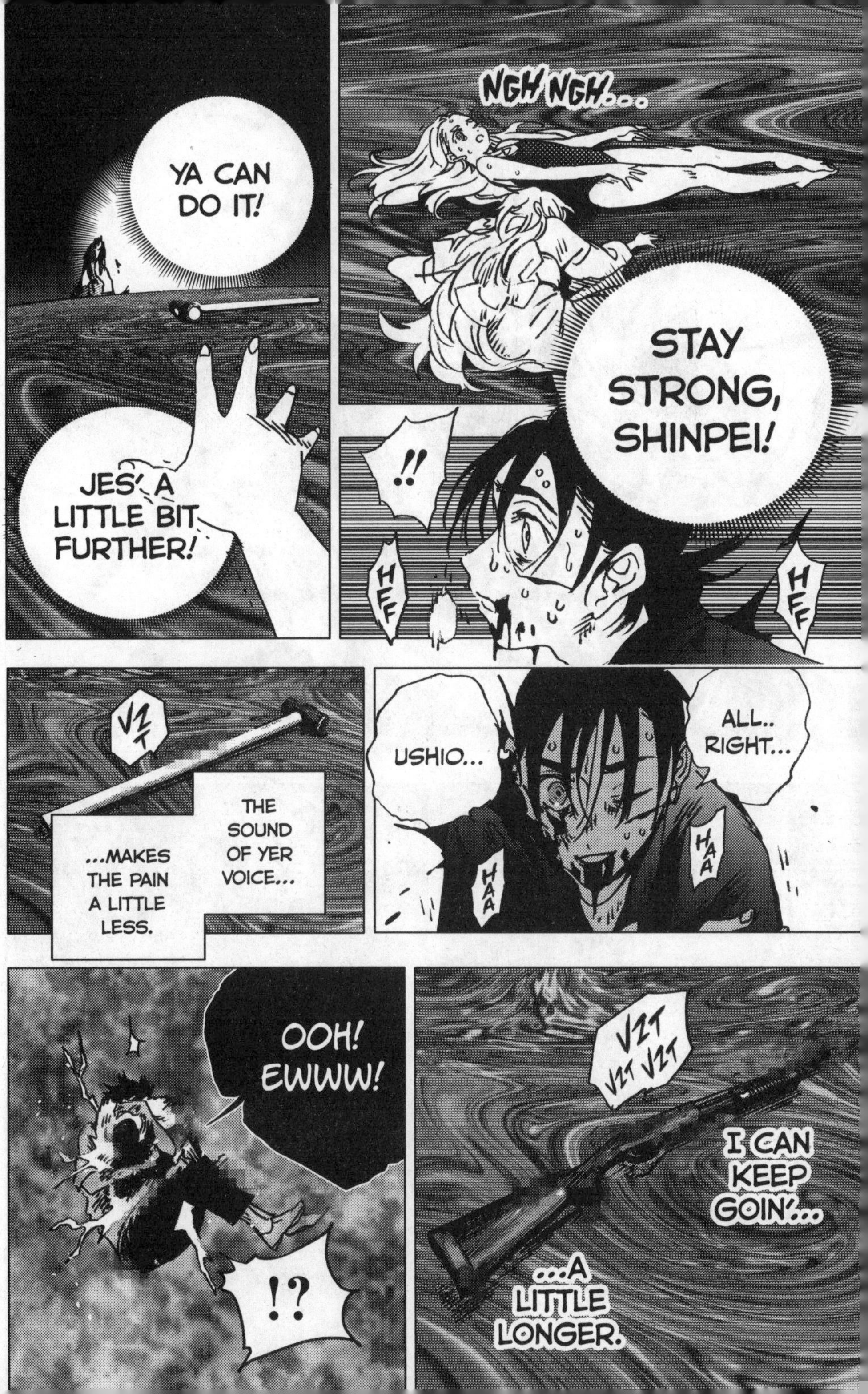
NGH NGH...
STAY STRONG, SHINPEI!
!!
HFF
HFF
YA CAN DO IT!
JES' A LITTLE BIT FURTHER!
ALL.. RIGHT...
USHIO...
HAA
HAA
VZT
THE SOUND OF YER VOICE...
...MAKES THE PAIN A LITTLE LESS.
VZT VZT VZT
I CAN KEEP GOIN'...
...A LITTLE LONGER.
OOH! EWWW!
!?

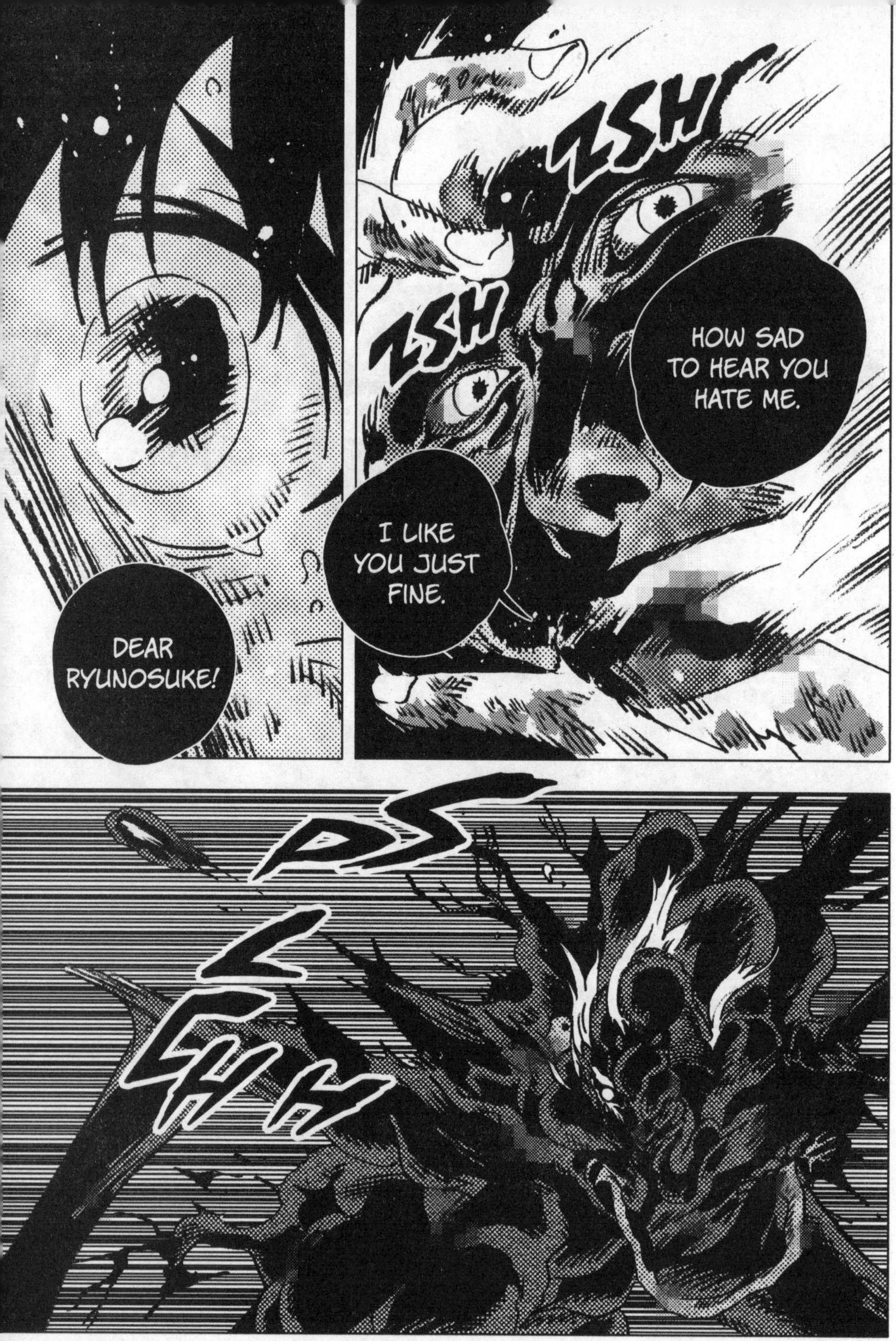
ZSH
ZSH
HOW SAD TO HEAR YOU HATE ME.
I LIKE YOU JUST FINE.
DEAR RYUNOSUKE!

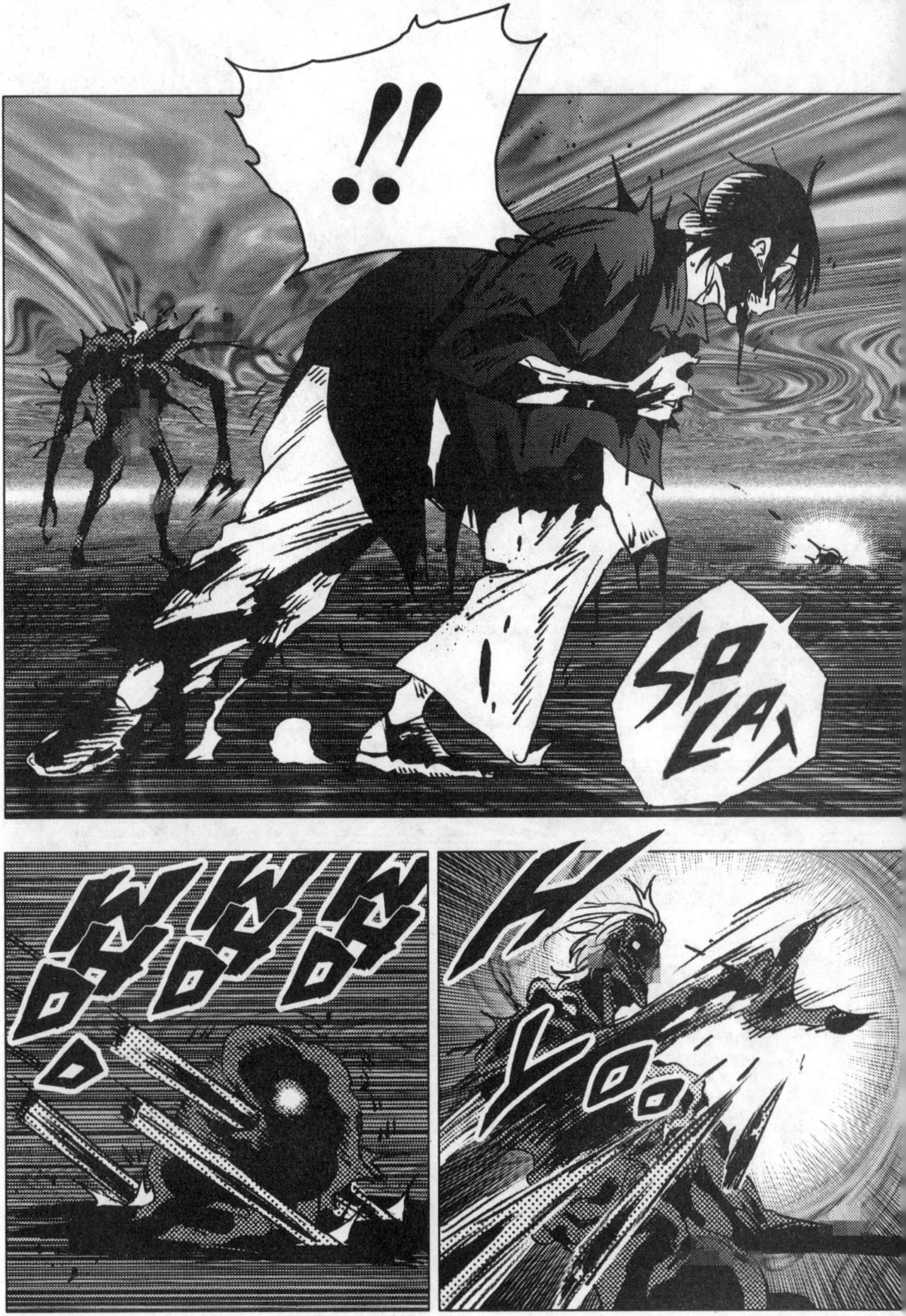
!!
SPLAT
HYOO

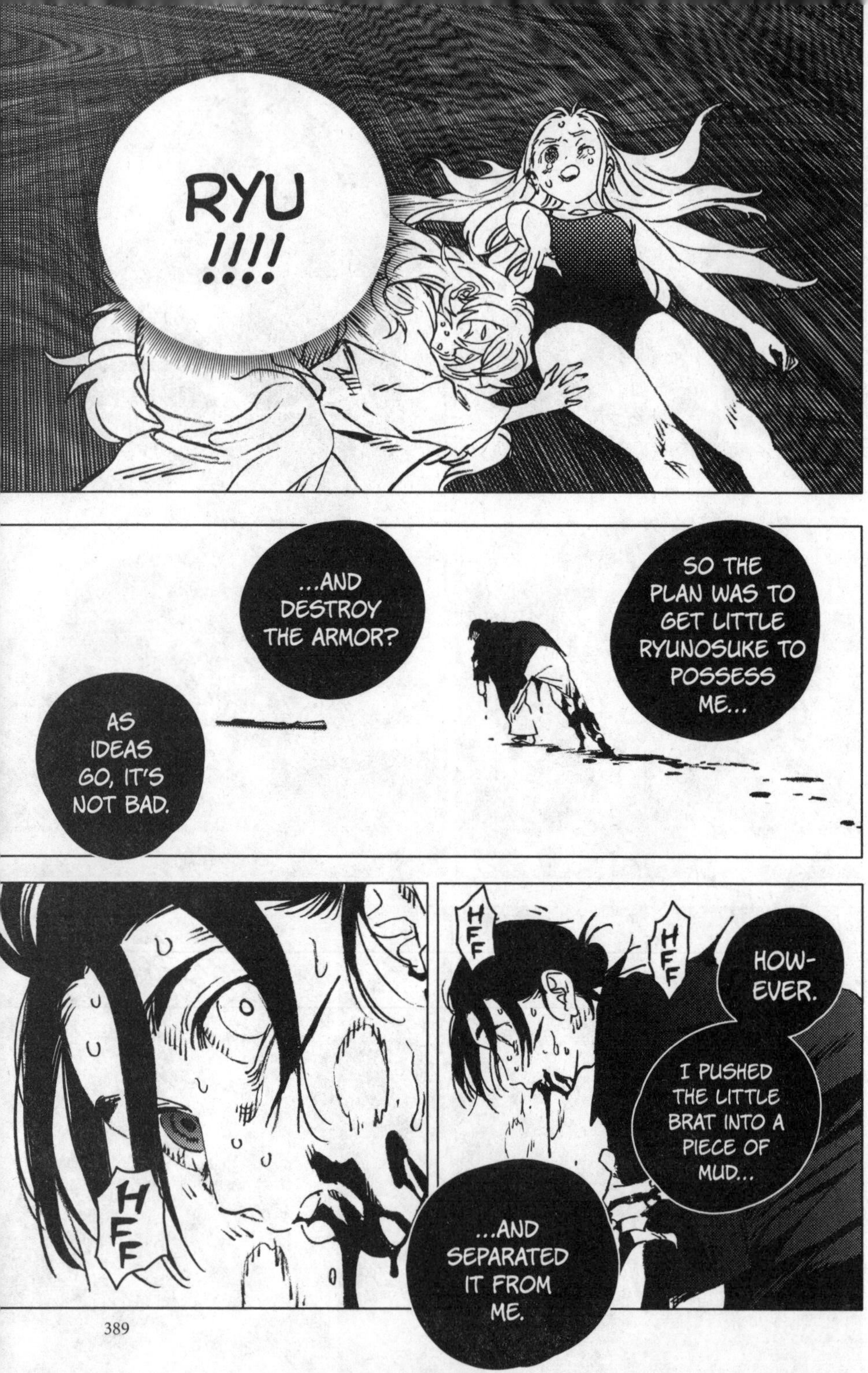
RYU !!!!
SO THE PLAN WAS TO GET LITTLE RYUNOSUKE TO POSSESS ME...
...AND DESTROY THE ARMOR?
AS IDEAS GO, IT'S NOT BAD.
HFF
HFF
HOW-EVER.
I PUSHED THE LITTLE BRAT INTO A PIECE OF MUD...
...AND SEPARATED IT FROM ME.
HFF

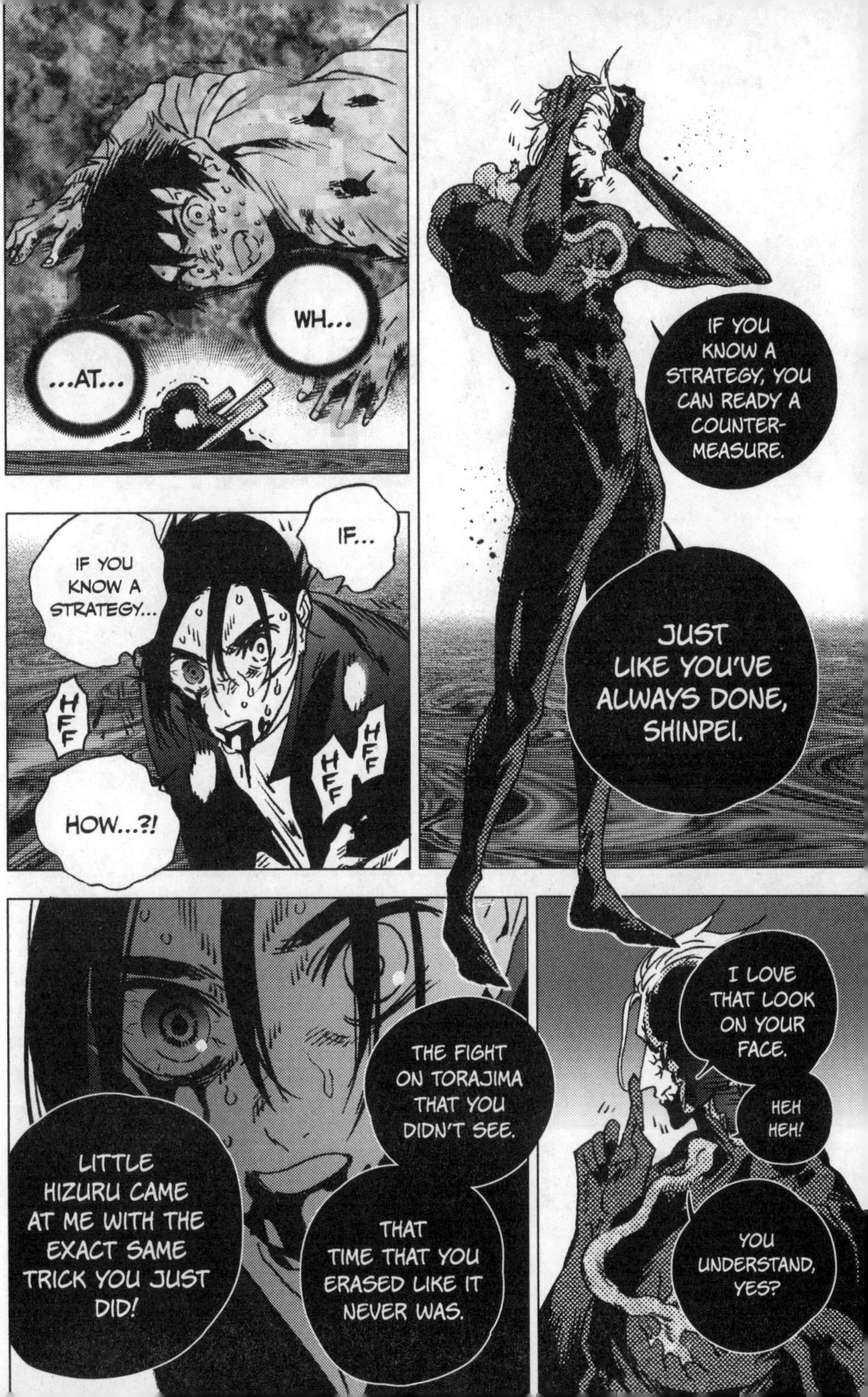
IF YOU KNOW A STRATEGY, YOU CAN READY A COUNTER-MEASURE.
JUST LIKE YOU'VE ALWAYS DONE, SHINPEI.
WH...
...AT...
IF...
IF YOU KNOW A STRATEGY...
HFF
HFF
HFF
HOW...?!
I LOVE THAT LOOK ON YOUR FACE.
HEH HEH!
YOU UNDERSTAND, YES?
THE FIGHT ON TORAJIMA THAT YOU DIDN'T SEE.
THAT TIME THAT YOU ERASED LIKE IT NEVER WAS.
LITTLE HIZURU CAME AT ME WITH THE EXACT SAME TRICK YOU JUST DID!

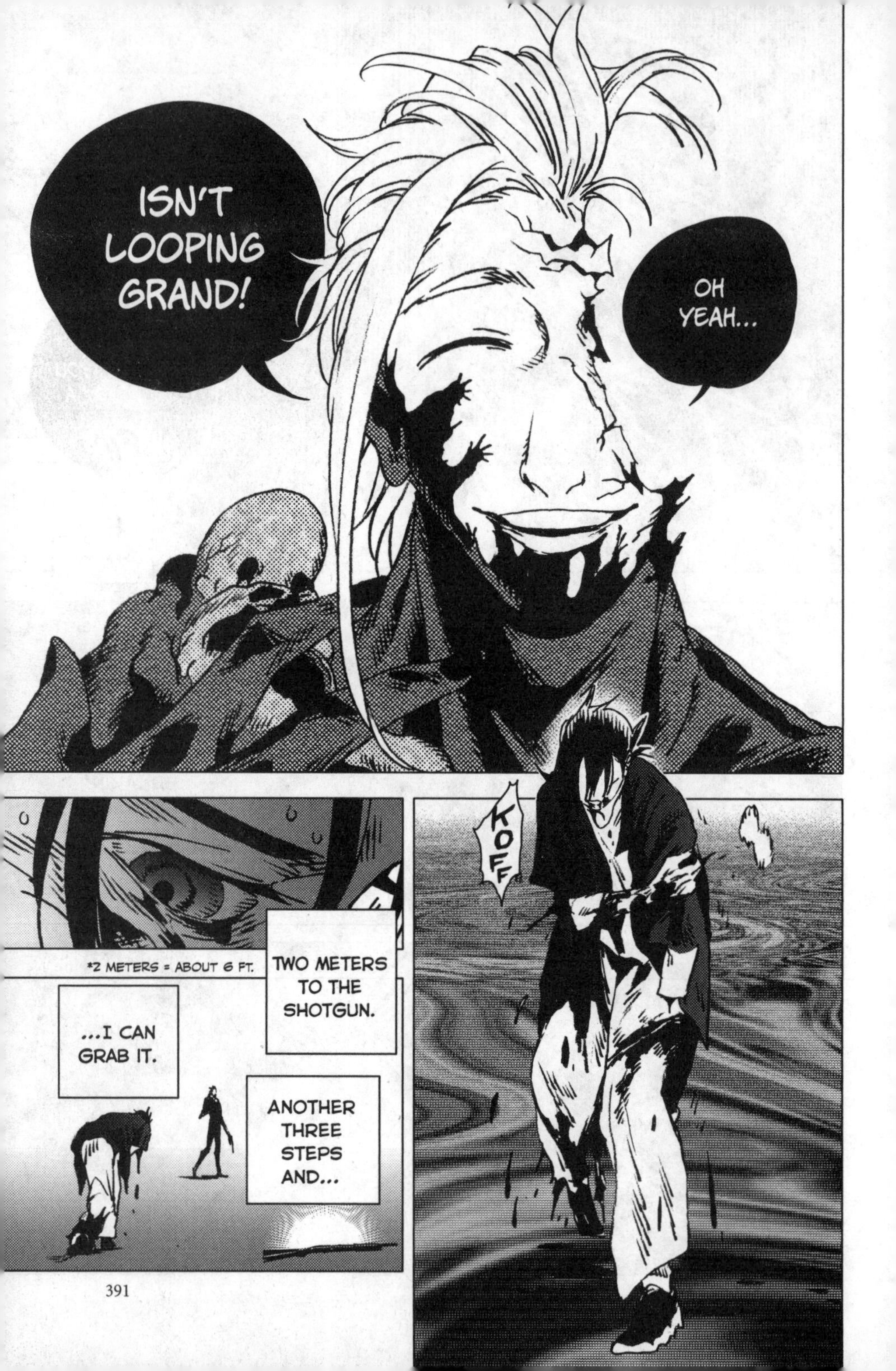

ISN'T LOOPING GRAND!
OH YEAH...
KOFF
TWO METERS TO THE SHOTGUN.
*2 METERS = ABOUT 6 FT.
ANOTHER THREE STEPS AND...
...I CAN GRAB IT.

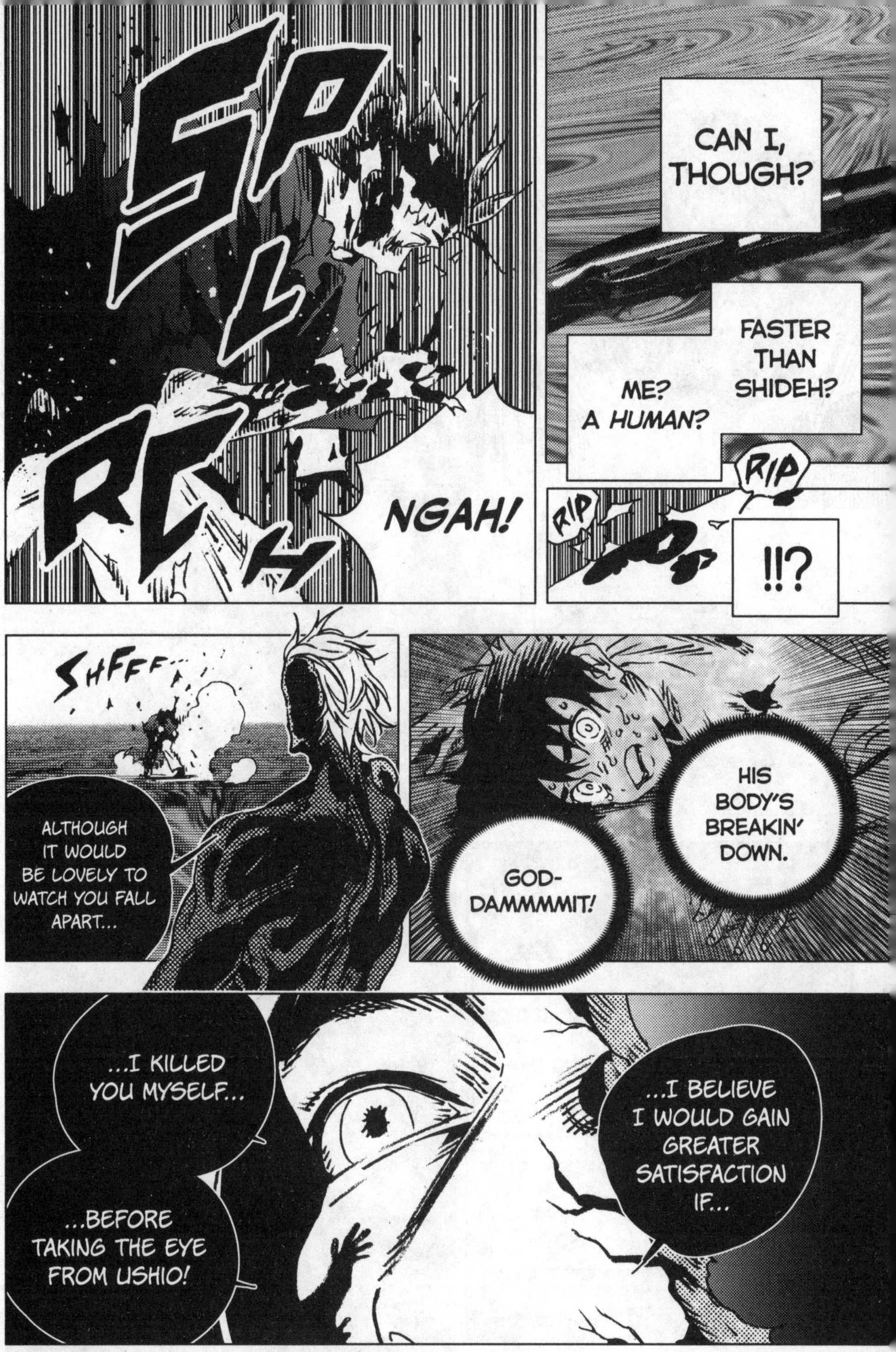
CAN I, THOUGH?
FASTER THAN SHIDEH?
ME? A HUMAN?
RIP
RIP
!!?
SPLRCH
NGAH!
HIS BODY'S BREAKIN' DOWN.
GOD-DAMMMMIT!
SHFFF...
ALTHOUGH IT WOULD BE LOVELY TO WATCH YOU FALL APART...
...I BELIEVE I WOULD GAIN GREATER SATISFACTION IF...
...I KILLED YOU MYSELF...
...BEFORE TAKING THE EYE FROM USHIO!

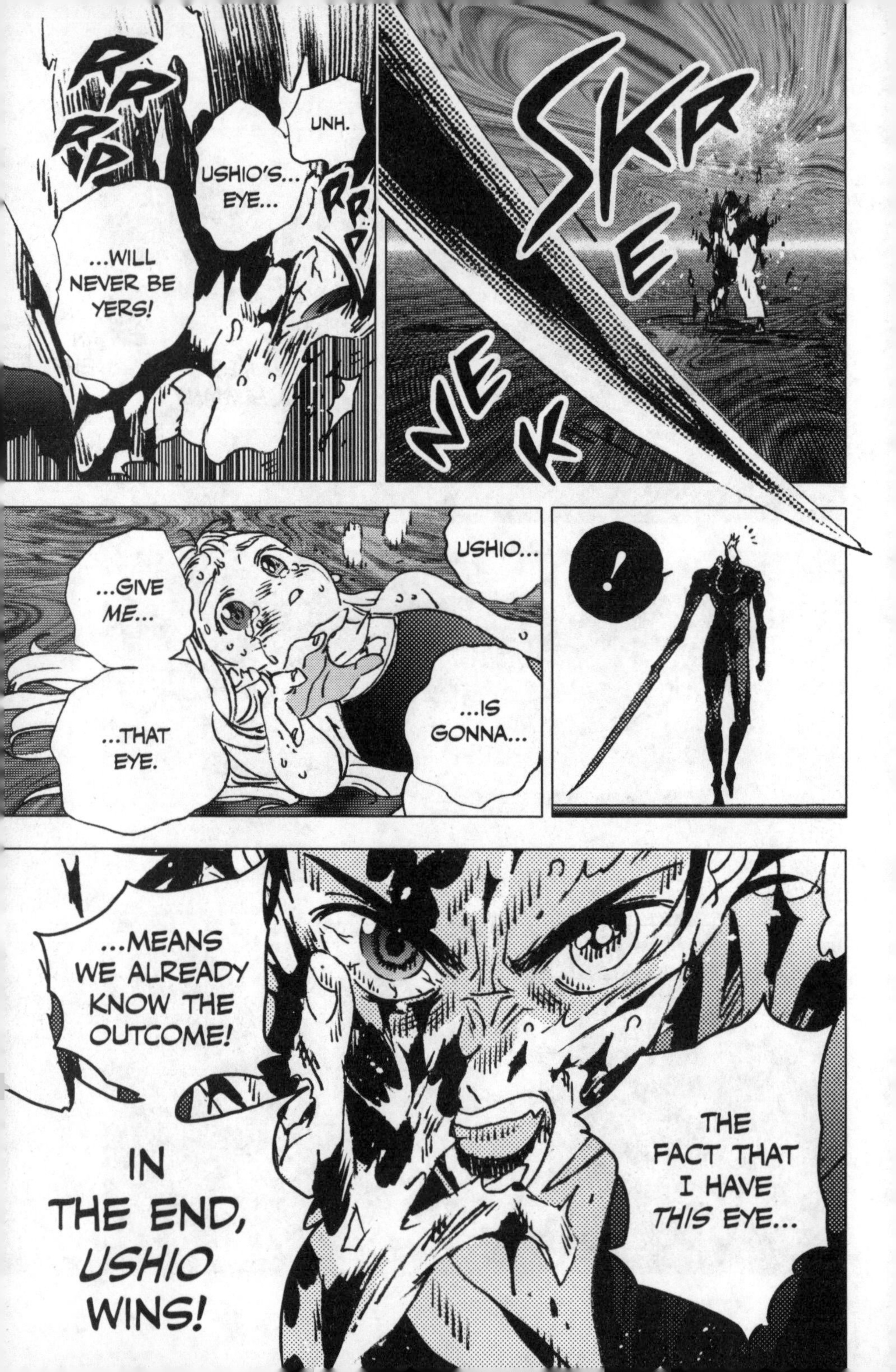
UNH.
USHIO'S... EYE...
...WILL NEVER BE YERS!
!
USHIO...
...IS GONNA...
...GIVE ME...
...THAT EYE.
THE FACT THAT I HAVE *THIS* EYE...
...MEANS WE ALREADY KNOW THE OUTCOME!
IN THE END, *USHIO* WINS!

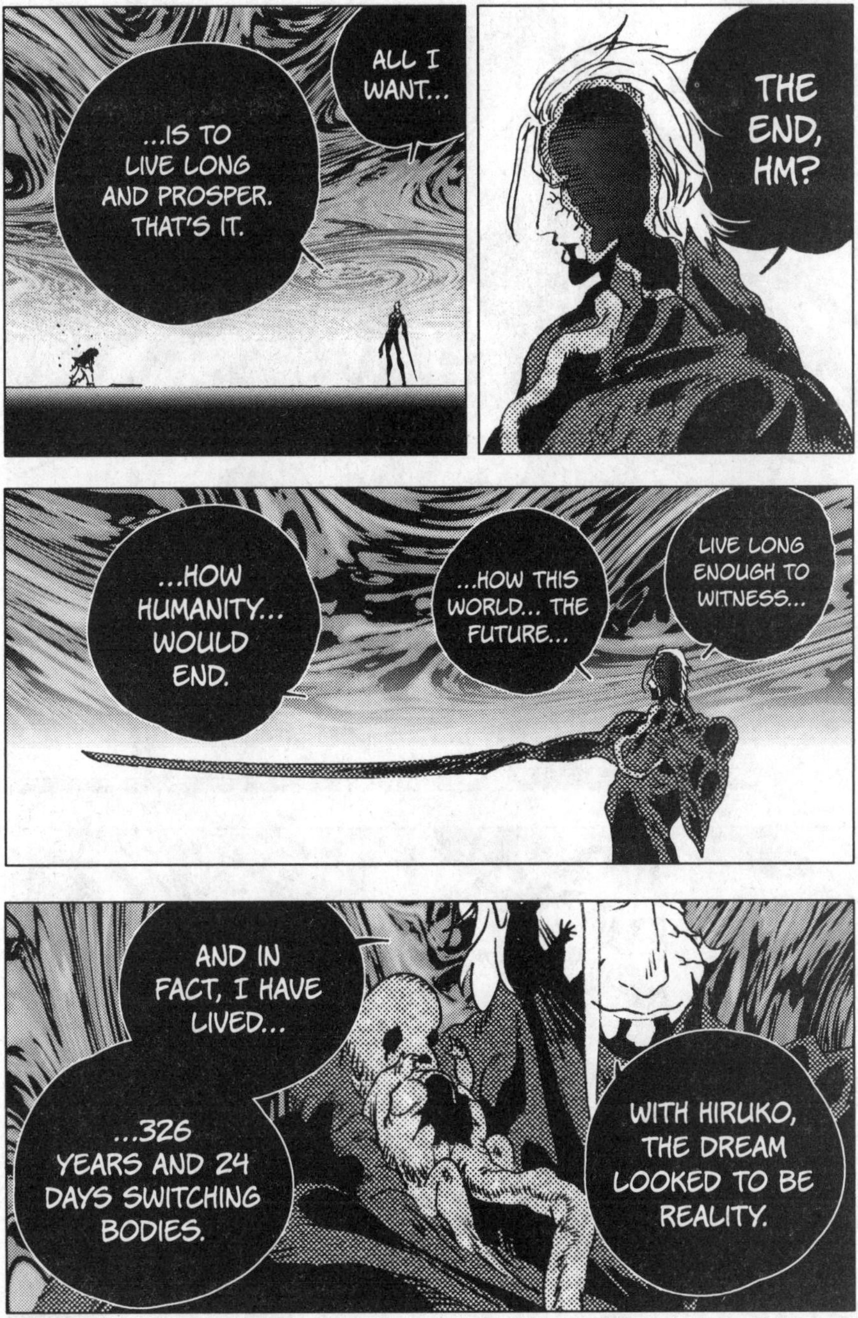
THE END, HM?
ALL I WANT...
...IS TO LIVE LONG AND PROSPER. THAT'S IT.
LIVE LONG ENOUGH TO WITNESS...
...HOW THIS WORLD... THE FUTURE...
...HOW HUMANITY... WOULD END.
AND IN FACT, I HAVE LIVED...
...326 YEARS AND 24 DAYS SWITCHING BODIES.
WITH HIRUKO, THE DREAM LOOKED TO BE REALITY.

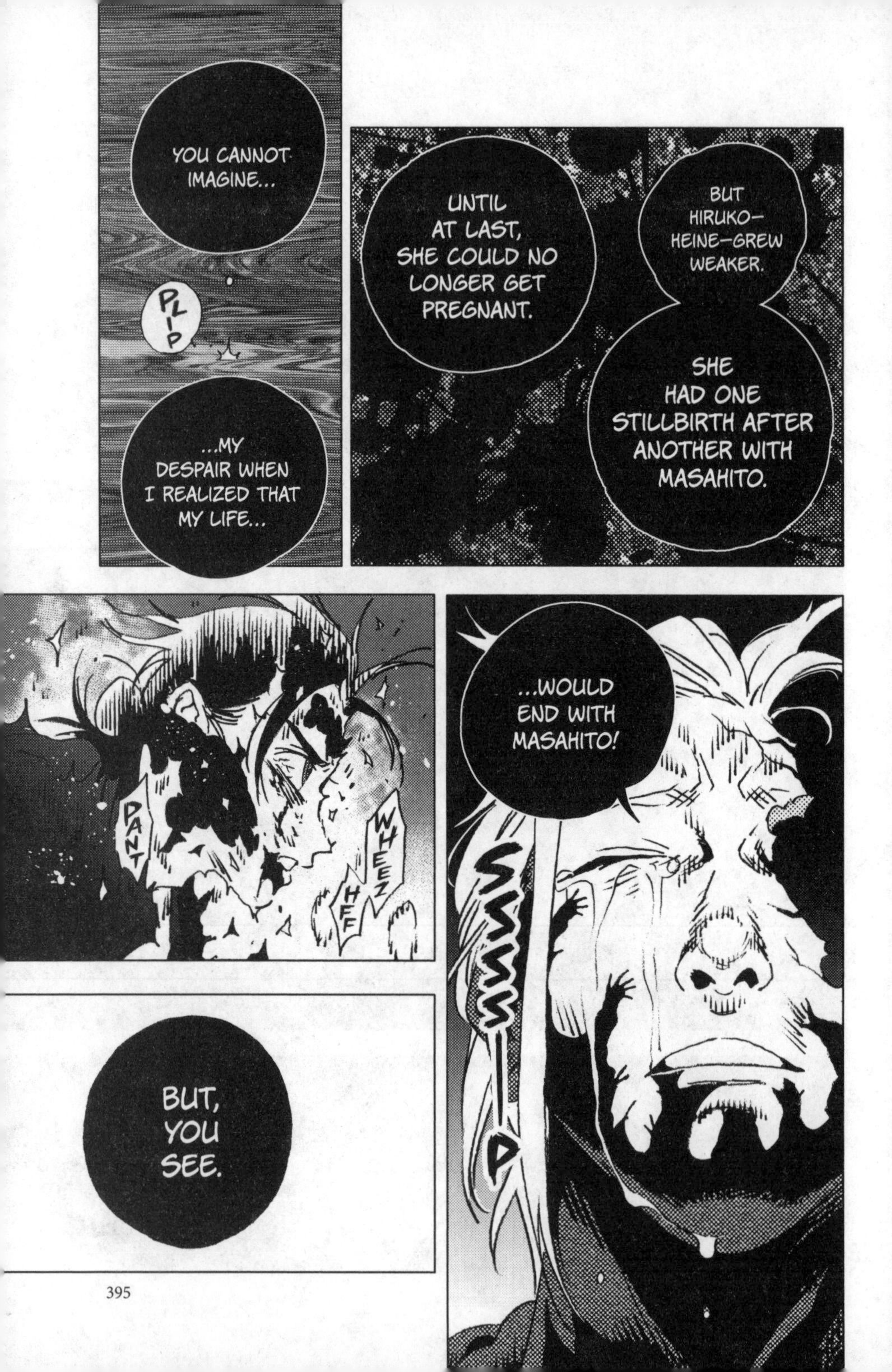
BUT HIRUKO—HEINE—GREW WEAKER.
SHE HAD ONE STILLBIRTH AFTER ANOTHER WITH MASAHITO.
UNTIL AT LAST, SHE COULD NO LONGER GET PREGNANT.
YOU CANNOT IMAGINE...
PLIP
...MY DESPAIR WHEN I REALIZED THAT MY LIFE...
...WOULD END WITH MASAHITO!
SSSSP
WHEEZ
HFF
PANT
BUT, YOU SEE.

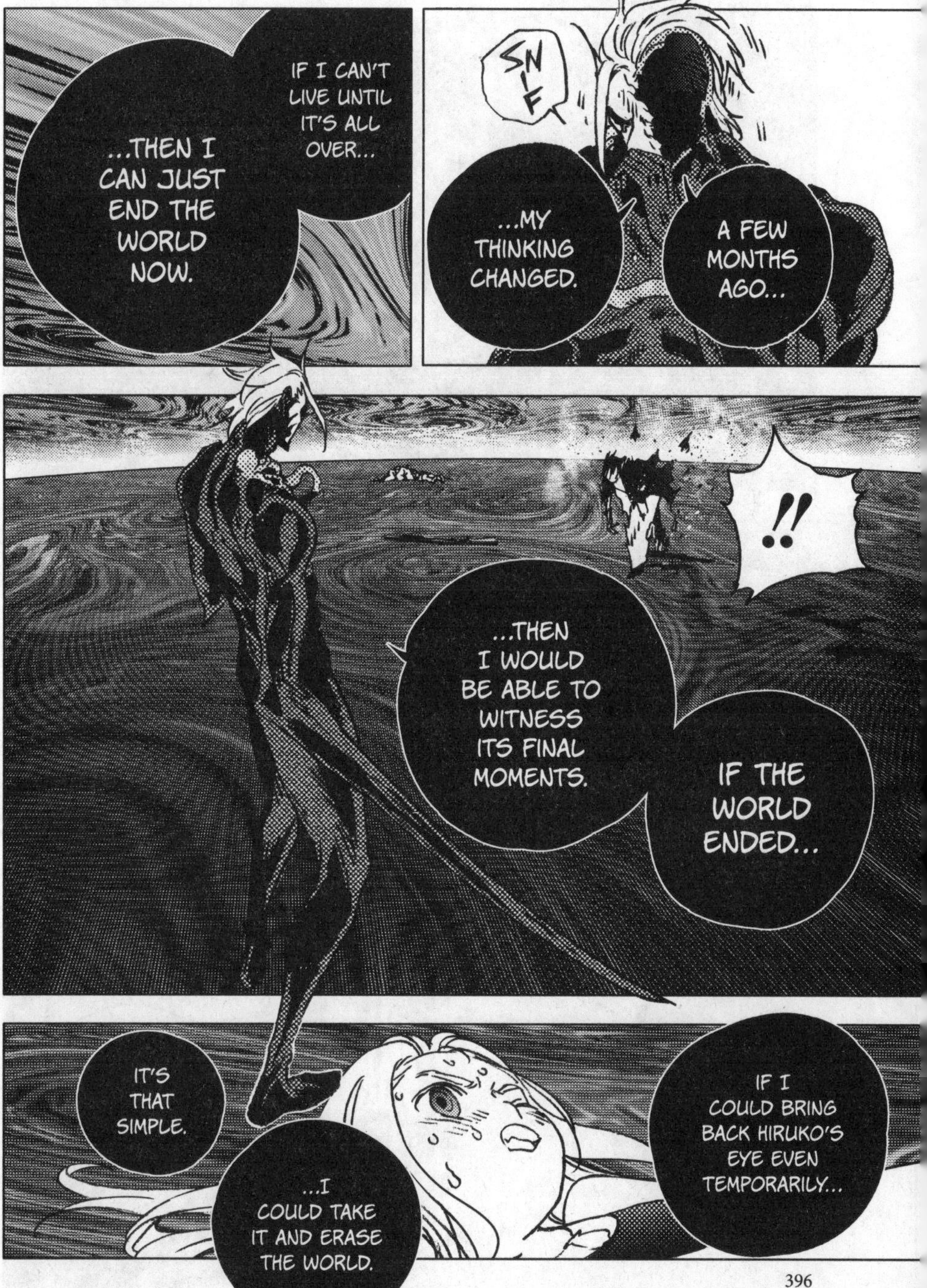
SNIF
A FEW MONTHS AGO...
...MY THINKING CHANGED.
IF I CAN'T LIVE UNTIL IT'S ALL OVER...
...THEN I CAN JUST END THE WORLD NOW.
!!
IF THE WORLD ENDED...
...THEN I WOULD BE ABLE TO WITNESS ITS FINAL MOMENTS.
IF I COULD BRING BACK HIRUKO'S EYE EVEN TEMPORARILY...
...I COULD TAKE IT AND ERASE THE WORLD.
IT'S THAT SIMPLE.

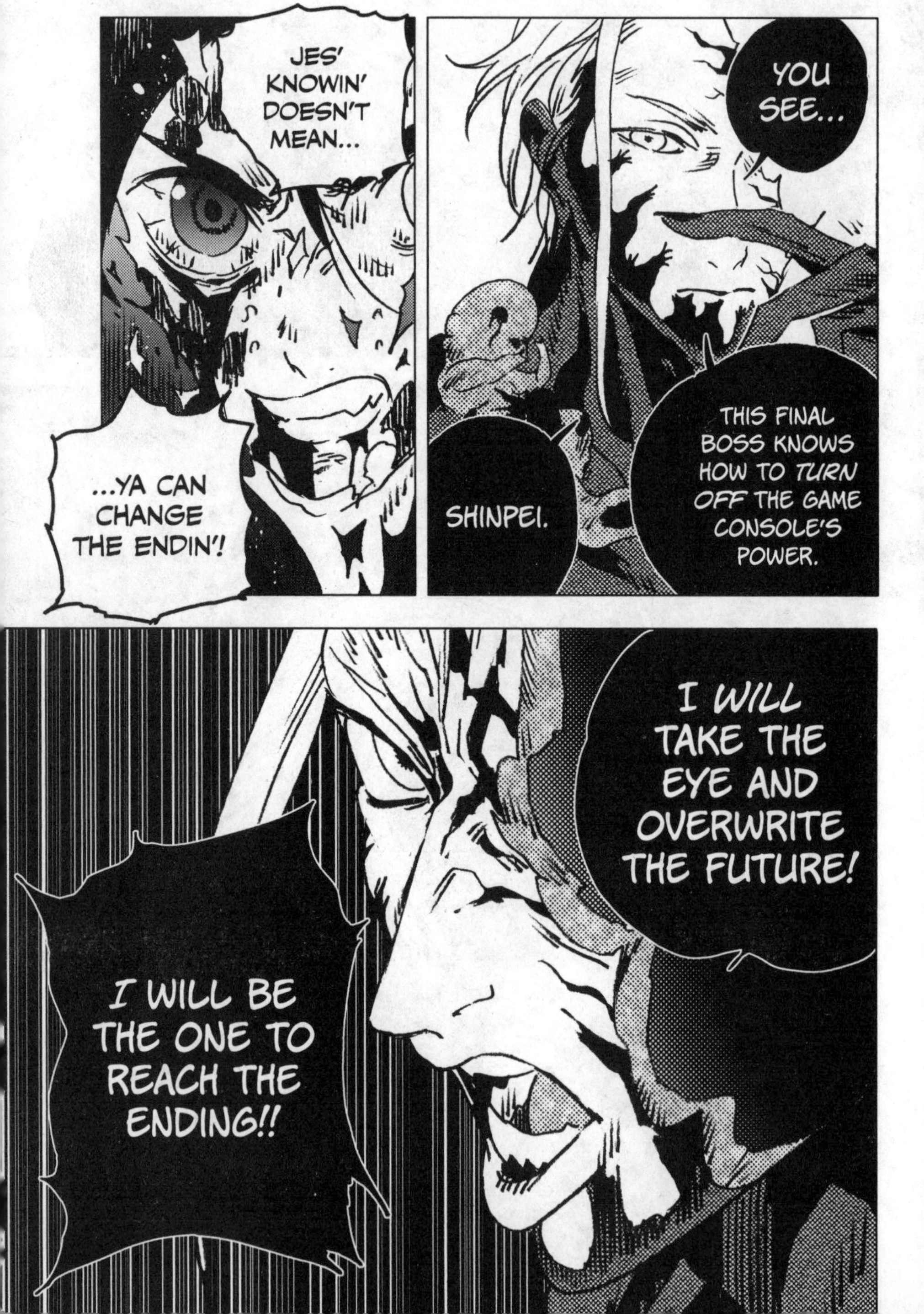
YOU SEE...
THIS FINAL BOSS KNOWS HOW TO *TURN OFF* THE GAME CONSOLE'S POWER.
SHINPEI.
JES' KNOWIN' DOESN'T MEAN...
...YA CAN CHANGE THE ENDIN'!
I *WILL* TAKE THE EYE AND OVERWRITE THE FUTURE!
I WILL BE THE ONE TO REACH THE ENDING!!

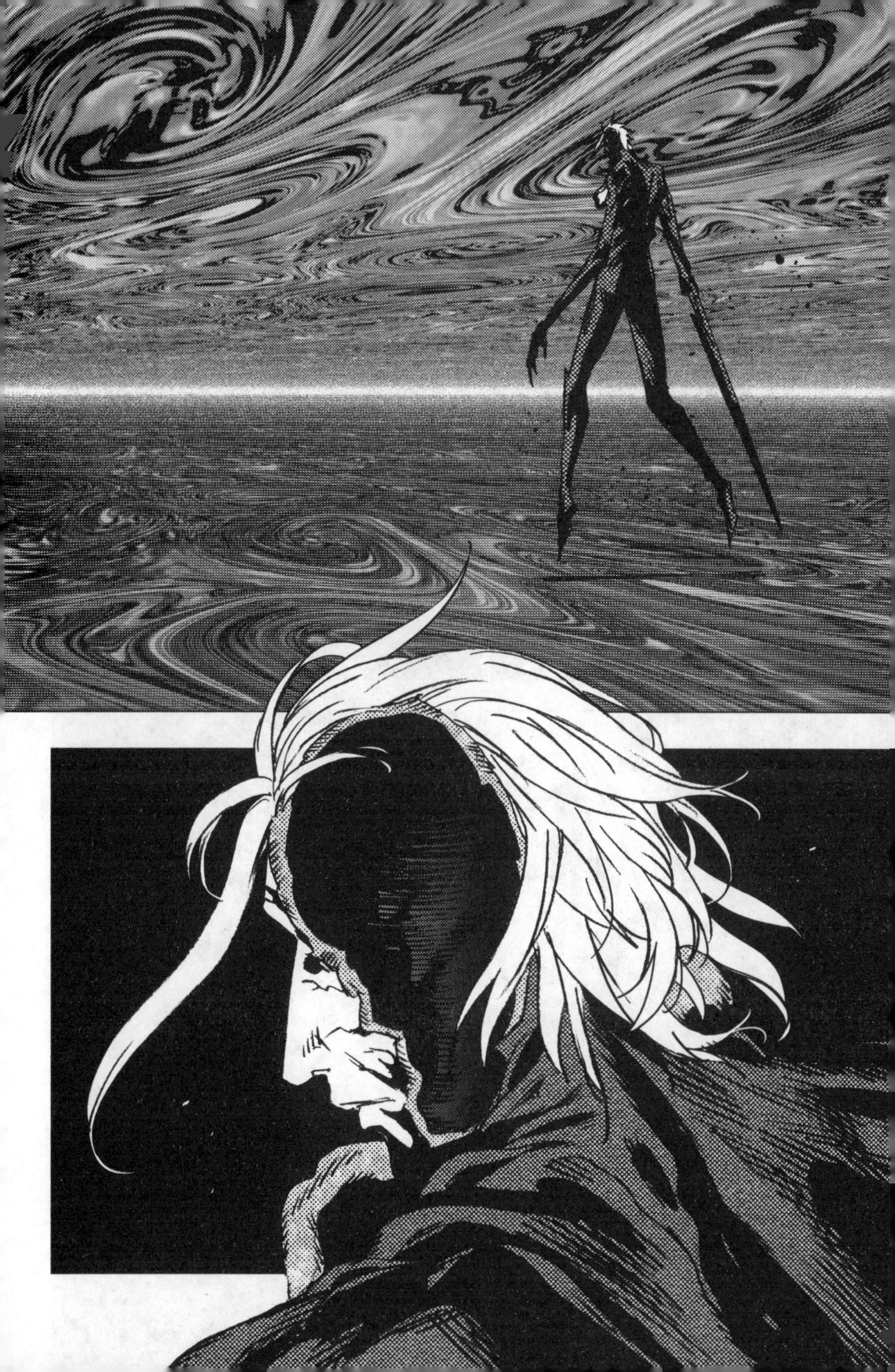

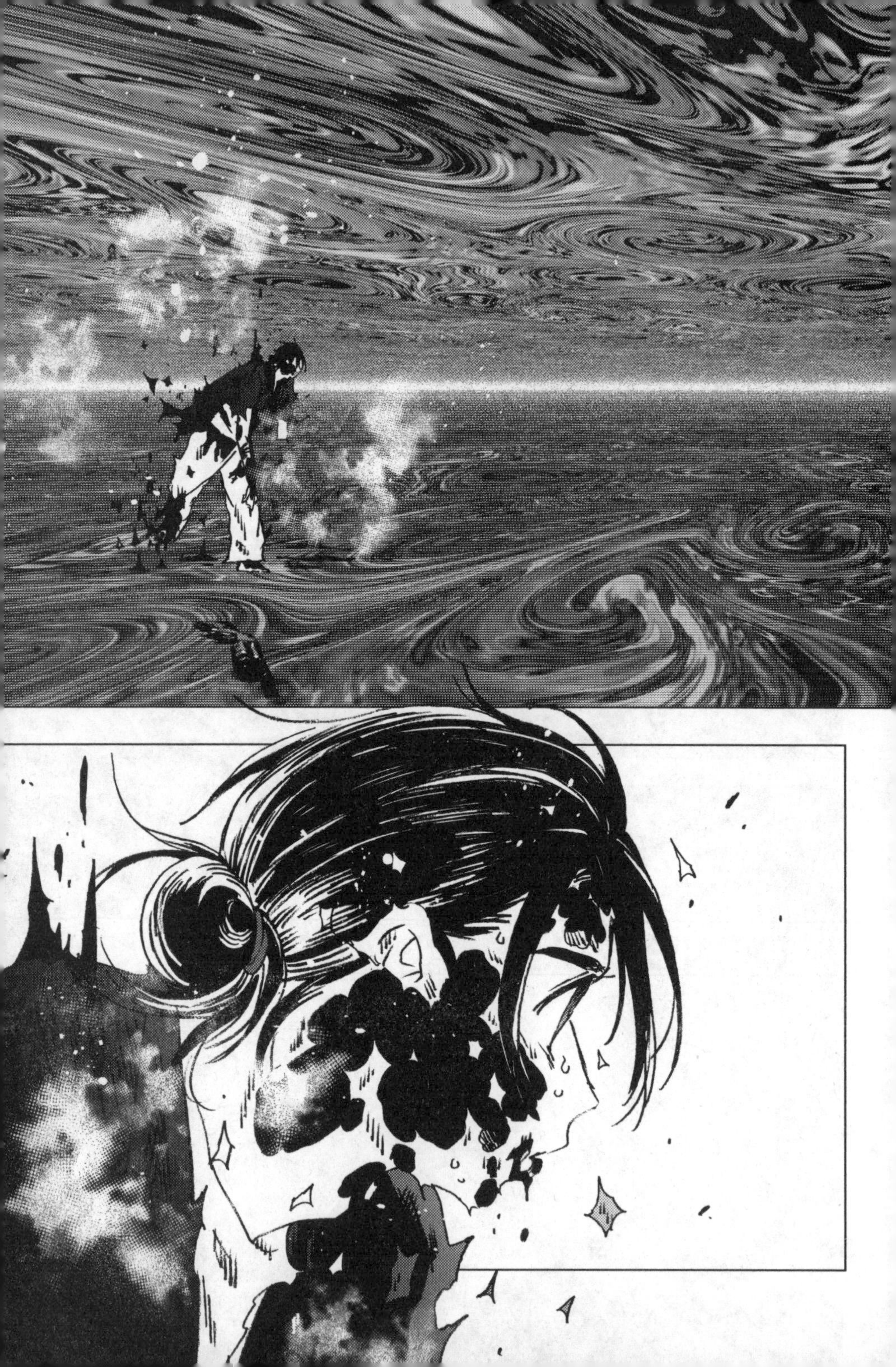

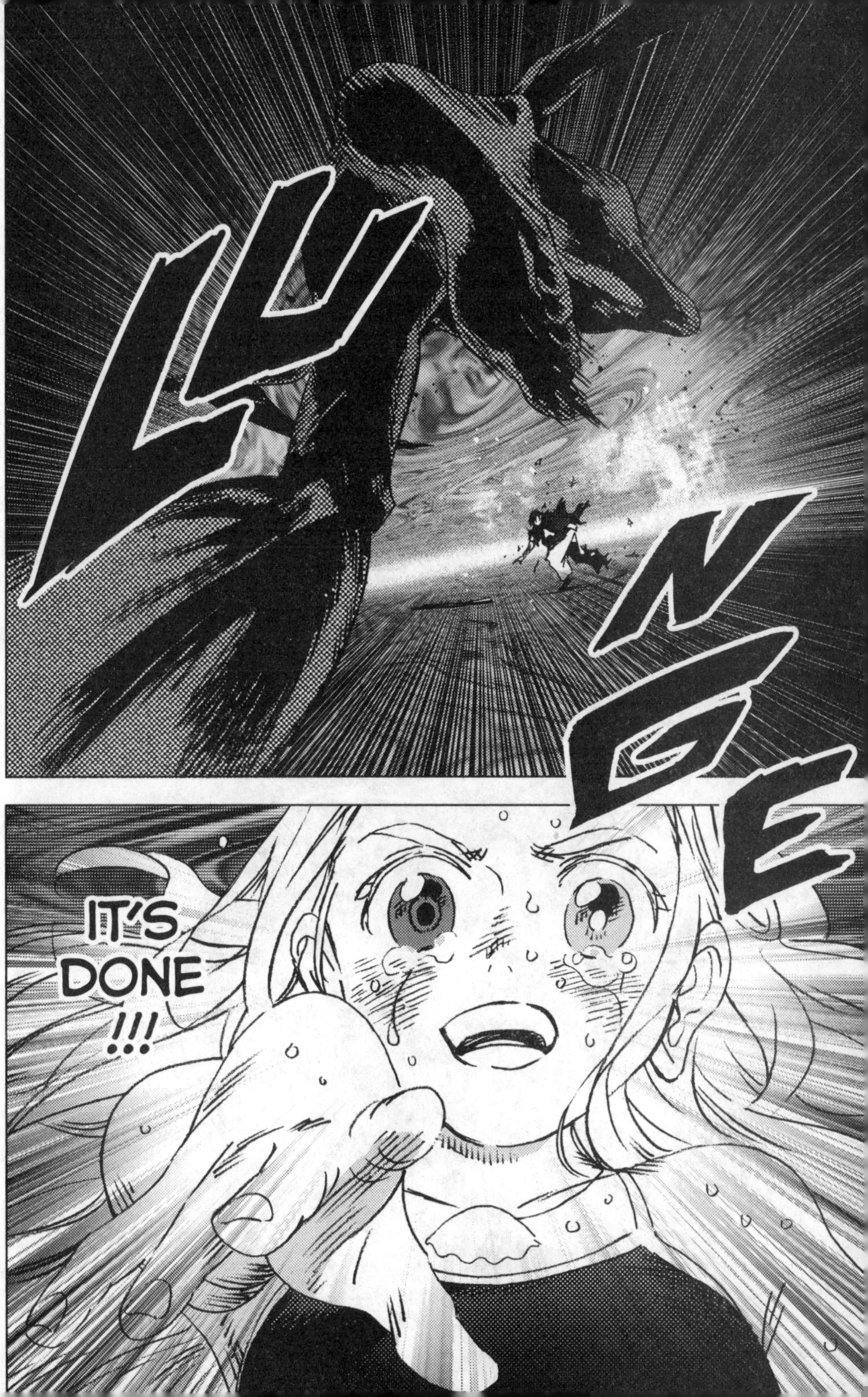
LUNGE
IT'S DONE !!!

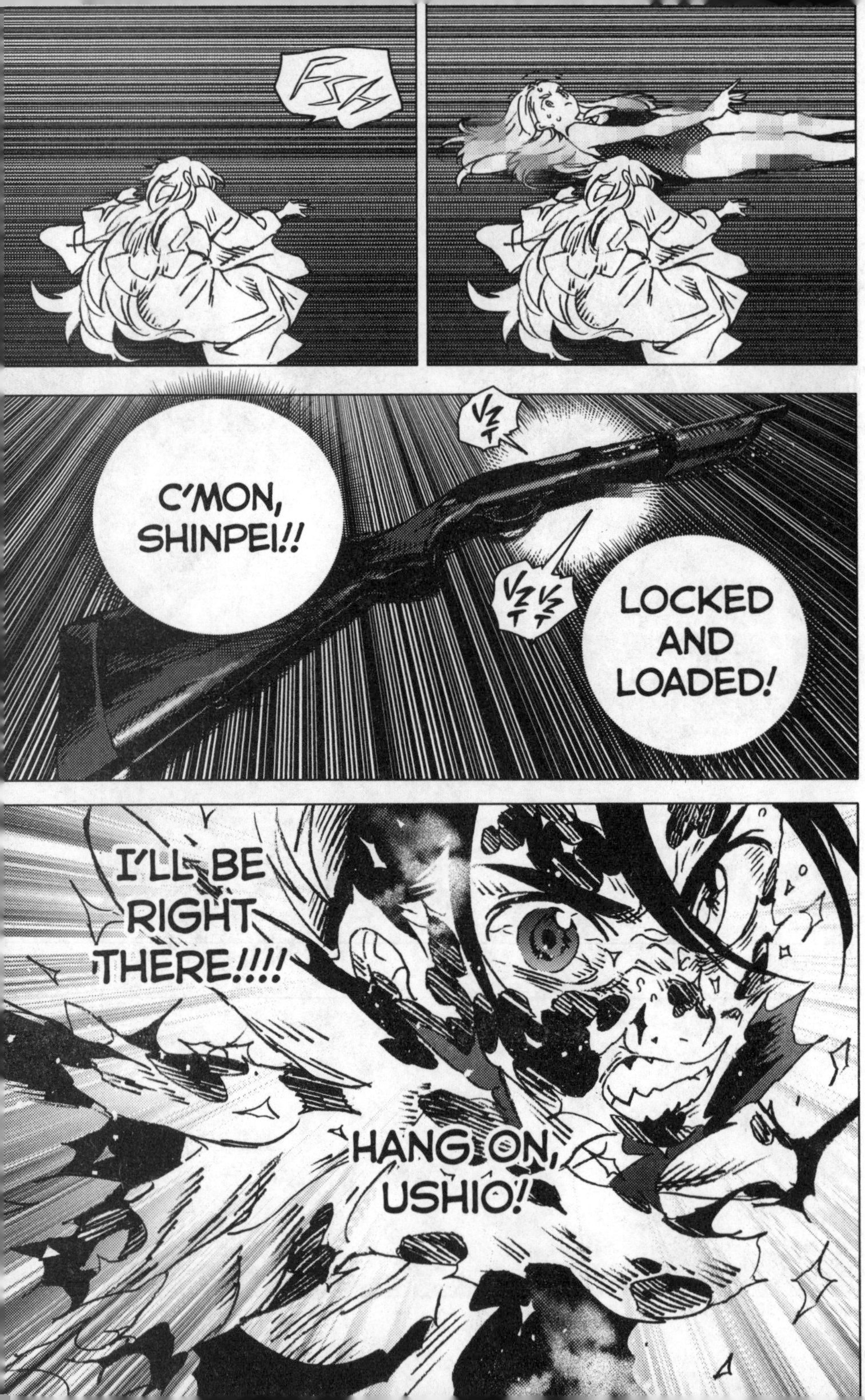
FSH
VZT
VZT VZT
LOCKED AND LOADED!
C'MON, SHINPEI!!
I'LL BE RIGHT THERE!!!!
HANG ON, USHIO!

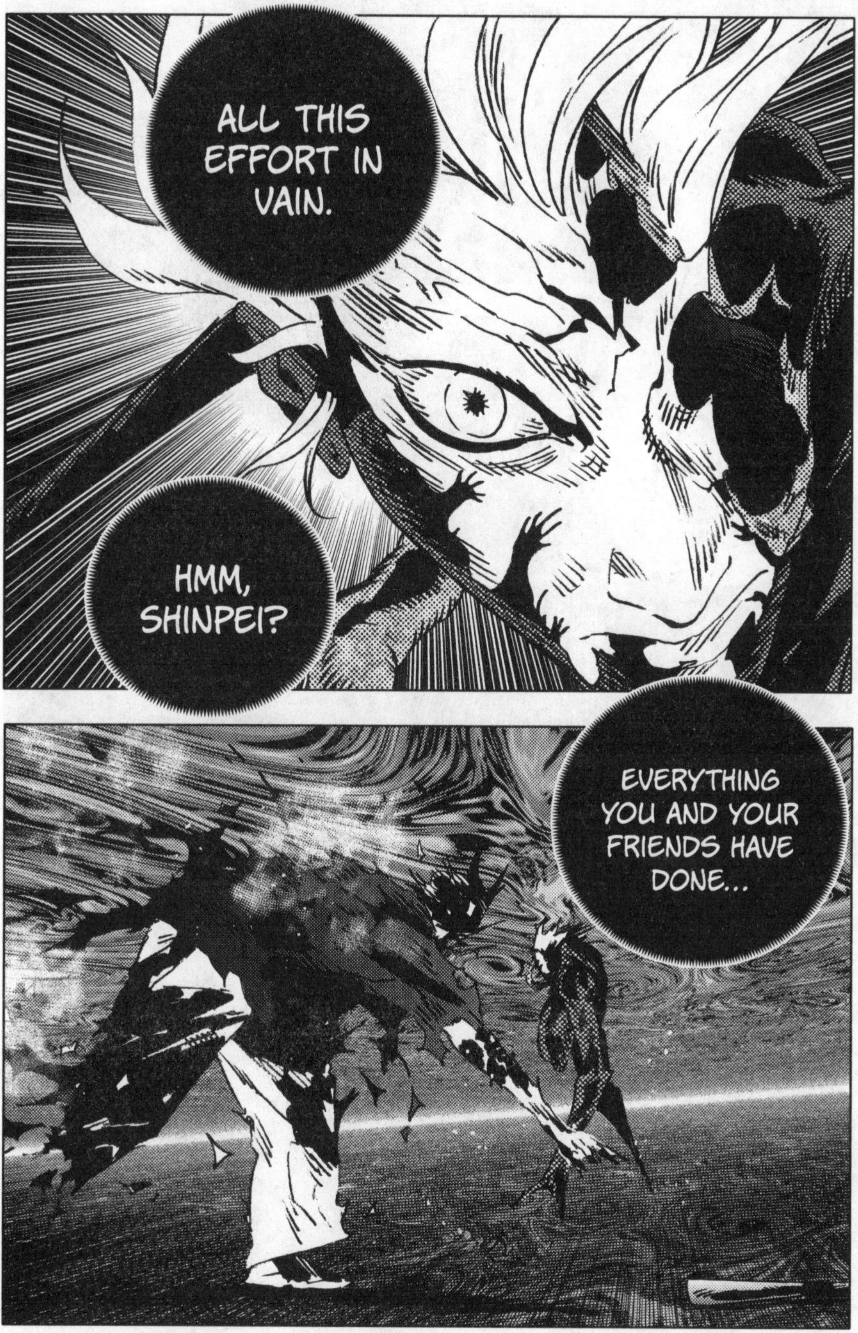
ALL THIS EFFORT IN VAIN.
HMM, SHINPEI?
EVERYTHING YOU AND YOUR FRIENDS HAVE DONE...

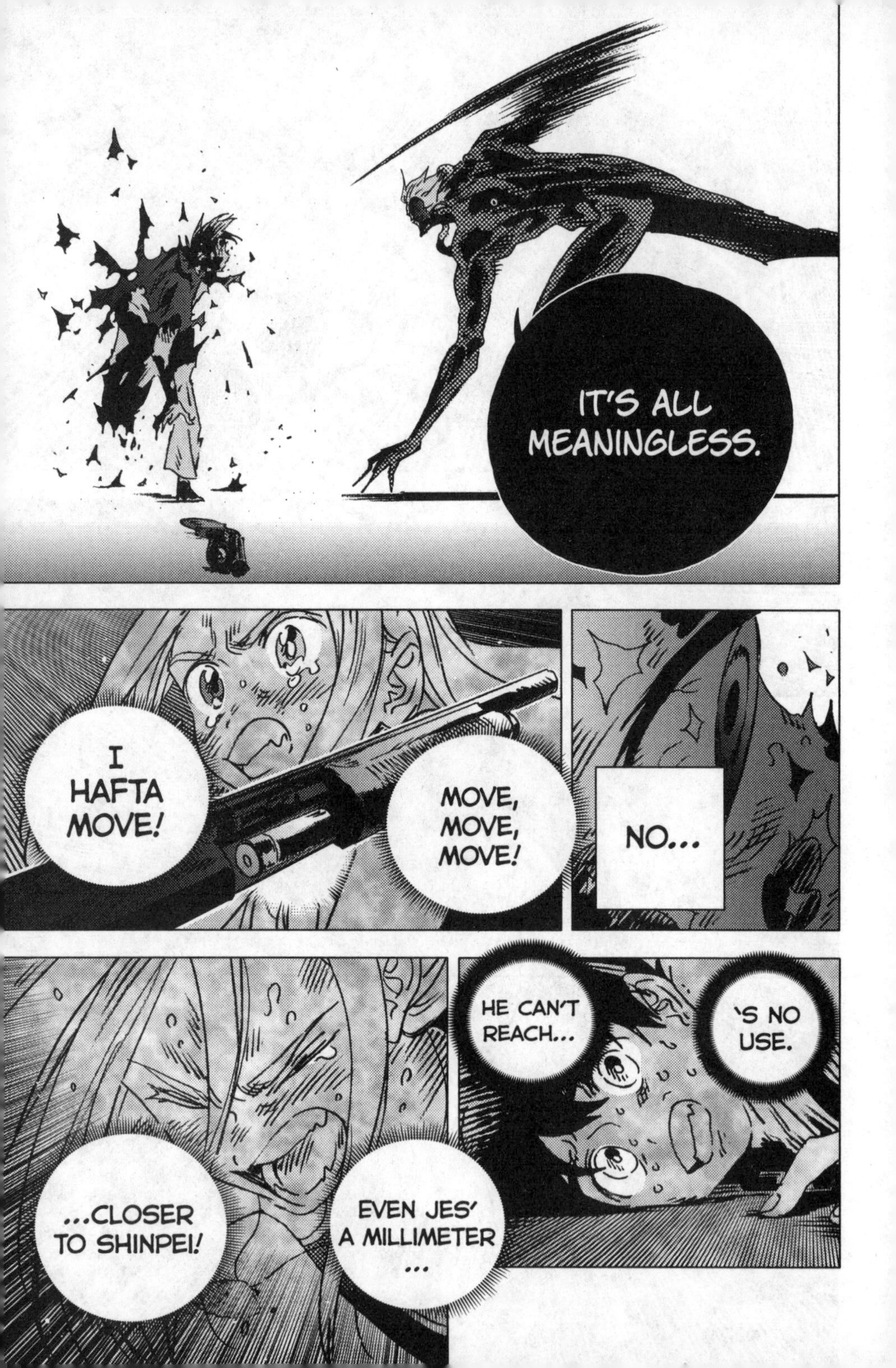
IT'S ALL MEANINGLESS.
NO...
MOVE, MOVE, MOVE!
I HAFTA MOVE!
'S NO USE.
HE CAN'T REACH...
EVEN JES' A MILLIMETER ...
...CLOSER TO SHINPEI!

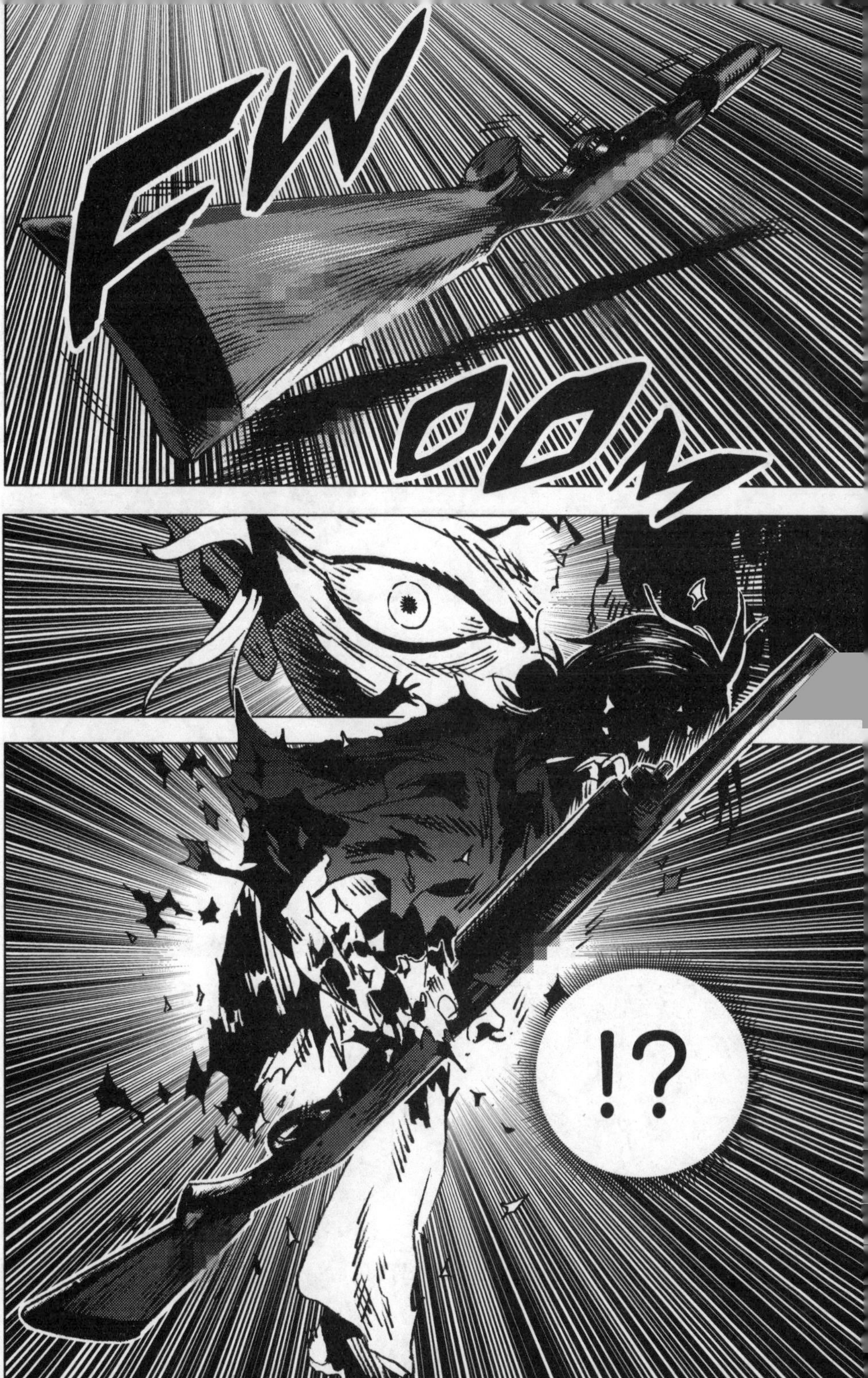
FWOOM
!?

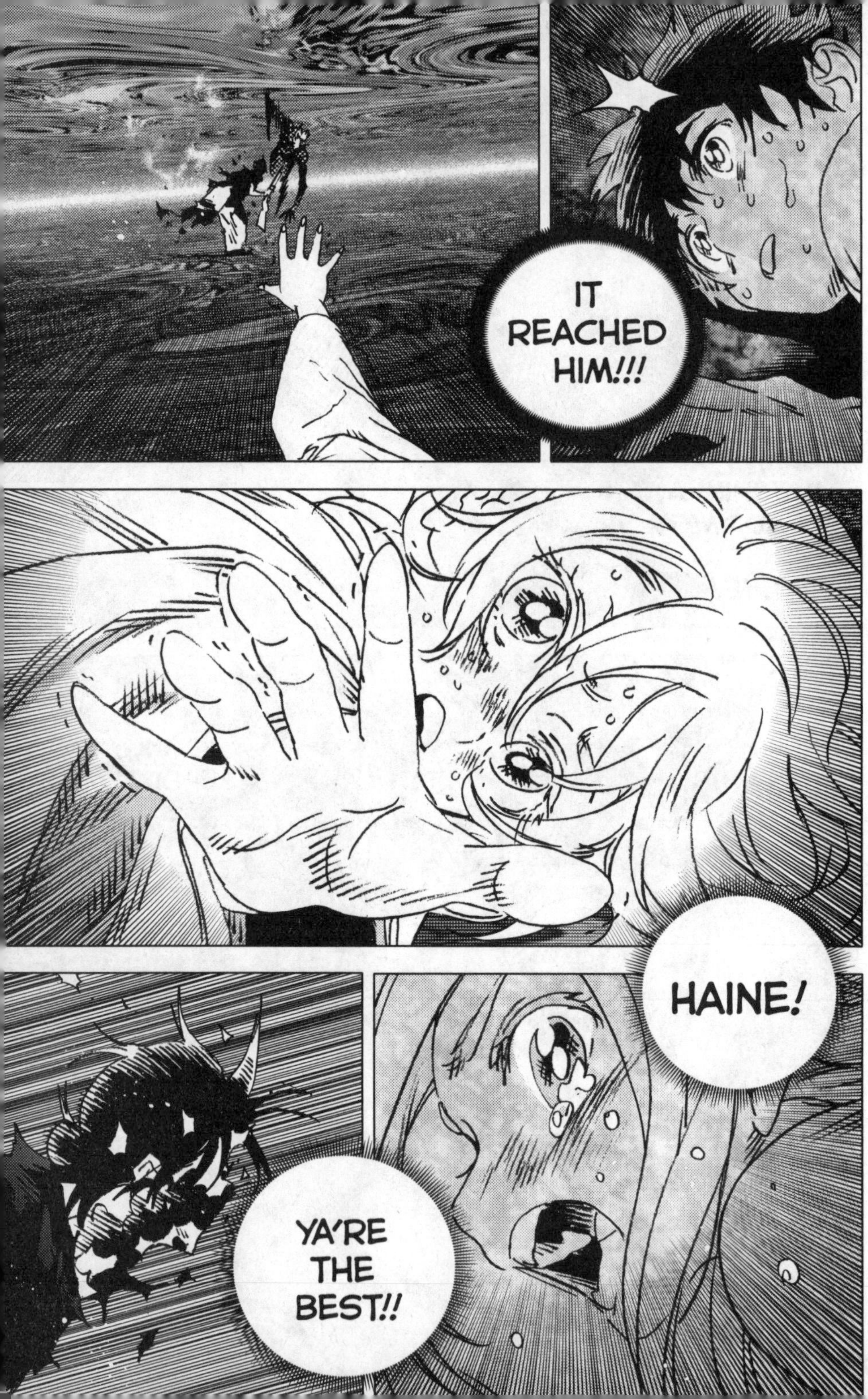
IT REACHED HIM!!!
HAINE!
YA'RE THE BEST!!

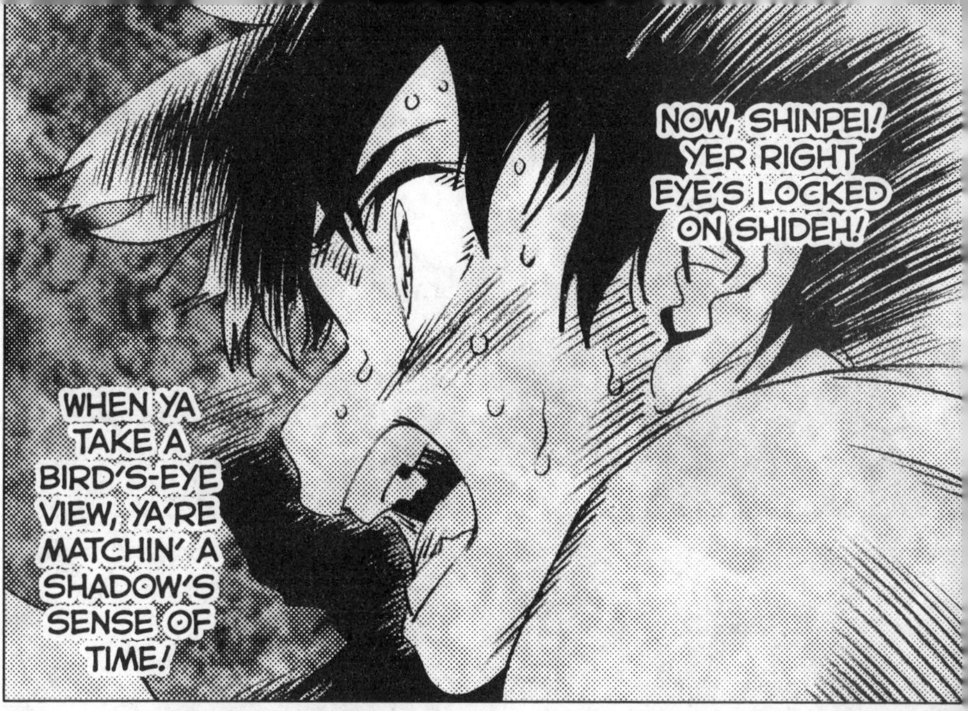
NOW, SHINPEI! YER RIGHT EYE'S LOCKED ON SHIDEH!
WHEN YA TAKE A BIRD'S-EYE VIEW, YA'RE MATCHIN' A SHADOW'S SENSE OF TIME!

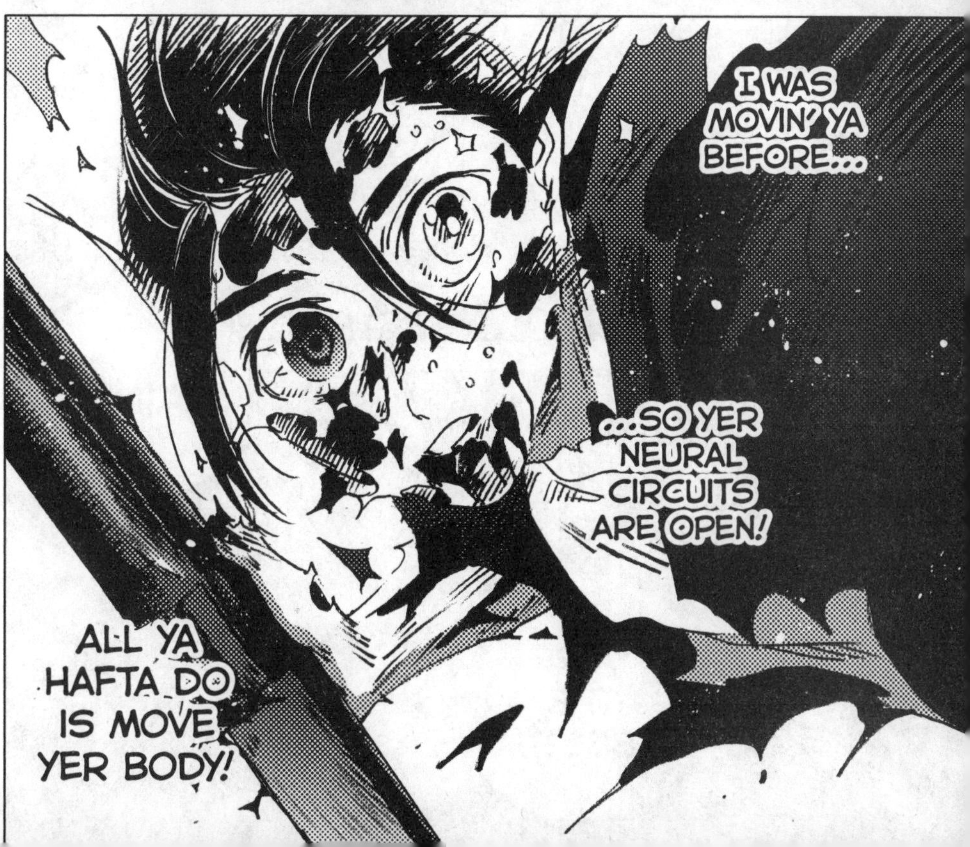
I WAS MOVIN' YA BEFORE...
...SO YER NEURAL CIRCUITS ARE OPEN!
ALL YA HAFTA DO IS MOVE YER BODY!

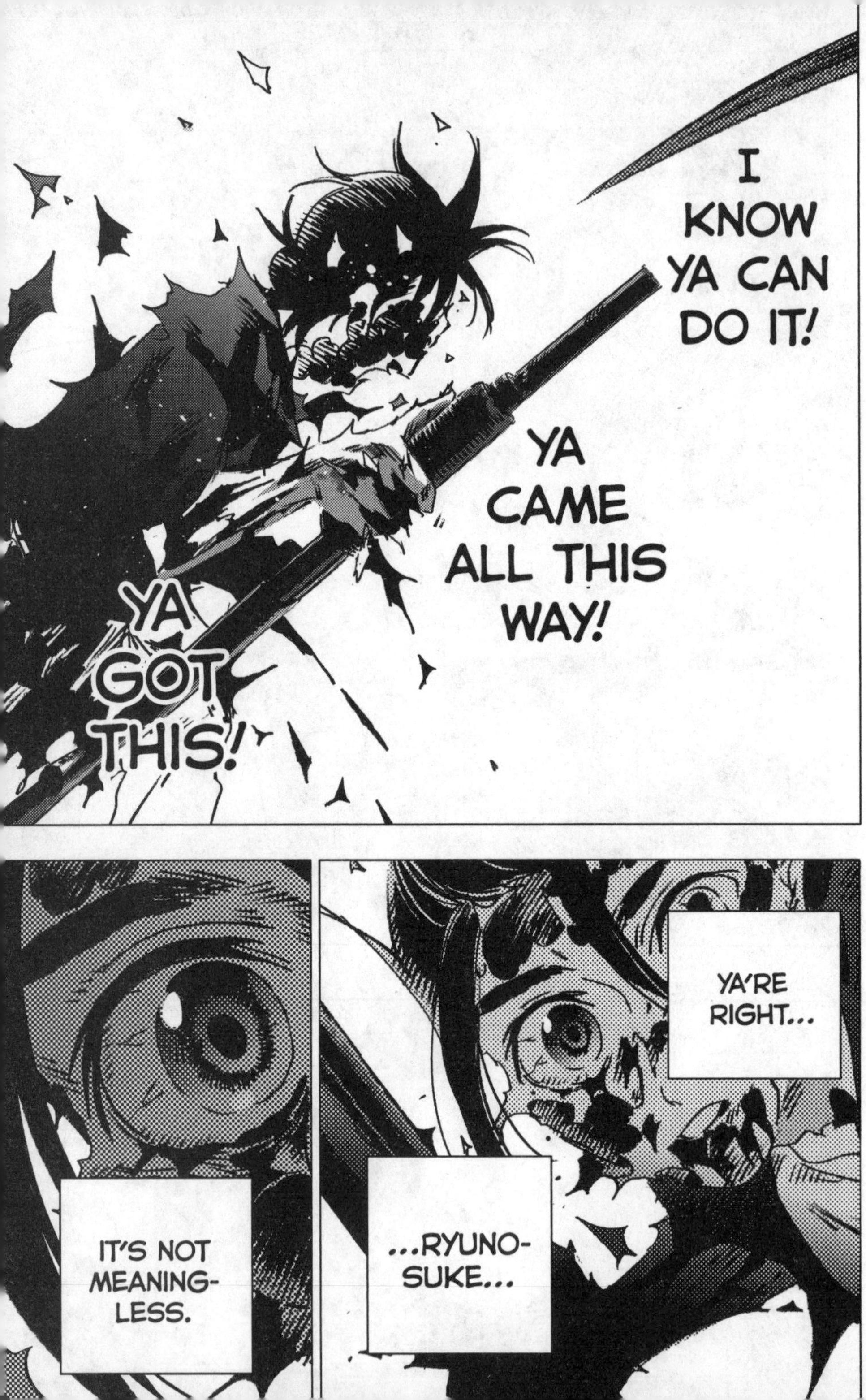
I KNOW YA CAN DO IT!
YA CAME ALL THIS WAY!
YA GOT THIS!
YA'RE RIGHT...
...RYUNO-SUKE...
IT'S NOT MEANING-LESS.

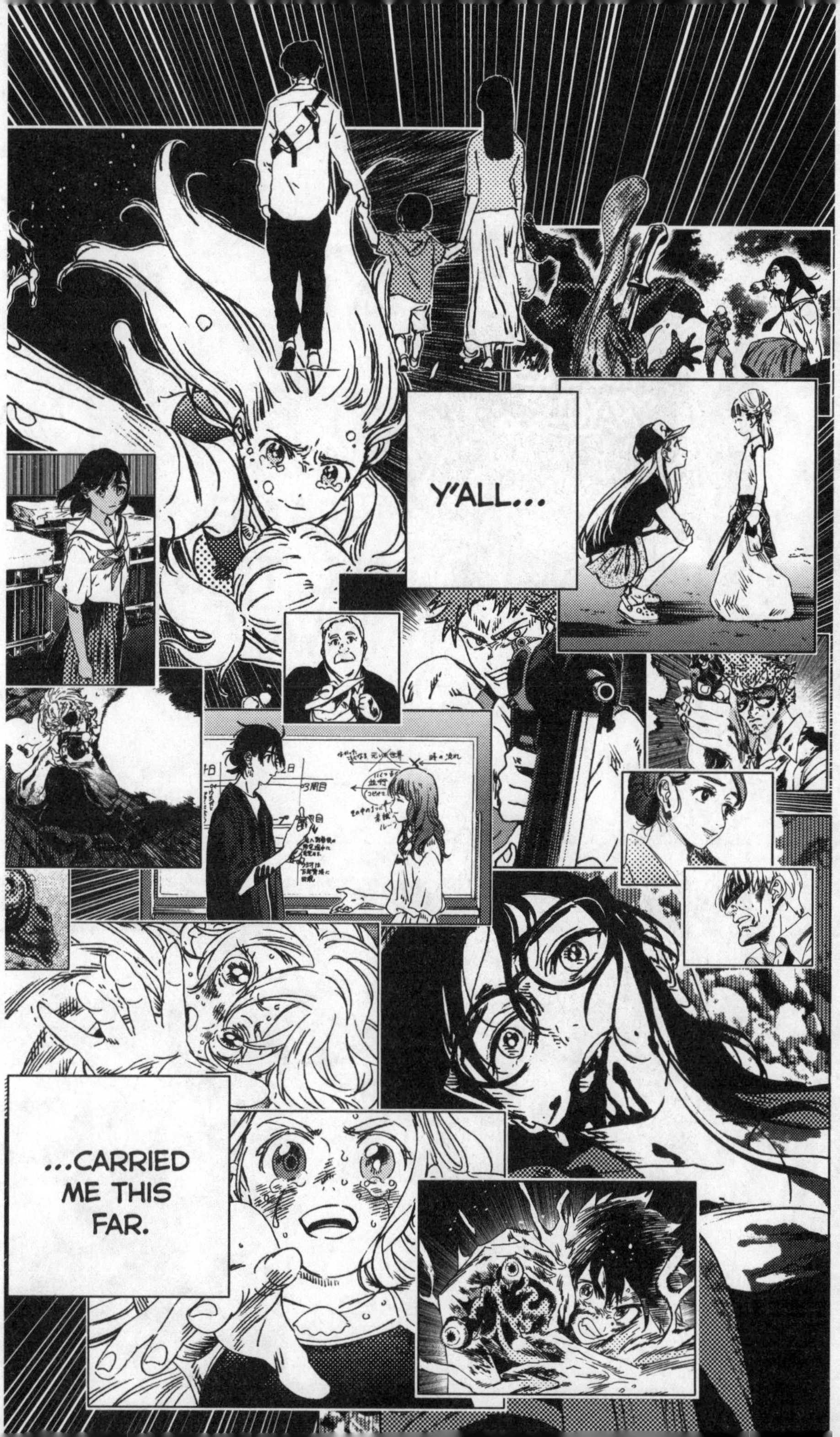
Y'ALL...
...CARRIED ME THIS FAR.

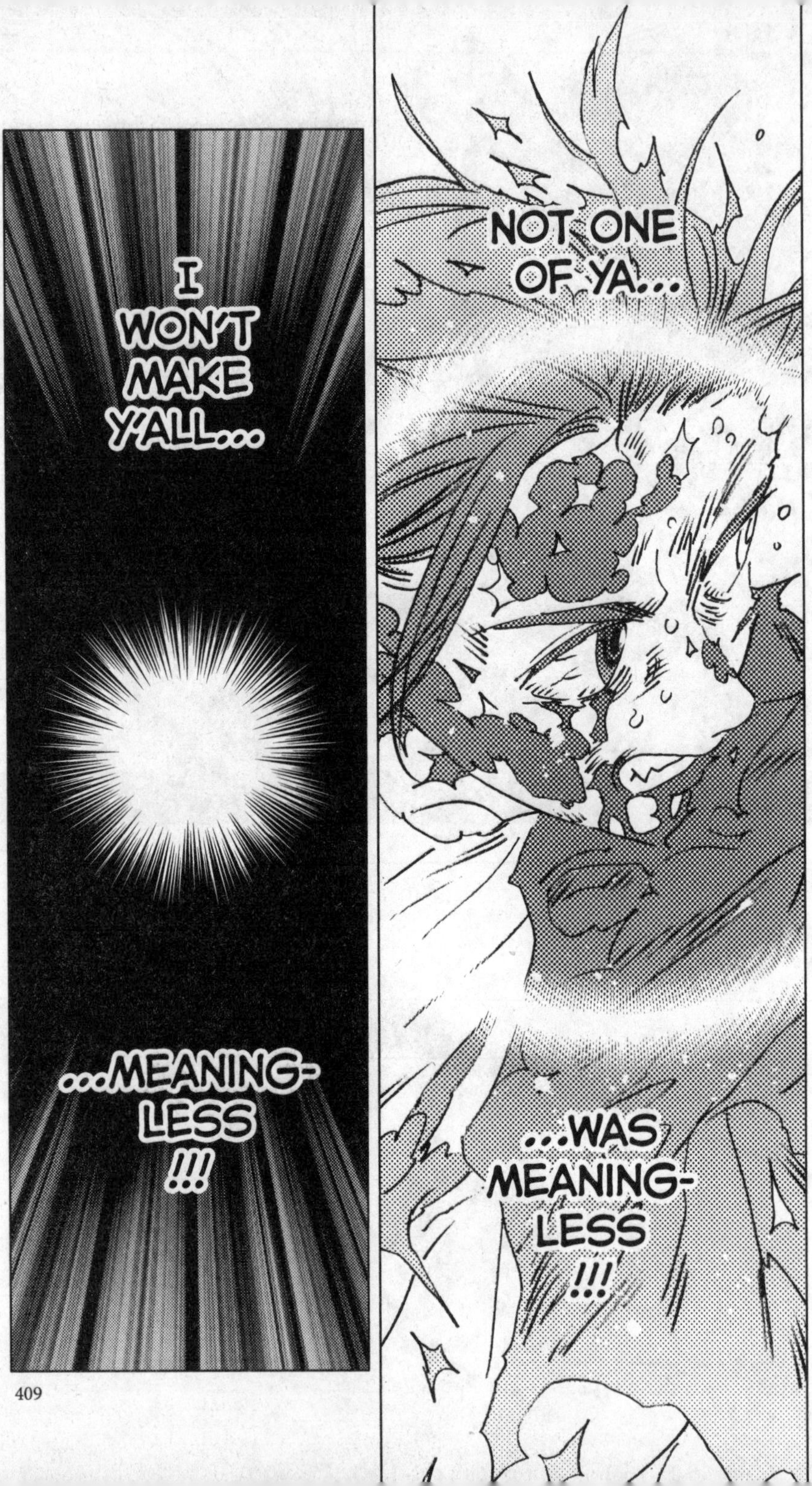
NOT ONE OF YA...
...WAS MEANING-LESS !!!
I WON'T MAKE Y'ALL...
...MEANING-LESS !!!

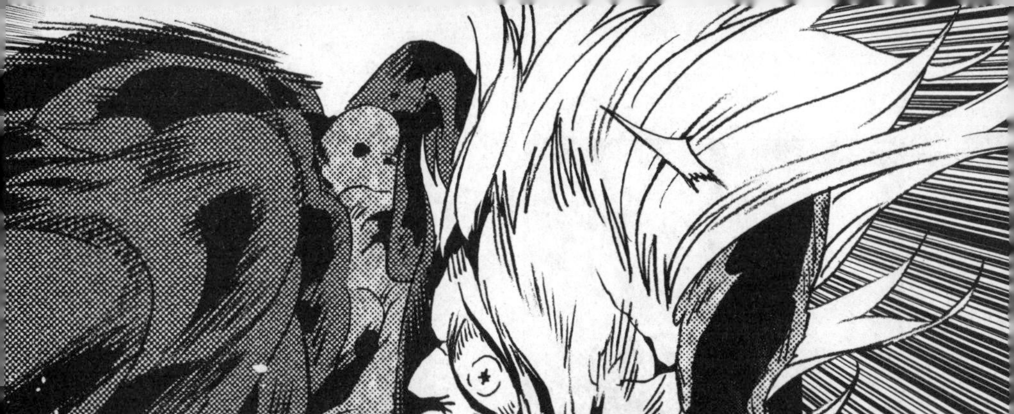
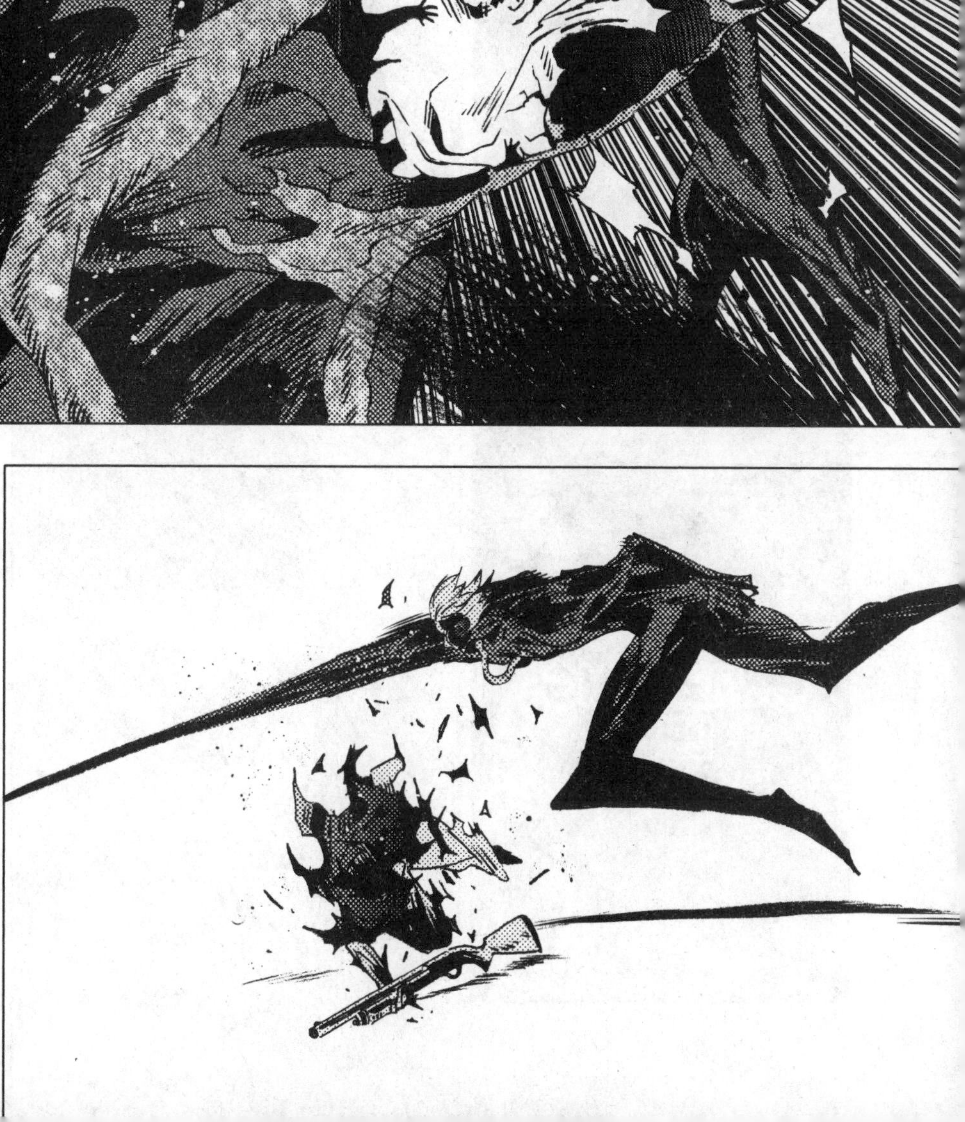

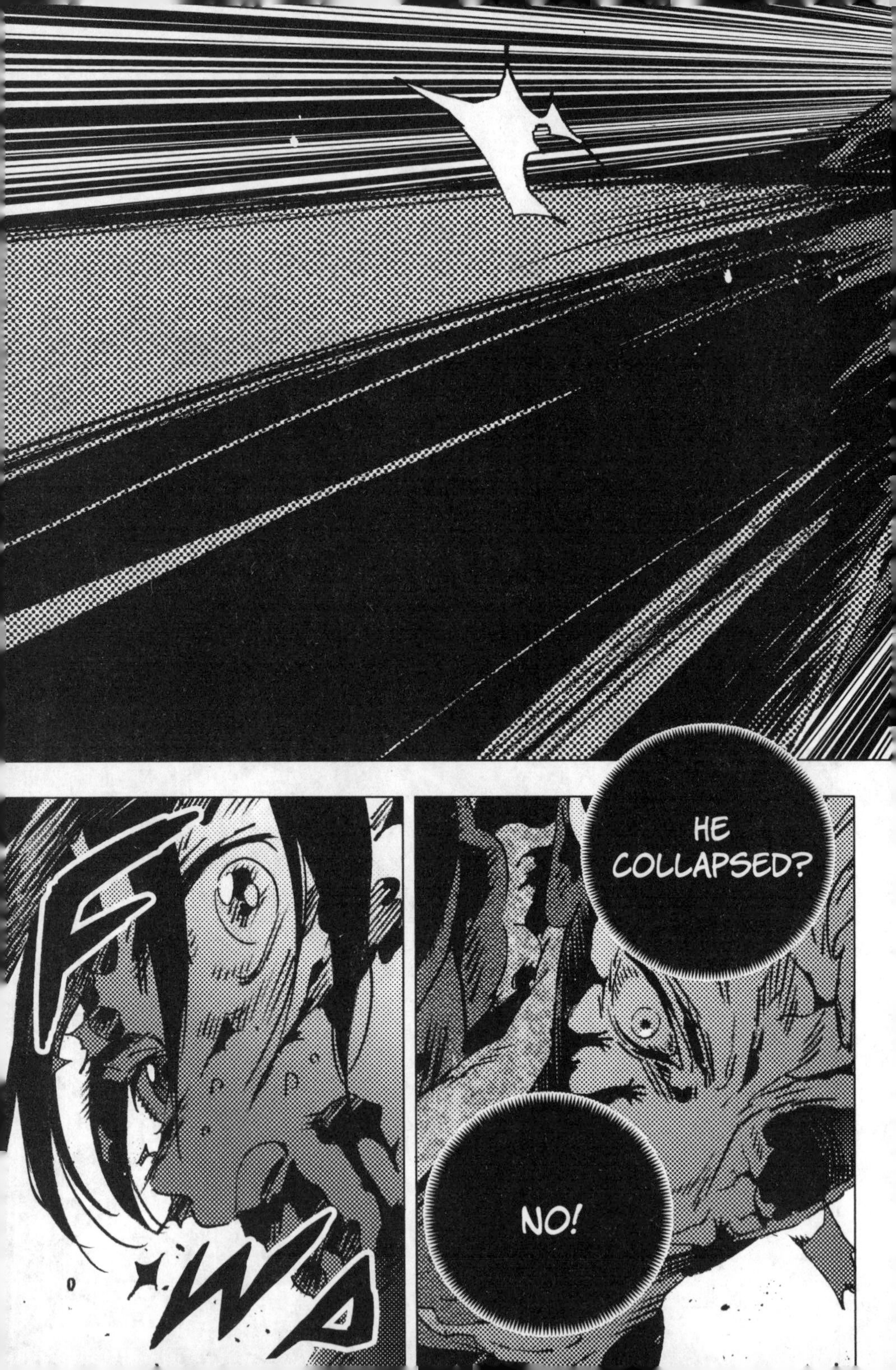
HE COLLAPSED?
NO!

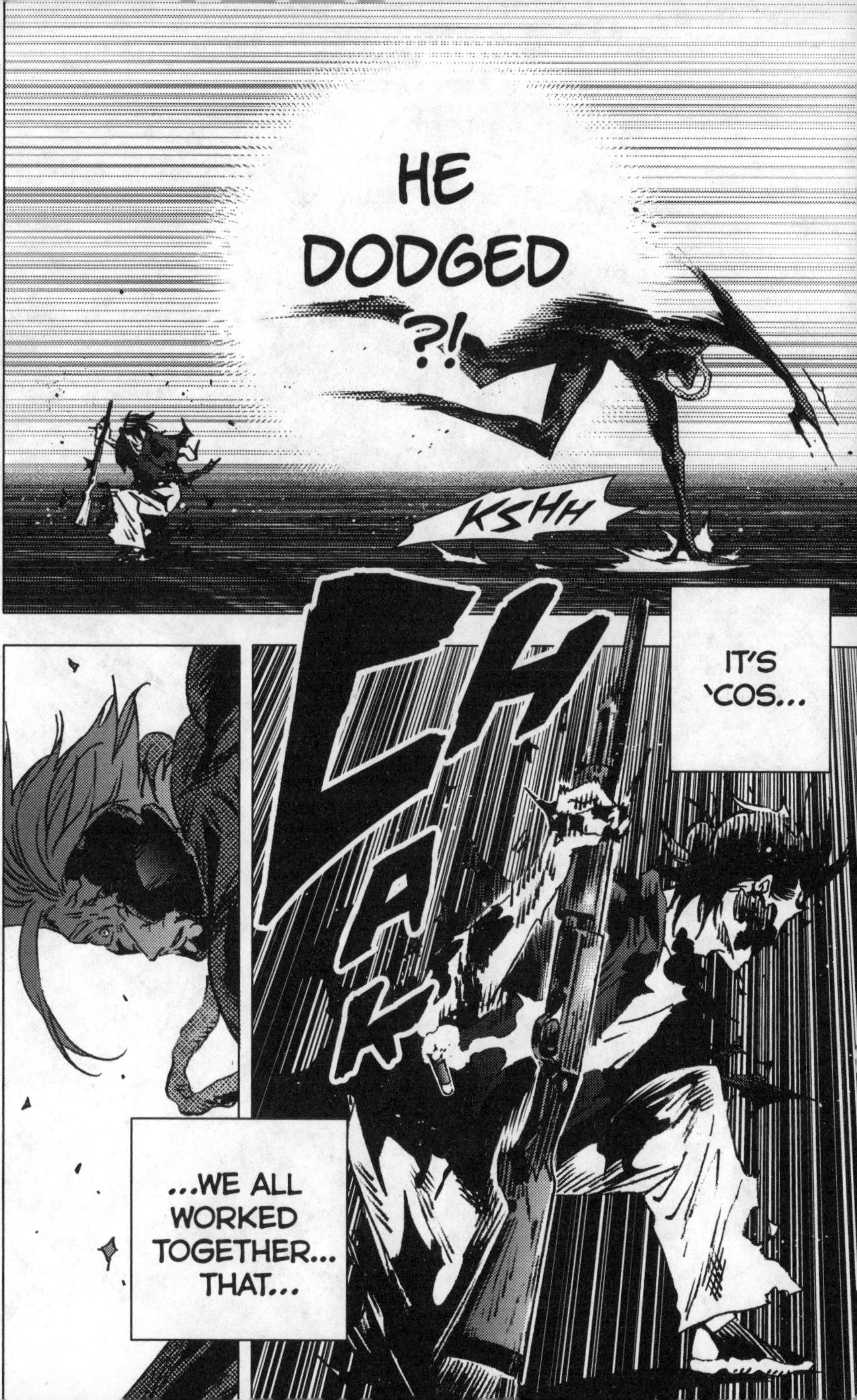
HE DODGED ?!
KSHH
IT'S 'COS...
...WE ALL WORKED TOGETHER... THAT...

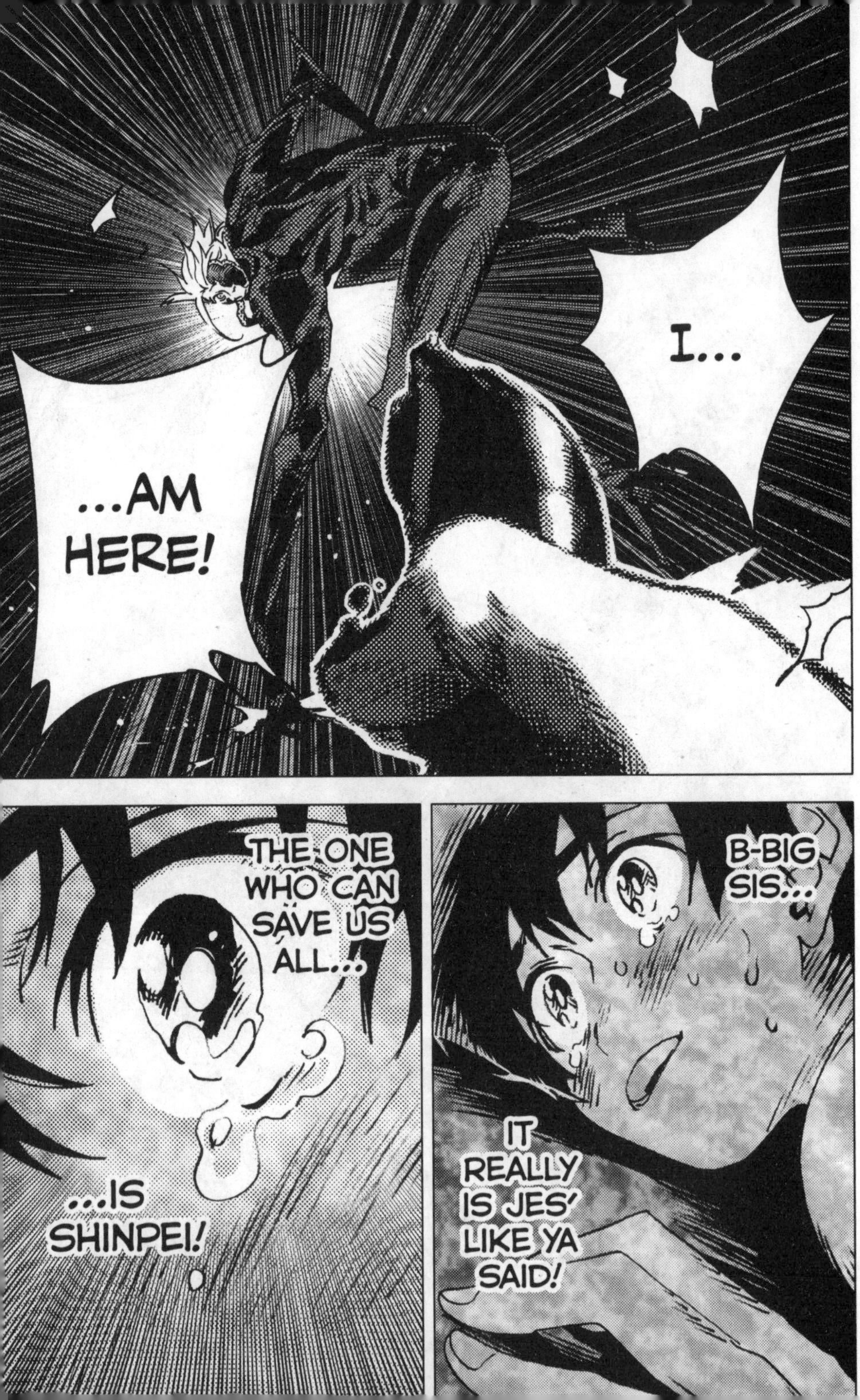
I...
...AM HERE!
B-BIG SIS...
IT REALLY IS JES' LIKE YA SAID!
THE ONE WHO CAN SAVE US ALL...
...IS SHINPEI!

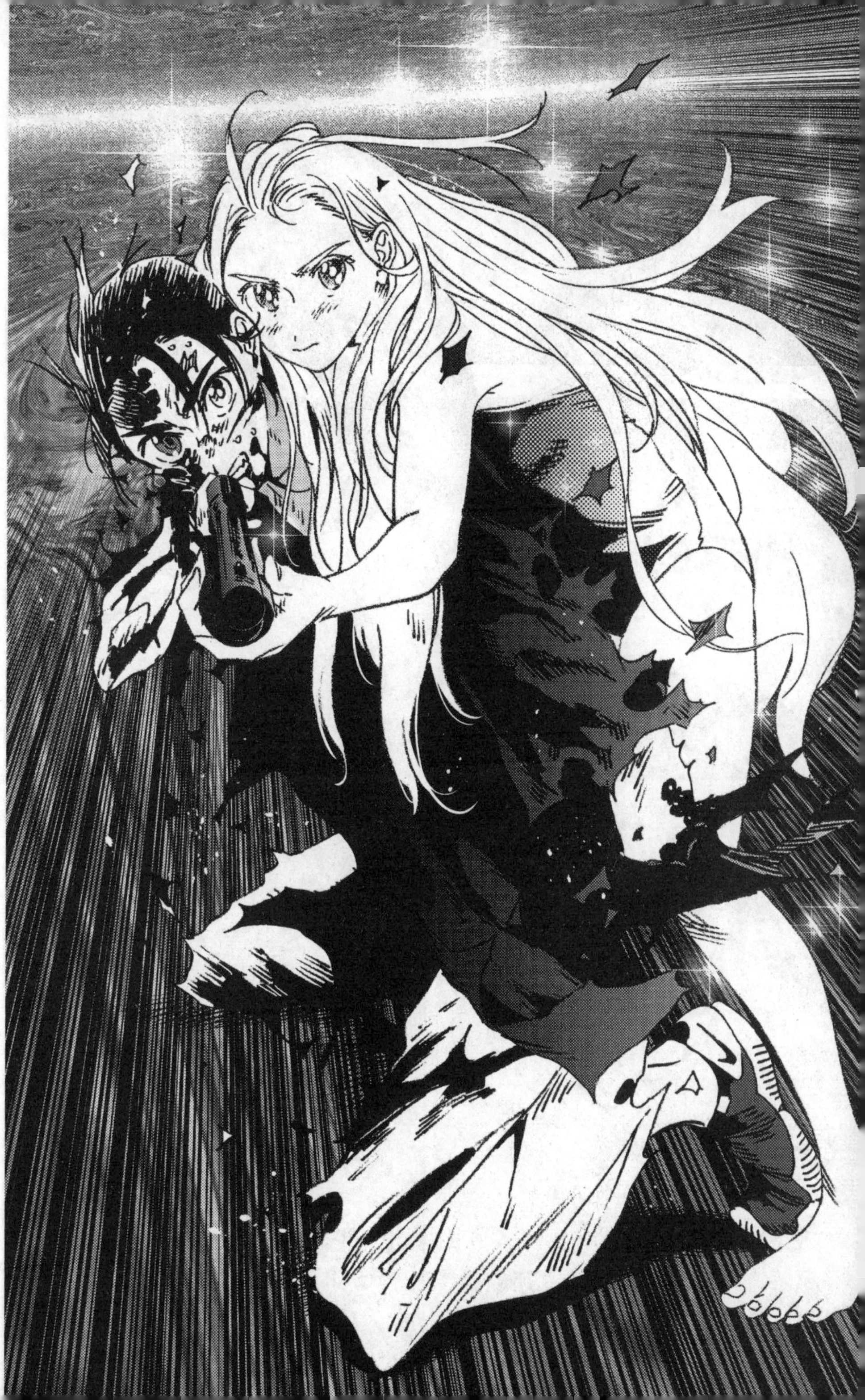

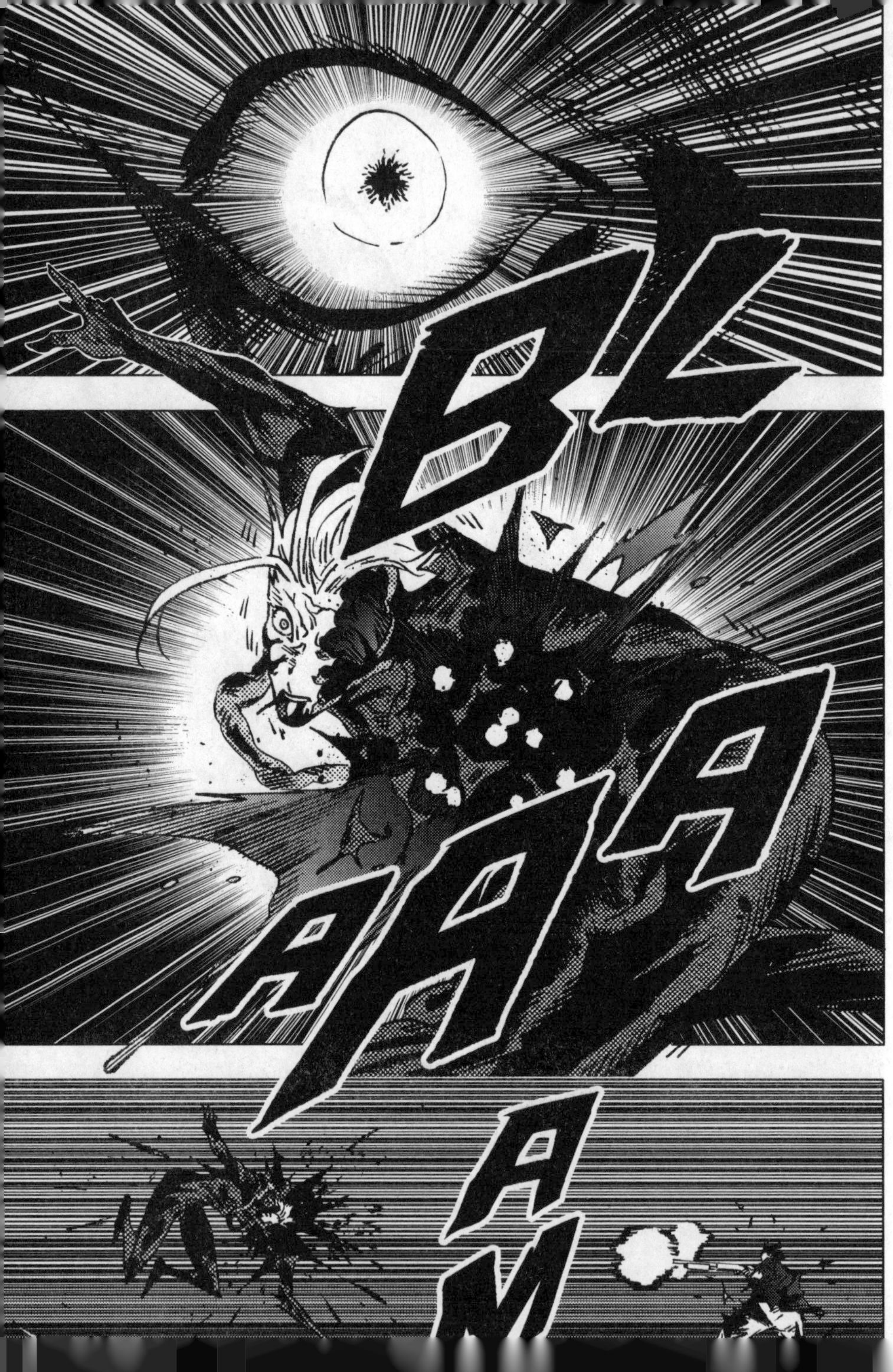
BLAAAAM

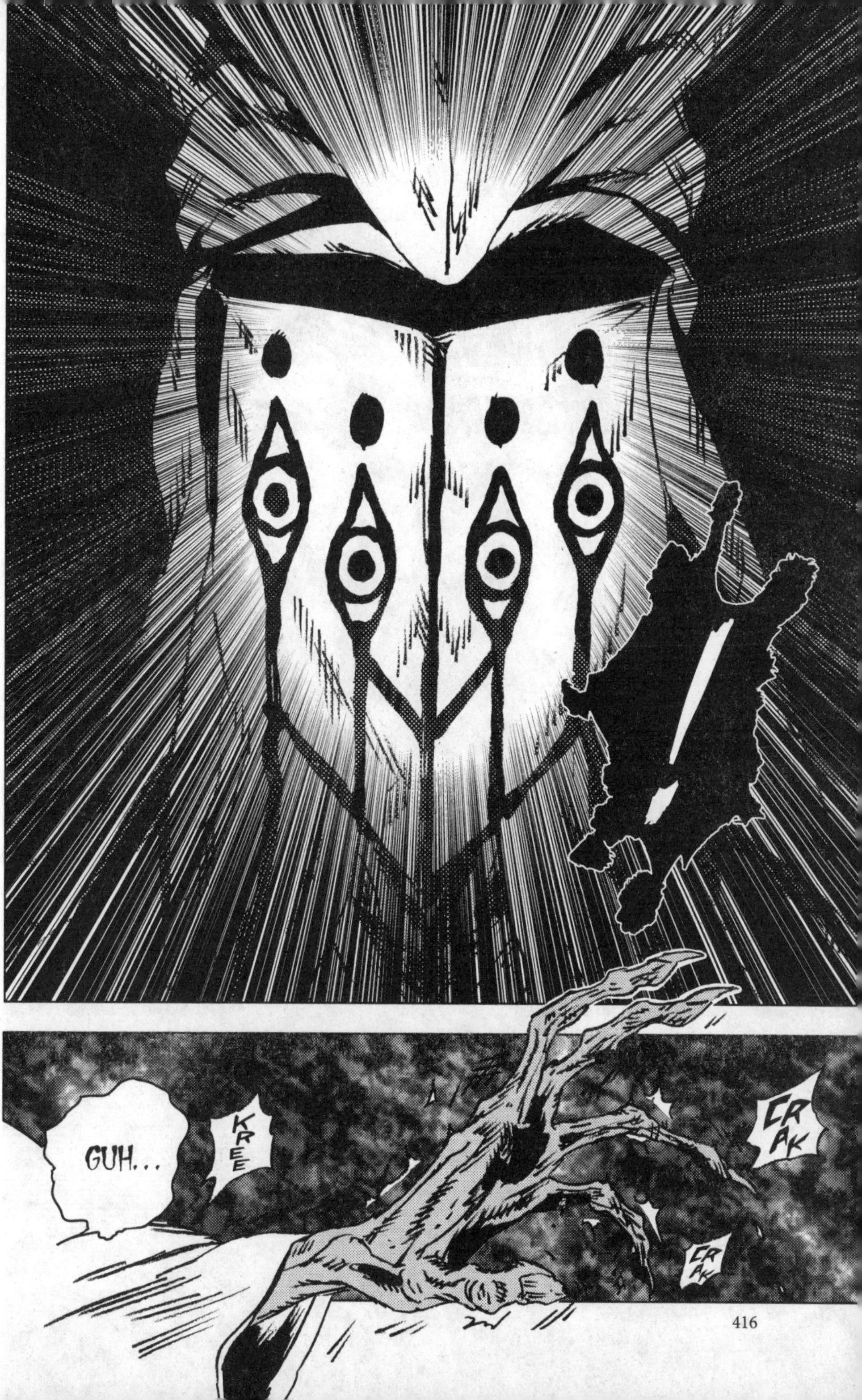
CRAK
CRAK
KREE
GUH...

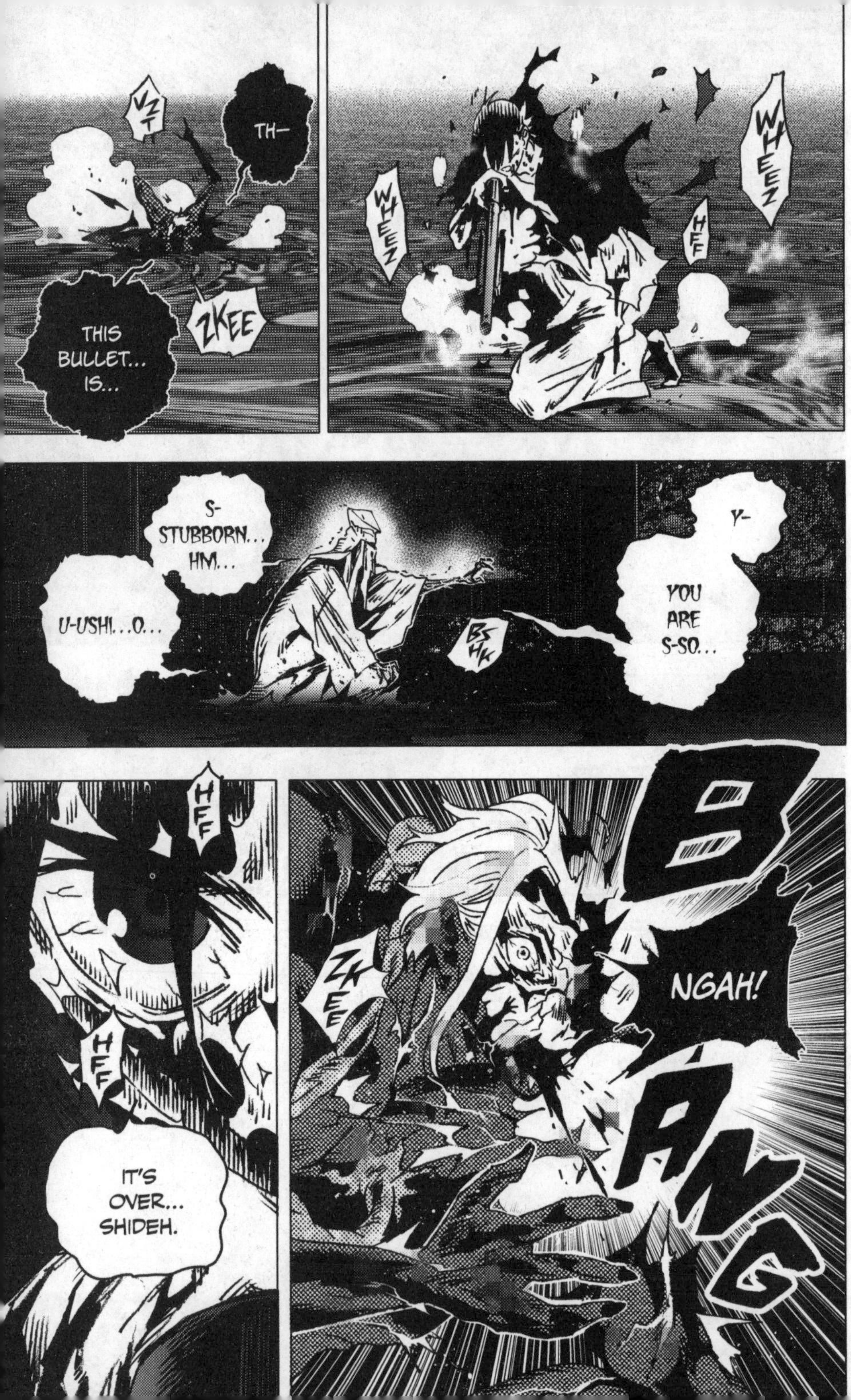
WHEEZ
HFF
WHEEZ
TH-
VZZT
ZKEE
THIS BULLET... IS...
Y-
YOU ARE S-SO...
BSHK
S-STUBBORN... HM...
U-USHI...O...
BANG
NGAH!
ZKEE
HFF
HFF
IT'S OVER... SHIDEH.

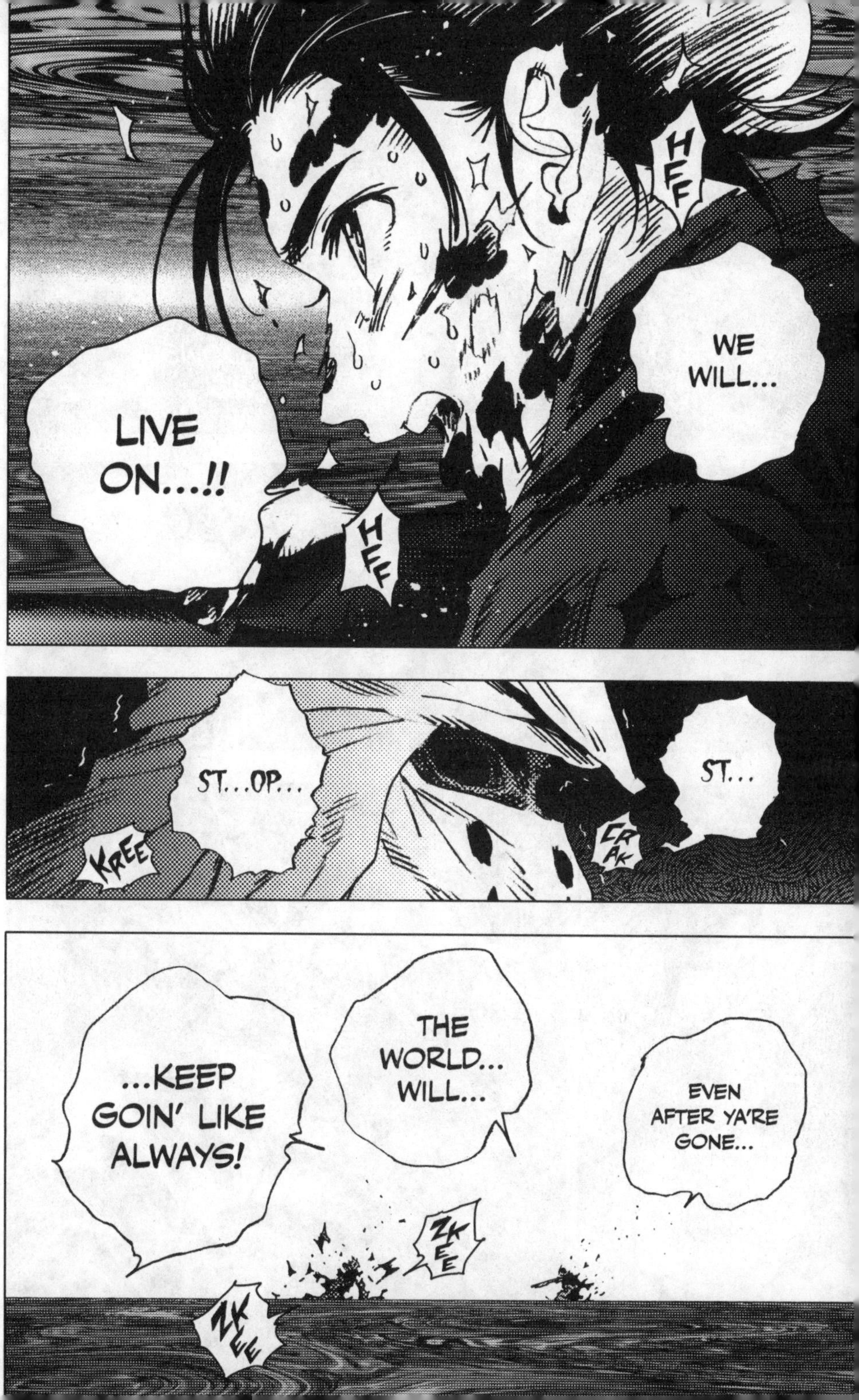
HFF
WE WILL...
LIVE ON...!!
HFF
ST...
CRAK
ST...OP...
KREE
EVEN AFTER YA'RE GONE...
THE WORLD... WILL...
...KEEP GOIN' LIKE ALWAYS!
ZKEE
ZKEE

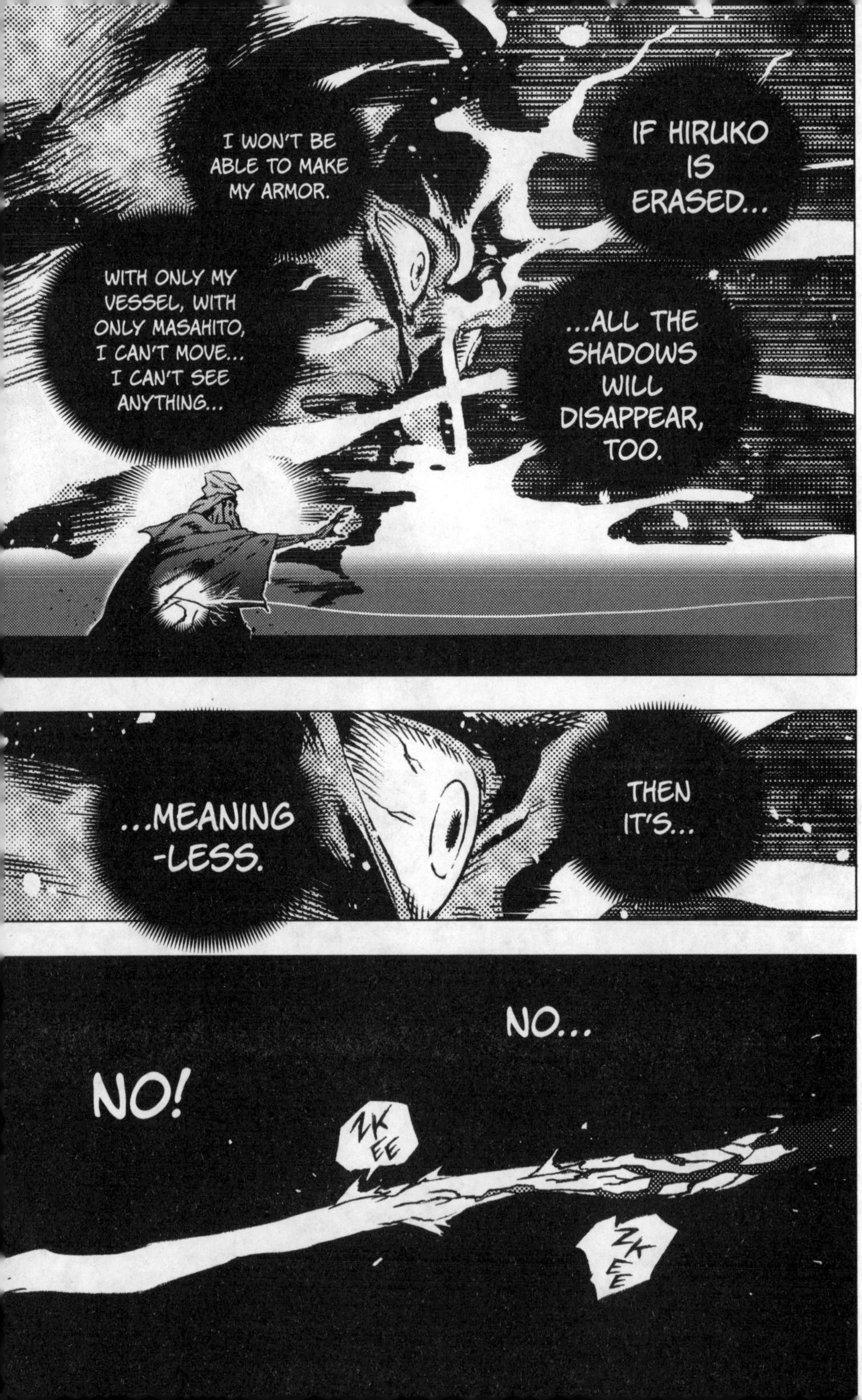
IF HIRUKO IS ERASED...
...ALL THE SHADOWS WILL DISAPPEAR, TOO.
I WON'T BE ABLE TO MAKE MY ARMOR.
WITH ONLY MY VESSEL, WITH ONLY MASAHITO, I CAN'T MOVE... I CAN'T SEE ANYTHING...
THEN IT'S...
...MEANING-LESS.
NO...
NO!
ZKEE
ZKEE

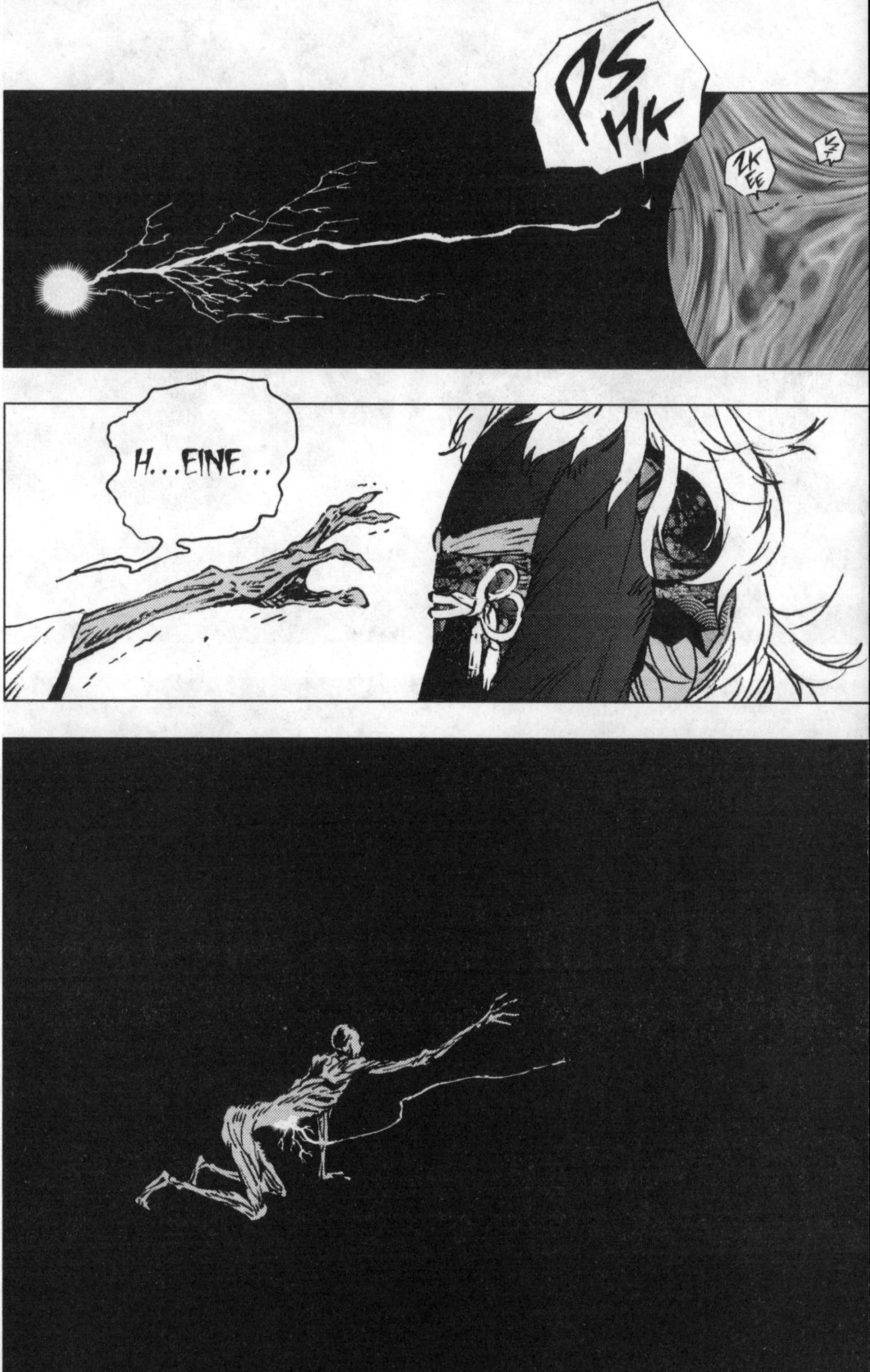
PSHK
VZT
ZKEE
H...EINE...

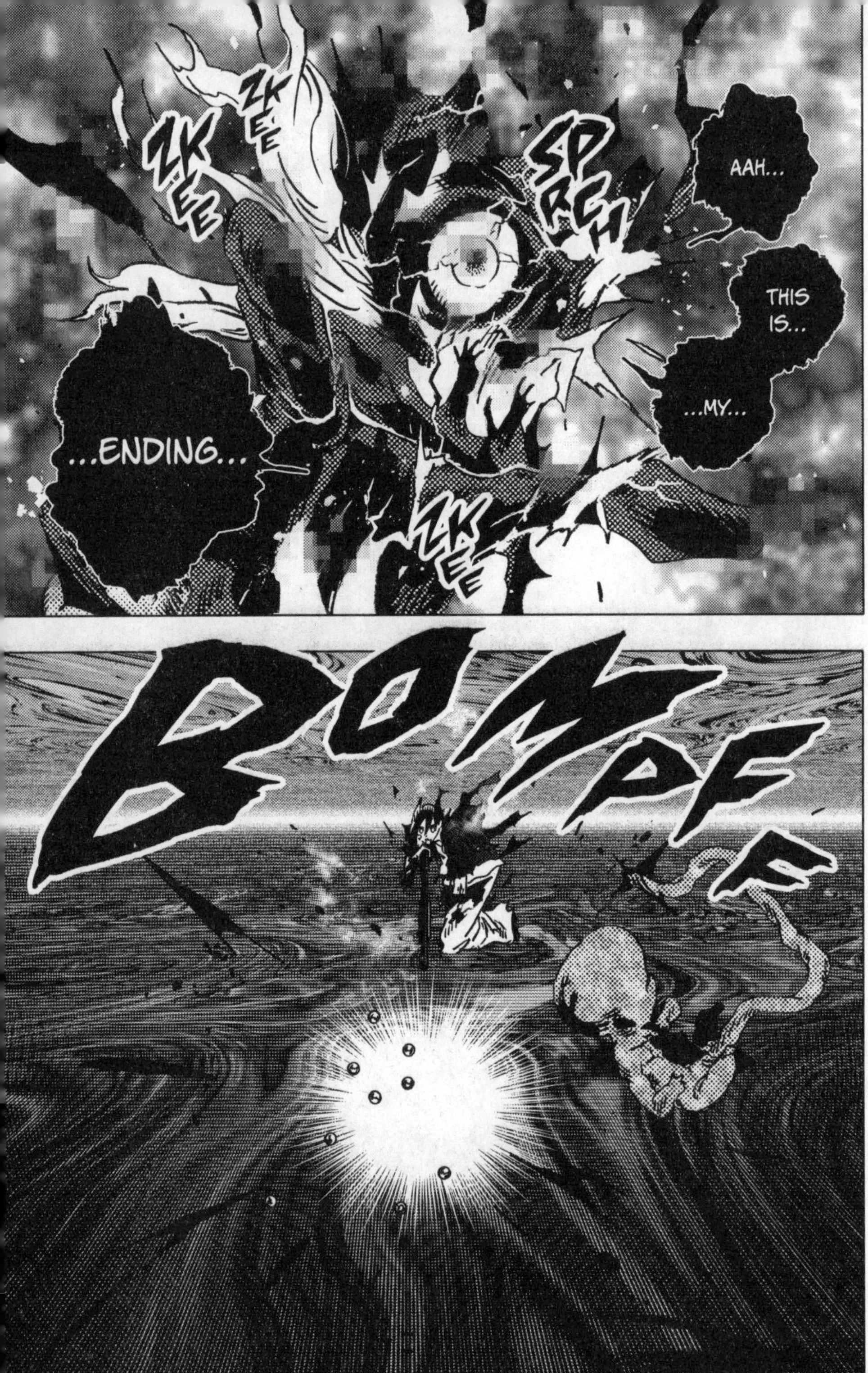
AAH...
SPRCH
THIS IS...
...MY...
ZKEE
ZKEE
...ENDING...
ZKEE
BOMPF

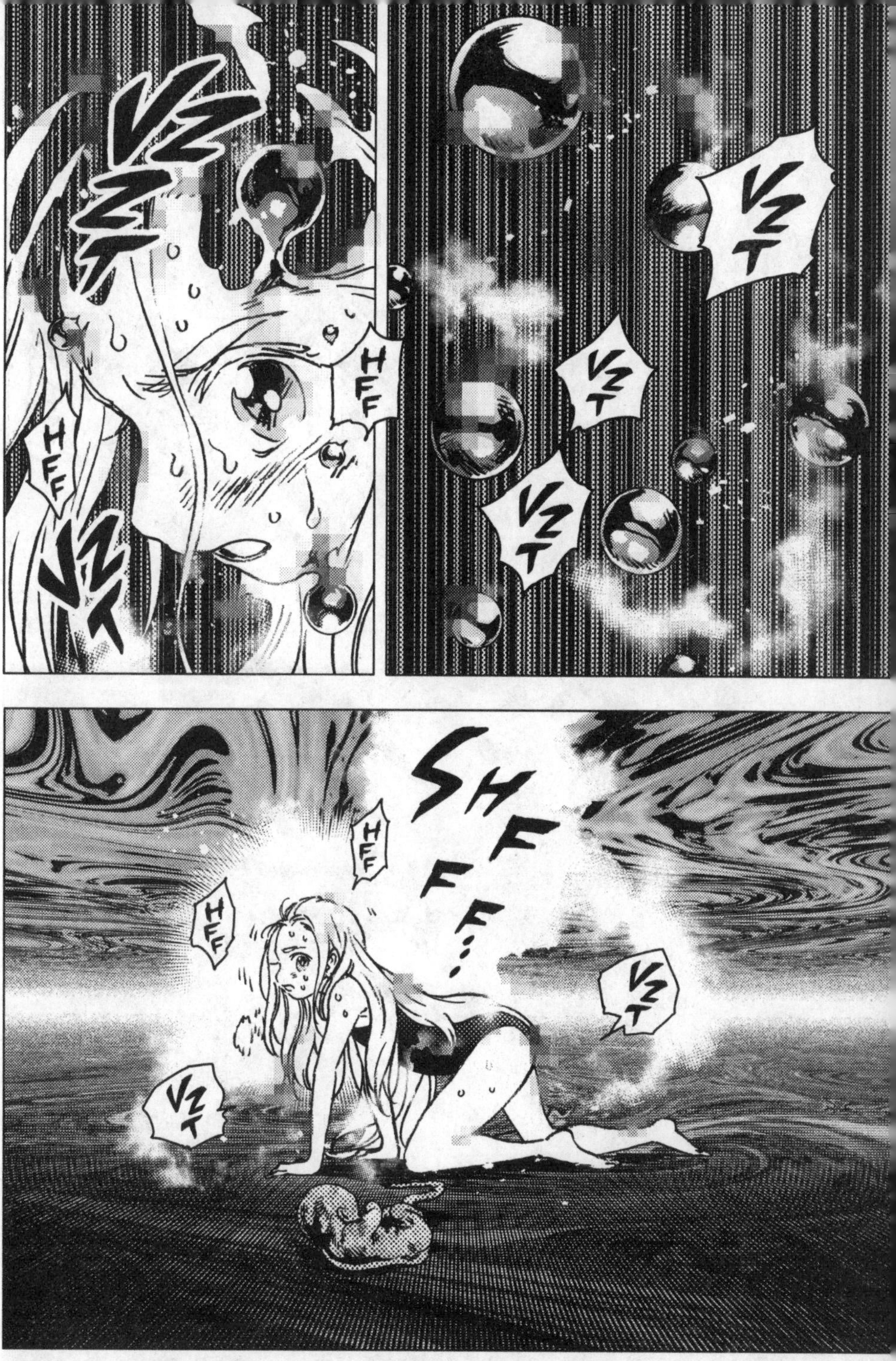
VZT
VZT
VZT
VZT
HFF
HFF
VZT
SHFFF...
HFF
HFF
VZT
VZT

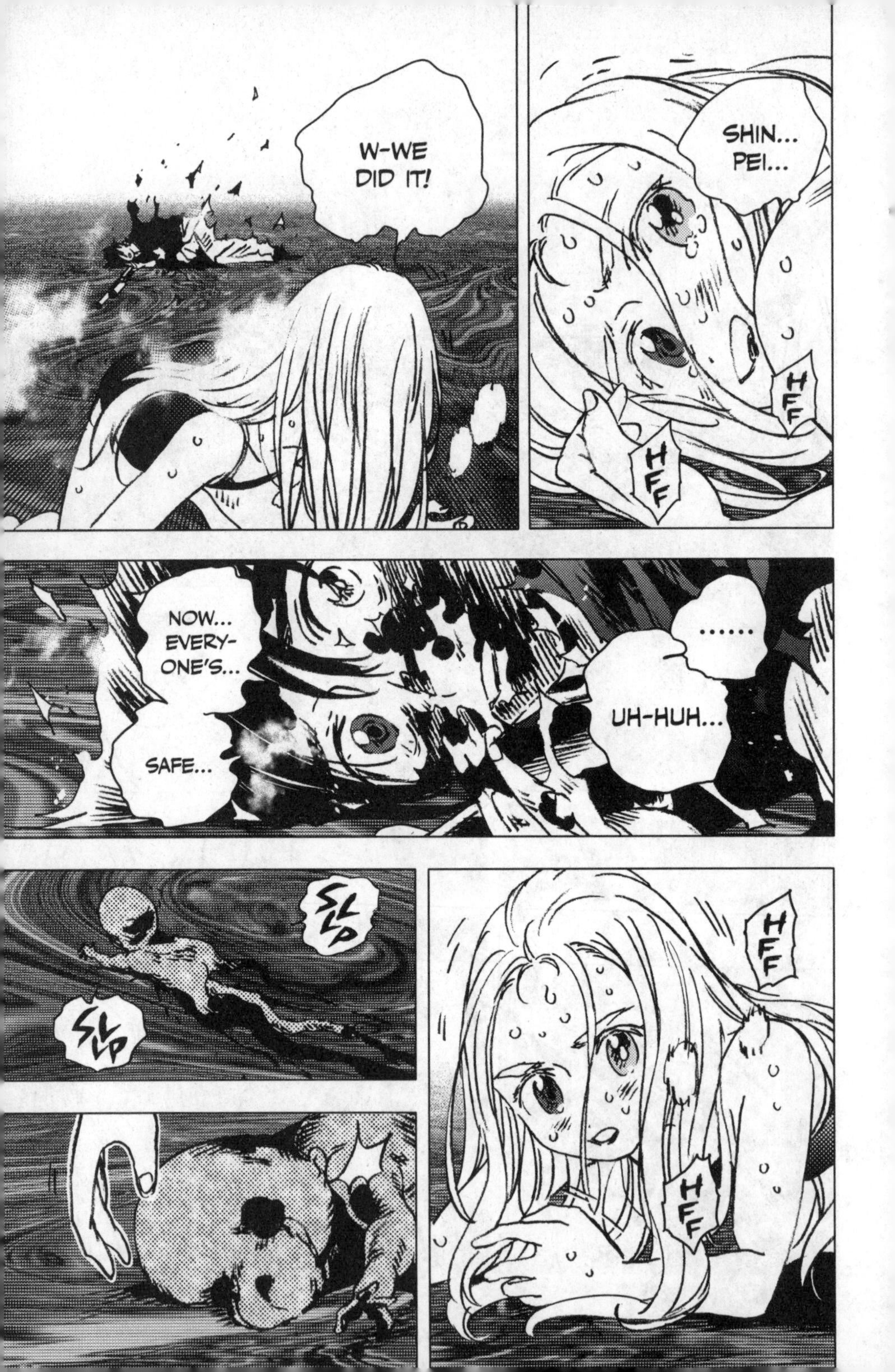
SHIN... PEI...
HFF
HFF
W-WE DID IT!
....
UH-HUH...
NOW... EVERY-ONE'S...
SAFE...
HFF
HFF
SLLP
SLLP

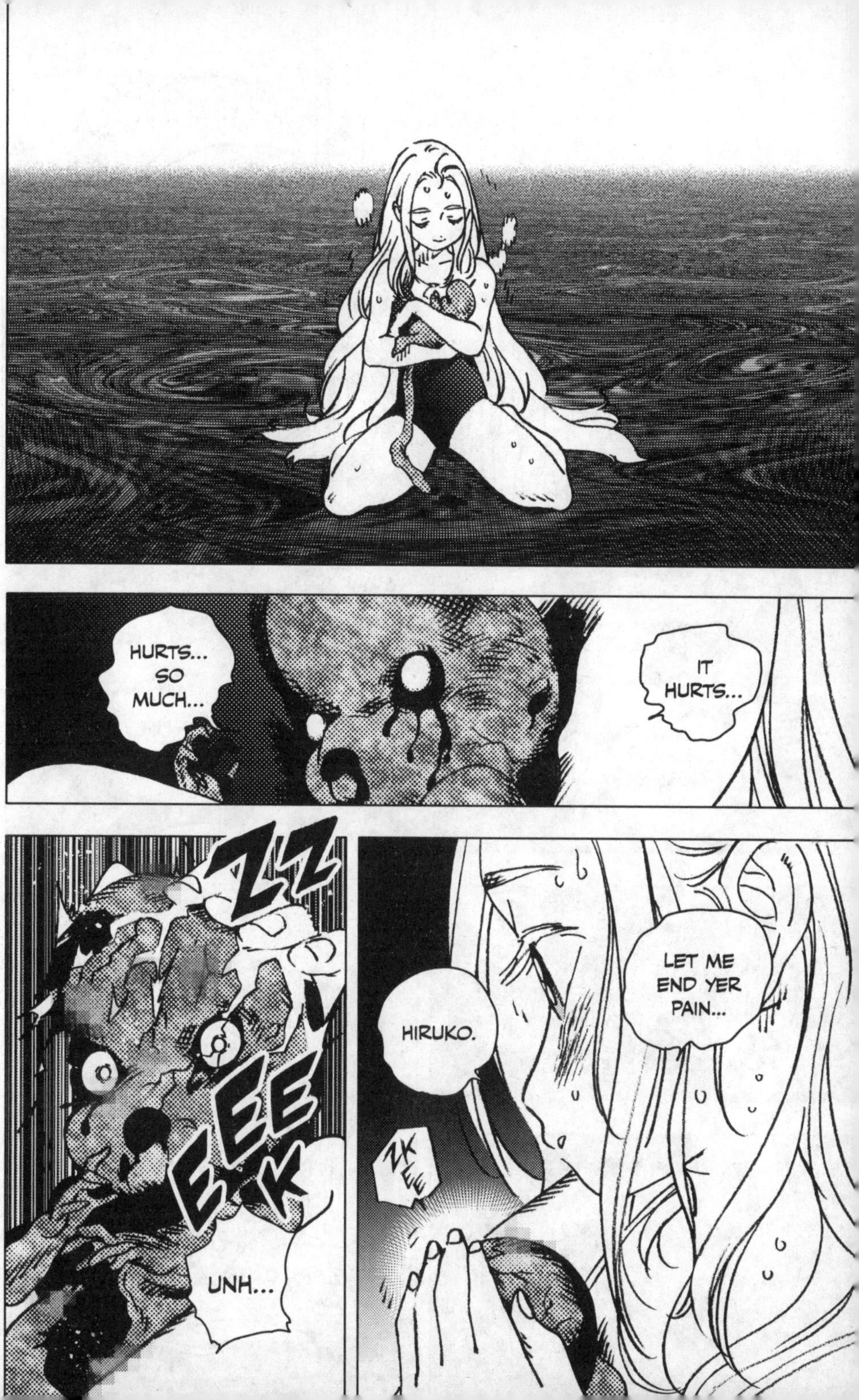
IT HURTS...
HURTS... SO MUCH...
LET ME END YER PAIN...
HIRUKO.
ZKEE
ZZEEEK
UNH...

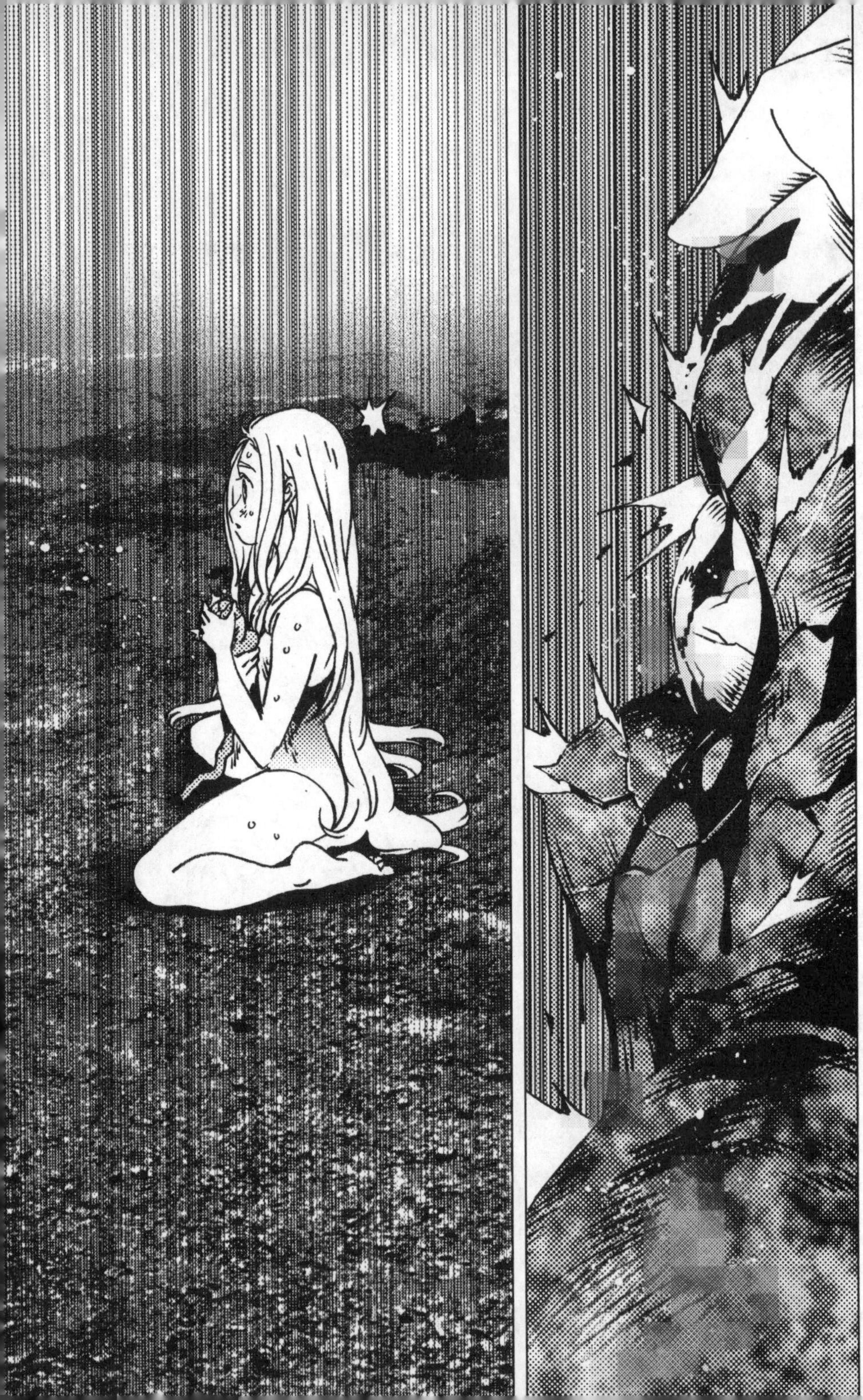

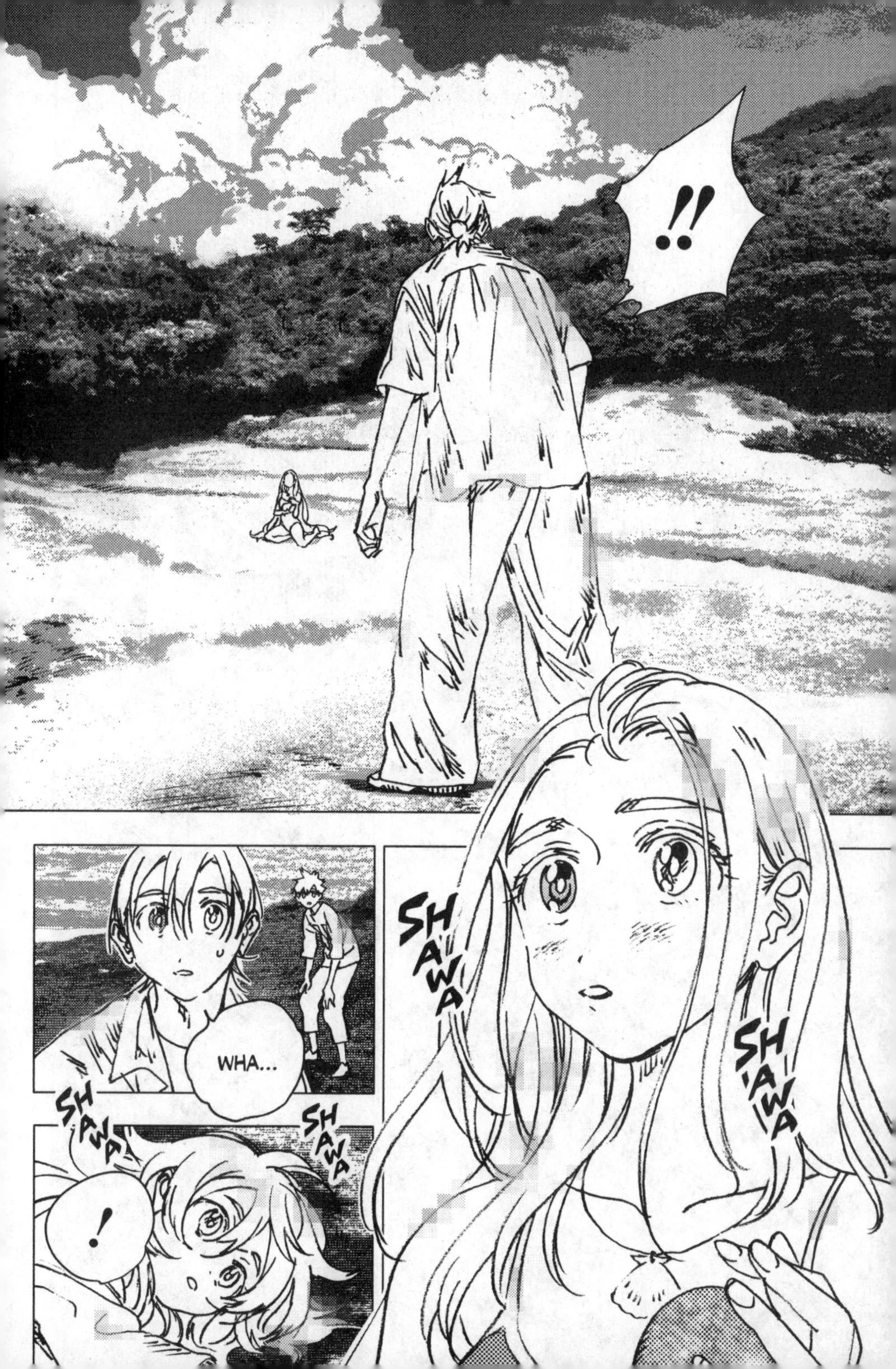
!!
SHAWA
SHAWA
WHA...
SHAWA
SHAWA
!

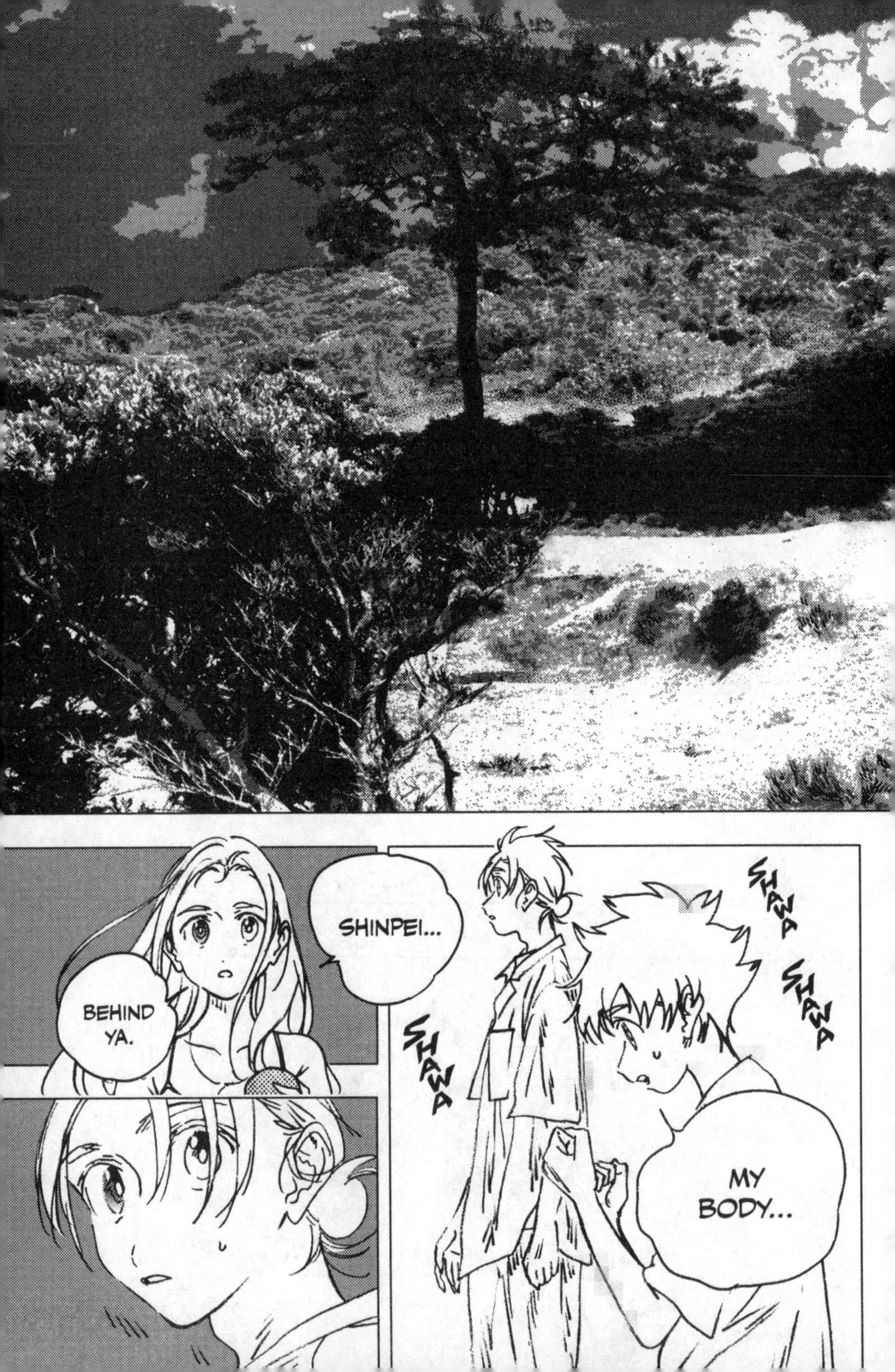
SHAWA
SHAWA
SHAWA
MY BODY...
SHINPEI...
BEHIND YA.

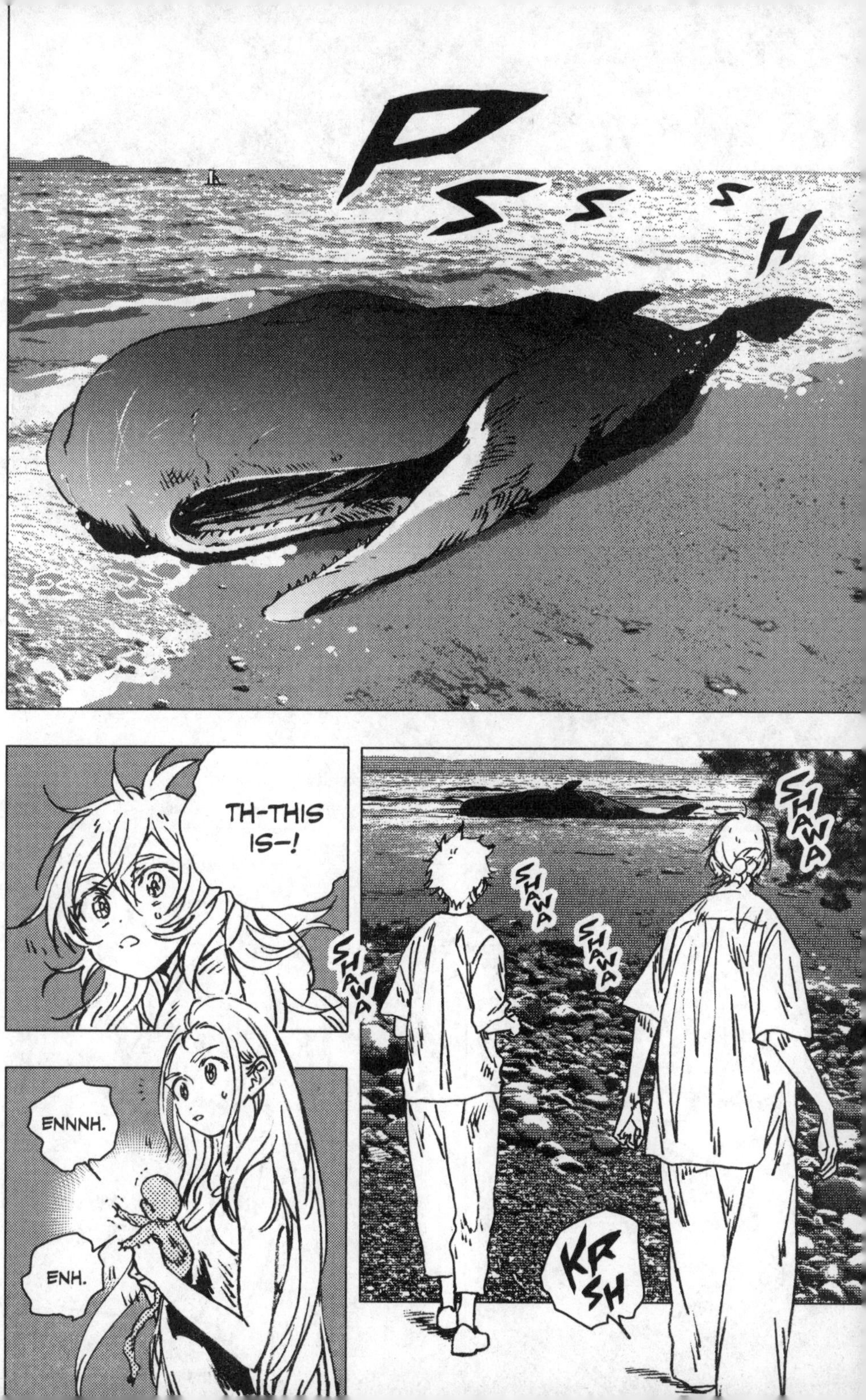
PSSSH
SHAWA
SHAWA
SHAWA
SHAWA
KRSH
TH-THIS IS—!
ENNNH.
ENH.

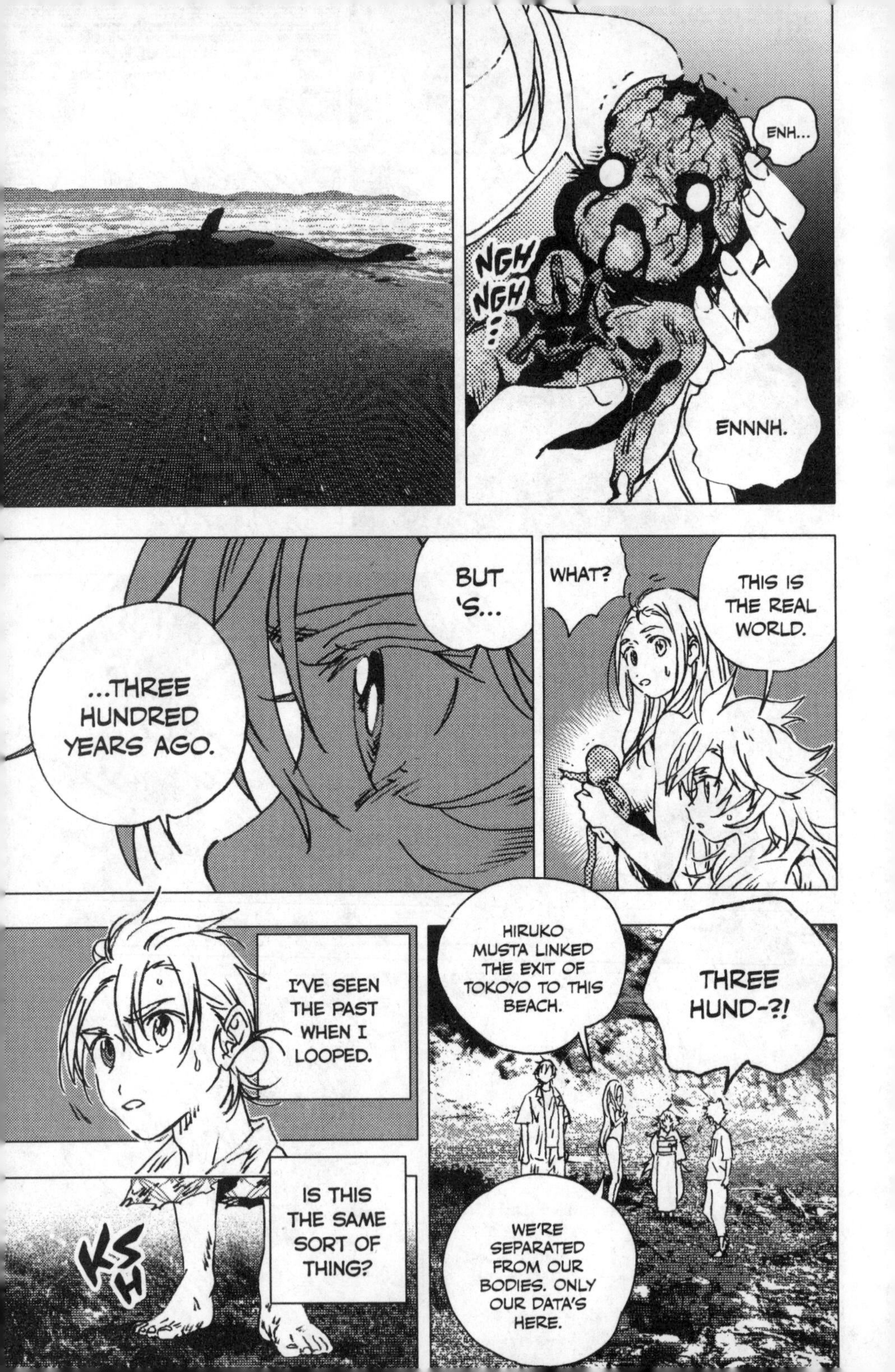
ENH...
NGH NGH...
ENNNH.
THIS IS THE REAL WORLD.
WHAT?
BUT 'S...
...THREE HUNDRED YEARS AGO.
THREE HUND-?!
HIRUKO MUSTA LINKED THE EXIT OF TOKOYO TO THIS BEACH.
WE'RE SEPARATED FROM OUR BODIES. ONLY OUR DATA'S HERE.
I'VE SEEN THE PAST WHEN I LOOPED.
IS THIS THE SAME SORT OF THING?
KSH

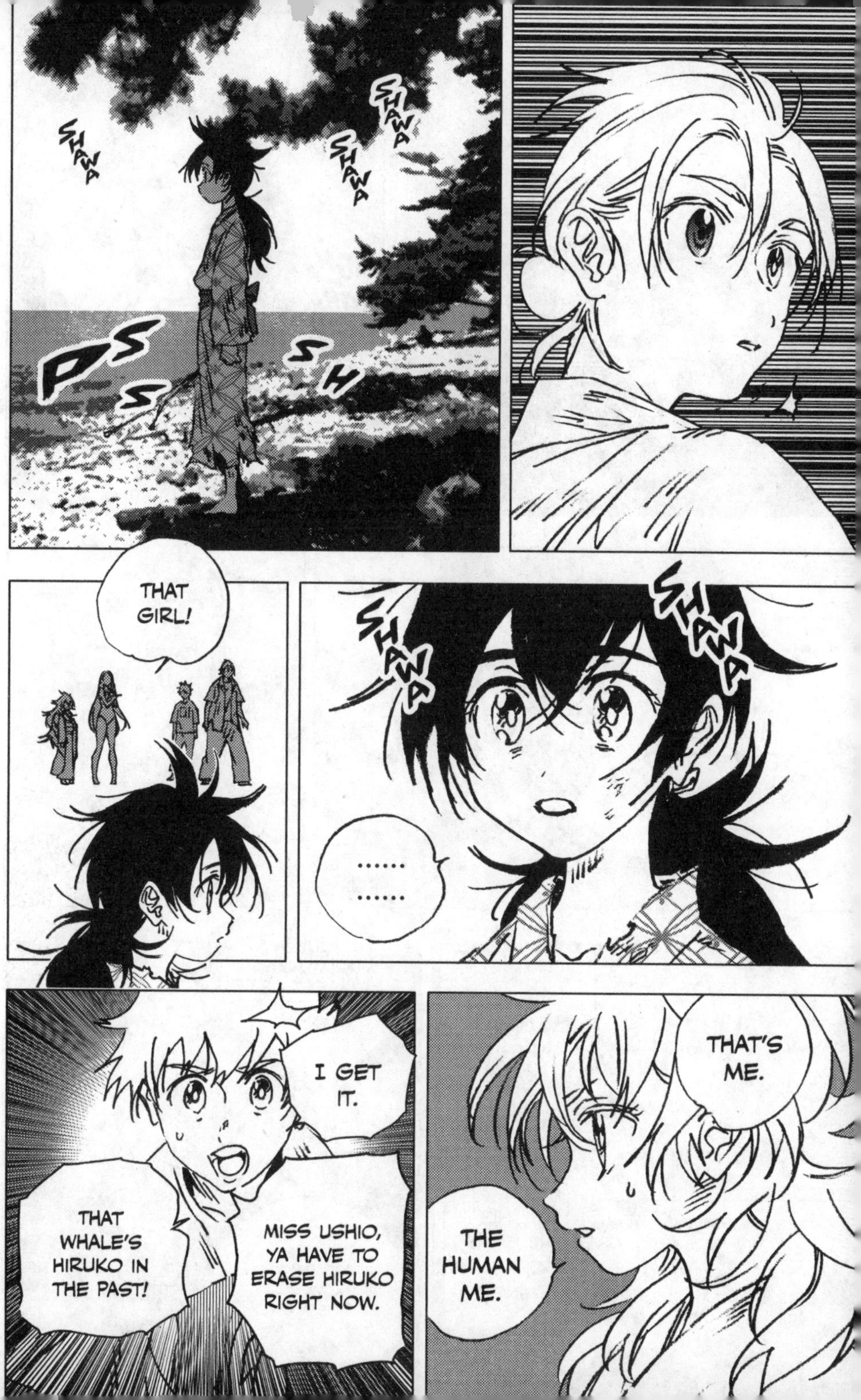
SHAWA
SHAWA
SHAWA
PSSSH
SHAWA
SHAWA
......
......
THAT GIRL!
THAT'S ME.
THE HUMAN ME.
I GET IT.
MISS USHIO, YA HAVE TO ERASE HIRUKO RIGHT NOW.
THAT WHALE'S HIRUKO IN THE PAST!

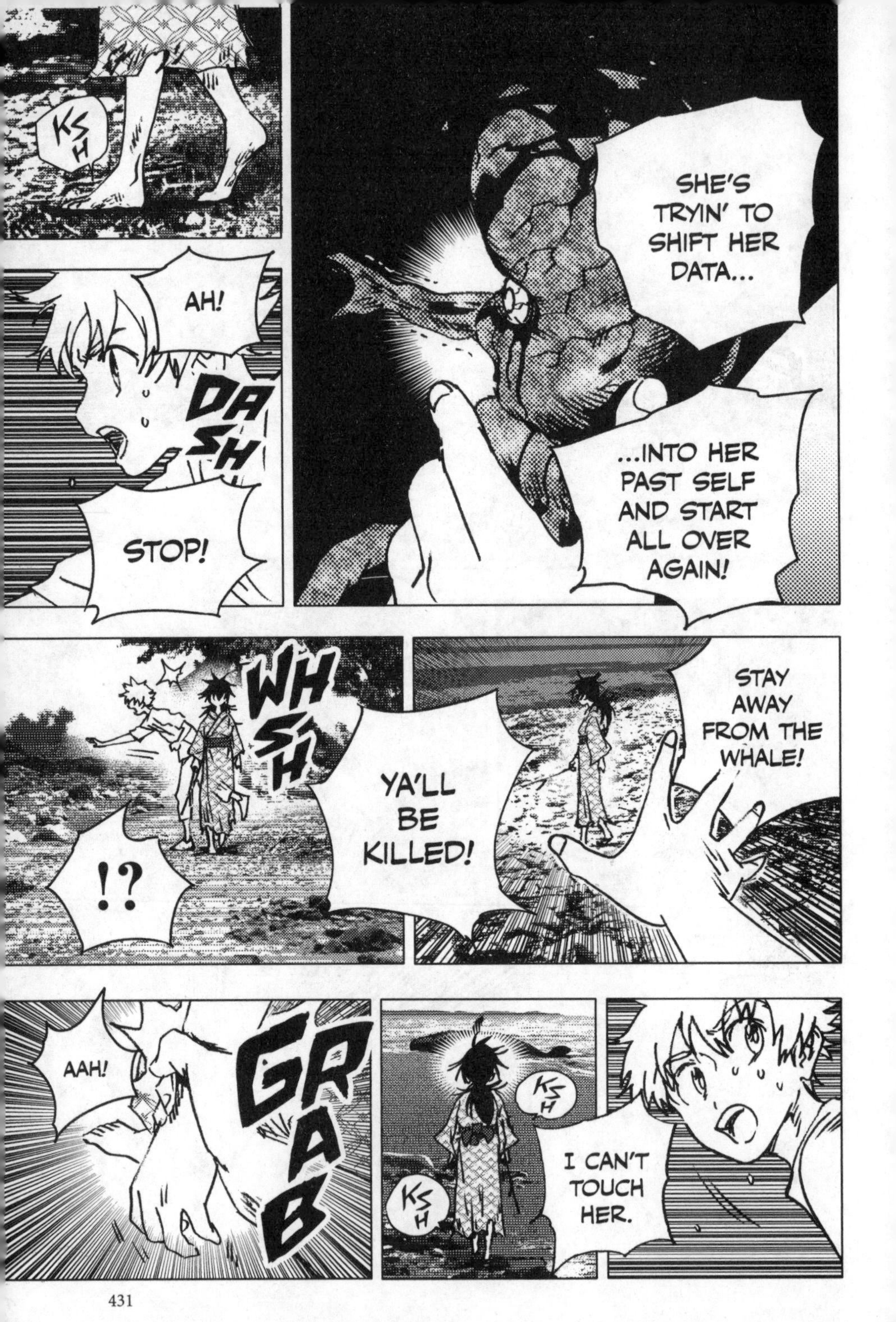
SHE'S TRYIN' TO SHIFT HER DATA...
...INTO HER PAST SELF AND START ALL OVER AGAIN!
KSH
AH!
DASH
STOP!
STAY AWAY FROM THE WHALE!
YA'LL BE KILLED!
WHSH
!?
I CAN'T TOUCH HER.
KSH
KSH
GRAB
AAH!

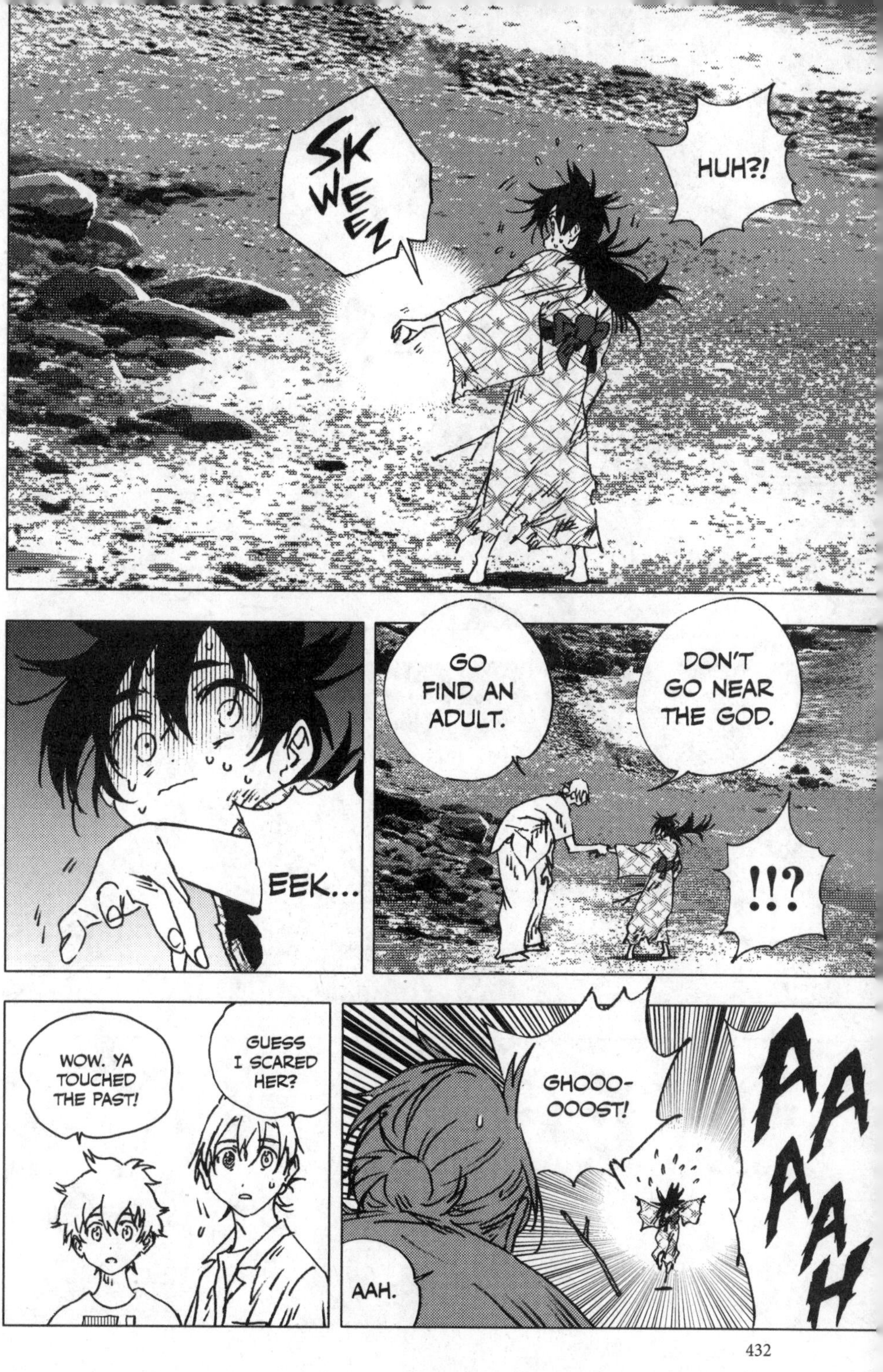
HUH?!
SKWEEZ
DON'T GO NEAR THE GOD.
GO FIND AN ADULT.
!!?
EEK...
AAAAH
GHOOOOOOST!
AAH.
GUESS I SCARED HER?
WOW. YA TOUCHED THE PAST!

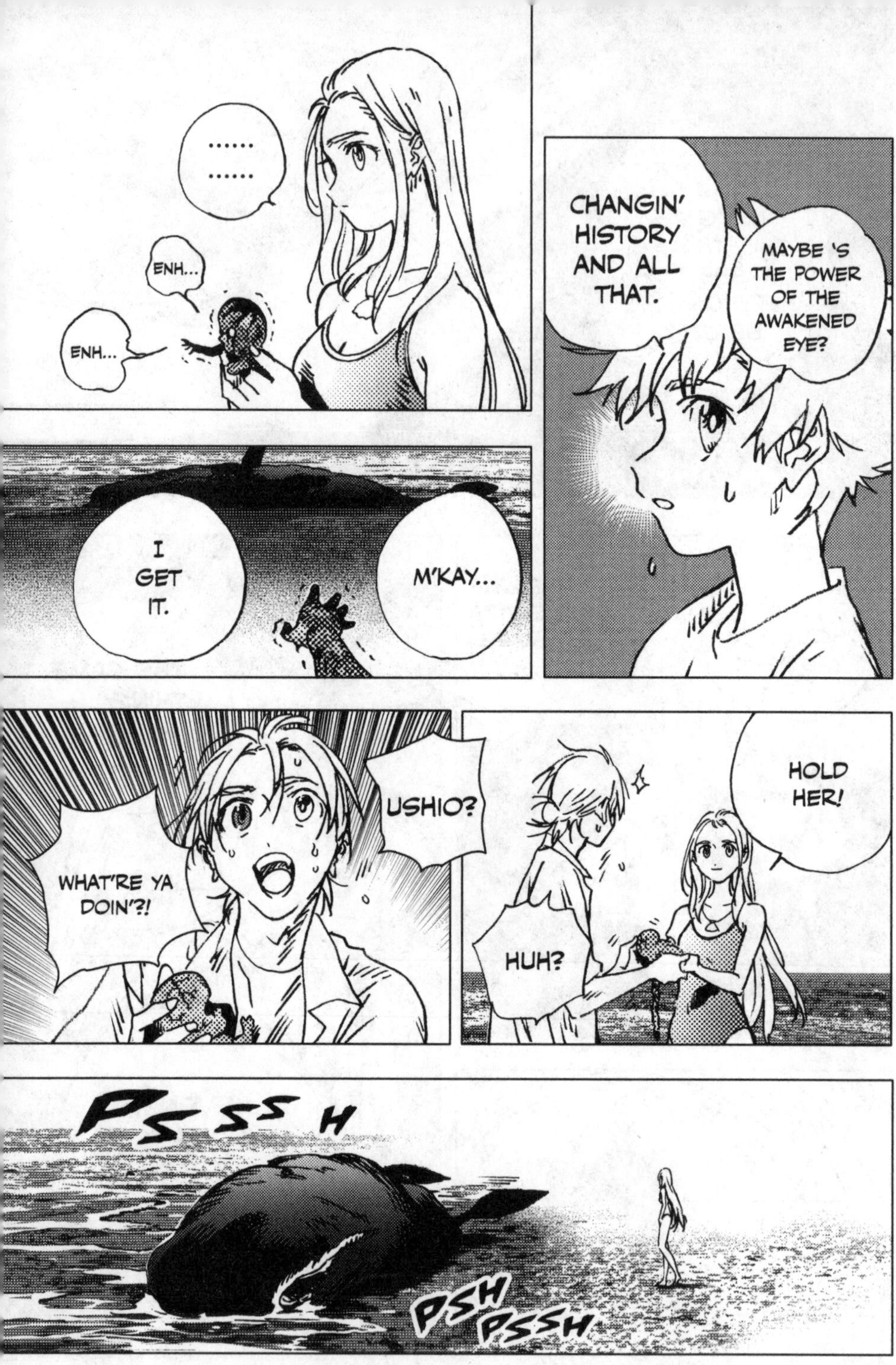
MAYBE 'S THE POWER OF THE AWAKENED EYE?
CHANGIN' HISTORY AND ALL THAT.
......
......
ENH...
ENH...
M'KAY...
I GET IT.
HOLD HER!
HUH?
USHIO?
WHAT'RE YA DOIN'?!
PSSSH
PSH PSSH

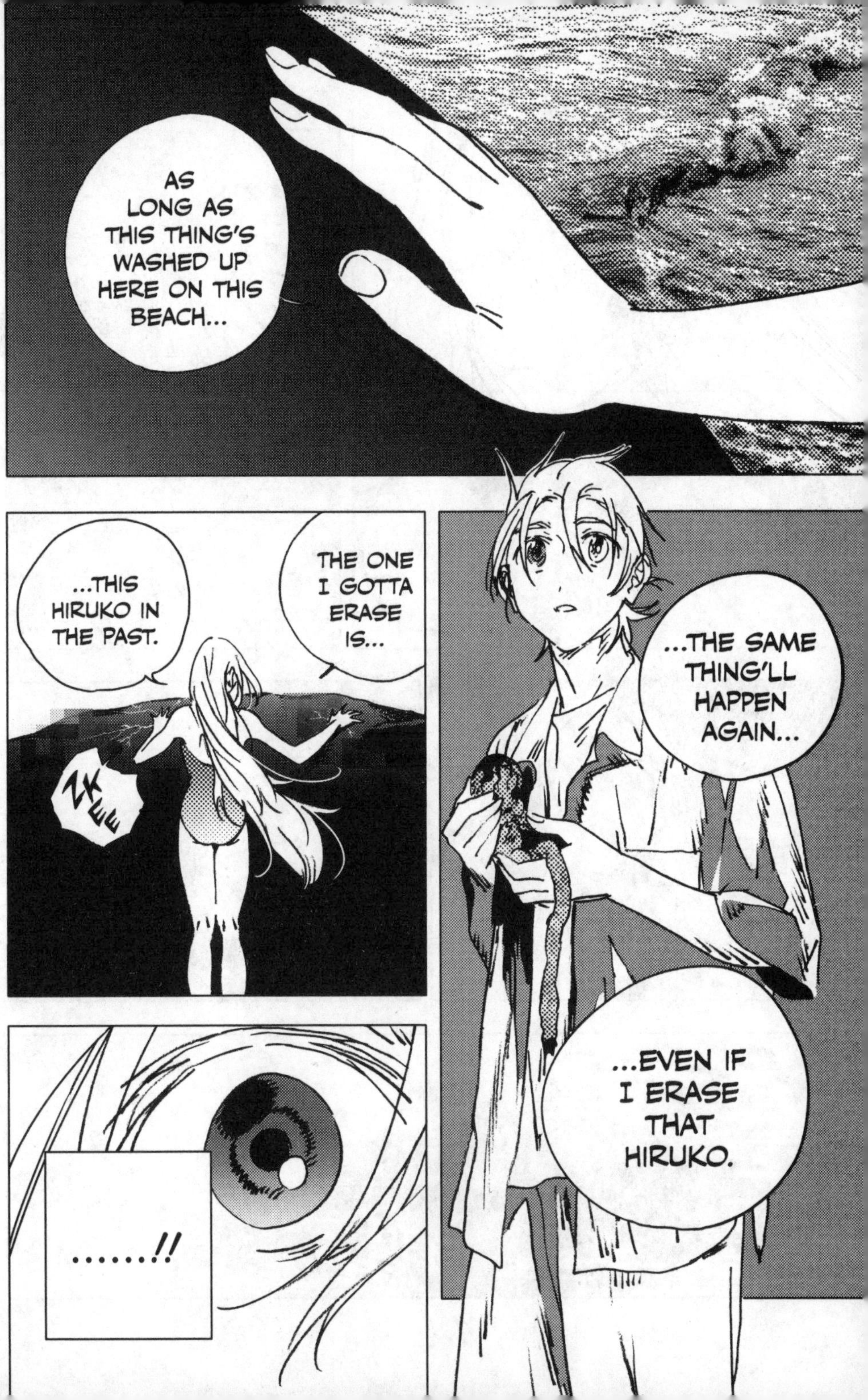
AS LONG AS THIS THING'S WASHED UP HERE ON THIS BEACH...
...THE SAME THING'LL HAPPEN AGAIN...
...EVEN IF I ERASE THAT HIRUKO.
THE ONE I GOTTA ERASE IS...
...THIS HIRUKO IN THE PAST.
ZKEE
......!!

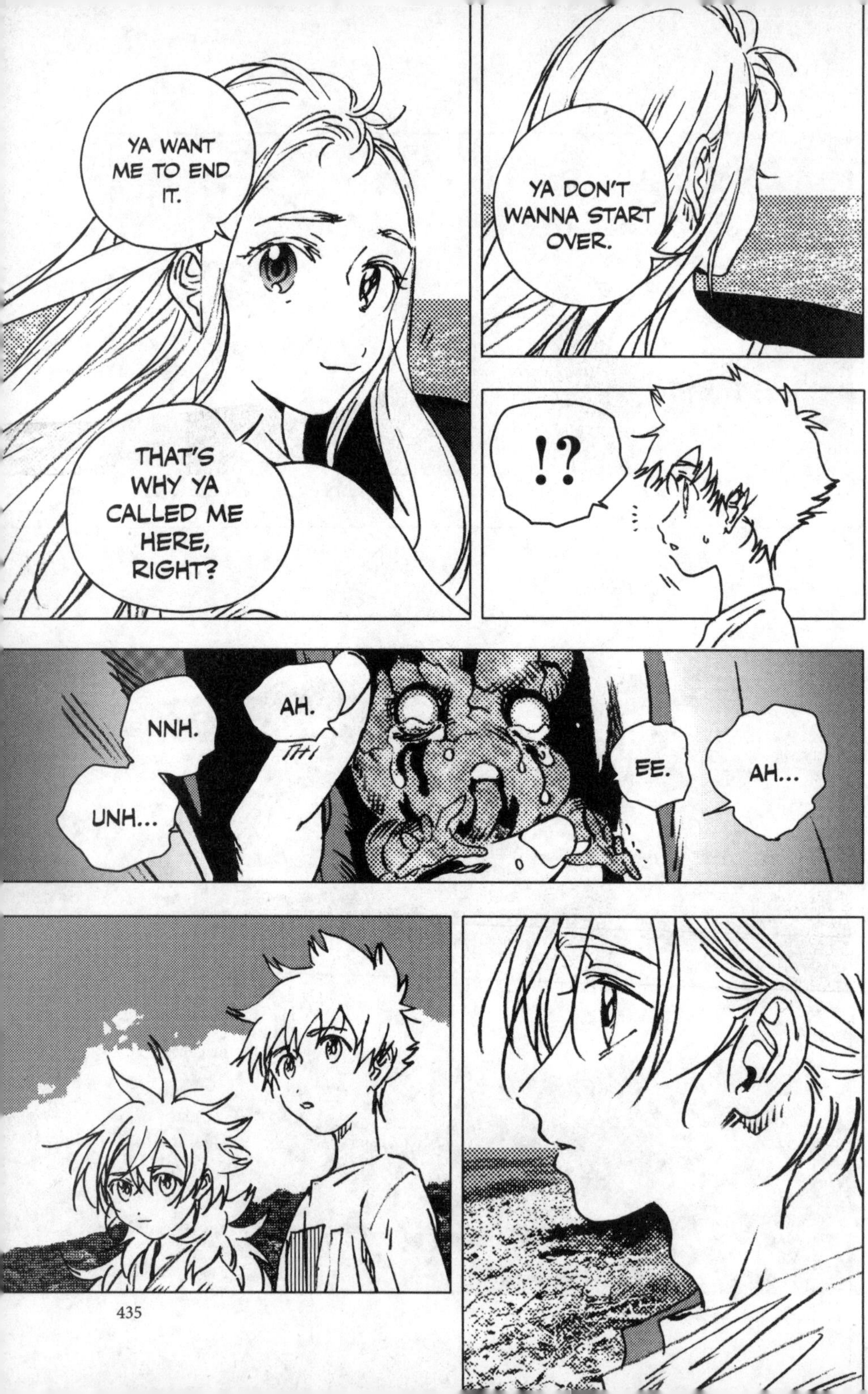

YA DON'T WANNA START OVER.
!?
YA WANT ME TO END IT.
THAT'S WHY YA CALLED ME HERE, RIGHT?
AH...
EE.
AH.
NNH.
UNH...

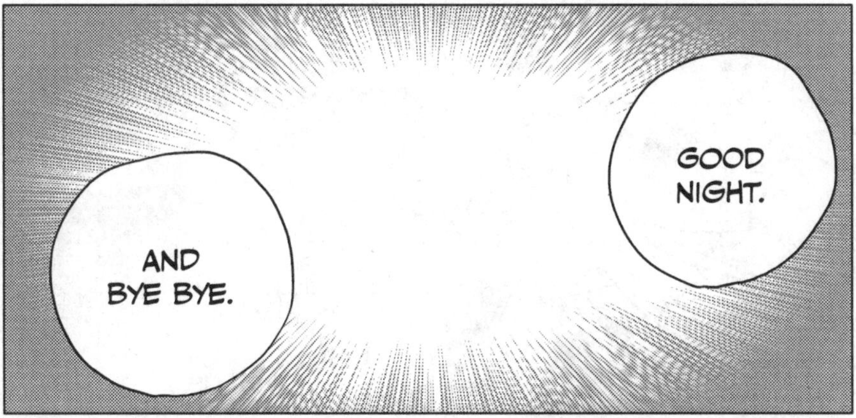
GOOD NIGHT.
AND BYE BYE.

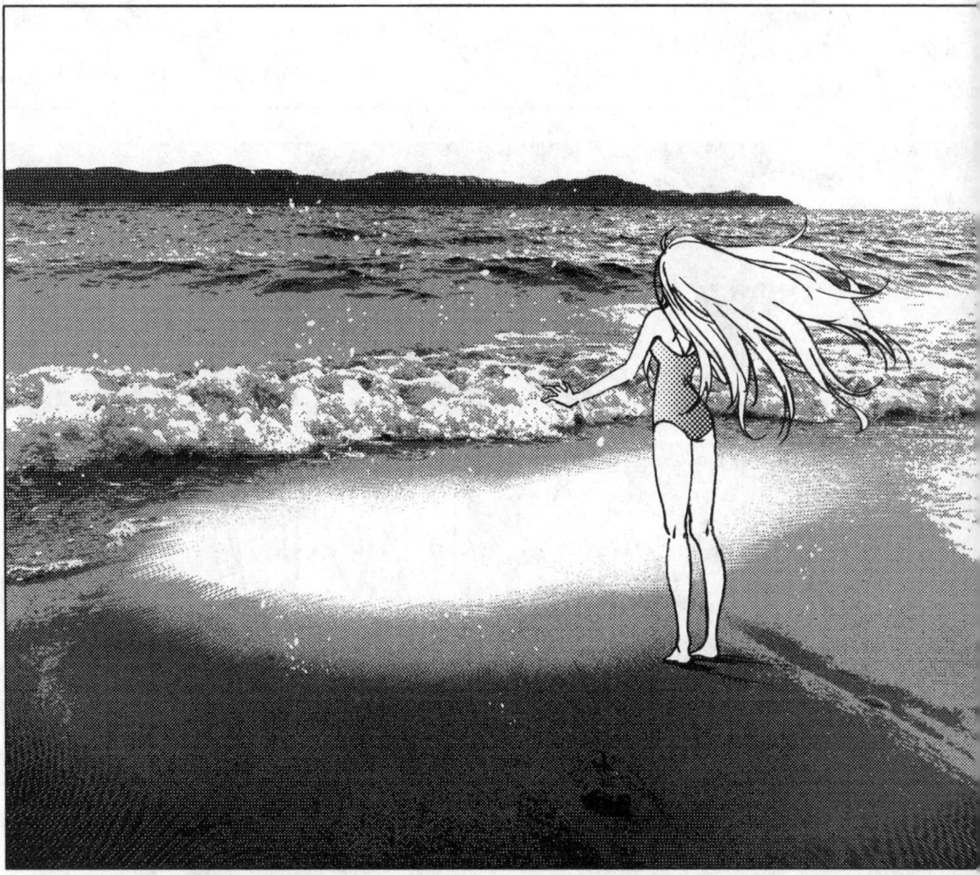

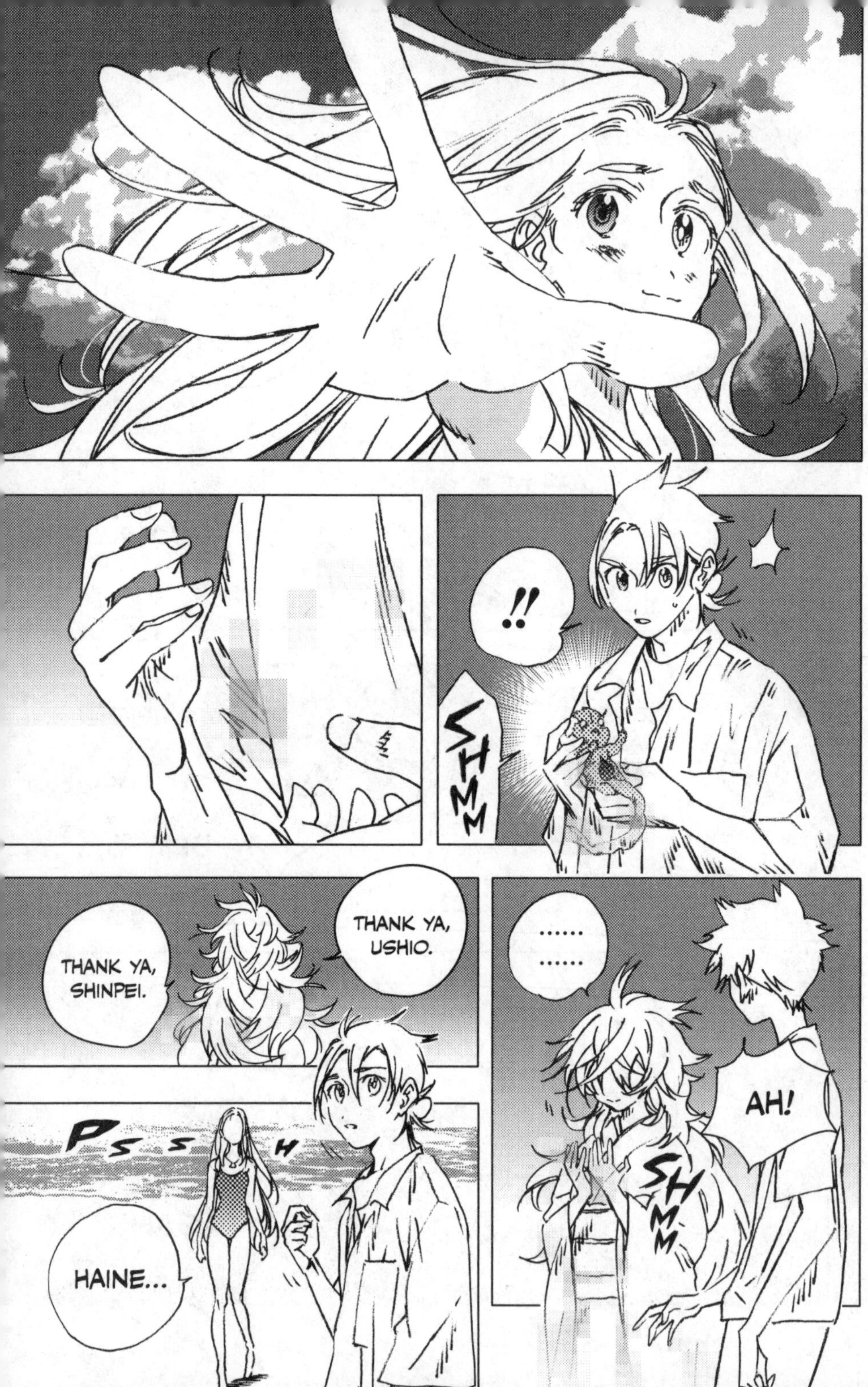
!!
SHMMM
......
......
AH!
SHMMM
THANK YA, USHIO.
THANK YA, SHINPEI.
PSSSH
HAINE...

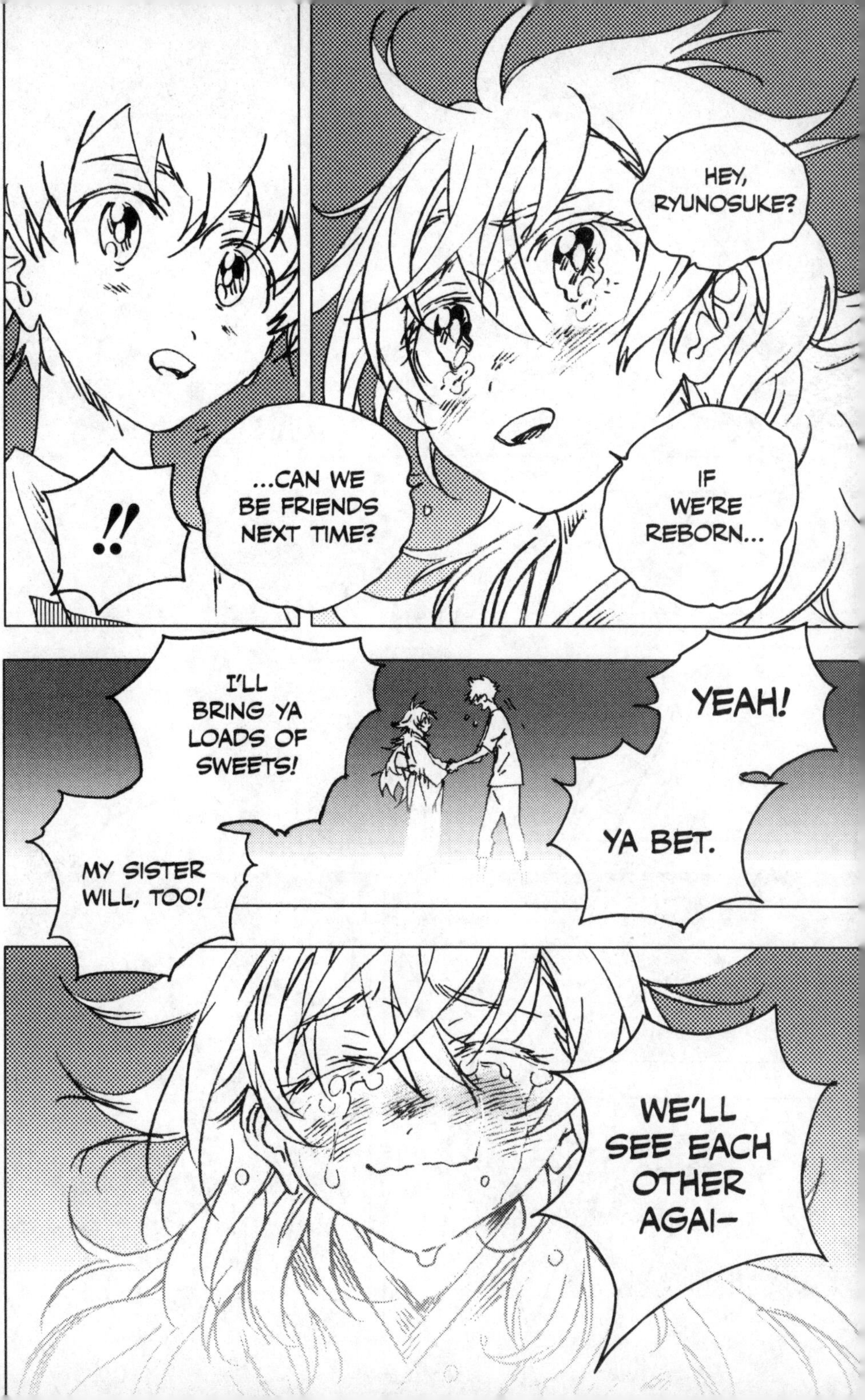
HEY, RYUNOSUKE?
IF WE'RE REBORN...
...CAN WE BE FRIENDS NEXT TIME?
!!
YEAH!
YA BET.
I'LL BRING YA LOADS OF SWEETS!
MY SISTER WILL, TOO!
WE'LL SEE EACH OTHER AGAI–

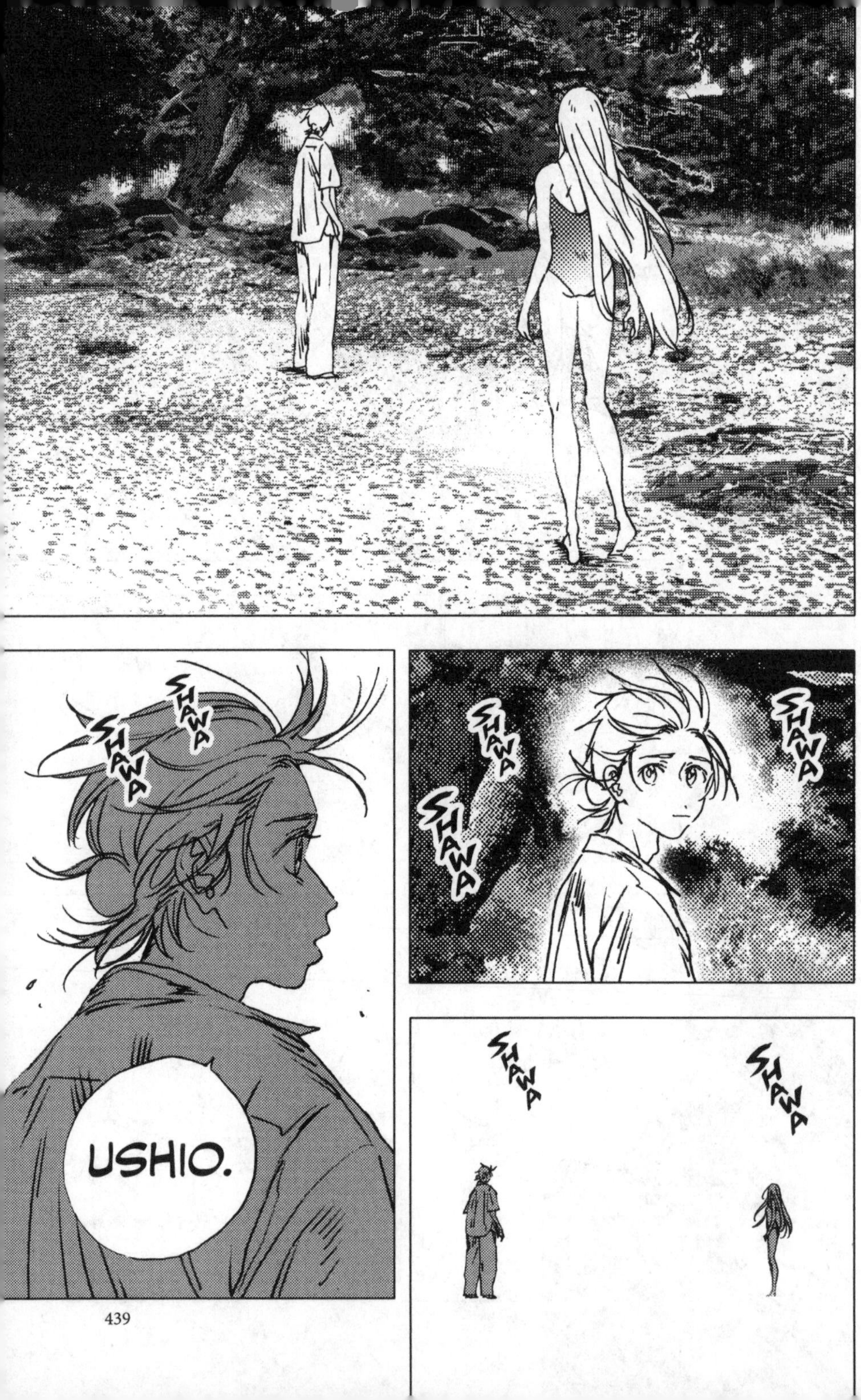
SHAWA
SHAWA
SHAWA
SHAWA
SHAWA
SHAWA
SHAWA
USHIO.

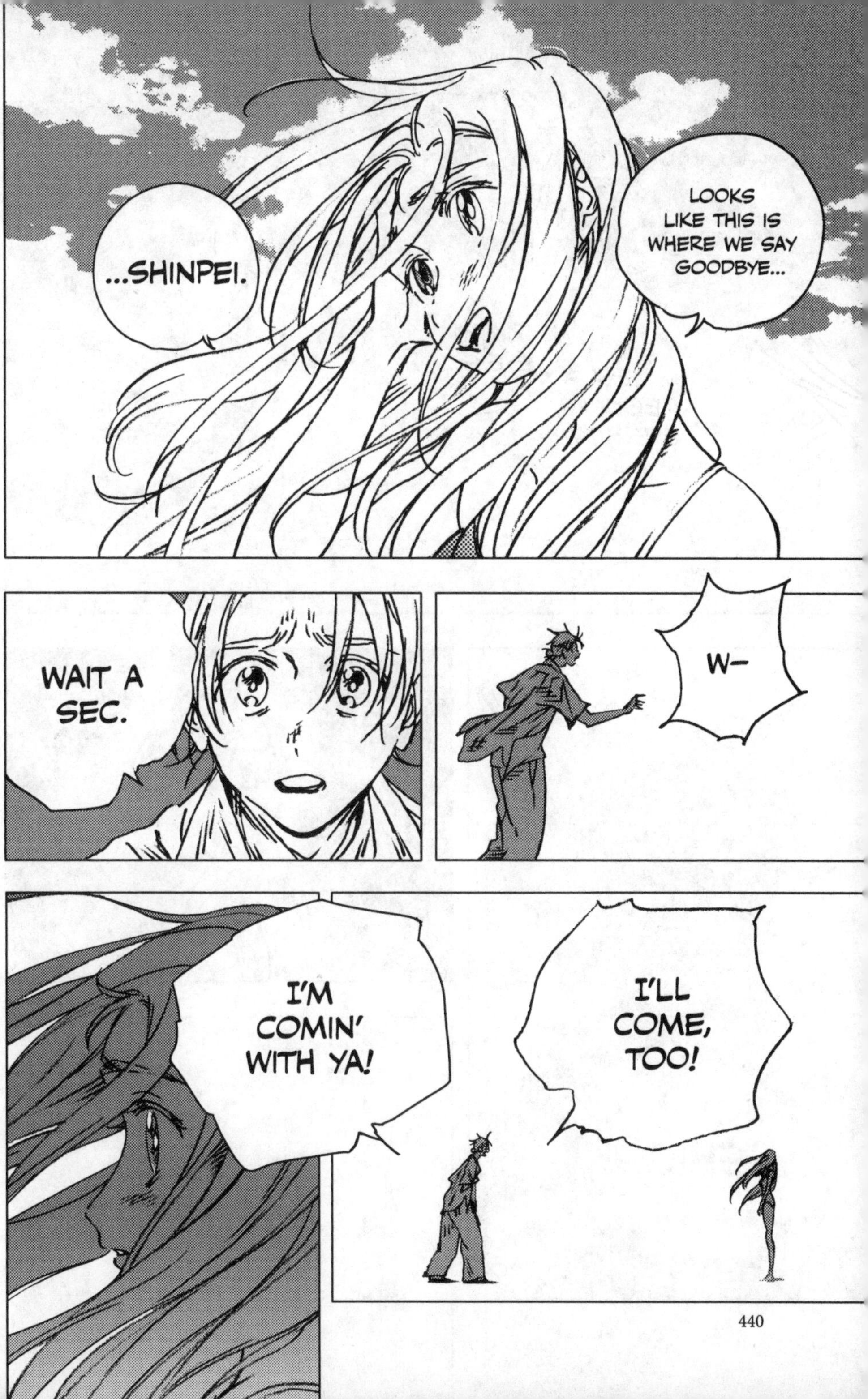
LOOKS LIKE THIS IS WHERE WE SAY GOODBYE...
...SHINPEI.
W-
WAIT A SEC.
I'LL COME, TOO!
I'M COMIN' WITH YA!

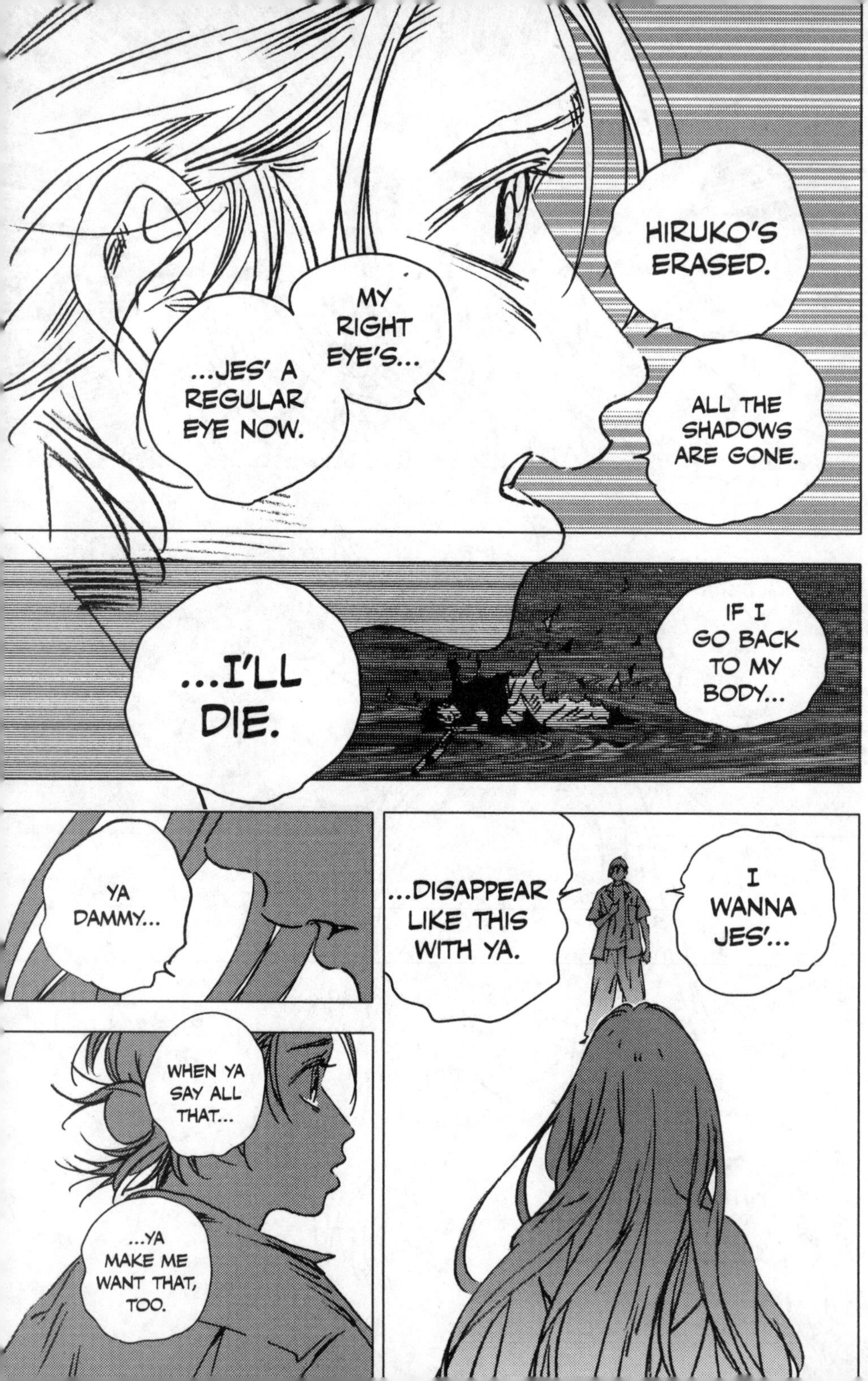
HIRUKO'S ERASED.
ALL THE SHADOWS ARE GONE.
MY RIGHT EYE'S...
...JES' A REGULAR EYE NOW.
IF I GO BACK TO MY BODY...
...I'LL DIE.
I WANNA JES'...
...DISAPPEAR LIKE THIS WITH YA.
YA DAMMY...
WHEN YA SAY ALL THAT...
...YA MAKE ME WANT THAT, TOO.

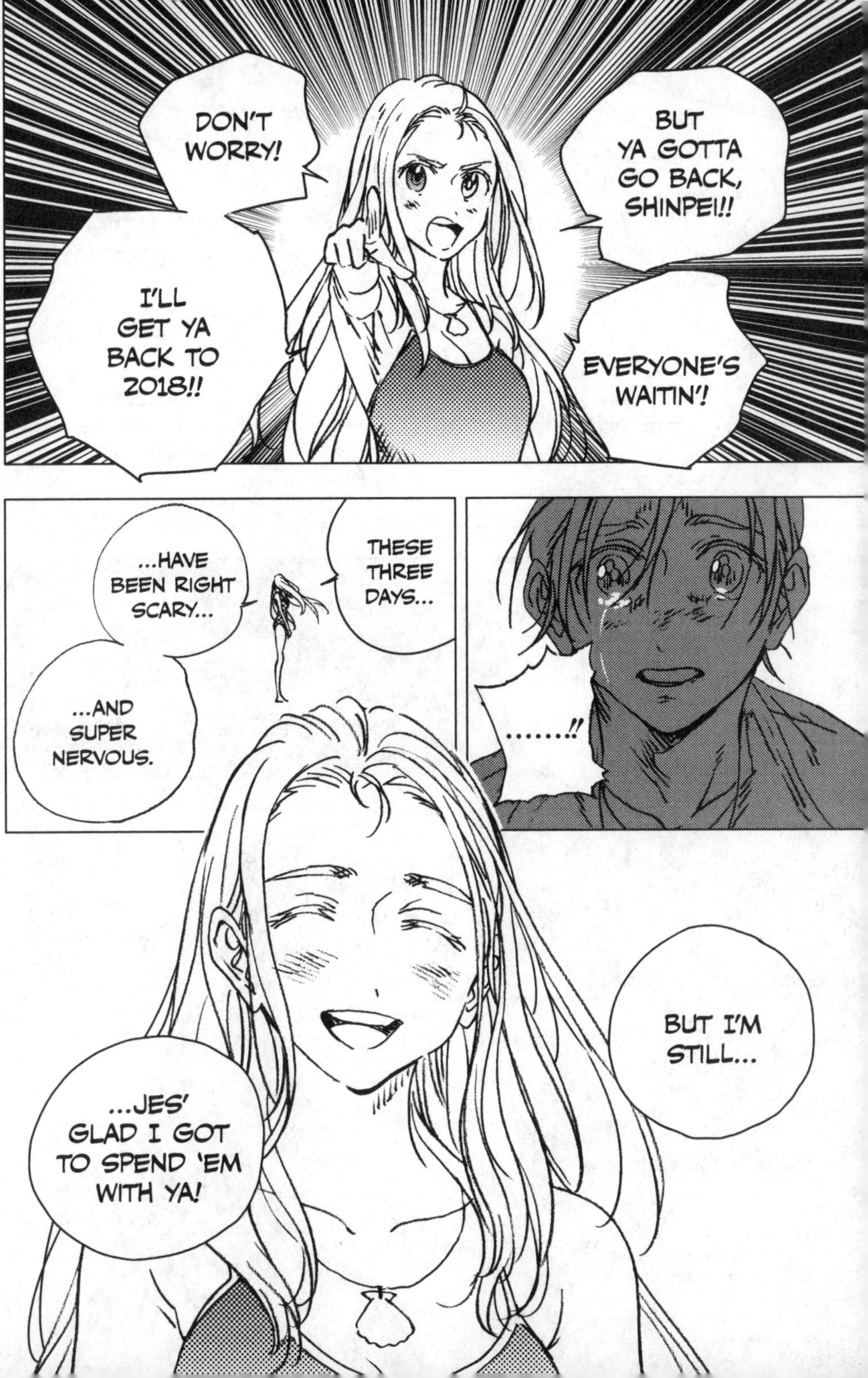
BUT YA GOTTA GO BACK, SHINPEI!!
EVERYONE'S WAITIN'!
DON'T WORRY!
I'LL GET YA BACK TO 2018!!
.......!!
THESE THREE DAYS...
...HAVE BEEN RIGHT SCARY...
...AND SUPER NERVOUS.
BUT I'M STILL...
...JES' GLAD I GOT TO SPEND 'EM WITH YA!

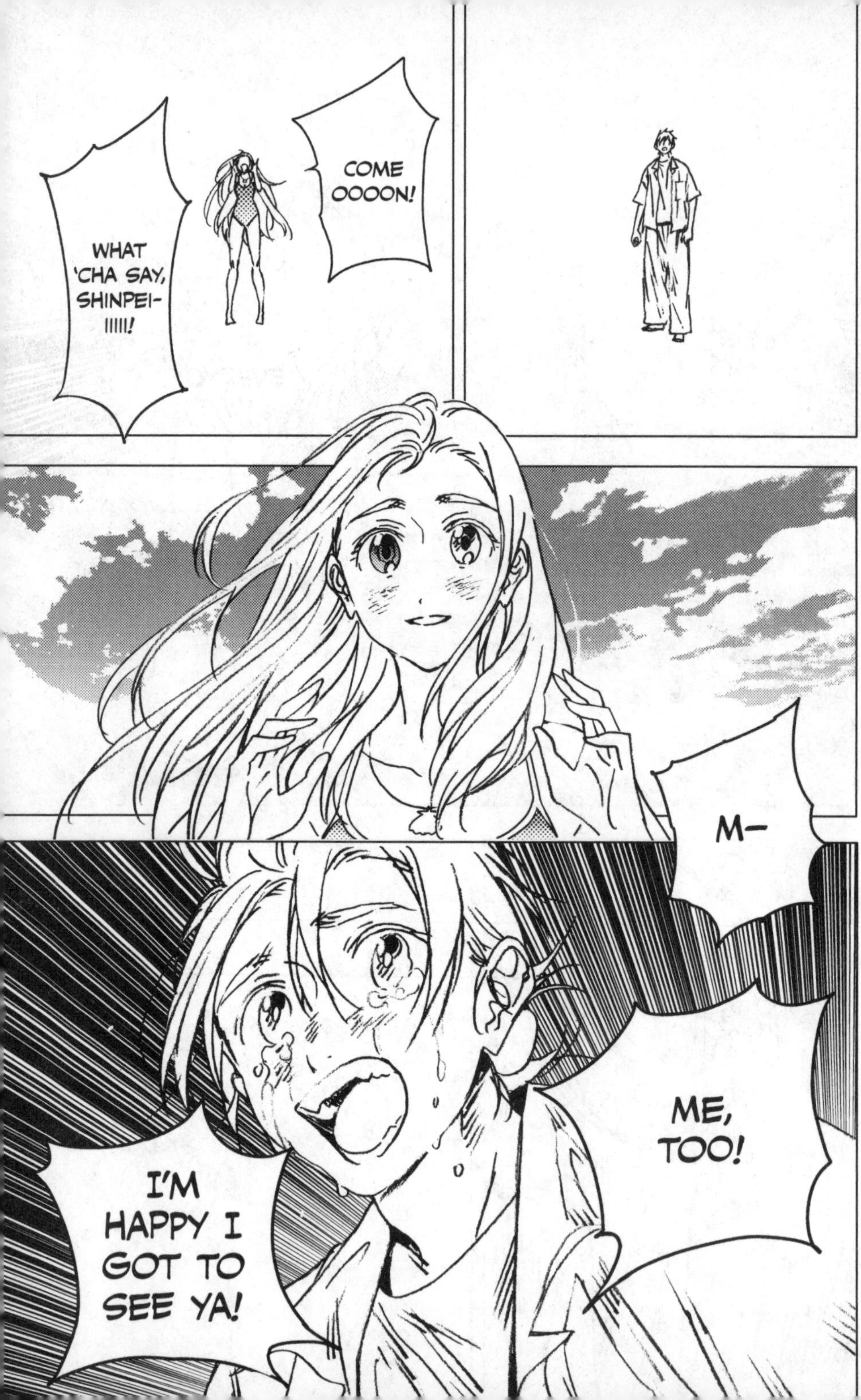
COME OOOON!
WHAT 'CHA SAY, SHINPEI-IIIII!
M—
ME, TOO!
I'M HAPPY I GOT TO SEE YA!

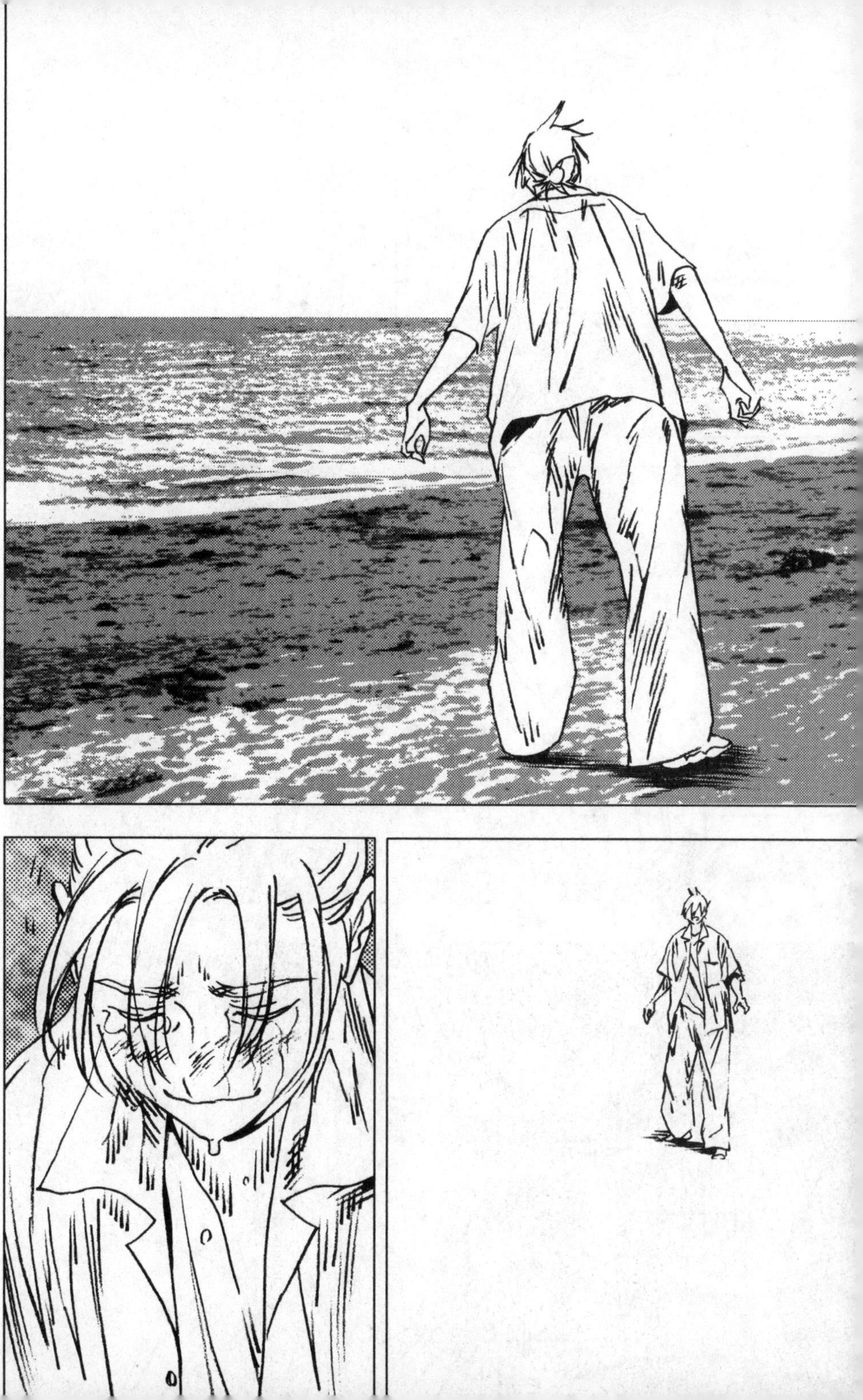

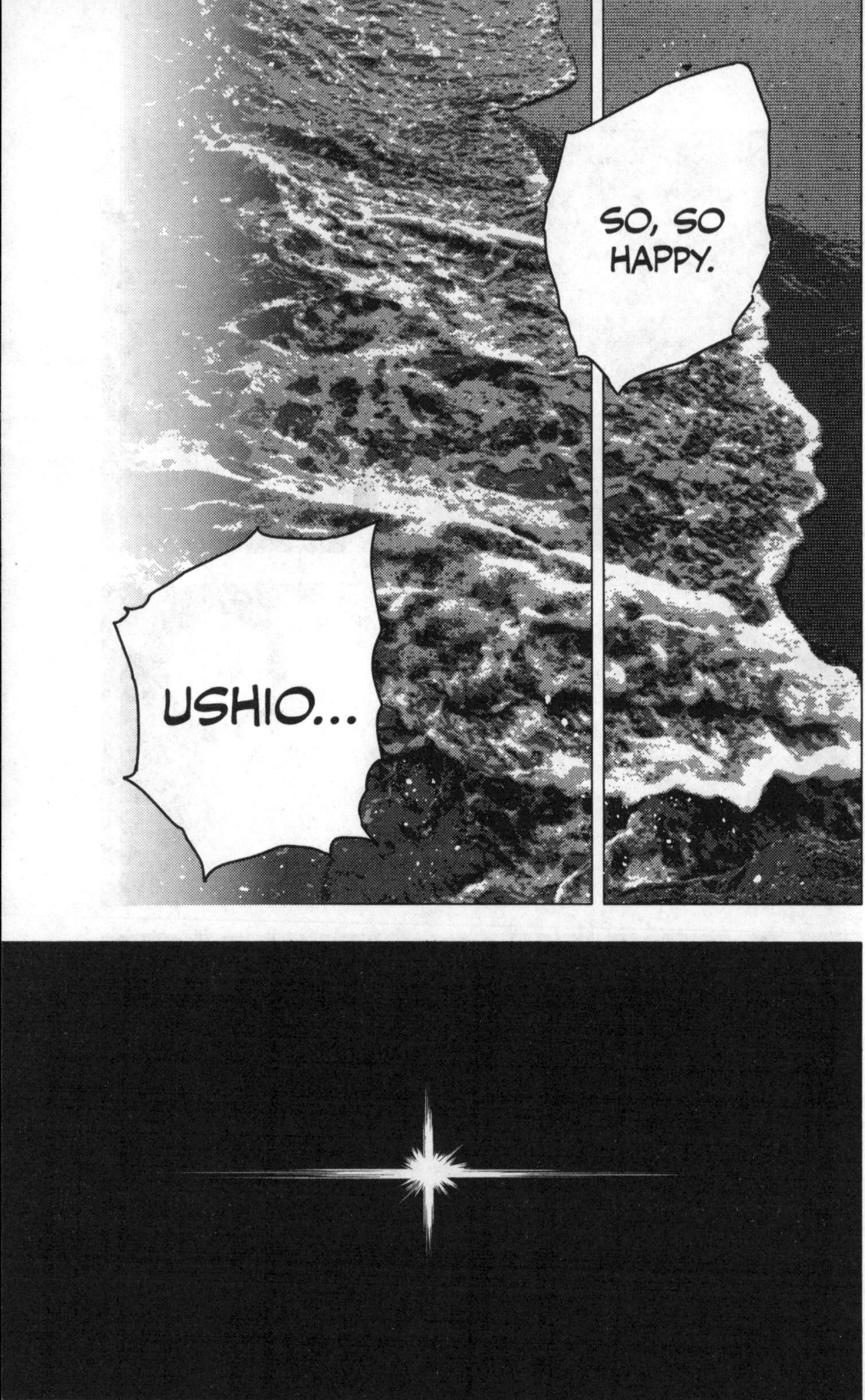
SO, SO HAPPY.
USHIO...

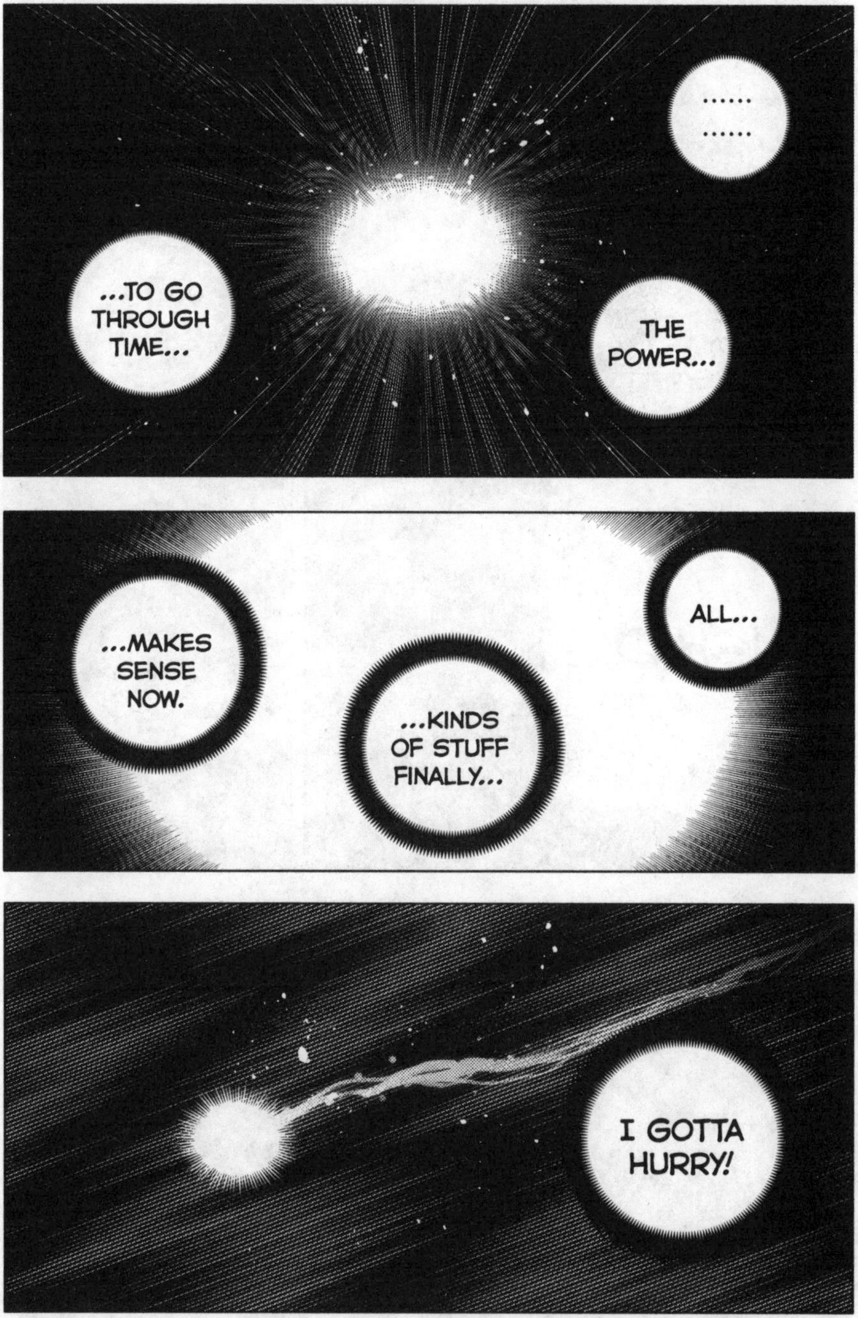
......
......
THE POWER...
...TO GO THROUGH TIME...
ALL...
...KINDS OF STUFF FINALLY...
...MAKES SENSE NOW.
I GOTTA HURRY!

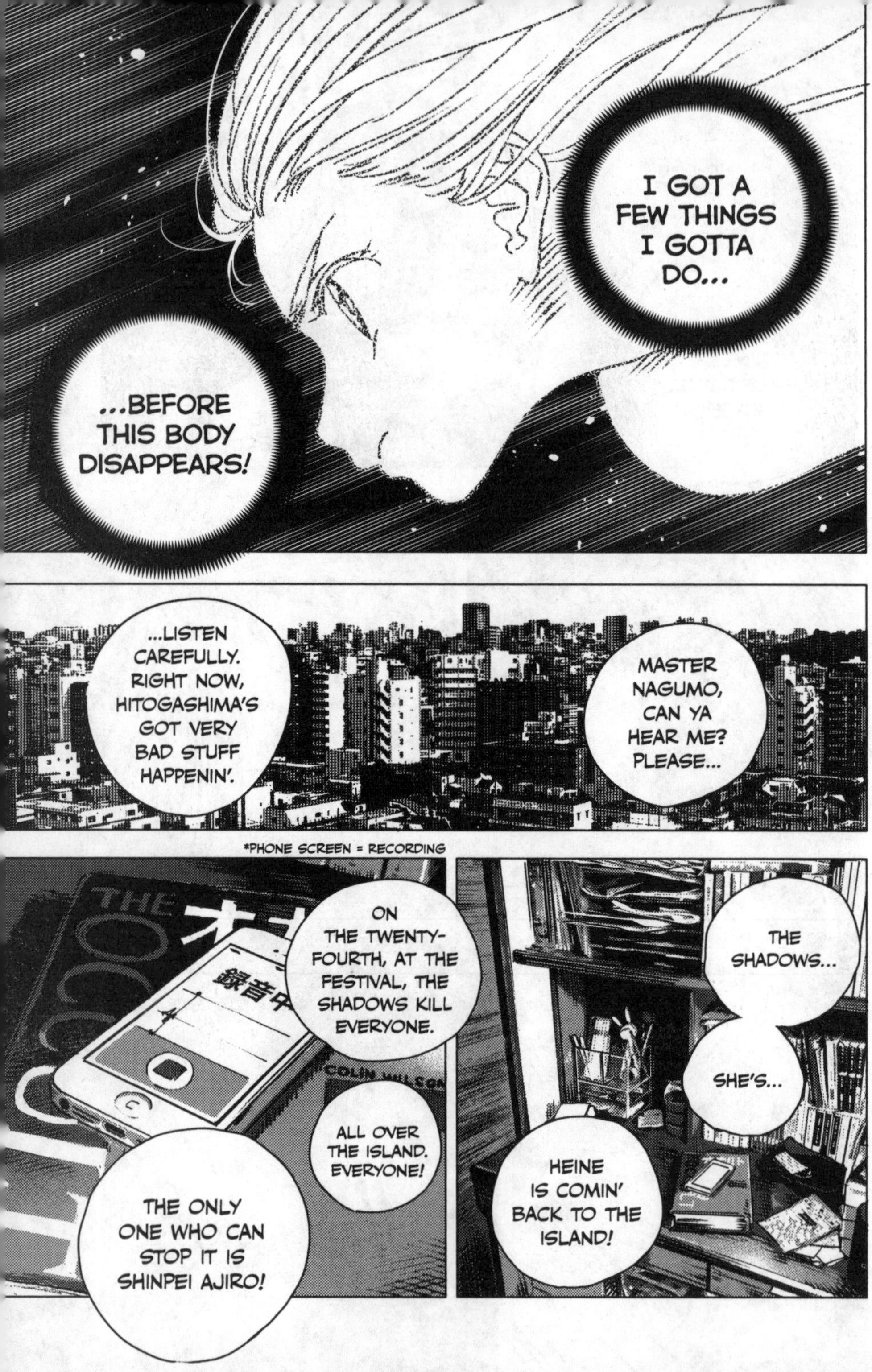
I GOT A FEW THINGS I GOTTA DO...
...BEFORE THIS BODY DISAPPEARS!
MASTER NAGUMO, CAN YA HEAR ME? PLEASE...
...LISTEN CAREFULLY. RIGHT NOW, HITOGASHIMA'S GOT VERY BAD STUFF HAPPENIN'.
*PHONE SCREEN = RECORDING
THE SHADOWS...
SHE'S...
HEINE IS COMIN' BACK TO THE ISLAND!
録音中
ON THE TWENTY-FOURTH, AT THE FESTIVAL, THE SHADOWS KILL EVERYONE.
ALL OVER THE ISLAND. EVERYONE!
THE ONLY ONE WHO CAN STOP IT IS SHINPEI AJIRO!

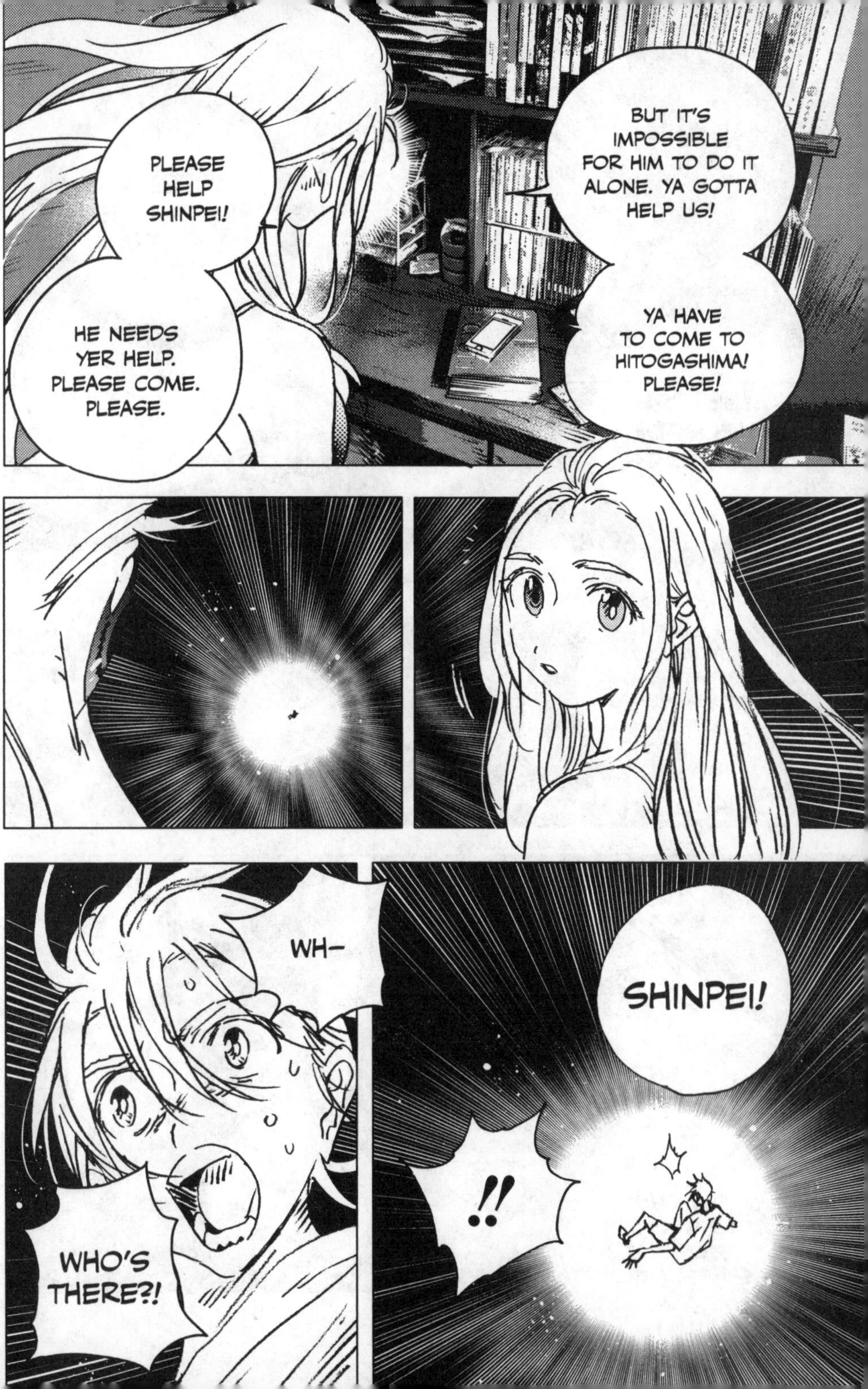
BUT IT'S IMPOSSIBLE FOR HIM TO DO IT ALONE. YA GOTTA HELP US!
YA HAVE TO COME TO HITOGASHIMA! PLEASE!
PLEASE HELP SHINPEI!
HE NEEDS YER HELP. PLEASE COME. PLEASE.
SHINPEI!
!!
WH-
WHO'S THERE?!

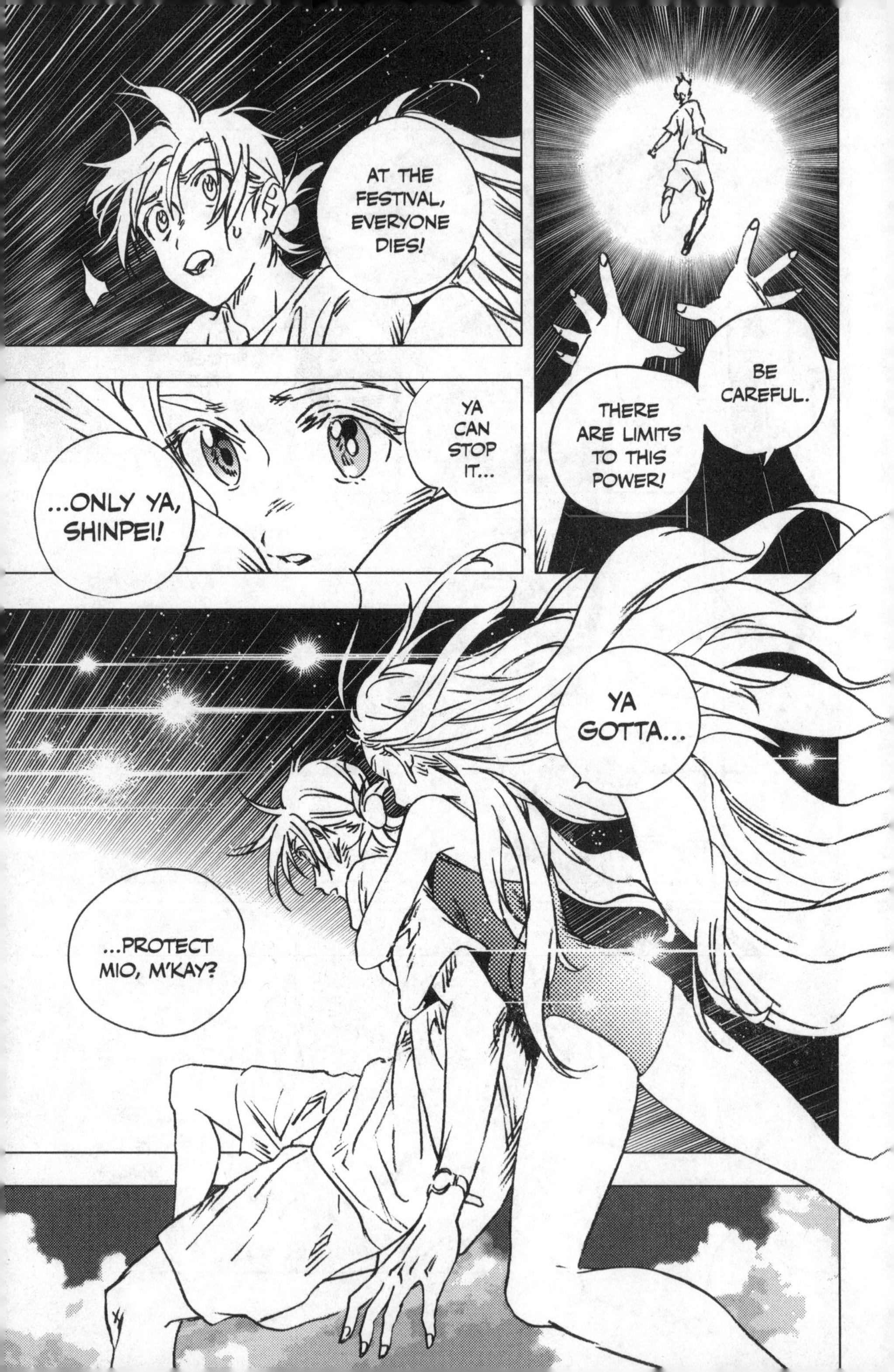
BE CAREFUL.
THERE ARE LIMITS TO THIS POWER!
AT THE FESTIVAL, EVERYONE DIES!
YA CAN STOP IT...
...ONLY YA, SHINPEI!
YA GOTTA...
...PROTECT MIO, M'KAY?

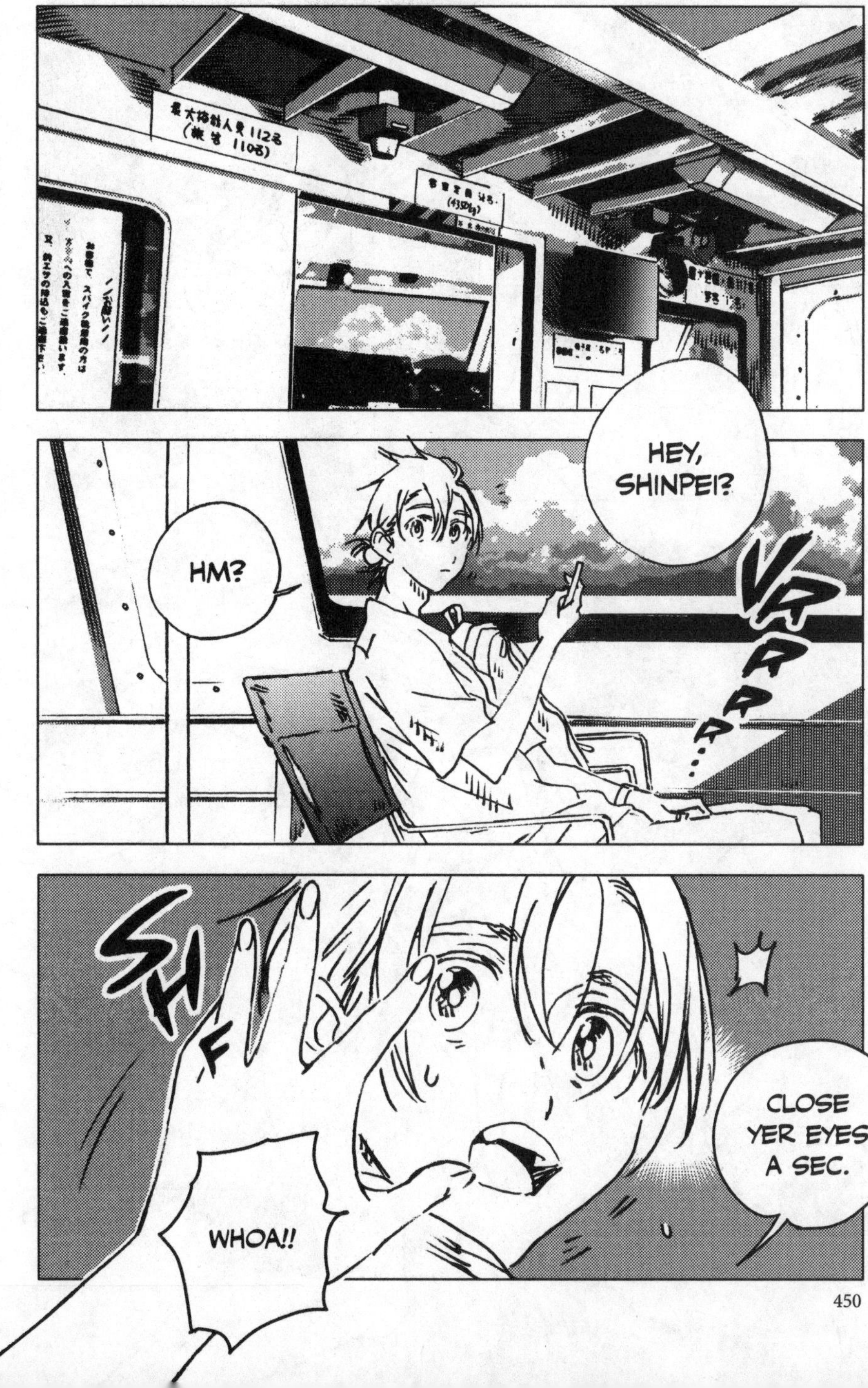

HEY, SHINPEI?
VRRRRR...
HM?
CLOSE YER EYES A SEC.
SHF
WHOA!!

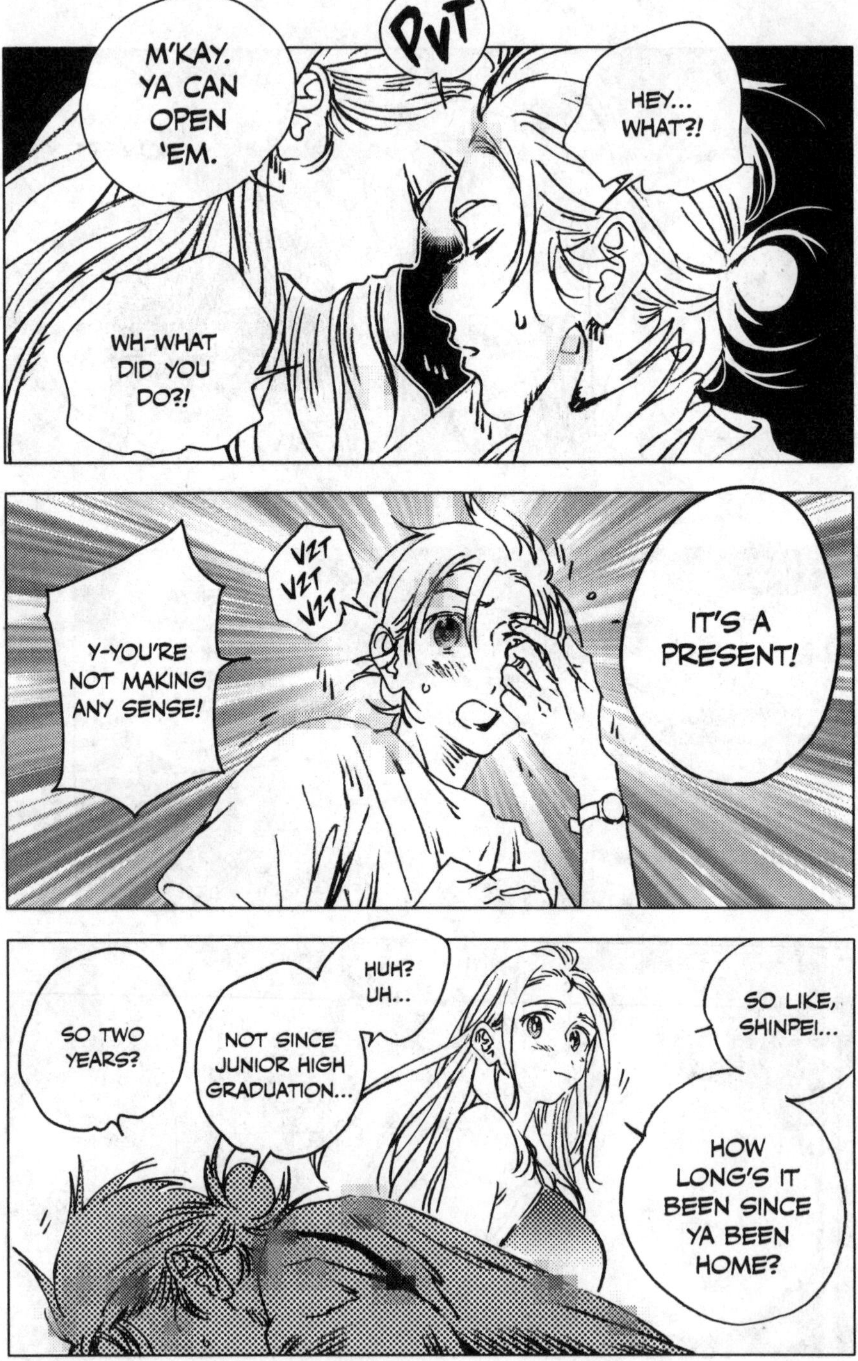
HEY... WHAT?!
PVT
M'KAY. YA CAN OPEN 'EM.
WH-WHAT DID YOU DO?!
IT'S A PRESENT!
VZT VZT VZT
Y-YOU'RE NOT MAKING ANY SENSE!
SO LIKE, SHINPEI...
HOW LONG'S IT BEEN SINCE YA BEEN HOME?
HUH? UH...
NOT SINCE JUNIOR HIGH GRADUATION...
SO TWO YEARS?

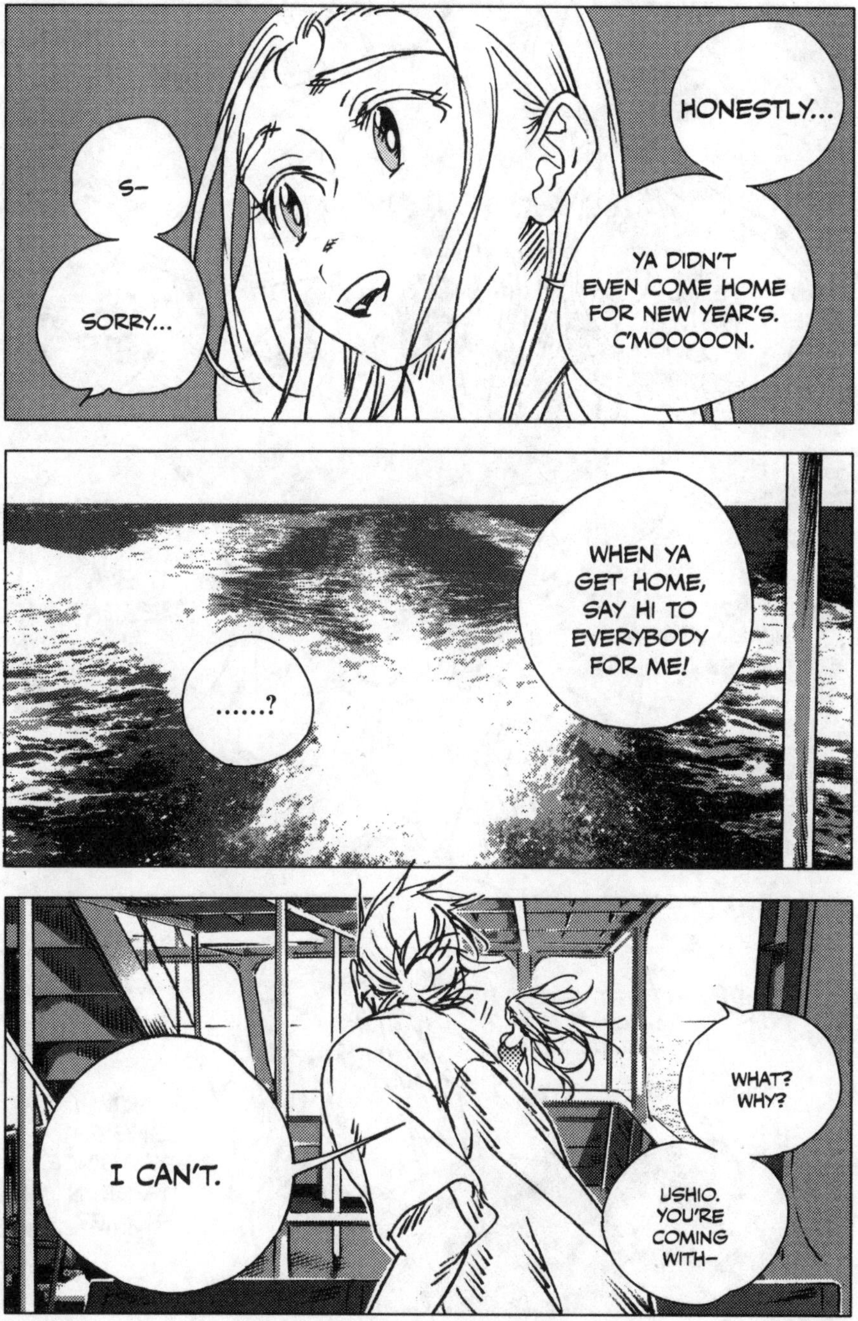
HONESTLY...
YA DIDN'T EVEN COME HOME FOR NEW YEAR'S. C'MOOOOON.
S-
SORRY...
WHEN YA GET HOME, SAY HI TO EVERYBODY FOR ME!
......?
WHAT? WHY?
USHIO. YOU'RE COMING WITH–
I CAN'T.

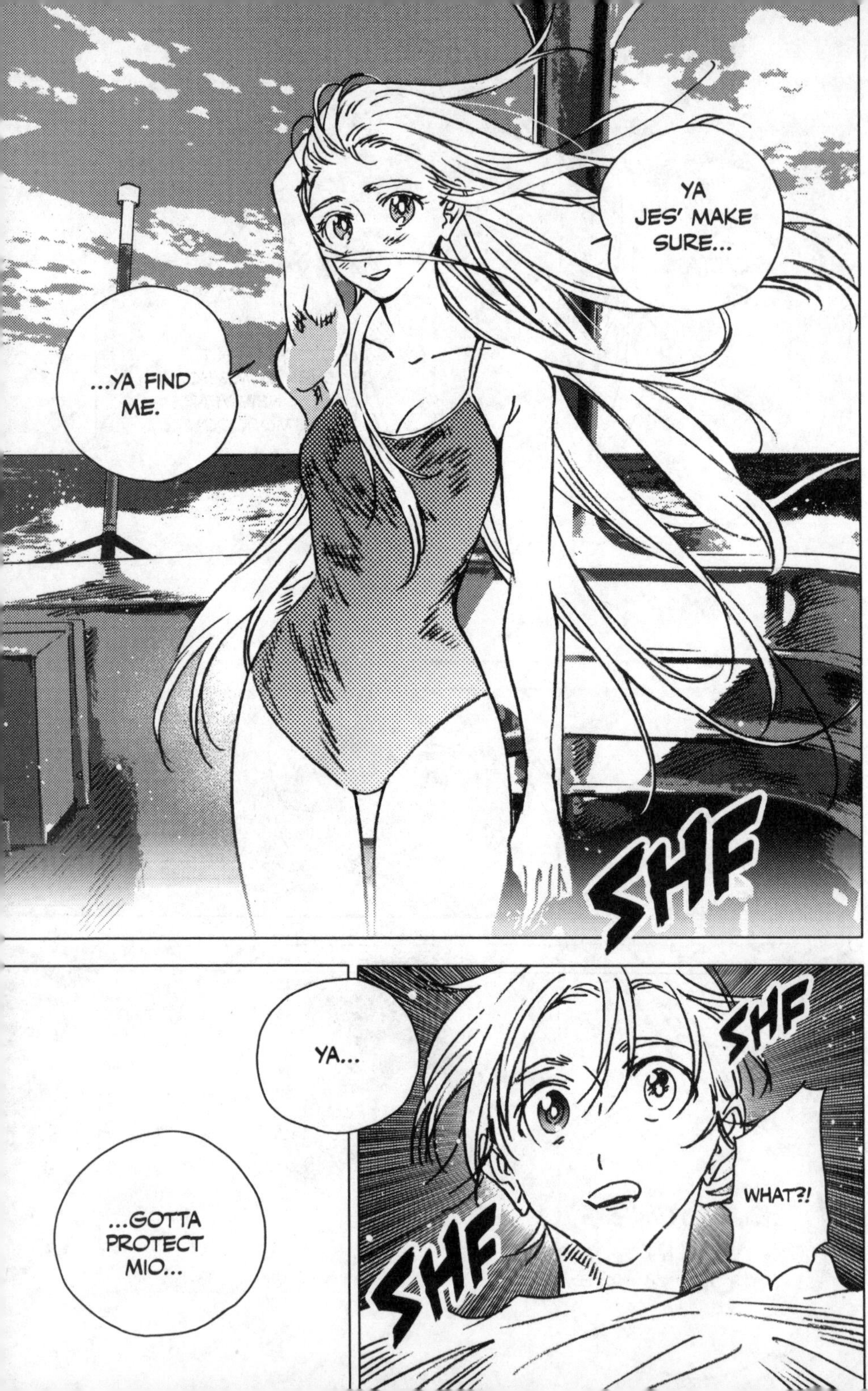
YA JES' MAKE SURE...
...YA FIND ME.
SHF
SHF
WHAT?!
SHF
YA...
...GOTTA PROTECT MIO...

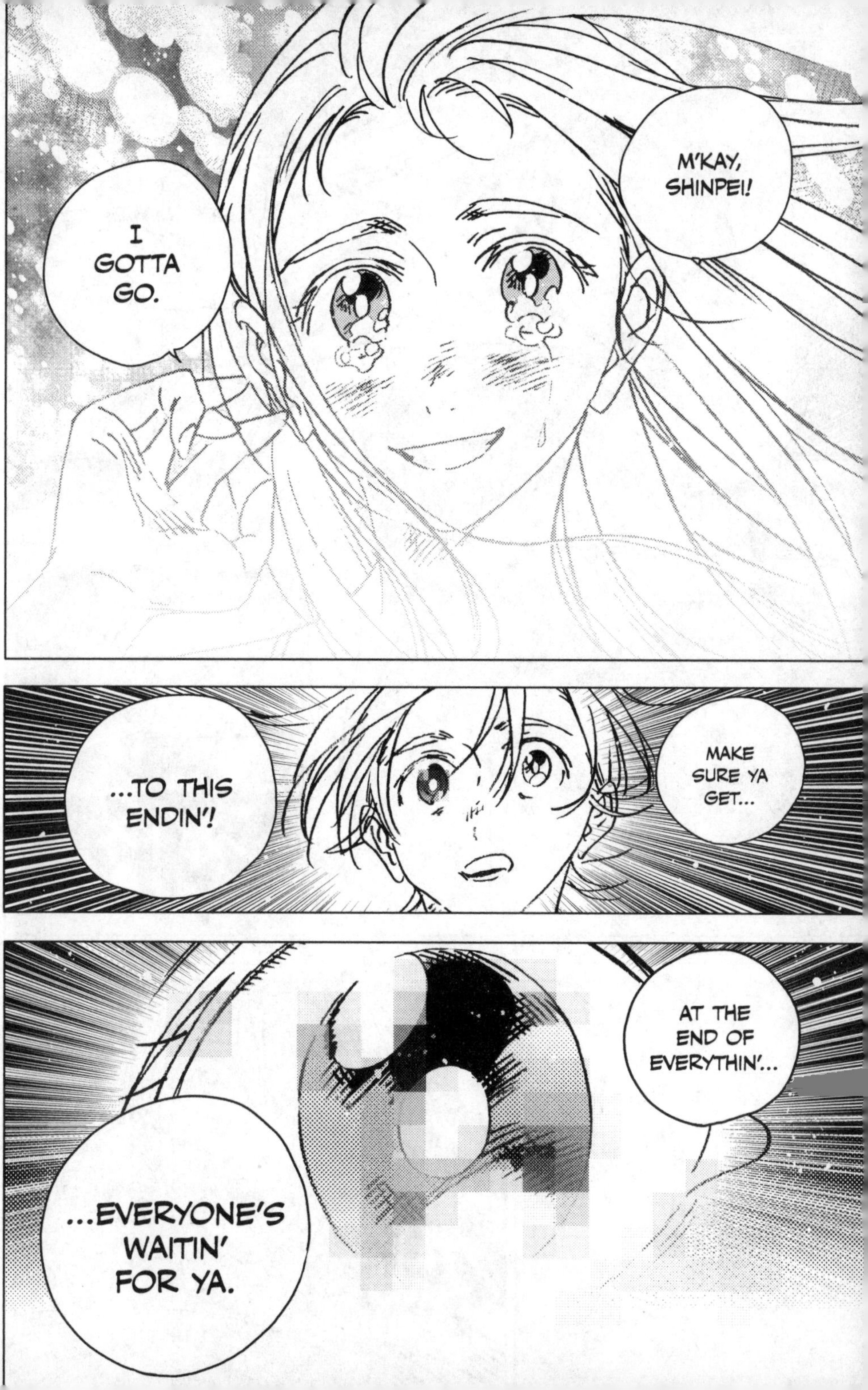
M'KAY, SHINPEI!
I GOTTA GO.
MAKE SURE YA GET...
...TO THIS ENDIN'!
AT THE END OF EVERYTHIN'...
...EVERYONE'S WAITIN' FOR YA.

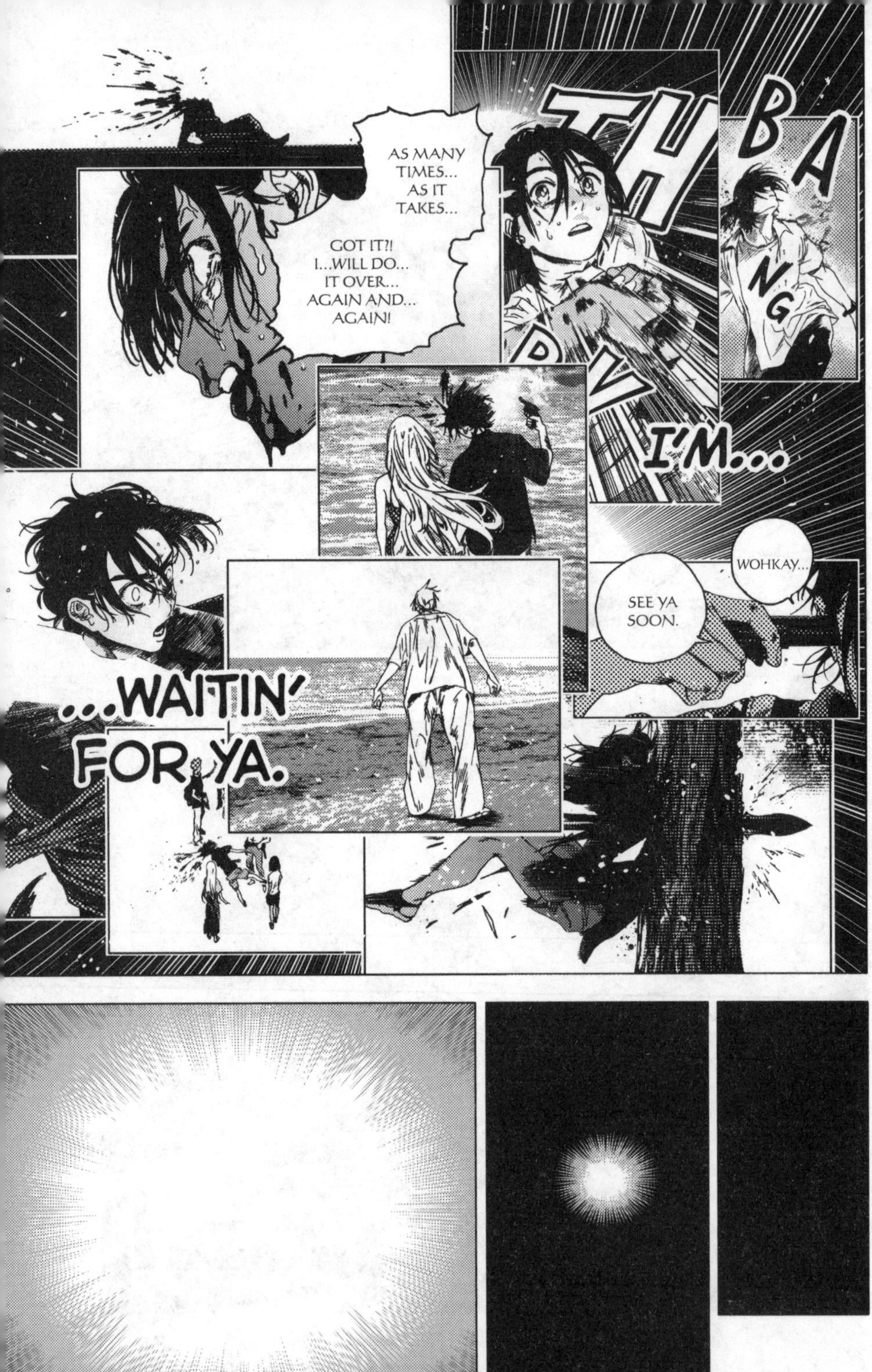
BANG
AS MANY TIMES... AS IT TAKES...
GOT IT?! I...WILL DO... IT OVER... AGAIN AND... AGAIN!
I'M...
WOHKAY...
SEE YA SOON.
...WAITIN' FOR YA.

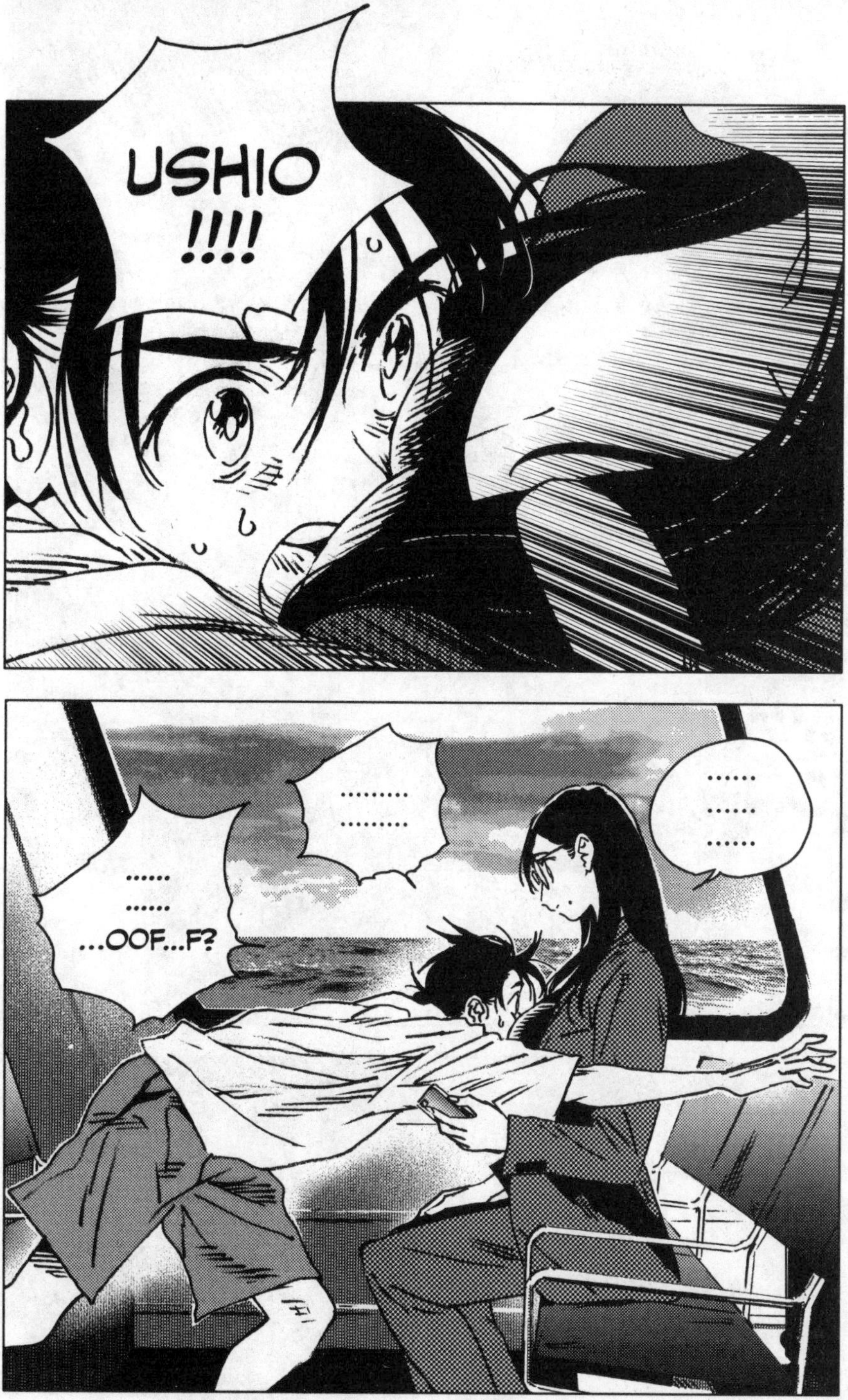
USHIO !!!!
......
......
......
....
....
......
......
...OOF...F?

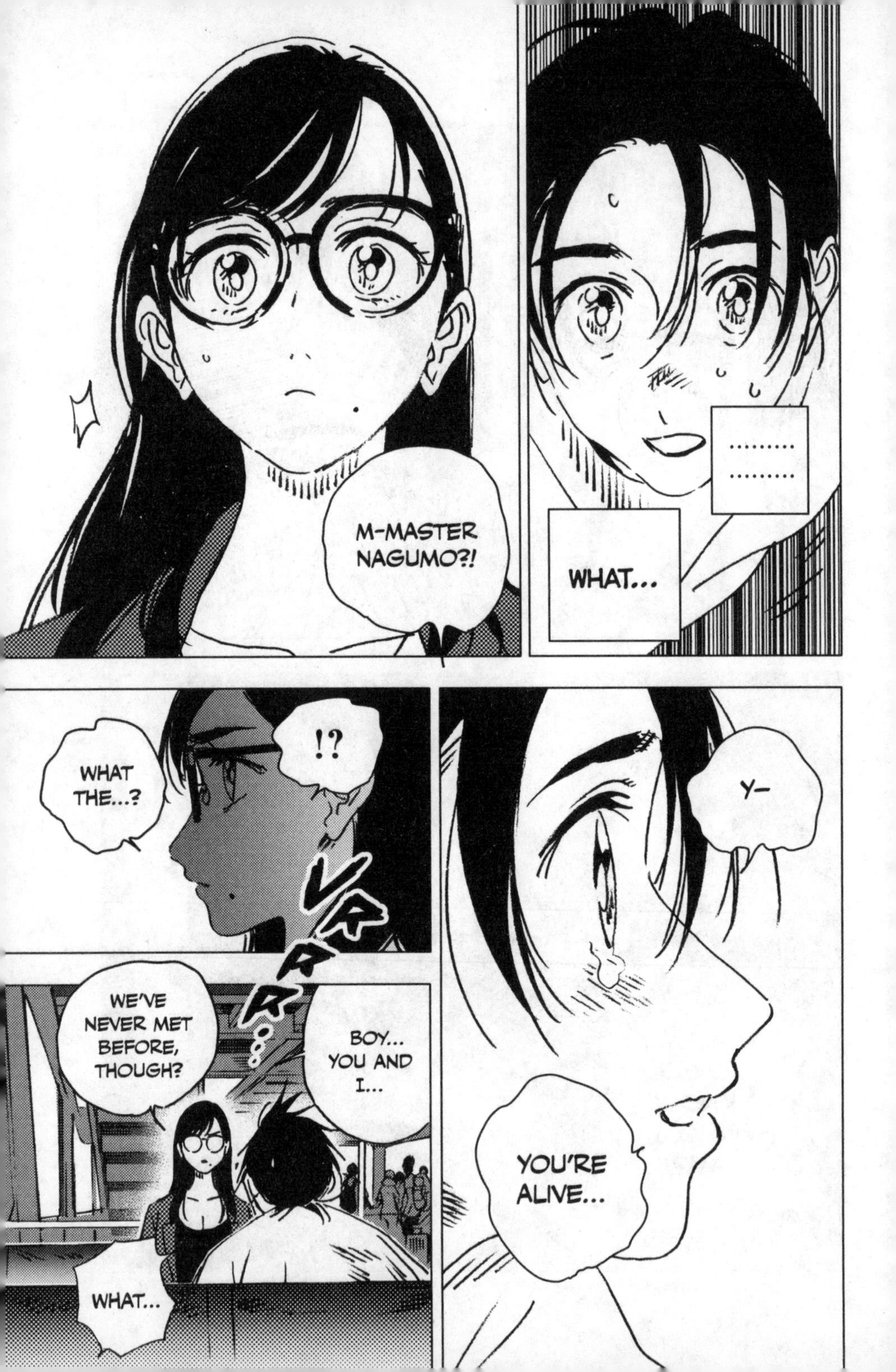

....
WHAT...
M-MASTER NAGUMO?!
Y-
YOU'RE ALIVE...
!?
WHAT THE...?
VRRRR...
BOY... YOU AND I...
WE'VE NEVER MET BEFORE, THOUGH?
WHAT...

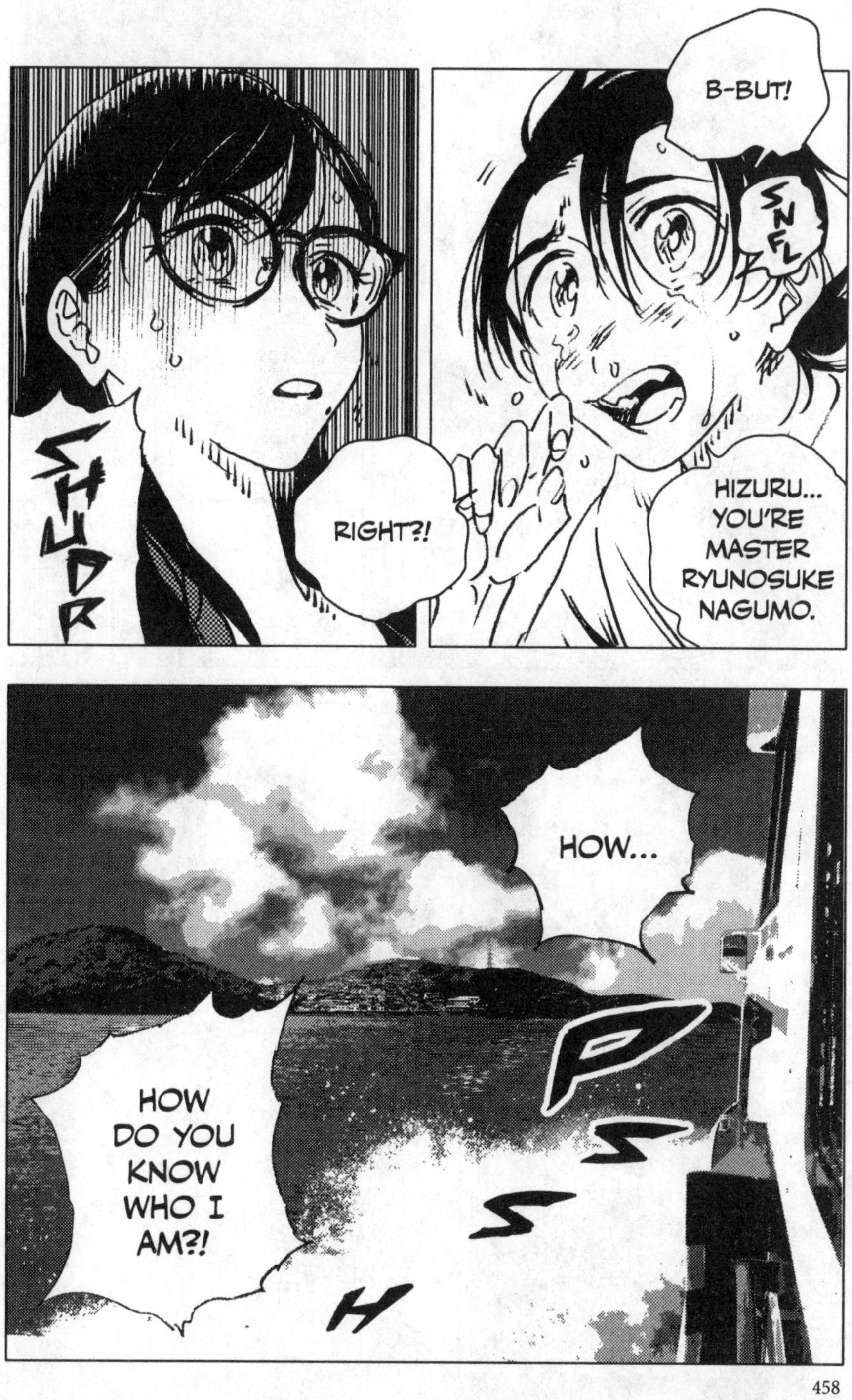

B-BUT!
SNFL
HIZURU... YOU'RE MASTER RYUNOSUKE NAGUMO.
RIGHT?!
SHUDR
HOW...
PSSH
HOW DO YOU KNOW WHO I AM?!

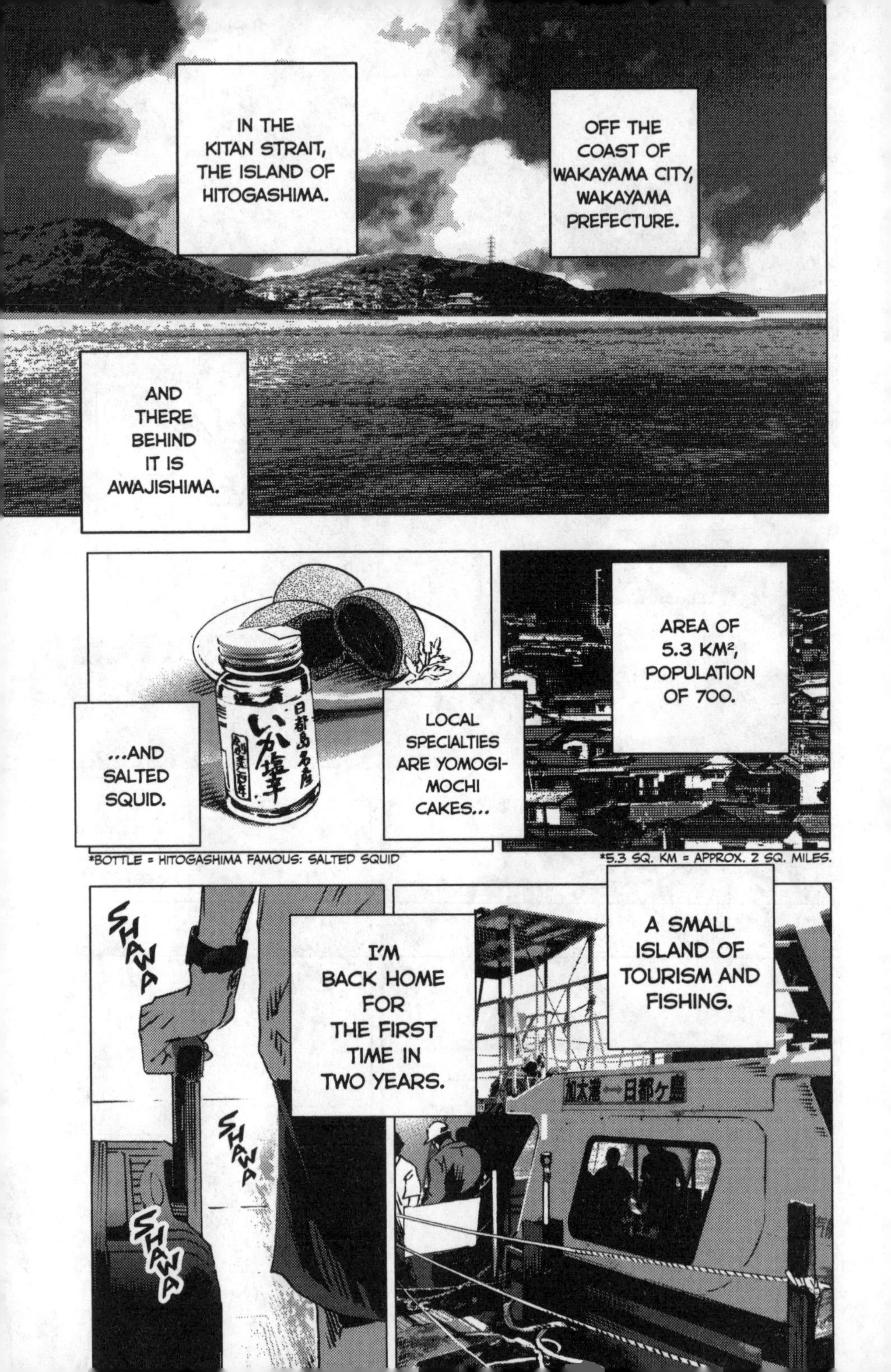
OFF THE COAST OF WAKAYAMA CITY, WAKAYAMA PREFECTURE.
IN THE KITAN STRAIT, THE ISLAND OF HITOGASHIMA.
AND THERE BEHIND IT IS AWAJISHIMA.
AREA OF 5.3 KM^2, POPULATION OF 700.
*5.3 SQ. KM = APPROX. 2 SQ. MILES.
LOCAL SPECIALTIES ARE YOMOGI-MOCHI CAKES...
...AND SALTED SQUID.
*BOTTLE = HITOGASHIMA FAMOUS: SALTED SQUID
A SMALL ISLAND OF TOURISM AND FISHING.
I'M BACK HOME FOR THE FIRST TIME IN TWO YEARS.
SHAWA
SHAWA
SHAWA

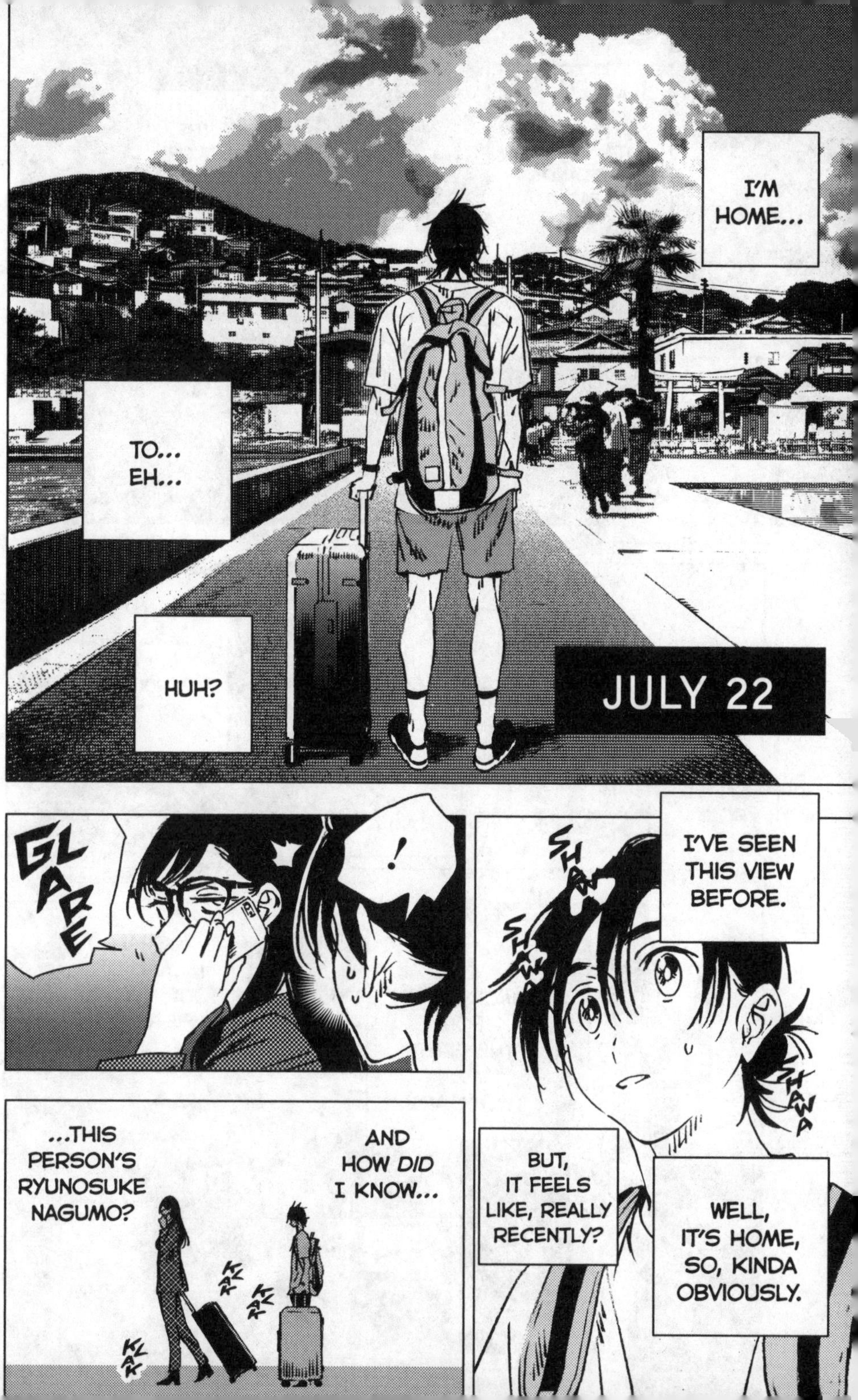
I'M HOME...
TO... EH...
HUH?
JULY 22
I'VE SEEN THIS VIEW BEFORE.
SHAW
SHAW
BUT, IT FEELS LIKE, REALLY RECENTLY?
SHAWA
WELL, IT'S HOME, SO, KINDA OBVIOUSLY.
!
GLARE
AND HOW *DID* I KNOW...
...THIS PERSON'S RYUNOSUKE NAGUMO?
KLAK
KLAK
KLAK

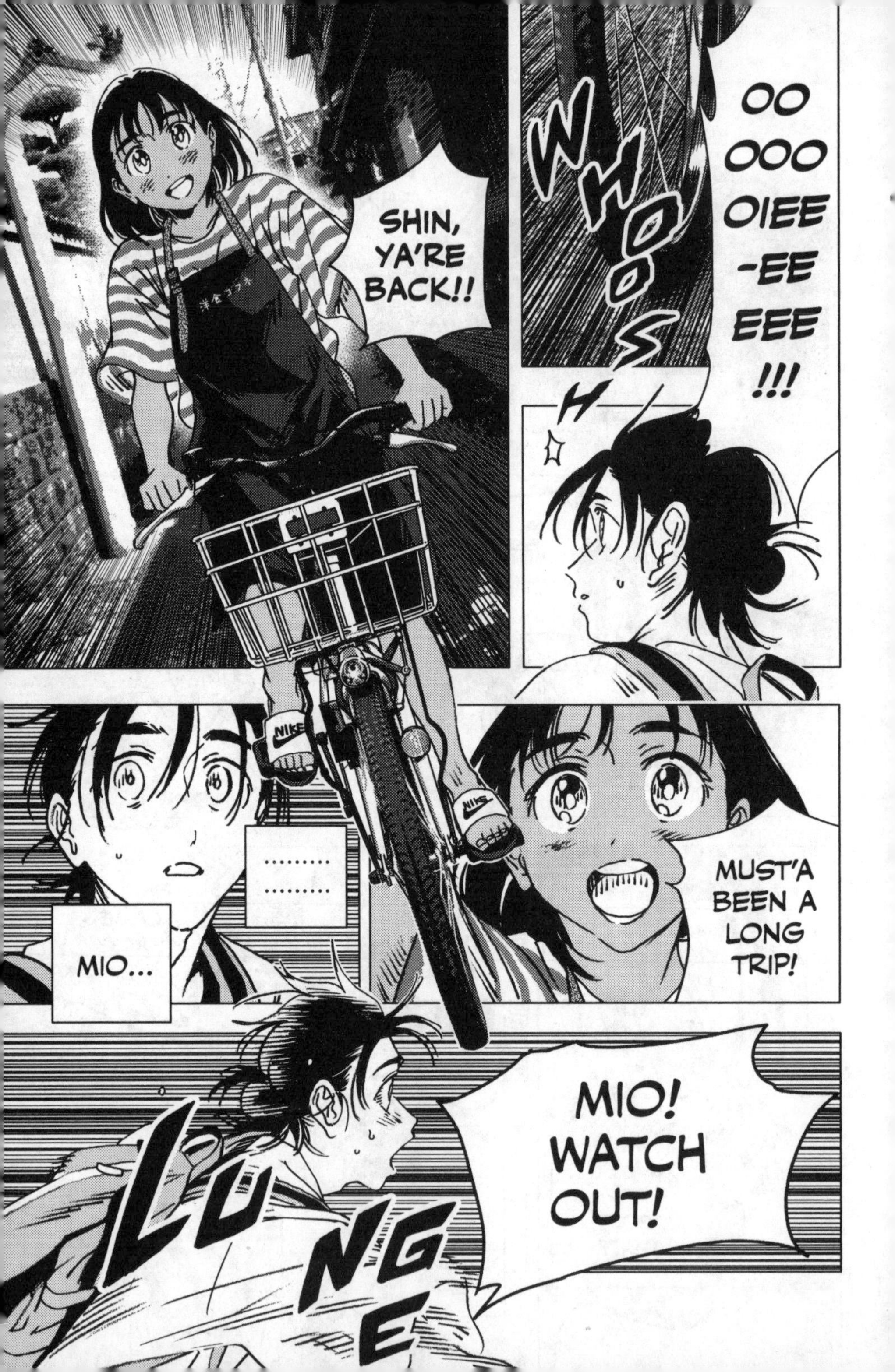
OO OOO OIEEE -EE EEE !!!
WHOOSH
SHIN, YA'RE BACK!!
MUST'A BEEN A LONG TRIP!
....
....
MIO...
MIO! WATCH OUT!
LUNGE

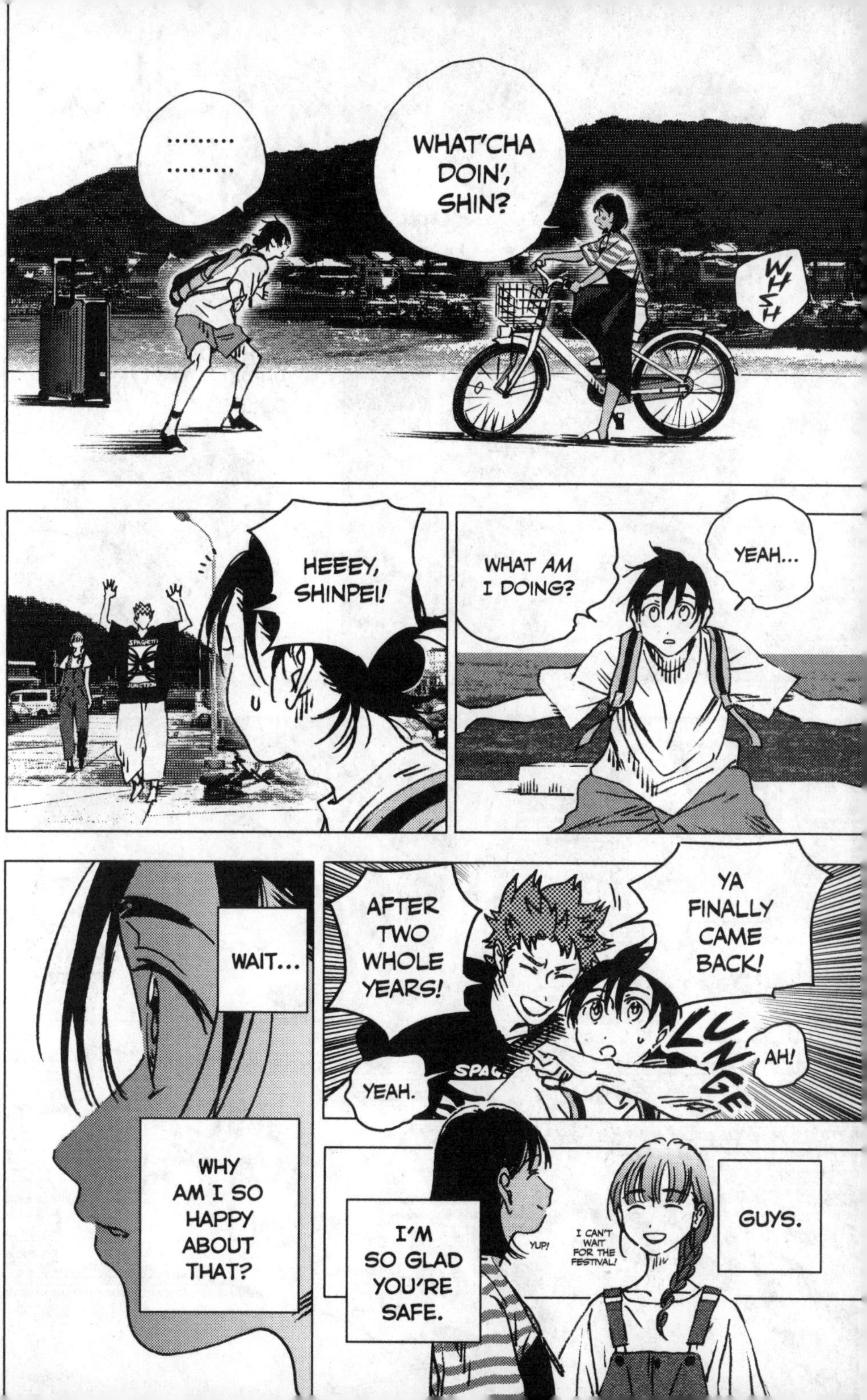
WHAT'CHA DOIN', SHIN?
WHSH
....
....
YEAH...
WHAT AM I DOING?
HEEEY, SHINPEI!
YA FINALLY CAME BACK!
AFTER TWO WHOLE YEARS!
LUNGE
AH!
YEAH.
GUYS.
I CAN'T WAIT FOR THE FESTIVAL!
YUP!
I'M SO GLAD YOU'RE SAFE.
WAIT...
WHY AM I SO HAPPY ABOUT THAT?

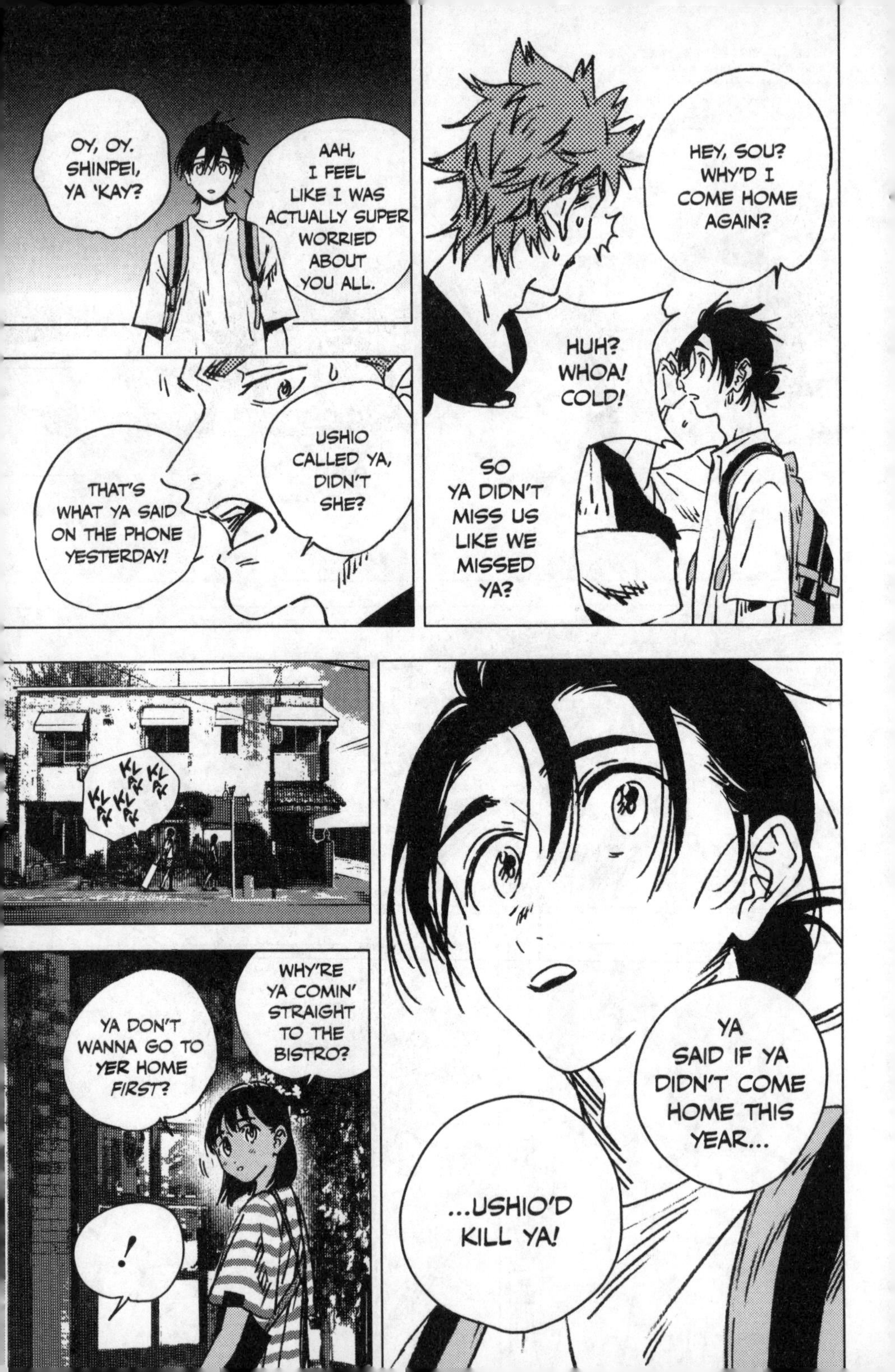
HEY, SOU? WHY'D I COME HOME AGAIN?
HUH? WHOA! COLD!
SO YA DIDN'T MISS US LIKE WE MISSED YA?
AAH, I FEEL LIKE I WAS ACTUALLY SUPER WORRIED ABOUT YOU ALL.
OY, OY. SHINPEI, YA 'KAY?
USHIO CALLED YA, DIDN'T SHE?
THAT'S WHAT YA SAID ON THE PHONE YESTERDAY!
YA SAID IF YA DIDN'T COME HOME THIS YEAR...
...USHIO'D KILL YA!
WHY'RE YA COMIN' STRAIGHT TO THE BISTRO?
YA DON'T WANNA GO TO YER HOME FIRST?
!

*PHONE CONVERSATION BETWEEN SHINPEI AND HIS DAD -
Shinpei: It's kinda sudden, but I am coming back to Hitogashima today. Will be arriving at 10am.
Dad: Ehhh!! We need to go to Osaka today. Need to do a lecture at the university's symposium. Be back tomorrow night. Can you cook for yourself?
Shinpei: That's ok! Will make something proper myself. Sorry for the short notice. Good luck with your lecture!
Dad: All good! Happy to see you soon.

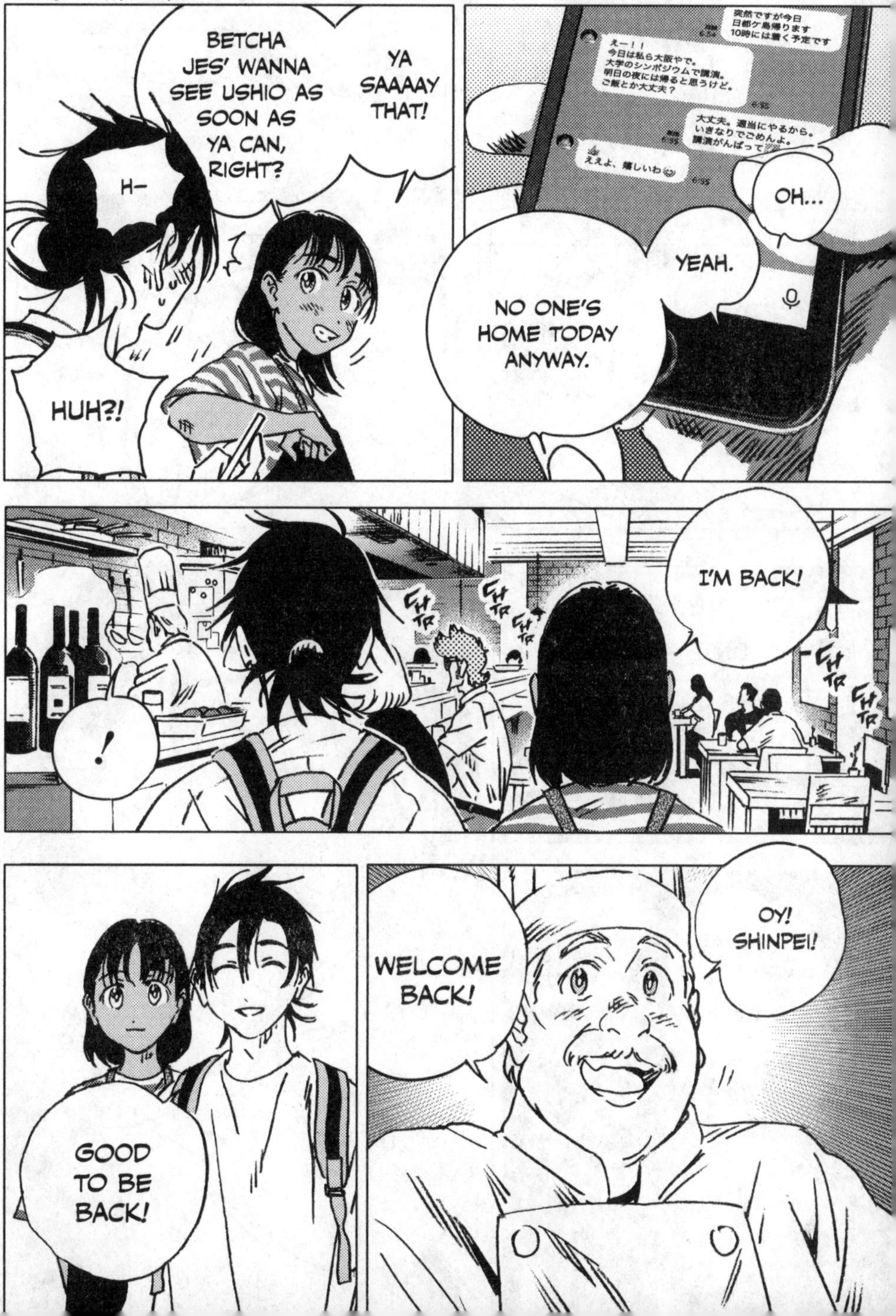

突然ですが今日 日都ケ島帰ります 10時には着く予定です
えー！！ 今日は私ら大阪やで。大学のシンポジウムで講演。明日の夜には帰ると思うけど。ご飯とか大丈夫？
大丈夫。適当にやるから。いきなりでごめんよ。講演がんばって
ええよ、嬉しいわ
OH...
YEAH.
NO ONE'S HOME TODAY ANYWAY.
BETCHA JES' WANNA SEE USHIO AS SOON AS YA CAN, RIGHT?
YA SAAAAY THAT!
H-
HUH?!
I'M BACK!
CHTR
CHTR
CHTR
CHTR
CHTR
CHTR
!
OY! SHINPEI!
WELCOME BACK!
GOOD TO BE BACK!

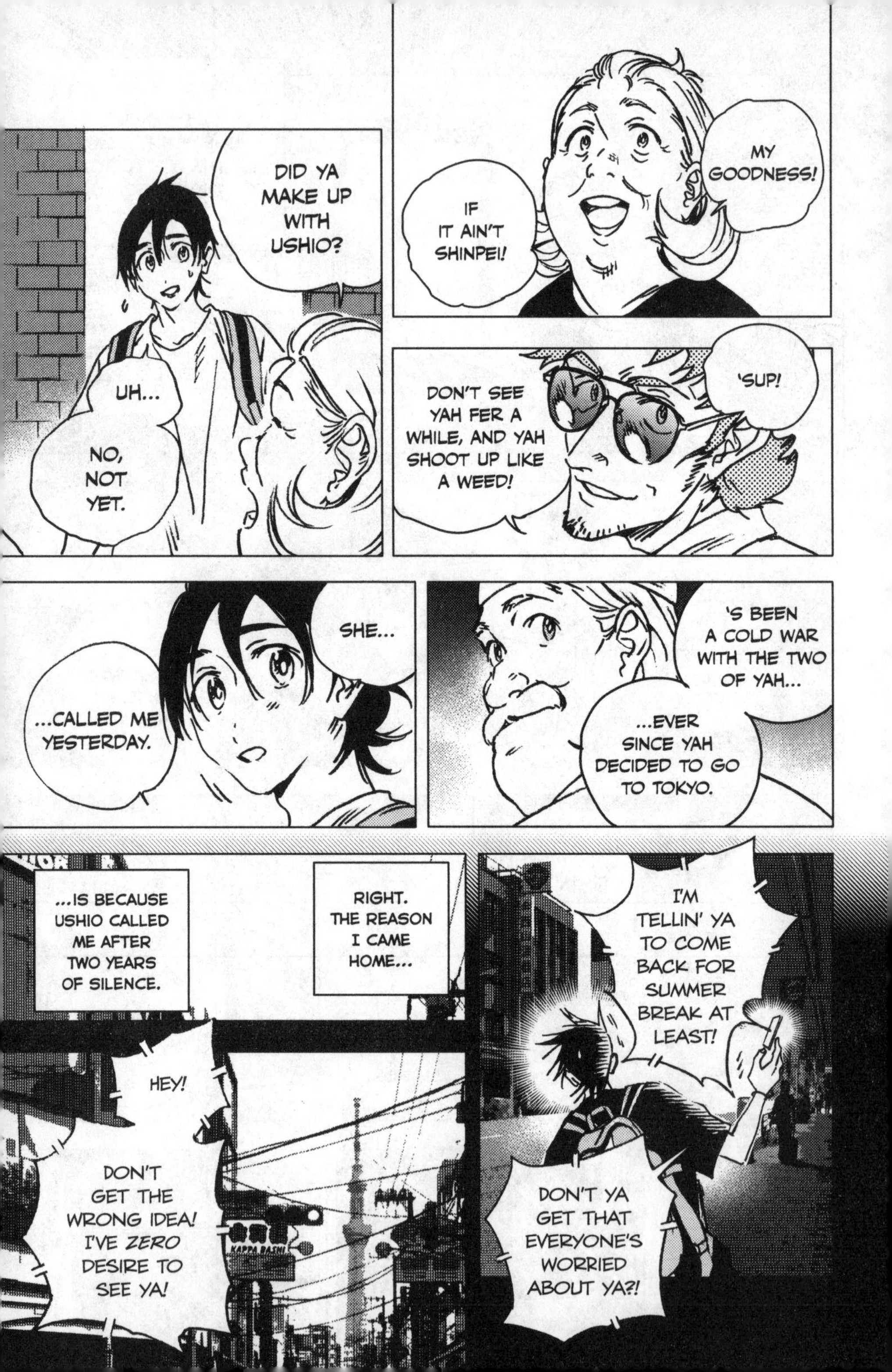
MY GOODNESS!
IF IT AIN'T SHINPEI!
'SUP!
DON'T SEE YAH FER A WHILE, AND YAH SHOOT UP LIKE A WEED!
DID YA MAKE UP WITH USHIO?
UH...
NO, NOT YET.
'S BEEN A COLD WAR WITH THE TWO OF YAH...
...EVER SINCE YAH DECIDED TO GO TO TOKYO.
SHE...
...CALLED ME YESTERDAY.
I'M TELLIN' YA TO COME BACK FOR SUMMER BREAK AT LEAST!
DON'T YA GET THAT EVERYONE'S WORRIED ABOUT YA?!
RIGHT. THE REASON I CAME HOME...
...IS BECAUSE USHIO CALLED ME AFTER TWO YEARS OF SILENCE.
HEY!
DON'T GET THE WRONG IDEA! I'VE ZERO DESIRE TO SEE YA!
KAPPA BASHI

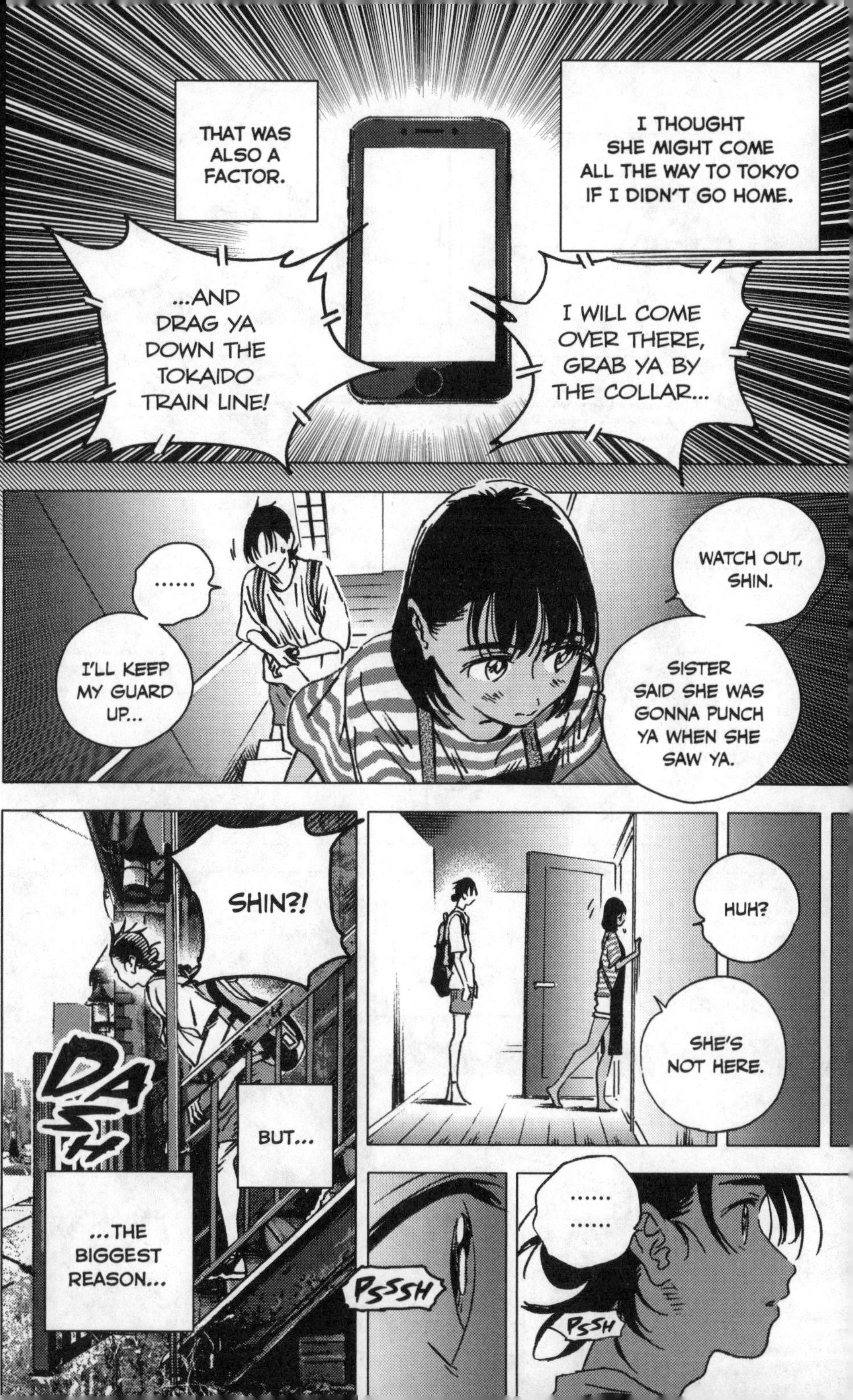
I THOUGHT SHE MIGHT COME ALL THE WAY TO TOKYO IF I DIDN'T GO HOME.
THAT WAS ALSO A FACTOR.
I WILL COME OVER THERE, GRAB YA BY THE COLLAR...
...AND DRAG YA DOWN THE TOKAIDO TRAIN LINE!
WATCH OUT, SHIN.
SISTER SAID SHE WAS GONNA PUNCH YA WHEN SHE SAW YA.
......
I'LL KEEP MY GUARD UP...
HUH?
SHE'S NOT HERE.
SHIN?!
DASH
BUT...
...THE BIGGEST REASON...
......
......
PSSH
PSSSH

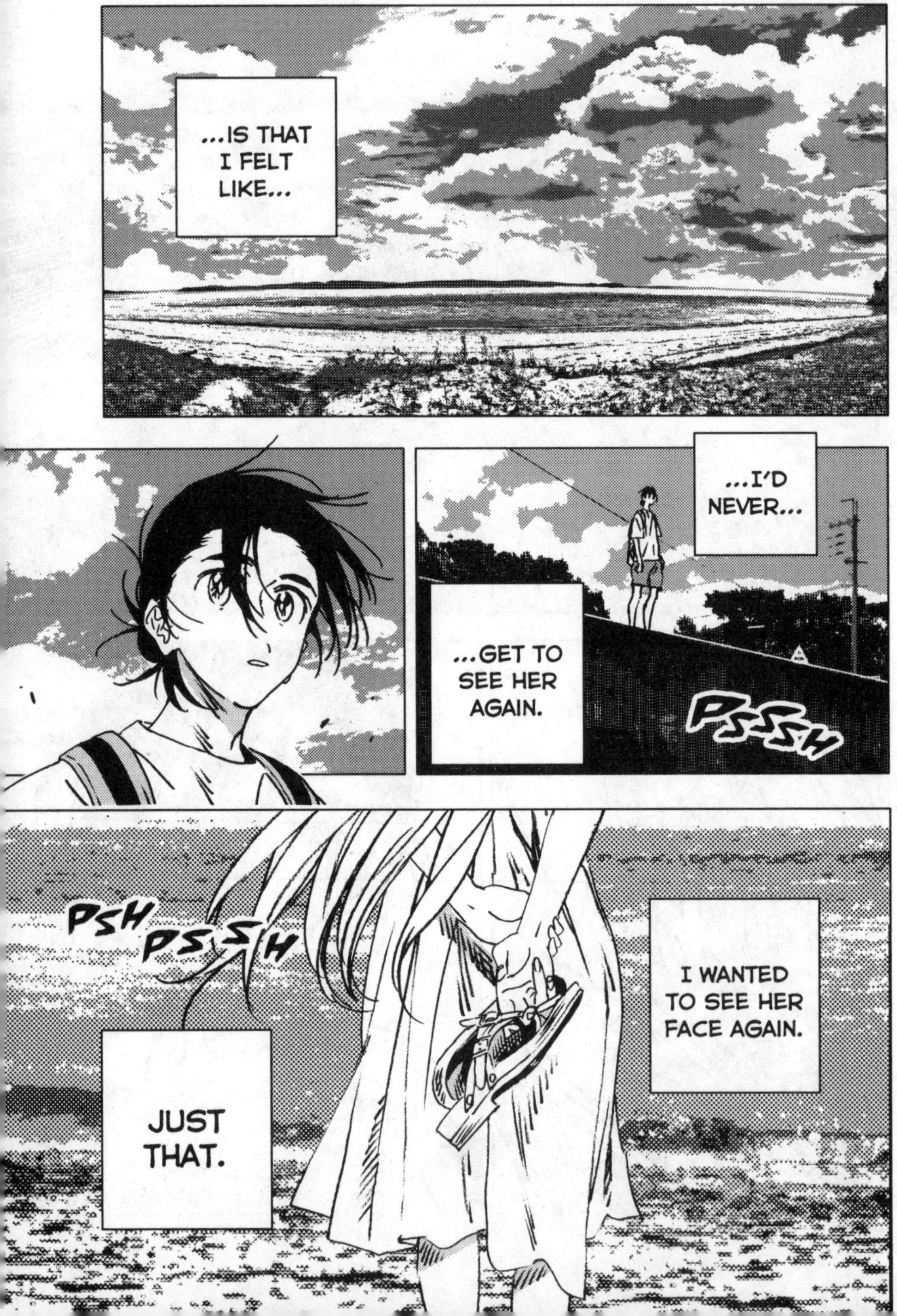
...IS THAT I FELT LIKE...
...I'D NEVER...
...GET TO SEE HER AGAIN.
PS-SSH
I WANTED TO SEE HER FACE AGAIN.
PSH
PS-SSH
JUST THAT.

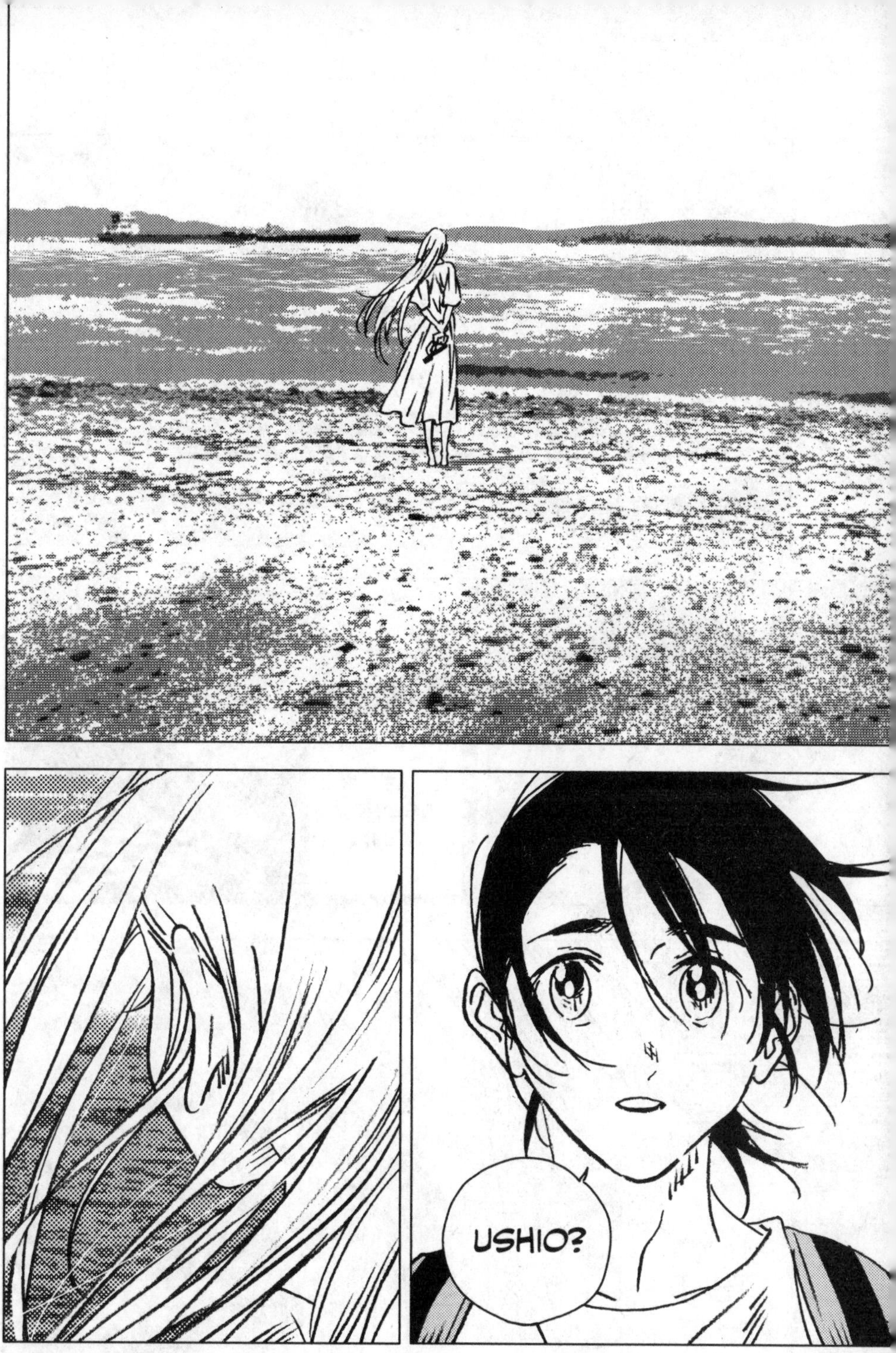
USHIO?

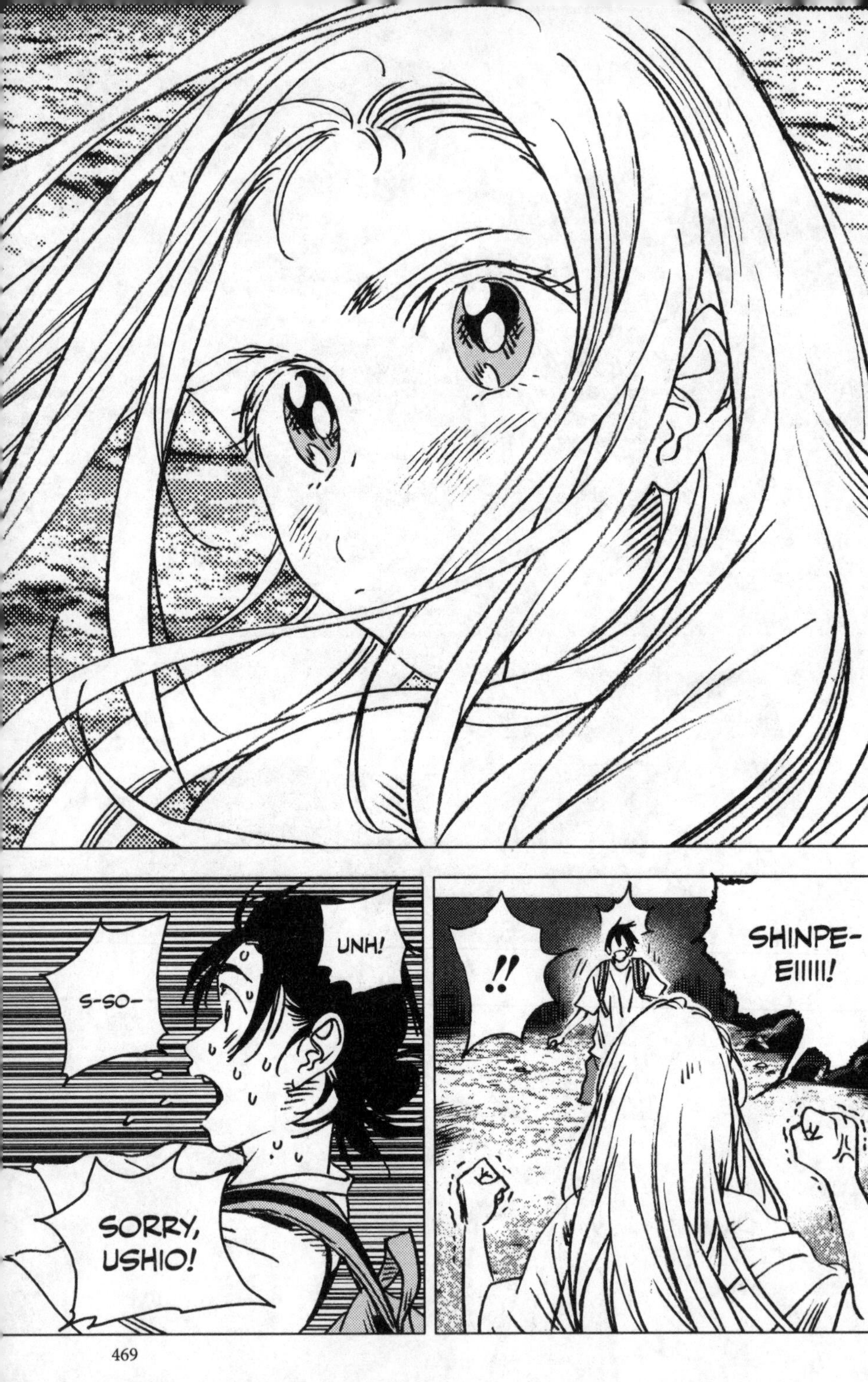
SHINPE-EIIIII!
!!
UNH!
S-SO-
SORRY, USHIO!

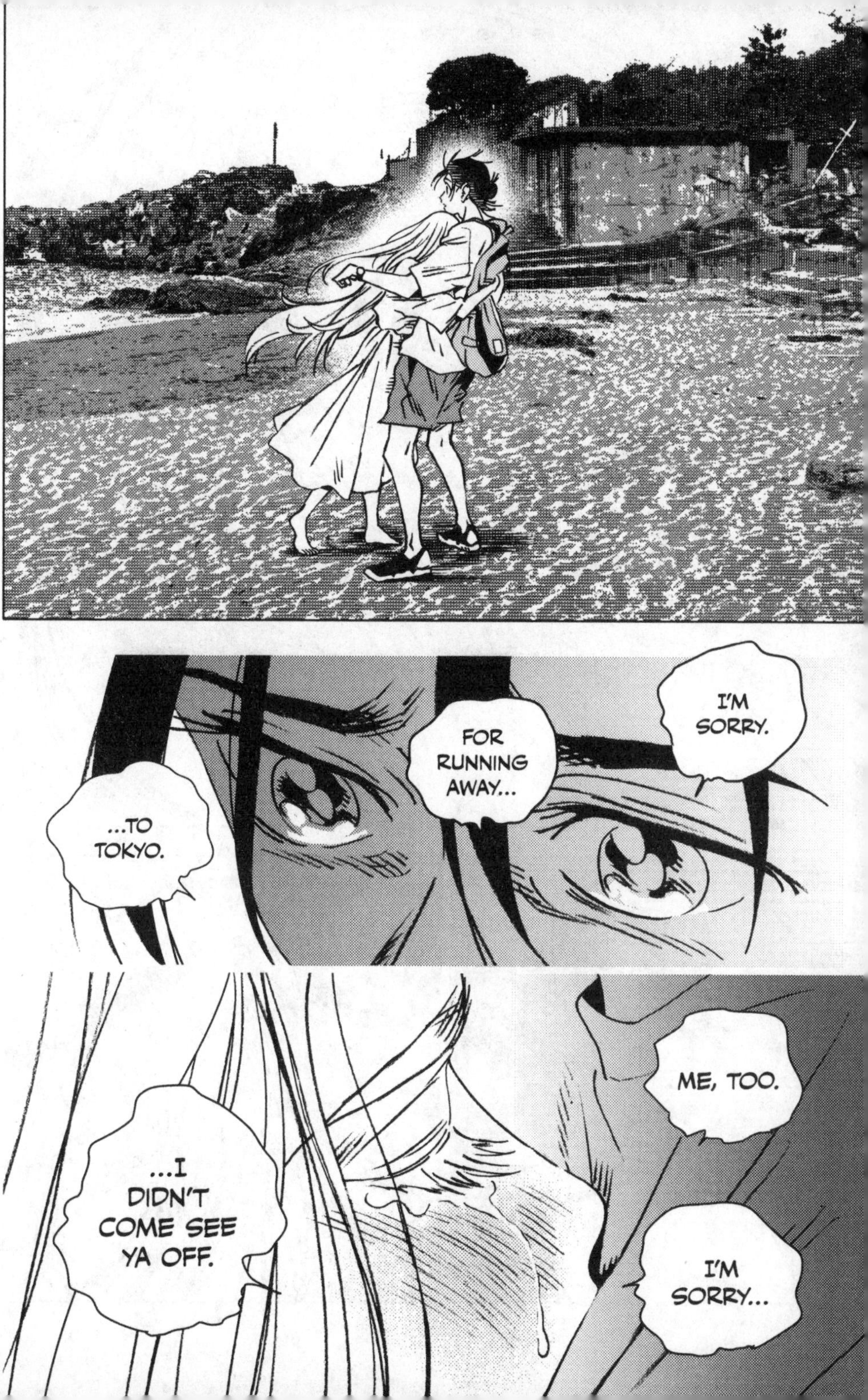
I'M SORRY.
FOR RUNNING AWAY...
...TO TOKYO.
ME, TOO.
...I DIDN'T COME SEE YA OFF.
I'M SORRY...

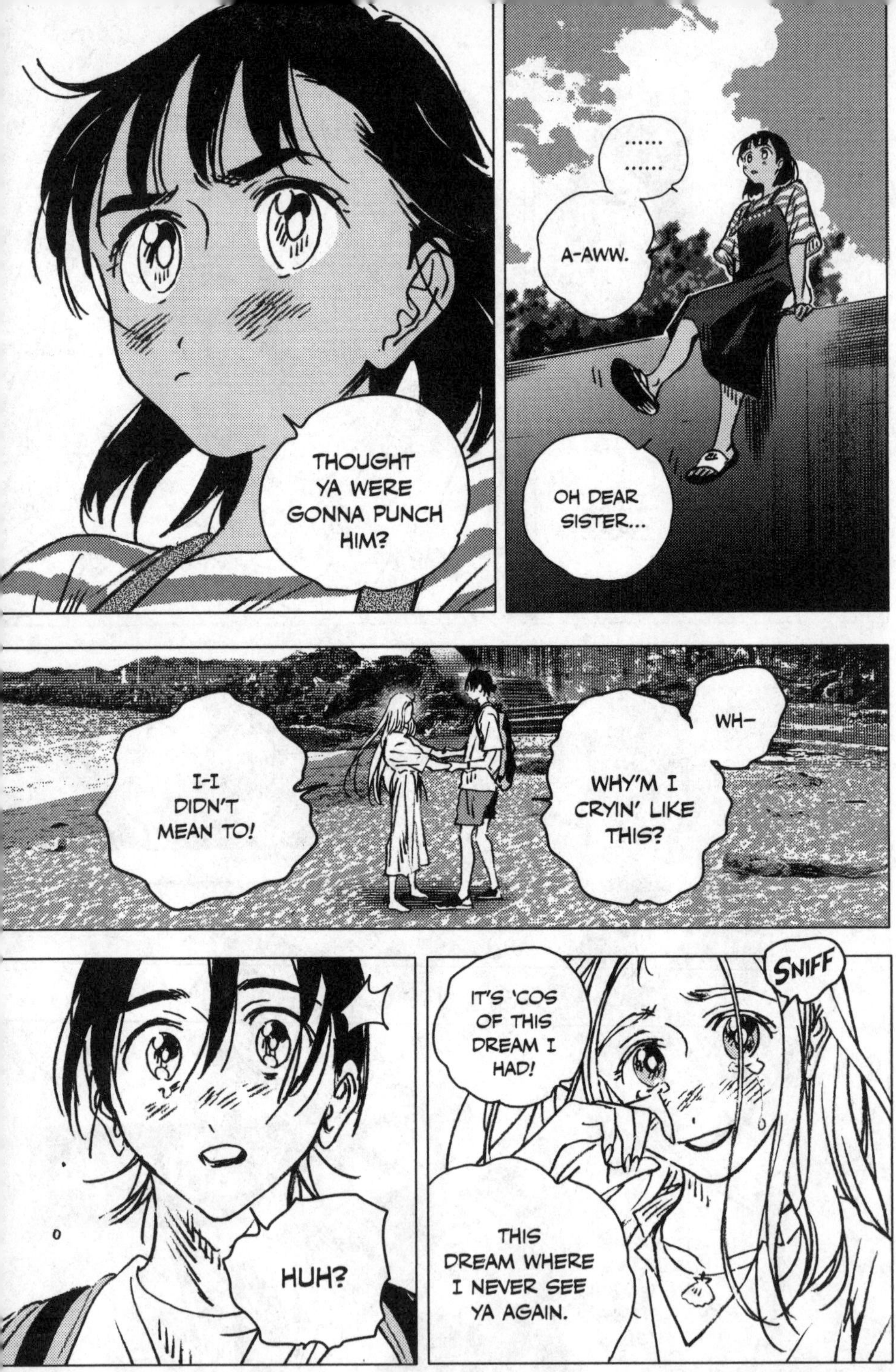
......
......
A-AWW.
OH DEAR SISTER...
THOUGHT YA WERE GONNA PUNCH HIM?
WH-
WHY'M I CRYIN' LIKE THIS?
I-I DIDN'T MEAN TO!
SNIFF
IT'S 'COS OF THIS DREAM I HAD!
THIS DREAM WHERE I NEVER SEE YA AGAIN.
HUH?

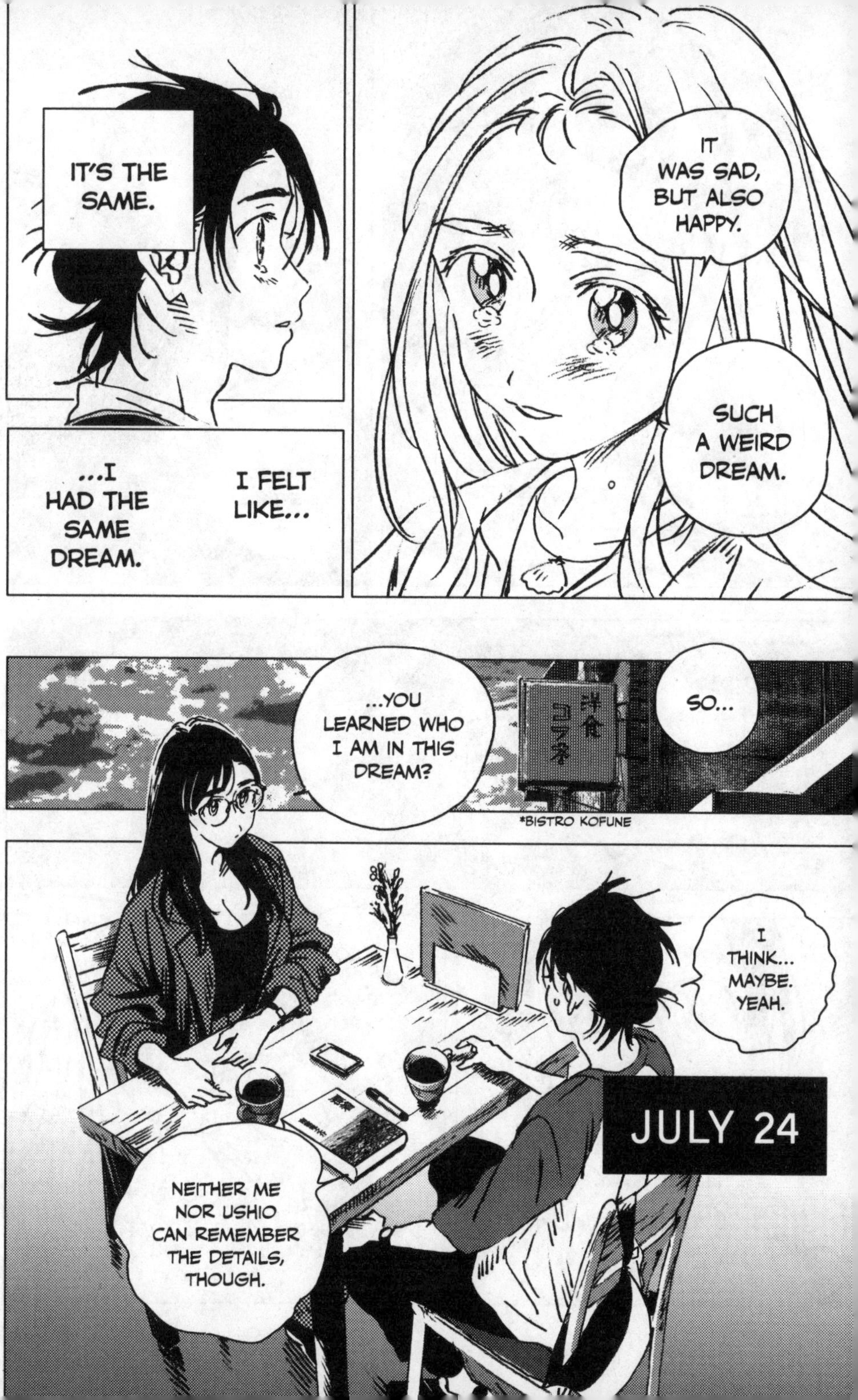
IT WAS SAD, BUT ALSO HAPPY.
SUCH A WEIRD DREAM.
IT'S THE SAME.
I FELT LIKE...
...I HAD THE SAME DREAM.
SO...
...YOU LEARNED WHO I AM IN THIS DREAM?
*BISTRO KOFUNE
I THINK... MAYBE. YEAH.
JULY 24
NEITHER ME NOR USHIO CAN REMEMBER THE DETAILS, THOUGH.

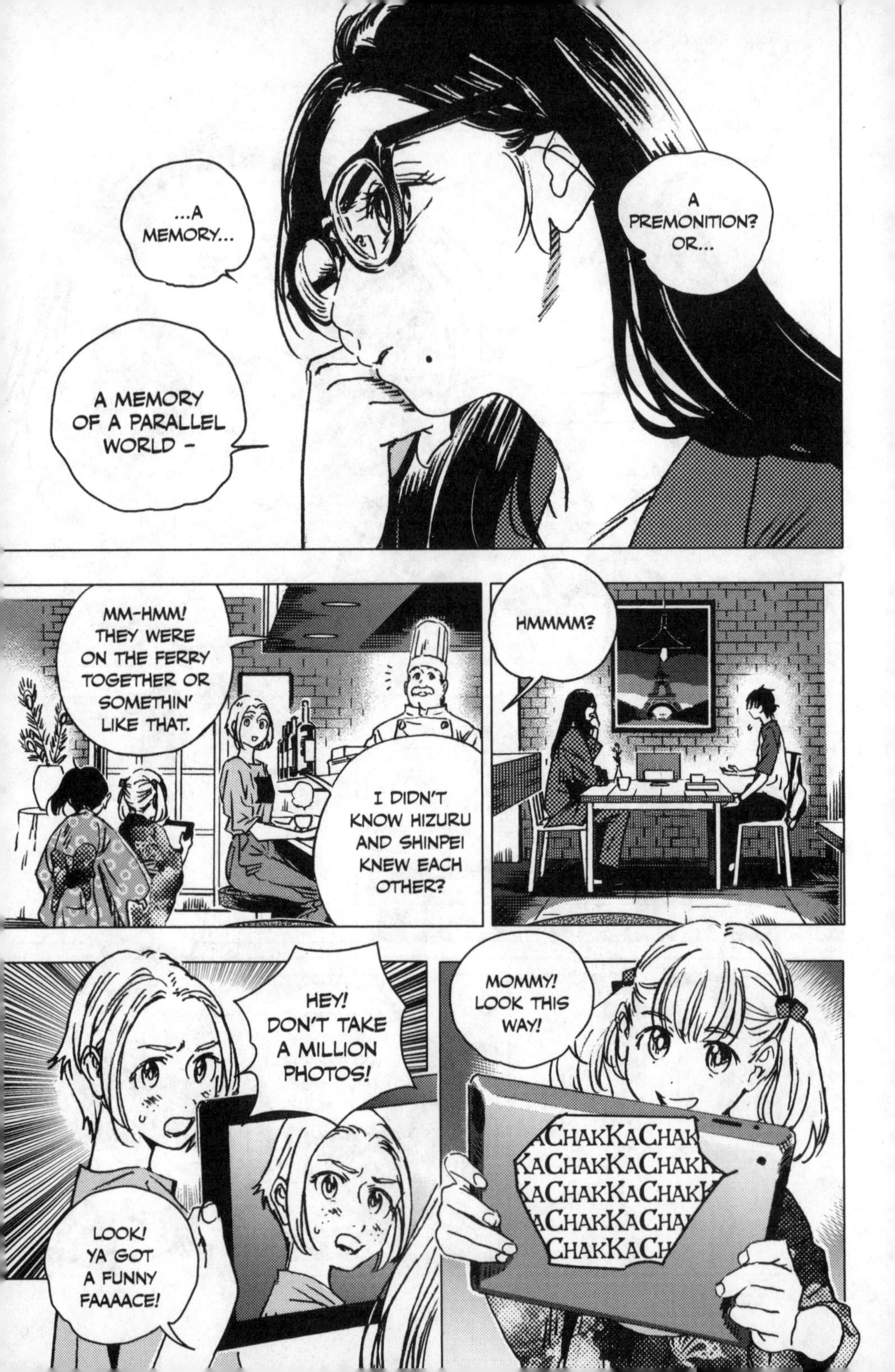
A PREMONITION? OR...
...A MEMORY...
A MEMORY OF A PARALLEL WORLD -
HMMMM?
I DIDN'T KNOW HIZURU AND SHINPEI KNEW EACH OTHER?
MM-HMM! THEY WERE ON THE FERRY TOGETHER OR SOMETHIN' LIKE THAT.
MOMMY! LOOK THIS WAY!
KaChakKaChak KaChakKaChak KaChakKaChak KaChakKaChak KaChakKaCh
HEY! DON'T TAKE A MILLION PHOTOS!
LOOK! YA GOT A FUNNY FAAAACE!

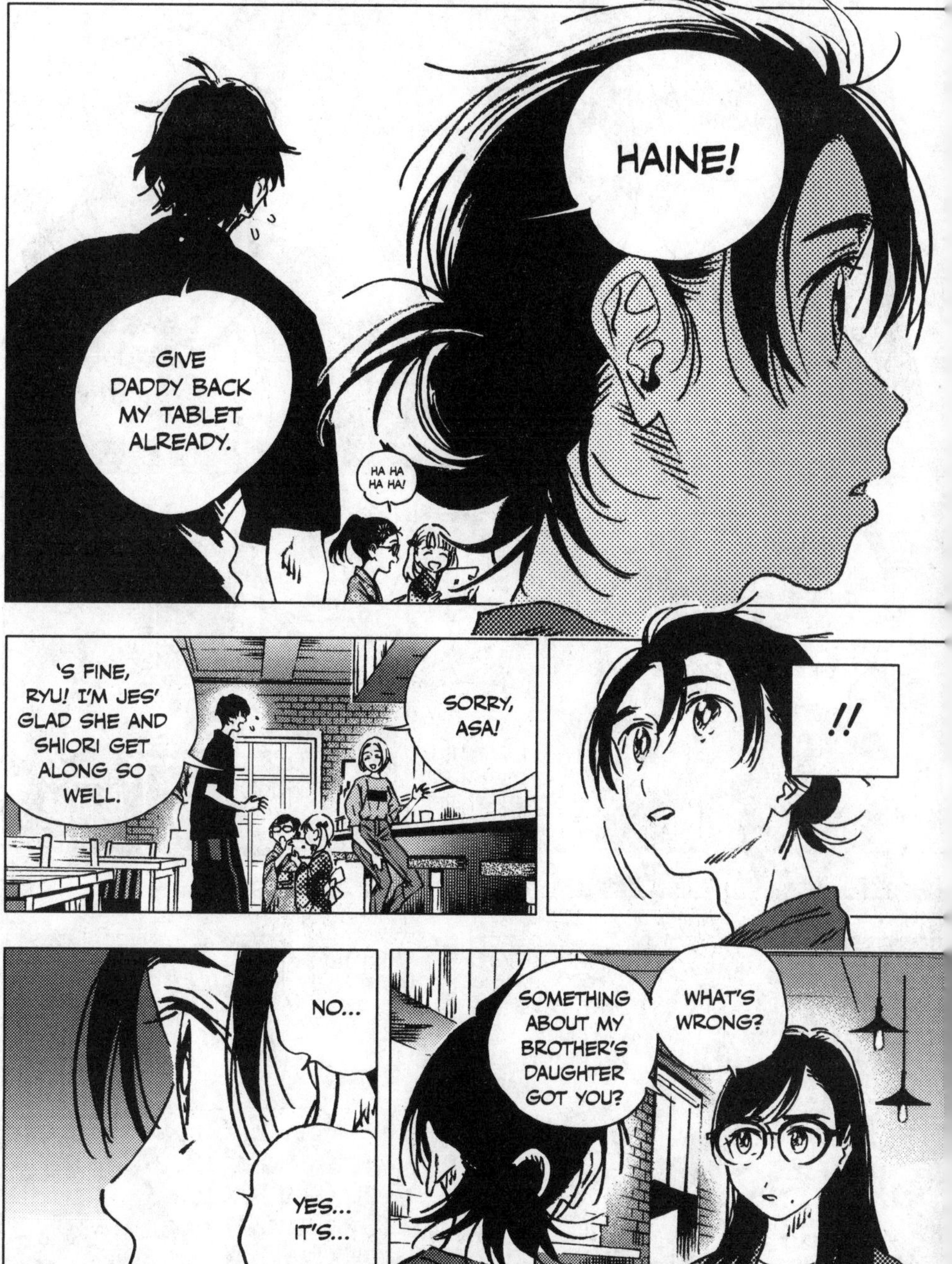
HAINE!
GIVE DADDY BACK MY TABLET ALREADY.
HA HA HA HA!
!!
SORRY, ASA!
'S FINE, RYU! I'M JES' GLAD SHE AND SHIORI GET ALONG SO WELL.
WHAT'S WRONG?
SOMETHING ABOUT MY BROTHER'S DAUGHTER GOT YOU?
NO...
YES... IT'S...

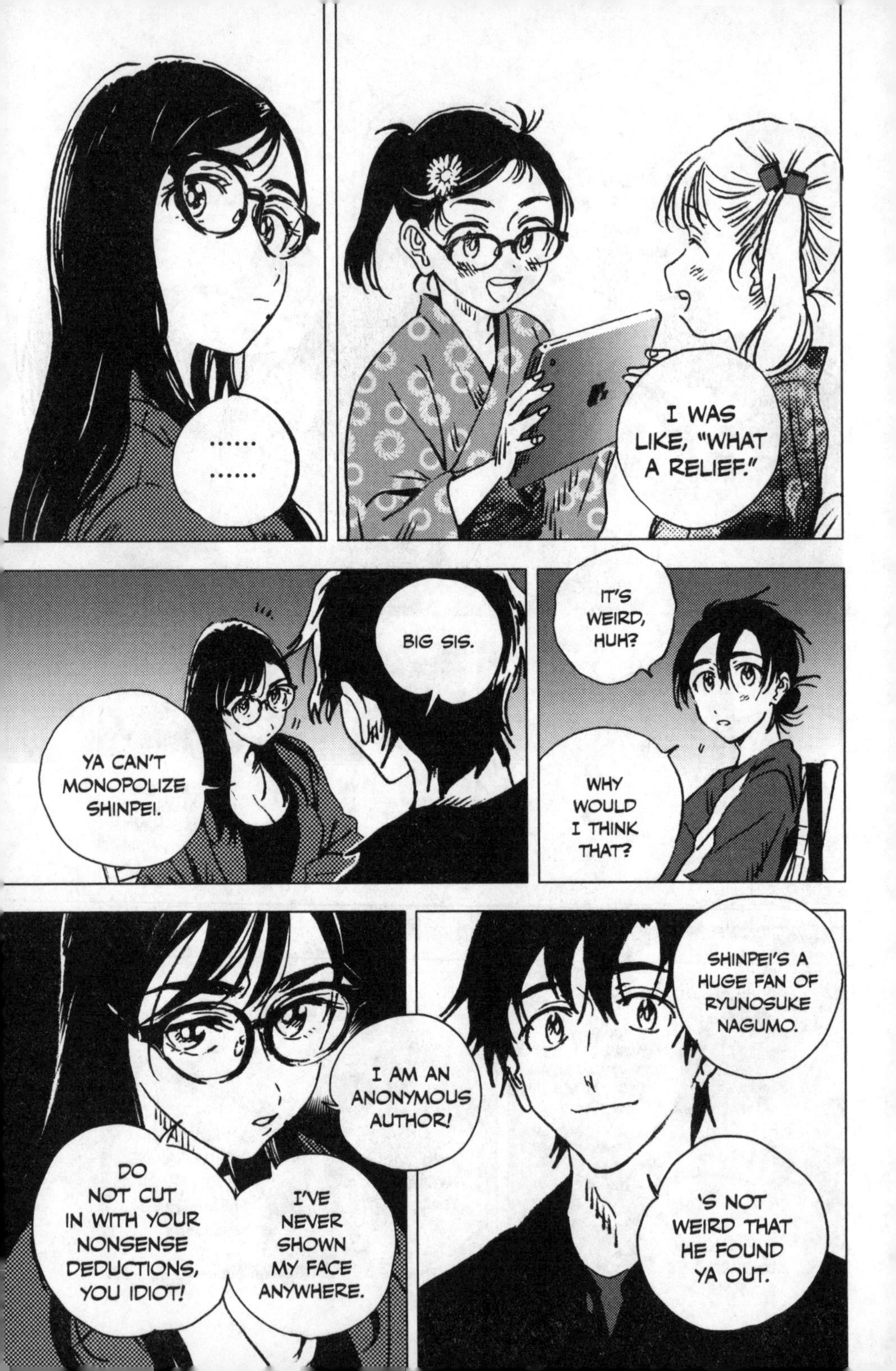
I WAS LIKE, "WHAT A RELIEF."
…… ……
IT'S WEIRD, HUH?
WHY WOULD I THINK THAT?
BIG SIS.
YA CAN'T MONOPOLIZE SHINPEI.
SHINPEI'S A HUGE FAN OF RYUNOSUKE NAGUMO.
'S NOT WEIRD THAT HE FOUND YA OUT.
I AM AN ANONYMOUS AUTHOR!
I'VE NEVER SHOWN MY FACE ANYWHERE.
DO NOT CUT IN WITH YOUR NONSENSE DEDUCTIONS, YOU IDIOT!

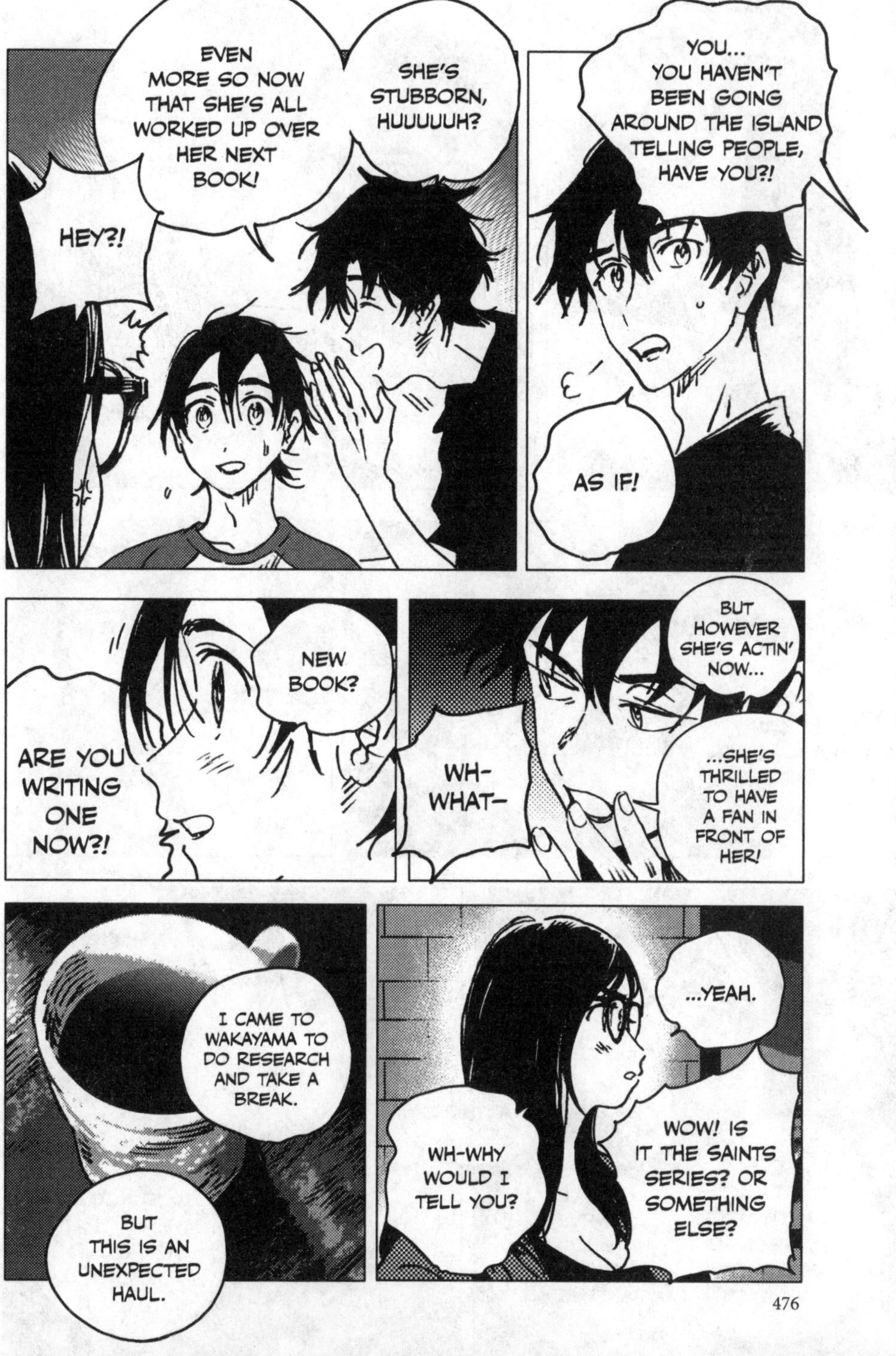
YOU... YOU HAVEN'T BEEN GOING AROUND THE ISLAND TELLING PEOPLE, HAVE YOU?!
AS IF!
SHE'S STUBBORN, HUUUUUH?
EVEN MORE SO NOW THAT SHE'S ALL WORKED UP OVER HER NEXT BOOK!
HEY?!
BUT HOWEVER SHE'S ACTIN' NOW...
...SHE'S THRILLED TO HAVE A FAN IN FRONT OF HER!
WH- WHAT-
NEW BOOK?
ARE YOU WRITING ONE NOW?!
...YEAH.
WOW! IS IT THE SAINTS SERIES? OR SOMETHING ELSE?
WH-WHY WOULD I TELL YOU?
I CAME TO WAKAYAMA TO DO RESEARCH AND TAKE A BREAK.
BUT THIS IS AN UNEXPECTED HAUL.

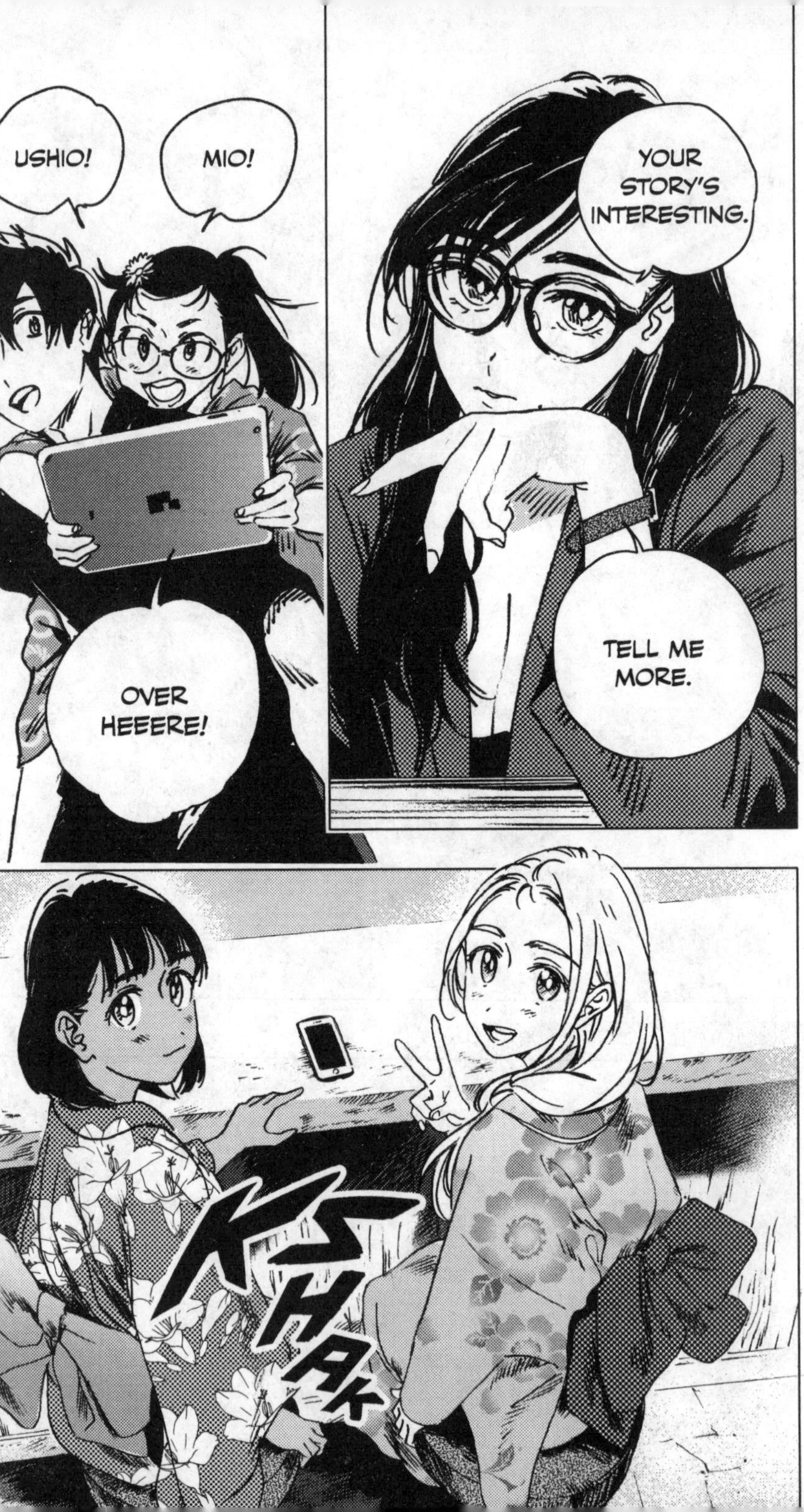
YOUR STORY'S INTERESTING.
TELL ME MORE.
MIO!
USHIO!
OVER HEEERE!
KSHAK

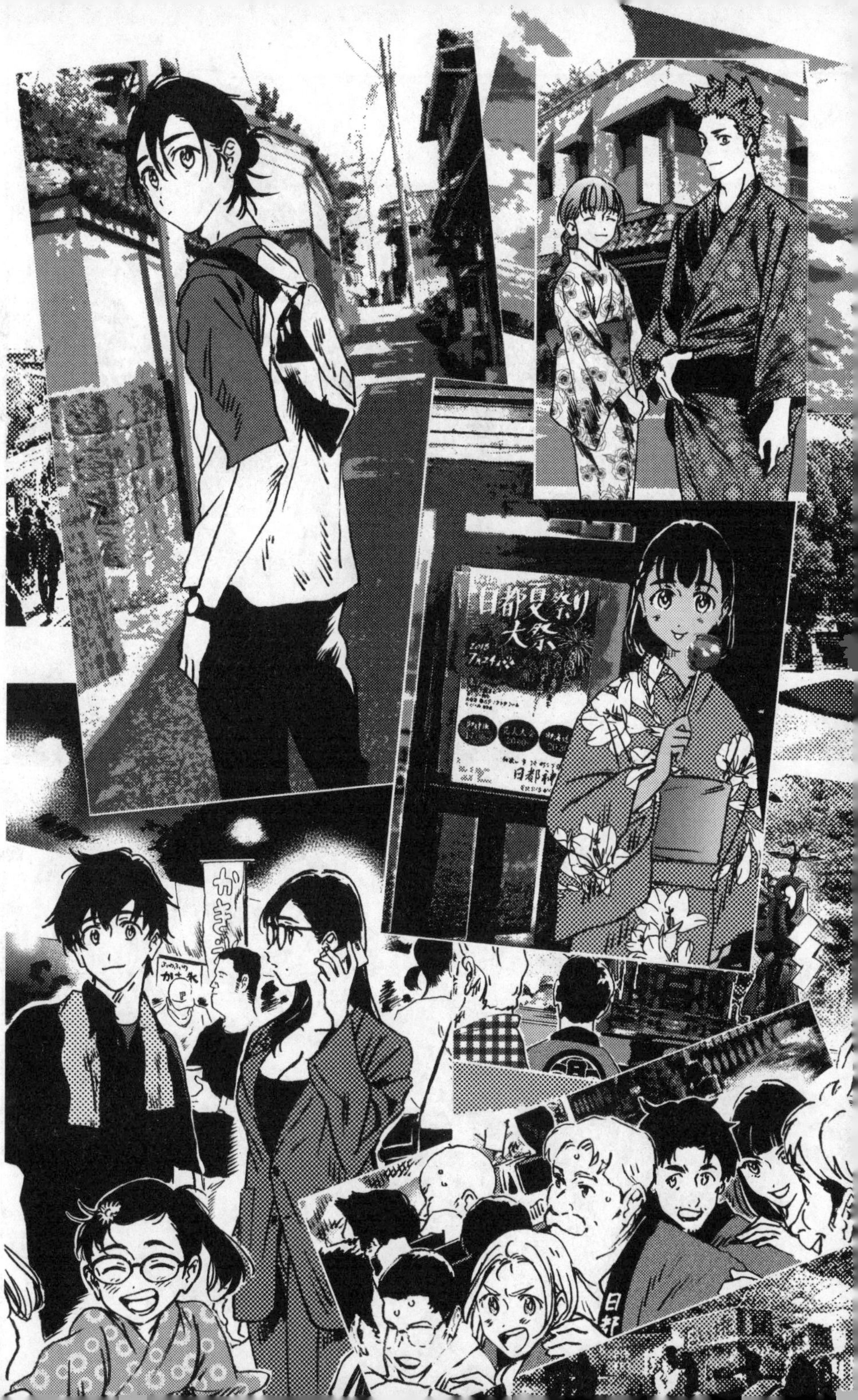
日都夏祭り
大祭
2015
日都神
かき
日都

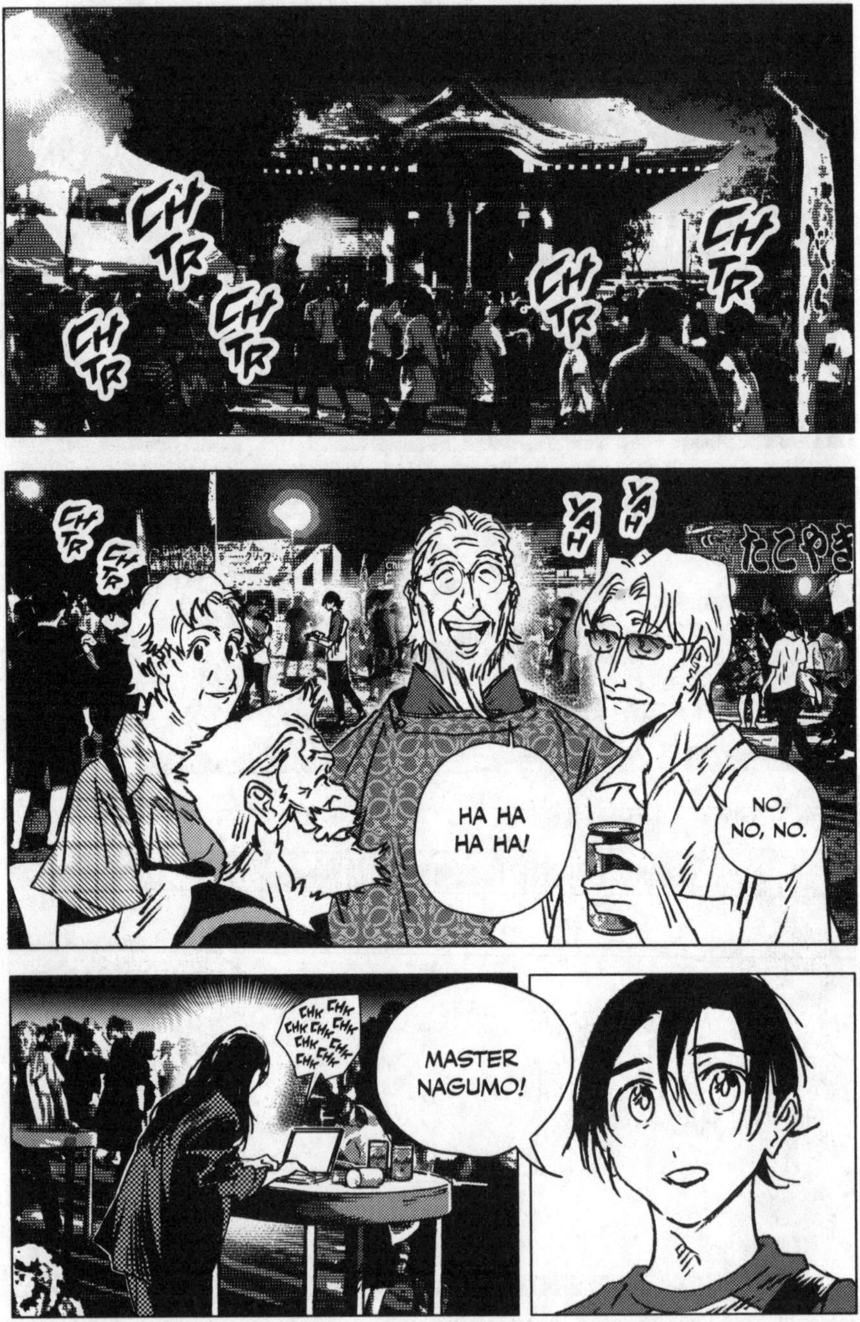
CH TR
CH TR
CH TR
CH TR
たこやき
YAH YAH
NO, NO, NO.
HA HA HA HA!
CH TR CH TR
MASTER NAGUMO!
CHK CHK CHK CHK CHK CHK CHK CHK CHK

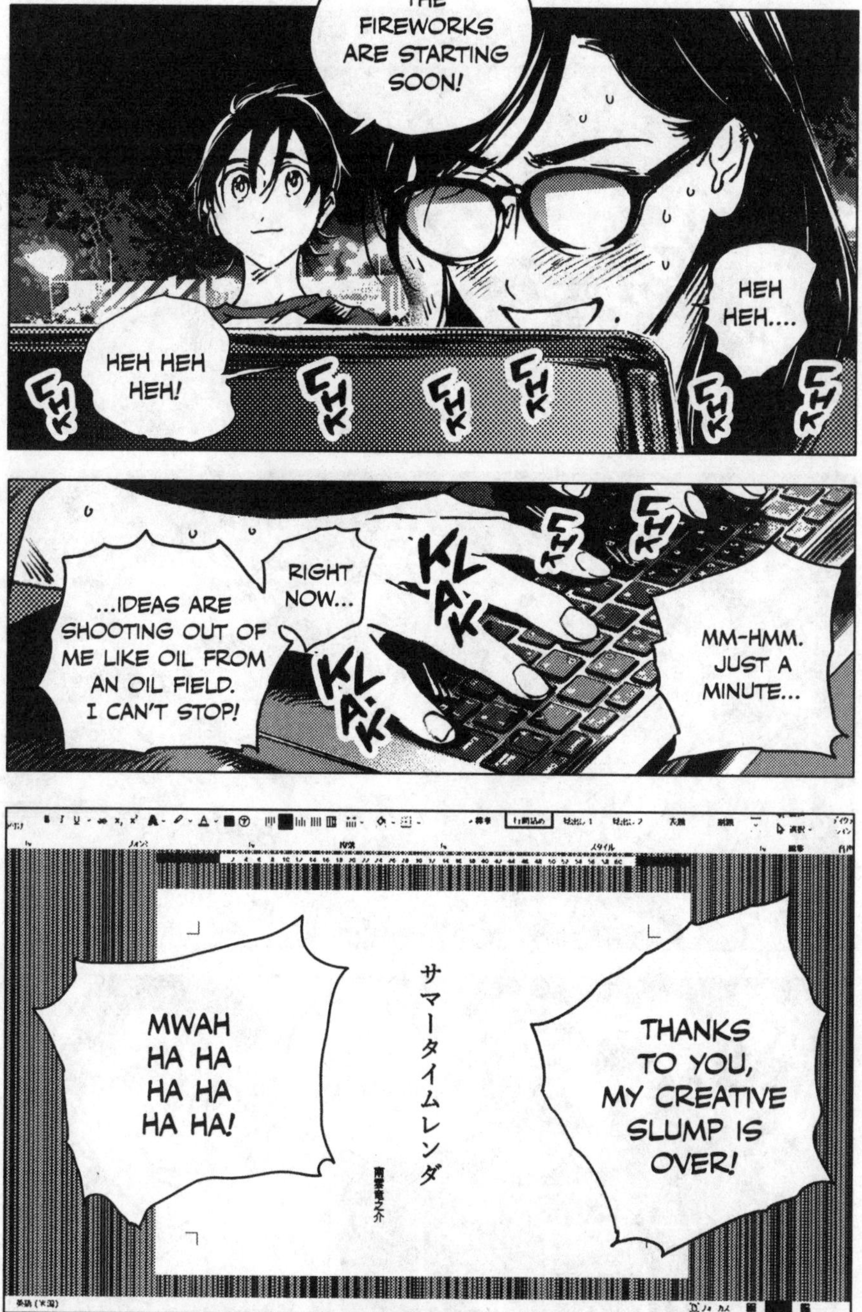
THE FIREWORKS ARE STARTING SOON!
HEH HEH....
CHK CHK CHK CHK CHK CHK
HEH HEH HEH!
CHK CHK
MM-HMM. JUST A MINUTE...
KLAK KLAK
RIGHT NOW...
...IDEAS ARE SHOOTING OUT OF ME LIKE OIL FROM AN OIL FIELD. I CAN'T STOP!
THANKS TO YOU, MY CREATIVE SLUMP IS OVER!
サマータイムレンダ
南雲竜之介
MWAH HA HA HA HA HA HA!

*SCREEN = SUMMER TIME RENDERING - RYUNOSUKE NAGUMO

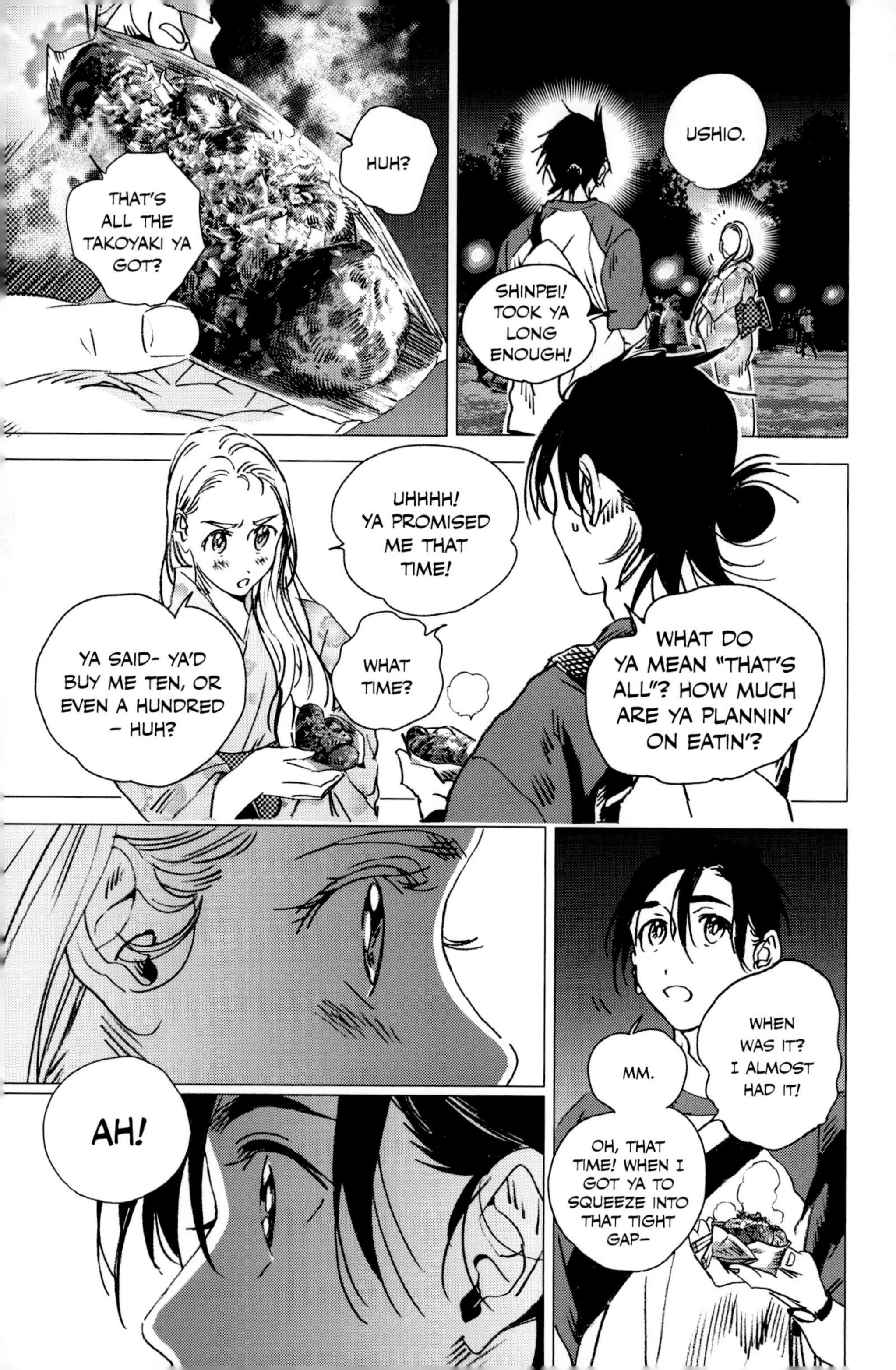
USHIO.
SHINPEI! TOOK YA LONG ENOUGH!
HUH?
THAT'S ALL THE TAKOYAKI YA GOT?
WHAT DO YA MEAN "THAT'S ALL"? HOW MUCH ARE YA PLANNIN' ON EATIN'?
UHHHH! YA PROMISED ME THAT TIME!
WHAT TIME?
YA SAID- YA'D BUY ME TEN, OR EVEN A HUNDRED – HUH?
WHEN WAS IT? I ALMOST HAD IT!
MM.
OH, THAT TIME! WHEN I GOT YA TO SQUEEZE INTO THAT TIGHT GAP–
AH!

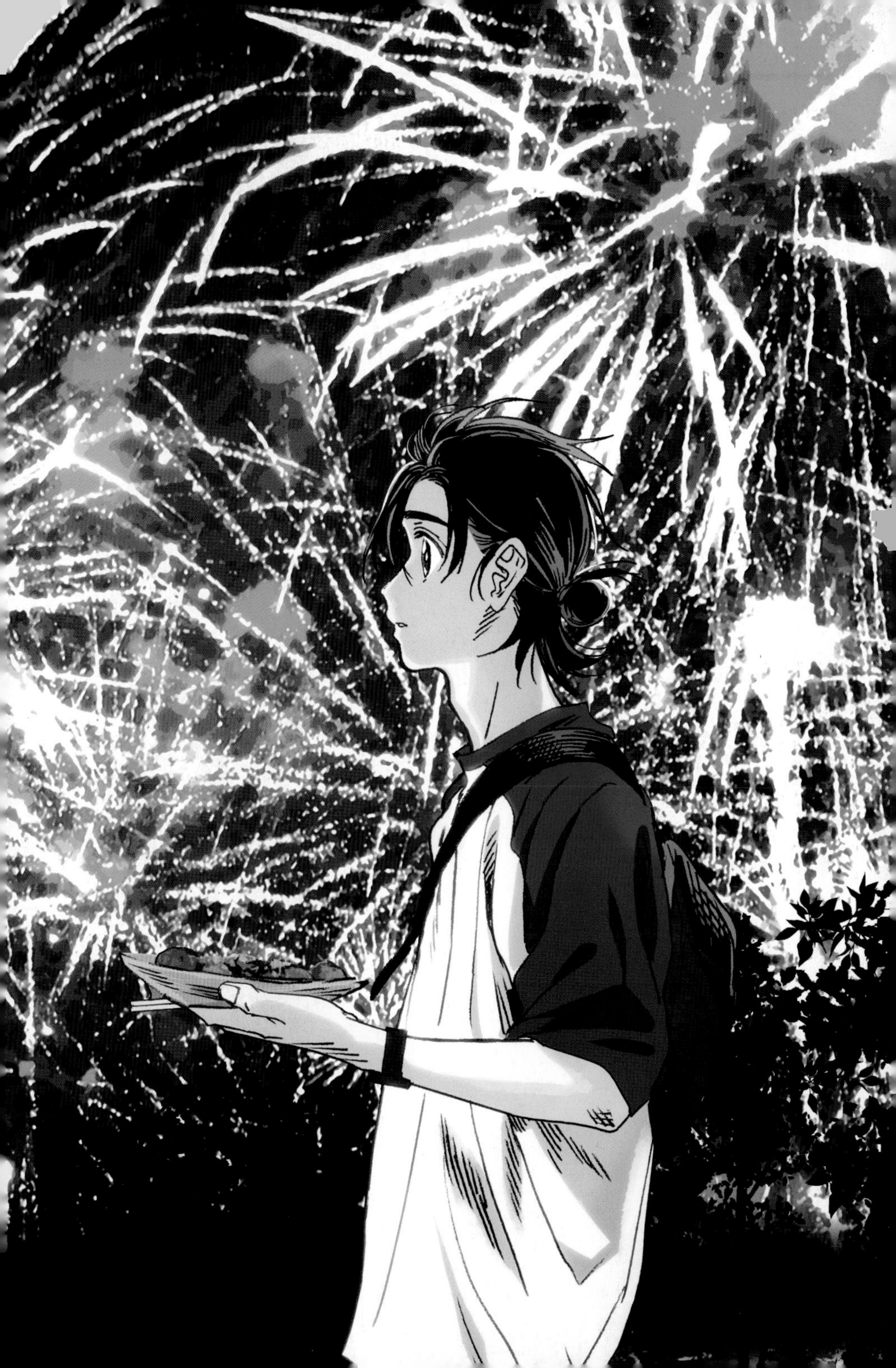

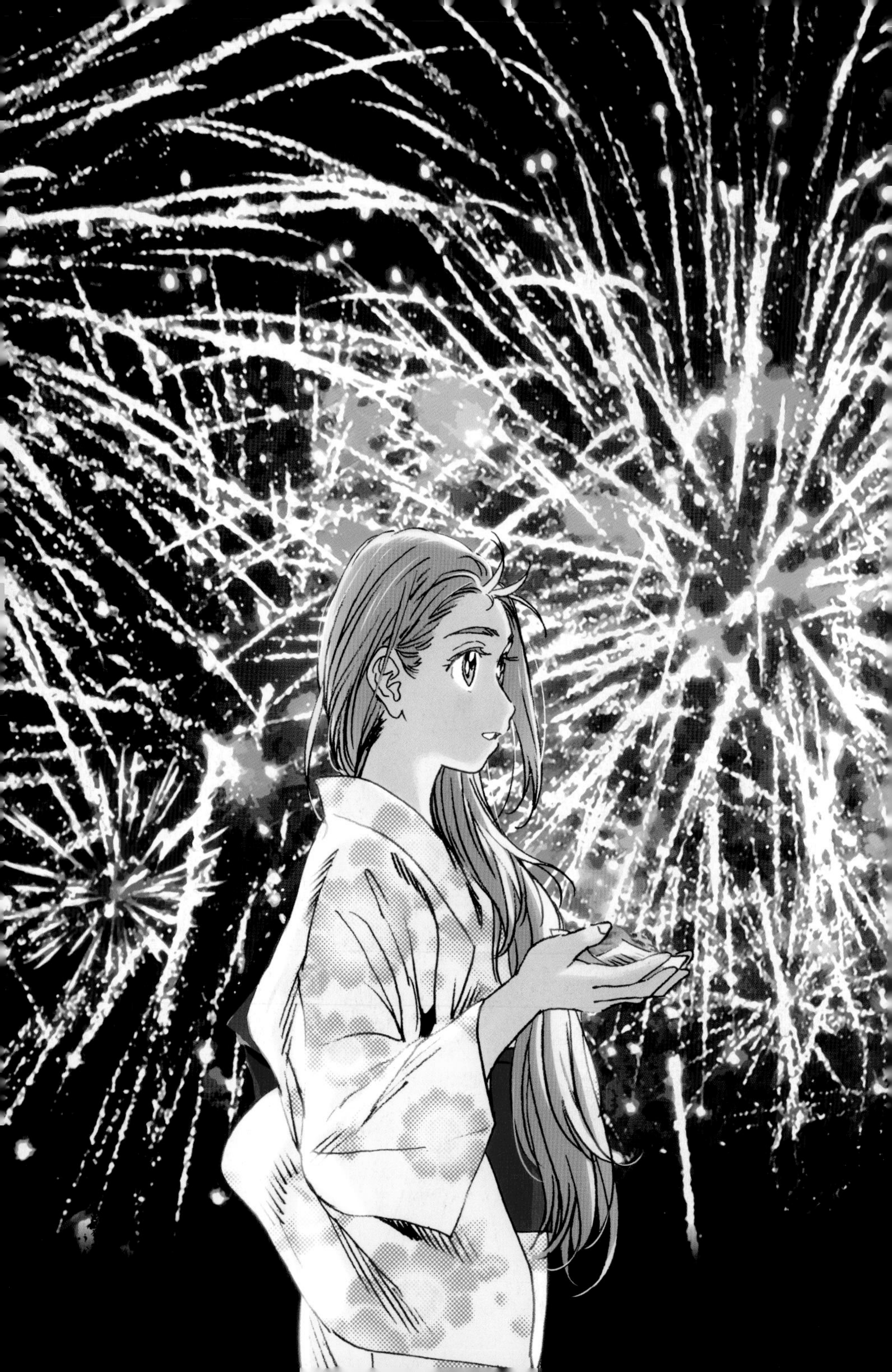

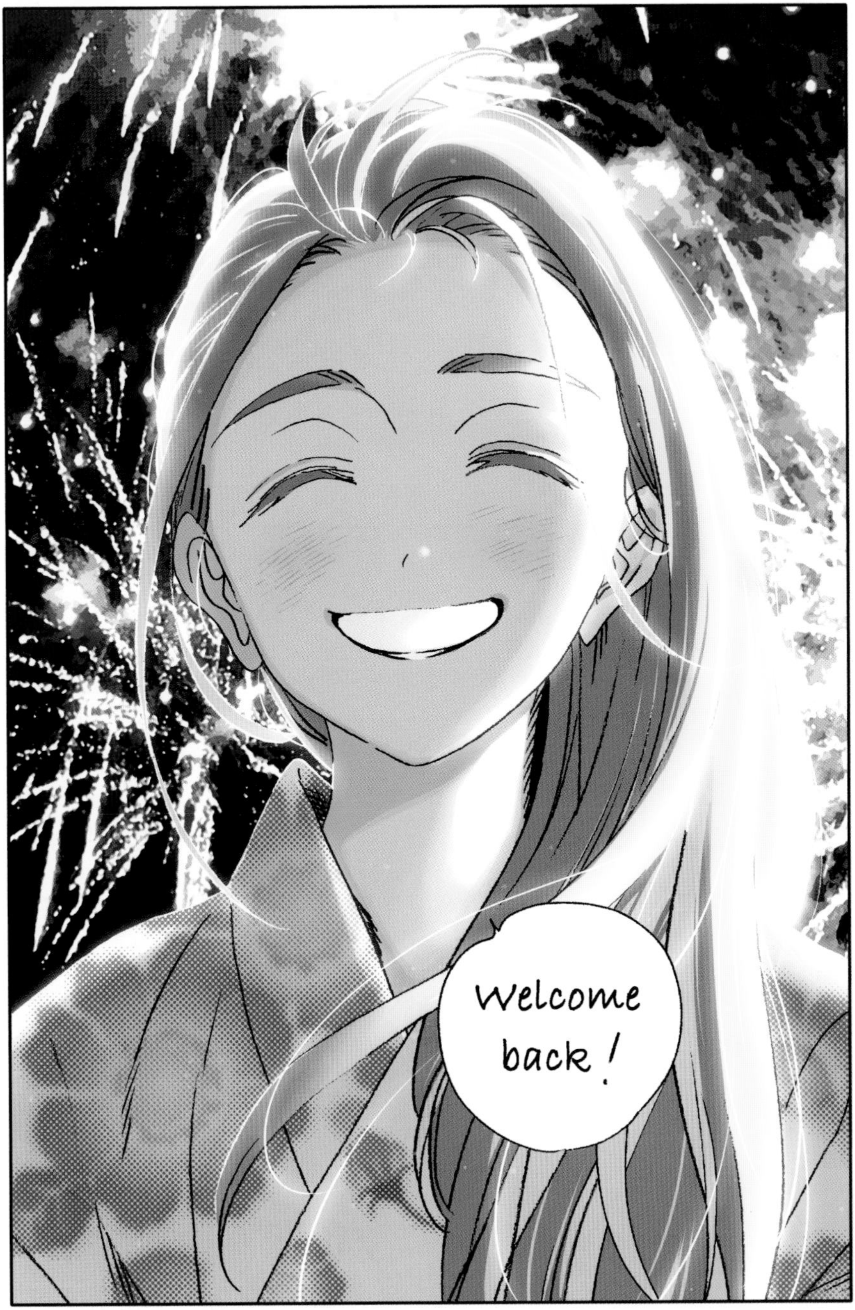
Welcome back!

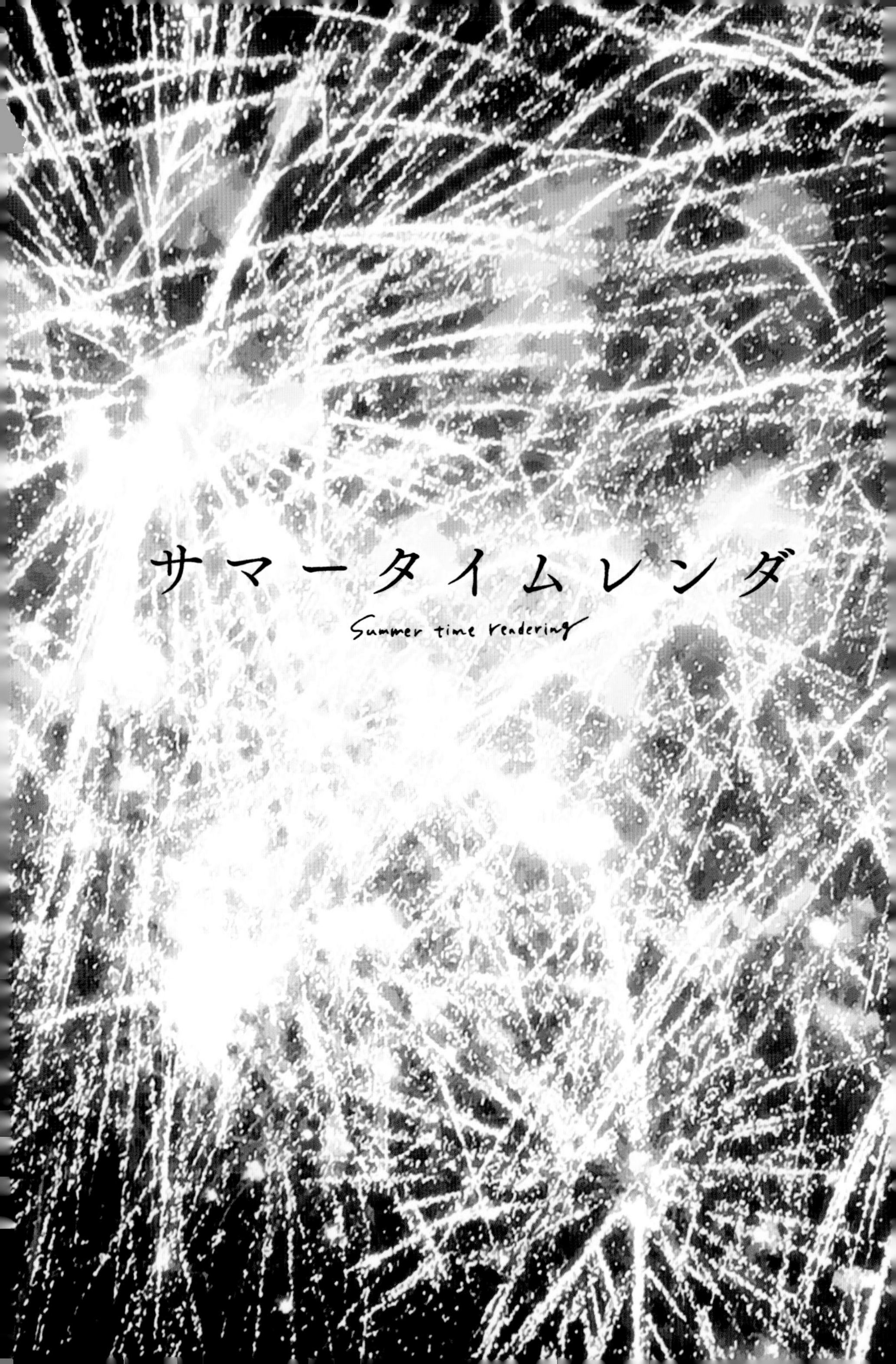
サマータイムレンダ
Summer time rendering

BOOK EDITOR
MITSUNORI KAWAMOTO

JAPANESE LOGO AND COVER DESIGN
YURI SUGAWARA

I'm so deeply grateful to everyone involved in the production of this manga, to my family who helped with making the little things and the photography, and to all the people who have supported me all this time.

Thank you so much!

2021. 2.3 田中靖規

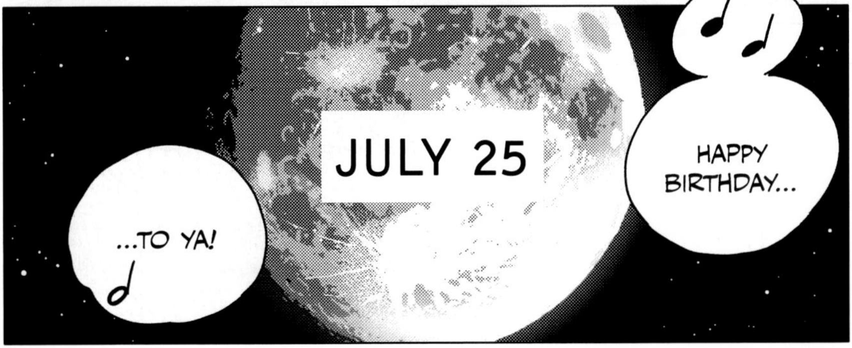

HAPPY BIRTHDAY...
JULY 25
...TO YA!

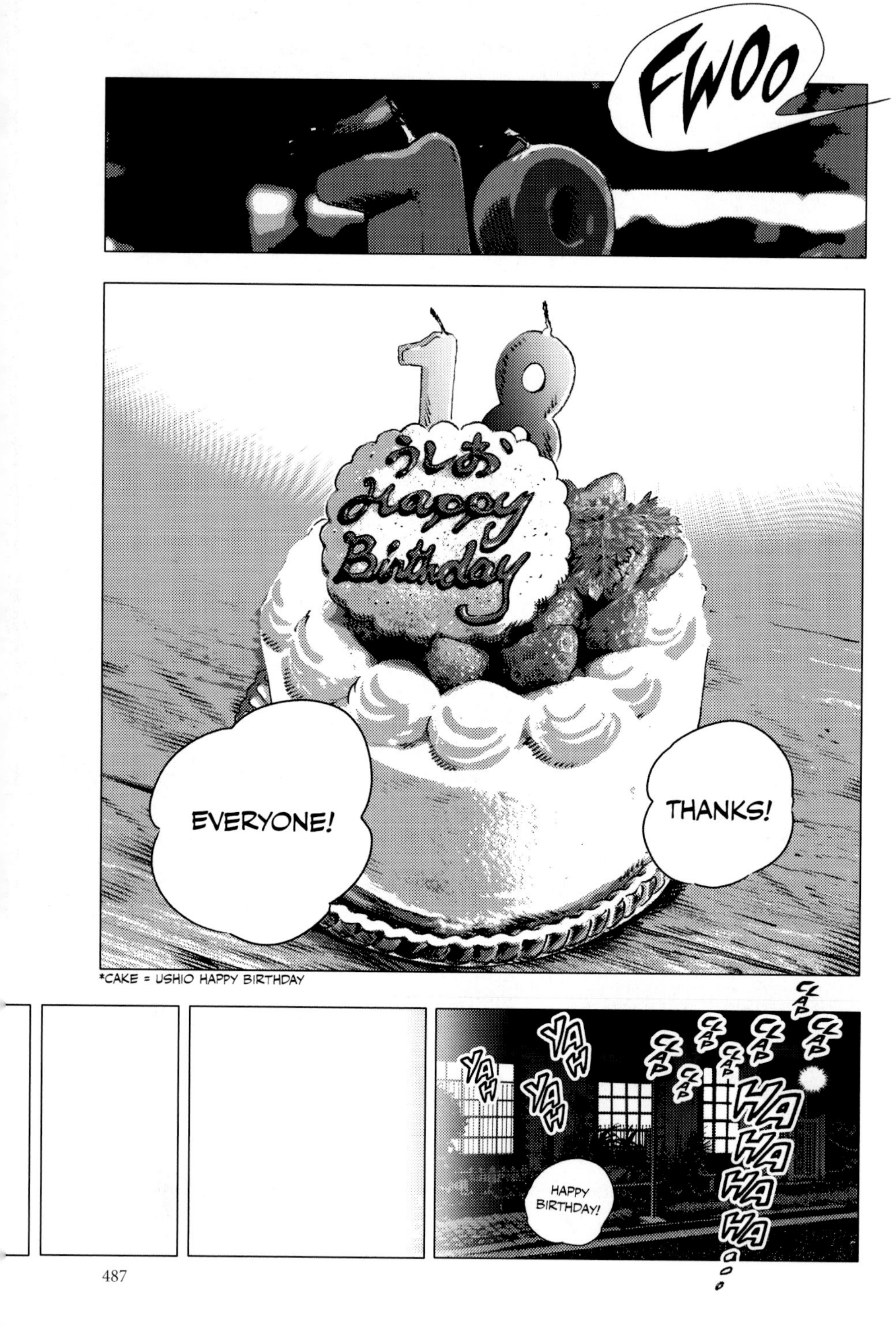
FWOO
うしお
Happy Birthday
THANKS!
EVERYONE!
*CAKE = USHIO HAPPY BIRTHDAY
CLAP CLAP
CLAP CLAP
CLAP CLAP
CLAP CLAP
HA HA HA HA...
YAH YAH
YAH YAH
HAPPY BIRTHDAY!

AFTERWORDS

ORIGINALLY PUBLISHED IN VOL. 12 OF THE JAPANESE EDITION.

I never usually look back at what I drew before, because it reminds me of how awkward and inexperienced I was. I have to ask myself, "Why did you think this was okay?" And I get mad.

However, Summertime Rendering is a "looping time travel" story and I have to draw the same scenes over and over. Sometimes I have to go back and check what the background looked like or how the character was dressed and stuff. I have to check so many times!!! (It's my fault for drawing a manga like this...)

What I imagined in my head for Shinpei and Ushio hasn't changed, but the art might have changed.

The image is being transmitted from the brain to the arm and output through the fingers to the pencil and some kind of misalignment occurs. I think I have been able to draw exactly what I imagined in my head, but if I look back in a few years (or even the next day...), I might think, "Something is wrong!"

If only I could print out the image in my brain on paper without using my arm, fingers and pencil!

I am trying my best to give my best performance, but there is always a gap.

However, I can now detect the difference, so it might be a sign of growth, so it's okay.

If I can't feel a difference, that means my growth has stopped... that would be the worst.

Then I face the helpless reality.

At some point, I will recognize the difference. Even if I draw something good today and am happy, that's just a temporary illusion. If I don't recognize the difference that would be my ceiling.

There is only despair. No matter how high you go... only despair.

So even if it's just an illusion I just repeat each instance of my self-satisfaction and live in the brief moment. Is there any other way to live? I just want to move forward until I die.

What I mean is...

I am looking forward to the day the PS5 comes out ——————————— !!!
I want to play the remake of Demon's Souls soon ———————— !!!
Also Resident Evil Village and FF16... I can't wait to play them all ——————— !!!!!!

··· that's all for now.

2020. 9. 27 田中靖規

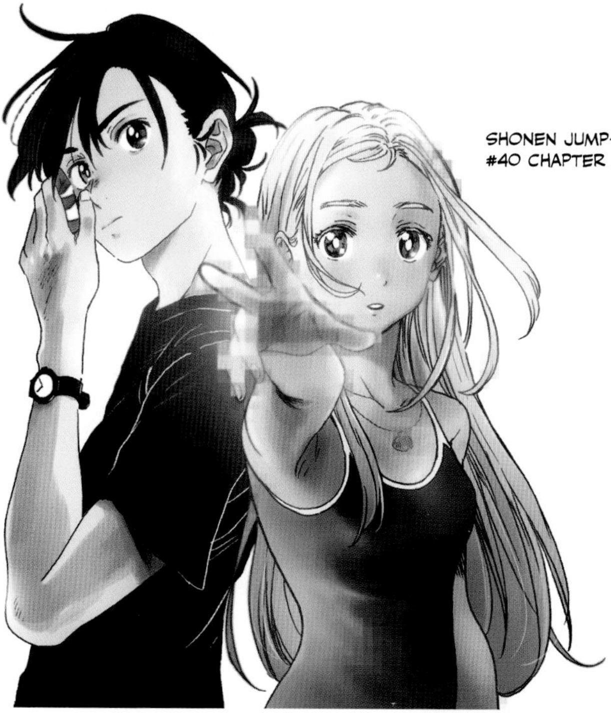

SHONEN JUMP+
#40 CHAPTER ART

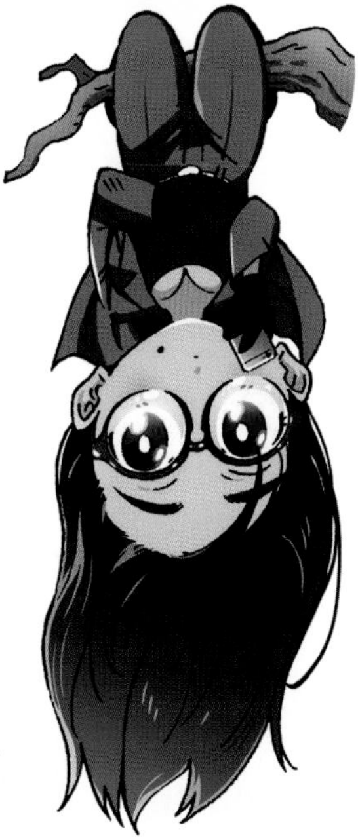

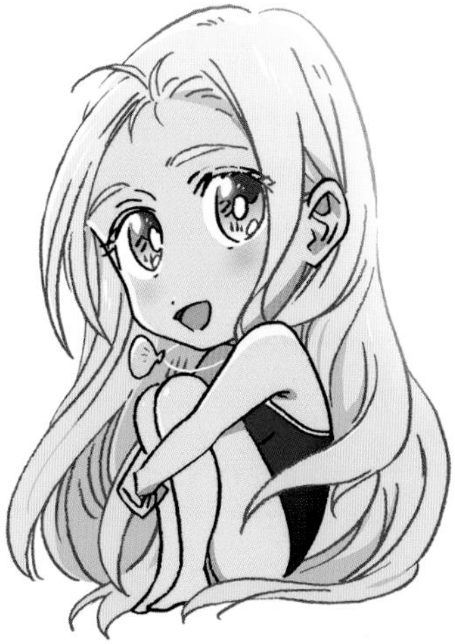

REAL ESCAPE GAME X SUMMERTIME RENDERING
"ESCAPE FROM THE SHADOW INFESTED ISLAND"
SUPER DEFORMED ILLUSTRATIONS

SUMMERTIME RENDERING

SIGNED: YASUKI TANAKA

USHIO KOFUNE (ELDER SISTER): WE SISTERS ARE STARRIN' IN THAT MANGA HAPPENIN' ON A REMOTE ISLAND IN WAKAYAMA.

MIO KOFUNE (YOUNGER SISTER): PLEASE READ IT ~ !

SHINPEI: HOW 'BOUT ME...?

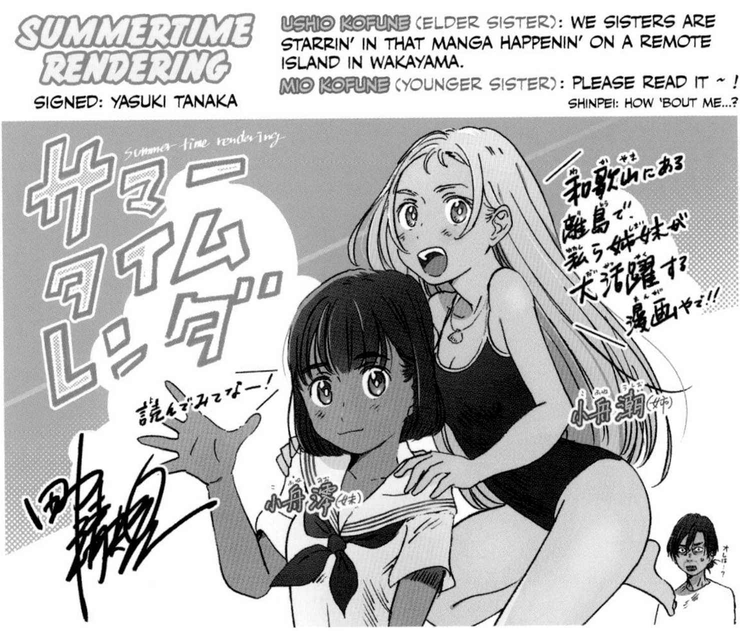

サマータイムレンダ
summer-time rendering
和歌山にある離島で、私ら姉妹が大活躍する漫画やで!!
小舟潮(姉)
読んでみてなー!
小舟澪(妹)

VOLUME 3 COMMEMORATIVE ILLUSTRATION FOR TSUTAYA SHOP'S POP DISPLAY

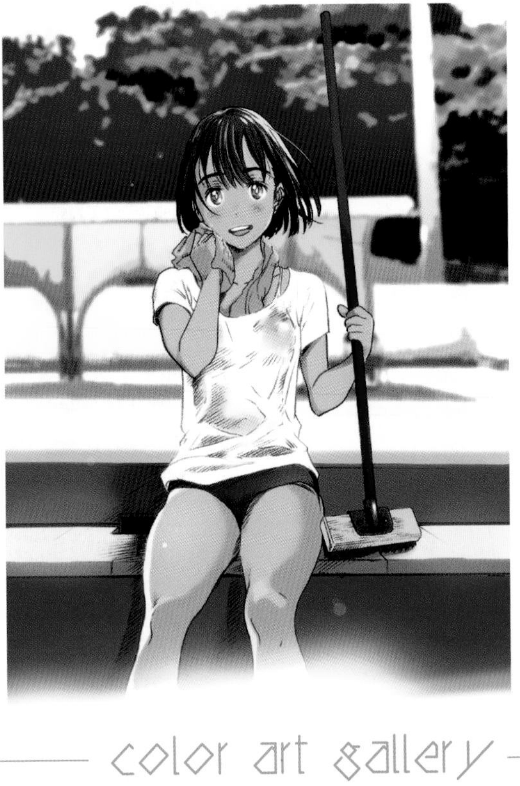

VOLUME 1 PURCHASING BONUS ILLUSTRATION CARD ART FOR COMIC TORANOANA

HAPPY NEW YEAR

HI READERS! THANKS FOR YA SUPPORT ♥♥♥♥
PLEASE KEEP FOLLOWIN' SHINPEI AND GANG'S ADVENTURES IN THE NEW YEAR ☺
NO MATTER WHAT! I WILL KEEP DOIN' MY BEST!

JANUARY 1, 2020 - USHIO KOFUNE

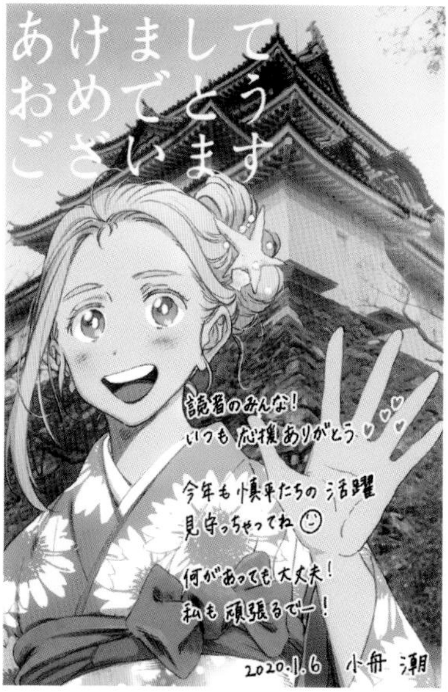

あけましておめでとうございます
読者のみんな!
いつも応援ありがとう♡
今年も慎平たちの活躍見守っちゃってね☺
何があっても大丈夫!
私も頑張るでー!
2020.1.6 小舟潮

SHONEN JUMP+ NEW YEAR'S GREETING ILLUSTRATION (JANUARY 2020)

WINTER SEASON'S GREETINGS

I HOPE TO ENJOY CONTINUING DRAWING SHINPEI AND GANG'S ADVENTURES. THE COLD WEATHER CONTINUES, SO EVERYONE PLEASE TAKE CARE OF YOURSELF! LOOKING FORWARD TO YOUR SUPPORT IN THE NEW YEAR!

JANUARY 31, 2019 - YASUKI TANAKA

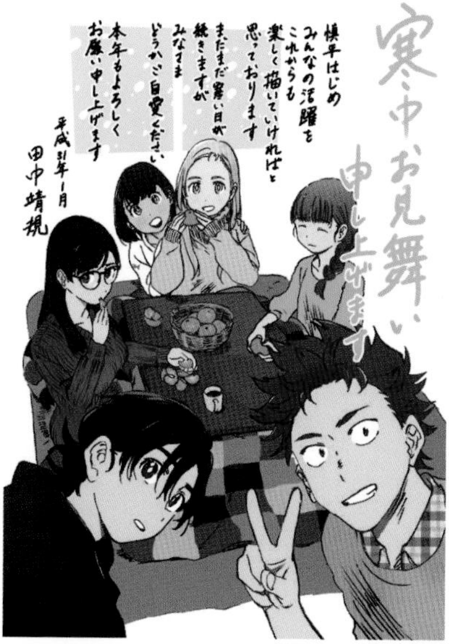

寒中お見舞い申し上げます
慎平はじめみんなの活躍をこれからも楽しく描いていければと思っております
まだまだ寒い日が続きますがみなさまどうかご自愛ください
本年もよろしくお願い申し上げます
平成31年1月
田中靖規

SHONEN JUMP+ WINTER SEASON'S GREETING ILLUSTRATION (JANUARY 2019)

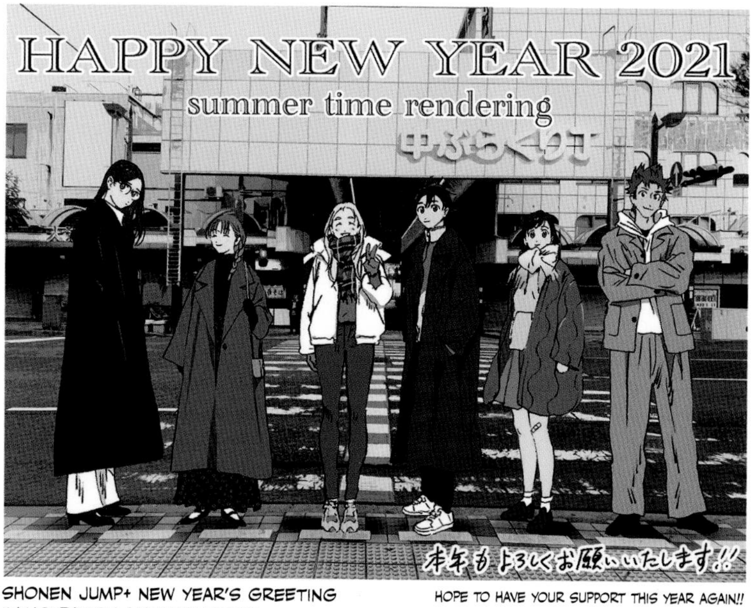

HAPPY NEW YEAR 2021
summer time rendering
中ぶらくり丁
本年もよろしくお願いいたします!!

SHONEN JUMP+ NEW YEAR'S GREETING ILLUSTRATION (JANUARY 2021)

HOPE TO HAVE YOUR SUPPORT THIS YEAR AGAIN!!

SHONEN JUMP+
LAUNCHING ILLUSTRATION
(MARCH 2018)

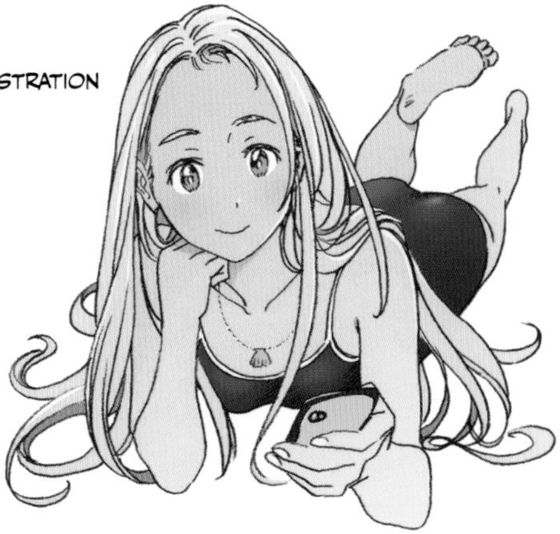

SHONEN JUMP+
LAUNCHING ILLUSTRATION
(NOVEMBER 2018)

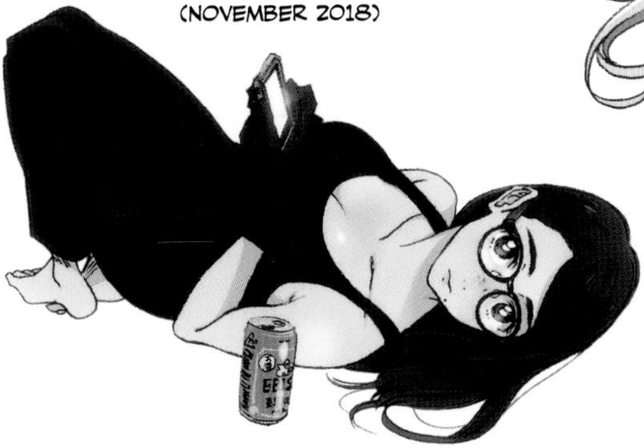

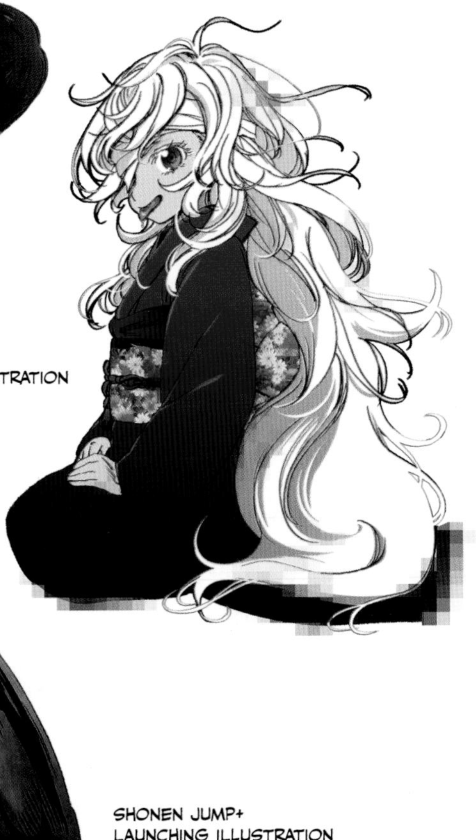

SHONEN JUMP+
LAUNCHING ILLUSTRATION
(MARCH 2019)

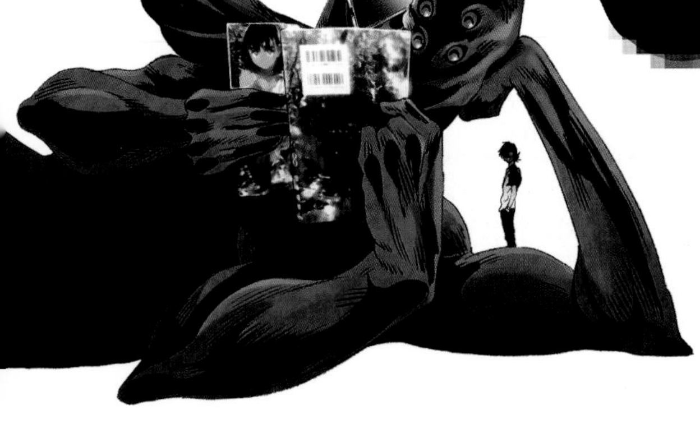

SHONEN JUMP+
LAUNCHING ILLUSTRATION
(FEBRUARY 2020)

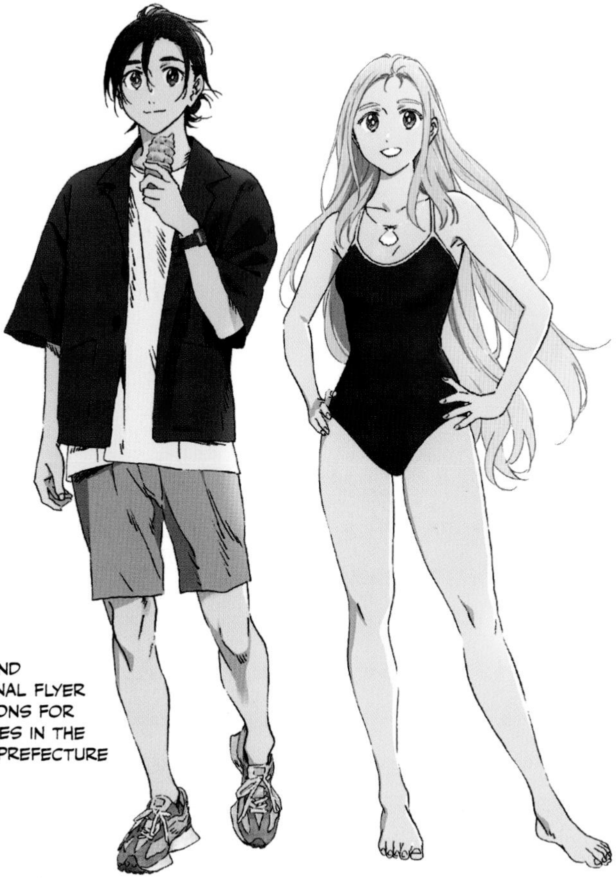

STANDEE AND PROMOTIONAL FLYER ILLUSTRATIONS FOR BOOKSTORES IN THE WAKAYAMA PREFECTURE

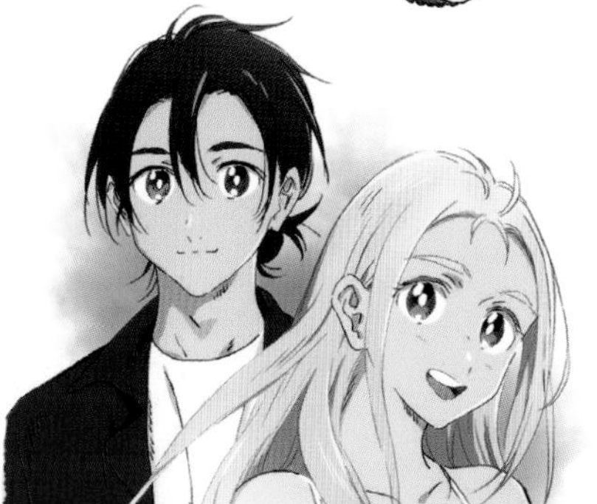

FRENCH ONLINE EVENT - PAM!
SIGNING BOARD ART

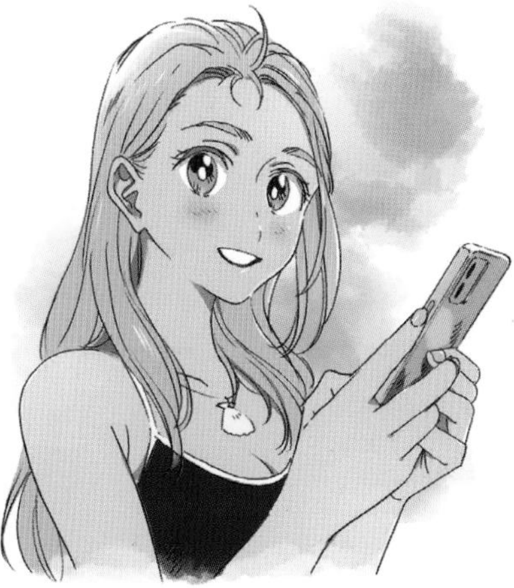

SMARTNEWS
SIGNING BOARD ART

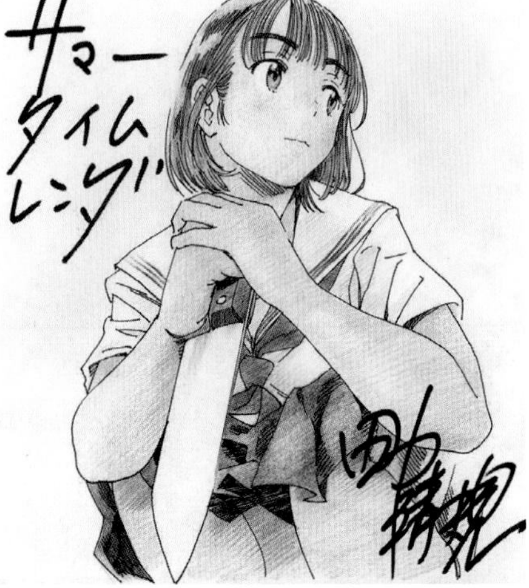
サマータイムレンダ

JUMP FESTA 2018
SIGNING BOARD ILLUSTRATION

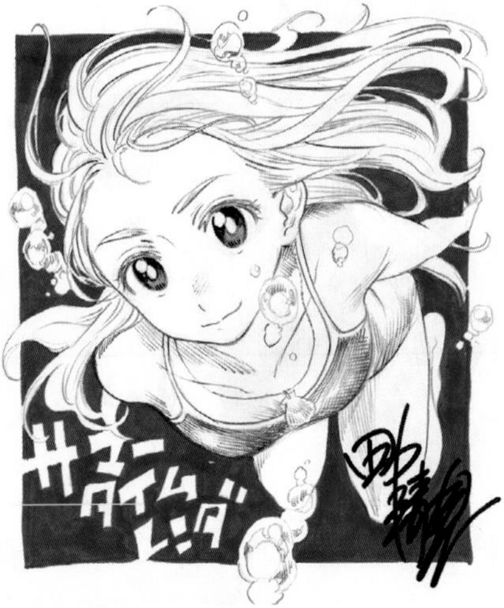
サマータイムレンダ

JUMP FESTA 2019
SIGNING BOARD ILLUSTRATION

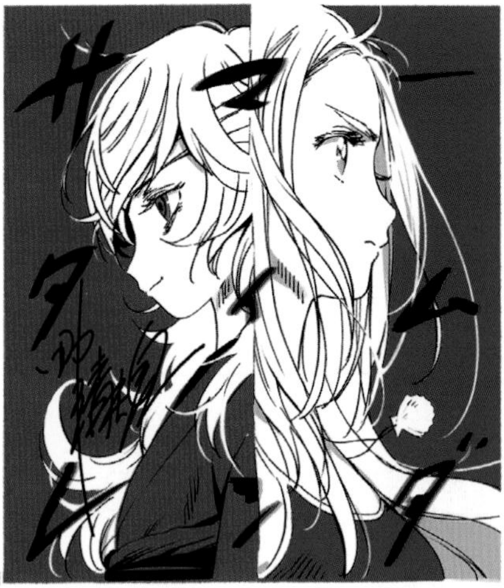
サマータイムレンダ

JUMP FESTA 2020
SIGNING BOARD ILLUSTRATION

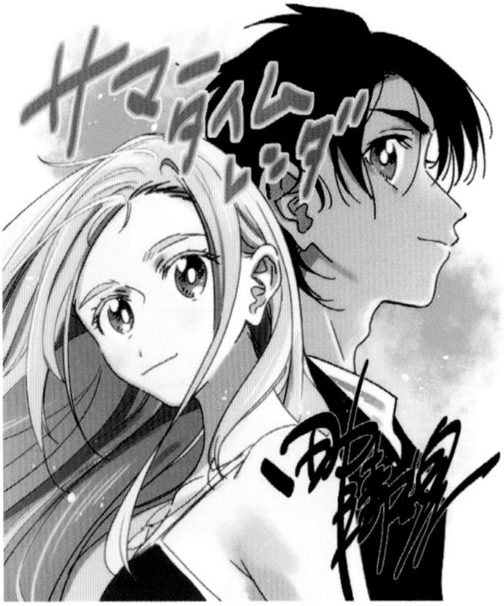
サマータイムレンダ

JUMP FESTA 2021
SIGNING BOARD ILLUSTRATION

SUMMERTIME RENDERING 6

Story & Illustration by: Yasuki Tanaka

English Edition
Translation: Jocelyne Allen
Additional Translation: Megumi Cummings & Anna Kawashima
Lettering: Janice Leung
Sound Effects & Touch Up: Jeannie Lee, EK Weaver, & Phil Christie.
Touch Up Assist: Kimmy N, & ABBASSI Ameur
Copy Editor: Claudia McGivney
Associate Editor: M. Chandler
Graphic & Cover Design: W.T. Francis

UDON Staff
Chief of Operations: Erik Ko
Director of Publishing: Matt Moylan
VP of Business Development: Cory Casoni
Director of Marketing: Megan Maiden
Japanese Liaisons: Steven Cummings & Anna Kawashima

SUMMER TIME RENDER

©2017 by Yasuki Tanaka

All rights reserved.

First published in Japan in 2017 by SHUEISHA Inc., Tokyo.

English translation rights arranged by SHUEISHA Inc.
through Tohan Corporation, Tokyo.

This volume contains contents originally published in サマータイムレンダ 11, 12, 13

English language version published by UDON Entertainment Inc.
118 Tower Hill Road, C1, PO Box 20008
RIchmond Hill, Ontario, L4K 0K0, Canada

www.UDONentertainment.com

Second printing: October 2022
Hard Cover ISBN: 978-1-772942-43-9
Paperback ISBN: 978-1-772942-37-8

Printed in Canada

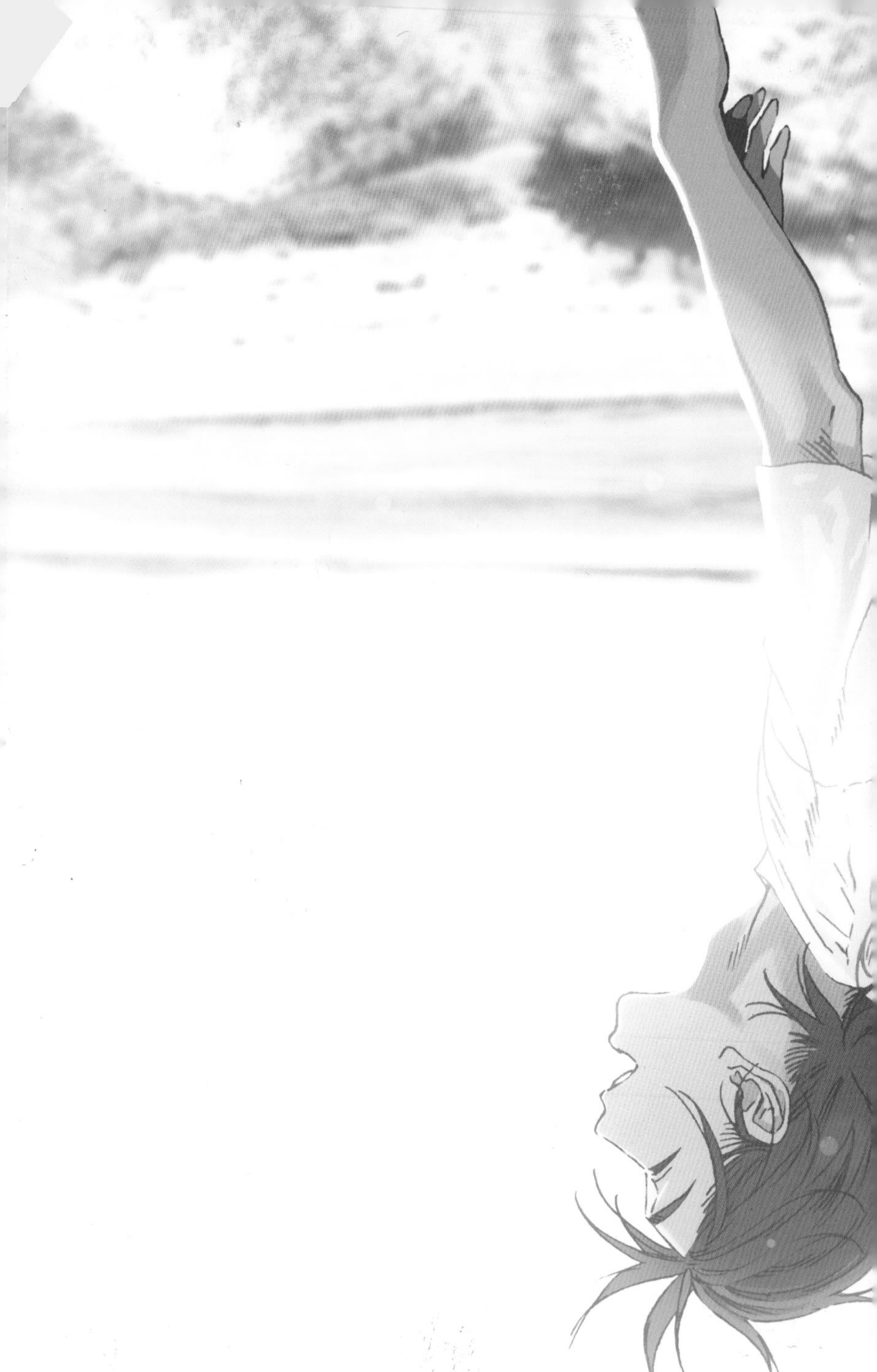

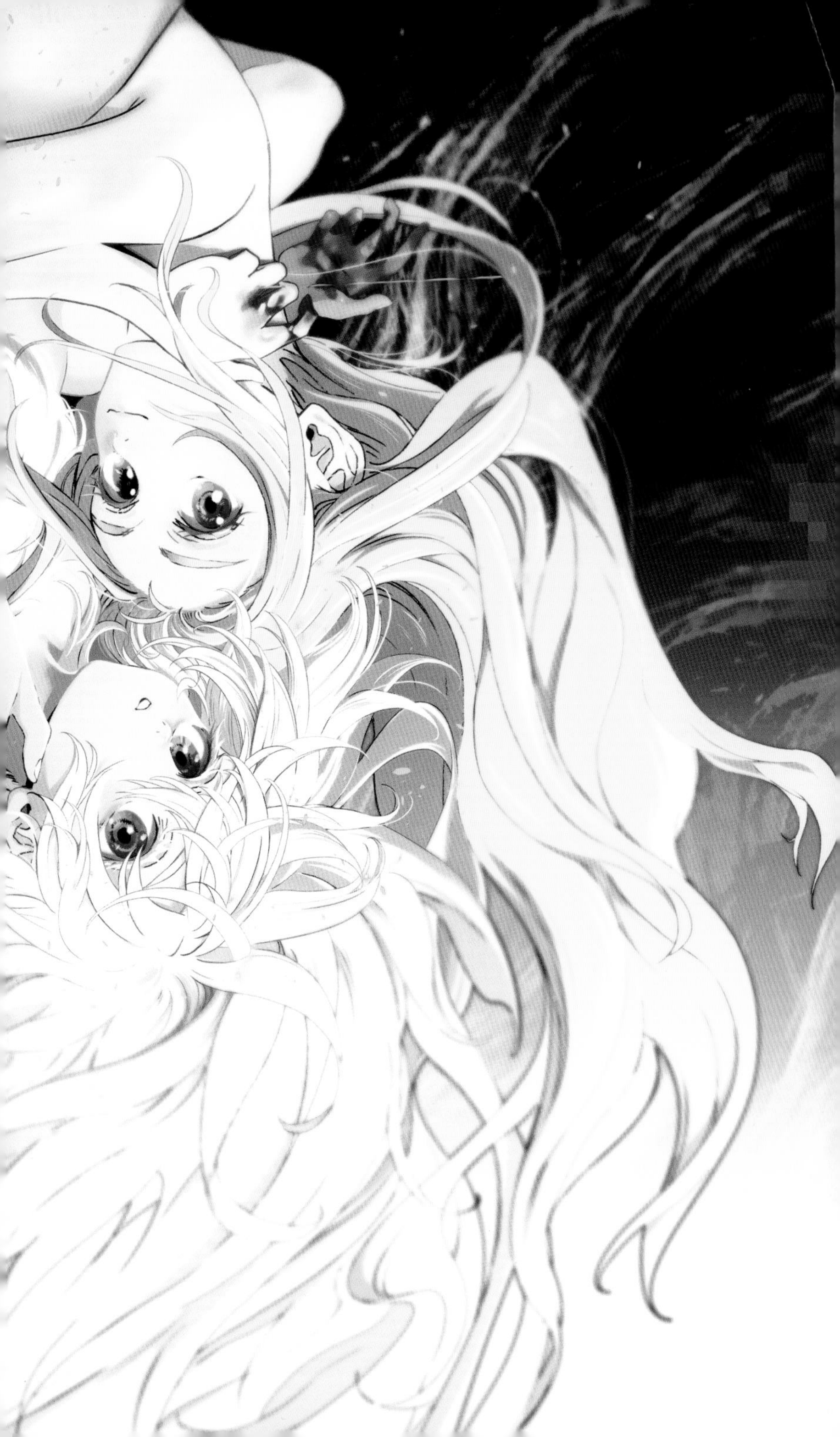

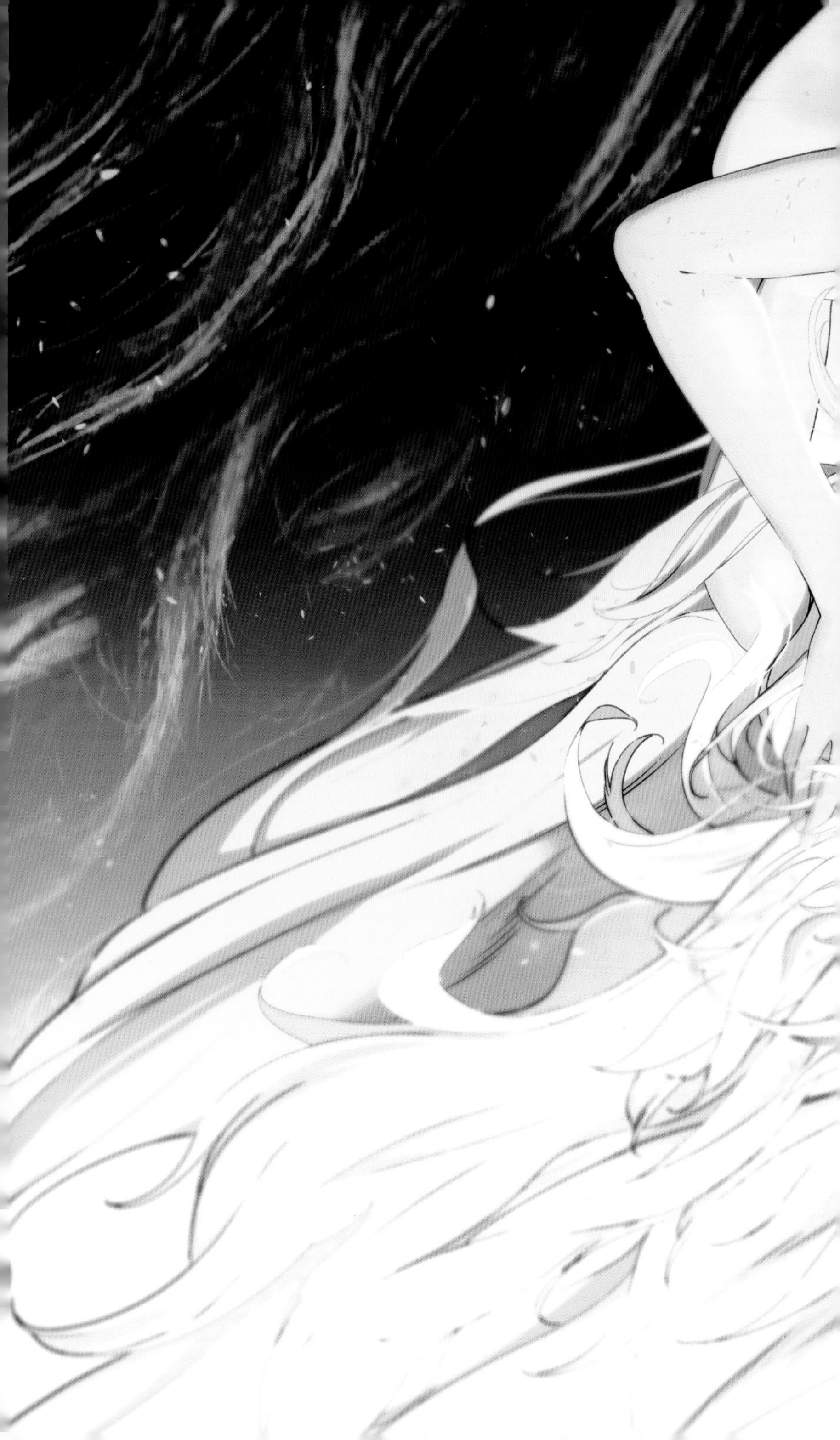

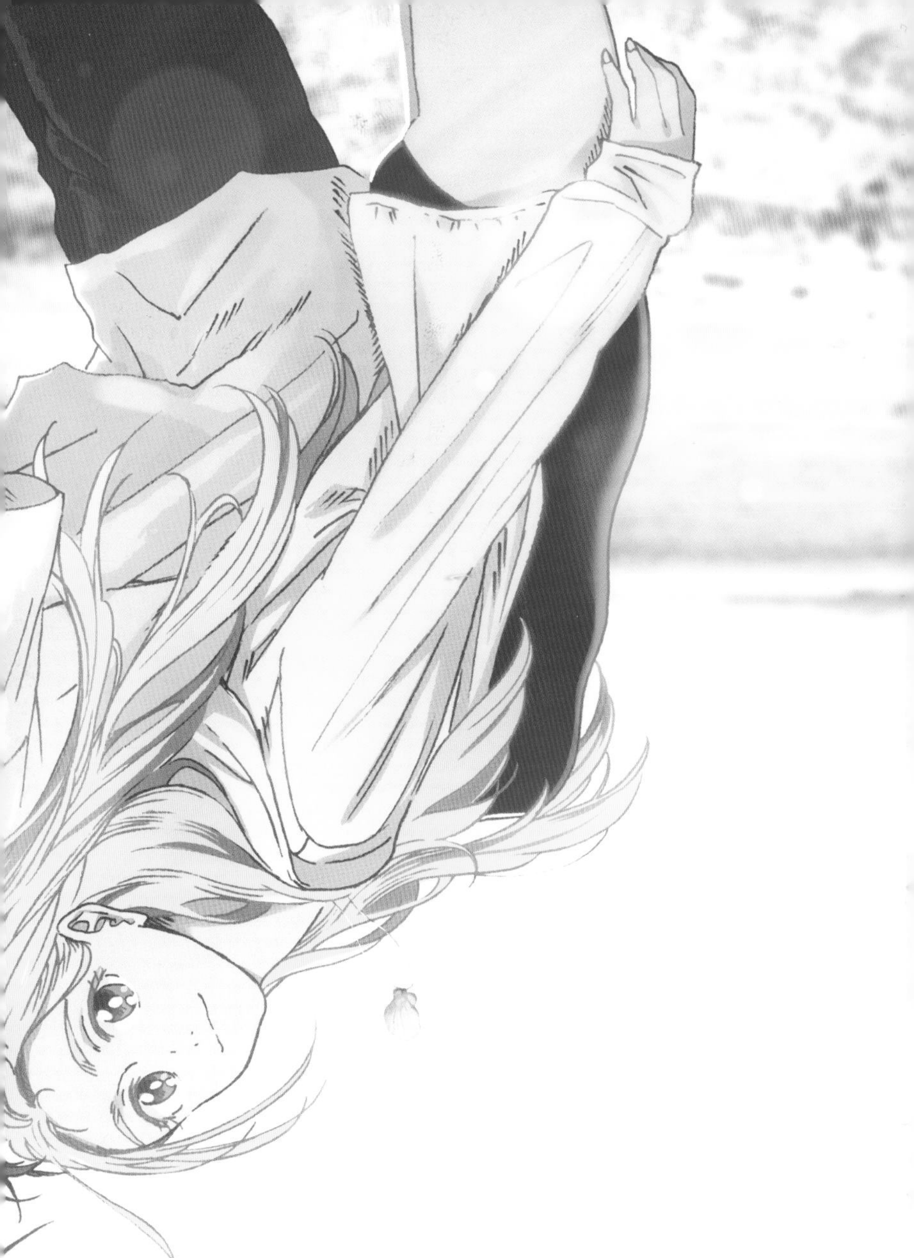